Physical/Political Map of the United States
0 150 300 mi
0 150 300 km
Puerto Rico
Atlantic Ocean
San Juan
PUERTO RICO
St. Thomas
Tortola (U.K.)
St. John
U.S. Virgin Islands
St. Croix
Caribbean Sea
0 50 mi
0 50 km
Hawaii
Kauai
Niihau
Kaulakahi Channel
Kauai Channel
Oahu
Honolulu
Kaiwi Channel
Molokai
Maui
Lanai
Kahoolawe
Alenuihaha Channel
Pacific Ocean
HAWAII
Mauna Kea
Mauna Loa
Hilo
Hawaii
0 100 mi
0 100 km
Alaska
Chukchi Sea
Beaufort Sea
North Slope
BROOKS RANGE
Kotzebue Sound
Seward Peninsula
St. Lawrence Island
Norton Sound
Yukon R.
Fairbanks
ALASKA
CANADA
ALASKA RANGE
Kuskokwim Mountains
Nunivak Island
Anchorage
St. Elias Mountains
Juneau
Kuskokwim Bay
Iliamna Lake
Cook Inlet
Kenai Peninsula
Bering Sea
Bristol Bay
Alaska Peninsula
Gulf of Alaska
Alexander Archipelago
Kodiak Island
Aleutian Islands
0 400 mi
0 400 km
Queen Charlotte Islands
Vancouver Island
Vancouver
Str. of Juan de Fuca
Cape Flattery
Victoria
Calgary
Bow R.
S. Saskatchewan R.
Kootenay R.
Columbia R.
Seattle
Tacoma
Olympia
Cape Disappointment
WASHINGTON
Spokane
Coeur d'Alene
Snake R.
Walla Walla
Portland
Columbia R.
Salem
Willamette R.
Eugene
Cape Blanco
OREGON
COLUMBIA PLATEAU
CASCADE RANGE
COAST RANGES
Milk R.
Missouri R.
Missoula
Helena
MONTANA
Yellowstone
Billings
Salmon R.
IDAHO
Boise
Idaho Falls
Snake R.
Pocatello
Owyhee R.
ROCKY MOUNTAINS
Bighorn R.
Jackson
WYOMING
Casper
Laramie
Klamath R.
Cape Mendocino
Sacramento R.
SIERRA NEVADA
Reno
Carson City
Lake Tahoe
Sacramento
GREAT BASIN
NEVADA
Great Salt Lake Desert
Great Salt Lake
Salt Lake City
Point Reyes
San Francisco
Oakland
San Jose
San Joaquin R.
Monterey Bay
Monterey
Salinas
Fresno
CALIFORNIA
Death Valley
MOJAVE DESERT
UTAH
Green R.
Colorado R.
Moab
St. George
Lake Powell
Steamboat Springs
Glenwood Springs
COLORADO
Las Vegas
Bakersfield
Point Conception
Santa Barbara
Lancaster
Oxnard
Pasadena
Channel Islands
Los Angeles
Long Beach
Lake Mead
COLORADO PLATEAU
Little Colorado R.
Flagstaff
ARIZONA
Salton Sea
Oceanside
Escondido
San Diego
Tijuana
SONORAN DESERT
Gila R.
Phoenix
Tucson
Rio Grande
Santa Fe
Albuquerque
NEW MEXICO
Pecos R.
El Paso
Ciudad Juárez
Pacific Ocean
BAJA CALIFORNIA
Vizcaino Bay
Gulf of California
Mulegé
Hermosillo
SIERRA MADRE OCCIDENTAL
MEXICO

CANADA
CANADIAN SHIELD
LAURENTIDE SCARP
James Bay
Albany R.
Missinaibi R.
Gulf of St. Lawrence
Assiniboine R.
Winnipeg
Lake of the Woods
St. John R.
Fredericton
Québec
Ottawa R.
Ottawa
Montréal
St. Lawrence R.
Isle Royale
Lake Superior
Sault Ste. Marie
Georgian Bay
Lake Huron
Lake Michigan
Lake Ontario
Lake Erie
Lake St. Clair
Upper Peninsula
Lower Peninsula
International Falls
Red R. of the North
NORTH DAKOTA
Bismarck
Fargo
James R.
Duluth
MINNESOTA
SOUTH DAKOTA
Pierre
Huron
Minneapolis
St. Paul
Minnesota R.
Mississippi R.
Sioux Falls
WISCONSIN
Green Bay
Oshkosh
Lake Winebago
Wisconsin R.
Madison
Milwaukee
Traverse City
MICHIGAN
Lansing
Detroit
Port Huron
Toronto
Niagara Falls
Buffalo
NEW YORK
Albany
Watertown
Adirondack Mountains
Burlington
Lake Champlain
Montpelier
VT
White Mts.
NH
Concord
MAINE
Bangor
Augusta
Penobscot R.
Kennebec R.
Portland
Gulf of Maine
Boston
MASS.
Cape Cod
Providence
Hartford
New Haven
Connecticut R.
Hudson R.
RHODE ISLAND
CONNECTICUT
Long Island
New York
Newark
Trenton
NEW JERSEY
Atlantic City
Delaware R.
PENNSYLVANIA
Erie
Pittsburgh
Harrisburg
Philadelphia
Cleveland
Akron
Toledo
OHIO
Columbus
Ohio R.
Cincinnati
Sioux City
IOWA
Cedar Rapids
Des Moines
Des Moines R.
Missouri R.
NEBRASKA
Loup R.
Platte R.
Omaha
Lincoln
CENTRAL LOWLAND
Chicago
Gary
Illinois R.
Peoria
Springfield
ILLINOIS
Fort Wayne
Wabash R.
INDIANA
Indianapolis
KANSAS
Kansas R.
Kansas City
Topeka
Independence
Hannibal
MISSOURI
Jefferson City
St. Louis
Osage R.
Lake of the Ozarks
Springfield
Ozark Plateau
Wichita
Louisville
Frankfort
Lexington
Ohio R.
KENTUCKY
Cumberland R.
WEST VIRGINIA
Charleston
Baltimore
Annapolis
Dover
Washington, D.C.
Delaware Bay
DELAWARE
MARYLAND
VIRGINIA
Richmond
Roanoke
Norfolk
Chesapeake Bay
Great Dismal Swamp
Roanoke R.
APPALACHIAN PLATEAU
APPALACHIAN MOUNTAINS
PIEDMONT
Nashville
Knoxville
Great Smoky Mountains
TENNESSEE
Tennessee R.
Chattanooga
Memphis
Asheville
Charlotte
Raleigh
NORTH CAROLINA
Wilmington
Cape Hatteras
Cape Lookout
Cape Fear
Pee Dee R.
Columbia
SOUTH CAROLINA
Charleston
Savannah R.
OKLAHOMA
Tulsa
Oklahoma City
Arkansas R.
ARKANSAS
White R.
Jonesboro
Little Rock
Red R.
Texarkana
Ouachita R.
Tupelo
MISSISSIPPI
Jackson
Birmingham
ALABAMA
Tombigbee R.
Alabama R.
Montgomery
Chattahoochee R.
Atlanta
GEORGIA
Macon
Columbus
Savannah
Altamaha R.
Okefenokee Swamp
Brazos R.
Fort Worth
Dallas
Sabine R.
Abilene
Colorado R.
Waco
TEXAS
Edwards Plateau
Austin
Beaumont
Houston
San Antonio
Galveston
Galveston Bay
Shreveport
Natchitoches
LOUISIANA
Baton Rouge
Lake Pontchartrain
Lafayette
New Orleans
Atchafalaya Bay
Breton Sound
Mississippi River Delta
Biloxi
Mobile
Pensacola
Tallahassee
Jacksonville
FLORIDA
Apalachee Bay
Cape San Blas
St. John's R.
Cape Canaveral
Orlando
Tampa
Lake Okeechobee
Fort Lauderdale
Miami
The Everglades
Cape Sable
Florida Keys
Key West
COASTAL PLAIN
Gulf of Mexico
Atlantic Ocean
Laredo
Corpus Christi
Brownsville
Matamoros
Nassau
BAHAMAS

SEVENTH EDITION

We the People

AN INTRODUCTION TO AMERICAN POLITICS

SEVENTH EDITION

We the People

AN INTRODUCTION TO AMERICAN POLITICS

Benjamin Ginsberg
THE JOHNS HOPKINS UNIVERSITY

Theodore J. Lowi
CORNELL UNIVERSITY

Margaret Weir
UNIVERSITY OF CALIFORNIA AT BERKELEY

W. W. NORTON & COMPANY
NEW YORK ★ LONDON

W. W. Norton & Company has been independent since its founding in 1923, when William Warder Norton and Mary D. Herter Norton first published lectures delivered at the People's Institute, the adult education division of New York City's Cooper Union. The Nortons soon expanded their program beyond the Institute, publishing books by celebrated academics from America and abroad. By mid-century, the two major pillars of Norton's publishing program—trade books and college texts—were firmly established. In the 1950s, the Norton family transferred control of the company to its employees, and today—with a staff of four hundred and a comparable number of trade, college, and professional titles published each year—W. W. Norton & Company stands as the largest and oldest publishing house owned wholly by its employees.

Printed in the United States of America

Editor: Ann Shin
Editorial assistant: Mollie Eisenberg
Project editor: Carla L. Talmadge
Senior production manager, College: Ben Reynolds
Book design: Rubina Yeh and Joan Greenfield
Figures: John McAusland
Managing editor, College: Marian Johnson
Composition: TSI Graphics
Manufacturing: R. R. Donnelley & Sons—Willard Division
Cover design: Joan Greenfield
Cover illustration: Mick Wiggins
Photo editor: Kelly Mitchell
Photo research: Patty Cateura, Elyse Rieder, and Rae Grant
E-media editor: Dan Jost

Library of Congress Cataloging-in-Publication Data

Ginsberg, Benjamin.
We the people : an introduction to American politics / Benjamin Ginsberg, Theodore J. Lowi, Margaret Weir.—7th ed.
p. cm.
Includes bibliographical references and index.

ISBN 978-0-393-93214-0 (hardcover)

1. United States—Politics and government—Textbooks. I. Lowi, Theodore J. II. Weir, Margaret, 1952– III. Title.

JK276.G55 2008
320.473—dc22 2008041985

W. W. Norton & Company, Inc., 500 Fifth Avenue, New York, N.Y. 10110
www.wwnorton.com

W. W. Norton & Company Ltd., Castle House, 75/76 Wells Street, London W1T 3QT

2 3 4 5 6 7 8 9 0

TO

SANDY, CINDY, AND ALEX GINSBERG

ANGELE, ANNA, AND JASON LOWI

NICHOLAS ZIEGLER

CONTENTS

4 ★ Civil Liberties *118*

5 ★ Civil Rights *156*

PART II Politics

6 ★ Public Opinion *204*

7 ★ The Media *246*

8 ★ Political Participation and Voting *282*

9 ★ Political Parties *318*

10 ★ Campaigns and Elections *362*

11 ★ Groups and Interests *416*

PART III Institutions

12 ★ Congress *454*

13 ★ The Presidency *502*

14 ★ Bureaucracy in a Democracy *544*

FREE SPEECH 4 STUDENTS
FREE SPEECH 4 STUDENTS
FREE SPEECH 4 STUDENTS

PROTECTING THE AMERICAN DREAM
PROTECTING THE AMERICAN DREAM

MEDICARE FOR ALL NOW
HEALTH CARE IS A HUMAN RIGHT
PNHP
Physicians for a National Health Program

PREFACE

This book has been and continues to be dedicated to developing a satisfactory response to the question more and more Americans are asking: Why should we be engaged with government and politics? Through the first six editions, we sought to answer this question by making the text directly relevant to the lives of the students who would be reading it. As a result, we tried to make politics interesting by demonstrating that students' interests are at stake and that they therefore need to take a personal, even selfish, interest in the outcomes of government. At the same time, we realized that students needed guidance in how to become politically engaged. Beyond providing students with a core of political knowledge, we needed to show them how they could apply that knowledge as participants in the political process. The "Get Involved" sections in each chapter help achieve that goal.

As events from the last several years have reminded us, "what government does" can be a matter of life and death. Recent events have reinforced the centrality of government in citizens' lives. The U.S. government has fought a war abroad, while claiming sweeping new powers at home that could compromise the liberties of its citizens. America's role in the world is discussed daily both inside and outside the classroom. Moreover, students and younger Americans have become more aware of and involved in politics, as the 2008 elections illustrated. Reflecting all of these trends, this new Seventh Edition shows more than any other book on the market (1) how students are connected to government; (2) how American government is connected to the world; and (3) why students should think critically about government and politics. These themes are incorporated in the following ways:

- **New "Get Involved" units show students how they can make a difference in politics.** The 2008 elections produced a surge in political participation among young Americans, as well as changes in the ways that they participated. These full-page boxes use contemporary examples to explain how young people (even those with busy lives!) can get involved in politics. Specific, step-by-step instructions guide students through a range of possible political activities related to each chapter's topic. These new boxes replace the "Get Involved" sections that appeared as part of the chapter text in the Sixth Edition and have been rewritten to take account of the Internet's growing prominence as an avenue for political participation.

- **"Politics and Popular Culture" boxes connect politics to topics students are interested in.** In each chapter "Politics and Popular Culture" boxes ask students to look critically at how politics intersects with television, film, music, cartoons, and the Internet. Drawing on a range of social science research, these boxes engage students in questions such as "Do non-news TV shows that include political content, like *The Daily Show with Jon Stewart*, have an effect on political knowledge?" "Is there a culture war?" and "Why do candidates sometimes prefer to be interviewed on talk shows rather than traditional news programs?"

- **Chapter introductions focus on "What Government Does and Why It Matters."** In recent decades, cynicism about "big government" has dominated the political zeitgeist. But critics of government often forget that governments do a great deal for citizens. Every year, Americans are the beneficiaries of billions of dollars of goods and services from government programs. Government "does" a lot, and what it does matters a great deal to everyone, including college students. At the start of each chapter, this theme is introduced and applied to the chapter's topic. The goal is to show students that government and politics mean something to their daily lives.

- **"America in the World" boxes show students how American government is connected to the world.** These one-page boxes in every chapter illustrate the important political role the United States plays abroad. Topics include "Should America Export Democracy?" "The American Constitution: A Model for the World?" "Participation and Democracy in Iraq," and "What Is Congress's Role in Foreign Policy?" These boxes exemplify the critical-analytical approach that characterizes the text and include "For Critical Analysis" questions.

- **"For Critical Analysis" questions are incorporated throughout the text.** "For Critical Analysis" questions in the margins of every chapter prompt students' own critical thinking about the material in the chapter, encouraging them to engage with the topic. The two "For Critical Analysis" questions that conclude each "America in the World" box get students to think more deeply about America's role in the world. The questions at the end of each "Politics and Popular Culture" box ask students to think critically about the intersection of politics and mass media. And the questions that follow the discussions of contending perspectives in each "Policy Debate" box invite students to reconsider their own perspective on the issue.

- **New "Politics Today" questions highlight discussions of current issues and recent events.** We believe that students value what they learn in the course more if they see how the course material relates to the issues and events in today's headlines. This Seventh Edition has been extensively updated with new sections on major events like the 2008 elections and the government's response to the recent housing and financial crisis, as well as contemporary examples throughout. New "Politics Today" questions in the margins of each chapter draw students' attention to discussions of recent events and ask questions to get them thinking critically about contemporary issues and events.

We continue to hope that our book will itself be accepted as a form of enlightened political action. This Seventh Edition is another chance. It is an advancement toward our goal. We promise to keep trying.

ACKNOWLEDGMENTS

Our students at Cornell, Johns Hopkins, Harvard, and Berkeley have been an essential factor in the writing and revising of this book. They have been our most immediate intellectual community, a hospitable one indeed. Another part of our community, perhaps a large suburb, is the discipline of political science itself. Our debt to the scholarship of our colleagues is scientifically measurable, probably to several decimal points, in the endnotes of each chapter. Despite many complaints that the field is too scientific or not scientific enough, political science is alive and well in the United States. It is an aspect of democracy itself, and it has grown and changed in response to the developments in government and politics that we have chronicled in our book. If we did a "time line" on the history of political science, it would show a close association with developments in "the American state." Sometimes the discipline has been out of phase and critical; at other times, it has been in phase and perhaps apologetic. But political science has never been at a loss for relevant literature, and without it, our job would have been impossible.

We are especially pleased to acknowledge our debt to the many colleagues who had a direct and active role in criticism and preparation of the manuscript. Our thanks go to:

FIRST EDITION REVIEWERS

Sarah Binder, Brookings Institution
Kathleen Gille, Office of Representative David Bonior
Rodney Hero, University of Colorado at Boulder
Robert Katzmann, Brookings Institution
Kathleen Knight, University of Houston
Robin Kolodny, Temple University
Nancy Kral, Tomball College
Robert C. Lieberman, Columbia University
David A. Marcum, University of Wyoming
Laura R. Winsky Mattei, State University of New York at Buffalo
Marilyn S. Mertens, Midwestern State University
Barbara Suhay, Henry Ford Community College
Carolyn Wong, Stanford University
Julian Zelizer, State University of New York at Albany

SECOND EDITION REVIEWERS

Lydia Andrade, University of North Texas
John Coleman, University of Wisconsin at Madison
Daphne Eastman, Odessa College
Otto Feinstein, Wayne State University
Elizabeth Flores, Delmar College
James Gimpel, University of Maryland at College Park
Jill Glaathar, Southwest Missouri State University

Shaun Herness, University of Florida
William Lyons, University of Tennessee at Knoxville
Andrew Polsky, Hunter College, City University of New York
Grant Reeher, Syracuse University
Richard Rich, Virginia Polytechnic
Bartholomew Sparrow, University of Texas at Austin

THIRD EDITION REVIEWERS

Bruce R. Drury, Lamar University
Andrew I. E. Ewoh, Prairie View A&M University
Amy Jasperson, University of Texas at San Antonio
Loch Johnson, University of Georgia
Mark Kann, University of Southern California
Robert L. Perry, University of Texas of the Permian Basin
Wayne Pryor, Brazosport College
Elizabeth A. Rexford, Wharton County Junior College
Andrea Simpson, University of Washington
Brian Smentkowski, Southeast Missouri State University
Nelson Wikstrom, Virginia Commonwealth University

FOURTH EDITION REVIEWERS

M. E. Banks, Virginia Commonwealth University
Lynn Brink, North Lake College
Mark Cichock, University of Texas at Arlington
Del Fields, St. Petersburg College
Nancy Kinney, Washtenaw Community College
William Klein, St. Petersburg College
Dana Morales, Montgomery College
Christopher Muste, Louisiana State University
Larry Norris, South Plains College
David Rankin, State University of New York at Fredonia
Paul Roesler, St. Charles Community College
J. Philip Rogers, San Antonio College
Greg Shaw, Illinois Wesleyan University
Tracy Skopek, Stephen F. Austin State University
Don Smith, University of North Texas
Terri Wright, Cal State, Fullerton

FIFTH EDITION REVIEWERS

Annie Benifield, Tomball College
Denise Dutton, Southwest Missouri State University
Rick Kurtz, Central Michigan University
Kelly McDaniel, Three Rivers Community College
Eric Plutzer, Pennsylvania State University
Daniel Smith, Northwest Missouri State University
Dara Strolovitch, University of Minnesota
Dennis Toombs, San Jacinto College–North
Stacy Ulbig, Southwest Missouri State University

SIXTH EDITION REVIEWERS

Janet Adamski, University of Mary Hardin-Baylor
Greg Andrews, St. Petersburg College
Louis Bolce, Baruch College
Darin Combs, Tulsa Community College
Sean Conroy, University of New Orleans
Paul Cooke, Cy Fair College
Vida Davoudi, Kingwood College
Robert DiClerico, West Virginia University
Corey Ditslear, University of North Texas
Kathy Dolan, University of Wisconsin, Milwaukee
Randy Glean, Midwestern State University
Nancy Kral, Tomball College
Mark Logas, Valencia Community College
Scott MacDougall, Diablo Valley College
David Mann, College of Charleston
Christopher Muste, University of Montana
Richard Pacelle, Georgia Southern University
Sarah Poggione, Florida International University
Richard Rich, Virginia Tech
Thomas Schmeling, Rhode Island College
Scott Spitzer, California State University–Fullerton
Dennis Toombs, San Jacinto College–North
John Vento, Antelope Valley College
Robert Wood, University of North Dakota

SEVENTH EDITION REVIEWERS

Molly Andolina, DePaul University
Nancy Bednar, Antelope Valley College
Paul Blakelock, Kingwood College
Amy Brandon, San Jacinto College
Jim Cauthen, John Jay College
Kevin Davis, North Central Texas College
Louis DeSipio, University of California–Irvine
Brandon Franke, Blinn College
Steve Garrison, Midwestern State University
Joseph Howard, University of Central Arkansas
Aaron Knight, Houston Community College
Paul Labedz, Valencia Community College
Elise Langan, John Jay College
Mark Logas, Valencia Community College
Eric Miller, Blinn College

Anthony O'Regan, Los Angeles Valley College
David Putz, Kingwood College
Chis Soper, Pepperdine University
Kevin Wagner, Florida Atlantic University
Laura Wood, Tarrant County College

We also must pay thanks to the many collaborators we have had on this project: Robert J. Spitzer of the State University of New York at Cortland; Mark Kann and Marcella Marlowe of the University of Southern California; Dannagal Young of the University of Delaware, who contributed the "Politics and Popular Culture" boxes; and, most recently, Molly Andolina of DePaul University and Krista Jenkins of Fairleigh Dickinson University, who together contributed the new "Get Involved" boxes.

We are also grateful for the talents and hard work of several research assistants, whose contributions can never be adequately compensated. In particular, for his work on this Seventh Edition, we thank Kevin Wallsten.

We would like to give special thanks to Jacqueline Pastore at Cornell University, who not only prepared portions of the manuscript but also helped to hold the entire project together. We especially thank her for her hard work and dedication.

Perhaps above all, we wish to thank those at W. W. Norton. For its first five editions, editor Steve Dunn helped us shape the book in countless ways. Our current editor, Ann Shin, has carried on the Norton tradition of splendid editorial work. We thank Kelly Mitchell, Patty Cateura, Elyse Rieder, and Rae Grant for devoting an enormous amount of time to finding new photos. For our student Web site and other media resources for the book, Dan Jost has been an energetic and visionary editor. Barbara Curialle copyedited the manuscript with Marian Johnson's superb direction, and project editor Carla Talmadge devoted countless hours keeping on top of myriad details. Ben Reynolds has been dedicated in managing production. Finally, we wish to thank Roby Harrington, the head of Norton's college department.

We are more than happy, however, to absolve all these contributors from any flaws, errors, and misjudgments that will inevitably be discovered. We wish the book could be free of all production errors, grammatical errors, misspellings, misquotes, missed citations, etc. From that standpoint, a book ought to try to be perfect. But substantively we have not tried to write a flawless book; we have not tried to write a book to please everyone. We have again tried to write an effective book, a book that cannot be taken lightly. Our goal was not to make every reader a political scientist or a political activist. Our goal was to restore politics as a subject matter of vigorous and enjoyable discourse, recapturing it from the bondage of the thirty-second sound bite and the thirty-page technical briefing. Every person can be knowledgeable because everything about politics is accessible. One does not have to be a television anchorperson to profit from political events. One does not have to be a philosopher to argue about the requisites of democracy, a lawyer to dispute constitutional interpretations, an economist to debate a public policy. We would be very proud if our book contributes in a small way to the restoration of the ancient art of political controversy.

BENJAMIN GINSBERG
THEODORE J. LOWI
MARGARET WEIR

November 2008

PART I

Foundations

1 American Political Culture

- What Americans Think about Government
- Citizenship: Knowledge and Participation
- Government
- Who Are Americans?
- Thinking Critically about American Political Culture

WHAT GOVERNMENT DOES AND WHY IT MATTERS

Americans sometimes appear to believe that the government is an institution that does things *to* them and from which they need protection. Business owners complain that federal health and safety regulations threaten their ability to make a profit. Farmers and ranchers complain that federal and state environmental rules intrude on their property rights. Motorists allege that municipal "red light" cameras, designed to photograph traffic violators, represent the intrusion of "Big Brother" into their lives. Civil libertarians—including groups such as the American Civil Liberties Union (ACLU), organized to defend First Amendment freedoms—express concern over what they view as sometimes overly aggressive police and prosecutorial practices. Everyone complains about federal, state, and local taxes.

Yet many of the same individuals who complain about what the government does *to* them also want the government to do a great deal *for* them. When the mortgage and banking crisis in 2008 threatened to throw the world economy into depression, all eyes turned to the federal government for help. The Treasury Department and the Federal Reserve responded with an unprecedented $700 billion rescue plan that they hoped would restore confidence in financial institutions and prevent a major economic downturn. Americans also look to government for assistance with more routine matters. Farmers are the beneficiaries of billions in federal subsidies and research programs. Motorists would have no roads on which to be photographed by those hated cameras if not for the tens of billions of dollars spent each year on road construction and maintenance by federal, state, and municipal authorities. Individuals accused of crimes benefit from procedural safeguards and state-funded defense attorneys. Most Americans would not be here at all if it were not for federal immigration policies, which set the terms for entry into the United States and for obtaining citizenship. And, as for those detested taxes, without them there would be no government benefits at all.

Americans' dependence on the government is brought into particularly sharp focus during times of danger. When Pearl Harbor was bombed on December 7, 1941,

Americans listened to their radios, waiting for President Franklin D. Roosevelt to tell them how he intended to defend Americans' lives and property. In a similar vein, after the September 11, 2001 terrorist attacks on the World Trade Center and the Pentagon, Americans demanded government action. President George W. Bush responded by mobilizing powerful military forces and organizing an international coalition for what he defined as a lengthy and worldwide campaign against terrorism. Bush also created an Office of Homeland Security (later reorganized as a cabinet department) and instituted massive new law-enforcement measures to combat terrorism. Congress authorized tens of billions of dollars in new federal expenditures to combat terrorism and to repair the damage already caused by terrorists. The states mobilized their own police and national guard forces for duties such as airport security, and local police and public safety departments were placed on high alert.

As the government seeks to protect its citizens it faces the challenge of doing so in ways that are true to American values. Liberty, equality, and democracy are key American political values. Liberty means personal freedom and a government whose powers are limited by law. Equality is the idea that all individuals should have the right to participate in political life and society on equivalent terms. Democracy implies placing considerable political power in the hands of ordinary people. Most Americans find it easy to affirm all three values in principle. In practice, however, matters are not always so clear. Policies and practices that seem to affirm one of these values may contradict another. Americans, moreover, are sometimes willing to subordinate liberty to security and have frequently tolerated significant departures from the principles of equality and democracy.

› **In this chapter, we will explore the relationship between the government and the people it governs. First, we will assess what Americans think about their government.** Although Americans rely on government for many of their needs, trust in government and the belief that individuals can influence government have both been in decline.

› **Second, we will explore the principle of democratic citizenship.** We believe that good citizenship begins with political knowledge—knowledge of government, of politics, and of democratic principles. With this knowledge, citizens can identify their interests and take advantage of their opportunities to influence politics.

› **Next, we will look at the principles of government and politics.** The relationship between a government and its citizens is especially dependent on the form that a government takes. We will look at alternative forms of government and key differences among them. We will also examine the factors that led to the emergence of representative democracy in the United States and elsewhere around the world.

› **Then, we will look at who the American people are,** and how the changing characteristics of the population have consistently contributed to political debates. We will conclude by assessing how well the American political system upholds the values of liberty, equality, and democracy for all Americans.

› **Finally, we will look at American political culture.** Here, we will examine the political principles that serve as the basis for American government.

What Americans Think about Government

Since the United States was established as a nation, Americans have been reluctant to grant government too much power, and they have often been suspicious of politicians. But over the course of the nation's history, Americans have also turned to government for assistance in times of need and have strongly supported the government in periods of war. In 1933, the power of the government began to expand to meet the crises created by the stock market crash of 1929, the Great Depression, and the run on banks of 1933. Congress passed legislation that brought the government into the businesses of home mortgages, farm mortgages, credit, and relief of personal distress. Today, the national government is an enormous institution with programs and policies reaching into every corner of American life. It oversees the nation's economy; it is the nation's largest employer; it provides citizens with a host of services; it controls the world's most formidable military establishment; and it regulates a wide range of social and commercial activities in which Americans engage.

Citizens are so dependent on government today that much of what they have come to take for granted—as, somehow, part of the natural environment—is in fact created by government. Take the example of a typical college student's day. Throughout the day, every student relies on a host of services and activities organized by national, state, and local government agencies. The extent of this dependence on government is illustrated by Box 1.1.

Government plays a role in everyone's activities and, by the same token, regulates almost everything we do. Figure 1.1 is a diagram of some of the governmental services received by and controls exerted on any recent college graduate. Some of these governmental activities are federal; others are the province of state and local governments.

When the financial crisis threatened the U.S. economy in 2008, Americans looked to the government to take extraordinary action. As Congress debated a $700 billion rescue plan, executives from failing companies, like the AIG insurance company, were called to testify.

BOX 1.1 The Presence of Government in the Daily Life of a Student at "State University"

TIME OF DAY	SCHEDULE
7:00 A.M.	Wake up. Standard time set by the national government.
7:10 A.M.	Shower. Water courtesy of local government, either a public entity or a regulated private company. Brush your teeth with toothpaste whose cavity-fighting claims have been verified by federal agency. Dry your hair with electric dryer, manufactured according to federal government agency guidelines.
7:30 A.M.	Have a bowl of cereal with milk for breakfast. "Nutrition Facts" on food labels are a federal requirement, pasteurization of milk required by state law, freshness dating on milk based on state and federal standards, recycling the empty cereal box and milk carton enabled by state or local laws.
8:30 A.M.	Drive or take public transportation to campus. Air bags and seat belts required by federal and state laws. Roads and bridges paid for by state and local governments, speed and traffic laws set by state and local governments, public transportation subsidized by all levels of government.
8:45 A.M.	Arrive on campus of large public university. Buildings are 70 percent financed by state taxpayers.
9:00 A.M.	First class: Chemistry 101. Tuition partially paid by a federal loan (more than half the cost of university instruction is paid for by taxpayers), chemistry lab paid for with grants from the National Science Foundation (a federal agency) and smaller grants from business corporations made possible by federal income tax deductions for charitable contributions.
Noon	Eat lunch. College cafeteria financed by state dormitory authority on land grant from federal Department of Agriculture.
2:00 P.M.	Second class: American Government 101 (your favorite class!). You may be taking this class because it's required by the state legislature or because it fulfills a university requirement.
4:00 P.M.	Third class: Computer lab. Free computers, software, and Internet access courtesy of state subsidies plus grants and discounts from IBM and Microsoft, the costs of which are deducted from their corporate income taxes; Internet built in part by federal government. Duplication of software protected by federal copyright laws.
6:00 P.M.	Eat dinner: hamburger and french fries. Meat inspected for bacteria by federal agencies.
7:00 P.M.	Work at part-time job at the campus library. Minimum wage set by federal government, books and journals in library paid for by state taxpayers.
10:00 P.M.	Go home. Street lighting paid for by county and city governments, police patrols by city government.
10:15 P.M.	Watch TV. Networks regulated by federal government, cable public-access channels required by city law. Weather forecast provided to broadcasters by a federal agency.
Midnight	Put out the garbage before going to bed. Garbage collected by city sanitation department, financed by "user charges."

Trust in Government

Ironically, even as popular dependence on it has grown, the American public's view of government has turned more sour. Public trust in government has declined, and Americans are now more likely to feel that they can do little to influence the government's actions. The decline in public trust among Americans is striking. In the early 1960s, three-quarters of Americans said they trusted government most of the time. By 1994, only one-quarter of Americans expressed trust in government; three-quarters stated that they did not trust government most of the time.[1] Different groups vary somewhat in their levels of trust: African Americans and Latinos express more confidence in the federal government than do whites. But even among the most supportive groups, more than half do not trust the government.[2] These developments are important because politically engaged citizens and public confidence in government are vital for the health of a democracy.

In the aftermath of the September 11 terrorist attacks, a number of studies reported a substantial increase in popular trust in government. For example, in October 2001, 60 percent of American college students surveyed said they trusted the government to "do the right thing" all or most of the time. Before September 11, only 36 percent expressed a similar view. In addition, 75 percent said they trusted the military, 69 percent expressed trust in the president, and 62 percent trusted Congress.[3] These views, expressed during a period of national crisis, may be indicative less of a renewed *trust* in government to do the right thing than of a fervent *hope* that it will. And, indeed, by July 2003, trust in government had returned to its pre–September 11 level, with only 36 percent of Americans indicating that they trusted the government most or all of the time (see Figure 1.2). During the same period, 48 percent said they would prefer a smaller government offering fewer services.[4] By 2007, trust in government had dropped even lower, with only 24 percent trusting the government in Washington "to do what is right" all or most of the time.[5] With the apparent waning of the emergency, mistrust of government was free to reassert itself.

By 2007, revelations about the faulty information that led up to the war in Iraq and ongoing concern about the war contributed to Americans' mistrust of government. In March 2007, 54 percent of those surveyed believed that the Bush administration had deliberately misled the American public about whether Iraq had weapons of mass destruction. In 2003, only 31 percent of Americans believed that the administration had misled the public. Mistrust about the origins of the war spilled over into public doubts about the information people were receiving about the progress of the war. In 2007, an NBC/Wall Street Journal Poll showed that only 28 percent of those surveyed believed that what they were hearing from the Bush administration about the situation in Iraq was mostly accurate.[6] Americans had mixed views about the financial bailout of 2008. Right after the Secretary of the Treasury, Hank Paulson, proposed the plan, a majority of the public thought it was the right thing to do. A few weeks later, however, opposition to the plan had mounted. Even those who believed the bailout was necessary were not happy about it: 60 percent reported being angry, according to a Pew Research Center poll. Despite the mixed feelings, a majority of those questioned expressed confidence that the government would be able to fix the economy.

Politics Today

What recent events have affected Americans' trust in government? Did the federal government's efforts to save the financial system in 2008 increase the public's trust in government?

Does it matter if Americans trust their government? For the most part, the answer is yes. As we have seen, most Americans rely on government for a wide range of services and laws that they simply take for granted. But long-term distrust in

FIGURE 1.1 ★ The Role of Government in Your Life

Government is a pervasive force in the lives of all Americans, especially at the state and local levels. Think of the many ways in which government affects your life every day.

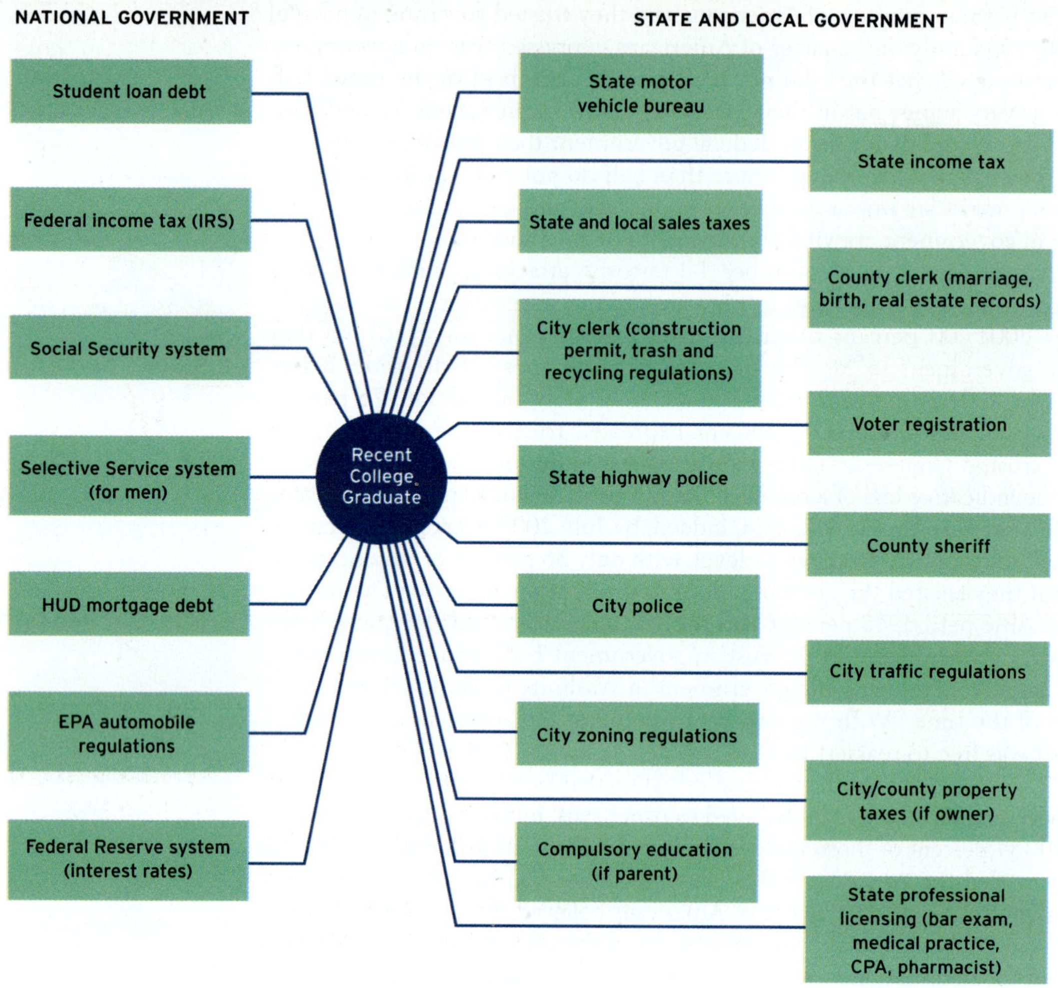

government can result in public refusal to pay taxes adequate to support such widely approved public activities. Low levels of confidence may also make it difficult for government to attract talented and effective workers to public service.[7] The weakening of government as a result of prolonged levels of distrust may ultimately harm our capacity to defend our national interest in the world economy and may jeopardize our national security. Likewise, a weak government can do little to assist citizens who need help in weathering periods of sharp economic or technological change.

FIGURE 1.2 ★ Trust in Government, 1958–2007

Participants in these polls were asked if they trusted the government to "do the right thing" always, most of the time, or only some of the time.

Since the 1960s, general levels of public trust in government have declined, though there was some increase in trust during the 1990s. What factors might help to account for changes in the public's trust in government? Why has confidence in government dropped again since September 11, 2001?

SOURCES: *The National Election Studies*, 1958–2004; and iPOLL Databank, www.ropercenter.uconn.edu/ipoll.html (accessed 2/25/08).

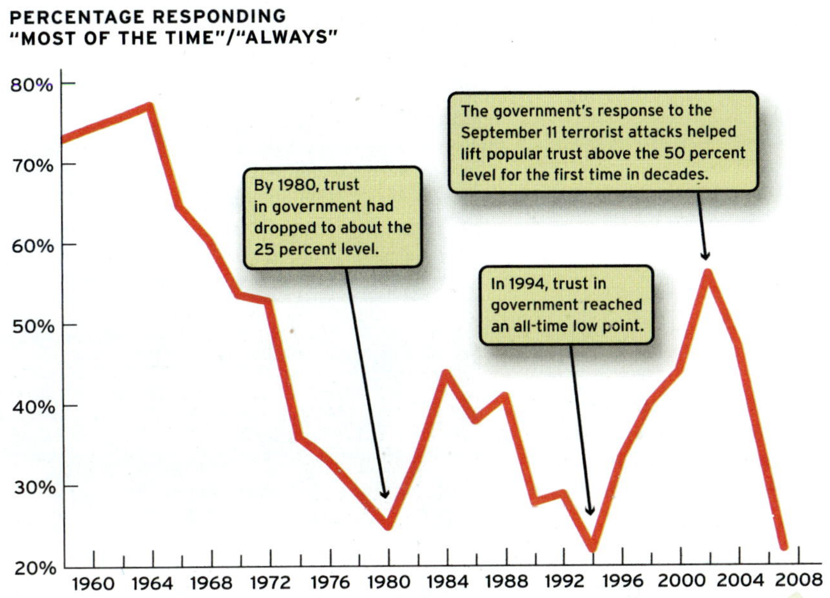

Political Efficacy

Another important trend in American views about government has been a declining sense of **political efficacy,** the belief that citizens can affect what government does, that they can take action to make government listen to them. In recent decades, the public belief that government is responsive to ordinary citizens has declined. In 2007, 62 percent of Americans said that elected officials don't care what people like them think; in 1960, only 25 percent felt so shut out of government. Accompanying this sense that ordinary people can't get heard is a growing belief—held by 56 percent of the public in 2007—that government is not run for the benefit of all the people. In 2007, 52 percent of the public disagreed with the idea that the "government is really run for the benefit of all the people."[8] These views are widely shared across the age spectrum.

political efficacy the ability to influence government and politics

This widely felt loss of political efficacy is bad news for American democracy. The feeling that you can't affect government decisions can lead to a self-perpetuating cycle of apathy, declining political participation, and withdrawal from political life. Why bother to participate if you believe it makes no difference? Yet the belief that you can be effective is the first step needed to influence government. Not every effort of ordinary citizens to influence government will succeed, but without any such efforts, government decisions will be made by a smaller and smaller circle of powerful people. Such loss of broad popular influence over government actions undermines the key feature of American democracy—government by the people.

In response to the terrorist attacks of September 11, 2001, Americans rallied around government officials and offered unprecedented support.

Citizenship: Knowledge and Participation

The first prerequisite to achieving an increased sense of political efficacy is knowledge. Political indifference is often simply a habit that stems from a lack of knowledge about how your interests are affected by politics and from a sense that you can do nothing to affect politics. But political efficacy is a self-fulfilling prophecy: if you think you cannot be effective, chances are you will never try. Most research suggests that people active in politics have a high sense of their efficacy. This means they believe they can make a difference—even if they do not win all the time. Most people do not want to be politically active every day of their lives, but it is essential to our political ideals that all citizens be informed and able to act.

Sadly, the state of political knowledge in the United States today is spotty. Most Americans know little about current issues or debates. Numerous surveys indicate that the majority of Americans know very little about their government or politics. For example, a 2007 poll showed that only 49 percent of Americans could identify Nancy Pelosi, the first female Speaker of the House of Representatives; only a paltry 15 percent could identify her Senate counterpart, Majority Leader Harry Reid. Celebrity politicians fare better, as the 93 percent name recognition of the California governor Arnold Schwarzenegger indicates (see Table 1.1). But rather than dwell on the widespread political ignorance of many Americans, we prefer to view this as an opportunity for the readers of this book. Those of you who make the effort to become among the knowledgeable few will be much better prepared to influence the political system regarding the issues and concerns that you care most about.

After September 11, many commentators noted a revival in Americans' sense of citizenship, as manifested by ubiquitous flag displays and other demonstrations of patriotic sentiment. There seems to be little doubt that millions of Americans

Following the 2003 Iraq war, Americans' trust in government declined sharply, as questions were raised about the Bush administration's justification for the war, and as American soldiers and Iraqi civilians continued to be killed. Many Americans complained that the government had no clear plan to end the fighting.

experienced a renewed sense of identification with their nation. Citizenship, however, has a broader meaning than just patriotism.

Beginning with the ancient Greeks, citizenship has meant membership in one's community. To the Greeks, citizenship entailed involvement in public discussion, debate, and activity designed to improve the welfare of the community. Our meaning for **citizenship** derives from the Greek ideal: enlightened political engagement.[9] To be politically engaged in a meaningful way, citizens require resources, especially political knowledge and information. Democracy functions best when citizens are informed. But to be a citizen in the full sense, as understood first by the ancient Greeks, requires more than an occasional visit to a voting booth. A true citizen must have the knowledge needed to participate in political debate.

citizenship informed and active membership in a political community

The Necessity of Political Knowledge

Political knowledge means more than having a few opinions to offer the pollster or to guide your decisions in a voting booth. It is important to know the rules and strategies that govern political institutions and the principles on which they are based, but it is more important to know them in ways that relate to your own interests. Citizens need knowledge in order to assess their interests and to know when to act on them. Knowledgeable citizens are more attentive to and more engaged in politics because they understand how and why politics is relevant to their lives.

Without political knowledge, no citizen can be aware of her interests or stake in a political dispute. In the year preceding the 2008 presidential election, for example, many of the prospective Democratic candidates presented rather detailed proposals on ways to change the current American health care system. How many voters paid enough attention to the discussion to be able to distinguish meaningfully among the various proposals and their implications? Did you attempt to ascertain whether you and your family would be better off under the health care system envisioned by Clinton, Obama, or Edwards rather than the system favored by Giuliani,

TABLE 1.1 ★ What Americans Know about Government

RESPONDENTS WHO:	PERCENTAGE
Knew that only citizens can vote in federal elections	48
Could identify two members of the president's cabinet and name their department	46
Knew how much of a majority is required for the U.S. Senate and House to override a presidential veto	38
Felt that in national politics, the Republican Party is more conservative than the Democratic Party	47
Felt that the government spends more on social security than foreign aid	18
Could identify California Governor Arnold Schwarzenegger	93
Could identify House Speaker Nancy Pelosi	49
Could identify Senate Majority Leader Harry Reid	15

SOURCES: Center for Information and Research on Civic Learning and Engagement, www.civicyouth.org/PopUps/2006_CPHS_Toplines.pdf; and Pew Research Center for People and the Press, http://people-press.org/reports/display.php3?ReportID-319 (accessed 2/4/08).

Romney, or McCain? How could you participate intelligently without this knowledge? Interestingly, various public and private interest groups devote enormous time and energy to understanding alternative policy proposals and their implications so they will know whom to support. Interest groups understand something that every citizen should also understand: effective participation requires knowledge.

Citizens also need political knowledge to identify the best ways to act on their interests. If your street is rendered impassable by snow, what can you do? Is snow removal the responsibility of the federal government? Is it a state or municipal responsibility? Knowing that you have a stake in a clear road does not help much if you do not know that snow removal is a city or a county responsibility and you cannot identify the municipal agency that deals with the problem. Americans are fond of complaining that government is not responsive to their needs, but in some cases, it is possible that citizens simply lack the information they need to present their problems to the appropriate government officials.

Citizens need political knowledge, as well, to ascertain what they cannot or should not ask of politicians and the government. We need to balance our need for protection and service with our equally pressing need for liberty. Particularly during periods when the nation's safety is threatened, Americans may be inclined to accept increased governmental intrusion into their lives in the name of national security. Since 2001, for example, Americans have accepted unprecedented levels of governmental surveillance and the erosion of some traditional restrictions on police powers in the name of preventing terrorism. It remains to be seen whether this exchange of liberty for the promise of security was a wise choice. Political knowledge includes knowing the limits on, as well as the possibilities for pursuing,

For Critical Analysis

Many studies seem to show that most Americans know very little about government and politics. Can we have democratic government without knowledgeable and aware citizens?

Political Knowledge and Comedy Television

Political knowledge is at the core of a healthy democracy. Historically, newspapers, news magazines, television news programs, and speeches and debates have been the most common sources for political information. However, in recent years more Americans—especially young Americans—report receiving political information from entertainment programs such as late-night comedy shows.

A report released by the Pew Research Center in 2004 showed that 21 percent of young people (aged eighteen to twenty-nine) reported regularly learning about the 2004 presidential campaign from comedy shows such as *The Daily Show with Jon Stewart* and *Saturday Night Live.* When these findings caught the public's attention, many journalists were openly critical of the apparent trend. Ted Koppel stated, "A lot of television viewers, more, quite frankly, than I'm comfortable with, get their news from the comedy channel on a program called *The Daily Show.*"

Many critics of the trend are concerned that the information conveyed through late-night comedy shows is not a good basis for political decision making. Although one-liners by Jay Leno and David Letterman do cover politics, these jokes tend to focus on the personal weaknesses of public officials rather than on complex issues of public policy.[a] The late-night comedians themselves generally do not accept the premise that they are the main source of political information for some young people. In October 2004, Jon Stewart explained, "The truth is I know most kids are not [getting their news from us] because you can't—because we just don't do it."

But could political content on comedy shows provide at least some information to viewers who are not receiving political news elsewhere? Scholars such as Matthew Baum argue that this "piggybacking" of politics on top of entertainment content does have the effect of informing typically apolitical viewers. Some research has shown that for late-night comedy viewers without a lot of political knowledge, watching these comedy shows can shape their impressions of the candidates. For example, one study found that viewers of late-night comedy shows who did not know a lot about politics rated Al Gore as less inspiring over the course of the 2000 campaign in keeping with his cardboard caricature from late-night jokes.[b]

Another way of assessing learning from late-night comedy is by testing the political knowledge of people who watch late-night comedy shows. A 2007 study by the Pew Research Center for People and the Press found that the audience of *The Daily Show with Jon Stewart* and *The Colbert Report* tied with the audiences of major newspaper Web sites as the most knowledgeable about politics and world affairs, with 54 percent of their audiences falling into a "high knowledge group." This compares with 34 percent for network morning shows, 38 percent for network evening news audiences, and 43 percent for local daily newspaper audiences.

The question of whether or not late-night comedy shows inform and influence viewers is illustrative of a larger phenomenon in the political-information environment—the blurring of the lines between entertainment and information. Popular culture has always been a part of political life, from political cartoons to movies about war. But in today's complex media environment, popular culture and politics are more intertwined than ever. From *South Park* to *The West Wing*, Rush Limbaugh to Michael Moore, YouTube to Facebook, a discussion about contemporary American politics would be incomplete without considering the role played by popular culture.

FOR CRITICAL ANALYSIS

1. Could the political content on late-night comedy television have a beneficial effect on political knowledge?
2. Does the blurring of the line between news and entertainment mean Americans are less politically engaged or more so?

a. D. Niven, S. R. Lichter, and D. Amundson, "The Political Content of Late Night Comedy," *Press/Politics* 8 (2003), pp. 118–33.

b. Dannagal Goldthwaite Young, "Late Night Comedy in Election 2000: Its Influence on Candidate Trait Ratings and the Moderating Effects of Political Knowledge and Partisanship," *Journal of Broadcasting and Electronic Media* 48(1) (2004), pp. 1–22.

one's own individual interests through political action. This is, perhaps, the most difficult form of political knowledge to acquire.

The rest of this chapter will look at the forms of political knowledge that we believe are most critical for a citizen to possess. In the next section, we will examine the principles of government and politics. Following that, we will review the democratic principles on which the United States is based and assess how well American government fulfills these principles. We will conclude with suggestions of what you and other ordinary citizens can do to become more knowledgeable and more engaged.

Government

government institutions and procedures through which a territory and its people are ruled

Government is the term generally used to describe the formal institutions through which a land and its people are ruled. To govern is to rule. A government may be as simple as a tribal council that meets occasionally to advise the chief, or as complex as its elaborate vast establishment, with procedures, laws, and bureaucracies. In the history of civilization, governments have not been difficult to establish. There have been thousands of them. The hard part is establishing a government that lasts. Even more difficult is developing a stable government that is compatible with liberty, equality, and democracy.

Is Government Needed?

Americans have always harbored some suspicion of government and have wondered how extensive a role it should play in their lives. Thomas Jefferson famously observed that the best government was one that "governed least." Generally speaking, a government is needed to provide those services, sometimes called "public goods," that all citizens need but are not likely to be able to provide adequately for themselves. These might include defense against foreign aggression, maintenance of public order, enforcement of contractual obligations and property rights, and a guarantee of some measure of social justice. The precise extent to which government involvement in our society is needed has been debated throughout our history and will continue to be a central focus of political contention in America.

autocracy a form of government in which a single individual—a king, queen, or dictator—rules

oligarchy a form of government in which a small group—landowners, military officers, or wealthy merchants—controls most of the governing decisions

democracy a system of rule that permits citizens to play a significant part in the governmental process, usually through the election of key public officials

Forms of Government

Governments vary in their structure, in their size, and in the way they operate. Two questions are of special importance in determining how governments differ: Who governs? And how much government control is permitted?

Some nations are governed by a single individual—a king or dictator, for example. This state of affairs is called **autocracy.** Where a small group—perhaps landowners, military officers, or wealthy merchants—controls most of the governing decisions, that government is said to be an **oligarchy.** If more people participate and have some influence over decision making, that government is a **democracy.**

Governments also vary considerably in terms of how they govern. In the United States and a small number of other nations, governments are limited as to what they are permitted to control (substantive limits), as well as how they go about it (procedural limits). Governments that are limited in this way are called **constitutional governments,** or liberal governments. In other nations, including many in Europe as well as in South America, Asia, and Africa, though the law imposes few real limits, the government is nevertheless kept in check by other political and social institutions that it is unable to control and must come to terms with—such as autonomous territories, an organized religion, organized business groups, or organized labor unions. Such governments are generally called **authoritarian.** In a third group of nations, including the Soviet Union under Joseph Stalin, Nazi Germany, and perhaps prewar Japan and Italy, governments not only are free of legal limits but also seek to eliminate those organized social groups that might challenge or limit their authority. These governments typically attempt to dominate or control every sphere of political, economic, and social life and, as a result, are called **totalitarian.**

constitutional government a system of rule in which formal and effective limits are placed on the powers of the government

authoritarian government a system of rule in which the government recognizes no formal limits but may nevertheless be restrained by the power of other social institutions

totalitarian government a system of rule in which the government recognizes no formal limits on its power and seeks to absorb or eliminate other social institutions that might challenge it

Americans have the good fortune to live in a nation in which limits are placed on what governments can do and how they can do it. But such constitutional democracies are relatively rare in today's world; it is estimated that only twenty or so of the world's nearly 200 governments could be included in this category. And constitutional democracies were unheard of before the modern era. Prior to the eighteenth and nineteenth centuries, governments seldom sought—and rarely received—the support of their ordinary subjects. The available evidence strongly suggests that the ordinary people had little love for the government or for the social order. After all, they had no stake in it. They equated government with the police officer, the bailiff, and the tax collector.[10]

Beginning in the seventeenth century, in a handful of Western nations, two important changes began to take place in the character and conduct of government. First, governments began to acknowledge formal limits on their power. Second, a small number of governments began to provide ordinary citizens with a formal voice in public affairs—through the vote. Obviously, the desirability of limits on government and the expansion of popular influence were at the heart of the American Revolution in 1776. "No taxation without representation," as we shall see in Chapter 2, was hotly debated from the beginning of the Revolution through the Founding in 1789. But even before the Revolution, a tradition of limiting government and expanding participation in the political process had developed throughout western Europe.

Limiting Government

The key force behind the imposition of limits on government power was a new social class, the bourgeoisie, which became an important political force in the sixteenth and seventeenth centuries. *Bourgeois* is a French word for "freeman of the city," or *bourg.* Being part of the bourgeoisie later became associated with being "middle class" and with being in commerce or industry. In order to gain a share of control of government, joining or even displacing the kings, aristocrats, and gentry who had dominated government for centuries, the bourgeoisie sought to change existing institutions—especially parliaments—into instruments of real political participation. Parliaments had existed for centuries, but were generally aristocratic institutions. The bourgeoisie embraced parliaments as means by which they could exert the weight of their superior numbers and growing economic advantage against their aristocratic rivals. At the same time, the bourgeoisie sought to place

America's founders were influenced by the English thinker John Locke (1632–1704). Locke argued that governments need the consent of the people.

John Stuart Mill (1806–1873) presented a ringing defense of individual freedom in his famous treatise On Liberty. *Mill's work influenced Americans' evolving ideas about the relationship between government and the individual.*

politics conflict over the leadership, structure, and policies of governments

restraints on the capacity of governments to threaten these economic and political interests by placing formal or constitutional limits on governmental power.

Although motivated primarily by the need to protect and defend their own interests, the bourgeoisie advanced many of the principles that became the central underpinnings of individual liberty for all citizens—freedom of speech, freedom of assembly, freedom of conscience, and freedom from arbitrary search and seizure. The work of political theorists such as John Locke (1632–1704) and John Stuart Mill (1806–1873) helped shape these ideas about liberty and political rights. However, it is important to note that the bourgeoisie generally did not favor democracy as we know it. They were advocates of electoral and representative institutions, but they favored property requirements and other restrictions so as to limit participation to the middle and upper classes. Yet once these institutions of politics and the protection of the right to engage in politics were established, it was difficult to limit them to the bourgeoisie.

Access to Government: The Expansion of Participation

The expansion of participation from the bourgeoisie to ever-larger segments of society took two paths. In some nations, popular participation was expanded by the crown or the aristocracy, which ironically saw common people as potential political allies against the bourgeoisie. Thus in nineteenth-century Prussia, for example, it was the emperor and his great minister Otto von Bismarck who expanded popular participation in order to build political support among the lower orders.

In other nations, participation expanded because competing segments of the bourgeoisie sought to gain political advantage by reaching out and mobilizing the support of working- and lower-class groups that craved the opportunity to take part in politics—"lining up the unwashed," as one American historian put it.[11] To be sure, excluded groups often agitated for greater participation. But seldom was such agitation, by itself, enough to secure the right to participate. Usually, expansion of voting rights resulted from a combination of pressure from below and help from above.

The gradual expansion of voting rights by groups hoping to derive some political advantage has been typical of American history. After the Civil War, one of the chief reasons that Republicans moved to enfranchise newly freed slaves was to use the support of the former slaves to maintain Republican control over the defeated southern states. Similarly, in the early twentieth century, upper-middle-class Progressives advocated women's suffrage because they believed that women were likely to support the reforms espoused by the Progressive movement.

Influencing the Government through Participation: Politics

Expansion of participation means that more and more people have a legal right to take part in politics. *Politics* is an important term. In its broadest sense, "politics" refers to conflicts over the character, membership, and policies of any organization to which people belong. As Harold Lasswell, a famous political scientist, once put it, politics is the struggle over "who gets what, when, how."[12] Although politics is a phenomenon that can be found in any organization, our concern in this book is narrower. Here, **politics** will be used to refer only to conflicts and struggles over the leadership, structure, and policies of governments. The goal of politics, as we define it, is to have a share or a say in the composition of the government's leadership, how the government is organized, or what its policies are going to be. Having a share is called having **power** or influence.

power influence over a government's leadership, organization, or policies

Politics can take many forms, including everything from sending letters to government officials to voting, lobbying legislators on behalf of particular programs, and participating in protest marches and even violent demonstrations. A system of government that gives citizens a regular opportunity to elect the top government officials is usually called a **representative democracy** or **republic.** A system that permits citizens to vote directly on laws and policies is often called a **direct democracy.** At the national level, America is a representative democracy in which citizens select government officials but do not vote on legislation. Some states and cities, however, have provisions for direct legislation through popular initiative and ballot referendum. These procedures allow citizens to collect petitions requiring an issue to be brought directly to the voters for a decision. In 2008, more than 150 initiatives appeared on state ballots. Recent initiatives have dealt with matters ranging from taxes and education to animal cruelty and affirmative action. Many hot-button issues are decided by initiatives. For example, Michigan voters approved a measure that prohibits public institutions such as the University of Michigan from giving preferential treatment on the basis of race; in Colorado, voters passed a referendum that called on the state to sue the federal government to enforce immigration laws. Often broad public campaigns promote controversial referenda, attempting to persuade voters to change existing laws. For example, a campaign by the American Civil Liberties Union and other groups helped persuade Rhode Island voters to support a measure allowing people with a felony conviction to vote as soon as they are released from prison. The initiative changed the existing law, which barred those with a felony conviction from voting until they had completed probation or parole. Other measures, such as animal-rights proposals, reach the ballot due to a small but dedicated set of activists. One example occurred in Arizona, where voters approved an initiative guaranteeing a minimum living space for pregnant pigs and cows.

representative democracy/republic a system of government in which the populace selects representatives, who play a significant role in governmental decision making

direct democracy a system of rule that permits citizens to vote directly on laws and policies

Groups and organized interests do not vote (although their members do), but they certainly do participate in politics. Their political activities usually consist of such endeavors as providing funds for candidates, lobbying, and trying to influence public opinion. The pattern of struggles among interests is called group politics, or **pluralism.** Americans have always been ambivalent about pluralist politics. On one hand, the right of groups to press their views and compete for influence in the government is the essence of liberty. On the other hand, Americans often fear that organized groups may sometimes exert too much influence, advancing special interests at the expense of larger public interests. We will return to this problem in Chapter 11.

pluralism the theory that all interests are and should be free to compete for influence in the government. The outcome of this competition is compromise and moderation

Sometimes, of course, politics does not take place through formal channels at all but instead involves direct action. Direct-action politics can include either violent politics or civil disobedience, both of which attempt to shock rulers into behaving more responsibly. Direct action can also be a form of revolutionary politics, which rejects the system entirely and attempts to replace it with a new ruling group and a new set of rules. In recent years in the United States, groups ranging from animal-rights activists to right-to-life advocates to protesters against the war in Iraq have used direct action to underline their demands. Direct political action is protected by the U.S. Constitution. The country's Founders knew that the right to protest is essential to the maintenance of political freedom, even where the ballot box is available.

Who Are Americans?

While American democracy aims to give the people a voice in government, the meaning of "we the people" has changed over time. Who are Americans? Over the course of American history, politicians, religious leaders, prominent scholars, and ordinary Americans have puzzled over and fought about the answer to this fundamental question. It is not surprising that such a simple question could provoke so much conflict: since the Founding, the American population has been a moving target, growing from 3.9 million in 1790, the year of the first official census, to 305 million in 2008 (see Figure 1.3). As the American population has grown, it has become more diverse on nearly every dimension imaginable.[13]

At the time of the Founding, when the United States consisted of thirteen states arrayed along the Eastern Seaboard, 81 percent of Americans traced their roots to Europe, mostly England and northern Europe; nearly one in five were of African origin, the vast majority of whom had been brought to the United States against their wills to work as slaves.[14] Only 1.5 percent of the black population was free. There was also an unknown number of Native Americans, the original inhabitants of the land, not counted by the census because the government did not consider them Americans. The first estimates of Native Americans and Hispanics in the mid-1800s showed that each group made up less than 1 percent of the total population.[15]

Flash forward to 1900. The country, now stretched out across the continent, had a sharply altered racial and ethnic composition. Waves of immigrants, mainly from Europe, boosted the population to 76 million. In 1900, the United States was predominantly composed of whites of European ancestry; the black population stood

FIGURE 1.3 ★
U.S. Population, 1790–2008

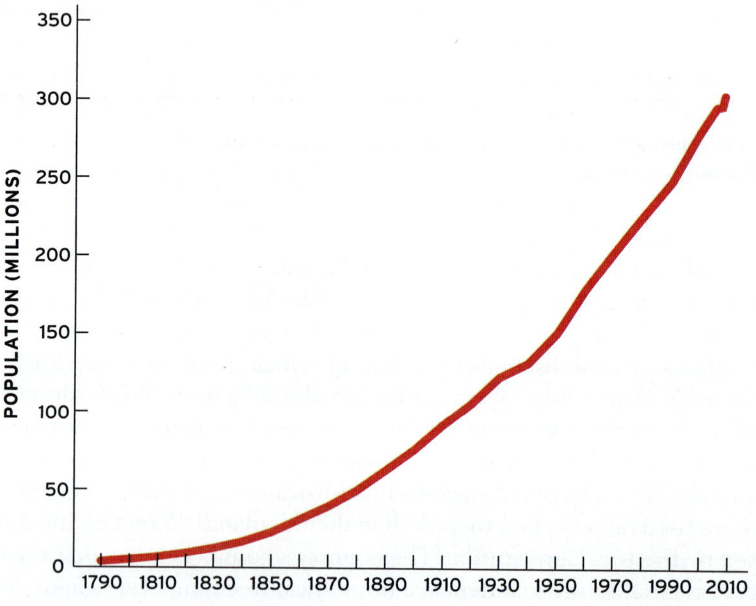

SOURCES: U.S. Census Bureau, www.census.gov/compendia/statab/tables/08s0001.pdf; www.census.gov/compendia/statab/tables/08s0002.pdf; and http://factfinder.census.gov/servlet/SAFFPopulation?_submenuID=population_0&_sse=on (accessed 3/20/08).

Native American societies, with their own forms of government, had existed for thousands of years before the first European settlers arrived. By the time this photo of Red Cloud and other Sioux warriors was taken around 1870, Native Americans made up about 1 percent of the American population.

at 12 percent. Residents who traced their origin to Latin America or Asia each accounted for less than 1 percent of the entire population (see Figure 1.4).[16] Although principally of European origin, the American population had become much more ethnically diverse as immigrants, first from Germany, then Ireland, and finally from southern and eastern Europe, made their way to the United States. The large number of new immigrants was reflected in the high proportion of foreign-born people in the United States: the foreign-born population reached its height at 14.7 percent in 1910.[17]

FIGURE 1.4 ★
Race in the United States, 1900 and 2007

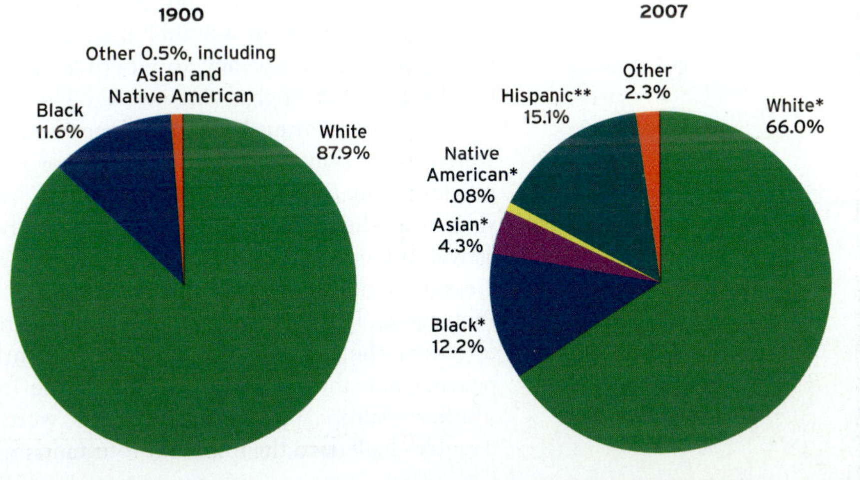

*Not Hispanic.
**May be of any race.
SOURCES: U.S. Census Bureau, www2.census.gov/prod2/decennial/documents/33973538v2p1ch2.pdf; and www.census.gov/popest/national/asrh/NC-EST2007-srh.html (accessed 7/13/08).

Millions of immigrants from Europe came to the United States in the early 1900s. Most passed through New York's Ellis Island, where they were checked for diseases before being admitted. Today, many Americans trace their family history to an immigrant who passed through Ellis Island.

Immigration and Ethnic Diversity

As the European-origin population grew more diverse, anxiety about Americans' ethnic identity mounted. In 1900, the author of a *New York Times* front-page article answered his own question—"Are Americans an Anglo-Saxon People?"—in the affirmative.[18] But the growing numbers of immigrants from southern and eastern Europe who were crowding into American cities spurred heated debates about how long Anglo-Saxons could dominate. Much as today, politicians and scholars argued about whether the country could absorb such large numbers of immigrants. Concerns ranged from whether their political and social values were compatible with American democracy, to whether they would learn English, to alarm about the diseases they might bring into the United States.

The distinct ethnic backgrounds and language differences of the new immigrants were not the only characteristics that worried the Anglo-Saxon natives; immigrant religious affiliations also aroused concern. The first immigrants to the United States were overwhelmingly Protestant, many of them fleeing religious persecution. The arrival of Germans and Irish in the mid-1800s began to shift that balance with increasing numbers of Catholics. Even so, in 1900, four in five Americans were still Protestants. The large-scale immigration of the early twentieth century threatened to reduce the ranks of Protestants significantly. The eastern European immigrants pouring into the country, especially those from Russia, were heavily Jewish; the southern Europeans, especially Italians, were Catholic. A more religiously diverse country challenged the implicit Protestantism embedded in many aspects of Ameri-

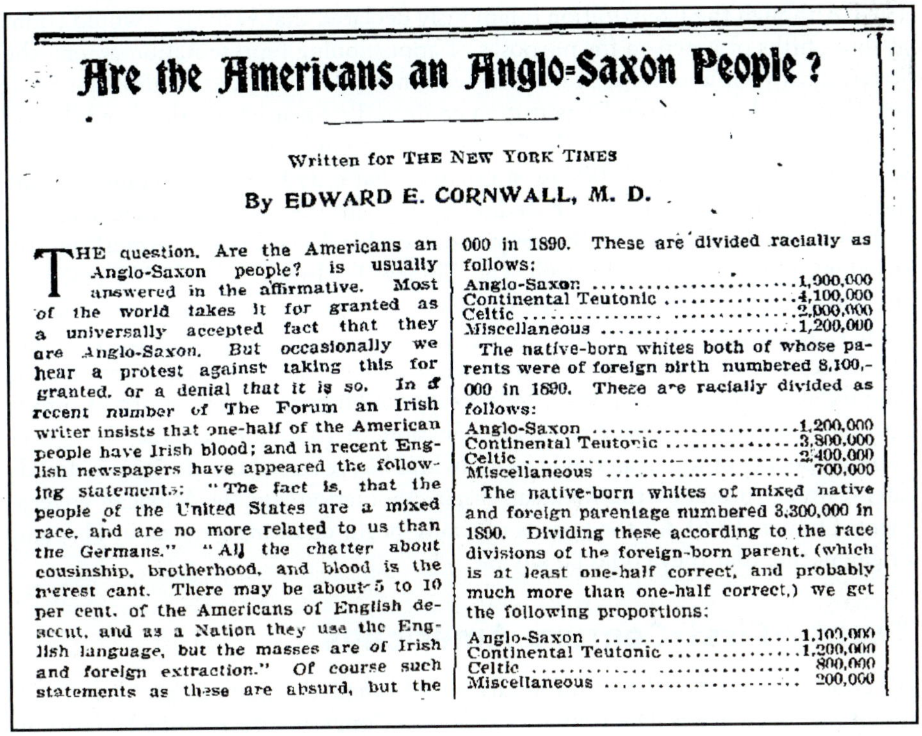
Are the Americans an Anglo-Saxon People?

Written for THE NEW YORK TIMES

By EDWARD E. CORNWALL, M. D.

THE question, Are the Americans an Anglo-Saxon people? is usually answered in the affirmative. Most of the world takes it for granted as a universally accepted fact that they are Anglo-Saxon. But occasionally we hear a protest against taking this for granted, or a denial that it is so. In a recent number of The Forum an Irish writer insists that one-half of the American people have Irish blood; and in recent English newspapers have appeared the following statements: "The fact is, that the people of the United States are a mixed race, and are no more related to us than the Germans." "All the chatter about cousinship, brotherhood, and blood is the merest cant. There may be about 5 to 10 per cent. of the Americans of English descent, and as a Nation they use the English language, but the masses are of Irish and foreign extraction." Of course such statements as these are absurd, but the

000 in 1890. These are divided racially as follows:

Anglo-Saxon	1,900,000
Continental Teutonic	4,100,000
Celtic	2,000,000
Miscellaneous	1,200,000

The native-born whites both of whose parents were of foreign birth numbered 8,100,000 in 1890. These are racially divided as follows:

Anglo-Saxon	1,200,000
Continental Teutonic	3,800,000
Celtic	2,400,000
Miscellaneous	700,000

The native-born whites of mixed native and foreign parentage numbered 3,300,000 in 1890. Dividing these according to the race divisions of the foreign-born parent, (which is at least one-half correct, and probably much more than one-half correct,) we get the following proportions:

Anglo-Saxon	1,100,000
Continental Teutonic	1,200,000
Celtic	800,000
Miscellaneous	200,000

The influx of immigrants from southern and eastern Europe set off debates about Americans' ethnic identity and social and political values. This New York Times *article from 1900 argued that Americans were an Anglo-Saxon people, and in the 1920s strict quotas were placed on immigration from areas other than northern Europe.*

can public life. For example, religious diversity introduced new conflicts into public schooling, as Catholics sought public funding for parochial schools and dissident Protestant sects lobbied to eliminate Bible reading and prayer in the schools.

Anxieties about immigration sparked intense debate about whether the numbers of immigrants entering the country should be limited and whether restrictions should be placed on which types of immigrants should be granted entry. After World War I, Congress responded to the fears swirling around immigration with new laws that sharply limited the number who could enter the country each year. Not only did Congress limit the number of new immigrants, it also established a new National Origins Quota System, based on the nation's population in 1890 before the wave of immigrants from eastern and southern Europe arrived.[19] Supporters of ethnic quotas hoped to turn back the clock and return to an earlier America in which northern Europeans dominated. The new system set up a hierarchy of admissions: northern European countries received generous quotas for new immigrants, whereas eastern and southern European countries were granted very small quotas. These restrictions ratcheted down the numbers of immigrants so that by 1970, the foreign-born population in the United States reached an all-time low of 5 percent.

Immigration and Race

Official efforts to use racial and ethnic criteria to restrict the American population were not new but had been used to draw boundaries around the American community from the start. The very first census, as we have seen, did not count Native Americans; in fact, Native Americans were not granted the right to vote until

1924. Although the Constitution infamously declared that each slave would count as three-fifths of a person for purposes of apportioning representation among the states, most people of African descent were not officially citizens until the Fourteenth Amendment to the Constitution conferred citizenship on the freed slaves.

Over half a century earlier, the federal government had sought to limit the nonwhite population with a 1790 law stipulating that only free whites could become naturalized citizens. Not until 1870 did Congress lift the ban on the naturalization of nonwhites. In addition to the restrictions on blacks and Native Americans, restrictions applied to Asians as well. The Chinese Exclusion Act of 1882 outlawed the entry of Chinese laborers to the United States. These provisions were not lifted until 1943, when China became America's ally during World War II. Additional barriers enacted after World War I meant that virtually no Asians entered the country as immigrants until the 1940s. People of Hispanic origin do not fit simply into the American system of racial classification. In 1930, for example, the census counted people of Mexican origin as nonwhite but reversed this decision a decade later—after protests by the Mexican-origin population and the Mexican government. Only in 1970 did the census officially begin counting persons of Hispanic origin, noting that they could be any race.[20]

Twenty-First-Century Americans

By 2000, immigration had profoundly transformed the nation's racial and ethnic profile once again. The primary cause was Congress's decision in 1965 to lift the tight restrictions of the 1920s, allowing for much expanded immigration from Asia and Latin America. One consequence of the shift has been the growth in the Hispanic, or Latino, population. Census estimates for 2007 show that the total Hispanic proportion of the population is now 15 percent; the black or African American population is under 13 percent of the total population. Asians made up 4 percent of the population (see Figure 1.4). European Americans accounted for only two-thirds of the population in 2007—their lowest share ever. Moreover, 1.6 percent of the population now identified itself as of "two or more races," a new category that the census added in 2000.[21] Although it is only a small percentage of the population, the biracial category points toward a future in which the traditional labels of racial identification may be blurring, marking a major shift in the long-standing American tradition of strict racial categorization. The blurring of racial categories poses challenges to a host of policies—many of them put in place to remedy past discrimination—that rely on racial counts of the population.

Politics Today

In 2008, most Americans, including the leading presidential candidates from both parties, agreed that the country needed new immigration laws. How does immigration today compare to immigration in 1900?

Large-scale immigration means that many more residents are foreign born. In 2005, 12 percent of the population was born outside the United States, a figure comparable to foreign-born rates at the turn of the previous century. Over half of the foreign born came from Latin America: one in ten from the Caribbean, nearly four in ten from Central America (including Mexico), and 6 percent from South America. Those born in Asia constituted the next largest group, making up one quarter of foreign-born residents. In sharp contrast to the immigration patterns of a century earlier, fewer immigrants came from Europe (see Figure 1.5). By 2004, only 14 percent of those born outside the United States came from Europe.[22]

These figures represent only legally authorized immigrants. One new feature of American society in recent years is the very large number of immigrants who live in the country without legal authorization. Estimates put the number of unauthorized immigrants at 11.5 to 12 million, the majority of whom are from Mexico and

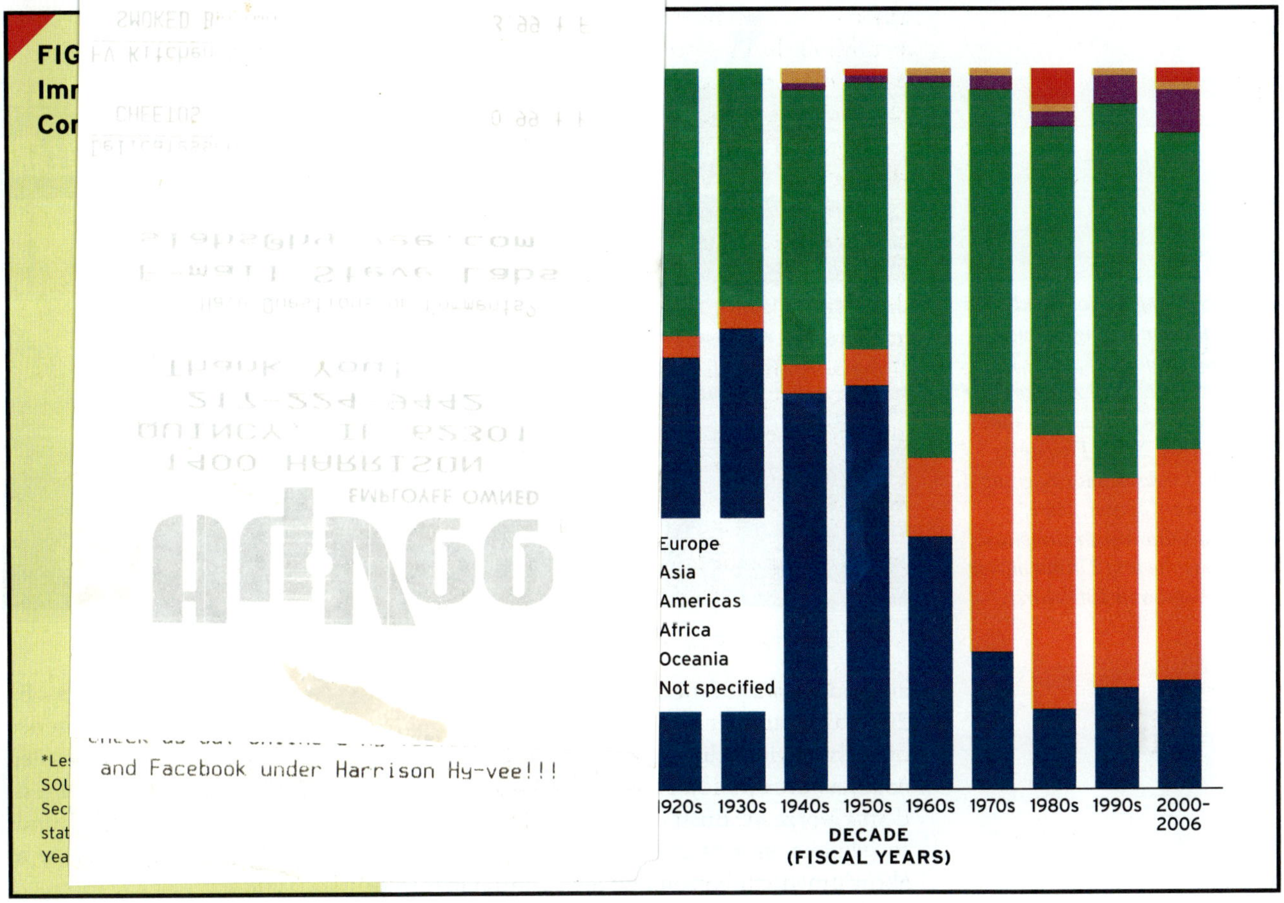

Central America.[23] The large unauthorized population has become a flashpoint for controversy as states and cities have passed a variety of conflicting laws. Some states have offered driver's licenses to undocumented immigrants, while others have sought to bar them from public services, such as education and emergency health care, both of which are constitutionally guaranteed to unauthorized immigrants.[24] The presence of such a significant proportion of residents who are barred from participating in American politics also poses troubling questions about the health of our democracy.

The new patterns of immigration combined with differences in birth rates and underlying social changes to alter the religious affiliations of Americans. In 1900, 80 percent of the American population was Protestant; by 2000 only a little over half of Americans identified themselves as Protestants.[25] Catholics now made up a quarter of the population, and Jews accounted for close to 2 percent. A small Muslim population had also grown, with nearly one half of 1 percent of the population. One of the most important shifts in religious affiliation during the latter half of the twentieth century was the percentage of people who professed no organized religion. In 2006, 12 percent of the population was not affiliated with an organized church. These changes suggest an important shift in American religious identity: although the United States thinks of itself as a "Judeo-Christian" nation—

In 1965, Congress loosened restrictions on immigration, allowing millions of people from Latin America and Asia to enter the country in the decades that followed. By 2002, Hispanics were the largest minority group in the United States. Here, Antonio Villaraigosa campaigns to become the first Latino mayor of Los Angeles in 130 years.

and indeed was 95 percent Protestant, Catholic, or Jewish from 1900 to 1968—by 2006, this number had fallen to only 83 percent of the population.[26] The presence of such religious diversity and a growing secular population sets the stage for deep conflicts over policy. For example, many religious groups welcomed former President George W. Bush's faith-based initiative, which sought to channel more funds to religious groups to administer social services. Secularists viewed the policy as abrogating the division between church and state.

As America grew and its population expanded and diversified, the country's age profile shifted with it. In 1900 only 4 percent of the population was over sixty-five. As life expectancy increased, the number of older Americans grew with it: by 2006, 12 percent of the population was over sixty-five (see Figure 1.6). The percent of children under the age of eighteen also changed; in 1900 this group comprised 43 percent of the American population; by 2006, children eighteen and under had fallen to less than a quarter of the population.[27] Another way to think about the age of Americans is that in 1800, the median age of the population was 16 years; by 1900, it was 22.9 years, and by 2000 it was 35.3 years. Even though the average age of Americans has grown older, Americans tend to be younger than citizens of many industrialized countries, mainly because of the large immigrant population in the United States. In most European countries, the median age was above forty in 2000.[28] But an aging population poses challenges to the United States as well. As the elderly population grows and the working aged population shrinks, questions arise about how we will fund programs for the elderly, such as Social Security.

Over the course of the nation's history, Americans have changed in other ways as well, moving from mostly rural settings and small towns to large urban areas. The idealization of country life in American culture traces its roots to the long period in which the majority of Americans lived in rural areas. Before 1920 less than half the population lived in urban areas; today three-quarters of Americans do.[29] Critics charge that the American political system—created when America was a

FIGURE 1.6 ★
Americans Aged 65 and Older

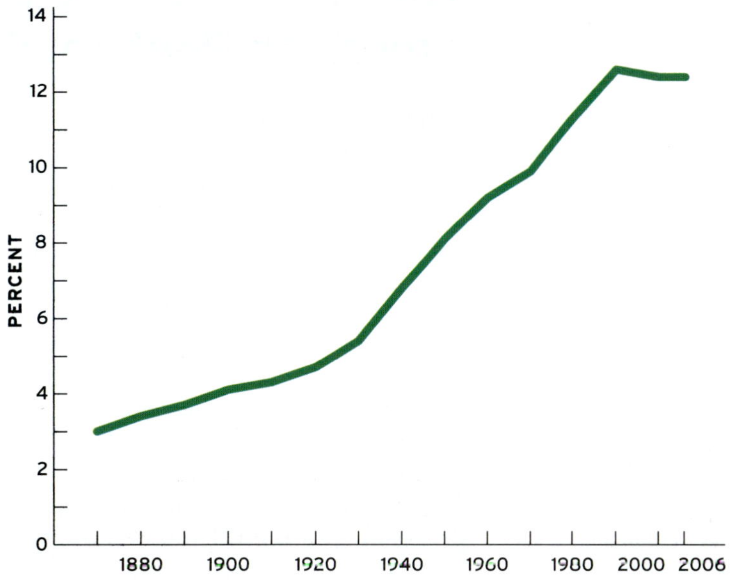

SOURCES: U.S. Census Bureau, www2.census.gov/prod2/statcomp/documents/CT1970p1-02.pdf; www.census.gov/prod/2002pubs/censr-4.pdf; and www.census.gov/compendia/statab/tables/08s0006.pdf (accessed 3/20/08)

largely rural society—underrepresents urban areas. The constitutional provision allocating each state two senators, for example, overrepresents sparsely populated rural states and underrepresents urban states, where the population is far more concentrated. In addition to becoming more urban over time, the American population has shifted regionally. During the past fifty years especially, many Americans left the Northeast and Midwest and moved to the South and Southwest. As congressional seats have been reapportioned to reflect the population shift, many problems that particularly plague the Midwest and Northeast—such as the decline of manufacturing jobs—receive less attention in national politics.

The shifting contours of the American people have regularly raised challenging questions about our politics and governing arrangements. Population growth has spurred politically charged debates about how the population should be apportioned among congressional districts. These conflicts have major implications for the representation of different regions of the country and for the balance of representation between urban and rural areas. Population growth has also transformed the close democratic relationship between congressional representatives and their constituents envisioned by the framers. For example, the framers stipulated that the number of representatives in the House of Representatives "shall not exceed one for every thirty Thousand . . ." constituents; today the average member of Congress represents 646,952 constituents.[30] Immigration and the cultural and religious changes it entails provoked heated disputes a hundred years ago and sparks passionate debate today. The different languages and customs that immigrants bring to the United States trigger fears that the country is changing in ways that may undermine American values and alter fundamental identities. The large number of unauthorized immigrants in the country today makes these anxieties even more acute. Yet a changing population has been one of the constants of American history. Indeed, each generation has confronted the myriad political challenges associated with answering anew "Who are Americans?"

Thinking Critically about American Political Culture

Underlying and framing political life in the United States are agreements on basic political values but disagreements over the ends or goals of government. Most Americans share the values of liberty, equality, and democracy. Values shape citizens' views of the world and define their sense of what is right and wrong, just and unjust, possible and impossible. If Americans shared no values, they would have difficulty communicating, much less agreeing on a common system of government and politics. On the other hand, sharing broad values does not guarantee political consensus. We can agree on principles but disagree over their application.

For example, some critics claim that measures such as affirmative action have not promoted political inclusion and instead have condoned reverse discrimination and a segmented society. Far from fulfilling American ideals, they argue, these policies represent a movement away from our most fundamental values. An opposing perspective questions the progress that has been made in promoting equality. Pointing to the disproportionately high rates of poverty among women and minorities and continuing evidence of discrimination against these groups, this side questions whether Americans are serious about equality. Much of the debate over the role of government has been over what government should do and how far it should go to reduce the inequalities within our society and political system.

political culture broadly shared values, beliefs, and attitudes about how the government should function. American political culture emphasizes the values of liberty, equality, and democracy

Even though Americans have disagreed over the meaning of such political ideals as equality, they still agree on the importance of these ideals. The shared values, beliefs, and attitudes that form our **political culture** and hold the United States and its people together date back to the time of the founding of the Union.

The essential documents of the American Founding—the Declaration of Independence and the Constitution—enunciated a set of political principles about the purposes of the new republic. In contrast with many other democracies, in the United States these political ideals did not just remain words on dusty documents. Americans actively embraced the principles of the Founders and made them central to the national identity. Let us look more closely at three of these ideals: liberty, equality, and democracy.

Patrick Henry's famous "Give me liberty, or give me death" speech demanded freedom at any cost and has resonated with Americans throughout the nation's history.

Liberty

No ideal is more central to American values than liberty. The Declaration of Independence defined three inalienable rights: "life, liberty and the pursuit of happiness." The preamble of the Constitution likewise identified the need to secure "the blessings of liberty" as one of the key reasons for drawing up the Constitution. For Americans, **liberty** means both personal freedom and economic freedom. Both are closely linked to the idea of **limited government.**

The Constitution's first ten amendments, known collectively as the Bill of Rights, above all preserve individual personal liberties and rights. In fact, liberty has come to mean many of the freedoms guaranteed in the Bill of Rights: freedom of speech and writing, the right to assemble freely, and the right to practice religious beliefs without interference from the government. Over the course of American history, the scope of personal liberties has expanded, as laws have become more tolerant and as individuals have successfully used the courts to challenge restrictions on their individual freedoms. Far fewer restrictions exist today on the press, political speech, and individual moral behavior than in the early years of the nation. Even so, conflicts persist over how personal liberties should be extended and when personal liberties violate community norms. For example, one of the most contentious issues in the last forty years has been that of abortion. Whereas defenders of the right to choose abortion view it as an essential personal freedom for women, opponents view it as murder—something that no society should allow.

liberty freedom from governmental control

limited government a principle of constitutional government; a government whose powers are defined and limited by a constitution

In addition to personal freedom, the American concept of liberty means economic freedom. Since the Founding, economic freedom has been linked to capitalism, free markets, and the protection of private property. Free competition, unfettered movement of goods, and the right to enjoy the fruits of one's labor are all essential aspects of economic freedom and American capitalism.[31] In the first century of the Republic, support for capitalism often meant support for the doctrine of *laissez-faire* (translated literally as to "leave alone"). **Laissez-faire capitalism** allowed very little room for the national government to regulate trade or restrict the use of private property, even in the public interest. Americans still strongly support capitalism and economic liberty, but they now also endorse some restrictions on economic freedoms to protect the public. Federal and state governments now deploy a wide array of regulations in the name of public protection. These include health and safety laws, environmental rules, and workplace regulations. Not surprisingly, fierce disagreements often erupt over what the proper scope of government regulation should be. What some people regard as protecting the public, others see as an infringement on their own freedom to run their businesses and use their property as they see fit.

laissez-faire capitalism an economic system in which the means of production and distribution are privately owned and operated for profit with minimal or no government interference

The new country did not meet Henry's demand for freedom, at least not for all people. Samuel Jennings painted this work, Liberty Displaying the Arts and Sciences, *in 1792. The books, instruments, and classical columns at the left of the painting contrast with the kneeling slaves at the right—illustrating the divide between America's rhetoric of liberty and equality, and the political and economic reality of slavery.*

Equality

The Declaration of Independence declares as its first "self-evident" truth that "all men are created equal." As central as it is to the American political creed, however, equality has been a less well-defined ideal than liberty because people interpret "equality" in different ways. Few Americans have wholeheartedly embraced full equality of results, but most Americans share the ideal of **equality of opportunity**—that is, the notion that each person should be given a fair chance to go as far as his or her talents will allow. Yet it is hard for Americans to reach agreement about what constitutes equality of opportunity. Must *past* inequalities be remedied in order to ensure equal opportunity in the *present*? Should inequalities in the legal, political, and economic spheres be given the same weight? In contrast to liberty, which requires limits on the role of government, equality implies an *obligation* of the government to the people.[32]

equality of opportunity a widely shared American ideal that all people should have the freedom to use whatever talents and wealth they have to reach their fullest potential

political equality the right to participate in politics equally, based on the principle of "one person, one vote"

popular sovereignty a principle of democracy in which political authority rests ultimately in the hands of the people

Americans do make clear distinctions between political equality and social or economic equality. **Political equality** means that members of the American political community have the right to participate in politics on equal terms. Beginning from a very restricted definition of political community, which originally included only propertied white men, the United States has moved much closer to an ideal of political equality that can be summed up as "one person, one vote." Broad support for the ideal of political equality has helped expand the American political community and extend the right to participate to all. Although considerable conflict remains over whether the political system makes it harder for some people to participate and easier for others and whether the role of money in politics has drowned out the public voice, Americans agree that all citizens should have an equal right to participate and that government should enforce that right.

The issue of freedom plays out in a personal way in abortion rights. In political terms, the debate hinges on the extent of government control over personal liberty.

In part because Americans believe that individuals are free to work as hard as they choose, they have always been less concerned about social or economic inequality. Many Americans regard economic differences as the consequence of individual choices, virtues, or failures. Because of this, Americans tend to be less supportive than most Europeans of government action to ensure equality. Yet when major economic forces, such as the Great Depression of the 1930s, affect many people or when systematic barriers appear to block equality of opportunity, Americans support government action to promote equality. Even then, however, Americans have endorsed only a limited government role designed to help people get back on their feet or to open up opportunity.

Democracy

The essence of democracy is the participation of the people in choosing their rulers and the people's ability to influence what those rulers do. In a democracy, political power ultimately comes from the people. The idea of placing power in the hands of the people is known as **popular sovereignty.** In the United States, popular sovereignty and political equality make politicians accountable to the people. Ideally, democracy envisions an engaged citizenry prepared to exercise its power over rulers. As we saw earlier, the United States is a representative democracy, meaning that the people do not rule directly but instead exercise power through elected representatives. Forms of participation in a democracy vary greatly, but voting is a key element of the representative democracy that the American Founders established.

Political participation was greatest during the nineteenth century. But as this 1854 painting indicates, white men were virtually the only people who could vote at the time.

American democracy rests on the principle of **majority rule** with **minority rights.** Majority rule means that the wishes of the majority determine what government does. The House of Representatives—a large body elected directly by the people—was designed in particular to ensure majority rule. But the Founders feared that popular majorities could turn government into a "tyranny of the majority" in which individual liberties would be violated. Concern for individual rights has thus been a part of American democracy from the beginning. The rights enumerated in the Bill of Rights and enforced through the courts provide an important check on the power of the majority.

majority rule, minority rights the democratic principle that a government follows the preferences of the majority of voters but protects the interests of the minority

Does the System Uphold American Political Values? Thinking Critically about Liberty, Equality, and Democracy

Liberty, equality, and democracy are core American ideals. But like many abstract ideals, they are not always easy to put into practice. Americans have always hotly debated the meaning and implications of each ideal as well as the proper balance among them.

LIBERTY The central historical conflict regarding liberty in the United States was about the enslavement of blacks. The facts of slavery and the differential treatment of the races have cast a long shadow over all of American history. In fact, scholars today note that the American definition of freedom has been formed in relation to the concept of slavery. The right to control one's labor and the right to receive rewards for that labor have been central elements of our definition of freedom precisely because these freedoms were denied to slaves.[33]

For Critical Analysis

What type of government does the United States have? Is it the most democratic government possible? Do citizens make the decisions of government, or do they merely influence them?

Should America Export Democracy?

Americans are justifiably proud of their democratic political institutions and often believe that the people of all nations would benefit from living under American-style democratic rule. Indeed, on a number of occasions Americans have sought to transform other nations into democracies—a policy called "democratization." In the aftermath of World War II, American military forces occupied Japan and the western portion of Germany, imposing new democratic governments to replace the dictatorial regimes blamed for launching the war. More recently, after successful American military campaigns to overthrow the governments of Afghanistan and Iraq, the United States has undertaken an effort to build democratic governments in those nations.

Exporting democracy might be seen as a desirable goal for three reasons. The first of these is humanitarian. Generally speaking, individuals are better off when they possess civil liberties and political rights. Indeed, former president George W. Bush asserted that one of the main purposes of American policy in the Middle East was to bring democracy to the people of the region. "It is the calling of our country," Bush said.

A second reason sometimes given in support of American efforts to export democracy is the promotion of political stability. In a democracy, competing economic and social forces have a chance to work out their differences through lawful political struggle. Dictatorial regimes, by contrast, seldom provide opportunities for lawful political activity and usually seek to quash expressions of political dissent or opposition. Lacking lawful channels, political grievances in nations ruled by dictatorships usually manifest themselves in such forms as public protest, political violence, and terrorism. Instability and violence in one country can easily spread beyond borders to pose threats elsewhere. As former President Bush put it, "As long as the Middle East remains a place where freedom does not flourish, it will remain a place of stagnation, resentment and violence ready for export."

A third reason Americans might wish to support policies of democratization is that the spread of democracy may promote world peace. In his famous 1795 essay "Toward Perpetual Peace," the German philosopher Immanuel Kant observed that democratic regimes seldom made war on each other. Thus, he argued, the expansion of democracy would enhance the prospects for world peace. In recent years, a good deal of empirical research has supported Kant's hypothesis.

Although a more democratic world might, indeed, be more humane, stable, and peaceful, a policy of democratization faces daunting prospects. First, a huge percentage of the world's population lives in nations that are not democracies. It seems unlikely that America could actually democratize so much of the globe. Second, many nations might not be capable of sustaining democratic regimes even if they were established. Democracy is most likely to flourish where there are vigorous social institutions and a stable economy—conditions that do not exist in many regions of the world. Finally, the process of democratization can, itself, be dangerous for American interests because it may lead to political instability or the election of hostile governments. By 2008, some observers were questioning whether it would be possible to build democracies in Iraq and Afghanistan, where corruption and security challenges were undermining government stability. With the threat from the Taliban mounting in Afghanistan, the British ambassador there went so far as to suggest that it would take "an acceptable dictator" to unite the country.

FOR CRITICAL ANALYSIS

1. What are some of the factors that might help to determine whether democratic politics can take root in a country that has not previously experienced democracy?
2. Is it appropriate for America to try to shape the governments and political arrangements of other countries?

Concerns about the meaning of liberty also arise in connection with government regulation of economic and social activity. Economic regulations imposed to ensure public health and safety are often decried by the affected businesses as infringements on their freedom. For example, in 2003 and 2005, the Occupational Safety and Health Administration (OSHA) adopted rules limiting the number of consecutive hours that long-distance truck drivers were permitted to operate their vehicles. In a twenty-four-hour period, drivers may work for only eleven consecutive hours. From OSHA's perspective, such regulations are needed to prevent sleepy truckers from endangering themselves and other motorists. From the truckers' perspective, though, the government is limiting their freedom and their ability to earn a living.

Government regulations intended to protect the public, such as the National Do Not Call Registry, are sometimes viewed by business as infringements on economic liberty.

Social regulations prompt similar disputes. Some citizens believe that government should enforce certain standards of behavior or instill particular values in citizens. Examples of such activity abound: welfare rules that once denied benefits to women who were found with a "man in the house," the practice of saying prayers in school, and laws that require citizens to wear seat belts are just a few examples. Deciding the proper scope of economic and social regulation is a topic of great concern and much conflict among Americans today.

More recently, concerns about liberty have arisen in relation to the government's efforts to combat terrorism. In November 2001, President Bush issued an executive order mandating that suspected foreign terrorists be tried before special military tribunals rather than in the regular federal courts. Hypothetically, such tribunals could impose severe penalties—on the basis of evidence that might not be admitted in civilian courts. In the months following September 11, hundreds of individuals—mainly of Middle Eastern origin—were arrested by federal authorities and held on immigration charges or by material witness warrants that allowed the government to incarcerate them without having to show any evidence they were linked to terrorist activities. Also in the immediate aftermath of September 11, President Bush issued secret orders to the National Security Agency, authorizing the agency to monitor domestic phone traffic in search of possible communications among terrorist groups. This program meant that the calls of millions of Americans were secretly intercepted without a court warrant. The events of September 11 leave us with an extraordinary dilemma. On the one hand, we treasure liberty, but on the other hand, we recognize that the lives of thousands of Americans have already been lost and countless others are threatened by terrorism. Can we reconcile liberty and security? Liberty and order? In previous national emergencies, Americans accepted restrictions on liberty with the understanding that these would be temporary. For example, military tribunals were established during World War II to try German saboteurs who landed on the East Coast. President Bush, however, has said that the war against terrorism will last years and years. Clearly, the implications for American liberty will be profound.

Politics Today

Have Americans become less supportive of the limitations on liberty put into place after the terror attacks in 2001? Or do they still think it makes sense to give up some liberties in order to feel more secure?

EQUALITY Because equality is such an elusive concept, many conflicts have arisen over what it should mean in practice. Americans have engaged in three kinds of controversies about the public role in addressing inequality. The first is determining what constitutes equality of access to public institutions. In 1896, the Supreme Court ruled in *Plessy v. Ferguson* that "separate but equal" accommodations for blacks and whites were constitutional. In 1954, in a major legal victory for the civil rights movement, the Supreme Court overturned the "separate but equal" doctrine in *Brown v. Board of Education* (see Chapter 5). Today, new questions have been raised about what constitutes equal access to public institutions. Some argue that the unequal financing of public schools in cities, suburbs, and rural districts is a violation of the right to equal education. To date, these claims have not been supported by the federal courts, which have rejected the notion that the unequal economic impacts of public policy outcomes are a constitutional matter.[34] Lawsuits arguing a right to "economic equal protection" stalled in 1973 when the Supreme Court ruled that a Texas school-financing law did not violate the Constitution even though the law affected rich and poor students differently.[35]

A second debate concerns the public role in ensuring equality of opportunity in private life. Although Americans generally agree that discrimination should not be tolerated, people disagree over what should be done to ensure equality of opportunity (see Table 1.2). Controversies about affirmative action programs reflect these disputes. Supporters of affirmative action claim that such programs are necessary to compensate for past discrimination in order to establish true equality of opportunity today. Opponents maintain that affirmative action amounts to reverse discrimination and that a society that espouses true equality should not acknowledge gender or racial differences. The question of the public responsibility for private inequalities is central to gender issues. The traditional view, still held by many today, sees the special responsibilities of women in the family as falling outside the range of public concern. Indeed, from this perspective, the role of women within families

Politics Today

Economic inequality among Americans is now as high as it was a hundred years ago. Many politicians and news commentators say that inequality is threatening the middle class. Is there any evidence that the American public is worried about the growth in inequality?

TABLE 1.2 ★ Equality and Public Opinion

Americans believe in some forms of equality more than others. How do these survey results reflect disagreement about what equality means in practice?

STATEMENT	PERCENTAGE WHO AGREE
Male and female citizens of the United States have equal rights.	97
Our society should do what is necessary to make sure that everyone has an equal opportunity to succeed.	91
Homosexuals should have equal rights in terms of job opportunities.	89
Marriages between same-sex couples should be recognized by the law as valid, with the same rights as traditional marriages.	46
It's ok to have a country where the races are basically separate from one another, as long as they have equal opportunity.	36
The opportunity for equal justice under the law is equal for blacks and whites (according to whites).	53
The opportunity for equal justice under the law is equal for blacks and whites (according to blacks).	21

SOURCES: Opinion Research Corporation, 2001; Pew, 2006; Gallup, 2007; Foundation for Ethnic Understanding, 2005; and National Conference for Community and Justice, 2005.

Voting rights expanded dramatically during the civil rights movement, which forced the government to allow people to vote regardless of their race. Here, residents of Wilcox County, Alabama, line up to vote in 1966. Prior to the passage of the Voting Rights Act of 1965, Wilcox County had no registered black voters.

is essential to the functioning of a democratic society. In the past thirty years, especially, these traditional views have come under fire, as advocates for women have argued that women occupy a subordinate place within the family and that such private inequalities *are* a topic of public concern.[36]

A third debate about equality concerns differences in income and wealth. Unlike in other countries, income inequality has not been an enduring topic of political controversy in the United States, which currently has the largest gap in income and wealth between rich and poor citizens of any developed nation. But Americans have generally tolerated great differences among rich and poor citizens, in part because of a pervasive belief that mobility is possible and that economic success is the product of individual effort.[37] This tolerance for inequality is reflected in America's tax code, which is more advantageous to wealthy taxpayers than that of almost any other Western nation. Indeed, tax changes enacted in recent years have sharply reduced the tax burdens of upper-income Americans. Debate about taxes dominated the closing days of the 2008 presidential race. John McCain promised to enact no new taxes and accused Barack Obama of being a socialist for commenting that he wanted to "spread the wealth around." Obama for his part pledged to reduce taxes for the 97 percent of Americans who made less than $250,000 a year. He defended the need to raise the marginal tax rate of upper-income Americans to support programs that benefit the middle class.[38]

Although Americans are no longer legally barred from voting on the basis of sex or race, political participation is minimal for most people. In the 2008 election, initial estimates indicated that only 62 percent of eligible voters came to the polls.

DEMOCRACY Despite Americans' deep attachment to the *ideal* of democracy, many questions can be raised about our *practice* of democracy. The first is the restricted definition of the political community during much of American history. The United States was not a full democracy until the 1960s, when African Americans were at last guaranteed the right to vote. Property restrictions on the right to vote were eliminated by 1828; in 1870, the Fifteenth Amendment to the Constitution granted African Americans the

Honing Your Political Radar

Numerous surveys have shown that the vast majority of college students view the world of government as a remote, far-off land dominated by "old white guys in suits." For many people politics seems like something that doesn't really have an impact on their lives, largely because the political system does so little to help younger Americans recognize how important government can be.

As you'll see throughout this book, the political decisions that government officials make can have a real impact on your life. Whom you can and cannot marry, how clean the environment is where you live—these are just two of many examples.

Even though you may never become a politician or a full-time activist, it's important to spend some time thinking through where you fit into the broader political debates that may affect your life. Doing so requires you to recognize that even core American political values—liberty, equality, and democracy—mean different things to different people. After all, it's one thing to say that everyone should be entitled to equal treatment under the law, but as the current debate over gay marriage and civil unions demonstrates, equality doesn't always mean the same thing to everyone.

The same thing can be said regarding government and the environment. Even though most Americans believe government has a role to play in protecting the environment, many also fear that their personal liberties are at stake if the government starts passing legislation that penalizes people for the kinds of cars they drive.

The following are a few steps you can take to better understand where you fit into policy debates today and how core political values play out in the real world.

- ★ Investigate a political or social issue that you have an opinion on yet know little about. This sounds odd at first, but we are often asked to offer opinions on things that we haven't had time to examine carefully, simply because our lives are already consumed with work, school, family, and friends. Try doing an Internet search of the issue of your choice and reading up on it. Be sure to read things that both contradict and reinforce your opinion. As you do this, think about how your interpretation of one or more core political values (liberty, equality, or democracy) shapes your understanding of this issue. Did thinking through other people's opinions change yours?
- ★ Talk to friends and family about a political or social issue that tends to promote a variety of opinions, such as abortion laws, the environment, health care, or the "right to die." Ask questions about their positions and listen to what differences of opinion emerge in your conversations. Do the differences have anything to do with disagreements over liberty and equality?
- ★ Watch a TV show with political content, like *The Daily Show with Jon Stewart* or *The Colbert Report*, and examine an issue that's covered in the broadcast. What you hear may be just one side of the issue, but a good place to explore other sides to many controversial issues is the Public Agenda Foundation Web site (www.publicagenda.org). If you click on the "Issue Guides" link at the top of the page, you can see what others say about an issue and how political values are interpreted differently when applied to this issue.
- ★ Read the other "Get Involved" sections in this book for specific ways that you can influence government and politics at the national level, the state level, on your campus, and in your community. As you consider getting involved in a particular issue, think about how it relates to core values such as liberty, equality, and democracy, and why government should (or should not) assume more responsibility in addressing this issue.

vote, although later exclusionary practices denied them that right; in 1920, the Nineteenth Amendment guaranteed women the right to vote; and in 1965, the Voting Rights Act finally secured the right of African Americans to vote.

Just securing the right to vote does not end concerns about democracy, however. The organization of electoral institutions can have a significant impact on access to elections and on who can get elected. During the first two decades of the twentieth century, states and cities enacted many reforms that made it harder to vote, including strict registration requirements and scheduling of elections. The aim was to rid politics of corruption, but the consequence was to reduce participation. Other institutional decisions affect which candidates stand the best chance of getting elected (see Chapter 10).

A further consideration about democracy concerns the relationship between economic power and political power. Money has always played an important role in elections and governing in the United States. Many argue that the pervasive influence of money in American electoral campaigns today undermines democracy. With the decline of locally based political parties that depended on party loyalists to turn out the vote, and the rise of political action committees, political consultants, and expensive media campaigns, money has become the central fact of life in American politics. Money often determines who runs for office; it can exert a heavy influence on who wins; and, some argue, money affects what politicians do once they are in office.[39]

Low turnout for elections and a pervasive sense of apathy and cynicism characterized American politics for much of the past half-century. The widespread interest in the 2008 election and the near-record levels of voter turnout reversed this trend. Millions of new voters—many of them young or immigrants—registered and voted for the first time. Volunteers found ways to become personally involved in politics. These developments are a hopeful sign for those wishing to revitalize American democracy.

For Critical Analysis

Think of some examples that demonstrate the gaps between the ideals of America's core political values and the practice of American politics. How might these discrepancies be reconciled?

Who Benefits from Government?

Government is not a neutral force in any society. Some groups always benefit more than others from the government's actions. Some regimes are run by small cliques or even by families for their own benefit. Our government is dominated by shifting coalitions of electoral forces along with interest groups; local, state, and national politicians; civic leaders; labor groups; ethnic and religious groups; professional associations; and a host of others. Almost every piece of legislation or governmental regulation bears the stamp of some set of interests that pushed for its enactment because it seemed to serve their purposes. In some instances, interests have turned getting what they want into a science. For example, the Enron Corporation, a now-bankrupt Texas energy giant, developed a computer program named Matrix that could evaluate the net impact on the company of any proposed federal energy regulation. This information, in turn, guided the firm's lobbying efforts and campaign contributions, which were designed to influence the government's activities.[40]

Special interests have been all too willing to influence government in the absence of popular political participation. Lobbyists not only attempt to convince politicians with their arguments; they also control large donations to political campaigns.

Although we know that most pieces of legislation and many regulations have particular beneficiaries, we hope that the benefits and costs of our government's policies are not narrowly defined. That is, we hope that the net benefits of government do not always flow to the same groups. James Madison, the principal author of the U.S. Constitution, argued that in a large and diverse republic so many groups would be fighting for power that no one group or coalition of groups would always prevail. Today, we call this idea pluralism, and we fervently hope that in our society some benefits of government accrue to all citizens—or at least to all participants in the political process. We can certainly observe that even apparently powerful forces are sometimes defeated in the political arena and that for most political actors, power is short lived. The once-mighty Enron Corporation was destroyed despite its grasp of sophisticated political techniques. Perhaps this is the best outcome for which we can hope—that political power will be dispersed and brief, so that government will benefit many and favor few for very long.

FOR FURTHER READING

Dahl, Robert. *Democracy and Its Critics.* New Haven, CT: Yale University Press, 1989.

Delli Carpini, Michael X., and Scott Keeter. *What Americans Know about Politics and Why It Matters.* New Haven, CT: Yale University Press, 1996.

Fischer, Claude S., and Michael Hout. *A Century of Difference: How America Changed in the Last One Hundred Years.* New York: Russell Sage Foundation, 2006.

Hibbing, John R., and Elizabeth Theiss-Morse. *Stealth Democracy: Americans' Belief about How Government Should Work.* New York: Cambridge University Press, 2002.

Huntington, Samuel. *Who Are We: The Challenges to America's National Identity.* New York: Simon & Schuster, 2004.

Jamieson, Kathleen Hall. *Everything You Think You Know About Politics . . . and Why You're Wrong.* New York: Basic Books, 2000.

Lasswell, Harold. *Politics: Who Gets What, When, How.* New York: Meridian Books, 1958.

Putnam, Robert. *Making Democracy Work: Civic Traditions in Modern Italy.* Princeton, NJ: Princeton University Press, 1993.

Tocqueville, Alexis de. *Democracy in America.* Trans. Phillips Bradley. New York: Knopf, Vintage Books, 1945; orig. published 1835.

Zakaria, Fareed. *The Future of Freedom.* New York: Norton, 2003.

RECOMMENDED WEB SITES

American Democracy Project
www.aascu.org/programs/adp/
This is an effort by the Association of State Colleges and Universities to increase political engagement among college students. See what opportunities are available for you to become politically active.

Americans for Informed Democracy
www.aidemocracy.org/
A nonpartisan organization that promotes democracy and seeks to build a new generation of globally conscious leaders. Find out how you can be politically active and coordinate a town hall meeting on campus, attend a leadership retreat, or publish your opinions on democracy.

DiversityInc
http://diversityinc.com
This site is dedicated to the promotion of American diversity and education. Here you can read about the issues that directly affect American minorities.

For Democracy
www.fordemocracy.com
Most Americans know little about our government. Log on to this independent site to find a plethora of information on the history of American democracy and related current events.

Future of Freedom Foundation
www.fff.org
This organization promotes individual liberty, free markets, private property, and limited government. Find out how some people are trying to protect freedom in the United States.

Institute for Learning Technologies
www.ilt.columbia.edu/publications/digitext.html#

Columbia University's Institute for Learning Technologies provides general information on early political thinkers such as Aristotle, Hobbes, Locke, and Rousseau. Take a moment to read some of the writings on topics such as popular sovereignty, democracy, and limited government.

Mobilize.org
http://mobilize.org

This all-partisan network is dedicated to educating, empowering, and energizing young people. Find out how politics affects America's youth and what they are doing about it by being engaged and active.

SpeakOut.com
www.speakout.com

This site encourages citizens to be politically informed and active. Visitors with a sense of political efficacy can participate in online polls, contact public officials, and sign petitions on important political issues.

U.S. Census Bureau
www.census.gov

The Web site for the Bureau of the Census offers a statistical look at our country's population and economy. Check out some of the statistics to get a better idea of American diversity.

STUDY OUTLINE

www.wwnorton.com/wtp7e

What Americans Think about Government

1. In recent decades, the public's trust in government has declined considerably. Some Americans believe that government has grown too large and that government programs do not benefit them. As public distrust of government has increased, so has public dissatisfaction with the government's performance.
2. Americans today are less likely to think that they can influence what the government does. This view has led to increased apathy and cynicism among the citizenry.

Citizenship: Knowledge and Participation

1. Informed and active membership in a political community is the basis for citizenship. Citizens require political knowledge in order to be aware of their interests in a political dispute, to identify the best ways of acting on their interests, and to know what political action can and cannot achieve. However, today many Americans have little political knowledge.

Government

1. Governments vary in their structure, in their size, and in the way they operate.
2. Beginning in the seventeenth century, two important changes began to take place in the governance of some Western nations: governments began to acknowledge formal limits on their power, and governments began to give citizens a formal voice in politics through the vote.
3. Political participation can take many forms: the vote, group activities, and even direct action, such as violent opposition or civil disobedience.

Who Are Americans?

1. As the American population has grown it has become more diverse. In the early years of the Republic, the majority of Americans were European settlers, mainly from northern Europe. One in five Americans were of African origin, the vast majority of whom had been brought to the United States against their will to work as slaves. There was also an unknown number of Indians, the original inhabitants of the land, who were not initially counted by the census.
2. In the 1800s and early 1900s, a large wave of immigrants from Germany, Ireland, and later from southern and eastern Europe changed the demographic profile of the United States. As the percent of foreign-born residents reached 14.7 percent in 1910, a movement to limit immigration gained ground. After World War I, Congress placed sharp limits on immigration. It also established a National Origins Quota System designed to limit the numbers of immigrants from eastern and southern Europe.
3. From the start, the American government used racial and ethnic criteria to draw boundaries around the American population. Until 1870, nonwhites could not become naturalized citizens. The Chinese Exclusion Act of 1882 outlawed the entry of Chinese laborers to the United States, a restriction that was not reversed until 1943.
4. In 1965, Congress opened the doors to immigrants once again. At the same time, it greatly expanded the number of immigrants who could come from Asia and Latin America. The American population has become much more diverse as a result. European Americans accounted for only two-thirds of the population in 2007. The African American

population stood at 12.2 percent, and reflecting the new immigration, Hispanics accounted for close to 15 percent, with Asian Americans at 4 percent of the American population. In 2005, 12 percent of the population was foreign-born.

Thinking Critically about American Political Culture

1. Three important political values in American politics are liberty, equality, and democracy.
2. At times in American history there have been large gaps between the ideals embodied in Americans' core values and the practice of American government.
3. Many of the important dilemmas of American politics revolve around conflicts over fundamental political values. One such conflict involves the ideals of liberty and equality. Over time, efforts to promote equality may threaten liberty.

PRACTICE QUIZ

www.wwnorton.com/wtp7e

1. Political efficacy is the belief that
   a) government operates efficiently.
   b) government has grown too large.
   c) government cannot be trusted.
   d) one can influence what government does.
2. The famous political scientist Harold Lasswell defined politics as the struggle over
   a) who gets elected.
   b) who gets what, when, how.
   c) who protests.
   d) who gets to vote.
3. What is the basic difference between autocracy and oligarchy?
   a) the extent to which the average citizen has a say in government affairs
   b) the means of collecting taxes and conscripting soldiers
   c) the number of people who control governing decisions
   d) They are fundamentally the same thing.
4. According to the authors, good citizenship requires
   a) political knowledge.
   b) political engagement.
   c) a good education.
   d) both a and b
5. The principle of political equality can be best summed up as
   a) "equality of results."
   b) "equality of opportunity."
   c) "one person, one vote."
   d) "equality between the sexes."
6. Which of the following is an important principle of American democracy?
   a) popular sovereignty
   b) majority rule, minority rights
   c) limited government
   d) All of the above are important principles of American democracy.
7. Which of the following is *not* related to the American conception of "liberty"?
   a) freedom of speech
   b) free enterprise
   c) freedom of religion
   d) All of the above are related to liberty.
8. Which of the following is *not* part of American political culture?
   a) belief in equality of results
   b) belief in equality of opportunity
   c) belief in individual liberty
   d) belief in free competition
9. Which of the following does *not* represent a current discrepancy between the ideal and practice of democracy in America?
   a) the use of property restrictions for voting in three remaining states
   b) the influence of money in electoral politics
   c) the low voter turnout in American elections
   d) All of the above are discrepancies between the ideal and practice of democracy in modern America.
10. Americans' trust in their government
    a) declined steadily from the early 1960s to the mid-1990s but has risen slightly since then.
    b) declined during Watergate but rose again during the 1980s.
    c) rose in the 1990s but dropped again after September 11, 2001.
    d) rose during the 1970s and 1980s but has declined since 1992.

KEY TERMS

www.wwnorton.com/wtp7e

authoritarian government (p. 15)
autocracy (p. 14)
citizenship (p. 11)
constitutional government (p. 15)
democracy (p. 14)
direct democracy (p. 17)
equality of opportunity (p. 28)
government (p. 14)
laissez-faire capitalism (p. 27)
liberty (p. 26)
limited government (p. 26)
majority rule, minority rights (p. 29)
oligarchy (p. 14)
pluralism (p. 17)
political culture (p. 26)
political efficacy (p. 9)
political equality (p. 28)
politics (p. 16)
popular sovereignty (p. 28)
power (p. 17)
representative democracy/republic (p. 17)
totalitarian government (p. 15)

2 The Founding and the Constitution

- ★ The First Founding: Interests and Conflicts
- ★ The Second Founding: From Compromise to Constitution
- ★ The Constitution
- ★ The Fight for Ratification
- ★ The Citizen's Role and the Changing Constitution
- ★ Thinking Critically about Liberty, Equality, and Democracy

WHAT GOVERNMENT DOES AND WHY IT MATTERS

The story of America's Founding and the Constitution is generally presented as something both inevitable and glorious: it was inevitable that the American colonies would break away from Great Britain to establish their own country; and it was glorious in that the country established the best of all possible forms of government under a new constitution, which was easily adopted and quickly embraced, even by its critics. In reality, though, America's successful breakaway from Britain was by no means assured, and the Constitution that we revere today as one of the most brilliant creations of any nation was in fact highly controversial. Moreover, its ratification and durability were often in doubt. George Washington, the man chosen to preside over the Constitutional Convention of 1787, thought the document produced that hot summer in Philadelphia would probably last no more than twenty years, at which time leaders would have to convene again to come up with something new.

That Washington's expectation proved wrong is, indeed, a testament to the enduring strength of the Constitution. However, the Constitution was a product of political bargaining and compromise, formed in very much the same way political decisions are made today. This fact is often overlooked because of what the historian Michael Kammen has called the "cult of the Constitution"—a tendency of Americans, going back more than a century, to venerate, sometimes to the point of near worship, the Founders and the document they created.[1] As this chapter will show, the Constitution reflects high principle, but political self-interest, too. It also defines the relationship between American citizens and their government.

Liberty, equality, and democracy were all major themes of the founding period and are all elements of the U.S. Constitution. Often, the story of the Founding and the Constitution is written to emphasize the framers' concerns regarding individual liberty and limits on government. And, of course, the framers had such concerns. It is important to note, however, that the primary goal of the framers was the creation of an *effective* government. They sought a government with the capacity to provide for the nation's safety in a sometimes hostile world: "Among the many objects to which a wise and free people find it necessary to direct their attention," wrote John Jay in *Federalist 3*, "that of providing for their safety seems to be the first." The framers endeavored to create a government with the power to maintain public order, promote prosperity, and secure the nation's independence, powers that the government under the Articles of Confederation lacked.

Some writers have also suggested that the framers were not so deeply committed to democracy and point to their tolerance of extreme inequality, including human slavery. There is, of course, some truth to both accusations. Some of the framers feared that "excessive" democracy would threaten property rights; several were themselves slaveholders. Nevertheless, the framers believed that a powerful government required a broad popular base and, hence, opened the way for direct popular election of members of the House of Representatives. And, although the framers—products of a particular time and place—certainly did not share today's notions of racial and gender equality, they did provide equal political rights for white males, regardless of wealth or social class background. By asserting this principle of equality, the framers made it more difficult to defend denying equal rights to African Americans, women, and others in subsequent centuries.

› **In this chapter, we will first assess the political backdrop of the American Revolution, which led to the Declaration of Independence and the Articles of Confederation.**

› **We will then consider the conditions that led to the Constitutional Convention of 1787 and the great issues that the framers debated.** To understand the character of the Founding and the meaning of the Constitution, it is essential to look beyond the myths and rhetoric and to explore the conflicting interests and forces at work during the period.

› **Next, we will examine the Constitution that ultimately emerged as the basis for the national government.** The framers sought to create a powerful national government, but guarded against possible misuse of that power through the separation of powers, federalism, and the Bill of Rights.

› **We will then examine the first hurdle that the Constitution faced, the fight for ratification.** Two sides, the Federalists and the Antifederalists, vigorously debated the great political issues and principles at stake.

› **We will then look at how the Constitution has changed over the past two centuries.** The framers designed an amendment process so that the Constitution could be changed, but the process has succeeded only on rare occasions.

› **Finally, we will ask what liberty, equality, and democracy meant to the framers of the Constitution.** Although the framers established a system of government that would eventually allow each of these political values to thrive, they championed liberty as the most important of the three.

The First Founding: Interests and Conflicts

Competing ideals and principles often reflect competing interests, and so it was in Revolutionary America. The American Revolution and the American Constitution were outgrowths and expressions of a struggle among economic and political forces within the colonies. Five sectors of society had interests that were important in colonial politics: (1) the New England merchants; (2) the southern planters; (3) the "royalists"—holders of royal lands, offices, and patents (licenses to engage in a profession or business activity); (4) shopkeepers, artisans, and laborers; and (5) small farmers. Throughout the eighteenth century, these groups were in conflict over issues of taxation, trade, and commerce. For the most part, however, the southern planters, the New England merchants, and the royal office and patent holders—groups that together made up the colonial elite—were able to maintain a political alliance that held in check the more radical forces representing shopkeepers, laborers, and small farmers. After 1760, however, by seriously threatening the interests of New England merchants and southern planters, British tax and trade policies split the colonial elite, permitting radical forces to expand their political influence, and set into motion a chain of events that culminated in the American Revolution.[2]

British Taxes and Colonial Interests

Beginning in the 1760s, the debts and other financial problems confronting the British government forced it to search for new revenue sources. This search rather quickly led to the Crown's North American colonies, which, on the whole, paid remarkably little in taxes to their parent country. The British government reasoned that a sizable fraction of its debt was, in fact, attributable to the expenses it had incurred in defense of the colonies during the French and Indian wars, which ended in 1763, as well as to the continuing protection that British forces were giving the colonists from Indian attacks and that the British navy was providing for colonial shipping. Thus, during the 1760s, Britain sought to impose new, though relatively modest, taxes on the colonists.

Like most governments of the period, the British regime had limited ways in which to collect revenues. The income tax, which in the twentieth century became the single most important source of governmental revenues, had not yet been developed. For the most part, in the mid-eighteenth century, governments relied on tariffs, duties, and other taxes on commerce, and it was to such taxes, including the Stamp Act, that the British turned during the 1760s.

The Stamp Act and other taxes on commerce, such as the Sugar Act of 1764, which taxed sugar, molasses, and other commodities, most heavily affected the two groups in colonial society whose commercial interests and activities were most extensive—the New England merchants and the southern planters. Under the famous slogan "no taxation without representation," the merchants and planters together sought to organize opposition to these new taxes. In the course of the struggle against British tax measures, the planters and merchants broke with their royalist allies and turned to their former adversaries—the shopkeepers, small farmers, laborers, and artisans—for help. With the assistance of these groups, the

This picture of a segmented snake, printed in Benjamin Franklin's newspaper, urged the colonies to unite during the French and Indian War of the 1750s. Again during the Revolutionary War, cooperation among the states was crucial to the independence movement.

The British helped radicalize colonists through bad policy decisions in the years before the Revolution. For example, Britain gave the ailing East India Company a monopoly on the tea trade in the American colonies. Colonists feared the monopoly would hurt colonial merchants' business and protested by throwing East India Company tea into Boston Harbor in 1773.

Politics Today

Conflicts over taxes did not end with the American Revolution. When Congress extended President Bush's 2001 and 2003 tax cuts through 2010, critics charged that they unfairly benefited the wealthy. Why is tax policy almost always controversial?

merchants and planters organized demonstrations and a boycott of British goods that ultimately forced the Crown to rescind most of its new taxes.

From the perspective of the merchants and planters, however, the British government's decision to eliminate most of the hated taxes brought a victorious conclusion to their struggle with the mother country. They were anxious to end the unrest they had helped to arouse, and they supported the British government's efforts to restore order. Indeed, most respectable Bostonians supported the actions of the British soldiers involved in the Boston Massacre. In their subsequent trial, the soldiers were defended by John Adams, a pillar of Boston society and a future president of the United States. Adams asserted that the soldiers' actions were entirely justified, provoked by "a motley rabble of saucy boys, Negroes and mulattos, Irish teagues and outlandish Jack tars." All but two of the soldiers were acquitted.[3]

Despite the efforts of the British government and the better-to-do strata of colonial society, it proved difficult to bring an end to the political strife. The more radical forces representing shopkeepers, artisans, laborers, and small farmers, who had been mobilized and energized by the struggle over taxes, continued to agitate for political and social change within the colonies. These radicals, led by individuals such as Samuel Adams, a cousin of John Adams, asserted that British power supported an unjust political and social structure within the colonies, and began to advocate an end to British rule.[4]

Political Strife and the Radicalizing of the Colonists

The political strife within the colonies was the background for the events of 1773–74. In 1773, the British government granted the politically powerful East India Company a monopoly on the export of tea from Britain, eliminating a lucrative form of trade for colonial merchants. To add to the injury, the East India Company sought to sell the tea directly in the colonies instead of working through the colonial merchants. Tea was an extremely important commodity during the 1770s, and these British actions posed a serious threat to the New England merchants. Together with their southern allies, the merchants once again called on their radical adversaries for support. The most dramatic result was the Boston Tea Party of 1773, led by Samuel Adams.

This event was of decisive importance in American history. The merchants had hoped to force the British government to rescind the Tea Act, but they did not support any demands beyond this one. They did not seek independence from Britain. Samuel Adams and the other radicals, however, hoped to provoke the British government to take actions that would alienate its colonial supporters and pave the way for a rebellion. This was precisely the purpose of the Boston Tea Party, and it succeeded. By dumping the East India Company's tea into Boston Harbor, Adams and his followers goaded the British into enacting a number of harsh reprisals. Within five months after the incident in Boston, the House of Commons passed a series of acts that closed the port of Boston to commerce, changed the provincial government of Massachusetts, provided for the removal of accused persons to Britain for trial, and most important, restricted movement to the West—further alienating the southern planters, who depended on access to new western lands. These acts of retaliation confirmed the worst criticisms of Britain and helped radicalize Americans. Radicals such as Samuel Adams and Christopher Gadsden of South Carolina had been agitating for more violent measures to deal with Britain. But ultimately they needed Britain's political repression to create widespread support for independence.

Thus, the Boston Tea Party set into motion a cycle of provocation and retaliation that in 1774 resulted in the convening of the First Continental Congress—an assembly of delegates from all parts of the country—that called for a total boycott of British goods and, under the prodding of the radicals, began to consider the possibility of independence from British rule. The eventual result was the Declaration of Independence.

The Declaration of Independence

In 1776, the Second Continental Congress appointed a committee consisting of Thomas Jefferson of Virginia, Benjamin Franklin of Pennsylvania, Roger Sherman of Connecticut, John Adams of Massachusetts, and Robert Livingston of New York to draft a statement of American independence from British rule. The Declaration of Independence, written by Jefferson and adopted by the Second Continental Congress, was an extraordinary document in both philosophical and political terms. In philosophic terms, the Declaration was remarkable for its assertion that certain rights, called "unalienable rights"—including life, liberty, and the pursuit of happiness—could not be abridged by governments. In the world of 1776, a world in which some kings still claimed to rule by divine right, this was a dramatic statement. In political terms, the Declaration was remarkable because, despite the differences of interest that divided the colonists along economic, regional, and philosophical lines, it identified and focused on problems, grievances, aspirations, and principles that might unify the various colonial groups. The Declaration was an attempt to identify and articulate a history and set of principles that might help to forge national unity.[5]

Britain eventually sent troops to subdue the American colonists. Grant Wood's Midnight Ride of Paul Revere *(1931) depicts Revere alerting colonists to the British army's arrival. The subsequent battle between colonial and British forces at Concord and Lexington began the Revolutionary War.*

The Articles of Confederation

Articles of Confederation America's first written constitution; served as the basis for America's national government until 1789

confederation a system of government in which states retain sovereign authority except for the powers expressly delegated to the national government

Having declared their independence, the colonies needed to establish a governmental structure. In November of 1777, the Continental Congress adopted the **Articles of Confederation and Perpetual Union**—the United States's first written constitution. Although it was not ratified by all the states until 1781, it was the country's operative constitution for almost twelve years, until March 1789.

However, from almost the moment of adoption, moves were afoot to reform and strengthen the Articles. The first goal of the Articles had been to limit the powers of the central government. The relationship between the national government and the states was called a **confederation;** as provided under Article II, "each state retains its sovereignty, freedom, and independence . . ." It was not unlike the contemporary relationship between the United Nations and its member states. The central government was given no president or any other presiding officer. The entire national government was vested in a Congress, with execution of its few laws to be left to the individual states. And the Articles gave Congress very little power to exercise. Its members were not much more than delegates or messengers from the state legislatures: their salaries were paid out of the state treasuries; they were subject to immediate recall by state authorities; and each state, regardless of its size, had only one vote.

Under the Articles of Confederation, Congress was given the power to declare war and make peace, to make treaties and alliances, to coin or borrow money, and to regulate trade with the Native Americans. It could also appoint the senior officers of the United States Army, but the national government had no army for those officers to command because the nation's armed forces were composed of the state militias. Moreover, the central government could not prevent one state

The year after fighting began between American colonists and the British army, the Continental Congress voted for independence on July 2, 1776 and approved the Declaration of Independence two days later, on July 4.

from discriminating against other states in the competition for foreign commerce. These extreme limits on the power of the national government made the Articles of Confederation hopelessly impractical.[6]

The Second Founding: From Compromise to Constitution

The Declaration of Independence and the Articles of Confederation were not sufficient to hold the new nation together as an independent and effective nation-state. A series of developments following the armistice with the British in 1783 highlighted the shortcomings of the Articles of Confederation.

International Standing and Balance of Power

There was a special concern for the country's international position. Competition among the states for foreign commerce allowed the European powers to play the states off against each other, which created confusion on both sides of the Atlantic. At one point during the winter of 1786–87, John Adams of Massachusetts, a leader in the independence struggle, was sent to negotiate a new treaty with the British, one that would cover disputes left over from the war. The British government responded that since the United States under the Articles of Confederation was unable to enforce existing treaties, it would negotiate with each of the thirteen states separately.

At the same time, the United States faced a threat from Spain, which still held vast territories in North and South America. Well-to-do Americans—in particular the New England merchants and southern planters—were especially troubled by the influence that "radical" forces exercised in the Continental Congress and in the governments of several of the states. The colonists' victory in the Revolutionary War had not only ended British rule but also significantly changed the balance of political power within the new states. As a result of the Revolution, one key segment of the colonial elite—the royal land, office, and patent holders—was stripped of its economic and political privileges. In fact, many of these individuals, along with tens of thousands of other colonists who considered themselves loyal British subjects, left for Canada after the British surrender. And although the pre-Revolutionary elite was weakened, the pre-Revolutionary radicals were now better organized than ever before and were the controlling forces in such states as Pennsylvania and Rhode Island, where they pursued economic and political policies that struck terror into the hearts of the pre-Revolutionary political establishment. In Rhode Island, for example, between 1783 and 1785, a legislature dominated by representatives of small farmers, artisans, and shopkeepers had instituted economic policies, including drastic currency inflation, that frightened business and property owners throughout the country. Of course, the central government under the Articles of Confederation was powerless to intervene.

The Annapolis Convention

The continuation of international weakness and domestic economic turmoil led many Americans to consider whether their newly adopted form of government might not already require revision. In the fall of 1786, many state leaders accepted an invitation from the Virginia legislature for a conference of representatives of all the states. Delegates from five states actually attended. This conference, held in Annapolis, Maryland, was the first step toward the second founding. The one positive thing that came out of the Annapolis Convention was a carefully worded resolution calling on the Congress to send commissioners to Philadelphia at a later time "to devise such further provisions as shall appear to them necessary to render the Constitution of the Federal Government adequate to the exigencies of the Union."[7] This resolution was drafted by Alexander Hamilton, a thirty-four-year-old New York lawyer who had played a significant role in the Revolution as George Washington's secretary and who would play a still more significant role in framing the Constitution and forming the new government in the 1790s. But the resolution did not necessarily imply any desire to do more than improve and reform the Articles of Confederation.

Shays's Rebellion

It is quite possible that the Constitutional Convention of 1787 in Philadelphia would never have taken place at all except for a single event that occurred during the winter following the Annapolis Convention: Shays's Rebellion.

Daniel Shays, a former army captain, led a mob of farmers in a rebellion against the government of Massachusetts. The purpose of the rebellion was to prevent foreclosures on their debt-ridden land by keeping the county courts of western Massachusetts from sitting until after the next election. The state militia dispersed the mob, but for several days Shays and his followers terrified the state government by attempting to capture the federal arsenal at Springfield, provoking an appeal to the Congress to help restore order. Within a few days, the state government regained control and captured fourteen of the rebels. (All were eventually pardoned.) In 1787, a newly elected Massachusetts legislature granted some of the farmers' demands.

In the winter of 1787, Daniel Shays led a makeshift army against the federal arsenal at Springfield to protest heavy taxes levied by the Massachusetts legislature. The rebellion proved the Articles of Confederation too weak to protect the fledgling nation.

Although the incident ended peacefully, its effects lingered and spread. Washington summed it up: "I am mortified beyond expression that in the moment of our acknowledged independence we should by our conduct verify the predictions of our transatlantic foe, and render ourselves ridiculous and contemptible in the eyes of all Europe."[8]

The Congress under the Confederation had been unable to act decisively in a time of crisis. This provided critics of the Articles of Confederation with precisely the evidence they needed to push Hamilton's Annapolis resolution through the Congress. Thus, the states were asked to send representatives to Philadelphia to discuss constitutional revision. Delegates were eventually sent by every state except Rhode Island.

The Constitutional Convention

Delegates selected by the state governments convened in Philadelphia in May 1787, with political strife, international embarrassment, national weakness, and local rebellion fixed in their minds. Recognizing that these issues were symptoms of fundamental flaws in the Articles of Confederation, the delegates soon abandoned the plan to revise the Articles and committed themselves to a second founding—a second, and ultimately successful, attempt to create a legitimate and effective national system of government. This effort occupied the convention for the next five months.

A MARRIAGE OF INTEREST AND PRINCIPLE For years, scholars have disagreed about the motives of the Founders in Philadelphia. Among the most controversial views of the framers' motives is the "economic interpretation" put forward by the historian Charles Beard and his disciples.[9] According to Beard's account, America's Founders were a collection of securities speculators and property owners whose only aim was personal enrichment. From this perspective, the Constitution's lofty principles were little more than sophisticated masks behind which the most venal interests sought to enrich themselves.

Contrary to Beard's approach is the view that the framers of the Constitution *were* concerned with philosophical and ethical principles. Indeed, the framers sought to devise a system of government consistent with the dominant philosophical and moral principles of the day. But in fact, these two views belong together; the Founders' interests were reinforced by their principles. The convention that drafted the American Constitution was chiefly organized by the New England merchants and southern planters. Although the delegates representing these groups did not all hope to profit personally from an increase in the value of their securities, as Beard would have it, they did hope to benefit in the broadest political and economic sense by breaking the power of their radical foes and establishing a system of government more compatible with their long-term economic and political interests. Thus, the framers sought to create a new government capable of promoting commerce and protecting property from radical state legislatures. At the same time, they hoped to fashion a government less susceptible than the existing state and national regimes to populist forces hostile to the interests of the commercial and propertied classes.

THE GREAT COMPROMISE The proponents of a new government fired their opening shot on May 29, 1787, when Edmund Randolph of Virginia offered a resolution that proposed corrections and enlargements in the Articles of Confederation. The proposal, which showed the strong influence of James Madison, was not a simple motion. It provided for virtually every aspect of a new government.

Opponents of the Articles called for a new Constitutional Convention to explore a stronger form of national government. George Washington, a hero of the Revolution, presided over the convention.

(There is no verbatim record of the debates, but Madison was present during virtually all of the deliberations and kept full notes on them.)[10]

Virginia Plan a framework for the Constitution, introduced by Edmund Randolph, which called for representation in the national legislature based on the population of each state

The portion of Randolph's motion that became most controversial was called the **Virginia Plan.** This plan provided for a system of representation in the national legislature based on the population of each state or the proportion of each state's revenue contribution to the national government, or both. (Randolph also proposed a second branch of the legislature, but it was to be elected by the members of the first branch.) Since the states varied enormously in size and wealth, the Virginia Plan was thought to be heavily biased in favor of the large states.

New Jersey Plan a framework for the Constitution, introduced by William Paterson, which called for equal state representation in the national legislature regardless of population

While the convention was debating the Virginia Plan, additional delegates were arriving in Philadelphia and were beginning to mount opposition to it. Their resolution, introduced by William Paterson of New Jersey and known as the **New Jersey Plan,** did not oppose the Virginia Plan point for point. Instead, it concentrated on specific weaknesses in the Articles of Confederation, in the spirit of revision rather than radical replacement of that document. Supporters of the New Jersey Plan did not seriously question the convention's commitment to replacing the Articles. But their opposition to the Virginia Plan's scheme of representation was sufficient to send its proposals back to committee for reworking into a common document. In particular, delegates from the less populous states, which included Delaware, New Jersey, Connecticut, and New York, asserted that the more populous states, such as Virginia, Pennsylvania, North Carolina, Massachusetts, and Georgia, would dominate the new government if representation were determined by population. The smaller states argued that each state should be equally represented in the new regime regardless of that state's population.

The issue of representation threatened to wreck the entire constitutional enterprise. Delegates conferred, factions maneuvered, and tempers flared. James Wilson of Pennsylvania told the small-state delegates that if they wanted to disrupt the union they should go ahead. The separation could, he said, "never happen on better grounds." Small-state delegates were equally blunt. Gunning Bedford of Delaware declared that the small states might look elsewhere for friends if they were forced. "The large states," he said, "dare not dissolve the confederation. If they do the small ones will find some foreign ally of more honor and good faith, who will take them by the hand and do them justice." These sentiments were widely shared. The union, as Oliver Ellsworth of Connecticut put it, was "on the verge of dissolution, scarcely held together by the strength of a hair."

Great Compromise the agreement reached at the Constitutional Convention of 1787 that gave each state an equal number of senators regardless of its population, but linked representation in the House of Representatives to population

The outcome of this debate was the Connecticut Compromise, also known as the **Great Compromise.** Under the terms of this compromise, in the first branch of Congress—the House of Representatives—the representatives would be apportioned according to the number of inhabitants in each state. This, of course, was what delegates from the large states had sought. But in the second branch—the Senate—each state would have an equal vote regardless of its size; this provision addressed the concerns of the small states. This compromise was not immediately satisfactory to all the delegates. Indeed, two of the most vocal members of the small-state faction, John Lansing and Robert Yates of New York, were so incensed by the concession that their colleagues had made to the large-state forces that they stormed out of the convention. In the end, however, both sets of forces preferred compromise to the breakup of the Union, and the plan was accepted.

THE QUESTION OF SLAVERY: THE THREE-FIFTHS COMPROMISE The story so far is too neat, too easy, and too anticlimactic. If it were left here, it would

The Looking Glass for 1787 *showcases Connecticut's debate about the newly drafted Constitution. In the cartoon, Federalists stand for trade and commerce. Antifederalists say "Tax Luxary" [sic]and "Success to Shays"—showing the cartoonist's Federalist leaning.*

only contribute to American mythology. After all, the notion of a **bicameral** (two-chambered) legislature was very much in the air in 1787. Some of the states had had bicameral legislatures for years. The Philadelphia delegates might well have gone straight to the adoption of two chambers based on two different principles of representation even without the dramatic interplay of conflict and compromise. But a far more fundamental issue had to be confronted before the Great Compromise could take place: the issue of slavery.

bicameral having a legislative assembly composed of two chambers or houses

Many of the conflicts that emerged during the Constitutional Convention were reflections of the fundamental differences between the slave and the nonslave states—differences that pitted the southern planters and New England merchants against one another. This was the first premonition of a conflict that would almost destroy the Republic in later years. In the midst of debate over large versus small states, Madison observed,

> The great danger to our general government is the great southern and northern interests of the continent, being opposed to each other. Look to the votes in Congress, and most of them stand divided by the geography of the country, not according to the size of the states.[11]

More than 90 percent of the country's slaves resided in five states—Georgia, Maryland, North Carolina, South Carolina, and Virginia—where they accounted for 30 percent of the total population. In some places, slaves outnumbered nonslaves by as much as ten to one. If the Constitution were to embody any principle of national supremacy, some basic decisions would have to be made about the place of slavery in the general scheme. Madison hit on this point on several occasions as different aspects of the Constitution were being discussed. For example, he observed,

> It seemed now to be pretty well understood that the real difference of interests lay, not between the large and small but between the northern and southern states. The institution of slavery and its consequences formed the line of discrimination. There were five states on the South, eight on the northern side of this line. Should a proportional representation take place it was true, the northern side would still outnumber the other: but not in the same degree, at this time; and every day would tend towards an equilibrium.[12]

Three-fifths Compromise the agreement reached at the Constitutional Convention of 1787 that stipulated that for purposes of the apportionment of congressional seats, every slave would be counted as three-fifths of a person

Northerners and southerners eventually reached agreement through the **Three-fifths Compromise.** The seats in the House of Representatives would be apportioned according to a "population" in which five slaves would count as three free persons. The slaves would not be allowed to vote, of course, but the number of representatives would be apportioned accordingly.

The issue of slavery was the most difficult one faced by the framers, and it nearly destroyed the Union. Although some delegates believed slavery to be morally wrong, an evil and oppressive institution that made a mockery of the ideals and values espoused in the Constitution, morality was not the issue that caused the framers to support or oppose the Three-fifths Compromise. Whatever they thought of the institution of slavery, most delegates from the northern states opposed counting slaves in the distribution of congressional seats. Wilson of Pennsylvania, for example, argued that if slaves were citizens they should be treated and counted like other citizens. If, on the other hand, they were property, then why should not other forms of property be counted toward the apportionment of representatives? But southern delegates made it clear that if the northerners refused to give in, they would never agree to the new government. William R. Davie of North Carolina heatedly said that it was time "to speak out." He asserted that the people of North Carolina would never enter the Union if slaves were not counted as part of the basis for representation. Without such agreement, he asserted ominously, "the business was at an end." Even southerners such as Edmund Randolph of Virginia, who conceded that slavery was immoral, insisted on including slaves in the

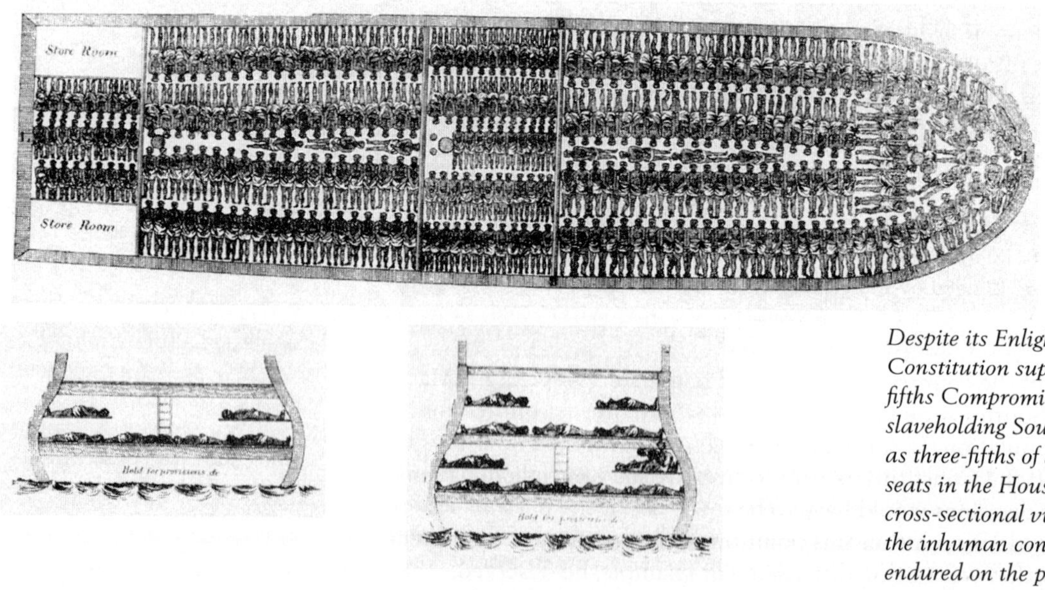

Despite its Enlightenment language, the new Constitution supported slavery. The Three-fifths Compromise made a concession to the slaveholding South by counting each slave as three-fifths of a person in apportioning seats in the House of Representatives. These cross-sectional views of a slave ship show the inhuman conditions that African slaves endured on the passage to America.

allocation of congressional seats. This conflict between the southern and northern delegates was so divisive that many came to question the possibility of creating and maintaining a union of the two. Pierce Butler of South Carolina declared that the North and South were as different as Russia and Turkey. Eventually, the North and South compromised on the issue of slavery and representation. Indeed, northerners even agreed to permit a continuation of the odious slave trade to keep the South in the Union. But in due course, Butler proved to be correct, and a bloody war was fought when the disparate interests of the North and the South could no longer be reconciled.

The Constitution

The political significance of the Great Compromise and the Three-fifths Compromise was to reinforce the unity of the mercantile and planter forces that sought to create a new government. The Great Compromise reassured those who feared that a new governmental framework would reduce the importance of their own local or regional influence. The Three-fifths Compromise temporarily defused the rivalry between the merchants and planters. Their unity secured, members of the alliance supporting the establishment of a new government moved to fashion a constitutional framework consistent with their economic and political interests.

In particular, the framers sought a new government that, first, would be strong enough to promote commerce and protect property from radical state legislatures such as Rhode Island's. This became the constitutional basis for national control over commerce and finance, as well as for the establishment of national judicial supremacy and the effort to construct a strong presidency. Second, the framers sought to prevent what they saw as the threat posed by the "excessive democracy" of the state and national governments under the Articles of Confederation. This led to such constitutional principles as bicameralism (division of the Congress into two chambers), **checks and balances,** staggered terms in office, and indirect election (selection of the president by an **electoral college** rather than directly by voters). Third, the framers, lacking the power to force the states or the public at large to accept the new form of government, sought to identify principles that would help to secure support. This became the basis of the constitutional provision for direct popular election of representatives and, subsequently, for the addition of the **Bill of Rights** to the Constitution. Finally, the framers wanted to be certain that the government they created did not pose even more of a threat to its citizens' liberties and property rights than did the radical state legislatures they feared and despised. To prevent the new government from abusing its power, the framers incorporated principles such as the **separation of powers** and **federalism** into the Constitution. Let us assess the major provisions of the Constitution's seven articles (listed in Box 2.1) to see how each relates to these objectives.

checks and balances mechanisms through which each branch of government is able to participate in and influence the activities of the other branches. Major examples include the presidential veto power over congressional legislation, the power of the Senate to approve presidential appointments, and judicial review of congressional enactments

electoral college the presidential electors from each state who meet after the popular election to cast ballots for president and vice president

Bill of Rights the first ten amendments to the U.S. Constitution, ratified in 1791; they ensure certain rights and liberties to the people

separation of powers the division of governmental power among several institutions that must cooperate in decision making

federalism a system of government in which power is divided, by a constitution, between a central government and regional governments

The Legislative Branch

In Article I, Sections 1–7, the Constitution provided for a Congress consisting of two chambers—a House of Representatives and a Senate. Members of the House of Representatives were given two-year terms in office and were to be elected directly by the people. Members of the Senate were to be appointed by the state

BOX 2.1 The Seven Articles of the Constitution

1. The Legislative Branch
House: two-year terms, elected directly by the people.
Senate: six-year terms (staggered so that only one-third of the Senate changes in any given election), appointed by state legislature (changed in 1913 to direct election).
Expressed powers of the national government: collecting taxes, borrowing money, regulating commerce, declaring war, and maintaining an army and a navy; all other power belongs to the states, unless deemed otherwise by the elastic (necessary and proper) clause.
Exclusive powers of the national government: states are expressly forbidden to issue their own paper money, tax imports and exports, regulate trade outside their own borders, and impair the obligation of contracts; these powers are the exclusive domain of the national government.

2. The Executive Branch
Presidency: four-year terms (limited in 1951 to a maximum of two terms), elected indirectly by the electoral college.
Powers: can recognize other countries, negotiate treaties, grant reprieves and pardons, convene Congress in special sessions, and veto congressional enactment.

3. The Judicial Branch
Supreme Court: lifetime terms, appointed by the president with the approval of the Senate.
Powers: include resolving conflicts between federal and state laws, determining whether power belongs to the national government or the states, and settling controversies between citizens of different states.

4. National Unity and Power
Reciprocity among states: establishes that each state must give "full faith and credit" to official acts of other states, and guarantees citizens of any state the "privileges and immunities" of every other state.

5. Amending the Constitution
Procedure: requires approval by two-thirds of Congress and adoption by three-fourths of the states.

6. National Supremacy
The Constitution and national law are the supreme law of the land and cannot be overruled by state law.

7. Ratification
The Constitution became effective when approved by nine states.

legislatures (this was changed in 1913 by the Seventeenth Amendment, which instituted direct election of senators) for six-year terms. These terms were staggered so that the appointments of one-third of the senators would expire every two years. The Constitution assigned somewhat different tasks to the House and Senate. Though the approval of each body was required for the enactment of a law, the Senate alone was given the power to ratify treaties and approve presidential appointments. The House, on the other hand, was given the sole power to originate revenue bills.

The character of the legislative branch was directly related to the framers' major goals. The House of Representatives was designed to be directly responsible to the people in order to encourage popular consent for the new Constitution and to help enhance the power of the new government. At the same time, to guard against "excessive democracy," the power of the House of Representatives was checked by the Senate, whose members were to be appointed by the states for long terms rather than be elected directly by the people. The purpose of this provision, according to Alexander Hamilton, was to avoid "an unqualified complaisance to every sudden breeze of passion, or to every transient impulse which the people may receive."[13] Staggered terms of service in the Senate, moreover, were intended to make that body even more resistant to popular pressure. Since only one-third of the senators would be selected at any given time, the composition of the institution would be protected from changes in popular preferences transmitted by the state legislatures. This would prevent what James Madison called "mutability in the public councils arising from a rapid succession of new members."[14] Thus, the structure of the legislative branch was designed to contribute to governmental power, to promote popular consent for the new government, and at the same time to place limits on the popular political currents that many of the framers saw as a radical threat to the economic and social order.

The issues of power and consent were important throughout the Constitution. Section 8 of Article I specifically listed the powers of Congress, which include the authority to collect taxes, to borrow money, to regulate commerce, to declare war, and to maintain an army and navy. By granting Congress these powers, the framers indicated very clearly that they intended the new government to be far more influential than its predecessor. At the same time, by defining the new government's most important powers as belonging to Congress, the framers sought to promote popular acceptance of this critical change by reassuring citizens that their views would be fully represented whenever the government exercised its new powers.

As a further guarantee to the people that the new government would pose no threat to them, the Constitution implied that any powers not listed were not granted at all. This is the doctrine of **expressed powers.** The Constitution grants only those powers specifically expressed in its text. But the framers intended to create an active and powerful government, and so they included the **elastic clause,** sometimes known as the necessary and proper clause, which signified that the enumerated powers were meant to be a source of strength to the national government, not a limitation on it. The national government could exercise each power with the utmost vigor, but it could seize no new powers without a constitutional amendment. In the absence of such an amendment, any power not enumerated was conceived to be "reserved" to the states (or the people).

expressed powers specific powers granted by the Constitution to Congress (Article I, Section 8) and to the president (Article II)

elastic clause Article I, Section 8, of the Constitution (also known as the necessary and proper clause), which enumerates the powers of Congress and provides Congress with the authority to make all laws "necessary and proper" to carry them out

The Executive Branch

The Constitution provided for the establishment of the presidency in Article II. As Alexander Hamilton commented, the presidential article aimed toward "energy in the Executive." It did so in an effort to overcome the natural tendency toward stalemate that was built into the bicameral legislature as well as into the separation of powers among the three branches. The Constitution afforded the president a measure of independence from the people and from the other branches of government—particularly the Congress.

In line with the framers' goal of increased power to the national government, the president was granted the unconditional power to accept ambassadors from other countries; this amounted to the power to "recognize" other countries. The president was also given the power to negotiate treaties, although their acceptance required the approval of the Senate by a two-thirds vote. The president was given the unconditional right to grant reprieves and pardons, except in cases of impeachment. And the president was provided with the power to appoint major departmental personnel, to convene Congress in special session, and to veto congressional enactments. (The veto power is formidable, but it is not absolute, since Congress can override it by a two-thirds vote.)

The framers hoped to create a presidency that would make the federal government rather than the states the agency capable of timely and decisive action to deal with public issues and problems. This was the meaning of the "energy" that Hamilton hoped to impart to the executive branch.[15] At the same time, however, the framers sought to help the president withstand excessively democratic pressures by creating a system of indirect rather than direct election through a separate electoral college.

Politics Today

The framers sought to create an "energetic" presidency, but some observers believe that the presidency has become too powerful. For example, in 2002 President Bush made it clear that he would go to war in Iraq with or without congressional approval. Has the presidency become too powerful?

The Judicial Branch

In establishing the judicial branch in Article III, the Constitution reflected the framers' preoccupations with nationalizing governmental power and checking radical democratic impulses while guarding against potential interference with liberty and property from the new national government itself.

Under the provisions of Article III, the framers created a court that was to be literally a supreme court of the United States, and not merely the highest court of the national government. The most important expression of this intention was granting the Supreme Court the power to resolve any conflicts that might emerge between federal and state laws. In particular, the Supreme Court was given the right to determine whether a power was exclusive to the national government, concurrent with the states, or exclusive to the states. In addition, the Supreme Court was assigned jurisdiction over controversies between citizens of different states. The long-term significance of this provision was that as the country developed a national economy, it came to rely increasingly on the federal judiciary, rather than on the state courts, for the resolution of disputes.

Judges were given lifetime appointments in order to protect them from popular politics and from interference by the other branches. This, however, did not mean that the judiciary would remain totally impartial to political considerations or to the other branches, for the president was to appoint the judges, and the Senate to approve the appointments. Congress would also have the power to create inferior (lower) courts, to change the jurisdiction of the federal courts, to add or subtract federal judges, and even to change the size of the Supreme Court.

No explicit mention is made in the Constitution of **judicial review**—the power of the courts to render the final decision when there is a conflict of interpretation of the Constitution or of laws between the courts and Congress, the courts and the executive branch, or the courts and the states. The Supreme Court eventually assumed the power of judicial review. Its assumption of this power, as we shall see in Chapter 15, was based not on the Constitution itself but on the politics of later decades and the membership of the Court.

judicial review the power of the courts to review and, if necessary, declare actions of the legislative and executive branches invalid or unconstitutional. The Supreme Court asserted this power in *Marbury v. Madison*

National Unity and Power

Various provisions in the Constitution addressed the framers' concern with national unity and power, including Article IV's provisions for comity (reciprocity) among states and among citizens of all states. Each state was prohibited from discriminating against the citizens of other states in favor of its own citizens. The

Supreme Court was charged with deciding in each case whether a state had discriminated against goods or people from another state. The Constitution restricted the power of the states in favor of ensuring enough power to the national government to give the country a free-flowing national economy.

The framers' concern with national supremacy was also expressed in Article VI, in the **supremacy clause,** which provided that national laws and treaties "shall be the supreme Law of the Land." This meant that all laws made under the "Authority of the United States" would be superior to all laws adopted by any state or any other subdivision, and the states would be expected to respect all treaties made under that authority. The supremacy clause also bound the officials of all governments—state and local as well as federal—to take an oath of office to support the national Constitution. This meant that every action taken by the United States Congress would have to be applied within each state as though the action were in fact state law.

supremacy clause Article VI of the Constitution, which states that laws passed by the national government and all treaties are the supreme law of the land and superior to all laws adopted by any state or any subdivision

Amending the Constitution

The Constitution established procedures for its own revision in Article V. Its provisions are so difficult that Americans have availed themselves of the amending process only seventeen times since 1791, when the first ten amendments were adopted. Many other amendments have been proposed in Congress, but fewer than forty of them have even come close to fulfilling the Constitution's requirement of a two-thirds vote in Congress, and only a fraction have gotten anywhere near adoption by three-fourths of the states. Article V also provides that the Constitution can be amended by a constitutional convention. Occasionally, proponents of particular measures, such as a balanced-budget amendment, have called for a constitutional convention to consider their proposals. Whatever the purpose for which it were called, however, such a convention would presumably have the authority to revise America's entire system of government.

Ratifying the Constitution

The rules for the ratification of the Constitution were set forth in Article VII. Nine of the thirteen states would have to ratify, or agree on, the terms in order for the Constitution to be formally adopted.

Constitutional Limits on the National Government's Power

As we have indicated, although the framers sought to create a powerful national government, they also wanted to guard against possible misuse of that power. To that end, the framers incorporated two key principles into the Constitution—the separation of powers and federalism. A third set of limitations, in the form of the Bill of Rights, was added to the Constitution to help secure its ratification when opponents of the document charged that it paid insufficient attention to citizens' rights.

Although there was much acrimonious debate and necessary compromise as the new Constitution was written, this print suggests that farmers, artisans, and "gentlemen" alike supported it after its ratification.

THE SEPARATION OF POWERS No principle of politics was more widely shared at the time of the 1787 founding than the principle that power must be used to balance power. The French political theorist Baron de la Brède et de Montesquieu (1689–1755) believed that this balance was an indispensable defense against tyranny. His writings, especially his major work, *The Spirit of the Laws,* "were taken as political gospel" at the Philadelphia Convention.[16] Although the principle of the separation of powers was not explicitly stated in the Constitution, the entire structure of the national government was built precisely on Article I, the legislature; Article II, the executive; and Article III, the judiciary (see Figure 2.1).

However, separation of powers is nothing but mere words on parchment without a method to maintain the separation. The method became known by the popular label "checks and balances" (see Figure 2.2). Each branch is given not only its own powers but also some power over the other two branches. Among the most familiar checks and balances are the president's veto as a power over Congress and Congress's power over the president through its control of appointments to high executive posts and to the judiciary. Congress also has power over the president with its control of appropriations and (by the Senate) the right of approval of treaties. The judiciary was assumed to have the power of judicial review over the other two branches.

Another important feature of the separation of powers is the principle of giving each of the branches a distinctly different constituency. Theorists such as Montesquieu called this a "mixed regime," with the president chosen indirectly by electors, the House by popular vote, the Senate (originally) by state legislature, and the judiciary by presidential appointment. By these means, the occupants of each

FIGURE 2.1 ★ The Separation of Powers

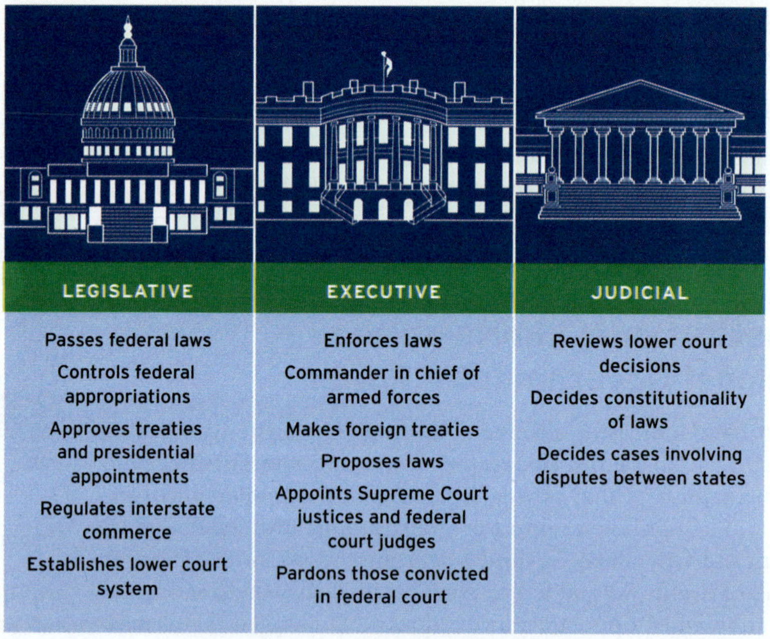

FIGURE 2.2 ★ Checks and Balances

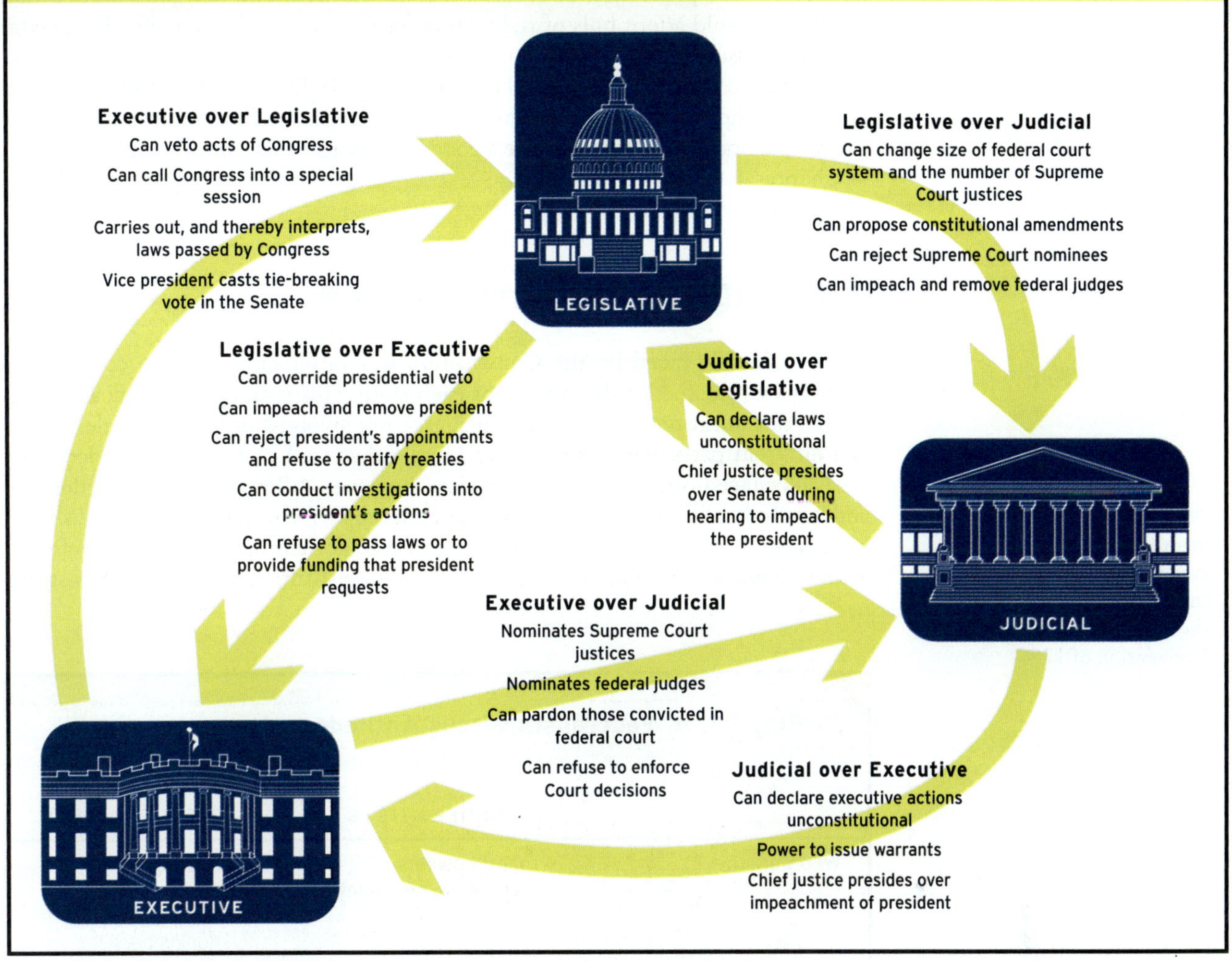

branch would tend to develop very different outlooks on how to govern, different definitions of the public interest, and different alliances with private interests.

FEDERALISM Compared with the confederation principle of the Articles of Confederation, federalism was a step toward greater centralization of power. The delegates agreed that they needed to place more power at the national level, without completely undermining the power of the state governments. Thus, they devised a system of two sovereigns—the states and the nation—with the hope that competition between the two would be an effective limitation on the power of both.

THE BILL OF RIGHTS Late in the Philadelphia Convention, a motion was made to include a list of citizens' rights in the Constitution. After a brief debate in which hardly a word was said in its favor and only one speech was made against it, the motion was almost unanimously turned down. Most delegates sincerely believed that since the federal government was already limited to its expressed powers, further protection of citizens was not needed. The delegates argued that the states should adopt bills of rights because their greater powers needed greater limitations. But almost immediately after the Constitution was ratified, a movement arose to adopt a national bill of rights. This is why the Bill of Rights, adopted in 1791, comprises the first ten amendments to the Constitution rather than being part of the body of it. We will have a good deal more to say about the Bill of Rights in Chapter 4.

The Fight for Ratification

The first hurdle faced by the Constitution was ratification by state conventions of delegates elected by the people of each state. This struggle for ratification was carried out in thirteen separate campaigns. Each involved different people, moved at a different pace, and was influenced by local as well as national considerations. Two sides faced off throughout the states, however, calling themselves Federalists and Antifederalists (see Table 2.1). The **Federalists** (who more accurately should have called themselves "Nationalists," but who took their name to appear to follow in the revolutionary tradition) supported the Constitution and preferred a strong

Federalists those who favored a strong national government and supported the Constitution proposed at the American Constitutional Convention of 1787

TABLE 2.1 ★ Federalists versus Antifederalists

	FEDERALISTS	ANTIFEDERALISTS
Who were they?	Property owners, creditors, merchants	Small farmers, frontiersmen, debtors, shopkeepers
What did they believe?	Believed that elites were most fit to govern; feared "excessive democracy"	Believed that government should be closer to the people; feared concentration of power in hands of the elites
What system of government did they favor?	Favored strong national government; believed in "filtration" so that only elites would obtain governmental power	Favored retention of power by state governments and protection of individual rights
Who were their leaders?	Alexander Hamilton, James Madison, George Washington	Patrick Henry, George Mason, Elbridge Gerry, George Clinton

national government. The **Antifederalists** opposed the Constitution and preferred a federal system of government that was decentralized; they took their name by default, in reaction to their better-organized opponents. The Federalists were united in their support of the Constitution, whereas the Antifederalists were divided over what they believed the alternative to the Constitution should be.

Antifederalists those who favored strong state governments and a weak national government and who were opponents of the Constitution proposed at the American Constitutional Convention of 1787

During the struggle over ratification of the Constitution, Americans argued about great political issues and principles. How much power should the national government be given? What safeguards were most likely to prevent the abuse of power? What institutional arrangements could best ensure adequate representation for all Americans? Was tyranny of the many to be feared more than tyranny of the few?

Federalists versus Antifederalists

During the ratification struggle, thousands of essays, speeches, pamphlets, and letters were presented in support of and in opposition to the proposed Constitution. The best-known pieces supporting ratification of the Constitution were the eighty-five essays written, under the name of "Publius," by Alexander Hamilton, James Madison, and John Jay between the fall of 1787 and the spring of 1788. These ***Federalist Papers,*** as they are collectively known today, defended the principles of the Constitution and sought to dispel fears of a national authority. The Antifederalists published essays of their own, arguing that the new Constitution betrayed the Revolution and was a step toward monarchy. Among the best of the Antifederalist works were the essays, usually attributed to the New York State Supreme Court justice Robert Yates, that were written under the name of "Brutus" and published in the *New York Journal* at the same time the *Federalist Papers* appeared. The Antifederalist view was also ably presented in the pamphlets and letters written by a former delegate to the Continental Congress and future U.S. senator, Richard Henry Lee of Virginia, using the pen name "The Federal Farmer." These essays highlight the major differences of opinion between Federalists and Antifederalists. Federalists appealed to basic principles of government in support of their nationalist vision. Antifederalists cited equally fundamental precepts to support their vision of a looser confederacy of small republics.

Federalist Papers a series of essays written by Alexander Hamilton, James Madison, and John Jay supporting the ratification of the Constitution

REPRESENTATION One major area of contention between the two sides was the question of representation. The Antifederalists asserted that representatives must be "a true picture of the people, . . . [possessing] the knowledge of their circumstances and their wants."[17] This could be achieved, argued the Antifederalists, only in small, relatively homogeneous republics such as the existing states. In their view, the size and extent of the entire nation precluded the construction of a truly representative form of government. As Brutus put it, "Is it practicable for a country so large and so numerous . . . to elect a representation that will speak their sentiments? . . . It certainly is not."[18]

Federalists, for their part, saw no reason that representatives should be precisely like those they represented. In the Federalist view, one of the great advantages of representative government over direct democracy was precisely the possibility that the people would choose as their representatives individuals possessing ability, experience, and talent superior to their own. In Madison's words, rather than serving as a mirror or reflection of society, representatives must be "[those] who possess [the] most wisdom to discern, and [the] most virtue to pursue, the common good of the society."[19]

Federalists versus Antifederalists: The Debate Gets Personal

Historians often cite the *Federalist Papers* and the letters by "Brutus" as the venues where the philosophies of Federalists and Antifederalists were debated. However, the issues surrounding the debate and the personal rivalries that emerged were also prevalent in popular culture in the form of cartoons, poems, and letters to newspaper editors. The feud between the Federalist Representative Roger Griswold of Connecticut and the Antifederalist Representative Matthew Lyon of Vermont in early 1798 illustrates how popular culture has always been a means to communicate political information and opinions to the American public.

Matthew Lyon was an Irish immigrant who advocated direct democracy and, like many Antifederalists, was suspicious of the intentions of elected representatives. During informal discussions in the House of Representatives on January 30, 1798, Lyon spoke loudly about ill-intentioned Connecticut representatives who, he argued, were not interested in carrying out the wishes of their constituents, but rather in maintaining their own power and pursuing their own selfish goals.[a]

The Connecticut Representative Roger Griswold, who was within earshot of Lyon's comments, responded by approaching Lyon and asking if he would march into Connecticut wearing his "wooden sword." Griswold's comments were an allusion to Lyon's dishonorable discharge from the military during the Revolutionary War.

Lyon's response was simple. He spit on Griswold. For several weeks following this episode, Federalist newspapers included various accounts as well as articles criticizing Lyon for violating the congressional honor code. Most argued that some retaliation for Griswold's personally humiliating comments might have been warranted, but not spitting. When Congress took a vote on whether to expel Lyon, the Federalists did not have the two-thirds majority necessary to do so. So Roger Griswold attempted to take matters into his own hands—literally. Armed with a new hickory walking stick, on February 15, 1798, Griswold rose from his seat in the Congress, approached Lyon, and bludgeoned him approximately twenty times in the head while calling him a "scoundrel."

The ongoing saga was the topic of many cartoons, editorials, and poems, including one detailed cartoon, "Congressional Pugilists" (another word for boxers). The cartoon shows Griswold holding a hickory cane above his head and attempting to hit Lyon, who is grasping at a set of fireplace tongs in his own defense. Perhaps most interesting to note are the expressions of onlookers who are either clearly pleased or outraged by the attack, illustrating the extremely partisan environment in Congress at the time.

Some poems and cartoons criticized Congress and expressed alarm over the health of the nation and its developing government. Of particular concern was the young nation's reputation around the world. Other cartoons and poems caricatured Griswold or Lyon, taking one side or the other. One cartoon, for example, compared Griswold with Hercules bravely slaying a lion. A popular poem at the time criticized Griswold's attacking an older man: "A Yankee young dog! to strike a bold paddy, A man old enough to be his grand daddy."[b]

The Griswold-Lyon affair illustrates that popular culture's prominent role in American politics is not a modern phenomenon. Although this feud dominated the headlines of traditional Federalist and Antifederalist publications, rumor of the scuffle spread quickly through other, more accessible avenues such as cartoons and poetry.

FOR CRITICAL ANALYSIS

1. Did cartoons and poetry spread the news of the Griswold-Lyon affair in a way that traditional newspapers could not? How might popular media facilitate quick dissemination of information?
2. Are cartoons, poetry, or political humor capable of communicating complex ideas? Or do they reduce politics to mere caricatures? How might the cartoon "Congressional Pugilists" have enlightened citizens? Or, in contrast, how might it have oversimplified the issues involved?

a. Brian T. Neff, "Fracas in Congress: The Battle of Honor between Matthew Lyon and Roger Griswold," *Essays in History* 41 (1999), http://etext.lib.virginia.edu/journals/EH/EH41/Neff41.html (accessed 2/8/08).

b. "1798: Two Hundred Years Ago; A Congressional Fistfight," *American Heritage* 49, no. 1 (1998), www.americanheritage.com/articles/magazine/ah/1998/1/1998_1_94.shtml (accessed 2/8/08).

Although the terms of discussion have changed, this debate over representation continues today. Some argue that representatives must be very close in life experience, race, and ethnic background to their constituents to truly understand the needs and interests of those constituents. This argument is made by contemporary proponents of giving the states more control over social programs. This argument is also made by proponents of "minority districts"—legislative districts whose boundaries are drawn so as to guarantee that minorities will be able to elect their own representative to Congress. Opponents of this practice, which we will explore further in Chapter 10, have argued in court that it is discriminatory and unnecessary; blacks, they say, can be represented by whites and vice versa. Who is correct? It would appear that this question can never be answered to everyone's complete satisfaction.

TYRANNY OF THE MAJORITY A second important issue dividing Federalists and Antifederalists was the threat of **tyranny**—unjust rule by the group in power. Both opponents and defenders of the Constitution frequently affirmed their fear of tyrannical rule. Each side, however, had a different view of the most likely source of tyranny and, hence, of the way in which to forestall the threat.

tyranny oppressive government that employs cruel and unjust use of power and authority

From the Antifederalist perspective, the great danger was the tendency of all governments—including republican governments—to become gradually more and more "aristocratic" in character, wherein the small number of individuals in positions of authority would use their stations to gain more and more power over the general citizenry. In essence, the few would use their power to tyrannize the many. For this reason, Antifederalists were sharply critical of those features of the Constitution that divorced governmental institutions from direct responsibility to the people—institutions such as the Senate, the executive, and the federal judiciary. The latter, appointed for life, presented a particular threat: "I wonder if the world ever saw . . . a court of justice invested with such immense powers, and yet placed in a situation so little responsible," protested Brutus.[20]

The Federalists, too, recognized the threat of tyranny, but they believed that the danger particularly associated with republican governments was not aristocracy, but instead, majority tyranny. The Federalists were concerned that a popular majority, "united and actuated by some common impulse of passion, or of interest, adverse to the rights of other citizens," would endeavor to "trample on the rules of justice."[21] From the Federalist perspective, it was precisely those features of the Constitution that the Antifederalists attacked as potential sources of tyranny that actually offered the best hope of averting the threat of oppression. The size and extent of the nation, for instance, was for the Federalists a bulwark against tyranny because a majority would have difficulty uniting in a large and populous nation.

GOVERNMENTAL POWER A third major difference between Federalists and Antifederalists was the issue of governmental power. Both opponents and proponents of the Constitution agreed on the principle of **limited government.** They differed, however, on the fundamentally important question of how to place limits on governmental action. Antifederalists favored limiting and enumerating the powers granted to the national government in relation both to the states and to the people at large. To them, the powers given the national government ought to be "confined to certain defined national objects.[22] Otherwise, the national government would "swallow up all the power of the state governments."[23] Antifederalists bitterly attacked the

limited government a government whose powers are defined and limited by a constitution supremacy clause and the elastic clause of the Constitution as unlimited and dangerous grants of power to the national government.[24] Antifederalists also demanded that a bill of rights be added to the Constitution to place limits on the government's exercise of power over the citizenry.

Federalists favored the construction of a government with broad powers. They wanted a government that had the capacity to defend the nation against foreign foes, guard against domestic strife and insurrection, promote commerce, and expand the nation's economy. Antifederalists shared some of these goals but still feared governmental power. Hamilton pointed out, however, that these goals could not be achieved without allowing the government to exercise the necessary power. Federalists acknowledged that every power could be abused but argued that the way to prevent misuse of power was not by depriving the government of the powers needed to achieve national goals. Instead, they argued that the threat of abuse of power would be mitigated by the Constitution's internal checks and controls. As Madison put it, "the power surrendered by the people is first divided between two distinct governments, and then the portion allotted to each subdivided among distinct and separate departments. Hence, a double security arises to the rights of the people. The different governments will control each other, at the same time that each will be controlled by itself."[25] The Federalists' concern with avoiding unwarranted limits on governmental power led them to oppose a bill of rights, which they saw as nothing more than a set of unnecessary restrictions on the government.

The Federalists acknowledged that abuse of power remained a possibility, but felt that the risk had to be taken because of the goals to be achieved. "The very idea of power included a possibility of doing harm," said the Federalist John Rutledge during the South Carolina ratification debates. "If the gentleman would show the power that could do no harm," Rutledge continued, "he would at once discover it to be a power that could do no good."[26] This aspect of the debate between the Federalists and the Antifederalists, perhaps more than any other, continues to reverberate through American politics. Should the nation limit the federal government's power to tax and spend? Should Congress limit the capacity of federal agencies to issue new regulations? Should the government endeavor to create new rights for minorities, the disabled, and others? What is the proper balance between promoting equality and protecting liberty? Though the details have changed, these are the same great questions that have been debated since the Founding.

Politics Today

Today the federal government is stronger than even the Federalists would have envisioned. How might the Federalists and Antifederalists each have reacted to the federal government's intervention into the economy in the wake of the 2008 financial crisis?

Reflections on the Founding

The final product of the Constitutional Convention would have to be considered an extraordinary victory for the groups that had most forcefully called for the creation of a new system of government to replace the Articles of Confederation. Antifederalist criticisms forced the Constitution's proponents to accept the addition of a bill of rights designed to limit the powers of the national government. In general, however, it was the Federalist vision of America that triumphed. The Constitution adopted in 1789 created the framework for a powerful national government that for more than 200 years has defended the nation's interests, promoted its commerce, and maintained national unity. In one notable instance, the national government fought and won a bloody war to prevent the nation from breaking apart. And despite this powerful government, the system of internal checks and balances has functioned reasonably well, as the Federalists predicted, to prevent the national government from tyrannizing its citizens.

The American Constitution: A Model for the World?

The U.S. Constitution is often said to be both the world's oldest written constitution and a continuing model for the nations of the world. Both of these assertions are *partly* accurate. Nearly two millennia before the delegates to America's Constitutional Convention met in Philadelphia, a number of Greek city-states had produced written constitutions.[a] And closer to home, all the first American states possessed written constitutions. Nevertheless, it might be said that the U.S. Constitution is the world's oldest written document that formally organizes the governmental processes of an entire nation. What is sometimes called America's first constitution—the Articles of Confederation—was more a compact among sovereign entities, the states, than an organic statute for a nation.

As to the second assertion, the U.S. Constitution has indeed frequently been a model for others, but other nations' constitution writers often consciously sought to avoid rather than imitate American-style institutions and practices. One important American idea that has been widely copied is that of having a written constitution. After America wrote its constitution in 1789, both Poland and France adopted written constitutions in 1791. The French became so enamored of constitution writing that they put forth four different constitutions during the 1790s alone, as successive revolutionary governments seized power.[b] As revolutions swept Europe during the nineteenth and early twentieth centuries, every new government viewed a written constitution both as an important legitimating instrument and as a declaration that the new regime categorically rejected the despotic and arbitrary practices of its predecessor. Today, virtually all the world's democracies have written constitutions. Britain, Israel, and New Zealand remain important exceptions.[c] Ironically, possession of a written constitution has become such an important attribute of political legitimacy and symbol of freedom that even some despotic regimes have sham constitutions to provide the appearance, albeit not the substance, of popular government. For example, the former Soviet Union often boasted that it possessed the world's most democratic constitution.

Among the world's constitutional democracies, some have copied elements of the American Constitution, but most have chosen patterns of government quite different from the American model. Judicial review of statutes, an American political innovation, has been adopted by most democracies. In a number of instances, too, new constitutions have incorporated the principle of federalism to deal with the problem of ethnic or regional divisions. For example, with American encouragement, both Iraq and Afghanistan have made federalism an important principle in their new constitutional documents. However, it remains to be seen if these constitutions will survive after American troops leave. Few democracies have copied the American system of separation of powers and checks and balances, with most opting, instead, for parliamentary government. Even the Japanese and German constitutions, written under the supervision of American occupation authorities following World War II, created parliamentary systems.

In addition to providing for parliamentary government, most of the world's constitutions have departed from the American model by providing extensive lists of political, social, cultural, and economic rights. For example, the constitution of the Czech Republic includes a lengthy "Charter of Fundamental Rights and Freedoms."

Thus, although the U.S. Constitution inspired many other nations to develop a written constitution, the precise form that national constitutions take can diverge considerably from the American model.

FOR CRITICAL ANALYSIS

1. Is America's Constitution appropriate for every nation? Which elements of the American Constitution might have universal validity? Which features of the American Constitution might be relevant mainly to the United States?
2. The U.S. Constitution is a very brief document, whereas many new constitutions are lengthy documents containing long lists of governmental duties and citizens' rights. What are the advantages and disadvantages of America's constitutional model?

a. Kim Lane Scheppele, "Constitutions Around the World," www.constitutioncenter.org/explore/ThreePerspectivesontheConstitution/ConstitutionsAroundtheWorld.shtml (accessed 2/9/08).

b. Scheppele, "Constitutions."

c. Scheppele, "Constitutions."

Of course, the groups whose interests were served by the Constitution in 1789, mainly the merchants and planters, are not the same groups that benefit from the Constitution's provisions today. Once incorporated into the law, political principles often take on lives of their own and have consequences that were never anticipated by their original champions. Indeed, many of the groups that benefit from constitutional provisions today did not even exist in 1789. Who would have thought that the principle of free speech would influence the transmission of data on the Internet? Who would have predicted that commercial interests that once sought a powerful government might come, two centuries later, to denounce governmental activism as "socialistic"? Perhaps one secret of the Constitution's longevity is that it did not confer permanent advantage on any one set of economic or social forces.

Although they were defeated in 1789, the Antifederalists present us with an important picture of a road not taken and of an America that might have been. Would the country have been worse off if it had been governed by a confederacy of small republics linked by a national administration with severely limited powers? Were the Antifederalists correct in predicting that a government given great power in the hope that it might do good would, through "insensible progress," inevitably turn to evil purposes? Two hundred years of government under the federal Constitution are not necessarily enough to answer these questions definitively. Time must tell.

The Citizen's Role and the Changing Constitution

The Constitution has endured for more than two centuries as the framework of government. But it has not endured without change. Without change, the Constitution might have become merely a sacred text, stored under glass.

Amendments: Many Are Called, Few Are Chosen

amendment a change added to a bill, law, or constitution

The need for change was recognized by the framers of the Constitution, and provisions for **amendment** were incorporated into Article V. Four methods of amendment are provided for in Article V:

1. Passage in House and Senate by two-thirds vote; then ratification by majority vote of the legislatures of three-fourths (thirty-eight) of the states.
2. Passage in House and Senate by two-thirds vote; then ratification by conventions called for the purpose in three-fourths of the states.
3. Passage in a national convention called by Congress in response to petitions by two-thirds of the states; ratification by majority vote of the legislatures of three-fourths of the states.
4. Passage in a national convention, as in (3); then ratification by conventions called for the purpose in three-fourths of the states.

Figure 2.3 illustrates each of these possible methods. Since no amendment has ever been proposed by national convention, however, methods (3) and (4)

In 2003, some conservatives, in an attempt to override several states' laws permitting gay marriage, began a push to add the Federal Marriage Amendment, a Constitutional amendment that defined marriage as a union legal only between a man and a woman.

have never been employed. And method (2) has only been employed once (the Twenty-first Amendment, which repealed the Eighteenth, or Prohibition, Amendment). Thus, method (1) has been used for all the others.

The Constitution has proven to be extremely difficult to amend. In the history of efforts to amend the Constitution, the most appropriate characterization is "many are called, few are chosen." Since 1789, more than 11,000 amendments have been formally offered in Congress. Of these, Congress officially proposed only twenty-nine, and twenty-seven of these were eventually ratified by the states. Two of these—Prohibition and its repeal—cancel each other out, so that for all practical purposes, only twenty-five amendments have been added to the Constitution since 1791.

For Critical Analysis

It is very difficult to amend the Constitution. Should it be made easier? Would our system of government be more democratic if our Constitution could be revised more easily?

The Case of the Equal Rights Amendment

The Equal Rights Amendment (ERA) is a case study of a proposed amendment that almost succeeded. In fact, the ERA is one of the very few proposals that got the necessary two-thirds vote in Congress yet failed to obtain the ratification of the requisite thirty-eight states.

On October 12, 1971, the U.S. House of Representatives approved the Equal Rights Amendment by the required two-thirds majority; the Senate followed suit on March 22, 1972. The amendment was simple:

> Sec. 1. Equality of rights under the law shall not be denied or abridged by the United States or by any State on account of sex.
>
> Sec. 2. The Congress shall have the power to enforce, by appropriate legislation, the provisions of this article.
>
> Sec. 3. This amendment shall take effect two years after the date of ratification.

A Federal Marriage Amendment?

The idea that all Americans are entitled to equal treatment is today a widely accepted principle. More controversial, however, is the matter of how that principle ought to apply to homosexuals. Most Americans embrace a live-and-let-live philosophy regarding homosexuality; at the same time, however, many Americans are uneasy with some highly publicized efforts to extend civil rights for gays. Central to this debate has been the question of whether the government should sanction gay marriage. Some conservatives have proposed amending the Constitution to define marriage as a union of one man and one woman.

Complicating this debate is the full faith and credit clause of the Constitution (Article IV, Section 1), which says that all states must honor the public acts of any other state, including marriage licenses. Thus, if gay marriage is recognized in even one state, other states are obliged to recognize its legality, too. In 1996, Congress enacted the Defense of Marriage Act, which provided that no state was required to recognize a same-sex marriage performed in another state. Vermont has legalized same-sex marriage, and in November 2003, the Massachusetts supreme court ruled that same-sex couples had the right to marry under the state's constitution. As a result, a constitutional test of the Defense of Marriage Act is likely to come before the Supreme Court.

Supporters of gay marriage point out that homosexuality is neither a fad nor a choice, but an involuntary condition. Given this, loving relationships are inevitable, and it is a denial of equality to discriminate against gays because they seek the same bond of marriage as heterosexuals. Civil marriage for gays would amount to formal public recognition of a homosexual union, making it in principle the same as a heterosexual marriage. Such recognition would actually encourage traditional values of fidelity and stability among homosexuals. It would also ease financial, insurance, and other problems, because gay partners could receive health and/or life insurance, and pension benefits, and it would clarify such matters as inheritance, property, and adoption rights. Some localities have extended such rights through domestic-partnership laws, but these enactments are relatively uncommon and vary in their applicability.

Opponents of gay marriage argue that marriage, as it is traditionally defined by law and religion, does and ought to apply only to heterosexual unions. If state governments officially sanctioned gay marriage, they would, in effect, be endorsing a lifestyle that society simply does not equate with heterosexual marriage. Some opponents of gay marriage support a constitutional amendment that would prevent the states from allowing same-sex marriage. Law reflects society's moral values, and those values do not countenance gay unions. Furthermore, a traditional purpose of marriage is the creation of children, and that cannot occur within the confines of a gay marriage (without the intervention of a third person). Many gay couples would seek to adopt children, but not enough research exists to demonstrate whether children would be harmed by such a situation.

The issue of same-sex marriage has posed difficulties for all politicians. Democrats want to please their liberal core constituencies, which favor gay marriage, but are reluctant to alienate moderate voters. At the same time, Republicans need to please their conservative core constituents, who oppose gay marriage, without alienating moderate voters. Former president George W. Bush declared his opposition to gay marriage and his support for the proposed constitutional amendment that would define marriage as a union between a man and a woman. During the 2008 presidential campaign, both Barack Obama and John McCain indicated that they were opposed to gay marriage but said they supported the idea that same-sex partners should be entitled to all the legal rights and privileges of heterosexual married partners.

FOR CRITICAL ANALYSIS

1. Rules governing marriage have traditionally been the province of the states, but the proposed constitutional amendment would remove that right from the states. Should marriage become a federal matter? Why or why not?
2. Why has gay marriage become an important political issue? What are the positions of your senators and congressional representatives on the topic? Perhaps their Web sites or calls to their offices can provide the answer.

FIGURE 2.3 ★
Four Ways the Constitution Can Be Amended

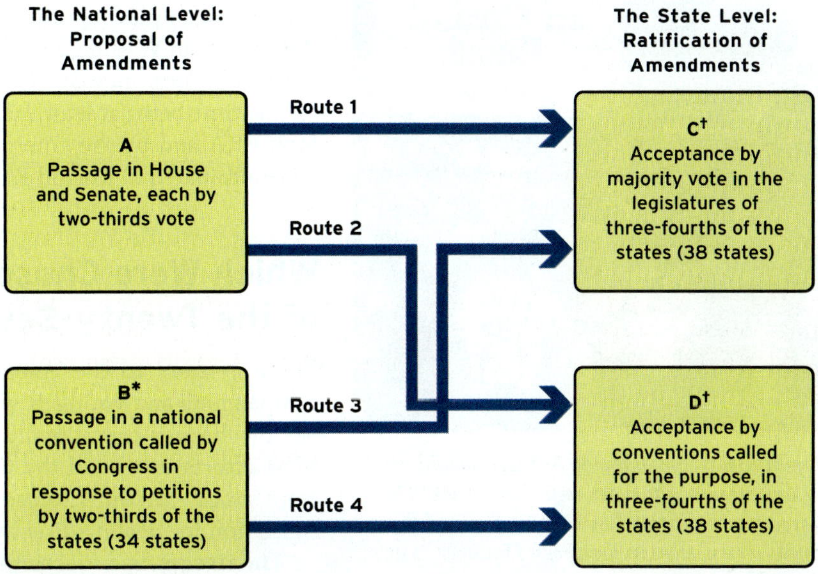

*This method of proposal has never been employed. Thus amendment routes 3 and 4 have never been attempted.
†For each amendment proposal, Congress has the power to choose the method of ratification, the time limit for consideration by the states, and other conditions of ratification. The movement to repeal Prohibition in the Twenty-first Amendment was the only occasion in which route 2 was used successfully. See Richard B. Bernstein, *Amending America: If We Love the Constitution So Much, Why Do We Keep Trying to Change It?* (Lawrence: University of Kansas Press, 1993), 176–77.

The congressional resolution provided for the accustomed method of ratification through the state legislatures rather than by state conventions—route (1) rather than route (2) in Figure 2.3—and that it had to be completed within seven years, by March 22, 1979.

Since the amendment was the culmination of nearly a half-century of efforts, and since the women's movement had spread its struggle for several years prior to 1971, the amendment was ratified by twenty-eight state legislatures during the very first year. But opposition forces who saw the ERA as an expression of radical feminism, quickly organized into the "Stop ERA" movement. By the end of 1974, five more states had ratified the amendment, but three states that had ratified it in 1973—Idaho, Nebraska, and Tennessee—had afterward voted to rescind their ratification. This posed an unprecedented problem: whether a state legislature had the right to rescind its approval. The Supreme Court refused to deal with this question, insisting that it was a political question to be settled by Congress. If the ERA had been ratified by the thirty-eight-state minimum, Congress would have had to decide whether to respect the rescissions or to count them as ratifications.

This point was rendered moot by events. By the end of 1978, thirty-five state legislatures had ratified the ERA—counting the three rescinding legislatures as ratifiers. But even counting them, the three additional state ratifications necessary to reach thirty-eight became increasingly difficult to get. In each of the remaining fifteen states, the amendment had already been rejected at least once. The only hope of the ERA forces was that the 1978 elections would change the composition of some of those state legislatures. Pinning their hopes on that, the ERA forces turned back to

The Equal Rights Amendment, or ERA, would have guaranteed equal rights regardless of sex. The amendment was proposed in 1971 and gained the two-thirds vote needed in Congress. However, it was not ratified by enough states and so did not become part of the Constitution.

Congress and succeeded in getting an extension of the ratification deadline to June 30, 1982. This was an especially significant victory, because it was the first time Congress had extended the time limit since it began placing time restrictions on ratification in 1917. But this victory in Washington failed to impress any of the fifteen holdout legislatures. June 30, 1982, came and went, and the ERA was, for the time being at least, laid to rest. It was beaten by the efforts of Stop ERA and by the emergence of conservatism generally, which had culminated in Ronald Reagan's election as president.[27]

Which Were Chosen? An Analysis of the Twenty-Seven

There is more to the amending difficulties than the politics of campaigning and voting. It would appear that only a limited number of changes can actually be made through the Constitution. Most efforts to amend the Constitution have failed because they were simply attempts to use the Constitution as an alternative to legislation for dealing directly with a public problem.

The twenty-five successful amendments on the other hand, are concerned with the structure or composition of government (see Table 2.2). This is consistent with the dictionary, which defines *constitution* as the makeup or composition of something. And it is consistent with the concept of a constitution as "higher law," because the whole point and purpose of a higher law is to establish a framework within which government and the process of making ordinary law can take place. Even those who would have preferred more changes in the Constitution have to agree that there is great wisdom in this principle. A constitution ought to enable legislation and public policies to take place, but it should not determine what that legislation or those public policies ought to be.

For those whose hopes for change center on the Constitution, it must be emphasized that the amendment route to social change is, and always will be, extremely limited. Through a constitution it is possible to establish a working structure of government, and through a constitution it is possible to establish basic rights of citizens by placing limitations on the powers of that government. Once these things have been accomplished, the real problem is how to extend rights to those people who do not already enjoy them. Of course, the Constitution cannot enforce itself. But it can and does have a real influence on everyday life because a right or an obligation set forth in the Constitution can become a cause of action in the hands of an otherwise powerless person.

Politics Today

In recent years, amendments to prohibit flag burning and to limit marriage to one man and one woman have frequently been proposed in Congress. Given the history of which proposed amendments have succeeded, what challenges do these proposals face?

Private property is an excellent example. Property is one of the most fundamental and well-established rights in the United States; but it is well established not because it is recognized in so many words in the Constitution, but because legislatures and courts have made it a crime for anyone, including the government, to trespass or to take away property without compensation.

A constitution is good if it produces the cause of action that leads to good legislation, good case law, and appropriate police behavior. A constitution cannot eliminate power. But its principles can be a citizen's dependable defense against the abuse of power.

TABLE 2.2 ★ Amendments to the Constitution

AMENDMENT	PURPOSE	YEAR PROPOSED	YEAR ADOPTED
I	*Limits on Congress:* Congress is not to make any law establishing a religion or abridging speech, press, assembly, or petition freedoms.		
II, III, IV	*Limits on Executive:* The executive branch is not to infringe on the right of people to keep arms (II), is not arbitrarily to take houses for a militia (III), and is not to engage in the search or seizure of evidence without a court warrant swearing to belief in the probable existence of a crime (IV).		
V, VI, VII, VIII	*Limits on Courts*:* The courts are not to hold trials for serious offenses without provision for a grand jury (V), a petit (trial) jury (VII) a speedy trial (VI), presentation of charges (VI), confrontation of hostile witnesses (VI), immunity from testimony against oneself (V), and immunity from more than one trial for the same offense (V). Neither bail nor punishment can be excessive (VIII), and no property can be taken without just compensation (V).		
IX, X	*Limits on National Government:* All rights not enumerated are reserved to the states or the people.		
XI	Limited jurisdiction of federal courts over suits involving the states.	1794	1798
XII	Provided separate ballot for vice president in the electoral college.	1803	1804
XIII	Eliminated slavery and eliminated the right of states to allow property in persons.	1865†	1865
XIV	(Part 1) Provided a national definition of citizenship.‡	1866	1868
XIV	(Part 2) Applied due process of Bill of Rights to the states.	1866	1868
XV	Extended voting rights to all races.	1869	1870
XVI	Established national power to tax incomes.	1909	1913
XVII**	Provided direct election of senators.	1911	1913
XIX	Extended voting rights to women.	1919	1920
XX	Eliminated "lame duck" session of Congress.	1932	1933
XXII	Limited presidential term.	1947	1951
XXIII	Extended voting rights to residents of the District of Columbia.	1960	1961

(continued)

TABLE 2.2 ★ Amendments to the Constitution (continued)

AMENDMENT	PURPOSE	YEAR PROPOSED	YEAR ADOPTED
XXIV	Extended voting rights to all classes by abolition of poll taxes.	1962	1964
XXV	Provided presidential succession in case of disability.	1965	1967
XXVI	Extended voting rights to citizens aged 18 and over.	1971	1971[††]
XXVII	Limited Congress's power to raise its own salary.	1789	1992

*These amendments also impose limits on the law-enforcement powers of federal (and especially) state and local executive branches.
†The Thirteenth Amendment was proposed January 31, 1865, and adopted less than a year later, on December 18, 1865.
‡In defining *citizenship*, the Fourteenth Amendment actually provided the constitutional basis for expanding the electorate to include all races, women, and residents of the District of Columbia. Only the "eighteen-year-olds' amendment" should have been necessary, since it changed the definition of citizenship. The fact that additional amendments were required following the Fourteenth suggests that voting is not considered an inherent right of U.S. citizenship. Instead, it is viewed as a privilege.
**The Eighteenth Amendment, ratified in 1919, outlawed the sale and transportation of liquor. It was repealed by the Twenty-first Amendment ratified in 1933.
††The Twenty-sixth Amendment holds the record for speed of adoption. It was proposed on March 23, 1971, and adopted on July 5, 1971.

The Supreme Court and Constitutional Amendment

Although the process of constitutional amendment outlined in Article V has seldom been used successfully, another form of constitutional revision is constantly at work in the United States. This is, of course, judicial interpretation of the Constitution. As the Supreme Court reviews cases, it interprets the meaning of the Constitution and its amendments. In some instances, the Court may give concrete definition to abstract constitutional principles. For example, the Constitution's Fifth Amendment asserts in general terms that individuals accused of crimes are entitled to procedural rights. The Supreme Court, in a series of decisions, established principles giving effect to those rights. Every viewer of television crime programs knows that, when arrested, individuals must receive *Miranda* warnings informing them of their right to refuse to speak and their right to counsel. These warnings are the result of a 1966 Supreme Court decision interpreting the meaning and implications of the Fifth Amendment.

In some instances, the Supreme Court does more than interpret or flesh out constitutional provisions. It seems to modify or augment the text itself. For example, in 1965 and 1973 decisions involving birth control and abortion, the Court said that Americans were constitutionally entitled to a right of privacy. No such right is mentioned anywhere in the Constitution. Similarly, the Court has held that the First Amendment prohibits many forms of government support for religion as well as many forms of religious exercise in public institutions such as schools. The framers of the First Amendment simply meant that the government was prohibited from declaring one religion to be the nation's official faith. They did not intend to prohibit nondenominational school prayer.

Of course, much of the Supreme Court's power is itself based on constitutional interpretation rather than the text of the document. The Supreme Court claims the power of judicial review—the power to render the final decision when there is a conflict of interpretations of the Constitution or federal law among the courts, Congress, the executive branch, or the states. Nowhere does the Constitution mention this power. In a number of early cases, the Supreme Court asserted that the Constitution gave it the power of judicial review, and it was able to rewrite the Constitution to enhance its own power.

Some commentators denounce constitutional amendment by the judiciary and demand that judges limit themselves to "strict construction" of the Constitution, adhering closely to the words of the document's text. Critics of this perspective, on the other hand, assert that the Constitution is a living document subject to change as conditions warrant. Proponents of the idea of the *living Constitution* argue that the judiciary is the institution best qualified to adjust the Constitution's principles to new problems and times. Advocates of strict construction and champions of the living Constitution disagree about the desirability of constitutional amendment by the courts, but both acknowledge its reality.

Thinking Critically about Liberty, Equality, and Democracy

The Constitution's framers placed individual liberty ahead of all other political values. Their concern for liberty led many of the framers to distrust both democracy and equality. They feared that democracy could degenerate into a majority tyranny in which the populace, perhaps led by a rabble-rousing demagogue, would trample on liberty. As to equality, the framers were products of their time and place; our contemporary ideas of racial and gender equality would have been foreign to them. The framers were concerned primarily with another manifestation of equality: they feared that those without property or position might be driven by what some called a "leveling spirit" to infringe on liberty in the name of greater economic or social equality. Indeed, the framers believed that this leveling spirit was most likely to produce demagoguery and majority tyranny. As a result, the basic structure of the Constitution—separated powers, internal checks and balances, and federalism—was designed to safeguard liberty, and the Bill of Rights created further safeguards for liberty. At the same time, however, many of the Constitution's other key provisions, such as indirect election of senators and the president, as well as the appointment of judges for life, were designed to limit democracy and, hence, the threat of majority tyranny.

For Critical Analysis

What are our Constitution's greatest strengths? What are its most pronounced weaknesses? If you were a framer, what changes would you make in the Constitution? Why?

By championing liberty, however, the framers virtually guaranteed that democracy and even a measure of equality would sooner or later evolve in the United States. For liberty promotes the growth of political activity and the expansion of political participation. In James Madison's famous phrase, "Liberty is to faction as air is to fire."[28] Where they have liberty, more and more people, groups, and interests will almost inevitably engage in politics and gradually overcome whatever restrictions might have been placed on participation. This is precisely what happened in the early years of the American Republic. During the Jeffersonian period, political parties formed. During the Jacksonian period, many state suffrage restrictions were

Amending the Constitution

On March 23, 1971, Congress passed a joint resolution in support of the Twenty-sixth Amendment, which lowered the legal voting age from twenty-one to eighteen. Less than four months later, the amendment was ratified by the states, achieving this status faster than any other amendment in U.S. history. Key to the success of the Twenty-sixth Amendment, which effectively enfranchised 11 million new voters aged eighteen to twenty, was a groundswell of activism by America's youth. Angry about the U.S. war in Vietnam, young Americans pushed for ratification with the slogan "Old enough to fight, old enough to vote." Members of Congress and representatives in the state legislatures heard their outcry. By the time the 1972 elections rolled around, young people finally had a constitutionally protected right to participate.

Although only one other amendment has been ratified since the Twenty-sixth, countless others have been introduced by members of Congress or promoted by interested members of the public. All of them have the potential to affect the lives of Americans of all ages. Some of the better-known proposals include:

- ★ The Federal Marriage Amendment, which would define marriage as a union between a man and a woman and expressly prohibit gay marriage.
- ★ The Every Vote Counts Amendment, which would replace the Electoral College with the direct election of the president and vice president.
- ★ The Religious Equality Amendment, which would permit prayer in public school ceremonies and class meetings and protect the teaching of creationism in public schools.
- ★ The English Language Amendment, which would make English the official language of the United States.
- ★ The Flag Desecration Amendment, which would prohibit the desecration (including burning) of the American flag.

If you get involved in these debates, either by pushing for passage of an amendment or working to defeat a proposal, you can have an impact on the actual content of our Constitution. There are several ways to get involved:

- ★ To see exactly what amendments have been proposed in Congress, you can search the Library of Congress archives (at www.thomas.gov.) using the phrase "proposing an amendment to the Constitution" (since most resolutions begin this way).
- ★ When you see the sponsor of the bill, you can contact him or her directly to voice your support or opposition via telephone, letter, or e-mail. An alphabetical list of all members of the House is available at www.house.gov. You can contact senators at www.senate.gov.
- ★ Find an organization that is working on your side of this issue with a quick Internet search of the amendment, or by searching for news articles about the amendment on Lexis/Nexis, a service that is available through most college and university library systems. Once you identify an organization, you can decide if you want to contribute money to the group, or perhaps sign an online petition, or participate in one of their rallies or meetings.
- ★ Each of the fifty states is governed by a constitution, most of which are much easier to amend than the U.S. Constitution. For example, while the Federal Marriage Amendment has not passed in Congress, at least a dozen states have amended their constitutions to ban same-sex marriage. Getting involved at the state level can have a true impact. A good resource on state-level policy is the Pew Research Center's www.stateline.org.

The Eighteenth Amendment was passed in 1919 and prohibited the manufacture, transportation, and sale of alcoholic beverages. Repealed in 1933 by the Twenty-first Amendment, the Prohibition Amendment can be seen as an attempt to legislate through the amendment process.

removed and popular participation greatly expanded. Over time, liberty is conducive to democracy.

Liberty does not guarantee that everyone will be equal. It does, however, reduce the threat of inequality in one very important way. Historically, the greatest inequalities of wealth, power, and privilege have arisen where governments have used their power to allocate status and opportunity among individuals or groups. From the aristocracies of the early modern period to twentieth-century despotisms, the most extreme cases of inequality are associated with the most tyrannical regimes.

The other side of the coin, however, is that the absence of government intervention in economic affairs—in the name of liberty—may mean that there is no antidote to the inevitable inequalities of wealth produced by the marketplace. Economic inequalities, in turn, may lead to inequalities in political power as wealthy groups and individuals use their superior resources to elect politicians friendly to them and their aims and to influence the legislative process. Thus, liberty is a complex matter. In the absence of liberty, inequality is virtually certain. The existence of liberty, however, poses its own threat to political equality. Can we fully reconcile liberty and equality? Doing so remains a constant challenge in a democratic society.

Another limitation of liberty as a political principle is that the idea of limits on government action can also inhibit effective government. Take one of the basic tasks of government, the protection of citizens' lives and property. A government limited by concerns over the rights of those accused of crimes may be limited in its ability to maintain public order. Currently, the U.S. government is asserting that protecting the nation against terrorists requires law enforcement measures that seem at odds with legal and constitutional formalities. The conflict between liberty and governmental effectiveness is another tension at the heart of the American constitutional system.

FOR FURTHER READING

Amar, Akhil Reed. *America's Constitution: A Biography.* New York: Random House, 2006.

Beard, Charles. *An Economic Interpretation of the Constitution of the United States.* New York: Macmillan, 1913.

Dahl, Robert A. *How Democratic Is the American Constitution?* 2nd ed. New Haven, CT: Yale University Press, 2002.

Ellis, Joseph. *American Creation: Triumphs and Tragedies at the Founding of the Republic.* New York: Knopf, 2007.

Hamilton, Alexander, James Madison, and John Jay. *The Federalist Papers.* Edited by Isaac Kramnick. New York: Viking, 1987.

Holton, Woody. *Unruly Americans and the Origins of the Constitution.* New York: Hill and Wang, 2007.

Jensen, Merrill. *The Articles of Confederation.* Madison: University of Wisconsin Press, 1963.

Main, Jackson Turner. *The Social Structure of Revolutionary America.* Princeton, NJ: Princeton University Press, 1965.

Rossiter, Clinton. *1787: Grand Convention.* New York: Macmillan, 1966.

Storing, Herbert, ed. *The Complete Anti-Federalist.* 7 vols. Chicago: University of Chicago Press, 1981.

Winik, Jay. *The Great Upheaval: America and the Birth of the Modern World, 1788–1800.* New York: HarperCollins, 2007.

RECOMMENDED WEB SITES

The American Civil Liberties Union
www.aclu.org
The ACLU is committed to protecting, for all individuals, the freedoms found in the Bill of Rights. This sometimes controversial organization continuously monitors the government for violations of liberty and encourages its members to take political action.

Archiving Early America
www.earlyamerica.com
Revolutionary Americans were motivated by a variety of competing ideals, principles, and interests. Visit this Web site to learn more about the early colonists and the founding of our government.

Constitution Finder
http://confinder.richmond.edu/
Is the American Constitution a model for the world? Explore the constitutions of many different nations and see what elements of the U.S. Constitution can be found in the governing documents of other countries.

FindLaw
http://findlaw.com/casecode/state.html
The Find Law Web site provides all fifty states' constitutions. Click on your state and try to identify such constitutional principles as bicameralism, staggered terms of office, checks and balances, or separation of powers.

The National Archives
www.archives.gov/
This government site provides information about and actual digital images of such founding documents as the Declaration of Independence, the U.S. Constitution, and the Bill of Rights.

The National Constitution Center
www.constitutioncenter.org
The National Constitution Center in Philadelphia maintains a Web site that provides in-depth instructional analysis of the U.S. Constitution. Check out the Interactive Constitution function and follow the document from its Preamble through the Twenty-seventh Amendment.

Oyez
www.oyez.org
This Web site for U.S. Supreme Court Media has a great search engine for finding information on Supreme Court cases. See how the Court has interpreted the Constitution over time.

The PBS *Liberty!* Series
www.pbs.org/ktca/liberty
The PBS *Liberty!* series on the American Revolution offers an in-depth look at the Revolutionary War and includes information on historical events such as the Constitutional Convention.

The Supreme Court of the United States
www.supremecourtus.gov
The Web site for the U.S. Supreme Court provides information on recent decisions. Take a moment to read some oral arguments, briefs, or opinions.

STUDY OUTLINE

www.wwnorton.com/wtp7e

The First Founding: Interests and Conflicts

1. In an effort to alleviate financial problems, including considerable debt, the British government sought to raise revenue by taxing its North American colonies. This energized New England merchants and southern planters, who then organized colonial resistance.
2. Colonial resistance set into motion a cycle of provocation and reaction that resulted in the First Continental Congress and eventually the Declaration of Independence.
3. The Declaration of Independence was an attempt to identify and articulate a history and set of principles that might help to forge national unity.
4. The colonies established the Articles of Confederation and Perpetual Union. Under the Articles, the central government was based entirely in Congress, yet Congress had little power.

The Second Founding: From Compromise to Constitution

1. Concern over America's precarious position in the international community coupled with domestic concern that "radical forces" had too much influence in Congress and in state governments led to the Annapolis Convention in 1786.
2. Shays's Rebellion in Massachusetts provided critics of the Articles of Confederation with the evidence they needed to push for constitutional revision.
3. Recognizing fundamental flaws in the Articles, the delegates to the Philadelphia Convention abandoned the plan to revise the Articles and committed themselves to a second founding.
4. Conflict between large and small states over the issue of representation in Congress led to the Great Compromise, which created a bicameral legislature based on two different principles of representation.
5. The Three-fifths Compromise addressed the question of slavery by apportioning the seats in the House of Representatives according to a population in which five slaves would count as three persons.

The Constitution

1. The new government was to be strong enough to defend the nation's interests internationally, promote commerce and protect property, and prevent the threat posed by "excessive democracy."
2. The House of Representatives was designed to be directly responsible to the people in order to encourage popular consent for the Constitution. The Senate was designed to guard against the potential for excessive democracy in the House.
3. The Constitution grants Congress important and influential powers, but any power not specifically enumerated in its text is reserved specifically to the states.
4. The framers hoped to create a presidency with energy—a president who would be capable of timely and decisive action to deal with public issues and problems.
5. The establishment of the Supreme Court reflected the framers' preoccupations with nationalizing governmental power and checking radical democratic impulses while guarding against potential interference with liberty and property from the new national government itself.
6. Various provisions in the Constitution addressed the framers' concern with national unity and power. Such provisions included clauses promoting reciprocity among states.
7. Procedures for amending the Constitution are provided in Article V. These procedures are so difficult that amendments are quite rare in American history.
8. To guard against possible misuse of national government power, the framers incorporated the principles of the separation of powers and federalism, as well as a Bill of Rights, in the Constitution.
9. The separation of powers was based on the principle that power must be used to balance power.
10. Although the framers' move to federalism was a step toward greater centralization of national government power, they retained state power by devising a system of two sovereigns.
11. The Bill of Rights was adopted as the first ten amendments to the Constitution in 1791.

The Fight for Ratification

1. The struggle for ratification was carried out in thirteen separate campaigns—one in each state.
2. The Federalists supported the Constitution and a stronger national government. The Antifederalists, on the other hand, preferred a more decentralized system of government and fought against ratification.

3. Federalists and Antifederalists had differing views regarding issues such as representation and the prevention of tyranny.
4. Antifederalist criticisms helped to shape the Constitution and the national government, but it was the Federalist vision of America that triumphed.

The Citizen's Role and the Changing Constitution

1. Provisions for amending the Constitution, incorporated into Article V, have proven to be difficult criteria to meet. Relatively few amendments have been made to the Constitution.
2. Most of the amendments to the Constitution deal with the structure or composition of the government.

Thinking Critically about Liberty, Equality, and Democracy

1. The Constitution's framers placed individual liberty ahead of all other political values. But by emphasizing liberty, the framers virtually guaranteed that democracy and equality would evolve in the United States.

PRACTICE QUIZ

www.wwnorton.com/wtp7e

1. In the Revolutionary struggles, which of the following groups was allied with the New England merchants?
   a) artisans
   b) southern planters
   c) western speculators
   d) laborers
2. How did the British attempt to raise revenue in the North American colonies?
   a) income tax
   b) taxes on commerce
   c) expropriation and government sale of land
   d) government asset sales
3. The first governing document in the United States was
   a) the Declaration of Independence.
   b) the Articles of Confederation and Perpetual Union.
   c) the Constitution.
   d) none of the above.
4. Which state's proposal embodied a principle of representing states in the Congress according to their size and wealth?
   a) Connecticut
   b) Maryland
   c) New Jersey
   d) Virginia
5. Where was the execution of laws conducted under the Articles of Confederation?
   a) the presidency
   b) the Congress
   c) the states
   d) the expanding federal bureaucracy
6. Which of the following was *not* a reason that the Articles of Confederation seemed too weak?
   a) the lack of a single voice in international affairs
   b) the power of radical forces in the Congress
   c) the impending "tyranny of the states"
   d) the power of radical forces in several states
7. What mechanism was instituted in the Congress to guard against "excessive democracy"?
   a) bicameralism
   b) staggered Senate terms
   c) appointment of senators for long terms
   d) all of the above
8. Which of the following best describes the Supreme Court as understood by the Founders?
   a) the highest court of the national government
   b) arbiter of disputes within the Congress
   c) a figurehead commission of elders
   d) a supreme court of the nation and its states
9. Which of the following were the Antifederalists most concerned with?
   a) interstate commerce
   b) the protection of property
   c) the distinction between principles and interests
   d) the potential for tyranny in the central government
10. The draft constitution that was introduced at the start of the Constitutional Convention was authored by
    a) Edmund Randolph.
    b) Thomas Jefferson.
    c) James Madison.
    d) George Clinton.

KEY TERMS

www.wwnorton.com/wtp7e

amendment (p. 66)
Antifederalists (p. 61)
Articles of Confederation (p. 46)
bicameral (p. 51)
Bill of Rights (p. 53)
checks and balances (p. 53)
confederation (p. 46)
elastic clause (p. 55)
electoral college (p. 53)
expressed powers (p. 55)
federalism (p. 53)
Federalist Papers (p. 61)
Federalists (p. 60)
Great Compromise (p. 50)
judicial review (p. 56)
limited government (p. 63)
New Jersey Plan (p. 50)
separation of powers (p. 53)
supremacy clause (p. 57)
Three-fifths Compromise (p. 52)
tyranny (p. 63)
Virginia Plan (p. 50)

3 Federalism

- ★ The Federal Framework
- ★ Who Does What? The Changing Federal Framework
- ★ Thinking Critically about Liberty versus Equality in the Federal System

WHAT GOVERNMENT DOES AND WHY IT MATTERS

After Hurricane Katrina slammed into the Gulf Coast in August 2005, thousands of residents of New Orleans—many of them elderly and sick—remained stranded for days on rooftops or in the Louisiana Superdome. Bodies floated in the streets, and looters emptied stores. Meanwhile, officials from local, state, and the federal government pointed fingers at each other for the massive failure of the public response. President Bush used his weekly radio address to imply that the problem was caused by strained state and local capacities. State and local officials in turn charged that the federal government was at fault because it did not take the hurricane warnings seriously or move quickly to provide assistance after the hurricane struck. The response to Katrina revealed the worst of what can happen when local governments, states, and the federal government fail to cooperate.

More than three years after the hurricane, the finger pointing had not stopped. The Federal Emergency Management Agency (FEMA) came in for the toughest criticism for failing to respond swiftly once the scope of the disaster became apparent. But critics also pointed to the poor performance of state and local officials, who in hindsight should have ordered mandatory evacuations sooner. In many cases it was simply unclear what responsibilities the state and federal government each had in such a situation, and when and under what circumstances the federal government should step in.[1] This ambiguity persisted as New Orleans struggled to recover in the years following the storm. Many neighborhoods remained in ruins, and the lack of housing meant that many residents—including a large number of sick and disabled people—were still without homes. The state of Louisiana proposed numerous plans but needed to work with the national government in order to make them a reality, and disagreements over responsibility for these aid programs slowed the recovery.

The United States is a federal system, in which the national government shares power with lower levels of government. Throughout American history, lawmakers, politicians, and citizens have wrestled with questions about how responsibilities should be allocated across the different levels of government. Some responsibilities, such as international relations, clearly lie with the federal government. Others, such as divorce laws, are controlled by state governments. In fact, most of the rules and regulations that Americans face in their daily lives are set by state and local governments. However, many government responsibilities are shared in American federalism and require cooperation among local, state, and federal governments. These include such activities as responding to natural disasters, including hurricanes; building transportation systems that include roads, bridges, airports, and mass transit; providing education; protecting the health and safety of citizens; providing social benefits; protecting civil liberties; and administering criminal justice.

The debate about "who should do what" remains one of the most important discussions in American politics. Much is at stake in how authority is divided up among national, state, and local governments. Reflecting the Founders' mistrust of centralized power and Americans' long-standing preference for local self-government, American federalism promotes the value of democracy by allowing states to set their own standards for many of the issues that most affect people's lives. Variations in state laws reflect the distinctive priorities of each state. Yet since the 1930s, the federal government has played an expanded role in ensuring democracy, equality, and liberty. During the 1960s, it outlawed many obstacles to political participation in the American South. By funding social welfare programs and setting national standards, the federal government helps to limit inequality across the states. Federal laws also ensure that basic liberties are enforced in every state. In recent years, a trend to return more power to the states has allowed greater differences in the laws and social protections in the states. Though this trend has slowed the move toward greater equality, its proponents believe that it has in fact enhanced democracy.

- **In this chapter, we will first look at how federalism was defined in the Constitution.** The framers sought to limit national power by giving states enough power to check the federal government.

- **We will then examine how the federal framework has changed in recent years, and how the national government's power grew.** After the 1930s, the national government began to expand, yet the states maintained most of their traditional powers.

- **We will next assess how changes in federalism reflect the changes in how Americans perceive liberty, equality, and democracy.** American federalism has always been a work in progress. As federal, state, and local governments change, questions about the relationship between American political values and federalism continue to emerge.

- **Finally, we examine current conflicts over federalism.** In recent years, politicians and advocates who want to expand government's role on issues such as health care and immigration have pressed their agenda in the states.

The Federal Framework

The Constitution has had its most fundamental influence on American life through federalism. **Federalism** can be defined as the division of powers and functions between the national government and the state governments. Governments can organize power in a variety of ways. One of the most important distinctions is between unitary and federal governments. In a **unitary system,** the central government makes the important decisions, and lower levels of government have little independent power. In such systems, lower levels of government primarily implement decisions made by the central government. In France, for example, the central government was once so involved in the smallest details of local activity that the minister of education boasted that by looking at his watch he could tell what all French schoolchildren were learning at that time because the central government set the school curriculum. In a **federal system,** by contrast, the central government shares power or functions with lower levels of government, such as regions or states. Nations with diverse ethnic or language groupings, such as Switzerland and Canada, are most likely to have federal arrangements. In federal systems, lower levels of government often have significant independent power to set policy in some areas, such as education and social programs, and to impose taxes. Yet the specific ways in which power is shared vary greatly: no two federal systems are exactly the same.

federalism a system of government in which power is divided, by a constitution, between a central government and regional governments

unitary system a centralized government system in which lower levels of government have little power independent of the national government

federal system a system of government in which the national government shares power with lower levels of government, such as states

Federalism in the Constitution

The United States was the first nation to adopt federalism as its governing framework. With federalism, the framers sought to limit the national government by creating a second layer of state governments. American federalism recognized two sovereigns in the original Constitution and reinforced the principle in the Bill of Rights by granting a few "expressed powers" to the national government and reserving all the rest to the states.

THE POWERS OF THE NATIONAL GOVERNMENT As we saw in Chapter 2, the **expressed powers** granted to the national government are found in Article I, Section 8, of the Constitution. These seventeen powers include the power to collect taxes, to coin money, to declare war, and to regulate commerce (which, as we will see, became a very important power for the national government). Article I, Section 8, also contains another important source of power for the national government: the **implied powers** that enable Congress "to make all Laws which shall be necessary and proper for carrying into Execution the foregoing Powers." Not until several decades after the Founding did the Supreme Court allow Congress to exercise the power granted in this **necessary and proper clause,** but, as we shall see later in this chapter, this doctrine allowed the national government to expand considerably the scope of its authority, although the process was a slow one. In addition to these expressed and implied powers, the Constitution affirmed the power of the national government in the supremacy clause (Article VI), which made all national laws and treaties "the supreme Law of the Land."

The Constitution defines certain powers of the federal government and reserves all others to the states. Town and city governments are not granted any powers in the Constitution. Debates have often erupted when federal laws conflict with state and local laws, as when Hazleton, Pennsylvania passed several ordinances that diverged from federal immigration laws.

expressed powers specific powers granted by the Constitution to Congress (Article I, Section 8), and to the president (Article II)

implied powers powers derived from the necessary and proper clause of Article I, Section 8, of the Constitution. Such powers are not specifically expressed, but are implied through the expansive interpretation of delegated powers

necessary and proper clause Article I, Section 8, of the Constitution, it provides Congress with the authority to make all laws "necessary and proper" to carry out its expressed powers

reserved powers powers, derived from the Tenth Amendment to the Constitution, that are not specifically delegated to the national government or denied to the states

police power power reserved to the state government to regulate the health, safety, and morals of its citizens

concurrent powers authority possessed by *both* state and national governments, such as the power to levy taxes

THE POWERS OF STATE GOVERNMENT One way in which the framers sought to preserve a strong role for the states was through the Tenth Amendment to the Constitution. The Tenth Amendment states that the powers that the Constitution does not delegate to the national government or prohibit to the states are "reserved to the States respectively, or to the people." The Antifederalists, who feared that a strong central government would encroach on individual liberty, repeatedly pressed for such an amendment as a way of limiting national power. Federalists agreed to the amendment because they did not think it would do much harm, given the powers of the Constitution already granted to the national government. The Tenth Amendment is also called the **reserved powers** amendment because it aims to reserve powers to the states.

The most fundamental power that the states retain is that of coercion—the power to develop and enforce criminal codes, to administer health and safety rules, to regulate the family via marriage and divorce laws. The states have the power to regulate individuals' livelihoods; if you're a doctor or a lawyer or a plumber or a barber, you must be licensed by the state. Even more fundamental, the states had the power to define private property—private property exists because state laws against trespass define who is and is not entitled to use a piece of property. If you own a car, your ownership isn't worth much unless the state is willing to enforce your right to possession by making it a crime for anyone else to drive your car without your consent. These are fundamental matters, and the powers of the states regarding these domestic issues are much greater than the powers of the national government, even today.

A state's authority to regulate these fundamental matters is commonly referred to as the **police power** of the state and encompasses the state's power to regulate the health, safety, welfare, and morals of its citizens. Policing is what states do—they coerce you in the name of the community in order to maintain public order. And this was exactly the type of power that the Founders intended the states to exercise.

In some areas, the states share **concurrent powers** with the national government, whereby they retain and share some power to regulate commerce and to affect the currency—for example, by being able to charter banks, grant or deny corporate charters, grant or deny licenses to engage in a business or practice a trade, and regulate the quality of products or the conditions of labor. This issue of concurrent versus exclusive power has come up from time to time in our history, but wherever there is a direct conflict of laws between the federal and the state levels, the issue will most likely be resolved in favor of national supremacy.

full faith and credit clause provision from Article IV, Section 1, of the Constitution, requiring that the states normally honor the public acts and judicial decisions that take place in another state

STATE OBLIGATIONS TO EACH OTHER The Constitution also creates obligations among the states. These obligations, spelled out in Article IV, were intended to promote national unity. By requiring the states to recognize actions and decisions taken in other states as legal and proper, the framers aimed to make the states less like independent countries and more like components of a single nation.

Article IV, Section I, calls for "Full Faith and Credit" among states, meaning that each state is normally expected to honor the "public Acts, Records, and judicial Proceedings" that take place in any other state. So, for example, if a couple is married in Texas—marriage being regulated by state law—Missouri must also recognize that marriage, even though the couple was not married under Missouri state law.

This **full faith and credit clause** has recently become embroiled in the controversy over gay and lesbian marriage. In December 1999, the Vermont Supreme Court ruled that gay and lesbian couples should have the same rights as heterosex-

From the Entertainment World to State and Local Politics

Under the American version of federalism, state governments have considerable power, and states and regions have their own lively political cultures. For example, in states, cities, and towns across the country, popular entertainers occasionally enter political life, drawing on their fame to get elected and to maintain their appeal while in office. These candidates often reflect the popular culture most prominent in their regions. In the South, for example, country music stars who run for office may have the advantage of widespread name recognition. In California, Hollywood stars have played an important role in state politics for decades.

Perhaps the most famous country music star to hold high state office was Jimmie Davis, known for his song "You Are My Sunshine." Recorded in 1940, the song became an international hit and propelled Davis into superstardom. Although he had held only minor public offices prior to 1944, Davis was easily elected governor of Louisiana.

Film and television stars have used their fame to win office most frequently in California. When rumors began to circulate in 2003 that the action film star Arnold Schwarzenegger might run for governor of California, many found the idea far-fetched. Yet, Schwarzenegger very effectively used his fame to build excitement and energy around his candidacy. Schwarzenegger drew on his show-business skills throughout the campaign, attracting enormous crowds and regularly using his most famous one-liners, "hasta la vista, baby" and "I'll be back." Although the glow of stardom faded after a few years in office, Schwarzenegger—now "the Governator"—was re-elected in 2006.

Other actors have also won office in California. The most famous actor-turned-politician was Ronald Reagan, who was elected governor in 1966 and went on to become president in 1980. At the local level, Clint Eastwood, of spaghetti westerns and Dirty Harry fame, and the singer Sonny Bono have both served as mayors. Although Eastwood decided to leave politics after one term, Bono went on to make politics his career, serving two terms in the House of Representatives.

In Minnesota, the pro wrestler Jesse "The Body" Ventura shocked the political establishment when he won election as governor in 1998. Known for his bad-boy persona as a wrestler, Ventura launched his political career by winning election as mayor of a Minneapolis suburb. He ran for governor as a third-party candidate who promised a big departure from politics as usual.

In 2006, the country musician and comic Kinky Friedman ran for governor of Texas on a similar platform, bringing in Ventura to help him campaign. Although he stood little chance of winning, Friedman attracted considerable media attention and distinguished himself from the career politicians in the race with slogans like "How Hard Could It Be?" and "Why The Hell Not?"

Entertainers have the advantage of name recognition when they enter politics. In state and local elections, such recognition alone may be enough to offset charges of inexperience. However, once in office, popular entertainers who enter state and local politics have varied careers. While some leave office after one term, others go on to make a career in politics. Popular entertainers who start their careers in state and local politics may also find it hard to attain sufficient stature to enter the national political arena. Moreover, the broad (but shallow) appeal that allows celebrities to win office may make it difficult for them to govern effectively. Research shows that celebrities often lack the firm base of political support needed to govern.[a]

FOR CRITICAL ANALYSIS

1. Why have more entertainers sought political office at the state and local level, rather than the national level?
2. Have entertainers won office in your state or local governments? How did their careers in show business affect their ability to govern?

---

a. Darrell M. West and John M. Orman, *Celebrity Politics* (Upper Saddle River, NJ: Prentice Hall, 2003).

uals. The Vermont legislature responded with a new law that allowed gays and lesbians to form "civil unions." Although not legally considered marriages, such unions allow gay and lesbian couples most of the benefits of marriage, such as eligibility for the partner's health insurance, inheritance rights, and the right to transfer property. In 2003, the Massachusetts Supreme Court went further, ruling that gays and lesbians have the right to marry under state law. The Court directed the state legislature to amend state law to allow such marriages. In 2006, a Massachusetts court ruled that same-sex couples from states that do not explicitly outlaw gay marriage can be married in Massachusetts. Only two states—New Mexico and Rhode Island—were affected by the ruling. Neither has agreed to legally recognize the marriages, although Rhode Island's state attorney general recommended that Rhode Island do so. In 2008, a New York court ruled that valid out-of-state marriages must be recognized as legal. In the case considered, the couple had married in Ontario, Canada.[2] However, the new law does not mean that same-sex couples from New York can cross into Massachusetts to marry and return to New York with a marriage that must be legally recognized. This is because Massachusetts only allows couples to marry if their home states don't ban gay marriage, which New York does. After Massachusetts legalized gay marriage, several other states including Connecticut, New Jersey, and New Hampshire approved civil unions among gays and lesbians. By 2008, a total of nine states (in addition to Massachusetts) had approved some spousal rights for same-sex partners. Advocates supporting gay and lesbian marriage have launched legal efforts to overturn bans in states across the country. They appeared to have some success in 2007, when an Iowa judge struck down that state's defense of marriage act. However, four hours later the judge issued a stay against issuing marriage licenses to same-sex couples pending legal appeals. During the few hours that gay marriage was legal in Iowa, one same sex couple tied the knot.[3] Such state-level legal efforts to legalize gay marriage were dealt a blow in 2007, when Maryland's Supreme Court—considered liberal—ruled that the ban on gay marriage was legal. The decisions by the high courts in California and Connecticut to legalize same-sex marriage in 2008 reopened the questions about whether other states would have to recognize such marriages. Although some legal analysts believed that other states would not have to recognize these marriages, all agreed that the issue would generate lawsuits in states across the country if gay marriage remained legal.

Politics Today

In 2008 the California and Connecticut supreme courts ruled that gays and lesbians had the right to marry under state law, following a similar decision in Massachusetts. Do other states have to recognize same-sex marriages performed in these states under the full faith and credit clause?

Advocates of gay marriage are not the only groups active in state politics; opponents of gay marriage have also mobilized in states across the country. By 2008, forty-one states had passed "defense of marriage acts" that define marriage as a union between one man and one woman only. Most of these states also outlaw recognition of gay marriages in other states. Anxious to show its disapproval of gay marriage, Congress passed the Defense of Marriage Act in 1996, which declared that states will *not* have to recognize a same-sex marriage, even if it is legal in one state. The act also said that the federal government will not recognize gay marriage—even if it is legal under state law—and that gay marriage partners will not be eligible for the federal benefits, such as Medicare and Social Security, normally available to spouses.[4]

Gay marriage is not the only issue in which the "full faith and credit" clause has come into play. It has also played a role in conflicts over gay adoption. In these cases, however, the courts have so far ruled that the full faith and credit clause requires states to accept the legal decisions of other states. Three states—Florida, Mississippi, and Utah—explicitly ban gay adoption and several other states sharply restrict it. An Oklahoma law banned state agencies from recognizing adoption orders to gay and lesbian couples approved in states that permit such adoption. Effectively, this meant that Oklahoma refused to issue birth certificates for children born in Oklahoma but legally adopted by same sex couples from other states. In 2007 a federal appeals court struck down the Oklahoma law, ruling that full faith and credit clause required Oklahoma to honor adoption orders approved by courts in other states.[5] For a further discussion of gay and lesbian marriage, see Chapter 5.

Article IV, Section 2, known as the "comity clause," also seeks to promote national unity. It provides that citizens enjoying the **privileges and immunities** of one state should be entitled to similar treatment in other states. What this has come to mean is that a state cannot discriminate against someone from another state or give special privileges to its own residents. For example, in the 1970s, when Alaska passed a law that gave residents preference over nonresidents in obtaining work on the state's oil and gas pipelines, the Supreme Court ruled the law illegal because it discriminated against citizens of other states.[6] This clause also regulates criminal justice among the states by requiring states to return fugitives to the states from which they have fled. Thus, in 1952, when an inmate escaped from an Alabama prison and sought to avoid being returned to Alabama on the grounds that he was being subjected to "cruel and unusual punishment" there, the Supreme Court ruled that he must be returned according to Article IV, Section 2.[7] This example highlights the difference between the obligations among states and those among different countries. In 1997, France refused to return an American fugitive because he might be subject to the death penalty, which does not exist in France.[8] The Constitution clearly forbids states from doing something similar.

privileges and immunities clause provision from Article IV, Section 2, of the Constitution, that a state cannot discriminate against someone from another state or give its own residents special privileges

States' relationships with each other are also governed by the interstate compact clause (Article I, Section 10), which states that "No State shall, without the Consent of Congress . . . enter into any Agreement or Compact with another State." The Court has interpreted the clause to mean that states may enter into agreements with each other, subject to congressional approval. Compacts are a way for two or more states to reach a legally binding agreement about how to solve a problem that crosses state lines. In the early years of the Republic, states turned to compacts primarily to settle border disputes. Today compacts are used for a wide range of issues but are especially important in regulating the distribution of river water, addressing environmental concerns, and operating transportation systems that cross state lines.[9]

TABLE 3.1 ★ 89,527 Governments in the United States

TYPE	NUMBER
National	1
State	50
County	3,033
Municipal	19,492
Townships	16,519
School districts	13,051
Other special districts	37,381

SOURCE: U.S. Census Bureau, www.census.gov/govs/cog/GovOrgTab03ss.html (accessed 7/14/08).

LOCAL GOVERNMENT AND THE CONSTITUTION Local government occupies a peculiar but very important place in the American system. In fact, the status of American local government is probably unique in world experience. First, it must be pointed out that local government has no status in the American Constitution. *State* legislatures created local governments, and *state* constitutions and laws permit local governments to take on some of the responsibilities of the state governments. Most states amended their own constitutions to give their larger cities **home rule**—a guarantee of noninterference in various areas of local affairs. But local governments enjoy no such recognition in the Constitution. Local governments have always been mere conveniences of the states.[10]

home rule power delegated by the state to a local unit of government to manage its own affairs

Local governments became administratively important in the early years of the Republic because the states possessed little administrative capability. They relied on local governments—cities and counties—to implement the laws of the state. Local government was an alternative to a statewide bureaucracy (see Table 3.1).

Restraining National Power with Dual Federalism, 1789–1937

dual federalism the system of government that prevailed in the United States from 1789 to 1937, in which most fundamental governmental powers were shared between the federal and state governments

As we have noted, the Constitution created two layers of government: the national government and the state governments. The consequences of this **dual federalism** are fundamental to the American system of government in theory and in practice; they have meant that states have done most of the fundamental governing. For evidence, look at Table 3.2. It lists the major types of public policies by which Ameri-

TABLE 3.2 ★ The Federal System: Specialization of Governmental Functions in the Traditional System (1800–1933)

NATIONAL GOVERNMENT POLICIES (DOMESTIC)	STATE GOVERNMENT POLICIES	LOCAL GOVERNMENT POLICIES
Internal improvements	Property laws (including slavery)	Adaptation of state laws to local conditions ("variances")
Subsidies	Estate and inheritance laws	Public works
Tariffs	Commerce laws	Contracts for public works
Public lands disposal	Banking and credit laws	Licensing of public accommodations
Patents	Corporate laws	Assessible improvements
Currency	Insurance laws	Basic public services
	Family laws	
	Morality laws	
	Public health laws	
	Education laws	
	General penal laws	
	Eminent domain laws	
	Construction codes	
	Land-use laws	
	Water and mineral laws	
	Criminal procedure laws	
	Electoral and political parties laws	
	Local government laws	
	Civil service laws	
	Occupations and professions laws	

In 1815, President James Madison called for a federally funded program of "internal improvements," which was one of the few policy roles for the national government during the first half of the nineteenth century. By improving transportation through the construction of roads and canals, the government fostered the growth of the market economy and boosted federal power.

cans were governed for the first century and a half under the Constitution. We call it the "traditional system" because it prevailed for much of American history and because it closely approximates the intentions of the framers of the Constitution.

Under the traditional system, the national government was quite small compared with both the state governments and the governments of other Western nations. Not only was it smaller than most governments of that time, but it was also actually very narrowly specialized in the functions it performed. The national government built or sponsored the construction of roads, canals, and bridges (internal improvements). It provided cash subsidies to shippers and shipbuilders and distributed free or low-priced public land to encourage western settlement and business ventures. It placed relatively heavy taxes on imported goods (tariffs), not only to raise revenues but also to protect "infant industries" from competition from the more advanced European enterprises. It protected patents and provided for a common currency, also to encourage and facilitate enterprises and to expand markets.

What do these functions of the national government reveal? First, virtually all the functions were aimed at assisting commerce. It is quite appropriate to refer to the traditional American system as a "commercial republic." Second, virtually none of the national government's policies directly coerced citizens. The emphasis of governmental programs was on assistance, promotion, and encouragement—the allocation of land or capital where they were insufficiently available for economic development.

Meanwhile, state legislatures were actively involved in economic regulation during the nineteenth century. In the United States, then and now, private property exists only in state laws and state court decisions regarding property, trespass, and real estate. American capitalism took its form from state property and trespass laws, as well as from state laws and court decisions regarding contracts, markets, credit, banking, incorporation, and insurance. Laws concerning slavery were a subdivision of property law in states where slavery existed. The practice of important professions, such as law and medicine, was and is illegal, except as provided for by state law.

In 1916, the national government passed the Keating-Owen Child Labor Act, which excluded from interstate commerce all goods manufactured by children under fourteen. The act was ruled unconstitutional by the Supreme Court, and the regulation of child labor remained in the hands of state governments until the 1930s.

Marriage, divorce, the registration of births and adoption of a child have always been regulated by state law. To educate or not to educate a child has been a decision governed more by state laws than by parents, and not at all by national law. It is important to note also that virtually all criminal laws—regarding everything from trespass to murder—have been state laws. Most of the criminal laws adopted by Congress are concerned with the District of Columbia and other federal territories.

All this (and more, as shown in the middle column of Table 3.2) demonstrates that most of the fundamental governing in the United States was done by the states. The contrast between national and state policies, as shown by Table 3.2, demonstrates the difference in the power vested in each. The list of items in the middle column could actually have been made longer. Moreover, each item on the list is a category of law that fills many volumes of statutes and court decisions.

This contrast between national and state governments is all the more impressive because it is basically what the framers of the Constitution intended. Since the 1930s, the national government has expanded into local and intrastate matters, far beyond what anyone could have foreseen in 1790, 1890, or even in the 1920s. But this significant expansion of the national government did not alter the basic framework. The national government has become much larger, but the states have continued to be central to the American system of government.

Herein lies probably the most important point of all: the fundamental impact of federalism on the way the United States is governed comes not from any particular provision of the Constitution but from the framework itself, which has determined the flow of government functions and, through that, the political development of the country. By allowing state governments to do most of the fundamental governing, the Constitution saved the national government from many policy decisions that might have proven too divisive for a large and very young country. There is no doubt that if the Constitution had provided for a unitary rather than a federal system, the war over slavery would have come in 1789 or 1809 rather than in 1860; and if it had come that early, the South might very well have seceded and established a separate and permanent slaveholding nation.

In helping the national government remain small and aloof from the most divisive issues of the day, federalism contributed significantly to the political stability of the nation, even as the social, economic, and political systems of many of the states and regions of the country were undergoing tremendous, profound, and sometimes violent, change.[11] As we shall see, some important aspects of federalism have changed, but the federal framework has survived two centuries and a devastating civil war.

Federalism and the Slow Growth of the National Government's Power

Having created the national government, and recognizing the potential for abuse of power, the states sought through federalism to constrain the national government. The "traditional system" of a weak national government prevailed for over a century despite economic forces favoring its expansion and despite Supreme Court cases giving a pro-national interpretation to Article I, Section 8, of the Constitution.

That article delegates to Congress the power "to regulate commerce with foreign nations, and among the several States and with the Indian tribes." This **commerce clause** was consistently interpreted *in favor* of national power by the Supreme Court for most of the nineteenth century. The first and most important case favoring national power over the economy was *McCulloch v. Maryland*.[12] This case involved the question of whether Congress had the power to charter a national bank, since such an explicit grant of power was nowhere to be found in Article I, Section 8. Chief Justice John Marshall answered that the power could be "implied" from other powers that were expressly delegated to Congress, such as the "powers to lay and collect taxes; to borrow money; to regulate commerce; and to declare and conduct a war."

commerce clause Article I, Section 8, of the Constitution, which delegates to Congress the power "to regulate commerce with foreign nations, and among the several States and with the Indian tribes." This clause was interpreted by the Supreme Court in favor of national power over the economy

By allowing Congress to use the necessary and proper clause to interpret its delegated powers expansively, the Supreme Court created the potential for an unprecedented increase in national government power. Marshall also concluded that whenever a state law conflicted with a federal law (as in the case of *McCulloch v. Maryland*, the state law would be deemed invalid since the Constitution states that "the Laws of the United States . . . shall be the supreme Law of the Land." Both parts of this great case are pro-national, yet Congress did not immediately seek to expand the policies of the national government.

Another major case, *Gibbons v. Ogden* in 1824, reinforced this nationalistic interpretation of the Constitution. The important but relatively narrow issue was whether the state of New York could grant a monopoly to Robert Fulton's steamboat company to operate an exclusive service between New York and New Jersey. Chief Justice Marshall argued that New York State did not have the power to grant this particular monopoly. In order to reach this decision, Marshall had to define what Article I, Section 8, meant by "commerce among the several states." He insisted that the definition was "comprehensive," extending to "every species of commercial intercourse." He did say that this comprehensiveness was limited "to that commerce which concerns more states than one," giving rise to what later came to be called "interstate commerce." *Gibbons* is important because it established the supremacy of the national government in all matters affecting interstate commerce.[13] But what would remain uncertain during several decades of constitutional discourse was the precise meaning of interstate commerce.

Backed by the implied powers decision in *McCulloch* and by the broad definition of "interstate commerce" in *Gibbons*, Article I, Section 8, was a source of power for the national government as long as Congress sought to facilitate commerce through subsidies, services, and land grants. But later in the nineteenth century, when the national government sought to use those powers to *regulate* the economy rather than merely to promote economic development, federalism and the concept of interstate commerce began to operate as restraints on, rather than sources of, national power. Any effort of the national government to regulate commerce in such areas as fraud, the production of impure goods, the use of child labor, or the existence of dangerous working conditions or long hours was declared unconstitutional by the Supreme Court as a violation of the concept of interstate commerce. Such legislation meant that the federal government was entering the factory and the workplace—local areas—and was attempting to regulate goods that had not passed into commerce. To enter these local workplaces was to exercise police power—the power reserved to the states for the protection of the health, safety, and morals of their citizens. No one questioned the power of the national government to regulate businesses that intrinsically involved interstate commerce, such as railroads, gas pipelines, and waterway transportation. But well into the twentieth century, the Supreme Court used the concept of interstate commerce as a barrier against most efforts by Congress to regulate local conditions.

This aspect of federalism was alive and well during an epoch of tremendous economic development, the period between the Civil War and the 1930s. It gave the American economy a freedom from federal government control that closely approximated the ideal of free enterprise. The economy was never entirely free, of course; in fact, entrepreneurs themselves did not want complete freedom from government. They needed law and order. They needed a stable currency. They needed courts and police to enforce contracts and prevent trespass. They needed roads, canals, and railroads. But federalism, as interpreted by the Supreme Court for seventy years after the Civil War, made it possible for business to have its cake and eat it, too. Entrepreneurs enjoyed the benefits of national policies facilitating commerce and were protected by the courts from policies regulating commerce.[14]

All this changed after 1937, when the Supreme Court issued a series of decisions that laid the groundwork for a much stronger federal government. Most significant was the Court's dramatic expansion of the commerce clause. By throwing out the old distinction between interstate and intrastate commerce, the Court converted the commerce clause from a source of limitations to a source of power for the national government. The Court upheld acts of Congress protecting the rights of employees to organize and engage in collective bargaining, regulating the amount of farmland in cultivation, extending low-interest credit to small businesses and farmers, and restricting the activities of corporations dealing in the stock market. The Court also upheld many other laws that contributed to the construction of the "welfare state."[15] With these rulings, the Court decisively signaled that the era of dual federalism was over. In the future, Congress would have very broad powers to regulate activity in the states.

The Changing Role of the States

states' rights the principle that the states should oppose the increasing authority of the national government. This principle was most popular in the period before the Civil War

As we have seen, the Constitution contained the seeds of a very expansive national government—in the commerce clause. For much of the nineteenth century, federal power remained limited. The Tenth Amendment was used to bolster arguments in favor of **states' rights,** which in their extreme version claimed that the states did not have to submit to national laws when they believed the national government had exceeded its authority. These arguments in favor of states' rights were voiced less often after the Civil War. But the Supreme Court continued to use the Tenth

AMERICA IN THE WORLD

International Trade Agreements and the States

The Constitution reserves for the federal government the power to make foreign policy and to enter into treaties. Yet the expansion of the global economy over the past three decades has also increased the importance of the international arena for state and local governments. For states, the expansion of international trade offers new opportunities to promote economic development but also presents enormous frustrations. This is because international trade agreements may tie the hands of states and because states have little formal voice in the provisions of these agreements.

One of the most important such trade agreements is the North American Free Trade Act (NAFTA), a treaty signed by Canada, the United States, and Mexico in 1992 to open trade across the national borders of these three countries. It also created new trade rules that each national government is obligated to follow. Although American state governments were not involved in creating these trade rules, the new rules may significantly restrict their own policies. Other trade agreements, such as those negotiated through the World Trade Organization (WTO), also may limit what states can do. Other trade agreements that have recently aroused concern in the states are proposed rulings that would label many common state procurement policies as barriers to trade, and therefore unenforceable. Procurement policies determine who can sell goods and provide services to the state. States often impose conditions on the companies with which they do business. For example, some states have policies requiring them to buy local or American-made products in an effort to reduce the offshoring of jobs. Other states impose requirements aimed at improving the environment, including provisions for buying goods with recycled content, or doing business with firms that use renewable energy sources. These conditions vary from state to state and are a product of the political process in different states. As Governor John Baldacci of Maine noted in a 2006 letter to the U.S. trade representative, "The state of Maine's procurement laws have been developed to protect the interests of Maine's citizens and businesses and to reflect the state's commitment to spend its citizens' tax dollars in a socially and environmentally responsible way."[a]

The states have challenged these proposed rulings as an infringement on state sovereignty. And some states have started to pass legislation to ensure that trade agreements are scrutinized by the state legislature. For example, in 2007, the Hawaii state legislature passed legislation—over the governor's veto—to ensure that only the state legislature can approve or reject the terms relating to procurement in international trade agreements. It became the third state to pass such legislation, joining Rhode Island and Maryland.

One of the major complaints that states have is that they have no voice in the process of formulating trade agreement provisions even when such agreements significantly limit their sovereignty and regulatory authority. Five state legislatures (California, Washington, Maine, North Carolina, and Minnesota) have created formal committees on international trade and federalism. These committees aim to give their state greater capacity to assess the impact of trade agreements, and to gain expert and constituency views about the trade and state economic development policies. These committees are also a point of contact between the state legislatures and the U.S. trade representative and the members of Congress on issues related to trade and economic development. The potential for trade agreements to restrict the traditional democratic decision-making powers of the states means that in the future, states will have to consider the international repercussions of their actions as a normal part of state lawmaking.

FOR CRITICAL ANALYSIS

1. How do international treaties such as NAFTA and international organizations such as the World Trade Organization affect the sovereign powers of the states?
2. What are states doing to ensure that their interests are considered when the federal government enters into international trade agreements?

---

a. www.citizens.org/documents/Baldacci_to_Portman_32006.pdf (accessed 9/25/07).

States' rights have been embraced by many causes in the past fifty years. Governor George Wallace of Alabama, a vocal supporter of states' rights, defiantly turned back U.S. Attorney General Nicholas Katzenbach, who tried to enroll two black students at the University of Alabama at Tuscaloosa in 1963.

Amendment to strike down laws that it thought exceeded national power, including the Civil Rights Act passed in 1875.

In the early twentieth century, however, the Tenth Amendment appeared to lose its force. Reformers began to press for national regulations to limit the power of large corporations and to preserve the health and welfare of citizens. The Supreme Court approved some of these laws but it struck others down, including a law combating child labor. The Court stated that the law violated the Tenth Amendment because only states should have the power to regulate conditions of employment. By the late 1930s, however, the Supreme Court had approved such an expansion of federal power that the Tenth Amendment appeared irrelevant. The desire to promote equal conditions across the country had elevated the federal government over the states. In fact, in 1941, Justice Harlan Fiske Stone declared that the Tenth Amendment was simply a "truism," that it had no real meaning.[16]

Yet the idea that some powers should be reserved to the states did not go away. One reason is that groups with substantive policy interests often support states' rights as a means for achieving their policy goals. For example, in the 1950s, southern opponents of the civil rights movement revived the idea of states' rights to support racial segregation. In 1956, ninety-six southern members of Congress issued a "Southern Manifesto" in which they declared that southern states were not constitutionally bound by Supreme Court decisions outlawing racial segregation. They believed that states' rights should override individual rights to liberty and formal equality. With the triumph of the civil rights movement, the slogan of "states' rights" became tarnished by its association with racial inequality.

devolution a policy to remove a program from one level of government by delegating it or passing it down to a lower level of government, such as from the national government to the state and local governments

The 1990s saw a revival of interest in the Tenth Amendment and important Supreme Court decisions limiting federal power. Much of the interest in the Tenth Amendment stemmed from conservatives who believed that a strong federal government encroaches on individual liberties. They believed such freedoms are better protected by returning more power to the states through the process of **devolution.** In 1996, the Republican presidential candidate Bob Dole carried a copy of the Tenth Amendment in his pocket as he campaigned, pulling it out to read at rallies.[17] The

Especially since the mid-1990s, Republican Party leaders have contended that the national government has grown too powerful at the expense of the states and argue that the Tenth Amendment should restrict the growth of national power.

Supreme Court's ruling in *United States v. Lopez* in 1995 fueled further interest in the Tenth Amendment.[18] In that case, the Court, stating that Congress had exceeded its authority under the commerce clause, struck down a federal law that barred handguns near schools. This was the first time since the New Deal that the Court had limited congressional powers in this way. In 1997, the Court again relied on the Tenth Amendment to limit federal power in *Printz v. United States.*[19] The decision declared unconstitutional a provision of the Brady Handgun Violence Prevention Act that required state and local law enforcement officials to conduct background checks on handgun purchasers. The Court declared that this provision violated state sovereignty guaranteed in the Tenth Amendment because it required state and local officials to administer a federal regulatory program. The Court also limited the power of the federal government over the states in a 1996 ruling that prevented Native Americans from the Seminole tribe from suing the state of Florida in federal court. A 1988 law had given Indian tribes the right to sue a state in federal court if the state did not negotiate in good faith over issues related to gambling casinos on tribal land. The Supreme Court's ruling appeared to signal a much broader limitation on national power by raising new questions about whether individuals can sue a state if it fails to uphold federal law.[20]

In 2003, the Court surprised many observers by ruling against the state of Nevada's challenge to the application of the federal Family and Medical Leave Act to Nevada state employees. The act guarantees workers time off (without pay) for family care responsibilities. The Court's decision, which required Nevada state government to abide by the Family and Medical Leave Act, appeared to conflict with earlier decisions immunizing states against lawsuits on the basis of age and disability discrimination. Perhaps most surprising was the support of former Chief Justice William Rehnquist, a strong proponent of states' rights. In his opinion, Rehnquist argued that family care issues were so strongly gender related that the Family and Medical Leave Act was necessary to prevent unconstitutional discrimination against women. Such protection against unconstitutional discrimination justified overriding state immunity in Rehnquist's view. Some analysts viewed the decision, in which the Court showed that on fundamental matters of civil rights federal law would supersede state sovereignty, as potentially a key turning point in judicial rulings on federalism.

The expansion of the power of the national government has not left the states powerless. The state governments continue to make important laws. No better demonstration of the continuing influence of the federal framework can be offered than that the middle column of Table 3.2 is still a fairly accurate characterization of state government today. In each of these domains, however, states must now share power with the federal government.

For Critical Analysis

How have Supreme Court decisions affected the balance of power between the federal government and the states? Has the Supreme Court favored the federal government or the states?

Who Does What? The Changing Federal Framework

Questions about how to divide responsibilities between the states and the national government first arose more than 200 years ago, when the framers wrote the Constitution to create a stronger union. But they did not solve the issue of who should do what. There is no "right" answer to that question; each generation of Americans has provided its own answer. In recent decades, Americans have grown distrustful of the federal government and have supported giving more responsibility to the states.[21] Even so, they still want the federal government to set standards, promote equality, and provide security.

Political debates about the division of responsibility often take sides: some people argue for a strong federal role to set national standards, whereas others say the states should do more. These two goals are not necessarily at odds. The key is to find the right balance. During the first 150 years of American history, that balance favored state power. But the balance began to shift toward Washington in the 1930s. In this section, we will look at how the balance shifted, and then we will consider current efforts to reshape the relationship between the national government and the states.

Expansion of the National Government

The New Deal of the 1930s signaled the rise of a more active national government. The door to increased federal action opened when states proved unable to cope with the demands brought on by the Great Depression. Before the depression, states and localities took responsibility for addressing the needs of the poor, usually through private charity. But the extent of the need created by the depression quickly exhausted local and state capacities. By 1932, 25 percent of the workforce was unemployed. The jobless lost their homes and settled into camps all over the country, called "Hoovervilles," after President Herbert Hoover. Elected in 1928, the year before the depression hit, Hoover steadfastly maintained that the federal government could do little to alleviate the misery caused by the depression. It was a matter for state and local governments, he said.

Yet demands mounted for the federal government to take action. In Congress, some Democrats proposed that the federal government finance public works to aid the economy and put people back to work. Other members of Congress introduced legislation to provide federal grants to the states to assist them in their relief efforts. None of these measures passed while Hoover remained in the White House.

When Franklin D. Roosevelt took office in 1933, he energetically threw the federal government into the business of fighting the depression. He proposed a variety of temporary measures to provide federal relief and work programs. Most of the programs he proposed were to be financed by the federal government but administered by the states. In addition to these temporary measures, Roosevelt presided over the creation of several important federal programs designed to provide future economic security for Americans.

During the Great Depression, the national government became more active in regulating the economy and supporting the poor. New Deal programs sought to aid those affected by the depression, such as residents of this Hooverville outside of Seattle, which was photographed in 1933.

Federal Grants

For the most part, the new national programs that the Roosevelt administration developed did not directly take power away from the states. Instead, Washington typically redirected states by offering them **grants-in-aid,** whereby Congress appropriates money to state and local governments on the condition that the money be spent for a particular purpose defined by Congress.

The principle of the grant-in-aid can be traced back to the nineteenth-century land grants that the national government made to the states for the improvement of agriculture and farm-related education. Since farms were not in "interstate commerce," it was unclear whether the Constitution permitted the national government to provide direct assistance to agriculture. Grants made to the states, but designated for farmers, presented a way of avoiding the question of constitutionality while pursuing what was recognized in Congress as a national goal.

grants-in-aid programs through which Congress provides money to state and local governments on the condition that the funds be employed for purposes defined by the federal government

Franklin Roosevelt's New Deal expanded the range of grants-in-aid into social programs, providing grants to the states for financial assistance to poor children. Congress added more grants after World War II, creating new programs to help states fund activities such as providing school lunches and building highways. Sometimes the national government required state or local governments to match the national contribution dollar for dollar, but in some programs, such as the development of the interstate highway system, the congressional grants provided 90 percent of the cost of the program.

These types of federal grants-in-aid are also called **categorical grants,** because the national government determines the purposes, or categories, for which the money can be used. For the most part, the categorical grants created before the 1960s simply helped the states perform their traditional functions.[22] During the 1960s, however, the national role expanded and the number of categorical grants increased dramatically. For example, during the 89th Congress (1965–66) alone, the number of categorical grant-in-aid programs grew from 221 to 379.[23] The value of categorical grants also has risen dramatically, increasing in value from $2.3 billion in 1950 to an estimated $467 billion in 2008. The grants authorized during the 1960s announced national purposes much more strongly than did earlier grants. One of the most important—and expensive—was the federal Medicaid program, which provides states with grants to pay for medical care for the poor, the disabled, and many nursing home residents (see Figure 3.1).

categorical grants congressional grants given to states and localities on the condition that expenditures be limited to a problem or group specified by law

project grants grant programs in which state and local governments submit proposals to federal agencies and for which funding is provided on a competitive basis

formula grants grants-in-aid in which a formula is used to determine the amount of federal funds a state or local government will receive

Many of the categorical grants enacted during the 1960s were **project grants,** which require state and local governments to submit proposals to federal agencies. In contrast to the older **formula grants,** which used a formula (composed of such

FIGURE 3.1 ★ Historical Trend of Federal Grants-in-Aid,* 1950–2008

Spending on federal grants-in-aid to the states has grown dramatically since 1990. These increases reflect the growing public expectations about what government should do. What is the most important cause of the steady increase in these grants?

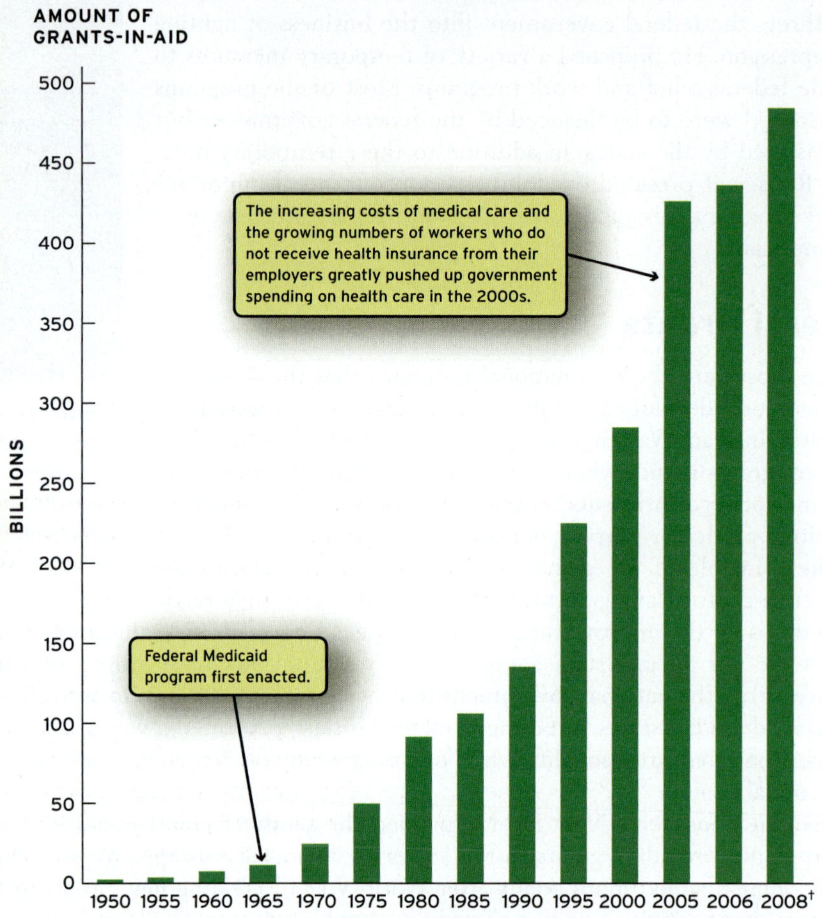

*Excludes outlays for national defense, international affairs, and net interest.

†Estimate

SOURCE: Office of Management and Budget, www.gpoaccess.gov/usbudget/fy09/pdf/spec.pdf (accessed 3/26/08).

elements as need and state and local capacities) to distribute funds, the new project grants made funding available on a competitive basis. Federal agencies would give grants to the proposals they judged to be the best. In this way, the national government acquired substantial control over which state and local governments got money, how much they got, and how they spent it.

Cooperative Federalism

cooperative federalism a type of federalism existing since the New Deal era in which grants-in-aid have been used strategically to encourage states and localities (without commanding them) to pursue nationally defined goals. Also known as "intergovernmental cooperation"

The growth of categorical grants created a new kind of federalism. If the traditional system of two sovereigns performing highly different functions could be called dual federalism, historians of federalism suggest that the system since the New Deal could be called **cooperative federalism.** The political scientist Morton Grozdins characterized this as a move from "layer-cake federalism" to "marble-cake federalism,"[24] in which intergovernmental cooperation and sharing have blurred a once-clear distinguishing line, making it difficult to say where the national government ends and the state and local governments begin (see Figure 3.2). Figure 3.3 demonstrates the financial basis of the marble-cake idea.

FIGURE 3.2 ★
Dual versus Cooperative Federalism

In layer-cake federalism, the responsibilities of the national government and state governments are clearly separated. In marble-cake federalism, national policies, state policies, and local policies overlap in many areas.

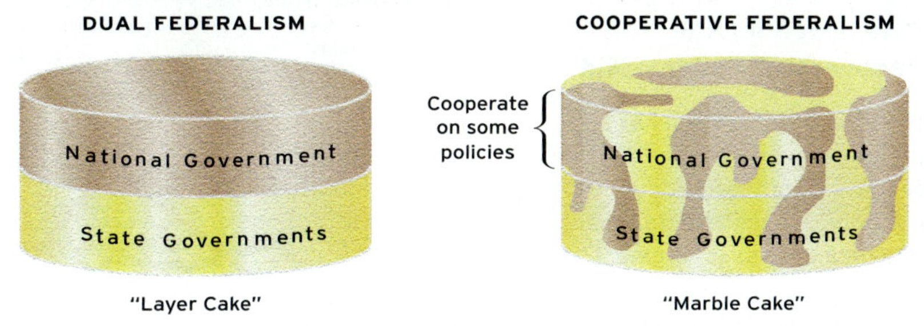

For a while in the 1960s, however, it appeared as if the state governments would become increasingly irrelevant to American federalism. Many of the new federal grants bypassed the states and instead sent money directly to local governments and even to local nonprofit organizations. The theme heard repeatedly in Washington was that the states simply could not be trusted to carry out national purposes.[25]

One of the reasons that Washington distrusted the states was because of the way African American citizens were treated in the South. The southern states' forthright defense of segregation, justified on the grounds of states' rights, helped to tarnish the image of the states as the civil rights movement gained momentum. The national officials who planned the War on Poverty during the 1960s pointed to the racial exclusion practiced in the southern states as a reason for bypassing state governments. The political scientist James Sundquist described how the "Alabama syndrome" affected the War on Poverty: "In the drafting of the Economic Opportunity Act, an 'Alabama syndrome' developed. Any suggestion within the poverty task force that the states be given a role in the administration of the act was met with the question, 'Do you want to give that kind of power to [the Alabama governor] George Wallace?' "[26]

Yet even though many national policies of the 1960s bypassed the states, other new programs, such as Medicaid—the health program for the poor—relied on state governments for their implementation. In addition, as the national government expanded existing programs run by the states, states had to take on more responsibility. These new responsibilities meant that the states were playing a very important role in the federal system.

Regulated Federalism and National Standards

The question of who decides what each level of government should do goes to the very heart of what it means to be an American citizen. How different should things be when one crosses a state line? In what policy areas is it acceptable for states to differ? In what areas should states be similar? How much inequality across the states is acceptable? Supreme Court decisions about the fundamental rights of American citizens provide the most important answers to these questions. Over time, the Court has pushed for greater uniformity across the states. In addition to

FIGURE 3.3 ★ The Rise, Decline, and Recovery of Federal Aid

The level of federal aid has varied over the past several decades as program costs and politics have affected the role the national government plays in funding state and local services. The data in this figure show a rise, decline, and recovery of federal aid. What factors contributed to each of these trends?

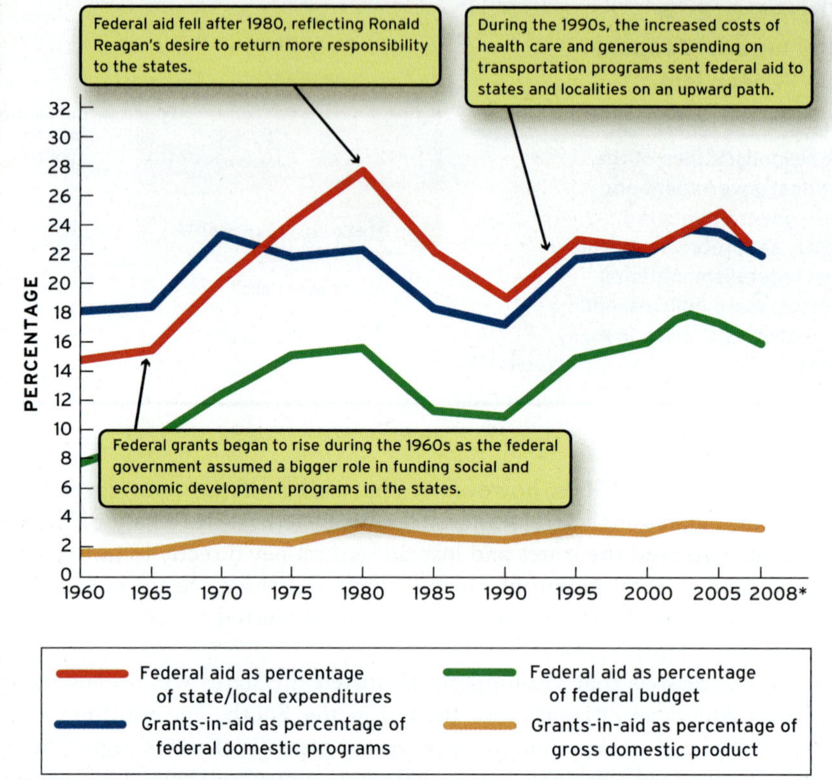

*Estimate

SOURCE: Office of Management and Budget, www.gpoaccess.gov/usbudget/fy09/pdf/spec.pdf (accessed 3/26/08).

legal decisions, the national government uses two other tools to create similarities across the states: grants-in-aid and regulations.

Grants-in-aid, as we have seen, are a little like bribes: Congress gives money to state and local governments if they agree to spend it for the purposes Congress specifies. But as Congress began to enact legislation in new areas, such as environmental policy, it also imposed additional regulations on states and localities. Some political scientists call this a move toward **regulated federalism.**[27] The national government began to set standards of conduct or required the states to set standards that met national guidelines. The effect of these national standards is that state and local policies in the areas of environmental protection, social services, and education are more uniform from coast to coast than are other nationally funded policies.

regulated federalism a form of federalism in which Congress imposes legislation on states and localities, requiring them to meet national standards

Some national standards require the federal government to take over areas of regulation formerly overseen by state or local governments. Such **preemption** occurs when state and local actions are found to be inconsistent with federal requirements. In some cases, federal laws and regulations are more stringent than state laws. For example, as federal regulations proliferated after the 1970s, Washington increasingly preempted state and local action in many different policy areas. These preemptions required the states to abide by tougher federal rules in policies as diverse as air and water pollution, occupational health and safety, and access for the handicapped. The regulated industries often oppose such laws because they increase the cost of doing business. More recently, the federal gov-

preemption the principle that allows the national government to override state or local actions in certain policy areas

In 2005, the Supreme Court ruled that the federal government had the right to prosecute individuals for using medical marijuana, even in states that had made such use legal. Despite the Court's ruling, some states have continued to permit the dispensing and use of medical marijuana.

ernment has used it preemption power in business's favor, limiting the ability of states to tax and regulate industry. For example, the Internet Tax Freedom Act (ITFA), first enacted by Congress in 1998 and then renewed in 2001 and 2004, prohibits states and localities from taxing Internet access services. Congress is not the only federal body that can preempt the states; federal regulatory agencies can also issue rules that override state law. One recent controversial case involves a 2006 Food and Drug Administration drug-labeling rule preempting state laws that allow individuals to sue drug companies in state courts. Opponents—many of them trial lawyers—charged that such rules amount to "stealth preemption" that "will deprive consumers of their right to hold negligent corporations accountable for injuries caused by defective products."[28] Supporters claimed that the rules were a proper use of federal authority. Preemption by federal agency rules attracted the attention of the Democratic Congress in 2007, prompting the Senate Judiciary Committee to hold hearings to investigate whether federal agencies were "usurping congressional and state authority."[29] This preemption has escalated since 1995, when Republicans gained control of Congress. Although the Republicans came to power promising to grant more responsibility to the states, they ended up reducing state control in many areas by preemption.

For Critical Analysis

Is federal preemption of local laws desirable? Is preemption justified for some issues more than for others?

State and local governments often contest federal preemptions. For example, in 2001, Attorney General John Ashcroft declared that Oregon's law permitting doctor-assisted suicide was illegal under federal drug regulations. Oregon took the Justice Department to federal court, which ruled in favor of the local law, stating that the federal government had overstepped its boundaries. In January 2006, the Supreme Court ruled in a 6-to-3 vote that the attorney general did not have the authority to outlaw the Oregon law. In other recent cases, federal preemption of local laws has been more successful, as in federal efforts to nullify the medical marijuana statutes passed by several states. Although voters in eleven states have approved medical use of marijuana, the federal government has conducted raids on dispensers of medical marijuana, charging that they violate federal law. In 2005, the Supreme Court ruled that the federal government can prosecute people who use medical marijuana, although it did not strike down the state laws sanctioning use of medical marijuana.

unfunded mandates regulations or conditions for receiving grants that impose costs on state and local governments for which they are not reimbursed by the federal government

The growth of national standards has created some new problems and has raised questions about how far federal standardization should go. One problem that emerged in the 1980s was the increase in **unfunded mandates**—regulations or new conditions for receiving grants that impose costs on state and local governments for which they are not reimbursed by the national government. The growth of unfunded mandates was the product of a Democratic Congress, which wanted to achieve liberal social objectives, and a Republican president, who opposed increased social spending. Between 1983 and 1991, Congress mandated standards in many policy areas, including social services and environmental regulations, without providing additional funds to meet those standards. Altogether, Congress enacted twenty-seven laws that imposed new regulations or required states to expand existing programs.[30] For example, in the late 1980s, Congress ordered the states to extend the coverage provided by Medicaid, the medical insurance program for the poor. The aim was to make the program serve more people, particularly poor children, and to expand services. But Congress did not supply additional funding to help states meet these new requirements; the states had to shoulder the increased financial burden themselves.

States and localities quickly began to protest the cost of unfunded mandates. Although it is very hard to determine the exact cost of federal regulations, the Congressional Budget Office estimated that between 1983 and 1990, new federal regulations cost states and localities between $8.9 and $12.7 billion.[31] States complained that mandates took up so much of their budgets that they were not able to set their own priorities.

These burdens became part of a rallying cry to reduce the power of the federal government—a cry that took center stage when a Republican Congress was elected in 1994. One of the first measures the new Congress passed was an act to limit the cost of unfunded mandates, the Unfunded Mandate Reform Act (UMRA). Under this law, Congress must estimate the cost of any proposal it believes will cost more than $50 million. It must then vote to approve the regulation, acknowledging the expenditure. At most, UMRA was an effort to move the national-state relationship a bit further to the state side. But it has had no significant impact on mandates. The act does not prevent congressional members from passing unfunded mandates but only makes them think twice before they do. Moreover, the act exempts several areas of regulation. States must still enforce antidiscrimination laws and meet other requirements to receive federal assistance.

For Critical Analysis

Should states be required to implement unfunded mandates? Are Americans better off or worse off as a result of devolution?

Despite considerable talk about unfunded mandates, the federal government has not acted to help states pay for existing mandates, many of which have grown very costly over the years. New national problems inevitably raise the question of "who pays?" Since the terrorist attacks of 2001, state governments have grown deeply concerned about the costs of security. Although ensuring the common defense is traditionally a federal responsibility, where responsibility for homeland security lies is not clear. This is not surprising because no one had ever used the term *homeland security* before the terror attacks. Since 2001, the costs of homeland security have fallen heavily on the states. In 2003, states, faced with their worst fiscal crises in sixty years, complained that the federal assistance provided for homeland security was far too little. At its annual meetings that year, the National Governors' Association declared homeland security an unfunded mandate

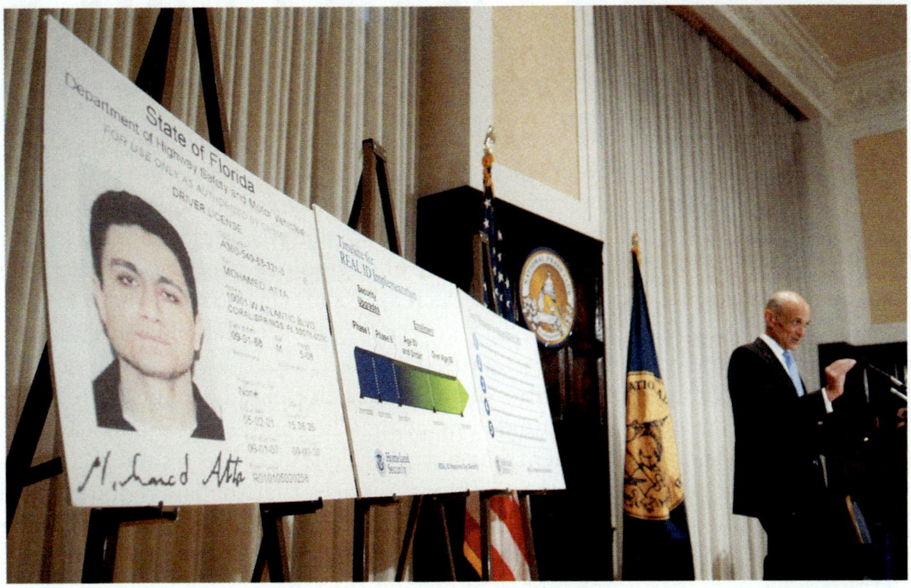

In 2005, Congress enacted the Real ID Act as a national security measure. Some states have complained that it forces them to make costly changes in their procedures for issuing drivers' licenses without providing funding to cover these costs. Opponents also argue that it may violate citizens' privacy.

with which the federal government should help more. The relationship between national security needs and state and local capabilities remains an unsettled area.

Among the most controversial of the state costs associated with national security is the Real ID Act of 2005, which created, among other things, minimum national standards for state-issued driver's licenses. The law, enacted as an antiterrorism measure, requires that state-issued licenses include specific information and stipulates that the information be digitized into a bar code. Many states claim that the measure is an unfunded mandate that will not only cost states money but will also invade citizens' privacy and make them vulnerable to ID theft. A number of states passed laws refusing to implement the act; others have passed resolutions announcing their opposition. For example, in 2007, the Maine legislature overwhelmingly passed a resolution refusing to implement the law although it backed down a year later. Soon after, the lower house of the Utah legislature unanimously passed a resolution opposing the act, charging that it is "in opposition to the Jeffersonian principles of individual liberty, free markets, and limited government."[32] The law was scheduled to go into effect on May 11, 2008, but states could request an extension to January 1, 2010. After that date, individuals in noncompliant states will have to use federal identification, such as a passport, for activities where federal agencies require an ID, including entry into national parks and domestic air travel.[33]

New Federalism and State Control

In 1970, the mayor of Oakland, California, told Congress that his city had twenty-two separate employment and training programs but that few poor residents were being trained for jobs that were available in the local labor market.[34] National programs had proliferated as Congress enacted many small grants, but little effort was made to coordinate or adapt programs to local needs. Today many governors argue for more control over such national grant programs. They complain that

The States, the Federal Government, and Public Education

The United States stands out among developed nations for its early and strong support of free public education. The provision of primary and secondary education has historically been the responsibility of state and local governments. Not until the 1960s did the federal government provide substantial funding for public schools. Even so, primary and secondary education remains largely funded by state and local governments: today, the federal government provides only 10 percent of the total spending on K–12 education. Since the 1980s, presidents have sought to respond to widespread concerns about the quality of American public education. Despite all the talk about education in Washington, the federal effort to improve public education remained primarily symbolic until 2002, with the passage of President George W. Bush's No Child Left Behind law.

No Child Left Behind dramatically expanded the federal role in public education. The goal of the law is to improve the quality of education by holding schools accountable for results. It requires testing in reading and math from the third to the eighth grades. The test results, which are reported to parents and to the federal government, have to be broken down by school, grade, race, ethnicity, and income level. Schools that fail to show steady progress in all subgroups of students are required to take remedial actions, which include extra tutoring for students and additional professional training for teachers. Schools that continue to fail can ultimately be closed and their staffs replaced. The goal is to move all students up to proficiency in math and reading by 2014. The law provides extra funding to help schools meet this goal.

Defenders of the strong federal role in the No Child Left Behind act point out that many states and localities have failed to deliver quality education and have especially neglected low-income students. Federal action is needed because an educated population is an important national resource. The country needs an educated population in order to compete internationally.

Moreover, supporters of the law believe that the federal government is in the best position to enforce educational standards because many state and local governments are unduly influenced by teachers' unions, which have long resisted standards and accountability in the schools. Federal action is particularly needed to ensure that low-income and minority students receive a quality education. Because their parents are not powerful and because their school districts are often resource poor, these students are frequently neglected by state and local districts. It is up to the federal government to see that all children have a chance to succeed.

Critics of No Child Left Behind denounce the law as an unfunded mandate. They argue that the federal government has not provided adequate resources to support the additional services that the law requires. Even though many of the services mandated in the law for failing schools are desirable, states simply do not have the money to pick up the tab.

Opponents also argue that No Child Left Behind is an intrusive law. It imposes a "one size fits all" model on schools, which should respond to local needs. Many suburban parents and educators, for example, reject the law's emphasis on testing. They believe that education should promote critical thinking, not the rote learning required to succeed on standardized tests. Because needs are so diverse, education policy demands the kind of flexibility that only states and localities can ensure. Critics claim that in usurping the state role, No Child Left Behind not only undermines state sovereignty but also threatens the future of public education.

Intense disagreements about how to reform the law prevented Congress from agreeing on a reauthorization plan for No Child Left Behind in 2007. It will fall to President Obama and the Democratic Congress to craft a revised law that can win wide support.

FOR CRITICAL ANALYSIS

1. Why do critics call the No Child Left Behind law an unfunded mandate that will harm low-income and minority students?
2. Why do supporters of the No Child Left Behind law believe that the federal government is better able than state and local governments to ensure that all children receive a high-quality education?

FIGURE 3.4 ★ Regulated versus New Federalism

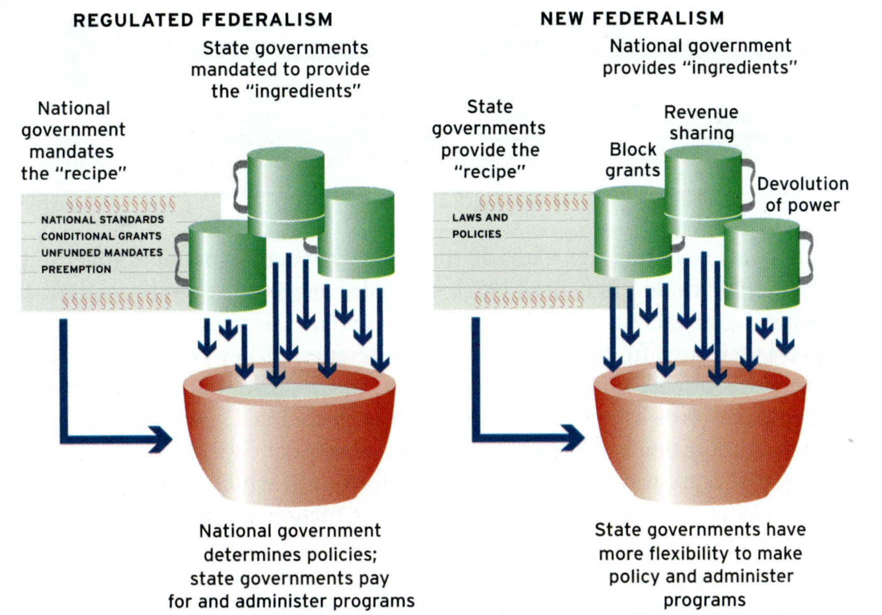

national grants do not allow for enough local flexibility and instead take a "one size fits all" approach.[35] These criticisms point to a fundamental problem in American federalism: how to get the best results for the money spent. Do some divisions of responsibility between states and the federal government work better than others? Since the 1970s, as states have become more capable of administering large-scale programs, the idea of devolution—transferring responsibility for policy from the federal government to the states and localities—has become popular.

Proponents of more state authority have looked to **block grants** as a way of reducing federal control. Block grants are federal grants that allow the states considerable leeway in spending federal money. President Nixon led the first push for block grants in the early 1970s, as part of his **New Federalism.** Nixon's block grants consolidated programs in the areas of job training, community development, and social services into three large block grants. These grants imposed some conditions on states and localities as to how the money should be spent, but not the narrow regulations contained in the categorical grants. In addition, Congress provided an important new form of federal assistance to state and local governments called **general revenue sharing.** Revenue sharing provided money to local governments and counties with no strings attached; localities could spend the money as they wished. In enacting revenue sharing, Washington acknowledged both the critical role that state and local governments play in implementing national priorities and their need for increased funding and enhanced flexibility in order to carry out that role (see Figure 3.4). Reagan's version of New Federalism also looked to block grants. Like Nixon, Reagan wanted to reduce the national government's control and return power to the states. In all, Congress created twelve new block grants between 1981 and 1990.[36]

block grants federal grants-in-aid that allow states considerable discretion in how the funds are spent

New Federalism attempts by Presidents Nixon and Reagan to return power to the states through block grants

general revenue sharing the process by which one unit of government yields a portion of its tax income to another unit of government, according to an established formula. Revenue sharing typically involves the national government providing money to state governments

FIGURE 3.5 ★ The Changing Federal Framework

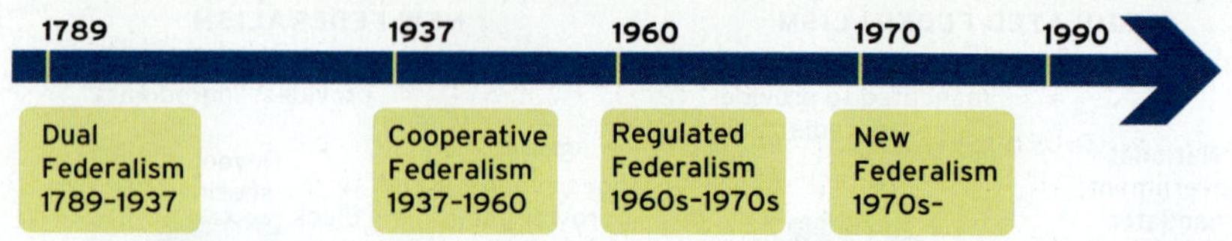

Another way of letting the states do more is by having the national government do less. When Nixon implemented block grants he increased federal spending. But Reagan's block grants cut federal funding by 12 percent. His view was that the states could spend their own funds to make up the difference, if they chose to do so. Revenue sharing was also eliminated during the Reagan administration, leaving localities to fend for themselves. The Republican Congress elected in 1994 took this strategy even further, supporting block grants as well as substantial cuts in federal programs. Their biggest success was the 1996 welfare reform law, which delegated to states important new responsibilities. Most of the other major proposed block grants or spending reductions failed to pass Congress or were vetoed by President Clinton. The Republican congressional leadership had found that it was much easier to promise a "devolution revolution" than to deliver on that promise.[37]

Neither block grants nor reduced federal funding have proven to be magic solutions to the problems of federalism. For one thing, there is always a trade-off between accountability—that is, whether the states are using funds for the purposes intended—and flexibility. Accountability and proper use of funds continue to be troublesome issues. Even after block grants were created, Congress reimposed regulations in order to increase the states' accountability. If the objective is to have accountable and efficient government, it is not clear that state bureaucracies are any more efficient or more capable than national agencies. In Mississippi, for example, the state Department of Human Services spent money from the child care block grant for office furniture and designer salt and pepper shakers that cost $37.50 a pair. As one Mississippi state legislator said, "I've seen too many years of good ol' boy politics to know they shouldn't [transfer money to the states] without stricter controls and requirements."[38]

Most discussion of New Federalism has focused on increased state control over government spending programs. On balance, we have seen, states did gain more power over spending policies during the 1980s and 1990s. But recently the federal government has moved to limit state discretion over spending in cases where it thinks states are too generous. For example, in 2007, President Bush issued regulations that prevented states from providing benefits under the State Child Health Insurance Program (SCHIP) to children in families well above the poverty line. New federal rulings also barred states from providing chemotherapy to illegal immigrants, who are guaranteed emergency medical treatment under Medicaid, the federal and state health program for the poor.[39] These new rules have embroiled states and the federal government in sharp conflicts over state discretion in spending decisions, once the hallmark of New Federalism. As Figure 3.5 indicates, federalism has changed dramatically over the course of American history. Finding the right balance among states and the federal government is an evolving challenge for American democracy.

Devolution: For Whose Benefit?

Since the expansion of the national government in the 1930s, questions about "who does what" have frequently provoked conflict in American politics. Why does such an apparently simple choice set off such highly charged political debate? One reason is that many decisions about federal versus state responsibility have implications for who benefits from government action.

Let's consider the benefits of federal control versus devolution in the realm of **redistributive programs.** These are programs designed primarily for the benefit of the poor. Many political scientists and economists maintain that states and localities should not be in charge of redistributive programs. They argue that since states and local governments have to compete with each other, they do not have the incentive to spend their money on the needy people in their areas. Instead, they want to keep taxes low and spend money on things that promote economic development.[40] In this situation, states might engage in a "race to the bottom": if one state cuts assistance to the poor, neighboring states will institute similar or deeper cuts both to reduce expenditures and to discourage poorer people from moving into their states. As one New York legislator put it, "The concern we have is that unless we make our welfare system and our tax and regulatory system competitive with the states around us, we will have too many disincentives for business to move here. Welfare is a big part of that."[41]

redistributive programs economic policies designed to control the economy through taxing and spending, with the goal of benefiting the poor

In 1996, when Congress enacted a major welfare reform law, it followed a different logic. By changing welfare from a combined federal-state program into a block grant to the states, Congress gave the states more responsibility for programs that serve the poor. Most of those who initially supported the law opposed the current welfare system and hoped to reduce welfare spending. They defended their decision to devolve significant responsibility to the states by arguing that states could act as "laboratories of democracy" by experimenting with many different approaches to find those that best met the needs of their citizens.[42] As states altered their welfare programs in the wake of the new law, they did indeed design diverse approaches. For example, Minnesota adopted an incentive-based approach that offers extra assistance to families that take low-wage jobs. Other states have more "sticks" than "carrots" in their welfare programs. For example, six states impose very strict time limits on receiving welfare, allowing recipients less than the five-year limit in the federal legislation. After the passage of the law, welfare rolls declined dramatically. On average they declined by more than half from their peak in 1994; in twelve states the decline was 70 percent or higher. Politicians have cited these statistics to claim that the poor have benefited from greater state control of welfare, yet analysts caution that the reality is more complex. Most studies have found that the majority of those leaving welfare remain in poverty.

For Critical Analysis

What would be the advantages and disadvantages of a unitary system in which the federal government had all power? What would be the advantages and disadvantages of a fully decentralized system in which states had all the power?

Because states are so diverse politically, devolution does not always mean fewer benefits for low-income people. As the number of people without health insurance has grown over the past decade, some states have sought to extend public health benefits to as many residents as possible. To cover more children, eighteen high-cost states raised the family income level necessary to qualify for benefits under the state and federal State Child Health Insurance Program (SCHIP). For example, California allows children in families with incomes up to 250 percent of the poverty line ($51,625 for a family of four) to receive SCHIP benefits if they lack private insurance. In 2007, however, the Bush administration sought to limit states' freedom to extend benefits by requiring that states cover 95 percent of eligible children under 200 percent of

The debate over national versus state control of speed limits arose in 1973, when gas prices skyrocketed and supplies became scarce. Drivers nationwide were forced to wait in long lines at gas stations. The federal government responded to the gas crisis by instituting a national 55-mile-per-hour speed limit.

the poverty line before they could offer benefits to families with higher incomes. It also required that children wait a year after losing private insurance before they could enroll in SCHIP. The move attracted widespread opposition from state officials. Governor Jon Corzine of New Jersey, for example, declared that he would not implement the new federal rules, warning of "the devastating impact that this misguided policy will have on our efforts to address the growing problem of the uninsured."[43] Yet because key health programs are jointly funded by the state and the federal government, the federal government has the power to restrict the ways states spend their money.

In some decisions about federalism, local concerns are overridden in the name of the national interest. The question of speed limits provides an example. Speed limits had traditionally been a state and local responsibility. But in 1973, at the height of the oil shortage, Congress passed legislation to withhold federal highway funds from states that did not adopt a maximum speed limit of 55 miles per hour (mph). The lower speed limit, it was argued, would reduce energy consumption by cars. Although Congress had not formally taken over the authority to set speed limits, the power of its purse was so important that every state adopted the new speed limit. The national interest in energy conservation had outweighed local preferences for higher speed limits. As the crisis faded, concern about energy conservation diminished. The national speed limit lost much of its support, even though it was found to have reduced the number of traffic deaths. In 1995, Congress repealed the penalties for higher speed limits, and states once again became free to set their own speed limits. Many states with large rural areas raised their maximum to 75 mph; Montana initially set unlimited speeds in the rural areas during daylight hours. Research indicates that numbers of highway deaths have indeed risen in the states that increased the limits.[44]

For Critical Analysis

The role of the national government has changed significantly from the Founding era to the present. Do you think the framers of the Constitution would be pleased with the current balance of power between the national government and the state governments?

Because the division of responsibility in the federal system has important implications for who benefits, few conflicts over state versus national control will ever be settled once and for all. As new evidence becomes available about the costs and benefits of different arrangements, it provides fuel for ongoing debates about what are properly the states' responsibilities and what the federal government should do. Likewise, changes in the political control of the national government usually provoke a rethinking of responsibilities as new leaders seek to alter federal arrangements for the benefit of the groups they represent.

In 1995, Congress removed its speed limit restrictions and gave the states the right to determine their own road speeds. As a result, speed limits went up on many highways.

Federalism since 2000

During the past ten years, many of the most controversial issues in American politics—including the appropriate size of public social spending, the rights and benefits of immigrants (legal as well as undocumented), what government should do about global warming, and questions about whether and how government should regulate business and moral behavior—have been fought out through the federal system. Politicians of all stripes regularly turn to the federal government in order to override decisions made by states. Likewise, when the federal government proves unable or unwilling to act, advocates and politicians try to achieve their goals in states and localities. In many cases, it is up to the courts to decide which level of government should have the final say.

Although conservatives proclaim their preference for a small federal government and their support for more state autonomy, in fact, they often expand the federal government and limit state autonomy. During the presidency of George W. Bush the growth of government, the activist free-spending Republican Congress, and a series of Supreme Court rulings supporting federal power over the states made it clear that conservatives do not always support small government, nor do they always favor returning power to the states. Once in power, many conservatives not only discovered that they needed a strong federal government to respond to public demands, but also found that they could use federal power to advance conservative policy goals.

For the president, the importance of a strong federal government dawned with force after the terrorist attacks in 2001. Aware that the American public was looking to Washington for protection, Bush worked with Congress to pass the USA PATRIOT Act, which greatly increased the surveillance powers of the federal government. A year later, he created the enormous new federal Department of Homeland Security. By 2006, the president had increased defense spending by 47 percent. Because national security had long been a conservative priority and because the terrorist attacks represented a frightening new danger, the increased federal role did not seem out of step with traditional conservative approaches to government.

But President Bush also expanded federal control and enhanced spending in policy areas far removed from concerns about security. The 2001 No Child Left Behind Act introduced unprecedented federal intervention in public education, traditionally a state and local responsibility. New, detailed federal testing requirements and provisions stipulating how states should treat failing schools were major expansions of federal authority in education. When a number of states threatened to defy some of the new federal requirements, Bush's Department of Education relaxed its tough stance and became more flexible in enforcing the act. But the administration did not back down entirely, leading to several legal challenges to different aspects of the law.

At times, federal officials who oppose what states are doing have directly overridden state decisions or deliberately reduced the scope for state action. In 2005, the case of Terri Schiavo, a brain-damaged woman who had been in a coma for fifteen years, attracted widespread attention. After more than a decade of court rulings, the Florida state court decreed in 2005 that Schiavo's feeding tube should be removed in accordance with her husband's wishes. Unwilling to let the state court's decision stand, congressional leaders unleashed a major campaign to circumvent it. The fanfare surrounding the case—with Senate Majority Leader (and medical doctor) Bill Frist pronouncing Schiavo conscious after watching her on videotape—led to widespread charges that Congress had greatly overstepped its role. Conservatives themselves were split on the issue, with one Republican charging, "My party is demonstrating that they are for states' rights unless they don't like what the states are doing."[45]

In the Supreme Court, too, many decisions began to support a stronger federal role over the states. This was surprising to many observers because in the 1990s, it had appeared that the Rehnquist Court was embarked on a "federalism revolution" designed to return more power to the states. Instead, in several key decisions, the Court reaffirmed the power of the federal government. Decisions to uphold the federal Family and Medical Leave Act and the Americans with Disabilities Act asserted federal authority against state claims of immunity from the acts. In one important 2005 case, the Court upheld the right of Congress to ban medical marijuana, even though eleven states had legalized its use. Overturning a lower court ruling that said that Congress did not have authority to regulate marijuana when it had been grown for noncommercial purposes in a single state, the Supreme Court ruled that the federal government did have the power to regulate use of all marijuana under the commerce clause.

States may also pressure the federal government to take more responsibility for some issues. In 2006, several states petitioned the Environmental Protection Agency to regulate emissions from new motor vehicles.

Perhaps the most closely watched federalism case in 2006 was the challenge to Oregon's "right to die" law, which allows doctors to prescribe lethal doses of medicine for terminally ill patients who request it. Challengers claimed the law was illegal because Congress has the right to outlaw such use of drugs under the Controlled Substances Act, which regulates prescription drugs. In a 6-to-3 decision, the Court ruled in Oregon's favor. Despite this victory for states, the narrow focus of the ruling and the dissenting opinion by new Chief Justice John G. Roberts, Jr., indicated that the power of the federal government over the states would continue to be a contentious legal issue.

In recent years, federalism has also involved state and local efforts to pressure the federal government to act. In 2006, Massachusetts and several other states (as well as a number of organizations) petitioned the Environmental Protection Agency (EPA), asking the EPA to regulate emissions of carbon dioxide and other gases that contribute to global warming from new motor vehicles.[46] Massachusetts argued that the EPA was required to regulate these "greenhouse gases" by the Clean Air Act, which states that Congress must regulate "any air pollutant" that can "reasonably be anticipated to endanger public health or welfare." The Court ruled that the Environmental Protection Agency has the authority to regulate heat-trapping gases in automobile emissions. The court further ruled that the agency could not sidestep its authority to regulate the greenhouse gases that contribute to global climate changes unless it could provide a scientific basis for its refusal.

In other policy areas, states and localities have forged their own policies because the federal government has not acted. One of the most controversial of these issues is immigration legislation, which Congress considered in 2007 but failed to enact. In 2007, state legislatures introduced more than 1,400 bills related to immigration, of which 170 were enacted; over one hundred ordinances related to immigration have been introduced in municipalities.

The presence of an estimated 12 million unauthorized immigrants in communities across the country is an especially volatile issue that affects many aspects of state lawmaking. Conflicts have emerged over requirements for obtaining a driver's license. In 2007, for example, New York's former governor Eliot Spitzer issued a rule that Social Security numbers would not be required to apply for driver's licenses, effectively allowing all residents, citizens, noncitizens, and legal and illegal immigrants to obtain licenses. However, the measure drew sharp public opposition and the governor rescinded the rule. The conflict in New York led other states that had issued driver's licenses to immigrants or were considering such a plan, to change course. Oregon and Michigan stopped issuing licenses to illegal immigrants, and Maryland dropped a plan to create a two-tiered license system. By 2008, only Hawaii, Maine, New Mexico, Utah, and Washington continued to provide licenses to unauthorized immigrants. However in all of these states except Hawaii, the laws were being challenged.[47] Other states such as California have considered legislation to allow driver's licenses for all residents but have failed to reach agreement on the issue. Although issuing driver's licenses has long been a state responsibility, the federal 2005 Real ID Act, referred to on page 103, encroaches on state authority by requiring all states to determine legal status before issuing driver's licenses.

Politics Today

How does the Real ID Act that went into effect in 2008 affect undocumented immigrants? Why has the act put some state policies in conflict with federal standards?

In many cases, the courts have become the final arbiters of whether state and local laws are legal. States have an uncontested right to issue driver's licenses, but many of the laws that states and localities have passed have not been found legal. One of the most publicized of the local rulings meant to address illegal immigrants was a Hazelton, Pennsylvania ordinance that denied business licenses to employers that hire illegal workers and fined landlords who rented to them. In 2007, a federal judge struck down the ordinance, on the grounds that the city did not have the power to regulate immigration. In his ruling the judge stated that, "Whatever frustrations officials of the City of Hazelton may feel about the current state of federal immigration enforcement, the nature of the political system in the United States prohibits the City from enacting ordinances that disrupt a carefully drawn federal statutory scheme."[48]

Thinking Critically about Liberty versus Equality in the Federal System

It is often argued that liberals prefer a strong federal government because they value equality more than liberty. Conservatives are said to prefer granting more power to states and localities because they care most about liberty. Although this greatly oversimplifies liberal and conservative views about government, such arguments

Take Action at the State Level

College campuses across the country are largely alcohol-free zones, as the majority of their student populations are under twenty-one and thus ineligible to purchase alcoholic drinks. This national standard is a relatively new phenomenon. The legal drinking age had traditionally been a state-level issue, with Congress unable to legislate directly on age requirements. However, in 1984, Congress threatened to withhold national transportation funds from any state that refused to pass a law prohibiting the sale of alcohol to those under twenty-one. Because most states relied heavily on these federal funds, every state except Louisiana quickly raised its legal drinking age (Louisiana signed on in 1995).

The debate over the legal drinking age illustrates the essence of federalism—determining which policy areas should be the domain of the federal government and which issues should be reserved to the states. Many of the key issues currently facing us as a nation have been caught in this struggle between federal and state power.

The No Child Left Behind (NCLB) Act, for example, requires states to test all children in grades 3 through 8 on math and reading and imposes penalties on schools that fail to improve over time. Proponents of these national mandates argue that they are necessary to ensure that all children in the country, regardless of their home state, are provided quality education. Yet others, including many local and state officials, complain that the federal government requirements are too narrow or do not address the needs of their states.

State policy on stem-cell research is similarly charged. Under the Bush administration, the federal government imposed limits on federally funded embryonic-stem-cell research. Some state governments responded to these limitations by attempting to set even stricter guidelines in their own states (often banning it outright). Others took the opposite position, passing legislation that specifically guarantees the right to conduct such research or appropriating state funds to support stem-cell studies.

These examples illustrate the ways in which federal and state policies can overlap, sometimes creating a web of legislation, and other times resulting in a national standard. Untangling this web can be tricky, but fortunately resources are available that can help you learn more about an issue, contact groups involved in the debate, and lend your own voice to the discussion.

- ★ To begin, you can educate yourself about how your state addresses a host of issues ranging from health to the environment to civil rights by visiting the Pew Research Center's Web site www.stateline.org/live/. This Web site provides an in-depth look at key issues facing the states, presents comparisons among various state policies, and sometimes offers links to advocacy groups on different sides of the debate.
- ★ After learning more about the issue from a state perspective, you can read comments from other readers, post your own comment, or share the entire article with friends.
- ★ If one of these issues captures your interest or passion or anger, you might have a better chance of affecting policy at the state level (where there is generally greater access to legislators and fewer competing activists) than on the national level.
- ★ In the abortion debate, for example, you might choose to write a letter or e-mail to your state representative or senator advocating either an expansion or restriction of abortion rights in your state.
- ★ You might even want to circulate a petition to get an initiative on the ballot that will set state law on the issue. The Initiative and Referendum Institute at the University of Southern California (www.iandrinstitute.org) has information on this process.

Whatever your choice—to educate yourself, to express your opinion, or to join with others in action—the states provide fifty different arenas for affecting political change.

underscore the reality that ideas about federalism are linked to different views about the purposes of government. For what ends should government powers be used? What happens when widely shared national values conflict in practice? The connections between federalism and our fundamental national values have made federalism a focus of political contention throughout our nation's history.

The Constitution limited the power of the federal government in order to promote liberty. This decision reflected the framers' suspicions of centralized power, based on their experience with the British Crown. The American suspicion of centralized power lives on today in widespread dislike of "big government," which generally evokes a picture of a bloated federal government. But over the course of our history we have come to realize that the federal government is also an important guarantor of liberty. As we'll see in Chapter 4, it took enhanced federal power to ensure that local and state governments adhered to the fundamental constitutional freedoms in the Bill of Rights.

One of the most important continuing arguments for a strong federal government is its role in ensuring equality. A key puzzle of federalism is deciding when differences across states represent the proper democratic decisions of the states and when such differences represent inequalities that should not be tolerated. Sometimes a decision to eliminate differences is made on the grounds of equality and individual rights, as in the Civil Rights Act of 1964, which outlawed legal segregation. At other times, a stronger federal role is justified on the grounds of national interest, as in the case of the oil shortage and the institution of a 55-mph speed limit in the 1970s. Advocates of a more limited federal role often point to the value of democracy. Public actions can more easily be tailored to fit distinctive local or state desires if states and localities have more power to make policy. Viewed this way, variation across states can be an expression of democratic will.

A decade ago, many Americans had grown disillusioned with the federal government and supported efforts to give the states more responsibilities. A 1997 poll, for example, found that Americans tended to have the most confidence in governments that were closest to them. Thirty-eight percent expressed "a great deal" of confidence in local government, 32 percent in state government, and 22 percent in the federal government. Nearly two-thirds of those polled believed that shifting some responsibility to states and localities would help achieve excellence in government. After the terrorist attacks of 2001, however, support for the federal government soared. With issues of security topping the list of citizens' concerns, the federal government, which had seemed less important with the waning of the Cold War, suddenly reemerged as the central actor in American politics. As one observer put it, "Federalism was a luxury of peaceful times."[49] Yet recent polls suggest that support for the federal government may be slipping: in a 2004 Gallup poll, 63 percent of those surveyed that they trusted the federal government "a great deal" or "a fair amount" on international issues and 61 percent on domestic issues. By February 2007, those percentages had dropped to 53 percent and 52 percent, respectively.[50] The financial bailout in 2008 did not improve the public's views of government: 77 percent of Americans rated the government's actions as only fair or poor.

American federalism remains a work in progress. As public problems shift and as local, state, and federal governments change, questions about the relationship between American values and federalism naturally emerge. The different views that people bring to this discussion suggest that concerns about federalism will remain a central issue in American democracy.

Politics Today

Immediately after September 11, 2001, support for the federal government shot up, but it now appears to be declining. What factors influence whether Americans prefer to hand responsibilities to state and local governments, or whether they want to increase the authority of the federal government?

FOR FURTHER READING

Bensel, Richard. *Sectionalism and American Political Development: 1880–1980.* Madison: University of Wisconsin Press, 1984.

Bowman, Ann O'M., and Richard Kearny. *The Resurgence of the States.* Englewood Cliffs, NJ: Prentice-Hall, 1986.

Derthick, Martha. *Keeping the Compound Republic: Essays on American Federalism.* Washington, DC: Brookings Institution Press, 2001.

Donahue, John D. *Disunited States.* New York: Basic Books, 1997.

Elazar, Daniel. *American Federalism: A View from the States.* 3rd ed. New York: Harper & Row, 1984.

Gerston, Larry N. *American Federalism: A Concise Introduction.* Armonk, NY: M. E. Sharpe, 2007.

Grodzins, Morton. *The American System.* Chicago: Rand McNally, 1974.

Johnson, Kimberly S. *Governing the American State: Congress and the New Federalism, 1877–1929.* Princeton, NJ: Princeton University Press, 2007.

Kettl, Donald. *The Regulation of American Federalism.* Baltimore: Johns Hopkins University Press, 1987.

Van Horn, Carl E. *The State of the States.* 4th ed. Washington DC: Congressional Quarterly Press, 2005.

Walker, David B. *The Rebirth of Federalism: Slouching toward Washington.* 2nd ed. Washington, DC: Congressional Quarterly Press, 1999.

RECOMMENDED WEB SITES

Constitution Finder
http://confinder.richmond.edu/

Governments can organize power in either unitary or federal systems. Examine the constitutions of different countries throughout the world and try to identify how those governments organize power.

Council of State Governments
www.csg.org

This organization provides information on a variety of state-federal policy areas. See what current issues concerning federalism are of prime importance to the state governments on this site.

Federalism Project
www.federalismproject.org

The Federalism Project of the American Enterprise Institute advocates competitive federalism and the empowering of states through devolution.

Governing.com
www.governing.com

See what state-federal issues are important to your local government officials on the Web site for *Governing* magazine.

National Conference of State Legislatures
www.ncsl.org
National Governors Association
www.nga.org

These are two of the largest organizations dedicated to representing state and local government interests at the federal level.

Oyez: U.S. Supreme Court Media
www.oyez.org/cases/1792-1850/1819/1819_0/

Read here about one of the most important U.S. Supreme Court decisions regarding the division of federal and state power in the case of *McCulloch v. Maryland.*

Urban Institute
www.newfederalism.urban.org

New Federalism gives state governments more flexibility to make public policy and administer programs. The Urban Institute's "Assessing the New Federalism" policy center takes a statistical look at the success and failure of recent government programs.

U.S. Census Bureau
www.census.gov

The Census Bureau maintains one of the largest collections of data about social and economic conditions of the nation's fifty states.

World Federalist Movement
www.wfm.org

This international organization is dedicated to the division of power and authority among all local, state, and international governmental agencies. Generally, it promotes federalism and constitutional democracy throughout the world.

STUDY OUTLINE

www.wwnorton.com/wtp7e

The Federal Framework

1. In an effort to limit national power, the framers of the Constitution established a system of dual federalism, wherein both the national and state governments would have sovereignty.
2. The Constitution granted a few "expressed powers" to the national government and, through the Tenth Amendment, reserved all the rest to the states.
3. The Constitution also created obligations among the states in the full faith and credit clause and the privileges and immunities clause.
4. Federalism and a restrictive definition of "interstate commerce" limited the national government's control over the economy.
5. Federalism allows a great deal of variation between states.
6. Under the traditional system of federalism, the national government was small and very narrowly specialized in its functions compared with other Western nations. Most of its functions were aimed at promoting commerce.
7. Under the traditional system, states rather than the national government did most of the fundamental governing in the country.
8. The system of federalism limited the expansion of the national government despite economic forces and expansive interpretations of the Constitution in cases such as *McCulloch v. Maryland* and *Gibbons v. Ogden*.
9. For most of U.S. history, the concept of interstate commerce kept the national government from regulating the economy. But in 1937, the Supreme Court converted the commerce clause from a source of limitations to a source of power for the national government.
10. Recent years have seen a revival of interest in returning more power to the states through devolution.

Who Does What? The Changing Federal Framework

1. The rise of national government activity after the New Deal did not necessarily mean that states lost power directly. Rather, the national government paid states through grants-in-aid to administer federal programs.
2. Some federal programs bypass the states by sending money directly to local governments or local organizations. The states are most important, however; they are integral to federal programs such as Medicaid.
3. The national government also imposed regulations on states and localities in areas such as environmental policy in order to guarantee national standards.
4. Under President Nixon, many categorical grants were combined into larger block grants that offered greater flexibility in the use of the money. The Nixon administration also developed revenue sharing that was not tied to any specific programs.
5. As states have become more capable of administering large-scale programs, the idea of devolution has become popular.

Thinking Critically about Liberty versus Equality in the Federal System

1. Some of the sharpest tensions among liberty, equality, and democracy are visible in debates over federalism.
2. The Constitution limited the power of the national government in order to safeguard liberty, but over the course of American history, a strong national government has been an important guarantor of liberty.
3. A key puzzle of federalism is deciding when differences across states represent the proper democratic decisions of the states and when such differences represent inequalities that should not be tolerated.

PRACTICE QUIZ

www.wwnorton.com/wtp7e

1. Which term describes the sharing of powers between the national government and the state governments?
   a) separation of powers
   b) federalism
   c) checks and balances
   d) shared powers

2. The system of federalism that allowed states to do most of the fundamental governing from 1789 to 1937 was
   a) home rule.
   b) regulated federalism.
   c) dual federalism.
   d) cooperative federalism.

3. Which of the following resulted from the federal system?
   a) It limited the power of the national government in relation to the states.
   b) It restrained the power of the national government over the economy.
   c) It allowed variation among the states.
   d) all of the above
4. The overall effect of the growth of national policies has been
   a) to weaken state government.
   b) to strengthen state government.
   c) to provide uniform laws in the nation.
   d) to make the states more diverse culturally.
5. Which amendment to the Constitution stated that the powers not delegated to the national government or prohibited to the states were "reserved to the states"?
   a) First Amendment
   b) Fifth Amendment
   c) Tenth Amendment
   d) Twenty-sixth Amendment
6. The process of returning more of the responsibilities of governing from the national level to the state level is known as
   a) dual federalism.
   b) devolution.
   c) preemption.
   d) home rule.
7. One of the most powerful tools by which the federal government has attempted to get the states to act in ways that are desired by the federal government is by
   a) providing grants-in-aid.
   b) requiring licensing.
   c) granting home rule.
   d) defending states' rights.
8. The form of regulated federalism that allows the federal government to take over areas of regulation formerly overseen by states or local governments is called
   a) categorical grants.
   b) formula grants.
   c) project grants.
   d) preemption.
9. To what does the term *New Federalism* refer?
   a) the national government's regulation of state action through grants-in-aid
   b) the type of federalism relying on categorical grants
   c) efforts to return more policy-making discretion to the states through the use of block grants
   d) the recent emergence of local governments as important political actors
10. A recent notable example of the process of giving the states more responsibility for administering government programs is
   a) campaign finance reform.
   b) prison reform.
   c) trade reform.
   d) welfare reform.

KEY TERMS

www.wwnorton.com/wtp7e

block grants (p. 105)
categorical grants (p. 97)
commerce clause (p. 91)
concurrent powers (p. 84)
cooperative federalism (p. 98)
devolution (p. 94)
dual federalism (p. 88)
expressed powers (p. 83)
federal system (p. 83)
federalism (p. 83)
formula grants (p. 97)
full faith and credit clause (p. 84)
general revenue sharing (p. 105)
grants-in-aid (p. 97)
home rule (p. 88)
implied powers (p. 83)
necessary and proper clause (p. 83)
New Federalism (p. 105)
police power (p. 84)
preemption (p. 100)
privileges and immunities clause (p. 87)
project grants (p. 97)
redistributive programs (p. 107)
regulated federalism (p. 100)
reserved powers (p. 84)
states' rights (p. 92)
unfunded mandates (p. 102)
unitary system (p. 83)

4 Civil Liberties

- A Brief History of the Bill of Rights
- The First Amendment and Freedom of Religion
- The First Amendment and Freedom of Speech and the Press
- The Second Amendment and the Right to Bear Arms
- Due Process of Law
- The Right to Privacy
- Thinking Critically about the Future of Civil Liberties

WHAT GOVERNMENT DOES AND WHY IT MATTERS

Today in the United States, we often take the liberties contained within the Bill of Rights for granted. Few citizens of other countries can make such a claim. In fact, few people in recorded history have enjoyed such protections, including American citizens before the 1960s. For more than 170 years after its ratification by the states in 1791 the Bill of Rights meant little to most Americans. As we shall see in this chapter, guaranteeing the liberties articulated in the Bill of Rights to all Americans required a long struggle. As recently as the early 1960s, criminal suspects in state cases did not have to be informed of their rights, some states required daily Bible readings and prayers in their public schools, and some communities regularly censored reading material that they deemed to be obscene.

Thomas Jefferson said that, a bill of rights "is what people are entitled to against every government on earth. . . ." Note the emphasis—people *against* government. Civil liberties are *protections from* improper government action. Some of these restraints are substantive liberties, which put limits on *what* the government shall and shall not have power to do—such as establishing a religion, quartering troops in private homes without consent, or seizing private property without just compensation. Other restraints are procedural liberties, which deal with *how* the government is supposed to act. Civil liberties require a delicate balance between governmental power and governmental restraint. The government must be kept in check, with severe limits on its powers; yet, at the same time, the government must be given enough power to defend liberty and its benefits from those who seek to deprive others of them. This chapter will explore how this balance is struck. We will also see how the Supreme Court, an undemocratic institution, is especially important in establishing the balance. Civil liberties also reflect how well the democratic principle of majority rule with minority rights works. The rights enumerated in the Bill of Rights and enforced through the courts can provide an important check on the power of the majority.

Often, civil liberties come under pressure during times of war or national emergency when many Americans are willing to forgo some personal freedoms in order to feel safer and more secure. For example, few Americans have objected to being questioned and searched at airports in the wake of the 2001 terrorist attacks that killed thousands of people in New York, Washington, and Pennsylvania. In a similar vein, the federal government has been conducting massive electronic eavesdropping campaigns designed to pick out potential terrorist communications from the hundreds of millions of phone conversations in which Americans engage every year. Civil libertarians have argued that electronic eavesdropping constitutes an invasion of Americans' right to privacy. Many Americans, however, are willing to allow the government to listen if this helps foil a dangerous terrorist plot.

During previous periods of national emergency, such as the First and Second World Wars, the government temporarily intruded upon some civil liberties. These wars, however, came to an end and, in due course, civil liberties were restored. The "war on terror," may be different. Terrorism is likely to remain a threat for decades to come and future governments may assert that they must continue to exercise emergency powers to keep the nation secure. Will Americans be willing to trade liberties for security or will we find a way to have both?

› **In this chapter, our first task is to define the Bill of Rights and establish its relationship to personal liberty.** As we shall see, it is through the Bill of Rights that Americans are protected from government.

› **We then turn to the process by which the Bill of Rights was applied, not only to the national government, but also to the state governments.** This nationalizing process has been long and selective in applying only certain provisions of the Bill of Rights.

› **The bulk of this chapter is an analysis of the state of civil liberties today, beginning with the First Amendment.** The First Amendment guarantees regarding the freedoms of religion, of speech, and of the press continue to be a focal point of judicial interpretation of the Bill of Rights.

› **After briefly reviewing the Second Amendment right to bear arms, we move on to the rights of those accused of a crime.** These rights, contained in the Fourth, Fifth, Sixth, and Eighth Amendments, make up the due process of law.

› **We then turn to a right that has become increasingly important in recent decades, the right to privacy.** This right takes many forms and, like the freedoms specifically named in the Bill of Rights, has been subject to new judicial interpretations.

› **We conclude by pondering the future of civil liberties in the United States.** As we emphasize throughout this chapter, the Bill of Rights is constantly subject to the interpretations of the Supreme Court. Will the Court try to limit the extent of civil liberties in the near future?

A Brief History of the Bill of Rights

When the first Congress under the newly ratified Constitution met in late April of 1789, the most important item of business was the consideration of a proposal to add a bill of rights to the Constitution. Such a proposal had been turned down with little debate in the waning days of the Philadelphia Constitutional Convention in 1787, not because the delegates were against rights, but because, as the Federalists, led by Alexander Hamilton, later argued, it was "not only unnecessary in the proposed Constitution but would even be dangerous."[1] First, according to Hamilton, a bill of rights would be irrelevant to a national government that was given only delegated powers in the first place. To put restraints on "powers which are not granted" could provide a pretext for governments to claim more powers than were in fact granted: "For why declare that things shall not be done which there is no power to do?"[2] Second, the Constitution was to Hamilton and the Federalists a bill of rights in itself, or contained provisions that amounted to a bill of rights without requiring additional amendments (see Table 4.1). For example, Article I, Section 9, included the right of ***habeas corpus,*** which prohibits the government from depriving a person of liberty without an open trial before a judge.

Despite the power of Hamilton's arguments, when the Constitution was submitted to the states for ratification, Antifederalists, most of whom had not been delegates in Philadelphia, picked up on the argument of Thomas Jefferson (who also had not been a delegate) that the omission of a bill of rights was a major imperfection of the new Constitution. The Federalists conceded that in order to gain ratification they would have to make an "unwritten but unequivocal pledge" to add a bill of rights that would include a confirmation (in what became the Tenth Amendment) of the understanding that all powers not expressly delegated to the national government or explicitly prohibited to the states were reserved to the states.[3]

"After much discussion and manipulation . . . at the delicate prompting of Washington and under the masterful prodding of Madison," the House of Representatives adopted seventeen amendments; of these, the Senate adopted twelve. Ten of the amendments were ratified by the necessary three-fourths of the states on December 15, 1791; from the start these ten were called the **Bill of Rights** (see Box 4.1).[4] The protections against improper government action contained in the Constitution and the Bill of Rights represent important **civil liberties.**

habeas corpus a court order demanding that an individual in custody be brought into court and shown the cause for detention

Bill of Rights the first ten amendments to the U.S. Constitution, ratified in 1791; they ensure certain rights and liberties to the people

civil liberties areas of personal freedom with which governments are constrained from interfering

Although the Bill of Rights has specified certain rights and liberties since it was ratified in 1791, the interpretation and protection of those rights and liberties has evolved over time. Many feared that the government's actions in the fight against terrorism following September 11, 2001 represented a turn away from protecting civil liberties.

Nationalizing the Bill of Rights

The First Amendment provides that "Congress shall make no law . . ." But this is the only amendment in the Bill of Rights that addresses itself exclusively to the national government. For example, the Second Amendment provides that "the right of the people to keep and bear Arms, shall not be infringed." And the Fifth Amendment says, among other things, that "no person shall . . . be twice put in jeopardy of life or limb" for the same crime. Since the First Amendment is the only part of the Bill of Rights that is explicit in its intention to put limits on Congress and therefore on the national government, a fundamental question inevitably arises: do

bill of attainder a law that declares a person guilty of a crime without a trial

***ex post facto* law** a law that declares an action to be illegal after it has been committed

TABLE 4.1 ★ Rights in the Original Constitution (Not in the Bill of Rights)

CLAUSE	RIGHT ESTABLISHED
Article I, Sec. 9	guarantee of *habeas corpus*
Article I, Sec. 9	prohibition of **bills of attainder**
Article I, Sec. 9	prohibition of ***ex post facto* laws**
Article I, Sec. 9	prohibition against acceptance of titles of nobility, etc., from any foreign state
Article III	guarantee of trial by jury in state where crime was committed
Article III	treason defined and limited to the life of the person convicted, not to the person's heirs

the remaining provisions of the Bill of Rights put limits only on the national government, or do they limit the state governments as well?

The Supreme Court first answered this question in 1833 by ruling that the Bill of Rights limited only the national government and not the state governments.[5] But in 1868, when the Fourteenth Amendment was added to the Constitution, the question arose once again. The Fourteenth Amendment reads as if it were meant to impose the Bill of Rights on the states:

> No *State* shall make or enforce any law which shall abridge the privileges or immunities of citizens of the United States; nor shall any *State* deprive any person of life, liberty, or property, without due process of law; nor deny to any person within its jurisdiction the equal protection of the laws [emphasis added].

This language sounds like an effort to extend the Bill of Rights in its entirety to all citizens, wherever they might reside.[6] Yet this was not the Supreme Court's interpretation of the amendment for nearly a hundred years. Within five years of ratification of the Fourteenth Amendment, the Court was making decisions as though the amendment had never been adopted.[7]

The only change in civil liberties during the first fifty-odd years following the adoption of the Fourteenth Amendment came in 1897, when the Supreme Court held that the due-process clause of the Fourteenth Amendment did in fact prohibit states from taking property for a public use without just compensation.[8] However, the Supreme Court had selectively "incorporated" into the Fourteenth Amendment only the property protection provision of the Fifth Amendment and no other clause of the Fifth or any other amendment of the Bill of Rights. In other words, although according to the Fifth Amendment "due process" applied to the taking of life and liberty as well as property, only property was incorporated into the Fourteenth Amendment as a limitation on state power.

No further expansion of civil liberties via the Fourteenth Amendment occurred until 1925, when the Supreme Court held that freedom of speech is "among the fundamental personal rights and 'liberties' protected by the due process clause of the Fourteenth Amendment from impairment by the states."[9] In 1931, the Court

BOX 4.1 The Bill of Rights

Amendment I: Limits on Congress Congress cannot make any law establishing a religion or abridging freedoms of religious exercise, speech, assembly, or petition.
Amendments II, III, IV: Limits on the Executive The executive branch cannot infringe on the right of the people to keep arms (II), cannot arbitrarily take houses for militia (III), and cannot search for or seize evidence without a court warrant swearing to the probable existence of a crime (IV).
Amendments V, VI, VII, VIII: Limits on the Judiciary The courts cannot hold trials for serious offenses without provision for a grand jury (V), a trial jury (VII), a speedy trial (VI), presentation of charges and confrontation by the accused of hostile witnesses (VI), and immunity from testimony against oneself and immunity from trial more than once for the same offense (V). Furthermore, neither bail nor punishment can be excessive (VIII), and no property can be taken without "just compensation" (V).
Amendments IX, X: Limits on the National Government Any rights not enumerated are reserved to the state or the people (X), but the enumeration of certain rights in the Constitution should not be interpreted to mean that those are the only rights the people have (IX).

added freedom of the press to that short list protected by the Bill of Rights from state action; in 1939, it added freedom of assembly.[10]

But that was as far as the Court was willing to go. As late as 1937, the Supreme Court was still unwilling to nationalize civil liberties beyond the First Amendment. The Constitution, as interpreted by the Supreme Court in *Palko v. Connecticut*, left standing the framework in which the states had the power to determine their own law on a number of fundamental issues. *Palko* established the principle of **selective incorporation,** by which the provisions of the Bill of Rights were to be considered one by one and selectively applied as limits on the states through the Fourteenth Amendment.[11] In order to make clear that "selective incorporation" should be narrowly interpreted, Justice Benjamin Cardozo, writing for an 8-to-1 majority, asserted that although many rights have value and importance, not all are of the same value and importance:

selective incorporation the process by which different protections in the Bill of Rights were incorporated into the Fourteenth Amendment, thus guaranteeing citizens protection from state as well as national governments

> [Not all rights are of] the very essence of a scheme of ordered liberty. To abolish them is not to violate a "principle of justice so rooted in the traditions and conscience of our people as to be ranked as fundamental." . . . What is true of jury trials and indictments is true also . . . of the immunity from compulsory self-incrimination [as in *Palko*]. . . . This too might be lost, and justice still be done. . . . If the Fourteenth Amendment has absorbed them [for example, freedom of thought and speech], the process of absorption has had its source in the belief that neither liberty nor justice would exist if they were sacrificed.

Palko left states with most of the powers they had possessed even before the adoption of the Fourteenth Amendment, including the power to pass laws segregating the races—a power in fact that the thirteen former Confederate states chose to continue to exercise on into the 1960s, despite *Brown v. Board of Education* in 1954. The constitutional framework also left states with the power to engage in searches and seizures without a warrant, to indict accused persons without a grand jury, to deprive accused persons of trial by jury, to deprive persons of their right not to have to testify against themselves, to deprive accused persons of their right to confront adverse witnesses, and to prosecute accused persons more than once for the same crime.[12] Few states chose to use these kinds of powers, but some states did, and the power to do so was available for any state whose legislative majority or courts so chose.

So, until 1961, only the First Amendment and one clause of the Fifth Amendment had been clearly incorporated into the Fourteenth Amendment as binding on the states as well as on the national government.[13] After that, one by one, most of the important provisions of the Bill of Rights were incorporated into the Fourteenth Amendment and applied to the states. Table 4.2 shows the progress of this revolution in the interpretation of the Constitution.

TABLE 4.2 ★ Incorporation of the Bill of Rights into the Fourteenth Amendment

SELECTED PROVISIONS AND AMENDMENTS	NOT INCORPORATED UNTIL	KEY CASE
Eminent domain (V)	1897	*Chicago, Burlington, and Quincy R.R. v. Chicago*
Freedom of speech (I)	1925	*Gitlow v. New York*
Freedom of press (I)	1931	*Near v. Minnesota*
Free exercise of religion (I)	1934	*Hamilton v. Regents of the University of California*
Freedom of assembly (I)	1939	*Hague v. CIO*
Freedom from unnecessary search and seizure (IV)	1949	*Wolf v. Colorado*
Freedom from warrantless search and seizure (IV) ("exclusionary rule")	1961	*Mapp v. Ohio*
Freedom from cruel and unusual punishment (VIII)	1962	*Robinson v. California*
Right to counsel in any criminal trial (VI)	1963	*Gideon v. Wainwright*
Right against self-incrimination and forced confessions (V)	1964	*Mallory v. Hogan* *Escobedo v. Illinois*
Right to privacy (III, IV, & V)	1965	*Griswold v. Connecticut*
Right to remain silent (V)	1966	*Miranda v. Arizona*
Right against double jeopardy (V)	1969	*Benton v. Maryland*

One notable provision of the Bill of Rights that has never been incorporated by the Supreme Court is the Second Amendment, which protects the right to bear arms. Thus, the Constitution does not prohibit states and localities from regulating or even prohibiting firearms possession. The only exception is the District of Columbia. A U.S. Appeals Court recently affirmed that since the district is an entity of the federal government, it is precluded by the Second Amendment from banning hand gun possession by district residents.[14]

The best way to examine the Bill of Rights today is the simplest way—to take the major provisions one at a time. Some of these provisions are settled areas of law, and others are not. The Court can reinterpret any one of them at any time.

The First Amendment affects everyday life in a multitude of ways. Because of its ban on state-sanctioned religion, the Supreme Court ruled in 2000 that student-initiated public prayer at school is illegal. Pregame prayer at public schools violates the establishment clause of the First Amendment.

The First Amendment and Freedom of Religion

> Congress shall make no law respecting an establishment of religion, or prohibiting the free exercise thereof; or abridging the freedom of speech, or of the press; or the right of the people peaceably to assemble, and to petition the Government for a redress of grievances.

The Bill of Rights begins by guaranteeing freedom, and the First Amendment provides for that freedom in two distinct clauses: "Congress shall make no law [1] respecting an establishment of religion, or [2] prohibiting the free exercise thereof." The first clause is called the "establishment clause," and the second is called the "free exercise clause."

Separation between Church and State

establishment clause the First Amendment clause that says that "Congress shall make no law respecting an establishment of religion." This law means that a "wall of separation" exists between church and state

The **establishment clause** has been interpreted quite strictly to mean that a virtual "wall of separation" exists between church and state. The separation of church and state was especially important to the great numbers of American colonists who had sought refuge from persecution for having rejected membership in state-sponsored churches. The concept of a "wall of separation" was Jefferson's own formulation, and this concept has figured in all of the modern Supreme Court cases arising under the establishment clause.

Despite the seeming absoluteness of the phrase "wall of separation," there is ample room to disagree on how high the wall is or of what materials it is composed. For example, the Court has been consistently strict in cases of school prayer, striking down such practices as Bible reading,[15] nondenominational prayer,[16] a moment of silence for meditation, and pregame prayer at public sporting events.[17] In each of these cases, the Court reasoned that school-sponsored observations, even of an apparently nondenominational character, are highly suggestive of school sponsorship and therefore violate the prohibition against establishment of religion. On the other hand, the Court has been quite permissive (and some would say inconsistent) about the public display of religious symbols, such as city-sponsored Nativity scenes in commercial or municipal areas.[18] And although the Court has consistently disapproved of government financial support for religious schools, even when the purpose has been purely educational and secular, the Court has permitted certain direct aid to students of such schools in the form of busing, for example. In 1971, after thirty years of cases involving religious schools, the Court attempted to specify some criteria to guide its decisions and those of lower courts, indicating, for example, in a decision invalidating state payments for the teaching of secular subjects in parochial schools, circumstances under which the Court might allow certain financial assistance. The case was *Lemon v. Kurtzman;* in its decision, the Supreme Court established three criteria to guide future cases, in what came to be called the ***Lemon* test.** The Court held that government aid to religious schools would be accepted as constitutional if (1) it had a secular purpose, (2) its effect was neither to advance nor to inhibit religion, and (3) it did not entangle government and religious institutions in each other's affairs.[19]

***Lemon* test** a rule articulated in *Lemon v. Kurtzman* that government action toward religion is permissible if it is secular in purpose, neither promotes nor inhibits the practice of religion, and does not lead to "excessive entanglement" with religion

Although these restrictions make the *Lemon* test hard to pass, imaginative authorities are finding ways to do so, and the Supreme Court has demonstrated a willingness to let them. For example, in 1995, the Court narrowly ruled that a student religious group at the University of Virginia could not be denied student activities funds merely because it was a religious group espousing a particular viewpoint about a deity. The Court called the denial "viewpoint discrimination" that violated the free speech rights of the group.[20] This led two years later to a new, more conservative approach to the "separation of church and state." In 1997, the Court accepted the practice of sending public school teachers into parochial (religious) schools to provide remedial education to disadvantaged children.[21]

More recently, the establishment clause has been put under pressure by the school-voucher and charter-school movements. Vouchers financed by public revenues are supporting student tuitions at religious schools, where common prayer and religious instruction are known parts of the curriculum. In addition, many financially needy church schools are actively recruiting students with tax-supported vouchers, considering them an essential source of revenue to keep their schools operating. In 2002, in the case of *Zelman v. Simmons-Harris,* the Supreme Court said that tax-supported vouchers could be used at religious schools so long as parents had a choice between religious and secular institutions.[22]

For Critical Analysis

Despite the establishment clause, the United States still uses the motto "In God We Trust" and calls itself "one nation, under God." This South Carolina license plate was introduced in 2002. Do you think this license plate is a violation of the separation of church and state?

In 2004, the question of whether the phrase "under God" in the Pledge of Allegiance violates the "establishment clause" was brought before the Court. Written in 1892, the pledge had been used in schools without any religious references. But in 1954, in the midst of the Cold War, Congress voted to change the Pledge, in response to the "godless Communism" of the Soviet Union. The conversion was made by adding two key words, so that the revised version read: "I pledge allegiance to the flag of the United States of America and to the Republic for which it stands, one nation *under God,* indivisible, with liberty and justice for all."

Ever since the change was made, there has been a consistent murmuring of discontent from those who object to an officially sanctioned profession of belief in a deity as a violation of the religious freedom clause of the First Amendment. When saying the pledge, those who object to the phrase have often simply stayed silent during the two key words and then resumed for the rest of the pledge. In 2003, Michael A. Newdow, the atheist father of a kindergarten student in a California elementary school, forced the issue to the surface when he brought suit against the local school district. Newdow argued that the reference to God turned the daily recitation of the pledge into a religious exercise. A federal court ruled that

In 2005, the Supreme Court ruled that this display of the Ten Commandments at the Texas State Capitol in Austin did not violate the separation of church and state. However, the Court found that displays of the Ten Commandments inside two courthouses in Kentucky were unconstitutional.

although students were not required to recite the pledge at all, having to stand and listen to "under God" still violated the First Amendment's "establishment clause." The case was appealed to the Supreme Court and on June 14, 2004—exactly fifty years to the day after the adoption of "under God" in the pledge—the Court ruled that Newdow lacked a sufficient personal stake in the case to bring the complaint. This inconclusive decision by the Supreme Court left "under God" in the pledge while keeping the issue alive for possible resolution in a future case.

In 2005 the Supreme Court ruled, also inconclusively, on government-sponsored displays of religious symbols. Two 2005 cases involved displays of the Ten Commandments. In *Van Orden v. Perry,* the Court decided by a 5-to-4 margin that a display of the Ten Commandments at the Texas state capital did not violate the Constitution.[23] However, in *McCreary v. ACLU,* decided at the same time and also by a 5-to-4 margin, the Court determined that a display of the Ten Commandments inside two Kentucky court houses was unconstitutional.[24] Justice Stephen Breyer, the swing vote in the two cases, said that the display in *Van Orden* had a secular purpose, whereas the displays in *McCreary* had a purely religious purpose. Most observers saw little difference between the two cases. Even Breyer was hard pressed to explain his shifting votes except to say that *Van Orden* was a "borderline" case. Obviously, the issue of government-sponsored displays of religious symbols has not been settled.

Free Exercise of Religion

The **free exercise clause** protects the right to believe and to practice whatever religion one chooses; it also protects the right to be a nonbeliever. The precedent-setting case involving free exercise is *West Virginia State Board of Education v. Barnette* (1943), which involved the children of a family of Jehovah's Witnesses who refused to salute and pledge allegiance to the American flag on the grounds that their religious faith did not permit it. Three years earlier, the Court had upheld such a requirement and had permitted schools to expel students for refusing to

free exercise clause the First Amendment clause that protects a citizen's right to believe and practice whatever religion he or she chooses salute the flag. But the entry of the United States into a war to defend democracy coupled with the ugly treatment to which the Jehovah's Witnesses' children had been subjected induced the Court to reverse itself and to endorse the free exercise of religion even when it may be offensive to the beliefs of the majority.[25]

Although the Supreme Court has been fairly consistent and strict in protecting the free exercise of religious belief, it has taken pains to distinguish between religious beliefs and *actions* based on those beliefs. In one case, for example, two Native Americans had been fired from their jobs for smoking peyote, an illegal drug. They claimed that they had been fired from their jobs illegally because smoking peyote was a religious sacrament protected by the free exercise clause. The Court disagreed with their claim in an important 1990 decision,[26] but Congress supported the claim and it went on to engage in an unusual controversy with the Court, involving the separation of powers as well as the proper application of the separation of church and state. Congress literally reversed the Court's 1990 decision with the enactment of the Religious Freedom Restoration Act of 1993 (RFRA), forbidding any federal agency or state government to restrict a person's free exercise of religion unless the federal agency or state government demonstrates that its action "furthers a compelling government interest" and "is the least restrictive means of furthering that compelling governmental interest." One of the first applications of the RFRA was to a case brought by St. Peter's Catholic Church against the city of Boerne, Texas, which had denied permission to the church to enlarge its building because the building had been declared a historic landmark. The case went to federal court on the argument that the city had violated the church's religious freedom as guaranteed by Congress in RFRA. The Supreme Court declared RFRA unconstitutional, but on grounds rarely utilized, if not unique to this case: Congress had violated the separation of powers principle, infringing on the powers of the judiciary by going so far beyond its law-making powers that it ended up actually expanding the scope of religious rights rather than just enforcing them. The Court thereby implied that questions requiring a balancing of religious claims against public policy claims were reserved strictly to the judiciary.[27]

The *City of Boerne* case did settle some matters of constitutional controversy over the religious exercise and the establishment clauses of the First Amendment but left a lot more unsettled. What about polygamy, a practice allowed in the Mormon faith? Or the refusal of Amish parents to send their children to school beyond eighth grade because exposing their children to "modern values" would undermine their religious commitment? In this last example, the Court decided in favor of the Amish and endorsed a very strong interpretation of the protection of free exercise.[28]

The First Amendment and Freedom of Speech and the Press

> Congress shall make no law . . . abridging the freedom of speech, or of the press. . . .

Freedom of speech and of the press have a special place in American political thought. To begin with, democracy depends on the ability of individuals to talk to each other and to disseminate information and ideas. It would be difficult to conceive how democratic politics could function without free and open debate. Such debate, moreover, is seen as an essential mechanism for determining the quality or validity of competing ideas. As Justice Oliver Wendell Holmes said, "the best test of truth is the power of the thought to get itself accepted in the competition of the market. . . . [t]hat at any rate is the theory of our Constitution."[29] What is sometimes called the "marketplace of ideas" receives a good deal of protection from the courts. In 1938 the Supreme Court held that any legislation that attempts to restrict speech "is to be subjected to a more exacting judicial scrutiny . . . than are most other types of legislation."[30] This higher standard of judicial review came to be called strict scrutiny.

The doctrine of strict scrutiny places a heavy burden of proof on the government if it seeks to regulate or restrict speech. Americans are assumed to have the right to speak and to broadcast their ideas unless some compelling reason can be identified to stop them. But strict scrutiny does not mean that speech can never be regulated. Over the past 200 years, the courts have scrutinized many different forms of speech and constructed different principles and guidelines for each. According to the courts, although virtually all speech is protected by the Constitution, some forms of speech are entitled to a greater degree of protection than others. Let us examine what the federal courts have said about some of the major forms of speech.

POLITICAL SPEECH Political speech was the activity of greatest concern to the framers of the Constitution, even though some found it the most difficult form of speech to tolerate. Within seven years of the ratification of the Bill of Rights in 1791, Congress adopted the infamous Alien and Sedition Acts, which, among other things, made it a crime to say or publish anything that might tend to defame or bring into disrepute the government of the United States. Quite clearly, the acts' intentions were to criminalize the very conduct given absolute protection by the First Amendment (see also Chapter 9). Fifteen violators—including several newspaper editors—were indicted, and a few were actually convicted before the relevant portions of the acts were allowed to expire.

The first modern free speech case arose immediately after World War I. It involved persons who had been convicted under the federal Espionage Act of 1917 for opposing U.S. involvement in the war. The Supreme Court upheld the Espionage Act and refused to protect the speech rights of the defendants on the grounds that their activities—appeals to draftees to resist the draft—constituted a **"clear and present danger"** to security.[31] This is the first and most famous "test" for when government intervention or censorship can be permitted.

"clear and present danger" test test to determine whether speech is protected or unprotected, based on its capacity to present a "clear and present danger" to society

It was only after the 1920s that real progress toward a genuinely effective First Amendment was made. Since then, political speech has been consistently protected by the courts even when it has been deemed "insulting" or "outrageous." Here is the way the Supreme Court put it in one of its most important statements on the subject:

> The constitutional guarantees of free speech and free press do not permit a State to forbid or proscribe advocacy of the use of force or of law violation *except where such advocacy is directed to inciting or producing imminent lawless action and is likely to incite or produce such action* [emphasis added].[32]

In other words, so long as speech falls short of actually inciting action, it cannot be prohibited, even if it is hostile to or subversive of the government and its policies. This statement was made in the case of a Ku Klux Klan leader, Charles Brandenburg, who had been arrested and convicted of advocating "revengent" action against the president, Congress, and the Supreme Court, among others, if they continued "to suppress the white, Caucasian race. . . ." Although Brandenburg was not carrying a weapon, some of the members of his audience were. Nevertheless, the Supreme Court reversed the state courts and freed Brandenburg while also declaring Ohio's Criminal Syndicalism Act unconstitutional because it punished persons who "advocate, or teach the duty, necessity, or propriety [of violence] as a means of accomplishing industrial or political reform . . ."; or who publish materials or "voluntarily assemble . . . to teach or advocate the doctrines of criminal syndicalism." The Supreme Court argued that the statute did not distinguish "mere advocacy" from "incitement to imminent lawless action." It would be difficult to go much further in protecting freedom of speech.

Another area of recent expansion of political speech—the participation of wealthy persons and corporations in political campaigns—was opened up in 1976, with the Supreme Court's decision in *Buckley v. Valeo.* Campaign finance reform laws of the early 1970s, arising out of the Watergate scandal, sought to put severe limits on campaign spending. A number of important provisions were declared unconstitutional on the basis of a new principle that spending money by or on behalf of candidates is a form of speech protected by the First Amendment. (For more details, see Chapter 10.) The issue came up again in 2003, with passage of a new and still more severe campaign finance law, the Bipartisan Campaign Reform Act (BCRA). In *McConnell v. FEC* (Federal Election Commission), the 5-to-4 majority seriously reduced the area of speech protected by the *Buckley v. Valeo* decision by holding that Congress was well within its power to put limits on the amounts individuals could spend, and to put severe limits on the amounts of "soft money" that corporations and their PACs could spend. The Court argued that "the selling of access . . . has given rise to the appearance of undue influence [that justifies] regulations impinging on First Amendment rights . . . in order to curb corruption or the appearance of corruption."[33] In the *McConnell* case, the Court also upheld BCRA's limitations on "issue advertising." The Act prohibited political advocacy groups from running ads that mentioned a candidate within thirty days of a primary election and sixty days of a general election. This ban was justified on the argument that wealthy special interests could affect election outcomes with last-minute ad campaigns. However, in its 2007 decision in the case of *Federal Election Commission v. Wisconsin Right to Life,* the Court reversed itself, declaring that such ads were protected speech and could not be prohibited so long as they focused mainly on issues and were not simply appeals to vote for or against a specific candidate.[34]

The Supreme Court has interpreted the freedom of speech as extending to symbolic acts of political protest, such as flag burning. On several occasions—most recently in 2006—a resolution for a constitutional amendment to ban flag burning has passed in the House of Representatives but never found enough support in the Senate.

SYMBOLIC SPEECH, SPEECH PLUS, AND THE RIGHTS OF ASSEMBLY AND PETITION The First Amendment treats the freedoms of assembly and petition as equal to the freedoms of religion and political speech. Freedom of assembly and freedom of petition are closely associated with speech but go beyond it to speech associated with action. Since at least 1931, the Supreme Court has sought to protect actions that are designed to send a political message. (Usually the purpose of a symbolic act is not only to send a direct message but also to draw a crowd—to do something spectacular in order to attract spectators to the action and thus strengthen the message.) Therefore the Court held unconstitutional a California statute making it a felony to display a red flag "as a sign, symbol or emblem of opposition to organized government."[35] Although today there are limits on how far one can go with actions that symbolically convey a message, the protection of such action is very broad. Thus, although the Court upheld a federal statute making it a crime to burn draft cards to protest the Vietnam War on the grounds that the government had a compelling interest in preserving draft cards as part of the conduct of the war itself, it considered the wearing of black armbands to school a protected form of assembly for symbolic action.

Politics Today

In October 2007, following a rash of incidents in which nooses were displayed, apparently to symbolize the lynchings of blacks in the Old South, the New York State legislature moved to make it a felony to display a noose in a threatening manner. Do you think such a law is constitutional?

Another example is the burning of the American flag as a symbol of protest. In 1984, at a political rally held during the Republican National Convention in Dallas, Texas, a political protester burned an American flag in violation of a Texas statute that prohibited desecration of a venerated object. In a 5-to-4 decision, the Supreme Court declared the Texas law unconstitutional on the grounds that flag burning was expressive conduct protected by the First Amendment.[36] Congress reacted immediately with a proposal for a constitutional amendment reversing the Court's Texas decision, and when the amendment failed to receive the necessary two-thirds majority in the Senate, Congress passed the Flag Protection Act of 1989. Protesters promptly violated this act, and their prosecution moved quickly into the federal district court, which declared the new law unconstitutional. The Supreme Court, in another 5-to-4 decision, affirmed the lower court decision.[37] A renewed effort began in Congress to propose a constitutional amendment that would reverse the Supreme Court and place this form of expressive conduct outside the realm of protected speech or assembly. Since 1995, the House of Representatives has four times passed a resolution for a constitutional amendment to ban flag burning, but each time the Senate has failed to go along.[38] In a 2003 decision the Supreme Court struck down a Virginia cross-burning statute. In that case, the Court ruled that states could make cross burning a crime as long as the statute requires prosecutors to prove that the act of setting fire to the cross was intended to intimidate. Former Justice Sandra Day O'Connor wrote for the majority that the First Amendment permits the government to forbid cross burning as a "particularly virulent form of intimidation" but not when the act was "a form of symbolic expression."[39] This decision will almost inevitably become a more generalized First Amendment protection of any conduct, including flag burning, that can be shown to be a form of symbolic expression.

Closer to the original intent of the assembly and petition clause is the category of **"speech plus"**—following speech with physical activity such as picketing, distributing leaflets, and other forms of peaceful demonstration or assembly. Such assemblies are consistently protected by courts under the First Amendment; state and local laws regulating such activities are closely scrutinized and frequently overturned. But the same assembly on private property is quite another matter and can in many circumstances be regulated. For example, the directors of a shopping center can lawfully prohibit an assembly protesting a war or supporting a ban on abortion. Assemblies in public areas can also be restricted under some circumstances, especially when the assembly or demonstration jeopardizes the health, safety, or rights of others. This condition was the basis of the Supreme Court's decision to uphold a lower court order that restricted the access abortion protesters had to the entrances of abortion clinics.[40]

"speech plus" speech accompanied by conduct such as sit-ins, picketing, and demonstrations; protection of this form of speech under the First Amendment is conditional, and restrictions imposed by state or local authorities are acceptable if properly balanced by considerations of public order

POLITICS & POPULAR CULTURE

Freedom of Speech—on the Airwaves, Too?

Freedom of speech is one of the cornerstones of the Bill of Rights. But freedom of speech as it exists today is freedom from *government* punishment or censorship. It does not protect speech—even political speech—from restrictions imposed by media owners or others. There are numerous examples, even within entertainment programming, of media executives canceling programs as a result of contentious political expression or avoiding airing political speech. Whether or not these decisions constitute "censorship" is an area of ongoing debate.

Often, when controversial political views are communicated on television, people who oppose those ideas put pressure on advertisers—who then pressure network executives—to avoid such programs. One illustration of this process is the case of the program *Politically Incorrect*. The program, which aired on ABC, featured the comedian/commentator Bill Maher discussing current events with celebrity guests. After the terrorist attacks on the World Trade Center in 2001, Maher angered many Americans when he stated that the act of flying planes into the towers was not "cowardly." "We have been the cowards lobbing cruise missiles from 2,000 miles away," he said on the show. Viewers and nonviewers alike began pressuring advertisers through email petitions and phone calls, and within days, advertisers such as Sears and Federal Express had withdrawn their ads. When *Politically Incorrect* was canceled a few months later, many people in the industry believed that the cancellation was due in large part to Maher's post–September 11 statements and the response by viewers and advertisers.

Interest groups often play a central role in organizing advertiser boycotts. In early 2000, Paramount announced that it would be creating a daytime television talk show starring the conservative radio host Dr. Laura Schlessinger. The Gay & Lesbian Alliance Against Defamation (GLAAD) and other gay rights groups critical of Dr. Laura's statements concerning homosexuality (including her comment that being gay was a "biological error") began a campaign to pressure advertisers not to buy time during her show. In March 2001, Paramount announced the cancellation of the program.

Although advertiser dollars often play a role, sometimes decisions to avoid controversial political content are made internally, as media executives make predictions about public opinion. In the week after September 11, 2001, for example, ClearChannel Communications circulated a memo to its 1,200 plus stations listing over 150 "questionable" songs that radio stations should avoid. Among the songs were Peter, Paul and Mary's "Leaving on a Jet Plane" and the Beastie Boys' "Sabotage."[a] More recently, record industry executives at Interscope Records made the decision to provide altered versions of Jadakiss's rap song "Why?" to radio stations and MTV due to the song's controversial lyrics. The song suggests that President Bush himself had something to do with the events of September 11: "Why did bush [*sic*] knock down the towers?"[b]

Do these acts constitute a form of censorship? Free-speech advocates argue that this process has the effect of censoring certain points of view. By staying away from controversial fare that leans either too far left or too far right, the media may support mainstream opinion and the status quo—limiting the opportunities for people holding minority opinions to be heard. On the other hand, some argue that the Bill of Rights guarantees only the right to express one's opinion—not access to the airwaves.

FOR CRITICAL ANALYSIS

1. What is the difference between government censorship and, say, a radio station's decision not to play a controversial song?
2. Should we be concerned if well-organized interest groups are able to influence television and radio programming to coincide more closely with their views?

a. James Sullivan, "Radio Employee Circulates Don't-play List," *San Francisco Chronicle*, September 18, 2001, p. E-1.
b. Joe Heim, "Rapper Ups the Anti on Bush and 9/11," *Washington Post*, July 17, 2004, p. C01.

An unusual "speech plus" case decided in 2006 was *Rumsfeld v. FAIR*.[41] A number of law schools had banned military recruiters from their campuses to protest the military's antigay policies. The government responded by threatening to cut off federal funding to schools that joined the ban. The schools argued, in turn, that the government was violating their constitutional right to voice opposition to its policies. The Supreme Court ruled that the government could require schools to host recruiters as a condition for funding. Recruitment, said the Court, was not a form of expression protected by the Constitution; schools remained completely free to voice their opposition to the military's policies even as they hosted the recruiters.

Freedom of the Press

For all practical purposes, freedom of speech implies and includes freedom of the press. With the exception of the broadcast media, which are subject to federal regulation, the press is protected under the doctrine against **prior restraint.** Beginning with the landmark 1931 case of *Near v. Minnesota*, the U.S. Supreme Court has held that, except under the most extraordinary circumstances, the First Amendment of the Constitution prohibits government agencies from seeking to prevent newspapers or magazines from publishing whatever they wish.[42] Indeed, in the case of *New York Times v. U.S.*, the so-called *Pentagon Papers* case, the Supreme Court ruled that the government could not even block publication of secret Defense Department documents furnished to the *New York Times* by an opponent of the Vietnam War who had obtained the documents illegally.[43] In a 1990 case, however, the Supreme Court upheld a lower-court order restraining Cable News Network (CNN) from broadcasting tapes of conversations between the former Panamanian dictator Manuel Noriega and his lawyer, supposedly recorded by the U.S. government. By a vote of 7 to 2, the Court held that CNN could be restrained from broadcasting the tapes until the trial court in the Noriega case had listened to the tapes and had decided whether their broadcast would violate Noriega's right to a fair trial.

prior restraint an effort by a governmental agency to block the publication of material it deems libelous or harmful in some other way; censorship. In the United States, the courts forbid prior restraint except under the most extraordinary circumstances

Another press freedom issue that the courts have often been asked to decide is the question of whether journalists can be compelled to reveal their sources of information. Journalists assert that if they cannot assure sources of confidentiality, the flow of information will be reduced and press freedom effectively curtailed. Government agencies, however, aver that names of news sources may be relevant to criminal or even national-security investigations. More than thirty states have "shield laws," which to varying degrees, protect journalistic sources. There is, however, no federal shield law. The Supreme Court has held that the press has no constitutional right to withhold information in court.[44] In 2005, a *New York Times* reporter, Judith Miller, was jailed for contempt of court for refusing to tell a federal grand jury the name of a confidential source in a case involving the leaked identity of the CIA analyst Valerie Plame. Plame's husband, Joseph Wilson, had been critical of the Bush administration's Iraq policies.

libel a written statement made in "reckless disregard of the truth" that is considered damaging to a victim because it is "malicious, scandalous, and defamatory"

LIBEL AND SLANDER Some speech is not protected at all. If a written statement is made in "reckless disregard of the truth" and is considered damaging to the victim because it is "malicious, scandalous, and defamatory," it can be punished as **libel.** If an oral statement of such nature is made, it can be punished as **slander.**

slander an oral statement, made in "reckless disregard of the truth," which is considered damaging to the victim because it is "malicious, scandalous, and defamatory"

Today, most libel suits involve freedom of the press, and the realm of free press is enormous. Historically, newspapers were subject to the law of libel, which

BANNED BOOKS

One of the more visible issues of free speech has been the banning of certain books in public schools. For example, Nobel Prize-winner Toni Morrison's novel, *The Bluest Eye*, has frequently been banned.

Following is a list of the most-censored books of 2006:

1. *And Tango Makes Three*, by Justin Richardson and Peter Parnell, for homosexuality, antifamily, and unsuited to age group
2. *Gossip Girls*, series by Cecily Von Ziegesar for homosexuality, sexual content, drugs, unsuited to age group, and offensive language
3. *Alice*, series by Phyllis Reynolds Naylor for sexual content and offensive language
4. *The Earth, My Butt, and Other Big Round Things*, by Carolyn Mackler for sexual content, antifamily, offensive language, and unsuited to age group
5. *The Bluest Eye*, by Toni Morrison for sexual content, offensive language, and unsuited to age group
6. *Scary Stories*, series by Alvin Schwartz for occult/Santanism, unsuited to age group, violence, and insensitivity
7. *Athletic Shorts*, by Chris Crutcher for homosexuality and offensive language
8. *The Perks of Being a Wallflower, by* Stephen Chbosky for homosexuality, sexually explicit, offensive language, and unsuited to age group
9. *Beloved*, by Toni Morrison for offensive language, sexual content, and unsuited to age group
10. *The Chocolate War, by* Robert Cormier: for sexual content, offensive language, and violence

SOURCE: American Library Association.

provided that newspapers that printed false and malicious stories could be compelled to pay damages to those they defamed. In recent years, however, American courts have greatly narrowed the meaning of libel and made it extremely difficult, particularly for politicians or other public figures, to win a libel case against a newspaper. In the important 1964 case of *New York Times v. Sullivan*, the Court held that to be deemed libelous, a story about a public official not only had to be untrue, but also had to result from "actual malice" or "reckless disregard" for the truth.[45] In other words, the newspaper had to print false and malicious material *deliberately*. In practice, it is nearly impossible to prove that a paper deliberately printed maliciously false information, and it is especially difficult for a politician or other public figure to win a libel case. Essentially, the print media have been able to publish anything they want about a public figure.

However, in at least one case, the Court has opened up the possibility for public officials to file libel suits against the press. In 1985, the Court held that the press was immune to libel only when the printed material was "a matter of public concern." In other words, in future cases a newspaper would have to show that the public official was engaged in activities that were indeed *public*. This new principle has made the press more vulnerable to libel suits, but it still leaves an enormous realm of freedom for the press. For example, the Reverend Jerry Falwell, the leader of the Moral Majority, lost his libel suit against *Hustler* magazine even though the magazine had published a cartoon of Falwell showing him having drunken intercourse with his mother in an outhouse. A unanimous Supreme Court rejected a jury verdict in favor of damages for "emotional distress" on the grounds that parodies, no matter how outrageous, are protected because "outrageousness" is too subjective a test and thus would interfere with the free flow of ideas protected by the First Amendment.[46]

With the emergence of the Internet as an important communications medium, the courts have had to decide how traditional libel law applies to Internet content. In 1995, the New York courts held that an on-line bulletin board could be held responsible for the libelous content of material posted by a third party. To protect Internet service providers, Congress subsequently enacted legislation absolving service providers of responsibility for third-party posts. The federal courts have generally upheld this law and declared that providers are immune to suits regarding the content of material posted by others.[47]

OBSCENITY AND PORNOGRAPHY If libel and slander cases can be difficult because of the problem of determining the truth of statements and whether those statements are malicious and damaging, cases involving pornography and obscenity can be even stickier. It is easy to say that pornography and obscenity fall outside the realm of protected speech, but it is impossible to draw a clear line defining exactly where protection ends and unprotected speech begins. Not until 1957 did the Supreme Court confront this problem, and it did so with a definition of obscenity that may have caused more confusion than it cleared up. In writing the Court's opinion, Justice William Brennan defined obscenity as speech or writing that appeals to the "prurient interest"—that is, books, magazines, films, and other material whose purpose is to excite lust as this appears "to the average person, applying contemporary community standards." Even so, Brennan added, the work should be judged obscene only when it is "utterly without redeeming social importance."[48] Instead of clarifying the Court's view, Brennan's definition actually caused more confusion. In 1964, Justice Potter Stewart confessed that, although he found pornography impossible to define, "I know it when I see it."[49]

All attempts by the courts to define pornography and obscenity have proved impractical, because each instance required courts to screen thousands of pages of print material and feet of film alleged to be pornographic. The vague and impractical standards that had been developed meant ultimately that almost nothing could be banned on the grounds that it was pornographic and obscene. An effort was made to strengthen the restrictions in 1973, when the Supreme Court expressed its willingness to define pornography as a work that (1) as a whole, is deemed prurient by the "average person" according to "community standards"; (2) depicts sexual conduct "in a patently offensive way"; and (3) lacks "serious literary, artistic, political, or scientific value." This definition meant that pornography would be determined by local rather than national standards. Thus, a local bookseller might be prosecuted for selling a volume that was a best-seller nationally but that was deemed pornographic locally.[50] This new definition of standards did not help much either, and not long after 1973 the Court began again to review all such community antipornography laws, reversing most of them.

In recent years, the battle against obscene speech has been against "cyberporn"—pornography on the Internet. Opponents of this form of expression argue that it should be banned because of the easy access children have to the Internet. The first major effort to regulate the content of the Internet occurred on February 1, 1996, when the 104th Congress passed major telecommunications legislation. Attached to the Telecommunications Act was an amendment, called the Communications Decency Act (CDA), that was designed to regulate the online transmission of obscene material. The constitutionality of the CDA was immediately challenged in court by a coalition of interests led by the American Civil Liberties Union (ACLU). In the 1997 case of *Reno v. ACLU,* the Supreme Court struck down the CDA, ruling that it suppressed speech that "adults have a constitutional right to receive" and that governments may not limit the adult population to messages that are fit for children. Supreme Court Justice John Paul Stevens described the Internet as the "town crier" of the modern age and said that the Internet was entitled to the greatest degree of First Amendment protection possible.[51] Congress again tried limiting children's access to Internet pornography with the 2001 Children's Internet Protection Act, which required public libraries to install antipornography filters on all library computers with Internet access. Though the act made cooperation a condition for receiving federal subsidies, it did permit librarians to unblock a site at the request of an adult patron. The law was challenged, and in 2003 the Court upheld it, asserting that its provisions did not violate library patrons' First Amendment rights.[52]

In 2000, the Supreme Court also extended the highest degree of First Amendment protection to cable (not broadcast) television. In *U.S. v. Playboy Entertainment Group,* the Court struck down a portion of the Telecommunications Act of 1996 that required cable TV companies to limit the broadcast of sexually explicit programming to late night hours. In its decision, the Court noted that the law already provided parents with the means to restrict access to sexually explicit cable channels through various blocking devices. Moreover, such programming could come into the home only if parents decided to purchase such channels in the first place.

FIGHTING WORDS AND HATE SPEECH Speech can also lose its protected position when it moves toward the sphere of action. "Expressive speech," for example, is protected until it moves from the symbolic realm to the realm of actual conduct—to direct incitement of damaging conduct with the use of so-called **fighting words.** In 1942, the Supreme Court upheld the arrest and conviction of a man who had violated a state law forbidding the use of offensive language in public. He had called the arresting officer a "goddamned racketeer" and "a damn Fascist." When his case reached the Supreme Court, the arrest was upheld on the grounds that the First Amendment provides no protection for such offensive language because such words "are no essential part of any exposition of ideas."[53] This case was reaffirmed in a much more famous and important case decided at the height of the Cold War, when the Supreme Court held that "there is no substantial public interest in permitting certain kinds of utterances: the lewd and obscene, the profane, the libelous, and the insulting or 'fighting' words—those which by their very utterance inflict injury or tend to incite an immediate breach of the peace."[54]

fighting words speech that directly incites damaging conduct

Since that time, however, the Supreme Court has reversed almost every conviction based on arguments that the speaker had used "fighting words." But again, that does not mean that this is an absolutely settled area. In recent years, increased activism of minority and women's groups prompted a movement against words that might be construed as offensive to members of a particular group. Sometimes this is called "hate speech." In response, many organizations have attempted to impose codes of etiquette that acknowledge enhanced sensitivities. Efforts to formalize restraints on the use of certain words in public have caused great concern over their possible infringement of freedom of speech. But how should we determine what words are "fighting words" that fall outside the protections of the freedom of speech?

The Supreme Court has often upheld limits on speech by public school students. With the help of the ACLU, these high school students filed a lawsuit against their school district after their principal censored student newspaper articles on homosexuality.

Some universities have tried to regulate speech by establishing "speech codes" or "harassment codes," to suppress racial, ethnic, or gender slurs. What these universities have found, however, is that speech codes often produce more problems than they solve. One instructive case happened at the University of Pennsylvania. Soon after the university adopted its "Harassment Code," a student hurled some rude comments at a group of black sorority members whose noisy party had interrupted his studies. Although it wasn't clear that his remarks were racist, the student was brought up on charges of racial harassment that violated the university's code, and the sorority members went much further by bringing civil charges of racial harassment. Eventually all charges were dropped, and the university promptly revoked its entire code. Similar codes at other universities were struck down by federal judges as unconstitutional infringements of speech.[55]

Such concerns are not limited to universities. Similar developments have taken place in large corporations, both public and private, against which many successful complaints and lawsuits have been brought, alleging that the words of employers or their supervisors create a "hostile or abusive working environment." These cases arise out of the civil rights laws and will be addressed in more detail in Chapter 5. The Supreme Court has held that "sexual harassment" that creates a "hostile working environment" includes "unwelcome sexual advances, requests for sexual favors, and other *verbal* or physical conduct of a sexual nature" (emphasis added).[56] A fundamental free speech issue is involved in these regulations of hostile speech. So far, the assumption favoring the regulation of hostile speech in universities and other workplaces is that "some speech must be shut down in the name of free speech because it tends to silence those disparaged by it,"[57] even though a threat of hostile action (usually embodied in "fighting words") is not present. However, the courts have been reluctant to draw a precise line between the right to express hostile views and the protection of the sensitivities of minorities and women.

For Critical Analysis

Should hate speech be protected? Is it contradictory that many who strongly support free thought and expression draw the line on protecting "thought we hate"?

SPEECH BY PUBLIC SCHOOL STUDENTS One group that seems to enjoy only a limited right of free speech is public school students. In 1986, the Supreme Court upheld the punishment of a high school student for making sexually suggestive speech. The Court opinion held that such speech interfered with the school's goal of teaching students the limits of socially acceptable behavior.[58] Two years later, the Supreme Court restricted student speech and press rights even further by defining them as part of the educational process not to be treated with the same standard as adult speech in a regular public forum.[59] In 2007, in the case of *Morse v. Frederick*, the Court held that a principal did not violate a student's free speech rights by suspending him for displaying a banner proclaiming "Bong Hits For Jesus."[60] The decision affirmed the principle that school officials can censor student speech that advocates or celebrates the use of illegal drugs.

COMMERCIAL SPEECH Commercial speech, such as newspaper or television advertisements, does not have full First Amendment protection because it cannot be considered political speech. Initially considered to be entirely outside the protection of the First Amendment, commercial speech made gains during the twentieth century. However, some commercial speech is still unprotected and therefore regulated. For example, the regulation of false and misleading advertising by the Federal Trade Commission is an old and well-established power of the federal government. The Supreme Court long ago approved the constitutionality of laws prohibiting the electronic media from carrying cigarette advertising.[61] The Court has upheld a state university ban on Tupperware parties in college dormitories.[62] It has upheld city ordinances prohibiting the posting of all commercial signs on public property (as long as the ban is total, so that there is no hint of censorship).[63] And the Supreme Court, in a heated 5-to-4 decision written by Chief Justice William Rehnquist, upheld Puerto Rico's statute restricting gambling advertising aimed at residents of Puerto Rico.[64]

However, the gains far outweigh the losses in the effort to expand the protection commercial speech enjoys under the First Amendment. "In part, this reflects the growing appreciation that commercial speech is part of the free flow of information necessary for informed choice and democratic participation."[65] For example, the Court in 1975 struck down a state statute making it a misdemeanor to sell or circulate newspapers encouraging abortions; the Court ruled that the statute infringed on constitutionally protected speech and on the right of the reader to make informed choices.[66] On a similar basis, the Court reversed its own earlier decisions upholding laws that prohibited dentists and other professionals from advertising their services. For the Court, medical service advertising was a matter of health that could be advanced by the free flow of information.[67] In a 1983 case, the Supreme Court struck down a congressional statute that prohibited the unsolicited mailing of advertisements for contraceptives. In 1996, the Supreme Court struck down Rhode Island laws and regulations banning the advertisement of liquor prices as a violation of the First Amendment.[68] And in a 2001 case, the Supreme Court ruled that a Massachusetts ban on all cigarette advertising violated the First Amendment right of the tobacco industry to advertise its products to adult consumers.[69] These instances of commercial speech are significant in themselves, but they are all the more significant because they indicate the breadth and depth of the freedom existing today to direct appeals to a large public, not only to sell goods and services but also to mobilize people for political purposes.

The Second Amendment arouses at least as much controversy as the First. The right to bear arms is constitutionally guaranteed, although an estimated 80 percent of Americans support some form of gun control.

The Second Amendment and the Right to Bear Arms

> A well regulated Militia, being necessary to the security of a free State, the right of the people to keep and bear Arms, shall not be infringed.

The point and purpose of the Second Amendment is the provision for militias; they were to be the backing of the government for the maintenance of local public order. "Militia" was understood at the time of the Founding to be a military or police resource for state governments, and militias were specifically distinguished from armies and troops, which came within the sole constitutional jurisdiction of Congress.

Thus, the right of the people "to keep and bear Arms" is based on and associated with participation in state militias. The reference to citizens keeping arms underscored the fact that in the 1700s,

A loophole in gun purchase laws allowed a student at Virginia Tech with a history of mental illness to purchase the handguns that he used to kill thirty-two fellow students and wound many others. Following the tragedy, both the state of Virginia and the national government strengthened the requirements for background checks on gun buyers.

state governments could not be relied on to provide firearms to militia members, so citizens eligible to serve in militias (white males between the ages of eighteen and forty-five) were expected to keep their own firearms at the ready. In the late nineteenth century, some citizens sought to form their own *private* militias, but the Supreme Court cut that short with a ruling that militias are a military or police resource of state governments.[70] In 2008, the U.S. Supreme Court declared that the Second Amendment also protected an individual's right to possess a firearm for private use.[71] In the *Heller* case, the Court struck down a District of Columbia law that was designed to make it nearly impossible for private individuals to legally purchase firearms. Because the District of Columbia is an agency of the federal government, the Court's decision does not mean that the states cannot ban gun ownership. The Court would have to decide in subsequent cases whether the Second Amendment applies to the states.

Politics Today

In 2007, a student with a history of mental illness shot and killed thirty-two people and wounded a number of others on the Virginia Tech University campus. Could a ban on the sale and possession of firearms prevent this type of tragedy? What, if any, restrictions would you support on the private possession of firearms?

Due Process of Law

Except for the First Amendment, most of the battle to apply the Bill of Rights to the states was fought over the various protections granted to individuals who are accused of a crime, who are suspects in the commission of a crime, or who are brought before the court as a witness to a crime. The Fourth, Fifth, Sixth, and Eighth Amendments, taken together, are the essence of the **due process of law,** even though this fundamental concept does not appear until the very last words of the Fifth Amendment. In the next sections we will look at specific cases that illuminate the dynamics of this important constitutional issue. The procedural

due process of law the right of every citizen against arbitrary action by national or state governments

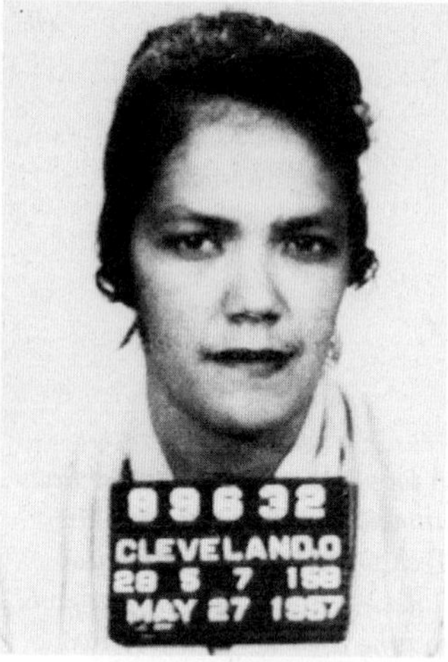

In the case of Dollree Mapp v. Ohio, *the Supreme Court interpreted the Fourth Amendment to mean that if incriminating material is found through illegal search and seizure, it cannot be used as evidence in court.*

exclusionary rule the ability of courts to exclude evidence obtained in violation of the Fourth Amendment

safeguards that we will discuss may seem remote to most law-abiding citizens, but they help define the limits of government action against the personal liberty of every citizen. Many Americans believe that "legal technicalities" are responsible for setting many actual criminals free. In many cases, that is absolutely true. In fact, setting defendants free is the very purpose of the requirements that constitute due process. One of America's traditional and most strongly held juridical values is that "it is far worse to convict an innocent man than to let a guilty man go free."[72] In civil suits, verdicts rest on "the preponderance of the evidence"; in criminal cases, guilt has to be proven "beyond a reasonable doubt"—a far higher standard. The provisions for due process in the Bill of Rights were added in order to improve the probability that the standard of "reasonable doubt" will be respected.

The Fourth Amendment and Searches and Seizures

> The right of the people to be secure in their persons, houses, papers, and effects, against unreasonable searches and seizures, shall not be violated, and no Warrants shall issue, but upon probable cause, supported by Oath or affirmation, and particularly describing the place to be searched, and the persons or things to be seized.

The purpose of the Fourth Amendment is to guarantee the security of citizens against unreasonable (i.e., improper) searches and seizures. In 1990, the Supreme Court summarized its understanding of the Fourth Amendment brilliantly and succinctly: "A search compromises the individual interest in privacy; a seizure deprives the individual of dominion over his or her person or property."[73] But how are we to define what is reasonable and what is unreasonable?

The 1961 case of *Mapp v. Ohio* illustrates the beauty and the agony of one of the most important of the procedures that have grown out of the Fourth Amendment—the **exclusionary rule,** which prohibits evidence obtained during an illegal search from being introduced in a trial. Acting on a tip that Dollree (Dolly) Mapp was harboring a suspect in a bombing incident, several policemen forcibly entered Ms. Mapp's house, claiming they had a warrant to look for the bombing suspect. The police did not find the bombing suspect but did find some materials connected to a local numbers racket (an illegal gambling operation) and a quantity of "obscene materials," in violation of an Ohio law banning possession of such materials. Although the warrant was never produced, the evidence that had been seized was admitted by a court, and Ms. Mapp was charged and convicted of illegal possession of obscene materials.

By the time Ms. Mapp's appeal reached the Supreme Court, the issue of obscene materials had faded into obscurity, and the question before the Court was whether any evidence produced under the circumstances of the search of her home was admissible. The Court's opinion affirmed the exclusionary rule: under the Fourth Amendment (applied to the states through the Fourteenth Amendment), "all evidence obtained by searches and seizures in violation of the Constitution . . . is inadmissible."[74] This means that even people who are clearly guilty of the crime of which they are accused must not be convicted if the only evidence for their conviction was obtained illegally. This idea was expressed by Supreme Court Justice Benjamin Cardozo nearly a century ago when he wrote that "the criminal is to go free because the constable has blundered."

The exclusionary rule is the most severe restraint ever imposed by the Constitution and the courts on the behavior of the police. The exclusionary rule is a dramatic restriction because it rules out precisely the evidence that produces a conviction; it frees those people who are *known* to have committed the crime of which they have been accused. Because it works so dramatically in favor of persons known to have committed a crime, the Court has since softened the application of the rule. In recent years, the federal courts have relied on a discretionary use of the exclusionary rule, whereby they make a judgment as to the "nature and quality of the intrusion." It is thus difficult to know ahead of time whether a defendant will or will not be protected from an illegal search under the Fourth Amendment.[75]

In a number of instances, such as in the course of an arrest, the authorities can conduct searches without obtaining warrants. In other instances, the authorities may obtain warrants in anticipation of some subsequent need. In 2006, in the case of *U.S. v. Grubbs*, the Supreme Court ruled that the police could conduct searches using such "anticipatory warrants."[76] These warrants are issued when the police know that incriminating material is not yet present but have reason to believe that it will eventually arrive at a particular premises. The warrant is held until the police are ready to conduct their search.

Another recent issue involving the Fourth Amendment is the controversy over mandatory drug testing. Such tests are most widely applied to public employees, and in an important case the Supreme Court has upheld the U.S. Customs Service's drug-testing program for its employees.[77] The same year the Court approved drug and alcohol tests for railroad workers if they were involved in serious accidents.[78] After Court approvals of those two cases in 1989, more than forty federal agencies initiated mandatory employee drug tests. The practice of drug testing was reinforced by a presidential executive order widely touted as the "campaign for a drug-free federal workplace." These growing practices gave rise to public appeals against the general practice of "suspicionless testing" of employees. Regardless of any need to limit the spread of drug abuse, working in this manner through public employees seemed patently unconstitutional, in violation of the Fourth Amendment. A 1995 case, in which the Court upheld a public school district's policy requiring all students participating in interscholastic sports to submit to random drug tests, surely contributed to the efforts of federal, state, and local agencies to initiate random and suspicionless drug and alcohol testing.[79] The most recent cases suggest, however, that the Court is beginning to consider limits on the war against drugs. In a decisive 8-to-1 decision, the Court applied the Fourth Amendment as a shield against "state action that diminishes personal privacy" when the officials in question are not performing high-risk or safety-sensitive tasks.[80] Using random and suspicionless drug testing as a symbol to fight drug use was, in the Court's opinion, carrying the exceptions to the Fourth Amendment too far.

More recently, the Court found it unconstitutional for police to use trained dogs in roadblocks set up to look for drugs in cars. Unlike drunk-driving roadblocks, where public safety is directly involved, narcotics roadblocks "cannot escape the Fourth Amendment's requirement that searches be based on suspicion of individual wrongdoing."[81] In 2007, the Court extended protection against unlawful searches to passengers in cars that have been stopped by the police. Passengers, said the Court, have the same right as drivers to challenge the validity of a search.[82]

THE RIGHTS OF THE ACCUSED FROM ARREST TO TRIAL

No improper searches and seizures (Fourth Amendment)
No arrest without probable cause (Fourth Amendment)
Right to remain silent (Fifth Amendment)
No self-incrimination during arrest or trial (Fifth Amendment)
Right to be informed of charges (Sixth Amendment)
Right to counsel (Sixth Amendment)
No excessive bail (Eighth Amendment)
Right to grand jury (Fifth Amendment)
Right to open trial before a judge (Article I, Section 9)
Right to speedy and public trial before an impartial jury (Sixth Amendment)
Evidence obtained by illegal search not admissible during trial (Fourth Amendment)
Right to confront witnesses (Sixth Amendment)
No double jeopardy (Fifth Amendment)
No cruel and unusual punishment (Eighth Amendment)

The Court also ruled that a public hospital cannot constitutionally test maternity patients for illegal drug use without their consent.[83] Finally, the Court found that the police may not use thermal imaging devices to detect suspicious patterns of heat emerging from private homes without obtaining the usual search warrant.[84]

The Fifth Amendment

> No person shall be held to answer for a capital, or otherwise infamous crime, unless on a presentment or indictment of a Grand Jury, except in cases arising in the land or naval forces, or in the Militia, when in actual service in time of War or public danger; nor shall any person be subject for the same offence to be twice put in jeopardy of life or limb; nor shall be compelled in any criminal case to be a witness against himself, nor be deprived of life, liberty, or property, without due process of law; nor shall private property be taken for public use, without just compensation.

grand jury jury that determines whether sufficient evidence is available to justify a trial; grand juries do not rule on the accused's guilt or innocence

double jeopardy the Fifth Amendment right providing that a person cannot be tried twice for the same crime

GRAND JURIES The first clause of the Fifth Amendment, the right to a **grand jury** to determine whether a trial is warranted, is considered "the oldest institution known to the Constitution."[85] Grand juries play an important role in federal criminal cases. However, the provision for a grand jury is the one important civil liberties provision of the Bill of Rights that was not incorporated by the Fourteenth Amendment to apply to state criminal prosecutions. Thus, some states operate without grand juries. In such states, the prosecuting attorney simply files a "bill of information" affirming that there is sufficient evidence available to justify a trial. If the accused person is to be held in custody, the prosecutor must take the available information before a judge to determine that the evidence shows probable cause.

DOUBLE JEOPARDY "Nor shall any person be subject for the same offence to be twice put in jeopardy of life or limb" is the constitutional protection from **double jeopardy,** or being tried more than once for the same crime. The protection from double jeopardy was at the heart of the *Palko* case in 1937, which, as we saw earlier in this chapter, also established the principle of selective incorporation of the Bill of Rights. In that case, the state of Connecticut had indicted Frank Palko for first-degree murder, but a lower court had found him guilty of only second-degree murder and sentenced him to life in prison. Unhappy with the verdict, the state of Connecticut appealed the conviction to its highest court, won the appeal, got a new trial, and then succeeded in getting Palko convicted of first-degree murder. Palko appealed to the Supreme Court on what seemed an open-and-shut case of double jeopardy. Yet, although the majority of the Court agreed that this could indeed be considered a case of double jeopardy, they decided that double jeopardy was *not* one of the provisions of the Bill of Rights incorporated in the Fourteenth Amendment as a restriction on the powers of the states. It took more than thirty years for the Court to nationalize the constitutional protection against double jeopardy. Palko was eventually executed for the crime, because he lived in the state of Connecticut rather than in a state whose constitution included a guarantee against double jeopardy.

The modern interpretation of the Fifth Amendment was shaped by the 1966 case Miranda v. Arizona. *Ernesto Miranda confessed to kidnapping and rape. Since he was never told that he was not required to answer police questions, his case was appealed on the grounds that his right against self-incrimination had been violated.*

SELF-INCRIMINATION Perhaps the most significant liberty found in the Fifth Amendment, and the one most familiar to many Americans who watch television crime shows, is the guarantee that no citizen "shall be compelled in any criminal case to be a witness against himself." The most famous case concerning self-incrimination is one of such importance that Chief Justice Earl Warren assessed its results as going "to the very root of our concepts of American criminal jurisprudence."[86] Twenty-three-year-old Ernesto Miranda was sentenced to between twenty and thirty years in prison for the kidnapping and rape of an eighteen-year-old woman. The woman had identified him in a police lineup, and, after two hours of questioning, Miranda confessed, subsequently signing a statement that his confession had been made voluntarily, without threats or promises of immunity. These confessions were admitted into evidence, served as the basis for Miranda's conviction, and also served as the basis of the appeal of his conviction all the way to the Supreme Court. In one of the most intensely and widely criticized decisions ever handed down by the Supreme Court, Ernesto Miranda's case produced the rules the police must follow before questioning an arrested criminal suspect. The reading of a person's "*Miranda* rights" became a standard scene in every police station and on virtually every dramatization of police action on television and in the movies. *Miranda* advanced the civil liberties of accused persons not only by expanding the scope of the Fifth Amendment clause covering coerced confessions and self-incrimination, but also by confirming the right to counsel (discussed later). The Supreme Court under Burger and Rehnquist considerably softened the *Miranda* restrictions, making the job of the police a little easier, but the ***Miranda* rule** still stands as a protection against egregious police abuses of arrested persons. The Supreme Court reaffirmed *Miranda* in *Dickerson v. United States* (2000).

***Miranda* rule** the requirement, articulated by the Supreme Court in *Miranda v. Arizona*, that persons under arrest must be informed prior to police interrogation of their rights to remain silent and to have the benefit of legal counsel

EMINENT DOMAIN The other fundamental clause of the Fifth Amendment is the "takings clause," which extends to each citizen a protection against the "taking" of private property "without just compensation." Although this part of the

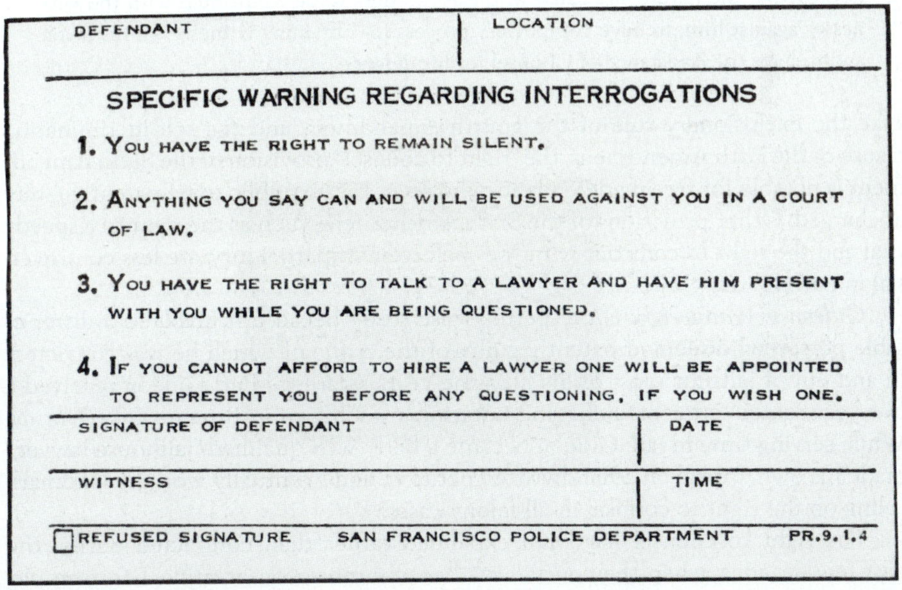

DEFENDANT | LOCATION

SPECIFIC WARNING REGARDING INTERROGATIONS

1. YOU HAVE THE RIGHT TO REMAIN SILENT.

2. ANYTHING YOU SAY CAN AND WILL BE USED AGAINST YOU IN A COURT OF LAW.

3. YOU HAVE THE RIGHT TO TALK TO A LAWYER AND HAVE HIM PRESENT WITH YOU WHILE YOU ARE BEING QUESTIONED.

4. IF YOU CANNOT AFFORD TO HIRE A LAWYER ONE WILL BE APPOINTED TO REPRESENT YOU BEFORE ANY QUESTIONING, IF YOU WISH ONE.

SIGNATURE OF DEFENDANT | DATE

WITNESS | TIME

☐ REFUSED SIGNATURE   SAN FRANCISCO POLICE DEPARTMENT   PR.9.1.4

The case of Ernesto Miranda resulted in the creation of Miranda *rights, which must be read to those arrested to make them aware of their constitutional rights.*

Fifth Amendment is not specifically concerned with protecting persons accused of crimes, it is nevertheless a fundamentally important instance where the government and the citizen are adversaries. The power of any government to take private property for a public use is called **eminent domain.** This power is essential to the very concept of sovereignty. The Fifth Amendment neither invents eminent domain nor takes it away; its purpose is to put limits on that inherent power through procedures that require a showing of a public purpose and the provision of fair payment for the taking of someone's property. This provision is now universally observed in all U.S. principalities, but it has not always been meticulously observed.

eminent domain the right of government to take private property for public use

The first modern case confronting the issue of public use involved a "mom and pop" grocery store in a run-down neighborhood on the southwest side of the District of Columbia. In carrying out a vast urban redevelopment program, the city government of Washington, D.C., took the property as one of a large number of privately owned lots to be cleared for new housing and business construction. The owner of the grocery store, and his successors after his death, took the government to court on the grounds that it was an unconstitutional use of eminent domain to take property from one private owner and eventually to turn that property back, in altered form, to another private owner. The store owners lost their case. The Supreme Court's argument was a curious but very important one: the "public interest" can mean virtually anything a legislature says it means. In other words, since the overall slum clearance and redevelopment project was in the public interest, according to the legislature, the eventual transfers of property that were going to take place were justified.[87] This principle was reaffirmed in the 2005 case of *Kelo v. City of New London*, where the Court held that the city could seize land from one private owner and transfer it to another as part of a redevelopment plan.[88]

The Sixth Amendment and the Right to Counsel

> In all criminal prosecutions, the accused shall enjoy the right to a speedy and public trial, by an impartial jury of the State and district wherein the crime shall have been committed, which district shall have been previously ascertained by law, and to be informed of the nature and cause of the accusation; to be confronted with the witnesses against him; to have compulsory process for obtaining witnesses in his favor, and to have the Assistance of Counsel for his defence.

Like the exclusionary rule of the Fourth Amendment and the self-incrimination clause of the Fifth Amendment, the "right to counsel" provision of the Sixth Amendment is notable for freeing defendants who seem to the public to be patently guilty as charged. Other provisions of the Sixth Amendment, such as the right to a speedy trial and the right to confront witnesses before an impartial jury, are less controversial in nature.

Gideon v. Wainwright is the perfect case study because it involved a disreputable person who seemed patently guilty of the crime of which he was convicted. In and out of jails for most of his fifty-one years, Clarence Earl Gideon received a five-year sentence for breaking and entering a poolroom in Panama City, Florida. While serving time in jail, Gideon became a fairly well qualified "jailhouse lawyer," made his own appeal on a handwritten petition, and eventually won the landmark ruling on the right to counsel in all felony cases.[89]

The right to counsel has been expanded rather than contracted during the past few decades, when the courts have become more conservative. For example,

The USA PATRIOT Act

The objective of civil liberties is to create a "private sphere" in which individuals are autonomous and free from government interference. There is also a presumption that people have the right to be left alone, to have privacy.

Few would argue, however, that the right of privacy is absolute. No right is absolute, and we regularly compromise our privacy in return for something we value even more. Every new communications technology reduces our privacy. Note how casually we compromise our private lives every time we use our credit cards, subscribe to a periodical, run a red light, or send and receive e-mails, whether for business, personal, confidential, or illegal affairs. Even our Social Security and bank account numbers are up for grabs.

The most ardent civil libertarian would find it difficult to disagree with former Attorney General John Ashcroft when he said that "liberty is meaningless without security," in his defense of the USA PATRIOT Act. War is the most fundamental threat to liberty. President Lincoln abruptly and unilaterally suspended the power of our judiciary to issue writs of *habeas corpus* (requiring a show of cause why an individual is in custody). President Washington, as well as Lincoln and Franklin Roosevelt, set up military tribunals to try, without right of counsel, persons believed to be collaborators with, or merely sympathizers of, the enemy. Most dramatically, in 1942 Presidential Roosevelt ordered over 120,000 Japanese-Americans (most of them U.S. citizens) to internment camps for the duration of World War II, without consulting Congress and without accusing the internees of any sort of crime.

Six weeks after September 11, 2001, President Bush submitted to Congress the USA PATRIOT Act—"*U*niting and *S*trengthening *A*merica by *P*roviding *A*ppropriate *T*ools *R*equired to *I*ntercept and *O*bstruct *T*errorism Act." The 342-page act gave the federal government power over many different types of beliefs and associations as well as over activities that could be interpreted as sympathetic to terrorism from whatever source.

Although Americans across the ideological spectrum are still willing to support the USA PATRIOT Act as a hedge against terrorism, there is also an unmistakable growth of opposition to many of its provisions, especially those that give the attorney general immense discretionary power to detain and imprison "on suspicion" and to use information technology to engage in "fishing expeditions" within the United States, as though America were a foreign country. In 2001 many politicians voted for the act as an emergency measure and accompanied their support with the assertion that the act "can be fixed" by Justice Department interpretations, by judicial review, and even by Congress itself.

Many of the provisions in the USA PATRIOT Act came under a "sunset clause" that provided for their termination in 2005. In 2006, Congress voted to extend these provisions but also added several new provisions designed to protect civil liberties.

Both American liberals and American conservatives fear an excessively strong state. If we give up the "eternal vigilance" Jefferson counseled as the price of liberty, we will be giving the terrorists their victory without their having to fire another shot or explode another suicide bomb.

FOR CRITICAL ANALYSIS

1. What should be the proper balance between liberty and security? Where does the USA PATRIOT Act fall on this spectrum?
2. Do you agree with John Ashcroft that civil libertarians concerned about lost liberties "threatened by the USA PATRIOT Act are just aiding terrorists"? Why or why not?

although at first the right to counsel was met by judges assigning lawyers from the community as a formal public obligation, most states and cities now have created an office of public defender; these state-employed professional defense lawyers typically provide poor defendants with much better legal representation. And, although these defendants cannot choose their private defense attorney, they do have the right to appeal a conviction on the grounds that the counsel provided by the state was deficient. For example, in 2003 the Supreme Court overturned the death sentence of a Maryland death-row inmate, holding that the defense lawyer had failed to fully inform the jury of the defendant's history of "horrendous childhood abuse."[90] Moreover, the right to counsel extends beyond serious crimes to any trial, with or without jury, that holds the possibility of imprisonment.[91] In the 2006 case of *U.S. v. Gonzalez-Lopez*, the Court held that a defendant had been deprived of his Sixth Amendment rights because the trial court had refused to allow him to make use of the particular counsel of his own choosing.[92]

The Eighth Amendment and Cruel and Unusual Punishment

The Eighth Amendment prohibits "excessive bail," "excessive fines," and "cruel and unusual punishment." Virtually all the debate over Eighth Amendment issues focuses on the last clause of the amendment: the protection from "cruel and unusual punishment." One of the greatest challenges in interpreting this provision consistently is that what is considered "cruel and unusual" varies from culture to culture and from generation to generation. And, unfortunately, it also varies by class and race.

Politics Today

In 2008, the Supreme Court upheld Kentucky's practice of execution by lethal injection, despite arguments that it may cause severe pain. Why do opponents of the death penalty argue that it is unconstitutional?

By far the biggest issue of class and race inconsistency as constituting cruel and unusual punishment arises over the death penalty. In 1972, the Supreme Court overturned several state death penalty laws, not because they were cruel and unusual, but because they were being applied in a capricious manner—that is, blacks were much more likely than whites to be sentenced to death, and the poor more likely than the rich, and men more likely than women.[93] Very soon after that decision, a majority of states revised their capital-punishment provisions to meet the Court's standards.[94] Since 1976, the Court has consistently upheld state laws providing for capital punishment, although the Court also continues to review numerous death-penalty appeals each year.

Between 1976 and 2008, states executed 1,109 people. Most of those executions occurred in southern states, with Texas leading the way at 406. As of 2008, thirty-six states had adopted some form of capital punishment, a move approved of by about three-quarters of all Americans.

Although virtually all criminal conduct is regulated by the states, Congress has also jumped on the bandwagon, imposing capital punishment for more than fifty federal crimes. Despite the seeming popularity of the death penalty, the debate has become, if anything, more intense. In 1997, for example, the American Bar Association passed a resolution calling for a halt to the death penalty until concerns about its fairness—that is, whether its application violates the principle of equality—and about ensuring due process are addressed. In 2000, the governor of Illinois imposed a moratorium on the death penalty and created a commission to review the capital punishment system. After a two-year study by the commission, Illinois adopted a number of reforms, including a ban on executions of the mentally retarded. In June 2002, the U.S. Supreme Court banned all executions of mentally retarded defendants. In 2007, the Supreme Court blocked the execution of a mentally ill convicted murderer who was delusional and lacked a "rational understanding" of why the state had sentenced him to death.[95] And in the same year, the Supreme Court stopped the execution of a Virginia man hours before he was to be put to death to allow time to decide whether lethal injection, the mode of execution used by most states, caused sufficient pain to violate constitutional standards.[96]

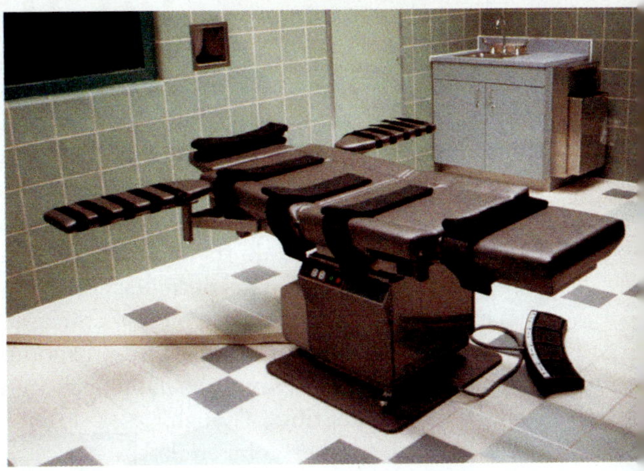

Thirty-six states currently have the death penalty for the most serious crimes. Although a majority of Americans support the death penalty, it has always been controversial and is sometimes seen as a violation of the Eighth Amendment.

The Right to Privacy

Some of the people all of the time and all of the people some of the time would just like to be left alone, to have their own private domain into which no one—friends, family, government, church, or employer—has the right to enter without permission.

A **right to privacy** was not granted in the Bill of Rights, but a clause in the Fourth Amendment provides for "the right of the people to be secure in their persons, houses, papers, and effects, against unreasonable searches and seizures." In a 1928 case, Justice Louis Brandeis argued in a dissent that the Fourth Amendment should be extended to a more general principle of "privacy in the home."[97] Another step in this direction was taken when several Jehovah's Witnesses directed their children not to salute the flag or say the Pledge of Allegiance in school because the first of the Ten Commandments prohibits the worship of "graven images." They lost their case in 1940, but the Supreme Court reversed itself in 1943, holding that the 1940 case was "wrongly decided." The Court recognized "a right to be left alone" as part of the free-speech clause of the First Amendment.[98] Another small step was taken in 1958, when the Supreme Court recognized "privacy in one's association" in its decision that the state of Alabama could not use the membership list of the National Association for the Advancement of Colored People (NAACP) in state investigations.[99]

right to privacy the right to be left alone, which has been interpreted by the Supreme Court to entail free access to birth control and abortions

BIRTH CONTROL The sphere of privacy was formally recognized in 1965, when the Court ruled that a Connecticut statute forbidding the use of contraceptives violated the right of marital privacy. Estelle Griswold, the executive director of the Planned Parenthood League of Connecticut, was arrested by the state of Connecticut for providing information, instruction, and medical advice about contraception to married couples. She and her associates were found guilty as accessories to the crime and fined $100 each. The Supreme Court reversed the lower court decisions and declared the Connecticut law unconstitutional because it violated "a right of privacy older than the Bill of Rights—older than our political parties, older than our school system."[100] Justice William O. Douglas, author of the majority decision in the *Griswold* case, argued that this right of privacy is also grounded in the Constitution, because it fits into a "zone of privacy" created by a combination of the Third, Fourth, and Fifth Amendments. A concurring opinion, written by Justice Arthur Goldberg, attempted to strengthen Douglas's argument by adding that "the concept of liberty . . . embraces the right of marital privacy though that right is not mentioned explicitly in the

The Death Penalty

The United States is the only Western democracy that continues to make use of capital punishment as a form of criminal sanction. Thirty-seven of the fifty states provide for the death penalty, as do the federal government and the military, though no federal or military executions have been carried out for more than fifty years. Since 1976, the states have executed more than one thousand convicted criminals. In 2007 alone, forty-two individuals were put to death by state authorities. Though this is a small number compared with, say, China, which may have executed as many as 8,000 persons for a variety of crimes in 2006, it was enough executions to rank the United States sixth, just behind Sudan, in its use of execution as a form of punishment.

Though a majority of Americans support capital punishment, America's continuing use of the death penalty has put the United States at odds with its European allies and with Canada and Mexico, which have all abolished capital punishment. One area of conflict concerns the extradition of criminals. If an individual charged with or convicted of a crime flees to another country, the fugitive's home country may ask that he or she be returned home to face trial or punishment. The United States has extradition treaties with many nations. In recent years, however, a number of European nations have resisted extraditing fugitives to the United States if there has been a possibility that they might face a death sentence on their return.

One of the most important of these cases involved Jens Soering. Soering was arrested in the United Kingdom in 1986 on a U.S. extradition warrant charging that he and his girlfriend had murdered her parents in Virginia. The European Court of Human Rights ruled that Soering's extradition to the United States would violate the European Convention on Human Rights, which prohibited torture or other degrading forms of punishment, because, if convicted in Virginia, he could be sentenced to death. To obtain Soering's extradition, the United States had to assure Britain that he would not be prosecuted for capital murder. Subsequently, Soering was returned, tried, and sentenced to ninety-nine years in prison. Since the Soering case, European authorities have generally made extradition to the United States conditional on American assurances that the individual sought by American authorities would not face capital charges if he or she was returned.

A second realm in which America's continuing use of capital punishment has created conflict with other nations stems from the 1963 Vienna Convention on Consular Relations. This treaty, signed by the United States and 162 other nations, requires the authorities to notify foreign nationals in their custody of their right to contact their own consulates for assistance before they are brought to trial. Police and courts in the United States often fail to comply with this obligation. As a result, a number of foreigners have been convicted of capital crimes and sentenced to death without having been allowed to contact their consulates for help. In 2001, the International Court of Justice ruled that the United States violated its treaty obligations with Germany by executing a German citizen, Walter LaGrand, without notifying him of his treaty rights. In recent years, the Mexican government has challenged the convictions and death sentences of several Mexican nationals in the United States on the grounds that they were not allowed to contact the Mexican consulate in a timely manner. In 2003, Mexico won a judgment against the United States in the International Court of Justice. Generally, U.S. courts have not been particularly hospitable to Vienna Convention claims.

FOR CRITICAL ANALYSIS

1. America's continued use of capital punishment has complicated its relations with its neighbors and allies. Should the United States adjust its laws to accommodate the wishes of other nations?
2. What might explain why the United States continues to use capital punishment, whereas other Western nations have abandoned the practice?

SOURCE: William A. Schabas, "Indirect Abolition: Capital Punishment's Role in Extradition Law and Practice," *Loyola Los Angeles International and Comparative Law Review* 25 (2003): 581–604.

Constitution [and] is supported by numerous decisions of this Court . . . and *by the language and history of the Ninth Amendment*" (emphasis added).[101]

ABORTION The right to privacy was confirmed and extended in 1973 in the most important of all privacy decisions, and one of the most important Supreme Court decisions in American history: *Roe v. Wade.* This decision established a woman's right to seek an abortion and prohibited states from making abortion a criminal act.[102] The Burger Court's decision in *Roe* took a revolutionary step toward establishing the right to privacy. It is important to emphasize that the preference for privacy rights and for their extension to include the rights of women to control their own bodies was not something the Supreme Court invented in a vacuum. Most states did not regulate abortions in any fashion until the 1840s, at which time only six of the twenty-six existing states had any regulations governing abortion. In addition, many states had begun to ease their abortion restrictions well before the 1973 *Roe* decision, although in recent years a number of states have reinstated some restrictions on abortion.

By extending the umbrella of privacy, this sweeping ruling dramatically changed abortion practices in America. In addition, it galvanized and nationalized the abortion debate. Groups opposed to abortion, such as the National Right to Life Committee, organized to fight the new liberal standard, while abortion rights groups sought to maintain that protection. In recent years, the legal standard shifted against abortion rights supporters in two key Supreme Court cases.

In *Webster v. Reproductive Health Services* (1989), the Court narrowly upheld (by a 5-to-4 majority) the constitutionality of restrictions on the use of public medical facilities for abortion.[103] And in the 1992 case of *Planned Parenthood v. Casey,* another 5-to-4 majority of the Court upheld *Roe* but narrowed its scope, refusing to invalidate a Pennsylvania law that significantly limits freedom of choice. The Court's decision defined the right to an abortion as a "limited or qualified" right subject to regulation by the states as long as the regulation does not constitute an "undue burden."[104] More recently, the Court had another opportunity to rule on what constitutes an undue burden. In the 2000 case of *Stenberg v. Carhart,* the Court, by a vote of 5-to-4, struck down Nebraska's ban on partial-birth abortions because the law had the "effect of placing a substantial obstacle in the path of a woman seeking an abortion."[105] However, in the 2006 case *Ayotte v. Planned Parenthood,* the Court held that a law requiring parental notification before a minor could obtain an abortion was not an undue burden.[106] And, in *Gonzales v. Carhart,* the Court effectively reversed its earlier *Carhart* decision by upholding the federal partial-birth abortion ban, which was virtually identical to the Nebraska law it had struck down in 2000.[107]

For Critical Analysis

Read the Third, Fourth, Fifth, and Ninth Amendments in the Appendix at the end of this book. In your opinion, do American citizens have a right to privacy?

HOMOSEXUALITY In the last two decades, the right to be left alone began to include the privacy rights of homosexuals. One morning in Atlanta, Georgia, in the mid-1980s, Michael Hardwick was arrested by a police officer who discovered him in bed with another man. The officer had come to serve a warrant for Hardwick's arrest for failure to appear in court to answer charges of drinking in public. One of Hardwick's unknowing housemates invited the officer to look in Hardwick's room, where he found Hardwick and another man engaging in "consensual sexual behavior." He was then arrested under Georgia's laws against heterosexual and homosexual sodomy. Hardwick filed a lawsuit against the state, challenging the constitutionality of the Georgia law. Hardwick won his case in

Free Speech on Campus

In September 1964, administrators from the University of California at Berkeley prohibited student civil rights activists from distributing information and collecting donations on campus, even though other less controversial groups were allowed to do so. Students reacted strongly and passionately to the administration's actions. Hundreds participated in a series of protests and sit-ins over the course of several months. Their collective action, known as the Free Speech Movement, ultimately resulted in the restoration of their civil liberties.

Free-speech issues continue to be debated on college campuses today. For example, student groups opposed to affirmative action have recently staged satirical bake sales, where the purchase price for baked goods is adjusted based on the buyer's race and ethnicity. Basically, Caucasians and Asians are asked to pay more and African Americans and Latinos are charged less. College administrators—acting with the support of other student groups—have shut down these bake sales, arguing that they violate university discrimination policies. These universities have asserted that their obligation to protect individuals from discrimination is greater than the need to protect free speech.

If you are interested in this debate—or concerned about the protection of civil liberties in general—there are many ways to get involved. As a first step, you might want to explore the free-speech provisions on your campus. Will the school tolerate *all* speech, or just speech that does not violate certain community standards? Who has the power to make these decisions? Where do you stand? To find out more, you could:

- ★ Find out what rights are guaranteed to you in the student handbook. Most colleges and universities provide online access to their handbooks.
- ★ E-mail or call the editor of the campus newspaper and find out if it has ever been censored by the administration or if the staff has freedom-of-press issues.

Once you learn what rights you have, you can move on to informing and motivating your fellow students about any issue or issues of concern to you. Here are some of the kinds of activities and events you can organize on your own or with a group of students who share your concern:

- ★ Host prominent speakers who will talk about your issue and address questions from the audience. Talk to some professors who you think might be interested in this issue. They may have suggestions for speakers, and their department might help you by contacting the speaker, providing money or making arrangements. If they can't help you, chances are they can connect you with an on-campus organization that can.
- ★ Plan or participate in debates with students or campus groups that have different views on your issue. Contact leaders of the groups to invite them to a public debate. For example, if your campus has had an affirmative action bake sale, you could contact leaders of the sale and their key opponents about coming together for a discussion.
- ★ Invite professors and students to participate in a roundtable discussion about a civil-liberties issue. National Constitution Day (September 17) is a good day to plan such a discussion. Many political science departments have money set aside to host activities on this day. The chair of the department can provide you with information about their plans.
- ★ Set up tables in high-traffic locations at lunchtime to disseminate information or to gather signatures for a petition relevant to your issue.
- ★ Make contact with national political groups that share your position. They may be able to provide you with materials for dissemination and other resources.

the federal court of appeals. The state of Georgia, in an unusual move, appealed the court's decision to the Supreme Court. The majority of the Court reversed the lower court decision, holding against Mr. Hardwick, on the grounds that "the federal Constitution confers [no] fundamental right upon homosexuals to engage in sodomy," and that therefore there was no basis to invalidate "the laws of the many states that still make such conduct illegal and have done so for a very long time."[108] The Court majority concluded its opinion with a warning that it ought not and would not use its power to "discover new fundamental rights embedded in the Due Process Clause." In other words, the Court under Chief Justice Rehnquist was expressing its determination to restrict quite severely the expansion of the Ninth Amendment and the development of new substantive rights. The four dissenters argued that the case was not about a fundamental right to engage in homosexual sodomy, but was in fact about "the most comprehensive of rights and the right most valued by civilized men, [namely,] the right to be let alone."[109]

The case of Terri Schiavo brought out strong reactions on both sides of the debate over the "right to die." Schiavo's husband ultimately won the right to remove the feeding tubes that had kept her alive in a vegetative state for many years, but this area of the law is still unsettled and highly controversial.

Seventeen years later and to almost everyone's surprise, the Court overturned *Bowers v. Hardwick* with a dramatic pronouncement that gays are "entitled to respect for their private lives" as a matter of constitutional due process. With *Lawrence v. Texas* (2003), the state legislatures no longer had the authority to make private sexual behavior a crime.[110] Drawing from the tradition of negative liberty, the Court maintained: "In our tradition the State is not omnipresent in the home. And there are other spheres of our lives and existence outside the home, where the State should not be a dominant presence." Explicitly encompassing lesbians and gay men within the umbrella of privacy, the Court concluded that the "petitioners are entitled to respect for their private lives. The State cannot demean their existence or control their destiny by making their private sexual conduct a crime." This decision added substance to the "right of privacy."[111]

THE RIGHT TO DIE Another area ripe for litigation and public discourse is the so-called right to die. A number of highly publicized physician-assisted suicides in the 1990s focused attention on whether people have a right to choose their own death and to receive assistance in carrying it out. Can this become part of the privacy right? Or is it a new substantive right? The Supreme Court has not definitively answered this question. However, the Court refused to intervene in the well-publicized case of Terri Schiavo, a woman who, as described in Chapter 3, suffered irreversible brain damage and was kept alive in a vegetative state via feeding tubes for fifteen years. During this period, Schiavo's husband, who wanted to withdraw life support, battled her parents, who wanted support continued indefinitely. The case was heard multiple times in the Florida state courts and the federal courts. In 2005, Schiavo's husband finally prevailed, and she was removed from life support and subsequently died. In the 2006 case of *Gonzales v. Oregon*, however, the Supreme Court did intervene to uphold an assisted-suicide law. The law allowed doctors to use drugs to facilitate the deaths of terminally ill patients who requested such assistance.[112] Thus, although the Court has not ruled definitively on the right-to-die question, it does not seem hostile to the idea.

Thinking Critically about the Future of Civil Liberties

Politics Today

As a senator, Barack Obama was sharply critical of the Bush administration's civil liberties record, saying "It's time to show the world we're not a country that ships prisoners in the dead of night to be tortured in far off countries." How is the Obama administration attempting to reconcile civil liberties and security in the war on terror?

In the months after the September 11, 2001 terrorists attacks against the United States, President George W. Bush issued a series of executive orders to combat the threat of terrorism. The president authorized the indefinite detention of individuals whom he designated enemy combatants at the Guantánamo Bay military prison in Cuba, the creation of special military tribunals to try enemy combatants, and the initiation of a massive warrantless surveillance program by the National Security Agency to monitor communications into and out of the United States in search of indications of terrorist activity. The president averred that these policies were necessary to protect the nation, but each of the president's orders was denounced by civil libertarians as an intrusion on constitutional rights and was challenged in the courts. Though the legal battle continues, as of the end of 2007 neither the president nor his critics had won a decisive victory.

In the 2004 case of *Hamdi v. Rumsfeld*, the Supreme Court declared that those declared enemy combatants could challenge their detention before a judge, but the Court affirmed the president's power to declare even U.S. citizens to be enemy combatants.[113] In 2006, in the case of *Hamdan v. Rumsfeld*, the Court invalidated the military tribunals established by presidential order because their procedures were not in accord with current law. The Court, however, accepted the principle that the president could order the creation of such tribunals so long as their procedures had some statutory basis. Congress provided that basis in the 2006 Military Commissions Act, which mainly reaffirmed the procedures that had been devised by the president.[114] The act also seemed partially to reverse the *Hamdi* decision by declaring that prisoners at Guantánamo could not present *habeas corpus* petitions to the federal courts challenging their detention. The legality of that portion of the act is currently being debated in the federal courts.

As for the NSA surveillance program, in 2007 the Sixth Circuit Court of Appeals upheld the validity of the program, but the American Civil Liberties Union has appealed the decision to the supreme Court.[115] Under new rules announced by President Bush, the NSA is to request warrants from the Foreign Intelligence Surveillance (FISA) Court, a secretive panel established to hear top-secret cases. The president, however, reserved the right to order warrantless searches if he deemed them to be necessary. As these war on terror cases illustrate, battles over civil liberties are not abstract, historical matters. They are part or our lives today.

The Obama administration is currently revisiting these issues. Most Democrats believe that America's reputation in the world has been hurt by the image of prisoners held without proper legal process and are eager to find ways to restore America's reputation as a bastion of liberty. At the same time, however, the administration does not wish to see dangerous foes of the United States to do harm to Americans. The dilemma of liberty versus security is never easy to resolve.

FOR FURTHER READING

Barendt, Eric. *Freedom of Speech*. 2nd ed. New York: Oxford University Press, 2007.

Brandon, Mark. *The Constitution in Wartime.* Durham, NC: Duke University Press, 2005.

Cook, Byrne. *Reporting the War: Freedom of the Press from the American Revolution to the War on Terror.* New York: Palgrave, Macmillan, 2007.

Dworkin, Ronald. *Justice in Robes.* Cambridge, MA: Belknap Press, 2006.

Fisher, Louis. *Military Tribunals and Presidential Power.* Lawrence: University Press of Kansas, 2005.

Friendly, Fred W. *Minnesota Rag: The Dramatic Story of the Landmark Supreme Court Case that Gave New Meaning to Freedom of the Press.* New York: Vintage, 1982.

Glendon, Mary Ann. *Rights Talk: The Impoverishment of Political Discourse.* New York: Free Press, 1991.

Hentoff, Nat. *The First Freedom: The Tumultuous History of Free Speech in America.* New York: Basic Books, 1994.

Lewis, Anthony. *Gideon's Trumpet.* New York: Random House, 1964.

Orth, John. *Due Process of Law: A Brief History.* Lawrence: University Press of Kansas, 2003.

Sundby, Scott. *A Life and Death Decision: A Jury Weighs the Death Penalty.* New York: Palgrave Macmillan, 2007.

Sunstein, Cass. *Radicals in Robes.* New York: Basic Books, 2005.

RECOMMENDED WEB SITES

The American Civil Liberties Union (ACLU)
www.aclu.org

The ACLU is committed in protecting for all individuals the freedoms found in the Bill of Rights. This sometimes controversial organization continuously monitors the government for violations of liberty and encourages its members to take political action.

Department of Justice Life and Liberty Page
www.lifeandliberty.gov/
ACLU Safe and Free Page www.aclu.org/safefree/resources/17343res20031114.html

What should be the proper balance between liberty and security? At these two Web sites you will find alternative perspectives on the USA PATRIOT Act provided by the U.S. Department of Justice and the American Civil Liberties Union. Read some of the information and make up your own mind.

Electronic Privacy Information Center
http://epic.org/privacy

For an extensive list of privacy issues, go to the Web page for Electronic Privacy Information Center. Here you will find civil liberties concerns as they relate to all forms of information technology, including the Internet.

The Free Expression Network
www.freeexpression.org

The Free Expression Network is an organization "dedicated to preserving the right to free expression." On its Web site you can find links to important First Amendment issues and organizations.

Freedom Forum
www.freedomforum.org

Freedom of speech and freedom of the press are considered critical in any democracy; however, only some kinds of speech are fully protected against restrictions. Freedom Forum is a nonpartisan agency that investigates and analyzes such First Amendment restrictions.

National Abortion and Reproductive Rights Action League
www.naral.org
National Right to Life Committee
www.nlrc.org

The National Abortion and Reproductive Rights Action League and the National Right to Life Committee are two of the nation's largest interest groups weighing in on the abortion issue. See what these opposing groups have to say about privacy rights.

Religious Freedom Page
http://religiousfreedom.lib.virginia.edu/

The establishment clause of the U.S. Constitution has been interpreted to mean a "wall of separation" between government and religion. On the Religious Freedom Page you can find information on a variety of issues pertaining to religious freedom in the United States and around the world.

U.S. Supreme Court Media
www.oyez.org

This Web site for U.S. Supreme Court media has a great search engine for finding information on cases affecting civil liberties, such as *Lemon v. Kurtzman*, *Miranda v. Arizona*, *Mapp v. Ohio*, and *New York Times v. Sullivan*, to name only a few.

STUDY OUTLINE

www.wwnorton.com/wtp7e

A Brief History of the Bill of Rights

1. Despite the insistence of Alexander Hamilton that a bill of rights was both unnecessary and dangerous, adding a list of explicit rights was the most important item of business for the 1st Congress in 1789.
2. The Bill of Rights would have been more aptly named the "Bill of Liberties," because it is made up of provisions that protect citizens from improper government action.
3. Civil rights did not become part of the Constitution until 1868 with the adoption of the Fourteenth Amendment, which sought to provide for each citizen "the equal protection of the laws."
4. In 1833, the Supreme Court found that the Bill of Rights limited only the national government and not state governments.
5. Although the language of the Fourteenth Amendment seems to indicate that the protections of the Bill of Rights apply to state governments as well as the national government, for the remainder of the nineteenth century the Supreme Court (with only one exception) made decisions as if the Fourteenth Amendment had never been adopted.
6. As of 1961, only the First Amendment and one clause of the Fifth Amendment had been "selectively incorporated" into the Fourteenth Amendment. After 1961, however, most of the provisions of the Bill of Rights were incorporated into the Fourteenth Amendment and applied to the states.

The First Amendment and Freedom of Religion

1. The "establishment clause" of the First Amendment has been interpreted to mean the strict separation of church and state.
2. The "free exercise clause" protects the right to believe and to practice whatever religion one chooses; it also involves protection of the right to be a nonbeliever.

The First Amendment and Freedom of Speech and the Press

1. Although freedom of speech and freedom of the press hold an important place in the Bill of Rights, the extent and nature of certain types of expression are subject to constitutional debate.
2. Among the forms of speech that are absolutely protected are the truth, political speech, symbolic speech, and "speech plus," which is speech plus a physical activity such as picketing. The forms of speech that are currently only conditionally protected include libel and slander; obscenity and pornography; fighting words; and commercial speech.

The Second Amendment and the Right to Bear Arms

1. In constitutional terms, the Second Amendment unquestionably protects citizens' rights to bear arms, but this right can be regulated by both state and federal law.

Due Process of Law

1. The purpose of due process is to equalize the playing field between the accused individual and the all-powerful state.
2. The Fourth Amendment protects against unreasonable searches and seizures.
3. The Fifth Amendment requires a grand jury for most crimes, protects against double jeopardy, and provides that you cannot be forced to testify against yourself.
4. The Sixth Amendment requires a speedy trial and the right to witnesses and counsel.
5. The Eighth Amendment prohibits cruel and unusual punishment.

The Right to Privacy

1. In the case of *Griswold v. Connecticut*, the Supreme Court found a right of privacy in the Constitution. This right was confirmed and extended in 1973 in the case of *Roe v. Wade*.

Thinking Critically about the Future of Civil Liberties

1. Under former Chief Justice William Rehnquist, the Court somewhat restricted civil liberties without actually overturning any of the important decisions from the 1960s and 1970s that established many of the liberties we enjoy today.

PRACTICE QUIZ

www.wwnorton.com/wtp7e

1. From 1789 until the 1960s, the Bill of Rights put limits on
   a) the national government only.
   b) the state government only.
   c) both the national and state governments.
   d) neither the national nor the state governments.
2. The amendment that provided the basis for the modern understanding of the government's obligation to protect civil rights was the
   a) First Amendment.
   b) Ninth Amendment.
   c) Fourteenth Amendment.
   d) Twenty-second Amendment.
3. The so-called *Lemon* test, derived from the Supreme Court's ruling in *Lemon v. Kurtzman*, concerns the issue of
   a) school desegregation.
   b) aid to religious schools.
   c) prayer in school.
   d) obscenity.
4. The process by which some of the liberties in the Bill of Rights were applied to the states (or nationalized) is known as
   a) selective incorporation.
   b) judicial activism.
   c) civil liberties.
   d) establishment.
5. Which of the following provided that all of the protections contained in the Bill of Rights applied to the states as well as the national government?
   a) the Fourteenth Amendment
   b) *Palko v. Connecticut*
   c) *Gitlow v. New York*
   d) none of the above
6. Which of the following protections are *not* contained in the First Amendment?
   a) the establishment clause
   b) the free exercise clause
   c) freedom of the press
   d) All of the above are First Amendment protections.
7. Which of the following describes a written statement made in "reckless disregard of the truth" that is considered damaging to a victim because it is "malicious, scandalous, and defamatory"?
   a) slander
   b) libel
   c) fighting words
   d) expressive speech
8. The Fourth, Fifth, Sixth, and Eighth Amendments, taken together, define:
   a) due process of law.
   b) free speech.
   c) the right to bear arms.
   d) civil rights of minorities.
9. In what case was a right to privacy first found in the Constitution?
   a) *Griswold v. Connecticut*
   b) *Roe v. Wade*
   c) *Baker v. Carr*
   d) *Planned Parenthood v. Casey*
10. Which famous case deals with Sixth Amendment issues?
    a) *Miranda v. Arizona*
    b) *Mapp v. Ohio*
    c) *Gideon v. Wainwright*
    d) *Terry v. Ohio*

KEY TERMS

www.wwnorton.com/wtp7e

bill of attainder (p. 122)
Bill of Rights (p. 121)
civil liberties (p. 121)
"clear and present danger" test (p. 129)
double jeopardy (p. 142)
due process of law (p. 139)
eminent domain (p. 144)
establishment clause (p. 125)
ex post facto law (p. 122)
exclusionary rule (p. 140)
fighting words (p. 136)
free exercise clause (p. 127)
grand jury (p. 142)
habeas corpus (p. 121)
Lemon test (p. 126)
libel (p. 133)
Miranda rule (p. 143)
prior restraint (p. 133)
right to privacy (p. 147)
selective incorporation (p. 123)
slander (p. 133)
"speech plus" (p. 131)

5 Civil Rights

- The Struggle for Civil Rights
- The Universalization of Civil Rights
- Affirmative Action

WHAT GOVERNMENT DOES AND WHY IT MATTERS

In 1960, four black students from North Carolina A&T State University made history: the four freshmen sat down at Woolworth's whites-only lunch counter in Greensboro, North Carolina, challenging the policies of segregation that kept blacks and whites in separate public and private accommodations across the South. Day after day the students sat at the counter, ignoring the taunts of onlookers, determined to break the system of segregation. Their actions and those of many other students, clergy members, and ordinary citizens finally did abolish such practices as separate white and black park benches, water fountains, and waiting rooms; the end of segregation meant opening access to public and private institutions on equal terms to all. But the victories of the civil rights movement did not come cheaply: many marchers, freedom riders, and sit-in participants were beaten; some were murdered.

Today, the Greensboro lunch counter is a part of history, on display at the Smithsonian Institution in Washington, D.C. Many goals of the civil rights movement that aroused such controversy in 1960 are now widely accepted as the proper expression of the American commitment to equal rights. But the question of what is meant by "equal rights" is hardly settled. Although most Americans reject the idea that government should create equal outcomes for its citizens, they do widely endorse government action to prohibit public and private discrimination, and they support the idea of equality of opportunity. However, even this concept is elusive. When past denial of rights creates unequal starting points for some groups, should government take additional steps to ensure equal opportunity? What kinds of groups should be specially protected against discrimination? Should the disabled receive special protection? Should gays and lesbians? Finally, what kinds of steps are acceptable to remedy discrimination, and who should bear the costs? These questions are at the heart of contemporary debates over civil rights, the obligation imposed on government to *take positive action* to protect citizens from any illegal action of government agencies as well as of other private citizens.

The answers that Americans give to these questions have shifted dramatically over the course of our nation's history. But ideas about civil rights did not change easily; advocates who challenged barriers to civil rights often encountered strong resistance. As a consequence, efforts to expand civil rights have often relied on social movements and nontraditional political tactics, as well as the courts, to achieve their goals. The movement for women's suffrage in the early 1900s sent women marching in the streets and picketing the White House to call attention to their movement. The civil rights activists of the 1950s and 60s staged sit-ins, marches, "freedom rides" on buses across the South, and other forms of nonviolent civil disobedience in order to build broad support for their goals. At the same time, civil rights advocates challenged racial segregation in the courts. The black civil rights movement inspired a new wave of movements for equality as groups including women, gays and lesbians, Native Americans, Latinos, and the disabled launched campaigns for equal rights.

This chapter will show how inequalities between races and genders were tolerated, and even enforced by law during much of our country's history. Although the United States was founded on the ideals of liberty, equality, and democracy, its history of civil rights reveals a gap between these principles and actual practice. This history also reveals how the struggle to attain those ideals has helped narrow this gap. Closer to the present day, the struggle for political and social equality also shows how liberty and equality are not mutually supportive. In fact, these principles are often in conflict with one another. This chapter's concluding discussion of affirmative action illustrates this conflict.

> **In this chapter, we first review the legal developments and political movements that have expanded the scope of civil rights.** We look at the establishment of legal segregation in the South and the civil rights movement that overthrew it.

> **Second, we trace the broad impact that civil rights legislation has had on American life.** The Civil Rights Act of 1964 was especially critical in guaranteeing the "equal protection of the laws" set forth in the Fourteenth Amendment almost 100 years earlier.

> **We then explore how other groups, including women, Native Americans, Latinos, the disabled, and gays and lesbians, formed movements to win active protection of their rights as well.**

> **Finally, we turn to the development of affirmative action and the controversies surrounding it.** The debate over affirmative action has intensified in recent years, revealing the ways in which Americans differ over the meaning of equality.

The Struggle for Civil Rights

In the United States, the history of slavery and legalized racial **discrimination** against African Americans coexists uneasily with a strong tradition of individual liberty. Indeed, for much of our history Americans have struggled to reconcile such exclusionary racial practices with our notions of individual rights. With the adoption of the Fourteenth Amendment in 1868, **civil rights** became part of the Constitution, guaranteed to each citizen through "equal protection of the laws." This **equal protection clause** launched a century of political movements and legal efforts to press for racial equality.

discrimination use of any unreasonable and unjust criterion of exclusion

civil rights obligation imposed on government to take positive action to protect citizens from any illegal action of government agencies as well as of other private citizens

equal protection clause provision of the Fourteenth Amendment guaranteeing citizens "the equal protection of the laws." This clause has been the basis for the civil rights of African Americans, women, and other groups

For African Americans, the central fact of political life has been a denial of full citizenship rights for most of American history. By accepting the institution of slavery, the Founders embraced a system fundamentally at odds with the "Blessings of Liberty" promised in the Constitution. Their decision set the stage for two centuries of African American struggles to achieve full citizenship. For women as well, electoral politics was a decidedly masculine world. Until 1920, not only were women barred from voting in national politics, but electoral politics was closely tied to such male social institutions as lodges, bars, and clubs. Yet the exclusion of women from this political world did not prevent them from engaging in public life. Instead, women carved out a "separate sphere" for their public activities. Emphasizing female stewardship of the moral realm, women became important voices in social reform well before they won the right to vote.[1] For example, prior to the Civil War, women played leading roles in the abolitionist movement.

Slavery and the Abolitionist Movement

No issue in the nation's history so deeply divided Americans as that of the abolition of slavery. The importation and subjugation of Africans kidnapped from their native lands was a practice virtually as old as the country itself: the first slaves brought to what became the United States arrived in 1619, a year before the Plymouth colony

African American men won the right to vote after the Civil War, and many former slaves began registering and voting in state elections as early as 1867. This political influence soon evaporated in the face of Jim Crow laws and the end of Reconstruction.

was established in Massachusetts. White southerners built their agricultural economy (especially cotton production) on a large slave labor force. By 1840, for example, nearly half of the populations of Alabama and Louisiana consisted of black slaves. Even so, only about a quarter of southern white families owned slaves.

The subjugation of blacks through slavery was so much a part of southern culture that efforts to restrict or abolish slavery were met with fierce resistance. Despite the manifest cruelties of the slave system, southerners referred to the system by the quaint term *peculiar institution*. The label meant little to slavery's opponents, however, and an abolitionist movement grew and spread among northerners in the 1830s (although abolitionist sentiment could be traced back to the pre-Revolutionary era). The movement was most closely identified with the writing of William Lloyd Garrison. Slavery had been all but eliminated in the North by this time, but few northerners favored outright abolition. In fact, most whites held attitudes toward blacks that would be considered racist today.

The abolitionist movement spread primarily through local organizations in the North. Antislavery groups coalesced in New York, Ohio, New Hampshire, Pennsylvania, New Jersey, and Michigan. In addition to forming antislavery societies, the movement spawned two political parties: the Liberty Party, a staunchly antislavery party, and the Free Soil Party, a larger but more moderate party that sought primarily to restrict the spread of slavery into new western territories. In 1857, the infamous case of *Dred Scott v. Sandford* "roused passions as never before"[2] by splitting the country deeply with its holding that Scott had no due process rights because as a slave he was his master's permanent property regardless of his master's having taken him to a free state or territory.[3]

Some opponents of slavery took matters into their own hands, aiding in the escape of runaway slaves along the Underground Railroad. Even today, private homes and churches scattered throughout the Northeast that were used to hide blacks on their trips to Canada attest to the involvement of local citizenry. In the South, a similar, if contrary, fervor prompted mobs to break into post offices in order to seize and destroy antislavery literature.

The emotional power of the slavery issue was such that it precipitated the nation's bloodiest conflict, the Civil War. From the ashes of the Civil War came the Thirteenth, Fourteenth, and Fifteenth Amendments, which would redefine civil rights from that time on.

The Link to the Women's Rights Movement

The quiet upstate New York town of Seneca Falls played host to what would later come to be known as the starting point of the modern women's movement. Convened in July 1848 and organized by the activists Elizabeth Cady Stanton (who lived in Seneca Falls) and Lucretia Mott, the Seneca Falls Convention drew three hundred delegates to discuss and formulate plans to advance the political and social rights of women.

The centerpiece of the convention was its Declaration of Sentiments and Resolutions. Patterned after the Declaration of Independence, the Seneca Falls document declared, "We hold these truths to be self-evident: that all men and women are created equal," and "The history of mankind is a history of repeated injuries and usurpations on the part of man toward woman, having in direct object the establishment of an absolute tyranny over her." The most controversial provision of the declaration, nearly rejected as too radical, was the call for the right to vote

Although a few women could vote in the early American republic, such as these New Jersey women who satisfied state property qualifications, laws were soon enacted to block women from the ballot box. At the beginning of the nineteenth century, no American woman could legally vote.

for women. Although most of the delegates were women, about forty men participated, including the renowned abolitionist Frederick Douglass.

The link to the antislavery movement was not new. Stanton and Mott had attended the World Anti-slavery Convention in London in 1840, but had been denied delegate seats because of their sex. This rebuke helped precipitate the 1848 convention. The movements for women's rights and the abolition of slavery were also closely linked with the temperance movement (because alcohol abuse was closely linked to male abuses of women). The convergence of the antislavery, temperance, and suffrage movements was reflected in the views and actions of other women's movement leaders, such as Susan B. Anthony.

The convention and its participants were subjected to widespread ridicule, but similar conventions were organized in other states, and in the same year, New York State passed the Married Women's Property Act in order to restore the right of a married woman to own property.

The Civil War Amendments to the Constitution

The hopes of African Americans for achieving full citizenship rights initially seemed fulfilled when three constitutional amendments were adopted after the Civil War: the **Thirteenth Amendment** abolished slavery; the **Fourteenth Amendment** guaranteed equal protection under the law; and the **Fifteenth Amendment** guaranteed voting rights for blacks. Protected by the presence of federal troops, African American men were able to exercise their political rights immediately after the war. During Reconstruction, blacks were elected to many political offices: two black senators were elected from Mississippi and a total of fourteen African Americans were elected to the House of Representatives between 1869 and 1877. African Americans also held many state-level political offices. As voters and public officials, black citizens found a home in the Republican Party, which had secured the ratification of the three constitutional amendments guaranteeing black rights. After the war, the Republican Party

Thirteenth Amendment one of three Civil War amendments; abolished slavery

Fourteenth Amendment one of three Civil War amendments; guaranteed equal protection and due process

Fifteenth Amendment one of three Civil War amendments; guaranteed voting rights for African American men continued to reach out to black voters as a means to build party strength in the South.[4]

This political equality was short-lived, however. The national government withdrew its troops from the South and turned its back on African Americans in 1877. In the Compromise of 1877, southern Democrats agreed to allow the Republican candidate, Rutherford B. Hayes, to become president after a disputed election. In exchange, northern Republicans dropped their support for the civil liberties and political participation of African Americans. After that, southern states erected a **"Jim Crow"** system of social, political, and economic inequality that made a mockery of the promises in the Constitution. The first Jim Crow laws were adopted in the 1870s in each southern state to criminalize intermarriage of the races and to segregate trains and depots. These were promptly followed by laws segregating all public accommodations, and within ten years all southern states had adopted laws segregating the schools.

"Jim Crow" laws laws enacted by southern states following Reconstruction that discriminated against African Americans

Around the same time, some women pressed for the right to vote at the national level immediately after the Civil War, when male ex-slaves won the franchise. Politicians in both parties rejected women's suffrage as disruptive and unrealistic. Women also started to press for the vote at the state level in 1867 when a referendum to give women the vote in Kansas failed. Frustration with the general failure to win reforms in other states accelerated suffrage activism. In 1872, Susan B. Anthony and several other women were arrested in Rochester, New York, for illegally registering and voting in that year's national election. (The men who allowed the women to register and vote were also indicted; Anthony paid their expenses and eventually won presidential pardons for them.) At her trial, Judge Ward Hunt ordered the jury to find her guilty without deliberation. Yet Anthony was allowed to address the court, saying, "Your denial of my citizen's right to vote is the denial of my right of consent as one of the governed, the denial of my right of representation as one of the taxed, the denial of my right to a trial of my peers as an offender against the law."[5] Hunt assessed Anthony a fine of $100 but did not sentence her to jail. Anthony refused to pay the fine.

The 1896 Supreme Court case of Plessy v. Ferguson *upheld legal segregation and created the "separate but equal" rule, which fostered national segregation. Overt discrimination in public accommodations was common.*

Civil Rights and the Supreme Court: "Separate but Equal"

Resistance to equality for African Americans in the South led Congress to adopt the Civil Rights Act of 1875, which attempted to protect blacks from discrimination by proprietors of hotels, theaters, and other public accommodations. But the Court declared the Civil Rights Act of 1875 unconstitutional on the grounds that the act sought to protect blacks against discrimination by *private* businesses, whereas the Fourteenth Amendment, according to the Court's interpretation, was intended to protect individuals from discrimination only against actions by *public* officials of state and local governments.

In 1896, the Court went still further, in the infamous case of *Plessy v. Ferguson*, by upholding a Louisiana statute that *required* segregation of the races on trolleys and other public carriers (and by implication in all public facilities, including schools). Homer Plessy, a man defined as "one-eighth black," had violated a Louisiana law that provided for "equal but separate accommodations" on trains and a $25 fine for any white passenger who sat in a car reserved for blacks or any black passenger who sat in a car reserved for whites. The Supreme Court held that the Fourteenth Amendment's "equal protection of the laws" was not violated by racial distinction as long as the facilities were equal, thus establishing the **"separate but equal" rule** that prevailed through the mid-twentieth century. People generally pretended that segregated accommodations were equal as long as some accommodation for blacks existed. The Court said that although "the object of the [Fourteenth] Amendment was undoubtedly to enforce the absolute equality of the two races before the law, . . . it could not have intended to abolish distinctions based on color, or to enforce social, as distinguished from political, equality, or a commingling of the two races upon terms unsatisfactory to either."[6] What the Court was saying in effect was that the use of race as a criterion of exclusion in public matters was not unreasonable.

"separate but equal" rule doctrine that public accommodations could be segregated by race but still be equal

Organizing for Equality

THE NATIONAL ASSOCIATION FOR THE ADVANCEMENT OF COLORED PEOPLE (NAACP) The creation of a "Jim Crow" system in the southern states and the lack of a legal basis for "equal protection under the laws" prompted the beginning of a long process in which African Americans built organizations and devised strategies for asserting their constitutional rights.

One such strategy sought to win political rights through political pressure and litigation. This approach was championed by the NAACP, established by a group of black and white reformers in 1909. Among the NAACP's founders was W. E. B. Du Bois, one of the most influential and creative thinkers on racial issues of the twentieth century. Because the northern black vote was so small in the early decades of the twentieth century, the organization primarily relied on the courts to press for black political rights. After the 1920s, the NAACP built a strong membership base, with some strength in the South, which would be critical when the civil rights movement gained momentum in the 1950s.

The great migration of blacks to the North beginning around World War I enlivened a protest strategy. Although protest organizations had existed in the nineteenth century, the continuing migration of blacks to the North made protest an increasingly useful tool. The black labor leader A. Philip Randolph forced the federal government to address racial discrimination in hiring practices during World War II by threatening a massive march on Washington. The federal government also grew more attentive to blacks as their voting strength increased as a result of the northward migration. By the 1940s, the black vote had swung away from Republicans, but the Democratic hold on black votes was by no means absolute.

The NAACP was formed in 1909 to promote the political rights of blacks. In the decades following the 1920s, the NAACP expanded its membership significantly and played an important role in the civil rights movement of the 1950s and 1960s.

WOMEN'S ORGANIZATIONS AND THE RIGHT TO SUFFRAGE Suffragists used the occasion of the Constitution's centennial in 1887 to protest the continued denial of their rights. For these women, the centennial represented "a century of injustice." The unveiling of the Statue of Liberty, depicting liberty as a woman, in New York Harbor in 1886 prompted women's rights advocates to call it "the greatest hypocrisy of the nineteenth century," in that "not one single woman throughout the length and breadth of the Land is as yet in possession of political Liberty."[7]

The climactic movement toward suffrage was formally launched in 1878 with the introduction of a proposed constitutional amendment in Congress. Parallel efforts were made in the states. Many states granted women the right to vote before the national government did; western states with less entrenched political systems opened politics to women earliest. When Wyoming became a state in 1890, it was the first state to grant full suffrage to women. Colorado, Utah, and Idaho all followed suit in the next several years. Suffrage organizations grew—the National American Woman Suffrage Association (NAWSA), formed in 1890, claimed two million members by 1917—and staged mass meetings, parades, petitions, and protests. NAWSA organized state-by-state efforts to win the right for women to vote. A more militant group, the National Woman's Party, staged pickets and got arrested in front of the White House to pro-

People had been agitating for women's right to vote since the 1830s, especially during the Civil War era. Here, a police officer arrests two early-twentieth-century suffragists in front of the White House. Women finally gained the constitutional right to vote in 1920.

test President Wilson's opposition to a constitutional amendment granting women this right. Finally in 1920, the Nineteenth Amendment was ratified, guaranteeing women the right to vote.

Litigating for Equality after World War II

The shame of discrimination against black military personnel during World War II, plus revelations of Nazi racial atrocities, moved President Harry S. Truman finally to bring the problem to the White House and national attention, with the appointment in 1946 of the President's Commission on Civil Rights. In 1948, the commission submitted its report, *To Secure These Rights*, which laid bare the extent of the problem of racial discrimination and its consequences. The report also revealed the success of experiments with racial integration in the armed forces during World War II to demonstrate to southern society that it had nothing to fear. But the committee recognized that the national government had no clear constitutional authority to pass and implement civil rights legislation. The committee proposed tying civil rights legislation to the commerce power, although it was clear that discrimination was not itself part of the flow of interstate commerce.[8] The committee even suggested using the treaty power as a source of constitutional authority for civil rights legislation.[9]

As for the Supreme Court, it had begun to change its position on racial discrimination before World War II by being stricter about the criterion of equal facilities in the "separate but equal" rule. In 1938, for example, the Court rejected Missouri's policy of paying the tuition of qualified blacks to out-of-state law schools rather than admitting them to the University of Missouri Law School.[10]

After the war, modest progress resumed. In 1950, the Court rejected Texas's claim that its new "law school for Negroes" afforded education equal to that of the all-white University of Texas Law School. Without confronting the "separate but equal" principle itself, the Court's decision anticipated its future civil rights rulings by opening the question of whether *any* segregated facilities could be truly equal.[11]

But in ordering the admission of blacks to all-white state law schools, the Supreme Court did not directly confront the "separate but equal" rule because the Court needed only to recognize the absence of any *equal* law school for blacks. The same was true in 1944, when the Supreme Court struck down the southern practice of "white primaries," which legally excluded blacks from participation in the nominating process. Here the Court simply recognized that primaries could no longer be regarded as the private affairs of the parties but were an integral aspect of the electoral process. This made parties "an agency of the State," and therefore any practice of discrimination against blacks was "state action within the meaning of the Fifteenth Amendment."[12] The most important pre-1954 decision was probably *Shelley v. Kraemer*, in which the Court ruled against the widespread practice of "restrictive covenants," whereby the seller of a home added a clause to the sales contract requiring the buyer to agree not to sell the home later to any non-Caucasian, non-Christian, and so on. The Court ruled that although private persons could sign such restrictive covenants, they could not be judicially enforced, since the Fourteenth Amendment prohibits any organ of the state, including the courts, from denying equal protection of its laws.[13]

Although none of those pre-1954 cases confronted "separate but equal" and the principle of racial discrimination as such, they were extremely significant to black leaders in the 1940s and gave them encouragement enough to believe that at last they had an opportunity and enough legal precedent to change the constitutional framework itself. Much of this legal work was done by the Legal Defense and Educational Fund of the NAACP. Until the late 1940s, lawyers working for the Legal Defense Fund had concentrated on winning small victories within that framework. Then, in 1948, the Legal Defense Fund upgraded its approach by simultaneously filing suits in different federal districts and through each level of schooling from unequal provision of kindergarten for blacks to unequal sports and science facilities in all-black high schools. After nearly two years of these mostly successful equalization suits, the lawyers decided the time was ripe to confront the "separate but equal" rule head-on, but they felt they needed some heavier artillery to lead the attack. Their choice was the African American lawyer Thurgood Marshall, who had been fighting, and often winning, equalization suits since the early 1930s. Marshall was pessimistic about the readiness of the Supreme Court for a full confrontation with segregation itself and the constitutional principle sustaining it. But the unwillingness of Congress after the 1948 election to consider fair employment legislation seems to have convinced Marshall that the courts were the only hope.

The Supreme Court must have come to the same conclusion because during the four years following 1948 there emerged a clear impression that the Court was willing to take more civil rights cases on appeal. Yet this was no guarantee that the Court would reverse *on principle* the separate but equal precedent of *Plessy v. Ferguson*. All through 1951 and 1952, as cases were winding slowly through the lower-court litigation maze, intense discussions and disagreements arose among NAACP lawyers as to whether a full-scale assault on *Plessy* was good strategy or whether it might not be better to continue with specific cases alleging unequal treatment and demanding relief with a Court-imposed policy of equalization.[14] But for some lawyers such as Marshall, these kinds of victories could amount to a defeat. For example, under the leadership of Governor James F. Byrnes, a former Supreme Court justice, South Carolina had undertaken a strategy of equalization of school services on a large scale in order to satisfy the *Plessy* rule and to head off or render moot litigation against the principle of separate but equal.

In the fall of 1952, the Court had on its docket cases from Kansas, South Carolina, Virginia, Delaware, and the District of Columbia challenging the constitutionality of school segregation. Of these, the case filed in Kansas became the chosen one. It seemed to be ahead of the pack in its district court, and it had the special advantage of being located in a state outside the Deep South.[15]

Oliver Brown, the father of three girls, lived "across the tracks" in a low-income, racially mixed Topeka neighborhood. Every school-day morning, Linda Brown took the school bus to the Monroe School for black children about a mile away. In September 1950, Oliver Brown took Linda to the all-white Sumner School, which was closer to home, to enter her into the third grade in defiance of state law and local segregation rules. When they were refused, Brown took his case to the NAACP, and soon thereafter ***Brown v. Board of Education*** was born. In mid-1953, the Court announced that the several cases on their way up would be reargued within a set of questions having to do with the intent of the Fourteenth Amendment. Almost exactly a year later, the Court responded to those questions in one of the most important decisions in its history.

Brown v. Board of Education the 1954 Supreme Court decision that struck down the "separate but equal" doctrine as fundamentally unequal. This case eliminated state power to use race as a criterion of discrimination in law and provided the national government with the power to intervene by exercising strict regulatory policies against discriminatory actions

In deciding the *Brown* case, the Court, to the surprise of many, basically rejected as inconclusive all the learned arguments about the intent and the history of the Fourteenth Amendment and committed itself to considering only the consequences of segregation:

> Does segregation of children in public schools solely on the basis of race, even though the physical facilities and other "tangible" factors may be equal, deprive the children of the minority group of equal educational opportunities? We believe that it does. . . . We conclude that in the field of public education the doctrine of "separate but equal" has no place. Separate educational facilities are inherently unequal.[16]

The *Brown* decision altered the constitutional framework in two fundamental respects. First, after *Brown*, the states no longer had the power to use race as a criterion of discrimination in law. Second, the national government from then on had the power (and eventually the obligation) to intervene with strict regulatory policies against the discriminatory actions of state or local governments, school boards, employers, and many others in the private sector.

Civil Rights after *Brown v. Board of Education*

Brown v. Board of Education withdrew all constitutional authority to use race as a criterion of exclusion, and it signaled more clearly the Court's determination to use the **strict scrutiny** test in cases related to racial discrimination. This meant that the burden of proof would fall on the government—not on the challengers—to show that the law in question *was* constitutional.[17] Although the use of strict scrutiny in cases relating to racial discrimination would give an advantage to those attacking racial discrimination, the historic decision in *Brown v. Board of Education* was merely a small opening move. First, most states refused to cooperate until sued, and many ingenious schemes were employed to delay obedience (such as paying

strict scrutiny test used by the Supreme Court in racial discrimination cases and other cases involving civil liberties and civil rights, which places the burden of proof on the government rather than on the challengers to show that the law in question is constitutional

"Massive resistance" among white southerners attempted to block the desegregation attempts of the national government. For example, at Little Rock Central High School in 1957, an angry mob of white students prevented black students from entering the school.

de jure literally, "by law"; legally enforced practices, such as school segregation in the South before the 1960s

de facto literally, "by fact"; practices that occur even when there is no legal enforcement, such as school segregation in much of the United States today

the tuition for white students to attend newly created "private" academies). Second, even as southern school boards began to cooperate by eliminating their legally enforced **(de jure)** school segregation, extensive actual **(de facto)** school segregation remained in the North as well as in the South, as a consequence of racially segregated housing that could not be reached by the 1954–55 *Brown* principles. Third, discrimination in employment, public accommodations, juries, voting, and other areas of social and economic activity were not directly touched by *Brown*.

SCHOOL DESEGREGATION, PHASE ONE Although the District of Columbia and some of the school districts in the border states began to respond almost immediately to court-ordered desegregation, the states of the Deep South responded with a carefully planned delaying tactic commonly called "massive resistance" by the more demagogic southern leaders and "nullification" and "interposition" by the centrists. Either way, southern politicians stood shoulder to shoulder to declare that the Supreme Court's decisions and orders were without effect. The legislatures in these states enacted statutes ordering school districts to maintain segregated schools and state superintendents to terminate state funding wherever there was racial mixing in the classroom. Some southern states violated their own long traditions of local school autonomy by centralizing public school authority under the governor or the state board of education and gave themselves the power to close the schools and to provide alternative private schooling wherever local school boards might be tending to obey the Supreme Court.

For Critical Analysis

Describe the changes in American society between the *Plessy v. Ferguson* and the *Brown v. Board of Education* decisions. How might changes in society have interacted with the changes in civil rights policy in America since the *Brown* case?

Most of these plans of "massive resistance" were tested in the federal courts and were struck down as unconstitutional.[18] But southern resistance was not confined to legislation. For example, in Arkansas in 1957, Governor Orval Faubus mobilized the Arkansas National Guard to intercede against enforcement of a federal court order to integrate Little Rock Central High School, and President Eisenhower was forced to deploy U.S. troops and literally place the city under martial law. The Supreme Court considered the Little Rock confrontation so historically important that the opinion it rendered in that case was not only agreed to unanimously but was, unprecedentedly, signed personally by every one of the justices.[19] The end of massive resistance, however, became simply the beginning of still another southern strategy. "Pupil placement" laws authorized school districts to place each pupil in a school according to a whole variety of academic, personal, and psychological considerations, never mentioning race at all. This put the burden of transferring to an all-white school on the nonwhite children and their parents, making it almost impossible for a single court order to cover a whole district, let alone a whole state. This delayed desegregation a while longer.[20]

SOCIAL PROTEST AND CONGRESSIONAL ACTION Ten years after *Brown*, fewer than 1 percent of black school-age children in the Deep South were attending schools with whites.[21] A decade of frustration made it fairly obvious to all observers that adjudication alone would not succeed. The goal of "equal protection" required positive, or affirmative, action by Congress and by administrative agencies. And given massive southern resistance and a generally negative national public opinion toward racial integration, progress would not be made through courts, Congress, or federal agencies without intense, well-organized support. Figure 5.1 shows the increase in civil rights demonstrations for voting rights and public accommodations during the fourteen years following *Brown*. Organized civil rights demonstrations began to mount slowly but surely after *Brown v. Board*

FIGURE 5.1 ★
Peaceful Civil Rights Demonstrations, 1954–68

Peaceful demonstrations were an important part of the civil rights movement. Why did the number of demonstrations grow after 1955? Why do you think the focus shifted from public accommodations to voting rights after 1964?

NOTE: The data are drawn from a search of the *New York Times* index for all references to civil rights demonstrations.
SOURCE: Jonathan D. Casper, *The Politics of Civil Liberties* (New York: Harper & Row, 1972), 90.

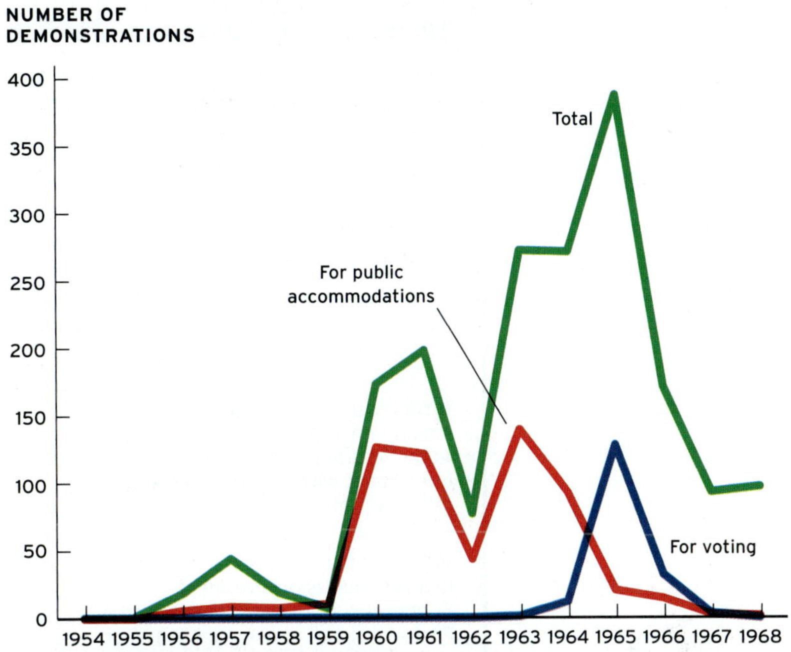

of Education. By the 1960s, the many organizations that made up the civil rights movement had accumulated experience and built networks capable of launching large-scale direct-action campaigns against southern segregationists. The Southern Christian Leadership Conference, the Student Nonviolent Coordinating Committee, and many other organizations had built a movement that stretched across the South. The movement used the media to attract nationwide attention and support. In the massive March on Washington in 1963, the Reverend Martin Luther King, Jr. staked out the movement's moral claims in his famous "I Have a Dream" speech. The image of protesters being beaten, attacked by police dogs, and set on with fire hoses did much to win broad sympathy for the cause of black civil rights and to discredit state and local governments in the South. In this way, the movement created intense pressure for a reluctant federal government to take more assertive steps to defend black civil rights.

The first modern effort to legislate in the field of civil rights was made in 1957, but the law contained only a federal guarantee of voting rights, without any powers of enforcement, although it did create the Civil Rights Commission to study abuses. Much more important legislation for civil rights followed, especially the Civil Rights Act of 1964. It is important to observe here the mutual dependence of the courts and legislatures: the legislatures need constitutional authority to act, and the courts need legislative assistance to implement court orders and focus political support. Consequently, even as the U.S. Congress finally moved into the field of school desegregation (and other areas of "equal protection"), the courts continued to exercise their powers, not only by placing court orders against recalcitrant school districts, but also by extending and reinterpreting aspects of the "equal protection" clause to support legislative and administrative actions (see Table 5.1).

TABLE 5.1 ★ Cause and Effect in the Civil Rights Movement

Political action and government action spurred each other to produce dramatic changes in American civil rights policies.

JUDICIAL AND LEGAL ACTION	POLITICAL ACTION
1954 *Brown v. Board of Education*	
	1955 Montgomery, Alabama, bus boycott
1956 Federal courts order school integration, especially one ordering Autherine Lucy admitted to University of Alabama, with Governor Wallace officially protesting	
1957 Civil Rights Act creating Civil Rights Commission; President Eisenhower sends paratroops to Little Rock, Arkansas, to enforce integration of Central High School	**1957** Southern Christian Leadership Conference (SCLC) formed, with Martin Luther King, Jr. as president
1960 First substantive Civil Rights Act, primarily voting rights	**1960** Student Nonviolent Coordinating Committee formed to organize protests, sit-ins, freedom rides
1961 Interstate Commerce Commission orders desegregation on all buses and trains, and in terminals	
1961 JFK favors executive action over civil rights legislation	
1963 JFK shifts, supports strong civil rights law; assassination; LBJ asserts strong support for civil rights	**1963** Nonviolent demonstrations in Birmingham, Alabama, lead to King's arrest and his "Letter from the Birmingham Jail"
	1963 March on Washington
1964 Congress passes historic Civil Rights Act covering voting, employment, public accommodations, education	
1965 Voting Rights Act	**1965** King announces drive to register 3 million blacks in the South
1966 War on Poverty in full swing	**Late 1960s** Movement dissipates: part toward litigation, part toward community action programs, part toward war protest, part toward more militant "Black Power" actions

The Civil Rights Acts

The right to equal protection of the laws could be established and, to a certain extent, implemented by the courts. But after a decade of very frustrating efforts, the courts and Congress ultimately came to the conclusion that the federal courts alone were not adequate to the task of changing the social rules, and that legislation and administrative action would be needed.

Three civil rights acts were passed during the first decade after the 1954 Supreme Court decision in *Brown v. Board of Education*. But these acts were of only marginal importance. The first two, in 1957 and 1960, established that the Fourteenth Amendment of the Constitution, adopted almost a century earlier, could no longer be disregarded, particularly with regard to voting. The third, the Equal Pay Act of 1963, was more important, but it was concerned with women, did not touch the question of racial discrimination, and had no enforcement mechanisms.

By far the most important piece of legislation passed by Congress concerning equal opportunity was the Civil Rights Act of 1964. It not only put some teeth in the voting rights provisions of the 1957 and 1960 acts but also went far beyond voting to attack discrimination in public accommodations, segregation in the schools, and at long last, the discriminatory conduct of employers in hiring, promoting, and laying off their employees. Discrimination against women was also included, extending the important 1963 provisions. The 1964 act seemed bold at the time, but it was enacted ten years after the Supreme Court had declared racial discrimination "inherently unequal" under the Fifth and Fourteenth Amendments. And it was enacted long after blacks had demonstrated that discrimination was no longer acceptable. The choice in 1964 was not between congressional action or inaction but between legal action and expanded violence.

PUBLIC ACCOMMODATIONS After the passage of the 1964 Civil Rights Act, public accommodations quickly removed some of the most blatant forms of racial discrimination. Signs defining "colored" and "white" restrooms, water fountains, waiting rooms, and seating arrangements were removed and a host of other practices that relegated black people to separate and inferior arrangements were ended. In addition, the federal government filed more than 400 antidiscrimination suits in federal courts against hotels, restaurants, taverns, gas stations, and other "public accommodations."

Many aspects of legalized racial segregation—such as separate Bibles in the courtroom—seem like ancient history today. But the issue of racial discrimination in public settings is by no means over. In 1993, six African American Secret Service agents filed charges against the Denny's restaurant chain for failing to serve them; white Secret Service agents at a nearby table had received prompt service. Similar charges citing discriminatory service at Denny's restaurants surfaced across the country. Faced with evidence of a pattern of systematic discrimination and numerous lawsuits, Denny's paid $45 million in damages to plaintiffs in Maryland and California in what is said to be the largest settlement ever in a public accommodation case.[22] The Denny's case shows how effective the Civil Rights Act of 1964 can be in challenging racial discrimination. In addition to the settlement, the chain vowed to expand employment and management opportunities for minorities in Denny's restaurants. Other forms of racial discrimination in public accommodations are harder to challenge, however. For example, there is considerable evidence that taxicabs often refuse to pick up black passengers.[23] Such practices may be common, but they are difficult to prove and remedy through the law.

Politics Today

If airport security personnel were permitted to detain and inspect people who appear to be from the Middle East, would it be "ethnic profiling," in violation of civil rights laws? Or would it be a reasonable exception to civil rights under the equal protection clause?

The 1964 Civil Rights Act made desegregation a legal requirement. The policy of busing from black neighborhoods to white schools bitterly divided the black and white communities in Boston. In 1976, a mob of white protesters sought to impale this innocent black bystander—a lawyer on his way to his office—on a flag.

SCHOOL DESEGREGATION, PHASE TWO The 1964 Civil Rights Act also declared discrimination by private employers and state governments (school boards, etc.) illegal, then went further to provide for administrative agencies to help the courts implement these laws. Title IV of the act, for example, authorized the executive branch, through the Justice Department, to implement federal court orders to desegregate schools, and to do so without having to wait for individual parents to bring complaints. Title VI of the act vastly strengthened the role of the executive branch and the credibility of court orders by providing that federal grants-in-aid to state and local governments for education must be withheld from any school system practicing racial segregation. Title VI became the most effective weapon for desegregating schools outside the South, because the situation in northern communities was more subtle and difficult to reach. In the South, the problem was segregation by law coupled with overt resistance to the national government's efforts to change the situation. In contrast, outside the South, segregated facilities were the outcome of hundreds of thousands of housing choices made by individuals and families. Once racial residential patterns emerged, racial homogeneity, property values, and neighborhood schools and churches were defended by realtors, neighborhood organizations, and the like. Thus, in order to eliminate discrimination nationwide, the 1964 Civil Rights Act (1) gave the president through the Office for Civil Rights of the Justice Department the power to withhold federal education grants,[24] and (2) gave the attorney general of the United States the power to initiate suits (rather than having to await complaints) wherever there was a "pattern or practice" of discrimination.[25]

In the decade following the 1964 Civil Rights Act, the Justice Department brought legal action against more than 500 school districts. During the same period, administrative agencies filed actions against 600 school districts, threatening to suspend federal aid to education unless real desegregation steps were taken.

BUSING One step taken toward desegregation was busing children from poor urban school districts to wealthier suburban ones. In 1971, the Supreme Court held that state-imposed desegregation could be brought about by busing children across school districts, even where relatively long distances were involved:

> If school authorities fail in their affirmative obligations, judicial authority may be invoked. Once a right and a violation have been shown, the scope of a district court's equitable powers to remedy past wrongs is broad. . . . Bus transportation [is] a normal and accepted tool of educational policy.[26]

But the decision went beyond that, adding that under certain limited circumstances even racial quotas could be used as the "starting point in shaping a remedy to correct past constitutional violations," and that pairing or grouping of schools and reorganizing school attendance zones would also be acceptable.

Three years later, however, this principle was severely restricted when the Supreme Court determined that only cities found guilty of deliberate and de jure racial segregation would have to desegregate their schools.[27] This ruling had the effect of exempting most northern states and cities from busing because school segregation in northern cities is generally de facto segregation that results from segregated housing and from thousands of acts of private discrimination against blacks and other minorities.

Boston provides the best illustration of the agonizing problem of making further progress in civil rights in the schools under the constitutional framework established by these decisions. Boston school authorities were found guilty of deliberately building school facilities and drawing school districts "to increase racial segregation." After vain efforts by Boston school authorities to draw up an acceptable plan to remedy the segregation, federal judge W. Arthur Garrity ordered an elaborate desegregation plan of his own, involving busing between the all-black neighborhood of Roxbury and the nearby white, working-class community of South Boston. Opponents of this plan were organized and eventually took the case to the Supreme Court, where *certiorari* (the Court's device for accepting appeals; see Chapter 15) was denied; this had the effect of approving Judge Garrity's order. The city's schools were so segregated and uncooperative that even the conservative administration of President Richard Nixon had already initiated a punitive cutoff of funds. But many liberals also criticized Judge Garrity's plan as being badly conceived, because it involved two neighboring communities with a history of tension and mutual resentment. The plan worked well at the elementary school level but proved so explosive at the high school level that it generated a continuing crisis for the city of Boston and for the whole nation over court-ordered, federally directed desegregation in the North.[28]

Additional progress in the desegregation of schools is likely to be extremely slow unless the Supreme Court decides to permit federal action against de facto segregation and against the varieties of private schools and academies that have sprung up for the purpose of avoiding integration. The prospects for further school integration diminished with a Supreme Court decision handed down on January 15, 1991. The opinion, written for the Court by Chief Justice William Rehnquist, held that lower federal courts could end supervision of local school boards if those boards could show compliance "in good faith" with court orders to desegregate and could show that "vestiges of past discrimination" had been eliminated "to the extent practicable."[29] It is not necessarily easy for a school board to prove that the new standard has been met, but this was the first time since *Brown* and the 1964 Civil Rights Act that the Court had opened the door at all to retreat.

That door of retreat was opened further by a 1995 decision in which the Court ruled that the remedies being applied in Kansas City, Missouri, were improper.[30] In accordance with a lower-court ruling, the state was pouring additional funding into salaries and remedial programs for Kansas City schools, which had a history of segregation. The aim of the spending was to improve student performance and to attract white students from the suburbs into the city schools. The Supreme Court declared the interdistrict goal improper and reiterated its earlier ruling that states can free themselves of court orders by showing a good-faith effort. This decision indicated the Court's new willingness to end desegregation plans even when predominantly minority schools continue to lag significantly behind white suburban schools. In 2007, the Court's ruling in *Parents Involved in Community Schools v. Seattle School District No. 1* limited still further the measures that can be used to promote school integration. The case involved school-assignment plans voluntarily initiated by the cities of Seattle and Louisville. By making race one factor in assigning students to schools, the cities hoped to achieve greater racial balance across the public schools. The court ruled that these plans—even though the cities voluntarily adopted them—were unconstitutional because they discriminated against white students on the basis of race. Many observers described the decision as the end of the *Brown* era because it eliminated one of the few public strategies left to promote racial integration. Others argued that Justice Anthony Kennedy's concurring opinion, which recognized the harm of racial isolation, may provide the basis for new efforts to promote integration in the future.[31]

Politics Today

After the 2007 ruling in the Seattle *Parents* case, are there still ways that the government can work to promote racial integration in the schools? Should Americans be concerned if schools become more racially segregated after the rulings restricting the use of racial criteria in school assignments?

OUTLAWING DISCRIMINATION IN EMPLOYMENT Despite the agonizingly slow progress of school desegregation, some progress was made in other areas of civil rights during the 1960s and 1970s. Voting rights were established and fairly quickly began to revolutionize southern politics. Service on juries was no longer denied to minorities. But progress in the right to participate in politics and government dramatized the relative lack of progress in the economic domain, and it was in this area that battles over civil rights were increasingly fought.

The federal courts and the Justice Department entered this area through Title VII of the Civil Rights Act of 1964, which outlawed job discrimination by all private and public employers, including governmental agencies (such as fire and police departments) that employed more than fifteen workers. We have already seen (in Chapter 3) that the Supreme Court gave "interstate commerce" such a broad definition that Congress had the constitutional authority to cover discrimination by virtually any local employers.[32] Title VII makes it unlawful to discriminate in employment on the basis of color, religion, sex, or national origin, as well as race.

Title VII delegated some of the powers to enforce fair-employment practices to the Justice Department's Civil Rights Division and others to a new agency created in the 1964 act, the Equal Employment Opportunity Commission (EEOC). By executive order, these agencies had the power of the national government to revoke public contracts for goods and services and to refuse to engage in contracts for goods and services with any private company that could not guarantee that its rules for hiring, promotion, and firing were nondiscriminatory. Executive orders in 1965, 1967, and 1969 by Presidents Johnson and Nixon extended and reaffirmed nondiscrimination practices in employment and promotion in the federal government service. And in 1972, President Nixon and a Democratic Congress cooperated to strengthen the EEOC by giving it authority to initiate suits rather than waiting for grievances.

In 2007, the Supreme Court ruled that public school systems in Seattle and Louisville could not use race as a factor in assigning students to schools, because this practice discriminated against white students. Critics of this decision argued that it would lead to racial segregation.

But one problem with Title VII was that the complaining party had to show that deliberate discrimination was the cause of the failure to get a job or a training opportunity. Rarely does an employer explicitly admit discrimination on the basis of race, sex, or any other illegal reason. Recognizing the rarity of such an admission, the courts have allowed aggrieved parties (the plaintiffs) to make their case if they can show that an employer's hiring practices had the *effect* of exclusion. A leading case in 1971 involved a "class action" by several black employees in North Carolina attempting to show with statistical evidence that blacks had been relegated to only one department in the Duke Power Company, which involved the least desirable, manual-labor jobs, and that they had been kept out of contention for the better jobs because the employer had added attainment of a high school education and the passing of specially prepared aptitude tests as qualifications for higher jobs. The Supreme Court held that although the statistical evidence did not prove intentional discrimination, and although the requirements were race-neutral in appearance, their effects were sufficient to shift the burden of justification to the employer to show that the requirements were a "business necessity" that bore "a demonstrable relationship to successful performance."[33] The ruling in this case was subsequently applied to other hiring, promotion, and training programs.[34]

VOTING RIGHTS Although 1964 was the *most* important year for civil rights legislation, it was not the only important year. In 1965, Congress significantly strengthened legislation protecting voting rights by barring literacy and other tests as a condition for voting in six southern states,[35] by setting criminal penalties for interference with efforts to vote, and by providing for the replacement of local registrars with federally appointed registrars in counties designated by the attorney general as significantly resistant to registering eligible blacks to vote. The right to vote was further strengthened with ratification in 1964 of the Twenty-fourth Amendment, which abolished the poll tax, and in 1975 with legislation permanently outlawing literacy tests in all fifty states and mandating bilingual ballots or oral assistance for Spanish-speakers, Chinese, Japanese, Koreans, Native Americans, and Eskimos.

In the long run, the laws extending and protecting voting rights could prove to be the most effective of all the great civil rights legislation, because the progress in black political participation produced by these acts has altered the shape of American politics. In 1965, in the seven states of the Old Confederacy covered by the Voting Rights Act (VRA), 29.3 percent of the eligible black residents were registered to vote, compared with 73.4 percent of the white residents (see Table 5.2). Mississippi was the extreme case, with 6.7 percent black and 69.9 percent white registration. In 1967, a mere two years after implementation of the voting rights laws, 52.1 percent of the eligible blacks in the seven states were registered, comparing favorably with 79.5 percent of the eligible whites, a gap of 27.4 points. By 1972, the gap between black and white registration in the seven states was only 11.2 points, and in Mississippi the gap had been reduced to 9.4 points. At one time, white leaders in Mississippi attempted to dilute the influence of this growing black vote by **gerrymandering** districts to ensure that no blacks would be elected to Congress. But the black voters changed Mississippi before Mississippi could change them. In 1988, 11 percent of all elected officials in Mississippi were black. This was up one full percentage point from 1987 and closely approximates the size of the national black electorate, which at the time was just over 11 percent of the American voting-age population. Mississippi's blacks had made significant gains (as

gerrymandering
apportionment of voters in districts in such a way as to give unfair advantage to one racial or ethnic group or political party

TABLE 5.2 ★ Registration by Race and State in Southern States Covered by the Voting Rights Act (VRA)

The VRA had a direct impact on the rate of black voter registration in the southern states, as measured by the gap between white and black voters in each state. Further insights can be gained by examining changes in white registration rates before and after passage of the VRA as well as by comparing the gaps between white and black registration. Why do you think registration rates for whites increased significantly in some states and dropped in others? What impact could the increase in black registration have had on public policy?

	BEFORE THE ACT*			AFTER THE ACT* 1971–72		
	WHITE	BLACK	GAP†	WHITE	BLACK	GAP
Alabama	69.2%	19.3%	49.9%	80.7%	57.1%	23.6%
Georgia	62.6	27.4	35.2	70.6	67.8	2.8
Louisiana	80.5	31.6	48.9	80.0	59.1	20.9
Mississippi	69.9	6.7	63.2	71.6	62.2	9.4
North Carolina	96.8	46.8	50.0	62.2	46.3	15.9
South Carolina	75.7	37.3	38.4	51.2	48.0	3.2
Virginia	61.1	38.3	22.8	61.2	54.0	7.2
TOTAL	73.4	29.3	44.1	67.8	56.6	11.2

*Available registration data as of March 1965 and 1971–72.

†The gap is the percentage-point difference between white and black registration rates.

SOURCE: U.S. Commission on Civil Rights, *Political Participation* (1968), Appendix VII: Voter Education Project, Attachment to Press Release, October 3, 1972.

they had in other Deep South states) as elected state and local representatives, and Mississippi was one of only eight states in the country in which a black judge presided over the highest state court. (Four of the eight were Deep South states.)[36]

Several provisions of the 1965 Act had been scheduled to expire in 2007. However, in 2006, responding to charges that black voters still faced discrimination at the polls, Congress renewed the Act for another twenty-five years. Pressure for renewal of the Act had been intense since the disputed 2000 presidential election. The U.S. Commission on Civil Rights conducted hearings on the election in Florida, at which black voters testified about being turned away from the polls, about being wrongly purged from the voting rolls, and about the unreliable voting technology in their neighborhoods. On the basis of this testimony and after an analysis of the vote, the Commission charged that there had been extensive racial discrimination.[37]

HOUSING The Civil Rights Act of 1964 did not address housing, but in 1968, Congress passed another civil rights act specifically to outlaw housing discrimination. Called the Fair Housing Act, the law prohibited discrimination in the sale or rental of most housing—eventually covering nearly all the nation's housing. Housing was among the most controversial of discrimination issues because of deeply entrenched patterns of residential segregation across the United States. Such segregation was not simply a product of individual choice. Local housing authorities deliberately segregated public housing, and federal guidelines had sanctioned discrimination in Federal Housing Administration mortgage lending, effectively preventing blacks from joining the exodus to the suburbs in the 1950s and 1960s. Nonetheless, Congress had been reluctant to tackle housing discrimination, fearing the tremendous controversy it could arouse. But just as the housing legislation was being considered in April 1968, the civil rights leader Martin Luther King, Jr. was assassinated; this tragedy brought the measure unexpected support in Congress.

Although it pronounced sweeping goals, the Fair Housing Act had little effect on housing segregation because its enforcement mechanisms were so weak. Individuals believing they had been discriminated against had to file suit themselves. The burden was on the individual to prove that housing discrimination had occurred, even though such discrimination is often subtle and difficult to document. Although local fair-housing groups emerged to assist individuals in their court claims, the procedures for proving discrimination proved a formidable barrier to effective change. These procedures were not altered until 1988, when Congress passed the Fair Housing Amendments Act. This new law put more teeth in the enforcement procedures and allowed the Department of Housing and Urban Development (HUD) to initiate legal action in cases of discrimination. With vigorous use, these provisions may prove more successful than past efforts at combating housing discrimination.[38]

For Critical Analysis

Many people believe that despite the significance of the *Brown v. Board of Education* decision, it has failed to fulfill its promise. What did *Brown* really accomplish? Can courts bring about social change?

Other avenues for challenging residential segregation also had mixed success. HUD tried briefly in the early 1970s to create racially "open communities" by withholding federal funds to suburbs that refused to accept subsidized housing. Confronted with charges of "forced integration" and bitter local protests, however, the administration quickly backed down. Efforts to prohibit discrimination in lending have been somewhat more promising. Several laws passed in the 1970s required banks to report information about their mortgage lending patterns, making it more difficult for them to engage in **redlining,** the practice of refusing to lend to entire neighborhoods. The 1977 Community Reinvestment Act required banks to lend in neighborhoods in which they do business. Through vigorous use of this act, many neighborhood organizations have reached agreements with banks that, as a result, have significantly increased investment in some poor neighborhoods. Even so, racial discrimination in home-mortgage lending remains a significant issue. In 2007, the issue of predatory lending—offering loans well above market rates, often with complex provisions that borrowers do not understand—attracted nationwide attention as the number of home foreclosures skyrocketed. Several lawsuits charged that these loans were particularly targeted at minority borrowers.[39]

redlining a practice in which banks refuse to make loans to people living in certain geographic locations

The Universalization of Civil Rights

Even before equal employment laws began to have a positive effect on the economic situation of blacks, something far more dramatic began happening—the universalization of civil rights. The right not to be discriminated against was being successfully claimed by the other groups listed in Title VII of the 1964 Civil Rights Act—those defined by sex, religion, or national origin—and eventually by still other groups defined by age or sexual preference. This universalization of civil rights has become the new frontier of the civil rights struggle.

Political equality did not end discrimination against women in the workplace or in society at large. African Americans' struggle for civil rights in the 1950s and 1960s spurred a parallel equal rights movement for women in the 1960s and 1970s.

Once gender discrimination began to be seen as an important civil rights issue, other groups arose to demand recognition and active protection of their civil rights. Under Title VII, any group or individual can try, and in fact is encouraged to try, to convert goals and grievances into questions of rights and of the deprivation of those rights. A plaintiff must establish only that his or her membership in a group is an unreasonable basis for discrimination—that is, that it cannot be proven to be a "job-related" or otherwise clearly reasonable and relevant decision. In America today, the list of individuals and groups claiming illegal discrimination is lengthy.

Women and Gender Discrimination

Title VII provided a valuable tool for the growing women's movement in the 1960s and 1970s. In fact, in many ways the law fostered the growth of the women's movement. The first major campaign of the National Organization for Women (NOW) involved picketing the Equal Employment Opportunity Commission for its refusal to ban sex-segregated employment advertisements. NOW also sued the *New York Times* for continuing to publish such ads after the passage of Title VII. Another organization, the Women's Equity Action League (WEAL), pursued legal action on a wide range of sex-discrimination issues, filing lawsuits against law schools and medical schools for discriminatory admission policies, for example.

Building on these victories and the growth of the women's movement, feminist activists sought an "Equal Rights Amendment" (ERA) to the Constitution. The proposed amendment was short: its substantive passage stated that "equality of rights under the law shall not be denied or abridged by the United States or by any State on account of sex." The amendment's supporters believed that such a sweeping guarantee of equal rights was a necessary tool for ending all discrimination against women and for making gender roles more equal. Opponents charged that it would be socially disruptive and would introduce changes—such as coed restrooms—that most Americans did not want. The amendment easily passed

Congress in 1972 and won quick approval in many state legislatures, but it fell three states short of the thirty-eight needed to ratify the amendment by the 1982 deadline for its ratification.[40]

Despite the failure of the ERA, gender discrimination expanded dramatically as an area of civil rights law. In the 1970s, the conservative Burger Court (under Chief Justice Warren Burger) helped to establish gender discrimination as a major and highly visible civil rights issue. Although the Burger Court refused to treat gender discrimination as the equivalent of racial discrimination,[41] it did make it easier for plaintiffs to file and win suits on the basis of gender discrimination by applying an "intermediate" level of review to these cases.[42] This **intermediate scrutiny** is midway between traditional rules of evidence, which put the burden of proof on the plaintiff, and the doctrine of strict scrutiny, which requires the defendant to show not only that a particular classification is reasonable but also that there is a need or compelling interest for it. Intermediate scrutiny shifts the burden of proof partially onto the defendant, rather than leaving it entirely on the plaintiff.

intermediate scrutiny test used by the Supreme Court in gender discrimination cases, which places the burden of proof partially on the government and partially on the challengers to show that the law in question is unconstitutional

One major step was taken in 1992, when the Court decided in *Franklin v. Gwinnett County Public Schools* that violations of Title IX of the 1972 Education Act could be remedied with monetary damages.[43] Title IX forbade gender discrimination in education, but it initially sparked little litigation because of its weak enforcement provisions. The Court's 1992 ruling that monetary damages could be awarded for gender discrimination opened the door for more legal action in the area of education. The greatest impact has been in the areas of sexual harassment—the subject of the *Franklin* case—and in equal treatment of women's athletic programs. The potential for monetary damages has made universities and public schools take the problem of sexual harassment more seriously. Colleges and universities have also started to pay more attention to women's athletic programs. In the two years after the *Franklin* case, complaints to the Education Department's Office for Civil Rights about unequal treatment of women's athletic programs nearly tripled. In several high-profile legal cases, some prominent universities were ordered to create more women's sports programs; many other colleges and universities have begun to add more women's programs in order to avoid potential litigation.[44] In 1997, the Supreme Court refused to hear a petition by Brown University challenging a lower court ruling that the university establish strict sex equity in its athletic programs. The Court's decision meant that in colleges and universities across the country, varsity athletic positions for men and women must reflect their overall enrollment numbers.[45]

In 1996, the Supreme Court made another important decision about gender and education by putting an end to all-male schools supported by public funds. It ruled that the Virginia Military Institute's policy of not admitting women was unconstitutional.[46] Along with the Citadel, another all-male military college in South Carolina, VMI had never admitted women in its 157-year history. VMI argued that the unique educational experience it offered—including intense physical training and the harsh treatment of freshmen—would be destroyed if women students were admitted. The Court, however, ruled that the male-only policy denied "substantial equality" to women. Two days after the Court's ruling, the Citadel announced that it would accept women. VMI considered becoming a private institution in order to remain all-male, but in September 1996, the school board finally voted to admit women. The legal decisions may have removed formal barriers to entry, but the experience of the new female cadets at these schools was not easy. The first female cadet at the Citadel, Shannon Faulkner, won admission in 1995 under a

Kim Messer, pictured here with a group of male cadets, was one of the first women admitted to the Citadel, a military college in South Carolina. The Supreme Court ruled in 1996 that state-sponsored schools must be open to both men and women.

federal court order but quit after four days. Although four women were admitted to the Citadel after the Supreme Court decision, two of the four quit several months later. They charged harassment from male students, including attempts to set the female cadets on fire.[47]

Courts began to find sexual harassment a form of sex discrimination during the late 1970s. Although sexual harassment law applies to education, most of the law of sexual harassment has been developed by courts through interpretation of Title VII of the Civil Rights Act of 1964. In 1986, the Supreme Court recognized two forms of sexual harassment. One type is "quid pro quo" harassment, which involves an explicit or strongly implied threat that submission is a condition of continued employment. The second is harassment that creates offensive or intimidating employment conditions that amount to a "hostile environment."[48]

Employers and many employees have worried that hostile-environment sexual harassment is too ambiguous. When can an employee bring charges? When is the employer liable? In 1986, the Court said that sexual harassment may be legally actionable even if the employee did not suffer tangible economic or job-related losses in relation to it. In 1993, the Court said that sexual harassment may be legally actionable even if the employee did not suffer tangible psychological costs as a result of it.[49] In two 1998 cases, the Court further strengthened the law when it said that whether or not sexual harassment results in economic harm to the employee, an employer is liable for the harassment if it was committed by someone with authority over the employee—by a supervisor, for example. But the Court also said that an employer may defend itself by showing that it had a sexual harassment prevention and grievance policy in effect.[50]

The development of gender discrimination as an important part of the civil rights struggle has coincided with the rise of women's politics as a discrete movement in American politics. As with the struggle for racial equality, the relationship between changes in government policies and political action suggests that changes in government policies to a great degree produce political action. Today,

Human Rights and America's War on Terror

In 2007, President George W. Bush appeared before the annual opening session of the United Nations to affirm America's support for human rights. The president condemned dictatorships, declaring that "every civilized nation . . . has a responsibility to stand up for the people suffering under dictatorship." Among the countries singled out in his speech was Myanmar (formerly Burma), where the ruling regime had just brutally stamped out peaceful prodemocracy protests led by Buddhist monks. Bush blasted the regime's Myanmar as a place where "basic freedoms of speech, assembly and worship are severely restricted. . . . [E]thnic minorities are persecuted. Forced child labor, human trafficking and rape are common." Announcing a tightening of sanctions, the president declared that those "responsible for the most egregious violations of human rights" would be denied visas to the United States.[a]

To many in the audience, however, the president's words rang hollow. Under the auspices of the "war on terror," the United States has engaged in a variety of practices that seem to violate basic human rights. These include the treatment of terrorism suspects being held at Guantánamo Bay, Cuba, the use of extraordinary rendition, and the defense of torture. Guantánamo detainees were held for years without formal charges levied against them and without access to lawyers. The trials were conducted in secret under rules in which defendants and their lawyers were not allowed access to the evidence against them. The rights to *habeas corpus* and public trials in an established court of law were instituted centuries ago in England as cornerstones of basic human rights. Countries around the globe have condemned the use of extraordinary rendition, whereby American intelligence agents kidnap suspected terrorists and send them to secret detention centers, often in countries that are known to practice torture. Finally, the Bush administration's defense of harsh interrogation tactics—such as simulated drowning, or "waterboarding"—put it at odds with long-standing international human rights agreements that ban the use of torture.

Although the administration defended these methods as essential to American security, critics believe that the cost has been too high because it has undermined America's moral authority in the world. As an advocate from Human Rights Watch put it, "I believe the president should be championing human rights at the U.N., but he's lost his authority and credibility as a world leader because of his policies on rendition and Guantanamo. . . . His remarks would be more effective if the U.S. was practicing what it's preaching."[b] During congressional hearings about the repression of protest in Myanmar, where the regime is accused of using waterboarding techniques against dissidents, critics noted the difficulties created by the gap between American words and practices.

After September 11, 2001, many Americans agreed that new measures would be needed to ensure American security against the threat of terrorism. However, the American decision to embrace techniques that violate basic human rights has been a costly one. America's moral stature and its ability to be a world leader in support of human rights have suffered. The challenge of addressing the need for security with a commitment to respecting basic human rights is a fundamental dilemma that all American leaders will confront in the years to come.

FOR CRITICAL ANALYSIS

1. Are there some circumstances where violations of human rights are an unavoidable necessity for the United States?
2. Do you think that the human rights violations associated with the war on terror prevent the United States from using its power to support human rights? If the United States can impose sanctions on human rights violators in foreign countries, does it matter if America's moral authority is weakened in international venues?

a. Steven Lee Myers, "Bush, at U.N., Announces Stricter Burmese Sanctions," *New York Times*, September 26, 2007, p. 12.

b. William Douglas, "Bush Astounds Activists, Supports Human Rights," McClatchy Washington Bureau, September 25, 2007, http://mcclatchydc.com/227/story/19964.html (accessed 2/17/08).

the existence of a powerful women's movement derives in large measure from the enactment of Title VII of the Civil Rights Act of 1964 and from the Burger Court's vital steps in applying that law to protect women. The recognition of women's civil rights has become an issue that in many ways transcends the usual distinctions of American political debate. In the heavily partisan debate over the federal crime bill enacted in 1994, for instance, the section of the bill that enjoyed the widest support was the Violence Against Women Act, whose most important feature was that it defined gender-biased violent crimes as a matter of civil rights, and created a civil rights remedy for women who have been the victims of such crimes. The Supreme Court's 2000 decision ruling the act unconstitutional signaled a defeat for women's rights. Another setback occurred in 2007, when the Court ruled against a claim of pay discrimination at work. The case, *Ledbetter v. Goodyear Tire and Rubber Co.*, involved a woman supervisor named Lily Ledbetter who learned late in her career that she was being paid up to 40 percent less than male supervisors, including those with less seniority. Ledbetter filed a grievance with the Equal Employment Opportunity Commission charging sex discrimination. The Supreme Court denied her claim, ruling that according to the law, workers must file their grievance 180 days after the discrimination occurs. Many observers found the ruling unfair because workers often do not know about pay differentials until well after the initial decision to discriminate has been made. Justice Ruth Bader Ginsburg, the only female member of the Court, marked her disagreement by reading her dissent aloud, a rare occurrence. The fair-pay issue will provoke ongoing political debate as Congress considers bills to greatly extend the time limits for filing pay grievances.

Latinos

The labels "Latino" and "Hispanic" encompass a wide range of groups with diverse national origins, distinctive cultural identities, and particular experiences. As a result, the civil rights issues have varied considerably by group and by place. For example, the early political experiences of Mexican Americans were shaped by race and by region. For the earliest Mexican Americans in the Southwest, the United States came to them, rather than the other way around. In 1848, under the Treaty of Guadalupe Hidalgo, Mexico ceded to the United States territory that now comprises Arizona, California, New Mexico, and parts of Colorado, Nevada, and Utah, as well as extending the Texas border to the Rio Grande. Although the treaty guaranteed full civil rights to the residents of these territories, Mexican Americans in fact experienced ongoing discrimination, which they sought to remedy through the courts. In 1898 the courts reconfirmed Mexican Americans' formal political rights, including the right to vote. In many places, however, and especially in Texas, Mexican Americans were segregated and prevented from voting through such means as the white primary and the poll tax.[51] There were regional differences too. In contrast to the northeastern and midwestern cities to which most European ethnics immigrated, the Southwest did not have a tradition of ethnic mobilization associated with machine politics. Particularly after the political reforms enacted in the first decade of the twentieth century, city politics in the Southwest was dominated by a small group of Anglo elites. In the countryside, when Mexican Americans participated in politics, it was often as part of a political organization dominated by a white landowner, or *patrón*.

The 1947 Mendez v. Westminister *case challenged segregation of Mexican American students in California and was an important precursor to later school segregation cases. In 2007, a U.S. postal stamp was issued to commemorate the* Mendez *case.*

The earliest Mexican American independent political organizations included the League of United Latin American Citizens (LULAC), founded in 1929, and the GI Forum, created in 1948. Both groups worked to stem discrimination against Mexican Americans. LULAC pursued a legal strategy like the NAACP's to eliminate the segregation of Mexican American students. One of its earliest victories came in 1931, when it successfully challenged a Texas school district's decision to establish separate schools for Anglos and Mexicans.[52] LULAC also litigated the 1947 *Mendez v. Westminister* case, which overturned school segregation in Orange County, California. This case was an important precursor to *Brown v. Board of Education*, and many of the same actors were involved. For example, Thurgood Marshall of the NAACP, the lead attorney on *Brown* (and later a Supreme Court justice), filed a brief supporting desegregation in the *Mendez* case. Moreover, the California governor Earl Warren, who signed the legislation outlawing school segregation there after the *Mendez* decision, served as chief justice when the Supreme Court ruled on *Brown* seven years later. In 2007, the *Mendez* case received national recognition as an important landmark in civil rights with a U.S. postal stamp bearing the words "toward equality in our schools."[53] By the late 1950s, the first Mexican American was elected to Congress, and four others followed in the 1960s. In the late 1960s a new kind of Mexican American political movement was born. Inspired by the black civil rights movement, Mexican American students launched boycotts of high school classes in East Los Angeles, Denver, and San Antonio. Students in colleges and universities across California joined in as well. Among their demands were bilingual education, an end to discrimination, and more cultural recognition. In Crystal City, Texas, which had been dominated by Anglo politicians despite a population that was overwhelmingly Mexican American, the newly formed La Raza Unida Party took over the city government.[54]

Since that time, Latino political strategy has developed along two tracks. One is a traditional ethnic-group path of voter registration and voting along ethnic lines. The second is a legal strategy using the various civil rights laws designed to ensure fair access to the political system. The Mexican American Legal Defense and Education Fund (MALDEF), founded in 1968, has played a key role in designing and pursuing the latter strategy.

Asian Americans

Like the term "Latino," the label "Asian American" encompasses a wide range of people from very different national backgrounds who came to the United States at different moments in history. As a consequence, they have had very diverse experiences.

The early Asian experience in the United States was shaped by a series of naturalization laws dating back to 1790, the first of which declared that only white aliens were eligible for citizenship. Chinese immigrants began arriving in California in the 1850s, drawn by the boom of the gold rush, but they were immediately met with hostility. The virulent antagonism toward Chinese immigrants in California led Congress to declare Chinese immigrants ineligible for citizenship in 1870. In 1882, the first Chinese Exclusion Act suspended the entry of Chinese laborers.

At the time of the Exclusion Act, the Chinese community was composed predominantly of single male laborers, with few women and children. The few Chinese children in San Francisco were initially denied entry to the public schools; only after parents of American-born Chinese children pressed legal action were the children allowed to attend public school. Even then, however, they were segregated into a separate Chinese school. American-born Chinese children could not be denied citizenship, however; this right was confirmed by the Supreme Court in 1898, when it ruled in *United States v. Wong Kim Ark* that anyone born in the

Asian immigrants faced discrimination throughout much of American history. During World War II, Americans of Japanese descent were forced from their homes and confined in internment camps. At the time, the Supreme Court supported this denial of civil rights as a necessary security measure.

United States was entitled to full citizenship.[55] Still, new Chinese immigrants were barred from the United States until 1943, after China had become a key wartime ally and Congress repealed the Chinese Exclusion Act and permitted Chinese residents to become citizens.

The earliest Japanese immigrants, who came to California in the 1880s at the height of the anti-Chinese movement, faced similar discrimination. Like Chinese immigrants, Japanese immigrants were ineligible to become citizens because of their race. During the first part of the twentieth century, California and several other western states enacted laws that denied Japanese immigrants the right to own property. The denial of basic civil rights to Japanese Americans culminated in the decision to remove forcibly Americans of Japanese descent as well as Japanese noncitizen residents from their homes and confine them in internment camps during World War II. Despite a vigorous legal challenge, the Supreme Court ruled that the internment was constitutional on the grounds of military necessity.[56] Not until the Civil Liberties Act of 1988 did the federal government formally acknowledge this denial of civil rights as a "grave injustice" that had been "motivated largely by racial prejudice, wartime hysteria, and a failure of political leadership."[57] Along with a formal apology from the president, Congress issued each person interned a $20,000 check.

Asian immigration increased rapidly after the 1965 Immigration Act, which lifted discriminatory quotas. In spite of this and other developments, limited English proficiency barred many new Asian American and Latino immigrants from full participation in American life. Two developments in the 1970s, however, established rights for language minorities. In 1974, the Supreme Court ruled in *Lau v. Nichols,* a suit filed on behalf of Chinese students in San Francisco, that school districts have to provide education for students whose English is limited.[58] It did not mandate bilingual education, but it established a duty to provide instruction that the students could understand. As we saw earlier, the 1970 amendments to the Voting Rights Act permanently outlawed literacy tests in all fifty states and mandated bilingual ballots or oral assistance for those who speak Spanish, Chinese, Japanese, Korean, Native American languages, or Eskimo languages.

IMMIGRANTS AND CIVIL RIGHTS Asian Americans and Latinos have also been among the groups concerned about the impact of immigration laws on civil rights. Many Asian American and Latino organizations opposed the Immigration Reform and Control Act of 1986 because it imposed sanctions on employers who hire undocumented workers. Such sanctions, they feared, would lead employers to discriminate against Latinos and Asian Americans. These suspicions were confirmed in a 1990 report by the General Accounting Office that found employer sanctions had created a "widespread pattern of discrimination" against Latinos and others who appear foreign.[59] Organizations such as MALDEF and the Asian Law Caucus monitor and challenge such discrimination. These groups have turned their attention to the rights of legal and illegal immigrants, as anti-immigrant sentiment has grown in recent years.

The Supreme Court has ruled that unauthorized immigrants are eligible for education and medical care but can be denied other social benefits; legal immigrants are to be treated much the same as citizens. But growing immigration—including an estimated 300,000 unauthorized immigrants per year—and mounting economic insecurity have undermined these practices. Groups of voters across the country now strongly support drawing a sharper line between immigrants and citizens. The movement to deny benefits to noncitizens began

For Critical Analysis

Would newly legalized "guest workers" lower wages and deprive citizens of jobs? What policy might maintain some equity between the newly documented low-wage workers and the existing workforce?

in California, which experienced sharp economic distress in the early 1990s and has the highest levels of immigration of any state. In 1994, Californians voted in favor of Proposition 187, denying unauthorized immigrants all services except emergency medical care. Supporters of the measure hoped to discourage unauthorized immigration and to pressure those already in the country to leave. Opponents contended that denying basic services to unauthorized immigrants risked creating a subclass of residents in the United States whose lack of education and poor health would threaten all Americans. In 1994 and 1997, a federal court declared most of Proposition 187 unconstitutional, affirming previous rulings that unauthorized immigrants should be granted public education. A booming economy helped to reduce public concern about unauthorized immigration, but supporters of Proposition 187 promised to reintroduce similar measures in the future.

Questions about the rights of unauthorized immigrants became especially contentious in 2007. Former president Bush attempted in 2004 and again in 2006 to promote legislation to overhaul the nation's immigration law, which had not seen major revision since 1986. Since that time, the number of unauthorized immigrants had grown to an estimated 12 million. In 2007, Congress considered a complex compromise bill—running some 761 pages long—that attempted to accomplish three goals: increase border security to reduce the entrance of undocumented immigrants; provide unauthorized immigrants who had been in the country for at least five years with a pathway to legal citizenship; and ensure employers an adequate supply of temporary immigrant workers through a guest worker program. The compromise failed in the face of opposition from the Right, which disliked the provisions for creating a path to legal citizenship, and from the Left, which opposed the proposed guest worker program.

Politics Today

What do you think the federal government should do to address the issue of illegal immigration?

In the aftermath of the failed legislation, the federal government stepped up enforcement of existing laws. In 2007, federal immigration authorities warned employers that they would be subject to penalties if they could not vouch for the legal status of their employees. The authorities also increased raids on workplaces suspected of employing undocumented workers. At the same time, states and localities passed a wide assortment of new immigration measures, leading to a tangled array of conflicting laws. For example, in 2007 Illinois enacted legislation banning employers from using a federal database called E-Verify to determine the legal status of their employees. The state believed that E-Verify was unreliable and would lead employers to fire some legal employees. The federal Department of Homeland Security responded with a lawsuit that aimed to force Illinois to change its law. Oklahoma went in the opposite direction from Illinois, passing laws that made it a felony to transport or employ undocumented immigrants. The law also gave local police the right to check immigration status if they suspected that someone was not a legal immigrant.[60] Latino organizations, including the National Council of La Raza, initiated lawsuits against the Oklahoma laws on the grounds that they violate the civil rights of legal immigrants. In the absence of new federal legislation that addresses the large numbers of undocumented immigrants in the country, the conflicting policies and lawsuits are likely to continue, with no end in sight.

Native Americans

The political status of Native Americans was left unclear in the Constitution. But by the early 1800s, the courts had defined each of the Indian tribes as a nation.

As members of Indian nations, Native Americans were declared noncitizens of the United States. The political status of Native Americans changed in 1924, when congressional legislation granted citizenship to all persons born in the United States. A variety of changes in federal policy toward Native Americans during the 1930s paved the way for a later resurgence of their political power. Most important was the federal decision to encourage Native Americans on reservations to establish local self-government.[61]

The Native American political movement gathered force in the 1960s, as Native Americans began to use protest, litigation, and assertion of tribal rights to improve their situation. In 1968, Dennis Banks, Herb Powless, and Clyde Bellecourt cofounded the American Indian Movement (AIM), the most prominent Native American rights organization. AIM won national attention in 1969 when 200 of its members, representing twenty different tribes, took over the famous prison island of Alcatraz in San Francisco Bay, claiming it for Native Americans. The federal government responded to the rise in Indian activism with the Indian Self-Determination and Education Assistance Act, which began to give Indians more control over their own land.[62]

As a language minority, Native Americans were also affected by the 1975 amendments to the Voting Rights Act and the *Lau* decision. The *Lau* decision established the right of Native Americans to be taught in their own languages. This marked quite a change from the boarding schools once run by the Bureau of Indian Affairs, at which members of Indian tribes had been forbidden to speak their own languages. In addition to these language-related issues, Native Americans have sought to expand their rights on the basis of their sovereign status. Since the 1920s and 1930s, Native American tribes have sued the federal government for illegally seizing land, seeking monetary reparations and land as damages. Both types of damages have been awarded in such suits, but only in small amounts. Native American tribes have been more successful in winning federal recognition of their sovereignty. Sovereign status has, in turn, allowed them to exercise greater self-determination. Most significant in economic terms was a 1987 Supreme Court decision that freed Native American tribes from most state regulations prohibiting gambling. The establishment of casino gambling on Native American lands has brought a substantial flow of new income into desperately poor reservations.

Disabled Americans

The concept of rights for the disabled began to emerge in the 1970s as the civil rights model spread to other groups. The seed was planted in a little-noticed provision of the 1973 Rehabilitation Act, which outlawed discrimination against individuals on the basis of disabilities. As in many other cases, the law itself helped give rise to the movement demanding rights for the handicapped.[63] Modeling itself on the NAACP's Legal Defense Fund, the disability movement founded a Disability Rights Education and Defense Fund to press its legal claims. The movement achieved its greatest success with the

Same-sex couples lined up to obtain marriage licenses at San Francisco's city hall in 2004. The California Supreme Court eventually voided the marriages, but in 2008 it changed course, ruling that same-sex marriages were legal under the California constitution.

passage of the Americans with Disabilities Act (ADA) of 1990, which guarantees equal employment rights and access to public businesses for the disabled. Claims of discrimination in violation of this act are considered by the Equal Employment Opportunity Commission. The impact of the law has been far reaching, as businesses and public facilities have installed ramps, elevators, and other devices to meet the act's requirements.[64] In 1998, the Supreme Court interpreted the ADA to apply to people with HIV. Until then, ADA was interpreted as covering people with AIDS but not people with HIV. The case arose when a dentist was asked to fill a cavity for a woman with HIV; he refused unless the procedure was done in a hospital setting. The woman sued, and her complaint was that HIV had already disabled her because it was discouraging her from having children. (The act prohibits discrimination in employment, housing, and in health care.) Despite widespread concerns that the ADA was being expanded too broadly and the costs were becoming too burdensome, corporate America did not seem to be disturbed by the Court's ruling. Stephen Bokat, general counsel of the U.S. Chamber of Commerce, said businesses in general had already been accommodating people with HIV as well as with AIDS and that the case presented no serious problem.[65]

The Aged

Age discrimination in employment is illegal. The 1967 federal Age Discrimination in Employment Act (ADEA) makes age discrimination illegal when practiced by employers with at least twenty employees. Many states have added to the federal provisions with their own age discrimination laws, and some such state laws are stronger than the federal provisions. The major lobbyist for seniors, the AARP, formerly the American Association of Retired Persons (see Chapter 11), with its claim to over 30 million members, has been active in keeping these laws on the books and making sure that they are vigorously implemented.

Gays and Lesbians

In less than thirty years, the gay and lesbian movement has become one of the largest civil rights movements in contemporary America. Beginning with street protests in the 1960s, the movement has grown into a well-financed and sophisticated lobby. The Human Rights Campaign is the primary national political action committee (PAC) focused on gay rights; it provides campaign financing and volunteers to work for candidates endorsed by the group. The movement has also formed legal-rights organizations, including the Lambda Legal Defense and Education Fund.

Gay and lesbian rights drew national attention in 1993, when President Bill Clinton confronted the question of whether gays should be allowed to serve in the military. As a candidate, Clinton had said he favored lifting the ban on homosexuals in the military. The issue set off a huge controversy in the first months of Clinton's presidency. After nearly a year of deliberation, the administration enunciated a compromise: its "Don't ask, don't tell" policy. This policy allows gays and lesbians to serve in the military as long as they do not openly proclaim their sexual orientation or engage in homosexual activity. The administration maintained that the ruling would protect gays and lesbians against witchhunting investigations, but many gay and lesbian advocates expressed disappointment, charging the president with reneging on his campaign promise.

Affirmative action programs seek to overcome past discrimination against a group by practicing benign discrimination—providing additional opportunities for those who face discrimination. Here, women's rights advocates call for more opportunities for women and equal pay for equal work.

But until 1996, there was no Supreme Court ruling or national legislation explicitly protecting gays and lesbians from discrimination. The first gay-rights case that the Court decided, *Bowers v. Hardwick*, ruled against a right to privacy that would protect consensual homosexual activity.[66] After the *Bowers* decision, the gay and lesbian rights movement sought suitable legal cases to test the constitutionality of discrimination against gays and lesbians, much as the black civil rights movement had done in the late 1940s and 1950s. As one advocate put it, "lesbians and gay men are looking for their *Brown v. Board of Education*."[67] Test cases stemmed from local ordinances restricting gay rights (including the right to marry), job discrimination, and family law issues such as adoption and parental rights. In 1996, the Supreme Court, in *Romer v. Evans*, explicitly extended fundamental civil rights protections to gays and lesbians, by declaring unconstitutional a 1992 amendment to the Colorado state constitution that prohibited local governments from passing ordinances to protect gay rights.[68] The decision's forceful language highlighted the connection between gay rights and civil rights as it declared discrimination against gay people unconstitutional.

In *Lawrence v. Texas* (2003), the Court overturned *Bowers* and struck down a Texas statute criminalizing certain intimate sexual conduct between consenting partners of the same sex.[69] A victory for lesbians and gays every bit as significant as *Roe v. Wade* was for women, *Lawrence v. Texas* extends at least one aspect of civil liberties to sexual minorities: the right to privacy. However, this decision by itself does not undo the various exclusions that deprive lesbians and gays full civil rights, including the right to marry, which became a hot-button issue in 2004 and remains one today.

In San Francisco hundreds of gays and lesbians lined up to obtain marriage licenses after the mayor directed the county clerk to issue licenses to same-sex couples

Politics Today

In 2008, California's supreme court ruled that state law allowed gays and lesbians to marry. Do you think changing public attitudes will lead more states to enact laws legalizing gay marriage in the future?

Affirmative Action

The sweeping civil rights laws enacted in the 1960s officially ended state-sanctioned segregation. They did not, however, end racism or erase stark inequities between the races in such areas as employment and education. As a consequence, affirmative action policies were enacted to ensure some equality between the races.

Proponents of affirmative action cite the continued need for such programs, especially for African Americans, because of the nation's long history of discrimination and persecution. Racism was institutionalized throughout most of the country's history; indeed, the Constitution specifically recognized, and therefore countenanced, slavery. For example, it rewarded slave owners with the Three-fifths Compromise, giving slave owners extra representation in the House of Representatives, a provision excised from the Constitution only after the Civil War. Moreover, few would deny that racism still exists in America. Given these facts, it follows that equal treatment of unequals perpetuates inequality. Programs that give an extra boost to traditionally disadvantaged groups offer the only sure way to overcome structural inequality.

To take the example of university and college admissions, affirmative action opponents argue that admissions decisions should be based on merit, not race. Yet affirmative action does not disregard merit, and in any case, admissions does not operate purely on the basis of merit, however defined, for any college or university. Institutions of higher education rely on such measures as grade point average, board scores, and letters of recommendation. But they also consider such nonmerit factors as region, urban vs. rural background, family relationship to alumni and wealthy donors, athletic ability, and other specialized factors unrelated to the usual definition of merit. The inclusion of race as one of these many admissions criteria is as defensible as the inclusion of any other; moreover, it helps ensure a more diverse student body, which in itself is a laudable educational goal. In addition, such programs do not guarantee educational success, but simply assure that individuals from disadvantaged groups have a chance to succeed, an idea most Americans support. Affirmative action programs have in fact succeeded in providing opportunity to millions who would not otherwise have had it.

Opponents of affirmative action argue that such programs, while based on good intentions, do more harm than good. The belief that persons who gain employment or college admission from such programs did not earn their positions stigmatizes those who are supposed to benefit, creating self-doubt among the recipients and mistrust in others. In the realm of education, students admitted to colleges and universities under these special programs have lower graduation rates. Affirmative action also violates the fundamental American value of equality of opportunity. Although all may not possess the same opportunity, the effort expended to provide special advantages to some would be better directed toward making sure that the principles of equal opportunity and merit are followed.

America's history of discrimination, though reprehensible, should not be used as a basis for employment or educational decisions, because it is unreasonable to ask Americans today to pay for the mistakes of their ancestors. Moreover, the track record of affirmative action programs reveals another problem: the groups that have benefited most are middle-class African Americans and women. If anything, preferential programs should focus on *economic* disadvantage, regardless of race, and better education early in life. Good intentions notwithstanding, there are limits to what government social engineering can accomplish, and most Americans favor the abandonment of race-based preference programs.

FOR CRITICAL ANALYSIS

1. Supporters of affirmative action argue that it is intended to level an uneven playing field in which discrimination still exists. What do you think? To what extent is our society free from discrimination?
2. What is the impact of affirmative action on society today? What alternatives to affirmative action policies exist?

in defiance of California law. A significant victory came in 2004, when the Supreme Judicial Court of Massachusetts ruled that under that state's constitution, gay men and lesbians were entitled to marry. The state senate then requested the court to rule on whether a civil-union statute (avoiding the word "marriage") would, as it did in Vermont, satisfy the court's ruling. The court ruled negatively, asserting that civil unions were too much like the "separate but equal" doctrine that maintained legalized racial segregation from 1896 to 1954. In the years that followed, gay rights advocates in Massachusetts launched a large-scale political mobilization to defeat a legislative campaign to enact a constitutional ban on gay marriage. Their success in 2007 ensured the legality of gay marriage in Massachusetts. In 2008 California became the second state to make gay and lesbian marriage legal. The state supreme court ruled that marriage was a fundamental right and that marriage laws could not discriminate against same-sex couples. Once again couples lined up to marry in California, this time with the approval of the state's highest court. However, in November 2008, voters overturned the court's ruling by voting on an initiative declaring that only marriage between a man and a woman should be legally recognized. In 2008, Connecticut's high court also ruled in favor of gay marriage.

Affirmative Action

Not only has the politics of rights spread to increasing numbers of groups in American society since the 1960s, but it has also expanded its goal. The relatively narrow goal of equalizing opportunity by eliminating discriminatory barriers evolved into the far broader goal of **affirmative action**—compensatory action to overcome the consequences of past discrimination. Affirmative action policies take race or some other status into account in order to provide greater opportunities to groups that have previously been at a disadvantage due to discrimination.

affirmative action government policies or programs that seek to redress past injustices against specified groups by making special efforts to provide members of these groups with access to educational and employment opportunities

President Lyndon Johnson put the case emotionally in 1965: "You do not take a person who, for years, has been hobbled by chains . . . and then say you are free to compete with all the others, and still just believe that you have been completely fair."[70] Johnson attempted to inaugurate affirmative action by executive orders directing agency heads and personnel officers to pursue vigorously a policy of minority employment in the federal civil service and in companies doing business with the national government. But affirmative action did not become a prominent goal of the national government until the 1970s.

Affirmative action also took the form of efforts by the agencies in the Department of Health, Education, and Welfare to shift their focus from "desegregation" to "integration."[71] Federal agencies—sometimes with court orders and sometimes without them—required school districts to present plans for busing children across district lines, for pairing schools, for closing certain schools, and for redistributing faculties as well as students, under pain of loss of grants-in-aid from the federal government. The guidelines issued for such plans constituted preferential treatment to compensate for past discrimination, and without this legislatively assisted approach to integration orders, there would certainly not have been the dramatic increase in black children attending integrated classes. The yellow school bus became a symbol of hope for many and a signal of defeat for others.

Affirmative action was also initiated in the area of employment opportunity. The Equal Employment Opportunity Commission often has required plans whereby employers must attempt to increase the number of their minority employees,

TABLE 5.3 ★ Supreme Court Rulings on Affirmative Action	
CASE	COURT RULING
Regents of the University of California v. Bakke, 438 U.S. 265 (1978)	Affirmative action upheld, but quotas and separate admission for minorities rejected; burden of proof on defendant
Wards Cove v. Atonio, 490 U.S. 642 (1989)	All affirmative action programs put in doubt: burden of proof shifted from defendant to plaintiff (victim), then burden of proof shifted back to employers (defendants)
St. Mary's Honor Center v. Hicks, 113 S.Ct. 2742 (1993)	Required victim to prove discrimination was intentional
Adarand Constructors v. Pena, 515 U.S. 200 (1995)	All race-conscious policies must survive "strict scrutiny," with burden of proof on government to show the program serves "compelling interest" to redress past discrimination
Hopwood v. Texas, 78 F3d 932 (5th Cir., 1996)	Race can *never* be used as a factor in admission, even to promote diversity (Supreme Court refusal to review limited application to the Fifth Circuit—Texas, Louisiana, Mississippi)
Gratz v. Bollinger, 123 S.Ct. 2411 (2003)	Rejection of a "mechanical" point system favoring minority applicants to University of Michigan as tantamount to a quota; *Bakke* reaffirmed
Grutter v. Bollinger, 123 S.Ct. 2325 (2003)	Upheld race-conscious admission to Michigan Law School, passing strict scrutiny with diversity as a "compelling" state interest, as long as admission was "highly individualized" and not "mechanical" as in *Gratz*

and the Office of Federal Contract Compliance Programs in the Department of Labor has used the threat of contract revocation for the same purpose. Increases in the number of minorities did not require formal quotas.

The Supreme Court and the Burden of Proof

Efforts by the executive, legislative, and judicial branches to shape the meaning of affirmative action today tend to center on a key issue: what is the appropriate level of review in affirmative action cases—that is, on whom should the burden of proof be placed, the plaintiff or the defendant? Affirmative action was first addressed formally by the Supreme Court in the case of Allan Bakke (see Table 5.3). Bakke, a white male, brought suit against the University of California at Davis Medical School on the grounds that in denying him admission the school had discriminated against him on the basis of his race (that year the school had reserved 16 of 100 available slots for minority applicants). He argued that his grades and test scores had ranked him well above many students who had been accepted at the school and that the only possible explanation for his rejection was that those others accepted were black or Latino, whereas he was white. In 1978, Bakke won his case before the Supreme Court and was admitted to the medical school, but the Court stopped short of declaring affirmative action unconstitutional. The Court rejected the procedures at the University of California because its medical school had used both a quota *and* a separate admissions system for minorities. The Court accepted the argument that achieving "a diverse student body" was a "compelling public purpose," but found that the method of a rigid quota of student slots assigned on the basis of race was incompatible with the equal protection clause. Thus, the Court permitted universities (and presumably other schools, training programs, and hiring authorities) to continue to take minority status into consideration, but limited severely the use of quotas to situations in which (1) previous discrimination had been shown, and (2) it was used more as a guideline for social diversity than as a mathematically defined ratio.[72]

For nearly a decade after *Bakke*, the Supreme Court was tentative and permissive about efforts by universities, corporations, and governments to experiment with affirmative action programs.[73] But in 1989, with the case of *Wards Cove v. Atonio*, the Court backed away further from affirmative action by easing the way for employers to prefer white males, holding that the burden of proof of unlawful discrimination should be shifted from the defendant (the employer) to the plaintiff (the person claiming to be the victim of discrimination).[74] Congress reacted with the Civil Rights Act of 1991, which shifted the burden of proof in employment discrimination cases back to employers.

In 1995, the Supreme Court's ruling in *Adarand Constructors v. Pena* further weakened affirmative action. This decision stated that race-based policies, such as preferences given by the government to minority contractors, must survive strict scrutiny, placing the burden on the government to show that such affirmative action programs serve a compelling government interest and are narrowly tailored to address identifiable past discrimination.[75] President Clinton responded to the *Adarand* decision by ordering a review of all government affirmative action policies and practices and adopted an informal policy of trying to "mend, not end" affirmative action.

This betwixt and between status of affirmative action was how things stood in 2003, when the Supreme Court took two cases against the University of Michigan that were virtually certain to clarify, if not put closure on, affirmative action. The first suit, *Gratz v. Bollinger* (the university president), was against the University of Michigan's undergraduate admissions policy and practices, alleging that by using a point-based ranking system that automatically awarded 20 points (out of 150) to African American, Latino, and Native American applicants, the university discriminated unconstitutionally against white students of otherwise equal or superior academic qualifications. The Supreme Court agreed, 6-to-3, arguing that something tantamount to a quota was involved because undergraduate admissions lacked the necessary "individualized consideration," employing instead a "mechanical one," based too much on the favorable minority points.[76] The Court's ruling in *Gratz v. Bollinger* was not surprising, given *Bakke*'s (1978) holding against quotas and given recent decisions calling for strict scrutiny of all

Television and Public Opinion Regarding Minority Groups

Americans' support for the rights of minority groups often hinges on the way they perceive those groups, and some researchers believe that television plays a significant role in shaping people's perceptions of minority groups.

Depictions of African Americans in popular culture have a long and complicated history, from the mocking portrayals in early radio and television programs like *Amos 'n' Andy* to contemporary programs like *Everyone Hates Chris.* In the late 1980s, the sitcom *The Cosby Show* provoked concern that portrayals of upper-middle class African Americans could create a false perception of African American affluence. In 1989, the chair of Harvard's department of African American Studies, Henry Louis Gates, Jr., argued that there was a fundamental disconnect between the socioeconomic status of African Americans in programs such as *Cosby* and the actual status of most African Americans at the time. *The Cosby Show* starred Bill Cosby as a successful doctor married to a lawyer. The problem, according to critics such as Gates, was that, "As the dominant representation of blacks on TV, it suggests that blacks are solely responsible for their social conditions, with no acknowledgement of the severely constricted life opportunities that most black people face."[a] In fact, according to one study of white viewers, exposure to the affluent *Cosby* family led some to believe that affirmative action was unnecessary.

A different concern about television portrayals of African Americans is that the mass media may contribute to perceptions of black men as criminals. Some research has shown that news coverage of crime tends to portray African American suspects as more threatening than white suspects. Studies confirm that negative stereotypical portrayals of African Americans on television foster negative attitudes towards African Americans among white audience members. Similarly, recent research suggests that the television and film portrayal of Hispanics as drug lords may contribute to enduring public views that Latinos are susceptible of violence.

Public opinion about gays and lesbians may also be linked to recent trends in media. Traditionally, gays and lesbians in America have been one of the most marginalized minority groups. Yet, the political scientist Alan Yang has presented data showing that Americans are becoming more accepting of gays and lesbians and same-sex marriage. During this same time period, portrayals of gays and lesbians on television have become more diverse and more frequent. One recent example of a popular program featuring gay characters was the comedy *Will and Grace,* which debuted on NBC in 1998. While the show received criticism from some who said it reinforced gay stereotypes (the flamboyant character Jack in particular), other research suggests that the program had positive effects on the status of gays in society. As reality television shows have gained, gays and lesbians have also been well represented on such shows as *Top Chef, Project Runway,* and *Queer Eye for the Straight Guy.*

But how might these portrayals of minorities on television translate into public opinion and eventually policy concerning rights? According to one theory, viewing programs including minority characters is associated with lower levels of prejudice. Another view is that television portrayals of minority groups are influenced by public opinion, not the other way around.

FOR CRITICAL ANALYSIS

1. Do you think that the way minority groups are portrayed on television is likely to have a major effect on support for those groups' rights?
2. Even if public opinion toward gays and lesbians shifts dramatically over the next several years, will that necessarily translate into more rights for gays? What are some factors that might foster a gap between public opinion toward gays and public policy toward gay rights?

a. H. L. Gates, "TV's Black World Turns—But Stays Unreal," *New York Times,* November 12, 1989, sec. 2, p. 1.

racial classifications, even those that are intended to remedy past discrimination or promote future equality.

The second case, *Grutter v. Bollinger,* broke new ground. Grutter sued the law school on the grounds that it had discriminated in a race-conscious way against white applicants with equal or superior grades and law boards. A precarious majority of 5-to-4 aligned the majority of the Supreme Court with Justice Powell's lone plurality opinion in *Bakke* for the first time. In *Bakke,* Powell argued that (1) diversity in education is a compelling state interest and (2) race could be constitutionally considered as a plus factor in admissions decisions. In *Grutter,* the Court reiterated Powell's holding and, applying strict scrutiny to the law school's policy, found that the law school's admissions process is narrowly tailored to the school's compelling state interest in diversity because it gives a "highly individualized, holistic review of each applicant's file" in which race counts but is not used in a "mechanical" way.[77] The Court's ruling that racial categories can be deployed to serve a compelling state interest puts affirmative action on stronger ground. Even so, a 2006 state referendum (see below) outlawing affirmative action led the University of Michigan to abandon its affirmative action program in 2007.

Referenda on Affirmative Action

The courts have not been the only center of action: during the 1990s, challenges to affirmative action also emerged in state and local politics. One of the most significant state actions was the passage of the California Civil Rights Initiative, also known as Proposition 209, in 1996. Proposition 209 outlawed affirmative action programs in the state and local governments of California, thus prohibiting state and local governments from using race or gender preferences in their decisions about hiring, contracting, or university admissions. The political battle over Proposition 209 was heated, and supporters and defenders took to the streets as well as the airwaves to make their cases. When the referendum was held, the measure passed with 54 percent of the vote, including 27 percent of the black vote, 30 percent of the Latino vote, and 45 percent of the Asian American vote.[78] In 1997, the Supreme Court refused to hear a challenge to the new law. California's Proposition 209 was framed as a civil rights initiative: "the state shall not discriminate against, or grant preferential treatment to, any individual or group on the basis of race, sex, color, ethnicity, or national origin." Different wording can produce quite different outcomes, as a 1997 vote on affirmative action in Houston revealed. There, the ballot initiative asked voters whether they wanted to ban affirmative action in city contracting and hiring, not whether they wanted to end preferential treatment. Fifty-five percent of Houston voters decided in favor of affirmative action.[79] In 2006, 58 percent of Michigan voters voted to support a measure outlawing affirmative action in public education, contracting, and employment. Modeled after California's Proposition 209—and championed by the California anti-affirmative activist Ward Connerly—Michigan's Proposition 2 amended the state constitution to prohibit affirmative action. Although University of Michigan officials initially declared that they would continue to use affirmative action criteria in the admissions process until all legal appeals were exhausted, in early 2007 the university announced that it would stop using affirmative action procedures in admissions. Buoyed by their success in Michigan, affirmative action opponents planned to place similar initiatives on the ballot in Colorado, Missouri, Arizona, South Dakota, and Oklahoma in 2008.

TABLE 5.4 ★ Americans' Opinions on Racial Equality

Black and white Americans disagree somewhat on issues of affirmative action and progress toward racial equality. What factors explain their differing perceptions?

Dr. Martin Luther King gave his famous "I Have a Dream Speech" at a civil rights march in Washington in 1963. In your view, how much of Dr. King's "dream" that he talked about has been fulfilled today . . . ?

	ALL OF IT	A GREAT DEAL	A MODERATE AMOUNT	NOT VERY MUCH	NONE OF IT
All	6	37	45	10	1
Whites	6	37	47	8	1
Blacks	7	37	41	10	--

SOURCE: CNN/Opinion Research Corporation Poll, www.pollingreport.com/race.htm (accessed 3/28/09). Conducted January 14–January 17, 2008 and based on telephone interviews with a total of 513 African American respondents interviewed and 743 non-Hispanic whites. Results were weighted to be representative of a national adult population.

Thinking Critically about the Affirmative Action Debate

Affirmative action efforts have contributed to the polarization of the politics of civil rights. At the risk of grievous oversimplification, we can divide the sides by two labels: liberals and conservatives.[80] The conservatives' argument against affirmative action can be reduced to two major points. The first is that rights in the American tradition are *individual* rights, and affirmative action violates this concept by concerning itself with "group rights," an idea said to be alien to the American tradition. The second point has to do with quotas. Conservatives would argue that the Constitution is "color blind," and that any discrimination, even if it is called positive or benign discrimination, ultimately violates the equal protection clause.

The liberal side agrees that rights ultimately come down to individuals, but argues that since the essence of discrimination is the use of unreasonable and unjust criteria of exclusion to deprive *an entire group* of access to something valuable the society has to offer, then the phenomenon of discrimination itself has to be attacked on a group basis. Although many agree that there has been progress toward racial equality (see Table 5.4), liberals argue that race still matters. Liberals can also use Supreme Court history to support their side because the first definitive interpretation of the Fourteenth Amendment by the Court in 1873 stated explicitly that

> the existence of laws in the state where the newly emancipated Negroes resided, which discriminated with gross injustice and hardship against them *as a class*, was the evil to be remedied by this clause [emphasis added].[81]

Liberals also have a response to the other conservative argument concerning quotas. The liberal response is that the Supreme Court has already accepted ratios—a

Civil Rights on Campus

Imagine, for a moment, your campus as it might have been in 1950. The student body would be largely white because higher education for nonwhites was almost unthinkable unless they attended a handful of largely segregated minority institutions. The diverse faculty that you see today would be mostly absent. For example, women were discouraged from teaching and researching the subjects that they do today. If they did teach, women were often relegated to teaching home-economics related courses. The list of differences that would characterize your campus then versus now goes beyond these examples. But the point is simple—civil rights activism since 1950 has brought about significant social change.

Today there are many groups dedicated to advancing the cause of civil rights. For example, gay and lesbian groups argue that their civil rights are discriminated against on the basis of their sexuality. They believe, among other things, that their inability to marry in most states prevents them from enjoying many of the benefits that married heterosexual couples enjoy, such as tax deductions and the right to have a same-sex partner recognized by hospitals as a legal decision maker if the other partner is incapacitated.

Other groups advocating greater civil rights include undocumented immigrants and their supporters, who argue that despite their status as illegal citizens, they should still be afforded civil rights and legal protections because of the labor and financial contributions they make to society. For example, many immigrants pay Social Security taxes but never receive Social Security benefits. These and other groups have joined traditional civil rights organizations that continue to advocate for greater civil rights protections.

However, there is not always agreement that the civil rights of certain groups are being violated. For example, to many, the civil rights of women are not compromised by excluding them from certain combat positions in the military. For others this policy seems a clear civil rights violation.

Campuses often bring together diverse groups of people with different ideas regarding how society should function. The following ideas present ways that you can engage your fellow students on the issue of civil rights at your college or university.

- ★ Identify whether your college or university practices affirmative action in recruiting and admissions. For example, are certain racial and ethnic groups recruited more heavily, and do they receive different considerations during the admissions process? What about the consideration that's given to students whose parents are alumni of the same college?

- ★ Weigh in on what you think about your institution's affirmative action policies by writing a letter to the editor of your school newspaper, then see what kind of responses your letter generates. If your campus has a radio station, try using that as a venue for expressing your opinion about affirmative action at your college.

- ★ Find out what kind of groups on campus organize students with similar backgrounds. For example, the National Council of La Raza often has campus chapters for Latino students; the LGBT (lesbian, gay, bisexual, and transgendered) community may have a student organization on your campus. If you find one that you can identify with, consider joining and exploring the activism that group is engaged in to advocate for civil rights on campus.

- ★ Help organize a debate about civil rights on campus, perhaps through an organization such as those mentioned earlier. You can invite student panelists as well as representatives of interest groups on both sides of the issue that you'll be debating. The American Civil Liberties Union is one such group to contact for people who take a more liberal approach to civil rights issues. The American Conservative Union may be useful for putting you in touch with those who hold a conservative interpretation of civil rights.

form of quota—that are admitted as evidence to prove a "pattern or practice of discrimination" sufficient to reverse the burden of proof—to obligate the employer to show that there was *not* an intent to discriminate. Liberals can also argue that benign quotas often have been used by Americans both to compensate for some bad action in the past or to provide some desired distribution of social characteristics—sometimes called diversity. For example, a long and respected policy in the United States is that of "veteran's preference," on the basis of which the government automatically gives extra consideration in hiring to persons who have served the country in the armed forces. The justification is that ex-servicepeople deserve compensation for having made sacrifices for the good of the country. And the goal of social diversity has justified "positive discrimination," especially in higher education, the very institution where conservatives have most adamantly argued against positive quotas for blacks and women. For example, all of the Ivy League schools and many other private colleges and universities regularly and consistently reserve admissions places for some students whose qualifications in a strict academic sense are below those of others who are not admitted. These schools not only recruit students from minority groups, but they also set aside places for the children of loyal alumni and of their own faculty, even when, in a pure competition solely and exclusively based on test scores and high school records, many of those same children would not have been admitted. These practices are not conclusive justification in themselves, but they certainly underscore the liberal argument that affirmative or compensatory action for minorities who have been unjustly treated in the past is not alien to American experience.

If we think of the debate about affirmative action in terms of American political values, it is clear that conservatives emphasize liberty, whereas liberals stress equality. Conservatives believe that using government actively to promote equality for minorities and women infringes on the rights of white men. Lawsuits challenging affirmative action often cite this "reverse discrimination" as a justification. Liberals, on the other hand, traditionally have defended affirmative action as the best way to achieve equality. In recent years, however, the debate over affirmative action has become more complex and has created divisions among liberals. These divisions stem from growing doubts among some liberals about whether affirmative action can be defended as the best way to achieve equality and about the tensions between affirmative action and democratic values. One recent study of public opinion found that many self-identified liberals were angry about affirmative action.[82] These liberals felt that in the name of equality, affirmative action actually violates norms of fairness and equality of opportunity by giving special advantages to some. Moreover, it is argued, affirmative action is broadly unpopular and is therefore questionable in terms of democratic values. Because our nation has a history of slavery and legalized racial discrimination, and because discrimination continues to exist (although it has declined over time), the question of racial justice, more than any other issue, highlights the difficulty of reconciling our values in practice (see Table 5.4).

FOR FURTHER READING

Garrow, David J. *Bearing the Cross: Martin Luther King and the Southern Christian Leadership Conference: A Personal Portrait.* New York: Morrow, 1986.

Greenberg, Jack. *Crusaders in the Courts: How a Dedicated Band of Lawyers Fought for the Civil Rights Revolution.* New York: Basic Books, 1994.

Katznelson, Ira. *When Affirmative Action Was White: The Untold Story of Racial Inequality in Twentieth-Century America.* New York: Norton, 2006.

Klinkner, Philip A., and Rogers M. Smith. *The Unsteady March: The Rise and Decline of Racial Equality in America.* Chicago: University of Chicago Press, 1999.

Massey, Douglas S., and Nancy A. Denton. *American Apartheid: Segregation and the Making of the Underclass.* Cambridge, MA: Harvard University Press, 1993.

McClain, Paula D., and Joseph Stewart, Jr. *"Can We All Get Along?" Racial Minorities in American Politics.* 4th ed. Boulder, CO: Westview Press, 2005.

Mink, Gwendolyn. *Hostile Environment: The Political Betrayal of Sexually Harassed Women.* Ithaca, NY: Cornell University Press, 2000.

Nava, Michael. *Created Equal: Why Gay Rights Matter to America.* New York: St. Martin's, 1994.

Rosales, Francisco. *Chicano! The History of the Mexican American Civil Rights Movement.* Houston: Arte Público Press, 1997.

Rosenberg, Gerald N. *The Hollow Hope: Can Courts Bring About Social Change?* Chicago: University of Chicago Press, 1991.

Russell, Nancy. *Freedom is Not Enough: The Opening of the American Workplace.* Cambridge, MA: Harvard University Press, 2006.

Valelly, Richard. *The Voting Rights Act.* Washington, DC: CQ Press, 2005.

RECOMMENDED WEB SITES

ADA Home Page
www.ada.gov/

The Americans with Disabilities Act (ADA), enacted in 1990, guarantees equal employment rights and access to public businesses for the physically disabled. The U.S. Department of Justice maintains this Web site, which offers general information on ADA standards, changes in regulation, and policy enforcement.

Dr. Martin Luther King, Jr., Research and Education Institute
www.stanford.edu/group/King/

Dr. Martin Luther King, Jr. was a key leader in the fight for civil rights and desegregation. At this Web site you can find Dr. King's important speeches and papers, as well as other information about social injustice.

Equal Employment Opportunity Commission (EEOC)
www.eeoc.gov

This Web site provides information on the federal agency and current employment laws. At this site you can even find out how someone might file a harassment or discrimination charge against an employer.

Equality Now
www.equalitynow.org

This is an organization dedicated to ending gender discrimination around the world. Read about how this group is fighting for the rights of women in Africa or campaigning against female genital mutilation and sex trafficking.

Federal Bureau of Investigation
www.fbi.gov/hq/cid/civilrights/hate.htm

Civil rights violations fall under the jurisdiction of the Federal Bureau of Investigation. Find out what steps the FBI is taking to combat the problem of hate crimes and view some comprehensive statistical data.

Human Rights Campaign (HRC)
www.hrc.org
Gay and Lesbian Alliance Against Defamation (GLAAD)
www.glaad.org

These two prominent interest groups are dedicated to equal rights for gays and lesbians and ending gender discrimination.

League of United Latin American Citizens (LULAC)
www.mundo.com/lulac.html

LULAC has worked to stem discrimination against Mexican Americans since World War II and is now the largest and oldest Hispanic organization in the United States. See what this group is doing to guarantee racial equality based on the Fourteenth Amendment's equal protection clause.

Mexican American Legal Defense and Education Fund (MALDEF)
www.maldef.org/

MALDEF is the leading nonprofit Latino litigation, advocacy, and educational outreach institution in the United States. At this site, you will learn about litigation and other activities that MALDEF has initiated related to the rights of Latinos and of immigrants more generally.

NAACP
www.naacp.org

The NAACP is one of the oldest and largest civil rights organizations that is dedicated to equal rights and putting an end to racial discrimination. This group was particularly influential in the landmark case *Brown v. Board of Education*, which led to the desegregation of public schools.

National Organization for Women
www.now.org
Feminist Majority Foundation
www.feminist.org

These leading women's rights groups continue to fight for gender equality and equal rights.

U.S. Commission on Civil Rights
www.usccr.gov

The U.S. Commission on Civil Rights was created by Congress in the late 1950s and continues to investigate complaints of discrimination in American society.

U.S. Supreme Court Media
www.oyez.org

This Web site has a good search engine for finding information on such landmark civil rights cases as *Plessy v. Ferguson*, *Brown v. Board of Education*, *Lawrence v. Texas*, or *United States v. Wong Kim Ark*, to name only a few.

STUDY OUTLINE

www.wwnorton.com/wtp7e

The Struggle for Civil Rights

1. From 1896 until the end of World War II, the Supreme Court held that racial distinction did not violate the Fourteenth Amendment's equal protection clause as long as the facilities were equal.
2. After World War II, the Supreme Court began to undermine the separate but equal doctrine, eventually declaring it unconstitutional in *Brown v. Board of Education*.
3. The *Brown* decision marked the beginning of a difficult battle for equal protection in education, employment, housing, voting, and other areas of social and economic activity.
4. The first phase of school desegregation was met with such massive resistance in the South that ten years after *Brown*, fewer than 1 percent of black children in the South were attending schools with whites.
5. In 1971, the Supreme Court held that state-imposed desegregation could be brought about by busing children across school districts.
6. Title VII of the Civil Rights Act of 1964 outlawed job discrimination by all private and public employers, including governmental agencies, that employed more than fifteen workers.
7. In 1965, Congress significantly strengthened legislation protecting voting rights by barring literacy and other tests as a condition for voting in southern states. In the long run, the laws extending and protecting voting rights could prove to be the most effective of all civil rights legislation, because increased political participation by minorities has altered the shape of American politics.

The Universalization of Civil Rights

1. The protections won by the African American civil rights movement spilled over to protect other groups as well, including women, Latinos, Asian Americans, Native Americans, disabled Americans, and gays and lesbians.

Affirmative Action

1. By seeking to provide compensatory action to overcome the consequences of past discrimination, affirmative action has expanded the goals of groups championing minority rights.
2. Affirmative action has been a controversial policy. Opponents charge that affirmative action creates group rights and establishes quotas, both of which are inimical to the American tradition. Proponents of affirmative action argue that the long history of group discrimination makes affirmative action necessary and that efforts to compensate for some bad action in the past are well within the federal government's purview. Recent conflicts over affirmative action have raised questions about what is effective political action.

PRACTICE QUIZ

www.wwnorton.com/wtp7e

1. When did civil rights become part of the Constitution?
   a) in 1789 at the Founding
   b) with the adoption of the Fourteenth Amendment in 1868
   c) with the adoption of the Nineteenth Amendment in 1920
   d) in the 1954 *Brown v. Board of Education* case
2. Which civil rights case established the "separate but equal" rule?
   a) *Plessy v. Ferguson*
   b) *Brown v. Board of Education*
   c) *Regents of the University of California v. Bakke*
   d) *Adarand Constructors v. Pena*
3. "Massive resistance" refers to efforts by southern states during the late 1950s and early 1960s to
   a) build public housing for poor blacks.
   b) defy federal mandates to desegregate public schools.
   c) give women the right to have an abortion.
   d) bus black students to white schools.
4. Which of the following organizations established a Legal Defense Fund to challenge segregation?
   a) the Association of American Trial Lawyers
   b) the National Association for the Advancement of Colored People
   c) the Student Nonviolent Coordinating Committee
   d) the Southern Christian Leadership Council
5. Which of the following made discrimination by private employers and state governments illegal?
   a) the Fourteenth Amendment
   b) *Brown v. Board of Education*
   c) the 1964 Civil Rights Act
   d) *Regents of the University of California v. Bakke*
6. In what way does the struggle for gender equality most resemble the struggle for racial equality?
   a) There has been very little political action in realizing the goal.
   b) Changes in government policies to a great degree produced political action.
   c) The Supreme Court has not ruled on the issue.
   d) No legislation has passed adopting the aims of the movement.
7. Which of the following is *not* an example of an area in which women have made progress since the 1970s in guaranteeing certain civil rights?
   a) sexual harassment
   b) integration into all-male publicly supported universities
   c) more equal funding for college women's varsity athletic programs
   d) the passage of the Equal Rights Amendment
8. Which of the following civil rights measures dealt with access to public businesses and accommodations?
   a) the 1990 Americans with Disabilities Act
   b) the 1964 Civil Rights Act
   c) neither a nor b
   d) both a and b
9. Which of the following cases represents the *Brown v. Board of Education* case for lesbians and gay men?
   a) *Bowers v. Hardwick*
   b) *Lau v. Nichols*
   c) *Romer v. Evans*
   d) There has not been a Supreme Court ruling explicitly protecting gays and lesbians from discrimination.
10. In what case did the Supreme Court find that "rigid quotas" are incompatible with the equal protection clause of the Fourteenth Amendment?
    a) *Regents of the University of California v. Bakke*
    b) *Brown v. Board of Education*
    c) *United States v. Nixon*
    d) *Immigration and Naturalization Service v. Chadha*

KEY TERMS

www.wwnorton.com/wtp7e

affirmative action (p. 191)
Brown v. Board of Education (p. 166)
civil rights (p. 159)
de facto (p. 168)
de jure (p. 168)
discrimination (p. 159)
equal protection clause (p. 159)
Fifteenth Amendment (p. 161)
Fourteenth Amendment (p. 161)
gerrymandering (p. 175)
intermediate scrutiny (p. 179)
"Jim Crow" laws (p. 162)
redlining (p. 177)
"separate but equal" rule (p. 163)
strict scrutiny (p. 167)
Thirteenth Amendment (p. 161)

PART II

Politics

6 Public Opinion

- Understanding Public Opinion
- How We Form Political Opinions
- Measuring Public Opinion
- Thinking Critically about Public Opinion and Democracy

WHAT GOVERNMENT DOES AND WHY IT MATTERS

In a democracy, we expect the government to pay attention to public opinion. If the government's programs and policies do not seem consistent with popular preferences, we often begin to question the legitimacy of the government's actions. In 2007 and 2008, many Americans questioned why American forces remained in Iraq even though most Americans had concluded that it was time to bring the troops home. Americans also wonder why on issues ranging from gun control through health care, the government never seems to be able to do what the public wants. Policy makers reply that the people often speak with many voices that are hard to reconcile and interpret. Sometimes, say public officials, their job is to do what's right even if it is unpopular. President Bush, for example, once pointed to the fact that President Abraham Lincoln became quite unpopular as the Civil War dragged on. If Lincoln had allowed himself to be guided by public opinion, the United States might not exist today.

Another concern when we consider how closely government should follow public opinion is the fact that many Americans have very little knowledge about government. For example, 40 percent of the Americans responding to a recent survey did not know that every state has two senators; 71 percent could not name their own member of Congress; and a surprising 81 percent could not name both of their own state's senators.[1] Many Americans know even less about major policy issues, so their opinions on these issues may not be well informed.[2] Particularly troubling is that the opinions of the uninformed may be susceptible to manipulation by politicians, interest groups, and the government itself through public relations and advertising. Most Americans deny that they are affected by political advertising, but one study showed that many Americans' knowledge about politics is derived, in part, from biased (and sometimes inaccurate) information disseminated in political ads.[3]

Americans like to believe that public opinion is an important force in political life. The famous Austrian economist, Joseph Schumpeter, however, once observed that public opinion was the "product," not the "motive power" of the political process. By this comment he meant that public opinion was seldom, if ever, a driving force in politics. Instead, according to Schumpeter, politics was driven by the contending politicians, parties, and social forces that worked to win control of the government and to shape national policy. Such groups might seek to mold public opinion as part of their effort to bring about the policy and personnel changes they desired. So, for example, groups seeking changes in banking policy, farm policy, or military policy frequently mount public relations campaigns to secure public support for their goals. The appearance of popular support, in turn, might help these groups build a stronger case in Congress or even in the corridors of the White House. In this model of the political process, public opinion plays, at best, an intermediate role. It does not control policy. Instead, groups that hope to change policy find it useful—sometimes even essential—to change public opinion along the way.

Thus, when it comes to public opinion, the question of what the government does and why it matters is complicated. We certainly want the government to pay attention to public opinion. But, in some instances, when the government seems to be following public opinion it is actually responding to powerful forces that were able to shape opinion as they worked to control policy.

Moreover, the dictates of public opinions are not always obvious. In fall 2008, with the nation facing a serious financial crisis, public opinion was divided and offered little firm guidance to policy makers. According to a September 19, 2008, CNN poll, 79 percent of those Americans surveyed thought the government should take quick action to deal with the situation. The same poll, however, found that 77 percent resented the idea of government help for the banks and other financial institutions whom they held responsible for the economic downturn in the first place. Since a response to the crisis—which public opinion demanded—necessarily entailed government intervention on behalf of financial institutions—which public opinion opposed—policy makers found themselves in a difficult position.

› **In this chapter we will examine the role of public opinion in American politics. First, we examine the political values and beliefs that inform how Americans perceive the political process.** After reviewing the most basic American political values, we analyze how values and beliefs are formed and how certain processes and institutions influence their formation. We conclude this introductory section by looking at how a person's values and beliefs relate to political ideology.

› **Second, we turn to the process of how political opinions are formed.** We begin by assessing the relative importance of ideology in this process. We then look at how a person's knowledge of politics—and the influence of political leaders, private groups, and the media—affect the formation of political views.

› **Third, we describe the science of gathering and measuring public opinion.** The reliability of public opinion is directly related to the way in which it is gathered. Despite the limitations of public opinion polls, they remain an important part of the American political process.

Understanding Public Opinion

The term **public opinion** is used to denote the values and attitudes that people have about issues, events, and personalities. Although the terms are sometimes used interchangeably, it is useful to distinguish between values and beliefs on the one hand, and attitudes or opinions on the other. **Values (or beliefs)** are a person's basic orientations to politics. Values underlie deep-rooted goals, aspirations, and ideals that shape an individual's perceptions of political issues and events. Liberty, equality, and democracy are basic political values that most Americans hold. Another useful term for understanding public opinion is *ideology*. **Political ideology** refers to a complex set of beliefs and values that, as a whole, form a general philosophy about government. As we shall see, liberalism and conservatism are important ideologies in America today.

public opinion citizens' attitudes about political issues, leaders, institutions, and events

values (or beliefs) basic principles that shape a person's opinions about political issues and events

political ideology a cohesive set of beliefs that forms a general philosophy about the role of government

attitude (or opinion) a specific preference on a particular issue

For example, many Americans believe that governmental solutions to problems are inherently inferior to solutions offered by the private sector. This general belief, in turn, may lead individuals to have negative views of specific government programs even before they know much about them. An **attitude (or opinion)** is a specific view about a particular issue, personality, or event. An individual may have an opinion about Bill Clinton or an attitude toward American policy in Iraq. The attitude or opinion may have emerged from a broad belief about Democrats or military intervention, but an attitude itself is very specific. Some attitudes may be short-lived.

When we think of opinion, we often think in terms of differences of opinion. The media are fond of reporting and analyzing political differences between blacks and whites, men and women (the so-called gender gap), the young and old, and so on. Certainly, Americans differ on many issues, and often these differences do seem to be associated with race, religion, gender, age, or other social characteristics. Today, Americans seem sharply divided on truly fundamental questions about the role of government in American society, the proper place of religious and moral values in public life, and how best to deal with racial conflicts.

Political Values

As we review these differences, however, it is important to remember that Americans also agree on a number of matters.[4] Indeed, most Americans share a common set of values, including a belief in the principles—if not always the actual practice—of liberty, equality, and democracy. **Equality of opportunity** has always been an important theme in American society. Americans believe that all individuals should be allowed to seek personal and material success. Moreover, Americans generally believe that such success should be linked to personal effort and ability, rather than to family connections or other forms of special privilege. Similarly, Americans have always voiced strong support for the principle of individual **liberty.** They typically support the notion that governmental interference with individuals' lives and property should be kept to the minimum consistent with the general welfare (although in recent years Americans have grown accustomed to greater levels of governmental intervention than would have been deemed appropriate by the founders of liberal theory). And most Americans also believe in **democracy.** They presume that every person should have the opportunity to take part in the nation's governmental and policy-making processes and to have some say in determining how they are governed.[5] Figure 6.1

equality of opportunity a widely shared American ideal that all people should have the freedom to use whatever talents and wealth they have to reach their fullest potential

liberty freedom from governmental control

democracy a system of rule that permits citizens to play a significant part in the governmental process, usually through the election of key public officials

FIGURE 6.1 ★
American's Support for Fundamental Values

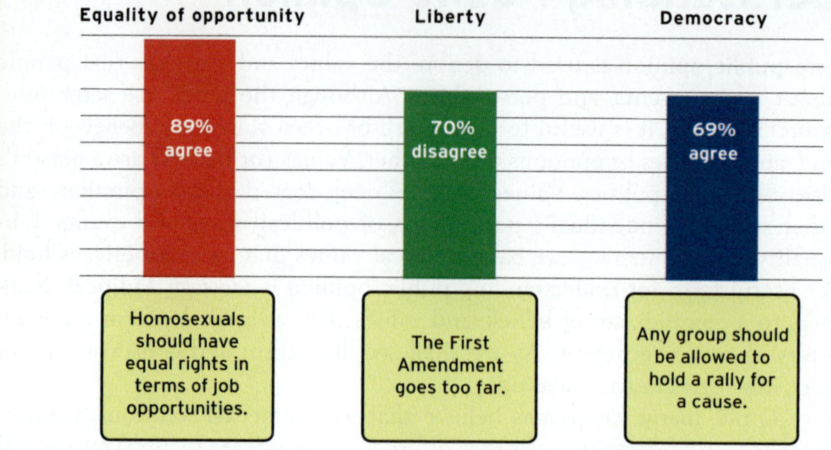

SOURCES: Gallup Poll, 2001, 2007; Roper Poll, 2002; and New England Survey Research Associates, 2007.

offers some indication of this American consensus on fundamental values: 89 percent believe that gays should have equal employment rights; 70 percent *disagree* that the First Amendment goes too far; and 69 percent agree that any group should be free to assemble.

One indication that Americans of all political stripes share these fundamental political values is the content of the speeches delivered by Barack Obama and John McCain on accepting their parties' presidential nominations in 2008. Obama and McCain differed on many issues and policies. Yet the political visions they presented reveal an underlying similarity: Both candidates placed major emphasis on equality of opportunity. Obama made opportunity a centerpiece in his speech, saying that his parents "weren't well-off or well-known but shared a belief that in America, their son could achieve whatever he put his mind to." Indeed, said Obama, "It is that promise that's always set this country apart; that through hard work and sacrifice; each of us can pursue our individual dreams . . . " McCain struck a similar note in his acceptance speech when he said, "We believe everyone has something to contribute and deserves the opportunity to reach their God-given potential from the boy whose descendants arrived on the Mayflower to the Latina daughter of migrant workers. We're all God's children and we're all Americans."

Obviously, the principles that Americans espouse have not always been put into practice. For two hundred years, Americans were able to believe in the principles of equality of opportunity and individual liberty while denying them in practice to generations of African Americans. Yet it is important to note that the strength of the principles ultimately helped to overcome practices that deviated from those principles. Proponents of slavery and, later, of segregation, were defeated in the arena of public opinion because their practices differed so sharply from the fundamental principles accepted by most Americans. Ironically, in contemporary politics, Americans' fundamental commitment to equality of opportunity has led to divisions over racial policy. In particular, both proponents and opponents of affirmative action programs cite their belief in equality of opportunity as the justification for their position. Proponents see these programs as necessary to ensure equality of opportunity, whereas opponents believe that affirmative action is a form of preferential treatment that violates basic American values.[6]

Gay marriage is another issue that provokes strong differences in opinion. In recent years, the debate over same-sex unions has sparked mass protests around the country.

Forms of Disagreement

Agreement on fundamentals by no means implies that Americans do not differ with each other on a wide variety of issues. American political life is characterized by vigorous debate on economic-policy, foreign-policy, and social-policy issues; race relations; environmental affairs; and a host of other matters.

As we will see later in this chapter, differences of political opinion are often associated with such variables as income, education, and occupation. Similarly, factors such as race, gender, ethnicity, age, religion, and region—which not only influence individuals' interests but also shape their experiences and upbringing—have enormous influence on their beliefs and opinions. For example, individuals whose incomes differ substantially have different views on the desirability of a number of important economic and social programs. In general, the poor—who are the chief beneficiaries of these programs—support them more strongly than do those who are wealthier and pay more of the taxes that fund the programs. Similarly, blacks and whites have different views on questions of civil rights and civil liberties—presumably reflecting differences of interest and historical experience. In recent years, many observers have begun to take note of a number of differences between the views expressed by men and those supported by women, especially on foreign-policy questions, where women appear to be much more concerned with the dangers of war. Let us see how such differences develop.

How Political Values Are Formed

People's attitudes about political issues and personalities tend to be shaped by their underlying political beliefs and values. For example, an individual who has basically negative feelings about government intervention into America's economy and society would probably be predisposed to oppose the development of new health-care and social programs. Similarly, someone who distrusts the military would likely be

political socialization the induction of individuals into the political culture; learning the underlying beliefs and values on which the political system is based

agencies of socialization social institutions, including families and schools, that help to shape individuals' basic political beliefs and values

suspicious of any call for the use of American troops. The processes through which these underlying political beliefs and values are formed are collectively called **political socialization.**

The process of political socialization is important. Probably no nation, and certainly no democracy, could survive if its citizens did not share some fundamental beliefs. If Americans had few common values or perspectives, it would be very difficult for them to reach agreement on particular issues. In contemporary America, some elements of the socialization process tend to produce differences in outlook, whereas others promote similarities. Four of the most important **agencies of socialization** that foster differences in political perspectives are the family, membership in social groups, education, and prevailing political conditions.

No inventory of agencies of socialization can fully explain the development of a given individual's basic political beliefs. In addition to the factors that are important for everyone, forces that are unique to each individual play a role in shaping political orientations. For one person, the character of an early encounter with a member of another racial group can have a lasting impact on that individual's view of the world. For another, a highly salient political event, such as the Vietnam War, can leave an indelible mark on that person's political consciousness. For a third person, some deep-seated personality characteristic, such as paranoia, for example, may strongly influence the formation of political beliefs. Nevertheless, knowing that we cannot fully explain the development of any given individual's political outlook, let us look at some of the most important agencies of socialization that do affect one's beliefs.

Influences on Our Political Values

THE FAMILY Most people acquire their initial orientation to politics from their families. As might be expected, differences in family background tend to produce divergent political outlooks. Although relatively few parents spend much time teaching their children about politics, political conversations occur in many households and children tend to absorb the political views of parents and other caregivers, perhaps without realizing it. Studies have suggested, for example, that party preferences are initially acquired at home. Children raised in households in which the primary caregivers are Democrats tend to become Democrats themselves, whereas children raised in homes where their caregivers are Republicans tend to favor the GOP (Grand Old Party, a traditional nickname for the Republican Party).[7] Similarly, children reared in politically liberal households are more likely than not to develop a liberal outlook, whereas children raised in politically conservative settings are likely to see the world through conservative lenses. Obviously, not all children absorb their parents' political views. Two of the late conservative Republican president Ronald Reagan's three children, for instance, rejected their parents' conservative values. Moreover, even those children whose views are initially shaped by parental values may change their minds as they mature and experience political life for themselves. Nevertheless, the family is an important initial source of political orientation for everyone.

SOCIAL GROUPS Another important source of divergent political orientations and values are the social groups to which individuals belong. Social groups include those to which individuals belong involuntarily—national, religious, gender and racial groups, for example—as well as those to which people belong voluntarily, such as political parties, labor unions, and educational and occupational groups.

Some social groups have both voluntary and involuntary attributes. For example, individuals are born with a particular social-class background, but as a result of their own efforts people may move up—or down—the class structure.

Membership in social groups can affect political values in a variety of ways. Membership in a particular group can give individuals important experiences and perspectives that shape their view of political and social life. In American society, for example, the experiences of blacks and whites can differ significantly. Blacks are a minority and have been victims of persecution and discrimination throughout American history. Blacks and whites also have different educational and occupational opportunities, often live in separate communities, and may attend separate schools. Such differences tend to produce distinctive political outlooks. For example, in 1995 blacks and whites had very different reactions to the murder trial of the former football star O. J. Simpson, who was accused of killing his ex-wife and one of her friends. Seventy percent of the white Americans surveyed believed that Simpson was guilty, on the basis of evidence presented by the police and prosecutors. But an identical 70 percent of black Americans surveyed immediately after the trial believed that the police had fabricated evidence and had sought to convict Simpson of a crime he had not committed; these beliefs were presumably based on blacks' experiences with and perceptions of the criminal justice system.[8] In a similar vein, Reverend Al Sharpton's 2003–04 campaign for the Democratic presidential nomination was not taken seriously by most white voters and received little attention from the mainstream news media. Black voters, on the other hand, were quite attuned to Sharpton's candidacy, which received considerable coverage in the African American news media. Indeed, Sharpton received considerable financial backing from black media executives.[9] In 2008, Senator Barack Obama's candidacy depended initially on strong support in the black community.

Politics Today

In 2008, African Americans strongly supported Barack Obama's presidential bid while whites were divided. What factors might help persuade voters to support a candidate who does not share their racial identity?

According to other recent surveys, blacks and whites in the United States differ on many issues. For example, among middle-income Americans (defined as those earning between $30,000 and $75,000 per year), 65 percent of black respondents and only 35 percent of white respondents thought racism was a major problem in the United States today. Within this same group of respondents, 63 percent of blacks and only 39 percent of whites thought the federal government should provide more services even at the cost of higher taxes.[10] Nearly three-quarters of white Americans but only one-third of black Americans favored going to war against Iraq in 2003. Other issues show a similar pattern of disagreement, reflecting the differences in experience, background, and interests between blacks and whites in America (see Figure 6.2).

Other racial and nationality groups—Asians and Latinos, for example—have histories and cultural orientations that give them unique attitudes. For example, although most voters in 2004 cited terrorism, the economy, or moral issues as the matters most affecting their vote, a majority of Hispanics said education was the most important issue facing America. Latinos view access to a good education as the necessary route to mobility and success in America and say so quite emphatically when pollsters query them.

Men and women have important differences of opinion as well. Reflecting differences in social roles, political experience, and occupational patterns, women tend to be less militaristic than men on issues of war and peace, more likely than men to favor measures to protect the environment, and more supportive than men of government social and health care programs (see Table 6.1). Perhaps because of these differences on issues, women are more likely than men to vote for Democratic candidates.[11] This tendency of men's and women's opinions to differ is called the **gender gap**.

gender gap a distinctive pattern of voting behavior reflecting the differences in views between women and men

FIGURE 6.2 ★ Disagreement among Blacks and Whites

In the United States, blacks and whites do not perceive race relations in precisely the same way. How, according to the data in this figure, do blacks and whites differ in their views on race relations? Which group is more likely to think that race relations are good? What factors help to account for these differences in perception?

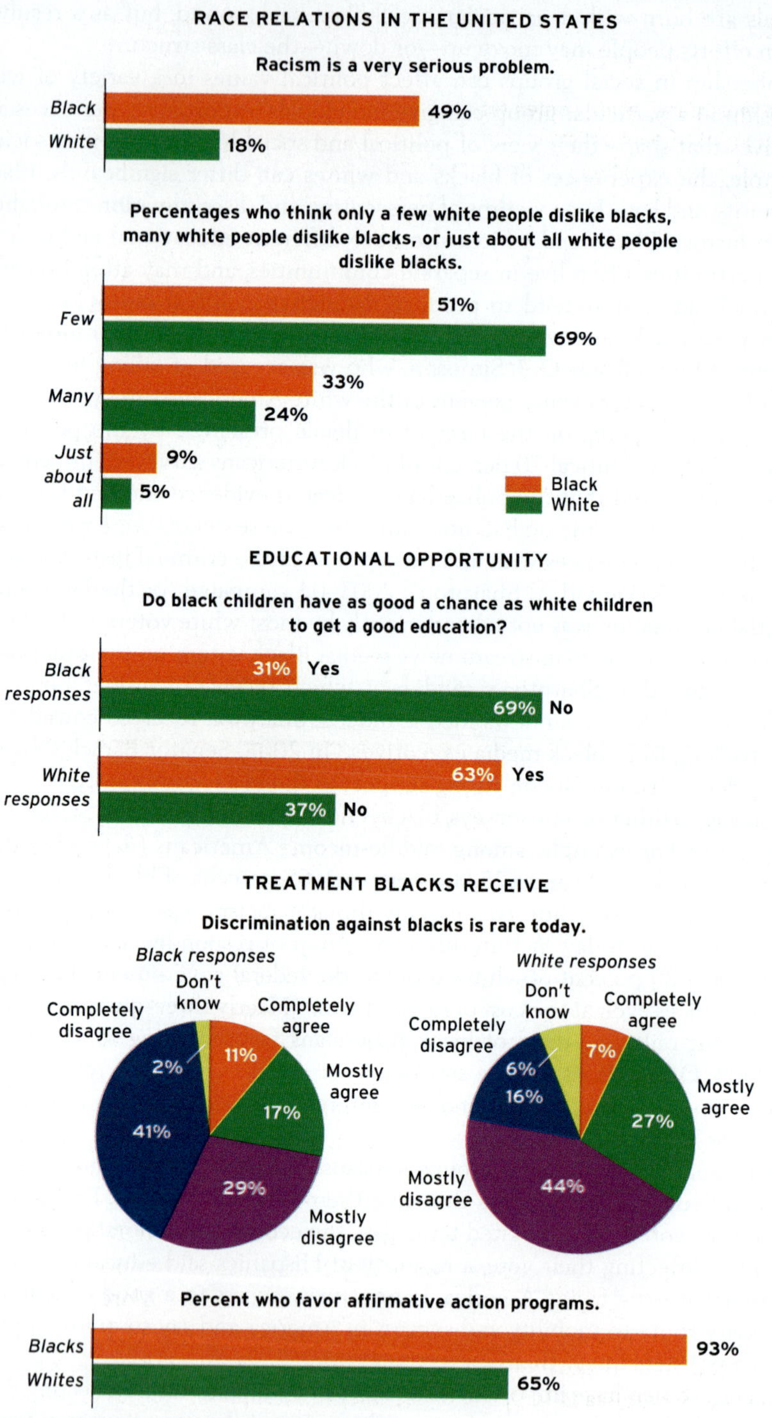

SOURCES: CNN, www.cnn.com/2006/US/12/12/racism.poll/index.html; Gallup, Inc., www.gallup.com/poll/11686/Race-Education-Years-After-Brown-Board-Education.aspx; and Pew Research Center Publications, http://pewresearch.org/pubs/531/democratic-debate (accessed 4/1/08).

TABLE 6.1 ★ Disagreements among Men and Women on National Security Issues

For the most part, fewer women than men favor the use of military force as an instrument of foreign policy. Is this pattern reflected consistently in the data? What might explain gender differences in this realm?

GOVERNMENT ACTION	PERCENTAGE APPROVING OF ACTION MEN	WOMEN
Agree that torture of terror suspects is acceptable	44	27
Favor withdrawing troops from Iraq within a year	43	55
Agree NSA surveillance program is needed	60	50
Oppose sending more troops to Iraq	52	69
Favor cutting off funding for Iraq war	48	57
Believe U.S. should mount long-term war in Afghanistan (2002)	64	42
Support going to war against Iraq (2003)	78	66

SOURCES: ABC, 2004; *Ms*, 2006; UPI/Zogby, 2007; *USA Today*, 2007; *Washington Post*/ABC, 2007; Gallup, 2002; and Gallup, 2003.

Political party membership can be another factor affecting political orientations.[12] Partisans tend to rely on party leaders and spokespersons for cues on the appropriate positions to take on major political issues. In recent years, congressional redistricting and partisan realignment in the South have reduced the number of conservative Democrats and all but eliminated liberal Republicans from the Congress and from positions of prominence in the party. As a result, the leadership of the Republican Party has become increasingly conservative, whereas that of the Democratic Party has become more and more liberal. These changes in the positions of party leaders have been reflected in the views of party adherents and sympathizers in the general public. According to recent studies, differences between Democratic and Republican partisans on a variety of political and policy questions are greater today than during any other period for which data are available. On issues of national security, for example, Republicans have become very "hawkish," whereas Democrats have become quite "dovish." In October 2003, for instance, 85 percent of Republicans compared with 39 percent of the Democrats surveyed thought America's war against Iraq had been a good idea.[13] By March 2006, only 34 percent of Democrats surveyed by the Pew Research Center thought the war would succeed, but 74 percent of Republicans remained optimistic. By 2007, 60 percent of all Republicans still supported the war. Gaps on domestic social and economic issues were nearly as broad.

Religion may also affect individuals' attitudes. Religions provide a historical experience and philosophical perspective that lead their members to see the world in different ways. In the United States, for example, members of America's Christian majority are not likely to be offended by the display of Christian symbols in schools

Politics Today

In 2008, religious conservatives were often called "values voters." What values did these voters support? Did their opponents lack values?

Religion may affect attitudes about political and social issues. In 2008, these Christian teenagers demanded more restrictions on popular culture content that they considered harmful to young people.

and other government buildings. Jews and members of other minority religious groups, on the other hand, often view such displays through their own historical lens as an effort to undermine their religions. Similarly, many commonplace elements of American secular culture, such as clothing styles, may be deeply offensive to an individual raised in a conservative Muslim tradition.

Politics Today

In 2008, Jewish Americans were among the Democratic Party's strongest supporters. On the basis of economic position, though, most Jews might be expected to be Republicans. What explains this peculiarity?

Membership in a social group can affect individuals' political orientations in another way: through the efforts of groups themselves to influence their members. Labor unions, for example, often seek to inform their members through meetings, rallies, and literature. These activities are designed to shape union members' understanding of politics and to make them more amenable to supporting the political positions favored by union leaders. Similarly, organization can sharpen the impact of membership in an involuntary group. Women's groups, black groups, religious groups, and the like usually endeavor to structure their members' political views through intensive educational programs. The importance of such group efforts can be seen in the impact of group membership on political opinion. Women who belong to women's organizations, for example, are likely to differ more from men in their political views than women without such group affiliation.[14] Other analysts have found that African Americans who belong to black organizations are likely to differ more from whites in their political orientations than blacks who lack such affiliations.[15]

In many cases, no particular efforts are required by groups to affect their members' beliefs and opinions. Often, individuals will consciously or unconsciously adapt their views to those of the groups with which they identify. For example, an African American who is dubious about affirmative action is likely to come under considerable peer pressure and internal pressure to modify his or her views. In this and other cases, dissenters are likely gradually to shift their own views to conform to those of the group. The political psychologist Elisabeth Noelle-Neumann has called this process the "spiral of silence."[16]

A third way that membership in social groups can affect political beliefs is through what might be called objective political interests. On many economic issues, for example, the interests of the rich and the poor differ significantly. Inevitably, these differences of interest will produce differences of political outlook. James Madison and other framers of the Constitution thought that the inherent gulf between the rich and the poor would always be the most important source of conflict in political life. Certainly today, struggles over tax policy, welfare policy, health care policy, and so forth are fueled by differences of interest between wealthier and poorer Americans. In a similar vein, objective differences of interest between senior citizens and younger Americans can lead to very different views on such diverse issues as health care policy, Social Security, and criminal justice. To take another example, in recent decades major differences of opinion and political orientation have developed between American civilians and members of the armed services. Military officers, in particular, are far more conservative in their domestic and foreign policy views than the public at large and are heavily Republican in their political leanings.[17] It is interesting to note that support for the Republicans among military officers climbed sharply during the 1980s and 1990s, decades in which the GOP championed large military budgets. Could this be another case of objective interests swaying ideology?

It is worth pointing out again that, like the other agencies of socialization, group membership can never fully explain a given individual's political views. One's unique personality and life experiences may produce political views very different from those of the group to which one might nominally belong. This is why some African Americans are conservative Republicans, or why an occasional wealthy businessperson is also a socialist. Group membership is conducive to particular outlooks, but it is not determinative.

DIFFERENCES IN EDUCATION A third important source of differences in political perspectives comes from a person's education. In some respects, of course, schooling is a great equalizer. Governments use public education to try to teach all children a common set of civic values. It is mainly in school that Americans acquire their basic belief in liberty, equality, and democracy. In history classes, students are taught that the Founders fought for the principle of liberty. Through participation in class elections and student government, students are taught the virtues of democracy. In the course of studying such topics as the Constitution, the Civil War, and the civil rights movement, students are taught the importance of equality. These lessons are repeated in every grade in a variety of contexts. It is no wonder they are such an important element in Americans' beliefs.

At the same time, however, differences in educational attainment are strongly associated with differences in political outlook. In particular, those who attend college are often exposed to philosophies and modes of thought that will forever distinguish them from their friends and neighbors who do not pursue college diplomas. Table 6.2 outlines some general differences of opinion that are found between college graduates and other Americans.

In recent years, conservatives have charged that liberal college professors indoctrinate their students with liberal ideas. College does seem to have some "liberalizing" effect on students, but, more significantly, college seems to convince students of the importance of political participation and of their own capacity for having an impact on politics and policy. Thus, one of the major differences between college graduates and other Americans can be seen in levels of political participation. College graduates vote, write "letters to the editor," join campaigns, take part in protests, and, generally, make their voices heard. Does this mean that college graduates are turned

TABLE 6.2 ★ Education and Public Opinion

The figures show the percentage of respondents in each category who agree with the statement. Are college graduates generally more or less liberal than other Americans? Which data support your claim? Can you think of economic or political explanations for these findings?

	EDUCATION			
ISSUES	GRADE SCHOOL	HIGH SCHOOL	SOME COLLEGE	COLLEGE GRAD.
1. Women and men should have equal roles.	38%	75%	83%	86%
2. Abortion should never be allowed.	21	10	7	4
3. The government should adopt national health insurance.	35	47	42	49
4. The United States should not concern itself with other nations' problems.	45	26	20	8
5. Government should see to fair treatment in jobs for African Americans.	49	28	30	45
6. Government should provide fewer services to reduce government spending.	8	17	19	27

SOURCE: The American National Election Studies, 2004 data, provided by the Inter-University Consortium for Political and Social Research, University of Michigan.

into dangerous radicals by liberal professors? Quite the contrary: college seems to convince individuals that it is important to involve themselves in the nation's politics. What perspective could be more conservative?

POLITICAL CONDITIONS A fourth set of factors that shape political orientations and values are the conditions under which individuals and groups are recruited into and involved in political life. Although political beliefs are influenced by family background and group membership, the precise content and character of these views is, to a large extent, determined by political circumstances. For example, in the nineteenth century, millions of southern Italian peasants left their homes. Some migrated to cities in northern Italy; others came to cities in the United States. Many of those who moved to northern Italy were recruited by socialist and communist parties and became mainstays of the forces of the Italian Left. At the same time, their cousins and neighbors who migrated to American cities were recruited by urban patronage machines and became mainstays of political conservatism. In both instances, group membership influenced political beliefs. Yet the character of those beliefs varied enormously with the political circumstances in which a given group found itself.

Is There a Culture War in America?

Around the recent elections, Americans listening to the news heard a lot about a "culture war" in America that was being waged between "blue states" (states won by Democratic presidential candidates) and "red states" (states won by Republican presidential candidates)—indicating to some that there were two Americas, the Republican one and the Democratic one. According to this view, Americans are deeply divided along lines drawn by their opinions on religion, morality, and certain political values.

The question of whether or not a true culture war exists in America is the subject of an ongoing battle among political scientists and other scholars, but the "two Americas" said to result from the culture war present clearly identifiable stereotypes in American popular culture. Perhaps the most often-cited example is the "NASCAR dad." As early as 1984, politicians (especially Republicans) understood the political importance of mobilizing NASCAR (National Association for Stock Car Auto Racing) fans, and that year Ronald Reagan started the Daytona 500 from inside Air Force One, announcing via telephone, "Gentlemen, start your engines." Twenty years later, in 2004, George W. Bush followed in Reagan's footsteps, starting the Daytona 500. Journalist Bill Schneider described the stereotype of the NASCAR fan as "male, southern, rural, blue collar and Republican."[a]

Stereotypes of liberal Americans also exist in popular culture. A political advertisement paid for by the conservative group Club for Growth that aired during the 2004 presidential primaries played on caricatures of liberals. In the ad, an older man (an actor) states, "I think Howard Dean should take his tax-hiking, government-expanding, latte-drinking, sushi-eating, Volvo-driving, *New York Times*-reading . . . ," and a woman completes the thought, "body-piercing, Hollywood-loving, left-wing freak show back to Vermont where it belongs."

One of the less predictable places that these two Americas intersect is in animated television programming. The writer Brian C. Anderson, for example, claims that Comedy Central's controversial program *South Park* is a clear attack on liberal elitism, hyper-environmentalism, and political correctness, through the program's characteristically shocking plotlines and language. The *New York Times* columnist Matt Bai suggests that the Fox series *King of the Hill*, on the other hand, is a more realistic and nuanced depiction of middle-American values. In *King of the Hill*, Hank Hill and his wife, Peggy, live in a suburban American town, and Hank—a NASCAR fan and gun owner—"finds himself struggling to adapt to new phenomena: art galleries and yoga studios, latte-sipping parents who ask their kids to call them by their first names and encourage them to drink responsibly."[b]

In 2008, Republicans chose Sarah Palin, a self-styled "hockey mom" to be their vice-presidential candidate partly on the assumption that Palin would appeal to the "Joe Six-Packs" in the electorate, the blue-collar families uneasy with the liberalism of the Democrats. Much was made of the fact that Palin liked to hunt and knew how to field dress a moose. Her husband Todd's blue-collar origins were also emphasized by Republican campaigners.

Latte-drinking, yoga-practicing liberals and moose-hunting, NASCAR-watching conservatives are extreme oversimplifications of a diverse and nuanced American population. Yet research from the 2004 elections indicates that what we buy and watch on television may be indicators of who we will vote for. After their victory in the 2004 election, Republican strategists explained that one of the keys to their success in mobilizing likely Republican voters was through the use of consumer data.

FOR CRITICAL ANALYSIS

1. Some commentators have pointed out that much of America is "purple" rather than "red" or "blue." To what extent do you believe that the red state/blue state stereotypes apply to your state?
2. What are some of the core political values that a majority of Americans agree on? What factors may account for differences in political values among Americans?

---

a. "George Bush Prepares to Campaign for Reelection," *Insight*, CNN Transcript, December 3, 2003, http://transcripts.cnn.com/TRANSCRIPTS/0312/03/i_ins.00.html (accessed 3/31/08).

b. M. Bai, "'King of the Hill' Democrats?" *New York Times*, June 26, 2005.

Similarly, the views held by members of a particular group can shift drastically over time, as political circumstances change. For example, American white southerners were staunch members of the Democratic Party from the Civil War through the 1960s. As members of this political group, they became key supporters of liberal New Deal and post–New Deal social programs that greatly expanded the size and power of the American national government. Since the 1960s, however, southern whites have shifted in large numbers to the Republican Party. Now they provide a major base of support for efforts to scale back social programs and to reduce sharply the size and power of the national government. The South's move from the Democratic to the Republican camp took place because of white southern opposition to the Democratic Party's racial policies and because of determined Republican efforts to win white southern support. It was not a change in the character of white southerners but a change in the political circumstances in which they found themselves that induced this major shift in political allegiances and outlooks in the South.

The moral of this story is that a group's views cannot be inferred simply from the character of the group. College students are not inherently radical or inherently conservative. Jews are not inherently liberal. Southerners are not inherently conservative. Men are not inherently supportive of the military. Any group's political outlooks and orientations are shaped by the political circumstances in which that group finds itself, and those outlooks can change as circumstances change. Quite probably, the generation of American students now coming of political age will have a very different view of the use of American military power than their parents—members of a generation that reached political consciousness during the 1960s, when opposition to the Vietnam War and military conscription was an important political phenomenon.

One of the hallmarks of American democracy has been vigorous debate on important policy issues. During the 1960s and early 1970s, anti–Vietnam War protestors staged numerous demonstrations across the nation.

From Political Values to Ideology

As we have seen, people's beliefs about government can vary widely. But for some individuals, this set of beliefs can fit together into a coherent philosophy about government. This set of underlying orientations, ideas, and beliefs through which we come to understand and interpret politics is called a political ideology. Ideologies take many different forms. Some people may view politics primarily in religious terms. During the course of European political history, for example, Protestantism and Catholicism were often political ideologies as much as they were religious creeds. Each set of beliefs not only included elements of religious practice but also involved ideas about secular authority and political action. Other people may see politics through racial lenses. Nazism was a political ideology that placed race at the center of political life and sought to interpret politics in terms of racial categories.

In America today, a variety of ideologies compete for attention and support. Libertarians, for example, argue that government is a wasteful and dangerous institution that should be limited to as few activities as possible. Socialists, on the other hand, argue that more government control is necessary to promote justice and reduce economic and political inequality. Environmentalists view global warming and other threats to the world's environment as the most important issues facing humanity today. Although many subscribe to these and other ideas, most Americans describe themselves as either liberals or conservatives. Liberalism and conservatism are political ideologies that include beliefs about the role of the government, ideas about public policies, and notions about which groups in society should properly exercise power (see Boxes 6.1 and 6.2). These ideologies can be seen as the end results of the process of political socialization that was discussed in the preceding section.

Today, the term **liberal** has come to imply support for political and social reform, extensive government intervention in the economy, the expansion of federal social services, and more vigorous efforts on behalf of the poor, minorities, and women, as well as greater concern for consumers and the environment. In social and cultural areas, liberals generally support abortion rights, are concerned with the rights of persons accused of crime, and oppose state involvement with religious institutions and religious expression. In international affairs, liberal positions are usually seen as including support for arms control, opposition to the development and testing of nuclear weapons, support for aid to poor nations, opposition to the use of American troops to influence the domestic affairs of developing nations, and support for international organizations such as the United Nations. Of course, liberalism is not monolithic. For example, among individuals who view themselves as liberal, many support American military intervention when it is tied to a humanitarian purpose, as in the case of America's military action in Kosovo in 1998–99. Most liberals supported the former president Bush's war on terrorism, even when some of the president's actions seemed to curtail civil liberties.

liberal today this term refers to those who generally support social and political reform; extensive governmental intervention in the economy; the expansion of federal social services; more vigorous efforts on behalf of the poor, minorities, and women; and greater concern for consumers and the environment

By contrast, the term **conservative** today is used to describe those who generally support the social and economic status quo and are suspicious of efforts to introduce new political formulae and economic arrangements. Conservatives believe strongly that a large and powerful government poses a threat to citizens' freedom.

conservative today this term refers to those who generally support the social and economic status quo and are suspicious of efforts to introduce new political formulae and economic arrangements. Conservatives believe that a large and powerful government poses a threat to citizens' freedom

BOX 6.1 Profile of a Liberal: House Speaker Nancy Pelosi

- Supports abortion rights.
- Opposes prayer in the public schools.
- Supports affirmative action.
- Favors expanded health coverage for all Americans.
- Wants to bring an end to the war in Iraq.
- Advocates increased funding for education.
- Supports further increases in the minimum wage.

BOX 6.2 Profile of a Conservative: House Republican Leader John Boehner

- Wants to trim the size of the federal government and transfer power to state and local governments.
- Wants to diminish government regulation of business.
- Favors prayer in the public schools.
- Opposes gay rights legislation.
- Favors making most abortions illegal.
- Supports harsher treatment of criminals.
- Opposes many affirmative action programs.
- Questions U.S. participation in international organizations.
- Favors tax cuts.
- Supports high levels of military spending.

Thus, in the domestic arena, conservatives generally oppose the expansion of governmental activity, asserting that solutions to social and economic problems can be developed in the private sector. Conservatives particularly oppose efforts to impose government regulation on business, pointing out that such regulation is frequently economically inefficient and costly and can ultimately lower the entire nation's standard of living. As for social and cultural positions, many conservatives oppose abortion, support school prayer, are more concerned for the victims than for the perpetrators of crimes, oppose school busing, and support traditional family arrangements. In international affairs, conservatism has come to mean support for the maintenance of American military power. Like liberalism, conservatism is far from a monolithic ideology. Some conservatives support many government social programs. The Republican George W. Bush called himself a "compassionate conservative" to indicate that he favored programs that assist the poor and needy. Other conservatives oppose efforts to outlaw abortion, arguing that government intrusion in this area is as misguided as government intervention in the economy. Such a position is sometimes called "libertarian." Pat Buchanan has angered many fellow conservatives by opposing government action in the form of American military intervention in other regions. Many conservatives charge Buchanan with advocating a form of American "isolationism" that runs counter to contemporary conservative doctrine. The real political world is far too complex to be seen in terms of a simple struggle between liberals and conservatives.

To some extent, contemporary liberalism and conservatism can be seen as differences of emphasis with regard to the fundamental American political values of liberty and equality. For liberals, equality is the most important of the core values. Liberals encourage government action in such areas as college admissions and business practices to enhance race, class, and gender equality. For conservatives, on the other hand, liberty is the core value. Conservatives oppose many efforts of the government, however well intentioned, to intrude into private life and the marketplace. For example, in October 2008, many conservative Republican members of Congress voted against the Bush administration's emergency plan to end the nation's financial crisis because they opposed the partial government takeover of banks and other financial institutions that would result from the plan. Some conservatives believed that even the risk of a financial meltdown did not justify the expansion of government power in the marketplace. This simple formula for distinguishing liberalism and conservatism, however, is not always accurate, because political ideologies seldom lend themselves to neat or logical characterizations. Often political observers search for logical connections among the various positions identified with liberalism or with conservatism, and they are disappointed or puzzled when they are unable to find a set of coherent philosophical principles that define and unite the several elements of either of these sets of beliefs. On the liberal side, for example, what is the logical connection between opposition to U.S. government intervention in the affairs of foreign nations and calls for greater intervention in America's economy and society? On the conservative side, what is the logical relationship between opposition to governmental regulation of business and support for a government ban on abortion? Indeed, the latter would seem to be just the sort of regulation of private conduct that conservatives claim to abhor.

Frequently, the relationships among the various elements of liberalism or of conservatism are political rather than logical. One underlying basis of liberal views is that all or most are criticisms of or attacks on the foreign and domestic policies and cultural values of the business and commercial strata that have been prominent in the United States for the past century. In some measure, the tenets of contemporary conservatism are this elite's defense of its positions against its enemies, who include organized labor, minority groups, and some intellectuals and professionals. Thus, liberals attack business and commercial elites by advocating more governmental regulation, including consumer protection and environmental regulation, opposing new military weapons programs, and supporting expensive social programs. Conservatives counterattack by asserting that governmental regulation of the economy is ruinous and that new military weapons are needed in a changing world, and they seek to stigmatize their opponents for showing no concern for the rights of "unborn" Americans.

For Critical Analysis

Describe the differences between liberal and conservative ideologies in American politics. Using one social or demographic group as an example, describe some of the factors that may have shaped the ideological orientation of that particular group.

Of course, it is important to note that many people who call themselves liberals or conservatives accept only part of the liberal or conservative ideology. During the 1980s, many political commentators asserted that Americans were becoming increasingly conservative. Indeed, it was partly in response to this view that the Democrats in 1992 selected a presidential candidate, Bill Clinton, drawn from the party's moderate wing. Although it appears that Americans have adopted more conservative outlooks on some issues, their views in most areas have remained largely unchanged or even have become more liberal in recent years. Thus, many individuals who are liberal on social issues are conservative on economic issues. There is nothing illogical about these mixed positions. They simply reflect the relatively open and fluid character of American political debate. As Figure 6.3 indicates, Americans are often likely to shift their ideological preferences.

How We Form Political Opinions

An individual's opinions on particular issues, events, and personalities emerge as he or she evaluates these phenomena through the lenses of the beliefs and orientations that, taken together, form his or her political ideology. Thus, if a conservative is confronted

FIGURE 6.3 ★
Americans' Shifting Ideology, 1972–2004

Over the past thirty years, the percentage of Americans claiming to be conservative or liberal has increased, whereas the percentage calling themselves moderates has not. Can you think of any reasons for this change? Would more moderates be better for democracy?

SOURCE: *National Election Studies Guide to Public Opinion and Electoral Behavior* (Ann Arbor, Michigan: Inter-University Consortium for Political and Social Research, 2006).

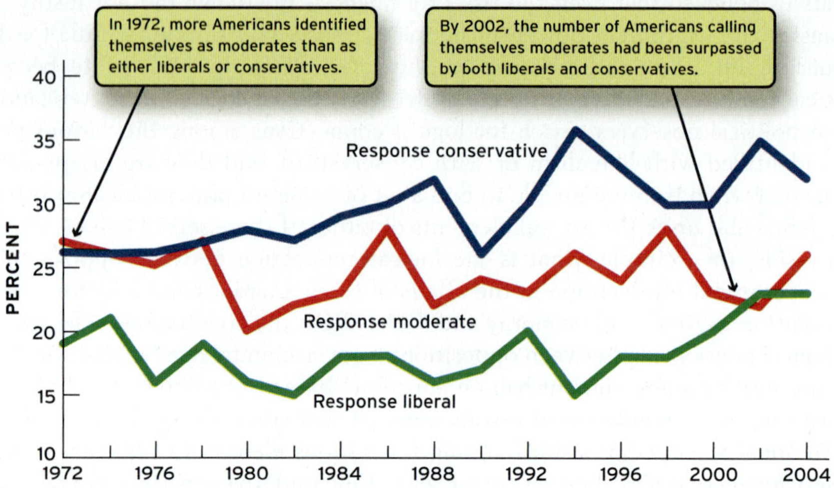

with a plan to expand federal social programs, he or she is likely to express opposition to the endeavor without spending too much time pondering the specific plan. Similarly, if a liberal is asked to comment on the late, conservative president Ronald Reagan, he or she is not likely to hesitate long before offering a negative view. Underlying beliefs and ideologies tend automatically to color people's perceptions and opinions about politics.

Opinions on particular issues, however, are seldom fully shaped by underlying ideologies. Few individuals possess ideologies so cohesive and intensely held that they will automatically shape all their opinions. Indeed, when we occasionally encounter individuals with rigid worldviews, who see everything through a particular political lens, we tend to dismiss them as "ideologues," or lacking common sense.

Although ideologies color our political perspectives, they seldom fully determine our views. This is true for a variety of reasons. First, as noted earlier, most individuals' ideologies contain internal contradictions. Take, for example, a conservative view of the issue of abortion. Should conservatives favor outlawing abortion as an appropriate means of preserving public morality, or should they oppose restrictions on abortion because these represent government intrusions into private life? Or take the issue of America's response to terrorism. Should conservatives support the government's eavesdropping, warrantless searches, and expanded surveillance of private citizens and businesses as needed to defend the nation, or should they be concerned about allowing the government so much power to intrude into private lives? In this instance, as in many others, ideology can point in different directions.

Second, individuals may have difficulty linking particular issues or personalities to their own underlying beliefs. Some issues defy ideological characterization. Should conservatives have supported or opposed the 1999 "Patient's Bill of Rights,"

School Prayer

One issue on which liberals and conservatives often disagree is school prayer. The First Amendment bars the government from establishing a state religion and from inhibiting the free exercise of religion by individuals. Thus, the government is barred from breaching the "wall of separation" between church and state, so that religious liberty may find full expression. Yet is that wall breached if individuals wish to express their religious beliefs in schools? At first glance, the answer would appear to be yes. In the 1962 case of *Engel v. Vitale*, the Supreme Court barred government-organized and -led religious prayer. Since then, proponents of prayer in school have marshaled much support for a more flexible approach, arguing in part that courts have misunderstood the framers' intent. Proponents have also pushed for a constitutional amendment guaranteeing free religious expression in public schools.

Proponents of prayer in school argue that the Constitution's framers were pious men who were not out to drive religion from schools or other aspects of public life. Every congress since the Founding has opened its daily session with a prayer. Supreme Court sessions begin with the words "God save the United States and this Honorable Court." By now shunning any form of religious expression at a time when children seem increasingly in need of moral and spiritual guidance, schools are sending the wrong message to the nation's children. Moreover, the absence of school religion implicitly encourages another belief system—secularism.

School prayer need not be led by teachers or administrators, nor need it be required. Voluntary prayer led by students would pose no threat to the First Amendment. Instead, it would reflect the proper extension of religious liberty into schools. In short, an enlightened approach to school prayer requires neither a government stamp of approval nor any form of coercion.

Opponents of school prayer argue that both the First Amendment and American respect for individual freedom require that schools avoid any role in religious teaching, instruction, or prayer. They generally oppose even student-run religious activities associated with school functions. For example, groups opposed to school prayer applauded the Supreme Court's decision in *Doe v. Santa Fe Independent School District* (2000), in which the Court ruled that a public school's policy of allowing students to read prayers over the public address system during football games violated the First Amendment's establishment clause. Government meddling in religion drove many European settlers to America, and the Founders understood that keeping government out of religious matters was not an expression of hostility to religion but a simple acknowledgment that both government and religion were better off if the former let the latter alone.

Opponents of school prayer point out that although most Americans hold some form of religious belief, the range of those beliefs is wide and growing, meaning that any form of religious teaching or prayer is bound to offend the sensibilities of some religious groups. Moreover, the rights of nonbelievers are equal to those of believers. School actions that ostracize, penalize, or stigmatize nonbelievers violate their right to equal treatment and their right not to be subjected to religious teachings in what is a public and secular institution.

FOR CRITICAL ANALYSIS

1. Why do you think conservatives often support school prayer? Why do liberals tend to oppose it?
2. The Constitution bans the establishment of state religion and also prohibits Congress from interfering with the free exercise of religion. Could these provisions ever come into conflict?

which made it easier for individuals to file suit against the widely unpopular health maintenance organizations (HMOs) that came to dominate American health care in the 1990s? What should liberals think about America's 1998–99 bombing campaign against Serbia, our 2001–02 war in Afghanistan, and the continued conflict in Iraq? Each of these policies combines a mix of issues and is too complex to be viewed through simple ideological lenses.

Finally, most people have at least some conflicting underlying attitudes. Most conservatives support *some* federal programs—defense, or tax deductions for businesses, for example—and wish to see them, and hence the government, expanded. Many liberals favor American military intervention in other nations for what they deem to be humanitarian purposes, but generally oppose American military intervention in the affairs of other nations.

Thus, most individuals' attitudes on particular issues do not spring automatically from their ideological predispositions. It is true that most people have deeply rooted beliefs that help to shape their opinions on particular issues, but two other factors are also important: a person's knowledge of political issues, and outside influences on that person's views.

Political Knowledge

As we have seen, general political beliefs can guide the formation of opinions on specific issues, but an individual's beliefs and opinions are not always consistent with each other. Studies of political opinion have shown that most people don't hold specific and clearly defined opinions on every political issue. As a result, they are easily influenced by others. What best explains whether citizens are generally consistent in their political views or inconsistent and open to the influence of others? The key is knowledge and information about political issues. In general, knowledgeable citizens are better able to evaluate new information and to determine whether it is relevant to and consistent with their beliefs and opinions. As a result, better-informed individuals can recognize their political interests and act consistently on behalf of them.

For Critical Analysis

Americans vary enormously in their knowledge about government and politics, yet we treat all opinions as having equal weight. Should all political opinions be treated equally?

One of the most obvious and important examples of this proposition is voting. Despite the predisposition of voters to support their own party's candidates (see Chapter 9 for a discussion of party identification), millions of voters are affected by the information they receive about candidates during a campaign. During the 2008 presidential campaign, for instance, voters weighed the arguments of Barack Obama against those of John McCain about who was more qualified to oversee the U.S. economy. Many Republican voters turned to Obama because they held the GOP responsible for the nation's financial crisis and found Obama's economic proposals more credible than those put forward by John McCain. Thus citizens can use information and judgment to overcome their predispositions. Without some political knowledge, citizens would have a difficult time making sense of the complex political world in which they live.

This point brings up two questions, however. First, how much political knowledge is necessary for one to act as an effective citizen? And second, how is political knowledge distributed throughout the population? In a recent study of political knowledge in the United States, the political scientists Michael X. Delli Carpini and Scott Keeter found that the average American exhibits little knowledge of political institutions, processes, leaders, and policy debates. Many Americans cannot even name their own congressional representative.[18] Does this ignorance of key political facts matter?

Another important concern is the character of those who possess and act on the political information that they acquire. Political knowledge is not evenly distributed throughout the population. Those with higher education, income, and occupational status and who are members of social or political organizations are more likely to know about and be active in politics. An interest in politics reinforces an individual's sense of **political efficacy** and provides more incentive to acquire additional knowledge and information about politics. Those who don't think they can have an effect on government tend not to be interested in learning about or participating in politics. As a result, individuals with a disproportionate share of income and education also have a disproportionate share of knowledge and influence and are better able to get what they want from government.

political efficacy the ability to influence government and politics

Because becoming truly knowledgeable about politics requires a substantial investment of time and energy, many Americans seek to acquire political information and to make political decisions "on the cheap," making use of shortcuts that seem to relieve them of having to engage in a lengthy process of information gathering and evaluation. One "inexpensive" way to become informed is to take cues from trusted others—the local minister, the television commentator or newspaper editorialist, an interest-group leader, friends and relatives.[19] Along the same lines, a common shortcut for political evaluation and decision making is to assess new issues and events through the lenses of one's more general beliefs and orientations. Thus, if a conservative learns of a plan to expand federal social programs, he or she might express opposition to the endeavor without spending too much time pondering the specific proposal. Similarly, if a liberal is told that Republican leaders are backing a major overhaul of the Social Security system, he or she will probably not need to read thousands of pages of economic projections before expressing disapproval of the GOP's efforts.

Neither of these shortcuts, however, is entirely reliable. Taking cues from others may lead individuals to accept positions they would not support if they had more information. And general ideological orientations are usually poor guides to decision making in concrete instances. For one thing, especially when applied to real issues, most individuals' beliefs turn out to be filled with contradictions. For example, what position should a liberal take on immigration? Should a liberal favor keeping America's borders open to poor people from all over the world? Or should a liberal be concerned that America's open borders create a pool of surplus labor that permits giant corporations to drive down the wages of poor American workers? Many other issues defy easy ideological characterization. What should liberals think about the nuclear cooperation pact between the United States and India enacted by Congress in 2008? How should conservatives view America's military actions in Iraq? Each of these policies combines a mix of issues and is too complex to lend itself to simple ideological interpretation.

Although understandable and, perhaps, inevitable, widespread inattentiveness to politics weakens American democracy in two ways. First, those who lack political information or resort to inadequate shortcuts to acquire and assess information cannot effectively defend their own political interests and can easily become victims or losers in political struggles. The presence, moreover, of large numbers of politically inattentive or ignorant individuals means that the political process can more easily be manipulated by the various institutions and forces that seek to shape public opinion.

POLITICAL KNOWLEDGE AND POLITICAL INEQUALITY If knowledge is power, lack of knowledge can be an enormous source of political weakness and contribute greatly to political inequality. When individuals are unaware of their

Governments frequently attempt to influence public opinion. This 1943 poster was intended to build support for World War II by associating it with the American Revolution.

interests or how to pursue them, it is virtually certain that political outcomes will not favor them. One example is in the realm of taxation. Over the past several decades, the United States has substantially reduced the rate of taxation paid by its wealthiest citizens. Most recently, tax cuts signed into law by President Bush provided a tax break mainly for the top 1 percent of the nation's wage earners; further tax cuts proposed by the president offer additional benefits to this privileged stratum. Surprisingly, however, polling data show that millions of middle-class and lower-middle-class Americans who do not stand to benefit from the president's tax cuts seem to favor them, nonetheless. The explanation for this odd state of affairs appears to be lack of political knowledge. Millions of individuals who are unlikely to derive much advantage from President Bush's tax policy think they will. The political scientist Larry Bartels has called this phenomenon "misplaced self-interest."[20] Upper-bracket taxpayers, who are usually served by an army of financial advisers, are unlikely to suffer from this problem.

The Influence of Political Leaders, Private Groups, and the Media

When individuals attempt to form opinions about particular political issues, events, and personalities, they seldom do so in isolation. Typically, they are confronted with—sometimes bombarded by—the efforts of a host of individuals and groups seeking to persuade them to adopt a particular point of view. Someone trying to decide what to think about Hillary Clinton, Barack Obama, or John McCain could hardly avoid an avalanche of opinions expressed through the media, in meetings, or in conversations with friends. The **marketplace of ideas** is the interplay of opinions and views that takes place as competing forces attempt to persuade as many people as possible to accept a particular position on a particular event. Given constant exposure to the ideas of others, it is virtually impossible for most individuals to resist some modification of their own beliefs. For example, as we saw earlier, African Americans and white Americans disagree on a number of matters. Yet as the political scientists Paul Sniderman and Edward Carmines have shown, considerable cross-racial agreement has evolved on fundamental issues of race and civil rights.[21]

marketplace of ideas the public forum in which beliefs and ideas are exchanged and compete

The marketplace of ideas has created a common ground on which the discussion of issues is encouraged, based on common understandings. Despite the many and often sharp divisions that exist in the twenty-first century—between liberals and conservatives or different income groups—most Americans see the world through similar lenses. This idea market makes it possible for ideas of all sorts to compete for attention and acceptance.

Few ideas spread spontaneously. Usually, whether they are matters of fashion, science, or politics, ideas must be vigorously promoted to become widely known and accepted. For example, the clothing, sports, and entertainment fads that occasionally seem to appear from nowhere and sweep the country before being replaced by some other new trend are almost always the product of careful marketing campaigns by some commercial interest, rather than spontaneous phenomena. Like their counterparts in fashion, successful—or at least widely held—political ideas are usually the products of carefully orchestrated campaigns by governments or by organized groups and interests, rather than the results of unheralded popular enthusiasm. In general, new ideas are presented in ways that make them seem consistent with, or even logical outgrowths of, Americans' more fundamental beliefs. For example, proponents of affirmative action generally present the policy as a necessary step toward racial equality. Or opponents of a proposed government regulation will vehemently assert that the rule is inconsistent with liberty. Both supporters and opponents of campaign finance reform seek to wrap their arguments in the cloak of democracy.[22]

Three forces that play important roles in shaping opinions are the government, private groups, and the news media.[23]

GOVERNMENT AND THE SHAPING OF PUBLIC OPINION All governments attempt, to a greater or lesser extent, to influence, manipulate, or manage their citizens' beliefs. But the extent to which public opinion is actually affected by governmental public-relations efforts is probably limited. The government—despite its size and power—is only one source of information and evaluation in the United States. Very often, governmental claims are disputed by the media, by interest groups, and at times by opposing forces within the government itself. Often, too, governmental efforts to manipulate public opinion backfire when the public is made aware of the government's tactics. Thus, in 1971, the United States government's efforts to build popular support for the Vietnam War were hurt when CBS News aired its documentary "The Selling of the Pentagon," which purported to reveal the extent and character of governmental efforts to sway popular sentiment. In this documentary, CBS demonstrated the techniques, including planted news stories and faked film footage, that the government had used to misrepresent its activities in Vietnam. These revelations, of course, undermined popular trust in all governmental claims.

A hallmark of the Clinton administration was the steady use of techniques like those used in election campaigns to bolster popular enthusiasm for White House initiatives. The president established a political "war room," similar to the one that operated in his campaign headquarters, where representatives from all departments met daily to discuss and coordinate the president's public-relations efforts. Many of the same consultants and pollsters who directed the successful Clinton campaign were also employed in the selling of the president's programs.[24]

Indeed, the Clinton White House made more sustained and systematic use of public-opinion polling than any previous administration. For example, during his presidency Bill Clinton relied heavily on the polling firm of Penn & Schoen to help him decide which issues to emphasize and what strategies to adopt. During the 1995–96 budget battle with Congress, the White House commissioned polls almost every night to chart changes in public perceptions about the struggle. Poll data suggested to Clinton that he should present himself as struggling to save

Politics Today

In October 2007, the Federal Emergency Management Agency (FEMA) staged a fake press conference with FEMA employees posing as reporters. How can the public protect itself from such forms of manipulation?

Medicare from Republican cuts. Clinton responded by launching a media attack against what he claimed were GOP efforts to hurt the elderly. This proved to be a successful strategy and helped Clinton defeat the Republican budget.[25]

After he assumed office in 2001, President George W. Bush asserted that political leaders should base their programs on their own conception of the public interest rather than the polls. This, however, did not mean that Bush ignored public opinion. Bush relied on the pollster Jan van Lohuizen to conduct a low-key operation, sufficiently removed from the limelight to allow the president to renounce polling while continuing to make use of survey data.[26] At the same time, the Bush White House developed an extensive public relations program, led by the former presidential aide Karen P. Hughes, to bolster popular support for the president's policies. Hughes, working with the conservative TV personality Mary Matalin, coordinated White House efforts to maintain popular support for the administration's war against terrorism. These efforts included presidential speeches, media appearances by administration officials, numerous press conferences, and thousands of press releases presenting the administration's views.[27] The White House also made a substantial effort to sway opinion in foreign countries, even sending officials to present the administration's views on television networks serving the Arab world.

For Critical Analysis

Bill Clinton polled public opinion on an almost daily basis. George W. Bush placed less emphasis on polling, apparently believing that leaders should follow their own judgment rather than popular sentiment. Which of these views is more appropriate in a democracy?

Another example of a Bush administration effort to shape public opinion is a series of commercials it produced at taxpayer expense in 2004 to promote the new Medicare prescription drug program. The commercials, prominently featuring the president, were designed to look like actual news stories and were aired in English and Spanish by hundreds of local television stations. Called a "video news release," this type of commercial is designed to give viewers the impression that they are watching a real news story. The presumption is that viewers are more likely to believe what they think is news coverage than material they know to be advertising. Democrats, of course, accused the administration of conducting a partisan propaganda campaign with public funds, but Republicans pointed out that the Clinton administration had engaged in similar practices.

PRIVATE GROUPS AND THE SHAPING OF PUBLIC OPINION We have already seen how the government tries to shape public opinion. But the ideas that become prominent in political life are also developed and spread by important economic and political groups searching for issues that will advance their causes. One example is the "right-to-life" issue, which has inflamed American politics over the past thirty years.

The notion of the right to life, whose proponents seek to outlaw abortion and overturn the Supreme Court's *Roe v. Wade* decision, was developed and heavily promoted by conservative politicians who saw the issue of abortion as a means of uniting Catholic and Protestant conservatives and linking both groups to the Republican Party. These politicians convinced Catholic and evangelical Protestant leaders that they shared similar views on the question of abortion, and they worked with religious leaders to focus public attention on the negative issues in the abortion debate. To advance their cause, leaders of the movement sponsored well-publicized Senate hearings, where testimony, photographs, and other exhibits were presented to illustrate the violent effects of abortion procedures. At the same time, publicists for the movement produced leaflets, articles, books, and films such as *The Silent Scream* to highlight the agony and pain ostensibly felt by the "unborn" when they were being aborted. All this underscored the movement's claim that abortion was nothing more or less than the murder of millions of innocent human beings. Finally, Catholic and evangelical Protestant religious leaders were organized to denounce abortion from their church pulpits and, increasingly, from their electronic pulpits on the Christian Broadcasting Network (CBN) and the various other television forums available for religious programming. Religious leaders also organized demonstrations, pickets, and disruptions at abortion clinics throughout the nation.[28] The abortion rights issue remains a potent one.

Because of the importance of public opinion, most presidents have made major efforts both to ascertain the public's views and to promote opinions favorable to themselves and their policies. Bill Clinton was often criticized for retaining a number of pollsters to chart shifts in public opinion on a daily basis.

Typically, ideas are marketed most effectively by groups with access to financial resources, public or private institutional support, and sufficient skill or education to select, develop, and draft ideas that will attract interest and support. Thus, the development and promotion of conservative themes and ideas in recent years have been greatly facilitated by the millions of dollars that conservative corporations and business organizations such as the Chamber of Commerce and the Public Affairs Council spend each year on public information and what is now called in corporate circles "issues management." In addition, conservative business leaders have contributed millions of dollars to such conservative institutions as the Heritage Foundation, the Hoover Institution, and the American Enterprise Institute.[29] Many of the ideas that helped those on the Right influence political debate were first developed and articulated by scholars associated with institutions such as these.

Although they do not usually have access to financial assets that match those available to their conservative opponents, liberal intellectuals and professionals have ample organizational skills; access to the media; and practice in creating, communicating, and using ideas. During the past three decades, the chief vehicle through which liberal intellectuals and professionals have advanced their ideas has been the "public interest group," an institution that relies heavily on voluntary contributions of time, effort, and interest on the part of its members. Through groups such as Common Cause, the National Organization for Women, the Sierra Club, Friends of the Earth, and Physicians for Social Responsibility, intellectuals and professionals have been able to apply their organizational skills and educational resources to developing and promoting ideas.[30] Often, research conducted in universities and in liberal "think tanks" such as the Brookings Institution provides the ideas on which liberal politicians rely. For example, the welfare reform plan introduced by the Clinton administration in 1994 originated with the work of a former Harvard professor, David Ellwood. Ellwood's academic research led him to the conclusion that the nation's welfare system would be improved if services to the poor were expanded in scope but limited in duration. His idea was adopted by the 1992 Clinton campaign, which was searching for a position on welfare that would appeal to both liberal and conservative Democrats. The Ellwood plan seemed perfect: it promised liberals an immediate expansion of welfare benefits, yet it held out to conservatives the idea that welfare recipients would receive benefits only for a limited period of time. The Clinton welfare reform plan even borrowed phrases from Ellwood's book *Poor Support*.[31]

The journalist and author Joe Queenan has correctly observed that although political ideas can erupt spontaneously, they almost never do. Instead, he says,

Opponents and proponents of a woman's right to choose often clash with one another. Large well-financed groups on both sides of the debate try to influence public opinion and government policy.

> issues are usually manufactured by tenured professors and obscure employees of think tanks. . . . It is inconceivable that the American people, all by themselves, could independently arrive at the conclusion that the depletion of the ozone layer poses a dire threat to our national well-being, or that an immediate, across-the-board cut in the capital-gains tax is the only thing that stands between us and the economic abyss. The American people do not have that kind of sophistication. They have to have help.[32]

THE MEDIA AND PUBLIC OPINION The communications media are among the most powerful forces operating in the marketplace of ideas. As we shall see in Chapter 7, the mass media are not simply neutral messengers for ideas developed by others. Instead, the media have an enormous impact on popular attitudes and opinions. Over time, the ways in which the mass media report political events help to shape the underlying attitudes and beliefs from which opinions emerge.[33] For example, for the past thirty years, the national news media have relentlessly investigated personal and official wrongdoing on the part of politicians and public officials. This continual media presentation of corruption in government and venality in politics has undoubtedly fostered the general attitude of cynicism and distrust that exists in the general public.

For Critical Analysis

Politicians, governments, and a host of groups endeavor to shape public perceptions of issues, events, and personalities. What are some of the ways these actors try to mold opinion? How can we distinguish between information and propaganda?

At the same time, the ways in which media coverage interprets or frames specific events can have a major impact on popular responses and opinions about these events.[34] Because media framing can be important, the Bush administration sought to persuade broadcasters to follow its lead in its coverage of terrorism and America's response to terrorism in the months following the September 11 attacks. Broadcasters, who found themselves targets of anthrax-contaminated letters apparently mailed by terrorists, needed little persuasion. For the most part, the media praised the president for his leadership and presented the administration's military campaign in Afghanistan and domestic antiterrorist efforts in a positive light. Even newspapers such as the *New York Times*, which had strongly opposed Bush in the 2000 election and questioned his fitness for the presidency, asserted that he had grown into the job. In the aftermath of the 2003 Iraq war, however, media coverage of the Bush administration became more critical. Formerly supportive media accused the president of failing both to anticipate the chaos and violence of postwar Iraq and to develop a strategy that would allow America to extricate itself from its involvement in Iraq. The president, for his part, accused the media of failing to present an accurate picture of his administration's successes in Iraq.

Measuring Public Opinion

As recently as fifty years ago, American political leaders gauged public opinion by people's applause and by the presence of crowds at meetings. This direct exposure to the people's views did not necessarily produce accurate knowledge of public opinion. It did, however, give political leaders confidence in their public support—and therefore confidence in their ability to govern by consent.

Abraham Lincoln and Stephen Douglas debated each other seven times during the summer and autumn of 1858, two years before they became presidential nominees. Their debates took place before audiences in parched cornfields and courthouse squares. A century later, the presidential debates, although seen by millions, take place before a few reporters, technicians, and audiences instructed not to applaud or make noise in television studios that might as well be on the moon. Only rarely can politicians experience the public's response directly. This distance between leaders and followers is one of the agonizing problems of modern democracy. The media send information to millions of people, but they are not yet as efficient at getting information back to leaders. Is government by consent possible where the scale of communication is so large and impersonal? In order to compensate for the decline in their ability to experience public opinion for themselves, leaders have turned to science, in particular to the science of opinion polling.

It is no secret that politicians and public officials make extensive use of **public-opinion polls** to help them decide whether to run for office, what policies to support, how to vote on important legislation, and what types of appeals to make in their campaigns. President Lyndon Johnson was famous for carrying the latest Gallup and Roper poll results in his pocket, and it is widely believed that he began to withdraw from politics because the polls reported losses in public support. All recent presidents and other major political figures have worked closely with polls and pollsters.

public-opinion polls scientific instruments for measuring public opinion

Constructing Public Opinion from Surveys

The population in which pollsters are interested is usually quite large. To conduct their polls they first choose a **sample** of the total population. The selection of this sample is important. Above all, it must be representative: the views of those in the sample must accurately and proportionately reflect the views of the whole. To a large extent, the validity of the poll's results depends on the sampling procedure used.

sample a small group selected by researchers to represent the most important characteristics of an entire population

probability sampling a method used by pollsters to select a representative sample in which every individual in the population has an equal probability of being selected as a respondent

SAMPLING TECHNIQUES AND SELECTION BIAS The most common techniques for choosing such a sample are probability sampling and random digit dialing. In **probability sampling,** the pollster begins with a listing of the population to be surveyed. This listing is called the "sampling frame." After each member of

Though public opinion is important, it is not always easy to interpret, and polls often fail to predict accurately how Americans will vote. In 1948, election-night polls showed Thomas Dewey defeating Harry S. Truman for the presidency.

the population is assigned a number, a table of random numbers or a computerized random selection process is used to select those to be surveyed. This technique is appropriate when the entire population can be identified. For example, all students registered at Texas colleges and universities can be identified from college records, and a sample of them can easily be drawn. When the pollster is interested in a national sample of Americans, however, this technique is not feasible, as no complete list of Americans exists.[35] National samples are usually drawn using a technique called **random digit dialing.** A computer random-number generator is used to produce a list of as many ten-digit numbers as the pollster deems necessary. Given that more than 95 percent of American households have telephones, this technique usually results in a random national sample. Similar techniques can be used to construct an Internet-based sample. Today, some polls contact respondents through the Internet. Still in its infancy, this form of polling is plagued by technical problems. In the years to come, though, Internet polling will very likely become common.[36]

random digit dialing a polling method in which respondents are selected at random from a list of ten-digit telephone numbers, with every effort made to avoid bias in the construction of the sample

The importance of sampling was brought home early in the history of political polling. A 1936 *Literary Digest* poll predicted that the Republican presidential candidate Alf Landon would defeat the Democrat Franklin D. Roosevelt in that year's presidential election. The actual election, of course, ended in a Roosevelt landslide. The main problem with the survey was what is called **selection bias** in drawing the sample. The pollsters had relied on telephone directories and automobile registration rosters to produce a sampling frame. During the Great Depression, only wealthier Americans owned telephones and automobiles. Thus, the millions of working-class Americans who constituted Roosevelt's principal base of support were excluded from the sample. A more recent instance of polling error caused by selection bias was the 1998 Minnesota gubernatorial election. A poll conducted by the *Minneapolis Star Tribune* just six weeks before the election showed Jesse Ventura running a distant

selection bias polling error that arises when the sample is not representative of the population being studied, which creates errors in overrepresenting or underrepresenting some opinions third to Democratic candidate Hubert Humphrey III, who seemed to have the support of 49 percent of the electorate, and the Republican Norm Coleman, whose support stood at 29 percent. Only 10 percent of those polled said they were planning to vote for Ventura. On election day, of course, Ventura outpolled both Humphrey and Coleman. Analysis of exit-poll data showed why the preelection polls had been so wrong. In an effort to be more accurate, preelection pollsters' predictions often take account of the likelihood that respondents will actually vote. This is accomplished by polling only people who have voted in the past or by correcting for past frequency of voting. The *Star Tribune* poll was conducted only among individuals who had voted in the previous election. Ventura, however, brought to the polls not only individuals who had not voted in the last election but also many people who had never voted before in their lives. Twelve percent of Minnesota's voters in 1998 said they came to the polls only because Ventura was on the ballot. This surge in turnout was facilitated by the fact that Minnesota permits same-day voter registration. (See Chapter 10 for a discussion of the consequences of registration rules.) Thus, the pollsters were wrong because Ventura changed the composition of the electorate.[37]

In recent years, the issue of selection bias has been further complicated by the fact that growing numbers of individuals refuse to answer pollsters' questions or use such devices as answering machines and "Caller ID" to screen unwanted callers. If pollsters could be certain that those who responded to their surveys simply reflected the views of those who refused to respond, there would be no problem. Some studies, however, suggest that the views of respondents and nonrespondents can differ, especially along social-class lines. Middle- and upper-middle-class individuals are more likely to be willing to respond to surveys than their working-class counterparts.[38] Thus far, "nonresponse bias" has not undermined a major national survey, but the possibility of a future *Literary Digest* fiasco should not be ignored.

SAMPLE SIZE The degree of reliability in polling is also a function of sample size. The same sample is needed to represent a small population as to represent a large population. The typical size of a sample ranges from 450 to 1,500 respondents. This number, however, reflects a trade-off between cost and degree of precision desired. The degree of accuracy that can be achieved with even a small sample can be seen from the polls' success in predicting election outcomes. The chance that the sample used does not accurately represent the population from which it is drawn is called the **sampling error** or *margin of error.* A typical survey of 1,500 respondents will have a sampling error of approximately 3 percent. When a preelection poll indicates 51 percent of voters surveyed favor the Republican candidate and 49 percent support the Democratic candidate, the outcome is too close to call because it is within the margin of error of the survey. A figure of 51 percent means that between 48 and 54 percent of voters in the population favor the Republicans, while a figure of 49 percent indicates that between 46 and 52 percent of all voters support the Democrats. Thus, in this example, a 52–48 percent Democratic victory would still be consistent with polls predicting a 51–49 percent Republican triumph.

sampling error polling error that arises based on the small size of the sample

Table 6.3 shows how accurate two of the major national polling organizations actually have been in predicting the outcomes of presidential elections. Pollsters have been mostly correct in their predictions.

SURVEY DESIGN Even with reliable sample procedures, surveys may fail to reflect the true distribution of opinion within a target population. One frequent source of **measurement error** is the wording of survey questions. The precise words

measurement error failure to identify the true distribution of opinion within a population because of errors such as ambiguous or poorly worded questions

TABLE 6.3 ★ Two Pollsters and Their Records (1948–2008)

Since their poor showing in 1948, the major pollsters have been close to the mark in every national presidential election. In 2000, though, neither Gallup nor Harris accurately predicted the outcome. From what you have learned about polling, what were some of the possible sources of error in these two national polls?

	HARRIS	GALLUP	ACTUAL OUTCOME
2008			
McCain	44%	43%	46%
Obama	50	51	53
2004			
Bush	49%	49%	51%
Kerry	48	49	48
Nader	1	1	0
2000			
Bush	47%	48%	48%
Gore	47	46	49
Nader	5	4	3
1996			
Clinton	51%	52%	49%
Dole	39	41	41
Perot	9	7	8
1992			
Clinton	44%	44%	43%
Bush	38	37	38
Perot	17	14	19
1988			
Bush	51%	53%	54%
Dukakis	47	42	46
1984			
Reagan	56%	59%	59%
Mondale	44	41	41
1980			
Reagan	48%	47%	51%
Carter	43	44	41
Anderson		8	
1976			
Carter	48%	48%	51%
Ford	45	49	48
1972			
Nixon	59%	62%	61%
McGovern	35	38	38
1968			
Nixon	40%	43%	43%
Humphrey	43	42	43
Wallace	13	15	14

(continued)

TABLE 6.3 ★ Two Pollsters and Their Records (1948–2008) (continued)

	HARRIS	GALLUP	ACTUAL OUTCOME
1964			
Johnson	62%	64%	61%
Goldwater	33	36	39
1960			
Kennedy	49%	51%	50%
Nixon	41	49	49
1956			
Eisenhower	NA	60%	58%
Stevenson		41	42
1952			
Eisenhower	47%	51%	55%
Stevenson	42	49	44
1948			
Truman	NA	44.5%	49.6%
Dewey		49.5	45.1

NOTE: All figures except those for 1948 are rounded. NA = Not asked.
SOURCES: Data from the Gallup Poll and the Harris Survey (New York: Chicago Tribune–New York News Syndicate, various press releases 1964–2004). Courtesy of the Gallup Organization and Louis Harris Associates.

used in a question can have an enormous impact on the answers it elicits. The validity of survey results can also be adversely affected by poor question format, faulty ordering of questions, inappropriate vocabulary, ambiguity of questions, or questions with built-in biases. Often, seemingly minor differences in the wording of a question can convey vastly different meanings to respondents and thus produce quite different response patterns (see Box 6.3). For example, for many years the University of Chicago's National Opinion Research Center has asked respondents whether they think the federal government is spending too much, too little, or about the right amount of money on "assistance for the poor." Answering the question posed this way, about two-thirds of all respondents seem to believe that the government is spending too little. However, the same survey also asks whether the government spends too much, too little, or about the right amount for "welfare." When the word "welfare" is substituted for "assistance for the poor," about half of all respondents indicate that too much is being spent.[39]

PUSH POLLING In recent years, a new form of bias has been introduced into surveys by the use of a technique called **push polling.** This technique is not intended to yield accurate information. Instead, it involves asking a respondent a loaded question about a political candidate designed to elicit the response sought by the pollster and, simultaneously, to shape the respondent's perception of the candidate in question. One of the most notorious uses of push polling occurred in the 2000 South Carolina Republican presidential primary, in which George W. Bush defeated John McCain and went on to win the presidency. Callers working

push polling a polling technique in which the questions are designed to shape the respondent's opinion

BOX 6.3 It Depends on How You Ask

The public's desire for tax cuts can be hard to measure. In 2000, pollsters asked what should be done with the nation's budget surplus and got different results depending on the specifics of the question.

THE QUESTION

President Clinton has proposed setting aside approximately two-thirds of an expected budget surplus to fix the Social Security system. What do you think the leaders in Washington should do with the remainder of the surplus?

VARIATION 1

Should the money be used for a tax cut, or should it be used to fund new government programs?

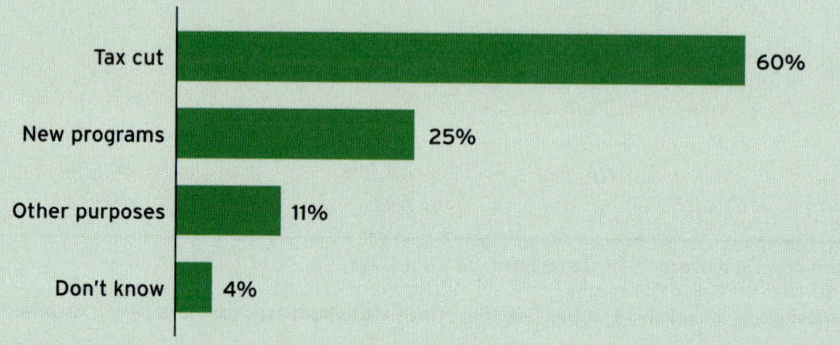

VARIATION 2

Should the money be used for a tax cut, or should it be spent on programs for education, the environment, health care, crime fighting, and military defense?

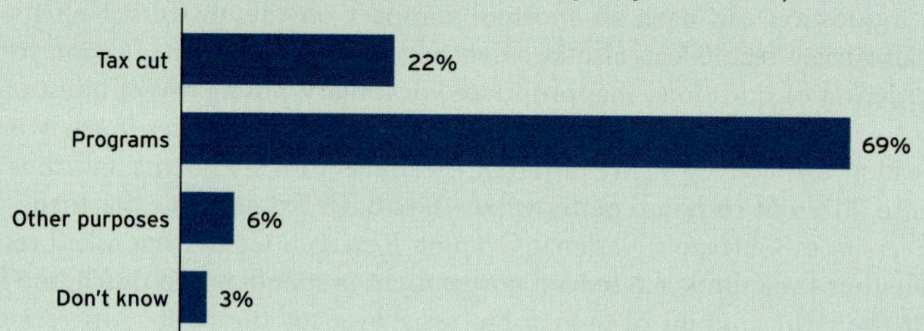

SOURCE: Pew Research Center, reported in the *New York Times,* January 30, 2000, p. WK 3.

for Bush supporters asked Conservative white voters if they would be more or less likely to vote for McCain if they knew that he had fathered an illegitimate black child. Because McCain often campaigned with a daughter whom he and his wife had adopted from Mother Teresa's orphanage in Bangladesh, many voters accepted the premise of the "poll." This push poll was often cited by McCain as one of the political smear tactics that had made him reluctant to expose his family to the stresses of the 2008 presidential race. More than one hundred consulting firms across the nation now specialize in push polling.[40] Calling push polling the "political equivalent of a drive-by shooting," Representative Joe Barton (R-Tex.) launched a congressional investigation into the practice.[41] Push polls may be one

In 2000, the major networks announced, on the basis of their exit polls, that Al Gore had defeated George W. Bush. Later, they were forced to retract their prediction.

reason that Americans are becoming increasingly skeptical about the practice of polling and increasingly unwilling to answer pollsters' questions.[42]

ILLUSION OF SALIENCY During the early days of a political campaign, when voters are asked which candidates they do, or do not, support, the answer they give often has little significance, because the choice is not yet important to them. Their preferences may change many times before the actual election. This is part of the explanation for the phenomenon of the postconvention "bounce" in the popularity of presidential candidates, which was observed after the Democratic and Republican national conventions in 1992 and 1996.[43] Respondents' preferences reflected the amount of attention a candidate had received during the conventions rather than strongly held views.

Salient interests are interests that stand out beyond others, that are of more than ordinary concern to respondents in a survey or to voters in the electorate. Politicians, social scientists, journalists, or pollsters who assume something is important to the public, when in fact it is not, create an **illusion of saliency.** This illusion can be created and fostered by polls despite careful controls over sampling, interviewing, and data analysis. In fact, the illusion is strengthened by the credibility that science gives survey results.

salient interests attitudes and views that are especially important to the individual holding them

illusion of saliency the impression conveyed by polls that something is important to the public when actually it is not

The problem of saliency has become especially acute as a result of the proliferation of media polls. The television networks and major national newspapers all make heavy use of opinion polls. Increasingly, polls are being commissioned by local television stations and local and regional newspapers as well.[44] On the positive side, polls allow journalists to make independent assessments of political realities—assessments not influenced by the partisan claims of politicians.

At the same time, however, media polls can allow journalists to make news when none really exists. Polling diminishes journalists' dependence on news makers. A poll commissioned by a news agency can provide the basis for a good story even when candidates, politicians, and other news makers refuse to cooperate by engaging in newsworthy activities. Thus, on days when little or nothing is actually

AMERICA IN THE WORLD

How Americans View the World and Vice Versa

When they are not being accused of seeking to conquer the world, Americans are often charged with failing to pay enough attention to international affairs. It is true that many Americans lack a basic knowledge of world history and geography and have considerable difficulty naming the leaders of other nations. Several surveys have indicated that some Americans think Canada is one of the 50 states. Nevertheless, Americans do have strong opinions about which foreign nations are America's friends in the world and which are its foes. Topping the list of friends is Great Britain, seen by 74 percent of recent poll respondents as a "close ally." Curiously, 2 percent of those surveyed viewed Britain as an enemy. Perhaps they have not forgotten King George's mistreatment of the colonists in 1775. When it comes to China, now one of America's most important trading partners, only 9 percent of Americans believe China is a close ally, whereas 54 percent think China is not friendly or even is America's enemy. It is interesting to note also that France, traditionally an American ally, came to be viewed less favorably than Russia, America's Cold War adversary, in the wake of vocal French opposition to America's Middle East policy.

Just as Americans have opinions about the world, citizens of other nations have their own opinions about America. Americans sometimes complain that their efforts on behalf of other nations are not properly appreciated and feel envied and disliked by the rest of the world. Only Kenyan, Nigerian, and Filipino respondents to a recent survey had an overwhelmingly positive view of America. Even normally friendly Europeans seem to have developed a negative view of the United States.

During the American occupation of Iraq, antagonism toward American foreign policy has hardened even more in most Muslim countries. An overwhelming majority of those polled in the Middle East expressed strongly anti-American sentiment. The enduring popularity of Osama bin Laden in these countries also reinforces Muslim attitudes generally toward the United States. Worldwide, a majority of people, believed that the United States' war on terror is actually an attempt to control the Middle East's oil or to dominate the world. The Bush administration's foreign policies earned few converts abroad and lost support at home as well.

FOR CRITICAL ANALYSIS

1. What are the factors shaping the ways Americans view other nations and how others view America?
2. Should Americans care about how they are seen around the world? Why or why not?

GLOBAL VIEWS OF THE UNITED STATES

	MOSTLY POSITIVE	MOSTLY NEGATIVE		MOSTLY POSITIVE	MOSTLY NEGATIVE
Argentina	13	64	Italy	35	47
Australia	29	60	Kenya	70	20
Brazil	29	57	Lebanon	34	58
Chile	33	51	Mexico	12	53
China	28	52	Nigeria	72	20
Egypt	11	59	Philippines	73	11
France	24	69	Poland	38	24
Germany	16	74	Portugal	29	55
Great Britain	33	57	Russia	19	59
Hungary	29	31	South Korea	35	54
India	30	28	Turkey	7	69
Indonesia	21	71	UAE	25	57

SOURCE: BBC/Globe Scan, 2007.

taking place in a political campaign, poll results, especially apparent changes in candidate popularity margins, can provide exciting news. Several times during the 2008 presidential campaign, for example, small changes in the relative standing of the Democratic and Republican candidates produced banner headlines around the country. Stories about what the candidates actually did or said often took second place to reporting the "horse race."

Interestingly, because rapid and dramatic shifts in candidate margins tend to take place when voters' preferences are least fully formed, horse-race news is most likely to make the headlines when it is actually least significant.[45] In other words, media interest in poll results is inversely related to the actual salience of voters' opinions and the significance of the polls' findings. However, by influencing perceptions, especially those of major contributors, media polls can influence political realities.

BANDWAGON EFFECT The most noted, but least serious, of polling problems is the **bandwagon effect,** which occurs when polling results influence people to support the candidate marked as the probable victor. Some scholars argue that this bandwagon effect can be offset by an "underdog effect" in favor of the candidate who is trailing in the polls.[46] However, a candidate who demonstrates a lead in the polls usually finds it considerably easier to raise campaign funds than a candidate whose poll standing is poor. With these additional funds, poll leaders can often afford to pay for television time and other campaign activities that will cement their advantage.

bandwagon effect a shift in electoral support to the candidate whom public opinion polls report as the front-runner

Thinking Critically about Public Opinion and Democracy

A major purpose of democratic government, with its participatory procedures and representative institutions, is to ensure that political leaders will heed public opinion. And, indeed, a good deal of evidence suggests that they do. There are many instances in which public policy and public opinion do not coincide, but in general the government's actions are consistent with citizens' preferences. One recent study, for example, found that between 1935 and 1979, in about two-thirds of all cases, significant changes in public opinion were followed within one year by changes in government policy consistent with the shift in the popular mood.[47] Other studies have come to similar conclusions about public opinion and government policy at the state level.[48] Some recent studies, however, have suggested that the responsiveness of government to public opinion has been declining, reaching an all-time low during President Clinton's first term. These findings imply that, contrary to popular beliefs, elected leaders don't always pander to the results of public opinion polls, but instead use polling to sell their policy proposals and shape the public's views.[49]

In addition, areas of disagreement always arise between opinion and policy. For example, the majority of Americans favored stricter governmental control of handguns for years before Congress finally adopted the modest restrictions on firearms purchases embodied in the Brady bill and the Violent Crime Control Act, passed in 1993 and 1994, respectively. Similarly, most Americans—blacks as well as whites—

For Critical Analysis

In what ways does the public, through opinion, control its political leaders? In what ways do political leaders control public opinion? What are the positive and negative consequences of governing by popular opinion?

Become a Savvy Consumer of Polls

In a recent *Washington Post* poll, 69 percent of respondents under age thirty said they preferred a "bigger government with bigger services" over a smaller one with fewer services. This preference stands in stark contrast to the opinions of Americans ages thirty and up, a majority of whom favor smaller government.

More important, this gap in opinion is not an isolated phenomenon. Similar disparities exist between the attitudes of young and older Americans on a host of other issues. For example, when compared with older adults, today's youth are more supportive of plans to privatize Social Security, more likely to argue that economic growth needs to be balanced by environmental concerns, more tolerant of the rights of gays and lesbians, and the most supportive of affirmative action programs.

As you read this, you may wonder if the public-opinion differences between young people and older Americans are real, or if they've been manufactured by pollsters, politicians, or pundits trying to push their various agendas. This is a legitimate concern. Indeed, although accurate polls can yield important information about public opinion, it is not uncommon for polls to be manipulated and distorted by those who have a stake in the findings. In this case, you can trust the numbers; the data cited above comes from scientific opinion polls, designed and fielded by reputable scholars or polling agencies.

But how do you know when to trust a poll? If you were buying a new computer or car or MP3 player, you'd learn something about its properties (or its manufacturer) in order to evaluate its worth. You can easily become a savvy consumer of polls as well. For the most part, this involves asking a few key questions, such as the ones listed below.

- ★ *Who's behind the poll?* This means asking not just who paid for the poll, but who actually conducted the interviews and published the results. Most news outlets include this information in their coverage, but if you find a reference to a poll in a candidate's promotional material or an interest group's solicitation, you may need to contact the campaign or group for more information.
- ★ *Who participated in the poll?* This includes determining how many people were interviewed, if they were chosen scientifically (rather than by self-selection, for example), and if the respondents were representative of a larger population. Bigger samples aren't necessarily better—it is more important that the sample was selected through a scientific (usually random) method and that the characteristics of the respondents generally match those of the group they are supposed to represent. For example, are there more women than men in the sample? Are respondents balanced in terms of region, religion, and ethnicity? Should they be?
- ★ *Is there a margin of error (also called sampling error) associated with the poll?* If this information is included in the description of the survey results, it is a good sign that the sample was drawn scientifically.
- ★ *Is the wording or the order of the questions suspicious?* Even a scientifically selected poll can be susceptible of other biases. For example, two questions about the same topic using similar, but not exactly the same, wording can elicit very different responses. Poll numbers can also be affected by the order in which questions were asked. Most polling organizations will include an exact copy of their questionnaire along with their analysis. Almost all on-line news outlets provide a link to the full set of questions.
- ★ *Could this be considered a pseudopoll or a push poll?* Both of these types of polls are problematic, for different reasons. Pseudopolls, often found on Web sites, are not accurate measures of public opinion because respondents simply decide for themselves that they want to participate, rather than being selected scientifically. As we saw in this chapter, push polls are not really polls at all, but an attempt to spread negative rumors or innuendos about a candidate for office under the guise of a poll.

oppose school busing to achieve racial balance, yet such busing continues to be used in many parts of the nation. Most Americans are far less concerned with the rights of the accused than the federal courts seem to be. Most Americans usually oppose U.S. military intervention in other nations' affairs, yet such interventions continue to take place in such regions as Bosnia, Haiti, and Iraq, where American troops are currently stationed, and often win public approval after the fact. Of course, the overwhelming majority of Americans supported the Bush administration's decision to attack Afghanistan after September 11.

George W. Bush's efforts to shape public opinion didn't always work. For instance, while onboard the aircraft carrier USS Abraham Lincoln *in 2003, President Bush declared "mission accomplished" at the end of major combat in Iraq. Yet the continuing guerrilla warfare and suicide bombings in Iraq contributed to a sharp decline in his public approval rating.*

Several factors can contribute to a lack of consistency between opinion and governmental policy. First, the nominal majority on a particular issue may not be as intensely committed to its preference as the adherents of the minority viewpoint. An intensely committed minority may often be more willing to commit its time, energy, efforts, and resources to the affirmation of its opinions than an apathetic, even if large, majority. In the case of firearms, for example, although the proponents of gun control are by a wide margin the majority, most do not regard the issue as one of critical importance to themselves and are not willing to commit much effort to advancing their cause. The opponents of gun control, by contrast, are intensely committed, well organized, and well financed, and as a result are usually able to carry the day.

A second important reason that public policy and public opinion may not coincide has to do with the character and structure of the American system of government. The framers of the American Constitution, as we saw in Chapter 2, sought to create a system of government that was based on popular consent but that did not invariably and automatically translate shifting popular sentiments into public policies. As a result, the American governmental process includes arrangements such as an appointed judiciary that can produce policy decisions that may run contrary to prevailing popular sentiment—at least for a time.

Perhaps the inconsistencies between opinion and policy could be resolved if we made broader use of a mechanism currently employed by a number of states—the initiative and referendum. This procedure allows propositions to be placed on the ballot and voted into law by the electorate, bypassing most of the normal machinery of representative government. In recent years, several important propositions sponsored by business and conservative groups have been enacted by voters in certain states.[50] For example, California's Proposition 209, approved by the state's voters in 1996, prohibited the state and local government agencies in California from using race or gender preferences in hiring, contracting, or university admissions decisions. Responding to conservatives' success, liberal groups launched a number of ballot initiatives in 2000. For example, in Washington state, voters were asked to consider propositions sponsored by teachers' unions that would have required annual cost-of-living raises for teachers and more than $1.8 billion in additional state spending over the next six years.[51] In 2004, voters in thirty-four states considered 162 ballot referenda. In eleven of these states, voters approved bans on same-sex marriage. In Montana, voters approved the use of marijuana for medical purposes. In Alaska, voters narrowly defeated a proposition to make marijuana use legal for all adults.

Initiatives such as these seem to provide the public with an opportunity to express its will. The major problem, however, is that government by initiative offers little opportunity for reflection and compromise. Voters are presented with a proposition, usually sponsored by a special-interest group, and are asked to take it or leave it. Perhaps the true will of the people, not to mention their best interest, might lie somewhere between the positions taken by various interest groups. Perhaps, for example, California voters might have wanted affirmative action programs to be modified but not scrapped altogether as Proposition 209 mandated. In a representative assembly, as opposed to a referendum campaign, a compromise position might have been achieved that was more satisfactory to all the residents of the state. This is one reason the framers of the U.S. Constitution strongly favored representative government rather than direct democracy.

When all is said and done, even without the initiative and the referendum, there can be little doubt that in general the actions of the American government do not remain out of line with popular sentiment for very long. We can take these as signs of a vital and thriving democracy.

FOR FURTHER READING

Althaus, Scott. *Collective Preferences in Democratic Politics.* New York: Cambridge University Press, 2003.

Berinsky, Adam. *Silent Voices: Public Opinion and Political Participation in America.* Princeton, NJ: Princeton University Press, 2005.

Bishop, George. *The Illusion of Public Opinion.* New York: Rowman and Littlefield, 2004.

Erikson, Robert, and Kent Tedin. *American Public Opinion.* 7th ed. New York: Longman, 2004.

Fiorina, Morris. *Culture War: The Myth of a Polarized America.* New York: Longman, 2005.

Gallup, George. *The Pulse of Democracy.* New York: Simon and Schuster, 1940.

Ginsberg, Benjamin. *The Captive Public: How Mass Opinion Promotes State Power.* New York: Basic Books, 1986.

Glynn, Carol, ed. *Public Opinion.* Boulder, CO: Westview, 2004.

Jacobs, Lawrence R., and Robert Y. Shapiro. *Politicians Don't Pander: Political Manipulation and the Loss of Democratic Responsiveness.* Chicago: University of Chicago Press, 2000.

Key, V. O. *Public Opinion and American Democracy.* New York: Knopf, 1961.

Lippman, Walter. *Public Opinion.* New York: Harcourt, Brace, 1922.

Stimson, James. *Tides of Consent: How Public Opinion Shapes American Politics.* New York: Cambridge University Press, 2004.

Zaller, John. *The Nature and Origins of Mass Opinion.* New York: Cambridge University Press, 1992.

RECOMMENDED WEB SITES

American Association for Public Opinion Research
www.aapor.org/
This is one of the premier academic sites for public opinion data on a host of political and social topics.

Etalkinghead
http://directory.etalkinghead.com/
Political blogs have become an increasingly popular way for Americans to express and discuss political opinions. This Web page provides a directory of political blogs by ideology and issue.

Gallup
www.gallup.com/
The Gallup Organization has been involved in the scientific study of public opinion for over seventy years and is very highly regarded. This Web site contains public-opinion data archives, video archives, and international polls.

The Political Compass
www.politicalcompass.org/

A political ideology is a cohesive set of beliefs that form a general philosophy about government; however, people are often unsure if they are liberal, moderate, or conservative. Go to the Web site for The Political Compass and take the test to see if it helps you identify your ideology.

Polling Report
http://pollingreport.com

This independent, nonpartisan resource tracks trends in American public opinion. On this site you will find countless political opinion polls by all of the major media outlets, all in one place.

Public Agenda
www.publicagenda.org/polling/polling_20q.cfm

Measuring public opinion from surveys can be problematic. Oftentimes samples contain selection bias, or surveys have measurement error. Public Agenda is an organization that studies public opinion on major policy issues. Its Web site contains critiques of public opinion.

ThisNation.com
www.thisnation.com/socialization.html

The process through which underlying political beliefs and values are formed is called political socialization. This civic-minded Web page offers a brief discussion of political socialization with some related Web links.

STUDY OUTLINE

www.wwnorton.com/wtp7e

Understanding Public Opinion

1. Although Americans have many political differences, they share a common set of values, including liberty, equality of opportunity, and democracy.
2. Agreement on fundamental political values is probably more widespread in the United States than anywhere else in the Western world.
3. Often for reasons associated with demographics, Americans' opinions do differ widely on a variety of issues.
4. Most people acquire their initial orientation to politics from their families.
5. Membership in both voluntary and involuntary social groups can affect an individual's political values through personal experience, the influence of group leaders, and recognition of political interests.
6. One's level of education is an important factor in shaping political beliefs.
7. Conditions under which individuals and groups are recruited into political life also shape political orientations.
8. Many Americans describe themselves as either liberal or conservative in political orientation.

How We Form Political Opinions

1. Although ideologies shape political opinions, they seldom fully determine one's views.
2. Political opinions are influenced by an individual's underlying values, knowledge of political issues, and external forces such as the government, private groups, and the media.

Measuring Public Opinion

1. In order to construct public opinion from surveys, a polling sample must be large, and the views of those in the sample must accurately and proportionately reflect the views of the whole.

Thinking Critically about Public Opinion and Democracy

1. Government policies in the United States are generally consistent with popular preferences. There are, however, always some inconsistencies.
2. Disagreements between opinion and policy come about because on some issues, such as gun control, an intensely committed minority can defeat a more apathetic majority. Moreover, the American system of government is not designed to quickly transform changes in opinion into changes in government programs.

PRACTICE QUIZ

www.wwnorton.com/wtp7e

1. The term *public opinion* is used to describe
   a) the collected speeches and writings made by a president during his or her term in office.
   b) the analysis of events broadcast by news reporters during the evening news.
   c) the beliefs and attitudes that people have about issues.
   d) decisions of the Supreme Court.
2. Variables such as income, education, race, gender, and ethnicity
   a) often create differences of political opinion in America.
   b) have consistently been a challenge to America's core political values.
   c) have little impact on political opinions.
   d) help explain why public opinion polls are so unreliable.
3. Which of the following is an agency of socialization?
   a) the family
   b) social groups
   c) education
   d) all of the above
4. When men and women respond differently to issues of public policy, they are demonstrating an example of
   a) liberalism.
   b) educational differences.
   c) the gender gap.
   d) party politics.
5. The process by which Americans learn political beliefs and values is called
   a) brainwashing.
   b) propaganda.
   c) indoctrination.
   d) political socialization.
6. In addition to one's basic political values, what other two factors influence one's political opinions?
   a) ideology and party identification
   b) political knowledge and the influence of political leaders, private groups, and the media
   c) the gender gap and the education gap
   d) sample size and the bandwagon effect
7. Which of the following is (are) *not* an important external influence on how political opinions are formed?
   a) the government and political leaders
   b) private interest groups
   c) the media
   d) the Constitution
8. Which of the following is the term used in public opinion polling to denote the small group representing the opinions of the whole population?
   a) control group
   b) sample
   c) micropopulation
   d) respondents
9. When politicians, pollsters, journalists, or social scientists assume something is important to the public when in fact it is not, they are creating
   a) an illusion of saliency.
   b) an illusion of responsibility.
   c) a gender gap.
   d) an elitist issue.
10. A familiar polling problem is the "bandwagon effect," which occurs when
    a) the same results are used over and over again.
    b) polling results influence people to support the candidate marked as the probable victor in a campaign.
    c) polling results influence people to support the candidate who is trailing in a campaign.
    d) background noise makes it difficult for a pollster and a respondent to communicate with each other.

KEY TERMS

www.wwnorton.com/wtp7e

agencies of socialization (p. 210)
attitude (or opinion) (p. 207)
bandwagon effect (p. 239)
conservative (p. 219)
democracy (p. 207)
equality of opportunity (p. 207)
gender gap (p. 211)
illusion of saliency (p. 237)
liberal (p. 219)
liberty (p. 207)
marketplace of ideas (p. 226)
measurement error (p. 233)
political efficacy (p. 225)
political ideology (p. 207)
political socialization (p. 210)
probability sampling (p. 231)
public opinion (p. 207)
public-opinion polls (p. 231)
push polling (p. 235)
random digit dialing (p. 232)
salient interests (p. 237)
sample (p. 231)
sampling error (p. 233)
selection bias (p. 232)
values (or beliefs) (p. 207)

7 The Media

Troop Readiness, Veteran
and Iraq Accountabili
Expand funding for vete
and hospitals
Bush Administration must
standards for troop readiness
Iraqi government must
benchmarks for
Strategic
troops by 2
Refocus
and fighting

★ The Media Industry and Government

★ News Coverage

★ Media Power in American Politics

★ Thinking Critically about Media Power and Democracy

WHAT GOVERNMENT DOES AND WHY IT MATTERS

One area in which our government's role is intended to be minimal is the realm of the news media. The Constitution's First Amendment guarantees freedom of the press, and most Americans believe that a free press is an essential condition for both liberty and democratic politics. Certainly, the press is usually ready to denounce any government action that smacks of censorship or news manipulation. Nevertheless, attempts to silence or discredit the opposition press have a long history in America. The infamous Alien and Sedition Acts were enacted by the Federalists in an attempt to silence the Republican press. In more recent times, during the McCarthy era of the 1950s, right-wing politicians used charges of communist infiltration to intimidate the liberal news media. During President Richard Nixon's administration, the White House attacked its critics in the media by threatening to take action to bar the television networks from owning local affiliates, as well as by illegally wiretapping the phones of government officials suspected of leaking information to the press. During the early 1980s, conservative groups financed a series of libel suits against CBS News, *Time* magazine, and other media organizations in an attempt to discourage them from publicizing material critical of Reagan administration policies.[1] In 2004, an article by the investigative reporter Seymour Hersh in the *New Yorker,* along with a story on *60 Minutes II,* revealed that American soldiers had abused Iraqi prisoners in their custody. The story prompted a televised apology from President Bush, congressional hearings, and calls for the resignation of Defense Secretary Donald Rumsfeld. The Bush administration was furious but, like previous presidencies, could do little to silence its media critics. In all these instances, attempts to browbeat and intimidate the press failed.

Candidates for political office also complain frequently about the media. During the 2008 primary campaign, Hillary Clinton frequently asserted that the media were treating her opponent, and eventual Democratic nominee, Senator Barack Obama with kid gloves while giving her candidacy generally negative treatment. Echoing Clinton's complaint, during a famous skit on *Saturday Night Live* (*SNL*), the Hillary

Clinton character was subjected to a good deal of indignity by reporters, while the Obama character was fawned over. Of course, the *SNL* skit belied its own point by demonstrating that Clinton, too, could count upon some segments of the media for support.

In a similar vein, during the general election campaign in 2008, Republicans complained that the media, MSNBC in particular, were strongly anti-McCain and pro-Obama in their coverage. Democrats replied that MSNBC was very fair while other media outlets, Fox in particular, evidenced constant anti-Obama and pro-McCain bias. Republican candidate John McCain normally had good relations with the press. During the course of the campaign, however, McCain began to attack the media regarding their alleged bias. Complaints from McCain and his advisers became especially sharp after the national media began to question his choice of Sarah Palin as the GOP's vice-presidential candidate. The media regarded Palin as unprepared and unqualified for the job and generally gave her negative coverage. During the 2008 vice-presidential debate, Palin made a point of expressing her gratitude to the debate's organizers for allowing her an opportunity to speak to the American people without the intervention of interviewers and commentators who, in her view, constantly distorted her comments to make her appear foolish and uninformed.

Presumably, the only way that the media might avoid charges of bias by one side or the other would be to avoid presenting negative information about either side. But, of course, we rely upon the media to "vet" candidates by digging into their public claims and private records to help ensure that the individuals we elect to office are sufficiently trustworthy to hold positions of responsibility. Politicians who are the subjects of media revelations, of course, declare that their private lives are not the public's business and castigate the media for prying. However, when the media reveal that a politician has lied, cheated, stolen, or engaged in inappropriate sexual relationships, they are warning us that this individual may not be suited to hold high office. By looking closely at the actions of politicians, the media give us an opportunity to choose a better government.

Without the media's investigations and exposés, citizens would be forced to rely entirely on the information politicians and the government provide to them. This would hardly afford citizens a proper opportunity to evaluate issues and form reasoned opinions. Critical media play an essential role in a nation whose citizens hope to govern themselves.

- **In this chapter, we will examine the place of the media in American politics. First, we will look at the organization and regulation of the American news media.** The media industry continues to grow larger but remains centralized, which results in little variety in what is reported about national issues. Despite the importance of freedom of the press in the United States, the media are still subject to some regulation by the government.

- **Second, we will discuss the factors that help to determine what's "news."** The agenda of issues and type of coverage that the media provide are affected most by those who create the news and those who consume the news.

- **Third, we will examine the scope of media power in politics.** What the media report can have far-reaching effects on public perceptions of political events, issues, leaders, and institutions.

The Media Industry and Government

The American news media are among the world's freest and most vast. Americans literally have thousands of available options to find political reporting. This wide variety of newspapers, newsmagazines, broadcast media, and Web sources regularly present information that is at odds with the government's claims, as well as editorial opinions sharply critical of high-ranking officials. The freedom to speak one's mind is one of the most cherished of American political values. Yet although thousands of media companies exist across the United States, surprisingly little variety appears in what is reported about national events and issues.

Types of Media

Americans get their news from three main sources: broadcast media (radio and television), print media (newspapers and magazines), and, increasingly, the Internet (see Figure 7.1). Each of these sources has distinctive characteristics. Television news reaches more Americans than any other single news source. Tens of millions of individuals watch national and local news programs every day. Television news, however, covers relatively few topics and provides little depth of coverage. It serves the extremely important function of alerting viewers to issues and events, but generally doesn't provide much more than a series of **sound bites,** brief quotes and short characterizations of the day's events. Because they are aware of the character of television news coverage, politicians and other news makers often seek to manipulate the news by providing the media with sound bites that will dominate news coverage for at least a few days. Thus, in 2007 Senator Barack Obama generated headlines when he accused his presidential rival Senator Hillary Clinton of duplicity. Obama said, "Senator Clinton votes like a hawk in Washington while talking like a dove in Iowa." Several years earlier, Hillary Clinton had portrayed the effort to impeach her husband as a "vast right-wing conspiracy." George H. W. Bush's famous 1988 sound bite, "Read my lips, no new taxes," received a great deal

sound bites short snippets of information aimed at dramatizing a story rather than explaining its substantive meaning

FIGURE 7.1 ★ Young Americans* and Political News

At one time, newspapers and the network news were the dominant news sources in the United States. However, this survey of young Americans about news sources during the 2008 elections indicates that first TV and now the Internet have become more important. What are some likely consequences of this shift?

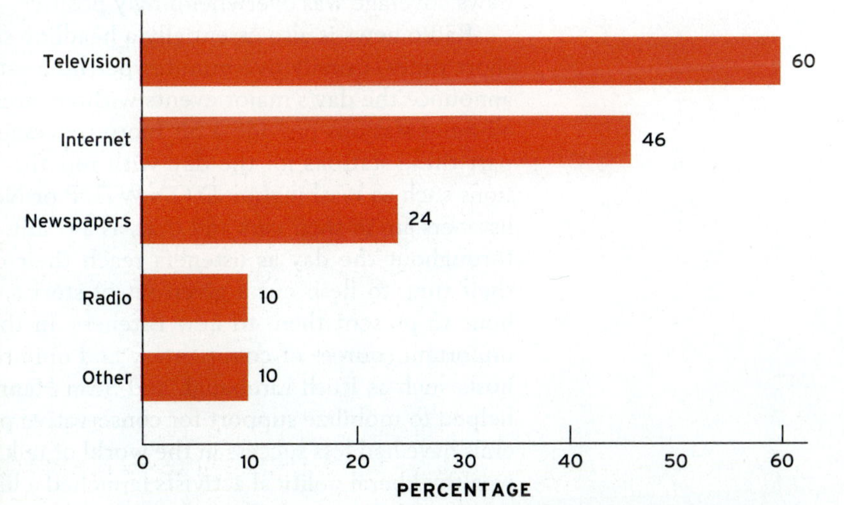

*Eighteen- to twenty-nine-year-olds.
SOURCE: Pew Internet and American Life Survey, 2008.

In 2007, President Bush used a nationally televised address to announce his plan to send a surge of 20,000 additional American troops to Iraq. Modern presidents have tended to use televised addresses to try to reassure the nation in times of controversy and crisis.

of media coverage. (Two years later he was, in effect, bitten by his own sound bite when he signed legislation that included new taxes.) Twenty-four-hour news stations such as Cable News Network (CNN) offer more detail and commentary than the networks' half-hour evening news shows. Even CNN and the others, however, offer more headlines than analysis, especially during their prime-time broadcasts.

Politicians generally consider local broadcast news a friendlier venue than the national news. National reporters are often inclined to criticize and question, whereas local reporters are more likely to accept the pronouncements of national leaders at face value. For this reason, presidents often introduce new proposals in a series of short visits to a number of cities—indeed, sometimes flying from airport stop to airport stop—in addition to or instead of making a national presentation. For example, in 2007 President George W. Bush announced his plan to reduce violence in Iraq, the so-called surge strategy, in a nationally televised speech and then made a number of local speeches around the country promoting the same theme. National reporters questioned the president's plans, but local news coverage was overwhelmingly positive.

Radio news is also essentially a headline service, but without pictures. In the short time—usually five minutes per hour—they devote to news, radio stations announce the day's major events without providing much detail. In major cities, all-news stations provide a bit more coverage of major stories, but for the most part these stations fill the day with repetition rather than detail. All-news stations such as Washington, D.C.'s WTOP or New York's WCBS assume that most listeners are in their cars and that, as a result, the people in the audience change throughout the day as listeners reach their destinations. Thus, rather than use their time to flesh out a given set of stories, they repeat the same stories each hour to present them to new listeners. In the 1990s, radio talk shows became important sources of commentary and opinion. A number of conservative radio hosts such as Rush Limbaugh and Sean Hannity have huge audiences and have helped to mobilize support for conservative political causes and candidates. Liberals have had less success in the world of talk radio. In 2003, however, a group of wealthy liberal political activists launched a liberal talk-radio network, Air America, designed to combat conservative dominance of this important medium.

The old-fashioned newspaper remains perhaps the most important source of news. Newspapers are critically important even though they are not the primary news source for most Americans. The print media are important for three reasons. First, as we shall see later in this chapter, the broadcast media rely on leading newspapers such as the *New York Times* and the *Washington Post* to set their news agenda. The broadcast media engage in very little actual reporting; they primarily cover stories that have been "broken," or initially reported, by the print media. For example, sensational charges that President Bill Clinton had an affair with a White House intern were reported first by the *Washington Post* and *Newsweek* before being trumpeted around the world by the broadcast media. It is only a slight exaggeration to observe that if an event is not covered in the *New York Times,* it is not likely to appear on the *CBS Evening News.* Second, the print media are important because they tend to provide more detailed and complete information, offering a better context for analysis. Third, the print media are important because they are the prime source of news for educated and influential individuals. The nation's economic, social, and political elites tend to rely on the detailed coverage provided by the print media to inform and influence their views about important public matters. The print media may have a smaller audience than their cousins in broadcasting, but they have an especially influential audience.

The Internet has been growing in importance as a news source. Every day, millions of Americans scan one of many news sites on the Internet for coverage of current events. Younger Americans are more likely to rely on the Internet than on almost any other news source (see Figure 7.1). One great advantage of the Internet is that it allows frequent updating. After the September 11 terrorist attacks, many Americans relied on the Internet for news about terrorism, bioterrorism, and the military campaign in Afghanistan.

In July 2007, candidates for the 2008 Democratic presidential nomination participated in a debate carried online on YouTube. This format allowed ordinary Americans from across the country to make comments and ask questions. One viewer played a guitar and sang a song that he had apparently composed about taxes. He then asked whether any of the famous politicians participating in the debate could help him deal with a recent speeding ticket. A lesbian couple asked whether any of the candidates would allow them to marry. Barack Obama was asked whether he was "authentically black" and replied that he proved he was black every time he tried to hail a cab in New York City.[2] As the 2008 campaign proceeded, candidates or their supporters placed a number of ads on YouTube that were seen by millions of viewers.[3] During the general election, John McCain developed a series of YouTube ads mocking Barack Obama and comparing him to empty-headed media celebrities like Paris Hilton. In August 2008, Hilton responded with her own YouTube videos comparing McCain to the wizened *Star Wars* character, Yoda.

Political entrepreneurs have also used the Internet to organize online advocacy groups to raise money, make their positions known through e-mail and letter campaigns, and provide support for politicians who accepted their views. For example, Chris Hughes, one of the founders of the social networking site Facebook, helped the Obama presidential campaign establish a Facebook site that allowed Obama supporters to register as the senator's "friends." At the site's resource center, the senator's friends could download flyers, videos, and other campaign materials. In the site's "groups" section, the senator's friends could create or join online groups to share

For Critical Analysis

Does news coverage on the Internet differ from news presented via the traditional media? What impact might the Internet have on American politics?

POLITICS & POPULAR CULTURE

The Internet, Blogs, and the Transformation of Political News

The American media are in the middle of a dramatic transformation. In 2005, Americans saw the last news broadcasts of Tom Brokaw, Dan Rather, and Peter Jennings, the three national network news anchors who had brought Americans the bulk of their political information every weeknight for over twenty years. As rates of traditional news consumption drop, use of the Internet as a source of political information is on the rise. In fact, the delivery of political information via the Internet—in particular through *Web logs*, or "blogs"—may be redefining contemporary journalism.

According to a 2008 study by the Pew Research Center, half of Americans under the age of fifty use the Internet as a source of political news. Although many of these users are turning to the Internet to read online versions of their favorite newspapers, a growing portion are turning to blogs. Political blogs often make use of articles, reports, statistics, and photos available on the Internet to research stories. These sites may provide personal commentary, links to various sources, and alternative versions of news stories that are reported in the mainstream media. They are updated frequently, usually with a series of relatively short entries.

In addition to growing readership, blogs have the potential to influence mainstream journalism and even political events. In December 2002, for example, both liberal and conservative bloggers vociferously criticized Senator Trent Lott for comments he made at Senator Strom Thurmond's hundredth-birthday party praising the segregationist Dixiecrats. Several days later, the mainstream press focused their attention on the story, and Lott soon resigned. In 2004, after a *60 Minutes* story claimed that George W. Bush received preferential treatment while serving in the Texas Air National Guard, conservative bloggers mounted a campaign against CBS and the news anchor Dan Rather for reporting a story that was based on forged documents. In the weeks that followed, CBS admitted that the documents had not been properly authenticated, and Dan Rather announced that he would resign. In 2008, a blogger recorded comments made by Barack Obama about "bitter" blue-collar workers and posted them online. This event became a major story, as Obama's ability to reach out to small-town voters came into question.

As blogs have attracted the attention of voters, and policy makers, many politicians have begun blogs of their own. In the 2004 election, Howard Dean's popular Blog for America was the first presidential-campaign-hosted Web log. In 2008, the Obama and McCain campaign Web sites both had blogs. Moreover, the candidates increasingly cultivated relationships with bloggers, and an unprecedented number of bloggers were authorized to cover the 2008 party conventions.

Although blog readership and influence appear to be on the rise, many Americans remain skeptical about the accuracy of information found on blogs. In fact, the Pew Internet and American Life Project reports that although a record 46 percent of Americans had used the Internet for campaign news in spring 2008, 60 percent of Internet users believed that "the internet is full of misinformation and propaganda" that mislead voters. The full impact of blogs on news media and American politics remains to be seen.

FOR CRITICAL ANALYSIS

1. What are some possible drawbacks of receiving political information mainly from blogs? What advantages might blog readers have over traditional news consumers?
2. Thanks in large part to the Internet, Americans can now get news from more sources than ever. Do you think this will have an effect on participation in politics?

SOURCE: Pew Internet & American Life Project, "The internet and the 2008 election," June 15, 2008, www.pewinternet.org/pdfs/PIP_2008_election.pdf (accessed 6/19/08).

In 2007, candidates for the Democratic and Republican presidential nominations participated in debates sponsored by YouTube and CNN. The questions for the candidates were submitted directly by voters, who posted videos of their questions on YouTube.

ideas and organize events and fund-raisers. The site's fund-raising section allowed the senator's friends to set personal fund-raising goals and to invite other registered friends to help them reach it. The Obama site attracted more than a million visitors during the campaign for the 2008 Democratic presidential nomination.[4]

In addition, a growing number of readers turn to informal sources of Internet news and commentary called *Web logs*, or "blogs." Blogs are published online and generally feature personal opinion and commentary on national and world events. Some "bloggers," as the authors of blogs are called, achieve fame, or at least notoriety, among online readers for their political and social views. In 2002 and 2003, the Howard Dean presidential campaign relied on hundreds of friendly bloggers to publicize the candidate's views and to help raise tens of millions of dollars in small contributions to finance his unsuccessful presidential bid.[5] Dean's tactics were a direct precursor to Barack Obama's 2008 campaign, which raised hundreds of millions of dollars in contributions via the Internet.

Inspired by Dean's example, two Democratic activists, Benjamin Rahn and Matt DeBergalis, created a Web site they called "ActBlue" to promote online Democratic fund-raising. ActBlue specializes in a practice called "bundling," which permits the campaign contributions of many individuals to be tied, or "bundled," together on behalf of a particular candidate. The practice is legal so long as no individual contribution exceeds the limits set by campaign-finance laws. As of October 2008, ActBlue had raised more than $50 million for Democratic candidates. Numerous, liberal Democratic candidates appealed for funds via YouTube videos that directed donors to ActBlue. For example, one campaigner posted a YouTube video in which he promised to subject himself to a variety of cyberspace humiliations if viewers met a series of donation targets. The video was watched more than 16,000 times on YouTube.[6] The ActBlue Web site lists the names of a number of Democratic candidates and allows users to decide to which ones they wish to donate. One analyst called it "one-stop shopping" for political donors.[7]

Although the Internet and the blogosphere are often seen as liberal and Democratic strongholds, conservatives have stepped up their efforts to make use of the new media. Over the past three years, conservative talk radio hosts and conservative bloggers have built an informal alliance to attack Democratic candidates and policies with which they disagree. In 2007, for example, conservative bloggers regularly posted material opposing the proposed immigration bill that wo uld have given legal status to many illegal immigrants currently in the United States. Conservative talk-radio hosts relied on the bloggers to provide critical commentary that they could broadcast on their radio programs.[8] This alliance also played a role in numerous attacks launched against Barack Obama in 2008, including the charge that Obama was closely associated with 1960s radical, William Ayers. Bloggers circulated claims that Obama and Ayers, a founder of the Weathermen group, had a long-standing relationship. Conservative commentators frequently used the bloggers' claims in their programs.

Regulation of the Broadcast Media

In some countries, the government controls media content. In other countries, the government owns the broadcast media (e.g., the BBC in Britain) but it does not tell the media what to say. In the United States, the government neither owns nor controls the communications networks, but it does regulate the content and ownership of the broadcast media.

As we saw in Chapter 4, in the United States, the print media are essentially free from government interference. The broadcast media, on the other hand, are subject to federal regulation. American radio and television are regulated by the Federal Communications Commission (FCC), an independent agency established in 1934. Radio and TV stations must have FCC licenses that must be renewed every five years. Licensing provides a mechanism for allocating radio and TV frequencies to prevent broadcasts from interfering with and garbling each other. License renewals are almost always granted automatically by the FCC. Indeed, renewal requests are now filed by postcard.

Federal Communications Commission (FCC) regulations prohibit obscenity, indecency, and profanity in American television and radio broadcasts. The radio personality Howard Stern incurred millions of dollars in FCC fines before moving to satellite radio, which is not regulated by the FCC.

Through regulations prohibiting obscenity, indecency, and profanity, the FCC has also sought to prohibit radio and television stations from airing explicit sexual and excretory references between 6 A.M. and 10 P.M. These are the hours when children are most likely to be in the audience. The FCC has enforced these rules haphazardly. Since 1990, nearly half the $5 million in fines levied by the agency have involved Howard Stern, a "shock jock" whose programs are built around sexually explicit material. In 2004, after another set of FCC fines, Stern's program was dropped by a major outlet, ClearChannel Communications. Stern charged that the Bush administration had singled him out for censure because of his known opposition to the president. Stern subsequently moved to Sirius satellite radio. Because, under the law, satellite radio is not a broadcast medium, Sirius is not subject to FCC regulation. In 2007, radio talker Don Imus was fired by CBS for racially offensive remarks about the Rutgers womens' basketball team. Later that year, Imus, who has a history of racist, sexist, and anti-Semitic, and generally offensive commentary was returned to the air by an ABC affiliate.

For more than sixty years, the FCC also sought to regulate and promote competition in the broadcast industry, but in 1996 Congress passed the Telecommunications Act, a broad effort to do away with most regulations in effect since 1934. The act loosened restrictions on media ownership and allowed for telephone companies, cable television providers, and broadcasters to compete with each other for telecommunication services. Following the passage of the act, several mergers between telephone and cable companies and among different segments of the entertainment media produced an even greater concentration of media ownership.

The Telecommunications Act of 1996 also included an attempt to regulate the content of material transmitted over the Internet. This law, known as the Communications Decency Act, made it illegal to make "indecent" sexual material on the Internet accessible to those under eighteen years old. The act was immediately denounced by civil libertarians and brought to court as an infringement of free speech. The case reached the Supreme Court in 1997, and the act was ruled an unconstitutional infringement of the First Amendment's right to freedom of speech (see Chapter 4).

Although the government's ability to regulate the content of the electronic media on the Internet has been questioned, the federal government has used its licensing power to impose several regulations that can affect the political content of radio and TV broadcasts. The first of these is the **equal time rule,** under which broadcasters must provide candidates for the same political office equal opportunities to communicate their messages to the public. If, for example, a television station sells commercial time to a state's Republican gubernatorial candidate, it may not refuse to sell time to the Democratic candidate for the same position.

equal time rule the requirement that broadcasters provide candidates for the same political office equal opportunities to communicate their messages to the public

The second regulation affecting the content of broadcasts is the **right of rebuttal,** which requires that individuals be given the opportunity to respond to personal attacks. In the 1969 case of *Red Lion Broadcasting Company v. FCC,* for example, the U.S. Supreme Court upheld the FCC's determination that a radio station was required to provide a liberal author with an opportunity to respond to a conservative commentator's attack that the station had aired.[9]

right of rebuttal a Federal Communications Commission regulation giving individuals the right to have the opportunity to respond to personal attacks made on a radio or television broadcast

For many years, a third important federal regulation was the **fairness doctrine.** Under this doctrine, broadcasters who aired programs on controversial issues were required to provide time for opposing views. In 1985, however, the FCC stopped enforcing the fairness doctrine on the grounds that there were so many radio and television stations—to say nothing of newspapers and newsmagazines—that in all likelihood many different viewpoints were already being presented without each station's being required to try to present all sides of an argument. Critics of this FCC decision charge that in many media markets the number of competing viewpoints is small. Nevertheless, a congressional effort to require the FCC to enforce the fairness doctrine was blocked by the Reagan administration in 1987.

fairness doctrine a Federal Communications Commission requirement for broadcasters who air programs on controversial issues to provide time for opposing views. The FCC ceased enforcing this doctrine in 1985

Organization and Ownership of the Media

The United States boasts more than 1,900 television stations, approximately 1,400 daily newspapers, and more than 13,000 radio stations (20 percent of which are devoted to news, talk, or public affairs).[10]

Even though the number of TV and radio stations and daily newspapers reporting news in the United States is enormous, the number of sources of national news is actually quite small—several wire services, four broadcast networks, public radio and television, two elite newspapers, three newsmagazines, and a scattering of other sources such as the national correspondents of a few large local papers and the small independent radio networks. More than three-fourths of the daily

Regulation of Media Ownership

In June 2003, the Federal Communications Commission (FCC) announced a set of rules that would permit major media corporations to expand their control of print and broadcast properties. Under the new rules, a company would be allowed to own newspapers and television stations that, together, could reach 45 percent of the nation's viewers (an increase from 35 percent under the old rule). A single company would also be permitted to own the most important newspaper and as many as three television and eight radio stations in a single market, effectively dominating news coverage within that market. Various public-interest groups and members of Congress were outraged by the FCC's action, charging that the commission was promoting the development of media monopolies. Both the House and the Senate considered legislation to reverse the FCC's decision, and several lawsuits were filed to block its enforcement. In 2004, a federal appeals court blocked implementation of the new rules, asserting that the agency had used faulty reasoning in determining how many media properties could be owned by a single corporate entity. After the U.S. Supreme Court refused to hear the agency's appeal, the FCC announced that it would begin developing a set of rules it hoped would pass judicial muster. As of 2007, the FCC was continuing to hold hearings on the issue.

Those who favor rules to limit the market power of media corporations make three major arguments. In the first of these arguments, proponents of rules regulating competition assert that the quality of the print and broadcast media is improved by vigorous competition among a large number of newspaper, radio, and television outlets, each striving to attract readers, listeners, or viewers. As the number of competitors diminishes, regulatory proponents argue, the quality of news and feature programming is reduced as media outlets feel less competitive incentive to aim for quality and innovation.

The second argument that proponents of regulation make concerns diversity of opinion. Regulation is needed, the argument goes, to ensure that the print and broadcast media will present as many different opinions and perspectives as possible. Concentration of ownership inevitably means that fewer perspectives will find their way into print or be presented on radio and television. This could mean that less popular views would seldom receive media coverage. For example, during the 2003 Iraq war, the five television networks all presented favorable accounts of American military efforts. Only viewers with access to foreign television coverage were presented with alternative perspectives.

The third argument concerns political competitiveness. If there were only a handful of media companies and they united behind a single party or candidate, their influence would be difficult to overcome.

Opponents of regulation, for their part, are not against quality, diversity, and political competitiveness. They argue, however, that regulation of media ownership is unnecessary and may be counterproductive. Quality, say opponents of regulation, is enhanced by open competition in the marketplace and not by rules that give small print and broadcast companies sheltered market niches where they are safe from powerful rivals. This, they say, is a recipe for mediocrity. And as for diversity of viewpoints, opponents of regulation note that so many media outlets exist in the United States, including online magazines and thousands of blogs, that there is no danger that a single media corporation or small number of corporations can dominate coverage. Regulation, rather than market competition, say opponents, poses a threat to political and ideological diversity.

FOR CRITICAL ANALYSIS

1. Why might we be concerned about media concentration? Should we seek government action to curb concentration? Or should we rely on market forces to maintain diversity?
2. Some nations restrict foreign ownership of major media outlets. Should the United States adopt such a policy?

newspapers in the United States are owned by large media conglomerates such as the Hearst, McClatchy, or Gannett corporations; thus the diversity of coverage and editorial opinion in American newspapers is not so broad as it might seem. Much of the national news that is published by local newspapers is provided by one wire service, the Associated Press, while additional coverage is provided by services run by several major newspapers such as the *New York Times* and the *Chicago Tribune*. More than five hundred of the nation's television stations are affiliated with one of the four networks and carry that network's evening news reports. Dozens of others carry PBS (Public Broadcasting System) news. Several hundred local radio stations also carry network news or National Public Radio news broadcasts. At the same time, although there are only three truly national newspapers, the *Wall Street Journal*, the *Christian Science Monitor*, and *USA Today*, two other papers, the *New York Times* and the *Washington Post*, are read by political leaders and other influential Americans throughout the nation. National news is also carried to millions of Americans by two major newsmagazines—*Time* and *Newsweek*. Beginning in the late 1980s, CNN became another major news source for Americans, especially after its spectacular coverage of the Persian Gulf war. At one point, CNN was able to provide live reports of American bombing raids on Baghdad, Iraq, after the major networks' correspondents had been forced to flee to bomb shelters. However, the number of news sources has remained essentially the same. Even the availability of new electronic media on the Internet has failed to expand the number of news sources. Most national news available on the World Wide Web, for example, consists of electronic versions of the conventional print or broadcast media.

The trend toward the homogenization of national news has been hastened by dramatic changes in media ownership, which became possible in large part due to the relaxation of government regulations in the 1980s and 1990s. The enactment of the 1996 Telecommunications Act opened the way for further consolidation in the media industry, and a wave of mergers and consolidations has further reduced the field of independent media across the country. Since that time, among the major news networks, ABC was bought by the Walt Disney corporation; CBS was bought by Westinghouse Electric and later merged with Viacom, the owner of MTV and Paramount Studios; and CNN was bought by Time Warner. General Electric has owned NBC since 1986. The Australian press baron Rupert Murdoch owns the Fox network plus a host of radio, television, and newspaper properties around the world. In 2007, Murdoch won control of the *Wall Street Journal*, making him one of the wold's most powerful publishers. A small number of giant corporations now controls a wide swath of media holdings, including television networks, movie studios, record companies, cable channels and local cable providers, book publishers, magazines, and newspapers. These developments have prompted questions about whether enough competition exists among the media to produce a diverse set of views on political and corporate matters or whether the United States has become the prisoner of media monopolies.[11]

For Critical Analysis

In recent years, a number of major media corporations have acquired numerous newspapers, television stations, and radio properties. Is media concentration a serious problem? Why or why not?

MEDIA OWNERSHIP AND POLITICAL EQUALITY Increasing concentration of media ownership raises a number of major issues (see this chapter's Policy Debate). One of the most important relates to political equality. Access to the print and broadcast media is such an important political resource that for all intents and purposes, political forces that lack media access have only a very limited opportunity to influence the political process. As major newspapers, television stations, and radio networks fall into fewer and fewer hands, the risk increases that less popular or minority viewpoints and the politicians who express them will have difficulty finding a public forum in which to disseminate their ideas. Increasingly, such individuals turn to the Internet and its numerous blogs and other Web sites to express their views. The problem, however, is that ideas presented on the Internet tend to be read mainly by those who already agree with them. The Internet can be an important mechanism for linking communities of adherents, but it is less effective than radio, television, and the print media for reaching new audiences. Hence, growing concentration and consolidation in the print and broadcast industries are important policy problems.

Nationalization of the News

In general, the national news media cover more or less the same sets of events, present similar information, and emphasize similar issues and problems. Indeed, the national news services watch each other quite carefully. It is very likely that a major story carried by one service will quickly find its way into the pages or programming of the others. As a result, in the United States a rather centralized national news has developed, through which a relatively uniform picture of events, issues, and problems is presented to the entire nation.[12] The nationalization of the news began in the early 1900s, was accelerated by the development of radio networks in the 1920s and 1930s and by the creation of the television networks after the 1950s, and has been further strengthened by the recent trends toward concentrated media ownership. This nationalization of news content has very important consequences for the American political system.

Nationalization of the news has contributed greatly to the nationalization of politics and of political perspectives in the United States. Prior to the development of the national media and the nationalization of news coverage, news traveled very slowly. Every region and city saw national issues and problems primarily through a local lens. Concerns and perspectives varied greatly from region to region, city to city, and village to village. Today, in large measure as a result of the nationalization of the media, residents of all parts of the country share similar pictures of the day's events.[13] They may not agree on everything, but most see the world in similar ways.

The exception to this pattern can be found with those Americans whose chief source of news is something other than the "mainstream" national media. Some radio stations and print media are aimed exclusively at specific racial, ethnic, or religious groups. These individuals are likely to develop and retain a perception of the news that is quite different from that of "mainstream" America. For example, the rural midwesterners who rely on the ultraconservative People's Radio Network for their news coverage may become concerned about the alleged efforts of the United Nations to subordinate the United States in a world government, a viewpoint unfamiliar to most Americans. In 2007, listeners to talk radio programs aimed at black audiences might have heard that the Atlanta Falcons quarterback Michael Vick, indicted on animal cruelty and dogfighting charges, was a victim of racism.

Web blogs are a form of news enclave for the like minded. Generally speaking, individuals seek out blogs with which they are likely to agree. The blogs function to reinforce people's preexisting ideas and to provide them with information to bol-

During the 2003 Iraq war, the Bush administration went to great lengths to influence media coverage so that the U.S. military's efforts were presented in a positive light. For example, the U.S. Central Command headquarters in Doha, Qatar, included an elaborate $1.5-million media center with multiple flat plasma television screens, high-speed telephone lines, and an espresso bar.

ster their established beliefs. Thus, liberals might turn to DailyKos, conservatives to Polipundit, those with an interest in military issues to Military.com, and so forth. It is unusual for individuals to venture into what they regard as unfriendly parts of the blogosphere.

News Coverage

Because of the important role the media can play in national politics, understanding the factors that affect media coverage is vitally important. What accounts for the media's agenda of issues and topics? What explains the character of coverage? Why does a politician receive good or bad press? What factors determine the interpretation, or "spin," that a particular story will receive? Although a host of minor factors plays a role, three major factors are important: (1) the journalists, or producers of the news; (2) the sources or topics of the news; and (3) the audience for the news.

Journalists

Media content and news coverage are inevitably affected by the views, ideals, and interests of those who seek out, write, and produce news and other stories. At one time, newspaper publishers exercised a great deal of influence over their papers' news content. Publishers such as William Randolph Hearst and Joseph Pulitzer became political powers through their manipulation of news coverage. Hearst, for example, almost single-handedly pushed the United States into war with Spain in 1898 through his newspapers' relentless coverage of the alleged

Prior to the Iraq war, the Bush administration invited more than one hundred news correspondents and photographers to accompany American forces into battle. These "embedded" journalists developed considerable rapport with the soldiers and provided generally sympathetic war coverage.

brutality employed by Spain in its efforts to suppress a rebellion in Cuba, at that time a Spanish colony. The sinking of the American battleship *Maine* in Havana harbor under mysterious circumstances gave Hearst the ammunition he needed to force a reluctant President McKinley to lead the nation into war.

More important than publishers, for the most part, are the reporters. Those who cover the news for the national media generally have a good deal of discretion or freedom to interpret stories and, as a result, have an opportunity to interject their views and ideals into news stories. For example, the personal friendship and respect that some reporters felt for Franklin Roosevelt or John Kennedy helped to generate more favorable news coverage for these presidents. Likewise, the dislike and distrust many reporters felt for Richard Nixon was also communicated to the public. In the case of Ronald Reagan, the disdain that many journalists felt for the president was communicated in stories suggesting that he was often asleep or inattentive when important decisions were made.

Conservatives have long charged that the liberal biases of reporters and journalists result in distorted news coverage. A 2004 survey conducted by the Pew Research Center found that 34 percent of national news reporters identified themselves as liberal, whereas only 7 percent said they were conservative.[14] In a similar vein, a 2005 study by the University of Connecticut found that 52 percent of the journalists surveyed voted Democratic, 19 percent voted Republican, and 21 percent refused to say.[15]

The linkage between journalists and liberal ideas is by no means absolute. Most reporters, to be sure, attempt to maintain some measure of balance or objectivity whatever their personal political views. In addition, a number of important newspaper owners and publishers have decidedly conservative views. These include such individuals as David Smith, president of the Sinclair Broadcast Group, which controls more than sixty U.S. television stations. During the 2004 presidential contest, Sinclair planned to air a documentary sharply critical of the Democratic candidate John Kerry but dropped the project in response to widespread criticism.

Conservative owners and publishers have built a set of conservative media entities to oppose what they perceive as the liberal media. This complex includes two newspapers, the *Wall Street Journal* and the *Washington Times*, several magazines such as the *American Spectator*, and a host of conservative radio and television talk programs. Also important is the media baron Rupert Murdoch, creator of Fox Network News and the financial force behind the *Weekly Standard*. Murdoch sees Fox as a conservative alternative to the more liberal networks and has staffed Fox with rather conservative broadcast personalities. To some extent, ideological diversity and polarization have also been encouraged by the proliferation of news sources. When there were few news sources, each appealed to the same broad national audience and, accordingly, maintained a middle-of-the-road stance. Now that there are many news sources, some seek to position themselves within a discrete ideological or partisan niche.

Probably more important than ideological bias is a selection bias in favor of news that the media view as having a great deal of audience appeal because of its dramatic or entertainment value. In practice, this bias often results in news coverage that focuses on crimes and scandals, especially those involving prominent individuals, despite the fact that the public obviously looks to the media for information about important political debates. For example, even though most journalists may be Democrats, this partisan predisposition did not prevent an enormous media frenzy in January 1998 when reports surfaced that President Clinton (a Democrat) might have had an affair with a White House intern, Monica Lewinsky. Once a hint of blood appeared in the water, partisanship and ideology were swept away by the piranha-like instincts journalists often manifest.

In addition to professional reporters, today's news is increasingly being covered by "citizen journalists" wielding digital cameras who post information and photos to blogs, YouTube, and other sites. The largest and most prominent group of citizen journalists calls itself OffTheBus.net, on online journalism project that has grown to a force of 7,500 volunteers who attend events, solicit interviews, and take pictures. One OffTheBus correspondent, Mayhill Fowler, broke two major stories in 2008, one involving a comment by Barack Obama about "bitter small-town voters," and the other, a story about former president Bill Clinton's criticism of a *Vanity Fair* writer.[16]

Subjects of the News

News coverage is also influenced by the individuals or groups who are subjects of the news or whose interests and activities are actual or potential news topics. The president, in particular, has the power to set the news agenda through speeches and actions. All politicians, for that matter, seek to shape or manipulate their media images by cultivating good relations with reporters as well as through news leaks and staged news events.

A *leak* is the disclosure of confidential information to the news media. Leaks may emanate from a variety of sources, including "whistle-blowers," lower-level officials who hope to publicize what they view as their bosses' improper activities. In 1971, for example, a minor Defense Department staffer named Daniel Ellsberg sought to discredit official justifications for America's involvement in Vietnam by leaking top-secret documents to the press. The "Pentagon Papers" were published by the *New York Times* and the *Washington Post* after the U.S. Supreme Court ruled that the government could not block their release.[17] Similarly, in 2005 President George W. Bush was infuriated when he learned that a still-unidentified source, presumed

For Critical Analysis

To what extent, do you think, are the media biased? As more news sources have become available, has this led to more or less bias in the media?

Politicians sometimes deliberately leak confidential information to the press, in the hope of influencing news coverage. In 2007, Vice President Cheney's chief of staff, Lewis "Scooter" Libby, was convicted of obstructing an investigation into the Bush administration's illegal leak of a covert CIA official's identity.

to be a whistle-blower, leaked information concerning the president's secret orders authorizing the National Security Agency to conduct clandestine surveillance of suspected terrorists without obtaining a warrant. Bush ordered the Justice Department to launch a probe of the leak. In 2006, another unidentified source leaked part of a secret intelligence summary that seemed to contradict the administration's claims of progress in the war in Iraq. The president was furious and claimed the leaked portion of the report did not accurately reflect the full report. The administration proceeded to declassify portions of the report that seemed to support its claims about the war.

Most leaks, though, originate not with low-level whistle-blowers but rather with senior government officials and prominent politicians and political activists. These individuals cultivate long-term relationships with journalists to whom they regularly leak confidential information, knowing that it is likely to be published on a priority basis in a form acceptable to them. Their confidence is based on the fact that journalists are likely to regard high-level sources of confidential information as valuable assets whose favor must be retained. For example, Lewis "Scooter" Libby, Vice President Cheney's former chief of staff, was apparently such a valuable source of leaks to so many prominent journalists that his name was seldom even mentioned in the newspapers, despite his prominence in Washington and his importance as a decision maker.[18] Further, the more that recipients of leaked information strive to keep their sources secret, the more difficulty other journalists will have in checking its validity.

Through such tacit alliances with journalists, prominent figures can manipulate news coverage and secure the publication of stories that serve their purposes. One recent case that revealed the complexities of this culture of leaks was the 2005 Valerie Plame affair. Plame was an undercover CIA analyst who happened to be married to Joseph Wilson, a prominent career diplomat. Wilson had angered the Bush White House by making a number of statements that were critical of the president's policies in Iraq. In an apparent effort to discredit Wilson, one or more administration officials informed prominent journalists that Plame had improperly used her position to help Wilson. In so doing, these officials may have violated a federal statute prohibiting disclosure of the identities of covert intelligence operatives. The subsequent investigation revealed that the story had been leaked to several journalists, including the *Washington Post*'s Bob Woodward, who did not use it; and the *New York Times*' Judith Miller, who did. Miller initially refused to name her source and spent several weeks in jail for contempt of court after refusing to testify before a federal grand jury looking into the leak. After Miller finally testified, Scooter Libby was charged with having been the source of the leak, though it later emerged that the leak actually came from a former State Department official, Richard Armitage. The leak in the Plame case came to light only because it was illegal. Thousands of other leaks each year are quietly and seamlessly incorporated into the news.

Also seamlessly incorporated into daily news reports each year are thousands of press releases. The press release, sometimes called a news release, is a story written by an advocate or publicist and distributed to the media in the hope that journalists will publish it with little or no revision and under their own bylines. The inventor of the press release was a famous New York public relations consultant named Ivy Lee. In 1906, a train operated by one of Lee's clients, the Pennsylvania Railroad, was involved in a serious wreck. Lee quickly wrote a story about the accident that presented the railroad in a favorable light and distributed the account to reporters. Many papers published Lee's slanted story as their own objective account of events and the railroad's reputation for quality and safety remained intact. Consistent with Lee's example, today's press release presents facts and perspectives that serve an advocate's interests, but is written in a way that mimics the factual news style of the paper, periodical, or television news program to which it has been sent. It is quite difficult for the audience to distinguish a well-designed press release from an actual news story. Newspapers, of course, realize that they are allowing themselves to be used, but they have a strong financial incentive to publish press releases that, in effect, allow them to fill their pages at little cost.

The capacity of news subjects to influence the news is hardly unlimited. Media consultants and issues managers may shape the news for a time, but it is generally not difficult for the media to penetrate the smoke screens thrown up by news sources if they have a reason to do so. Thus, for example, despite the administration's media management, by 2005, many news stories filed from combat zones in Iraq and Afghanistan emphasized American casualties and the administration's apparent inability to bring order to these turbulent nations. Opponents of the president's military policies scored a media coup of their own in 2005 by setting up a "peace camp" near Bush's Texas ranch. Here, antiwar activists such as Cindy Sheehan, the mother of a soldier killed in combat, were able to capture the attention of the news with their relentless criticism of the president. Also in 2005, Bush garnered a great deal of unfavorable publicity for his administration's apparent mishandling of relief efforts in the wake of Hurricane Katrina. The president sought to reverse negative reports by visiting the disaster site regularly, making a nationally televised speech in which he promised that New Orleans would be rebuilt, and, finally, dismissing the director of the Federal Emergency Management Agency (FEMA), who had been singled out for criticism by the press.

Occasionally, a politician proves incredibly adept at surviving repeated media attacks. Bill Clinton, for example, was able to survive repeated revelations of sexual improprieties, financial irregularities, lying to the public, and illegal campaign fund-raising activities. Clinton and his advisers crafted what the *Washington Post* called a "toolkit" for dealing with potentially damaging media revelations. This toolkit included techniques such as chiding the press, browbeating reporters, referring inquiries quickly to

During the late 1990s, President Bill Clinton was nearly driven from office by media revelations of his sexual misconduct with White House intern Monica Lewinsky. The media relentlessly pursued Clinton's evasions, lies, and indiscretions and provided fuel for a congressional effort to impeach the president. However, Clinton's skill in dealing with the media enabled him to survive the attacks.

lawyers who would not comment, and acting quickly to change the agenda. These techniques helped Clinton maintain a favorable public image despite the Monica Lewinsky scandal and even the humiliation of a formal impeachment and trial.

Adding a page to her husband's playbook, Senator Hillary Clinton in 2007 launched a Web site that would provide instantaneous rebuttals of charges or news reports that her presidential campaign deemed inaccurate or potentially damaging. Called The Fact Hub, the site allows Clinton staffers to attempt to shape the news by posting the senator's version of events. Thus, in November 2007, when the news media reported that Senator Clinton had failed to leave a tip at a diner in Iowa where she was campaigning, the senator's rebuttal site posted text and video, including statements from witnesses, asserting that Clinton had left a very generous tip. A GOP strategist said admiringly that the site was "the next evolution in rapid response."[19]

The Power of Consumers

The print and broadcast media are businesses that, in general, seek to show a profit. This means that like any other business, they must cater to the preferences of consumers. This has very important consequences for the content and character of the news media.

CATERING TO THE AUDIENCE In general, and especially in the political realm, the print and broadcast media and the publishing industry are not only responsive to the interests of consumers generally, but are particularly responsive to the interests and views of the better-educated and more affluent segments of their audience. The preferences of these audience segments have a profound effect on the content and orientation of the press, of radio and television programming, and of books, especially in the areas of news and public affairs.[20]

Although affluent consumers do watch television programs and read periodicals whose contents are designed simply to amuse or entertain, the one area that most directly appeals to the upscale audience is that of news and public affairs. The affluent—who are also typically well educated—are the core audience of newsmagazines, journals of opinion, books dealing with public affairs, such newspapers as the *New York Times* and the *Washington Post*, and broadcast news and weekend and evening public-affairs programs. Although other segments of the public also read newspapers and watch television news, their level of interest in world events, national political issues, and the like is closely related to their level of education. As a result, upscale Americans are overrepresented in the news and public-affairs audience. The concentration of these strata in the audience makes news, politics, and public affairs potentially very attractive topics to advertisers, publishers, radio broadcasters, and television executives. As a result, topics in which the upper-middle class is interested, such as the stock market, scientific and literary affairs, and international politics, receive extensive coverage.

At the same time, however, entire categories of events, issues, and phenomena of interest to lower-middle- and working-class Americans receive scant attention from the national print and broadcast media. For example, trade-union news and events are discussed only in the context of major strikes or revelations of corruption. No network or national periodical routinely covers labor organizations. Religious and church affairs receive little coverage. The activities of veterans', fraternal, ethnic, and patriotic organizations are also generally ignored.

During the 1960s, civil rights protesters learned a variety of techniques designed to elicit sympathetic media coverage. Television images of police brutality in Alabama led directly to the enactment of the 1965 Civil Rights Act.

THE MEDIA AND CONFLICT Although the media respond most to the upscale audience, groups that cannot afford the services of media consultants and issues managers can publicize their views and interests through protest. Frequently, the media are accused of encouraging conflict and even violence because the audience mostly watches news for the entertainment value that conflict can provide. Clearly, conflict can be an important vehicle for attracting the attention and interest of the media, and thus gives an opportunity for media attention to groups otherwise lacking the financial or organizational resources to broadcast their views. But although conflict and protest can succeed in drawing media attention, these methods ultimately do not allow groups from the bottom of the social ladder to compete effectively in the media.

The chief problem with protest as a media technique is that, in general, the media on which the protesters depend have considerable discretion in reporting and interpreting the events they cover. For example, should the media focus on the conflict itself, rather than the issues or concerns that created the conflict? The answer to this question is typically determined by the media, not by the protesters. This means that media interpretation of protest activities is more a reflection of the views of the groups and forces to which the media are responsive—as we have seen, usually segments of the upper-middle class—than it is a function of the wishes of the protesters themselves. It is worth noting that civil rights protesters received their most favorable media coverage during the 1960s, when a segment of the white upper-middle class saw blacks as potential political allies in the Democratic party.

Typically, upper-middle-class protesters—student demonstrators and the like—have little difficulty securing favorable publicity for themselves and their causes. Upper-middle-class protesters are often more skilled than their lower-class counterparts in the techniques of media manipulation. That is, they typically have a better sense—often as a result of formal courses on the subject—of how to package messages for media consumption. For example, it is important to know at what time of day a protest should occur if it is to be carried on the evening news. Similarly, the setting, definition of the issues, character of the rhetoric used, and so

Today, protesters continue to try to capture media attention as a way to publicize their views and interests. These supporters of Latinos' rights attracted media attention to their protest against recent immigration raids.

on all help to determine whether a protest will receive favorable media coverage, unfavorable coverage, or no coverage at all. Moreover, upper-middle-class protesters can often produce their own media coverage through "underground" newspapers, college newspapers, student radio and television stations, and, now, over the Internet. The same resources and skills that generally allow upper-middle-class people to publicize their ideas are usually not left behind when segments of this class choose to engage in disruptive forms of political action. This helps to explain why relatively small groups of demonstrators in Seattle, Washington, were able to garner enormous media coverage in the winter of 1999 for their protests against the World Trade Organization.

Media Power in American Politics

The content and character of news and public affairs programming—what the media choose to present and how they present it—can have far-reaching political consequences. Media disclosures can greatly enhance—or fatally damage—the careers of public officials. Media coverage can rally support for—or intensify opposition to—national policies. The media can shape and modify, if not fully form, public perceptions of events, issues, and institutions.

Shaping Events

In recent American political history, the media have played a central role in at least three major events. First, the media were a critically important factor in the civil rights movement of the 1950s and 1960s. Television images showing peaceful civil rights marchers attacked by club-swinging police helped to generate sympathy among northern whites for the civil rights struggle and greatly increased the pressure on Congress to bring an end to segregation.[21] Second, the media were instrumental in compelling the Nixon administration to negotiate an end to American involvement in the Vietnam War. Beginning in 1967, the national media, reacting in part to a shift in elite opinion, portrayed the war as misguided and unwinnable and, as a result, helped to turn popular sentiment against continued American involvement.[22]

Finally, the media were central actors in the Watergate affair, which ultimately forced President Richard Nixon, the landslide victor in the 1972 presidential election, to resign from office in disgrace. The relentless series of investigations launched by the *Washington Post*, the *New York Times*, and the television networks led to the disclosures of the various abuses of which Nixon was guilty and ultimately forced him to choose between resignation and almost certain impeachment.

The Sources of Media Power

AGENDA SETTING The power of the media stems from several sources. The first is **agenda setting,** which means that the media help to set the agenda for political discussion. Groups and forces that wish to bring their ideas before the public in order to generate support for policy proposals or political candidacies must somehow secure media coverage. If the media are persuaded that an idea is newsworthy, then they may declare it an "issue" that must be confronted or a "problem" to be solved, thus clearing the first hurdle in the policy-making process. On the other hand, if an idea lacks or loses media appeal, its chance of resulting in new programs or policies is diminished.

agenda setting the power of the media to bring public attention to particular issues and problems

For example, in 2003, the Democratic presidential candidate Al Sharpton sought to make poverty the central issue of his bid for office. Sharpton appeared at numerous events to speak out against poverty and offered a plan that he said would improve our national security by promoting education, health care, and housing. Sharpton also promised to raise the minimum wage and increase tax credits for the working poor. Although this topic was popular among some liberal and labor groups, the national media seemed to regard it as old hat and did not make Sharpton's plan a central theme in its coverage of the presidential race. Other candidates ignored the Sharpton effort, since the media failed to label it as a major issue in the race.

On the other hand, Democrats were able to persuade the media that regulation of health-maintenance organizations (HMOs) was an issue worthy of discussion. During well-publicized congressional hearings in the fall of 1999, Democrats presented many witnesses who testified that their HMOs had prevented them from receiving adequate treatment. Democrats called for a "Patient's Bill of Rights" to allow HMO physicians more autonomy and to permit unhappy patients redress in the courts. Republicans initially charged that the Democrats were simply doing the bidding of the trial lawyers, major contributors to the Democratic Party, who saw HMOs as rich targets for litigation. Media coverage of the disgruntled HMO patients, however, made it impossible for Republicans to dismiss the issue from the agenda and led eventually to the enactment of legislation close to the Democratic proposal.

Politics Today

What role have the media played in the Iraq war? What similarities and differences can you see between the role of the media in this most recent war and their role in past wars?

In the fall of 2001, President Bush had little difficulty convincing the media that terrorism and his administration's campaign to combat terrorist attacks merited a dominant place on the agenda. In 2002 and 2003, American military campaigns in Afghanistan and Iraq easily dominated the news. Some stories have such overwhelming significance that political leaders' main concern is not whether the story will receive attention but whether they will figure prominently and positively in media accounts. This was certainly true in 2005, when disastrous hurricanes struck the Gulf Coast. There was no question that these storms and the damage they caused would be on the national agenda. The question was how blame and credit would be apportioned. Local, state, and national leaders, including the president, sought to escape blame for the region's lack of preparedness and to take credit for emergency and relief efforts. Eventually, the Bush administration and the Federal Emergency Management Agency (FEMA) were blamed for the disaster. In 2007, when a series of huge fires struck Southern California, FEMA's director Michael Chertoff flew to the region and appeared on national television every evening to explain the evolving situation. Though FEMA actually played only a minor role in bringing the fires under control, because of Chertoff's presence and the appearance of federal action, the news media seemed to feel that the federal government had done a good job in California.

In many instances, the media serve as conduits for agenda-setting efforts by competing groups and forces. Occasionally, however, journalists themselves play an important role in setting the agenda of political discussion. For example, whereas many of the scandals and investigations surrounding President Clinton were initiated by his political opponents, the Watergate scandal that destroyed Nixon's presidency was in some measure initiated and driven by the *Washington Post* and the national television networks.

framing the power of the media to influence how events and issues are interpreted

FRAMING A second source of the media's power, known as **framing,** is their power to decide how the American people interpret political events and results. For example, during the 1995–96 struggle between President Clinton and congressional Republicans over the nation's budget—a struggle that led to several partial shutdowns of the federal government—the media's interpretation of events forced the Republicans to back down and agree to a budget on Clinton's terms. At the beginning of the crisis, congressional Republicans, led by then House Speaker Newt Gingrich, were confident that they could compel Clinton to accept their budget, which called for substantial cuts in domestic social programs. Republicans calculated that Clinton would fear being blamed for lengthy government shutdowns and would quickly accede to their demands, and that once Americans saw that life went on with government agencies closed, they would support the Republicans in asserting that the United States could get along with less government.

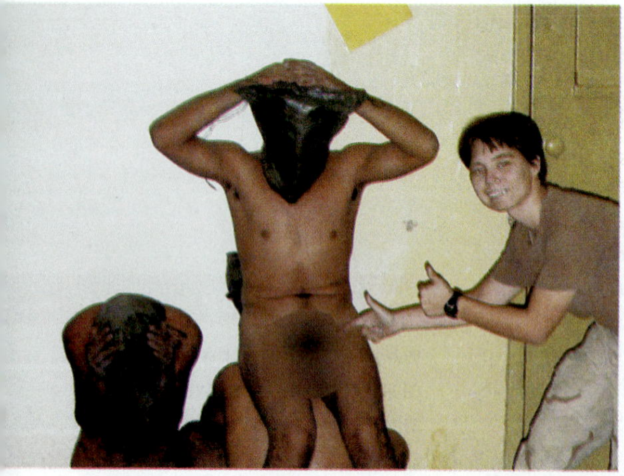

In April 2004, 60 Minutes II*'s broadcast of the story of American soldiers' abuse of Iraqi inmates at Abu Ghraib prison was seen around the world and led to accusations of brutality and torture. Initial efforts by the Bush administration to contain the Iraq prison scandal and limit the blame to a handful of soldiers and immediate senior officers failed.*

For the most part, however, the media did not cooperate with the GOP's plans. Media coverage of the several government shutdowns during this period emphasized the hardships imposed on federal workers who were being furloughed in the weeks before Christmas. Indeed, Newt Gingrich, who was generally portrayed as the villain who caused the crisis, came to be called the "Gin *grinch*" who stole Christmas from the children of hundreds of thousands of federal workers. Rather than suggest that the shutdown demonstrated that America could carry on with less government, media accounts focused on the difficulties encountered by Washington tourists unable to visit the capital's monuments, museums, and galleries. The woes of American travelers whose passports were delayed were given considerable attention. Thus, the "dominant frame" became the hardship and disruption caused by the Republicans. The GOP's "competing frame" was dismissed.[23] This sort of coverage eventually convinced most Americans that the govern-

This famous photograph of the aftermath of a napalm attack was one of many media images that shaped the American public's views on the Vietnam War. Media accounts critical of the war helped to turn public opinion against it and hastened the withdrawal of American troops.

ment shutdown was bad for the country. In the end, Gingrich and the congressional Republicans were forced to surrender and to accept a new budget reflecting many of Clinton's priorities. The Republicans' defeat in the budget showdown contributed to the unraveling of the GOP's legislative program and, ultimately, to the Republicans' poor showing in the 1996 presidential elections and 1998 congressional races. The character of media coverage of an event thus had enormous repercussions for how Americans interpreted it.

Media frames were quite important during the 2008 election. From the perspective of the national media, one of the most important aspects of the 2008 election was the fact that for the first time in American history an African American was making a serious bid for the presidency of the United States. The media appeared to regard this aspect of the campaign as more significant than Hillary Clinton's bid to become the first woman to serve as president. Partly because they regarded the fact that Obama was America's first significant black presidential candidate as supremely important, the media gave Obama much more attention and scrutiny than they afforded other candidates. This extra attention frequently allowed Obama to dominate the news and led his opponents constantly to charge that the media were biased in Obama's favor. It may be true that many reporters and commentators supported Obama. Nevertheless, if Obama had been an inept candidate, the extra coverage he received would only have amplified his weakness. Obama, however, was able to take full advantage of the extra media attention he was given to generate popular enthusiasm for his campaign and raise tens of millions of dollars in small contributions via the Internet. By devoting enormous quantities of ink and air time to Obama, the media were not so much exhibiting bias as reflecting what they saw as the historic importance of the story. Extra media

AMERICA IN THE WORLD

What the Media Tell Americans about the World and the World about America

It is often said that we live in an age of "globalization," when events anywhere in the world affect everyone in the world. Nevertheless, the American news media are surprisingly parochial in their orientation. Few news organizations have foreign bureaus or foreign correspondents. Indeed, in the face of globalization, the number of foreign bureaus operated by major news organizations has actually decreased. One veteran CBS reporter, Tom Fenton, said that when he joined the network in 1970, "I was one of three correspondents in the Rome bureau. We had bureaus in Paris, Bonn, Warsaw, Cairo, and Nairobi. Now you can count the number of foreign correspondents on two hands and have three fingers left over."[a] Despite vital American interests in the Middle East, most reporters know very little about the history, culture, and languages of the region. U.S. correspondents sent to cover the Iraq war could not speak directly with Iraqis or understand Arabic news media.[b]

A brief survey of recent American newspapers offers a sense of the character of news coverage of international affairs. On a typical Sunday, most American newspapers devote roughly 20 percent of their news coverage to international events. It is interesting to note that the bulk of the international news featured in these papers involved war, terrorism, and political violence. To the extent that Americans derive their understanding of the world from the newspapers, they might reasonably see much of it as a very dangerous place.

However, before we agree with Tom Fenton and dismiss the American news media as parochial, we should compare U.S. coverage of international events with that presented on the same day by one of the world's oldest and most famous newspapers, the *Times* of London. The *Times* did, indeed, devote a considerably greater portion of its news coverage to international events than did the American newspapers. Slightly more than 44 percent of the stories in the *Times* focused on world affairs—twice the percentage found in the typical American paper and considerably greater even than in the international-minded *New York Times*. And although the London *Times* hardly ignored war, revolution, and political turmoil, its international stories also dealt with more peaceful and prosaic items—political maneuvering in Sweden, marital customs in India, and other matters that might remind readers that the world outside their borders was filled with ordinary people like themselves.

The *Times* and other international newspapers devote enormous attention to the United States because America's economic and military power mean that American actions are likely to have important consequences throughout the world. In their news pages and editorial commentary, newspapers in Europe, Asia, Africa, Latin America, and the Middle East seek to dissect every nuance of American policy to understand its intentions and significance for their own nations. Often, this coverage is less than flattering, even when American policy appears to be successful. For example, one of France's most influential newspapers, *Le Monde*, saw the capture of Saddam Hussein as an act of revenge designed to allow America to present itself as "a righter of wrongs." Most European newspapers were sharply critical of the Bush administration's decision to go to war against Iraq without UN approval. The influential Jordanian daily *Al-Dustour* described American troops in Iraq as "a gang of murderers." Is the United States a malevolent force? Or is the world simply envious of America's wealth and power?

FOR CRITICAL ANALYSIS

1. In 2004, American news coverage of the abuse of Iraqi prisoners by U.S. soldiers shocked the world. Should the American media present a more positive image of the United States to foreigners?
2. American newspapers offer more coverage of local events than of world affairs. What factors might explain the local focus of the American press?

---

a. Michael Massing, "The Unseen War," *New York Review of Books*, May 29, 2003, p. 17.

b. Massing, "Unseen War," p. 17.

coverage, in turn, gave Obama an extra opportunity—which he seized—to display his intelligence and ability to the electorate.

In terms of media coverage, Sarah Palin's candidacy was almost the opposite of Obama's experience. One reason that John McCain chose Palin as his vice-presidential running mate was a calculation that the media would find Palin sufficiently new and interesting to divert their attention from Obama. Palin's acceptance speech at the Republican convention in which she described herself as a simple "hockey mom," and declared that the difference between a hockey mom and a pit bull was "lipstick," captured the media's interest and briefly gave the GOP a stage to rival Obama's. Palin, however, was not able to put her extra media exposure to good use. After two disastrous network interviews in which Palin appeared unable to answer the simplest questions, the media generally dismissed the Alaska governor as inept and uninformed, and resumed their focus on Obama.

PRIMING A third important media power is **priming.** This occurs when media coverage affects the way the public evaluates political leaders, issues, and events. For example, nearly unanimous media praise for President Bush's speeches to the nation in the wake of the September 11 terrorist attacks prepared, or *primed*, the public to view Bush's subsequent response to terrorism in an extremely positive light, even though some aspects of the administration's efforts, most notably those in the realm of bioterrorism, were quite problematic.

priming process of preparing the public to take a particular view of an event or political actor

In the case of political candidates, the media have considerable influence over whether a particular individual will receive public attention, whether a particular individual will be taken seriously as a viable contender, and whether the public will evaluate a candidate's performance favorably. Thus, if the media find a candidate interesting, they may treat him or her as a serious contender even though the facts of the matter seem to suggest otherwise. In a similar vein, the media may declare that a candidate has "momentum," a mythical property that the media confer on candidates if they happen to exceed the media's expectations. In 1992, when Bill Clinton's poll standings surged in the wake of the Democratic National Convention, the media determined that Clinton had enormous momentum. In fact, nothing that happened during the remainder of the race led the media to change its collective judgment.

Politics Today

In 2008, the McCain campaign charged that media bias led to more favorable coverage of Barack Obama. Has coverage of Obama been mostly positive or negative since he took office as president?

Typically, media coverage of election campaigns focuses on the "horse race" (that is, who is ahead and by how much) to the detriment of attention to issues and candidate records. In the year preceding the 2008 national elections, several candidates fought for the Democratic and Republican presidential nominations. From the outset, it appeared that Senator Hillary Clinton was nearly certain to become the Democratic nominee. Looking for a horse race, however, the national media gave enormous publicity to Senator Barack Obama. Newspapers and magazines ran hundreds of positive profiles of Obama, touting him as the first serious African American presidential contender. Hardly a negative word about Obama was uttered on the air or in print. Obama was even allowed to appear in a *Saturday Night Live* Halloween skit poking fun at Clinton, who was portrayed as a witch.[24] Months of positive coverage helped transform Obama into a serious presidential contender.

The media's power to influence people's evaluation of public figures is not absolute. Throughout the last decade, politicians implemented new techniques for communicating with the public and shaping their own images. For instance, Bill Clinton pioneered the use of town meetings and television entertainment programs as a means of communicating directly with voters in the 1992 election. During the

2000 presidential race between Bush and Gore, both candidates made use of town meetings, as well as talk shows and entertainment programs such as *The Oprah Winfrey Show, The Tonight Show with Jay Leno,* and *Saturday Night Live,* to reach mass audiences. During a town meeting, talk show, or entertainment program, politicians are free to craft their own images without interference from journalists.

In 2008, the McCain campaign quickly determined that vice-presidential nominee, Sarah Palin, was not quite ready for prime-time media exposure. Palin had little experience outside her own state and was not conversant with most national political issues. Accordingly, GOP strategists sought to limit Palin's media exposure to situations in which she would not be subjected to the sort of intensive questioning that might reveal her limitations. Palin was kept away from the media and refused almost all requests for interviews. The two interviews that Palin granted, with ABC's Charles Gibson and CBS's Katie Couric were public relations disasters. Gibson and Couric were chosen because neither is a particularly aggressive or incisive questioner. Nevertheless, Palin fumbled their simplest questions and convinced McCain staffers that the Alaska governor should stick to scripted appearances. During most of the campaign, Palin made speeches at which she took no questions from the media. In the opening moments of October's nationally televised vice-presidential debate, Palin announced that she would not necessarily be bound by the questions and would, instead, speak on matters she believed to be important. Palin then spent much of the debate ignoring the moderator's queries and, instead, continually reiterated the GOP "talking points," which had been prepared for her.

In the battle for the 2008 Democratic presidential nomination, favorable media coverage of Barack Obama contributed to his rise as a candidate and as a serious challenger to the early front-runner, Hillary Clinton.

The Rise of Adversarial Journalism

Politics Today

Before he left office in June, 2007, the long-time British prime minister Tony Blair called the news media a "feral beast." Why are many politicians hostile to media? Do you share their views?

The political power of the news media vis-à-vis the government has greatly increased in recent years through the growing prominence of "adversarial journalism"—a form of reporting in which the media adopt a hostile posture toward the government and public officials.

During the nineteenth century, American newspapers were completely subordinate to the political parties. Newspapers depended on official patronage—legal notice and party subsidies—for their financial survival and were controlled by party leaders. (A vestige of that era survived into the twentieth century in such newspaper names as the *Springfield Republican* and the *St. Louis Globe-Democrat.*) At the turn of the century, with the development of commercial advertising, newspapers became financially independent. This made possible the emergence of a formally nonpartisan press.

In an effort to avoid tough questions from interviewers on traditional news programs, politicians increasingly seek out opportunities to reach the public through entertainment or "soft news" programs. Bill Clinton played his saxophone on The Arsenio Hall Show *and discussed his choice of underwear with a teenage interviewer on MTV. George W. Bush also made good use of appearances on entertainment programs, appearing on* The Tonight Show with Jay Leno *and other programs.*

Presidents were the first national officials to see the opportunities in this development. By communicating directly to the electorate through newspapers and magazines, Theodore Roosevelt and Woodrow Wilson established political constituencies for themselves, independent of party organizations, and strengthened their own power relative to Congress. President Franklin Delano Roosevelt used the radio, most notably in his famous fireside chats, to reach out to voters throughout the nation and to make himself the center of American politics. FDR was also adept at developing close personal relationships with reporters that enabled him to obtain favorable news coverage despite the fact that in his day a majority of newspaper owners and publishers were staunch conservatives. Following Roosevelt's example, subsequent presidents have all sought to use the media to enhance their popularity and power. For example, through televised news conferences, President John F. Kennedy mobilized public support for his domestic and foreign-policy initiatives.

During the 1950s and early 1960s, a few members of Congress also made successful use of the media—especially television—to mobilize national support for their causes. Senator Estes Kefauver of Tennessee became a major contender for the presidency and won a place on the 1956 Democratic national ticket as a result of his dramatic televised hearings on organized crime. Senator Joseph McCarthy of Wisconsin made himself a powerful national figure through his well-publicized investigations of alleged communist infiltration of key American institutions. These senators, however, were more exceptional than typical. Through the mid-1960s, the executive branch continued to generate the bulk of news coverage, and the media became a cornerstone of presidential power.

The Vietnam War shattered this relationship between the press and the presidency. During the early stages of U.S. involvement, American officials in Vietnam who disapproved of the way the war was being conducted leaked information critical of administrative policy to reporters. Publication of this material infuriated the

Adversarial journalism has become common in politics as reporters aggressively pursue stories that are critical of politicians and their actions. In 2008, intense media coverage of inflammatory remarks made by Barack Obama's preacher Jeremiah Wright presented a challenge for the Obama campaign.

White House, which pressured publishers to block its release—on one occasion, President Kennedy went so far as to ask the *New York Times* to reassign its Saigon correspondent. However, the national print and broadcast media—the network news divisions, the national news weeklies, the *Washington Post*, and the *New York Times*—discovered an audience for critical coverage and investigative reporting among segments of the public skeptical of administration policy. As the Vietnam conflict dragged on, critical media coverage fanned antiwar sentiment. Moreover, growing opposition to the war among liberals encouraged some members of Congress, most notably Senator J. William Fulbright, chair of the Senate Foreign Relations Committee, to break with the president. In turn, these shifts in popular and congressional sentiment emboldened journalists and publishers to continue to present critical news reports. Through this process, journalists developed a commitment to adversarial journalism, while a constituency emerged that would rally to the defense of the media when it came under White House attack.

This pattern, established during the Vietnam War, endured through the 1970s and into the 1980s. Political forces opposed to presidential policies, many members of Congress, and the national news media began to find that their interests often overlapped. Opponents of the Nixon, Carter, Reagan, and Bush administrations welcomed news accounts critical of the conduct of executive agencies and officials in foreign affairs and in such domestic areas as race relations, the environment, and regulatory policy. In addition, many senators and representatives found it politically advantageous to champion causes favored by the antiwar, consumer, or environmental movements because, by conducting televised hearings on such issues, they were able to mobilize national constituencies, to become national figures, and in a number of instances to become serious contenders for their party's presidential nomination.

As for the national media, aggressive use of the techniques of investigation, publicity, and exposure allowed them to enhance their autonomy and carve out a prominent place for themselves in American government and politics. The power derived by the press from adversarial journalism is one of the reasons that the media seem to relish opportunities to attack political institutions and to publish damaging information about important public officials. Increasingly, media coverage has come to influence politicians' careers, the mobilization of political constituencies, and the fate of issues and causes.

Adversarial, or "attack," journalism has become commonplace in America, and some critics have suggested that the media have contributed to popular cynicism and the low levels of citizen participation that characterize contemporary American political processes. But before we begin to think about means of compelling the media to adopt a more positive view of politicians and political issues, we should consider the possibility that media criticism is one of the major mechanisms of political accountability in the American political process. Without aggressive media coverage would we have known of Bill Clinton's misdeeds or, for that matter, those of Richard Nixon? Without aggressive media coverage, would important questions be raised about the conduct of American foreign and domestic policy? It is easy to criticize the media for their aggressive tactics, but would our democracy function effectively without the critical role of the press? Vigorous and critical media are needed as the "watchdogs" of American politics. Of course, in October 2001, the adversarial relationship between the government and the media was at least temporarily transformed into a much more supportive association as the media helped rally the American people for the fight against terrorism.

For Critical Analysis

In wartime, can media criticism of government action aid the nation's enemies? Should there be limits on media criticism of the government during time of war? Or does criticism actually enhance the nation's strength?

Become an Informed and Vocal News Critic

Americans today are less trusting of what's being reported by major news outlets than they were in the not too distant past, and many of the traditional sources of news and information—newspapers and the nightly news on television—have seen sizable reductions in their audience. The number of Americans who tune into national news on TV is down by around half since the early 1970s.

Although dissatisfaction with the media is on the rise across all age groups, young people are among the most likely to have negative things to say about the news media. In fact, recent surveys have shown that around one in four young Americans get the majority of their news and information from comedy shows like *The Daily Show with Jon Stewart* and *The Colbert Report*, and similar numbers say a candidate endorsement by Jon Stewart could sway their votes on Election Day. The content of these shows, which satirize the sensational and melodramatic style of mainstream news programming, resonates with media-savvy young Americans.

In an attempt to make mainstream news more attractive to young people, news editors have instituted changes in recent years. For example, CNN created its "Headline News" channel, which features fast-paced news and allows viewers to "dip in and dip out," thus catering to the tendency among younger Americans to consume news quickly and to channel surf. Many networks have added younger and more diverse anchors to their news desks. Hiring anchors who don't fit the mold of the "older white guy" is an attempt to connect with younger, more diverse viewers. Moreover, news organizations have expanded their reach by offering free access to companion Web sites. For example, at NBC only about a quarter of the TV news audience for its national news program is under 34, but 54 percent of visitors to the network's MSNBC Web site fall into this age demographic.

Of course, changing the look of how news is delivered doesn't necessarily address the complaints voiced by young Americans about the news media. But what these steps do suggest is that media industry leaders take audience reaction seriously and are willing to adapt rather than lose influence with a generation of potential readers, listeners, and viewers.

If you're interested in digging a little deeper into the mass media's news coveage, here are some things that you can do to become a more informed consumer of news and information:

- ★ People often complain that the news media seem biased. Rather than adhering to norms of objectivity, the news is often reported from a liberal or conservative perspective. Instead of accepting this complaint at face value, try a little experiment yourself. Spend some time watching, reading, and listening to news from two sources, one that is considered "conservative" and the other "liberal" (for example, Fox News and NPR, or the editorial pages of the *Wall Street Journal* and *New York Times*). Do you agree with the characterization of these organizations as biased?
- ★ Make your voice heard if you have concerns about news that's presented in a partisan fashion. Let the editors, hosts, writers, and owners of the broadcast or print media know that you expect more objectivity in the news that's being presented.
- ★ Spend some time checking out "new" and "alternative" media. Many blogs provide readers with a portal to information across a variety of sources, often with commentary. A few to consider are: the Huffington Post (www.huffingtonpost.com), the DrudgeReport (www.drudgereport.com), the Daily Dish (andrewsullivan.theatlantic.com), and the Daily Kos: State of the Nation (www.dailykos.com).
- ★ If none of the above interest you, simply do an Internet search for "political blog" or "news blogs." Compare the blog's content with what's covered in national newspapers and broadcasts. Do the blogs provide better, more comprehensive, or more up-to-date information than what you'd get from traditional news sources? Are they more or less objective?

The adversarial relationship between the government and segments of the press, however, resumed in the wake of the 2003 Iraq war. Such newspapers as the *Washington Post* and the *New York Times* castigated President Bush for going to war without the support of some of America's major allies. When American forces failed to uncover evidence that Iraq possessed weapons of mass destruction—a major reason cited by the administration for launching the war—these newspapers intimated that the war had been based on intelligence failures, if not outright presidential deceptions. The president, as noted earlier, denounced the media for distorting his record. Thus, after a brief interlude of post–September 11 harmony, the customary hostilities between politicians and the press resumed.

This adversarial relationship is not confined to the national news media. Sometimes student journalists can be caught up in conflicts with politicians. In 2007, a University of North Carolina journalism student posted a report on YouTube that asked why the Edwards campaign, while emphasizing poverty as a central issue, had located its North Carolina headquarters in one of the most affluent sections of Chapel Hill. The Edwards press office furiously demanded that the story be removed and threatened to cut off all university access to Mr. Edwards and the campaign staff. The controversy, of course, increased interest in the video, which was viewed more than 2,000 times in a period of several days.[25]

Thinking Critically about Media Power and Democracy

The free media are an institution absolutely essential to democratic government. Ordinary citizens depend on the media to investigate wrongdoing, to publicize and explain governmental actions, to evaluate programs and politicians, and to bring to light matters that might otherwise be known to only a handful of governmental insiders. In short, without free and active media, popular government would be virtually impossible. Citizens would have few means through which to know or assess the government's actions—other than the claims or pronouncements of the government itself. Moreover, without active—indeed, aggressive—media, citizens would be hard pressed to make informed choices among competing candidates at the polls. Of course, by continually emphasizing deceptions and wrongdoing by political figures, the media encourage the public to become cynical and distrustful, not only of the people in office, but of the government and the political process themselves. A widespread sense that all politics is corrupt or deceptive can easily lead to a sense that nothing can be done. In this way, the media's adversarial posture may contribute to the low levels of political participation seen in America today.

Today's media are not only adversarial, but also increasingly partisan. Debates about the liberalism and conservatism of the mass media point up the fact that many readers and viewers perceive a growing bias in newspapers, radio, and television. Blogs and other Internet outlets, of course, are often unabashedly partisan. To some extent, increasing ideological and partisan stridency is an inevitable result of the expansion and proliferation of news sources. When the news was dominated by three networks and a handful of national papers, each sought to appeal to the entire national audience. This required a moderate and balanced tone so that consumers would not be offended and jump ship to a rival network or newspaper. Today, there are so many news sources that few can aim for a national audience. Instead, each targets a partisan or ideological niche and aims to develop a strong relationship with consumers in that audience segment by catering to their biases and predispositions. The end result may be to encourage greater division and disharmony among Americans.

At the same time, the declining power of party organizations (as we will see in Chapter 9) has made politicians ever more dependent on favorable media coverage. National political leaders and journalists have had symbiotic relationships, at least since FDR's presidency, but initially politicians were the senior partners. They benefited from media publicity, but they were not totally dependent on it as long as they could still rely on party organizations to mobilize votes. Journalists, on the other hand, depended on their relationships with politicians for access to information and would hesitate to report stories that might antagonize valuable sources for fear of being excluded from the flow of information in retaliation.

During President Richard Nixon's second term in office, media accounts of the president's complicity in a break-in at the 1972 Democratic campaign headquarters in Washington's Watergate Hotel led to congressional investigations that forced Nixon to resign from office. The Washington Post *reporters Robert Woodward and Carl Bernstein played an important role in uncovering the Watergate conspiracy.*

With the decline of party organizations, journalists have less fear that their access to information can be restricted in retaliation for negative coverage. Such freedom gives the media enormous power. The media can make or break reputations, help to launch or to destroy political careers, and build support for or rally opposition to programs and institutions.[26] Wherever there is so much power, at least the potential exists for its abuse or overly zealous use. All things considered, free media are so critically important to the maintenance of a democratic society that Americans must be prepared to take the risk that the media will occasionally abuse their power. The forms of governmental control that would prevent the media from misusing their power would also certainly destroy freedom. The ultimate beneficiaries of free and active media are the American people.

The Power of the New Media

Contemporary technology is opening new avenues for popular political participation. The Internet has become a powerful tool for political organization. Blogs and other Internet forums allow the rapid dissemination of information, ideas and opinions outside the control of the government or other institutions. To be sure, many of the ideas and opinions found in the various Web logs are unsupported by research or careful reasoning. Moreover, corporations and politicians have learned to create and use blogs for their own purposes. Blogs, nevertheless, sharply lower the technological and financial barriers that previously prevented all but a few individuals and interests from reaching mass audiences and potentially increase the ability of ordinary people to engage in effective political action. In 2003, for example, bloggers took the lead in publicizing a story that cost Senate Majority Leader Trent Lott his job. At Thurmond's 100th birthday party, Lott had praised Senator Strom Thurmond, a fervent segregationist, as a man who would have made a good president. Only after the blogs broke the story did the mainstream media seem to become aware of the significance of Lott's comments. In 2008, bloggers were responsible for some of the most negative aspects of the presidential campaign. While the candidates themselves generally took the high road, focusing on issues and problems, Democratic and Republican bloggers often focused on negative stories and even scurrilous rumors.

For Critical Analysis

How do the media distort political reality? How do politicians use the media for their own purposes? What are the consequences for American democracy when the electorate is informed through such a filter? How might the quality of political information in America be improved?

Thus, Republican bloggers circulated the unfounded claim that Barack Obama was a Muslim intent on subverting the U.S. government. Democratic bloggers circulated stories about John McCain's personal history and made much of an allegation that Sarah Palin's infant son was actually her daughter's baby. These blog-driven rumors became widespread and received attention in the mainstream media.

Magnifying the power of the Internet is the universal availability of digital cameras. Particularly since cell phones are now equipped with cameras, millions of Americans have the capacity to photograph or film events that they may witness. At the same time, Internet sites such as YouTube permit users to upload photos and video clips that are then viewed by hundreds of thousands of subscribers and are sometimes picked up by the mainstream media for even wider dissemination. In 2006, a YouTube video showing Senator George Allen making a racist comment to one of his opponent's campaign workers caused an uproar. Allen, who had been positioning himself for a possible 2008 presidential race, was defeated for reelection to the Senate from Virginia, when his victory had previously been seen as a sure thing. His presidential aspirations were dashed. With a bit of technology, citizens had ended the career of a once-powerful politician. This example illustrates the way in which technology can have a strong effect on popular politics.

FOR FURTHER READING

Armstorng, Jerome, and Markos Zuniga. *Crashing the Gate: Netroots, Grassroots, and the Rise of People-Powered Politics.* New York: Chelsea Green, 2006.

Cook, Timothy. *Governing with the News: The News Media as a Political Institution.* Chicago: University of Chicago Press, 1997.

Davis, Richard, and Diana Owen. *New Media and American Politics.* New York: Oxford University Press, 1998.

Fenton, Tom. *Bad News: The Decline of Reporting, the Business of News, and the Danger to Us All.* New York: HarperCollins, 2005.

Graber, Doris, ed. *Media Power in American Politics.* 5th ed. Washington, DC: CQ Press, 2006.

Hamilton, James T. *All the News That's Fit to Sell.* Princeton, NJ: Princeton University Press, 2004.

Jamieson, Kathleen, and Paul Waldman. *The Press Effect.* New York: Oxford University Press, 2004.

Kellner, Douglas. *Media Spectacle and the Crisis of Democracy.* Boulder, CO: Paradigm, 2005.

Kurtz, Howard. *Spin Cycle: Inside the Clinton Propaganda Machine.* New York: Free Press, 1998.

Merritt, Davis. *Knightfall: Knight Ridder and How the Erosion of Newspaper Journalism Is Putting Democracy at Risk.* New York: AMACOM, 2005.

Rich, Frank. *The Greatest Story Ever Sold.* New York: Penguin, 2006.

Rutherford, Paul. *Weapons of Mass Persuasion.* Toronto: University of Toronto Press, 2004.

Starr, Paul. *The Creation of the Media.* New York: Basic Books, 2004.

Weaver, David, et al. *The American Journalist in the 21st Century: U.S. News People at the Dawn of a New Millennium.* New York: Erlbaum, 2006.

RECOMMENDED WEB SITES

Accuracy in Media
www.aim.org
This non-profit, watchdog group attempts to ensure accuracy in media reporting by identifying botched or slanted stories and then "setting the record straight." Check out the media monitor, special reports, and press releases to see what current stories may be cause for concern.

Drudge Report
www.drudgereport.com
The site for the Drudge Report is a great source page for all the world's breaking news and most recent columns. Any consumer of the news will appreciate this handy guide to specific columnists and opinion pages of major publications.

Federal Communications Commission
www.fcc.gov/

The FCC is an independent regulatory agency established by the U.S. government in 1934 to regulate the broadcast media. On the official FCC Web site you can read about the rules and regulations that affect the media, along with other current topics of interest.

FOX News.com
www.foxnews.com/politics
CNN Politics.com
www.cnn.com/POLITICS
The New York Times
www.nytimes.com/pages/politics/index.html

Political news sites provide a good variety of perspectives on the news from conservative to liberal.

Journalism.org
www.journalism.org

This non-profit, non-political site, sponsored by the Project for Excellence in Journalism, examines the overall performance of the press as providers of information. Their aim is to help both consumers and producers of the news understand what the press is delivering and hopefully make it better.

National Newspaper Association
http://nna.org

The NNA is one of the oldest and largest professional associations in the print media today. As ownership of major newspapers fall into fewer and fewer hands, the NNA is trying to protect, promote, and enhance America's community newspapers.

Newseum
www.newseum.org

Newseum is the webpage for an interactive museum of news journalism. On this site you can browse the front pages of over 500 daily national and international newspapers and explore the galleries and theatres of the news museum in Washington, D.C.

The Pew Research Center for the People and the Press
http://people-press.org

This independent survey research organization studies attitudes towards the press and numerous political issues.

STUDY OUTLINE

www.wwnorton.com/wtp7e

The Media Industry and Government

1. Americans obtain their news from radio, television, newspapers, magazines, and the Internet. Even though television news reaches more Americans than any other single news source, the print media are still important because they often set the agenda for the broadcast media. Internet news sources are becoming increasingly popular.
2. Since the passage of the Telecommunications Act of 1996, a wave of mergers and consolidations in the media industry has reduced the number of independent media in the United States.
3. The nationalization of the American news media, through which a relatively uniform picture of events, issues, and problems is presented to the entire nation, has contributed greatly to the nationalization of politics and of political perspectives in the United States.
4. Despite the widespread nationalization of news in America, news enclaves exist in which some demographic and ideological groups receive alternative news coverage.
5. Part of the Telecommunications Act of 1996, known as the Communications Decency Act, attempted to regulate the content of material transmitted over the Internet, but the law was overruled by the Supreme Court in the 1997 case *Reno v. American Civil Liberties Union*.
6. Under federal regulations, broadcasters must provide candidates seeking the same political office equal time to communicate their messages to the public.
7. Regulations also require that individuals be granted the right to rebut personal attacks.
8. Although recently diminished in importance, the fairness doctrine for many years required that broadcasters that aired programs on controversial issues provide time for opposing views.

News Coverage

1. Media content and news coverage are inevitably affected by the views, ideals, and interests of the journalists who seek out, write, and produce news stories.
2. News coverage is also influenced by the individuals or groups who are subjects of the news or whose interests and activities are actual or potential news topics.

3. Because the print and broadcast media are businesses that generally seek to show a profit, they must cater to the preferences of consumers.
4. The print and broadcast media, as well as the publishing industry, are particularly responsive to the interests and views of the upscale segments of their audiences.
5. Protest is one way that groups who cannot afford the services of media consultants and "issues managers" can publicize their views and interests.

Media Power in American Politics

1. In recent political history, the media have played a central role in the civil rights movement, the ending of American involvement in the Vietnam War, and in the Watergate investigation.
2. The power of the media stems from several sources, all of which contribute to the media's great influence in setting the political agenda, shaping electoral outcomes, and interpreting events and political results.
3. The political power of the news media has greatly increased in recent years through the growing prominence of investigative reporting.
4. The "new media" can empower ordinary citizens.

Thinking Critically about Media Power and Democracy

1. Because the media provide the information citizens need for meaningful participation in the political process, they are essential to democratic government.
2. The decline of political parties has given the media enormous power, which creates a great potential for abuse.

PRACTICE QUIZ

www.wwnorton.com/wtp7e

1. The nationalization of the news has been influenced by which of the following trends in ownership of the media?
   a) the purchase of influential newspapers by foreign corporations
   b) the fragmentation of ownership of all media in the United States
   c) the wave of mergers and consolidations following the passage of the 1996 Telecommunications Act
   d) the purchase of the major news networks by the national government
2. Which of the following best describes national news in the United States?
   a) fragmented and localized
   b) nationalized and centralized
   c) centralized but still localized
   d) none of the above
3. Which of the following Supreme Court cases overruled the government's attempt to regulate the content of the Internet?
   a) *Near v. Minnesota*
   b) *New York Times v. United States*
   c) *Red Lion Broadcasting Company v. FCC*
   d) *Reno v. American Civil Liberties Union*
4. Which *two* of the following principles affect the political content of radio and television broadcasts?
   a) the equal time rule
   b) the right of rebuttal
   c) the fairness doctrine
   d) the indecency rule
5. Which of the following have an impact on the nature of media coverage of politics?
   a) reporters
   b) political actors
   c) news consumers
   d) all of the above
6. Which of the following is a strategy available to poor people to increase their coverage by the news media?
   a) protest
   b) media consultants
   c) television advertising
   d) newspaper advertising "time sharing"
7. The media's powers to determine what becomes a part of the political discussion and to shape how political events are interpreted by the American people are known as
   a) issue definition and protest power.
   b) agenda setting and framing.
   c) the illusion of saliency and the bandwagon effect.
   d) the equal time rule and the right of rebuttal.
8. Which of the following can be considered an example of a news enclave?
   a) Internet chat rooms
   b) letters to the editor
   c) readers of the *New York Times*
   d) people who watch CNN

9. Which of the following exemplifies the liberal bias in the news media?
   a) talk radio programs
   b) the *Wall Street Journal*
   c) the *American Spectator*
   d) none of the above

10. The newspaper publisher William Randolph Hearst was responsible for encouraging U.S. involvement in which war?
    a) the Spanish-American War
    b) the Vietnam War
    c) the U.S. war with Mexico
    d) the Gulf War

KEY TERMS

www.wwnorton.com/wtp7e

agenda setting (p. 267)
equal time rule (p. 255)
fairness doctrine (p. 255)
framing (p. 268)
priming (p. 271)
right of rebuttal (p. 255)
sound bites (p. 249)

8 Political Participation and Voting

- ★ Forms of Political Participation
- ★ Who Participates, and How?
- ★ Explaining Political Participation
- ★ Thinking Critically about Political Participation and Liberty, Equality, and Democracy

WHAT GOVERNMENT DOES AND WHY IT MATTERS

For much of American history, formal barriers restricted the right to vote and created a pattern of unequal participation in politics. By the 1960s, the political struggles of women and members of racial minorities had succeeded in extending voting rights to all citizens. The extension of the franchise to those eighteen and older in 1971 underscored the importance of political participation to our democratic values. Although most formal barriers to participation have been eliminated, voter turnout remains low, especially among younger voters. Registering, learning about the issues, and distinguishing among the candidates are often not easy tasks for first-time voters. For many young people, the decision to stay away from politics has been reinforced by their perception that politics is "a dirty, distance spectator sport, whose players don't seem interested in their ideas or their issues."[1]

The 2008 election proved to be an exception to this pattern of disinterest in American politics. From the start, the Obama campaign sought to mobilize new voters, reaching out especially to young voters. The campaign worked to register large numbers of first-time voters, especially among the young and among immigrants. As the first major-party African American candidate for president, Obama spurred a huge mobilization among black voters. Among Republicans, the nomination of Sarah Palin for vice president injected new energy into the election and motivated party loyalists to participate. In the 2004 election, Republicans held the advantage in recruiting volunteers and in mobilizing the electorate. In 2008, by contrast, Democrats had a much more extensive operation for registering new voters, contacting potential supporters, and turning them out to vote.

In many ways, the Obama campaign rewrote the rules for engaging supporters in electoral campaigns. The campaign paid special attention to young voters, seeking to replace cynicism and apathy with idealism and hope. Connecting through the Internet and other new technologies, volunteers found many opportunities to participate. The campaign opened many offices across the country, making it easier for potential supporters to connect with campaign activities. It also encouraged voters to take advantage of early voting, which was available in many states. An estimated one-third of voters cast their ballots in advance, easing the strain at the polls on Election Day. Obama's success ensures that these strategies of promoting broad political engagement in elections will be studied and likely emulated by future candidates from both political parties.

The combination of excitement and mobilization in the 2008 elections spurred more than 73 percent of eligible voters to register, a modern record. However, early analysis of the vote indicated that turnout did not reach the anticipated record levels, partly due to somewhat lower levels of turnout among Republicans. Participation did increase among many categories of voters. It was especially high among African Americans, inspired by the first major-party black presidential candidate in American history. Young voters also increased their turnout, adding to the growing levels of youth participation that began in 2004. However, initial analyses suggested that Obama's victory did not rest primarily on unprecedented turnout of young voters and African American voters, as election forecasters had predicted. Instead, higher support among all groups of voters allowed him to win a broad victory. Even so, the high turnout overall suggested that with the economy on the verge of a major recession, two wars still unresolved, and strong campaign efforts to encourage participation, many Americans wanted to make their voices heard in the election of 2008.

Who votes and participates in other ways affects the issues that candidates and elected officials put at the top of their agenda. Recent polls show that young people share many of the same concerns as older voters, but their views on how to address issues are often distinct. For example, young adults prefer more lenient immigration policies and are more likely to support Social Security privatization than are older voters. They also tend to be more positive about the role of government and express support for stronger environmental laws than older people do.[2] Yet young people's relatively lower rates of participation mean that a narrower set of policy options receives serious attention, while the approaches favored by a majority of younger people are neglected. When young people participate in greater numbers, the scope of public debate is broadened, and the possibilities of approaching old problems in new ways expand.

- **In this chapter, we will first examine patterns of contemporary political participation, discussing the different forms that participation can take.**
- **We then review the kinds of access to the political system that groups with different social backgrounds and cultural beliefs fought for and subsequently enjoyed.** We will see that such identities do not always provide the basis for shared political activity.
- **We will then consider the reasons for declining political participation in recent decades.** We will see that individual beliefs, such as a sense of efficacy, are important, but that most significant is the failure of our institutions to mobilize people into politics.
- **Finally, we will consider the implications of uneven political participation.** As the role of money in politics gives the wealthy a greater say in government, we ask if our institutions do enough to foster participation by all Americans.

Forms of Political Participation

Political participation refers to a wide range of activities, designed to influence government. Today, voting has come to be seen as the normal or typical form of citizen political activity. Yet ordinary people took part in politics long before the advent of the election or any other formal mechanism of popular involvement in political life. If there is any natural or spontaneous form of popular political participation, it is the riot rather than the election. The urban riot and the rural uprising were common in both Europe and America prior to the nineteenth century and not entirely uncommon even in the twentieth century. Urban riots played an important role in American politics in the 1960s and 1970s. Even as recently as 1999, riots during the Seattle, Washington, meeting of the World Trade Organization helped labor unions and other opponents of trade liberalization to slow the pace of change in the rules governing world trade.

political participation political activities, such as voting, contacting political officials, volunteering for a campaign, or participating in a protest, whose purpose is to influence government

Most Americans would not consider taking part in a riot. Yet in recent years, fewer numbers of Americans are exercising their right to vote. Participation in presidential elections has dropped significantly over the past forty years. In 1960, 64 percent of eligible voters cast ballots; in 1996, participation reached a new low when only 52 percent of eligible voters cast ballots. In 2004, major efforts to get out the vote brought turnout to over 60 percent. This was the first significant increase in voting in recent years. The trend continued in 2008, when initial estimates indicated that 62.6 percent of the voting-eligible population came out to vote. Turnout for midterm elections (that is, elections that fall between presidential elections) is typically lower; for local elections, even lower.[3]

Protests and rallies are forms of political participation. At this rally, demonstrators gathered in support of immigrants' rights. They hoped to draw attention to their cause and to influence the government to adopt policies that would result in better conditions for immigrant workers.

Of course, voting and rioting are not the only forms of participation available to Americans. Citizens can contact political officials, sign petitions, attend public meetings, join organizations, give money to a politician or a political organization, volunteer in a campaign, write a letter to the editor or write an article about an issue, or participate in a protest or rally. Such activities differ from voting because they can communicate much more detailed information to public officials than voting can. Voters may support a candidate for many reasons, but their actual votes do not indicate specifically what they like and don't like, nor do they tell officials how intensely voters feel about issues. A vote can convey only a general sense of approval or disapproval. By writing a letter or engaging in other kinds of political participation, people can convey much more specific information, telling public officials exactly what issues they care most about and what their views on those issues are. For that reason these other political activities are often more satisfying than voting. And citizens who engage in these other activities are more likely to try to influence state and local politics rather than national politics; in voting, people find the national scene more interesting than state and local politics.[4]

Nonelectoral political activity takes many forms: some of the most prominent in recent years include *lobbying, public relations, litigation*, and *protest*.

lobbying a strategy by which organized interests seek to influence the passage of legislation by exerting direct pressure on members of the legislature

Lobbying is an effort by groups or individuals to take their case directly to elected or appointed officials. By voting, citizens seek to determine who will govern. By lobbying, citizens attempt to determine what those in power will do. As we will see in Chapter 11, many interest groups employ professional lobbyists to bring their views to lawmakers. At the same time, however, thousands of volunteers lobby Congress and the bureaucracy each year on behalf of citizen groups such as the National Organization for Women (NOW), the Sierra Club, and the Home School Legal Defense Fund.[5] The hundreds of thousands of citizens who call or write to members of Congress each year, seeking to influence their votes, are also engaged in lobbying.

public relations an attempt, usually through the use of paid consultants, to establish a favorable relationship with the public and influence its political opinions

Public relations is an effort to sway public opinion on behalf of an issue or cause. Corporations and interest groups typically employ professional public relations firms to produce print, radio, and television advertising in support of their goals. At times, corporations use public relations strategies to influence specific pieces of legislation. For example, in 2006 the giant retailer Wal-Mart sought to fend off new regulations in Maryland requiring the company to offer more generous health care benefits to its workers. Wal-Mart aired ads accusing proponents of the legislation of unfairly singling out Wal-Mart for attack. Other advertisements warned that the company would be forced to cancel expansion plans, costing the state jobs. In other instances, corporations launch public relations efforts to create goodwill in the public and fend off possible future regulations. Oil companies routinely air television commercials and print advertisements that affirm their support for a clean environment. At the same time, public-relations tactics are also used by numerous citizen groups to promote issues and causes important to them.

In some cases efforts to influence public opinion can backfire. In September 2007, when General David Petraeus appeared before Congress to report on the progress of the war in Iraq, the progressive antiwar group MoveOn.org sought to challenge his positive account of the war with a public-relations strategy. Move-On bought a full-page advertisement in the *New York Times* bearing the headline, "General Petraeus or General Betray Us?" Although MoveOn's membership approved of the ad, it provoked an outcry of opposition among critics who charged that MoveOn was undermining the Iraq war effort and unfairly smearing an upstanding military leader. Both houses of Congress passed resolutions condemning the advertisement.

A favorite tactic of citizen groups is the press release designed to shape news coverage. In the aftermath of Hurricane Katrina in 2005, all types of groups produced press releases that sought to explain the disaster in terms that would benefit their policy priorities. For example, three days after the hurricane hit, Friends of the Earth, an environmental group, issued a press release blaming the storm's strength on global warming and urging the federal government to address the problem of climate change. A religious group called Repent America put out a press release with a very different message. Blaming the hurricane on the decadent lifestyles of New Orleans residents, the group advocated moral reform as the only way to prevent such disasters. Because of the intense press attention to Katrina, groups supporting a wide range of policies, including school vouchers, tax cuts, and increased aid to the poor, sought to link their issues to the hurricane.

Litigation is an attempt to use the courts to achieve a goal. In recent years, citizen groups and even individuals have used the federal courts more and more frequently to affect public policy. Using the so-called citizen-suit provisions of a number of federal statutes, citizen groups play an active role in shaping policy in such areas as air and water quality, preservation of endangered species, civil rights, and the rights of persons with disabilities. Use of the courts by citizen groups is encouraged by federal and state fee-shifting provisions that allow plaintiffs (those bringing a case in court) to recover legal fees from the government or the defendant, as well as by class-action rules that allow an individual to bring suit on behalf of large groups. We will learn more about this form of participation in Chapter 15.

litigation a lawsuit or legal proceeding; as a form of political participation, an attempt to seek relief in a court of law

Though most Americans reject violent **protest** or terrorism for political ends, peaceful protest is generally recognized as a legitimate and important form of political activity and is protected by the First Amendment. During the 1960s and 1970s, hundreds of thousands of Americans took part in peaceful protests that helped bring an end to legalized racial segregation. In recent years, peaceful marches and demonstrations have been employed by a host of groups ranging from opponents of the war in Iraq to antiabortion activists. Protest is widely valued as a strategy that is available to all groups. The largest public protests in recent years were staged by immigrants and their supporters in 2006. The spark for the protest was opposition to a House bill that branded unauthorized immigrants and those who assisted them as felons. The protest, which took place in cities across the country, drew unexpectedly large crowds, estimated at 500,000 in Los Angeles, 300,000 in Chicago, and tens of thousands in many other cities. Galvanized by Spanish-language radio and the organizational power of the Catholic church, the large numbers turning out to march across the country stunned even the organizers. As one organizer put it, "People are joining in so spontaneously, it's almost like the immigrants have risen. I would call it a civil rights movement reborn in this country."[6]

protest participation that involves assembling crowds to confront a government or other official organization

Alternative forms of political action generally require more time, effort, or money than voting does. It is not surprising, then, that far fewer people engage in these forms of political participation than vote. In a 2004 survey of participation, for example, 80 percent of those questioned reported voting in the last election. (This figure is higher than the percentages reported in exit polls because people tend to overstate their voting habits in surveys.) In contrast, fewer than a third said they had contacted a public official; 21 percent said they had been active in a political campaign; and fewer than 10 percent said they had made a campaign contribution (see Figure 8.1). Nearly 40 percent, however, said they were involved in an organization that took positions on political issues.[7]

FIGURE 8.1 ★ Political Participation

Political activities such as protests generally take more time and effort than voting. When asked about various forms of political participation, 80 percent of respondents said they voted in the most recent election. (This number is higher than the actual turnout because people tend to overstate their voting habits in surveys.)

SOURCE: Virginia Sapiro, Steven J. Rosenstone, and the National Election Studies, *American National Election Studies Cumulative Data File, 1948–2002*, 12th ICPSR version (Ann Arbor: University of Michigan, Center for Political Studies [producer], and Inter-University Consortium for Political and Social Research [distributor], 2004).

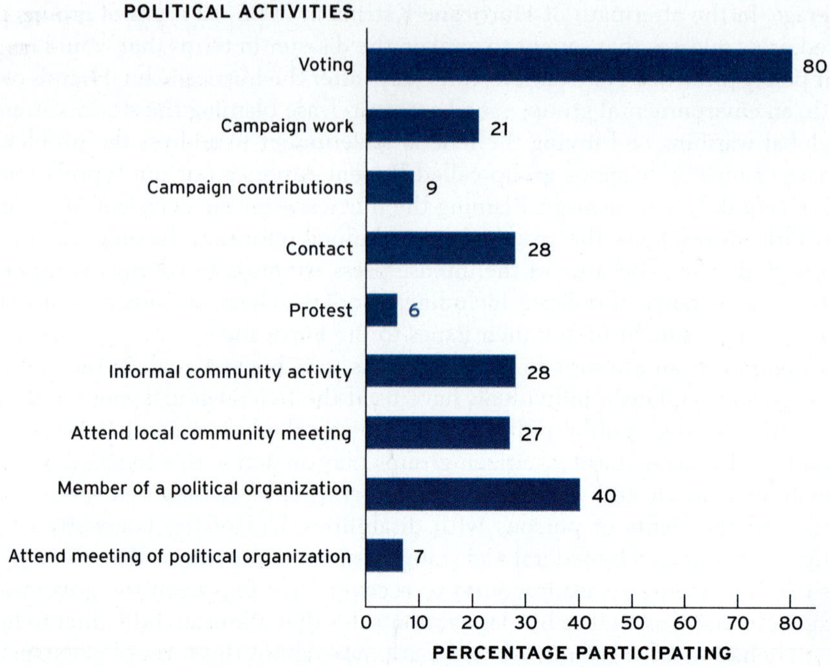

Whether voting is as effective or satisfying as these other forms of political action is an open question. It is clear, however, that for most Americans voting remains the most accessible and most important form of political activity. Moreover, precisely because of the time, energy, and money often required to lobby, litigate, and even demonstrate, these forms of political action are often, albeit not always, dominated by better-educated and wealthier Americans. As we will see, voting participation in America is also somewhat biased in favor of those with greater wealth and, especially, higher levels of education. Nevertheless, the right to vote gives ordinary Americans a more equal chance to participate in politics than almost any other form of political activity. In the remainder of this chapter, therefore, we will turn to voting in America.

Voting

Despite the availability of an array of alternatives, in practice citizen participation in American politics is generally limited to voting and a small number of other electoral activities (for example, campaigning). It is true that voter turnout in the United States is relatively low. But when, for one reason or another, Americans do seek to participate, their participation generally takes the form of voting.

suffrage the right to vote; also called franchise

The preeminent position of voting in the American political process is not surprising. The American legal and political environment is overwhelmingly weighted in favor of electoral participation. The availability of the right to vote, or **suffrage,** is, of course, a question of law. And civic education, also to a large extent mandated by law, encourages citizens to believe that electoral participation is the appropriate way to express opinions and grievances. Although all American citizens over the age of eighteen now have the right to vote and most learn about the importance of the vote in school, electoral participation has declined in recent decades. What

Voting is the most common way in which Americans participate in politics. Voter turnout is highest in presidential election years.

is most alarming about declining electoral participation is that the least well-off Americans are the least likely to vote, and the most advantaged are the most likely to vote. Because this pattern of class bias in participation conflicts so strongly with the American ideal of equal political rights, it has raised considerable concern.

VOTING RIGHTS In principle, states determine who is eligible to vote. During the nineteenth and early twentieth centuries, the right to vote was not distributed equally across the American population. Voter eligibility requirements often varied greatly from state to state. Some states openly abridged the right to vote on the basis of race; others did not. Some states imposed property restrictions on voting; others had no such restrictions. Most states mandated lengthy residency requirements, which meant that persons moving from one state to another sometimes lost their right to vote for as much as a year. In more recent years, however, constitutional amendments, federal statutes, and federal court decisions have limited states' discretion in the area of voting rights. Individual states may establish brief residency requirements, generally fifteen days, for record-keeping purposes. Beyond this, states have little or no power to regulate suffrage.

Today in the United States, all native-born or naturalized citizens over the age of eighteen, with the exception of those imprisoned for a felony in most states and, in many states, people who have a felony conviction even if they are not in prison, have the right to vote. During the colonial and early national periods of American history, the right to vote was generally restricted to white males over the age of twenty-one. Many states also limited voting to those who owned property or paid more than a specified amount of annual tax. Property and tax requirements began to be rescinded during the 1820s, however, and had generally disappeared by the end of the Civil War.

By the time of the Civil War, blacks had won the right to vote in most northern states. In the South, black voting rights were established by the Fifteenth Amendment, ratified in 1870, which prohibited denial of the right to vote on the basis of race. Despite the Fifteenth Amendment, the voting rights of African Americans were effectively rescinded during the 1880s by the states of the former Confederacy. During this period, the southern states created what was called the "Jim Crow" system of racial segregation. As part of this system, a variety of devices, such

poll tax a state-imposed tax on voters as a prerequisite for registration. Poll taxes were rendered unconstitutional in national elections by the Twenty-fourth Amendment, and in state elections by the Supreme Court in 1966

as **poll taxes** and literacy tests, were used to prevent virtually all blacks from voting. During the 1950s and 1960s, through the civil rights movement led by Dr. Martin Luther King, Jr., and others, African Americans demanded the restoration of their voting rights. Their goal was accomplished through the enactment of the 1965 Voting Rights Act, which provided for the federal government to register voters in states that discriminated against minority citizens. The result was the reenfranchisement of southern blacks for the first time since the 1860s.

Women won the right to vote in 1920, with the adoption of the Nineteenth Amendment. This amendment resulted primarily from the activities of the women's suffrage movement, led by Elizabeth Cady Stanton, Susan B. Anthony, and Carrie Chapman Catt during the late nineteenth and early twentieth centuries. The "suffragists," as they were called, held rallies, demonstrations, and protest marches for more than half a century before achieving their goal. The cause of women's suffrage was ultimately advanced by World War I. President Woodrow Wilson and members of Congress became convinced that women would be more likely to support the war effort if they were granted the right to vote. For this same reason, women were given the right to vote in Great Britain and Canada during World War I.

The most recent expansion of the right to vote in the United States took place in 1971, during the Vietnam War, when the Twenty-sixth Amendment was ratified, lowering the voting age from twenty-one to eighteen. Unlike black suffrage and women's suffrage, which came about in part because of the demands of groups that had been deprived of the right to vote, the Twenty-sixth Amendment was not a response to the demands of young people to be given the right to vote. Instead, many policy makers hoped that the right to vote would channel the disruptive protest activities of students involved in the anti–Vietnam War movement into peaceful participation at the ballot box.

For Critical Analysis

Describe the expansion of suffrage in the United States since the Founding. Why might the government have denied participation to so many for so long? What forces influenced the expansion of voting rights?

VOTING AND CIVIC EDUCATION Laws, of course, cannot completely explain why most people vote rather than rioting or lobbying. If public attitudes were completely unfavorable to elections, it is doubtful that legal remedies alone would have much impact.

Positive public attitudes about voting do not come into being in a completely spontaneous manner. Americans are taught to equate citizenship with electoral participation. Civic training, designed to give students an appreciation for the American system of government, is a legally required part of the curriculum in every elementary and secondary school. Although it is not so often required by law, civic education usually manages to find its way into college curricula as well.

turnout the percentage of eligible individuals who actually vote

VOTER PARTICIPATION Although the United States has developed a system of civic education and a legal basis for nearly universal suffrage, America's rate of voter participation, or **turnout,** is very low. About 50 percent of those eligible participate in national presidential elections. Barely one-third of eligible voters take part in midterm congressional elections (see Figure 8.2). Turnout in state and local races that do not coincide with national contests is typically even lower. In most European countries and other Western democracies, by contrast, national voter turnout is usually between 70 and 90 percent[8] (see Figure 8.3).

Figure 8.4 shows the marked differences in voter turnout linked to ethnic group, education level, employment status, and age. This trend has created a political process whose class bias is so obvious and egregious that, if it continues, Americans may have to begin adding a qualifier when they describe their politics as demo-

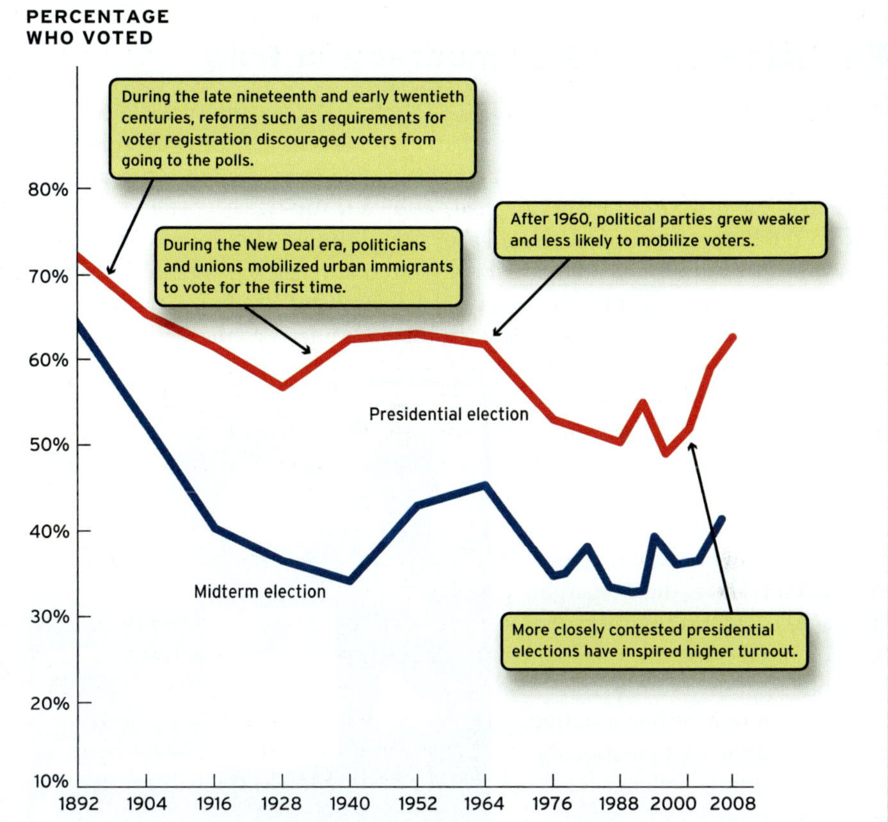

FIGURE 8.2 ★ Voter Turnout in Presidential and Midterm Elections, 1892–2008

Since the 1800s, participation in elections has declined substantially. One pattern is consistent across time: more Americans tend to vote in presidential election years than in years when only congressional and local elections are held. What are some of the reasons that participation rose and fell during the last century?

SOURCES: Erik Austin and Jerome Clubb, *Political Facts of the United States since 1789* (New York: Columbia University Press, 1986), 378–79; and U.S. Census Bureau, www.census.gov/compendia/statab/tables/08s0404.pdf (accessed 4/7/08).

cratic. Perhaps the terms "semidemocratic," "quasidemocratic," or "neodemocratic" are in order to describe a political process in which ordinary voters have as little influence as they do in contemporary America.

Who Participates, and How?

The original **American political community** consisted of a rather limited group of white male property holders. Over the ensuing two centuries, "we the people" became a larger and more inclusive body as a result of such forces as the abolitionist movement, the women's suffrage movement, and the civil rights movement (see Chapter 5). This expansion of the political community was marked by enormous conflicts involving questions of race, gender, religious identity, and age. Today, these conflicts continue in the form of struggles over such issues as affirmative action, welfare reform, abortion, the gender gap, the political mobilization of religious groups, and the rise and fall of minority voting districts. The ongoing participation of groups with distinctive social and cultural identities has transformed politics, altering political coalitions and changing political debates. This section examines the experiences of different kinds of cultural and social groups in American politics:

American political community citizens who are eligible to vote and who participate in American political life

Participation and Democracy in Iraq

When the United States first launched the war in Iraq in 2003, many Americans expected that Iraqi citizens would readily participate in a new democracy. Saddam Hussein's harsh authoritarian rule had, after all, suppressed the domestic population, led the country into a disastrous war with Iran, and made Iraq an international pariah. Instead, the effort to encourage participation and build democracy in Iraq presented a formidable challenge. At the heart of the difficulty were Iraq's ethnic divisions. In a country where 60 percent of the population were Shiite Muslims, 20 percent Kurds, and 20 percent Sunni Muslims, Sunnis feared that a majoritarian democracy would leave them marginalized. As the ethnic group that had benefited most from Saddam Hussein's rule, Sunnis had the most to lose in a democratic Iraq. Securing Sunni participation became the central challenge for the fledgling democracy: disaffected Sunnis were being drawn into the insurgency, which threatened to destroy democratic hopes and plunge the country into civil war.

After the invasion in 2003, Americans set up a complex multistage approach to promoting democratic participation. Unfortunately, this groundwork did little to allay the fears of Sunnis that they would be excluded from power in a new democracy. As a result, the vast majority of Sunnis boycotted the January 2005 elections in which Iraq's first national assembly was chosen. The boycott meant that this group initially had little influence in drawing up the constitution, the main task of the new national assembly. Instead, the constitution reflected a deal between the majority Shiites and the Kurds, leaving Sunnis fearful that the country could be partitioned, with its vast oil wealth going to Shiites and Kurds.

Only with American prodding were Sunnis included in the drafting of the constitution. Although last-minute changes made the constitution more acceptable to Sunni leaders, many of them urged their followers to vote against the constitution when it was presented for voter approval in October 2005. In fact, the overwhelming majority of the Sunnis rejected the document. Yet because their opposition fell short in one of the three Sunni-dominated provinces, the constitution, which received strong support in Iraq's fifteen other provinces, passed with the support of 78 percent of the voters.

The question of Sunni participation was of paramount concern during the campaigning for the National Assembly elections in December 2005, the final phase in the transition to democracy. American leaders stressed the importance of greater inclusiveness in Iraqi democracy and urged Sunnis to participate. Although Sunnis did participate in the elections, sharp divisions among the different ethnic groups continued to hamper the emergence of a strong democratic government. The newly elected parliament could not agree on selecting the prime minister and other cabinet positions for five months.

As concerns over the security situation grew, the U.S. Congress tied its funding for the war to a series of benchmarks that the Iraqi government was expected to meet in its path toward national reconciliation. The benchmarks included approval of laws for sharing oil revenues and reining in sectarian militias as well as for holding provincial elections and returning provincial power to the Iraqis. By August 2007, the government in Baghdad had established an Independent High Electoral Commission, but had not managed to pass a law establishing a date for provincial elections. With the next set of national elections not scheduled until 2009, many observers wondered whether the security situation on the ground might do as much as direct channels of electoral participation to determine the future of Iraqi democracy.

FOR CRITICAL ANALYSIS

1. Why did Americans think that Iraqis would want to participate in a new democracy? Why has it been difficult to transplant American-style democracy to Iraq?
2. Why is it so important to secure Sunni participation in Iraqi elections? Why did Sunni leaders boycott the first elections to the National Assembly and then work to defeat adoption of the Iraqi constitution? Can participation in elections undermine support for the insurgency in Iraq?

FIGURE 8.3 ★
Voter Turnout around the World, 1945–2006

Although the United States is the oldest mass democracy, rates of voter turnout are substantially higher in other countries. In many of these countries, election days are holidays and voting is compulsory. Do you think that either of these reforms would increase voting in the United States?

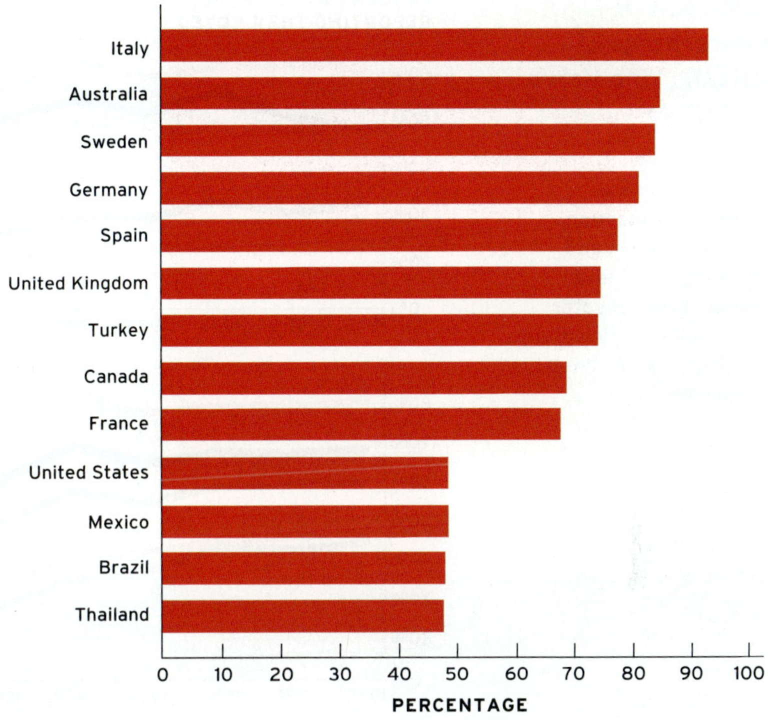

NOTE: Average between 1945 and 2006.
SOURCE: International Institute of Democracy and Electoral Assistance.

racial and ethnic, gender, religious, and age-based groups. It asks to what extent members of these particular groups have recognized common interests and have sought to act politically on those interests.

African Americans

As we saw in Chapter 5, political and legal pressure and protest all played a part in the modern civil rights movement, which took off in the 1950s. The movement drew on an organizational base and network of communication rooted in black churches, the NAACP, and black colleges.

The nonviolent protest tactics adopted by local clergy members, including Rev. Martin Luther King, Jr., eventually spread across the South and brought national attention to the movement. The clergy organized into a group called the Southern Christian Leadership Conference (SCLC). Students also played a key role. The most important student organization was the Student Nonviolent Coordinating Committee (SNCC). In 1960, four black students sat down at the lunch counter of the Greensboro, North Carolina, Woolworth's department store, which like most southern establishments did not serve African Americans. Their sit-in was the first of many. Through a combination of protest, legal action, and political pressure, the civil rights movement compelled a reluctant federal government to enforce black civil and political rights.

The victories of the civil rights movement made blacks full citizens and stimulated a tremendous growth in the number of black public officials at all levels of government, as blacks exercised their newfound political rights. Yet despite these

FIGURE 8.4 ★ The Percentage of Americans Who Voted, 1976–2004*

Voting rates vary substantially by race and ethnicity, education, employment status, and age. Which groups have the highest rates of voter turnout? Among which groups has participation declined the most since 1992?

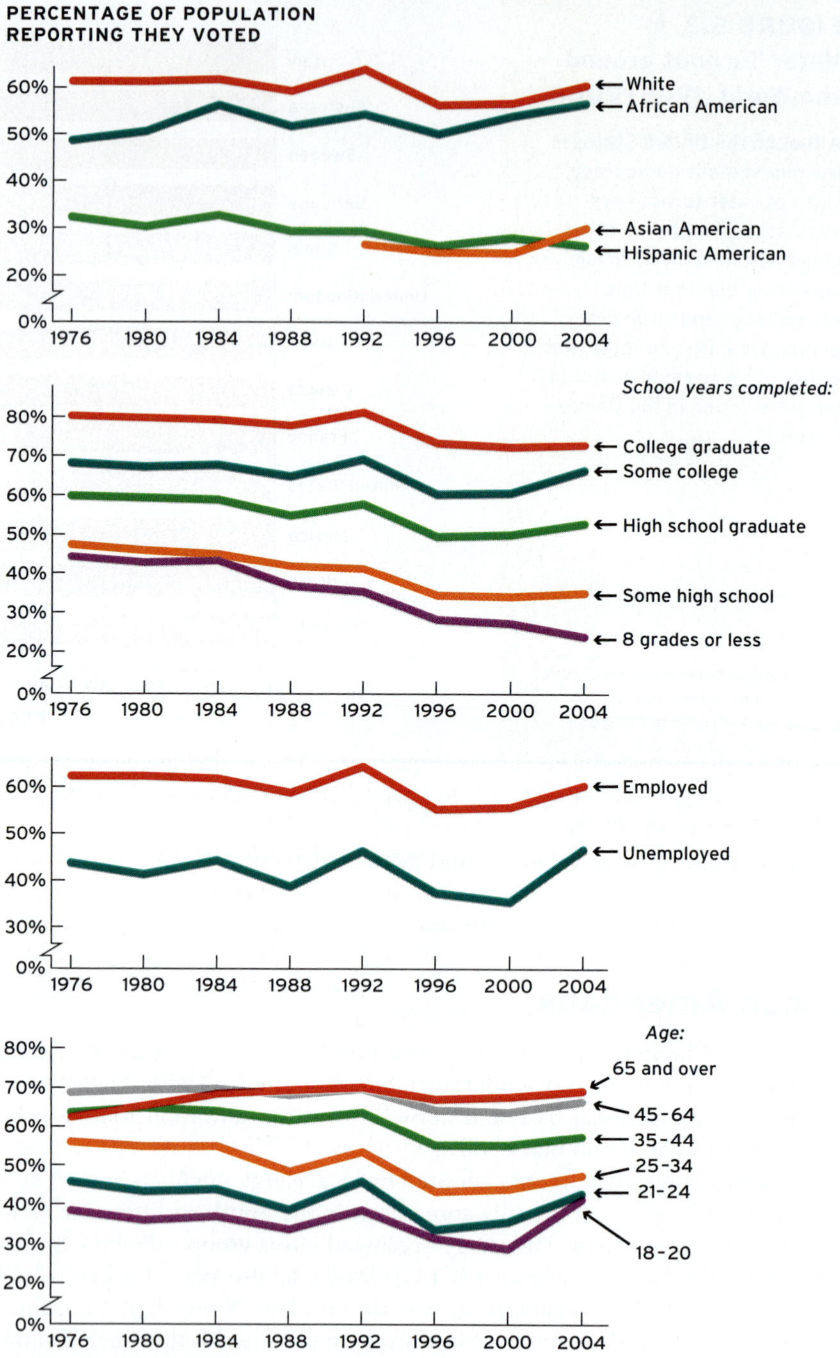

SOURCES: U.S. Census Bureau, www2.census.gov/prod2/statcomp/documents/1994-03.pdf; and www.census.gov/compendia/statab/tables/08s0404.pdf (accessed 4/8/08).

successes, racial segregation remains a fact of life in the United States, and new problems have emerged. Most troubling is the persistence of black urban poverty, now coupled with deep social and economic isolation.[9] These conditions raise new questions about African American political participation. One question concerns black political cohesion: Will blacks continue to vote as a bloc, given the sharp economic differences that now divide a large black middle class from an equally large

After the Civil War, the Fifteenth Amendment to the Constitution appeared to guarantee black voting rights, and blacks were elected to many political offices during Reconstruction. But with the end of Reconstruction in the 1870s, African Americans were effectively deprived of the right to vote in most southern states.

group of deeply impoverished African Americans? A second question concerns the benefits of participation: How can political participation improve the lives of African Americans, especially of the poor?

Public opinion and voting evidence indicate that African Americans continue to vote as a bloc despite their economic differences.[10] Surveys of black voters show that blacks across the income spectrum believe that their fates are linked because of their race. This sense of shared experience and a common fate has united blacks at the polls and in politics.[11] Since the 1960s, blacks have overwhelmingly chosen Democratic candidates, and black candidates have sought election under the Democratic banner. Republican hostility to affirmative action and other programs of racial preference is likely to sharply check any large-scale black migration to the Republican Party. After Hurricane Katrina, President George W. Bush's popularity among blacks fell to new lows. The rap singer Kanye West caused a stir when he went off script at a fund-raising telethon for hurricane relief, declaring that the poor federal response to the hurricane showed that "George Bush doesn't care about black people." Despite the controversy that surrounded West's remarks, his sentiments were echoed weeks later in polls showing that only 2 percent of blacks approved of the job that President Bush was doing.

At the same time, however, the black community and its political leadership have been considerably frustrated about the benefits of loyalty to the Democratic Party. Some analysts argue that the structure of party competition makes it difficult for African Americans to win policy benefits through political participation. Because Republicans have not sought to win the black vote and Democrats take it for granted, neither party is willing to support bold measures to address the problems of poor African Americans. With Barack Obama running as the first black major-party candidate for president in 2008, African American interest in the election surged. Exit polls indicated that 95 percent of African Americans who voted cast ballots for Obama. Obama's historic victory engendered widespread pride among all Americans that a racial barrier as old as the country itself had finally fallen.

Although the Latino community has shown relatively low rates of voter turnout, increasing rates of naturalization and voter registration are beginning to make it a powerful force in American politics. In the 2008 elections, all of the major candidates tried to win the support of Hispanic voters.

Latinos

For many years, analysts called the Latino vote "the sleeping giant" because as a group Latinos had relatively low levels of political mobilization. Two important reasons for this were the low rates of voter registration and low rates of naturalization. Among those who were eligible to vote, registration and turnout rates were relatively low.

Today, Latinos are viewed as a political group of critical importance. Rapid population growth, increased political participation, and uncertain party attachment all magnify the importance of the Latino vote. The Latino population grew to an estimated 43 million by 2006, making Hispanics more numerous than African Americans. Moreover, Latino voters have begun to register and vote in unprecedented numbers. In 2006, Hispanics accounted for 5.8 percent of the total national vote. Latinos have traditionally voted heavily Democratic: Vice President Al Gore received two-thirds of the Hispanic vote in 2000. But Republicans also believe they can attract Hispanic voters because Democratic Hispanic voters tend to be more socially conservative than non-Hispanic Democrats. Many pollsters now see Latinos as a key "swing" vote that can tip elections toward either party. There is some controversy over what percentage of Latinos voted for Bush in 2004. Exit polls showed that he received an unprecedented 44 percent of the Latino vote. Some researchers have charged that this high figure was the result of bias in the exit poll sample; they estimate that the percent of Latinos voting for Bush was actually 39 percent.[12] In any case, there is little doubt that President Bush actively courted Hispanic voters. At rallies and meetings involving Hispanic groups, Bush routinely displayed his Spanish-speaking abilities. He also appointed Latinos to high-level cabinet positions and nominated conservative Hispanics for important judicial positions. Despite the former president's efforts to win Latino votes for Republicans during the 2006 congressional elections, the Hispanic vote swung to Democrats, with an estimated 69 percent of Latinos voting Democratic compared with 30 percent for Republicans. Most observers attributed the shift to the importance of the immigration debate, in which Republicans were seen as less sympathetic to immigrants than Democrats.[13] The move of Latino voters toward the Democratic Party continued in the 2008 elections, with exit polls showing that 67 percent of Latinos voted for Barack Obama and 31 percent for John McCain. Latino voter registration surged in 2008, and first-time voters went heavily for Obama. With the election focused more on the troubled economy than on social issues such as abortion, Latinos moved decisively to support Democrats.

Politics Today

How significant a factor was the Latino vote in the 2008 election? Why does the percent of eligible Latinos voting still lag behind that of other groups?

Asian Americans

The diversity of national backgrounds among Asian Americans has impeded the development of group-based political power. No one national group dominates among the Asian American population. This diversity means that Asian Americans—or, to use the broader census-based category, Asian Pacific Islanders (commonly referred to as Asian Pacific Americans or APAs)—often have different political concerns stemming from their different national backgrounds and experiences in the United States. Historically, these groups have united most effectively around common issues of ethnic discrimination or anti-Asian violence in the United States. For example, discriminatory immigration policies or discrimination in access to federal mortgage policies provided a common focus in the past.

With a population of 14.9 million in 2006, APAs are also a smaller group than whites, Hispanics, and African Americans. However, in particular states, such as California, where 40 percent of APAs live, this group has the potential to become an important political presence. In terms of political orientation, APAs are a diverse group, but they have been moving more toward the Democratic party during the past decade. Polls showed Asian Americans voting 55 percent Republican and 31 percent Democratic in 1992. By 2000, 54 percent of Asians voted Democratic, and 41 percent cast ballots for Republicans. The pro-Democratic vote increased in more recent elections, with 58 percent of Asians voting Democratic and 41 percent Republican in 2004 and 62 percent Democratic and 37 percent Republican in 2006.[14] In 2008, the exit polls showed that a growing majority of Asian Americans continued to support Democrats.

In recent years there have been efforts to mobilize a more united Asian American political presence. For example, a group initially called Chinese Americans United for Self-Empowerment (CAUSE) changed its name to the Center for Asian Americans United for Self-Empowerment to reflect a panethnic identity. In 2004, CAUSE produced a thirty-second video entitled "The Least Likely," which was shown on MTV. The video's title referred to the fact that Asian Pacific youth are the least likely to vote compared with other young voters. In the video, prominent Asian American actors urged Asian Pacific youth to vote. CAUSE launched a major effort to register Asian voters for the 2008 election. Since 2000, another group, called the 80–20 Initiative, has sought to mobilize Asian Americans to vote as a bloc in order to increase their

Although Asian Americans come from diverse national backgrounds and hold diverse political opinions, recent efforts have tried to increase overall turnout among Asian American voters and increase their influence as a group. In 2008, the Center for Asian Americans United for Self-Empowerment (CAUSE) undertook a major effort to register Asian Pacific voters.

Women won the right to vote with the adoption of the Nineteenth Amendment in 1920, in part because many officials were convinced that women's suffrage would increase female support for American involvement in World War I. Women have generally been less likely than men to support military activities.

political power. In 2000 and 2004, the 80–20 Initiative endorsed the Democratic candidates for president. In 2008, the 80–20 Initiative's national endorsement convention, which brings together delegates who are one-third Democrats, one-third Republican, and one-third Independents, voted to endorse Barack Obama.

Women versus Men

gender gap a distinctive pattern of voting behavior reflecting the differences in views between women and men

The ongoing significance of gender issues in American politics is best exemplified by the emergence of a **gender gap**—a distinctive pattern of male and female voting decisions—in electoral politics. Although proponents of women's suffrage had expected women to make a distinctive impact on politics as soon as they won the vote, not until the 1980s did voting patterns reveal a clear difference between male and female votes. In 1980, men voted heavily for the Republican candidate, Ronald Reagan; women divided their votes between Reagan and the incumbent Democratic president, Jimmy Carter. Since that election, gender differences have emerged in congressional and state elections as well. Women tend to vote in higher numbers for Democratic candidates, whereas Republicans win more male votes. In the 2004 election, George W. Bush narrowed the gender gap substantially, winning 48 percent of the female vote.[15] By 2006 the gender gap had reappeared, with 55 percent of women voting Democratic and only 43 percent Republician.[16] As the general election got under way in 2008, observers expressed doubt about how women would vote, especially the disappointed supporters of Hillary Clinton. Republicans hoped that the selection of Alaska governor Sarah Palin as vice-presidential candidate would draw support from women. In the end, women voted strongly Democratic in 2008, with exit polls showing that 58 percent of women cast their ballots for the Obama-Biden ticket and 43 percent for the McCain-Palin ticket.

Behind these voting patterns are differing assessments of key policy issues. For one thing, more women than men take liberal positions on political issues; women are more likely than men to oppose military activities and support social spending. For example, 54 percent of women approved of the U.S. decision to send troops to Saudi Arabia in 1991, compared with 78 percent of men. The military campaign in Afghanistan was a rare exception to this pattern of gender differences: 85 percent of women and 89 percent of men expressed support for the war in Afghanistan.[17] The gender gap returned with the war in Iraq. During the war, 79 percent of men supported the war, compared with 65 percent of women. This split continued during the debate about when to withdraw from Iraq. In 2007, 51 percent of men stated that they were in favor of keeping troops in Iraq until civil order was restored, whereas only 35 percent of women supported keeping troops there with such an indefinite time horizon.[18] On social programs, these trends reverse: 37 percent of men express satisfaction with the Social Security and Medicare system, whereas only 33 percent of women do; 45 percent of men were content with the quality of public education, whereas only 39 percent of women were. Men were also more likely to be satisfied that they could get ahead through hard work, with 73 percent satisfied, but only 65 percent of women agreed.[19] It is important to note that these differences do not mean that all women vote more liberally than all men. In fact, the voting differences between women who are homemakers and women who are in the workforce are almost as large as the differences between men and women. The sharpest differences are found between married men and single women, with single women tending to take the most liberal positions.[20]

Another key development in gender politics in recent years is the growing number of women in political office (see Figure 8.5). Journalists dubbed 1992 the "Year of the Woman" because so many women were elected to Congress: women doubled their numbers in the House and tripled them in the Senate. By 2008, women held 16.1 percent of the seats in the House of Representatives and 16 percent in the Senate; 23.5 percent of state legislators in 2008 were women.[21] Organizations supporting female candidates have worked to encourage more women to run for office and have supported them financially. In addition to the bipartisan National Women's Political Caucus (NWPC), the Women's Campaign Fund and EMILY's List provide prochoice Democratic women with early campaign financing, which is critical to establishing electoral momentum. (The acronym of the latter group stands for Early Money Is Like Yeast.) Recent research has shown that the key to increasing the numbers of women in political office is to encourage more women to run for election. Women are disadvantaged as candidates not because they are women but because male candidates are more likely to have the advantage of incumbency.[22] Although women in public office by no means take uniform positions on policy issues, surveys show that, on the whole, female legislators are more supportive of women's rights, health care spending, and children's and family issues.[23]

Women candidates gained special prominence in the 2008 elections, with Senator Hillary Clinton's spirited campaign for the Democratic presidential nomination and the selection of Alaska's governor Sarah Palin to run as vice president on the Republican ticket. Although neither succeeded in winning office, their campaigns marked important milestones in the road to power for women politicians. Clinton's near-miss for the Democratic presidential nomination, in particular, is likely to make it easier for women to be considered as credible presidential candidates in the future.

Religious Identity and Politics

Religious identity plays an important role in American life. For some people, religious groups provide an organizational infrastructure for participating in politics around issues of special group concern. Black churches, for example, were instrumental in the civil rights movement, and black religious leaders continue

FIGURE 8.5 ★
Increase in Number of Women in Elective Office, 1975–2008

The number of women holding elected office has always been larger in state offices than in Congress. When did the percentage of women elected to office begin to rise more rapidly?

*Governors, attorneys general, etc.
SOURCES: Cynthia Costello, Shari Miles, and Anne J. Stone, eds., *The American Woman, 2001–2002* (New York: Norton, 2002), 328; and Center for American Women and Politics, www.cawp.rutgers.edu/Facts/Officeholders/cawpfs.html (accessed 3/8/08).

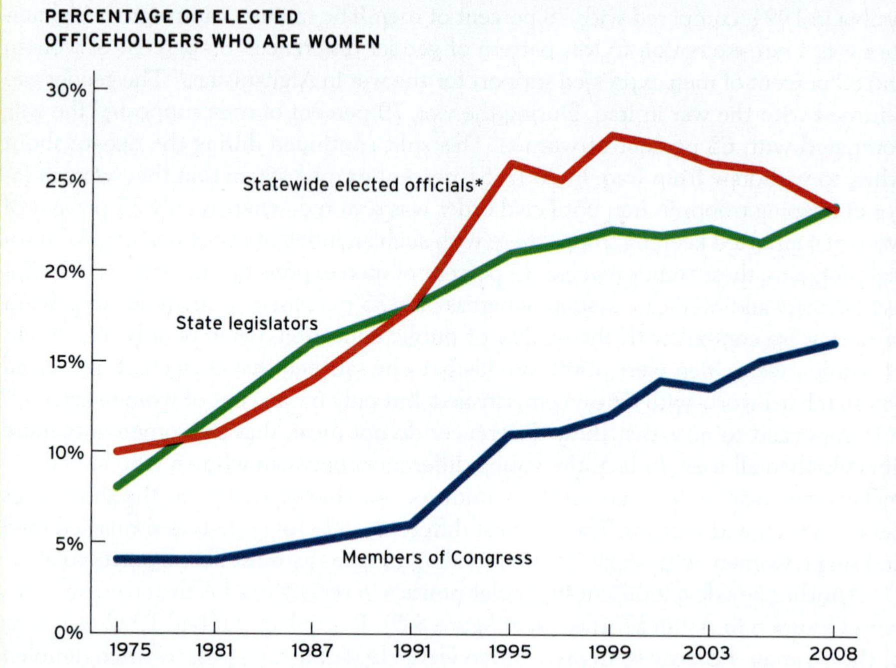

to play important roles in national and local politics. Jews have also been active as a group in politics, but less through religious bodies than through a variety of social-action agencies. Such agencies include the American Jewish Congress, the Anti-Defamation League, and the American Jewish Committee.

For most of American history, religious values have been woven deeply into the fabric of public life. Public-school students began the day with prayers or Bible reading; city halls displayed crèches during the Christmas season. Practices that were religiously proscribed—most notably abortion—were also forbidden under law. But over the past thirty-five years, a variety of court decisions greatly reduced this kind of religious influence on public life. In 1962, the Supreme Court ruled in *Engel v. Vitale* that prayer in public schools was unconstitutional—that government should not be in the business of sponsoring official prayers. Bible reading was prohibited the following year. By 1973, with *Roe v. Wade*, the Court had made abortion legal.[24]

These decisions drew the condemnation of many Catholic and Protestant leaders. They also helped to spawn a countermovement of religious activists seeking to roll back these decisions and to find a renewed role for religion in public life. The mobilization of religious organizations and other groups that aim to reintroduce their view of morality into public life has been one of the most significant political developments of the past two and a half decades. Some of the most divisive conflicts in politics today, such as those over abortion and gay marriage, hinge on differences over religious and moral issues. These divisions have become so significant and so broad that they now constitute a major clash of cultures with repercussions throughout the political system and across many different areas of policy.

One of the most significant elements of this new politics has been the mobilization of white evangelical Protestants into a cohesive and politically shrewd organization aligned with the Republican Party. The Moral Majority, the first broad political organization of evangelical Christians, became a notable political force in the 1980 election, when it aligned with the Republican Party, eventually backing Ronald Reagan for president. Over the next few years, evangelicals strengthened their movement by registering voters and mobilizing them with sophisticated, state-of-the-art political techniques. Their success was evident in the 1984 election, when 80 percent of evangelical Christian voters cast their ballots for Reagan. The 1988 election was a turning point in the political development of the Christian right. The televangelist Pat Robertson ran for president and, although his candidacy was unsuccessful, his effort laid the groundwork for future political strength. Robertson's supporters gained control of some state Republican parties and won positions of power in others. With this new organizational base and sharply honed political skills, Robertson formed a new organization, the Christian Coalition. This organization became one of the most important groups in American politics during the 1990s because of its ability to reach and mobilize a large grassroots base.

President George W. Bush was closely aligned with religious conservatives. Many analysts viewed the former president's faith-based initiative, which sought to funnel government assistance to religious groups engaged in charitable work, as a way to reward conservative Christian groups for supporting his election. In fact, conservative religious groups spoke out against the initiative at first because they feared that government control would accompany federal dollars.[25]

The religious right played an important role in mobilizing voters to support George W. Bush in the 2004 election. In 2008, the religious right was less excited about the candidacy of John McCain, who had clashed with these groups during the 2000 Republican primaries. The nomination of the more socially conservative Sarah Palin as vice-presidential candidate greatly increased the enthusiasm of the religious right for the Republican ticket. Although Barack Obama sought to win this group over, exit polls showed that Democrats made only marginal gains among white evangelical Christians, who voted overwhelmingly Republican.

Politics Today

Is the religious right still an important bloc vote in elections? Or has its influence diminished in recent years? What factors determine how influential the religious right is in politics?

Age and Participation

One of the most significant patterns in political participation is the generational divide. Older people have much higher rates of participation than young people. This division is especially apparent in the different voting rates of the two groups. In the 2006 midterm election, the overall turnout was 43.6 percent. The elderly were significantly above the average, with 60.5 percent of people over sixty-five voting. Young people were far below the average, with only 17.1 percent of people between the ages of eighteen and twenty reporting that they voted.[26] Although these two groups make up a similar portion of the population, the political voice of the elderly is much stronger because of their higher voting rates. When the Twenty-sixth Amendment to the Constitution granted eighteen- to twenty-year-olds the right to vote in 1971, many believed this group would be a significant new voice in politics. Instead, voting participation of the young declined quite dramatically. During recent elections, a major effort to mobilize young voters reversed this downward trend.

One reason that younger people vote less is that political campaigns have rarely targeted young voters. A study of political advertising in the 2000 elections found that 64 percent of campaign television advertising was directed at people over fifty. Only 14.2 percent of advertising was aimed at eighteen- to thirty-four-year-olds.[27] This creates a vicious cycle: the less political campaigns appeal to younger voters,

In 2004 and 2008, groups like Rock the Vote helped increase turnout among young voters. Rock the Vote works with musicians like The Black Eyed Peas (shown here) to encourage young Americans to register, learn about the issues, and vote. However, participation rates among young voters still lag behind those of older Americans.

the less likely they are to participate, and the less they participate, the less likely they will be targeted by political campaigns.

Another reason that political campaigns target older voters is that the elderly are better organized to participate than young people. The most important organization representing the elderly is the AARP, which has a membership of nearly 38 million. Although only a small fraction of the members are active in the organization, the AARP's ability to mobilize many thousands of individuals to weigh in on policy proposals has made the organization one of the most powerful in Washington, D.C. Young people have no comparable organization. The United States Student Association has represented college students since the 1950s, but its numbers are much smaller and it does not have the same organizational capacity to mobilize its members as the AARP. Other organizations, such as Third Millennium, have emerged to represent the voice of young people in politics. But like most advocacy organizations, these groups do not have a membership base and have little capacity to mobilize.

Politics Today

When the Twenty-sixth Amendment changed the voting age from 21 to 18 in 1971, observers expected that the youth vote would add a significant new voice to American politics. Why has the youth vote turned out to be less important than was hoped? What changes would engage more young people in the political system?

Since the early 1990s, several campaigns have been designed to increase the participation of young voters. Rock the Vote, which began in 1990, uses musicians and actors to urge young people to vote. It has spawned other initiatives aimed at young voters including Rap the Vote and Rock the Vote a lo Latino. Active mobilization by such groups helped the youth vote increase in every election since 2000. Aware of the potential importance of young voters, political campaigns in the 2008 election appealed to the youth vote by turning to new technologies. Candidates posted videos on YouTube and created MySpace and Facebook pages in order to be visible in media frequented by young people. Independent mobilization efforts also sought to register and mobilize young people to vote. Older organizations joined forces with new ones to devise the best strategies for reaching young people. For example, an organization called Young Voter Strategies, which launched a major registration and get-out-the-vote drive for the 2006 midterm elections, merged with Rock the Vote in 2007 in order to mobilize young voters in 2008.[28]

The Obama campaign made young voters central to its electoral strategy. The campaign sought to increase participation of young voters through a major voter registration campaign and turn them out to vote. Although predictions of a massive youth turnout did not prove true, early returns suggested that young people did indeed turn out in larger numbers than they did in 2004. Exit polls showed that two-thirds of these younger voters cast ballots for Barack Obama.

Although young people have been disengaged from politics, they have a strong record in community service. More than 70 percent of young people volunteer at some time in their own communities.[29] One recent national survey found that a majority of students believed that community service was the best way to deal with national problems. In contrast, they tended to view politics and politicians with cynicism.

Explaining Political Participation

Political participation is skewed toward those with more education and more money. To understand these current patterns we must go back to a basic question: Why do people participate in politics? Simple as it seems, there are different ways to answer this question.

Socioeconomic Status

The first explanation for political participation points to the characteristics of individuals. One of the most important and consistent results of surveys about participation is that Americans with higher levels of education, more income, and higher-level occupations—what social scientists call higher **socioeconomic status**—participate much more in politics than do those with less education and less income. Education level alone is the strongest predictor of most kinds of participation, but income becomes important—not surprisingly—when it comes to making contributions. In addition to education and income, other individual characteristics also affect participation. For example, African Americans and Latinos are less likely to participate than are whites, although when differences in education and income are taken into account, both groups participate at the same levels or higher levels than do whites. Finally, young people are far less likely to participate in politics than are older people. The proportion of young people that vote has declined in almost every single election since 1972. The jump in the participation of young voters in the 2004 and 2006 elections was a significant exception to this downward trend.[30] As we have seen, the 2008 elections continued the trend of increased participation among young people. Even with these substantial gains over the past four years, younger people continue to vote at lower rates than older people. Exit polls conducted during the 2008 elections also indicated that more affluent voters continued to vote in greater numbers than those with lower incomes.

socioeconomic status status in society based on level of education, income, and occupational prestige

Although they give us a picture of who participates and who does not, explanations based on individual characteristics leave many questions open. One of the biggest questions is why the relationship between education and participation—so strong in surveys—does not seem to hold true over time. As Americans have become more educated, with more people finishing high school and attending college, we would expect to see more people participating in politics. Yet participation has declined, not increased.[31] During the nineteenth century, participation in presidential elections was 20 percent higher than current levels. Moreover, politics was a much more vibrant and encompassing social activity: large numbers of people joined in

Does Higher Voter Participation Really Matter?

One of the great contradictions of American politics is the fact that our elections—the hallmark of democracy—are plagued by low, and declining, voter turnout. From a high point of about 65 percent turnout in 1960 to a seven-decade low of 49 percent in the 1996 presidential election, Americans are staying away from the polls in record numbers with just 00 percent turning out for the 2008 presidential election. By comparison, voter turnout in virtually every other democratic nation of the world is significantly higher, typically in the range of 70 to 90 percent in their comparable national elections. But is this anything to worry about?

Yes, say many. Part of the problem lies in the tangle of rules that regulate voting, which are more complicated than those found in almost any other nation. Most of these rules were enacted decades ago to discourage "undesirables"—African Americans, immigrants, the poor—from voting. In many nations, voting is easier because citizens are automatically registered to vote and do not have to worry about local residency requirements, and elections are held on the weekends. A government that cares about its elections should certainly do more to make the act of voting easier. Turnout matters to campaigns, because those who run for office tailor their campaign issues and strategies to those who are likely to vote. Thus, the needs and concerns of the nonvoters—generally those with lower incomes and less education and members of disadvantaged groups—are likely to be ignored, with the result that policy fails to address the nation's most pressing needs. In recent years, states have made voting easier. As of 2008 thirty-one states allowed some form of early voting in order to make voting easier. Oregon allows all voters to cast their ballots by mail. These changes demonstrate that the government could do more to make voting easier, and should do so, many argue, because the ever-declining percentage of voting casts a shadow over the very legitimacy of the government that is elected. How can a president, or other elected leaders, claim a mandate to govern when fewer than a quarter of eligible voters cast ballots for the winner?

Skeptics counter these arguments by asserting that the negative consequences of nonvoting have been greatly overstated. In 1993, Congress passed the "Motor Voter" law, which allowed citizens to register to vote when they applied for a driver's license. Even though millions of new voters registered by this means, it had little or no effect on voting rates, suggesting that existing election laws may have little to do with voting rates. Further, research has demonstrated that there is often less difference between voters and nonvoters than many assume. A study of the 1988 election, for example, showed that, contrary to expectations, nonvoters would have supported the winning presidential candidate, George H. W. Bush, over the challenger, Michael Dukakis. This and similar research supports the idea that the interests of nonvoters are not so different from those of voters. Beyond this, nonvoting is not necessarily a sign of alienation from the political system. To some extent at least, it can be interpreted as citizen satisfaction with the overall course of the country's affairs. Although indifference is a less than noble sentiment, it can at least be taken as a green light for the nation's political leaders. When crises have arisen in the past, from the Great Depression to the September 11 terrorist attacks, Americans have turned close attention to their political leaders. Finally, voting is only one method of political expression, and citizens with concerns ranging from race to abortion to gun control increasingly express their views through means other than the ballot box, from interest group activity to the Internet. Voting is still the most frequent political activity, but citizens are free to express themselves in an ever-wider array of methods.

FOR CRITICAL ANALYSIS

1. Why is it important to vote even if the voter feels that he or she is only choosing between the "lesser of two evils"?
2. Why do many Americans believe that it makes no difference if they vote? Does it make sense to avoid voting but concentrate on other forms of political activity?

parades, public meetings, and electioneering.[32] This puzzle suggests that we need to look beyond the characteristics of individuals to the larger social and political setting to understand changes in patterns of participation over time.

Civic Engagement

The social setting can affect political participation in a variety of ways. One recent study argued that participation depends on three elements: resources (including time, money, and know-how), **civic engagement** (are you concerned about public issues, and do you feel that you can make a difference?), and recruitment (are you asked to participate, especially by someone you know?).[33] Whether people have resources, feel engaged, and are recruited depends very much on their social setting—what their parents are like, whom they know, what associations they belong to. In the United States, churches are a particularly important social institution in helping to foster political participation. Through their church activities people learn the civic skills that prepare them to participate in the political world more broadly. It is often through church activities that people learn to run meetings, write newsletters, or give speeches and presentations. Churches are also an important setting for meeting people and creating networks for recruitment, since people are more likely to participate if asked by a friend or an acquaintance.

civic engagement a sense of concern among members of the political community about public, social, and political life, expressed through participation in social and political organizations

As this model suggests, if fewer people belong to social organizations, they may be less likely to participate in politics. The United States has often been called a nation of joiners because of our readiness to form local associations to address common problems. As early as the 1830s, the Frenchman Alexis de Tocqueville singled out this tendency to form associations as a most distinctive American trait.[34] There is evidence, however, that Americans no longer join organizations as much as they did in the past. This declining membership raises concerns that the civic engagement that ordinary Americans once had is deteriorating. These concerns are magnified by declining levels of social trust, which further contribute to the tendency to pull back from public engagement.[35] There are many possible reasons for the decline in organizational membership and social trust, and consequently in civic engagement. Television, for example, keeps people in their houses and away from meetings or other, more civic, engagements.[36] Crime can also reduce civic engagement by reducing social trust, making people suspicious and unwilling to take part in neighborhood activities.

Another way to explain the decline in civic engagement is to look at how the experiences of different generations might make them more or less oriented toward civic engagement. The generation that came of age during the Great Depression and World War II has been called the "long civic generation" because this group tends to participate in politics and associational life much more than previous or later generations. During the 1930s, people looked to government to help them with economic hardships, and in the 1940s, the same generation fought World War II, a popular war in which the entire country pulled together.[37] Later generations have not experienced such popular common causes to bring them together in the public sphere: their wars have been less popular and their great social causes more divisive. In addition, political life has seemed much less inspiring, filled with accusations of wrongdoing and constant investigations into possible scandal. Such a generational perspective makes sense because people form habits and beliefs in their early years that are very important in how they participate later in life. A generational perspective also helps explain why participation did not decline during the twentieth century, but instead started out low in the early 1900s, rose from the 1930s through the 1960s, and then began to fall once again.

Arguments about declining public trust and generational effects don't pay enough attention to the political setting in which participation takes place. The organization of politics itself plays a key role in channeling participation in particular directions and in encouraging or discouraging people from participating. Participation depends on whether there are formal obstacles in the political system, what people think political engagement has to offer them, and most important, whether political parties and politicians try to mobilize people into politics.

Formal Obstacles

Formal obstacles can greatly decrease participation. As we saw earlier in the chapter, in the South prior to the 1960s, the widespread use of the poll tax and other measures such as the white primary essentially deprived black Americans (and many poor whites) of the right to vote during the first part of the twentieth century. This system of legal segregation meant that black Americans in the South had few avenues for participating in politics. With the removal of these legal barriers in the 1960s, black political participation shot up, with rates of turnout approaching those of southern whites as early as 1968.[38]

Another important political factor reducing voter turnout in the United States is our nation's peculiar registration rules. In every American state but North Dakota, individuals who are eligible to vote must register with the state election board before they are actually allowed to vote. Registration requirements were introduced at the end of the nineteenth century in response to the demands of the Progressive movement. Progressives hoped to make voting more difficult both to reduce multiple voting and other forms of corruption, and to discourage immigrant and working-class voters from going to the polls. In some states, registration requirements reduced voter turnout by as much as 50 percent. Once voters are registered, they participate at very high levels—80 to 90 percent of those registered have voted in recent elections. Altering registration laws to allow same-day voting is one simple change that would boost voter turnout.

Registration requirements particularly depress the participation of those with little education and low incomes because registration requires a greater degree of political involvement and interest than does the act of voting itself. To vote, a person need be concerned only with the particular election campaign at hand. Requiring individuals to register before the next election forces them to make a decision to participate on the basis of an abstract interest in the electoral process rather than a simple concern with a specific campaign. Such an abstract interest in electoral politics is largely a product of education. Those with relatively little education may become interested in political events once the issues of a particular campaign become salient, but by that time it may be too late to register. Young people tend to assign a low priority to registration even if they are well educated. Moreover, because young people tend to move more often than older people, registration requirements place a greater burden on them. As a result, personal registration requirements not only diminish the size of the electorate but also tend to create an electorate that is, on average, better educated, higher in income and social status, and composed of fewer young people, African Americans, and other minorities than the citizenry as a whole (see Figure 8.6). In Europe, there is typically no registration burden on the individual voter; voter registration is handled automatically by the government. This is one reason that voter turnout rates in Europe are higher than those in the United States.

FIGURE 8.6 ★ Voter Registration Rates by Social Group, 2004

Some political analysts argue that registration requirements depress turnout. The percentage of the population that is registered to vote varies according to education level, employment status, race and ethnicity, and age. Are people with a lower income more or less likely to register to vote? Are less educated people more or less likely to register? Would the rates of participation among these groups change if registration requirements were altered?

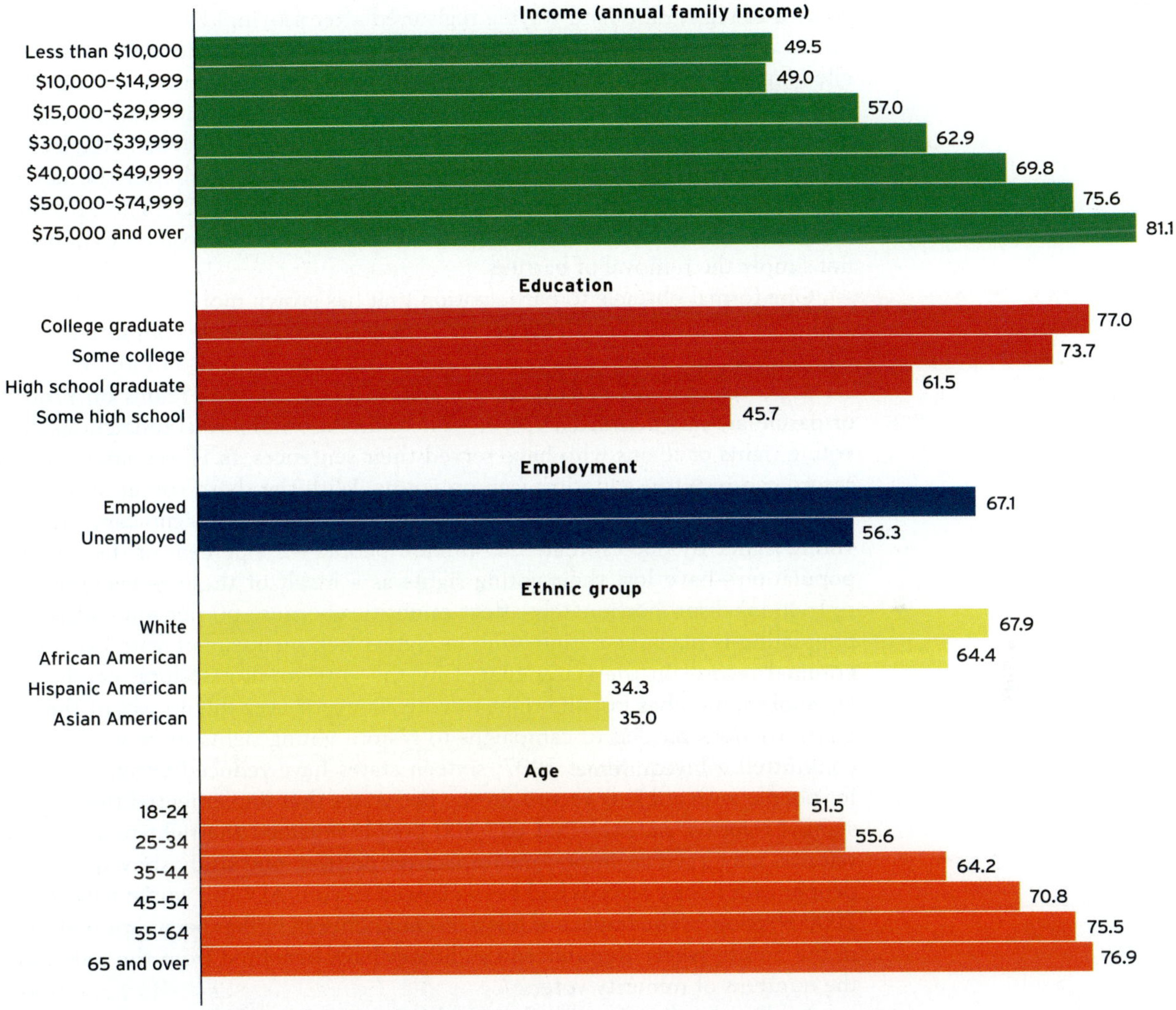

SOURCE: U.S. Bureau of the Census, www.census.gov/prod/2006pubs/p20-556.pdf (accessed 3/17/06).

As might be expected, in states that do not require registration (North Dakota) or that allow registration on the day of the election (Minnesota, Idaho, Maine, Montana, New Hampshire, Wisconsin, Iowa, and Wyoming), voter turnout is not only higher than average, but younger and less affluent voters turn out in larger percentages.[39] Minnesota's same-day rule played an important role in the surprise 1998 gubernatorial victory of the colorful former professional wrestler Jesse

Ventura. Ventura won the votes of many young men who had not been registered until they came to the polls on election day. Without same-day registration, Ventura's electoral chances would have been considerably smaller.

Over the years, voter registration restrictions have been modified somewhat to make registration easier. But the removal of formal obstacles is not enough to ensure that people participate, as the example of the National Voter Registration Act passed in 1993 shows. Popularly known as the Motor Voter Act, the law aimed to increase participation by making it easier to register to vote. The cumbersome process of registering (and staying registered after moving) has often been singled out as a barrier to participation. The new law aimed to remove this obstacle by allowing people to register when they apply for a driver's license and at other public facilities. Although voter registration increased, turnout did not. An estimated 3.4 million people registered to vote as a result of the Motor Voter Act, but turnout in the 1996 election—the first presidential election held after the law went into effect—actually declined by 6 percent from that in 1992.[40] The very limited success of the Motor Voter Act suggests that people need motivation to participate, not simply the removal of barriers.

One formal obstacle to participation that has grown more important in recent years is the restriction on the voting rights of people who have committed a felony. Forty-eight states and the District of Columbia prohibit prison inmates who are serving a felony sentence from voting.[41] In thirty-six states, felons on probation or parole are not permitted to vote. There are also numerous restrictions on the voting rights of felons who have served their sentences. In eleven states, a felony record can result in a lifetime ban on voting. With the sharp rise in incarceration rates in the 1980s and 1990s, these restrictions have had a significant impact on voting rights. By one estimate, 5.3 million people—2.4 percent of the voting-age population—have lost their voting rights as a result of these restrictions. These restrictions disproportionately affect minorities because 60 percent of the prison population is black or Latino. One in eight black men cannot vote because of a criminal record. In the states that deny the vote to all ex-felons, nearly one in three black men has lost the right to vote. Concern over the impact of these voting restrictions has led to campaigns to restore voting rights to people who have committed a felony. Since 1997, sixteen states have reduced voting restrictions for people with a felony record. In the five states that implemented the most substantial reforms, an estimated 621,400 people regained the right to vote.[42] Such reforms may have an important impact on politics: one study showed that if all people with felony records had been allowed to vote, Al Gore would have won the 2000 election.[43] The impact of felon disenfranchisement has been especially strong in the South, where Republican candidates have benefited from the reduction in the numbers of minority voters.

Another type of formal obstacle has received less attention. In the United States, elections are held on Tuesdays, regular working days. By contrast, in most European counties, elections are held on Sundays or holidays. In some countries, such as India, polls remain open for several days. The United States has addressed this problem somewhat by expanding the use of absentee ballots and instituting early voting or voting by mail. In states that promote the absentee ballot, such as Washington, 64.5 percent of the vote was cast via absentee ballot in the 2004 election.[44] Oregon has gone the furthest in instituting new ways of voting: in 1998, Oregon voters approved a measure allowing voters to cast their ballots by mail. Early and absentee voting reached unprecedented levels in the 2008 campaign, as Democrats in particular made early voting central to their campaign strategy. Although research prior to 2008 showed that early voting does not increase turnout, the success of the Obama campaign in promoting early voting suggests that it can be an important turnout tool.[45]

Political Mobilization

The political setting can play an important role in motivating people to vote. When elections are closely contested, more people tend to vote. And in political settings where they think their input will make a difference, people are more likely to participate. One study of black political participation, for example, found that blacks were more likely to vote, participate in campaigns, and contact public officials in cities run by a black mayor. Their greater attention to city politics and their belief that city government is more responsive to their concerns helps to spark participation.[46]

But the most significant factor affecting participation is whether people are mobilized by parties, candidates, interest groups, and social movements. A recent comprehensive study of the decline in participation in the United States found that fully half of the drop-off could be accounted for by reduced **mobilization** efforts.[47] People are much more likely to participate when someone—preferably someone they know—asks them to get involved.

mobilization the process by which large numbers of people are organized for a political activity

A series of experiments recently conducted by the political scientists Donald Green and Alan Gerber demonstrates the importance of personal contact for mobilizing voters. Evaluating the results of several get-out-the-vote drives, Gerber and Green showed that face-to-face interaction with a canvasser greatly increased the chances that the person contacted would go to the polls. They estimated that personal contact boosted turnout by 9.8 percent. The impact of direct mail was much smaller, causing only a 0.6 percent increase in voting.[48] Impersonal calls

During the nineteenth century, America's political parties worked hard to mobilize voters, using everything from barbecues to bribes to get out the vote. On the day of a presidential election, hundreds of thousands of party workers handed out leaflets, knocked on doors, and even provided free transportation to those unable to get to the polls on their own.

from a phone bank had no effect on voter turnout. Green and Gerber have also evaluated the impact of mobilization on young voters, studying a series of get-out-the-vote campaigns conducted near college campuses during the 2000 election. In these campaigns, phone contacts that were chattier and more informal than standard phone-bank messages increased turnout by an estimated 5 percent. Face-to-face contact again proved even more powerful, increasing turnout by 8.5 percent.[49] Recent research has shown that text messaging also has a positive impact on youth turnout. In the 2006 election, one study found that a text-message reminder boosted youth turnout by 4 percent.[50]

In previous decades, political parties, organizations, and social movements relied on personal contact to mobilize voters. As we will see in Chapter 9, during the nineteenth century, American political party machines employed hundreds of thousands of workers to organize and mobilize voters as well as to bring them to the polls. The result was an extremely high rate of turnout, typically more than 90 percent of eligible voters.[51] But political party machines began to decline in strength in the beginning of the twentieth century and by now have, for the most part, disappeared. Without party workers to encourage them to go to the polls and even to bring them there if necessary, many eligible voters will not participate.

For Critical Analysis

Why is voter turnout so low in the United States? What are the consequences of low levels of voter turnout?

Rather than mobilizers of people, political parties became essentially fund-raising and advertising organizations. The experience of a Connecticut woman during the 1996 election was typical. Hoping to participate in the campaign, she sent a check to the Democratic Party and asked how she could volunteer. She subsequently received many more requests to donate money but she was never informed of any other way to become involved.[52] Interest groups also reduced their efforts at direct mobilization. Although the number of interest groups has grown dramatically in recent decades, the connection that most interest-group members had to these groups often extended no further than their checkbook. Rather than being a means for contact by a friend or an acquaintance to take part in a political activity, belonging to an organization was likely to bring requests through the mail for donations. And

In recent elections, political parties have begun to focus again on mobilizing voters, using a combination of old approaches and new technologies. In 2008, Republican Party workers knocked on doors, phoned potential voters, and held rallies in their efforts to get Republicans to the polls. Like the Democrats, they also used the Internet as a way to reach out directly to potential voters.

POLITICS & POPULAR CULTURE

Television, Digital Media, and the Decline of Civic Culture

In recent years, political scientists have tried to explain why fewer and fewer Americans are participating in politics and other civic activities. Participation in everything from local government to grassroots organizations and bowling leagues has generally declined over the past several decades. Although society has changed substantially since the 1960s, suggesting myriad explanations to account for eroding participation, much attention has focused on the possible role of television and electronic media.

In an extensive analysis of the decline in civic participation titled *Bowling Alone,* Robert D. Putnam proposed that one of the culprits in this trend was the rise of television. "[I]t is precisely those Americans most marked by a dependence on televised entertainment who were most likely to have dropped out of civic and social life—who spent less time with friends, were less involved in community organizations, and were less likely to participate in public affairs."[a] Because watching television is a private and often solitary activity, Putnam argues that television's presence in the home discourages participation in political, community, or social groups outside the home.

Others theorize that the many choices of media content offered in the new digital world provide citizens the opportunity to disconnect completely from political life—simply tuning into something else instead of politics. The political communication scholar Markus Prior found that people who generally prefer entertainment programs over public-affairs programs are less likely to vote and are less knowledgeable about politics as their choice in media outlets increases.[b] If limited to only the three main broadcast networks, a person who prefers entertainment programming has fewer opportunities to avoid political content. If she turns on the television at 6:30 P.M., she has no other option than to watch the national news, since it airs at that time on all three networks. However, a viewer armed with an extensive digital cable package can watch many other entertainment-oriented programs at 6:30 and avoid the news altogether. According to Prior, digital media facilitate this avoidance of public affairs information and thus decrease political participation and political knowledge.

Yet optimists propose that the role played by television and other electronic media is not that dire. News and public-affairs programming offered on television and through digital media helps inform viewers about the important issues and events of the day. Even entertainment programs can enhance citizenship, some argue, because they sometimes provide cursory understanding of political issues. In addition, new digital media may promote political participation by allowing users to produce, rather than be mere recipients of political information. E-mail has made writing to public officials and editorial pages more efficient and has helped speed up the process of political petitioning. Web sites such as Meetup.com facilitate grassroots activities by linking people with similar political interests who can then meet face to face. In the 2004 election, Meetup .com became especially well known for its role in the Howard Dean campaign, enhancing volunteers' ability to organize campaign activities. A Pew Research report on the 2008 election found that online activism had doubled since the 2004 elections, as Americans were increasingly likely to use online forums, such as social networking sites like MySpace and Facebook, to share political views and connect with others who share those views.

FOR CRITICAL ANALYSIS

1. Do you believe that television and the Internet may be responsible for a decline in civic engagement? What anecdotal evidence can you find to support your position?
2. Do you agree with the premise that those who prefer entertainment over public affairs programming are less likely to participate in politics? What other factors influence who participates?

---

a. Robert D. Putnam, *Bowling Alone: The Collapse and Revival of American Community* (New York: Simon & Schuster, 2000), 246.

b. Markus Prior, "News vs. Entertainment: How Increasing Media Choice Widens Gaps in Political Knowledge and Turnout," *American Journal of Political Science* 49 (2005): 577–92.

rather than providing a venue for meeting new people and widening your circle of engagement, organizational membership was more likely to land your name on yet another mailing list, generating still more requests for funds. In the past, social movements, such as the labor movement in the 1930s and the civil rights movement of the 1960s, played an important role in mobilizing people into politics.

In recent elections, parties and candidates have begun to reemphasize direct voter mobilization using a blend of old and new technologies. In the 2002 midterm elections, for example, Georgia Republicans built strong support through traditional door-to-door political mobilization. For the last three days before the election, they organized a "72-hour task force" of volunteers who made sure their voters went to the polls. The spectacular success of the strategy—an unexpected Republican sweep in Georgia—meant that both parties sought to deploy such strategies in future elections.

For Critical Analysis

Why do efforts at direct mobilization seem to be more successful than television advertising in promoting voter turnout? How might the Internet become an important tool for increasing political participation?

In 2004 both parties launched major grassroots efforts to mobilize voters. Republicans built an organization with more than 1.4 million volunteers who were trained to make calls, go door to door to register voters, write letters to the editor in support of former president Bush, post blogs on the Web, and phone in to local radio talk shows. Groups aligned with the Democratic party, including organized labor, women's organizations, and environmental groups, coalesced to mobilize likely Democratic voters. These groups, known as 527 organizations because of their tax-code designation, constituted a virtual "shadow Democratic party."

During the 2008 campaign, efforts to mobilize voters reached new heights. This time, however, the Democrats built a more extensive organization to contact and turn out voters than did Republicans. Barack Obama's campaign made mobilization a centerpiece of its strategy from the start. Inspired by the Republican strategies of 2004 and by Obama's own experience as a community organizer, the campaign sought to build an organized base of volunteers to go door-to-door seeking support for their candidate. Many of Obama's crucial primary victories relied on direct voter mobilization, including his initial win in Iowa and his later success in states that used the caucus system to select presidential candidates.

These victories in the primaries led the Obama campaign to build a nationwide organization of paid staff and volunteers for the general election. The expansion of the electorate through mobilization became a central pillar of the Obama strategy. The campaign opened more than 700 offices in the battleground states, where paid staff coordinated the work of tens of thousands of volunteers. The Internet played a significant role in the mobilization strategy: text messages, e-mails, and the campaign Web site made it easy for volunteers to connect with mobilization efforts, either by signing up to join a neighborhood team or by securing a list of voters to be contacted by phone. The campaign paid special attention to registering and turning out new voters—especially young voters.

The McCain campaign put less emphasis on building an organization of paid staff and volunteers. McCain's reputation as a maverick in the Republican Party meant that many of the party's core voters—who accounted for the bulk of volunteers in past elections—were not initially enthusiastic about his candidacy. The selection of Alaska governor Sarah Palin as vice-presidential nominee sent a burst of energy though the party faithful, sparking a wave of volunteering. The McCain campaign fielded significant ground operations to mobilize voters in battleground states. Even so, the McCain campaign's capacity to mobilize voters remained far weaker and less extensive than that of the Democrats. Obama's significant fund-

Become a Voter (and More)

On a bitterly cold Tuesday night in early January 2008, more than 65,000 young adults left the warmth of their homes to attend presidential caucuses in small towns, midsized cities, and rural communities all over Iowa. Hours later, when they emerged, the rest of America learned that Republican Mike Huckabee and Democrat Barack Obama had each won his party's contest in Iowa. Both winners owed their success in large part to their popularity among voters under the age of thirty.

Pundits lauded the giant increase in youth turnout, which was three times the 2004 rate, and which continued throughout the 2008 primary season. Youth turnout was up in almost every state in the nation, also tripling in places like Missouri, Mississippi and Massachusetts, and quadrupling in Tennessee. And while young voters supported many different candidates in both parties, Obama continued to draw a disproportionate share of their support, which helped him win the Democratic nomination.

If you are a citizen and eighteen years old, you are eligible to vote in all federal, state, and local elections. In most states, however, you must register to vote approximately thirty days before Election Day. A growing number of states, including Maine, Minnesota, Wisconsin, Idaho, New Hampshire, Wyoming, Iowa, and Montana, allow for Election Day registration. This means you can show up at the polls and register on the spot. In general, registration is fairly simple, but it does require a bit of time and effort.

- ★ *Register.* The easiest method is to use several online resources to get you started. Various organizations such as the League of Women Voters (www.lwv.org), Rock the Vote (www.rockthevote.org), or the National Association of Secretaries of State (www.canivote.org) allow you to see the voter registration guidelines particular to your state. Most states require individuals to print out and complete a voter registration form that you must then mail to your local registrar's office, although some states ask that you complete a request for an official voter registration form that they mail to you.
- ★ *Request an absentee ballot.* If you go to college away from home, you can choose to register to vote at school or at your "home" address. If you choose to register at your home address, you will most likely have to vote absentee, which will require an additional request for an absentee ballot. Again, each state has somewhat different requirements for absentee ballots. The League of Women Voters and the National Association of Secretaries of States Web sites cited above can help you find the right paperwork for your state.

- ★ *Know where and when to vote.* Once you're registered to vote, you'll want to make sure you know where to go, when the polls are open, and what kind of identification is required of you. The League of Women Voters Web site can answer all of these questions for you.
- ★ *Sign up to be an election judge.* Local election officials are often desperate for young poll workers to help monitor and manage polling places on Election Day. (The average age of a poll worker is seventy-two!) With a little bit of training, you can participate in this process—and get paid for your work. There is no national program, but the National Association of Secretaries of State Web site has a link that will connect you to your local offices.
- ★ *Learn about the candidates and issues.* Deciding whom to vote for can be a difficult choice, especially when it comes to less publicized state and local races, initiatives and referendums, and the retention of judges. In some local races (such as school board elections), the candidates are not affiliated with political parties, which may make the decision even harder. However, with a little time on the Internet, you can learn a lot about the candidates and the ballot questions. Some election offices will send out sample ballots that will allow you to see ahead of time what you will be asked to vote on, including the names of various candidates. Other organizations (such as those listed in the first point above) provide information about candidates' stands on various issues. Or, armed with the candidates' names, you can check out their own Web sites. Often, local newspapers will publish a list of endorsements just prior to the election.

raising advantage allowed him to create a much larger field operation than McCain could support.

Early analyses of the 2008 election suggested that the organization and mobilization on the part of the Democrats helped Barack Obama win the White House. By mobilizing support in places where Democrats had not seriously contended in the past, the Obama campaign expanded the electoral map. Some of the new states won by Democrats, including North Carolina, substantially increased their turnout rates. The marriage of technology, money, and field organization that the Obama campaign assembled for the 2008 campaign is sure to be imitated in future elections.

Thinking Critically about Political Participation and Liberty, Equality, and Democracy

Over the course of our history, as we have seen, the American political community has expanded to make our politics more closely match our fundamental values of liberty, equality, and democracy. But more recently, our political institutions have ceased to mobilize an active citizenry. Furthermore, our uneven pattern of political participation is at odds with our notions of equality and democracy. These problems highlight the tension among our basic values and raise questions about whether our institutions could help provide a better balance among them. Two questions about institutions are particularly pressing: Is "checkbook democracy" enough? Do our public institutions do enough to bring us together to engage in common problem solving? Both questions raise a third: Does the contemporary pattern of political participation in the United States reinforce inequality by providing a stronger voice for more advantaged groups?

"Checkbook democracy" refers to the importance of money in politics, both in electoral campaigns and in interest-group activity. Checkbook democracy is a major aspect of inequality in politics because citizens with fatter wallets are much better positioned to participate in this form of politics. Because it has been associated with declining participation and a greater inequality in participation patterns, checkbook politics has been the target of reformers who want to limit the role of money in politics. But the Supreme Court greatly limited the scope for reform in an important decision in 1976, when it ruled that individual contributions to candidates were a form of free speech and that it would be a curtailment of liberty to forbid such spending so long as it was not formally connected with a political campaign.[53] Many reformers remain dissatisfied with the Court's decision because they believe that allowing money to play such an important role in politics undermines political equality. Critics also do not think that restricting direct spending on candidates is a significant infringement of liberty. The Bipartisan Campaign Finance Reform Act (upheld by the Supreme Court in 2003) limited donations to parties. But because interest groups quickly created new organizations to attract funds, the law did little to reduce the importance of money in campaigns. (See Chapter 10 for a discussion of this reform.)

The other charge against checkbook politics is that it saps the energy from democracy because most members have only very loose connections with the groups who receive their checks. This not only allows interest groups to lobby in Washington with little direct accountability to their memberships, it also fails to mobilize people directly and thus does not build the personal connections that promote broad political engagement. Defenders of this style of politics say it does not drain democracy, it only makes it more efficient. In other words, people no longer have to go to meetings; they can simply send a check to the organizations they like and avoid the organizations they dislike.[54] These different views provoke questions about whether we need more direct participation to promote political equality and a vibrant democracy. They also cause us to ask what kinds of changes in social and political institutions would promote more direct participation.

Public institutions can play an important role in helping people understand our values in practice and find acceptable balances among them. Yet there are indications that our institutions are increasingly less able to perform this role. Some people argue that the behavior of American elites—the upper-middle class and the corporate community—has been the driving factor in the weakening of American democracy. Many American elites no longer participate in broad public institutions; instead, they send their children to private schools, obtain their medical care from generous private insurance plans, and hire private police to ensure their security. This "secession of the rich" has had damaging consequences for American democracy because these groups no longer have a stake in what happens in the public sector. Their main interest is in keeping taxes low and protecting themselves from public problems.[55] Yet clearly individuals have the right to participate as they wish and to purchase the services they think they need. But what happens when these individual choices undermine our ability to bring people together to hammer out their differences about what our values should mean in practice?

American political culture has supplied a core set of values that has helped knit together a culturally diverse nation. But the scope and meaning of these values has shifted over the course of history. In the past, these values were applied selectively, and some people were excluded from the definition of the American political community. Today, a more inclusive definition has evolved. Nonetheless, new questions about the role of our institutions in promoting political engagement and broad-based participation have emerged. We now face serious questions about what our values mean in a political system that seems irrelevant to many people and in which higher-income citizens have a disproportionately strong voice. The answers given to these questions today will shape the meaning of the American dream for future generations.

For Critical Analysis

As voter turnout has declined since its peak in the late 1800s, inequality in political participation has become more severe. Why are upper-income Americans more likely to be voters than lower-income Americans?

FOR FURTHER READING

Crenson, Matthew A., and Benjamin Ginsberg. *Downsizing Democracy: How America Sidelined Its Citizens and Privatized Its Public.* Baltimore: Johns Hopkins University Press, 2004.

Dalton, Russell J. *The Good Citizen: How a Younger Generation is Reshaping American Politics.* Washington, DC: CQ Press, 2007.

Green, Donald P., and Alan S. Gerber. *Get Out the Vote! How to Increase Voter Turnout.* Washington, DC: Brookings Institution Press, 2004.

Manza, Jeff, and Christopher Uggen. *Locked Out: Felon Disenfranchisement and American Democracy.* New York: Oxford University Press, 2006.

Patterson, Thomas E. *The Vanishing Voter: Public Involvement in an Age of Uncertainty.* New York: Vintage, 2003.

Putnam, Robert D. *Bowling Alone: The Collapse and Revival of American Community.* New York: Simon & Schuster, 2000.

Rosenstone, Steven J., and John Mark Hansen. *Mobilization, Participation and Democracy in America.* New York: Macmillan, 1993.

Schudson, Michael. *The Good Citizen: A History of American Civic Life.* New York: Free Press, 1998.

Verba, Sidney, Kay Lehman Schlotzman, and Henry Brady. *Voice and Equality: Civic Voluntarism in American Politics.* Cambridge, MA: Harvard University Press, 1995.

Zukin, Cliff, Scott Keeter, Molly Andolina, Krista Jenkins, and Michael X. Delli Carpini. *A New Engagement? Political Participation, Civic Life and the Changing American Citizen.* New York: Oxford University Press, 2006.

RECOMMENDED WEB SITES

Association of Community Organizations for Reform Now
www.acorn.org/

In the 2008 elections, ACORN's voter registration efforts drew criticism for registering invalid voters. Republicans accused the organization of promoting voter fraud. Supporters argued that the faulty registrations did not lead to voter fraud and defended ACORN's activities as important for ensuring broad political participation.

CQ MoneyLine
http://moneyline.cq.com/pml/home.do

Campaign contributions are a form of political participation that is both necessary and controversial. This Web site uses data from the Federal Election Commission (FEC) to publish those who give elected officials campaign money and those who may be receiving preferential treatment.

Declare Yourself
http://declareyourself.com

Statistics on political participation show that older people are much more likely to vote than are young people. Declare Yourself is a national nonpartisan, nonprofit campaign dedicated to closing the intergenerational divide by energizing and empowering a new movement of young voters.

League of Women Voters
www.lwv.org

Established in 1920 as part of the women's suffrage movement, the League of Women Voters encourages informed and active participation in government by women.

Project Vote Smart
www.votesmart.com

This nonpartisan site is dedicated to providing citizens with information on political candidates and elected officials. Here you can easily view candidates' biographical information, positions on issues, and voting records, so that you can make an informed choice on election day.

SpeakOut.com
www.speakout.com/activism/politics/

Levels of political participation in America are quite low. This Web site is the place to go to make a difference. SpeakOut.com tries to educate citizens on a variety of political issues and to mobilize individual participation via the Internet.

U.S. Census Bureau: Voting and Registration
www.census.gov/population/www/socdemo/voting.html

The U.S. Census Bureau collects statistics on voting and registration by various demographic and socioeconomic characteristics. See if you can find differences in voter turnout by race, age, sex, or socioeconomic status.

STUDY OUTLINE

www.wwnorton.com/wtp7e

Forms of Political Participation

1. Political participation can take many forms. The most common today are lobbying, public relations, litigation, protest, and, most important, voting.
2. Throughout American history, there has been a progressive, if uneven, expansion of suffrage to groups such as African Americans, women, and youths.
3. Americans are taught to equate citizenship with electoral participation.
4. Though the United States now has a system of universal suffrage, voter turnout continues to be low.

Who Participates, and How?

1. Several strategies of mobilization emerged to guide African Americans' quest for equality in the twentieth century, including political pressure, legal strategies, and protest. But the question remains whether political participation can improve the lives of African Americans, especially the poor.
2. In recent years, Latino political organizations have attempted to mobilize members of their community. This effort, if successful, would tap a "sleeping giant" of political influence.
3. The diversity of national backgrounds among Asian Americans has impeded the development of group-based political power.
4. The ongoing significance of gender issues in American politics is indicated by three trends: the gender gap, the increase in the number of women holding public office, and the continued importance of political issues of special concern to women.
5. A significant element of modern religious politics has been the mobilization of evangelical Protestants into a cohesive and politically active organization aligned with the Republican party.
6. One of the most significant patterns in political participation is that older people have much higher rates of participation than young people.

Explaining Political Participation

1. Several factors explain political participation. They include socioeconomic status, levels of civic engagement, formal obstacles, and efforts by political institutions to mobilize people. The most significant political factor affecting participation is whether people are mobilized by parties, candidates, interest groups, or social movements.
2. In recent decades, political institutions have ceased to mobilize an active citizenry. As a result, the ties between elected leaders and members of the upper and middle classes, who tend to vote more regularly, have been strengthened.
3. The quasi-democratic features of the American electoral system reveal its inherent inequality.

PRACTICE QUIZ

www.wwnorton.com/wtp7e

1. Which of the following is *not* a form of political participation?
   a) volunteering in a campaign
   b) attending an abortion-rights rally
   c) contributing to the Democratic Party
   d) watching the news on television
2. What is the most common form of political participation?
   a) lobbying
   b) contributing money to a campaign
   c) protesting
   d) voting
3. Which of the following best describes the electorate in the United States prior to the 1820s?
   a) landowning white males over the age of twenty-one
   b) all white males
   c) all literate males
   d) "universal suffrage"
4. Women won the right to vote in ________ with the adoption of the ________ Amendment.
   a) 1791; Fifth
   b) 1868; Fourteenth
   c) 1920; Nineteenth
   d) 1971; Twenty-sixth
5. Civic education takes place during
   a) elementary school.
   b) high school.
   c) election campaigns.
   d) all of the above
6. Which of the following negatively affects voter turnout in the United States?
   a) registration requirements
   b) weak parties
   c) neither a nor b
   d) both a and b
7. Of all the factors explaining political participation, which is the most important?
   a) the mobilization of people by political institutions
   b) socioeconomic status
   c) civic engagement
   d) level of education
8. Which of the following are examples of obstacles to political participation for African Americans?
   a) mobilization and levels of civic engagement
   b) the Civil Rights Acts of 1957 and 1964
   c) poll taxes and white primaries
   d) churches and community centers
9. After passage of the Motor Voter Act in 1993, participation in the 1996 elections
   a) increased dramatically.
   b) increased somewhat.
   c) declined somewhat.
   d) was not affected, since few people registered to vote as a result of the act.
10. Americans who do vote tend to be ________ than the population as a whole.
   a) wealthier
   b) whiter
   c) more educated
   d) all of the above

KEY TERMS

www.wwnorton.com/wtp7e

American political community (p. 291)
civic engagement (p. 305)
gender gap (p. 298)
litigation (p. 287)
lobbying (p. 286)
mobilization (p. 309)
political participation (p. 285)
poll tax (p. 290)
protest (p. 287)
public relations (p. 286)
socioeconomic status (p. 303)
suffrage (p. 288)
turnout (p. 290)

9 Political Parties

- What Are Political Parties?
- The Two-Party System in America
- Party Organization
- Parties and the Electorate
- Parties and Elections
- Parties and Government
- Thinking Critically about the Role of Parties in a Democracy

WHAT GOVERNMENT DOES AND WHY IT MATTERS

In the United States, political parties force the government to concern itself with the needs of its citizens. Strong parties and energetic party competition make it more likely that the political system will support basic American values.

Liberty requires coherent and well-organized opposition to those in power. Political equality is enhanced when parties organize the collective political energies of those who, as individuals, might lack the resources and knowledge to compete with elites and interest groups. Democracy is promoted when parties mobilize large numbers of individuals to participate in the political arena.

Unfortunately, political parties in America today may not be sufficiently vigorous or well organized to bolster participation or to provide a democratic counterweight to the power of special interests. The consequence is that policy may be designed to benefit powerful special interests at the expense of the majority of Americans. However, when parties compete with one another, policy may be more responsive to the public. The student-loan industry provides an example. For many years, the student-loan industry benefited from subsidies and high interest rates, which translated into costly loans and large payments for students. But in the 2006 midterm elections, the issue became a target of party competition, with Democrats supporting far-reaching reforms. The reforms aimed to limit the profits of loan providers and offer students financial aid at much better rates. After the Democrats won control of Congress in 2006, they sought to pass legislation that would reduce subsidies to lenders and cut student interest rates in half. Many congressional Republicans opposed the proposed reform, citing the harm to lenders. Former president Bush promised to veto the measure. However, fear that Democrats would use the issue against them in the 2008 elections ultimately drove many Republicans to support the College Cost Reduction and Access Act, which the president signed into law in 2007.[1] Party competition was the spur to a major reform in financial aid for students.

Over the past 200 years, Americans' conception of political parties has changed considerably. In the early years of the Republic, parties were seen as threats to the social order. In his 1796 "Farewell Address," President George Washington warned his countrymen to shun partisan politics. Nonetheless, the party-building activities of the Jeffersonians, Jacksonians, and their successors made American politics more egalitarian and democratic. Today, political parties are a core feature of the American political system. They play central roles in mobilizing citizens to vote and, through their competition, help to ensure that the public voice is heard in policymaking.

During the 2008 election, parties directed and financed the core campaign activities, including media advertisements for candidates and direct mobilization of voters. The centrality of parties in 2008 marked a shift from the 2004 campaign, when outside groups played much more prominent roles in the campaigns. Candidates and their parties dominated in the 2008 campaigns in part because both McCain and Obama expressed reservations about the negative advertising associated with outside groups. Another important factor was Obama's massive fund-raising and his decision to forego public financing and the limits it places on campaign spending. Obama's fund-raising advantage allowed his campaign to dominate the airwaves during the general election. McCain's campaign benefited from the fund-raising muscle of the Republican National Committee, but the constraints of public funding put McCain at a disadvantage in the general election.

The 2008 election also featured new party strategies. In the past, images of "red" and "blue" America—states that reliably voted Republican and Democratic, respectively—led parties to concentrate their activities in a handful of swing states, such as Ohio and Florida. The 2008 election was notable for the efforts of the Democratic Party to expand the electoral map by mobilizing supporters in formerly "red" states, such as Virginia and Colorado. The 2008 elections created a new map that marks the starting point for parties as they contemplate their strategies for the 2010 and 2012 elections.

- **In this chapter, we begin by explaining why political parties exist.** In doing so, we will see that parties play a significant role in the political process.
- **We then examine the history of the American two-party system.** As we will see, the history of parties has followed an interesting pattern that has had important consequences for governance.
- **In the next three sections, we look at parties as organizations, parties in the electorate, and the role of parties in the campaign process.** We will see that although party organizations remain strong, the electorate's identification with parties and the role of parties in the electoral process have been declining in recent decades.
- **We then assess the impact of parties on government and the policy-making process.** We will see that the differences between the two major parties can and do have an effect on policy.

What Are Political Parties?

political parties organized groups that attempt to influence the government by electing their members to important government offices

Political parties, like interest groups, are organizations that seek influence over government. Ordinarily, they can be distinguished from interest groups on the basis of their orientation. A party seeks to control the government by electing its members to office and thereby controlling the government's personnel. Interest groups usually accept government and its personnel as givens and try to influence government policies through them.

In the United States today, the relationship between parties and government is more complex than this basic definition suggests. Political parties have been the chief points of contact between government, on the one side, and groups and forces in society, on the other. Through organized political parties, social forces can gain some control over governmental policies and personnel. Simultaneously, the government often seeks to organize and influence important groups in society through political parties. All political parties have this dual character: they are instruments through which citizens and government attempt to influence one another.

As long as political parties have existed, they have been criticized for introducing selfish, "partisan" concerns into public debate and national policy. Yet political parties are extremely important to the proper functioning of a democracy. As we will see, parties expand popular political participation, promote more effective choice, and smooth the flow of public business in the Congress. Our problem in America today is not that political life is too partisan but that our parties are not strong enough to function effectively. This is one reason that America has such low levels of popular political involvement. Unfortunately, some reforms currently being implemented, such as restrictions on so-called soft money, might further erode party strength in America.

The Democratic Party of the United States is the world's oldest political party. It can trace its history back to Thomas Jefferson's Jeffersonian Republicans and, later, to Andrew Jackson's Jacksonian Democrats. The Jacksonians expanded voter participation and ushered in the political era of the common person, as shown in this image of Jackson's inauguration celebration.

The Two-Party System in America

two-party system a political system in which only two parties have a realistic opportunity to compete effectively for control

Although George Washington, and in fact many other leaders of his time, considered partisan politics unhealthy, the **two-party system** emerged early in the history of the new Republic. Beginning with the Federalists and the Jeffersonian Republicans in the late 1780s, two major parties have dominated national politics, although which particular two parties they were has changed with the times and issues. This two-party system has culminated in today's Democrats and Republicans (see Figure 9.1).

Historical Origins

Historically, parties form in one of two ways. The first, which could be called "internal mobilization," occurs when political conflicts break out and government officials and competing factions seek to mobilize popular support. This is precisely what happened during the early years of the American Republic. Competition in the Congress between northeastern merchants and southern agricultural factions led first the southerners and then the northeasterners to attempt to organize their supporters. The result was the foundation of America's first national parties—the Jeffersonians, whose primary base was in the South, and the Federalists, whose strength was greatest in the New England states.

The second way that parties may form, which could be called "external mobilization," takes place when a group of politicians outside government organizes popular support to win governmental power. For example, during the 1850s, a group of state politicians who opposed slavery, especially the expansion of slavery in America's territorial possessions, built what became the Republican Party by constructing party organizations and mobilizing popular support in the Northeast and West.

America's two major parties now, of course, are the Democrats and the Republicans. Both trace their roots back over 150 years to the nineteenth century and have evolved over time. Since they were formed, the two major parties have undergone significant shifts in their positions and goals, and their membership. These changes within the parties have been prompted by issues and events as well as by demographic and social developments. Let us consider the cases of each party in turn.

THE DEMOCRATS When the Jeffersonian Party splintered in 1824, Andrew Jackson emerged as the leader of one of its four factions. In 1830, Jackson's group became the Democratic Party. This new party had the strongest national organization of its time and presented itself as the party of the common man. Jacksonians supported reductions in the price of public lands and economic policies that would make it easier to borrow money. Laborers, immigrants, and western settlers were quickly attracted to this new party.

From 1828, when Jackson was elected president, to 1860, the Democratic Party was the dominant force in American politics. For all but eight of those years, the Democrats held the White House. In addition, a Democratic majority controlled the Senate for twenty-six years and the House for twenty-four years during the same time period. These nineteenth-century Democrats emphasized the importance of interpreting the Constitution literally, upholding states' rights, and limiting federal spending.

In 1860, the issue of slavery split the Democrats along geographic lines. In the South, many Democrats served in the Confederate government. Although most Democrats in

FIGURE 9.1 ★ How the Party System Evolved

During the nineteenth century, the Democrats and the Republicans emerged as the two dominant parties in American politics. As the American party system evolved, many third parties emerged, but few of them remained in existence for very long.

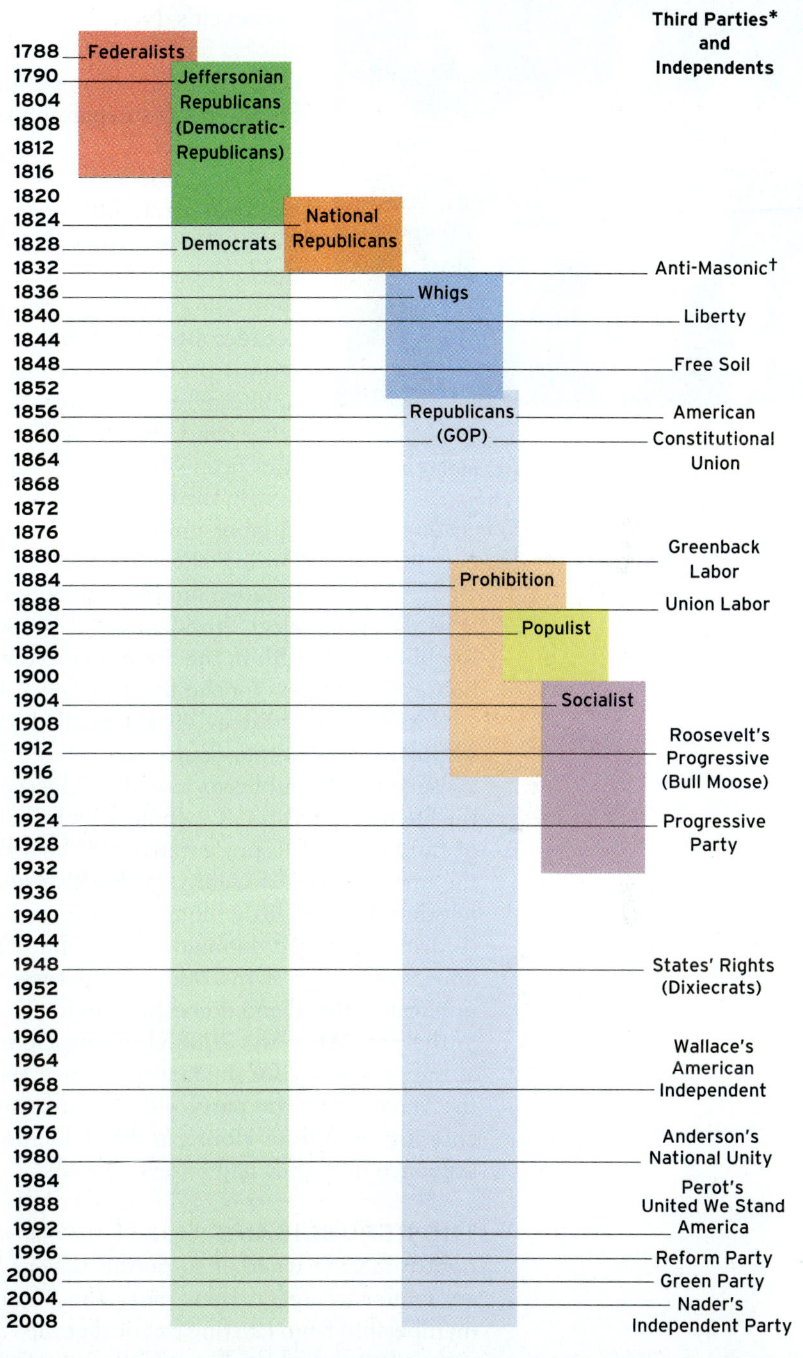

*Or in some cases, fourth parties; most of these parties lasted through only one term.

†The Anti-Masonics had the distinction of being not only the first third party, but also the first party to hold a national nominating convention and the first to announce a party platform.

the North were antislavery, one faction of the party (known as the Copperheads) opposed the Civil War and advocated negotiating a peace with the South. Thus, for years after the war, Republicans accused the Democrats of being the "party of treason."

The Democratic Party was not fully able to regain its political strength until the Great Depression. In 1933, the Democrat Franklin D. Roosevelt entered the

Following the 2006 elections, the Democrats won majorities in both houses of Congress, ending a twelve-year period of Republican domination. In 2008, the Democrats increased their majorities in both houses of Congress and won the presidency.

White House, and the Democrats won control of Congress as well. Roosevelt's New Deal coalition, composed of Catholics, Jews, blacks, farmers, intellectuals, and members of organized labor, dominated American politics until the 1970s and formed the basis for the party's expansion of federal power and efforts to remedy social problems.

The Democrats were never fully united. In Congress, southern Democrats often voted with Republicans in the "conservative coalition" rather than with members of their own party. But the Democratic Party remained America's majority party, usually controlling both Congress and the White House, for nearly four decades after 1932. By the 1980s, the Democratic coalition faced serious problems. The once-solid South often voted for the Republicans, as did many white, blue-collar northern voters. On the other hand, the Democrats increased their strength among African American voters and women. The Democrats maintained a strong base in the bureaucracies of the federal government and the states, in labor unions, and in the not-for-profit sector of the economy. During the 1980s and 1990s, moderate Democrats sought to broaden middle-class support. These efforts helped the Democrats elect President Bill Clinton in 1992. In 1994, however, growing Republican strength in the South led to the loss of the Democrats' control of both houses of Congress for the first time since 1954.

Employing a strategy his aides called "triangulation," President Clinton sought to pursue a moderate course that placed him midway between the positions of conservative Republicans and liberal Democrats. This strategy helped Clinton and the Democratic Party as a whole, which gained strength and nearly regained control of the House of Representatives in the 1998 national elections. However, during the first six years of George W. Bush's presidency, many congressional Democrats felt that they had little room to express a distinctive party view about the national-security issues that dominated the public agenda. After Democrats took back both houses of Congress in 2006, they became more vocal in their opposition to Republican national and domestic policies. They also became much more united than in the past. After the 2008 elections, Democrats controlled the Congress as well as the presidency for the first time since 1995. Democratic gains in the House and the Senate gave the party a sizable majority, and with Democrat Barack Obama entering the White House in 2009, Democrats appeared poised to exert greater influence than they had in several years.

THE REPUBLICANS In 1854, the Kansas-Nebraska Act gave each territory the right to decide whether to permit slavery. Opposition to this policy led antislavery groups to create a new party, the Republicans. The Republican Party drew its membership from existing political groups and antislavery Democrats. In 1856, the party's first presidential candidate, John C. Fremont, won one-third of the popular vote and carried eleven states.

The early Republican platforms appealed to commercial as well as antislavery interests. The Republicans favored homesteading, internal improvements such as the construction of a transcontinental railroad, and protective tariffs as well as the containment of slavery. In 1858, the Republican Party won control of the House of Representatives; in 1860, the Republican presidential candidate, Abraham Lincoln, was victorious in a four-way race.

For almost seventy-five years after the North's victory in the Civil War, the Republicans were America's dominant political party, especially after 1896. Between 1860 and 1932, Republicans occupied the White House and controlled Congress most of the time. During these years, the Republicans came to be closely associated with big business. The party of Lincoln became the party of Wall Street.

In 1994, Republicans took control of both houses of Congress for the first time in four decades and promised to implement a conservative agenda under the rubric of a "Contract with America." However, the GOP's campaign to impeach the Democratic president Bill Clinton diverted Republican energies from other tasks.

The Great Depression ended Republican dominance, however. The voters held President Herbert Hoover responsible for the depression, and by 1936, the party's popularity was so low that Republicans won only eighty-nine seats in the House and seventeen in the Senate. The Republican presidential candidate in 1936, Governor Alfred M. Landon of Kansas, carried only two states. The Republicans won only four presidential elections between 1932 and 1980, and they controlled Congress for only four of those years (1947–49 and 1953–55).

The Republican Party, also known as the GOP (which stands for "Grand Old Party"), widened its appeal in the second half of the twentieth century. Groups previously associated with the Democratic Party—particularly white, blue-collar workers and white southern Democrats—have been increasingly attracted to Republican presidential candidates (for example, Dwight D. Eisenhower, Richard Nixon, Ronald Reagan, George H. W. Bush, and George W. Bush). Yet Republicans generally did not do as well at the state and local levels until the 1990s. In 1994, however, the Republican Party finally won a majority in both houses of Congress, in large part because of the party's growing strength in the South.

During the 1990s, conservative religious groups, which had been attracted to the Republican camp by its opposition to abortion and support for school prayer, made a concerted effort to expand their influence within the party. This effort led to conflict between these members of the "religious right" and more traditional "country-club" Republicans, whose major concerns were economic matters such as taxes and federal regulation of business. The coalition between these two wings won control of both houses of Congress in 1994 and was able to retain control of both houses in 1996, despite President Clinton's re-election in that year. In 2000, George W. Bush sought to unite the party's centrist and right wings behind a program of tax cuts, education reform, military strength, and family values. However, by 2006, the public's disapproval of the Bush administration and the war in Iraq led to major losses for Republicans in both houses of Congress. Campaigning during the worst financial crisis since the 1930s and burdened with a president whose approval ratings had sunk to historic lows, Republicans fared poorly in the 2008 elections. With the party in disarray, contending factions sought to redefine a strategy that would allow Republicans to regain the influence they had enjoyed in the early days of George W. Bush's presidency.

Party Systems

Our understanding of American party history would be incomplete if we considered each party only in isolation. America's political parties compete with one another for offices, policies, and power, and the history of each party is inextricably linked to that of its major rival. Historians often refer to the set of parties that are important at any given time as a nation's "party system." The most obvious feature of a party system is the number of major parties competing for power. The United States has usually had a two-party system, meaning that only two parties have a serious chance to win national elections. Of course, we have not always had the same two parties, and, as we shall see below, minor parties often put forward candidates.

The term *party system*, however, refers to more than just the number of parties competing for power. It also includes the organization of the parties, the balance of power between and within party coalitions, the parties' social and institutional bases, and the issues and policies around which party competition is organized. Seen from this broader perspective, the character of a nation's party system can change even if the number of parties remains the same and even when the same two parties seem to be competing for power. Today's American party system is very different from the country's party system of fifty years ago, but the Democrats and Republicans continue to be the major competing forces. The character of a nation's party system can have profound consequences for the relative influences of social forces, the importance of political institutions, and even the types of issues and policies that reach the nation's political agenda. For example, the contemporary American political parties mainly compete for the support of different groups of middle-class Americans. As a result, issues that concern the middle and upper-middle classes, such as the environment, health care, retirement benefits, and taxation, are very much on the political agenda, whereas issues that concern working-class and poorer Americans, such as welfare and housing, receive short shrift from both parties.[2] Over the course of American history, changes in political forces and alignments have produced six distinctive party systems.

THE FIRST PARTY SYSTEM: FEDERALISTS AND JEFFERSONIAN REPUBLICANS The first party system emerged in the 1790s and pitted the Federalists against the Jeffersonian Republicans. The Federalists spoke mainly for New England merchants and supported a program of protective tariffs to encourage manufacturing, assumption of the states' Revolutionary War debts, the creation of a national bank, and resumption of commercial ties with Britain. The Jeffersonians, led by southern agricultural interests, opposed these policies and instead favored free trade, the promotion of agricultural over commercial interests, and friendship with France. The Federalists sought, unsuccessfully, to use the force of law against the Jeffersonians by enacting the Alien and Sedition Acts to outlaw criticism of the government. These acts, however, proved virtually impossible to enforce, and the Jeffersonians gradually expanded their base from the South into the Middle Atlantic states. In the election of 1800, Jefferson defeated the incumbent Federalist president, John Adams, and led his party to power. Over the following years, the Federalists gradually weakened. The party disappeared altogether after the pro-British sympathies of some Federalist leaders during the War of 1812 led to charges of treason against the party.

From the collapse of the Federalists until the 1830s, America had only one political party, the Jeffersonian Republicans, who gradually came to be known as the Democrats. This period of one-party politics is sometimes known as the "era of good feelings" to indicate the absence of party competition. Throughout this period, however, there was intense factional conflict within the Democratic Party, particularly between the supporters and opponents of General Andrew Jackson, America's great military hero of the War of 1812. Jackson's opponents united to deny him the presidency in 1824, but Jackson won election in 1828 and again in 1832. Jackson's base of support was in the South and in the West, and he generally espoused a program of free trade and policies that would make it easier to borrow money that appealed to those regions. During the 1830s, groups opposing Jackson united to form a new political force—the Whig Party—thus giving rise to the second American party system.

THE SECOND PARTY SYSTEM: DEMOCRATS AND WHIGS During the 1830s and 1840s, the Democrats and the Whigs built party organizations throughout the nation; they both sought to enlarge their bases of support by expanding the right to vote. They increased the number of eligible voters through the elimination of property restrictions and other barriers to voting—at least voting by white males. This was not the last time that party competition would pave the way for expansion of the electorate. Support for the new Whig Party was stronger in the Northeast than in the South and West and stronger among merchants than among small farmers. Hence, in some measure, the Whigs were the successors of the Federalists. Yet conflict between the two parties revolved more around personalities than policies. The Whigs were a diverse group united more by opposition to the Democrats than by agreement on programs. In 1840, the Whigs won their first presidential election under the leadership of General William Henry Harrison, a military hero known as "Old Tippecanoe." The Whig campaign carefully avoided issues—since the party could agree on almost none—and emphasized the personal qualities and heroism of the candidate. The Whigs also invested heavily in campaign rallies and entertainment to win the hearts, if not exactly the minds, of the voters. The 1840 campaign came to be called the "hard cider" campaign because of the practice of using food and especially drink to win votes.

During the late 1840s and early 1850s, conflicts over slavery produced sharp divisions within both the Whig and the Democratic parties despite the efforts of party leaders to develop compromises. By 1856, the Whig Party had all but disintegrated under the strain, and many Whig politicians and voters, along with

The Republican Party was formed during the 1850s as a coalition of antislavery and other forces. The party's nomination of Abraham Lincoln for the presidency at the 1860 convention sparked the secession of the South and of the Civil War.

Democratic Party support for the civil rights movement led many white southerners to the Republican camp. Starting in 1952, this bolstered the GOP's strength and gave it a decided edge in presidential elections. Between 1968 and 1988, Republicans won five of six presidential elections.

antislavery Democrats, joined the new Republican Party, which pledged to ban slavery from the western territories. In 1860, the Republicans nominated Abraham Lincoln for the presidency. Lincoln's victory strengthened southern calls for secession from the Union and, soon thereafter, for all-out civil war.

THE CIVIL WAR AND POST–CIVIL WAR PARTY SYSTEM: REPUBLICANS AND DEMOCRATS During the course of the war, President Lincoln depended heavily on Republican governors and state legislatures to raise troops, provide funding, and maintain popular support for a long and bloody military conflict. The secession of the South had stripped the Democratic Party of many of its leaders and supporters, but the Democrats remained politically competitive throughout the war and nearly won the 1864 presidential election because of war weariness on the part of the northern public. With the defeat of the Confederacy in 1865, some congressional Republicans sought to convert the South into a Republican bastion through a program of Reconstruction that enfranchised newly freed slaves. This Reconstruction program collapsed in the 1870s as a result of disagreement within the Republican Party in Congress and violent resistance to Reconstruction by southern whites. With the end of Reconstruction, the former Confederate states regained full membership in the Union and full control of their internal affairs. Throughout the South, African Americans were deprived of political rights, including the right to vote, despite post–Civil War constitutional guarantees to the contrary. The post–Civil War South was solidly Democratic in its political affiliation, and with a firm Southern base, the national Democratic Party was able to confront the Republicans on a more or less equal basis. From the end of the Civil War to the 1890s, the Republican Party remained the party of the North, with strong business and middle-class support, while the Democrats were the party of the South, with support from working-class and immigrant groups.

THE SYSTEM OF 1896: REPUBLICANS AND DEMOCRATS During the 1890s, profound and rapid social and economic changes led to the emergence of a variety of protest parties, including the Populist Party, which won the support of hundreds of thousands of voters in the South and West. The Populists appealed mainly to small farmers but also attracted western mining interests and urban workers as well. In the 1892 presidential election, the Populist Party carried four states and elected governors in eight. In 1896, the Populist Party effectively merged with the Democrats, who nominated William Jennings Bryan, a Democratic senator with pronounced Populist sympathies, for the presidency. The Republicans nominated the conservative senator William McKinley. In the ensuing campaign, northern and midwestern businesses made an all-out effort to defeat what they saw as a radical threat from the Populist-Democratic alliance. When the dust settled, the Republicans had won a resounding victory. The GOP had carried the more heavily populated northern and midwestern states and confined the Democrats to their smaller bases of support in the South and far West. For the next thirty-six years, the Republicans were the nation's majority party, carrying seven of nine presidential elections and controlling both houses of Congress in fifteen of eighteen contests. The Republican Party of this era was very much the party of American business, advocating low taxes, high tariffs on imports, and a minimum of government regulation. The Democrats were far too weak to offer much opposition. Southern Democrats, moreover, were too concerned with maintaining the region's autonomy on issues of race to challenge the Republicans on other fronts.

THE NEW DEAL PARTY SYSTEM: REVERSAL OF FORTUNE Soon after the Republican presidential candidate Herbert Hoover won the 1928 presidential election, the nation's economy collapsed. The Great Depression, which produced unprecedented economic hardship, stemmed from a variety of causes, but from the perspective of millions of Americans the Republican Party did not do enough to promote economic recovery. In 1932, Americans elected Franklin Delano Roosevelt (FDR) and a solidly Democratic Congress. FDR developed a program for economic recovery that he dubbed the "New Deal." Under the auspices of the New Deal, the size and reach of America's national government increased substantially. The federal government took responsibility for economic management and social welfare to an extent that was unprecedented in American history. Roosevelt designed many of his programs specifically to expand the political base of the Democratic Party. He rebuilt the party around a nucleus of unionized workers, upper-middle-class intellectuals and professionals, southern farmers, Jews, Catholics, and African Americans that revitalized the Democrats. This so-called New Deal coalition made the Democrats the nation's majority party for the next thirty-six years. Republicans groped for a response to the New Deal and often wound up supporting popular New Deal programs such as Social Security in what was sometimes derided as "me too" Republicanism.

The New Deal coalition was severely strained during the 1960s by conflicts over civil rights and the Vietnam War. The struggle over civil rights initially divided northern Democrats who supported the civil rights cause from white southern Democrats who defended the system of racial segregation. Subsequently, as the civil rights movement launched a northern campaign aimed at securing access to jobs and education and an end to racial discrimination in such realms as housing, northern Democrats also split, often along income lines. The struggle over the Vietnam War further divided the Democrats, with upper-income liberal Democrats strongly opposing the Johnson administration's decision to send U.S. forces to fight in Southeast Asia. These schisms within the Democratic Party provided an opportunity for the GOP, which returned to power in 1968 under the leadership of Richard Nixon.

THE CONTEMPORARY AMERICAN PARTY SYSTEM In the 1960s, conservative Republicans argued that "me-tooism" was a recipe for continual failure and sought to reposition the GOP as a genuine alternative to the Democrats. In 1964, for example, the Republican presidential candidate Barry Goldwater, author of a book entitled *Conscience of a Conservative,* argued in favor of substantially reduced levels of taxation and spending, less government regulation of the economy, and the elimination of many federal social programs. Though Goldwater was

In America's contemporary party system, the Republican party appeals to social conservatives and has also cast itself as the party best equipped to handle security issues. Throughout the 2008 campaigns, Americans consistently saw Republican John McCain as better qualified than Barack Obama to serve as commander in chief. However, voters were ultimately more concerned about the economy—a traditional Democratic strength—than security in 2008.

defeated by Lyndon Johnson, the ideas he espoused continued to be major themes for the Republican Party. It took Richard Nixon's "southern strategy" to give the GOP the votes it needed to end Democratic dominance of the political process. Nixon appealed strongly to disaffected white southerners, and with the help of the independent candidate and former Alabama governor George Wallace, he sparked the shift of voters that eventually gave the once-hated "party of Lincoln" a strong position in all the states of the former Confederacy. During the 1980s, under the leadership of Ronald Reagan, Republicans added two additional important groups to their coalition. The first were religious conservatives who were offended by Democratic support for abortion and gay rights as well as alleged Democratic disdain for traditional cultural and religious values. The second were working-class whites who were drawn to Reagan's tough approach to foreign policy as well as his positions against affirmative action.

While Republicans built a political base around economic and social conservatives and white southerners, the Democratic Party maintained its support among a majority of unionized workers and upper-middle-class intellectuals and professionals. Democrats also appealed strongly to racial minorities. The 1965 Voting Rights Act had greatly increased black voter participation in the South and helped the Democratic Party retain some House and Senate seats in southern states. And whereas the GOP appealed to social conservatives, the Democrats appealed strongly to Americans concerned with abortion rights, gay rights, feminism, environmentalism, and other progressive social causes. In 2008, Democrats sought to reach beyond their base by appealing to moderate voters in states that had once been Republican strongholds. Obama's post-partisan rhetoric of "one America" signaled the party's efforts to move beyond the social cleavages that had dominated politics since the 1960s. The Democrats' success in 2008 suggests that a new set of issues and a new alignment of groups may characterize future races.

Electoral Alignments and Realignments

electoral realignment the point in history when a new party supplants the ruling party, becoming in turn the dominant political force. In the United States, this has tended to occur roughly every thirty years

The points of transition between party systems in American history are sometimes called periods of **electoral realignment.** During these periods, the electoral coalitions that support the parties and the balance of power between the parties are redefined. Figure 9.2 charts the sequence of party systems and realignments in American history. Party loyalties in contemporary America continue to be in a state of flux, as party identification among some voters has grown stronger, but the percentage of voters who declare no party loyalty remains at an all-time high.[3]

Although scholars dispute the timing of realignments, there is some agreement that five have occurred since the Founding. The first took place around 1800, when the Jeffersonian Republicans defeated the Federalists and became the dominant force in American politics. The second realignment took place in about 1828, when the Jacksonian Democrats seized control of the White House and the Congress. The third period of realignment centered on 1860. During this period, the newly founded Republican party led by Abraham Lincoln won power, in the process destroying the Whig Party, which had been one of the nation's two major parties since the 1830s. During the fourth realignment, centered on the election of

FIGURE 9.2 ★
Electoral Realignments

Political scientists disagree over whether an electoral realignment occurred in 1968, because no one party clearly dominated the national government after that election. Although Republicans dominated the federal government between 2000 and 2006, their control fell short of a full-fledged realignment: Republicans never gained a majority of party identifiers, they failed to enact many of their key policy goals, and elections remained extremely close.

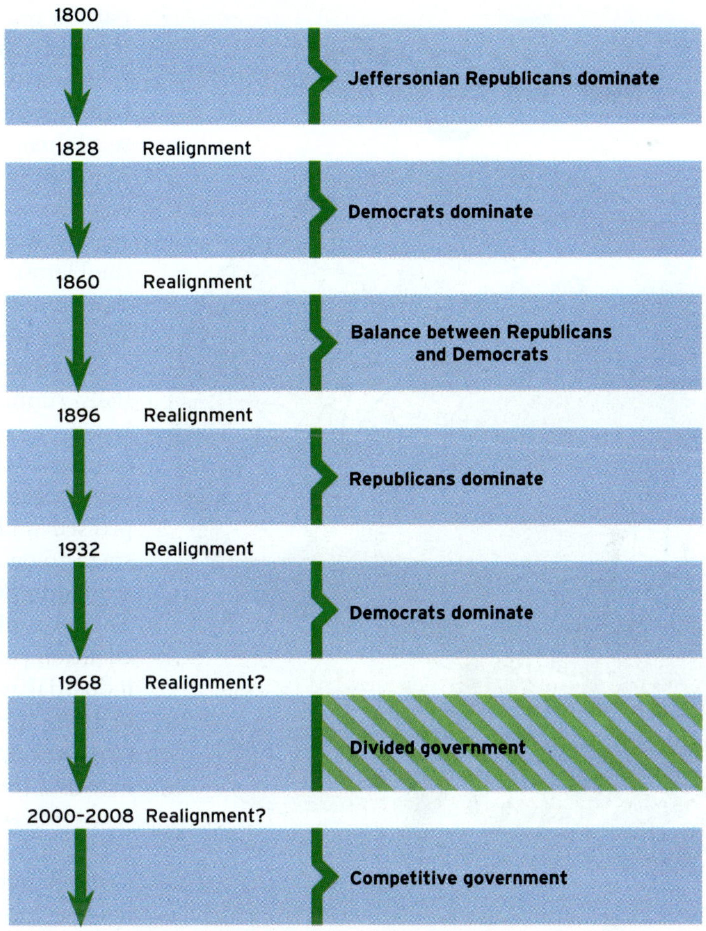

1896, the Republicans reasserted their dominance of the national government, a dominance that had been weakening since the 1880s. The fifth realignment took place during the period 1932–36, when the Democrats, led by Franklin Delano Roosevelt, took control of the White House and Congress and, despite sporadic interruptions, maintained control of both through the 1960s. After that time, American party politics was characterized primarily by **divided government,** wherein the presidency is controlled by one party while the other party controls one or both houses of Congress.

divided government the condition in American government wherein the presidency is controlled by one party while the opposing party controls one or both houses of Congress

In historical terms realignments occur when new issues, combined with economic or political crises, mobilize new voters and persuade large numbers of voters to reexamine their traditional partisan loyalties and permanently shift their support from one party to another. For example, during the 1850s, diverse regional, income, and business groups supported one of the two major parties, the Democrats or the Whigs, on the basis of their positions on various economic issues, such as internal improvements, the tariff, monetary policy, and banking. This economic alignment was shattered during the 1850s. The newly formed Republican Party campaigned on the basis of opposition to slavery and, in particular, opposition to the expansion of slavery into the territories. The issues of slavery and sectionalism produced

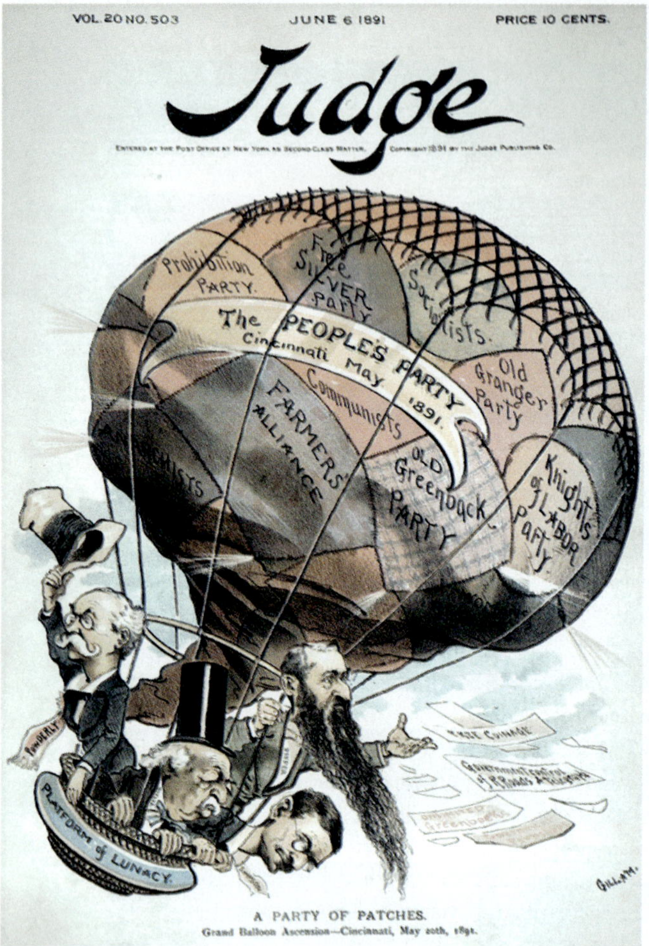

Although the Republicans and Democrats are America's dominant parties, many minor parties have presented candidates for political office throughout American history. Typically, third parties in the United States have been considered short-lived coalitions of disgruntled outsiders, as shown in this satiric view of the nineteenth-century People's Party as a "party of patches."

divisions within both the Democratic and the Whig parties, ultimately leading to the dissolution of the latter, and these issues compelled voters to reexamine their partisan allegiances. Many northern voters who had supported the Whigs or the Democrats on the basis of their economic stands shifted their support to the Republicans as slavery replaced tariffs and economic concerns as the central item on the nation's political agenda. Many southern Whigs shifted their support to the Democrats. The new sectional alignment of forces that emerged was solidified by the trauma of the Civil War and persisted almost to the turn of the century.

In 1896, this sectional alignment was at least partially supplanted by an alignment of political forces based on economic and cultural factors. During the economic crises of the 1880s and 1890s, the Democrats forged a coalition consisting of economically hard-pressed midwestern and southern farmers, as well as small-town and rural economic interests. These groups tended to be native-stock, fundamentalist Protestants. The Republicans, on the other hand, put together a coalition comprising most of the business community, industrial workers, and city dwellers. In the election of 1896, the Republican candidate William McKinley, emphasizing business, industry, and urban interests, defeated the Democrat William Jennings Bryan, who spoke for sectional interests, farmers, and fundamentalism. Republican dominance lasted until 1932.

Such periods of electoral realignment in American politics have had extremely important institutional and policy results. Realignments occur when new issue concerns, coupled with economic or political crises, weaken the established political elite and permit new groups of politicians to create coalitions of forces capable of capturing and holding the reins of governmental power. The construction of new governing coalitions during these realigning periods has effected major changes in American governmental institutions and policies. Each period of realignment was a turning point in American politics. The choices made by the national electorate during these periods have helped shape the course of American political history for the following generation.[4]

American Third Parties

third parties parties that organize to compete against the two major American political parties

Although the United States is said to have a two-party system, the country has always had more than two parties. Typically, **third parties** in the United States have represented social and economic interests that for one or another reason were not given voice by the two major parties.[5] Such parties have had a good deal of influence on ideas and elections in the United States. The Populists, a party centered in the rural areas of the West and Midwest, and the Progressives, spokesmen for the

TABLE 9.1 ★ Parties and Candidates in 2008

In the 2008 presidential election, in addition to the Democratic and Republican nominees, several candidates appeared on the ballot in one or more states.

CANDIDATE	PARTY	VOTE TOTAL*	PERCENTAGE OF VOTE*
Barack Obama	Democratic	64,629,649	53%
John McCain	Republican	56,887,996	46%
Ralph Nader	Independent	667, 045	0.5%
Robert L. Barr, Jr.	Libertarian	493,987	0.4%
Charles O. Baldwin	Independent	177,690	0.1%
Alan Keyes	Independent	35,299	0%

*With 99 percent of votes tallied.
SOURCE: http://elections.foxnews.com/tracker.html (accessed 11/6/08).

urban middle classes in the late nineteenth and early twentieth centuries, are the most important examples in the past 100 years. More recently, Ross Perot, who ran in 1992 as an independent and in 1996 as the Reform Party's nominee, impressed voters with his folksy style; he garnered almost 19 percent of the votes cast in the 1992 presidential election. Table 9.1 lists the top candidates in the presidential election of 2008, including the top third-party and independent candidates who ran. In addition to the candidates listed in Table 9.1, the Green Party, the Socialist Party, the Prohibition Party, and several other parties nominated candidates for the presidency in 2008. In order to have even any realistic chance of winning, a candidate needs to appear on the ballot in at least enough states to reach a total of 270 electoral votes. However, most of the third-party and independent candidates in 2008 did not appear on the ballot in enough states to have any hope of winning. Including Ralph Nader, the third-party and independent candidates gained no electoral votes for president, and most of them disappeared immediately after the presidential election. Third-party and independent candidacies also arise at the state and local levels. In New York, the Liberal and Conservative parties have been on the ballot for decades. In 1998, Minnesota elected a third-party governor, the former professional wrestler Jesse Ventura. In 2002, the Green Party candidate for governor in Massachusetts, Jill Stein, may have affected the race between Mitt Romney and his Democratic rival by drawing votes away from the Democrats in a close race. And in 2006, the entertainer Kinky Friedman mounted a somewhat credible campaign running as an independent candidate for the governorship of Texas.

Although the Republican Party was only the third American political party to make itself permanent (by replacing the Whigs), other third parties have enjoyed an influence far beyond their electoral size. This was because large parts of their programs were adopted by one or both of the major parties, which sought to appeal to the voters mobilized by the new party, and so to expand their own electoral

Politics Today

In historical terms third parties have developed in America when certain issues or constituencies have been ignored by the existing parties. Considering the similarities and differences between the Democratic and Republican parties, where might a budding third party find a constituency?

In 2000, Ralph Nader ran as the candidate of the Green Party and won 3 percent of the vote, mainly at the expense of Democratic candidate Al Gore. Many observers believed that Gore would have won the 2000 election had Nader dropped out. In 2004 and 2008, Nader ran again as an independent candidate, receiving less than 1 percent of the vote.

strength. The Democratic Party, for example, became a great deal more liberal when it adopted most of the Progressive program early in the twentieth century. Many socialists felt that President Roosevelt's New Deal had adopted most of their party's program, including old-age pensions, unemployment compensation, an agricultural marketing program, and laws guaranteeing workers the right to organize into unions.

This kind of influence explains the short lives of third parties. Their causes are usually eliminated when the major parties absorb their programs and draw their supporters into the mainstream. There are, of course, additional reasons for the short duration of most third parties. One is the usual limitation of their electoral support to one or two regions. Populist support, for example, was primarily midwestern. The 1948 Progressive Party, with Henry Wallace as its candidate, drew nearly half its votes from the state of New York. The American Independent Party polled nearly 10 million popular votes and forty-five electoral votes for George Wallace in 1968—the most electoral votes ever polled by a third-party candidate. But all of Wallace's electoral votes and the majority of his popular vote came from the states of the Deep South.

Americans usually assume that only the candidates nominated by one of the two major parties have any chance of winning an election. Thus, a vote cast for a third-party or independent candidate is often seen as a vote wasted. Voters who would prefer a third-party candidate may feel compelled to vote for the major-party candidate whom they regard as the "lesser of two evils" to avoid wasting their votes in a futile gesture. Third-party candidates must struggle—usually without success—to overcome the perception that they cannot win. Thus, in 1996, many voters who favored Ross Perot gave their votes to Bob Dole or Bill Clinton on the presumption that Perot was not really electable.

Under federal election law, any minor party receiving more than 5 percent of the national presidential vote is entitled to federal funds, though considerably less than the major parties receive. The Reform Party qualified by winning 8.2 percent in 1996. Ralph Nader, the Green Party candidate in 2000, hoped to win the 5 percent of the vote that would entitle the Green Party to federal funds. Though Nader may have drawn enough liberal votes in New Hampshire and Florida to give those states—and the national election—to the GOP, hopes of achieving the 5 percent threshold were dashed. Nader, nevertheless, resumed his presidential campaign in 2004 and 2008, although he had little impact in either race. The other third-party and independent candidates that ran in 2008 fell even farther from the 5 percent mark. Libertarian candidate Bob Barr, running on a platform of smaller government and more individual freedom, received less than half a percentage point of the vote and just under half a million votes. Independent candidates Charles Baldwin and Alan Keyes each received fewer than 200,000 votes in 2008.

Third parties are not active only in presidential races. During the 2002 off-year elections, third-party candidates ran for state office and for congressional seats in many states. Libertarian Party gubernatorial candidates received at least 2 percent of the vote in fifteen states, including a whopping 11 percent of the vote in Wisconsin. Green Party candidates also were active throughout the nation. Whereas the Green Party generally draws votes that might have been cast for Democrats, the Libertarians tend to be supported by individuals who might otherwise have voted for the GOP's candidate. Thus, the Libertarians' strong showing in Wisconsin helped to bring about a Democratic victory in that state in 2002.

As many scholars have pointed out, third-party prospects are also hampered by America's **single-member-district** plurality election system. In many other nations, several individuals can be elected to represent each legislative district. This is called a system of **multiple-member districts.** In this type of system, the candidates of weaker parties have a better chance of winning at least some seats, and voters, less concerned about wasting ballots, are usually more willing to support minor-party candidates.

Reinforcing the effects of the single-member district, the **plurality system** of voting (see Chapter 10) generally has the effect of setting what could be called a high threshold for victory. To win a plurality race, candidates usually must secure many more votes than they would need under most European systems of **proportional representation.** For example, to win an American plurality election in a single-member district where there are only two candidates, a politician must win more than 50 percent of the votes cast. To win a seat from a European multiple-member district under proportional rules, a candidate may need to win only 15 or 20 percent of the votes cast. This high American threshold discourages minor parties and encourages the various political factions that might otherwise form minor parties to minimize their differences and remain within the major-party coalitions.[6]

However, it is not strictly accurate to assert (as some scholars have) that America's single-member plurality election system is the major cause of its historical two-party pattern. All that can be said is that American election law depresses the number of parties likely to survive over long periods of time in the United States. There is nothing magical about two. Indeed, the single-member plurality system of election can also discourage second parties. After all, if one party consistently receives a large plurality of the vote, people may eventually come to see their vote *even for the second party* as a wasted effort. This happened to the Republican Party in the Deep South before World War II.

single-member district an electorate that is allowed to select only one representative from each district; the normal method of representation in the United States

multiple-member district an electorate that selects all candidates at large from the whole district; each voter is given the number of votes equivalent to the number of seats to be filled

plurality system a type of electoral system in which, to win a seat in the parliament or other representative body, a candidate need only receive the most votes in the election, not necessarily a majority of votes cast

proportional representation a multiple-member district system that allows each political party representation in proportion to its percentage of the total vote

party organization the formal structure of a political party, including its leadership, election committees, active members, and paid staff

caucus (political) a normally closed meeting of a political or legislative group to select candidates, plan strategy, or make decisions regarding legislative matters

national convention a national party political institution that nominates the party's presidential and vice presidential candidates, establishes party rules, and writes and ratifies the party's platform

Party Organization

In the United States, **party organizations** exist at virtually every level of government (see Figure 9.3). These organizations are usually committees made up of a number of active party members. State law and party rules prescribe how such committees are constituted. Usually, committee members are elected at local party meetings—called **caucuses**—or as part of the regular primary election. The best-known examples of these committees are at the national level—the Democratic National Committee and the Republican National Committee.

National Convention

At the national level, the party's most important institution is the **national convention.** The convention, held every four years, is attended by delegates from each of the states; as a group, they nominate the party's presidential and vice

FIGURE 9.3 ★ How American Parties Are Organized

presidential candidates, draft the party's campaign platform for the presidential race, and approve changes in the rules and regulations governing party procedures. Before World War II, presidential nominations occupied most of the time, energy, and effort expended at the national convention. The nomination process required days of negotiation and compromise among state party leaders and often required many ballots before a nominee was selected. In recent years, however, presidential candidates have essentially nominated themselves by capturing enough delegate support in primary elections to win the official nomination on the first ballot. The actual convention has played little or no role in selecting the candidates.

The convention's other two tasks, determining the party's rules and its platform, remain important. Party rules can determine the relative influence of competing factions within the party and can also increase or decrease the party's chances for electoral success. In 1972, for example, the Democratic National Convention adopted a new set of rules favored by the party's liberal wing. Under these rules, state delegations to the Democratic convention were required to include women and members of minority groups in rough proportion to those groups' representation among the party's membership in that state. Liberals correctly calculated that women and African Americans would generally support liberal ideas and candidates. The rules also called for the use of proportional representation—a voting system liberals thought would give them an advantage by allowing the election of more women and minority delegates. (Although Republican rules do not require proportional representation, some state legislatures have moved to compel both parties to use this system in their presidential primaries.)

The convention also approves the party **platform.** Platforms are often dismissed as documents filled with platitudes that voters seldom read. To some extent this criticism is well founded. Not one voter in a thousand so much as glances at the party platform, and even the news media pay little attention to the documents. Furthermore, the parties' presidential candidates make little use of the platforms in their campaigns; usually they prefer to develop and promote their own themes. Nonetheless, the platform can be an important document. The platform should be understood as a contract in which the various party factions attending the convention state their terms for supporting the ticket. For one faction, welfare reform may be a key issue. For another faction, tax reduction may be more important. For a third, the critical issue might be deficit reduction. When one of these "planks" is included in the platform, its promoters are asserting that this is what they want in exchange for their support for the ticket, while other party factions are agreeing that the position seems reasonable and appropriate. Thus, party platforms should be seen more as internal party documents than as public pledges. The 2008 Democratic platform, for example, included a plank aimed at cities, promising to "strengthen the federal commitment to cities." Urban areas have long formed the backbone of Democratic political strength. A party plank pledging aid to cities and metropolitan areas rewards a key constituency whose enthusiastic support is crucial to a Democratic victory. Because party platforms are written more for the delegates than for ordinary voters, they tend to be less centrist than the presidential candidates themselves. A presidential candidate hoping to win over "swing" voters in addition to the party faithful has to stake out more moderate positions. Thus, the 2008 Republican platform presented more extreme views on issues like environmental regulation and the rights of same-sex couples than candidate John McCain.

platform a party document, written at a national convention, that contains party philosophy, principles, and positions on issues

Delegates from each state attend the party's national convention. In 2008, Democratic Party delegates from Wisconsin supported Barack Obama after he won the Wisconsin primary.

National Committee

Between conventions, each national political party is technically headed by its national committee. For the Democrats and Republicans, these are called the Democratic National Committee (DNC) and the Republican National Committee (RNC), respectively. These national committees raise campaign funds, head off factional disputes within the party, and endeavor to enhance the party's media image. The actual work of each national committee is overseen by its chairperson. Mike Duncan, the chair of the Republican National Committee, was active in local, state, and national Republican politics before he became chair in 2007. The Democratic National Committee is chaired by the former presidential candidate Howard Dean, whose innovative grassroots presidential campaign and pledge to reinvent the Democratic Party led to his election as party chairperson in 2005. Other committee members are generally major party contributors or fund-raisers and serve in a largely ceremonial capacity. Prior to the enactment of campaign finance reforms in 2002, during every election cycle the DNC and RNC each raised tens of millions of dollars of so-called soft money that could be used to support party candidates throughout the nation. The 2002 Bipartisan Campaign Reform Act (BCRA), sometimes known as the McCain-Feingold Act, outlawed this practice. To circumvent BCRA, however, each party has established a set of "shadow parties." These are groups nominally organized to promote and publicize political issues and, as such, can claim tax-exempt status under Section 527 of the Internal Revenue Code, which defines and provides tax-exempt status for nonprofit political advocacy groups. Such groups are sometimes called **527 committees** because of this provision of the tax code.

527 committees nonprofit independent groups that receive and disburse funds to influence the nomination, election, or defeat of candidates. Named after Section 527 of the Internal Revenue Code, which defines and grants tax-exempt status to nonprofit advocacy groups

Under the law, 527 committees can raise and spend unlimited amounts of money as long as their activities are not coordinated with those of the formal party organizations. Although some 527 committees are actually independent, many are directed by former Republican and Democratic party officials and run shadow campaigns on behalf of the parties. On the Republican side, a major shadow is the Republican Club for Growth, which raises and spends millions of dollars for GOP television ads. Democratic shadows include such groups as Americans Coming Together (ACT) and the Media Fund, which together raised tens of millions of dollars in support of Senator John Kerry's presidential bid. In 2004 the Federal Election Commission (FEC) affirmed the legality of unlimited spending by 527 groups.[7] In the 2008 election cycle, more soft money was funneled through nonprofit organizations formed specifically to support particular candidates. This change was the result of a 2007 Supreme Court decision that overturned parts of the BCRA, allowing corporations, including nonprofits, to run issue advertisements in the days leading up to the primaries and general elections.[8] Soft money played a less prominent role in the 2008 election in part because the presidential candidates and their parties created such successful fund-raising operations. But a diverse array of outside groups, including the U.S. Chamber of Commerce, the National Rifle Association, and Defenders of Wildlife Action Fund, continued to raise and spend large sums of money on competitive congressional races.

Politics Today

Why did 527 committees play a less prominent role in the 2008 presidential race?

Whichever party controls the White House, the party's national committee chair is appointed by the president. Typically, this means that that party's national committee becomes little more than an adjunct to the White House staff. For a first-term president, the committee devotes the bulk of its energy to the re-election campaign. The national committee chair of the party not in control of the White House is selected by the committee itself and usually takes a broader view of the party's needs, raising money and performing other activities on behalf of the party's members in Congress and in the state legislatures.

Are More Parties Better Than Two Parties?

Despite occasionally strong performances by third parties, America is one of the few nations that has maintained an enduring two-party political system, beginning with the Federalist and Antifederalist parties in the postcolonial period. Today's Democratic Party is the world's oldest viable party; the younger Republican Party dates from the 1850s. America's stubborn loyalty to its two parties has been complicated by persistent criticisms of both of them, including charges that they are little different from one another and that they monopolize political power, choke off new ideas, and restrict the influx of new leaders with different ideas.

These and other criticisms have produced support for the idea of a multiparty system (any political system with three or more active parties is considered a multiparty system). American history supports the idea that third parties can help the political process. First, new parties can raise new and important issues ignored by the two major parties. In the pre–Civil War era, the Liberty and Free Soil parties advanced the cause of slavery abolition when the dominant Democratic and Whig parties were unable to come to grips with the issue. Early in the twentieth century, the Progressive Party advanced a vast array of social and political reforms that Democrats and Republicans eventually embraced. Ross Perot's Reform Party moved issues such as deficit spending and budgetary responsibility to center stage in 1992. Second, as these examples suggest, a third-party option gives voters more choices among candidates and issues, addressing a persistent voter complaint. Third, most democratic nations have a multiparty system, showing that the idea not only is viable, but is a routine part of the workings of democracy. Fourth, new parties might spark renewed voter interest in an electoral system that now attracts fewer than half of the eligible adult electorate to the voting booth. And fifth, states such as Minnesota and New York have maintained an active multiparty tradition (although in these states, the two major parties still dominate), suggesting that some version of the idea could indeed work on a national level.

Supporters of two-partyism argue that the virtues of the existing system are taken for granted. First and foremost, a two-party system produces automatic majorities, for the obvious reason that one will always receive over 50 percent of the vote. In a nation as large and diverse as America, governance could easily become impossible, or at least far more difficult, if multiple parties produced a bevy of candidates with no clear winner, or if American legislatures were populated with representatives from many different parties, barring any one party from organizing power. A second and related point is that the compromises that produce two candidates from two large parties also generally encourage moderation, compromise, and stability. Multiple parties might well heighten polarization and paralysis in America in a way that would make contemporary political gridlock seem tame by comparison. And although many democracies have multiparty systems, politics in those nations is often polarized and unstable. The Italian multiparty system, for example, produced over forty different governing coalitions in its first fifty years after the end of World War II. Third, the charge of exclusion of new factions and ideas by the two parties misses the fact that the two American parties are very large and diverse. In other nations, political conflict plays out among multiple parties. In America, much of that conflict occurs within the parties, especially during the nomination process. Fourth, America's enduring two-party system is a product of its political culture and historical development. The idea that a multiparty system could simply be transplanted onto the American political landscape is a leap of faith little supported by actual experience.

FOR CRITICAL ANALYSIS

1. Third parties are formed in the United States every year, but few last more than one or two electoral cycles. Why do third parties tend to be short lived?
2. Should voters support a third party that has no chance of winning? Or should they vote for the major party candidate they dislike least?

Congressional Campaign Committees

Each party also forms House and Senate campaign committees to raise funds for House and Senate election campaigns. Their efforts may or may not be coordinated with the activities of the national committees. Within the party that controls the White House, the national committee and the congressional campaign committees are often rivals, since both groups are seeking donations from the same people but for different candidates: the national committee seeks funds for the presidential race, while the congressional campaign committees approach the same contributors for support for the congressional contests. In recent years, the Republican Party has attempted to coordinate the fund-raising activities of all its committees. Republicans have sought to give the GOP's national institutions the capacity to invest funds in those close congressional, state, and local races where they can do the most good. The Democrats have been slower to coordinate their various committee activities, and this may have placed them at a disadvantage in recent congressional and local races.

State and Local Party Organizations

Each of the two major parties has a central committee in each state. The parties traditionally also have county committees and, in some instances, state senate district committees, judicial district committees, and in the case of larger cities, citywide party committees and local assembly district "ward" committees as well. Congressional districts also may have party committees.

Some cities also have precinct committees. Precincts are not districts from which any representative is elected but instead are legally defined subdivisions of wards that are used to register voters and set up ballot boxes or voting machines. A precinct is typically composed of 300 to 600 voters. Well-organized political parties—especially the famous old machines of New York, Chicago, and Boston—provided for "precinct captains" and a fairly tight group of party members around them. Precinct captains were usually members of long standing in neighborhood party clubhouses, which were important social centers as well as places for distributing favors to constituents.[9]

machines strong party organizations in late-nineteenth- and early-twentieth-century American cities. These machines were led by "bosses" who controlled party nominations and patronage

patronage the resources available to higher officials, usually opportunities to make partisan appointments to offices and to confer grants, licenses, or special favors to supporters

During the nineteenth and early twentieth centuries, many cities, counties, and occasionally even a few states had such well-organized parties that they were called **machines** and their leaders were called "bosses." Some of the great reform movements in American history were motivated by the excessive powers and abuses of these machines and their bosses. But few, if any, machines are left today. Traditional party machines depended heavily on **patronage,** their power to control government jobs. With thousands of jobs to dispense, party bosses were able to recruit armies of political workers who, in turn, mobilized millions of voters. Today, because of civil-service reform, party leaders no longer control many positions. Nevertheless, state and local party organizations are very active in recruiting candidates and conducting voter registration drives. In addition, under current federal law, state and local party organizations can spend unlimited amounts of money on "party-building" activities such as voter registration and get-out-the-vote drives (though in some states such practices are limited by state law). As a result, for many years the national party organizations, which have enormous fund-raising abilities but were restricted by law in how much they could spend on candidates, transferred millions of dollars to the state and local organizations. The state and local parties, in turn, spent these funds, sometimes called **"soft money,"** to promote national, as well as state and local, political activities. In this process, local organizations became linked financially to the national parties and American political parties became somewhat more integrated and nationalized than ever before. At the same time, the state and local party organizations came to control large financial resources and play important roles in elections despite the collapse of the old patronage machines.[10]

soft money money contributed directly to political parties for political activities that is not regulated by federal campaign spending laws

The Bipartisan Campaign Reform Act (McCain-Feingold) of 2002 prohibits soft-money contributions to national, state, and local political parties. Critics of the act argue that it weakens political parties and strengthens interest groups, which remain free to spend as much as they wish as long as their expenditures are not formally coordinated with a candidate's own campaign. In the 2008 election cycle, soft money groups played an important, though relatively low-profile role. For example, the National Rifle Association planned to spend $40 million on advertisements and efforts to turn gun owners out to vote. The Planned Parenthood Action Fund sponsored advertisements describing the candidates' positions on reproductive issues and aimed to contact and turn out sympathetic women voters in battleground states.

Parties and the Electorate

Party organizations are more than just organizations; they are made up of millions of rank-and-file members. Individual voters tend to develop **party identification** with one of the political parties. Although it is a psychological tie, party identification also has a rational component. Voters generally form attachments to parties that reflect their views and interests. Once those attachments are formed, however, they are likely to persist and even to be handed down to children, unless some very strong factors convince individuals that their party is no longer an appropriate object of their affections. In some sense, party identification is similar to brand loyalty

party identification an individual voter's psychological ties to one party or another

Party affiliations help voters decide whom and what to vote for when they are not familiiar with all of the candidates and issues. Parties provide information directly through voter guides and other materials, and indirectly through the party affiliations of the candidates.

in the marketplace: consumers choose a brand of automobile for its appearance or mechanical characteristics and stick with it out of loyalty, habit, and unwillingness to reexamine their choices constantly, but they may eventually change if the old brand no longer serves their interests.

Although the percentage of independents is high, most Americans continue to identify with either the Republican Party or the Democratic Party (see Figure 9.4). Party identification gives citizens a stake in election outcomes that goes beyond the particular race at hand. This is why strong party identifiers are more likely than other Americans to go to the polls and, of course, are more likely than others to support the party with which they identify. **Party activists** are drawn from the ranks of the strong identifiers. Activists are those who not only vote but also contribute their time, energy, and effort to party affairs. No party could succeed without the thousands of volunteers who undertake the mundane tasks needed to keep the organization going. Many party activists devote their time to politics because they have strong beliefs on particular policy issues. Across a range of issues, the views of party activists tend to be more extreme than the views of the party's rank-and-file voters. The views of Democratic activists are more liberal than those of Democratic voters, whereas the views of Republican activists are more conservative than those of Republican voters. One study that compared the views of party activists and rank-and-file voters across a range of issues found that since

party activists partisans who contribute time, energy, and effort to support their party and its candidates

FIGURE 9.4 ★ Americans' Party Identification, 1952–2008

Over time, the Democrats lost strength as more Americans identify themselves as Republicans and independents. However, the percent identifying as Democrats has grown in recent years. Why do you think the percentage of people identifying themselves as independents grew during the 1970s?

*From 2000–2007, Independent includes "No Preference."
SOURCES: From 1952–1996: American National Election Studies, www.electionstudies.org/nesguide/toptable/tab2a_1.htm; 2000–2006: The Pew Research Center for the People and the Press, www.people-press.org/reports/pdf/312.pdf; 2007–2008: http://people-press.org/report/?pageid=1340 (accessed 8/8/08).

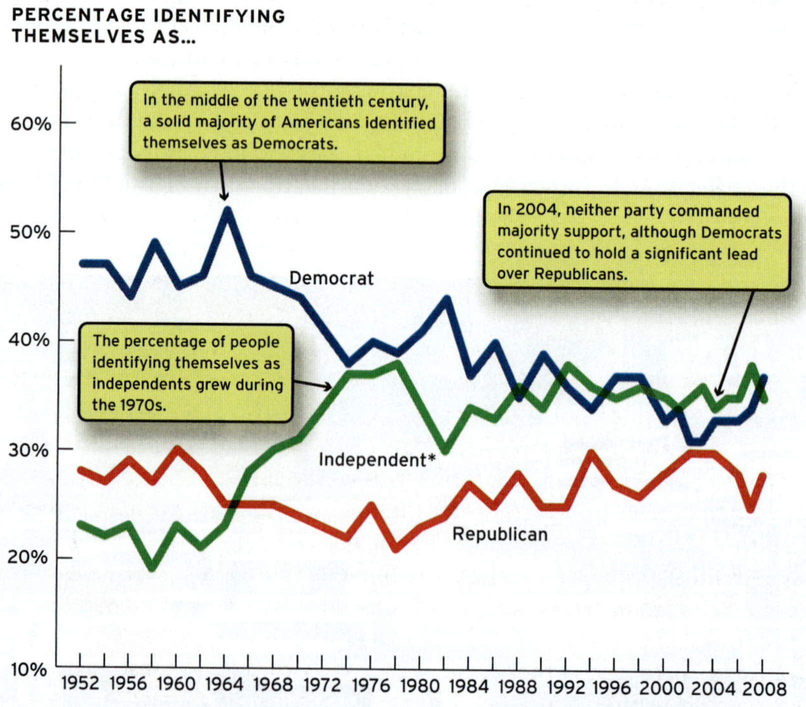

the 1990s, the views of Republican party activists have diverged most sharply from those of the average voter.[11]

Group Affiliations

The Democratic and Republican parties are currently America's only truly national parties. They are the only political organizations that draw support from most regions of the country and from Americans of every racial, economic, religious, and ethnic group. The two parties do not draw equal support from members of every social stratum, however. In the United States today, a variety of group characteristics are associated with party identification. These include race and ethnicity, gender, religion, class, ideology, region, and age.

RACE AND ETHNICITY Since the 1930s and Franklin Roosevelt's New Deal, African Americans have been overwhelmingly Democratic in their party identification. More than 90 percent of African Americans describe themselves as Democrats and support Democratic candidates in national, state, and local elections. In 2008, 95 percent of African Americans supported the Democratic candidate, Senator Barack Obama. Latino voters do not form a monolithic bloc, by contrast. Cuban Americans have generally leaned Republican in their party affiliations, whereas Mexican Americans favored the Democrats by a small margin. Other Latino voters, including those from Puerto Rico, have tended to be overwhelmingly Democratic. This mix of partisan preferences shifted strongly toward the Democrats in 2008, when the exit polls showed that 67 percent of Latinos supported Senator Obama, and 31 percent of Latinos voted for Senator McCain. The Latino vote is particularly important because it can help alter the electoral map. In 2008, the Latino vote in swing states such as Florida, Colorado, New Mexico, and Nevada helped bring the Democrats to victory. Asian Americans have been divided in past elections, but in 2008, 62 percent of Asian Americans voted for Barack Obama, and 35 percent voted for John McCain.

GENDER Women are somewhat more likely to support Democrats, and men are somewhat more likely to support Republicans, in surveys of party affiliation. This difference is known as the **gender gap.** The gender gap has varied between 6 and 11 percent since 1992. For example, in 1992, 47 percent of women voted for Bill Clinton compared to 41 percent of men. The gap grew to 11 percent in 1996, when 54 percent of women supported Clinton and only 43 percent of men did. George W. Bush's first election, in 2000, had a sizeable gender gap of 53 percent support among men and 43 percent among women. In 2004, the gender gap decreased slightly, with 55 percent of men voting for Bush compared with 48 percent of women. In 2008, the gap remained on the small side, with 56 percent of women and 49 percent of men supporting Barack Obama for president. Obama's near-majority support among men was the highest for a Democratic candidate in many years.

gender gap a distinctive pattern of voting behavior reflecting the differences in views between women and men

RELIGION Jews are among the Democratic Party's most loyal constituent groups and have been since the New Deal. Nearly 90 percent of all Jewish Americans describe themselves as Democrats. Catholics were also once a strongly pro-Democratic group but have been shifting toward the Republican Party since the

When the leading candidates in the 2008 presidential election emerged as Hillary Clinton—a woman, Barack Obama—an African American, and John McCain, who would be the oldest American president if elected, observers questioned how the traditional affiliations of racial, gender, and age groups would play out.

1970s, when the GOP began to focus on abortion and other social issues deemed to be important to Catholics. Protestants are more likely to identify with the Republicans than with the Democrats. Protestant fundamentalists, in particular, have been drawn to the GOP's conservative stands on social issues, such as school prayer and abortion. The importance of religious conservatives to the Republican Party became quite evident in 2001. After his victory in the November 2000 presidential election, George W. Bush announced that his administration would seek to award federal grants and contracts to religious groups. By using so-called faith-based groups as federal contractors, Bush was seeking to reward religious conservatives for their past loyalty to the GOP and to ensure that these groups would have a continuing stake in Republican success. Religious conservatives, particularly white born-again Christians, overwhelmingly supported President Bush in 2004, accounting for one-third of his votes. Almost 80 percent of white born-again Christians voted for President Bush; only 21 percent supported Kerry. Yet the 2004 election results also revealed that religiosity—as measured by frequency of attendance at religious services—had a larger impact on voting than denominational affiliation. Voters who attended religious services weekly were more likely to vote for Bush, regardless of their religion, than were voters who were less observant. In 2008 it appeared that the white evangelical vote might be somewhat more open to voting Democratic, and Barack Obama sought to appeal to this group.[12] However, exit polls showed that white evangelicals continued to vote overwhelmingly Republican, giving McCain 76 percent of their votes.

Politics Today

Which groups voted for Democrats and which for Republicans in 2008? Did this represent change or continuity in terms of past elections?

CLASS The patterns of class voting that emerged from the New Deal of the 1930s were simple: upper-income Americans were considerably more likely to affiliate with the Republicans, whereas lower-income Americans were far more likely to identify with the Democrats. This divide is reflected by the differences between the two parties on economic issues. In general, the Republicans support cutting taxes and social spending—positions that reflect the interests of the wealthy. The Democrats, however, favor increasing social spending, even if this requires increasing taxes—a position consistent with the interests of less-affluent Americans. These broad trends remain true today, but beginning in the 1970s, many white working class voters, concerned about "law and order" and racial liberalism, started voting Republican. Often called "Reagan Democrats" because so many voted for Reagan in the 1980s, some of these voters have remained in the Republican Party. Analysts disagree about the trend of class voting because there is no widely accepted definition of class. When the electorate is divided into thirds on the basis of income, the relationship between lower-income voters and Democratic allegiance remains strong. When class is measured by education, however, white workers without a college degree have voted heavily for Republicans in recent elections.[13]

A large majority of evangelical Christians identify with the Republican party. In 2008, John McCain sought the support of Reverend Jerry Falwell and other Christian leaders, attempting to reassure them that the Republicans would continue to support policies they favored.

IDEOLOGY Ideology and party identification are very closely linked. Most individuals who describe themselves as conservatives identify with the Republican Party, whereas most who call themselves liberals support the Democrats. This division has increased in recent years as the two parties have taken very different positions on social and economic issues. Before the 1970s, when party differences were more blurred, it was not uncommon to find Democratic conservatives and Republican liberals. Both of these species are rare today. Yet important differences remain among conservatives and among liberals. Economic conservatives care most about reducing government regulation and taxes. Social conservatives are concerned about social issues such as abortion and gay marriage. The Republican Party includes both groups, but at times the interests of these two kinds of conservatives conflict. Likewise, many Democrats who are economic liberals in favor of generous social spending, are conservative when it comes to matters such as gun control.

REGION After the 2000 election, red and blue maps appeared showing the regional distribution of the vote. Democrats, represented as "Blue America," were clustered on the coasts and the upper Midwest. Republicans, represented as "Red America," were concentrated in the Mountain West, the Southwest, and the South.

The explanations for these regional variations are complex. Between the Civil War and the 1960s, the "Solid South" was a Democratic bastion. Today the South is solidly Republican. Southern Republicanism has come about because conservative white southerners identify the Democratic Party with the civil rights movement and with liberal positions on abortion, school prayer, and other social issues. Republican strength in the South is also related to the weakness of organized labor in these regions, as well as to the dependence of the two regions on military programs supported by the Republicans. Democratic strength in the Northeast and Midwest is a function of the continuing influence of organized labor in the large cities of this region, as well as of the region's large population of minority and elderly voters, who benefit from Democratic social programs. The coastal West, especially California, shifted toward the Democrats in the 1990s, in part because of the growing importance of the Latino vote.

AGE Age is another factor associated with partisanship. In 2008, the shift toward the Democratic party affected all age groups but it was particularly strong among young voters. Polls showed that, while older voters preferred Democrats by 11–12 percent, those born after 1977 favored Democrats by 24 percent. There is nothing about a particular numerical age that leads to a particular party loyalty. Instead, individuals from the same age cohort are likely to have experienced a similar set of events during the period when their party loyalties were formed. Thus, Americans between the ages of fifty and sixty-four came of political age during the Cold War, Vietnam, and civil rights eras. Apparently among voters whose initial perceptions of politics were shaped during this period, more responded favorably to the role played by the Democrats than to the actions of the Republicans. Young people who came of age during the Bush presidency had the strongest Democratic party identification of any age group.

For Critical Analysis

What are the major components of each party's political coalition? What factors tie these groups to their respective parties?

Figure 9.5 indicates the relationship between party identification and a number of social criteria. Race, religion, and income seem to have the greatest influence on Americans' party affiliations. None of these social characteristics are inevitably linked to partisan identification, however. There are black Republicans, southern white Democrats, Jewish Republicans, and even an occasional conservative Democrat. The general party identifications just discussed are broad tendencies that both reflect and reinforce the issue and policy positions the two parties take in the national and local political arenas.

Parties and Elections

Parties play an important role in the electoral process. They provide the candidates for office, get out the vote, and facilitate mass electoral choice.

Recruiting Candidates

One of the most important but least noticed party activities is the recruitment of candidates for local, state, and national office. Each election year, candidates must be found for thousands of state and local offices as well as congressional seats. Where they do not have an incumbent running for re-election, party leaders attempt to identify strong candidates and to interest them in entering the campaign.

An ideal candidate will have an unblemished record and the capacity to raise enough money to mount a serious campaign. Party leaders are usually not willing to provide financial backing to candidates who are unable to raise substantial funds on their own. For a House seat this can mean several hundred thousand dollars; for a Senate seat a serious candidate must be able to raise several million dollars. Often, party leaders have difficulty finding attractive candidates and persuading them to run. Candidate recruitment is problematic in an era when political campaigns often involve mudslinging, and candidates must assume that their personal lives will be intensely scrutinized in the press.[14]

Nominations

Article I, Section 4, of the Constitution makes only a few provisions for elections. It delegates to the states the power to set the "times, places, and manner" of

FIGURE 9.5 ★
Party Identification by Social Groups, 2006

Party identification varies sharply by income, ideology, and race. Republicans are strongest among whites, higher-income voters, and those who identify themselves a conservatives. Democrats are strongest among those who identify themselves as liberals, lower-income voters and black people. Women are substantially more likely to identify as Democrats than are men. How do younger people differ from older people in their party identification? How does education affect party identification? Are there regional differences in the strength of the two parties?

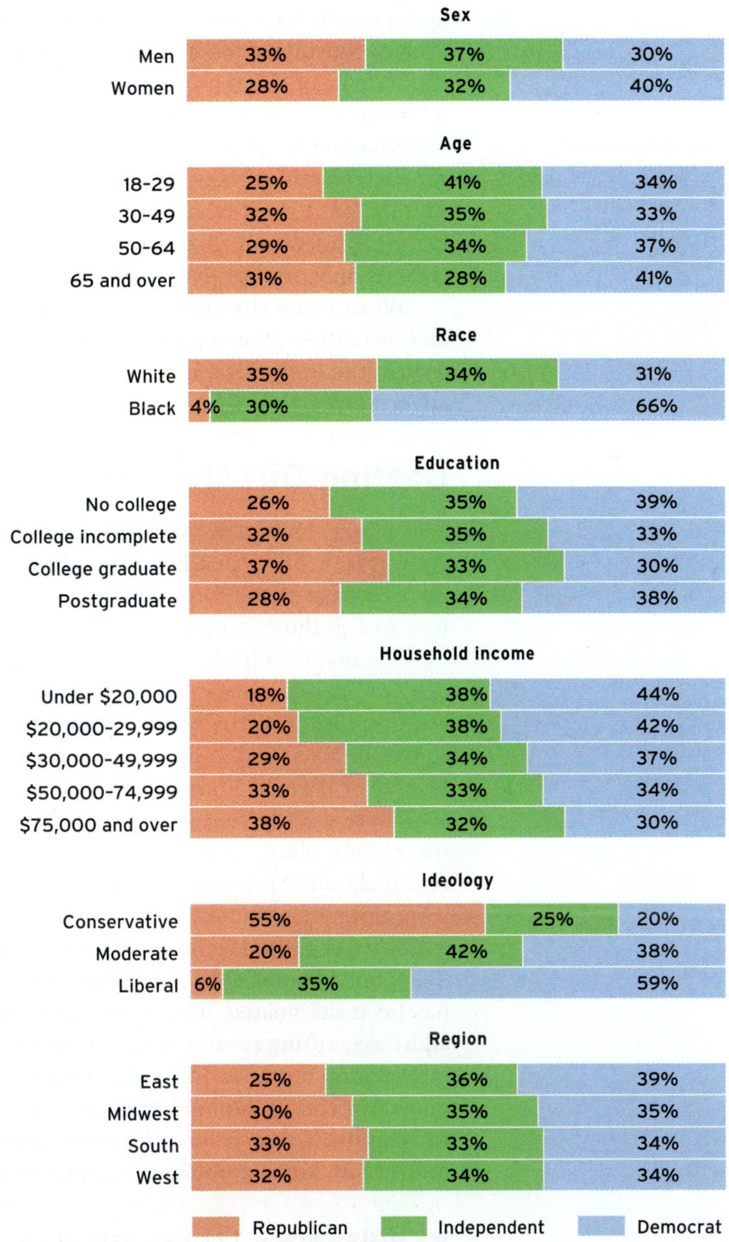

NOTE: Group percentages are rounded and may equal more than 100 percent in this graph.
SOURCE: Harold W. Stanley and Richard G. Niemi, *Vital Statistics on American Politics, 2007–2008* (Washington, DC: Congressional Quarterly Press, 2008), 122.

holding elections, even for U.S. senators and representatives. It does, however, reserve to Congress the power to make such laws if it chooses to do so. The Constitution has been amended from time to time to expand the right to participate in elections. Congress has also occasionally passed laws about elections, congressional districting, and campaign practices. But the Constitution and the laws are almost completely silent on nominations, setting only citizenship and age requirements for candidates. The president must be at least thirty-five years of age, a native-born citizen, and a resident of the United States for fourteen years. A senator must be at least thirty, a U.S. citizen for at least nine years, and a resident of the state he or she represents. A member of the House must be at least twenty-five, a U.S. citizen for seven years, and a resident of the state he or she represents.

nomination the process through which political parties select their candidates for election to public office

Nomination is the process by which a party selects a single candidate to run for each elective office. The nominating process can precede the election by many months, as it does when the many candidates for the presidency are eliminated from consideration through a grueling series of debates and state primaries until there is only one survivor in each party—the party's nominee.

When more than one person aspires to an office, the choice can divide friends and associates. In comparison to such an internal dispute, the electoral campaign against the opposition is almost fun, because there the fight is against the declared adversaries.

Getting Out the Vote

The actual election period begins immediately after the nominations. Throughout American history, this has been a time of glory for the political parties, whose popular base of support is fully displayed. All the paraphernalia of party committees and all the committee members are activated into local party work forces.

The first step in the electoral process involves voter registration. This aspect of the process takes place all year round. There was a time when party workers were responsible for virtually all of this kind of electoral activity, but they have been supplemented (and in many states virtually displaced) by civic groups such as the League of Women Voters, unions, and chambers of commerce.

Those who have registered have to decide on Election Day whether to go to the polling place, stand in line, and actually vote for the various candidates and referenda on the ballot. Political parties, candidates, and campaigning can make a big difference in convincing the voters to vote. In recent years, each of the two major parties has developed extensive data files on hundreds of millions of potential voters. The GOP has called its archive "Voter Vault," while the Democratic file has been designated "Demzilla." Democrats claim their files contain the names, addresses, voting preferences, contribution history, ethnic backgrounds, and other information on some 165 million Americans. Republican files contain similar data on nearly 200 million individuals. These elaborate data files allow the two parties to bring their search for votes, contributions, and campaign help down to named individuals. Voter mobilization, once an art, has now become a science.

Facilitating Voter Choice

On any general election ballot, there are likely to be only two or three candidacies where the nature of the office and the characteristics and positions of the candidates are well known to voters. But what about the choices for judges, the state comptroller, the state attorney general, and many other elective positions? And what about referenda? This method of making policy choices is being used more and more as a means of direct democracy. A referendum may ask: Should there be a new bond issue for financing the local schools? Should there be a constitutional amendment to increase the number of county judges? In 1996, Californians approved Proposition 209, a referendum that called for an end to most statewide affirmative action programs, including those employed for college admission. Another famous proposition on the 1978 California ballot was a referendum to reduce local property taxes. It started a taxpayer revolt that spread to many other states. By the time the revolt had spread, most voters knew where they stood on the issue. But the typical referendum question is one on which few voters have clear and knowledgeable positions. Parties and campaigns help most by providing information when voters must choose among obscure candidates and vote on unclear referenda.

Parties and Government

When the dust of the campaign has settled, does it matter which party has won? It can. When the parties are sharply divided ideologically, as they have been in recent years, the party that controls government can make significant changes moving policy in new directions.

Parties and Policy

One of the most familiar observations about American politics is that the two major parties try to be all things to all people and are therefore indistinguishable from each other. Data and experience give some support to this observation. Parties in the United States are not programmatic or ideological, as they have sometimes been in Britain or other parts of Europe. But this does not mean there are no differences between them. Since the 1980s, important differences have emerged between the positions of Democratic and Republican party leaders on a number of key issues, and these differences are still apparent today. For example, the national leadership of the Republican Party supports maintaining high levels of military spending, cuts in social programs, tax relief for middle- and upper-income voters, tax incentives for businesses, and the "social agenda" backed by members of conservative religious denominations. The national Democratic leadership, on the other hand, supports expanded social welfare spending, cuts in military spending, increased regulation of business, and a variety of consumer and environmental programs.

These differences reflect differences in philosophy and differences in the core constituencies to which the parties seek to appeal. The Democratic Party at the national level seeks to unite organized labor, the poor, members of racial minorities, and liberal upper-middle-class professionals. The Republicans, by contrast, appeal to business, upper-middle- and upper-class groups in the private sector, white working-class voters, and social conservatives. Often, party leaders will seek to develop issues they hope will add new groups to their party's constituent base. During the 1980s, for example, under the leadership of Ronald Reagan, the Republicans devised a series of "social issues," including support for school prayer, opposition to abortion, and opposition to affirmative action, designed to cultivate the support of white southerners. This effort was extremely successful in increasing Republican strength in the once solidly Democratic South. In the 1990s, under the leadership of Bill Clinton, who called himself a "new Democrat," the Democratic Party sought to develop new social programs designed to solidify the party's base among working-class and poor voters, and new, somewhat more conservative economic programs aimed at attracting the votes of middle- and upper-middle-class voters. In 2000, George W. Bush labeled himself a "compassionate conservative" to signal the Republican base that he was a conservative while seeking to reassure moderate and independent voters that he was not an opponent of federal social programs.

As these examples suggest, parties do not always support policies just because their constituents already favor those policies. Instead, party leaders can play the role of **policy entrepreneurs,** seeking ideas and programs that will expand their party's base of support while eroding that of the opposition. It is one of the essential characteristics of party politics in America that a party's programs and policies often lead, rather than follow, public opinion. Like their counterparts in the business world, party leaders seek to identify and develop "products" (programs and policies) that will appeal to the public. The public, of course, has the ultimate voice. With its votes it decides whether or not to "buy" new policy offerings.

policy entrepreneur an individual who identifies a problem as a political issue and brings a policy proposal into the political agenda

Thus, for example, in 2007, all the Democratic presidential hopefuls proposed new programs in the realms of health care, which they hoped would expand their own political bases as well as increase support for the Democratic Party.

Parties in Congress

The ultimate test of the party system is its relationship to and influence on the institutions of government. Congress, in particular, depends more on the party system than is generally recognized. For one thing, the speakership of the House is essentially a party office. All the members of the House take part in the election of the Speaker. But the actual selection is made by the **majority party,** that is, the party that holds a majority of seats in the House. (The other party is known as the **minority party.**) When the majority-party caucus presents a nominee to the entire House, its choice is then invariably ratified in a straight vote along party lines.

majority party the party that holds the majority of legislative seats in either the House or the Senate

minority party the party that holds a minority of legislative seats in either the House or the Senate

The committee system of both houses of Congress is also a product of the two-party system. Although the whole membership adopts the rules organizing committees and the rules defining the jurisdiction of each like ordinary legislation, parties shape all other features of the committees. For example, each party is assigned a quota of members for each committee, depending on the percentage of total seats held by the party. On the rare occasions when an independent or third-party candidate is elected, the leaders of the two parties must agree against whose quota this member's committee assignments will count. Presumably the member will not be able to serve on any committee until the question of quota is settled.

As we shall see in Chapter 12, the assignment of individual members to committees is a party decision. Each party has a "committee on committees" to make such decisions. Granting permission to transfer to another committee is also a party decision. Moreover, advancement up the committee ladder toward the chair is a party decision. Since the late nineteenth century, most advancements have been automatic—based on the length of continual service on the committee. This seniority system has existed only because of the support of the two parties, however, and either party can depart from it by a simple vote. During the 1970s, both parties reinstituted the practice of reviewing each chair—voting anew every two years on whether the same person would continue to hold each committee's chair. In their 1994 campaign document, the "Contract with America," House Republican candidates pledged to limit committee and subcommittee chairs to three two-year

Partisanship in the Media

Although partisan media figures like Rush Limbaugh and Michael Moore have no formal relationships with the Republican or Democratic parties, they often play a significant role in mobilizing party supporters. Strongly partisan media serve a useful function for the political parties, because while they speak to the party's base, party leaders can maintain a distance from polarizing figures such as Limbaugh and Moore and focus on appealing to people towards the middle of the political spectrum.

The conservative political talk radio host Rush Limbaugh began his career in 1988, soon after the Federal Communications Commission rescinded the Fairness Doctrine, allowing radio stations to air opinion commentary without giving equal attention to the opposing point of view. Limbaugh earned notoriety for his unapologetic criticism of liberal fiscal and social policies, and his colorful insults. Throughout the 1990s, *The Rush Limbaugh Show* grew in popularity and soon attracted the largest number of talk radio listeners in the country.

In 1996, the comedian and political satirist Al Franken wrote a book titled *Rush Limbaugh Is a Big Fat Idiot and Other Observations,* in which he criticized Limbaugh and Republican political leaders. In 2003, Franken published another satirical book, *Lies and the Lying Liars Who Tell Them: A Fair and Balanced Look at the Right*, that caused a legal battle with Fox News. In 2004, Franken became one of the founders of the Air America Radio Network, airing news and satire from a progressive liberal perspective.

In 2004, the filmmaker Michael Moore released his controversial documentary *Fahrenheit 9/11*, which criticized the Bush administration's response to the terrorist attacks of September 11. By the end of the film's first day in theaters, *Fahrenheit 9/11* was the top-grossing documentary in the nation's history. However, many accused the filmmaker of creating an unfair and inaccurate portrayal of the administration's policies, and some theater owners refused to show the documentary.[a]

The question often asked about strongly partisan programs, books, and films is, "Do these messages persuade the public?" Because their audiences tend to favor the creator's point of view in the first place, the persuasive power of overtly partisan media is limited. A study by the National Annenberg Election Survey found that the audiences of Rush Limbaugh's talk radio show and Michael Moore's documentary were about equivalent in size and about as far apart as they could be in terms of public opinion regarding George W. Bush, the Iraq war, and whether or not the country was moving "in the right direction." As the survey's director Kathleen Jamieson explained, "One-sided partisan communication tends to attract an audience of believers and reinforces their beliefs rather than change their minds."[b]

The legal scholar Cass Sunstein argues that the rise of such fragmented media may have negative consequences for the health of the democracy.

As digital media expand Americans' content options, it will become easier for citizens to only see and hear about the topics and points of view that they favor. Partisan media is not a negative in and of itself. If people listen to Rush Limbaugh in the morning and Air America in the afternoon, listeners might obtain the liberal and conservative perspectives, which could thwart the polarization effect. But how many liberals are listening to Limbaugh? How many conservatives are listening to Franken?

FOR CRITICAL ANALYSIS

1. If tuning in to partisan media that favors our preexisting opinions is bad for society, what is the answer? Should writers and producers be required to include opposing points of view?
2. Party leaders tend to distance themselves from highly partisan media figures, even as they rely on them to help maintain the support of their base. Why?

---

a. "Less Moore, *Fahrenheit 9/11* in Iowa," *Chicago Sun-Times,* July 5, 2004.

b. National Annenberg Election Survey, "*Fahrenheit 9/11* Viewers and Limbaugh Listeners about Equal in Size Even Though They Perceive Two Different Nations, Annenberg Data Show," press release, August 3, 2004, www.annenbergpublicpolicycenter.org/Downloads/Political_Communication/NAES/Release_fahrenheit_20040803.pdf (accessed 2/24/08).

terms if the GOP won control of Congress. For years, Republicans had argued that entrenched Democratic committee chairs had become powerful, arrogant, and indifferent to the popular will. When Republicans took control of Congress in 1994, they reaffirmed their pledge to limit the terms of committee and subcommittee chairs. As they approached the 2000 congressional elections, however, some GOP leaders came to regret the commitment they had made six years earlier. Powerful Republican committee chairs were not very enthusiastic about the idea of surrendering their positions if the GOP maintained control of the House. Some Republican committee chairs hoped to trade positions with each other and begin new stints in charge of new panels. Younger members who had hoped to benefit from the three-term rule by claiming the vacated chairs were prepared to fight for what they now regarded as their due. Thus, a pledge made in 1994 when the GOP was out of power seemed to portend sharp conflicts among Republican members if the GOP retained power in 2000. However, in 2001, Republicans lived up to their 1995 pledge to limit House committee chairs to three terms. Incumbent chairmen were forced to step down but were generally replaced by the most senior Republican member of each committee.

The continuing importance of parties in Congress became especially evident after the Republicans won control of Congress in 1994. During the first few months of the 104th Congress, the Republican leadership was able to maintain nearly unanimous support among party members on vote after vote as it sought to implement the GOP's legislative agenda. In recent years, Republicans have maintained a unified front on tax cuts; however, significant disputes remain within the party on Social Security reform, Medicare reform, and the expanding federal deficit. The unity began to fray as George W. Bush's popularity declined and Democrats won control of Congress in 2006. Congressional Democrats showed substantial party unity after 2006, although they were not so united as Republicans. We will discuss these legislative struggles further in Chapter 12.

President and Party

As we saw earlier, the party that wins the White House is always led, in title anyway, by the president. The president normally depends on fellow party members in Congress to support legislative initiatives. At the same time, members of the party in Congress hope that the president's programs and personal prestige will help them raise campaign funds and secure re-election. During his two terms in office, President Bill Clinton had a mixed record as party leader. Although Clinton proved to be an extremely successful fund-raiser, congressional Democrats often complained that he failed to share his largesse with them. At the same time, however, a number of Clinton's policy initiatives, such as his health care initiative, seemed calculated to strengthen the Democratic Party as a whole. But by the middle of Clinton's second term, the president's acknowledgment of his sexual affair with a White House intern threatened his position as party leader. Initially, Democratic candidates nationwide feared that the scandal would undermine their own chances for election, and many moved to distance themselves from the president. The Democrats' surprisingly good showing in the 1998 elections, however, strengthened Clinton's position and gave him another chance to shape the Democratic agenda.

Between the 1998 and 2000 elections, however, the president's initiatives on Social Security and nuclear disarmament failed to make much headway in

Political Parties and the World

Few Americans are aware of the international involvements of our two major political parties. Since the mid-1980s each political party has been associated with a formal foreign policy institute. The International Republican Institute (IRI) was founded in 1983, and the National Democratic Institute for International Affairs (NDI) was established in 1985. Each party's institute is led by a cadre of the party's former officials and elected officeholders.

Both the IRI and the NDI work to encourage citizen participation and democracy throughout the world, particularly in regions that lack a historical and institutional base for democratic politics. Both party institutes work with local politicians, civic leaders, and community activists to encourage understanding of democratic political techniques and respect for democratic values.

Although the programs of the party institutes have many similarities, they diverge in ways that reflect the differences between the two American political parties. NDI programs pay special attention to women and young people—groups cultivated by the Democratic Party in the United States—and to trade unions, another bulwark of the U.S. Democratic Party. Thus, for example, an NDI program in Senegal was designed to increase the involvement of women in local government and in the leadership of the nation's political parties.

The IRI, for its part, has emphasized cultivating relationships with government officials and business leaders, and whereas the NDI's approach is decidedly grass roots in character, the IRI, like the Republican Party, emphasizes political technology. For example, in Macedonia, the IRI has taught public officials the elements of media relations, public-opinion polling, and "message development." Differences are also evident in which countries each institute emphasizes. For example the IRI pays special attention to the issue of democracy in Cuba, reflecting the significance of the Cuban American vote to the Republican party.

Although promoting democracy sounds uncontroversial, intervention into the affairs of other countries can lead to results that are anything but democratic. The case of the IRI's activities in Haiti provide an example. A 2006 investigative article in the *New York Times* charged that the IRI deliberately worked to destabilize democracy in Haiti in 2003–04.[a] At the time, Haiti was in a political crisis, with two opposing sides seeking to reach a political reconciliation. According to interviews and public records, the IRI's representative in Haiti provided one-sided support to the opponents of the elected president, Bertrand Aristide. Aristide was a controversial leader who was seen as a voice for Haiti's poor. Although the U.S. ambassador to Haiti at the time protested the involvement of the IRI, the group continued to operate with little accountability. Aristide's opponents launched a coup in 2004, sending the country into chaos for years to come.

Despite criticism, the IRI has grown and in 2008 employed 400 people working on democracy projects in seventy countries.[b]

FOR CRITICAL ANALYSIS

1. What are the similarities and differences between the NDI and the IRI? Do these parallel the similarities and differences between the Democratic and Republican parties?
2. How can Americans ensure that the activities of groups such as the IRI and NDI are accountable to the taxpayers who fund them?

a. Walt Bogdanich and Jenny Nordberg, "Mixed U. S. Signals Helped Tilt Haiti toward Chaos," *New York Times*, January 29, 2006, p. 1.
b. Mike Mcintire, "Democracy Group Gives Donors Access to McCain," *New York Times*, July 28, 2008, p. A1.

a Republican-controlled Congress. The GOP was not prepared to give Clinton anything for which Democrats could claim credit in the 2000 elections. Lacking strong congressional leadership, however, the GOP did agree to many of Clinton's budgetary proposals in 1999 and dropped its own plan for large-scale cuts in federal taxes.

For Critical Analysis

Should parties refrain from criticizing each other's foreign policies for fear of presenting a picture of division to foreign foes? Most Democrats supported President Bush's campaign against terrorism, but many Democrats criticized the president's policies involving the war in Iraq. Is partisan politics compatible with effective governance?

When he assumed office in 2001, George W. Bush called for a new era of bipartisan cooperation. The new president did receive the support of some conservative Democrats, such as the Georgia senator Zell Miller, who spoke in favor of Bush at the 2004 GOP convention. Bush also enjoyed widespread bipartisan support for his education reform legislation, the No Child Left Behind Act. Generally, however, Bush depended on near-unanimous backing from his own party in Congress to implement his plans, which included a substantial cut in federal income taxes. After the September 11 terrorist attacks, both parties united behind the president's military response. Even then, however, the parties were divided on a number of matters. Ultimately, the Democrats prevailed, and the president signed into law a bill that federalized baggage inspection. Democrats and Republicans clashed over issues such as drilling in the Arctic National Wildlife Refuge, Medicare reform, federal judicial nominees, and Social Security reform. Once Democrats took over Congress after the 2006 elections, they clashed repeatedly with President Bush on a wide range of issues, including the Iraq war, expansions of children's health insurance, and federal spending levels. The 2008 financial bailout plan provided a notable example of cooperation between Bush and the Democratic Congress. Democratic victories in the 2008 elections set the stage for a new era of Democratic political dominance. Whether it would prove lasting or not depended in large measure on the ability of the Democratic Congress and President Obama to work well together.

Thinking Critically about the Role of Parties in a Democracy

Democracy and political parties arose together in the modern world. Without democracy, a system of competing political parties never could have emerged. At the same time, without a system of competing political parties, democracy never could have flourished. Without a strong opposition, rulers never would have surrendered power, and without well-organized parties, ordinary people never could have acquired or exercised the right to vote. It is because of this strong historical association between democracy and political parties that the current weakness of American political parties is a matter of concern.

Healthy political parties are extremely important for maintaining political equality, democracy, and liberty in America. First, strong parties are generally an essential ingredient for effective electoral competition by groups lacking substantial economic or institutional resources. Party building has typically been the strategy pursued by groups that must organize the collective energies of large numbers of individuals to counter their opponents' superior material means or institutional standing. Historically, disciplined and coherent party organizations were generally developed first by groups representing the political aspirations of the working classes. Parties, the French political scientist Maurice Duverger notes, "are always more developed on the Left than on the Right because they are always more necessary on the Left than on the Right."[15] In the United States, the first mass party was built by the Jeffersonians as a counterweight to the superior social, institutional, and economic resources that the incumbent Federalists could deploy. In a subsequent period of American history, a similar set of circumstances impelled the efforts of the Jacksonians to construct a coherent mass party organization. Only by organizing the power of numbers could the Jacksonian coalition hope to compete successfully against the superior resources that its adversaries could mobilize.

In the United States, the political success of party organizations forced their opponents to copy them in order to meet the challenge. It was, as Duverger points out, "contagion from the Left" that led politicians of the Center and Right to attempt to build strong party organizations.[16] These efforts were sometimes successful. In the United States during the 1830s, the Whig Party, which was led by northeastern business interests, carefully copied the effective organizational techniques the Jacksonians had devised. The Whigs won control of the national government in 1840. But even when groups nearer the top of the social scale responded in kind to organizational efforts by their inferiors, the net effect nonetheless was to give lower-class groups an opportunity to compete on a more equal footing. In the absence of coherent mass organization, middle- and upper-class factions almost inevitably have a substantial competitive edge over their lower-class rivals. When both sides organize, the net effect is erosion of the relative advantage of the well off.

Second, political parties are bulwarks of liberty. The Constitution certainly provides for freedom of speech, freedom of assembly, and freedom of the press. Maintaining these liberties, though, requires more than parchment guarantees. Of course, as long as freedom is not seriously threatened, abstract guarantees suffice to protect it. If, however, those in power actually threaten citizens' liberties, the preservation of freedom may come to depend on the presence of a coherent and well-organized opposition. As we saw earlier in this chapter, in the first years of the

At election time, party workers try to increase turnout among potential voters who are likely to support their candidates. By promoting political participation, parties contribute to a healthy democracy.

Republic, it was not the Constitution or the courts that preserved free speech in the face of Federalist efforts to silence the government's critics; it was the vigorous action of the Jeffersonian-Republican opposition that saved liberty. To this day, the presence of an opposition party is a fundamentally important check on attempts by those in power to skirt the law and infringe on citizens' liberties. For example, twenty-five years ago, although it was the news media that revealed President Richard Nixon's abuses of power, the concerted efforts of Nixon's Democratic opponents in Congress were required finally to drive the president from office. Most recently, the Democratic party has played this role in challenging President Bush's program to authorize domestic wiretaps without a warrant.

For Critical Analysis

What are the principal issues dividing the two major parties today? What are the chief areas of agreement between the two parties? Do the parties agree or disagree on questions of liberty and democracy?

Third, parties promote voter turnout. Party competition has long been known to be a key factor in stimulating voting. As the political scientists Stanley Kelley, Richard Ayres, and William Bowen note, competition gives citizens an incentive to vote and politicians an incentive to get them to vote.[17] The origins of the American national electorate can be traced to the competitive organizing activities of the Jeffersonian Republicans and the Federalists. According to the historian David Fischer,

> During the 1790s the Jeffersonians revolutionized electioneering. . . . Their opponents complained bitterly of endless "dinings," "drinkings," and celebrations; of handbills "industriously posted along every road"; of convoys of vehicles which brought voters to the polls by the carload; of candidates "in perpetual motion."[18]

The Federalists, although initially reluctant, soon learned the techniques of mobilizing voters: "mass meetings, barbecues, stump-speaking, festivals of many kinds, processions and parades, runners and riders, door-to-door canvassing, the distribution of tickets and ballots, . . . free transportation to the polls, outright bribery and corruption of other kinds."[19]

The result of this competition for votes was described by the historian Henry Jones Ford in his classic *Rise and Growth of American Politics.*[20] Ford examined the popular clamor against John Adams and Federalist policies in the 1790s that made government a "weak, shakey affair" and appeared to contemporary observers to mark the beginnings of a popular insurrection against the government.[21] Attempts by the Federalists initially to suppress mass discontent, Ford observed, might have "caused an explosion of force which would have blown up the government."[22] What intervened to prevent rebellion was Jefferson's "great unconscious achievement," the creation of an opposition party that served to "open constitutional channels of political agitation."[23] The creation of the Jeffersonian Republican Party diverted opposition to the administration into electoral channels. Party competition gave citizens a sense that their votes were valuable and that it was thus not necessary to take to the streets to have an impact upon political affairs. Whether or not Ford was correct in crediting party competition with an ability to curb civil unrest, it is clear that competition between the parties promoted voting.

Finally, political parties make democratic government possible. We often do not appreciate that democratic government is a contradiction in terms. Government implies policies, programs, and decisive action. Democracy, on the other hand, implies an opportunity for all citizens to participate fully in the governmental process. The contradiction is that full participation by everyone is often inconsistent with

Become a Party Activist

When Evan Blewett arrived as a student at DePaul University in September 2006, one of the first groups he joined was the DePaul Democrats. He quickly became actively involved—first serving as membership director, then as treasurer, and finally filling the job of political director. As a member of the DePaul Democrats, Evan has had countless opportunities to work in local, state, and federal elections. Officials in the Democratic Party and local Democratic candidates have turned to Evan and his fellow campus Democrats to help staff their campaigns. One candidate paid students $50 a day to help in her run for office, eventually paying more than $15,000 to DePaul students.

The DePaul Democrats have used their connections to Democratic Party officials to bring speakers to campus, including numerous local politicians, many members of Congress serving in the House and Senate, and even presidential candidate Barack Obama. And Evan has used these experiences to build his own political credentials. Indeed, using a network built through these experiences, Evan became a volunteer for Obama's campaign, coordinating the student invitations to the candidate's Chicago kickoff speech, traveling to key primary races, and finally landing a full-time paid position in Obama's headquarters for summer 2008.

Whether you want a lifetime of politics or simply want some exposure to the inside activities of a political party, an important first step may be to decide which political party best represents your own values. Most Americans who identify with a particular party choose the Democratic Party or the Republican Party, although others opt for minor parties such as the Green Party, the Natural Law Party, or the Peace and Freedom Party.

- ★ If you're unsure which party best represents your views, you can take several online "tests" (such as the one at www.politicalcompass.org/test) to see how your views line up with the policies espoused by the different political parties.
- ★ Once you've found out which party best represents your views, see if your campus has a student organization that is affiliated with this party. Most schools have campus chapters of the Democratic and Republican parties, and some even have organizations associated with minor parties. These campus chapters are likely to be in contact with groups on nearby campuses, as well as the local and state offices of the parties themselves.
- ★ If your campus does not currently have a College Republicans or College Democrats group, you can contact the national party committees for guidance on how to build your own chapter and helpful hints on reaching out to expand your membership. Visit www.crnc.org for the College Republican National Committee or www.collegedems.com for the College Democrats of America.
- ★ As a member of one of these student organizations, you can have party-affiliated speakers come to campus to speak to your group, or to a larger campus-wide event. The national organization will even contact the speaker and arrange the details for you.
- ★ You can also apply for an internship in local, state, or national party offices. Often you can do this directly through the party's Web site (which often has a link to an application), and many schools or political science departments also have internship coordinators who can help you find a position. You may even be able to receive academic credit for your involvement.

getting anything done. At what point should participation stop and governance begin? How can we make certain that popular participation will result in a government capable of making decisions and developing needed policies? The problem of democratic government is especially acute in the United States because of the system of separated powers bequeathed to us by the Constitution's framers. Our system of separated powers means that it is very difficult to link popular participation and effective decision making. Often, after the citizens have spoken and the dust has settled, no single set of political forces has been able to win control of enough of the scattered levers of power to actually do anything. Instead of government, we have a continual political struggle.

Strong political parties are a partial antidote to the inherent contradiction between participation and government. Strong parties can both encourage popular involvement and convert participation into effective government. In 1950, a committee of the academic American Political Science Association (APSA) called for the development of a more "responsible" party government. By **responsible party government,** the committee meant political parties that mobilized voters and were sufficiently well organized to develop and implement coherent programs and policies after the election. Strong parties can link democratic participation and government.

responsible party government a set of principles that idealizes a strong role for parties in defining their stance on issues, mobilizing voters, and fulfilling their campaign promises once in office

Although they are significant factors in politics and government, American political parties today are not so strong as the "responsible parties" advocated by the APSA. Many politicians are able to raise funds, attract volunteers, and win office without much help from local party organizations. Once in office, these politicians have no particular reason to submit to party discipline; instead, they steer independent courses. They are often supported by voters who see independence as a virtue and party discipline as "boss rule." Sometimes analysts refer to this pattern as a "candidate-centered" politics to distinguish it from a political process in which parties are the dominant forces. The problem with a candidate-centered politics is that it tends to be associated with low turnout, high levels of special-interest influence, and a lack of effective decision making. In short, many of the problems that have plagued American politics in recent years can be traced directly to the independence of American voters and politicians and the candidate-centered nature of American national politics.

For Critical Analysis

Describe the factors that have contributed to the overall weakening of political parties in America. What are the advantages of a political system with weak political parties? What are the disadvantages?

The health of America's parties should be a source of concern to all citizens who value liberty, equality, and democracy. Can political parties be strengthened? The answer is, in principle, yes. For example, political parties could be strengthened if the rules governing campaign finance were revised to make candidates more dependent financially on state and local party organizations rather than on personal resources or private contributors. Such a reform, to be sure, would require stricter regulation of party fund-raising practices. The potential benefit, however, of a greater party role in political finance could be substantial. If parties controlled the bulk of the campaign funds, they would become more coherent and disciplined, and might come to resemble the responsible parties the APSA envisioned. In 2002, Congress enacted campaign-finance reforms that diminished the role of the national party organizations in financing campaigns. Although some feared that the reform would undermine parties, parties continued to grow stronger in the years after the reform. Political parties have been such important features of American democratic politics that we need to think long and hard about how to preserve and strengthen them.

FOR FURTHER READING

Aldrich, John H. *Why Parties? The Origin and Transformation of Political Parties in America*. Chicago: University of Chicago Press, 1995.

Andersen, Kristi. *After Suffrage: Women in Partisan and Electoral Politics before the New Deal*. Chicago: University of Chicago Press, 1996.

Edsall, Thomas Byrne, and Mary D. Edsall. *Chain Reaction: The Impact of Race, Rights, and Taxes on American Politics*. New York: Norton, 1993.

Gerring, John. *Party Ideologies in America*. New York: Cambridge University Press, 1998.

Green, Donald, Bradley Palmquist, and Eric Schickler. *Partisan Hearts and Minds: Political Parties and the Social Identities of Voters*. New Haven, CT: Yale University Press, 2002.

Green, John C., and Paul S. Herrnson, eds. *Responsible Partisanship? The Evolution of American Political Parties since 1950*. Lawrence: University Press of Kansas, 2002.

Maisel, L. Sandy. *Political Parties and Elections: A Very Short Introduction*. New York: Oxford University Press, 2007.

McCarty, Nolan, Keith Poole, and Howard Rosenthal. *Polarized America: The Dance of Ideology and Unequal Riches*. Cambridge, MA: MIT Press, 2006.

Milkis, Sidney M. *Political Parties and Constitutional Government: Remaking American Democracy*. Baltimore: Johns Hopkins University Press, 1999.

Shefter, Martin. *Political Parties and the State: The American Historical Experience*. Princeton, NJ: Princeton University Press, 1994.

RECOMMENDED WEB SITES

D.C.'s Political Report
www.dcpoliticalreport.com/Disclaimer.htm

This is a great resource page for political parties, with a special focus on American third parties. Here you can find almost every organization that identifies itself as a political party, including such obscure groups as the American Beer Drinker's Party or the Scorched Earth Party.

Democratic Party
www.dnc.org
Republican Party
www.GOP.com, www.rnc.org

These are the official Web sites for the Democrats and Republicans. Compare the platforms of the two main U.S. parties and see if there's "not a dime's worth of difference" between the two of them.

Green Party
www.gp.org
Libertarian Party
www.lp.org
Reform Party National Committee
http://reformparty.org

The Green Party, Libertarian Party, and Reform Party are three of the largest and most successful third parties in recent years. Find out what these parties are trying to accomplish and why their candidates run when they have little or no chance of winning.

National Annenberg Election Survey
http://dev.annenbergpublicpolicycenter.org/ProjectDetails.aspx?myId=1

Individual voters tend to develop psychological ties to one party or another. The National Annenberg Election Survey (NAES) uses survey data to track party identification by state every two years. Find out if your state has more Democratic or Republican identifiers.

Politics1.com
www.politics1.com/parties.htm

Politics1 is a nonpartisan site that provides an extensive list of political parties in the United States. Here you will find numerous party links as well as an abundance of historical information on America's third parties and biographies of leading politicians.

PoliTxts: Party Platforms since 1840
http://janda.org/politxts/PartyPlatforms/listing.html

Party platforms contain the party philosophy, principles, and positions on issues and are customarily approved at a national convention. Compare and contrast major party platforms for every presidential election year since 1840 on this page, compiled by Kenneth Janda.

STUDY OUTLINE

www.wwnorton.com/wtp7e

1. In modern history, political parties have been the chief points of contact between governments and groups and forces in society. By organizing political parties, social forces attempt to gain some control over government policies and personnel.

What Are Political Parties?

1. Political parties as they are known today developed along with the expansion of suffrage, and actually took their shape from the electoral process.
2. Political parties, as coalitions of those with similar interests, are also important in making policy.

The Two-Party System in America

1. Historically, parties originate through either internal or external mobilization by those seeking to win governmental power.
2. The Democratic Party originated through a process of internal mobilization when the Jeffersonian Party splintered into four factions in 1824, and Andrew Jackson emerged as the leader of one of these four groups.
3. The Republican Party grew through a process of external mobilization as antislavery groups formed a new party to oppose the 1854 Kansas-Nebraska Act.
4. The United States has experienced five realigning eras, which occur when the established political elite weakens sufficiently to permit the creation of new coalitions of forces capable of capturing and holding the reins of government.
5. American third parties have always represented social and economic protests ignored by the other parties.

Party Organization

1. Party organizations exist at virtually every level of American government—usually taking the form of committees made up of active party members.
2. Although national party conventions no longer have the power to nominate presidential candidates, they are still important in determining the party's rules and platform.
3. The national committee and the congressional campaign committees play important roles in recruiting candidates and raising money.

Parties and the Electorate

1. Individuals tend to form psychological ties with parties in "party identification." This identification often follows demographic, ideological, and regional lines.

Parties and Elections

1. Parties are important in the electoral process for recruiting and nominating candidates for office.
2. Though not so important today as in the past, parties also can make a big difference in convincing voters to vote.
3. Parties also help voters choose among candidates.

Parties and Government

1. The differences between the two parties reflect a general difference in philosophy but also an attempt to appeal to core constituencies. The policy agenda that party leaders adopt often reflect these differences.
2. Political parties help to organize Congress. Congressional leadership and the committee system are both products of the two-party system.
3. The president serves as an informal party head by seeking support from congressional members of the party and by supporting their bids for re-election.

Thinking Critically about the Role of Parties in a Democracy

1. Democracy depends on strong parties, which promote electoral competition and voter turnout and enable governance through their organizations in Congress.
2. The ties that parties have to the electorate are currently weak; the resulting "candidate-centered" politics has some negative consequences, including lower voter turnout, increased influence of interest groups, and a lack of effective decision making by elected leaders.
3. Parties could be strengthened by changes in campaign-finance laws.

PRACTICE QUIZ

www.wwnorton.com/wtp7e

1. A political party is different from an interest group in that a political party
   a) seeks to control the entire government by electing its members to office and thereby controlling the government's personnel.
   b) seeks to control only limited, very specific, functions of government.
   c) is entirely nonprofit.
   d) has a much smaller membership.
2. The periodic episodes in American history in which an "old" dominant political party is replaced by a "new" dominant political party are called
   a) constitutional revolutions.
   b) party turnovers.
   c) presidential elections.
   d) electoral realignments.
3. Through which mechanism did party leaders in the late nineteenth and early twentieth centuries maintain their control?
   a) civil service reform
   b) soft money contributions
   c) machine politics
   d) electoral reform
4. On what level are U.S. political parties organized?
   a) national
   b) state
   c) county
   d) all of the above
5. Contemporary national party conventions are important because they
   a) determine the party's presidential candidate.
   b) determine the party's rules and platform.
   c) Both a and b are correct.
   d) Neither a nor b is correct.
6. Which party was founded as a political expression of the antislavery movement?
   a) American Independent
   b) Prohibition
   c) Republican
   d) Democratic
7. Historically, when do realignments occur?
   a) typically, every twenty years
   b) whenever a minority party takes over Congress
   c) when large numbers of voters permanently shift their support from one party to another
   d) in odd-numbered years
8. Parties today are most important in the electoral process in
   a) recruiting and nominating candidates for office.
   b) financing all of the campaign's spending.
   c) providing millions of volunteers to mobilize voters.
   d) creating a responsible party government.
9. What role do parties play in Congress?
   a) They select leaders, e.g., Speaker of the House.
   b) They assign members to committees.
   c) Both a and b are correct.
   d) Parties play no role in Congress.
10. Parties are important to democracy because they
    a) encourage electoral competition.
    b) promote voter turnout.
    c) make governance possible by organizing elected leaders into governing coalitions.
    d) all of the above.

KEY TERMS

www.wwnorton.com/wtp7e

caucus (political) (p. 335)
divided government (p. 331)
electoral realignment (p. 330)
527 committees (p. 338)
gender gap (p. 343)
machines (p. 340)
majority party (p. 350)
minority party (p. 350)
multiple-member district (p. 335)
national convention (p. 335)
nomination (p. 348)
party activists (p. 342)
party identification (p. 341)
party organization (p. 335)
patronage (p. 340)
platform (p. 337)
plurality system (p. 335)
policy entrepreneur (p. 350)
political parties (p. 321)
proportional representation (p. 335)
responsible party government (p. 358)
single-member district (p. 335)
soft money (p. 341)
third parties (p. 332)
two-party system (p. 322)

10 Campaigns and Elections

- Elections in America
- Election Campaigns
- Presidential Elections
- How Voters Decide
- The 2008 Election
- Money and Politics
- Thinking Critically about the Electoral Process

WHAT GOVERNMENT DOES AND WHY IT MATTERS

In November 2008, Americans chose Democrat Barack Obama to be their forty-fourth president. Obama defeated Republican senator, John McCain, by a margin of more than 7 million votes out of some 120 million votes cast, posting 53 percent of the popular vote to McCain's 46 percent. Little more than a half century after the enactment of the 1965 Voting Rights Act enfranchised millions of black voters, Obama became America's first nonwhite president.

The 2008 campaign was fought against a backdrop of continuing war in the Middle East and a host of domestic problems including a financial crisis and general economic uncertainty. During the campaign, Obama pledged that he would soon withdraw American forces from Iraq and concentrate, instead, on stabilizing Afghanistan. He also pledged to improve America's relations with its allies—relations that had been frayed by the unilateralism of the Bush administration. Obama's victory was welcomed in most parts of the world where he was seen as representing America's more cosmopolitan social forces and less bellicose nature than his predecessor, who had been widely disliked, even by America's strongest admirers.

On the domestic front, Obama pledged to enhance educational opportunities for America's youth; to reduce the nation's dependence on foreign energy suppliers by expanding the use of alternative fuels; and to develop a health-care system that would assure every American of access to high-quality, affordable care. Obama pledged significant tax reforms that would end the Bush administration's policies favoring wealthier Americans. Obama also promised regulatory reform, asserting that Republican efforts to deregulate the economy had gone too far and had allowed the reckless practices that paved the way for the nation's 2008 financial crisis.

Americans also elected an overwhelmingly Democratic Congress in 2008. The fact that the president's party held significant majorities in Congress increased the likelihood that the Democrats would be able to enact major new policies and programs. Obama had campaigned on a promise of change and, perhaps, the 2008 election would bring new political directions.

In the aftermath of these elections, most pundits focused on explaining voters' choices and their implications for the nation's politics and policies. These are important topics, but it is also worthwhile to think a bit about the overall significance of elections.

Over the past two centuries, elections have come to play a role in the political processes of most nations. The forms that elections take and the purposes they serve, however, vary greatly from nation to nation. The most important difference among national electoral systems is that some provide the opportunity for opposition, but others do not. Democratic electoral systems, such as those that have evolved in the United States and western Europe, allow opposing forces to compete against and even to replace current officeholders. Authoritarian electoral systems, by contrast, do not allow the defeat of those in power. In the authoritarian context, elections are used primarily to mobilize popular enthusiasm for the government, to provide an outlet for popular discontent, and to persuade foreigners that the regime is legitimate. In the former Soviet Union, for example, citizens were required to vote even though no opposition to Communist Party candidates was allowed.

In democracies, elections promote leadership accountability because the threat of defeat at the polls exerts pressure on those in power to conduct themselves in a responsible manner and to take account of popular interests and wishes when they make their decisions. It is because of this need to anticipate the dissatisfaction of their constituents that elected officials constantly monitor public-opinion polls as they decide what positions to take on policy issues.

Although elections allow citizens a chance to participate in politics, they also allow the government a chance to exert a good deal of control over when, where, how, and which of its citizens will participate. Electoral processes are governed by a variety of rules and procedures that allow those in power a significant opportunity to regulate the character—and perhaps also the consequences—of mass political participation.

› **In this chapter, we will examine the place of elections in American political life. We will first discuss some of the formal aspects of electoral participation in the United States.** These include types of elections, the ways that election winners are determined, electoral districts, the ballot, and the electoral college.

› **In the next two sections, we will see how election campaigns are conducted in the United States.** The campaign for any political office consists of a number of steps. Election campaigns are also becoming increasingly expensive to wage.

› **Next, we assess the various factors that influence voters' decisions.** Despite the growing importance of money to elections, it is still voters who decide the outcomes.

› **We then turn to the issue of money and elections.** Raising campaign funds is now a crucial factor for winning. Although attempts to reform campaign finance have been made, the money keeps pouring in. As we will see, this development produces a clash between liberty and equality.

Elections in America

In the United States, elections are held at regular intervals. National presidential elections take place every four years, on the first Tuesday in November; congressional elections are held every two years on the same Tuesday. (Congressional elections that do not coincide with a presidential election are sometimes called **midterm elections.**) Elections for state and local office also often coincide with national elections. Some states and municipalities, however, prefer to schedule their local elections in years that do not coincide with national contests to ensure that local results will not be affected by national trends.

In the American federal system, the responsibility for organizing elections rests largely with state and local governments. State laws specify how elections are to be administered, determine the boundaries of electoral districts, and specify candidate and voter qualifications. Elections are administered by state, county, and municipal election boards that are responsible for establishing and staffing polling places and verifying the eligibility of individuals who come to vote.

midterm elections congressional elections that do not coincide with a presidential election; also called off-year elections

primary elections elections held to select a party's candidate for the general election

closed primary a primary election in which voters can participate in the nomination of candidates, but only of the party in which they are enrolled for a period of time prior to primary day

open primary a primary election in which the voter can wait until the day of the primary to choose which party to enroll in to select candidates for the general election

Types of Elections

Three types of elections are held in the United States: primary elections, general elections, and runoff elections. Americans occasionally also participate in a fourth voting process, the referendum, but the referendum is not actually an election.

Primary elections are held to select each party's candidates for the general election. In the case of local and statewide offices, the winners of primary elections face one another as their parties' nominees in the general election. At the presidential level, however, primary elections are indirect; they are used to select state delegates to the national nominating conventions, at which the major party presidential candidates are chosen. America is one of the only nations in the world to hold primary elections. In most countries, nominations are controlled by party officials, as they once were in the United States. The primary system was introduced at the turn of the century by Progressive reformers who hoped to weaken the power of party leaders by taking candidate nominations out of their hands.

Under the laws of some states, only registered members of a political party may vote in a primary election to select that party's candidates. This is called a **closed primary.** Other states allow all registered voters to decide on the day of the primary in which party's primary they will participate. This is called an **open primary.**

The primary is followed by the general election—the decisive electoral contest. The winner of the general election is elected to office for a specified term. In some states, however, mainly in the Southeast, if no candidate wins an absolute majority in the primary, a runoff election is held before the general election. This situation is most likely to arise if there are more than two candidates, none of whom receives a majority of the votes cast. A runoff election is held between the two candidates who received the largest number of votes.

Although the referendum process is not an election, voters may decide on referenda at the same time that they cast their votes to elect public officials. In 2006, Wisconsin voters were asked to decide several referenda, including one that called for the withdrawal of troops from Iraq.

referendum the practice of referring a measure proposed or passed by a legislature to the vote of the electorate for approval or rejection

recall procedure to allow voters an opportunity to remove state officials from office before their terms expire

Twenty-four states also provide for referendum voting, as we saw in Chapter 1. The **referendum** process allows citizens to vote directly on proposed laws or other governmental actions. In recent years, voters in several states have voted to set limits on tax rates, to block state and local spending proposals, and to prohibit social services for illegal immigrants. Although it involves voting, a referendum is not an election. The election is an institution of representative government. Through an election, voters choose officials to act for them. The referendum, by contrast, is an institution of direct democracy; it allows voters to govern directly without intervention by government officials. The validity of referenda results, however, is subject to judicial action. If a court finds that a referendum outcome violates the state or national constitution, it can overturn the result. This happened in the case of a 1995 California referendum curtailing social services to illegal aliens.[1] More than 150 propositions appeared on November 2008 ballots. The most common were efforts to outlaw same-sex marriage and to place restrictions on abortion.

Eighteen states also have legal provisions for **recall** elections. The recall is an electoral device that allows voters to remove governors and other state officials from office prior to the expiration of their terms. Generally speaking, a recall effort begins with a petition campaign. For example, in California, if 12 percent of those who voted in the last general election sign petitions demanding a special recall election, one must be scheduled by the state board of elections. In 2003, California voters blamed Governor Gray Davis for the state's $38 billion budget deficit, allowing his opponents to secure enough signatures to force a vote. In October 2003, Davis became only the second governor in American history to be recalled by his state's electorate. Under California law, voters are also asked to choose a replacement for the official whom they dismiss. Californians in 2003 elected Arnold Schwarzenegger to be their governor. In 2008, a number of politicians faced recall elections. For example, Michigan voters were given an opportunity to recall House Speaker Andy Dillon who made enemies when he backed a state income tax increase. And, in an ironic twist, the California prison guards union launched an (unsuccessful) effort to recall Governor Arnold Schwarzenegger. Federal officials, such as the president and members of Congress, are not subject to recall.

majority system a type of electoral system in which, to win a seat in the parliament or other representative body, a candidate must receive a majority of all the votes cast in the relevant district

plurality system a type of electoral system in which, to win a seat in the parliament or other representative body, a candidate need only receive the most votes in the election, not necessarily a majority of votes cast

proportional representation a multiple-member district system that allows each political party representation in proportion to its percentage of the total vote

The Criteria for Winning

In some countries, to win a seat in the parliament or other governing body, a candidate must receive an absolute majority (50 percent plus 1) of all the votes cast in the relevant district. This type of electoral system is called a **majority system** and, in the United States, is used in primary elections by some southern states. Majority systems usually include a provision for a runoff election between the two top candidates, because if the initial race draws several candidates, there is little chance that any one will receive a majority.

In other nations, candidates for office need not win an absolute majority of the votes cast to win an election. Instead, victory is awarded to the candidate who receives the most votes, regardless of the actual percentage this represents. A candidate receiving 50 percent, 30 percent, or 20 percent of the vote can win if no other candidate received more votes. This type of electoral system is called a **plurality system** and is used in virtually all general elections in the United States.

Most European nations employ a third type of electoral system, called **proportional representation.** Under proportional rules, competing political parties are awarded legislative seats in rough proportion to the percentage of the popular votes cast that each party won. A party that wins 30 percent of the vote will receive roughly 30 percent of the seats in the parliament or other representative body. In the United States, proportional representation is used by many states in presidential primary elections.

In general, proportional representation works to the advantage of smaller or weaker groups in society, whereas plurality and majority rules tend to help larger and more powerful forces. Proportional representation benefits smaller or weaker groups because it usually allows a party to win legislative seats with fewer votes than would be required under a majority or plurality system. In Europe, for example, a party that wins 10 percent of the national vote might win 10 percent of the parliamentary seats. In the United States, by contrast, a party that wins 10 percent of the vote would probably win no seats in Congress. Because they give small parties little chance of success, plurality and majority systems tend to reduce the number of competitive political parties. Proportional representation, on the other hand, tends to increase the number of parties. In part because of its use of plurality elections, the United States has usually had only two significant political parties, whereas with proportional representation, many European countries have developed multiparty systems.

redistricting the process of redrawing election districts and redistributing legislative representatives. This happens every ten years to reflect shifts in population or in response to legal challenges in existing districts

Electoral Districts

The boundaries for congressional and state legislative districts in the United States are redrawn by the states usually every ten years in response to population changes determined by the census. This redrawing of district boundaries is called **redistricting.** The character of district boundaries is influenced by several factors. Some of

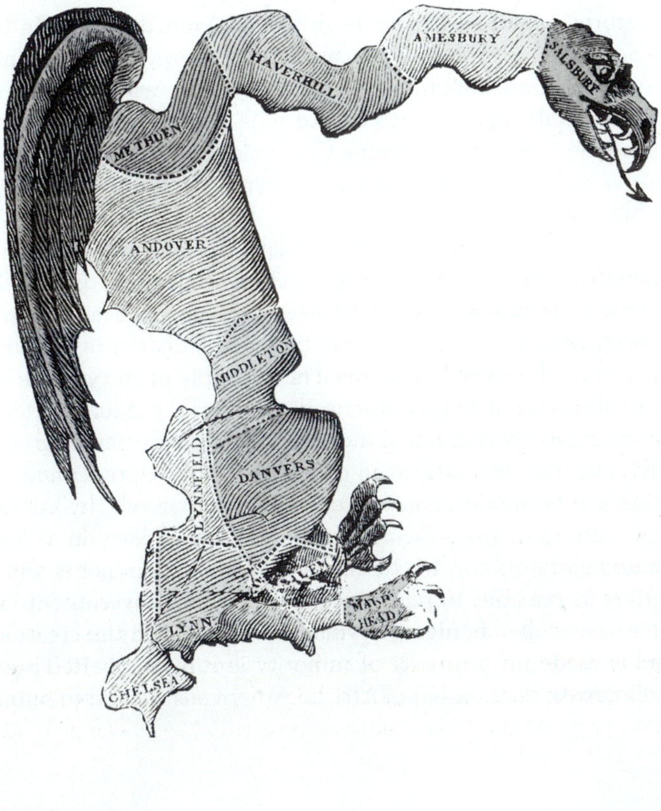

The drawing of electoral districts is always a matter of controversy, with opponents accusing one another of "gerrymandering"—drawing district boundaries in such a way as to serve a particular group's interests. The original gerrymander was a districting plan attributed to the Massachusetts governor Elbridge Gerry (1744–1814).

In a number of recent cases, black, white, and Hispanic voters have claimed to be the victims of racial gerrymanders. For instance, in 1995 the Supreme Court held that one Georgia district, which was 64 percent African American, was unfairly based on race. Meanwhile, no challenge was made to Texas's 6th District, which was predominantly white. In 2006, the Supreme Court rejected part of a Texas redistricting plan on the grounds that it suppressed minority votes, though the Court upheld most of the plan.

the most important influences have been federal court decisions. In the 1963 case of *Gray v. Sanders,* and in the 1964 cases of *Wesberry v. Sanders* and *Reynolds v. Sims,* the Supreme Court held that legislative districts within a state must include roughly equal populations, so as to accord with the principle of "one person, one vote."[2] During the 1980s, the Supreme Court also declared that legislative districts should, insofar as possible, be contiguous, compact, and consistent with existing political subdivisions.[3]

gerrymandering apportionment of voters in districts in such a way as to give unfair advantage to one racial or ethnic group or political party

benign gerrymandering attempts to draw district boundaries so as to create districts made up primarily of disadvantaged or underrepresented minorities

Despite judicial intervention, state legislators routinely seek to influence electoral outcomes by manipulating the organization of electoral districts. This strategy is called **gerrymandering,** named for a nineteenth-century Massachusetts governor, Elbridge Gerry, who was alleged to have designed a district in the shape of a salamander to promote his party's interests. The principle of gerrymandering is simple: different distributions of voters among districts can produce different electoral results. For example, by dispersing the members of a particular group across two or more districts, state legislators can dilute their voting power and prevent them from electing a representative in any district. Alternatively, by concentrating the members of a group or the adherents of the opposing party in as few districts as possible, state legislators can try to ensure that their opponents will elect as few representatives as possible. In recent years, the federal government has supported what is sometimes called **benign gerrymandering** through the creation of congressional districts made up primarily of minority group members. This practice was intended to increase the number of African Americans elected to public office. The

Supreme Court has viewed this effort as constitutionally dubious, however. Beginning with the 1993 case of *Shaw v. Reno,* the Court has generally rejected efforts to create such **majority-minority districts.**[4] The Court has asserted that districting based exclusively on racial criteria is unlawful.

majority-minority district a gerrymandered voting district that improves the chances of minority candidates by making selected minority groups the majority within the district

Traditionally, district boundaries have been redrawn only once a decade, following the national census. In recent years, however, the Republican Party has adopted an extremely aggressive redistricting strategy, in some instances not waiting for a new census before launching a redistricting effort that could serve its political interests. In Texas, for example, after the GOP took control of both houses of the state legislature in the 2002 elections, Republican lawmakers sought to enact a redistricting plan that promised to shift as many as five congressional seats to the Republican column. This Republican effort was masterminded by then–U.S. House majority leader Tom DeLay, who is himself a Texan. DeLay saw an opportunity to increase the Republican majority in the House and reduce Democratic prospects for regaining control of Congress. In an effort to block DeLay's plan, fifty-one Democratic legislators refused to attend state legislative sessions, leaving the Texas legislature without a quorum and unable to conduct its business. The legislature's Republican leadership ordered the state police to apprehend the missing Democrats and return them to the Capitol. The Democrats responded by escaping to Oklahoma, beyond the jurisdiction of the Texas police. Eventually, the Democrats capitulated and the GOP was able to enact its redistricting plan. In 2006, the U.S. Supreme Court upheld the legality of most of the DeLay plan. A similar GOP redistricting effort in Pennsylvania was also upheld by the United States Supreme Court in 2004.

The Ballot

Prior to the 1890s, voters cast ballots according to political parties. Each party printed its own ballots, listed only its own candidates for each office, and employed party workers to distribute its ballots at the polls. Because only one party's candidates appeared on any ballot, it was very difficult for a voter to cast anything other than a straight party vote.

The advent of a new, neutral ballot brought a significant change to electoral procedure. The new ballot was prepared and administered by the state rather than the parties. Each ballot was identical and included the names of all candidates for office. This ballot reform made it possible for voters to make their choices on the basis of the individual rather than the collective merits of a party's candidates. Because all candidates for the same office now appeared on the same ballot, voters were no longer forced to choose a straight party ticket. This gave rise to the phenomenon of split-ticket voting in American elections.

If a voter supports candidates from more than one party in the same election, he or she is said to be casting a split-ticket vote. Voters who support only one party's candidates are casting a straight-ticket vote. Straight-ticket voting occurs most often when a voter casts a ballot for a party's presidential candidate and then "automatically" votes for the rest of that party's candidates. The result of this voting pattern is known as the **coattail effect.**

coattail effect the result of voters casting their ballot for president or governor and "automatically" voting for the remainder of the party's ticket

Prior to the reform of the ballot, it was not uncommon for an entire incumbent administration to be swept from office and replaced by an entirely new set of officials. In the absence of a real possibility of split-ticket voting, the electorate could express any desire for change only as a vote against all candidates of the

Electoral Redistricting and Race

The process of redrawing election districts to take account of population shifts is both necessary and controversial. America's two major political parties have always vied to obtain political advantage through redistricting in the hope that redrawn district lines will help their candidates, or hurt the opposing candidates. Yet redistricting has also been used as a weapon to minimize the electoral influence of selected groups, especially African Americans, a process many consider an undemocratic denial of equality. To remedy this problem, Congress amended the 1965 Voting Rights Act in 1982 to compel states with significant African American and Latino populations to redraw district lines in such a way as to make more likely the election of representatives from these groups. This redistricting was carried out in thirteen states after the 1990 census, and it produced the desired effect. Before the 1990 reapportionment, the House of Representatives had a record-high twenty-five African American members (5.7 percent of members). After the reapportionment, which included the creation of districts having black majorities, thirty-nine African Americans were elected (9 percent of the House); Latino representatives increased from ten to seventeen. Yet many of these race-based reapportionment schemes were challenged in court.

Supporters of race-based redistricting argue that such drastic measures are necessary to overcome traditional white dominance. Southern blacks, in particular, traditionally have been frozen out of public office, since most American elections follow the winner-take-all system, meaning that election districts with substantial nonwhite populations could always be outvoted by a white majority. Indeed, studies have shown that race matters to voters. In a study from the 1980s, more than 80 percent of white North Carolina voters reported that they would not vote for an African American candidate, even if there was no other choice on the ballot. North Carolina did not elect an African American to Congress in the twentieth century until after the 1990 reapportionment, despite the fact that between one-fifth and one-third of the state's population was black.

Although race-based redistricting has produced some odd-shaped congressional districts, it increased not only the number of nonwhite representatives in Congress but also increased their political voice and clout. This larger number of representatives has exerted more influence over national policy making in such areas as crime and gun control. It also has increased the pool of potential office seekers. The persistence of racism, and the resistance of institutions to change, has made such "minority" districts necessary.

Critics have argued that race-based redistricting is nothing more than racial gerrymandering and that it perpetuates the very problem it claims to solve. Although the number of minority representatives in Congress has increased, race-based reapportionment has also purged surrounding districts of nonwhite voters, transforming many of these districts from racially and politically competitive to uniformly white and Republican, a fact reflected in the shift of twelve seats to Republican candidates in the thirteen states where these changes took place (because of the shifting of Democratic-voting blacks from these formerly competitive districts). Thus, black voters have been walled off from more conservative white voters.

The shoestring shape of many of these districts—some portions of some districts are no wider than an interstate highway—reveals their blatant gerrymandering. Even though the purpose of providing more representation for African Americans and Latinos may be praiseworthy, the method violates the principle of equal protection, as the Supreme Court has noted in recent decisions. Winner-take-all elections do often disguise the preferences of minority groups, but the remedy is stronger electoral competition and greater pressure from constituent groups. According to this view, reapportionment based on race is unacceptable, regardless of which race benefits.

FOR CRITICAL ANALYSIS

1. Is it ever appropriate to use race and ethnicity as criteria for drawing legislative district boundaries?
2. What are some of the most important U.S. Supreme Court decisions concerning race and districting? How has the Court's position changed over time?

SOURCES: Gary Cox and Jonathan Katz *Elbridge Gerry's Salamander: The Electoral Consequences of the Reapportionment Revolution* (New York: Cambridge University Press, 2002); and Mark Monmonier, *Bushmanders and Bullwinkles: How Politicians Manipulate Electronic Maps and Census Data to Win Elections* (Chicago: University of Chicago Press, 2001).

party in power. Because of this, the possibility always existed, particularly at the state and local levels, that an insurgent slate committed to policy change could be swept into power. The party ballot thus increased the potential impact of elections on the government's composition. Although this potential may not always have been realized, the party ballot at least increased the chance that electoral decisions could lead to policy changes. By contrast, because it permitted choice on the basis of candidates' individual appeals, ticket splitting led to increasingly divided partisan control of government.

The actual ballots used by voters vary from county to county across the United States. Some counties employ paper ballots; others use mechanical voting machines or computerized systems. Not surprisingly, the controversy surrounding Florida's presidential vote in 2000 led to a closer look at the different balloting systems, and it became apparent that some of them produced unreliable results. When many counties moved to introduce computerized voting systems, critics warned that they might be vulnerable to unauthorized use or "hacking." However, in 2006, with over a third of the nation's voters using electronic, touch-screen machines, few problems were reported. During the 2008 Ohio primaries a software error was discovered that potentially affected electronic voting machines used in thirty-four states. The machine's manufacturer, however, moved to correct the error before the November national elections.

The Electoral College

In the early history of popular voting, nations often made use of indirect elections. In these elections, voters would choose the members of an intermediate body. These members would, in turn, select public officials. The assumption underlying such processes was that ordinary citizens were not really qualified to choose their leaders and could not be trusted to do so directly. The last vestige of this procedure in America is the **electoral college,** the group of electors who formally select the president and vice president of the United States.

electoral college the presidential electors from each state who meet after the popular election to cast ballots for president and vice president

When Americans go to the polls on election day, they are technically not voting directly for presidential candidates. Instead, voters within each state are choosing among slates of electors selected by each state's party and pledged, if elected, to support that party's presidential candidate. In each state (except Maine and Nebraska), the slate that wins casts all the state's electoral votes for its party's candidate.[5] Each state is entitled to a number of electoral votes equal to the number of the state's senators and representatives combined, for a total of 538 electoral votes for the fifty states and the District of Columbia. Occasionally, an elector will break his or her pledge and vote for the other party's candidate. For example, in 1976, when the Republicans carried the state of Washington, one Republican elector from that state refused to vote for Gerald Ford, the Republican presidential nominee. Many states have now enacted statutes formally binding electors to their pledges, but some constitutional authorities doubt whether such statutes are enforceable.

In each state, the electors whose slate has won proceed to the state's capital on the Monday following the second Wednesday in December and formally cast their ballots. The ballots are sent to Washington and tallied by the Congress in January; then the name of the winner is formally announced. If no candidate were to receive a majority of all electoral votes, the names of the top three candidates would be submitted to the House, where each state would be able to cast one vote. Whether a state's vote would be decided by a majority, plurality, or some other

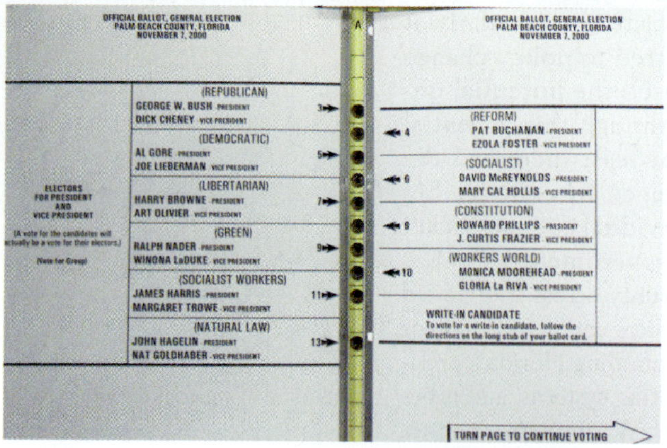

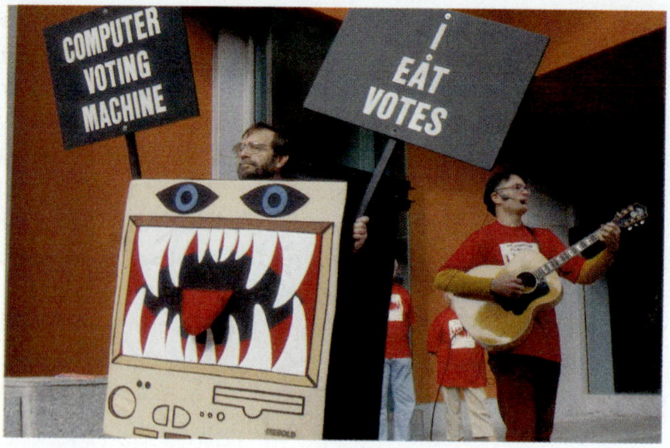

A number of the devices that have been used to record votes in the United States are notably prone to errors that can affect election results. For example, in the state of Florida, the cumbersome methods used to tally votes may have affected the result of the 2000 presidential election. Some voters were confused by the "butterfly ballot" in Palm Beach County, which made it difficult to match candidates and votes. In the 2008 elections, many of the nation's voters cast their ballots on electronic touch-screen machines. Critics of touch-screen voting systems, however, question the machines for their accuracy and security against fraud.

fraction of the state's delegates would be determined under rules established by the House.

In 1800 and 1824, the electoral college failed to produce a majority for any candidate. In the election of 1800, Thomas Jefferson, the Jeffersonian Republican Party's presidential candidate, and Aaron Burr, that party's vice-presidential candidate, received an equal number of votes in the electoral college, throwing the election into the House of Representatives. (The Constitution at that time made no distinction between presidential and vice-presidential candidates, specifying only that the individual receiving a majority of electoral votes would be named president.) Some members of the Federalist Party in Congress suggested that they should seize the opportunity to damage the Republican cause by supporting Burr and denying Jefferson the presidency. The Federalist leader Alexander Hamilton put a stop to this mischievous notion, however, and made certain that his party supported Jefferson. Hamilton's actions enraged Burr and helped lead to the infamous duel between the two men, in which Burr killed Hamilton. The Twelfth Amendment, ratified in 1804, was designed to prevent a repetition of such an inconclusive election by providing for separate electoral college votes for president and vice president.

In the 1824 election, four candidates—John Quincy Adams, Andrew Jackson, Henry Clay, and William H. Crawford—divided the electoral vote; no one of them received a majority. The House of Representatives eventually chose Adams over the others, even though Jackson had won more electoral and popular votes. After 1824, the two major political parties had begun to dominate presidential politics to such an extent that by December of each election year, only two candidates remained for the electors to choose between, thus ensuring that one would receive a majority. This freed the parties and the candidates from having to plan their campaigns to culminate in Congress, and Congress very quickly ceased to dominate the presidential selection process.

On all but three occasions since 1824, the electoral vote has simply ratified the nationwide popular vote. Since electoral votes are won on a state-by-state basis, it is mathematically possible for a candidate who receives a nationwide popular plurality to fail to carry states whose electoral votes would add up to a majority. Thus, in 1876, Rutherford B. Hayes was the winner in the electoral college despite receiving fewer popular votes than his rival, Samuel Tilden. In 1888, Grover Cleveland received more popular votes than Benjamin Harrison, but received fewer electoral votes. And in 2000, Al Gore outpolled his opponent, George W. Bush, by more than 500,000 votes, but narrowly lost the electoral college by a mere four electoral votes.

Election Campaigns

A **campaign** is an effort by political candidates and their supporters to win the backing of donors, political activists, and voters in their quest for political office. Campaigns precede every primary and general election. Because of the complexity of the campaign process, and because of the amount of money that candidates must raise, presidential campaigns usually begin almost two years before the November presidential elections. The campaign for any office consists of a number of steps. Candidates must first organize groups of supporters who will help them raise funds and bring their names to the attention of the media and potential donors. This step is relatively easy for a candidate currently in the office. The current officeholder is called an **incumbent.** Incumbents usually are already well known and have little difficulty attracting supporters and contributors, unless of course they have been subject to damaging publicity while in office.

campaign an effort by political candidates and their staffs to win the backing of donors, political activists, and voters in the quest for political office

incumbent a candidate running for re-election to a position that he or she already holds

Advisers

The next step in a typical campaign involves recruiting advisers and creating a formal campaign organization (see Figure 10.1). Most candidates, especially for national or statewide office, will need a campaign manager, a media consultant, a pollster, a financial adviser, and a press spokesperson, as well as a staff director to coordinate the activities of volunteer and paid workers. For a local campaign, candidates generally need hundreds of workers. State-level campaigns call for thousands of workers, and presidential campaigns require tens of thousands of workers nationwide.

Professional campaign workers, including the managers, consultants, and pollsters required in a modern campaign, prefer to work for candidates who seem to have a reasonable chance of winning. Candidates seen as having little chance of winning often have difficulty hiring the most experienced professional consultants. Professional political consultants have taken the place of the old-time party bosses who once controlled political campaigns. Most consultants who direct campaigns specialize in politics, although some are drawn from the ranks of corporate advertising and may work with commercial clients in addition to politicians. Campaign consultants conduct public opinion polls, produce television commercials, organize direct-mail campaigns, and develop the issues and advertising messages the candidate will use to mobilize support. George W. Bush's former chief political strategist, Karl Rove, not only played a key role in two presidential campaigns, but is also widely credited with crafting the strategy that brought about a Republican victory in the 2002 national congressional races.

FIGURE 10.1 ★ The Typical Organization of a National Political Campaign

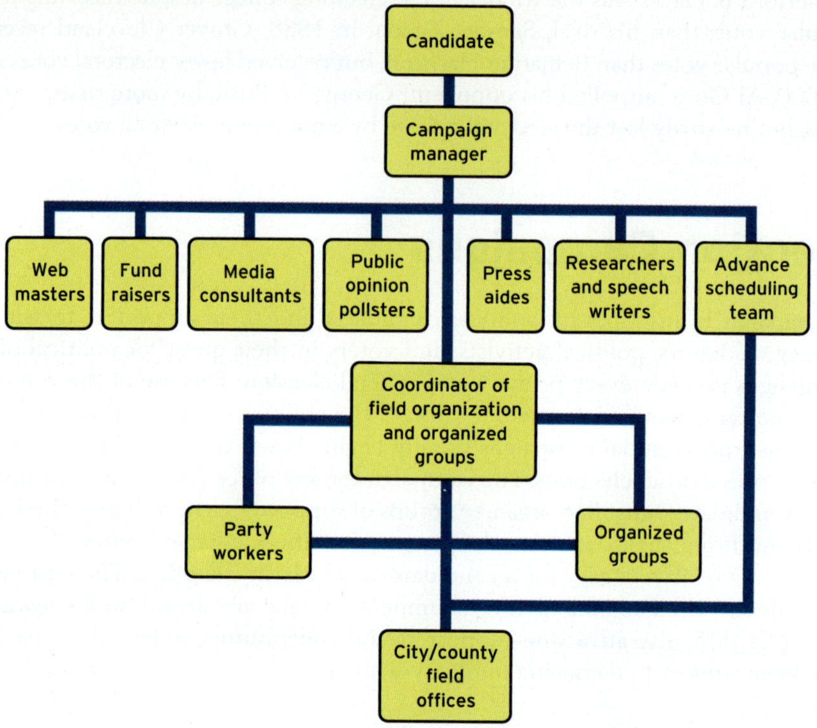

Together with their advisers, candidates must begin serious fund-raising efforts at an early stage in the campaign. To have a reasonable chance of winning a seat in the House of Representatives, a candidate may need to raise more than $500,000. To win a Senate seat, a candidate may need ten times that much. Candidates generally begin raising funds long before they face an election. Once in office, members of Congress find it much easier to raise campaign funds and are thus able to outspend their challengers (see Figure 10.2).[6] Members of the majority party in the House and Senate are particularly attractive to donors who want access to those in power.[7] Presidential candidates in particular must raise huge amounts of money. In 2008, Barack Obama set new fund-raising records. His early fund-raising produced more than $200 million, much of it in small contributions. Ultimately, Obama raised around $700 million, an unprecedented figure.

Polling

Another important element of a campaign is public-opinion polling. To be competitive, a candidate must collect voting and poll data to assess the electorate's needs, hopes, fears, and past behavior. Polls are conducted throughout most political campaigns. Surveys of voter opinion provide the basic information that candidates and

FIGURE 10.2 ★ Average House and Senate Campaign Expenditures, 1980–2006 (Net Dollars)

The average amount spent by House and Senate incumbents to secure reelection has risen sharply in recent years, whereas spending by challengers has remained more stable. What would you expect to see as a consequence of this trend? Is legislation needed to level the playing field?

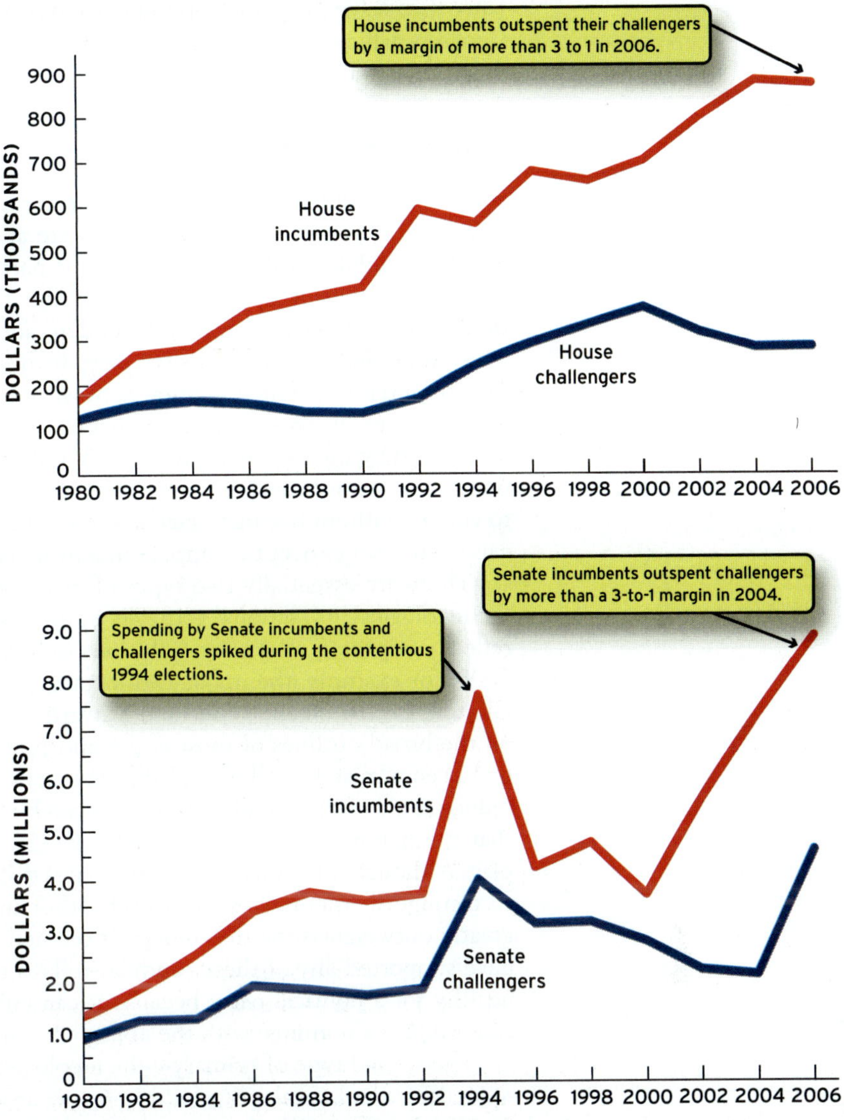

SOURCES: Norman J. Ornstein, Thomas E. Mann, and Michael J. Malbin. eds., *Vital Statistics on Congress, 2001–2002* (Washington DC: American Enterprise Institute, 2002), 87, 93; and Campaign Finance Institute, www.cfinst.org/data/congress.aspx (accessed 2/25/08).

their staffs use to craft campaign strategies—that is, to select issues, to assess their own strengths and weaknesses as well as those of the opposition, to check voter response to the campaign, and to measure the degree to which various constituent groups may respond to campaign appeals. The themes, issues, and messages that candidates present during a campaign are generally based on polls and smaller face-to-face sessions with voters, called "focus groups." In recent years, pollsters have become central figures in most national campaigns, and some have continued as advisers to their clients after they win the election.

In the months prior to the 2008 presidential contest, Democrats and Republicans conducted extensive polling on both foreign and domestic issues. On the basis of their poll data, Democrats judged that they should campaign against President Bush's record and emphasize such issues as health care reform and voters' misgivings about the economy. The GOP's poll data indicated that Republican candidates should distance themselves from the unpopular Bush administration and attack the Democratic Congress, which polls showed was even more unpopular with Republicans than the Bush administration.

The Primaries

For many candidates, the next step in a campaign is the primary election. In the case of all offices but the presidency, state and local primary elections determine which candidates will receive the major parties' official nominations. Of course, candidates can run for office without the Democratic or Republican nomination. In most states, however, independent and third-party candidates must obtain many thousands of petition signatures to qualify for the general election ballot. This requirement alone discourages most independent and third-party bids. More important, most Americans are reluctant to vote for candidates other than those nominated by the two major parties. Thus most of the time, a major party nomination is a necessary condition for electoral success. Some popular incumbents coast to victory without having to face a serious challenge. In most major races, however, candidates can expect to compete in a primary election.

There are essentially two types of primary contests: the personality clash and the ideological, or factional, struggle. In the first category are primaries that simply reflect competing efforts by ambitious individuals to secure election to office. In 2008, for example, the major Democratic presidential hopefuls, Hillary Rodham Clinton, Barack Obama, and John Edwards were all moderate liberals who agreed on the broad outlines of most issues and policies. All agreed that the war in Iraq had been a mistake. All agreed that the nation's tax system should be revised to reduce some of the tax advantages enjoyed by the wealthiest Americans. All agreed that the national government should develop a comprehensive health insurance plan. Although, of course, these candidates disagreed on some specifics and sought to distinguish themselves from each other in a variety of ways, the similarities greatly outweighed the differences. It seemed that most Democratic voters could have supported any of these candidates. This type of primary contest can be very healthy for a political party because it can enhance interest in the campaign and can produce a nominee with the ability to win the general election.

The second type of primary—the ideological struggle—can have different consequences. Ideological struggles usually occur when one wing or faction of a party decides that it is not willing to compromise its principles for the sake of the party's electoral success. Early in the 2008 race, religious conservatives backed a presidential bid by the former Arkansas governor Mike Huckabee, an evangelical minister. Huckabee's campaign brought the issue of religion and politics to the forefront, dividing the economic conservatives from the religious conservatives in the GOP coalition. In previous years, these groups had united behind such candidates as Ronald Reagan and George W. Bush, who appealed to both social and economic conservatives. Religious conservatives, however, concluded that they had gained little from their allegiance to the GOP in recent years and vowed to stage a fight for the soul of the party. When John McCain won the GOP nomination, religious conservatives threatened to sit out the general election. Religious conservatives viewed McCain as a "country club" Republican, indifferent to abortion and other social issues. However, when McCain designated Sarah Palin as his running mate, religious conservatives were pleased. Palin had strong religious ties and was a stalwart foe of abortion. In the wake of the Palin nomination, religious conservatives stopped denouncing McCain and rushed to embrace the Republican ticket.

Presidential Elections

Although they also involve primary elections, the major party presidential nominations follow a pattern that is quite different from the nominating process employed for other political offices. In some years, particularly when an incumbent president is running for re-election, one party's nomination may not be contested. If, however, the Democratic or Republican presidential nomination is contested, candidates typically compete in primaries or presidential nominating caucuses in all fifty states, attempting to capture national convention delegates. Most states hold primary elections to choose the delegates for national conventions. A few states hold the **caucus,** a nominating process that begins with precinct-level meetings throughout the state. Some caucuses, called **open caucuses,** are open to anyone wishing to attend. Other states use **closed caucuses,** open only to registered party members. Citizens attending the caucuses typically elect delegates to statewide conventions at which delegates to the national party conventions are chosen.

caucus (political) a normally closed meeting of a political or legislative group to select candidates, plan strategy, or make decisions regarding legislative matters

open caucus a presidential nominating caucus open to anyone who wishes to attend

closed caucus a presidential nominating caucus open only to registered party members

The primaries and caucuses begin in January of a presidential election year and end in June (see Figure 10.3). The early ones are most important because they can help front-running candidates secure media attention and financial support. Gradually, the primary and caucus process has become "front loaded," with states vying with each other to increase their political influence by holding their nominating processes first. Traditionally, the New Hampshire primary and the Iowa caucuses are considered the most important of the early events, and candidates spend months courting voter support in these two states. A candidate who performs well in Iowa and New Hampshire will usually be able to secure support and better media coverage for subsequent races. A candidate who fares badly in these two states may be written off as a loser. As they sought their parties' 2008 presidential nominations, the leading Democratic and Republican candidates campaigned intensely in Iowa and New Hampshire. The Democrats Hillary Clinton, Barack Obama, and John Edwards spent long hours in the two states, greeting voters, seeking endorsements and launching media blitzes. On the GOP side, John McCain, Rudy Guiliani, and Mike Huckabee fought tooth and nail for the support of Republican voters.

As noted in Chapter 9, the Democratic Party requires that state presidential primaries allocate delegates on the basis of proportional representation; Democratic candidates win delegates in rough proportion to their percentage of the primary vote. The Republican Party does not require proportional representation, but most states have now written proportional representation requirements into their election laws. A few states use the **winner-take-all system,** by which the candidate with the most votes wins all the party's delegates in that state.

winner-take-all system a system in which all of a state's presidential nominating delegates are awarded to the candidate who wins the most votes, while runners-up receive no delegates

When the primaries and caucuses are concluded, it is usually clear which candidates have won their parties' nominations. For example, in 2008, John McCain had effectively wrapped up the Republican nomination by the first week in March. Barack Obama and Hillary Clinton, though, fought for the Democratic nomination until the beginning of June.

FIGURE 10.3 ★ The 2008 Presidential Election Season

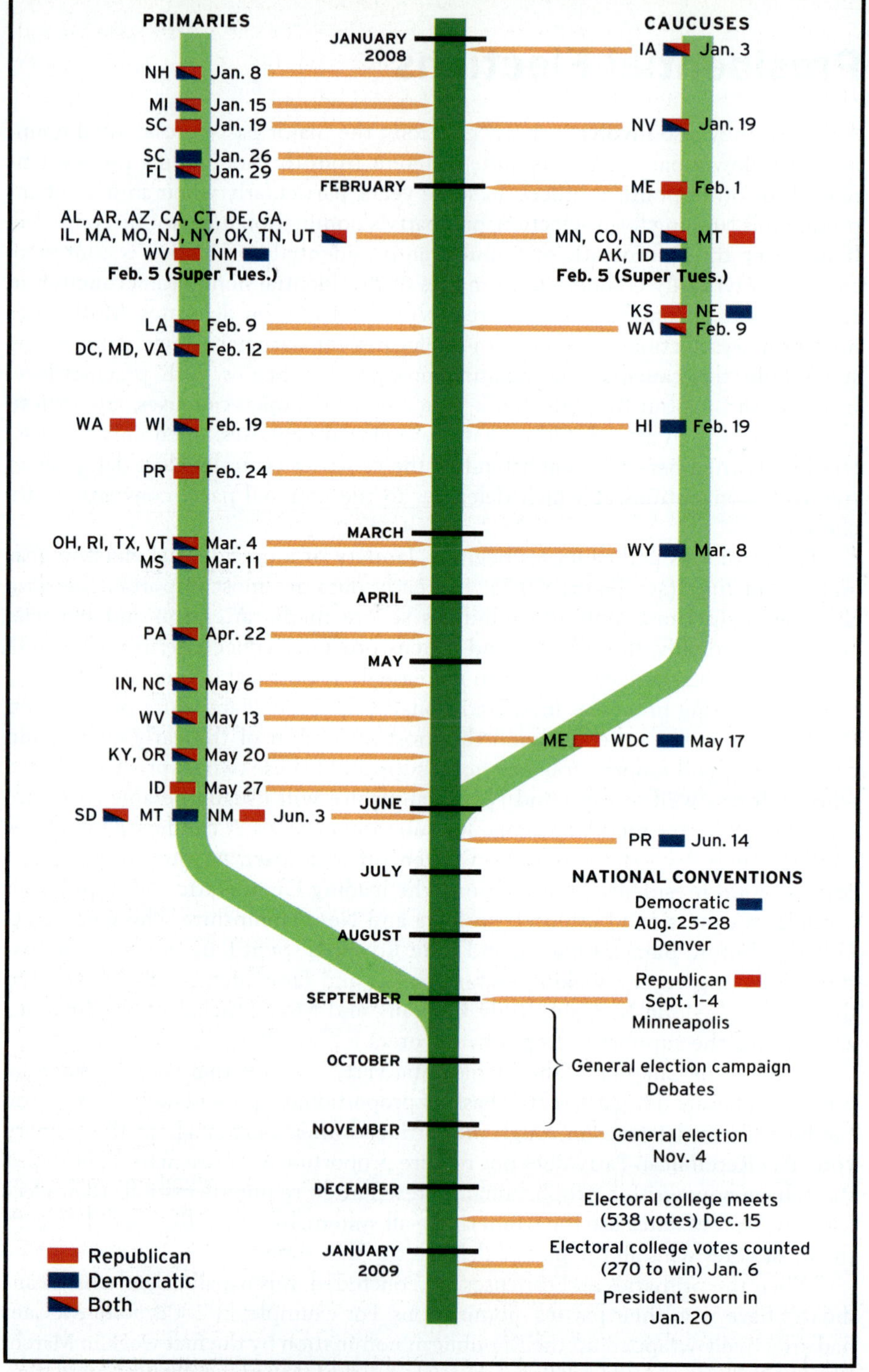

The Convention

The one major step that remains before a nomination is actually awarded is the national party convention. The Democratic and Republican national party conventions occur every four years to certify formally each party's presidential and vice-presidential nominees. In addition, the conventions draft a statement of party principles, called a **platform,** and determine the rules that will govern party activities for the next four years.

platform a party document, written at a national convention, that contains party philosophy, principles, and positions on issues

THE HISTORY OF POLITICAL CONVENTIONS For more than fifty years after America's founding, presidential nominations were controlled by each party's congressional caucus—all the party's members in the House and the Senate. Critics referred to this process as the "King Caucus" and charged that it did not take proper account of the views of party members throughout the nation. In 1824, the King Caucus method came under severe attack when the Democratic Party caucus failed to nominate Andrew Jackson, the candidate with the greatest support among both party members and activists outside the capital. In the 1830s, the party convention was devised as a way of allowing party leaders and activists throughout the nation to participate in selecting presidential candidates. The first party convention was held by the Anti-Masonic Party in 1831. The Democratic Party held its first convention in 1832, when Andrew Jackson was nominated for a second term.

As it developed during the course of the next century, the convention became the decisive institution in the presidential nominating processes of the two major parties. The convention was a genuine deliberative body in which party factions argued, negotiated, and eventually reached a decision. The convention was composed of delegations from each state. The size of a state's delegation depended on the state's population, and each delegate was allowed one vote for the purpose of nominating the party's presidential and vice-presidential candidates. Before 1936, victory required the support of two-thirds of the delegates. Until 1968, state delegations voted according to the unit rule, which meant that all the members of the state delegation would vote for the candidate favored by the majority of the state's delegates. This practice was designed to maximize a state's influence in the nominating process. The unit rule was abolished in 1968.

Between the 1830s and World War II, national convention delegates were generally selected by a state's party leaders. Usually the delegates were public officials, political activists, and party notables from all regions of the state, representing most major party factions. Some delegates would arrive at the convention having pledged in advance to give their support to a particular presidential candidate. Most delegates were uncommitted, however. This fact, coupled with the unit rule, allowed state party leaders (i.e., the delegates) to negotiate with each other and with presidential candidates for their support. State party leaders might agree to support a candidate in exchange for a promise to name them or their followers to important national positions, or in exchange for promises of federal programs and projects for their state. During the course of a convention, alliances of states would form, dissolve, and re-form in the course of tense negotiations. Typically, many votes were needed before the nomination could be decided. Often, deadlocks developed between the most powerful party factions, and state leaders would be forced to find a compromise, or "dark-horse," candidate. Among the more famous dark-horse nominees were James Polk in 1844 and Warren Harding in 1920. Although he was virtually unknown, Polk won the Democratic nomination when it

In the past, each party's nominees for president and vice president were chosen and announced at the national convention. Today, presidential and vice-presidential candidates are chosen in a series of primary elections and local caucuses, though they deliver acceptance speeches at the conventions.

became clear that none of the more established candidates could win. Similarly, Harding, another political unknown, won his nomination after the major candidates had fought one another to a standstill.

In its day, the convention was seen as a democratic reform. In later years, however, new generations of reformers came to view the convention as a symbol of rule by party leaders. The convention also strengthened the independence and power of the presidency by taking the nominating process out of the hands of Congress.

CONTEMPORARY PARTY CONVENTIONS Whereas the traditional party convention was a deliberative assembly, the contemporary convention acts more to ratify than to determine the party's presidential and vice-presidential nominations. Today, as we saw earlier in this chapter, the nomination is actually determined in a series of primary elections and local party caucuses held in virtually all fifty states during several months prior to the convention. These primaries and caucuses determine how each state's convention delegates will vote. Candidates now arrive at the convention knowing who has enough delegate support in hand to assure a victory in the first round of balloting. State party leaders no longer serve as power brokers, and the party's presidential and vice-presidential choices are made relatively quickly.

Even though the party convention no longer controls presidential nominations, it still has a number of important tasks. The first of these is the adoption of party rules concerning such matters as convention delegate selection and future presidential primary elections. In 1972, for example, the Democratic convention accepted rules requiring convention delegates to be broadly representative of the party's membership in terms of race and gender. After those rules were passed, the convention refused to seat several state delegations that were deemed not to meet this standard.

Another important task for the convention is the drafting of a party platform—a statement of principles and pledges around which the delegates can unite. Although the two major parties' platforms tend to contain many similar principles and platitudes, differences between the two platforms can be significant. In recent years, for example, the Republican platform has advocated tax cuts and taken strong positions on such social issues as affirmative action and abortion. The Democratic platforms, on the other hand, have focused on the importance of maintaining welfare and regulatory programs. A close reading of the party platforms can reveal some of the ideological differences between the parties.

CONVENTION DELEGATES Today, convention **delegates** are generally political activists with strong positions on social and political issues. Generally, Republican delegates tend to be more conservative than Republican voters as a whole, whereas Democratic delegates tend to be more liberal than the majority of Democratic voters. In states such as Michigan and Iowa, local party caucuses choose many of the delegates who will actually attend the national convention. In most of the remaining states, primary elections determine how a state's delegation will vote, but the actual delegates are selected by state party officials. Delegate votes won in primary elections are apportioned to candidates on the basis of proportional representation. Thus a candidate who received 30 percent of the vote in the California Democratic primary would receive roughly 30 percent of the state's delegate votes at the party's national convention.

delegates political activists selected to vote at a party's national convention

As was mentioned earlier, the Democratic Party requires that a state's convention delegation be representative of that state's Democratic electorate in terms of race, gender, and age. Republican delegates, by contrast, are more likely to be male and white. The Democrats also reserve slots for elected Democratic Party officials, called **superdelegates.** All the Democratic governors and about 80 percent of the party's members of Congress now attend the national convention as delegates.

superdelegate a convention delegate position, in Democratic conventions, reserved for party officials

CONVENTION PROCEDURE Each party convention lasts several days. The convention usually begins with the selection of party committees, including the credentials, rules, and platform committees, and the election of a temporary convention chairperson. This individual normally delivers a keynote address highlighting the party's appeals and concerns. After all the delegates have been seated by the credentials committee, a permanent chair is elected. This person presides over the presidential and vice-presidential nominations, the adoption of a party platform, and any votes on rules that are proposed by the rules committee.

Although the actual presidential nomination is effectively decided before the convention, the names of a number of candidates are generally put in nomination and speeches made on their behalf at the convention. To be nominated is considered an honor, and ambitious politicians are eager for the media attention, however brief, that such a nomination brings.

The nominating speeches, as well as speeches by party notables, are carefully scrutinized by the mass media, which report and analyze the major events of the convention. During the 1950s and 1960s, the television networks provided "gavel-to-gavel" coverage of the Democratic and Republican national conventions. Today, however, the major television networks carry convention highlights only. Because the parties are eager to receive as much media coverage as possible, they schedule convention events in order to reach large television audiences. The parties typically try to present the actual presidential nomination and the nominee's acceptance speech during prime viewing time, normally between 8:00 and 11:00 P.M. on a weeknight.

After the nominating speeches are concluded, the voting begins. The names of the states are called alphabetically and the state delegation's vote is reported by its chairperson. During this process, noisy and colorful demonstrations are staged in support of the nominees. When the nomination is formally decided, a lengthy demonstration ensues, with bands and colorful balloons celebrating the conclusion of the process. The party's vice-presidential candidate is usually nominated the next day. This individual is almost always selected by the presidential nominee, and the choice is merely ratified by the convention. In 2008, Barack Obama chose Senator Joseph Biden of Delaware, who brought extensive foreign policy experience to the ticket. John McCain chose Governor Sarah Palin of Alaska, partly in the hope that her very conservative stance on social issues would appeal to the religious right.

Once the nominations have been settled and most other party business has been resolved, the presidential and vice-presidential nominees deliver acceptance speeches. These speeches are opportunities for the nominees to begin their formal campaigns on a positive note, and they are usually meticulously crafted to make as positive an impression on the electorate as possible.

The General Election Campaign and High-Tech Politics

For those candidates lucky enough to survive the nominating process, the last hurdle is the general election. There are essentially two types of general election in the United States today. The first type is the organizationally driven, labor-intensive election. In general, local elections and many congressional races fall into this category. Candidates campaign in such elections by recruiting large numbers of volunteer workers to hand out leaflets and organize rallies. The candidates make appearances at receptions, community group meetings, and local events, and even in shopping malls and on busy street corners. Generally, local and congressional campaigns depend less on issues and policy proposals and more on hard work designed to make the candidate more visible than his or her opponent. Statewide campaigns, some congressional races, and, of course, the national presidential election fall into the second category: the media-driven, capital-intensive electoral campaign.

In the nineteenth and early twentieth centuries, political campaigns were waged by the parties' enormous armies of patronage workers. Throughout the year, party workers cultivated the support of voters by assisting them with legal problems, helping them find jobs, and serving as liaisons with local, state, and federal agencies. On Election Day, throughout the nation hundreds of thousands of party workers marched from house to house reminding their supporters to vote, helping the aged and infirm to reach the polls, and calling in the favors they had accrued during the year. Campaigns resembled the maneuvers of huge infantries vying for victory. Historians have, in fact, referred to this traditional style of party campaigning as "militarist."

Contemporary political campaigns rely less on infantries and more on "air power." That is, rather than deploying huge armies of workers, contemporary campaigns make use of a number of communications techniques to reach voters and bid for their support. Six techniques are especially important.

POLLING Surveys of voter opinion provide the information that candidates and their staffs use to craft campaign strategies. Candidates employ polls to select issues, to assess their own strengths and weaknesses (as well as those of the opposition), to check voter response to the campaign, and to determine the degree to

The Age of the Talk Show Campaign

Modern day political candidates are increasingly likely to seek out voters through non-news television programs such as talk shows, late-night comedy shows, or MTV. Not only do these programs provide candidates an opportunity to be seen by viewers who may not otherwise be following the campaign, but they also allow candidates to show a less formal side of their personalities and even poke fun at themselves.

In what is considered the first presidential candidate appearance on an entertainment show, in September 1968, Republican Richard Nixon delivered the catchphrase: "Sock it to me" on NBC's hit sketch comedy show *Laugh-In*. However, Nixon's successful appearance did not spark a wave of candidate appearances on entertainment shows. Most of the '70s and '80s found political candidates in their typical television forums: political advertisements, presidential debates, and network news programs. It wasn't until 1992 that the governor of Arkansas, Bill Clinton, became America's first talk-show presidential candidate, appearing on the popular late-night *Arsenio Hall Show* wearing sunglasses and playing the saxophone, and in a town hall style question and answer session on MTV. On MTV, Clinton responded to questions about what kind of underwear he wore, and about his past drug use.

Since the Clinton talk show campaign, Americans have come to expect their presidential candidates to show a softer and more humorous side of themselves on entertainment programs. In 2000, Al Gore and George Bush appeared separately on *Oprah*, *The Tonight Show with Jay Leno*, and *The Late Show with David Letterman*. In 2004, John Kerry made appearances with Leno and Letterman, and on *The Daily Show with Jon Stewart*. Both Bush and Kerry sat down separately with America's therapist Dr. Phil to respond to personal questions about family. Such intimate exchanges with potential leaders would have seemed inappropriate thirty years ago.

Late-night comedy programs also provide candidates an opportunity to poke fun at themselves. For example, several nights before the 2000 election, Bush and Gore appeared together on the sketch comedy show *Saturday Night Live* playing their own caricatures: Bush as bumbling fool who mispronounces words, and Gore as the stiff, dull, exaggerator who tells tall tales to make himself shine. In 2007, Barack Obama played himself in a *Saturday Night Live* skit mocking Hillary Rodham Clinton. The skit presented a Halloween party attended by masked characters portraying a number of Democratic politicians. When the Obama character removed his mask, he turned out to be Obama himself. Obama turned to the Hillary Clinton character and pointedly said, "You know, Hillary, I have nothing to hide." The Clinton character replied through clenched teeth, "That's great." The Hillary Clinton character was dressed as a bride, but the character portraying Bill Clinton said, "She's a witch."

Research shows that these appearances can help candidates. Studies have shown that when viewers see interviews with political candidates on late-night comedy programs, those viewers base evaluations of that candidate more on personal characteristics, like how much the candidate "cares about people like me." This can be particularly advantageous to political candidates whose policy positions are not popular, but whose personalities are warm or inspiring.

FOR CRITICAL ANALYSIS

1. If you were a presidential candidate, would you choose to be interviewed on talk shows? Why or why not?
2. Do you think presidential candidate appearances on talk shows contribute to a more informed electorate? Are they good for democracy? Why or why not?

SOURCES: Matthew Baum, "Talking the Vote: Why Presidential Candidates Hit the Talk Show Circuit," *American Journal of Political Science* 49, no. 2 (April 2005): 213–234(22); Elizabeth Kolbert, "Stooping to Conquer," *The New Yorker,* April 19, 2004; Patricia Moy, Michael A. Xenos, and Verena K. Hess, "Priming Effects of Late-Night Comedy," *International Journal of Public Opinion Research* (2006); and Katherine Q. Seelye, "Obama Plays Convincing Obama in a Skit Mocking Bill Clinton," *New York Times,* November 5, 2007, p. A17.

which various constituent groups are susceptible to campaign appeals. Virtually all contemporary campaigns for national and statewide office as well as many local campaigns make extensive use of opinion polling.

THE BROADCAST MEDIA Extensive use of the broadcast media, television in particular, has become the hallmark of the modern political campaign. Candidates endeavor to secure as much positive news and feature coverage as possible. This type of coverage is called *free media* because the cost of air time is borne by the media themselves. Candidates can secure free media coverage by participating in newsworthy events. Incumbents introduce legislation, sponsor hearings, undertake inspection tours of fires and floods, meet with delegations of foreign dignitaries, and so on, to capture the attention of the television cameras. Challengers announce new policy proposals, visit orphanages and senior centers, and demand that their opponent agree to a series of debates. Generally speaking, incumbents have the advantage in securing free media time.

spot advertisement a fifteen-, thirty-, or sixty-second television campaign commercial that permits a candidate's message to be delivered to a target audience

In addition to pursuing free media coverage, candidates spend millions of dollars for *paid media* time, in the form of television and radio ads. Many of these ads consist of fifteen-, thirty-, or sixty-second **spot advertisements** that permit a candidate's message to be delivered to a target audience before uninterested or hostile viewers can tune it out. Examples of extremely effective spot ads include George H. W. Bush's 1988 "Willie Horton" ad, which implied that Bush's opponent, Michael Dukakis, coddled criminals, and Lyndon Johnson's 1964 "daisy girl" ad, which suggested that his opponent, Barry Goldwater, would lead the United States into nuclear war. A successful 2008 spot ad promoting Hillary Clinton's candidacy presented an image of Senator Clinton surrounded by children and cradling a baby. "She changed our way of thinking when she introduced universal health care to America," the narrator intones. The ad ended with the often-repeated Clinton line, "If you're ready for change, she's ready to lead."[8] The ad was designed to soften Clinton's image while declaring her leadership experience in a realm that most Americans believe should be a legislative priority. Television spot ads are used to establish candidate name recognition, to create a favorable image of the candidate and a negative image of the opponent, to link the candidate with desirable groups in the community, and to communicate the candidate's stands on selected issues.

In a typical campaign, candidates will begin with biographical ads to acquaint voters with appealing aspects of their backgrounds. As the campaign progresses, candidates air ads dealing with important issues. In 2008, the presidential candidates presented ads focusing on taxes, foreign policy, health care, and Social Security during the middle rounds of the campaign. In the closing weeks of a campaign, candidates often unleash "attack ads," questioning the opponent's character or judgement. During their October 15, 2008, presidential debate, Obama and McCain criticized one another for running negative campaigns. McCain, however, insisted that his most controversial attack ads, accusing Obama of associating with 1960s radical, William Ayers, were completely fair and pointed to questions about Obama's character that merited consideration. In the same debate, McCain repeated questions about Obama's ties to ACORN, a liberal group accused of fraudulently registering large numbers of ineligible Democratic voters and other forms of election fraud.

The 1992 presidential campaign introduced two new media techniques that are still important today: the talk show interview and the "electronic town hall meeting." Candidates used interviews on television and radio talk shows to reach the large audiences drawn to this popular entertainment program format. The **town meeting** format allows candidates the opportunity to appear in an auditorium-like setting and interact with ordinary citizens, thus underlining the candidates' concern with the views and needs of the voters. Moreover, both talk-show appearances and town meetings allow candidates to deliver their messages to millions of Americans without the input of journalists or commentators who might criticize or question the candidates' assertions.

town meeting a media format in which candidates meet with ordinary citizens. Allows candidates to deliver messages without the presence of journalists or commentators

Another use of the broadcast media in contemporary campaigns is the televised candidate debate. Televised presidential debates began with the famous 1960 Kennedy-Nixon clash. Today, both presidential and vice-presidential candidates hold debates, as do candidates for statewide and even local offices. Debates allow candidates to reach voters who have not fully made up their minds about the election. Moreover, debates can increase the visibility of lesser-known candidates. In 1960, John F. Kennedy's strong performance in the presidential debate was a major factor in bringing about his victory over the much better known Richard Nixon.

PHONE BANKS Through the broadcast media, candidates communicate with voters en masse and impersonally. Phone banks, on the other hand, allow campaign workers to make personal contact with hundreds of thousands of voters. Personal contacts of this sort are thought to be extremely effective. Again, polling data identify the groups that will be targeted for phone calls. Computers select phone numbers from areas in which members of these groups are concentrated. Staffs of paid or volunteer callers, using computer-assisted dialing systems and prepared scripts, then place calls to deliver the candidate's message. The targeted groups are generally those identified by polls as either uncommitted or weakly committed, as well as strong supporters of the candidate who are contacted simply to encourage them to vote. In 2008, the campaigns also placed hundreds of thousands of automated "robo calls" urging voters to support their candidates.

DIRECT MAIL Direct mail is both a vehicle for communicating with voters and a mechanism for raising funds. The first step in a direct-mail campaign is the purchase or rental of a computerized mailing list of voters deemed to have some particular perspective or social characteristic. Often magazine subscription lists or lists of donors to various causes are employed. For example, a candidate interested in reaching conservative voters might rent subscription lists from the *National Review, Human Events,* or *Conservative Digest*; a candidate interested in appealing to liberals might rent subscription lists from the *New York Review of Books* or *The Nation.* Considerable fine-tuning is possible. After obtaining the appropriate mailing lists, candidates usually send pamphlets, letters, and brochures describing themselves and their views to voters believed to be sympathetic. Different types of mail appeals are made to different electoral subgroups. Often the letters sent to voters are personalized. The recipient is addressed by name in the text and the letter appears actually to have been signed by the candidate. Of course, these "personal" letters are written and even signed by a computer.

Despite the growing use of high-tech campaign techniques, candidates still rely on volunteer campaign workers to help get their messages out. Volunteers often go door to door, canvassing to encourage supporters of their candidate to get out and vote on Election Day.

In addition to its use as a political advertising medium, direct mail has also become an important source of campaign funds. Computerized mailing lists permit campaign strategists to pinpoint individuals whose interests, background, and activities suggest that they may be potential donors to the campaign. Letters of solicitation are sent to these potential donors. Some of the money raised is then used to purchase additional mailing lists. Direct-mail solicitation can be enormously effective.

PROFESSIONAL PUBLIC RELATIONS Modern campaigns and the complex technology they rely on are typically directed by professional public-relations consultants. Virtually all serious contenders for national and statewide office retain the services of professional campaign consultants. Increasingly, candidates for local office, too, have come to rely on professional campaign managers. Consultants offer candidates the expertise necessary to conduct accurate opinion polls, produce television commercials, organize direct-mail campaigns, and make use of sophisticated computer analyses.

The number of technologically oriented campaigns increased greatly after 1971. The Federal Election Campaign Act of 1971 prompted the creation of large numbers of political action committees (PACs) by a host of corporate and ideological groups. This development increased the availability of funds to political candidates—conservative candidates in particular—which meant in turn that the new technology could be used more extensively. Initially, the new techniques were employed mainly by individual candidates who often made little or no effort to coordinate their campaigns with those of other political aspirants sharing the same party label. For this reason, campaigns employing new technology sometimes came to be called "candidate-centered" efforts, as distinguished from the traditional party-coordinated campaign. Nothing about the new technology, however, precluded its use by political party leaders seeking to coordinate a number of campaigns. In recent years, party leaders have learned to make good use of modern campaign technology. The difference between the old and new political methods is not that the latter are inherently candidate-centered, whereas the former are strictly a party tool; it is a matter of the types of political resources on which each method depends.

THE INTERNET The Internet has become a major weapon in modern political campaigns. Although "netwar" has been a factor in politics since the 1990s, the 2008 campaigns made Internet tactics more central to their political strategies than ever before. Beginning with the primaries, every campaign developed a Web strategy for fund-raising, generating interest in the candidate, mobilizing supporters, and getting out the vote. The Clinton primary campaign made extensive use of the Internet to mobilize potential supporters and to raise money. The Edwards campaign used the Web to contact liberal activists who might have seen him as an alternative to Clinton and Obama. The Obama campaign, for its part, used the Internet to create events such as walkathons and fund-raisers all around the country. Obama, along with John McCain, created social networking sites that allow supporters to post information about themselves and to chat with each other. These sites help build enthusiasm and are potent fundraising tools. Obama's site was built by Thomas Gensemer and the company Blue State Digital. Obama's Web site played a major role in the Illinois senator's ability to raise money and build strong ties to supporters.[9]

AMERICA IN THE WORLD

American Campaign Techniques Conquer the World

Since the 1950s, American election campaigns have been characterized by a reliance on technology in place of organization and personnel and by the rise of a new type of campaigner, the professional political consultant, in place of the old-time party boss. More and more, these campaign methods and even the consultants who wield them have spread to other parts of the world. American campaign consultants with their polls and phone banks and spot ads have directed campaigns in Europe, Latin America, and Asia. One American consultant recently said, "[We have] worked a lot in South America, Israel, [and the] Philippines and one of the things that I've discovered through that work is that the tools and techniques and strategies that we have developed here are applicable everywhere."[a]

The foreign activities of American political consultants are depicted in a 2005 film documentary, *Our Brand Is Crisis*, which presents the story of a group of American consultants working in Bolivia in 2002. This phenomenon, which is sometimes called the Americanization of politics, has important political implications. For the most part, the substitution of technology for organization in political campaigns works to the advantage of politicians and political forces representing the upper ends of the social spectrum versus those representing the lower classes. Strong party organization was generally introduced by working-class parties as a way of maximizing their major political resource—the power of numbers. When politics is based mainly on organization and numbers, working-class parties can compete quite successfully. The growing use of technology in place of organization shifts the advantage to middle- and upper-class parties, which generally have better access to the financial resources needed to fuel the polls and television ads on which new-style campaigns depend. In the United States, the shift to high-tech politics was led by the Republicans. Democrats followed the GOP's lead but found themselves fighting on the opponents' terrain. Moreover, since technology is most effectively used by those Democrats with the best access to corporate and other financial resources, high-tech politics has generally served the interests of more moderate and conservative forces within the Democratic Party—Bill Clinton's "New Democrats," for example.

In Britain and France, new techniques were introduced first by conservative parties and then copied by their opponents. The development of the new technology in Europe and other parts of the world followed the American pattern.

This phenomenon is now becoming apparent in Africa, in particular in the nation of Kenya. In Kenya's 2008 presidential contest, for example, President Mwai Kibaki made use of consultants, opinion polls, and media technology in his nation's presidential race. The lynchpin of Kibaki's effort was the cell-phone campaign. Many Kenyan voters, especially in rural areas, lack Internet access or television service. Most, however, own cell phones. The president's ads, plastered on billboards throughout the nation, provided a cell-phone number and urged voters to call in their views. Voters were also likely to receive cell-phone calls and text messages from Kibaki supporters asking them to vote for the president. Not to be outdone, Kibaki's main rival, the populist Raila Odinga, hired Dick Morris, a former consultant to Bill Clinton, to offer advice to his campaign. Odinga used television ads designed by a media consultant and organized his own cell-phone campaign.[b]

Unfortunately, when Kibaki lost the election, he refused to cede power and a period of fighting ensued before a power-sharing agreement was reached. American consultants scurried for cover when the bullets flew.

FOR CRITICAL ANALYSIS

1. Which foreign political parties were first to adopt American-style campaign techniques? Why?
2. What are the political implications and consequences of the shift from old-fashioned campaign styles to American-style, technology-intensive politics?

---

a. Quoted in Paul Baines, Fritz Plasser, and Christian Scheucher, "Operationalising Political Marketing: A Comparison of US and Western European Consultants and Managers," Middlesex University Discussion Paper Series, No. 7, July 1999.

b. Stephanie McCrummen, "Kenya Tests New Style of Politicking," *Washington Post*, December 22, 2007, p. A10.

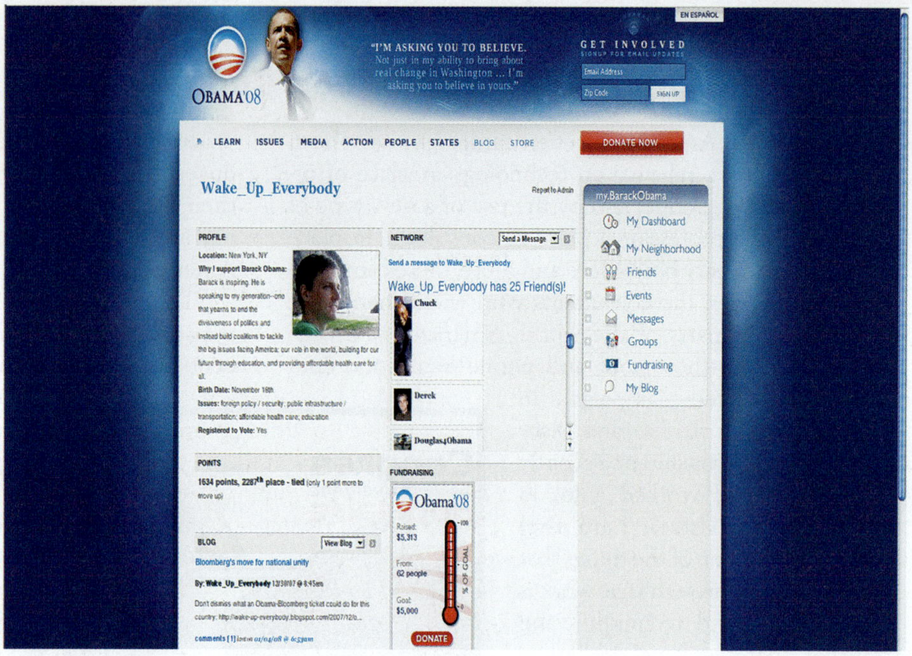

In the 2008 presidential race, the Obama campaign developed an innovative Web site with features based on social networking sites like Facebook. Obama supporters were able to create their own pages on the site for fund-raising and networking.

Campaigns and Political Equality: From Labor-Intensive to Capital-Intensive Politics

For Critical Analysis

In recent years, the Internet has become a prominent campaign tool. Does the Internet make electoral campaigns more democratic? Does it make them less democratic? Or are its effects neutral?

The displacement of organizational methods by technology is, in essence, a shift from labor-intensive to capital-intensive competitive electoral practices. Campaign tasks that were once performed by masses of party workers with some cash now require fewer personnel but a great deal more money, for the new political style depends on polls, computers, and other electronic paraphernalia. Of course, even when workers and organization were the key electoral tools, money had considerable political significance. Nevertheless, during the nineteenth century, national political campaigns in the United States employed millions of people. Indeed, as many as 2.5 million individuals did political work during the 1880s.[10] The direct cost of campaigns, therefore, was relatively low. For example, in 1860, Abraham Lincoln spent only $100,000—which was approximately twice the amount spent by his chief opponent, Stephen A. Douglas.

Modern campaigns depend heavily on money. Each element of contemporary political technology is enormously expensive. A sixty-second spot announcement on prime-time network television costs hundreds of thousands of dollars each time it is aired. Opinion surveys can be quite expensive; polling costs in a statewide race can easily reach or exceed the six-figure mark. Campaign consultants can charge substantial fees. The inauguration of a serious national direct-mail campaign requires at least $1 million in "front-end cash" to pay for mailing lists, brochures, letters, envelopes, and postage.[11] Even debate preparation requires substantial staff work, research, and, of course, money. It is the expense of new technology that accounts for the enormous cost of recent American national elections.

Certainly "people power" is not irrelevant to modern political campaigns. Candidates continue to utilize the political services of tens of thousands of volunteer workers. Nevertheless, in the contemporary era, even the recruitment of campaign workers has become a matter of electronic technology. Employing a technique called "instant organization," paid telephone callers use phone banks to contact individuals in areas targeted by a computer (which they do when contacting potential voters, as we discussed before). Volunteer workers are recruited from among these individuals. A number of campaigns—Richard Nixon's 1968 presidential campaign was the first—have successfully used this technique.

The displacement of organizational methods by technology has the farthest-reaching implications for the balance of power among contending political groups. Labor-intensive organizational tactics allowed parties whose chief support came from groups nearer the bottom of the social scale to use the numerical superiority of their forces as a partial counterweight to the institutional and economic resources more readily available to the opposition. The capital-intensive technological format, by contrast, has given a major boost to the political fortunes of those forces whose sympathizers are better able to furnish the large sums now needed to compete effectively.[12] Indeed, the new technology permits financial resources to be more effectively harnessed and exploited than was ever before possible.

Dominated by expensive technology, electoral politics has become a contest in which the wealthy and powerful have a decided advantage. Perhaps the use of the Internet is the only exception. Through the Internet, political candidates have been able to raise millions of dollars in small contributions from tens of thousands of donors. To maximize the power of online fund-raising, Internet "bundlers" such as ActBlue combine thousands of small contributions to make major donations to particular candidates. For example, in 2007 ActBlue raised over $4 million from 54,000 online donors for John Edwards's campaign for the Democratic presidential nomination.[13] Despite the potential of the Internet, online fund-raising produced only 5 to 10 percent of the more than $3 billion spent by or on behalf of candidates in the 2008 national elections. For the bulk of their funds, both political parties are compelled to rely heavily on the support of well-funded special interests—a situation that has become clear in the fund-raising scandals that have plagued both parties in recent years. We shall return to this topic later in this chapter.

How Voters Decide

Whatever the capacity of those with the money and power to influence the electoral process, it is the millions of individual decisions on Election Day that ultimately determine electoral outcomes. Sooner or later the choices of voters weigh more heavily than the schemes of campaign advisers or the leverage of interest groups.

Three factors influence voters' decisions at the polls: partisan loyalty, issues and policy concerns, and candidate characteristics.

Partisan Loyalty

Many studies have shown that most Americans identify more or less strongly with one or the other of the two major political parties. Partisan loyalty was considerably

FIGURE 10.4 ★
The Effect of Party Identification on the Vote, 2008

In 2008, nearly 90 percent of Democrats and Republicans supported their party's presidential candidate. Should candidates devote their resources to converting voters who identify with the opposition or to winning more support among independents? What factors might make it difficult for candidates to simultaneously pursue both courses of action?

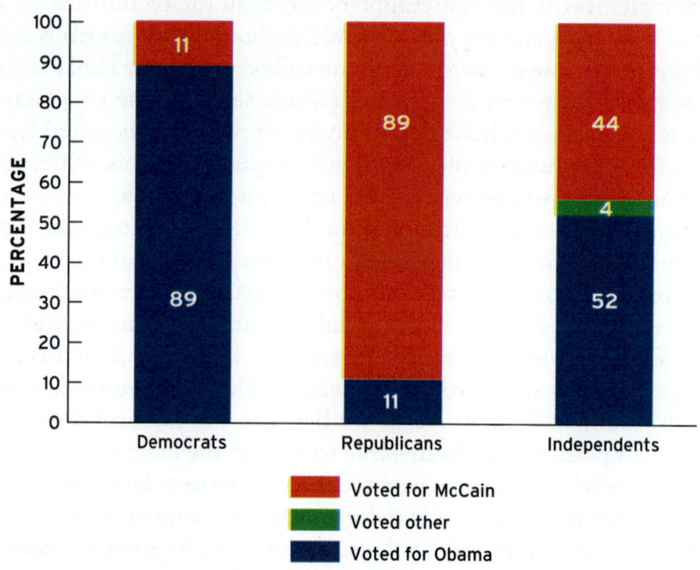

stronger during the 1940s and 1950s than it is today. But even now most voters feel a certain sense of identification or kinship with the Democratic or Republican party. This sense of identification is often handed down from parents to children and is reinforced by social and cultural ties. Partisan identification predisposes voters in favor of their party's candidates and against those of the opposing party (see Figure 10.4). At the level of the presidential contest, issues and candidate personalities may become very important, although even here many Americans supported John McCain or Barack Obama in the 2008 race only because of partisan loyalty. But partisanship is more likely to assert itself in the less-visible races, where issues and the candidates are not as well known. State legislative races, for example, are often decided by voters' party ties. Once formed, voters' partisan loyalties seldom change. Voters tend to keep their party affiliations unless some crisis causes them to reexamine the bases of their loyalties and to conclude that they have not given their support to the appropriate party. During these relatively infrequent periods of electoral change, millions of voters can change their party ties. For example, at the beginning of the New Deal era, between 1932 and 1936, millions of former Republicans transferred their allegiance to Franklin Roosevelt and the Democrats.

Issues

Issues and policy preferences are a second factor influencing voters' choices at the polls. Voters may cast their ballots for the candidate whose position on economic issues they believe to be closest to their own. Similarly, they may select the candidate who has what they believe to be the best record on foreign policy. Issues are more important in some races than others. If candidates actually "take issue" with each other, that is, articulate and publicize very different positions on important public questions, then voters are more likely to be able to identify and act on whatever policy preferences they may have.

The ability of voters to make choices on the basis of issue or policy preferences is diminished, however, if competing candidates do not differ substantially or do not focus their campaigns on policy matters. Very often, candidates deliberately take the safe course and emphasize topics that will not be offensive to any voters. Thus, candidates often trumpet their opposition to corruption, crime, and inflation. Presumably, few voters favor these things. Although it may be perfectly reasonable for candidates to take the safe course and remain as inoffensive as possible, this candidate strategy makes it extremely difficult for voters to make their issue or policy preferences the basis for their choices at the polls.

Voters' issue choices usually involve a mix of their judgments about the past behavior of competing parties and candidates and their hopes and fears about candidates' future behavior. Political scientists call choices that focus on future behavior **prospective voting,** whereas those based on past performance are called **retrospective voting.** To some extent, whether prospective or retrospective evaluation is more important in a particular election depends on the strategies of competing candidates. Candidates always endeavor to define the issues of an election in terms that will serve their interests. Incumbents running during a period of prosperity will seek to take credit for the economy's happy state and define the election as revolving around their record of success. This strategy encourages voters to make retrospective judgments. By contrast, an insurgent running during a period of economic uncertainty will tell voters it is time for a change and ask them to make prospective judgments. Thus, Bill Clinton focused on change in 1992 and prosperity in 1996, and through well-crafted media campaigns was able to define voters' agenda of choices.

prospective voting voting based on the imagined future performance of a candidate

retrospective voting voting based on the past performance of a candidate

In 2008, no incumbent was running for the presidency. Democrats, however, sought to portray Republican candidate, John McCain, as simply a continuation of the failed Bush administration and took every opportunity to link McCain to Bush's unpopular economic and foreign policies. McCain, for his part, portrayed himself as a "maverick" who had often disagreed with Bush and other Republicans. During one of their debates, McCain responded to a comment from Barack Obama linking McCain to Bush policies by saying that he was not George Bush and that if Obama had wanted to run against Bush he should have run in 2004. In the end, voters associated a Republican White House with their economic woes and took out their frustrations on the Republican candidate.

THE ECONOMY As we identify the strategies and tactics employed by opposing political candidates and parties, we should keep in mind that the best-laid plans of politicians often go awry. Election outcomes are affected by a variety of forces that candidates for office cannot fully control. Among the most important of these forces is the condition of the economy. If voters are satisfied with their economic prospects, they tend to support the party in power, while voter unease about the economy tends to favor the opposition. Thus, George H. W. Bush lost in 1992 during an economic downturn even though his victory in the Middle East had briefly given him a 90 percent favorable rating in the polls. And Bill Clinton won in 1996 during an economic boom even though voters had serious concerns about his moral fiber. As we shall see later in this chapter, the 2008 financial crisis gave Barack Obama and the Democrats a significant advantage.

FIGURE 10.5 ★
Consumer Confidence and Presidential Elections

Since 1968, the Consumer Confidence Index has been a reliable predictor of incumbents' political fortunes. Was the result of the 2008 election consistent with this trend? What issues other than the economy influenced the 2008 election?

*Survey was bimonthly prior to 1977 so figures for 1968, 1972, and 1976 are for October and they are for September from 1983 on.
†Gore won the popular vote but Bush was elected by the Electoral College.
SOURCE: Bloomberg Financial Markets.

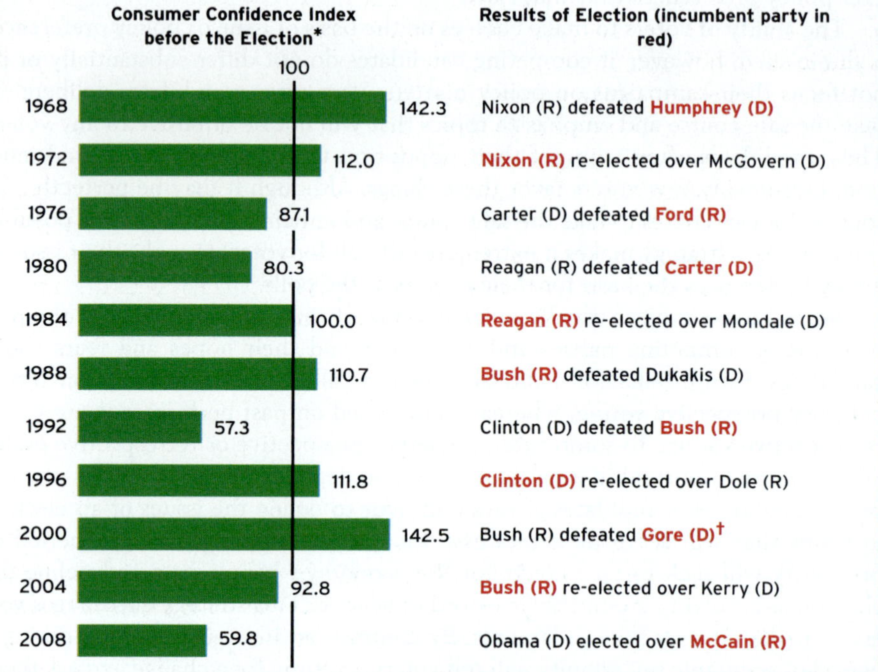

Over the past quarter-century, the "Consumer Confidence Index," calculated by the Conference Board, a business research group, has been a fairly accurate predictor of presidential outcomes. The index is based on surveys asking voters how optimistic they are about the future of the economy. It would appear that a generally rosy view, indicated by a score over 100, augurs well for the party in power. An index score under 100, suggesting that voters are pessimistic about the economy's trend, suggests that incumbents should worry about their own job prospects (see Figure 10.5).

Candidate Characteristics

Candidates' personal attributes always influence voters' decisions. Some analysts claim that voters prefer tall candidates to short ones, candidates with shorter names to candidates with longer names, and candidates with lighter hair to candidates with darker hair. Perhaps these rather frivolous criteria do play some role. But the more important candidate characteristics that affect voters' choices are race, ethnicity, religion, gender, geography, and social background. In general, voters prefer candidates who are closer to themselves in terms of these categories; voters presume that such candidates are likely to have views and perspectives close to their own. Moreover, they may be proud to see someone of their ethnic, religious, or geographic background in a position of leadership. This is why, for many years, politicians sought to "balance the ticket," making certain that their party's ticket included members of as many important groups as possible.

For Critical Analysis

Do American political campaigns help voters make decisions? Or do they produce more confusion than enlightenment?

Just as candidates' personal characteristics may attract some voters, they may repel others. Many voters are prejudiced against candidates of certain ethnic, racial, or religious groups. And for many years voters were reluctant to support the candidacies of women, although this appears to be changing. Indeed, the fact that in 2008 the Democratic candidate was a black man and the Republican vice-presidential candidate a woman indicates the ongoing collapse of previously rigid political barriers.

Voters also pay attention to candidates' personality characteristics, such as "decisiveness," "honesty," and "vigor." In recent years, integrity has become a key election issue. In 2008, Republicans frequently questioned Barack Obama's character, pointing to his association with 1960s radical, William Ayers, and with outspoken black minister, Rev. Jeremiah Wright. Democrats, for their part, attacked Sarah Palin for alleged abuses of power in Alaska. However, voters seemed less concerned with these matters than with the ability of the candidates to deal with the nation's economic woes. In hard times, the electorate tends to become impatient with partisan mudslinging.

The 2008 Election

The 2008 presidential election was in some ways predictable—voters wanted a change from a very unpopular Republican administration and, perhaps predictably, elected a Democrat—but in many ways the 2008 race was a groundbreaking departure from politics as usual. In 2008, for the first time in the nation's history, Americans elected an African American to the White House as Illinois senator Barack Obama led the Democratic Party to a solid electoral victory, securing 53 percent of the popular vote versus Republican candidate, Senator John McCain's 46 percent. Obama won a 365-to-173 majority in the Electoral College (see Figure 10.6), far more than the 270 electoral votes needed to claim the presidency. The 2008 presidential election was also notable because of the prominence of women candidates. Hillary Clinton's strong campaign for the Democratic nomination shattered the notion that a woman couldn't compete seriously for the nation's highest office, and John McCain's selection of Sarah Palin as his running mate seemed based at least partly on the advantages of having a woman on the ticket. The 2008 campaigns also brought about a significant shift in the electoral map, as states like Virginia and North Carolina that hadn't supported a Democratic candidate in decades went from "red" to "blue."

As noted above, the Democrats increased their strength in both houses of Congress, adding at least six seats in the Senate, giving them a larger majority, and four more seats still up for grabs pending recounts in the days after the election. Democrats had hoped to reach the magical sixty-seat total that would prevent GOP filibusters from blocking votes on Democratic bills. Democrats also gained at least twenty-two seats in the House of Representatives (eight were still undecided at the end of the night) to win a 254-to-173 majority in the lower chamber with more seats possible. Further embarrassing the Republicans, incumbent GOP senators in New Hampshire (John Sununu) and North Carolina (Elizabeth Dole) were ousted by Democratic challengers. Because of enormous interest in the campaign, the increasing use of absentee and pre-Election Day voting, and well-financed voter registration drives conducted mainly by the Democrats, more than 120 million Americans cast ballots in 2008, a number comparable to the level of turnout reached in 2004.

Politics Today

In 2006 and 2007 several states enacted "voter ID" laws requiring voters to produce photo identification at the polls. Republicans say such laws are needed to prevent fraud. Democrats charge these laws are intended to intimidate minority voters. What do you think about voter ID requirements?

The Path to 2008: Modern Electoral Politics and Race

At one level, the 2008 results are not so surprising. Outgoing Republican president George W. Bush had become one of the most unpopular chief executives in American history, the nation seemed mired in never-ending and inconclusive wars in the Middle East and, to make matters even worse, the nation's fall 2008 financial crisis appeared to presage a deep economic recession. Could there be any reason the GOP could even hope to survive the triple whammy of recession, war, and an extraordinarily unpopular Republican president? One reason Republicans might have hoped for survival in 2008 was the matter of race. Democrat Barack Obama is the son of a black African father and white Kansan mother, and was the first nonwhite major party presidential candidate in American history. Given America's tangled racial politics and sometimes violent racial antagonisms, many observers questioned whether white Americans were prepared to elect a black man to the highest office in the land. As late as September 2008, polls showed that more than one-third of white Democratic and independent voters harbored misgivings about the idea of a black president. That tens of millions of whites did vote for the Democratic candidate is a reflection both of Obama's unique attributes and of underlying changes in American race relations over the past several decades.

To understand the significance of the 2008 election, a bit of political history is in order. The roots of Obama's victory go back nearly a half century to the civil rights movement of the 1960s. The white South had been a solid Democratic bastion since the end of Reconstruction and was a lynchpin of Democratic power in the Congress and the White House. Indeed, during this era, many black Americans believed that the Republican Party, which had no ties to the South, was more likely to take up their cause than the Democrats. However, a younger generation of northern Democratic leaders saw support for the civil rights movement as a matter of moral necessity and, at the same time, came to believe that there were potential political advantages to be gotten from supporting the black cause. In particular, northern liberals believed that by allying themselves with blacks they would enhance their power within the Democratic Party vis-à-vis the southern barons and northern machine politicians, and labor leaders who were such dominant forces in Democratic leadership circles.

After President Kennedy's assassination, Democratic liberals secured the support of President Lyndon Johnson. Prodded by Johnson and against the backdrop of increasingly violent southern resistance to peaceful civil rights protests, Congress enacted the 1965 Voting Rights Act under whose auspices federal voting officials presided over the registration of millions of African American voters in the former Confederacy. Johnson also issued executive orders mandating "affirmative action," a term first coined by the Kennedy administration, in federal hiring and contracting. Johnson's orders began an era of affirmative action in hiring and education. Johnson justified affirmative action by saying that having been deprived of opportunity for so long, African Americans should, at least temporarily, be given extra opportunities until the playing field was leveled. These landmark efforts changed America's political landscape but, at least initially, not in the way that liberal Democrats had hoped.

THE GOP'S SOUTHERN STRATEGY Democratic support for black voting rights and affirmative action infuriated millions of white southerners and, at the

Barack Obama's candidacy energized Democratic voters, and especially young voters and African American voters. His rallies frequently drew enormous crowds, as when he spoke in St. Louis to a crowd that was reported to number around 100,000 people.

same time, angered many blue-collar northern Democrats over what they saw as preferential treatment for blacks when they themselves were engaged in day-to-day economic struggles. These resentments were exploited by an opportunistic southern governor, George Wallace of Alabama, who launched an independent presidential candidacy in 1968. Wallace won millions of votes, mainly in the South, and the electoral votes of five southern states. With the Democratic Party divided by racial conflicts and struggles over the Vietnam War, the 1968 election was won by Republican Richard Nixon, who launched what he called his "southern strategy," to bring disaffected southern whites who had supported Wallace into the Republican camp. Nixon attacked racial preferences and declared that the civil rights movement had gone too far in its demands. Nixon intimated that he spoke for a "silent majority" of American whites who were fed up with civil rights protestors and claims from other disaffected groups. In response to Nixon's appeals, millions of southern whites began to shift their political allegiance to the Republican Party. With the enfranchisement of southern blacks, Democrats had lost the support of the more numerous southern white community and the once solidly Democratic South was becoming the new solidly Republican South.

Ronald Reagan built upon but significantly modified Nixon's efforts. After taking office in 1980, Reagan eschewed the sorts of racial appeals that had been made by Nixon eight years earlier. Instead, Reagan made use of patriotic and religious symbols that would resonate not only among white southerners but also among blue-collar white northerners who might harbor racist sentiments but were uncomfortable with the sorts of overt race baiting that had been common in the South. Reagan wrapped the GOP in patriotism and the American flag and, in particular, Reagan and his advisers turned to "family values" issues, especially the

Although Barack Obama's victory in the 2008 presidential election seemed to signal a new era in race relations, there were some charges of racism during the campaign. These protesters demonstrated against FoxNews, not long after Fox referred to Obama's wife as his "baby mama" in a news heading.

issue of abortion, to appeal to Catholic and Protestant religious conservatives in the North and South. With this strategy, Reagan cemented the support of white southerners for the Republicans and made significant inroads among patriotic and religious blue-collar voters in the North, as well. These voters came to be known as the Republican "base" and every two years they were mobilized for political action by activist religious leaders and conservative radio personalties.

THE DEMOCRATS' RACIAL DILEMMA As for the Democrats during this period, the nation's racial politics and racial polarization posed significant political dilemmas, especially at the presidential level. Championing the cause of civil rights had helped Democratic liberals greatly expand their power within the Democratic Party but had undermined the party's fortunes in national presidential elections. Racial divisions were one reason that the Democrats lost seven of ten presidential elections between 1968 and 2004, electing only two presidents in a forty-year period. Efforts by Democratic presidential candidates to rebuild their party's support among southern whites and blue-collar northerners were hampered by the harsh racial arithmetic of American politics. In the wake of the Voting Rights Act, the Democratic Party depended upon African Americans for more than 20 percent of its votes in national presidential elections. Yet, at the same time, and for a somewhat larger percentage of Democratic and independent voters, the Democrats relied upon whites who, for one or another reason, were unfriendly to blacks.

THE 2000 AND 2004 ELECTIONS In 2000 and 2004, George W. Bush generally followed the electoral game plan developed by Ronald Reagan. In 2000, Bush's own ineptitude and general voter satisfaction with the economics, if not the public morality of the Clinton years, almost cost the Republicans the presidency. In fact, Bush lost the popular vote but thanks to the vagaries of the Electoral College system and the intervention of the Supreme Court, Bush became America's forty-third president.

As president, Bush reacted forcefully to the September 11, 2001 terrorist attacks against the United States and temporarily saw his standing in the polls rise to a stratospheric 90 percent level. Over the next two years, however, sluggish economic growth and the Bush administration's miscues in Iraq seemed to offer the Democrats an opportunity to reclaim the White House. Bush, however, made enormous efforts to register and mobilize the Republican base. During the November election, Republican campaign materials emphasized moral themes and the president's religious and moral commitments, and the GOP launched a series of ballot initiatives on such "hot button" issues as same-sex marriage and abortion. Though Bush's dismal performance in the 2004 presidential debates briefly seemed to threaten his re-election, the Republican base rallied to his side and handed him a solid electoral victory.

Virtually unnoticed during the 2000 and 2004 elections, and during Bush's years in office, was a decline in the racial polarization of American politics. Some Americans, to be sure, continued to harbor animosities toward one another, but race seemed to be less salient in the political arena. To some extent, the credit for this development should go to Ronald Reagan. Reagan had made a deliberate decision to drop the racially charged Republican rhetoric of the Nixon years in favor of a focus on patriotism and religious values. This shift in rhetoric was not total and absolute but it meant that the number of overtly racial appeals and even racial code words found in political debate gradually diminished, and that issues of race were gradually deemphasized on the national political battlefield. It was significant that George W. Bush, a conservative president, appointed African Americans, such as former secretaries of state Colin Powell and Condoleezza Rice, and other non-white candidates to high government positions. Democrats accused Bush and the Republicans of racial tokenism, but these tokens were important.

In an atmosphere in which racially charged rhetoric was on the decline, other social processes could begin to have an effect. After the civil rights revolution of the 1960s, and the erosion of America's many systems of segregation, both legal and customary, blacks and whites were more likely to live in the same neighborhoods, attend the same schools, work in the same factories and offices, serve in the military together, and frequent the same stores, restaurants, and entertainment venues. For many Americans the end of segregation opened the way for a gradual lessening of racial antagonisms over the course of several decades. The nation's demographics also changed during this period. A huge influx of immigrants from Latin America as well as Asia and the Middle East meant that America was no longer a land of black and white. It now included many shades of brown, as well, complicating the nation's once more clear-cut racial divisions. In this new America, explicitly racist appeals from politicians would seem out of step and illegitimate.

All these developments did not bring an end to white misgivings about blacks or, for that matter, black suspicions about whites. Nevertheless, over the decades following the civil rights movement, racial antagonisms in the United States had softened. Indeed, a growing number of white voters began to show a willingness to support blacks for political office. According to the Joint Center for Political and Economic Studies, by 2008 about 30 percent of the nation's black state legislators represented predominately white districts. This change, in turn, would make it possible for the Democrats to overcome the racial dilemma that had plagued them for decades.

The 2008 Campaigns

In this political landscape of shifting race relations and frustration with a Republican administration, Democrats saw that 2008 offered a major opportunity to reclaim the White House. Democratic strategists were determined not to repeat their errors in 2000 and 2004. In the 2006 congressional elections, the Democrats picked up momentum, winning majorities in both houses of Congress for the first time since 1994. By 2006, the electorate already blamed the GOP for a sluggish economy and seemingly endless war. As voters became increasingly dissatisfied with the policies promoted by President Bush and supported by his Republican allies in Congress, it appeared that the stage was set for a Democratic victory in 2008.

THE 2008 PRIMARIES The 2008 Democratic and Republican primaries and caucuses to select the parties' candidates for the presidency began January 3 with the Iowa Democratic caucuses. The actual campaigns, of course, began early in 2007 as ambitious politicians assessed their chances and started the long process needed to raise the tens of millions of dollars required to launch a presidential candidacy. On the Republican side, the front-runner was John McCain. The Arizona senator had campaigned for the Republican nomination in 2000 only to be defeated by Bush in a primary contest remembered for the victor's smear tactics. McCain, the son and grandson of U.S. Navy admirals, was a Vietnam War hero whose body still bore the marks of having been severely tortured by the North Vietnamese after he was captured when his plane was shot down during a bombing mission. McCain had a distinguished career in the Senate and was the chief sponsor of several major pieces of legislation including the McCain-Feingold campaign reform law. When the Republicans had last controlled the Senate, McCain had chaired the Foreign Relations Committee and was regarded in Washington as one of the Senate's foreign policy experts. Despite his national prominence, McCain was generally not well liked in Republican circles. The party's business wing was suspicious of McCain because of his reformist bent and often found him annoyingly hypocritical for continually denouncing the role of big money in politics while frequently approaching corporate donors and lobbyists to ask for their support. For its part, the GOP's social-conservative base distrusted McCain whom they saw as uninterested—at best—in the various social issues they regarded as having paramount political importance. Traditional Republicans might have preferred Mitt Romney, a successful businessperson and former governor of Massachusetts, but the GOP's evangelical Protestant cadres did not like the idea of Romney, a Mormon, as their party's candidate. Social conservatives supported former Arkansas governor and evangelical minister, Mike Huckabee, an articulate politician whose sense of humor made him a successful guest on *Saturday Night Live.* Other Republicans, Ron Paul, Rudy Guliani, and Fred Thompson, excited little interest.

After losing the Iowa caucuses to Huckabee and struggling to raise money, McCain regained his political and financial footing and was able to drive his opponents from the race. McCain had effectively secured the Republican nomination by the beginning of March. Though Republicans appeared to have no serious alternative to McCain, the Arizona senator's candidacy did not excite the party. A large segment of the GOP's conservative base was uninspired by McCain, and some saw him as a liberal in Republican clothing.

CLINTON VERSUS OBAMA On the Democratic side, the clear front-runner for the presidential nomination was New York senator and former first lady Hillary Rodham Clinton. Senator Clinton was famous, her husband was extraordinarily popular among Democrats, and her contacts and position as a New York senator meant that she would be able to count on tens of millions of dollars in campaign contributions. Most pundits predicted an easy Clinton victory. Other Democratic contenders included former North Carolina senator and 2004 vice-presidential candidate John Edwards, former New Mexico governor Bill Richardson, congressman Dennis Kucinich, former Alaska senator Mike Gravel, and senators Joe Biden, Chris Dodd, and Barack Obama. Biden, Dodd, and Richardson, along with Gravel and Kucinich, generated relatively little interest and quickly dropped out. Edwards was popular among his fellow trial lawyers who contributed enough money to his campaign to keep him in through the end of January, though with little chance of success. The surprise of the Democratic primary contest was, of course, Illinois senator Barack Obama.

Obama was a first-term senator, having arrived in Washington in 2004. He had won a measure of national celebrity by delivering a rousing keynote address at the 2004 Democratic national convention. Many Democrats' first opportunity to see Obama as a serious contender came in the Democratic debates. Prior to and during the primary contests, it has become conventional for each party's contenders to hold televised debates on various issues of national interest. Twenty-six debates between the Democratic hopefuls were scheduled, beginning in April 2007 with the last debate in April 2008. For the most part, the debaters acquitted themselves well, committing few gaffes. Media analysts generally thought Clinton had a somewhat stronger command of the issues, though some thought Edwards spoke more forcefully. However, the true winner of the primary-season debates was Obama. The Illinois senator was not necessarily more articulate, more knowledgeable, or more

Hillary Clinton was seen as the front-runner for the Democratic nomination in the months leading up to the primaries. How to address the ongoing war in Iraq was an issue debated by the Democratic candidates, and Clinton was criticized by some Democrats for initially supporting the war.

In his bid for the presidency, John McCain strived to distance himself from George W. Bush, whose popularity had reached record lows prior to the 2008 election. However, Americans' reluctance to elect another Republican after the Bush administration's poor performance contributed to McCain's defeat.

passionate about important issues than Clinton, Edwards, and the others, but observers were impressed that at debate after debate the virtually unknown senator stood toe to toe with his more seasoned and famous opponents and held his own. Obama's impressive performance electrified liberal Democrats, excited young voters, intrigued the media, and ignited the enthusiasm of black Democrats, even if most were initially dubious that Obama could succeed. This enthusiastic response to Obama's debate appearances swelled the ranks of Obama supporters, inspired donors to write checks, and gave Obama the means to compete against Clinton and Edwards.

Over the next six months, Clinton and Obama battled furiously in state after state. Edwards dropped out of the race, and Obama had established himself as a contender with the potential to defeat the once seemingly invincible Clinton. Obama was particularly popular with younger voters and with liberals who resented what they saw as Clinton's early equivocation on the Iraq war. Black politicians—many of whom considered Bill Clinton an important ally during his presidency—initially supported Hillary Clinton, assuming she would win. But, as their constituents rallied to Obama, and it became clear that Obama's candidacy actually had a chance, the Illinois senator was able to garner overwhelming black support. Some pundits said it was ironic that the first woman to mount a serious presidential bid and the first black person to mount such a bid were pitted against one another. For the news media, however, in this battle of the firsts, Obama's candidacy was the more important first. Clinton was seen as an established figure on the political scene—a powerful senator from New York, former first lady, and wife of perhaps the most powerful figure in the Democratic Party. Clinton's status in some ways worked against her. To some commentators it appeared that Clinton had already been co-president for eight years and was no longer a first.

By late spring, it became clear that Obama would be the Democratic presidential nominee. The result was close. Under Democratic rules, 2,118 delegates were needed to win the nomination. In the various primaries and caucuses, Obama had won 1,763 delegates to Clinton's 1,640. This effectively left the decision to the party's 796 "superdelegates," party officials and notables chosen to attend the convention. At the outset, most superdelegates had backed Clinton. As the race wore on, however, sentiment shifted toward Obama. Some saw Obama as the better candidate while others worried that black Democrats—20 percent of the party's electoral strength—would stay home on Election Day if Obama was denied the nomination. With 438 superdelegates supporting Obama, he could count on 2,201 votes. Clinton briefly weighed taking her candidacy to the floor of the convention to be decided there, but ultimately, on June 3, withdrew and announced that she and her husband would staunchly support Obama in the general election.

THE GENERAL ELECTION At the August 2008 Democratic national convention, speaker after speaker extolled Obama's virtues. Obama chose Delaware senator Joseph Biden as his vice-presidential running mate. Biden, chair of the Senate Foreign Relations Committee, was selected at least partly in response to questions about Obama's scant foreign policy experience. In addition, Biden had working-class roots in Pennsylvania. Democrats hoped that Biden would appeal to the so-called "Joe Six-pack" voters, blue-collar workers whom the Democrats needed in such battleground states as Ohio and Pennsylvania.

The Republican convention, which opened a few days after the Democratic convention ended, began without much fanfare. Hurricane Gustav, which was bearing down on the Gulf states, led the Republicans to cancel many of the first day's events, as they wanted to make clear that they were taking a possible natural disaster seriously. Rather than attending the convention, President Bush addressed the delegates via video. Moreover, although John McCain won the primary battle and was respected for his military service, he was not an especially beloved figure among rank-and-file Republicans. Nevertheless, McCain excited and energized Republicans when he chose little-known Alaska governor Sarah Palin as his vice-presidential running mate and "introduced" her to the GOP base at the convention. Palin, a religious conservative who opposed abortion, excited many Republicans who had been cool toward McCain.

Palin's vice-presidential acceptance speech, which might otherwise have been watched by a handful of diehard Republicans, attracted more than 50 million curious viewers when it was broadcast from the convention. Palin rose to the occasion and delivered a strong speech, filled with memorable quips and emphasizing issues of character and family values. "A star is born," declared conservative commentator Pat Buchanan after the speech. Unfortunately for the GOP, Palin's star faded rapidly as the inexperienced governor proved unequal to the demands of a national campaign. In television interviews, including one with Katie Couric on CBS, Palin seemed to know little about current political issues and problems, and could do no more than repeat Republican talking points that she seemed to have committed to memory. Despite her reasonably good performance in the nationally televised vice-presidential debate, Palin was declared "clearly out of her league," even by staunchly Republican commentators who wondered aloud if Palin could seriously be entrusted with the presidency if anything happened to McCain.

Republican voters were initially enthusiastic about McCain's choice of Governor Sarah Palin of Alaska as his running mate. However, Palin stumbled badly in television interviews, including an interview with CBS's Katie Couric in which Palin's answers sometimes seemed incoherent. Palin's poor performance was the subject of widely viewed skits on Saturday Night Live, *in which comedian Tina Fey impersonated Palin, in one case using Palin's own words from the interview with Katie Couric.*

Despite the brief surge of enthusiasm generated by the selection of Palin, the McCain ticket struggled throughout the campaign. From the beginning the deck seemed stacked against the Republicans. Despite his protestations of independence, the fact remained that McCain was a Republican and, hence, tied to the Bush administration. Obama and the Democrats, moreover, held an enormous fund-raising advantage over McCain and the Republicans. Knowing that he would have difficulty raising money from traditional GOP donors, McCain had decided to accept public funding for the general election. This would give his campaign some $84 million to spend on organizing, advertising, and voter registration. McCain hoped Republican Party fund-raising would add considerably to this figure. Obama, on the other hand, became the first major-party candidate since the law was enacted to forgo general election public funding. Obama was, instead, able to step up his Internet and conventional fund-raising, which eventually produced in the neighborhood of $700 million, an astonishing total that more than doubled the previous record set by the Republicans in 2004. His campaign's extraordinary fund-raising prowess gave Obama and the Democrats some $200 million more to spend than was available to McCain and the Republicans.

Lack of money was not McCain's only problem. Beginning in 2008, the nation experienced a serious financial crisis that began with a decline in home sales and a wave of mortgage foreclosures, and continued with billions of dollars of losses in mortgage-based securities. Toward the end of September, the stock market lost more than a third of its value, wiping out trillions of dollars in investments. Some of the nation's leading financial institutions, such as the venerable Lehman Brothers failed, and a host of others seemed poised to close their doors. Since all these events took place while the Republicans controlled the White House, the Democrats were quick to blame the Bush administration's economic policies for the crisis though, in truth, congressional Democrats had often protected such institutions as Fannie Mae and Freddie Mac that were at the root of the problem. Nevertheless, Republican presidential chances seemed to decline with the stock market as the GOP bore the brunt of the public's anger and concern.

THE DEBATES Obama helped his cause enormously in the three televised presidential debates held in September and October. He responded with evident knowledge and intelligence to questions on matters of domestic and foreign policy. So, for that matter, did McCain. But McCain, the Washington veteran, was expected to have answers to policy questions. Obama was the newcomer who had been chided for his inexperience. Like Kennedy, Reagan, and Clinton before him, Obama bore the burden of reassuring voters that he measured up to the job of being president. In the debates, Obama spoke clearly and incisively on education, economic policy, health policy, and the wars in Iraq and Afghanistan. McCain, to be sure, had actual experience in all these areas while Obama only spoke well, but the same had been true of—and enough for—Kennedy, Reagan, and Clinton.

Even more important was Obama's manner. By contrast with the often twitchy McCain, Obama was smooth, calm, and reassuring. Many commentators observed that Obama appeared "presidential," and that this helped more and more Americans feel comfortable with his candidacy. Following the debates, Obama's approval ratings rose steadily and the McCain campaign faltered. Republicans were reduced to efforts to portray Obama as the friend of 1960s radical William Ayers, with whom Obama had had a casual connection in the past. Obama easily parried these attacks by presenting his new friends, such establishment figures as billionaire investor Warren Buffett, former secretary of state Colin Powell, and former Federal Reserve head Paul Volcker.

OBAMA'S VICTORY Throughout October, Obama led consistently in the national polls, but by single-digit margins. Given the faltering economy, an unpopular president, and the Democrats' enormous financial advantage, the GOP should have been heading for a train wreck of epic proportions and yet, until late October when Obama's lead increased, McCain trailed only by three- to five-point margins in the polls. Some analysts of opinion data thought the problem was race. A white Democratic candidate, according to some mathematical models of public opinion, would have enjoyed a much stronger lead in the polls, perhaps an additional six or seven points. Some analysts worried whether Obama's lead was even as strong as it looked. These analysts pointed to the so-called "Bradley effect," a phantom lead in the polls produced when white voters, reluctant to display overt signs of racism, lie to pollsters about their intentions. This is allegedly what happened in 1982 when Los Angeles mayor, Tom Bradley, lost the California gubernatorial race after leading his white opponent in the polls. While asserting that race would not be a factor in the 2008 election, Obama cautioned his supporters not to be overconfident.

In the end, racial antipathy did not determine the outcome of the 2008 presidential election. Some voters undoubtedly opposed Obama because of his race while others supported him on the same grounds. But, given America's long history of slavery, segregation, and racial antagonism, the most important fact of the election was that tens of millions of white voters—some reluctantly—had voted

FIGURE 10.6 ★ Distribution of Electoral Votes in the 2008 Election

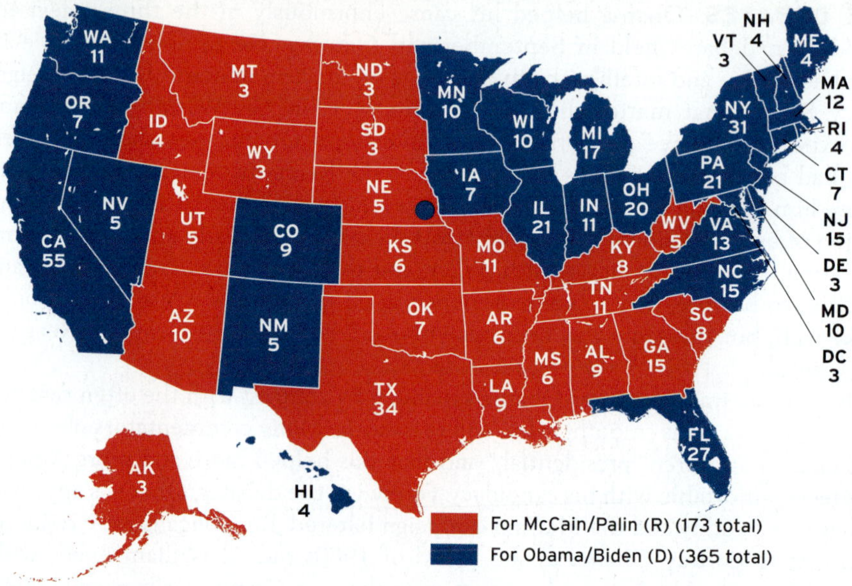

for a black man for the presidency of the United States. Remarkably, Obama ran better among white voters than Democratic candidate John Kerry had in 2004. Obama polled 43 percent of the white vote, two points more than the percentage polled by Kerry. Obama also ran well among Latinos (66 percent), young people (66 percent), and among black voters, where he took 95 percent of the vote. Two Democratic constituencies, women and Jews, who had favored Hillary Clinton in the primaries gave their support to Obama in the general election. Obama won 56 percent of the vote among women and 78 percent among Jews. The most important issue cited by voters who cast ballots for Obama was the economy. More than 60 percent said that their chief policy reason for supporting Obama over McCain was a belief that Obama and the Democrats would be better able to restore the nation's economic health.

Though many forces were at work in 2008, Obama's victory was made possible by the softening of racial antagonisms in the United States over the past half century and the delegitimation of overtly racist rhetoric in the public forum. But the election of a black president does not mean the end of racism in America. Obama is an exceptional individual—a graduate of the Harvard Law School with a white mother, an African rather than an African American father, and raised by white grandparents. Some Democratic canvassers emphasized these facts to white voters, describing their candidate as a man from a multiracial background whose father was an African intellectual, not an African American from the inner city. Does Obama's victory represent the end of racism and the birth of a new America? Or, is Obama an exception? Only time will help us to fully understand the meaning of the 2008 election.

Money and Politics

Modern national political campaigns are fueled by enormous amounts of money. In 2008, incumbent candidates in competitive races for the House of Representatives typically spent close to $2 million to hold on to their seats. In Senate races, the average winner spent more than $4 million. In recent years, some Senate contests have cost $25 million or more. In the 2008 presidential race, the two parties and their presidential candidates raised and spent more than $1.5 billion. Hundreds of millions more were spent by individuals and groups who ran independent ads seeking to influence the outcome of the presidential contest.

Sources of Campaign Funds

In 2008, according to the Center for Responsive Politics, roughly $3 billion was spent by candidates for federal offices. About 10 percent of this total came from political action committees (PACs), mainly in support of congressional races, and the remainder from individual donors. Several million individuals donated money to political campaigns in 2008, some in contributions of as little as five or ten dollars. One of the sources of Barack Obama's fund-raising advantage in the 2008 campaign was his ability to generate more than 2 million small- and medium-size contributions to his campaign.[14] Another $500 million in 2008 was raised and spent by individuals and advocacy groups—the so-called 527 and 501c(4) groups operating outside the structure of the Democratic and Republican campaigns.

INDIVIDUAL DONORS Politicians spend a great deal of time asking people for money. Money is solicited via direct mail, through the Internet, over the phone, and in numerous face-to-face meetings. Under federal law, individual donors may donate as much as $2,300 per candidate per election, $5,000 per PAC per calendar year (to a maximum of $65,500), $28,500 per national party committee per

Fund-raising is a major part of political campaigns. Candidates meet with individual donors and leaders of important groups in their efforts to amass a campaign "war chest." John McCain eventually accepted public funding for the 2008 general election, at which point he was barred from further fund-raising, although his party and other groups remained free to raise money to back his candidacy.

BOX 10.1 Federal Campaign Finance Regulation

Campaign Contributions

No individual may contribute more than $2,300 to any one candidate in any single election. Individuals may contribute as much as $28,500 to a national party committee and up to $5,000 to a political action committee. Full disclosure is required by candidates of all contributions over $100. Candidates may not accept cash contributions over $100. Contribution limits are raised for individuals facing "millionaire" opponents.

Political Action Committees

Any corporation, labor union, trade association, or other organization may establish a political action committee (PAC). PACs must contribute to the campaigns of at least five different candidates and may contribute as much as $5,000 per candidate in any given election.

Soft Money

The national parties are prohibited from raising campaign funds to be transferred to state party organizations.

Broadcast Advertising

Unions, corporations, and nonprofit agencies may not broadcast "issue ads" mentioning federal candidates within sixty days of a general election and thirty days of a primary election. In the 2007 case of *Wisconsin Right to Life v. FEC* (06-969, 2007), the Supreme Court ruled that issue ads that were not specific appeals to vote for or against a particular candidate could not constitutionally be banned, even if they mentioned candidates and their political records.

Presidential Elections

Candidates in presidential primaries may receive federal matching funds if they raise at least $5,000 in each of twenty states. The money raised must come in contributions of $250 or less. The amount raised by candidates in this way is matched by the federal government. Candidates who accept public funding in the primaries must adhere to an overall spending limit, which was set at $42 million for 2008. In the general election, candidates may accept public funding, currently $84 million. Candidates who accept such funding may spend no money beyond their federal allotments, though political parties may work to support their candidacies. Independent groups may spend money on behalf of a candidate so long as their efforts are not directly tied to the official campaign. Minor-party candidates may get partial federal funding.

Federal Election Commission (FEC)

The six-member FEC supervises federal elections, collects and publicizes campaign finance records, and investigates violations of federal campaign finance law.

calendar year, and $10,000 to state and local committees per calendar year (to a maximum of $42,700). Federal rules also impose an overall limit on individual contributors of $108,200 per election cycle. Individuals may also contribute freely to 527 committees and to 501c(4) groups. 527 donations are a matter of public record, but 501c(4)s are not required to disclose their donor lists. Individuals may also attempt to enhance their influence by raising and "bundling" their contributions with those of friends and associates. Many Washington lobbyists curry favor with politicians through vigorous bundling efforts.

political action committee (PAC) a private group that raises and distributes funds for use in election campaigns

POLITICAL ACTION COMMITTEES **Political action committees (PACs)** are organizations established by corporations, labor unions, or interest groups to channel the contributions of their members into political campaigns. Under the terms of the 1971 Federal Elections Campaign Act, which governs campaign finance in the United States, PACs are permitted to make larger contributions to any given candidate than individuals are allowed to make (see Box 10.1). As noted above, individuals cannot donate more than $2,300 to any single candidate, but a PAC may donate as much as $5,000 to each candidate. Moreover, allied or related PACs often coordinate their campaign contributions, greatly increasing the amount of money a candidate actually receives from the same interest group. More than 4,500 PACs are registered with the Federal Election Commission, which oversees campaign finance practices in the United States. Nearly two-thirds of all PACs represent corporations, trade associations, and other business and professional groups. Alliances of bankers, lawyers, doctors, and merchants all sponsor PACs. One example of a PAC is the National Beer Wholesalers' Association PAC, which for many years was known as "SixPAC." Labor unions also sponsor PACs, as do ideological, public interest, and nonprofit groups. The National Rifle Association sponsors a PAC, as does the Sierra Club. Many congressional and party leaders have established PACs, known as leadership PACs, to provide funding for their political allies.

THE CANDIDATES On the basis of the Supreme Court's 1976 decision in *Buckley v. Valeo,* the right of individuals to spend their *own* money to campaign for office is a constitutionally protected matter of free speech and is not subject to limitation. Thus, extremely wealthy candidates often contribute millions of dollars to their own campaigns. The Democrat Jon Corzine, for example, spent approximately $60 million of his own funds in a successful New Jersey Senate bid in 2000 and another $40 million when he ran for New Jersey Governor in 2005. The only exception to the *Buckley* rule concerns presidential candidates who accept federal funding for their general election campaigns. Such individuals are limited to $50,000 in personal spending.

INDEPENDENT SPENDING—527 COMMITTEES AND 501C(4)S Committees known as **527s** and **501c(4)s** are independent groups that are currently not covered by the campaign-spending restrictions imposed in 2002 by the Bipartisan Campaign Reform Act (BCRA). These groups, named for the sections of the tax code under which they are organized, can raise and spend unlimited amounts on political advocacy so long as their efforts are not coordinated with those of any candidate's campaign. A 527 is a group established specifically for the purpose of political advocacy, whereas a 501c(4) is a nonprofit group such as an environmental or other public interest group that also engages in advocacy. A 501c(4) may not spend more that half its revenues for political purposes, but many political activists favor this mode of organization. Unlike a 527, a 501c(4) is not required to disclose where it gets its funds or exactly what it does with them. As a result, it has become a common practice for wealthy and corporate donors to route campaign contributions far in excess of the legal limits through 501s. The donor makes a legal contribution to the 501, which keeps a cut and donates the remainder of the money to a designated "grassroots" campaign on behalf of the politician. In 2008, 527s and 501s raised and spent hundreds of millions of dollars on campaign ads and other activities promoting issues and discussing what they saw as the virtues and vices of various politicians. Because they are not subject to contribution or spending limits, 527s and 501s have been able to raise three times as much money as PACs. In the 2008 national elections the top 527s were mainly, but not exclusively, supportive of the Democrats. These included the Service Employees International Union,

527 committees nonprofit independent groups that receive and disburse funds to influence the nomination, election, or defeat of candidates. Named after Section 527 of the Internal Revenue Code, which defines and provides tax-exempt status for nonprofit advocacy groups

501c(4) committees nonprofit groups that also engage in issue advocacy. Under Section 501c(4) such a group may spend up to half its revenue for political purposes

TABLE 10.1 ★ Top Donors to 527 Committees, 2008

DONOR	TOTAL DONATIONS
Service Employees International Union	$30,999,124
American Federation of State, County, and Municipal Employees	$5,581,604
Soros Fund Management	$5,150,000
Shangri-La Entertainment	$4,850,000
Las Vegas Sands	$4,359,820
Fund for America	$4,020,000
Oak Spring Farms	$3,480,000
Friends of America Votes	$3,225,425
United Food and Commercial Workers	$3,179,000
United Brotherhood of Carpenters	$2,786,690
Pharmaceutical Product Development, Inc.	$2,740,790
Int. Union of Operating Engineers	$1,865,000
National Association of Realtors	$1,556,600
America Votes	$1,450,000
Democratic Governors Association	$1,265,000
Sheet Metal Workers	$1,225,000
Templeton Foundation	$1,086,200
Bonanza Oil	$1,050,000
Trust Asset Management	$1,000,000

SOURCE: Center for Responsive Politics, based on records released October 21, 2008.

America Votes, Emily's List, and Citizens United. Table 10.1 lists the top donors to 527 committees in 2008. However, 527 groups were less active in 2008 than they had been in 2004, in part because so much campaign money went directly to Obama.

POLITICAL PARTIES Before 2002, most campaign dollars took the form of soft money, or unregulated contributions to the national parties nominally to assist in party building or voter registration efforts rather than for particular campaigns. Federal campaign finance legislation crafted by Senators John McCain and Russell Feingold and enacted in 2002 sought to ban soft money by prohibiting the national parties from soliciting and receiving contributions from corporations, unions, or individuals and prevented them from directing such funds to their affiliated state parties. However, it did not reduce the overall importance of money in politics, and political parties continue to play a major role in financing political campaigns. Under federal rules, a national political party committee may make unlimited "independent expenditures" advocating support for its own presidential candidate or advocating the defeat of the opposing party's candidate so long as

During the 2004 presidential campaign, dozens of independent 527 committees spent hundreds of millions of dollars on television advertising. One of the most notorious of these ads was the "Swift Boat Veterans for Truth," which challenged John Kerry's military record and activism against the Vietnam War.

these expenditures are not coordinated with the candidate's own campaign. A national party committee may also spend up to $19 million in coordination with its presidential candidates' campaign even if its candidate has accepted public funding. Thus, for example, even though John McCain accepted full public funding, the national Republican Party helped fund McCain's advertising up to the federal limit. State and local party organizations may spend unlimited funds for grassroots presidential campaign activities such as voter registration drives, phone banks, and campaign materials. In 2008, Republican Party efforts partly, but not fully, offset Barack Obama's enormous fund-raising advantage over John McCain.

PUBLIC FUNDING The Federal Elections Campaign Act also provides for public funding of presidential campaigns. As they seek a major party presidential nomination, candidates become eligible for public funds by raising at least $5,000 in individual contributions of $250 or less in each of twenty states. Candidates who reach this threshold may apply for federal funds to match, on a dollar-for-dollar basis, all individual contributions of $250 or less they receive. Currently, candidates who accept matching funds may spend no more than $42 million, including matching funds, in their presidential primary campaigns. The funds are drawn from the Presidential Election Campaign Fund. Taxpayers can contribute $3 to this fund, at no additional cost to themselves, by checking a box on the first page of their federal income tax returns. Major party presidential candidates receive a lump sum (currently nearly $85 million) during the summer prior to the general election. They must meet all their general expenses from this money. Third-party candidates are eligible for public funding only if they received at least 5 percent of the vote in the previous presidential race. This stipulation effectively blocks preelection funding for third-party or independent candidates, although a third party that wins more than 5 percent of the vote can receive public funding after the election. In 1980, John Anderson convinced banks to lend him money for an independent candidacy on the strength of poll data showing that he would receive more than 5 percent of the vote and thus would obtain public funds with which to repay the loans. Under current law, no candidate is required to accept public

For Critical Analysis

Why do candidates for public office need to raise so much money? How has the government sought to balance the competing ideals of free expression and equal representation in regard to campaign financing?

funding for either the nominating races or general presidential election. Candidates who do not accept public funding are not affected by any expenditure limits. In 2008, John McCain accepted public funding for the general election campaign, receiving $84 million, but Barack Obama declined, choosing to rely on his own fund-raising prowess. Obama was ultimately able to outspend McCain by a wide margin. As a result, many observers believe that the 2008 race may be the last time that a major-party candidate will forgo their own fund-raising in favor of public funding. Candidates who accept public funding may not engage in fund-raising for their own campaigns with one exception: Publicly funded candidates may raise money to meet the costs of complying with federal campaign laws and other legal and accounting costs, up to a total of 5 percent of their campaign expenditures. Hence in 2008, John McCain raised more than $4 million for the "McCain-Palin Compliance Fund."

Implications for Democracy

The important role played by private funds in American politics affects the balance of power among contending social groups. Politicians need large amounts of money to campaign successfully for major offices. This fact inevitably ties their interests to the interests of the groups and forces that can provide this money. In a nation as large and diverse as the United States, to be sure, campaign contributors represent many different groups and often represent clashing interests. Business groups, labor groups, environmental groups, and pro-choice and right-to-life forces all contribute millions of dollars to political campaigns. One set of trade associations may contribute millions to win politicians' support for telecommunications reform, whereas another set may contribute just as much to block the same reform efforts. Insurance companies may contribute millions of dollars to Democrats to win their support for changes in the health care system, whereas physicians may contribute equal amounts to prevent the same changes from becoming law.

Interests that donate large amounts of money to campaigns expect and often receive favorable treatment from the beneficiaries of their largesse. For example, in 2000 a number of major interest groups with specific policy goals made substantial donations to the Bush presidential campaign. These interests included airlines, energy producers, banks, tobacco companies, and a number of others. After Bush's election, these interests pressed the new president to promote their legislative and regulatory agendas. For example, MBNA America Bank was a major donor to the 2000 Bush campaign. The bank and its executives gave Bush $1.3 million. The bank's president helped raise millions more for Bush and personally gave an additional $100,000 to the president's inaugural committee after the election. All told, MBNA and other banking companies donated $26 million to the GOP in 2000. Within weeks of his election, President Bush signed legislation providing MBNA and the others with something they had sought for years—bankruptcy laws making it more difficult for consumers to escape credit card debts. Such laws could potentially enhance the earnings of large credit card issuers like MBNA by tens of millions of dollars every year.

For Critical Analysis

Democratic elections are virtually an American invention, yet voter participation in the United States today is lower than voting rates in many other nations. What might be done to enhance the democratic character of American electoral politics?

Similarly, a coalition of manufacturers led by the U.S. Chamber of Commerce and the National Association of Manufacturers also provided considerable support for Bush's 2000 campaign. This coalition sought, among other things, the repeal of federal rules promulgated in 2000 by the federal Occupational Safety and Health

Influence Campaigns and Elections *Before* You Cast Your Vote

Although young Americans have been less likely to vote in elections than older Americans, there's plenty of historical evidence that demonstrates how young Americans have influenced the ways campaigns and elections are conducted.

For example, demonstrations that were driven largely by young protesters against the 1968 Democratic convention led directly to changes in the contemporary nomination system. Today, candidates for the party's presidential nomination must appeal directly to voters through primaries and caucuses. However, this was not the case in 1968 and before when party nominees were hand picked by party elites. Unhappy with the chosen candidate in 1968—Hubert Humphrey—young protesters turned out on the streets of Chicago to demonstrate against his nomination. Chicago police responded with force to the peaceful protests. The Democratic Party, fearing similar uprisings in subsequent elections, reformed their nominating process to give the people more of a say through primaries and caucuses. The Republican Party quickly followed suit.

Fast forward to more recent times. Even though it's conventional wisdom today to write off young people when it comes to electoral politics, the 2008 campaign for president was unique because of the campaign activism that it inspired among high school and college-aged youth. For example, CNN and YouTube partnered to present two debates in the 2008 primary elections—one for Democratic and the other for Republican candidates. Recognizing that young people are a driving force behind YouTube, allowing individuals to submit their own questions to the candidates this way was intended to bring a more youthful perspective to the debates. Moreover, candidates are increasingly turning to Internet sites like Facebook and MySpace for connecting with young voters. This move is likely driven by the increasing realization that voters can be found online, and young voters are among the most likely to be turning to the Internet to make political connections and getting political news.

These are just a few of many examples that demonstrate how young people have influenced campaigns and elections. If you're interested in ensuring that voices such as yours continue to shape campaigns and elections in this country, here are a few suggestions for getting involved.

- ★ Volunteer for a campaign! As simple as this sounds, this is one of the most direct things that you can do to take an active role in elections in this country and perhaps express your interests directly to a candidate. Whether the campaign is at the campus, local, or national level, candidates are always grateful for volunteers. One of the easiest ways to find out who to contact about volunteering is by visiting Project Vote Smart's Web site (www.votesmart.org). By entering your zip code, you can find out who is running for specific offices in your area. Contact information for each candidate is provided in the event you choose to volunteer.
- ★ Invite a candidate (or two or three) to your college in order to engage in either a one-on-one with interested students or a forum amongst a variety of candidates. The best way to go about this is to work with a campus organization, such as your student government association or the College Republicans or Democrats. In addition to congressional candidates, you can consider candidates running for statewide and local offices, like the state assembly or the city council.
- ★ Host a gathering to watch a debate. Debates are a key way for voters to gain information about where candidates stand on issues. However, most people who watch debates do so by themselves. You might consider checking out DebateWatch (www.debates.org/pages/dwoverview.html). It provides information about hosting a gathering of people to watch a debate together and discuss what they hear from the candidates.

Rules governing campaign finance have been the object of intense debate in recent years. Many Americans believe that government is "for sale to the highest bidder" and shudder when they watch political candidates raise millions of dollars from corporations, labor unions, lobby groups, and wealthy individuals.

Administration (OSHA), which were designed to protect workers from repetitive motion injuries. Again, within weeks of his election, the president approved a resolution rejecting the rules. In March 2001, the House and Senate both voted to kill the ergonomic regulations.

Despite the diversity of contributors, not all interests play a role in financing political campaigns. Only those interests that have a good deal of money to spend can make their interests known in this way. These interests are not monolithic, but they do not completely reflect the diversity of American society. The poor, the destitute, and the downtrodden also live in America and have an interest in the outcome of political campaigns. Who is to speak for them? Who benefits from the American system of private funding of campaigns?

Thinking Critically about the Electoral Process

As we have seen throughout this book, Americans' most fundamental values often clash, leaving us perplexed as to the best way to proceed. In the realm of electoral politics, the question of campaign finance produces such a clash of values. On the one hand, most Americans are wary of the high cost of campaigns and the apparently sinister role of campaign contributions in the political process. Through their contributions, wealthy individuals and well-funded interest groups seek to influence election outcomes, the behavior of elected officials, and, through so-called issue advertising, even the tenor of the political debate.

The problem, however, is that we find ourselves with a case of competing political ends. Although reform of spending practices might appear to advance the goal of political equality, it might do so at the expense of liberty. Don't we want to encourage vigorous and lively political debate—even though it may be expensive? Should not any group of citizens be free to promote its political ideas at its own expense? These are questions worth pondering, and as we often see in political life, they are dilemmas with no quick and easy solution.

FOR FURTHER READING

Ackerman, Bruce and Ian Avres. *Voting with Dollars.* New Haven: Yale University Press, 2004.

Browning, Graeme. *Electronic Democracy.* New York: Cyberage, 2002.

Caeser, James, and Andrew Busch. *Red over Blue.* New York: Rowman and Littlefield, 2005.

Ginsberg, Benjamin, and Martin Shefter. *Politics by Other Means: Institutional Conflict and the Declining Significance of Elections in America.* New York: Norton, 1999.

Johnson, Dennis W. *No Place for Amateurs: How Political Consultants Are Reshaping American Democracy.* New York: Routledge, 2001.

Nelson, Michael, ed. *The Elections of 2004*. Washington, DC: CQ Press, 2005.

Polsby, Nelson, Aaron Wildavsky, and David Hopkins. *Presidential Elections.* 12th ed. New York: Rowman and Littlefield, 2007.

Raymond, Allen, and Ian Spiegelman. *How to Rig an Election.* New York: Simon & Schuster, 2008.

Schier, Steven. *You Call This an Election?* Washington, DC: Georgetown University Press, 2003.

Wayne, Stephen. *Is This Any Way to Run A Democratic Election?* 3rd ed. Washington, DC: CQ Press, 2007.

RECOMMENDED WEB SITES

Center for Voting and Democracy
www.fairvote.org

The Center for Voting and Democracy is dedicated to open access to voting, equal representation, and a voice for all Americans. Read about some of their electoral reform proposals such as runoff elections, proportional representation, and alternatives to the electoral college.

The Color of Money
www.colorofmoney.org

Campaign funding affects the balance of power among contending social groups in America. Politicians are tied to groups that provide them with the large amounts of money needed to campaign for major office. This Web site examines federal campaign contributions with a focus on race and ethnicity to show how campaign money has the potential to skew government policy decisions.

ElectionMail.com
www.electionmail.com

Are you thinking about running for office? Whether you aspire to be student government president or president of the United States, here you can find links to affordable political printing including: political brochures, campaign literature, and campaign signs.

Federal Election Commission
www.fec.gov/

The Federal Election Commission (FEC) is an independent government agency that was created in 1975 to administer and enforce the Federal Election Campaign Act (FECA). At the official FEC Web site you can read about the rules and regulations that govern the financing of federal elections and other topics of interest.

JibJab.com
www.jibjab.com

This Web site became famous for its political video clips during the 2004 presidential campaign. For a good laugh check out some of the political jokes or rummage through the video archives to find one of the original Bush or Kerry clips.

MultiEducator.com
www.multied.com/elections/

MultiEducator's History Central Web site features a major section on elections. Here you can find the history of every U.S. national election, including popular and electoral votes, turnout, and a map of the states carried by each competing candidate.

National Archives and Records Administration
www.archives.gov/federal-register/electoral-college/index .html

The U.S. National Archives and Records Administration's Electoral College page is a great resource on presidential elections. Find answers to frequently asked questions about our electoral system, read about how electors vote, or try predicting who will win the next presidential election with the electoral college calculator.

OpenSecrets.org
www.opensecrets.org

Campaign funds come from a variety of sources including individual donors, political action committees (PACs), self-contributions, independent spending, parties, and public funding. At this site you can research funding for all federal officials, including your own members of Congress.

Project Vote Smart
www.votesmart.org

Project Vote Smart is a nonpartisan site dedicated to providing citizens with information on political candidates and elected officials. Here you can easily view a candidate's biographical information, position on issues, and voting record, so that you can make an informed choice on Election Day.

Voter Information Services
www.vis.org

Voter Information Services (VIS) is a nonpartisan, nonprofit organization dedicated to helping interested citizens learn about their elected members of Congress. Here you can obtain a Congressional Report Card for your members of Congress and find out where they stand on the issues.

STUDY OUTLINE

www.wwnorton.com/wtp7e

1. In democratic systems, elections can be used to replace current officeholders as well as being institutions of legitimation.
2. Elections also help to promote government accountability and are a source of protection for groups in society.

Elections in America

1. In the American federal system, the responsibility for organizing elections rests largely with state and local governments.
2. State legislators routinely seek to influence electoral outcomes by manipulating the organization of electoral districts.
3. Prior to the 1890s, voters cast ballots according to political parties. The advent of the neutral ballot allowed voters to choose individual candidates rather than a political party as a whole.
4. Americans do not vote directly for presidential candidates. Rather, they choose electors who are pledged to support a party's presidential candidate.

Election Campaigns

1. The first step in campaigning involves the organization of supporters to help the candidate raise funds and create public name recognition.
2. The next steps of campaigning involve hiring experts—campaign managers, media consultants, pollsters, and others—to aid in developing issues and a message and communicating them to the public.
3. Because most of the time a major-party nomination is necessary for electoral success, candidates must seek a party's nomination in primary elections.

Presidential Elections

1. Presidential candidates secure a party's nomination by running in state party primaries and caucuses.
2. Nominations of presidential candidates were first made in caucuses of a party's members of Congress. This system was replaced in the 1830s by nominating conventions, which were designed to be a more democratic, deliberative method of nominating candidates.
3. Contemporary conventions merely ratify a party's presidential and vice-presidential nominations, although conventions still draft the party platform and adopt rules governing the party and its future conventions.
4. In recent years, the role of the parties during the general campaign has been transformed by the introduction of high-tech campaign techniques, including polls, use of broadcast media, phone banks, direct mail, professional public relations, and the Internet.
5. In capital-intensive campaigns, the main technique is to use the broadcast media to present the electorate with themes and issues that will induce them to support one candidate over another.

How Voters Decide

1. Three factors influence voters' decisions at the polls: partisan loyalty, issues, and candidate characteristics.
2. Partisan loyalty predisposes voters in favor of their party's candidates and against those of the opposing party.
3. The impact of issues and policy preferences on electoral choice is diminished if competing candidates do not differ substantially or do not focus their campaigns on policy matters.
4. Candidates' attributes and personality characteristics always influence voters' decisions.
5. The salience of these three bases of electoral choice varies from contest to contest and from voter to voter.

Money and Politics

1. Campaign funds in the United States are provided by small, direct-mail contributions, large gifts, PACs, political parties, 527s, candidates' personal resources, and public funding. In 2000, some candidates also benefited from issue advocacy.
2. Campaign finance is regulated by the Federal Elections Campaign Act of 1971. Following the 1996 and 2000 elections, the role of soft money was scrutinized. The Bipartisan Campaign Reform Act, a bipartisan attempt to restrict soft money contributions and issue advocacy, became law in 2002.
3. The role played by private money in American politics affects the relative power of social groups. As a result, less affluent groups have considerably less power in the political system.

PRACTICE QUIZ

www.wwnorton.com/wtp7e

1. What is the most important difference between democratic and authoritarian electoral systems?
   a) The latter do not allow the defeat of those in power.
   b) There are no elections in authoritarian systems.
   c) Democratic systems use elections as a safety valve for social discontent.
   d) Authoritarian elections are not organized by party.
2. The neutral ballot made it possible for voters to
   a) vote the party line.
   b) vote for a split-ticket.
   c) send clear mandates for policy change.
   d) both a and b
3. What is the difference between an open and a closed primary?
   a) You must pay a poll tax to vote in a closed primary.
   b) Open primaries allow voters to split the ticket.
   c) In closed primaries, only registered members of a political party may vote to select that party's candidates.
   d) They are fundamentally the same thing.
4. What are the potential consequences of ideological struggles in primary contests?
   a) General election chances may be undermined.
   b) Party extremists may win the nomination.
   c) Typical party supporters may refuse to support the party's nominee.
   d) all of the above
5. What was the most fundamental change in national conventions in the twentieth century?
   a) They no longer nominate presidential candidates.
   b) Now party platforms are written at the convention.
   c) The participation of electoral officials in conventions has continued to decline.
   d) none of the above
6. Which of the following is *not* an example of a media technique introduced in the 1992 presidential campaign?
   a) the spot advertisement
   b) the town meeting
   c) the campaign website
   d) a, b, and c were all introduced in 1992.
7. In *Buckley v. Valeo*, the Supreme Court ruled that
   a) PAC donations to campaigns are constitutionally protected.
   b) the right of individuals to spend their own money to campaign is constitutionally protected.
   c) the political system is corrupt.
   d) the Federal Elections Campaign Act is unconstitutional.
8. Partisan loyalty
   a) is often handed down from parents to children.
   b) changes frequently.
   c) has little impact on electoral choice.
   d) is mandated in states with closed primaries.
9. Which of the following is *not* a factor that influences voters' decisions?
   a) partisanship
   b) issues
   c) candidate characteristics
   d) the electoral system used to determine the winner
10. If a state has ten members in the U.S. House of Representatives, how many electoral votes does that state have?
    a) two
    b) ten
    c) twelve
    d) can't tell from this information

KEY TERMS

www.wwnorton.com/wtp7e

benign gerrymandering (p. 368)
campaign (p. 373)
caucus (political) (p. 377)
closed caucus (p. 377)
closed primary (p. 365)
coattail effect (p. 369)
delegates (p. 381)
electoral college (p. 371)
501c(4) committees (p. 407)
527 committees (p. 407)
gerrymandering (p. 368)
incumbent (p. 373)
majority system (p. 366)
majority-minority district (p. 369)
midterm elections (p. 365)
open caucus (p. 377)
open primary (p. 365)
platform (p. 379)
plurality system (p. 366)
political action committee (PAC) (p. 406)
primary elections (p. 365)
proportional representation (p. 366)
prospective voting (p. 391)
recall (p. 366)
redistricting (p. 367)
referendum (p. 366)
retrospective voting (p. 391)
spot advertisement (p. 384)
superdelegate (p. 381)
town meeting (p. 385)
winner-take-all system (p. 377)

11 Groups and Interests

- The Character of Interest Groups
- The Proliferation of Groups
- Strategies: The Quest for Political Power
- Thinking Critically about Groups and Interests: The Dilemmas of Reform

WHAT GOVERNMENT DOES AND WHY IT MATTERS

In December 2007, Congress enacted a major energy bill mandating increased fuel-economy standards for motor vehicles and new subsidies for alternative fuels such as ethanol. The act, however, did not include two important provisions that were dropped at the last minute after a massive lobbying campaign by the energy industry. One provision would have imposed new taxes on the oil companies, which continue to post huge profits as energy costs to consumers have risen. Another provision would have established mandates and subsidies for the development of wind and solar power.

What happened to these provisions of the act? The oil industry lobbied vigorously against the tax increases, asserting that it needed more resources to identify and develop new sources of oil. "We made sure that everybody knew our point of view—the White House, the House, the Senate," said James Ford, a top oil industry lobbyist. "We told our story and told it thoroughly." The effort to increase the use of wind and solar power was defeated by a coalition of oil companies, utilities, and manufacturing groups that saw the provision as likely to have an adverse effect on their profits.[1] These groups collectively contribute tens of millions of dollars to political campaigns and employ hundreds of lobbyists. Thus, their voice is always heard in Washington.

The case of the energy bill exemplifies the power of interest groups in action. Tens of thousands of organized groups have formed in the United States, ranging from civic associations to huge nationwide groups such as the National Rifle Association (NRA), whose chief cause is opposition to restrictions on gun ownership, or Common Cause, a public-interest group that advocates a variety of liberal political reforms. Despite the array of interest groups in American politics, however, we can be sure neither that all interests are represented equally nor that the results of this group competition are consistent with the common good. Often, interest groups work hard to make us unaware of their self-interested activities. Some interest groups and organizations spend years and millions of dollars on what is called "institutional advertising" designed to create such a favorable public image of themselves and their activities that citizens will automatically view them as public-spirited rather than selfish entities. Take, for example, Fannie Mae (Federal National Mortgage Corporation) and Freddie Mac (Federal Home Loan Mortgage Corporation). These giant banks, whose risky speculative activities helped bring about a national financial crisis in 2008, were created by Congress during the 1930s to make more mortgage money more readily available to home buyers. Despite their nominal public purpose, Fannie and Freddie were independent, for-profit organizations that gradually shifted most of their activities from helping ordinary Americans get mortgages to more profitable venues. To hide their true character, however, Fannie and Freddie spent millions of dollars every year on institutional advertising and other forms of image polishing. Freddie's trademark slogan, plastered on thousands of billboards, magazine and newspaper pages, and TV ads was, "We make home possible." No wonder millions of Americans were shocked in September 2008, when the federal government took control of both Fannie and Freddie to prevent their collapse. Instead of making home possible, the two giant financial institutions had been making risky loans and issuing dubious securities in search of higher profit margins. A powerful interest group that affects millions of college students and their families but is all but invisible to them is the higher education lobby. America's colleges and universities are represented in Washington by more than fifty groups led by the American Council on Education (ACE). Larger institutions employ their own lobbyists as well. One major goal of the higher education lobby is continued expansion of the federally guaranteed student loan program that provides tuition assistance for millions of students. Education lobbyists aver that their purpose is to make college more affordable. To this end, education lobbyists constantly argue that students need to be able to borrow more in order to meet the rising cost of tuition. Of course, whenever the federal government allows students to borrow more, colleges are able to raise their tuitions to take advantage of students' greater ability to pay. The true beneficiary of increases in the loan limit is often the education industry rather than beleaguered students and their parents.

In this chapter we will examine the nature and consequences of interest group politics in the United States.

- **In this chapter, we will first seek to understand the character of interest groups.** We will look at types of interests, the organizational components of groups, and the characteristics of members. We will also examine the important question of why people join interest groups.
- **Second, we will assess the growth of interest-group activity in recent American political history.** The number of interest groups has proliferated in recent years, and we will examine the reasons.
- **Third, we will review and evaluate the strategies that competing groups use in their struggles for influence.** The quest for political influence takes many forms.

The Character of Interest Groups

The framers of the American Constitution feared the power that organized interests could wield. Yet they believed that interest groups thrived because of liberty—the freedom that all Americans enjoy to organize and to express their views. If the government were given the power to regulate or in any way to forbid efforts by organized interests to interfere in the political process, the government would in effect have the power to suppress liberty. The solution to this dilemma was presented by James Madison:

> Take in a greater variety of parties and interest [and] you make it less probable that a majority of the whole will have a common motive to invade the rights of other citizens. . . . [Hence the advantage] enjoyed by a large over a small republic.[2]

According to Madison, a good constitution encourages multitudes of interests so that no single interest, which he called a "faction," can ever tyrannize the others. The basic assumption is that competition among interests will produce balance, with all the interests regulating each other.[3] Today, this Madisonian principle of regulation is called **pluralism.** According to pluralist theory, all interests are and should be free to compete for influence in the United States. Moreover, according to pluralist doctrine, the outcome of this competition is compromise and moderation, since no group is likely to be able to achieve any of its goals without accommodating itself to some of the views of its many competitors.[4]

pluralism the theory that all interests are and should be free to compete for influence in the government. The outcome of this competition is compromise and moderation

interest group individuals who organize to influence the government's programs and policies

An **interest group** is an organized group of people that makes policy-related appeals to government. This definition of interest groups includes membership organizations as well as businesses, corporations, universities, and other institutions that do not accept members. Individuals form groups in order to increase the chance that their views will be heard and their interests treated favorably by the government. Interest groups are organized to influence governmental decisions.

Interest groups are sometimes referred to as "lobbies." Interest groups are also sometimes confused with political action committees, which are actually groups

As long as there is government, there will be interests trying to influence it. During the 1890s, for instance, business interests fought for protective tariffs from Congress and President McKinley. This 1897 cartoon satirizes their success in capturing Congress.

that focus on influencing elections rather than trying to influence the elected (see Chapter 10). One final distinction that we should make is that interest groups are also different from political parties: interest groups tend to concern themselves with the *policies* of government; parties tend to concern themselves with the *personnel* of government.

The number of interest groups in the United States is enormous, and millions of Americans are members of one or more groups, at least to the extent of paying dues or attending an occasional meeting. By representing the interests of such large numbers of people and encouraging political participation, organized groups can and do enhance American democracy. Organized groups educate their members about issues that affect them. Groups lobby members of Congress and the executive, engage in litigation, and generally represent their members' interests in the political arena. Groups mobilize their members for elections and grassroots lobbying efforts, thus encouraging participation. Interest groups also monitor government programs to make certain that their members are not adversely affected by these programs. In all these ways, organized interests can be said to promote democratic politics. But because not all interests are represented equally, interest-group politics works to the advantage of some and the disadvantage of others.

It is also important to remember that not all organized interests are successful. Struggles among interest groups have winners and losers, and even large groups well represented in Washington are sometimes defeated in political struggle. In recent years, for example, despite relentless lobbying, physicians' groups such as the American Medical Association (AMA) have been unable to persuade Congress to increase Medicare funding for physicians' services. One reason for this failure is that physicians are forced to compete for funding with insurers, drug companies, and hospitals. The doctors have simply been overmatched.

What Interests Are Represented?

BUSINESS AND AGRICULTURAL GROUPS Interest groups come in as many shapes and sizes as the interests they represent. When most people think about interest groups, they immediately think of groups with a direct economic interest in governmental actions. These groups are generally supported by groups of producers or manufacturers in a particular economic sector. Examples of this type of group include the National Petroleum Refiners Association and the American Farm Bureau Federation. At the same time that these types of broadly representative groups are active in Washington, specific companies, such as Exxon, IBM, and General Motors, may be active on certain issues that are of particular concern to them.

LABOR GROUPS Labor organizations are equally active lobbyists. The AFL-CIO, the United Mine Workers, and the Teamsters are all groups that lobby on behalf of organized labor. In recent years, groups have arisen to further the interests of public employees, the most significant among these being the American Federation of State, County, and Municipal Employees (AFSCME).

PROFESSIONAL ASSOCIATIONS Professional lobbies such as the American Bar Association and the American Medical Association have been particularly successful in furthering their members' interests in state and federal legislatures. Financial institutions, represented by organizations such as the American Bankers

Association and the National Savings & Loan League, although often less visible than other lobbies, also play an important role in shaping legislative policy.

PUBLIC INTEREST GROUPS Recent years have witnessed the growth of a powerful "public interest" lobby, purporting to represent interests whose concerns are not addressed by traditional lobbies. These groups have been most visible in the consumer protection and environmental policy areas, although public interest groups cover a broad range of issues. The Natural Resources Defense Council, the Sierra Club, the Union of Concerned Scientists, and Common Cause are all examples of public interest groups.

IDEOLOGICAL GROUPS Closely related to and overlapping public interest groups are ideological groups, organized in support of a particular political or philosophical perspective. People for the American Way, for example, promotes liberal values, whereas the Christian Coalition focuses on conservative social goals, and the National Taxpayers Union campaigns to reduce the size of the federal government.

PUBLIC-SECTOR GROUPS The perceived need for representation on Capitol Hill has generated a public-sector lobby in the past several years, including the National League of Cities and the "research" lobby. The latter group comprises think tanks and universities that have an interest in obtaining government funds for research and support, and it includes such institutions as Harvard University, the Brookings Institution, and the American Enterprise Institute. Indeed, universities

Politics Today

The 2007 energy bill increased subsidies for ethanol and other biofuels despite concerns that the costs of producing ethanol are greater than the savings generated by its use. What types of groups do you think are likely to be part of the "biofuels coalition" that lobbies for ethanol?

Public interest groups often advocate for interests that are not addressed by traditional lobbies. For example, in addition to many other activities, the Public Interest Research Group (PIRG) publishes an annual toy safety report to help protect consumers and to encourage policymakers to address problems in this area.

Do Foreign Interests Exert Influence in the United States?

Discussions of interest groups often focus on the efforts of competing domestic forces—business, labor, public interest groups and so on—to influence the government. Often, however, foreign interests and foreign governments also lobby vigorously to influence U.S. policy. Much of this lobbying is undertaken by foreign firms hoping to do business in the United States or directly with the U.S. government on favorable terms. For example, every year Americans purchase billions of dollars of goods manufactured in China. In some instances, these Chinese products have failed to comply with American health and safety standards, leading to demands that the United States restrict Chinese imports. To protect their access to the U.S. market, Chinese firms, like those from many other countries, retain the services of international trade lobbyists. These lobbyists guide foreign firms through the intricacies of U.S. laws and customs and introduce foreign executives to American power brokers, movers, and shakers. Some see international trade lobbyists as corporate traitors, but American lobbyists and their counterparts in other countries play an important role in promoting world trade and diminishing international rivalries.

Questions of loyalty are also often raised by the activities of another form of foreign lobby in the United States—the ethnic lobby. Many Americans retain a sense of identification with their family's country of origin or, in the case of Jewish Americans, with their coreligionists in another country. Individuals with such ethnic or religious ties to another country are often willing to lobby vigorously on its behalf. The best-known case is that of the pro-Israel lobby. Through such organizations as AIPAC, the American Israel Public Affairs Committee, Jewish Americans have worked to secure American military, financial, and economic support for Israel since that nation's founding. Largely because of the pro-Israel lobby's activities, Israel is the largest recipient of American foreign aid and is usually supported by the United States in its conflicts with the Arab nations of the Middle East. Interestingly, Jewish Americans are not the only pro-Israel lobbyists. Israel is also strongly supported by so-called Christian Zionists, evangelical Protestants who see Israel's existance as the fulfillment of biblical prophecy.

In addition to the pro-Israel lobby, a number of other ethnic lobbies are active in Washington. Americans from the Indian subcontinent lobby effectively for the improvement of U.S.–Indian relations. Some Irish Americans have lobbied against British rule in Northern Ireland and, recently, Armenian Americans have organized an effective Washington lobby. In 2007, despite a good deal of lobbying by Armenian Americans, Congress failed to pass a resolution condemning the murder of hundreds of thousands of Armenians by Turkish forces between 1914 and 1917. Turkey, an important U.S. military ally, was able to defeat the resolution with a lobbying campaign of its own.

Often, lobbying by foreign firms and governments is accompanied by extensive public-relations campaigns. One foreign government that lobbies vigorously in the United States and also spends tens of millions of dollars each year on public relations is the Kingdom of Saudi Arabia. For example, a recent issue of the *New Republic*—a magazine read mainly by upper-middle-class professionals and intellectuals in New York, Washington, and Boston—the Kingdom of Saudi Arabia sponsored a full-page ad promoting its efforts to combat terrorism.[a]

In point of fact, however, the Saudi government's longstanding practice has been to subsidize and support Islamic radicals so long as they do not make trouble within Saudi Arabia.[b] The Saudi ad campaign is designed to gloss over this rather embarrassing and politically inconvenient fact.

FOR CRITICAL ANALYSIS

1. Should foreign firms be allowed to lobby in the United States?
2. Is it un-American or disloyal for ethnic and religious groups to lobby on behalf of a foreign country with which they identify?

a. *New Republic*, December 5, 2005, back cover.
b. Craig Unger, *House of Bush, House of Saud* (New York: Scribners, 2004).

have expanded their lobbying efforts even as they have reduced faculty positions and course offerings.[5]

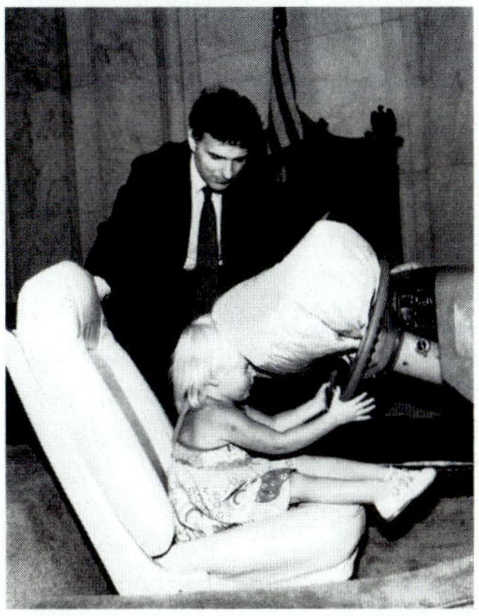

Although there have always been groups trying to influence the government, since the 1960s the number of organized interests in Washington, D.C., has increased substantially. For instance, the consumer activist Ralph Nader, shown here at a demonstration in support of mandatory airbags in cars, founded a network of consumer advocacy groups in the 1960s.

What Interests Are Not Represented?

It is difficult to categorize unrepresented interests precisely because they are not organized and are not able to present us (or governments) their identity and their demands. The political scientist David Truman referred to these interests as "potential interest groups."[6] And he is undoubtedly correct that at any time, as long as there is freedom, any interest shared by a lot of people can develop through "voluntary association" into a genuine interest group that can demand, usually successfully, to get some representation. But the fact remains that many interests—very widely shared interests—do not get organized and recognized. Such "potential interests" might include grandparents, tall people, or undergraduates.

Organizational Components

Although interest groups are many and varied, most share certain key organizational components. These include leadership, money, an agency or office, and members.

First, every group must have a leadership and decision-making structure. For some groups, this structure is very simple. For others, it can be quite elaborate and involve hundreds of local chapters that are melded into a national apparatus. Interest-group leadership is, in some respects, analogous to business leadership. Many interest groups are initially organized by political entrepreneurs with a strong commitment to a particular set of goals. Such entrepreneurs see the formation of a group as a means both for achieving those goals and for enhancing their own influence in the political process. Just as is true in the business world, however, successful groups often become bureaucratized; the initial entrepreneurial leadership is replaced by a paid professional staff. In the 1960s, for example, Ralph Nader led a loosely organized band of consumer advocates ("Nader's Raiders") in a crusade for product safety that resulted in the enactment of a number of pieces of legislation and numerous regulations, such as the requirement that all new cars be equipped with air bags. Today, Nader remains active in the consumer movement, and his ragtag band of raiders has been transformed into a well-organized and well-financed phalanx of interlocked groups, including Public Citizen, the Center for the Study of Responsive Law, and the Center for Science in the Public Interest. All of these groups are now led by professional staffs.

Second, every interest group must build a financial structure capable of sustaining an organization and funding the group's activities. Most interest groups rely on membership dues and voluntary contributions from sympathizers. Many also sell some ancillary services to members, such as insurance and vacation tours. Third, most groups establish an agency that actually carries out the group's tasks. This may be a research organization, a public relations office, or a lobbying office in Washington or a state capital.

Finally, almost all interest groups must attract and keep members. Somehow, groups must persuade individuals to invest the money, time, energy, or effort required to take part in the group's activities. Members play a larger role in some groups than in others. In **membership associations,** group members actually serve on committees and engage in projects. In the case of labor unions, members may march on picket lines; in the case of political or ideological groups, members may

membership association an organized group in which members actually play a substantial role, sitting on committees and engaging in group projects

staff organization a type of membership group in which a professional staff conducts most of the group's activities

participate in demonstrations and protests. In another set of groups, **staff organizations,** a professional staff conducts most of the group's activities; members are called on only to pay dues and make other contributions. Among the well-known public interest groups, some, such as the National Organization for Women (NOW), are membership groups; others, such as Defenders of Wildlife and the Children's Defense Fund, are staff organizations.

THE "FREE RIDER" PROBLEM Whether they need individuals to volunteer or merely to write checks, both types of groups need to recruit and retain members. Yet many groups find this task difficult, even when it comes to recruiting members who agree strongly with the group's goals. Why? As the economist Mancur Olson explains, the benefits of a group's success are often broadly available and cannot be denied to nonmembers.[7] Such benefits can be called **collective goods**. This term is usually associated with certain government benefits, but it can also be applied to beneficial outcomes of interest-group activity. Following Olson's own example, suppose a number of private property owners live near a mosquito-infested swamp. Each owner wants this swamp cleared. But if one or a few of the owners were to clear the swamp alone, their actions would benefit all the other owners as well, without any effort on the part of those other owners. Each of the inactive owners would be a **free rider** on the efforts of the ones who cleared the swamp. Thus, there is a disincentive for any of the owners to undertake the job alone.

collective goods benefits, sought by groups, that are broadly available and cannot be denied to nonmembers

free riders those who enjoy the benefits of collective goods but did not participate in acquiring them

Since the number of concerned owners is small in this particular case, they might eventually be able to organize themselves to share the costs as well as enjoy the benefits of clearing the swamp. But suppose the numbers of interested people are increased. Suppose the common concern is not the neighborhood swamp but polluted air or groundwater involving thousands of residents in a region, or in fact millions of residents in a whole nation. National defense is the most obvious collective good whose benefits are shared by every resident, regardless of the taxes they pay or the support they provide. As the number of involved persons increases, or as the size of the group increases, the free-rider phenomenon becomes more of a problem. Individuals do not have much incentive to become active members and supporters of a group that is already working more or less on their behalf. The group would no doubt be more influential if all concerned individuals were active members—if there were no free riders. But groups do not reduce their efforts just because free riders get the same benefits as dues-paying activists. In fact, groups may try even harder precisely because there are free riders, with the hope that the free riders will be encouraged to join in.

WHY JOIN? Despite the free-rider problem, interest groups offer numerous incentives to join. Most important, they make various "selective benefits" available only to group members. These benefits can be information related, material, solidary, or purposive. Of course, groups sometimes offer combinations of benefits. Membership in a community association, for example, can offer its members a sense of belonging (solidary benefit), involvement in community decision making (purposive benefit), and reduced rates on homeowners' insurance (material benefit). Table 11.1 gives some examples of the range of benefits in each of these categories.

informational benefits special newsletters, periodicals, training programs, conferences, and other information provided to members of groups to entice others to join

Informational benefits are the most widespread and important category of selective benefits offered to group members. Information is provided through conferences, training programs, and newsletters and other periodicals sent automatically to those who have paid membership dues.

TABLE 11.1 ★ Selective Benefits of Interest Group Membership

CATEGORY	BENEFITS
Informational benefits	Conferences Professional contacts Training programs Publications Coordination among organizations Research Legal help Professional codes Collective bargaining
Material benefits	Travel packages Insurance Discounts on consumer goods
Solidary benefits	Friendship Networking opportunities
Purposive benefits	Advocacy Representation before government Participation in public affairs

SOURCE: Adapted from Jack Walker, Jr., *Mobilizing Interest Groups in America: Patrons, Professions, and Social Movements* (Ann Arbor: University of Michigan Press, 1991), 86.

Material benefits include anything that can be measured monetarily, such as special services, goods, and even money. Groups can offer a broad range of material benefits to attract members. These benefits often include discount purchasing, shared advertising, and, perhaps most valuable of all, health and retirement insurance.

material benefits special goods, services, or money provided to members of groups to entice others to join

Another option identified on Table 11.1 is that of **solidary benefits.** The most notable of this class of benefits are the friendship and "networking" opportunities that membership provides. Another benefit that has become extremely important to many of the newer nonprofit and citizen groups is "consciousness raising." One example of this can be seen in the claims of many women's organizations that active participation conveys to each member of the organization an enhanced sense of her own value and a stronger ability to advance individual as well as collective rights. Members of associations based on ethnicity, race, or religion also derive solidary benefits from interacting with individuals they perceive as sharing their own histories, values, and perspectives.

solidary benefits selective benefits of group membership that emphasize friendship, networking, and consciousness raising

A fourth type of benefit involves the appeal of the purpose of an interest group. An example of these **purposive benefits** is businesses' joining trade associations to further their economic interests. Similarly, individuals join consumer, environmental, or other civic groups to pursue goals important to them. Many of the most successful interest groups of the past twenty years have been citizen groups or public interest groups, whose members are brought together largely around shared ideological goals, including government reform, election and campaign reform, civil rights, economic equality, "family values," or even opposition to government itself.

purposive benefits selective benefits of group membership that emphasize the purpose and accomplishments of the group

During the 2003 national debate over Medicare reform and prescription drug pricing, it was the support of senior citizen groups for a new Medicare bill that ultimately allowed the bill to prevail in Congress.

THE AARP AND THE BENEFITS OF MEMBERSHIP One group that has been extremely successful in recruiting members and mobilizing them for political action is the AARP (formerly called the American Association of Retired Persons). The AARP was founded in 1958 as a result of the efforts of a retired California high school principal, Ethel Percy Andrus, to find affordable health insurance for herself and for the thousands of members of the National Retired Teachers Association (NRTA). In 1955 she found an insurer who was willing to give NRTA members a low group rate. In 1958, partly at the urging of the insurer (who found that insuring the elderly was quite profitable), Andrus founded the AARP. For the insurer it provided an expanded market; for Andrus it was a way to serve the ever-growing elderly population, whose problems and needs were expanding along with their numbers and their life expectancy.

Today, the AARP is a large and powerful organization with 36 million members and an annual income of $900 million. In addition, the organization receives $90 million in federal grants. Its national headquarters in Washington, D.C., staffed by nearly 3,000 full-time employees, is so large that it has its own zip code. Its monthly periodical, *Modern Maturity*, has a circulation larger than the combined circulations of *Time*, *Newsweek*, and *US News & World Report*.[8]

How did this large organization overcome the free-rider problem and recruit 35 million older people as members? First, no other organization on earth has ever provided more successfully the selective benefits necessary to overcome the free-rider problem. It helps that the AARP began as an organization to provide affordable health insurance for aging members rather than as an organization to influence public policy. But that fact only strengthens the argument that members need short-term individual benefits if they are to invest effort in a longer-term and less concrete set of benefits. As the AARP evolved into a political interest group, its leadership also added more selective benefits for individual members. They provided guidance against consumer fraud, offered low-interest credit cards, evaluated and endorsed products that were deemed of best value to members, and provided auto insurance and a discounted mail-order pharmacy.

For Critical Analysis

Are all interests organized? Why does it seem that some interests are more amenable to organization than others?

In a group as large as the AARP, members are bound to disagree on particular subjects, often creating serious factional disputes. But the resources of the AARP are so extensive that its leadership has been able to mobilize itself for each issue of importance to the group. One of its most successful methods of mobilization for political action is the "telephone tree," with which AARP leaders can quickly mobilize thousands of members for and against proposals that affect Social Security, Medicare, and other questions of security for the aging. A "telephone tree" in each state enables the state AARP chair to phone all of the AARP district directors, who then can phone the presidents of the dozens of local chapters, who can call their local officers and individual members. Within twenty-four hours, thousands of individual AARP members can be contacting local, state, and national officials to express their opposition to proposed legislation. It is no wonder that the AARP is respected and feared throughout Washington, D.C. AARP support for the Bush administration's Medicare prescription drug plan made it virtually impossible for congressional Democrats to oppose the bill, even though many had misgivings about the bill's provisions and about handing the administration an important victory in the year before a presidential election.

The Characteristics of Members

Membership in interest groups is not randomly distributed in the population. People with higher incomes, higher levels of education, and management or professional occupations are much more likely to become members of groups than those who occupy the lower rungs on the socioeconomic ladder (see Figure 11.1).[9] Well-educated, upper-income business and professional people are more likely to have the time and the money and to have acquired through the educational process the concerns and skills needed to play a role in a group or association. Moreover, for business and professional people, group membership may provide personal contacts and access to information that can help advance their careers. At the same time, of course, corporate entities—businesses and the like—usually have ample resources to form or participate in groups that seek to advance their causes.

The result is that interest-group politics in the United States tends to have a very pronounced upper-class bias. Certainly, many interest groups and political associations have a working-class or lower-class membership—labor organizations or welfare-rights organizations, for example—but the great majority of interest groups and their members are drawn from the middle and upper-middle classes. In general, the "interests" served by interest groups are the interests of society's "haves." Even when interest groups take opposing positions on issues and policies, the conflicting positions they espouse usually reflect divisions among upper-income strata rather than conflicts between the upper and lower classes.

For Critical Analysis

Could college students be organized as an interest group? What would such a group advocate? What might be some impediments to the creation of a National Organization of College Students?

FIGURE 11.1 ★ Interest Group Membership by Income Level

The percentage of Americans who report that they are involved in an organization that takes a stand on political issues increases with income level. What are some reasons wealthier Americans are more likely than poorer citizens to join a group?

SOURCE: Kay Lehman Scholzman, "Voluntary Organizations in Politics: Who Gets Involved?" in *Representing Interest and Interest Group Representations*, ed. William Crotty, Mildred A. Schwartz, and John C. Green (Lanham, MD: University Press of America, 1994), 76.

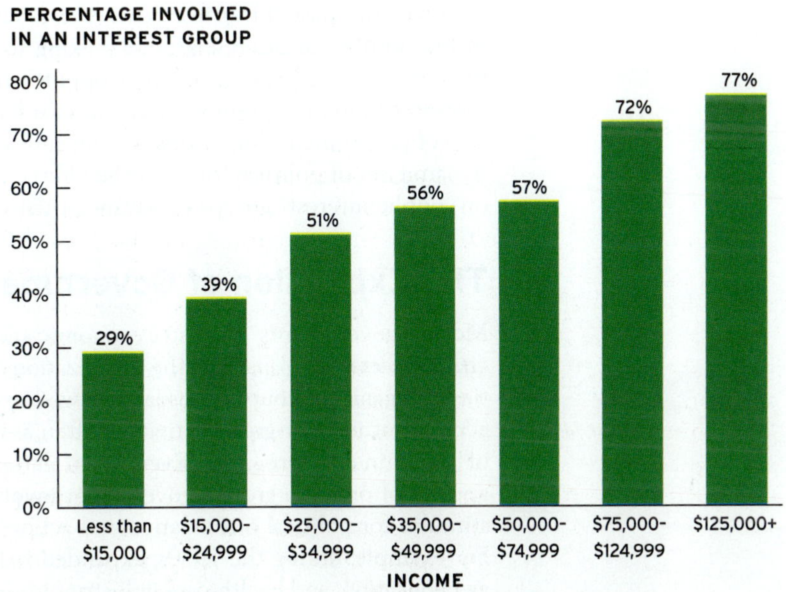

In general, to obtain adequate political representation, forces from the bottom rungs of the socioeconomic ladder must be organized on the massive scale associated with political parties. Parties can organize and mobilize the collective energies of large numbers of people who, as individuals, may have very limited resources. Interest groups, on the other hand, generally organize smaller numbers of the better-to-do. Thus, the relative importance of political parties and interest groups in American politics has far-ranging implications for the distribution of political power in the United States. As we saw in Chapter 9, political parties have declined in influence in recent years. Interest groups, on the other hand, as we shall see in the next section, have become much more numerous, more active, and more influential in American politics.

The Proliferation of Groups

Interest groups and concerns about them are not new phenomena. As long as there is government, as long as government makes policies that add value or impose costs, and as long as there is liberty to organize, interest groups will abound; and if government expands, so will interest groups. There was, for example, a spurt of growth in the national government during the 1880s and 1890s, arising largely from the first government efforts at economic intervention to fight large monopolies and to regulate some aspects of interstate commerce. In the latter decade, a parallel spurt of growth occurred in national interest groups, including the imposing National Association of Manufacturers (NAM) and numerous other trade associations. Many groups organized around specific agricultural commodities as well. This period also marked the beginning of the expansion of trade unions as interest groups. Later, in the 1930s, interest groups with headquarters and representation in Washington began to grow significantly, concurrent with that decade's historic and sustained expansion within the national government (see Chapter 3).

Over the past thirty-five years, there has been an even greater increase both in the number of interest groups seeking to play a role in the American political process and in the extent of their opportunity to influence that process. This explosion of interest-group activity has two basic origins: first, the expansion of the role of government during this period; and second, the coming of age of a new and dynamic set of political forces in the United States—forces that have relied heavily on "public interest" groups to advance their causes.

The Expansion of Government

Modern governments' extensive economic and social programs have powerful politicizing effects, often sparking the organization of new groups and interests. The activities of organized groups are usually viewed in terms of their effects on governmental action. But interest-group activity is often as much a consequence as an antecedent of governmental programs. Even when national policies begin as responses to the appeals of pressure groups, government involvement in any area can be a powerful stimulus for political organization and action by those whose interests are affected. For example, during the 1970s, expanded federal regulation of the automobile, oil, gas, education, and health-care industries impelled each of these interests to increase substantially its efforts to influence the government's behavior. These efforts, in turn, spurred the organization of other groups to augment or counter the activities of the first.[10] Similarly, federal social programs have occasionally sparked political organization and action on the part of clientele groups seeking to influence the distribution of benefits and, in turn, the organization of groups opposed to the programs or their cost. For example, federal programs and court decisions in such areas as abortion and school prayer were the stimuli for political organization and action by fundamentalist religious groups. Thus, the expansion of government in recent decades has also stimulated increased group activity and organization.

The New Politics Movement and Public Interest Groups

The second factor accounting for the explosion of interest-group activity in recent years has been the emergence of a new set of forces in American politics that can collectively be called the "New Politics" movement.

The **New Politics movement** is made up of upper-middle-class professionals and intellectuals for whom the civil rights and antiwar movements were formative experiences, just as the Great Depression and World War II had been for their parents. The crusade against racial discrimination and the Vietnam War led these young men and women to see themselves as a political force in opposition to the public policies and politicians associated with the nation's postwar regime. In more recent years, the forces of New Politics have focused their attention on such issues as environmental protection, women's rights, and nuclear disarmament.

New Politics movement a political movement that began in the 1960s and 1970s, made up of professionals and intellectuals for whom the civil rights and antiwar movements were formative experiences. The New Politics movement strengthened public interest groups

Members of the New Politics movement constructed or strengthened public interest groups such as Common Cause, the Sierra Club, the Environmental Defense Fund, Physicians for Social Responsibility, and the National Organization for Women. New Politics forces were able to influence the media, Congress, and even the judiciary and enjoyed a remarkable degree of success during the late 1960s and early 1970s in securing the enactment of policies they favored. New Politics activists played a major role in securing the enactment of environmental, consumer, and occupational health and safety legislation.

Among the factors contributing to the rise and success of New Politics forces was technology. In the 1970s and 1980s, computerized direct-mail campaigns allowed public interest groups to reach hundreds of thousands of potential sympathizers and contributors. Today, the Internet and e-mail serve the same function. Electronic communication allows relatively small groups efficiently to identify and mobilize their adherents throughout the nation. Individuals with perspectives that might be in the minority can become aware of each other and mobilize for national political action through the magic of electronic politics.

New Politics groups seek to distinguish themselves from other interest groups—business groups, in particular—by styling themselves as **public interest groups,** terminology that suggests they serve the general good rather than their own selfish interest. These groups' claims to represent *only* the public interest should be viewed with caution, however. It is not uncommon to find decidedly private interests seeking to hide behind the term "public interest." For example, the benign-sounding Partnership to Protect Consumer Credit is a coalition of credit-card companies fighting for less federal regulation of credit abuses, and Project Protect is a coalition of logging interests promoting increased timber cutting.[11] Citizens for a Better Medicare actually represents the pharmaceutical industry. A bill rejected by the Senate in 2006 would have required lobbying groups to disclose their actual identities but was attacked by the industry as a threat to free speech.

public interest groups groups that claim they serve the general good rather than only their own particular interest

Strategies: The Quest for Political Power

Politics Today

Interest groups often use aliases in their advertising. For example, "Americans for Balanced Energy Choices" is an alias for a coal-industry trade group. Should lobbying groups be required to disclose their actual identities?

Interest groups work to improve the probability that they and their policy interests will be heard and treated favorably by all branches and levels of the government. The quest for political influence or power takes many forms. Insider strategies include access to key decision makers and using the courts. Outsider strategies include going public and using electoral politics. These strategies do not exhaust all the possibilities, but they paint a broad picture of ways that groups utilize their resources in the fierce competition for power (see Figure 11.2).

Many groups employ a mix of insider and outsider strategies. For example, environmental groups such as the Sierra Club lobby members of Congress and key congressional staff members, participate in bureaucratic rule making by offer-

FIGURE 11.2 ★ How Interest Groups Influence Congress

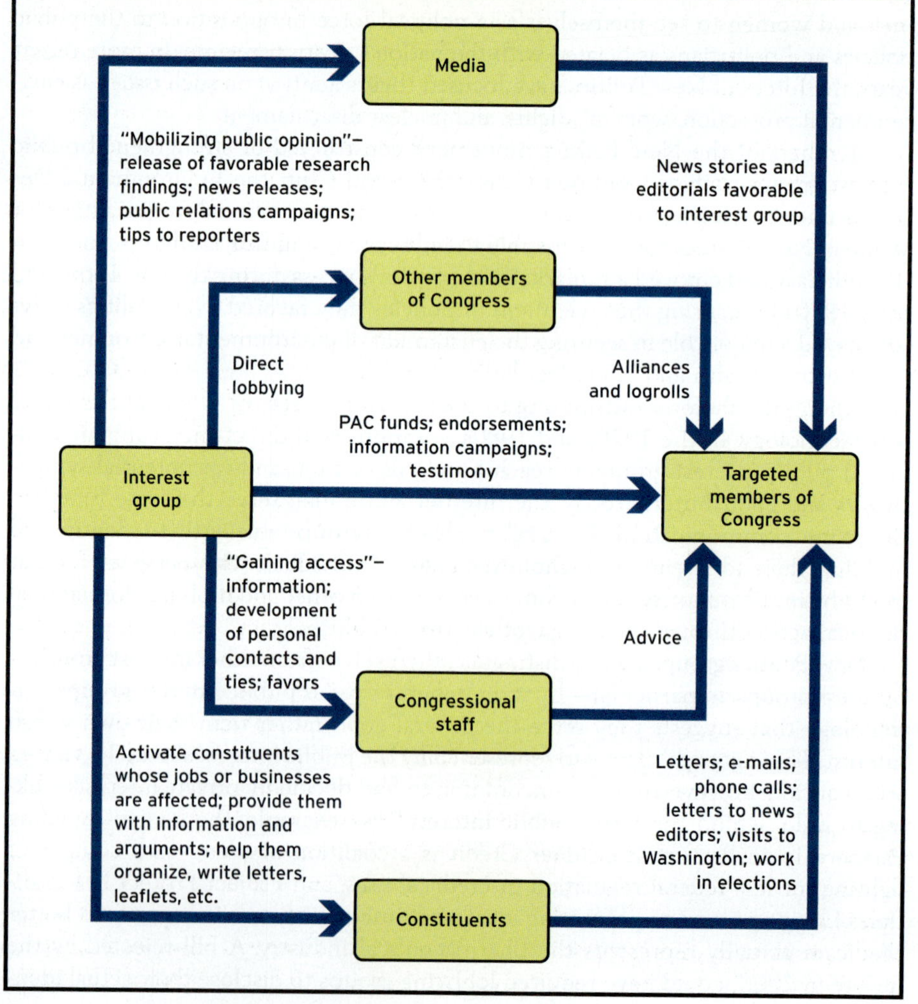

ing comments and suggestions to agencies on new environmental rules, and bring lawsuits under various environmental acts like the Endangered Species Act, which authorizes groups and citizens to come to court if they believe the act is being violated. At the same time, the Sierra Club attempts to influence public opinion through media campaigns and to influence electoral politics by supporting candidates whom they believe share their environmental views and opposing candidates whom they view as foes of environmentalism.

Direct Lobbying

lobbying a strategy by which organized interests seek to influence the passage of legislation by exerting direct pressure on members of the legislature

Lobbying is an attempt by a group to influence the policy process through persuasion of government officials. Most Americans tend to believe that interest groups exert their influence through direct contact with members of Congress, but lobbying encompasses a broad range of activities that groups engage in with all sorts of government officials and the public as a whole.

The 1946 Federal Regulation of Lobbying Act defines a lobbyist as "any person who shall engage himself for pay or any consideration for the purpose of attempting to influence the passage or defeat of any legislation of the Congress of the United States." The 1995 Lobbying Disclosure Act requires all organizations employing lobbyists to register with Congress and to disclose whom they represent, whom they lobby, what they are looking for, and how much they are paid. More than 34,000 lobbyists are currently registered.[12]

Lobbying involves a great deal of activity on the part of someone speaking for an interest. Lobbyists badger and buttonhole legislators, administrators, and committee staff members with facts about pertinent issues and facts or claims about public support of certain issues or facts.[13] Lobbyists can serve a useful purpose in the legislative and administrative processes by providing this kind of information. In 1978, during debate on a bill to expand the requirement for lobbying disclosures, the Democratic senators Edward Kennedy of Massachusetts and Dick Clark of Iowa joined with the Republican senator Robert Stafford of Vermont to issue the following statement: "Government without lobbying could not function. The flow of information to Congress and to every federal agency is a vital part of our democratic system."[14]

LOBBYING CONGRESS Today, lobbyists attempt to influence the policy process in a variety of ways.[15] Traditionally, however, the term *lobbyist* referred mainly to individuals who sought to influence the passage of legislation in the Congress. The First Amendment to the Constitution provides for the right to "petition the Government for a redress of grievances." But as early as the 1870s, "lobbying" became the common term for petitioning. Petitioning cannot take place on the floor of the House or Senate. Therefore, petitioners must confront members of Congress in the lobbies of the legislative chamber; this activity gave rise to the term "lobbying."

In many instances, the influence of lobbyists is based on networks of personal relationships and behind-the-scenes services that they are able to perform for lawmakers. For example, one of Washington's most successful lobbyists is J. Steven Hart, a senior partner at Williams & Jensen, a well-known Washington, D.C., lobbying and law firm. Hart's roster of clients includes such firms as Dell, Inc. and Bass Enterprises. What does Hart offer such clients? The most important service Hart provides is direct access to the leadership of Congress. Hart, as it happens, is the personal attorney for several members of the House leadership. Often, this

In 2008, the Senate Commerce and Labor Committee heard from lobbyists for the "payday loan" industry, which offers small loans at very high interest rates. Public advocacy groups complained that the payday lenders were taking advantage of consumers and should be regulated more closely by government. Lobbyists for the lenders argued that the industry provides a beneficial service to consumers and does not need stricter regulation.

legal work is performed at a nominal fee, as a "loss leader."[16] As a result of these personal relationships, Hart is able to promise clients that the nation's most important officials will hear their cases. Hart, for example, organized a meeting at former House majority leader Tom DeLay's office in September 2001 in which airline executives were able to convince congressional leaders of the need for an airline bailout package in the wake of September 11. On the whole, about 50 percent of Washington lobbyists have prior government experience. Other lobbyists present at the September meeting included Rebecca Cox, the wife of the influential former congressman of California and current SEC chariman Chris Cox. Ms. Cox is counsel for Continental Airlines, one of the firms that was seeking the bailout. Chris and Rebecca Cox are one example of a standard Washington phenomenon—a legislator married to a lobbyist. For instance, Hadassah Lieberman, the wife of the Connecticut senator Joseph Lieberman, was for many years a lobbyist for the pharmaceutical industry. Lobbyists married to powerful legislators can certainly promise their clients access to the highest level of government.

Interest groups also have substantial influence in setting the legislative agenda and in helping to craft specific language in legislation. Today, sophisticated lobbyists win influence by providing information about policies to busy members of Congress. As one lobbyist noted, "You can't get access without knowledge. . . . I can go in to see [the former Energy and Commerce Committee chair] John Dingell, but if I have nothing to offer or nothing to say, he's not going to want to see me."[17] In recent years, interest groups have also begun to build broader coalitions and comprehensive campaigns around particular policy issues.[18] These coalitions do not rise from the grass roots but instead are put together by Washington lobbyists who launch comprehensive lobbying campaigns that combine stimulated grass-roots activity with information and campaign funding for members of Congress. In recent years, the Republican leadership worked so closely with lobbyists that crit-

Lobbyists are a frequent sight in the halls of power. Although the most common image is that of a lobbyist meeting with a member of Congress, lobbyists also lobby the president. The former President George H. W. Bush is seen here with lobbyists from the group Citizens for a Sound Economy.

ics charged that the boundaries between lobbyists and legislators had been erased, and that lobbyists had become "adjunct staff to the Republican leadership."[19]

Lobbyists also often testify on behalf of their clients at congressional committee and agency hearings. Lobbyists talk to reporters, place ads in newspapers, and organize letter-writing and e-mail campaigns. Lobbyists also play an important role in fund-raising, helping to direct clients' contributions to members of Congress and presidential candidates.

What happens to interests that do not engage in extensive lobbying? They often find themselves "Microsofted." In 1998, the software giant was facing antitrust action from the Justice Department and had few friends in Congress. One member of the House, Representative Billy Tauzin (R-La.), told Microsoft's chairman, Bill Gates, that without an extensive investment in lobbying, the corporation would continue to be "demonized." Gates responded by quadrupling Microsoft's lobbying expenditures and hiring a group of lobbyists with strong ties to Congress. The result was congressional pressure on the Justice Department resulting in a settlement of the Microsoft suit on terms favorable to the company. Similarly, in 1999, members of Congress advised Wal-Mart that its efforts to win approval to operate savings and loans in its stores were doomed to failure if the retailer did not greatly increase its lobbying efforts. "They don't give money. They don't have congressional representation—so nobody here cares about them," said one influential member. Like Microsoft, Wal-Mart learned its lesson, hired more lobbyists, and got what it wanted.[20] By 2005, Wal-Mart had become a seasoned political player, creating a "war room" in its Arkansas headquarters. Staffed by a phalanx of veteran political operatives from both parties, the war room is the nerve center of the giant retailer's lobbying and public relations efforts.[21]

LOBBYING THE PRESIDENT So many individuals and groups clamor for the president's time and attention that only the most skilled and best-connected members of the lobbying community can hope to influence presidential decisions. One Washington lobbyist who fills this bill is Tom Kuhn, president of the Edison Electric

Concern about business having too much influence in Washington dates back to the early days of the country. Here, a mid-nineteenth-century cartoon lampoons the ease with which corporate executives could bribe members of Congress.

Institute, a lobbying organization representing the electric power industry. Kuhn is a friend and former college classmate of President George W. Bush. In 2000, Kuhn was among the leading "Pioneers"—individuals who raised at least $100,000 for the Bush election campaign. Later, the electric power companies represented by Kuhn gave nearly $20 million to congressional candidates in the 2001–02 election cycle. Kuhn's close relationship with the president and his efforts on behalf of the president's election have given Kuhn enormous leverage with the White House. During the 2000 transition, candidates for a presidential nomination to head the EPA felt compelled to pay "courtesy calls" to Kuhn. Subsequently, Kuhn led a successful effort to delay and weaken proposed new EPA controls on electric-power-plant emissions of mercury, a toxic substance linked to neurological damage, especially in children.[22] This was a victory for the electric power industry that promised to save the industry hundreds of millions of dollars a year and illustrates the influence that can be brought to bear by a powerful lobbyist.

LOBBYING THE EXECUTIVE BRANCH Even when an interest group is very successful at getting its bill passed by Congress and signed by the president, the prospect of full and faithful implementation of that law is not guaranteed. Often, a group and its allies do not pack up and go home as soon as the president turns their lobbied-for new law over to the appropriate agency. On average, 40 percent of interest-group representatives regularly contact both legislative and executive branch organizations, whereas 13 percent contact only the legislature and 16 percent only the executive branch.[23]

In some respects, interest-group access to the executive branch is promoted by federal law. The Administrative Procedure Act, first enacted in 1946 and frequently amended in subsequent years, requires most federal agencies to provide notice and an opportunity for comment before implementing proposed new rules and regulations. This "notice and comment rule-making" is designed to allow interests an opportunity to make their views known and to participate in the implementation of federal legislation that affects them. In 1990, Congress enacted the Negotiated Rulemaking Act to encourage administrative agencies to engage in direct and open negotiations with affected interests when developing new regulations. These two pieces of legislation—which have been strongly enforced by the federal courts—have played an important role in opening the bureaucratic process to interest-group influence. Today, few federal agencies would consider attempting to implement a new rule without consulting affected interests, who are sometimes known in Washington as "stakeholders."[24]

Cultivating Access

In 2005, one prominent Washington lobbyist, Jack Abramoff, was indicted on numerous charges of fraud and violations of federal lobbying laws. During the investigation of his activities, it was revealed that Abramoff, along with his associate, Michael Scanlon, had collected tens of millions of dollars from several American Indian tribes that operated lucrative gambling casinos. Indian gambling is currently a $16 billion industry in the United States. What Abramoff provided in exchange was access to key members of Congress who helped his clients shut down rival casino operators. Abramoff was closely associated with several House members, including the former House majority leader Tom DeLay as well as senators John Cornyn, Conrad Burns, and David Vitter. Millions of tribal dollars apparently found their way into the campaign war chests of Abramoff's friends in Congress. Thus, through a well-connected lobbyist, money effectively purchased access and influence. Abramoff and several of his associates subsequently pled guilty to federal bribery and fraud charges. Abramoff was sentenced to more than five years in prison.

For the most part, though, access to decision makers does not require bribes or other forms of illegal activity. In many areas, interest groups, government agencies, and congressional committees routinely work together for mutual benefit. The interest group provides campaign contributions for members of Congress and lobbies for larger budgets for the agency. The agency, in turn, provides government contracts for the interest group and constituency services for friendly members of Congress. The congressional committee or subcommittee supports the agency's budgetary requests and programs that the interest group favors. Figure 11.3 illustrates one of the most important access patterns

FIGURE 11.3 ★
The Iron Triangle in the Defense Sector

Defense contractors are powerful actors in shaping defense policy; they act in concert with defense committees and subcommittees in Congress and executive agencies concerned with defense.

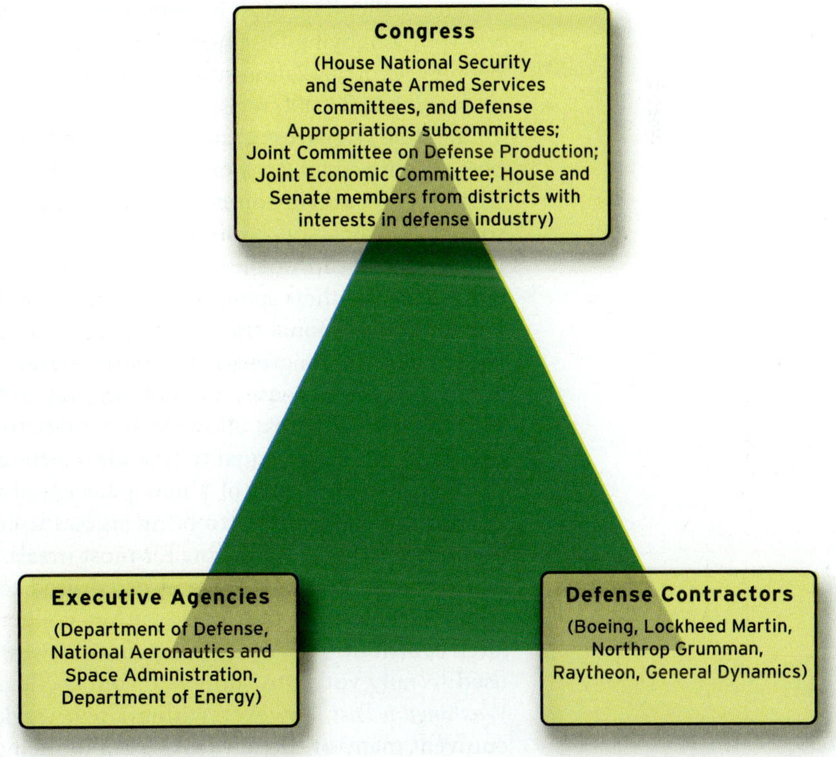

iron triangle the stable, cooperative relationship that often develops among a congressional committee, an administrative agency, and one or more supportive interest groups

issue network a loose network of elected leaders, public officials, activists, and interest groups drawn together by a specific policy issue

in recent American political history: that of the defense industry. Each such pattern, or **iron triangle,** is almost literally a triangular shape, with one point in an executive-branch program, another point in a Senate or House legislative committee or subcommittee, and a third point in some highly stable and well-organized interest group. The points in the triangular relationship are mutually supporting; they count as access only if they last over a long period of time. For example, access to a legislative committee or subcommittee requires that at least one member of it support the interest group in question. This member also must have built up considerable seniority in Congress. An interest cannot feel comfortable about its access to Congress until it has one or more of its "own" people with ten or more years of continuous service on the relevant committee or subcommittee.

A number of important policy domains, such as the environmental and welfare arenas, are controlled not by highly structured and unified iron triangles but by rival **issue networks.** These networks consist of like-minded politicians, consultants, public officials, political activists, and interest groups having some concern with the issue in question. Activists and interest groups recognized as being involved in the area, the "stakeholders," are customarily invited to testify before congressional committees or give their views to government agencies considering action in their domain.

With the growing influence of the lobbying industry, stricter guidelines regulating the actions of lobbyists have been adopted in the last decade. For example, as of 1993, businesses may no longer deduct lobbying costs as a business expense. Trade associations must report to members the proportion of their dues that goes to lobbying, and that proportion of the dues may not be reported as a business expense either. The most important attempt to limit the influence of lobbyists was the 1995 Lobbying Disclosure Act, which significantly broadened the definition of people and organizations that must register as lobbyists. This led, as we saw earlier, to more than 34,000 registrations today.

In 1996, Congress passed legislation limiting the size of gifts to its own members: no gift could be more than $50, and no member could receive more than $100 from a single source. It also banned the practice of honoraria for giving speeches, which special interests had used to supplement congressional salaries. But Congress did not limit payment by lobby groups for travel of representatives, senators, their spouses, or congressional staff members. Interest groups can pay for congressional travel as long as a trip is related to legislative business and is disclosed on congressional reports within 30 days. On these trips, meals and entertainment expenses are not limited to $50 per event and $100 annually. The rules of Congress allow its members to travel on corporate jets as long as they pay an amount equal to first-class airfare. In 2007, congressional Democrats secured the enactment of a new package of ethics rules designed to fulfill their 2006 campaign promise to bring an end to lobbying abuses. The new rules prohibited lobbyists from paying for most meals, trips, parties, and gifts for members of Congress. Lobbyists were also required to disclose the amounts and sources of small campaign contributions they collected from clients and "bundled" into large contributions. And interest groups were required to disclose the funds they used to rally voters to support or oppose legislative proposals. According to the *Washington Post*, however, within a few weeks lobbyists had learned how to circumvent many of the new rules, and lobbying firms were as busy as ever.[25]

After the Abramoff scandal, in which a prominent lobbyist pleaded guilty to conspiring to bribe members of Congress, both parties called for reform of the lobbying process. In 2007, Democrats in the House of Representatives passed new ethics rules designed to end lobbying abuses.

Using the Courts (Litigation)

Interest groups sometimes turn to litigation when they lack access or when they are dissatisfied with government in general or with a specific government program and feel they have insufficient influence to change the situation. Interest groups can use the courts to affect public policy in at least three ways: (1) by bringing suit directly on behalf of the group itself, (2) by financing suits brought by individuals, or (3) by filing a companion brief as an *amicus curiae* (literally "friend of the court") to an existing court case (see Chapter 15 for a discussion of *amicus curiae* briefs).

Among the most significant modern illustrations of the use of the courts as a strategy for political influence are those that accompanied the "sexual revolution" of the 1960s and the emergence of the movement for women's rights.

The 1973 Supreme Court case of *Roe v. Wade,* which took away a state's power to ban abortions, sparked a controversy that brought conservatives to the fore on a national level.[26] These conservative groups made extensive use of the courts to whittle away the scope of the privacy doctrine. They obtained rulings, for example, that prohibit the use of federal funds to pay for voluntary abortions. And in 1989, right-to-life groups were able to use a strategy of litigation that significantly undermined the *Roe v. Wade* decision, namely in the case of *Webster v. Reproductive Health Services* (see Chapter 4), which restored the right of states to place restrictions on abortion.[27] The *Webster* case brought more than 300 interest groups on both sides of the abortion issue to the Supreme Court's door.

Another extremely significant set of contemporary illustrations of the use of the courts as a strategy for political influence are those found in the history of the NAACP. The most important of these court cases was, of course, *Brown v. Board of Education of Topeka, Kansas,* in which the U.S. Supreme Court held that legal segregation of the schools was unconstitutional.[28]

Business groups are also frequent users of the courts because of the number of government programs applied to them. Litigation involving large businesses is most mountainous in such areas as taxation, antitrust, interstate transportation, patents, and product quality and standardization. Often a business is brought to litigation against its will by virtue of initiatives taken against it by other businesses or by government agencies. But many individual businesses bring suit themselves in order to influence government policy. Major corporations and their trade associations pay tremendous amounts of money each year in fees to the most prestigious Washington law firms. Some of this money is expended in gaining access. A great proportion of it, however, is used to keep the best and most experienced lawyers prepared to represent the corporations in court or before administrative agencies when necessary.

New Politics forces made significant use of the courts during the 1970s and 1980s, and judicial decisions were instrumental in advancing their goals. Facilitated by changes in the rules governing access to the courts ("standing" is discussed in Chapter 15), the New Politics agenda was clearly visible in court decisions handed down in several key policy areas. In the environmental policy area, New Politics groups were able to force federal agencies to pay attention to environmental issues, even when the agency was not directly involved in activities related to environmental quality. For example, the Federal Trade Commission (FTC) became very responsive to the demands of New Politics activists during the 1970s and 1980s. The FTC stepped up its activities considerably, litigating a series of claims arising under regulations prohibiting deceptive advertising in cases ranging from false claims for over-the-counter drugs to inflated claims about the nutritional value of children's cereal.

Feminists and equal rights activists enjoyed enormous success in litigating discrimination claims under Title VII of the Civil Rights Act of 1964, and anti–nuclear power activists succeeded in virtually shutting down the nuclear power industry. Challenges to power plant siting and licensing regulations were instrumental in discouraging energy companies from pursuing nuclear projects over the long term.[29]

Mobilizing Public Opinion

Going public is a strategy that attempts to mobilize the widest and most favorable climate of opinion. Many groups consider it imperative to maintain this climate at all times, even when they have no issue to fight about. An increased use of this kind of strategy is usually associated with modern advertising. As early as the 1930s, political analysts were distinguishing between the "old lobby" of direct group representation before Congress and the "new lobby" of public-relations professionals addressing the public at large to reach Congress.[30]

institutional advertising advertising designed to create a positive image of an organization

INSTITUTIONAL ADVERTISING One of the best-known ways of going public is the use of **institutional advertising.** A casual scanning of important mass-circulation magazines and newspapers will provide numerous examples of expensive and well-designed ads by the major oil companies, automobile and steel companies, other large corporations, and trade associations. The ads show how much these organizations are doing for the country, for the protection of the environment, or for the defense of the American way of life. Their purpose is to create and maintain a strongly positive association between the organization and the community at large in the hope that they can draw on these favorable feelings as needed for specific political campaigns later on.

Many interest groups stage protests and demonstrations in order to draw attention to their cause and mobilize public opinion. This Sierra Club demonstration in 2005 was intended to call attention to the problem of toxic pollution in Oregon's Willamette River.

PROTESTS AND DEMONSTRATIONS Many groups resort to going public because they lack the resources, the contacts, or the experience to use other political strategies. The sponsorship of boycotts, sit-ins, mass rallies, and marches by Martin Luther King, Jr.'s Southern Christian Leadership Conference (SCLC) and related organizations during the 1950s and 1960s is one of the most significant and successful cases of going public to create a more favorable climate of opinion by calling attention to abuses. The success of these events inspired similar efforts on the part of women. Organizations such as the National Organization for Women (NOW) used public strategies in their drive for legislation and in their efforts to gain ratification of the Equal Rights Amendment. In 2004 and 2005, antiwar groups demonstrated near President Bush's ranch in Crawford, Texas, to demand an end to the American military presence in Iraq. The protestors were led by Cindy Sheehan, whose son had been killed while serving in Iraq.

GRASSROOTS MOBILIZATION Another form of going public is **grassroots mobilization.** In such a campaign, a lobby group mobilizes its members and their families throughout the country to write to their elected representatives in support of the group's position.

grassroots mobilization a lobbying campaign in which a group mobilizes its membership to contact government officials in support of the group's position

Among the most effective users of the grassroots effort in contemporary American politics is the religious right. Networks of evangelical churches have the capacity to generate hundreds of thousands of letters and phone calls to Congress and the White House. For example, the religious right was outraged when President Clinton announced soon after taking office that he planned to end the military's ban on gay and lesbian soldiers. The Reverend Jerry Falwell, an evangelical leader, called on viewers of his television program to dial a telephone number that would add their names to a petition urging Clinton to retain the ban on gays in the military. Within a few hours, 24,000 people had called to support the petition.[31]

Grassroots campaigns have been so effective throughout the last few years that a number of Washington consulting firms have begun to specialize in this area. In 2007, for example, a grassroots firm called Grassfire.org led the drive to kill the immigration reform bill supported by President Bush and a number of congressional Democrats that would have legalized the status of many illegal immigrants. Grassfire.org used the Internet and talk radio programs to generate a campaign that yielded 700,000 signatures on petitions opposing the bill. The petitions, along with tens of thousands of phone calls, letters, and e-mails generated by Grassfire and several other groups led to the bill's defeat in the U.S. Senate.[32]

Grassroots lobbying has become more prevalent in Washington over the last couple of decades because the adoption of congressional rules limiting gifts to members has made traditional lobbying more difficult. This circumstance makes all the more compelling the question of whether grassroots campaigning has reached an intolerable extreme. One case in particular may have tipped it over: in 1992, ten giant companies in the financial-services, manufacturing, and technology industries began a grassroots campaign and spent untold millions of dollars over the next three years to influence a congressional decision that would limit their investors' ability to sue them for fraud. Retaining an expensive consulting firm, these corporations paid for the use of specialized computer software to persuade Congress that there was "an outpouring of popular support for the proposal." Thousands of letters from individuals flooded Capitol Hill. Many of those letters were written and sent by people who sincerely believed that investor lawsuits are often frivolous and should be curtailed. But much of the mail was phony, generated by the Washington-based campaign consultants; the letters came from people who had no strong feelings or even no opinion at all about the issue.

More and more people, including leading members of Congress, are becoming quite skeptical of such methods, charging that these are not genuine grassroots campaigns but instead represent "Astroturf lobbying" (a play on the name of an artificial grass used on many sports fields). Such Astroturf campaigns, often using e-mail, have increased in frequency in recent years as members of Congress have grown more and more skeptical of Washington lobbyists and far more concerned about demonstrations of support for a particular issue by their constituents. But after the firms mentioned above spent millions of dollars and generated thousands of letters to members of Congress, they came to the somber conclusion that "it's more effective to have one hundred letters from your district where constituents took the time to write and understand the issue," because "Congress is sophisticated enough to know the difference."[33]

Using Electoral Politics

In addition to attempting to influence members of Congress and other government officials, interest groups also seek to use the electoral process to elect the right legislators in the first place and to ensure that those who are elected will owe them a debt of gratitude for their support. If we view matters in perspective, groups invest far more resources in lobbying than in electoral politics. Nevertheless, financial support and campaign activism can be important tools for organized interests.

POLITICAL ACTION COMMITTEES By far the most common electoral strategy interest groups employ is that of giving financial support to the parties or to particular candidates. But such support can easily cross the threshold into outright bribery. Therefore, Congress has occasionally made an effort to regulate this strategy. For example, the Federal Election Campaign Act of 1971 (amended in 1974) limits campaign contributions and requires that each candidate or campaign committee itemize the full name and address, occupation, and principal business of each person who contributes more than $100. These provisions have been effective up to a point, considering the rather large number of embarrassments, indictments, resignations, and criminal convictions in the aftermath of the Watergate scandal.

Celebrity Involvement with Groups and Interests

Interest groups sometimes rely on the involvement of celebrities—such as actors, musicians, and sports figures—to help attract media attention and gain access to politicians. But, when Bono lobbies for debt relief for Africa or Angelina Jolie discusses the plight of refugees, do they actually help advance the causes that they represent?

Endorsing political candidates, making public statements for or against certain policies, and even becoming official representatives of certain groups have become common forms of political activism for entertainment-world celebrities. In their book *Celebrity Politics*, Darrell West and John Ormond argue that the American mass media pay attention to a celebrity's opinion on a political issue simply because it is the viewpoint of someone famous—not because of any special insight or expertise that person has. The perceived importance of what celebrities do and say is reinforced by the news-coverage style of "infotainment" shows like *Inside Edition* and *Extra*. West and Ormond argue that this trend encourages citizens to view politics as show business and spectacle rather than something in which they ought to participate.

Others are more positive about the role of celebrities in politics. Hans Reimer of Rock the Vote believes that the involvement of celebrities like rock stars in political life engages young Americans. "If musicians are politically engaged, then young people are going to be politically engaged," says Remier.[a] In fact, data from Harvard's Kennedy School of Government Vanishing Voter project suggests that the many celebrities involved in "get out the vote" campaigns did contribute to first time voters going to the polls in 2004.

Celebrities certainly bring media attention to the groups they support, as in the cases of Richard Gere's work for a free Tibet, Michael J. Fox's support for stem cell research, and Charleton Heston's involvement with the National Rifle Association. Members of Congress often invite celebrities to speak before committees to increase the chances of their policy negotiations getting on the news. Experiments by political scientists David Jackson and Thomas Darrow suggest that celebrity support can improve public opinion surrounding politicians or policies *if* those celebrities are well-liked. A problem for organizations represented by celebrities arises when those celebrities are not seen as likeable or credible. "Sometimes [celebrity representation] works against a cause if the general public perceives the celebrity as flaky or out of the mainstream," admits Bob Oettinger, president of Celebrity Outreach Foundation, an organization that helps coordinate charities and celebrity spokespeople.[b]

Celebrity involvement with specific interests seems likely to increase in the future, thanks in part to organizations like Oettinger's that match up celebrities with political groups. The dynamic is straightforward: celebrities want to enhance their reputations by being associated with good causes, and interest groups want media attention. But, as illustrated by the ongoing debates over the effectiveness of celebrities in politics, it is unclear whether this trend is ultimately good for the causes celebrities represent or for American democracy.

FOR CRITICAL ANALYSIS

1. Do you think "celebrity politics" discourages citizen participation by promoting a "sit down and watch" approach to political life? Or, do you believe celebrities can foster participation among people who might not otherwise pay attention to the causes they represent?
2. What are some of the other ways that interest groups can attract media attention and gain access to policy makers?

a. P. Brownfeld, "Musicians Try to Tune Fans In to Causes, Candidates," Foxnews.com, December 16, 2003, www.foxnews.com/story/0,2933,105844,00.html (accessed 4/28/08).

b. "Celebrities Use Status to Stump for Causes," Foxnews.com, January 9, 2002, www.foxnews.com/story/0,2933,44195,00.html (accessed 4/28/08).

TABLE 11.2 ★ Political Action Committee Spending, 1977–2006

Campaign spending by political action committees has increased nearly tenfold since the late 1970s. Why do interest groups form PACs? Should PAC spending be restricted or would restrictions prevent opposing groups and forces from making their views known in the political arena?

YEARS	CONTRIBUTIONS
1977–78 (est.)	$77,800,000
1979–80	131,153,384
1981–82	190,173,539
1983–84	266,822,476
1985–86	339,954,416
1987–88	364,201,275
1989–90	357,648,557
1991–92	394,785,896
1993–94	388,102,643
1995–96	429,887,819
1997–98	470,830,847
1999–2000	579,358,330
2001–02	685,305,553
2003–04	915,700,000
2005–06	1,086,000,000

SOURCE: Federal Election Commission, www.fec.gov.

The Watergate scandal was triggered by the illegal entry of Republican workers into the office of the Democratic National Committee in the Watergate apartment building. But an investigation quickly revealed numerous violations of campaign-finance laws, involving millions of dollars in unregistered cash from corporate executives to President Nixon's re-election committee. Many of these revelations were made by the famous Ervin Committee, named for its chair, Senator Sam J. Ervin (D-N.C.). The committee's official name and jurisdiction was the Senate Select Committee to Investigate the 1972 Presidential Campaign Activities.

Reaction to Watergate produced further legislation on campaign finance in 1974 and 1976, but the effect was to restrict individual rather than interest-group campaign activity. Today, individuals may contribute no more than $2,300 to any candidate for federal office in any primary or general election. A **political action committee (PAC),** however, can contribute $5,000, provided it contributes to at least five different federal candidates each year. Beyond this, the laws permit corporations, unions, and other interest groups to form PACs and to pay the costs of soliciting funds from private citizens for the PACs. In other words, PACs are interest groups that choose to operate in the electoral arena, in addition to whatever they do within the interest-group system. The option to form a PAC was made available by law only in the early 1970s. Until then, it was difficult—if not downright illegal—for corporations, including unions, to get directly involved in elections by supporting parties and candidates.

political action committee (PAC) a private group that raises and distributes funds for use in election campaigns

Electoral spending by interest groups has been increasing steadily despite the flurry of reform following Watergate. Table 11.2 presents a dramatic picture of the

FIGURE 11.4 ★
Growth of Political Action Committees, 1980–2008

The majority of political action committees represent corporations or trade associations. What accounts for business dominance of PACs? Would America be better off without PACs?

SOURCE: Federal Election Commission, www.fec.gov.

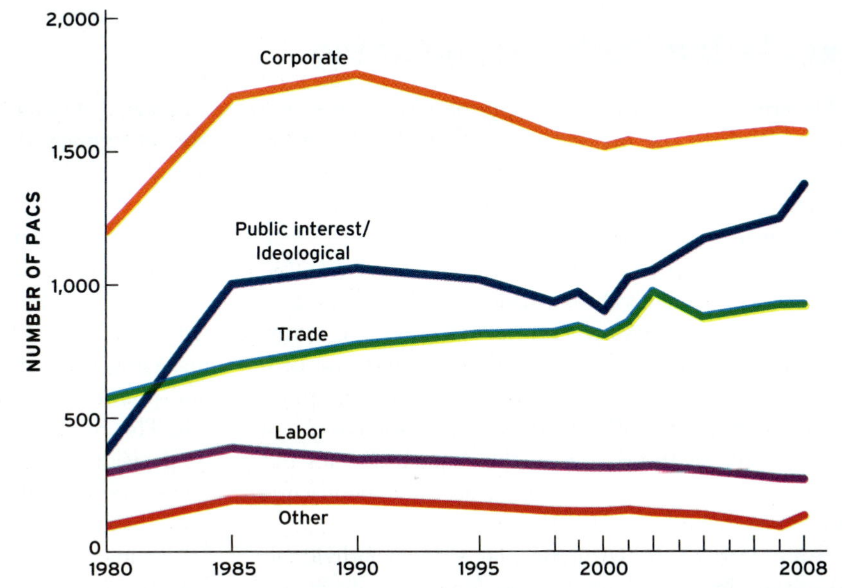

growth of PACs as the source of campaign contributions. The dollar amounts for each year reveal the growth in electoral spending. The number of PACs has also increased significantly—from 480 in 1972 to more than 5,000 in 2007 (see Figure 11.4). Although the reform legislation of the early and mid-1970s attempted to reduce the influence that special interests have over elections, the effect has been almost the exact opposite. Opportunities for legally influencing campaigns are now widespread. The total extent of spending on national elections for 2008 was approximately 3 billion. PACs contributed about one-third of this amount. Another third was contributed in soft money raised by 527 and 501(c) groups, which are not regulated by the Federal Election Commission.

Given the enormous costs of television commercials, polls, computers, and other elements of the new political technology (see Chapter 10), most politicians are eager to receive PAC contributions and are at least willing to give a friendly hearing to the needs and interests of contributors. Most politicians probably will not simply sell their services to the interests that fund their campaigns, but there is some evidence that interest groups' campaign contributions do influence the overall pattern of political behavior in Congress and in the state legislatures.

Indeed, PACs and campaign contributions provide organized interests with such a useful tool for gaining access to the political process that calls to abolish PACs have been quite frequent among political reformers. Concern about PACs grew through the 1980s and 1990s, creating a constant drumbeat for reform of federal election laws. Proposals were introduced in Congress on many occasions, perhaps the most celebrated being the McCain-Feingold bill, which became the Bipartisan Campaign Reform Act (BCRA) of 2002. When originally proposed in 1996, McCain-Feingold was aimed at reducing or eliminating PACs. But in a stunning about-face, when campaign finance reform was adopted in 2002, it did not restrict PACs in any significant way. Rather, it eliminated unrestricted "soft money" donations to the national political parties (see Chapter 10). One consequence of

For Critical Analysis

How do interest groups differ from political parties? In terms of America's core values of liberty and democracy, should we prefer a political process dominated by parties or one in which interest groups are more important?

POLICY DEBATE

Regulating Political Spending

In December 2003, the U.S. Supreme Court, in a 5–4 decision, upheld the major provisions of the Bipartisan Campaign Reform Act (BCRA). The Court upheld the act's restrictions on so-called soft-money contributions to the national party organizations as well as the act's ban on the use of unregulated funds for issue advertising that mentions a candidate's name within sixty days of a general election or thirty days of a primary election. The Court justified its decision on evidence that the electoral process was surrounded with the appearance of corruption and "the danger that officeholders will decide issues not on the merits or the desires of their constituencies but according to the wishes of those who have made large financial contributions valued by the officeholder."

Supporters of BCRA argue that affluent individuals and special interests have for too long been dominant forces in the American political process. In the 1970s, Congress enacted the Federal Elections Campaign Act (FECA) to deal with the corrupt practices revealed during the Watergate inquiry. FECA limited the amounts of money that individuals and political action committees were allowed to contribute to candidates. In the wake of FECA, however, tens of millions of dollars in unregulated or "soft" money began to flow into the coffers of the national political parties. Though this money was ostensibly to be used for voter registration and party-building activities, much of it was spent to elect candidates, circumventing FECA restrictions. In addition, wealthy individuals and groups discovered that they could launch campaign efforts on behalf of candidates without being limited by FECA restrictions as long as their efforts were not coordinated with the candidates' official campaigns. The intent of FECA had been to level the playing field and to prevent wealthy individuals and interests from essentially buying influence not available to ordinary voters. FECA clearly had failed. Thus, according to BCRA supporters, further reform was needed to restrict the use of soft money and to block deceptive issue advertising.

Critics of BCRA concede that money is a powerful force in the political process. They argue, however, that BCRA will be both ineffective and harmful. Critics note that BCRA is filled with loopholes. One loophole allows groups to raise and spend unlimited political funds as long as the groups are not formally affiliated with parties or candidates. BCRA proponents, of course, argue that loopholes can be dealt with as they come to light. They hope the law will be expanded and tightened over the years, perhaps leading to full public funding of election campaigns.

BCRA critics, however, assert that the law has fundamental defects that cannot be cured by further tinkering. First, say critics, BCRA interferes with free speech and political expression, most notably by limiting issue ads. The Supreme Court agreed with this argument in its decision in *Wisconsin Right to Life v. FEC*, which has weakened regulation of issue ads (see Chapter 10). Second, they see BCRA as undermining political parties by outlawing soft money while allowing "hard money" contributions directly to candidates. Third, critics claim that BCRA makes it more difficult for challengers to defeat incumbents. Challengers must raise and spend far more money than incumbents to have a chance to win a House or Senate seat. To the extent that it slows the flow of money into political contests, BCRA is characterized by its critics as "incumbent protection legislation." Finally, critics charge that BCRA is one more step in the direction of full public funding of elections. Whereas most BCRA supporters view this as a positive feature, critics say that full public funding would give those in power too much control over the electoral process and would lead to a system in which competing parties would have less incentive to pay attention to public preferences, since their funding would come from the government.

FOR CRITICAL ANALYSIS

1. Under BCRA, the government has placed limits on political advertising. Are these limits necessary? Or, do they constitute an infringement on First Amendment rights?
2. Many reformers advocate public funding of political campaigns, but critics charge that full public funding in Europe has made political parties less concerned with their constituents. Do the potential benefits of public funding justify the potential problems?

this reform, as we saw in Chapters 9 and 10, was the creation of a host of new organizations known as 527 committees. These are often directed by former party officials but nominally unaffiliated with the two parties. This change has had the effect of strengthening interest groups and weakening parties.

Activist groups carefully keep their campaign spending separate from party and candidate organizations to avoid the restrictions of federal campaign finance laws. As long as a group's campaign expenditures are not coordinated with those of a candidate's own campaign, the group is free to spend as much money as it wishes. Such expenditures are viewed as "issue advocacy" and are protected by the First Amendment. This view was reaffirmed by the Federal Election Commission, which ruled in May 2004 that spending by 527 committees was not limited by BCRA.

CAMPAIGN ACTIVISM Financial support is not the only way that organized groups seek influence through electoral politics. Sometimes, activism can be even more important than campaign contributions. Campaign activism on the part of conservative groups played a very important role in bringing about the Republican capture of both houses of Congress in the 1994 congressional elections. For example, Christian Coalition activists played a role in many races, including those in which Republican candidates were not overly identified with the religious right. One postelection study suggested that more than 60 percent of the more than 600 candidates supported by the Christian right were successful in state, local, and congressional races in 1994.[34] The efforts of conservative Republican activists to bring voters to the polls is one major reason that turnout among Republicans exceeded Democratic turnout in a midterm election for the first time since 1970. This increased turnout was especially marked in the South, where the Christian Coalition was most active. In many congressional districts, Christian Coalition efforts on behalf of the Republicans were augmented by grassroots campaigns launched by the NRA and the National Federation of Independent Business (NFIB). The NRA had been outraged by Democratic support for gun-control legislation, and the NFIB had been energized by its campaign against employer mandates in the failed Clinton health-care reform initiative. Both groups are well organized at the local level and were able to mobilize their members across the country to participate in congressional races.

One remarkable fact about the political activity of interest groups is how infrequently major interest groups have tried to form their own party. The fact that they have rarely done so is to a large extent attributable to the strength of the two-party tradition in the United States. But there is also a significant negative influence: the barriers erected by state laws regarding the formation of new political parties. As a consequence, significant interests such as "the working class," women, and African Americans have not been able to find clear expression in the electoral process. Their interests are always being adulterated by other interests within their chosen party. Yet this situation has a positive side: the two-party system has—unintentionally—softened social demarcations by cutting across classes, races, and other fundamental interests that deeply divide people. These interests are adulterated and softened, subduing what might otherwise become the kind of class conflict that we see so often in European history, where class, race, and ethnic interests have become radicalized when they are not forced to reconcile themselves with other interests in a broad political party.[35]

For Critical Analysis

Describe the different techniques of influence that organized interests employ. When is one technique preferable to another?

THE INITIATIVE Another political tactic that interest groups sometimes use is sponsorship of ballot initiatives at the state level. The initiative, a device adopted

Take an Interest in Interest Groups

The words "interest group" often conjure up images of powerful lobbyists working on behalf of people far removed from yourself and your peers. For example, AARP, or the American Association of Retired Persons, represents more than 35 million people who are fifty years of age and older and is one of the most politically powerful groups in existence today. It's probably safe to say that the effectiveness of AARP in influencing Social Security and Medicare reform doesn't strike most college students as something that's likely to change their lives anytime soon.

However, groups formed by young Americans lobbied successfully for the College Cost Reduction and Access Act, a measure that was ultimately passed by Congress in 2007. Among other things, the act increases Pell Grants, reduces interest on certain college loans, and makes the rate of loan repayment partially dependent on how much one earns. In short, it attempts to address one of the most vexing problems faced by young Americans today—affording a college education—especially as college increasingly seems a necessity in life rather than a choice. Students and other young people were at the forefront of activism around getting this bill passed.

Campus chapters of U.S. PIRG, a federation of state Public Interest Research Groups, were involved with mobilizing youth around this particular legislation. PIRG and the College Cost Reduction and Access Act is a terrific example of the power of interest groups in the United States and the ways in which youth are often involved in lobbying for solutions to social and political problems. As easy as it is to buy the conventional wisdom that interest groups are a political force used only by people older and wealthier than you, it's simply not the case.

The following ideas for getting involved will help you think through issues like interest group representation and influence. You don't necessarily need to become an activist yourself to gain a better understanding of what interest groups actually do in our democracy.

★ Identify what issues you care the most about in politics today and find out if there are any interest groups out there who advocate on behalf of those issues. You might consider joining one or two in order to show your support and to better understand the ways in which interest groups cultivate members and represent their interests in state and national governments. An easy way to learn about relevant issues of the day is to visit the Web site for Campus Activism (www.campusactivism.org) and check out their list of issues and campaigns that are going on around the country to help address them.

★ If you find a group for which you feel a close affinity, consider forming a campus chapter. There are a lot of groups out there who will gladly help students start campus chapters. Some that come to mind include the American Association for University Women (www.aauw.org) and Amnesty International (www.amnesty.org).

★ Find out how those who represent you in Congress measure up according to interest groups. As you'll see when you visit the link to interest group ratings on the Project Vote Smart Web site (www.votesmart.org), interest groups assess how consistently elected officials vote for legislation that's supportive of group interests. You may find a few surprising scores tied to those who represent you in Congress.

★ Interest groups often get a bad rap in American politics, mainly because people think they have too much influence over elected officials who end up responding to them more than average voters. These concerns are especially heightened during an election year because people believe that candidates are "bought and sold" by way of campaign donations from interest groups. Look up the McCain-Feingold Act, which was intended to reduce the influence of interest groups' money in elections. If you are still concerned about the influence of interest groups and think further reform is needed, e-mail your member of Congress, using the contact information at www.house.gov or www.senate.gov.

by a number of states around 1900, allows proposed laws to be placed on the general election ballot and submitted directly to the state's voters. This procedure bypasses the state legislature and the governor. The initiative was originally promoted by late-nineteenth-century Populists as a mechanism that would allow the people to govern directly. Populists saw the initiative as an antidote to interest group influence in the legislative process.

Many studies have suggested that, ironically, most initiative campaigns today are actually sponsored by interest groups seeking to circumvent legislative opposition to their goals. In recent years, for example, initiative campaigns have been sponsored by the insurance industry, trial lawyers' associations, and tobacco companies.[36] The role of interest groups in initiative campaigns should come as no surprise, since such campaigns can cost millions of dollars.

Thinking Critically about Groups and Interests: The Dilemmas of Reform

For Critical Analysis

How has the U.S. government sought to regulate interest-group activity in order to balance the competing values of liberty and equality? What else might government do to make group politics less biased?

We would like to think that policies are products of legislators' concepts of the public interest. Yet the truth of the matter is that few programs and policies ever reach the public agenda without the vigorous support of important national interest groups. In the realm of economic policy, social policy, international trade policy, and even such seemingly interest-free areas as criminal justice policy—where, in fact, private prison corporations lobby for longer sentences for lawbreakers—interest-group activity is a central feature. Of course, before we throw up our hands in dismay, we should remember that the untidy process and sometimes undesirable outcomes of interest-group politics are virtually inherent aspects of democratic politics.

James Madison wrote that "liberty is to faction as air is to fire."[37] By this he meant that the organization and proliferation of interests were inevitable in a free society. To seek to place limits on the organization of interests, in Madison's view, would be to limit liberty itself. Madison believed that interests should be permitted to regulate themselves by competing with each other. So long as competition among different interests was free, open, and vigorous—that is, so long as pluralism thrived—there would be some balance of power among them and no one interest would be able to dominate the political or governmental process.

There is considerable competition among organized groups in the United States. For example, prochoice and antiabortion forces continue to be locked in a bitter struggle. Nevertheless, interest-group politics is not as free of bias as Madisonian theory might suggest. Although the weak and poor do occasionally become organized to assert their rights, interest-group politics is generally a form of political competition in which the wealthy and powerful are best able to engage. In the realm of group politics, liberty seems inconsistent with equality.

Moreover, although groups sometimes organize to promote broad public concerns, interest groups more often represent relatively narrow, selfish interests. Small, self-interested groups can be organized much more easily than large and more diffuse collectives. For one thing, the members of a relatively small group—say, bankers or hunting enthusiasts—are usually able to recognize their shared interests and the need to pursue them in the political arena. Members of large and more diffuse groups—say, consumers or potential victims of firearms—often find it difficult to recognize their shared interests or the need to engage in collective action to achieve them.[38] This is why causes presented as public interests by their proponents often turn out, on examination, to be private interests wrapped in a public mantle. Thus, group politics often appears to be inconsistent with democracy.

To make matters still more complicated, group politics seems to go hand in hand with government. As we saw earlier, government programs often lead to a proliferation of interest groups as competing forces mobilize to support, oppose, or take advantage of the government's actions. Often, the government explicitly encourages the formation of interest groups. From the perspective of a government agency, nothing is more useful than a well-organized constituency for its programs. Agencies such as the Department of Veterans Affairs, the Social Security Administration, and the Department of Agriculture devote a great deal of energy to the organization and mobilization of groups of "stakeholders" to support the agencies and their efforts. This strategy, a variant of what is sometimes called "interest-group liberalism," can be very effective. One reason that the Social Security program is considered politically invulnerable despite its fiscal shortcomings is that it is so strongly supported by a powerful group—the AARP. Significantly, the Social Security Administration played an important early role in the formation of the AARP, precisely because agency executives realized that this group could become a useful ally.

The responsiveness of government agencies to interest groups is a challenge to democracy. Groups seem to have a greater impact than voters on the government's policies and programs. Yet, before we decide that we should do away with interest groups, we should think carefully: If there were no organized interests, would the government pay more attention to ordinary voters? Or would the government simply pay no attention to anyone? In his great work *Democracy in America*, Alexis de Tocqueville argued that the proliferation of groups promoted democracy by encouraging governmental responsiveness. Does group politics foster democracy or impede democracy? It does both.

The George W. Bush administration was frequently criticized for its close ties to the energy industry. For example, protesters outside of the annual stockholders meeting of Halliburton—the world's largest oil-and-gas services company, which Vice President Cheney led from 1995 to 2000—questioned the integrity of Halliburton's receiving up to $7 billion in government contracts for work in Iraq.

Thus, we have dilemmas for which there is no ideal answer. To regulate interest-group politics is, as Madison warned, to limit freedom and to expand governmental power. Not to regulate interest-group politics, on the other hand, may be to ignore equality and democracy. Those who believe that there are simple solutions to the issues of political life would do well to ponder this problem.

FOR FURTHER READING

Ainsworth, Scott. *Analyzing Interest Groups.* New York: Norton, 2002.

Alexander, Robert, ed. *The Classic of Interest Group Behavior.* New York: Wadsworth, 2005.

Berry, Jeffrey. *Interest Group Society.* 5th ed. New York: Longman, 2008.

Birnbaum, Jeffrey. *The Money Men.* New York: Crown, 2000.

Cigler, Allan J., and Burdett A. Loomis, eds. *Interest Group Politics.* 7th ed. Washington, DC: Congressional Quarterly Press, 2006.

Esterling, Kevin. *The Political Economy of Expertise.* Ann Arbor: University of Michigan Press, 2004.

Kollman, Kenneth W. *Outside Lobbying: Public Opinion and Interest Group Strategies.* Princeton, NJ: Princeton University Press, 1998.

Lowi, Theodore J. *The End of Liberalism: The Second Republic of the United States.* 2nd ed. New York: Norton, 1979.

Moe, Terry M. *The Organization of Interests: Incentives and the Internal Dynamics of Political Interest Groups.* Chicago: University of Chicago Press, 1980.

Nownes, Anthony. *Total Lobbying: What Lobbyists Want and How They Try to Get It.* New York: Cambridge University Press, 2006.

Olson, Mancur, Jr. *The Logic of Collective Action: Public Goods and the Theory of Groups.* Cambridge, MA: Harvard University Press, 1965.

Rosenthal, Alan. *The Third House: Lobbyists and Lobbying in the States.* Washington, DC: Congressional Quarterly Press, 2001.

Rozell, Mark, Clyde Wilcox, and David Madland. *Interest Groups in American Campaigns.* Washington, DC: Congressional Quarterly Press, 2005.

Sheingate, Adam. *The Rise of the Agricultural Welfare State: Institutions and Interest Groups Power in the United States, France, and Japan.* Princeton, NJ: Princeton University Press, 2003.

Skinner, Richard. *More Than Money.* New York: Rowman and Littlefield, 2006.

Truman, David B. *The Governmental Process: Political Interests and Public Opinion.* New York: Knopf, 1951.

RECOMMENDED WEB SITES

AARP
www.aarp.org/

AARP (formerly the American Association of Retired Persons) is one of the largest and most significant interest groups in the United States. Read about the history of this organization, its group benefits, and how it is affecting political issues and elections.

AFL-CIO Legislative Alert Center
www.aflcio.org/issues/legislativealert/

Created in 1955, the AFL-CIO represents over 10 million working men and women. See how this influential labor group is active and involved in political issues.

American Civil Liberties Union
www.aclu.org
American Conservative Union
www.conservative.org

The American Civil Liberties Union and the American Conservative Union are two of the nation's largest and most influential ideological interest groups. See what these opposing groups have to say about our government and current political issues.

American Israel Public Affairs Committee (AIPAC)
www.aipac.org

Due to globalization, interest groups cannot limit their activities to only one country. Decisions made in Washington, D.C. can affect countries around the world. The American Israel Public Affairs Committee (AIPAC) works with Republicans and Democrats to maintain a strong relationship between the United States and Israel.

MoveOn
www.moveon.org

This progressive interest group is dedicated to bringing ordinary citizens back into the political process and electing liberal members of government. See how this group uses electoral politics, via political action committees and campaign activism, to achieve its agenda.

National Rifle Association
www.nra.org
Coalition to Stop Gun Violence
www.csgv.org
Brady Campaign to Prevent Gun Violence
www.bradycampaign.org

Lobbying is an attempt by a group to influence the policy process by persuading government officials. These three groups employ a variety of lobbying techniques on the issue of gun control.

Political Advocacy Groups: A Directory of United States Lobbyists
www.csuchico.edu/~kfountain/

Kathi Fountain at California State University, Chico maintains this site, which lists political advocacy groups. This directory is a great place to find interest groups and lobbyists on most political issues.

U.S. PIRG (United States Public Interest Research Group)
www.uspirg.org/

This public interest group stands up for ordinary citizens. Its special emphasis is on consumer rights and the environment. U.S. PIRG mobilizes public opinion via institutional advertising, social movements, and grassroots efforts. PIRG chapters can be found in most states and at many colleges and universities.

World Wildlife Fund
www.wwf.org/

The World Wildlife Fund is dedicated to protecting nature. They provide information to policy makers about conservation and advocate policies to help preserve the natural environment.

STUDY OUTLINE

www.wwnorton.com/wtp7e

The Character of Interest Groups

1. An enormous number of diverse interest groups exist in the United States.
2. Most interest groups share key organizational components, such as mechanisms for member recruitment, financial and decision-making processes, and agencies that actually carry out group goals.
3. Interest-group politics in the United States tends to have a pronounced upper-class bias because of the characteristics of interest-group members.
4. Because of natural disincentives to join interest groups, groups offer material, informational, solidary, and purposive benefits to entice people to join.

The Proliferation of Groups

1. The modern expansion of governmental economic and social programs has contributed to the enormous increase in the number of groups seeking to influence the American political system.
2. The second factor accounting for the explosion of interest-group activity in recent years was the emergence of a new set of forces in American politics: the New Politics movement.

Strategies: The Quest for Political Power

1. Lobbying is an effort by outsiders to influence Congress or government agencies by providing them with information about issues, giving them support, and even threatening them with retaliation.
2. Access is actual involvement with and influence in the decision-making process.
3. Interest groups often turn to litigation when they lack access or feel they have insufficient influence over the formulation and implementation of public policy.
4. Going public is a strategy that attempts to mobilize the widest and most favorable climate of opinion.
5. Many groups employ a nonpartisan strategy in electoral politics to avoid giving up access to one party by embracing the other.

Thinking Critically about Groups and Interests: The Dilemmas of Reform

1. The organization of private interests into groups to advance their own views is a necessary and intrinsic element of the liberty of citizens to pursue their private lives and to express their views, individually and collectively.
2. The organization of private interests into groups is biased in favor of the wealthy and the powerful, who have superior knowledge, opportunity, and resources with which to organize.

PRACTICE QUIZ

www.wwnorton.com/wtp7e

1. The theory that competition among organized interests will produce balance with all the interests regulating one another is
   a) pluralism.
   b) elite power politics.
   c) democracy.
   d) socialism.
2. To overcome the free-rider problem, groups
   a) provide general benefits.
   b) litigate.
   c) go public.
   d) provide selective benefits.
3. Politically organized religious groups often make use of
   a) material benefits.
   b) solidary benefits.
   c) purposive benefits.
   d) none of the above.
4. Which of the following best describes the reputation of the AARP in the Washington community?
   a) It is respected and feared.
   b) It is supported and well liked by all political forces.
   c) It is believed to be ineffective.
   d) It wins the political battles it fights.
5. Which types of interest groups are most often associated with the New Politics movement?
   a) public-interest groups
   b) professional associations
   c) government groups
   d) labor groups
6. Access politics, exemplified by defense contractors acting in concert with congressional committees and executive agencies, is an example of
   a) campaign activism.
   b) public interest politics.
   c) an iron triangle.
   d) the role of conservative interest groups.
7. In which of the following ways do interest groups use the courts to affect public policy?
   a) filing *amicus* briefs
   b) bringing lawsuits
   c) financing those filing suit
   d) all of the above
8. According to this text, what is the limit a PAC can contribute to a primary or general election campaign?
   a) $1,000
   b) $5,000
   c) $10,000
   d) $50,000
9. Which of the following is *not* an activity in which interest groups frequently engage?
   a) starting their own political party
   b) litigation
   c) lobbying
   d) contributing to campaigns

KEY TERMS

www.wwnorton.com/wtp7e

collective goods (p. 424)
free riders (p. 424)
grassroots mobilization (p. 439)
informational benefits (p. 424)
institutional advertising (p. 438)
interest group (p. 419)
iron triangle (p. 436)
issue network (p. 436)
lobbying (p. 431)
material benefits (p. 425)
membership association (p. 423)
New Politics movement (p. 429)
pluralism (p. 419)
political action committee (PAC) (p. 442)
public interest groups (p. 429)
purposive benefits (p. 425)
solidary benefits (p. 425)
staff organization (p. 424)

PART III Institutions

12 Congress

WHAT GOVERNMENT DOES AND WHY IT MATTERS

Congress has vast authority over the two most important powers given to any government: the power of force (control over the nation's military forces); and the power over money. Specifically, in Article I, Section 8, Congress can "lay and collect Taxes," deal with indebtedness and bankruptcy, impose duties, borrow and coin money, and generally control the nation's purse strings. It also may "provide for the common Defense and general welfare," regulate interstate commerce, undertake public works, acquire and control federal lands, promote science and "useful Arts" (pertaining mostly to patents and copyrights), and regulate the militia. Thus, the most fundamental choices about the role that government plays in the lives of Americans—the quality and quantity of public services, the amount of income tax and other federal taxes, the health of the economy—rest with the Congress.

In the realm of foreign policy, Congress has the power to declare war, deal with piracy, regulate foreign commerce, and raise and regulate the armed forces and military installations. These powers over war and the military are supreme—even the president, as commander in chief of the military, must obey the laws and orders of Congress if Congress chooses to assert its constitutional authority. (In the past century, Congress has usually surrendered this authority to the president.) Congress could end our military engagement in foreign countries, such as Iraq, by cutting off funds for wars; it can also spread the burden of military engagement more broadly by reinstituting the draft. Further, the Senate has the power to approve treaties (by a two-thirds vote) and to approve the appointment of ambassadors. Capping these powers, Congress is charged to make laws that determine exactly how these powers—and all other powers of the government—will actually be implemented.

If it seems that many of these powers belong to the president, from war power to spending power, that is because modern presidents do exercise great authority in these areas. The modern presidency is a more powerful institution than it was 200 years ago, and much of that power has come from Congress, either because

Congress has delegated the power to the president by law, or because Congress has simply allowed, or even urged, presidents to be more active in these areas. This also helps explain why the executive branch often seems like a more important branch of government today than Congress. Still, the constitutional powers of Congress remain intact in the document. And Congress can exert important power over the executive branch by using its power of oversight. Congressional oversight hearings can lead to significant changes in the way the executive branch operates; at times these hearings lead to the resignation of public officials.

In addition to its lawmaking powers, Congress plays a critical role in American democracy as a representative institution. This is because Congress represents in Washington the voice of the people across America. Members of Congress pay close attention to the views of their local constituencies. Each congressional office has set up multiple channels for constituents to make their views known or to ask for help with a problem. Members of Congress maintain local offices and make sure to spend time in their home districts hearing from voters.

Yet some worry today that Congress does not represent all voices equally. Declining political participation among lower-income voters and the growing importance of money in politics may make Congress more responsive to higher-income voters and resource-rich interest groups. Congress can balance the tensions among liberty, equality, and democracy only when all groups are fairly represented. We will assess whether Congress fulfills these principles later in this chapter.

› **To understand the pivotal role that Congress plays in American democracy, we will first examine the concept of representation.** We will also look at how members of Congress act on behalf of their constituents and how the electoral process affects the relationship between Congress and the people.

› **Next, we will discuss the legislative process.** We will study the building blocks of congressional organization, including political parties, the committee system, congressional staff, and caucuses. We then turn to the rules of congressional procedure, through which laws are formulated.

› **We then look at congressional decision making, examining the influences on the legislation that Congress produces.** The complex legislative process is subject to a variety of influences from inside and outside government, including constituencies, interest groups, and party leaders.

› **We next turn to other powers that allow Congress to influence the process of government.** In addition to the power to make law, Congress has an array of instruments to use in its relationship with the president and the executive branch.

› **We conclude by taking a critical look at how well Congress represents the American people.** Congress embodies our democratic ideals by representing the public in government, but it's not always clear if or how members of Congress best represent their constituents' interests.

Congress: Representing the American People

Congress is the most important representative institution in American government. Each member's primary responsibility is to the district, to his or her **constituency,** not to the congressional leadership, a party, or even Congress itself. Yet the task of representation is not a simple one. Views about what constitutes fair and effective representation differ, and constituents may have very different expectations of their representatives. Members of Congress must consider these diverse views and expectations as they represent their districts.

constituency the residents in the area from which an official is elected

House and Senate: Differences in Representation

The framers of the Constitution provided for a **bicameral** legislature—that is, a legislative body consisting of two chambers. As we saw in Chapter 2, the framers intended each of these chambers, the House of Representatives and the Senate, to serve a different constituency. Members of the Senate, appointed by state legislatures for six-year terms, were to represent the elite members of society. Today, members of the House and Senate are elected directly by the people. The 435 members of the House are elected from districts apportioned according to population; the 100 members of the Senate are elected by state, with two senators from each. Senators continue to have much longer terms in office and usually represent much larger and more diverse constituencies than do their counterparts in the House (see Table 12.1).

bicameral having a legislative assembly composed of two chambers or houses

The House and Senate play different roles in the legislative process. In essence, the Senate is the more deliberative of the two bodies—the forum in which any and all ideas that senators raise can receive a thorough public airing. The House is the more centralized and organized of the two bodies—better equipped to play a routine role in the governmental process. In part, this difference stems from the different rules governing the two bodies. These rules give House leaders more control over the legislative process and allow House members to specialize in

TABLE 12.1 ★ Differences between the House and the Senate

	HOUSE	SENATE
Minimum age of member	25 years	30 years
U.S. citizenship	At least 7 years	At least 9 years
Length of term	2 years	6 years
Number representing each state	1–53 per state (depends on population)	2 per state
Constituency	Tends to be local	Both local and national

For its first 128 years, Congress was a decidedly masculine world. In 1917, three years before the ratification of the Nineteenth Amendment, Jeanette Rankin (R-Mont.) (pictured back row, far right) became the first woman to serve in Congress.

certain legislative areas. The rules of the much smaller Senate give its leadership relatively little power and discourage specialization.

Both formal and informal factors contribute to differences between the two chambers of Congress. Differences in the length of terms and requirements for holding office, specified by the Constitution, generate differences in how members of each body develop their constituencies and exercise their powers of office. The result is that members of the House most effectively and frequently serve as the agents of well-organized local interests with specific legislative agendas—for instance, used-car dealers seeking relief from regulation, labor unions seeking more favorable legislation, or farmers looking for higher subsidies. The small size and relative homogeneity of their constituencies and the frequency with which they must seek re-election make House members more attuned to the legislative needs of local interest groups.

Senators, on the other hand, serve larger and more heterogeneous constituencies. As a result, they are somewhat better able than members of the House to act as the agents for groups and interests organized on a statewide or national basis. Moreover, with longer terms in office, senators have more time to consider "new ideas" or to bring together new coalitions of interests, rather than simply serving existing ones.

Sociological versus Agency Representation

We have become so accustomed to the idea of representative government that we tend to forget what a peculiar concept representation really is. A representative claims to act or speak for some other person or group. But how can one person be trusted to speak for another? How do we know that those who call themselves our representatives are actually speaking on our behalf, rather than simply pursuing their own interests?

There are two circumstances under which one person reasonably might be trusted to speak for another. The first of these occurs if the two individuals are so similar in background, character, interests, and perspectives that anything said by one would very likely reflect the views of the other as well. This principle is at the heart of what is sometimes called **sociological representation**—the sort of representation that takes place when representatives have the same racial, gender, ethnic, religious, or educational backgrounds as their constituents. The assumption is that sociological similarity helps to promote good representation; thus, the composition of a properly constituted representative assembly should mirror the composition of society.

The second circumstance under which one person might be trusted to speak for another occurs if the two are formally bound together so that the representative is in some way accountable to those he or she is supposed to represent. If representatives can somehow be punished for failing to speak properly for their constituents, then we know they have an incentive to provide good representation even if their own personal backgrounds, views, and interests differ from those they represent. This principle is called **agency representation**—the sort of representation that takes place when constituents have the power to hire and fire their representatives.

sociological representation a type of representation in which representatives have the same racial, gender, ethnic, religious, or educational backgrounds as their constituents. It is based on the principle that if two individuals are similar in background, character, interests, and perspectives, then one could correctly represent the other's views

agency representation the type of representation in which a representative is held accountable to a constituency if he or she fails to represent that constituency properly

Both sociological and agency representation play a role in the relationship between members of Congress and their constituencies.

THE SOCIAL COMPOSITION OF THE U.S. CONGRESS

The extent to which the U.S. Congress is representative of the American people in a sociological sense can be seen by examining social characteristics of the House and Senate today. For example, the religious affiliations of members of both the House and Senate are overwhelmingly Protestant—the distribution is very close to the proportion in the population at large—although the Protestant category comprises more than fifteen denominations. Catholics are the second largest category of religious affiliation, and Jews a much smaller third category.[1] Religious affiliations directly affect congressional debate on a limited range of issues where different moral views are at stake, such as abortion.

African Americans, women, Hispanic Americans, and Asian Americans have increased their congressional representation in the past two decades (see Figure 12.1), but the representation of women and minorities in Congress is still not comparable to their proportions in the general population. In 2008, seventy-one women served in the House (up from only twenty-nine in 1990). After the Democrats won a majority in the House in November 2006, Nancy Pelosi (D-Calif.) became the first female Speaker of the House. In 2008, sixteen women served in the Senate. Since many important contemporary national issues cut along racial and gender lines, pressure for reform in the representative process is likely to continue until these groups are fully represented.

The increase in the number of African Americans in Congress in the last forty years is shown by the membership of the Congressional Black Caucus, which had forty-three members in 2008. Caucus members are shown here at a press conference about the government's response to Hurricane Katrina, which was especially devastating to the African American community in the Gulf states.

The occupational backgrounds of members of Congress have always been a matter of interest because so many issues split along economic lines that are relevant to occupations and industries. The legal profession is the dominant career of most members of Congress prior to their election. Public service or politics is also a significant background, with many members coming from positions in state and local government. In addition, many members of Congress also have important ties to business and industry.[2] Although Congress has become much more diverse in recent years, in 2008 it was still 84 percent male and 85 percent white. Moreover, members of Congress are much more highly educated than most Americans. More than nine in ten members hold university degrees, and close to half of them have law degrees.[3] This is not a portrait of the U.S. population. Congress is not a sociological microcosm of American society.

Can Congress still legislate fairly or take account of a diversity of views and interests if it is not a sociologically representative assembly? The task is certainly much more difficult. Yet there is reason to believe it can. Representatives, as we shall see shortly, can serve as the agents of their constituents, even if they do not precisely mirror their sociological attributes. Yet sociological representation is a matter of some importance, even if it is not an absolute prerequisite for fair legislation by members of the House and Senate. At the least, the social composition of a representative assembly is important for symbolic purposes—to demonstrate to groups in the population that the government takes them seriously. If Congress is not representative symbolically, then its own authority—and indeed that of the entire government—would be reduced.[4]

For Critical Analysis

Why is sociological representation important? If congressional representatives have racial, religious, or educational backgrounds similar to those of their constituents, are they better representatives? Why or why not?

FIGURE 12.1 ★ Women, African Americans, and Latinos in the U.S. Congress, 1971–2008

Congress has become much more socially diverse since the 1970s. After a gradual increase from 1971 to 1990, the number of women and African American members grew quickly during the first half of the 1990s. How does the pattern of growth for Latino representatives compare with that of women and African Americans?

SOURCES: Harold W. Stanley and Richard G. Niemi, eds., *Vital Statistics on American Politics 2003–2004* (Washington, DC: Congressional Quarterly Press, 2003), 207, Table 5-2; and CRS Report for Congress, http://assets.opencrs.com/rpts/RS22555_20061215.pdf (accessed 3/3/08).

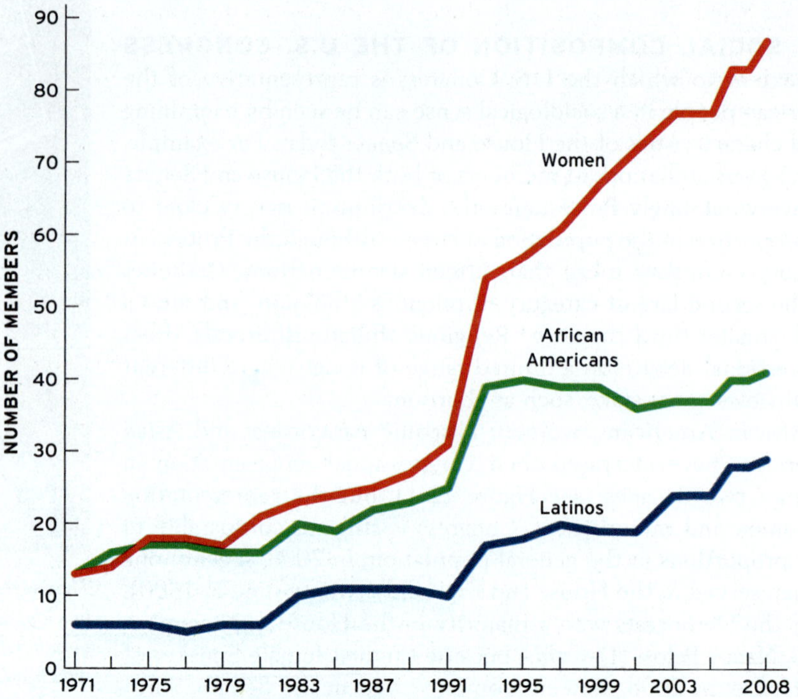

REPRESENTATIVES AS AGENTS A good deal of evidence indicates that whether or not members of Congress share their constituents' sociological characteristics, they *do* work very hard to speak for their constituents' views and serve their constituents' interests in the governmental process. The idea of representative as agent is similar to the relationship of lawyer and client. True, the relationship between the member of Congress and as many as 660,000 "clients" in the district, or the senator and millions of "clients" in the state, is very different from that of the lawyer and client. But the criteria of performance are comparable. One expects at the very least that each representative will constantly seek to discover the interests of the constituency and will speak for those interests in Congress and in other centers of government.[5]

There is constant communication between constituents and congressional offices, and communication has grown dramatically with the Internet. In 2006, Congress received 333 million communications: 20 million arrived by regular mail; e-mails accounted for 313 million communications.[6] Members of Congress, too, have found new ways to communicate with constituents. With a few exceptions, members have created Web sites describing their achievements and e-newsletters that alert constituents to timely issues. A handful have also set up blogs to establish a more informal style of communication with constituents.

The seriousness with which members of the House attempt to behave as representatives can be seen in the amount of time they spend on behalf of their constituents. Well over a quarter of their time and nearly two-thirds of the time of their staff members is devoted to constituency service (called "case work"). This service is not merely a matter of writing and mailing letters. It includes talking to constituents, providing them with minor services, presenting special bills for them, and attempting to influence decisions by regulatory commissions on their behalf.[7]

Although no members of Congress are above constituency pressures (and they would not want to be), on many issues constituents do not have very strong views, and representatives are free to act as they think best. Foreign policy issues often fall into this category, although that is less true since the Iraq war aroused strong feelings. But in many districts there are two or three issues on which constituents have such pronounced opinions that representatives feel they have little freedom of choice. For example, representatives from districts that grow wheat, cotton, or tobacco probably will not want to exercise a great deal of independence on relevant agricultural legislation. In oil-rich states such as Oklahoma and Texas, senators and members of the House are likely to be leading advocates of oil interests. For one thing, representatives are probably fearful of voting against their district interests; for another, the districts are unlikely to have elected representatives who would *want* to vote against them.

The influence of constituencies is so pervasive that both parties have strongly embraced the informal rule that nothing should be done to endanger the re-election chances of any member. Party leaders obey this rule fairly consistently by not asking any member to vote in a way that might conflict with a district interest.

The Electoral Connection

The sociological composition of Congress and the activities of representatives once they are in office are very much influenced by electoral considerations. Three factors related to the U.S. electoral system affect who gets elected and what they do once in office. The first set of issues concerns who decides to run for office and which candidates have an edge over others. The second issue is that of incumbency advantage. Finally, the way congressional district lines are drawn can greatly affect the outcome of an election. Let us examine more closely the impact that these considerations have on representation.

WHO RUNS FOR CONGRESS? Voters' choices are restricted from the start by who decides to run for office. In the past, decisions about who would run for a particular elected office were made by local party officials. A person who had a record of service to the party, or who was owed a favor, or whose "turn" had come up might be nominated by party leaders for an office. Today, few party organizations have the power to slate candidates in that way. Instead, parties try to ensure that well-qualified candidates run for Congress. During the 1990s, the Republican party developed "farm teams" of local officials who were groomed to run for Congress. Their success led Democrats to attempt a similar strategy. Even so, the decision to run for Congress is a personal choice. One of the most important factors determining who runs for office is a candidate's individual ambition.[8] A potential candidate may also assess whether he or she can attract enough money to mount a credible campaign. The ability to raise money depends on connections with other politicians, interest groups, and national party organizations. In the past, the difficulty of raising campaign funds posed a disadvantage to female candidates. Since the 1980s, however, a number of powerful political action committees (PACs) have emerged to recruit women and fund their campaigns. The largest of them, EMILY's List, has become one of the most powerful fund-raisers of all PACs. Recent research shows that money is no longer the barrier it once was to women running for office.[9]

Features distinctive to each congressional district also affect the field of candidates. Among them are the range of other political opportunities that may lure potential candidates away. In addition, the way the congressional district overlaps with state legislative boundaries may affect a candidate's decision to run. A state-level representative or senator who is considering running for the U.S. Congress is more likely to assess her prospects favorably if her state district coincides with the congressional district (because the voters will already know her). And for any candidate, decisions about running must be made early, because once money has been committed to already declared candidates, it is harder for new candidates to break into a race. Thus, the outcome of a November election is partially determined many months earlier, when decisions to run are finalized.

incumbency holding a political office for which one is running

INCUMBENCY Incumbency plays a very important role in the American electoral system and in the kind of representation citizens get in Washington. Once in office, members of Congress possess an array of tools that they can use to stack the deck in favor of their re-election. The most important of these is constituency service: taking care of the problems and requests of individual voters. Through such services and through regular newsletter mailings, the incumbent seeks to establish a "personal" relationship with his or her constituents. The success of this strategy is evident in the high rates of re-election for congressional incumbents: as high as 98 percent for House members and 90 percent for members of the Senate in recent years (see Figure 12.2). It is also evident in what is called "sophomore surge"—the tendency for candidates to win a higher percentage of the vote when seeking future terms in office. As in past elections, voters returned large numbers of congressional incumbents to office in 2004—specifically, 98.5 percent to the House and 96 percent to the Senate. These rates dropped significantly in the 2006 midterm elections as voters disenchanted with congressional scandals and the Iraq war turned incumbents out in greater numbers than usual. In 2006, 94 percent of incumbents were reelected to the House; 79 percent were reelected in the Senate.

Incumbency can help a candidate by scaring off potential challengers. In many races, potential candidates may decide not to run because they fear that the incumbent simply has too much money or is too well liked or too well known. Potential challengers may also decide that a district's partisan leanings are too unfavorable. It often takes exceptional circumstances to persuade strong candidates to run against well-established incumbents. In 2005, the Ohio Republican incumbent Deborah Pryce held the fourth most powerful leadership position in the House and was the highest-ranking Republican woman. In office since 1993, Pryce was a popular politician who used her powers of incumbency well, providing benefits for her district. She typically won elections by large margins and rarely faced strong opponents. The Democrats who ran against her were weak candidates viewed as "sacrificial lambs" by party leaders.[10] The 2006 race promised to be different. With congressional Republicans at a national disadvantage due to lobbying scandals and Republicans across the state tainted by unrelated statehouse scandals, Pryce attracted a strong opponent for the first time. Pryce won the 2006 race by a narrow margin. But with her seat considered among the most likely to go Democratic in the next election, Pryce announced in 2007 that

Politics Today

How did incumbents fare in the 2008 elections? Were Democrats successful in their effort to ensure that those first elected to Congress in 2006 would be re-elected in 2008?

FIGURE 12.2 ★
The Power of Incumbency

Members of Congress who run for re-election have a very good chance of winning. Senators have at times found it difficult to use the power of incumbency to protect their seats, as the sharp decline in Senate incumbency rates between 1974 and 1980 indicates. Has the incumbency advantage generally been greater in the House or in the Senate?

SOURCES: Norman J. Ornstein et al., eds., *Vital Statistics on Congress, 1999–2000* (Washington, DC: AEI Press, 2000), 57–58; and authors' update.

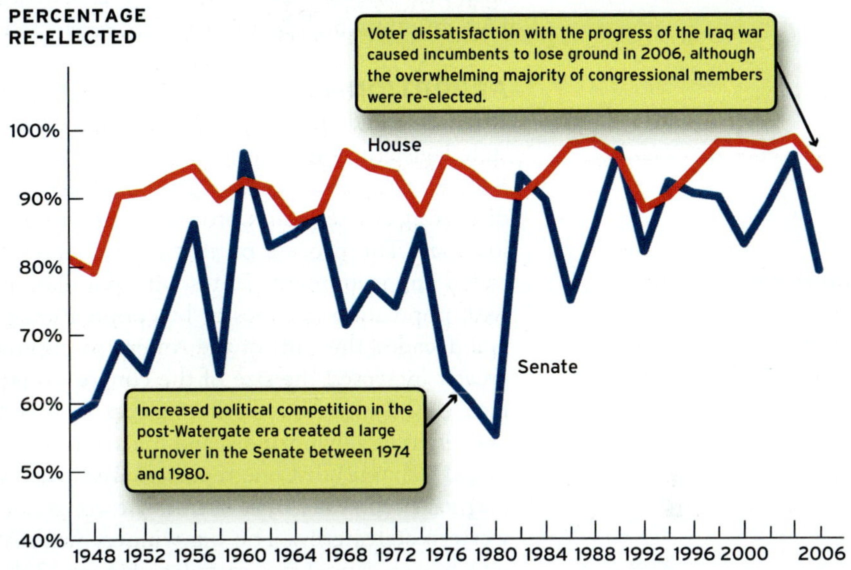

she would not seek another term. The efforts of incumbents to raise funds to ward off potential challengers start early. A Connecticut Democrat, Joe Courtney, who earned the nickname "Landslide Joe" with his ninety-one-vote margin of victory in 2006, began fund-raising for the 2008 election even before he was sworn in for his first term. In addition, the Democratic Congressional Campaign Committee placed him on its Frontline team, a group of the twenty-nine most vulnerable Democrats. The Democratic leadership took special efforts to raise the profile of these members of Congress. For example, Courtney and others in the Frontline team received high-profile speaking assignments on the floor of Congress and were appointed to key congressional committees.[11]

The advantage of incumbency thus tends to preserve the status quo in Congress. This fact has implications for the social composition of Congress. For example, incumbency advantage makes it harder for women to increase their numbers in Congress because most incumbents are men. Women who run for open seats (for which there are no incumbents) are just as likely to win as male candidates.[12] Supporters of **term limits** argue that such limits are the only way to get new faces into Congress. They believe that incumbency advantage and the tendency of many legislators to view politics as a career mean that very little turnover will occur in Congress unless limits are imposed on the number of terms a legislator can serve.

term limits legally prescribed limits on the number of terms an elected official can serve

Yet the percentage of incumbents who are returned to Congress after each election also depends on how many members decide to run again. Because each year some members decide to retire, turnover in Congress is greater than the re-election rates of incumbents suggest. On average, 10 percent of the House and Senate decide to retire each election. In some years, the number of retirements is higher, as in 1992, when 20 percent of House members decided to retire; thus, the 90 percent of incumbents who were re-elected that year were a subset of all the eligible incumbents (80 percent). Opponents of term limits argue that, over time, such retirements ensure that there is sufficient turnover in Congress despite the high rates at which incumbents are re-elected.

APPORTIONMENT AND REDISTRICTING The final factor that affects who wins a seat in Congress is the way congressional districts are drawn. Every ten years, state legislatures must redraw congressional districts to reflect population changes. Because the number of congressional seats has been fixed at 435 since 1929, redistricting is a zero-sum process; in order for one state to gain a seat, another must lose one. The process of allocating congressional seats among the fifty states is called **apportionment.** States with population growth gain additional seats; states with population declines or less population growth lose seats. Over the past several decades, the shift of the American population to the South and the West has greatly increased the size of the congressional delegations from these regions (see Figure 12.3). In the redistricting that followed the 2000 census, this trend continued: eight largely northern and midwestern states (the exceptions were Mississippi and Oklahoma) lost one representative, and two states (New York and Pennsylvania) lost two seats. By contrast, the congressional delegations from southern and western states grew. The big winners were Arizona, Texas, Florida, and Georgia, which each gained two seats (see Figure 12.4).

apportionment the process, occurring after every decennial census, that allocates congressional seats among the fifty states

redistricting the process of redrawing election districts and redistributing legislative representatives

Not surprisingly, **redistricting** is a highly political process: districts are shaped to create an advantage for the majority party in the state legislature, which controls the redistricting process. In this complex process, those charged with drawing districts use sophisticated computer technologies to come up with the most favorable

FIGURE 12.3 ★ Apportionment of House Seats by Region, 1910 and 2000

During the twentieth century, population movements greatly increased the number of congressional seats in the West and the South. Which areas have lost the most congressional representation over time?

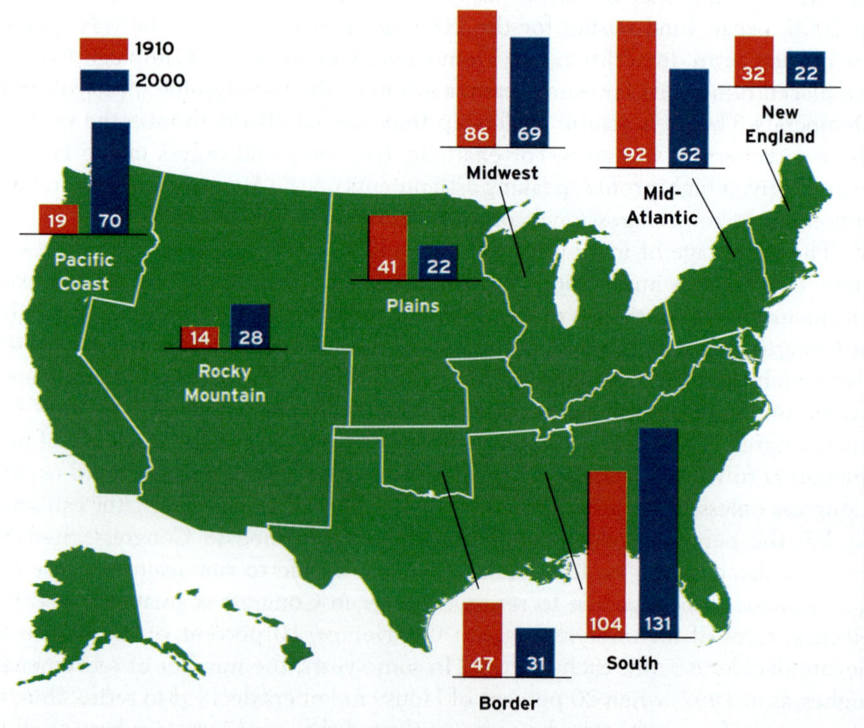

SOURCE: Norman J. Ornstein, Thomas E. Mann, and Michael J. Malbin, eds., *Vital Statistics on Congress, 2001–2002* (Washington, DC: AEI Press, 2002), 59.

FIGURE 12.4 ★

Results of Congressional Reapportionment, 2000

States in the West and parts of the South were the big winners in the reapportionment of House seats following the 2000 census. The old manufacturing states in the Midwest and mid-Atlantic regions were the biggest losers. Which states have the greatest number of House seats?

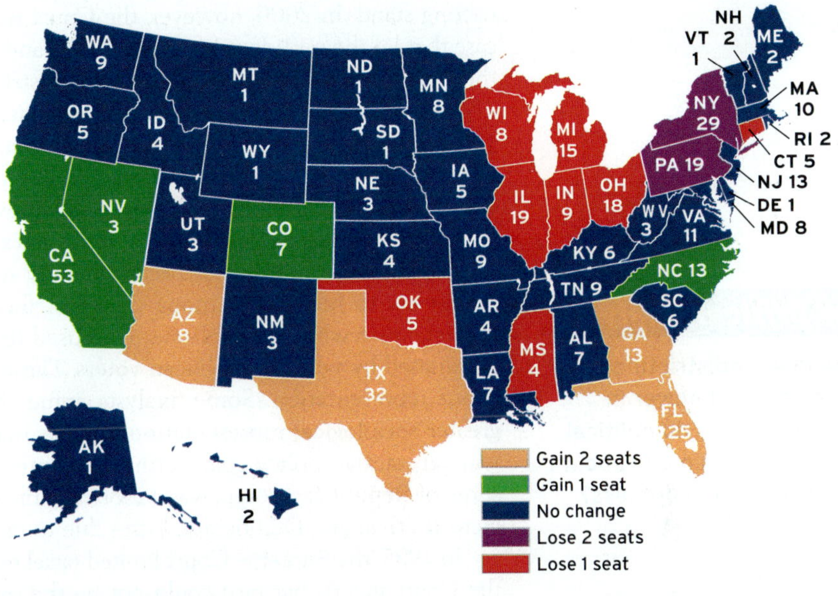

district boundaries. Redistricting can create open seats and may pit incumbents of the same party against one another, ensuring that one of them will lose. Redistricting can also give an advantage to one party by clustering voters with some ideological or sociological characteristics in a single district, or by separating those voters into two or more districts. The manipulation of electoral districts to serve the interests of a particular group is known as **gerrymandering** (see Chapter 10).

gerrymandering apportionment of voters in districts in such a way as to give unfair advantage to one racial or ethnic group or political party

In the redistricting following the 2000 census, the close balance of power in the House—with party control hinging on only six seats—made the process especially charged. Both Republicans and Democrats went to court to challenge remaps that they viewed as unfair. In 2003, Texas Republicans took the unprecedented step of redrawing the lines set in 2001 rather than waiting for the next census. The 2001 lines were drawn by a judicial panel when the politically divided legislature could not agree on a plan. In 2002, Texas elected seventeen Democrats and fifteen Republicans to the House. Republican leaders felt that the strong Democratic showing was the result of a flawed redistricting plan, since Republicans won the overall vote in Texas with 53 percent of the vote for House seats. Texas Republicans, who now controlled the state legislature as well as the governor's office, moved to redraw the map. The Republican congressional majority leader at the time, Tom DeLay (Tex.), played a central role in pushing the Texas legislature to take this step. As we saw in Chapter 11, the effort produced high drama when Texas Democratic legislators fled to first Oklahoma and later New Mexico to prevent passage of the plan. After forty-five days in New Mexico in July and August 2003, eleven state senators returned to Texas. The state legislature quickly approved the new map, which promised to be far more favorable to Republicans. It is unclear whether the strategy of additional redistricting in mid-decade will become a common practice across the states. Colorado's Supreme Court ruled against a similar redistricting effort in that state, writing that redistricting should occur only once a decade. In 2004, the U.S. Supreme Court refused to hear a challenge to the

Colorado decision, effectively letting the state court's rejection of additional redistricting stand. In 2006, however, the Court issued a ruling in the Texas redistricting case that let the mid-decade redistricting stand. The majority of the Court agreed that the Constitution did not prohibit such redistricting.

As we saw in Chapter 10, since the passage of the 1982 amendments to the 1964 Civil Rights Act, race has become a major—and controversial—consideration in drawing voting districts. These amendments, which encouraged the creation of districts in which members of racial minorities have decisive majorities, have greatly increased the number of minority representatives in Congress. After the 1991–92 redistricting, the number of predominantly minority districts doubled, rising from twenty-six to fifty-two. Among the most fervent supporters of the new minority districts were white Republicans, who used the opportunity to create more districts dominated by white Republican voters. These developments raise thorny questions about representation. Some analysts argue that the system may grant minorities greater sociological representation but has made it more difficult for minorities to win substantive policy goals. Others dispute this argument, noting that the strong surge of Republican voters was a more significant factor in Republican congressional victories than any Democratic losses due to racial redistricting.[13]

For Critical Analysis

How does redistricting alter the balance of power in Congress? Why do political parties care so much about the redistricting process?

In 1995, the Supreme Court limited racial redistricting in *Miller v. Johnson*, in which the Court stated that race could not be the predominant factor in creating electoral districts.[14] Yet concerns about redistricting and representation have not disappeared. The distinction between race being the "predominant" factor and its being one factor among many is very hazy. Because the drawing of district boundaries affects incumbents as well as the field of candidates who decide to run for office, it continues to be a key battleground on which political parties fight about the meaning of representation.

Direct Patronage

patronage the resources available to higher officials, usually opportunities to make partisan appointments to offices and to confer grants, licenses, or special favors to supporters

pork barrel (or pork) appropriations made by legislative bodies for local projects that are often not needed but that are created so that local representatives can win re-election in their home districts

As we saw in the preceding discussion, members of Congress often have an opportunity to provide direct benefits, or **patronage,** for their constituents. The most important of these opportunities for direct patronage is in legislation that has been described half-jokingly as the **pork barrel.** This type of legislation specifies a project to be funded within a particular district. Many observers of Congress argue that pork-barrel bills are the only ones that some members are serious about moving toward actual passage, because they are seen as so important to members' re-election bids.

A common form of pork barreling is the "earmark," the practice through which members of Congress insert into bills language that provides special benefits for their own constituents. When the Democrats took over Congress in 2007, they vowed to limit the use of earmarks, which had grown from 1,439 per year in 1995 to 15,268 in 2006. More troubling, earmarks were connected to congressional scandals. For example, the Republican House member Randy "Duke" Cunningham (R-Calif.) was sent to jail in 2005 for accepting bribes by companies hoping to receive earmarks in return.[15] The House passed a new rule requiring that those representatives supporting each earmark identify themselves and guarantee that they had no personal financial stake in the requested project. A new ethics law applied similar provisions to the Senate as well. The new requirements appear to have had some impact: the 2007 military bill, for example, cut in half the value of earmarks contained in the military bill passed in 2006. Even so, House and Senate lawmakers—Republicans and Democrats alike—included $8 billion in earmarks in the bill, many of them designated to benefit corporations and nonprofits that were important campaign contributors.[16]

Highway bills are a favorite vehicle for congressional pork-barrel spending. A 2005 highway bill was full of such items, containing more than 6,000 projects earmarked for specific congressional districts. Among them were such projects as $3.5 million for horse trails in Virginia and $5 million for a parking garage in downtown Bozeman, Montana. These measures often have little to do with transportation needs, instead serving as evidence that congressional members can bring federal dollars back home. Perhaps the most extravagant—and least needed for transportation—item in the 2005 bill was a bridge in Alaska designed to connect a barely populated island to the town of Ketchikan, population just under 8,000. At a cost that could soar to $2 billion, the bridge would replace an existing five-minute ferry ride. The Alaska representative Don Young (R) proudly claimed credit for such pork-barrel projects. At the suggestion that Alaska's senior senator, Ted Stevens (R), chairman of the Senate Appropriations committee, might be the reason Alaska got these projects, Young pretended to be offended, saying, "If he's the chief porker, I'm upset."[17] After Hurricane Katrina, growing concern about the rising budget deficit made "the bridge to nowhere" a symbol of wasteful congressional spending. Sensitive to this criticism, Congress removed the earmarks for the bridge from the final legislation. Even so, it allowed Alaska to keep the funds for other unspecified transportation projects. In 2007, the state quietly dropped the project.

A limited amount of other direct patronage also exists (see Figure 12.5). One important form of constituency service is intervention with federal administrative

Politics Today

In 2008, the Senate appropriations bill for the Department of Transportation and the Department of Housing and Urban Development contained 609 earmarks. Why are earmarks so difficult to eliminate?

FIGURE 12.5 ★ How Members of Congress Represent Their Districts

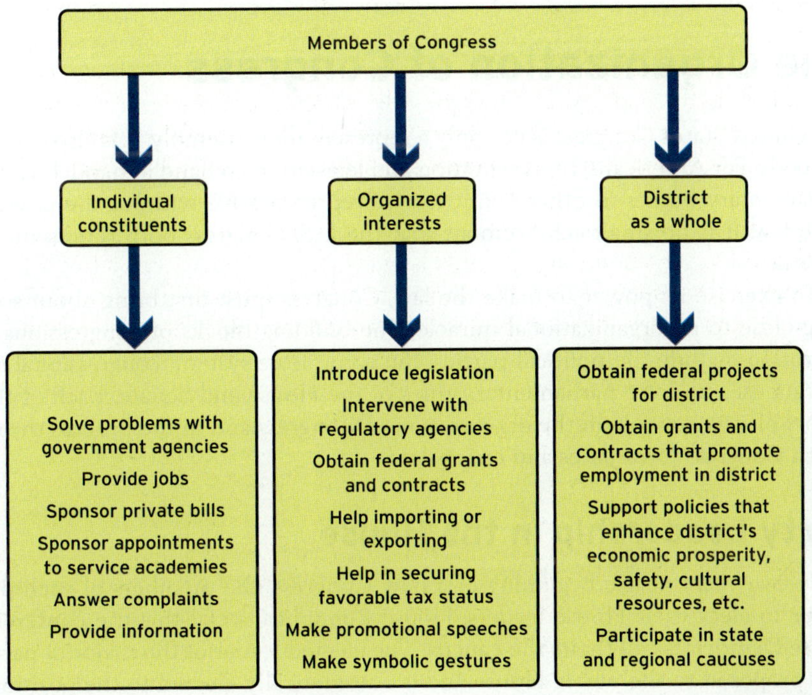

agencies on behalf of constituents. Members of the House and Senate and their staff members spend a great deal of time on the telephone and in administrative offices seeking to secure favorable treatment for constituents and supporters. Among the kinds of services that members of Congress offer to constituents is assistance for senior citizens who are having Social Security or Medicare benefit eligibility problems. They may also assist constituents in finding federal grants for which they may be eligible to apply. As Representative Pete Stark (D-Calif.) said on his Web site, "We cannot make the decision for a federal agency on such matters, but we can make sure that you get a fair shake."[18] A small but related form of patronage is getting an appointment to one of the military academies for the child of a constituent. Traditionally, these appointments are allocated one to a district.

private bill a proposal in Congress to provide a specific person with some kind of relief, such as a special exemption from immigration quotas

A different form of patronage is the **private bill**—a proposal to grant some kind of relief, special privilege, or exemption to the person named in the bill. The private bill is a type of legislation, but it is distinguished from a public bill, which is supposed to deal with general rules and categories of behavior, people, and institutions. As many as 75 percent of all private bills introduced (and one-third of the ones that pass) are concerned with providing relief for foreign nationals who do not have resident status in the United States but who the sponsoring member of Congress believes are deserving of citizenship. For example, in 2007 Gene Green (D-Tex.) sponsored a private bill to obtain legal status for an undocumented couple in danger of being deported but whose son died as a marine in Iraq.[19]

Private legislation is a congressional privilege that is often abused, but it is impossible to imagine members of Congress giving it up completely. It is one of the easiest, cheapest, and most effective forms of patronage available to each member. It can be defended as an indispensable part of the process by which members of Congress seek to fulfill their role as representatives. And obviously they like the privilege because it helps them win re-election.

The Organization of Congress

The United States Congress is not only a representative assembly. It is also a legislative body. For Americans, representation and legislation go hand in hand, but many parliamentary bodies in other countries are representative without the power to make law. It is no small achievement that the U.S. Congress both represents and governs.

To exercise its power to make the law, Congress must first bring about something close to an organizational miracle. The building blocks of congressional organization include the political parties, the committee system, congressional staff, the caucuses, and the parliamentary rules of the House and Senate. Each of these factors plays a key role in the organization of Congress and in the process through which Congress formulates and enacts laws.

conference a gathering of House Republicans every two years to elect their House leaders. Democrats call their gathering the caucus

caucus (political) a normally closed meeting of a political or legislative group to select candidates, plan strategy, or make decisions regarding legislative matters

Party Leadership in the House

Every two years, at the beginning of a new Congress, the members of each party gather to elect their House leaders. House Republicans call this the **conference.** House Democrats call theirs the **caucus.** The elected leader of the majority party is later proposed to the whole House and is automatically elected to the position of

Speaker of the House, with voting along straight party lines. The House majority conference or caucus then also elects a **majority leader.** The minority party goes through the same process and selects the **minority leader.** Both parties also elect **whips** to line up party members on important votes and to relay voting information to the leaders.

Next in order of importance for each party after the Speaker and majority or minority leader is its Committee on Committees (called the Steering and Policy Committee by the Democrats), whose tasks are to assign new legislators to committees and to deal with the requests of incumbent members for transfers from one committee to another. Currently, the Speaker serves as chair of the Democratic Steering and Policy Committee, while the minority leader chairs the Republican Committee on Committees. (The Republicans have a separate Policy Committee.) At one time, party leaders strictly controlled committee assignments, using them to enforce party discipline. Today, in principle, representatives receive the assignments they want. But several individuals often seek assignments to the most important committees, which gives the leadership an opportunity to cement alliances when it resolves conflicting requests.

Generally, representatives seek assignments that will allow them to influence decisions of special importance to their districts. Representatives from farm districts, for example, may request seats on the Agriculture Committee.[20] Seats on powerful committees such as Ways and Means, which is responsible for tax legislation, and Appropriations are especially popular.

Party Leadership in the Senate

Within the Senate, the president pro tempore exercises primarily ceremonial leadership. Usually, the majority party designates a member with the greatest seniority to serve in this capacity. Real power is in the hands of the majority leader and minority leader, each elected by party conference. Together they control the Senate's calendar, or agenda for legislation.

Speaker of the House the chief presiding officer of the House of Representatives. The Speaker is the most important party and House leader, and can influence the legislative agenda, the fate of individual pieces of legislation, and members' positions within the House

majority leader the elected leader of the majority party in the House of Representatives or in the Senate. In the House, the majority leader is subordinate in the party hierarchy to the Speaker of the House

minority leader the elected leader of the minority party in the House or Senate

whip a party member in the House or Senate responsible for coordinating the party's legislative strategy, building support for key issues, and counting votes

In 2003, Nancy Pelosi became the first woman to lead a major party in the U.S. Congress when the Democrats elected her as the House minority leader. After the Democrats won a majority of seats in 2006, she was the natural choice for Speaker.

In addition to the majority leader and the minority leader, the senators from each party elect a whip. Each party also elects a Policy Committee, which advises the leadership on legislative priorities. The structure of majority party leadership in the House and the Senate is shown in Figures 12.6 and 12.7.

Along with these tasks of organization, congressional party leaders may also seek to establish a legislative agenda. Since the New Deal, presidents have taken the lead in creating legislative agendas. (This trend will be discussed in Chapter 13.) When congressional leaders have been faced with a White House controlled by the opposing party, they have attempted to devise their own agendas. Democratic leaders of Congress sought to create a common Democratic perspective in 1981 when Ronald Reagan became president. The Republican Congress elected in 1994 expanded on this idea, calling its agenda the "Contract with America." From 2000 to 2006, with both houses of Congress in the hands of Republicans, congressional leaders worked closely with the Republican White House. President Bush's aggressive campaigning in the 2002 congressional elections helped to cement strong relationships with Republican members. In 2005, however, significant tensions between the White House and the Republican Congress emerged. Because congressional Republicans, unlike the president, faced elections in 2006, they were reluctant to endorse unpopular presidential initiatives such as Social Security reform. Republican members also broke with the president on several key national security matters, including the use of torture in interrogations and the surveillance provisions in the USA PATRIOT Act. In 2007, when Democrats took over Congress, the Democratic House Speaker Nancy Pelosi sought to promote party unity with a plan to pass six key pieces of legislation in the first hundred hours of Democratic congressional control. Although the House succeeded in passing the six measures, most of them died in the Senate, where at least sixty votes are required to enact legislation.[21] Perhaps Congress's most important achievement in 2008 was enacting the financial bailout plan, formally called the Emergency Economic Stabilization Act. Party leaders worked hard to win the support of skeptical members of Congress from both parties. After the House rejected the first version of the bill, congressional leaders worked with the Bush administration to revise the

FIGURE 12.6 ★ Majority Party Structure in the House of Representatives

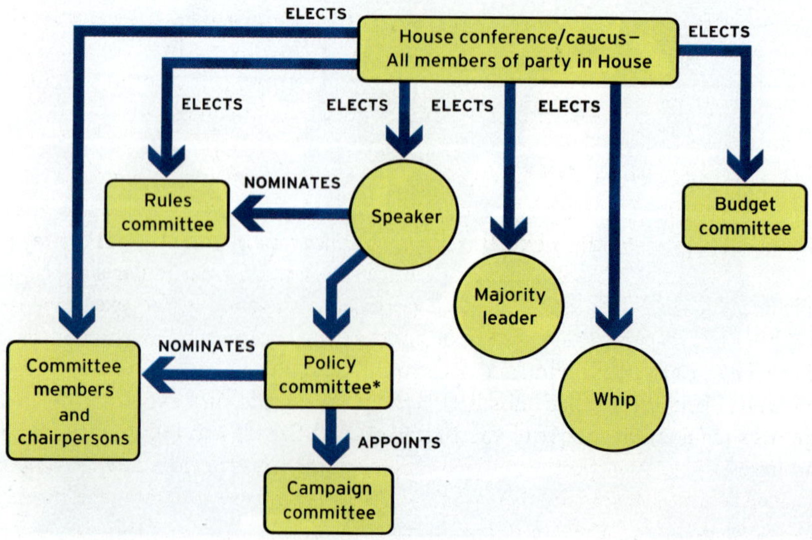

*Includes Speaker, majority leader, chief and deputy whips, caucus chair, chairs of five major committees, members elected by regional caucuses, members elected by recently elected representatives, and at-large members appointed by the Speaker.

FIGURE 12.7 ★ Majority Party Structure in the Senate

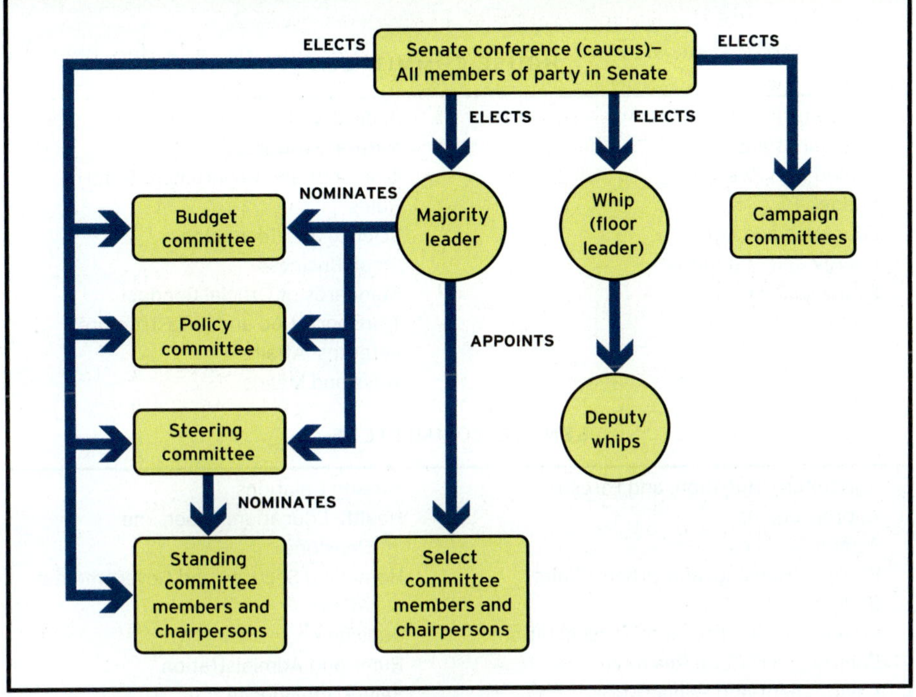

measure to include congressional oversight and other provisions that helped ensure the passage of the bailout plan through both houses of Congress.

The Committee System

The committee system is central to the operation of Congress. At each stage of the legislative process, Congress relies on committees and subcommittees to do the hard work of sorting through alternatives and writing legislation. There are several different kinds of congressional committees; these include standing committees, select committees, joint committees, and conference committees.

standing committee a permanent committee with the power to propose and write legislation that covers a particular subject, such as finance or agriculture

STANDING COMMITTEES The most important arenas of congressional policy making are **standing committees.** These committees continue in existence from one session of Congress to the next; they have the power to propose and write legislation. The jurisdiction of each standing committee covers a particular subject matter, which in most cases parallels a major department or agency in the executive branch (see Table 12.2). Among the most important standing committees are those in charge of finances. The House Ways and Means Committee and the Senate Finance Committee are powerful because of their jurisdiction over taxes, trade, and expensive entitlement programs such as Social Security and Medicare. The Senate and House Appropriations committees also play important ongoing roles because they decide how much funding various programs will actually receive; they also determine exactly how the money will be spent. A seat on an appropriations committee allows a member the opportunity to direct funds to a favored program—perhaps one in his or her home district.

TABLE 12.2 ★ Permanent Committees of Congress

HOUSE COMMITTEES	
Agriculture	Judiciary
Appropriations	Natural Resources
Armed Services	Oversight and Government Reform
Budget	Rules
Education and Labor	Science and Technology
Energy and Commerce	Small Business
Financial Services	Standards of Official Conduct
Foreign Affairs	Transportation and Infrastructure
Homeland Security	Veterans' Affairs
House Administration	Ways and Means

SENATE COMMITTEES	
Agriculture, Nutrition, and Forestry	Foreign Relations
Appropriations	Health, Education, Labor, and Pensions
Armed Services	Homeland Security and Governmental Affairs
Banking, Housing, and Urban Affairs	Judiciary
Budget	Rules and Administration
Commerce, Science, and Transportation	Select Intelligence
Energy and Natural Resources	Small Business and Entrepreneurship
Environment and Public Works	Veterans' Affairs
Finance	

Except for the House Rules Committee, all standing committees receive proposals for legislation and process them into official bills. The House Rules Committee decides the order in which bills come up for a vote on the House floor and determines the specific rules that govern the length of debate and opportunity for amendments. The Senate, which has less formal organization and fewer rules, does not have a rules committee.

select committee a (usually) temporary legislative committee set up to highlight or investigate a particular issue or address an issue not within the jurisdiction of existing committees

SELECT COMMITTEES **Select committees** are usually not permanent and usually do not have the power to present legislation to the full Congress. (The House and Senate Select Intelligence committees are permanent, however, and do have the power to report legislation.) These committees hold hearings and serve as focal points for the issues they are charged with considering. Congressional leaders form select committees when they want to take up issues that fall outside the jurisdictions of existing committees, to highlight an issue, or to investigate a particular problem. Examples of select committees investigating political scandals include the Senate Watergate Committee of 1973, the committees set up in 1987 to investigate the Iran-Contra affair, and the Whitewater Committee of 1995–96. Select committees set up to highlight ongoing issues have included the House Select Committee on Hunger, established in 1984, and the House Select Committee on Energy Independence and Global Warming, created in 2007. A few select com-

The House Select Committee on Energy Dependence and Global Warming was created in 2007. In 2008, with the cost of gasoline rising quickly, the committee held hearings on oil prices and asked energy companies to invest in alternative fuels.

mittees have remained in existence for many years, such as the select committees on aging; hunger; children, youth, and families; and narcotics abuse and control. In 1995, however, congressional Republicans abolished most of these select committees, both to streamline operations and to remove a forum used primarily by Democratic representatives and their allies. In 2003, an important select committee, the House Select Homeland Security Committee, was created to oversee the new Department of Homeland Security. Unlike most select committees, this one has the ability to present legislation. Initially the committee had only temporary status. It was made a permanent committee in 2005.

JOINT COMMITTEES **Joint committees** involve members from both the Senate and the House. There are four such committees: economic, taxation, library, and printing. These joint committees are permanent, but they do not have the power to present legislation. The Joint Economic Committee and the Joint Taxation Committee have often played important roles in collecting information and holding hearings on economic and financial issues.

joint committee a legislative committee formed of members of both the House and the Senate

CONFERENCE COMMITTEES Finally, **conference committees** are temporary committees whose members are appointed by the Speaker of the House and the presiding officer of the Senate. These committees are charged with reaching a compromise on legislation once it has been passed by the House and the Senate. Conference committees play an extremely important role in determining what laws are actually passed, because they must reconcile any differences in the legislation passed by the House and Senate.

conference committee a joint committee created to work out a compromise on House and Senate versions of a piece of legislation

In 2003, conference committees became controversial when Democrats prevented several of them from convening. The Democrats took this action to protest their near exclusion from conference committees on major energy, health care, and transportation laws. When control of Congress is divided between two parties, each is guaranteed significant representation in conference committees. When a single party controls both houses, the majority party is not obligated to offer such representation to the minority party. Democrats complained that Republicans took this power to the extreme by excluding Democrats and adding new provisions to legislation at the conference-committee stage. When the Democrats returned to power in 2007, they also largely bypassed the conference committees. When their early efforts to reach compromises in the conference were derailed by partisan differences, the Democrats began making closed-door agreements between top leaders in the House and the Senate. Although the process facilitated compromises across the two chambers, it meant that important changes to bills were made in private, without the transparency that would have been part of the conference committee process.[22]

seniority ranking given to an individual on the basis of length of continuous service on a committee in Congress

POLITICS AND THE ORGANIZATION OF COMMITTEES Within each committee, hierarchy has usually been based on seniority. **Seniority** is determined by years of continuous service on a particular committee, not years of service in the House or Senate. In general, each committee is chaired by the most senior member of the majority party. But the principle of seniority is not absolute. Both Democrats and Republicans have violated it on occasion. When the Republicans took over the House in 1995, they violated the principle of seniority in the selection of key committee chairs. Newt Gingrich, House Speaker at the time, defended the new practice with an allusion to football, saying that "You've got to carry the moral responsibility of fielding the team that can win or you cheat the whole conference."[23] Since then, Republicans continued to depart from the principle of seniority in selecting committee chairs, often choosing on the basis of loyalty or fund-raising abilities rather than seniority. In 2007, Democrats returned to the seniority principle for choosing committee chairs. However, they altered traditional practices in other ways by offering freshman Democrats choice committee assignments in order to increase their chances of re-election.[24]

Over the years, Congress has reformed its organizational structure and operating procedures. Most changes have been made to improve efficiency, but some reforms have also been a response to political considerations. In the 1970s, for example, a series of reforms substantially altered the organization of power in Congress. Among the most important changes put into place at that time were an increase in the number of subcommittees and greater autonomy for subcommittee chairs. Subcommittees are responsible for considering a specific subset of issues under a committee's jurisdiction. One of the driving impulses behind these reforms was an effort to reduce the power of committee chairs. In the past, committee chairs exercised considerable power; they determined hearing schedules, selected subcommittee members, and appointed committee staff. Some chairs used their power to block consideration of bills they opposed. By enhancing subcommittee power and allowing more members to chair subcommittees and appoint subcommittee staff, the reforms undercut the power of committee chairs.

Yet the reforms of the 1970s created new problems for Congress. As a consequence of the reforms, power became more fragmented, making it harder to reach agreement on legislation. The Republican leadership of the 104th Congress (1995–97) sought to reverse the fragmentation of congressional power and concentrate more authority in the party leadership. To this end they reduced the number of subcommittees and limited the time committee chairs could serve to three terms. They made good on this promise in 2001, when they replaced thirteen committee chairs. As a consequence of these changes, committees no longer have the central role they once held in policy making. When the Democrats took control of Congress in 2007, they decided to retain some of the Republican reforms, including the term limits on committee chairs. Even so, the Democratic leadership's deference to the long experience and expertise of some of the Democratic committee chairs gave committees more clout than during the Republican Congresses of previous years. But sharp partisan divisions among members of Congress have made it difficult for committees to deliberate and bring bipartisan expertise to bear on policy making as in the past. With committees less able to engage in effective decision making and often unable to act, it has become more common in recent years for party-driven legislation to go directly to the floor, bypassing committees.[25]

Members of Congress rely heavily on their personal staffs and on committee staffs, who often play an important role in the legislative process. Here, Senator Orrin Hatch talks with two aides during a Judiciary Committee meeting.

The Staff System: Staffers and Agencies

The congressional institution second in importance only to the committee system is the staff system. Every member of Congress employs many staff members whose tasks include handling constituency requests and, to a large extent, dealing with legislative details and the activities of administrative agencies. Staffers often bear the primary responsibility for formulating and drafting proposals, organizing hearings, dealing with administrative agencies, and negotiating with lobbyists. Indeed, legislators typically deal with each other through staff, rather than through direct personal contact. Representatives and senators together employ 11,500 staffers in their Washington and home offices. Staffers even develop policy ideas, draft legislation, and in some instances, have a good deal of influence over the legislative process.

In addition to the personal staffs of individual senators and representatives, Congress also employs roughly 2,000 committee staffers. These individuals make up the permanent staff who stay attached to every House and Senate committee regardless of turnover in Congress and who are responsible for organizing and administering the committee's work, including doing research, scheduling, organizing hearings, and drafting legislation. Committee staffers can play key roles in the legislative process. One example of the importance that members of Congress attach to committee staffers was the conflict over hiring a new staff director for the House Ethics Committee (officially known as the Committee on Standards of Official Conduct) in 2005. The Ethics Committee has the power to investigate members for unethical practices and can issue reprimands or censures when it finds members in violation of House rules. The staff director is critical in determining how energetically and effectively the committee investigates alleged ethics violations. With allegations of ethics violations swirling around the congressional leadership and criminal investigations into the congressional lobbyist Jack Abramoff underway, the Ethics Committee was in a pivotal position. But for the first half of 2005, the committee was at a standstill as Republicans and Democrats fought over who would have the job of staff director. Although the House rules call for the committee staff director to be nonpartisan, the committee chair, Doc Hastings (R-Wash.), initially sought to appoint a partisan Republican to the job. After nearly half a year of wrangling, Hastings agreed to appoint a staff director acceptable to both parties.

staff agency a legislative support agency responsible for policy analysis

Not only does Congress employ personal and committee staff, it has also established **staff agencies** designed to provide the legislative branch with resources and expertise independent of the executive branch. These agencies enhance Congress's capacity to oversee administrative agencies and to evaluate presidential programs and proposals. They include the Congressional Research Service, which performs research for legislators who wish to know the facts and competing arguments relevant to policy proposals or other legislative business; the Government Accountability Office, through which Congress can investigate the financial and administrative affairs of any government agency or program; and the Congressional Budget Office, which assesses the economic implications and likely costs of proposed federal programs, such as health-care reform proposals. A fourth agency, the Office of Technology Assessment, which provided Congress with analyses of scientific or technical issues, was abolished in 1995.

Informal Organization: The Caucuses

caucus (congressional) an association of members of Congress based on party, interest, or social group, such as gender or race

In addition to the official organization of Congress, an unofficial organizational structure also exists—the caucuses. **Caucuses** are groups of senators or representatives who share certain opinions, interests, or social characteristics. A large number of caucuses are composed of legislators representing particular economic or policy interests, such as the Travel and Tourism Caucus, the Steel Caucus, the Mushroom Caucus, and Concerned Senators for the Arts. Legislators who share common backgrounds or social characteristics have organized caucuses such as the Congressional Black Caucus, the Congressional Caucus for Women's Issues, and the Hispanic Caucus. All these caucuses seek to advance the interests of the groups they represent by promoting legislation, encouraging Congress to hold hearings, and pressing administrative agencies for favorable treatment. In recent years, some caucuses have evolved into powerful lobbying organizations, well funded by interest groups. For example, the Sportsmen's Caucus receives funds from a nonprofit foundation that itself benefits from donations from the National Rifle Association, sports equipment manufacturers, and firearms manufacturers.

Rules of Lawmaking: How a Bill Becomes a Law

bill a proposed law that has been sponsored by a member of Congress and submitted to the clerk of the House or Senate

The institutional structure of Congress is a key factor in shaping the legislative process. A second and equally important set of factors is the rules of congressional procedure. These rules govern everything from the introduction of a **bill** through its submission to the president for signing (see Figure 12.8). Not only do these regulations influence the fate of every bill, but they also help to determine the distribution of power in the Congress.

Committee Deliberation

The first step in getting a law passed is drafting legislation. Members of Congress, the White House, and federal agencies all take roles in developing and drafting initial legislation. These bills are then officially submitted by a senator or representative

FIGURE 12.8 ★ How a Bill Becomes a Law

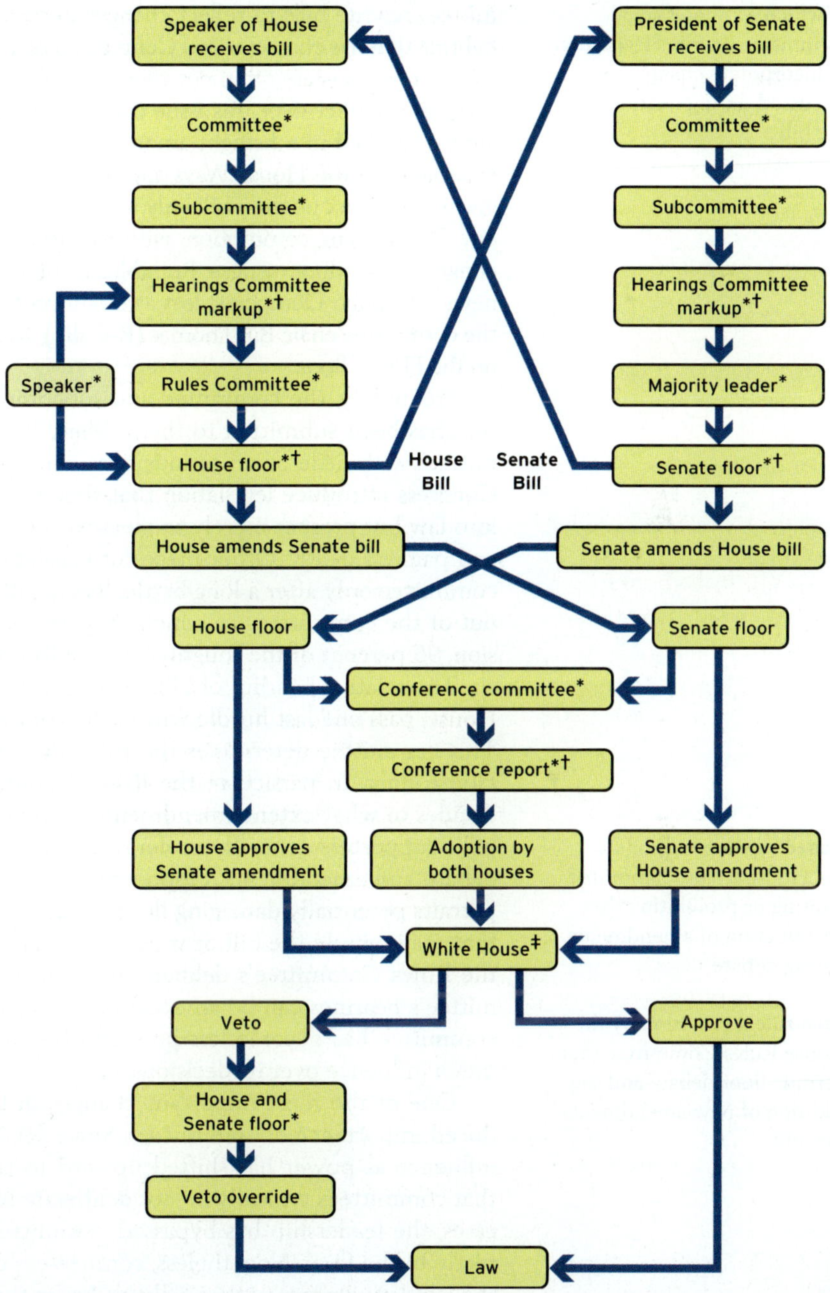

*Points at which a bill can be amended.
†Points at which a bill can die.
‡If the president neither signs nor vetoes a bill within ten days, it automatically becomes law.

to the clerk of the House or Senate and referred to the appropriate committee for deliberation. During the course of its deliberations, the committee typically refers the bill to one of its subcommittees, which may hold hearings, listen to expert testimony, and amend the proposed legislation before referring it to the full committee for consideration. The full committee may then accept the recommendation of the subcommittee or hold its own hearings and prepare its own amendments.

committee markup session in which a congressional committee rewrites legislation to incorporate changes discussed during hearings on the bill

The next steps in the process are the **committee markup** sessions, in which committees rewrite bills to reflect changes discussed during the hearings. In the partisan fighting that has characterized Congress in recent years, the minority party has charged that its members are often not given enough time to study proposed legislation before markup. Conflict over this issue drew the Capitol police to the House in 2003 and almost resulted in a fistfight among representatives when Democrats protested their treatment by the House Ways and Means Committee. Charging that they had been given a complex pension bill only ten hours before markup, House Democrats walked out. The ensuing commotion, with Republicans calling the police and a Democratic congressman threatening a Republican, presented a sorry spectacle for the nightly news. Although Democrats lost a resolution to censure the committee for its actions, the committee chair, Bill Thomas (R-Calif.), later broke down in tears as he apologized on the House floor.

Frequently, the committee and subcommittee do little or nothing with a bill that has been submitted to them. Many bills are simply allowed to "die in committee" with little or no serious consideration given to them. Often, members of Congress introduce legislation that they neither expect nor desire to see enacted into law but present merely to please a constituency group. These bills die a quick and painless death. Other pieces of legislation have ardent supporters and die in committee only after a long battle. But in either case, most bills are never reported out of the committees to which they are assigned. In a typical congressional session, 95 percent of the roughly 8,000 bills introduced die in committee.

The relative handful of bills that are presented out of committee must, in the House, pass one last hurdle within the committee system—the Rules Committee. This committee determines the rules that will govern action on the bill on the House floor. In particular, the Rules Committee allots the time for debate and decides to what extent amendments to the bill can be proposed from the floor. A bill's supporters generally prefer a **closed rule,** which puts severe limits on floor debate and amendments. Opponents of a bill usually prefer an **open rule,** which permits potentially damaging floor debate and makes it easier to add amendments that may cripple the bill or weaken its chances for passage. Thus, the outcome of the Rules Committee's deliberations can be extremely important, and the committee's hearings can be an occasion for sharp conflict. In recent years, the Rules committee has become less powerful because the House leadership exercises so much influence over its decisions.

closed rule a provision by the House Rules Committee limiting or prohibiting the introduction of amendments during debate

open rule a provision by the House Rules Committee that permits floor debate and the addition of new amendments to a bill

One of the most important changes in the way Congress operates is the reduced importance of committees. Since 1995, committees have lost considerable influence as power has shifted upward to the legislative leadership. This means that committees typically do not deliberate for very long or call witnesses. In some cases, the leadership has bypassed committees altogether, bringing legislation directly to the floor. Nonetheless, committees continue to play an important role in the legislative process, especially on issues that are not sharply partisan.[26]

Debate

The next step in getting a law passed is debate on the floor of the House and Senate. Party control of the agenda is reinforced by the rule giving the Speaker of the House and the president of the Senate the power of recognition during debate on a bill. Usually the chair knows the purpose for which a member intends to speak well in advance of the occasion. Spontaneous efforts to gain recognition are often

After a senator or representative proposes a new bill, it is referred to the appropriate committee for deliberation. Here, the Senate Foreign Relations Committee hears testimony from the U.S. ambassador in Baghdad via teleconference as they consider numerous proposals to address the ongoing conflict in Iraq.

foiled. For example, the Speaker may ask, "For what purpose does the member rise?" before deciding whether to grant recognition.

In the House, virtually all the time allotted by the Rules Committee for debate on a given bill is controlled by the bill's sponsor and by its leading opponent. In almost every case, these two people are the committee chair and the ranking minority member of the committee that processed the bill—or those they designate. These two participants are, by rule and tradition, granted the power to allocate most of the debate time in small amounts to members who are seeking to speak for or against the measure. Preference in the allocation of time goes to the members of the committee whose jurisdiction covers the bill.

In the Senate, the leadership has much less control over floor debate. Indeed, the Senate is unique among the world's legislative bodies for its commitment to unlimited debate. Once given the floor, a senator may speak as long as he or she wishes. On a number of memorable occasions, senators have used this right to prevent action on legislation that they oppose. Through this tactic, called the **filibuster,** small minorities or even one individual in the Senate can force the majority to give in. During the 1950s and 1960s, for example, opponents of civil rights legislation often sought to block its passage by staging a filibuster. Democrats used the threat of filibuster to block some of President George W. Bush's judicial nominees, much as Republicans used the same tactic to derail Clinton nominees. The votes of three-fifths of the Senate, or sixty votes, are needed to end a filibuster. This procedure is called **cloture.** The threat of a filibuster ensures that, in crafting legislation and proposing judicial appointments, the majority takes into account the viewpoint of the political minority. In 2005, Senate Republican leaders threatened to eliminate the use of the filibuster against judicial nominees. They planned to do this through a rule change—dubbed "the nuclear option"—that mandated a yes-or-no vote on all judicial appointments. Although a last-minute compromise dissuaded Senate leaders from pressing forward, the episode underscored the willingness of the leadership to alter a central feature of Senate decision making that guarantees the political minority a voice.

filibuster a tactic used by members of the Senate to prevent action on legislation they oppose by continuously holding the floor and speaking until the majority backs down. Once given the floor, senators have unlimited time to speak, and it requires a vote of three-fifths of the Senate to end a filibuster

cloture a rule allowing a majority of two-thirds or three-fifths of the members of a legislative body to set a time limit on debate over a given bill

Although it is the best known, the filibuster is not the only technique used to block Senate debate. Under Senate rules, members have a virtually unlimited ability to propose amendments to a pending bill. Each amendment must be voted on before the bill can come to a final vote. The introduction of new amendments can be stopped only by unanimous consent. This, in effect, can permit a determined minority to filibuster by amendment, indefinitely delaying the passage of a bill. Senators can also place "holds," or stalling devices, on bills to delay debate. Senators place holds on bills when they fear that openly opposing them will be unpopular. Because holds are kept secret, the senators placing the holds do not have to take public responsibility for their actions. There have been several efforts to eliminate holds. In 1997, opponents of this practice introduced an amendment that would have required publicizing the identity of the senator putting a bill on hold. But when the Senate voted on the measure, the proposal to end the practice of anonymous holds had "mysteriously disappeared."[27] Although no one took credit for killing the measure, it was evident that the majority of senators wanted to maintain the practice. In 2007, reformers succeeded in passing the Honest Leadership and Open Government Act. Although the new law did not eliminate holds, it contained provisions requiring Senators who impose a hold to identify themselves in the *Congressional Record* after six days and state the reasons for the hold.[28] The first hold made public after the legislation was a hold imposed by Senator John Ensign (R-Nev.), head of the Republican Senatorial Committee, the group responsible for fund-raising for Senate candidates. Ensign had placed a hold on popular reform legislation requiring senators to file their campaign finance reports electronically, as presidential candidates and candidates for the House do.[29]

Once a bill is debated on the floor of the House and the Senate, the leaders schedule it for a vote on the floor of each chamber. By this time, congressional leaders know what the vote will be; leaders do not bring legislation to the floor unless they are fairly certain it is going to pass. As a consequence, it is unusual for the leadership to lose a bill on the floor. On rare occasions, the last moments of the floor vote can be very dramatic, as each party's leadership puts its whip organization into action to make sure that wavering members vote with the party. The passage of Medicare reform in 2003 was one such occasion. Republican party leaders took the unprecedented step of keeping the vote open for two hours and fifty-one minutes while they looked high and low for the remaining votes needed to pass the law. It was nearly 6:00 A.M. by the time the bill passed.

Conference Committee: Reconciling House and Senate Versions of Legislation

Once a bill is out of committee and through both houses of Congress, it must be considered by a conference committee. Getting a bill out of committee and through one of the houses of Congress is no guarantee that the bill will be enacted into law. Frequently, bills that began with similar provisions in both chambers emerge with little resemblance to each other. Alternatively, a bill may be passed by one chamber but undergo substantial revision in the other chamber. In such cases, a conference committee composed of the senior members of the committees or subcommittees that initiated the bills may be required to iron out differences between the two pieces of legislation. Sometimes members or leaders will let objectionable provisions pass on the floor, knowing that they will get the chance to change what they

Grand Theft Auto and Video-Game Legislation

Before formally introducing a bill, members of Congress often try to bring the issues involved to the public's attention in order to build popular support for the proposed legislation. One issue that several members of Congress have sought to address recently is violence and sexual content in video games. In 2005, revelations about some particularly explicit features in the game Grand Theft Auto: San Andreas provided senators such as Hillary Rodham Clinton (D-N.Y.) a bold example to help direct the attention of news media and the public to the issue.

Public officials and special interest groups such as the National Institute of Media and the Family argue that regulating and restricting sales of violent video games will protect the health of American youth. They cite studies showing that exposure to violent content desensitizes video game users to violence, rendering them more likely to act aggressively in real life. In March 2005, Senator Clinton vented her frustration that "we have this data that demonstrates there is a clear public health connection between exposure to violence and increased aggression that we have been as a society unable to come up with any adequate public health response."[a] In June 2005, Democratic Senator Chuck Schumer (N.Y.) argued that retailers should choose not to carry the violent game 25 to Life. "Games that are aimed and marketed at kids shouldn't desensitize them to death and destruction," he stated.[b] These announcements were designed to attract public attention to the issue. Rather than simply introducing regulatory legislation, Clinton and Schumer used the media to make statements and raise awareness of the problem.

Supporters of video game regulation found a significant opportunity to build public support for legislation in July 2005, when the public learned that users of the game Grand Theft Auto: San Andreas could employ code obtained through the Internet to unlock graphic sex scenes. Soon after the Grand Theft Auto scandal, Senator Clinton urged the Federal Trade Commission to investigate the case. After discussing the issue at various press conferences throughout the year, on December 16, 2005 Senator Clinton, along with Senator Joseph Lieberman (D-Conn.) of Connecticut and Senator Evan Bayh (D-Ind.) of Indiana introduced a bill to regulate the sales of video games in the United States. However, none of the seven bills introduced that year were enacted. Congressional interest in video-game legislation declined by 2007 after the courts struck down several state laws that sought to impose similar types of regulation.

Even so, several members of Congress continued to introduce acts to regulate violent and sexually explicit video games. In 2007, Republican Senator Sam Brownback of Kansas, proposed a Truth in Video Game Rating Act, which would punish companies for misrepresenting the content on their games in order to get less restrictive ratings.

The battle over violence and sexual content in video games is a good example of how legislators work to attract attention to issues and then introduce legislation into the House and Senate. Even when a bill stands little chance of passage, members of Congress often find that the publicity they attract when they introduce legislation is politically beneficial. Proposals to regulate video games allow members of Congress to express their concern about children and identify themselves as champions of public morality. If the legislation ever does pass in both houses, its fate will undoubtedly rest in the hands of the courts.

FOR CRITICAL ANALYSIS

1. What do you think the role of Congress should be in the regulation of the content of popular culture such as video games, television, music, or music videos?
2. Can you think of other examples of specific events that allowed members of Congress an opportunity to advance legislation related to that event or story?

---

a. R. Hernandez, "Clinton Seeks Uniform Ratings In Entertainment for Children," *New York Times*, March 10, 2005, p. B5.

b. "Schumer: New 'Cop-Killer' Video Game Is All Time Low; Urges New York Retailers, Distributers Not to Stock, Sell in Stores," press release, June 19, 2005, http://schumer.senate.gov/SchumerWebsite/pressroom/press_releases/2005/PR41733.25tolife.061905.html (accessed 3/3/08).

want in conference. Usually, conference committees meet behind closed doors. Agreement requires a majority of each of the two delegations. Legislation that emerges successfully from a conference committee is more often a compromise than a clear victory of one set of forces over another.

When a bill comes out of conference, it faces one more hurdle. Before a bill can be sent to the president for signing, the House-Senate conference committee's version of the bill must be approved on the floor of each chamber. Usually such approval is given quickly. Occasionally, however, a bill's opponents use this round of approval as one last opportunity to defeat a piece of legislation.

Presidential Action

The final step in passing a law is presidential approval. Once adopted by the House and Senate, a bill goes to the president, who may choose to sign the bill into law or **veto** it. The veto is the president's constitutional power to reject a piece of legislation. To veto a bill, the president returns it unsigned within ten days to the house of Congress in which it originated. If Congress adjourns during the ten-day period, and the president has taken no action, the bill is also considered to be vetoed. This latter method is known as the **pocket veto.** The possibility of a presidential veto affects how willing members of Congress are to push for different pieces of legislation at different times. If they think a proposal is likely to be vetoed they might shelve it until a later time.

veto the president's constitutional power to turn down acts of Congress. A presidential veto may be overridden by a two-thirds vote of each house of Congress

pocket veto a presidential veto that is automatically triggered if the president does not act on a given piece of legislation passed during the final ten days of a legislative session

A presidential veto may be overridden by a two-thirds vote in both the House and Senate. A veto override says much about the support that a president can expect from Congress, and it can deliver a stinging blow to the executive branch. Presidents will often back down from a veto threat if they believe that Congress will override the veto.

How Congress Decides

What determines the kinds of legislation that Congress ultimately produces? According to the simplest theories of representation, members of Congress would respond to the views of their constituents. In fact, the process of creating a legislative agenda, drawing up a list of possible measures, and deciding among them is a very complex process, in which a variety of influences from inside and outside government play important roles. External influences include a legislator's constituency and various interest groups. Influences from inside government include party leadership, congressional colleagues, and the president. Let us examine each of these influences individually and then consider how they interact to produce congressional policy decisions.

Constituency

Because members of Congress, for the most part, want to be re-elected, we would expect the views of their constituents to be a primary influence on the decisions that legislators make. Yet constituency influence is not so straightforward. In fact, most constituents do not even know what policies their representatives support. The number of citizens who do pay attention to such matters—the attentive public—is usually very small. Nonetheless, members of Congress spend a lot of time worrying about what their constituents think, because these representatives realize that the choices they make may be scrutinized in a future election and used as ammunition by an opposing candidate. Because of this possibility, members of Congress try to anticipate their constituents' policy views.[30] Legislators are more likely to act in accordance with those views if they think that voters will take them into account during elections. In October 1998, for example, thirty-one House Democrats broke party ranks and voted in favor of an impeachment inquiry against President Clinton because they believed a "no" vote could cost them re-election that November. The White House successfully pressed to schedule the vote authorizing the use of force in Iraq right before the 2002 elections in order to pressure members to vote for it. In this way, constituents may affect congressional policy choices even when there is little direct evidence of their influence.

Members often spend a great deal of time in their electoral districts meeting with constituents. Congressman Elijah E. Cummings of Maryland is shown here greeting constituents at an event in Baltimore.

Interest Groups

Interest groups are another important external influence on the policies that Congress produces. When members of Congress are making voting decisions, those interest groups that have some connection to constituents in particular members' districts are most likely to be influential. For this reason, interest groups with the ability to mobilize followers in many congressional districts may be especially influential in Congress. In recent years, Washington-based interest groups with little grassroots strength have recognized the importance of locally generated activity. They have, accordingly, sought to simulate grassroots pressure, using a strategy that has been nicknamed "Astroturf lobbying" (see Chapter 11). Such campaigns encourage constituents to sign form letters or postcards, which are then sent to congressional representatives. Campaigns set up toll-free telephone numbers for a system in which simply reporting your name and address to the listening computer will generate a letter to your congressional representative. One Senate office estimated that such organized campaigns to demonstrate "grassroots" support account for two-thirds of the mail the office received. As such campaigns increase, however, they become less influential, because members of Congress are aware of how rare constituent interest actually is.[31]

Many interest groups now also use legislative "scorecards" that rate how members of Congress vote on issues of importance to that group. A high or low rating by an important interest group may provide a potent weapon in the next election. Interest groups can increase their influence over a particular piece of legislation by signaling their intention to include it in their scoring. Among the most influential groups that use scorecards, often posting them on their Web sites for members to see, are the National Federation of Independent Business, the AFL-CIO, National Right to Life, the League of Conservation Voters, and the National Rifle Association.

Interest groups also have substantial influence in setting the legislative agenda and in helping to craft specific language in legislation. Today, sophisticated lobbyists win influence by providing information about policies to busy members of Congress. In recent years, interest groups have also begun to build broader coalitions and comprehensive campaigns around particular policy issues. These coalitions do not rise from the grass roots, but instead are put together by Washington lobbyists who launch comprehensive lobbying campaigns that combine simulated grassroots activity with information and campaign funding for members of Congress.

Although party discipline in Congress has declined in the past century, recent years have seen a new increase in party unity. In 2008, House and Senate Republicans appeared together to show that they were united in their support of a proposal for property tax relief.

Close financial ties between members of Congress and interest-group lobbyists often raise eyebrows because they suggest that interest groups get special treatment in exchange for political donations. In 2008, longtime Alaska senator Ted Stevens (R) was indicted for concealing gifts that he received from an oil company that was also an important donor to his political campaigns. Concerns about the influence of lobbyists in Congress mounted in the early 2000s when the former majority leader Tom DeLay (R-Tex.) sought to tighten the connection between interest groups and the congressional Republicans with his K Street Project, named after the street in Washington where many high-powered lobbyists have offices. The K Street Project placed former Republican staffers in key lobbying positions and ensured a large flow of corporate cash into Republican coffers. Congressional relationships to lobbyists came under close scrutiny in 2005 as the activities of the lobbyist Jack Abramoff—a self-proclaimed big supporter of the K Street Project—were investigated. When Abramoff pled guilty in early 2006 to charges of conspiracy, mail fraud, and tax evasion in connection with his lobbying activities, and it became clear that he would "name names" as part of a plea deal, a group of House Republicans mobilized against the powerful DeLay, who was already under indictment in Texas for misusing campaign funds. In the face of mounting pressure, DeLay resigned his post as majority leader in January 2006 and left Congress later that year.

Concern over such corruption led Congress to enact new ethics legislation in 2007. The new law set new restrictions on the gifts lobbyists can bestow on lawmakers and limited privately funded travel. The law also prohibited members of Congress from lobbying for two years after they retire and required lawmakers to identify the earmarks they insert in legislation. It also aimed to shine light on the practice of "bundling," whereby lobbyists assemble money from a number of clients to make a single political donation. Now, lobbyists will be required to disclose the names of the individual contributors to these political donations. Although the new law provides additional transparency, allowing the public to learn more about the relationship between lobbyists and members of Congress, it does not fundamentally alter the fact that wealthy interest groups will continue to exercise tremendous influence in Congress.

party unity vote a roll-call vote in the House or Senate in which at least 50 percent of the members of one party take a particular position and are opposed by at least 50 percent of the members of the other party

roll-call vote a vote in which each legislator's yes or no vote is recorded as the clerk calls the names of the members alphabetically

Party Discipline

In both the House and Senate, party leaders have a good deal of influence over the behavior of their party members. This influence, sometimes called "party discipline," was once so powerful that it dominated the lawmaking process. At the turn of the century, party leaders could often command the allegiance of more than 90 percent of their members. A vote on which 50 percent or more of the members of one party take one position while at least 50 percent of the members of the other party take the opposing position is called a **party unity vote.** At the

FIGURE 12.9 ★
Party Unity Votes by Chamber

Party unity votes are roll-call votes in which a majority of one party lines up against a majority of the other party. Party unity votes increase when the parties are polarized and when the party leadership can enforce discipline. Why did the percentage of party unity votes decline in the 1970s? Why has it risen in recent years?

SOURCE: *Congressional Quarterly Weekly Report*, January 14, 2008, p. 143.

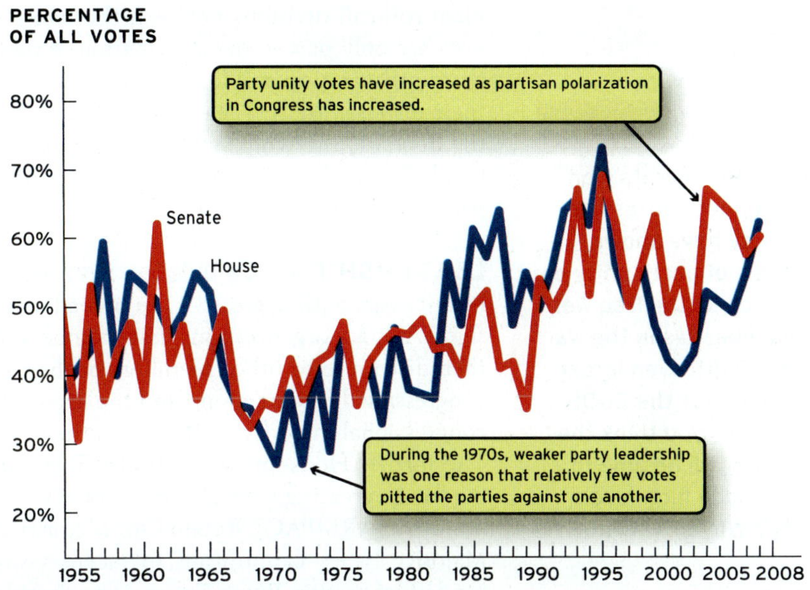

beginning of the twentieth century, nearly half of all **roll-call votes** in the House of Representatives were party votes. For much of the twentieth century, the number of party votes declined as bipartisan legislation became more common. The 1990s witnessed a return to strong party discipline as partisan polarization drew sharper lines between Democrats and Republicans, and congressional party leaders aggressively used their powers to promote party discipline. In 2005 party discipline was close to its all-time high.

Typically, party unity is greater in the House than in the Senate. House rules grant greater procedural control of business to the majority party leaders, which gives them more influence over House members. In the Senate, however, the leadership has few sanctions over its members. The former Senate minority leader Tom Daschle once observed that a Senate leader seeking to influence other senators has as incentives "a bushel full of carrots and a few twigs."[32]

Though it has not reached nineteenth-century levels, party unity has been on the rise in recent years because the divisions between the parties have deepened on many high-profile issues such as abortion, affirmative action, the minimum wage, and school vouchers (see Figure 12.9). Party unity scores rise when congressional leaders try to put a partisan stamp on legislation. For example, in 1995, then Speaker Newt Gingrich sought to enact a Republican Contract with America that few Democrats supported. The result was more party unity in the House than in any year since 1954. Republicans, especially in the House, exhibited very high party unity scores after they came to power in 1995. For example, in 2005, 90 percent of House Republicans voted with their leadership on votes that divided the two parties. In 2006 and 2007, Democrats showed unusually high levels of party unity, close to the levels that Republicans had achieved at the height of their power in Congress.

To some extent, party unity is based on ideology and background. Republican members of Congress are more likely than Democrats to be drawn from rural or suburban areas. Democrats are likely to be more liberal on economic and social questions than their Republican colleagues. These differences certainly help to explain roll-call divisions between the two parties. Ideology and background, however, are only part of the explanation of party unity. The other part has to do with party organization and leadership. Among the resources that party leaders have at their disposal are: (1) leadership PACs, (2) committee assignments, (3) access to the floor, (4) the whip system, (5) logrolling, and (6) the presidency. Party leaders regularly use these resources, which are often effective in securing the support of party members.

Politics Today

Since the Democrats won a majority in Congress in 2006, they have shown high levels of party unity on issues such as the Iraq war and civil liberties in the war on terror. With even larger majorities after the 2008 elections, do you think the Democrats will be able to maintain such high levels of unity? Why or why not?

LEADERSHIP PACS Leaders have increased their influence over members in recent years with aggressive use of leadership political action committees. Leadership PACs are organizations that members of Congress use to raise funds that they then distribute to other members of their party running for election. Republican congressional leaders pioneered the aggressive use of leadership PACs to win their congressional majority in 1995, and the practice has spread widely since that time. The former House majority leader Tom DeLay was especially aggressive in raising funds, creating several important PACs, including Americans for a Republican Majority (ARMPAC), Retain Our Majority Program (ROMP), and the Republican Majority Issues Committee. In recent years, Democrats have also formed well-funded leadership PACs. For aspiring presidential candidates, leadership PACs can provide an initial infrastructure for the campaign and can help fund precampaign travel. This is how Hillary Clinton used her leadership PAC, HILLPAC, before she formally announced her candidacy in 2007. Money from leadership PACs can be directed to the most vulnerable candidates or to candidates who are having trouble raising money. The PACs enhance the power of the party and create a bond between the leaders and the members who receive their help.[33]

COMMITTEE ASSIGNMENTS Leaders can create debts among members by helping them get favorable committee assignments. These assignments are made early in the congressional careers of most members and cannot be taken from them if they later balk at party discipline. Nevertheless, if the leadership goes out of its way to get the right assignment for a member, this effort is likely to create a bond of obligation that can be called on without any other payments or favors. This is one reason the Republican leadership gave freshmen favorable assignments when the Republicans took over Congress in 1995. When she assumed the position of Speaker in 2007, Nancy Pelosi sought to spread power more widely by limiting the number of committees that any one member could chair. She also gave freshmen representatives access to key committees that would raise their political stature.[34] By offering attractive committee assignments to members in competitive races, especially to new members, she sought to boost her party's chances in the 2008 election.

ACCESS TO THE FLOOR The most important everyday resource available to the parties is control over access to the floor. With thousands of bills awaiting passage and most members clamoring for access in order to influence a bill or to publicize themselves, floor time is precious. In the Senate, the leadership allows ranking committee members to influence the allocation of floor time—who will speak for how long; in the House, the Speaker, as head of the majority party (in consultation with the minority leader), allocates large blocks of floor time. Thus, floor time is allocated in both houses of Congress by the majority and minority leaders. More important, the Speaker of the House and the majority leader in the Senate possess the power of recognition. Although this power may not appear to be substantial, it is a formidable authority and can be used to stymie a piece of legislation completely or to frustrate a member's attempts to speak on a particular issue. Because the power is significant, members of Congress usually attempt to stay on good terms with the Speaker and the majority leader to ensure that they will continue to be recognized.

In 2007, House Speaker Nancy Pelosi was particularly generous in offering freshmen Democrats and other especially vulnerable Democrats an opportunity to speak on the floor. As the House considered the six signature pieces of legislation in their first hundred hours, Pelosi ensured that twenty-nine of the most vulnerable Democrats—designated as the Frontline team—received prime-time speaking assignments.[35]

Party leaders may use their power of recognition to give new members from their party a chance to gain visibility. Higher visibility helps the new senators and representatives, like freshman congresswoman Kathy Castor (D-Fla.), a member of the powerful Rules Committee, pictured here in 2007, get re-elected.

THE WHIP SYSTEM Some influence accrues to party leaders through the whip system, which is primarily a communications network. Between twelve and twenty assistant and regional whips are selected to operate at the direction of the majority or minority leader and the whip. They take polls of all the members in order to learn their intentions on specific bills. This enables the leaders to know if they have enough support to allow a vote as well as whether the vote is so close that they need to put pressure on a few undecided members. Leaders also use the whip system to convey their wishes and plans to the members, but only in very close votes do they actually exert pressure on a member. In those instances, the Speaker or a lieutenant will go to a few party members who have indicated they will switch if their vote is essential. The whip system helps the leaders limit pressuring members to a few times per session.

The whip system helps maintain party unity in both houses of Congress, but it is particularly critical in the House of Representatives because of the large number of legislators whose positions and votes must be accounted for. The majority and minority whips and their assistants must be adept at inducing compromise among legislators who hold widely differing viewpoints. The whips' personal styles and their perception of their function significantly affect the development of legislative coalitions and influence the compromises that emerge. As Republican House whip from 1995 to 2002, Tom DeLay established a reputation as an effective vote counter and a tough leader, earning the nickname the Hammer. DeLay also expanded the reach of the whip, building alliances with Republicans outside of Congress, particularly those in ideological and business-oriented groups. Under DeLay's leadership these lobbyists effectively worked as part of the whip operation. As whip, DeLay also began a campaign to pressure trade associations to hire Republicans as their lobbyists, which was continued by his successor Roy Blunt (R-Mo.). These relationships opened the congressional Republican leadership to accusations of corruption and led to DeLay's downfall as majority leader in 2006. Under the Democrats the whip system returned to its former status as an instrument of the Speaker. Speaker Pelosi uses the whip system to promote diversity and strengthen party loyalty.

LOGROLLING An agreement between two or more members of Congress who have nothing in common except the need for support is called **logrolling.** The agreement states, in effect, "You support me on bill X and I'll support you on another bill of your choice." Since party leaders are the center of the communications

logrolling a legislative practice whereby agreements are made between legislators in voting for or against a bill; vote trading networks in the two chambers, they can help members create large logrolling coalitions. Hundreds of logrolling deals are made each year, and although there are no official record-keeping books, it would be a poor party leader whose whips did not know who owed what to whom. In some instances, logrolling produces strange alliances. A most unlikely alliance emerged in Congress in October 1991, which one commentator dubbed "the corn for porn plot."[36] The alliance joined Senate supporters of the National Endowment for the Arts (NEA) with senators seeking limits on the cost of grazing rights on federal lands. The NEA, which provides federal funding to the arts, had been under fire from the conservative senator Jesse Helms (R-N.C.) for funding some controversial artists whose work Helms believed to be indecent. In an effort to prevent federal support for such works, Helms attached a provision to the NEA's funding that would have prohibited the agency from awarding grants to any work that in a "patently offensive way" depicted "sexual or excretory activities or organs." Supporters of the NEA condemned such restrictions as a violation of free speech and pointed out that many famous works of art could not have been funded under such restrictions. When it appeared that the amendment would pass, NEA supporters offered western senators a deal. In exchange for voting down the Helms amendment, they would eliminate a planned hike in grazing fees. Republican senators from sixteen western states switched their votes and defeated the Helms amendment. Although Helms called his defeat the product of "back-room deals and parliamentary flimflam," his amendment was simply the victim of the time-honored congressional practice of logrolling.[37]

THE PRESIDENCY Of all the influences that maintain the clarity of party lines in Congress, the influence of the presidency is probably the most important. Indeed, the office is a touchstone of party discipline in Congress. Since the late 1940s, under President Harry Truman, presidents each year have identified a number of bills that they want to be considered part of their administration's program. By the mid-1950s, both parties in Congress began to look to the president for these proposals, which became the most significant part of Congress's agenda. The presi-

The president is often an important influence on congressional decision making. President George W. Bush meets here with members of Congress to discuss a law related to wiretapping in the war on terror.

Congress and Global Warming Policy

Over the past decade, scientific evidence has mounted that global warming is accelerating and that it is caused by human activity. For much of his presidency, the former President George W. Bush dismissed concerns about global warming as an unproven theory. Although the former president's position had softened by 2007, the executive branch did little to develop policies that would reduce global warming. Congress stepped into this policy vacuum in 2007 as members introduced bills aimed at curbing global warming. To highlight the importance of the issue to Democrats, House Speaker Nancy Pelosi (D-Calif.) created a new House Select Committee on Energy Independence and Global Warming. The creation of the new committee signaled Democratic Congress's intention to lead the way in devising policies to address global warming.

Yet there is significant disagreement on what the best policies are for addressing global warming. How much regulation is necessary and how tough should regulations be? What impact would strict regulation have on economic growth? These are the questions that Congress confronts as it seeks to act on global warming.

Those favoring tougher regulations emphasize the need for quick and strong action to stop global warming. Speaker Pelosi sought to highlight these arguments soon after she took office. In early 2007, Pelosi took the unusual step of testifying before the House Committee on Science and Technology to urge passage of a mandatory "cap-and-trade system." Mandatory caps would limit the amount of greenhouse gas emissions that industries could put into the air. Under such a system, industries that exceed their caps can buy emissions credits from industries whose emissions are lower than the amount allowed. Those favoring tough regulation also supported higher mileage standards for automobiles.

On the other side of the issue are members of Congress who oppose government regulation and point to the potential economic damage that such regulations can cause. One of the most influential opponents of Pelosi's regulatory approach to global warming was her fellow Democrat John Dingell (Mich.), chair of the critically important House Energy and Commerce Committee. A powerful advocate for the automobile industry throughout his fifty-plus years in Congress, Dingell vociferously opposed Pelosi's agenda. Anxious to avoid any competition against his committee, Dingell demanded that the new Select Committee on Energy Independence and Global Warming have no power to propose legislation. When Pelosi conceded to his demand, Dingell derided the new committee as "about as useful as side pockets on a cow."[a] Although Dingell came to support a cap-and-trade system for regulating greenhouse gasses, he continued to resist higher mileage-per-gallon standards for automobiles, on the grounds that they would cause the auto industry to bear a disproportionate cost of addressing global warming.

These divisions made it difficult for Congress to reach agreement on an energy bill in 2007, as the Senate and House passed bills with conflicting provisions, and proponents of the cap-and-trade system introduced separate legislation. The new select committee held hearings to highlight the issue of global warming and to keep it on the agenda, but it could do little else. In the face of these disagreements, Congress acted where it found common ground by increasing spending to promote "green technologies." Although this spending conveyed a new sense of purpose in addressing climate change, the hard work of crafting a forceful set of policies to address climate change still lay ahead.

FOR CRITICAL ANALYSIS

1. Why is it so difficult for members of the same party—in this case Democrats—to agree on a policy to address global warming?
2. What is the purpose of a select congressional committee that cannot introduce legislation?

a. Joanna Neuman, "The Nation: Detroit's Bullying Angel is Set to Fight: Longtime Democratic Rep John Dingell Digs in Against His Party's Environmental Agenda," *Los Angeles Times*, August 11, 2007, p. A1.

dent's support is a criterion for party loyalty, and party leaders are able to use it to rally some members.

Weighing Diverse Influences

Clearly, many different factors affect congressional decisions. But at various points in the decision-making process, some factors are likely to be more influential than others. For example, interest groups may be more effective at the committee stage, when their expertise is especially valued and they are less obviously visible. Because committees play a key role in deciding what legislation actually reaches the floor of the House or Senate, interest groups can often put a halt to bills they dislike, or they can ensure that the options that do reach the floor are those that the groups' members support.

Once legislation reaches the floor and members of Congress are deciding among alternatives, constituent opinion will become more important. Legislators are also influenced very much by other legislators: many of their assessments about the substance and politics of legislation come from fellow members of Congress.

For Critical Analysis

Are there stages at which the legislative process is more democratic than it is at others? Are there stages at which the people have less influence? In your judgment, is the overall process democratic?

The influence of the external and internal forces described in the preceding section also varies according to the kind of issue being considered. On policies of great importance to powerful interest groups—farm subsidies, for example—those groups are likely to have considerable influence. On other issues, members of Congress may be less attentive to narrow interest groups and more willing to consider what they see as the general interest.

Finally, the mix of influences varies according to the historical moment. The close balance in Congress between Republicans and Democrats during the past fifteen years has made party leaders especially important in decision making.

The appropriations process is one of Congress's essential functions. Without funding, government cannot operate. In December 1995, when Congress and the president could not agree on a budget bill, a partial shutdown of the federal government occurred.

Beyond Legislation: Other Congressional Powers

In addition to the power to make the law, Congress has at its disposal an array of other instruments through which to influence the process of government. The Constitution gives the Senate the power to approve treaties and appointments. And Congress has a number of other powers through which it can share with the other branches the capacity to administer the laws.

Oversight

Oversight, as applied to Congress, refers to the effort to oversee or to supervise how the executive branch carries out legislation. Oversight is carried out by committees or subcommittees of the Senate or the House, which conduct hearings and investigations in order to analyze and evaluate bureaucratic agencies and the effectiveness of their programs. Their purpose may be to locate inefficiencies or abuses of power, to explore the relationship between what an agency does and what a law intended, or to change or abolish a program. Most programs and agencies are subject to some oversight every year during the course of hearings on **appropriations,** that is, the funding of agencies and government programs.

oversight the effort by Congress, through hearings, investigations, and other techniques, to exercise control over the activities of executive agencies

appropriations the amounts of money approved by Congress in statutes (bills) that each unit or agency of government can spend

Committees or subcommittees have the power to subpoena witnesses, take oaths, cross-examine, compel testimony, and bring criminal charges for contempt (refusing to cooperate) and perjury (lying under oath). Hearings and investigations are similar in many ways, but they differ on one fundamental point. A hearing is usually held on a specific bill, and the questions asked are usually intended to build a record with regard to that bill. In an investigation, the committee or subcommittee does not begin with a particular bill, but examines a broad area or problem and then concludes its investigation with one or more proposed bills.

In recent years, congressional oversight power has increasingly been used as a tool of partisan politics. The Republican Congress aggressively investigated President

In 2006, the Senate Judiciary Committee responded to concerns about President Bush's authorization of secret domestic surveillance by holding hearings on the program.

AMERICA IN THE WORLD

What Is Congress's Role in Foreign Policy?

During World War II, national security dominated the congressional agenda. With the massive mobilization of American troops and economic production geared to support the war effort, domestic policy commanded only modest attention in Congress. Congress focused on supporting the president as the nation faced total mobilization for war. During other periods, Congress has been much less supportive of the president's foreign policy. For example, in the late 1960s, as widespread doubts about the wisdom of the Vietnam War began to grow, Congress convened hearings that questioned administration assumptions and priorities.

Americans disagree about Congress's proper role in foreign policy. Such disagreements become especially salient in times of war. Should Congress primarily support the president as commander in chief of the armed forces? Or should Congress play the role of watchdog, delving into the details of foreign policy to ensure that the president's policies best serve the public interest? These questions become particularly hard to answer in prolonged "shadow wars" such as the Cold War and the current war on terrorism, when the nature and degree of the danger we confront is uncertain.

Intensive congressional scrutiny of the president's foreign policy is counterproductive, say those who believe Congress should unite behind the president. In order to manage the nation's defense effectively, the national government must speak with one voice. Congressional objections to the president's priorities only strengthen the nation's enemies by weakening our resolve to take the measures needed to ensure our defense. There is always the danger that sensitive foreign policy matters are easily turned into political footballs in the hands of Congress. Congress is more likely than the president to adopt a short-term, politicized perspective. Congress is also more likely to put domestic concerns ahead of foreign-policy priorities. These tensions grew more pronounced after public disenchantment with the war in Iraq gave control of Congress to the Democrats in the 2006 midterm election. House and Senate leaders pressed the president to announce a new strategy for reducing American forces in Iraq. The president insisted, however, that U.S. troops needed to stay in Iraq to end sectarian violence. In the end, presidents are better equipped than Congress to know what needs to be done to conduct a successful foreign policy. They have a large national security apparatus with extensive expertise, and they are able to keep the big picture in mind.

Critics disagree, arguing that Congress has a vital role to play in foreign policy. The absence of ongoing congressional scrutiny can lead to poor policy, detached from democratic accountability. The continuing violence in Iraq and the lack of progress toward political stability provided only one example where congressional leaders claimed the Bush administration had lost touch with the electorate. From this viewpoint, democratic checks and balances must extend to foreign policy. If the executive branch refuses to adjust its foreign policies in response to public opinion, then Congress may have to exercise its power of the purse by cutting off funds for foreign policies that it considers misguided. Ultimately, Congress must closely monitor the executive to ensure that the arguments and evidence for U.S. foreign policy are sound.

Former president Bush's handling of the war in Iraq and the threat of terrorism brought tensions between Congress and the White House to a level not seen since the Vietnam War. A new president will not, however, be immune from these tensions. The president's reputation rests far more heavily on success or failure in foreign policy than do the reputations of members of Congress. Meanwhile, Congress is more responsive to popular pressures that also have a place in foreign policy. A democracy must be responsive to the wishes of the people. Foreign policy is no exception.

FOR CRITICAL ANALYSIS

1. Why is the president better equipped than Congress to conduct foreign policy, especially in matters such as the war against terrorism?
2. Why is congressional oversight essential to good foreign policy? How does the experience of the war in Iraq point to the importance of strong congressional involvement in foreign policy?

Clinton, racking up 140 hours of sworn testimony on whether the president had used the White House Christmas card list for partisan purposes. By contrast, the Republican-controlled Congress failed to scrutinize seriously the actions of the Bush administration during Bush's first six years in office. The investigation into the abuse of prisoners in Iraq's Abu Ghraib prison, for example, entailed only twelve hours of sworn testimony. Moreover, the few oversight hearings that the Republican Congress held mainly sought to support the leadership's policy goals—during a hearing on Arctic oil drilling, for example, much testimony was devoted to the benefits of such drilling. Congress also convened oversight hearings on issues that had nothing to do with the executive branch, such as the high profile hearings on steroid use in Major League Baseball in 2005 and 2008.[38]

When the Democrats took control of Congress in 2007, the congressional oversight role increased dramatically. To highlight the importance of oversight, Democrats renamed the House Government Reform Committee to be the House Oversight and Government Reform Committee and added four new subcommittees dedicated to oversight. They also hired over 200 new investigative staffers.[39] Armed with these resources, Congress stepped up the number of oversight hearings: during its first six months in power, the Democratic Congress held 942 oversight hearings, compared with 579 for the same period when Republicans controlled Congress in 2005.[40] The hearings dealt with a wide range of issues, including inquiries into government contracting, the activities of the private contractor Blackwater in Iraq, the revelation of the identity of the CIA officer Valerie Plame, and the firing of nine U.S. attorneys. Many of the hearings created high drama as once-powerful former administration officials, such as former Secretary of Defense Donald Rumsfeld and Attorney General Alberto Gozales, were called to account for their actions in office. Some Republicans agreed that oversight had been neglected in previous Congresses but warned, in the words of the Republican senator Charles E. Grassley (Iowa), that "the most credible oversight is nonpartisan."[41] Congress also held hearings on the financial crisis in 2008, sharply questioning the fallen titans of Wall Street. Members wanted to know whether the executives withheld information from their shareholders or protected their own salaries at the expense of their employees.

Presidential appointments are sometimes given high levels of scrutiny by the Senate. For instance, when Clarence Thomas was nominated to the Supreme Court by George H. W. Bush, the Senate Judiciary Committee brought in numerous witnesses, including Anita Hill, who claimed that she had been sexually harassed by Thomas.

Advice and Consent: Special Senate Powers

The Constitution has given the Senate a special power, one that is not based on lawmaking. The president has the power to make treaties and to appoint top executive officers, ambassadors, and federal judges—but only "with the Advice and Consent of the Senate" (Article II, Section 2). For treaties, two-thirds of those present must concur; for appointments, a simple majority is required.

The power to approve or reject presidential requests also involves the power to set conditions. The Senate only occasionally exercises its power to reject treaties and appointments. Despite the recent debate surrounding judicial nominees, only a handful of judicial nominees have been rejected by the Senate during the past century, whereas hundreds have been approved.

Most presidents make every effort to take potential Senate opposition into account in treaty negotiations and will frequently resort to **executive agreements** with foreign powers instead of treaties. The Supreme Court has held that such agreements are equivalent to treaties, but they do not need Senate approval.[42] In the past, presidents sometimes concluded secret agreements without informing Congress of the agreements' contents, or even their existence. For example, American involvement in the Vietnam War grew in part out of a series of secret arrangements made between American presidents and the South Vietnamese during the

executive agreement an agreement, made between the president and another country, that has the force of a treaty but does not require the Senate's "advice and consent"

1950s and 1960s. Congress did not even learn of the existence of these agreements until 1969. In 1972, Congress passed the Case Act, which requires that the president inform Congress of any executive agreement within sixty days of its having been reached. This provides Congress with the opportunity to cancel agreements that it opposes. In addition, Congress can limit the president's ability to conduct foreign policy through executive agreement by refusing to appropriate the funds needed to implement an agreement. In this way, for example, Congress can modify or even cancel executive agreements to provide American economic or military assistance to foreign governments.

Impeachment

impeachment the formal charge by the House of Representatives that a government official has committed "Treason, Bribery, or other high Crimes and Misdemeanors"

The Constitution also grants Congress the power of **impeachment** over the president, vice president, and other executive officials. Impeachment means to charge a government official (president or otherwise) with "Treason, Bribery, or other high Crimes and Misdemeanors" and bring them before Congress to determine their guilt. Impeachment is thus like a criminal indictment in which the House of Representatives acts like a grand jury, voting (by simple majority) on whether the accused ought to be impeached. If a majority of the House votes to impeach, the impeachment trial moves to the Senate, which acts like a trial jury by voting whether to convict and forcibly remove the person from office (this vote requires a two-thirds majority of the Senate).

Controversy over Congress's impeachment power has arisen over the grounds for impeachment, especially the meaning of "high Crimes and Misdemeanors." A strict reading of the Constitution suggests that the only impeachable offense is an actual crime. But a more commonly agreed on definition is that "an impeachable offense is whatever the majority of the House of Representatives considers it to be at a given moment in history."[43] In other words, impeachment, especially impeachment of a president, is a political decision.

The Senate possesses the power to impeach federal officials. In American history, sixteen federal officials have been impeached, including two presidents, Andrew Johnson and Bill Clinton. During Clinton's trial in the House, Bill McCollum (R-Fla.), argued that lying under oath was sufficient grounds for removing Clinton from office.

The political nature of impeachment was very clear in the two instances of impeachment that have occurred in American history. In the first, in 1867, President Andrew Johnson, a southern Democrat who had battled a congressional Republican majority over Reconstruction, was impeached by the House but saved from conviction by one vote in the Senate. In 1998, the House impeached President Bill Clinton on two counts, for lying under oath and obstructing justice, in the investigation into his sexual affair with the White House intern Monica Lewinsky. The vote was highly partisan, with only five Democrats voting for impeachment on each charge. In the Senate, where a two-thirds majority was needed to convict the president, only forty-five senators voted to convict on the first count of lying and fifty voted to convict on the second charge of obstructing justice. As in the House, the vote for impeachment was highly partisan, with all Democrats and only five Republicans supporting the president's ultimate acquittal.

The impeachment power is a considerable one; its very existence in the hands of Congress is a highly effective safeguard against the executive tyranny so greatly feared by the framers of the Constitution.

Thinking Critically about Congress and Democracy

Much of this chapter has described the major institutional components of Congress and has shown how they work as Congress makes policy. But what do these institutional features mean for how Congress represents the American public? Does the organization of Congress promote the equal representation of all Americans? Or are there institutional features of Congress that allow some interests more access and influence than others?

As we noted at the beginning of this chapter, Congress instituted a number of reforms in the 1970s to make itself more accessible and to distribute power more widely within the institution. These reforms sought to respond to public views that Congress had become a stodgy institution ruled by a powerful elite that made decisions in private. We have seen that these reforms increased the number of subcommittees, prohibited most secret hearings, and increased the staff support for Congress. These reforms spread power more evenly throughout the institution and opened new avenues for the public to contact and influence Congress.

But the opening of Congress ultimately did not benefit the broad American public, as reformers had envisioned. In fact the congressional reforms enacted during the 1970s actually made Congress less effective and, ironically, more permeable to special interests. Open committee meetings made it possible for sophisticated interest groups to monitor and influence every aspect of developing legislation. The unanticipated, negative consequences of these reforms highlighted the trade-off between representation and effectiveness in Congress.[44] Efforts to improve representation by opening Congress up made it difficult for Congress to be effective.

For Critical Analysis

Two of Congress's chief responsibilities are representation and lawmaking. How do these responsibilities support and reinforce one another? How might they also conflict with one another?

During the first six years of the Bush administration, the concern about congressional effectiveness waned because of the ability of the Republican-controlled Congress to enact much of the president's agenda. Yet concerns about congressional representativeness have persisted. For the Founders, Congress was the national institution that best embodied the ideals of representative democracy. Throughout our history, Congress has symbolized the American commitment to democratic values. Members of Congress, working to represent their constituents, bring these democratic values to life. A member of Congress can interpret his job as representative in two different ways: as a delegate or as a trustee. As a **delegate,** a member of Congress acts on the express preferences of his constituents; as a **trustee,** the member is more loosely tied to constituents and makes the decisions he thinks best. The delegate role appears to be the more democratic because it forces the representative to heed the desires of his constituents. But this requires the representative to be in constant touch with constituents; it also requires constituents to follow each policy issue very closely. The problem with this form of representation is that most people do not follow every issue so carefully; instead they focus only on extremely important issues or issues of particular interest to them. Many people are too busy to get the information necessary to make informed judgments even on issues they care about. Thus, adhering to the delegate form of representation takes the risk that the voices of only a few active and informed constituents get heard. Although it seems more democratic at first glance, the delegate form of representation may actually open Congress up even more to the influence of the voices of special interests.

delegate a representative who votes according to the preferences of his or her constituency

trustee a representative who votes based on what he or she thinks is best for his or her constituency

Get Your Representatives in Congress Working for You

Most students in college today are receiving some sort of federal financial assistance in the form of Pell grants or subsidized loans. With college tuition rising faster than inflation, many students (and their families) view such assistance as absolutely essential to their ability to stay in school. Members of Congress are well aware of these concerns, thanks in part to the letters, e-mails, and personal visits from many young people who have contacted their representatives and senators and urged them to continue (or extend) such help. As the Get Involved box in Chapter 11 described, in 2007, Congress responded by passing the College Cost Reduction and Access Act, which overhauls the federal student aid program and raises the level of grants.

Voicing your opinion on issues that matter to you may seem difficult, but it is actually relatively easy. Members of Congress have strong incentives to listen to their constituents, and there are several ways that you can let them know how they can represent you better.

- ★ You first need to know who is representing you in the House and Senate. To locate your senators, simply go to the official U.S. Senate Web site (www.senate.gov) and use the drop-down menu to enter your state. You can find out who your representative is by visiting the U.S. House of Representatives Web site (www.house.gov) and entering your zip code.
- ★ *Learn about past votes.* You can also use the Web sites of the two chambers to look up how your member may have voted in the past. You can see if he or she supported the invasion of Iraq, funding for financial aid, or to reauthorize the Patriot Act, among many others.
- ★ *Follow current policymaking.* Both the House and Senate Web sites have links to allow you to check what legislation is currently on the floor or in committee. You can also use the Library of Congress's Web site (www.thomas.loc.gov) to search for bills currently in Congress or to "browse" by sponsor to see what legislation has been introduced by your senators and representative this session. Contacting your member of Congress about an issue may be especially effective if a proposal related to that issue is currently under consideration.
- ★ *Contact Congress directly.* You can phone Congress by calling the U.S. Capitol Switchboard at (202) 224-3121 and ask to be connected to your senators or your representative. You can send them e-mails through links on their home Web sites. Or, you can send them a letter to their Washington, D.C., office (the address will be found on their Web site). You don't have to be an expert on the topic—you can simply ask them to "vote no" or "please support," or you can write a more detailed request. The Web site www.congress.org has tips on how to address your letters and e-mails, as well as guidance on what to write.
- ★ *See your representative or senator in person.* Members of Congress spend a lot of time in their home districts and states, holding town hall meetings and listening to the concerns of their constituents. You can find out their schedules by e-mailing or calling their office, and then simply show up at a local event. Because many of these events are sparsely attended, they offer unique opportunities to personally meet your elected officials.
- ★ *Apply for an internship.* Most members of Congress have internships that run either for a school term or for the summer. Your university's internship coordinator (and sometimes even the political science department) has probably worked with local congressional offices in the past and can help facilitate your application.

If a congressional member acts as a trustee, on the other hand, there is a danger that she will not pay sufficient attention to the wishes of constituents. In this scenario, the only way the public can exercise influence is by voting every two years for representatives or every six years for senators. Yet most members of Congress take this electoral check very seriously. They try to anticipate the wishes of their constituents even when they don't know exactly what those interests are, because they know that unpopular decisions can be used against them in the coming election.

The public understands the trade-offs entailed in these different forms of representation and is, in fact, divided on how members of Congress should represent it. In a recent poll, 69 percent of respondents agreed that when a congressional representative votes, the views of the district should be the most important; only 25 percent believed that the representative's own principles and judgment should prevail. Yet the public also recognizes that representatives are often better informed about issues than the public. On a different survey, 65 percent of respondents agreed that, in making a decision, members of Congress should ask themselves how the majority of the public would think if they were well informed on all sides of the issue; only 29 percent said the representative should be guided instead by what the majority actually thinks.[45]

What the public dislikes most about Congress stems from suspicions that Congress acts as neither a trustee nor a delegate of the broad public interest, but instead is swayed by narrow special interests with lots of money.[46] The former majority leader Tom DeLay's K Street Project, aimed at creating closer ties between lobbyists and the Republican Congress, reinforced the suspicions. After the lobbyist Jack Abramoff pled guilty in relation to his dealings with members of Congress in 2006, it was widely anticipated that many members of Congress would be implicated in lobbying scandals. Indeed, immediately after Abramoff's guilty plea, some eighty members of Congress either returned Abramoff's political contributions or donated them to charity in order to avoid an association with the lobbyist. Such corruption scandals greatly damage Congress's reputation with the American people by creating the impression that it is for sale. In 2007, Congress enacted a package of ethics reform designed to restore public confidence. Among its provisions were new regulations restricting members of Congress from lobbying for two years after they retire. The law was credited with spurring several members of Congress looking forward to lucrative lobbying careers—including the number-two Senate Republican, Trent Lott—to retire before the new restrictions took effect in 2008.[47] Some research also shows that senators are far more responsive to their affluent constituents.[48] Drawing on survey data that gauged the views of constituents in different income categories, one study showed that on key pieces of legislation, such as those dealing with the minimum wage and civil rights, the views of constituents in the top quarter of income distribution were far more likely to be represented than were the views of those in the bottom quarter of income distribution.

For Critical Analysis

Why is it so hard to make the voice of the public heard over the special interests in Congress? What reforms can enhance the public's influence in congressional deliberations?

For Critical Analysis

What are the reasons that members of Congress may be more responsive to upper-income Americans? What would it take to alter this bias in responsiveness?

Although political scientists have not been able to pinpoint the causes of such unequal representation, it is clear that interest group lobbying and the role of money in politics are important factors skewing congressional responsiveness toward the affluent. As we saw in Chapter 11, high-income people are far more likely to become active in an interest group. Interest groups that represent business have grown stronger over the past three decades, whereas groups that represent labor have weakened. And as we saw in Chapter 8, higher-income people are more likely to vote and to contact their congressional representatives. These patterns of group representation and political participation mean that members of Congress are more likely to hear the voices of higher-income Americans than of those who are less well off. For most of the past half century, class politics was a prominent feature of European politics but not of the more fluid American politics. The United States has long prided itself on having a political system that responds to all Americans regardless of income. The sharp bias in our contemporary patterns of interest representation and participation raise questions about whether the American political system is contributing to new forms of inequality.

Ideally, representative democracy grants all citizens equal opportunity to select their leaders and to communicate their preferences to these elected representatives. Yet, in reality, some citizens have more wealth, are more politically savvy, or belong to more effective organizations. Despite past efforts to reform Congress, these advantages provide special access to some interests even as they mute the voice of much of the American public. The dilemma that congressional reformers confront is how to devise safeguards that reduce the voices of special interests while allowing Congress to remain open to public influence.

FOR FURTHER READING

Adler, E. Scott. *Why Congressional Reforms Fail.* Chicago: University of Chicago Press, 2002.

Burrell, Barbara C. *A Woman's Place Is in the House: Campaigning for Congress in the Feminist Era.* Ann Arbor: University of Michigan Press, 1994.

Dodd, Lawrence, and Bruce I. Oppenheimer, eds. *Congress Reconsidered.* 8th ed. Washington, DC: Congressional Quarterly Press, 2005.

Dodson, Debra L. *The Impact of Women in Congress.* New York: Oxford University Press, 2006.

Fenno, Richard F. *Homestyle: House Members in Their Districts.* Boston: Little, Brown, 1978.

Fiorina, Morris. *Congress: Keystone of the Washington Establishment.* 2nd ed. New Haven, CT: Yale University Press, 1989.

Fowler, Linda, and Robert McClure. *Political Ambition: Who Decides to Run for Congress?* New Haven, CT: Yale University Press, 1989.

Hamilton, Lee. *How Congress Works.* Bloomington: Indiana University Press, 2004.

Mann, Thomas E., and Norman J. Ornstein. *The Broken Branch: How Congress Is Failing America and How to Get It Back on Track.* New York: Oxford University Press, 2006.

Mayhew, David R. *Congress: The Electoral Connection.* New Haven, CT: Yale University Press, 1974.

Polsby, Nelson. *How Congress Evolves.* New York: Oxford University Press, 2005.

Redman, Eric. *The Dance of Legislation.* Seattle: University of Washington Press, 2001.

RECOMMENDED WEB SITES

Capitol Hearings
www.capitolhearings.org
Congressional committees are essential to the lawmaking process. They do most of the legislative work by gathering information and writing bills. Read about congressional committees at C-SPAN's Capitol Hearings page.

Cook Political Report
www.cookpolitical.com
The Cook Political Report, by Charlie Cook, is a nonpartisan analysis of electoral politics. Check out current House and Senate races for an in-depth analysis of past and future congressional elections.

Library of Congress: Thomas
http://thomas.loc.gov
The Library of Congress's "Thomas" Web site is a superb place to find information about the U.S. Congress. Roll-call votes, current legislation, and the full text of the *Congressional Record*, and committee reports are just a few of the archives you will find.

National Committee for an Effective Congress
www.ourcampaigns.com/InfoLinkDetail.html?InfoLinkID=1212
Congressional redistricting is the process of redrawing House districts every ten years to account for shifts in population. For information about redistricting in your state, log on to the Redistricting Resource Center, provided by the National Committee for an Effective Congress.

Project Vote Smart
www.vote-smart.org/resource_govt101_02.php

The legislative process is very complicated. For a detailed description of how a bill becomes a law, refer to this Web page from Project Vote Smart.

Roll Call
www.rollcall.com

Roll Call, the newspaper of Capitol Hill, provides daily coverage on the members, legislation, and events taking place in and around the U.S. legislature.

The Sunlight Foundation and Taxpayers for Common Sense
http://earmarkwatch.org

Earmarks are language that members of Congress put into legislation that dedicates funds for specific uses, many whose broad benefits can be questioned. The Sunlight Foundation and Taxpayers for Common Sense are two watchdog groups that have joined forces to publish a database of congressional earmarks. Earmarks can be searched by state, congressional sponsor, recipient, and description of the project.

U.S. House of Representatives
www.house.gov
U.S. Senate
www.senate.gov

These are the official Web sites for the U.S. House of Representatives and the U.S. Senate. Here you can find information on your members of Congress, key congressional leaders, bills currently under consideration, and legislative committees.

STUDY OUTLINE

www.wwnorton.com/wtp7e

Congress: Representing the American People

1. The House and Senate play different roles in the legislative process. The Senate is more deliberative, whereas the House is characterized by greater centralization and organization.
2. House members are more attuned to localized narrow interests in society, whereas senators are more able than House members to represent statewide or national interests.
3. In recent years, the House has exhibited more partisanship and ideological division than the Senate.
4. Congress is not fully representative because it is not a sociological microcosm of American society.
5. Members of Congress frequently communicate with constituents and devote a great deal of staff time to constituency service.
6. Electoral motivations have a strong impact on both sociological and agency representation in Congress.
7. Incumbency affords members of Congress resources such as constituency service and mailing to help secure re-election.
8. In recent years, turnover rates in Congress have increased, although this is due more to incumbent retirement than to the defeat of incumbents in elections.
9. Members of Congress can supply benefits to constituents by passing pork-barrel legislation. Members of Congress exchange pork-barrel votes for votes on other issues.

The Organization of Congress

1. At the beginning of each Congress, Democrats and Republicans gather to select their leaders. The leader of the majority party in the House of Representatives is elected Speaker of the House by a strict party vote.
2. In the Senate, the president pro tempore is the presiding officer, although the majority and minority leaders control the calendar and agenda of the Senate.
3. The committee system provides Congress with a second organizational structure that is more a division of labor than the party-based hierarchies of power.
4. With specific jurisdiction over certain policy areas and the task of processing proposals of legislation into bills for floor consideration, standing committees are the most important arenas of congressional policy making.
5. Power within committees is based on seniority, although the seniority principle is not absolute.
6. During the 1970s, reforms fragmented power in Congress—the committee system, specifically—by increasing both the number of subcommittees and the autonomy of subcommittee chairpersons.
7. Each member of Congress has a personal staff that deals with constituency requests and, increasingly, with the details of legislative and administrative oversight.
8. Groups of senators or representatives who share certain opinions, interests, or social characteristics form informal organizations called caucuses.

Rules of Lawmaking: How a Bill Becomes a Law

1. Committee deliberation is necessary before floor action on any bill.
2. Many bills receive little or no committee or subcommittee action; they are allowed to "die in committee."
3. Bills presented out of committee in the House must go through the House Rules Committee before they can be debated on the floor. The Rules Committee allots the time for floor debate on a bill and the conditions under which a bill may (or may not) be amended.
4. In the Senate, rules of debate are much less rigid. In fact, senators may delay Senate action on legislation by refusing to yield the floor; this is known as a filibuster.
5. Conference committees are often required to reconcile House and Senate versions of bills that began with similar provisions but emerged with significant differences.
6. After being adopted by the House and the Senate, a bill is sent to the president, who may choose to sign the bill or veto it. Congress can override a president's veto by a two-thirds vote in both the House and the Senate.

How Congress Decides

1. Creating a legislative agenda, drawing up a list of possible measures, and deciding among them is a complex process in which a variety of influences from inside and outside government play important roles.
2. Interest groups can influence congressional decision making by mobilizing followers in congressional districts, setting the agenda, or writing legislative language.
3. Party discipline is still an important factor in congressional voting, despite its decline throughout the twentieth century.
4. Party unity is typically greater in the House than in the Senate. Party unity on roll-call votes has increased in recent sessions of Congress.
5. Party unity is a result of a combination of the ideology and background of individual members and the resources party leaders have at their disposal.
6. The influence of the presidency is probably the most important of all the resources that maintain party discipline in Congress.

Beyond Legislation: Other Congressional Powers

1. Congress has increasingly relied on legislative oversight of administrators.
2. The Senate also has the power of approving or rejecting presidential treaties and appointments.
3. Congress has the power to impeach executive officials.

Thinking Critically about Congress and Democracy

1. Congressional reforms of the 1970s fragmented power in Congress and made it more open to special interests.
2. What the public dislikes most about Congress stems from suspicions that Congress does not act as a trustee or as a delegate of any broad interest but that it is swayed by narrow special interests with money.

PRACTICE QUIZ

www.wwnorton.com/wtp7e

1. Members of Congress can work as agents of their constituents by
   a) providing direct patronage.
   b) taking part in a party vote.
   c) joining a caucus.
   d) supporting term limits.
2. Why has public approval of Congress as an institution declined since the 1970s?
   a) Constituents don't like their own representatives in Congress.
   b) Congress has become increasingly inaccessible to the public since the 1970s.
   c) Citizens can now see members of Congress on television every night.
   d) Congress has increasingly opened itself up to the control of special interests.
3. Because they have larger and more heterogeneous constituencies, senators
   a) are more attuned to the needs of localized interest groups.
   b) care more about re-election than House members.
   c) can better represent the national interest.
   d) face less competition in elections than House members.
4. Sociological representation is important in understanding the U.S. Congress because
   a) members often vote on the basis of their religion.
   b) Congress is a microcosm of American society.
   c) the symbolic composition of Congress is important for the political stability of the United States.
   d) there is a distinct "congressional sociology."

5. What type of representation is described when constituents have the power to hire and fire their representative?
   a) agency representation
   b) sociological representation
   c) democratic representation
   d) trustee representation
6. Incumbency is an important factor in deciding who is elected to Congress because
   a) incumbents have tools they can use to help ensure re-election.
   b) potentially strong challengers may be dissuaded from running because of the strength of the incumbent.
   c) Both a and b are true.
   d) Neither a nor b is true.
7. Some have argued that the creation of minority congressional districts has
   a) lessened the sociological representation of minorities in Congress.
   b) made it more difficult for minorities to win substantive policy goals.
   c) been a result of the media's impact on state legislative politics.
   d) lessened the problem of "pork-barrel" politics.
8. Which of the following is not an important influence on how members of Congress vote on legislation?
   a) the media
   b) constituency
   c) interest groups
   d) party leaders
9. Which of the following types of committees does not include members of both the House and the Senate?
   a) standing committee
   b) joint committee
   c) conference committee
   d) No committees include both House members and senators.
10. An agreement between members of Congress to trade support for each other's bill is known as
    a) oversight.
    b) filibuster.
    c) logrolling.
    d) patronage.

KEY TERMS

www.wwnorton.com/wtp7e

agency representation (p. 458)
apportionment (p. 464)
appropriations (p. 491)
bicameral (p. 457)
bill (p. 476)
caucus (congressional) (p. 476)
caucus (political) (p. 468)
closed rule (p. 478)
cloture (p. 479)
committee markup (p. 478)
conference (p. 468)
conference committee (p. 473)
constituency (p. 457)
delegate (p. 495)
executive agreement (p. 493)
filibuster (p. 479)
gerrymandering (p. 465)
impeachment (p. 494)
incumbency (p. 462)
joint committee (p. 473)
logrolling (p. 487)
majority leader (p. 469)
minority leader (p. 469)
open rule (p. 478)
oversight (p. 491)
party unity vote (p. 484)
patronage (p. 466)
pocket veto (p. 482)
pork barrel (or pork) (p. 466)
private bill (p. 468)
redistricting (p. 464)
roll-call vote (p. 484)
select committee (p. 472)
seniority (p. 474)
sociological representation (p. 458)
Speaker of the House (p. 469)
staff agency (p. 476)
standing committee (p. 471)
term limits (p. 463)
trustee (p. 495)
veto (p. 482)
whip (p. 469)

13 The Presidency

- ★ The Constitutional Basis of the Presidency
- ★ The Constitutional Powers of the Presidency
- ★ The Presidency as an Institution
- ★ The Contemporary Bases of Presidential Power
- ★ Thinking Critically about Presidential Power and Democracy

WHAT GOVERNMENT DOES AND WHY IT MATTERS

In November 2008, Americans elected Barack Obama to serve as the nation's forty-fourth president. The new administration inherited a host of problems and powers from its predecessor. Among the most important of these problems were the ongoing wars in Iraq and Afghanistan, continuing fears of terrorism, and the economic woes afflicting America and the world. During the campaign, all the candidates had pledged to find new solutions to the global challenges facing America. And with the election over, Americans hoped for the best. During times of trouble, after all, Americans have always looked to their government for protection. Yet many Americans continued to fear that war and terrorism had become permanent features of our national life and would continue to threaten our safety despite the best efforts of the new administration.

The new president also inherited a presidency vastly more powerful than the institution imagined by the framers of America's Constitution. Ironically, the same wars that presented such an enormous challenge to the new administration also had the potential to enhance its power.

Presidential power generally seems to increase during times of war. For example, President Abraham Lincoln's 1862 declaration of martial law and Congress's 1863 legislation giving the president the power to make arrests and imprisonments through military tribunals amounted to a "constitutional dictatorship" that lasted through the war and Lincoln's re-election in 1864. But these measures were viewed as emergency powers that could be revoked once the crisis of union was resolved. In less than a year after Lincoln's death, Congress had reasserted its power, leaving the presidency in many respects the same as, if not weaker than, it had been before the war.

During World War II, Franklin D. Roosevelt, like Lincoln, did not bother to wait for Congress but took executive action first and expected Congress to follow. Roosevelt brought the United States into an undeclared naval war against Germany a year before Pearl Harbor, and he ordered the unauthorized use of wiretaps and other surveillance as well as the investigation of suspicious persons for reasons not clearly specified. The most egregious (and revealing) of these was his segregation and eventual confinement of 120,000 individuals of Japanese descent, many of whom were American citizens. Even worse, the Supreme Court validated Roosevelt's treatment of the Japanese on the flimsy grounds of military necessity. One dissenter on the Court called the president's assumption of emergency powers "a loaded weapon ready for the hand of any authority that can bring forward a plausible claim of an urgent need."

The "loaded weapon" was seized again on September 14, 2001, when Congress defined the World Trade Center and Pentagon attacks as an act of war and proceeded to adopt a joint resolution authorizing the president to use "all necessary and appropriate force against those nations, organizations or persons he determines planned, authorized, committed or aided the terrorist attacks that occurred on September 11, 2001, or harbored such organizations or persons. . . ." On the basis of this authorization, President Bush ordered the invasion of Afghanistan and began the reorganization of the nation's "homeland security." If history is any guide, our new president is unlikely to relinquish the powers seized by President Bush and his predecessors. Each president uses power differently, but thus far, none has relinquished any of the powers claimed by his/her forebears.

In this chapter, we will examine the foundations of the American presidency and assess the origins and character of presidential power in the twenty-first century. National emergencies are one source of presidential power, but presidents are also empowered by democratic political processes and, increasingly, by their ability to control and expand the institutional resources of the office. This chapter explains why the American system of government could be described as presidential government and how it got to be that way. We also explore how and why the president, however powerful, is particularly vulnerable to the popular will. In other words, as the presidency became a powerful center of government, its foundation rested on a virtually untamable mass popular democracy.

- **The first two parts of this chapter explore the constitutional basis and resources of presidential power.** The Constitution provides an array of expressed powers to the president. The Constitution also allows for Congress to delegate to the president the power to implement or execute its will. Some presidents have asserted, especially during times of war or national emergency, that the office also includes inherent powers.
- **We turn next to the institutional resources that presidents use as tools of management.** Without these resources, such as the Cabinet, presidents would be unable to exercise the powers provided by the Constitution.
- **We will then examine the contemporary bases of presidential power.** Presidents rely on their party, the media, and public opinion to build support for their programs and persuade Congress to cooperate. These resources offer great strength to the president but, as we will see, can also be a great liability. As a result, contemporary presidents have increasingly turned to their administrative capabilities in order to increase the power of their office.

The Constitutional Basis of the Presidency

The presidency was established by Article II of the Constitution. Article II begins by asserting, "The executive power shall be vested in a President of the United States of America." It goes on to describe the manner in which the president is to be chosen and defines the basic powers of the presidency. By vesting the executive power in a single president, the framers were emphatically rejecting proposals for various forms of collective leadership. Some delegates to the Constitutional Convention had argued in favor of a multiheaded executive or an "executive council" in order to avoid undue concentration of power in the hands of one individual. Most of the framers, however, were anxious to provide for "energy" in the executive. They hoped to have a president capable of taking quick and aggressive action. These framers thought a unitary executive would be more energetic than some form of collective leadership. They believed that a powerful executive would help to protect the nation's interests vis-à-vis other nations and promote the federal government's interests relative to the states.

Immediately following the first sentence of Section 1, Article II of the Constitution defines the manner in which the president is to be chosen. The selection process defined by Article II resulted from a struggle between those delegates who wanted the president to be selected by, and thus be responsible to, Congress and those delegates who preferred that the president be elected directly by the people. Direct popular election would create a more independent and more powerful presidency. With the adoption of a scheme of indirect election through an electoral college in which the electors would be selected by the state legislatures (and close elections would be resolved in the House of Representatives), the framers hoped to achieve a "republican" solution: a strong president responsible to state and national legislators rather than directly to the electorate.

The framers of the Constitution wanted an "energetic" presidency, capable of quick, decisive action. However, when George Washington was sworn in as the first president in 1876, the presidency was a less powerful office than it is today.

This indirect method of electing the president probably did dampen the power of most presidents in the nineteenth century.

The presidency was strengthened somewhat in the 1830s with the introduction of the national convention system of nominating presidential candidates. Until then, presidential candidates had been nominated by their party's congressional delegates. This was the **caucus** system of nominating candidates, derisively called "King Caucus" because any candidate for president was beholden to the party's leaders in Congress to get the party's nomination and the support of the party's congressional delegation in the presidential election. The national nominating convention arose outside Congress to provide some representation for a party's voters who lived in districts where they weren't numerous enough to elect a member of Congress. The political party in each state made its own provisions for selecting delegates to attend the presidential nominating convention, and in virtually all states the selection was dominated by the party leaders. Only in recent decades have state laws intervened to regularize the selection process and to provide (in all but a few instances) for open election of delegates. The convention system quickly became the most popular method of nominating candidates for all elective offices and remained so until well into the twentieth century, when it succumbed to the criticism that it was a nondemocratic method dominated by a few leaders in a "smoke-filled room." But during the nineteenth century, it was seen as a victory for democracy against the congressional elite. And the national convention gave the presidency a base of power independent of Congress.

caucus (political) a normally closed meeting of a political or legislative group to select candidates, plan strategy, or make decisions regarding legislative matters

Politics Today

In 2008, the Democratic Party ruled that neither Michigan's nor Florida's Democratic convention delegates would be allowed to vote because these states had scheduled their Democratic primaries earlier than the party wanted. Should a political party be allowed to determine whether and how its supporters' votes will count in the presidential nominating process?

This additional independence did not immediately transform the presidency into the office familiar to us today, but the national convention did begin to open the presidency to larger social forces and newly organized interests in society. In other words, it gave the presidency a mass popular base that would eventually support and demand increased presidential power. Improvements in the telephone, the telegraph, and other forms of mass communication allowed individuals to share their complaints and allowed national leaders—especially presidents and presidential candidates—to reach out directly to people to ally themselves with, and even sometimes to create, popular groups and forces. Eventually, though more slowly, the presidential selection process began to be further democratized, with the adoption of primary elections through which millions of ordinary citizens were given an opportunity to take part in the presidential nominating process by popular selection of convention delegates.

But despite political and social conditions favoring the enhancement of the presidency, the development of presidential government as we know it today did not mature until the middle of the twentieth century. For a long period, even as the national government began to grow, Congress was careful to keep tight reins on the president's power. The real turning point in the history of American national government came during the administration of Franklin Delano Roosevelt. Since FDR and his "New Deal" of the 1930s, every president has been strong whether he was committed to the strong presidency or not.

The Constitutional Powers of the Presidency

Whereas Section I of Article II explains how the president is to be chosen, Sections 2 and 3 outline the powers and duties of the president. These two sections identify two sources of presidential power. Some presidential powers are specifically established by the language of the Constitution. For example, the president is authorized to make treaties, grant pardons, and nominate judges and other public officials. These specifically defined powers are called the **expressed powers** of the office and cannot be revoked by Congress or any other agency without an amendment to the Constitution. Other expressed powers include the power to receive ambassadors and the command of the military forces of the United States.

expressed powers specific powers granted by the Constitution to Congress (Article I, Section 8), and to the president (Article II)

In addition to the president's expressed powers, Article II declares that the president, "shall take Care that the Laws be faithfully executed." Since the laws are enacted by Congress, this language implies that Congress is to delegate to the president the power to implement or execute its will. Powers given to the president by Congress are called **delegated powers.** In principle, Congress delegates to the president only the power to identify or develop the means through which to carry out its decisions. So, for example, if Congress determines that air quality should be improved, it might delegate to a bureaucratic agency in the executive branch the power to identify the best means of bringing about such an improvement as well as the power actually to implement the cleanup process. In practice, of course, decisions about how to clean the air are likely to have an enormous impact on businesses, organizations, and individuals throughout the nation. As it delegates power to the executive, Congress substantially enhances the importance of the presidency and the executive branch. In most cases, Congress delegates power to bureaucratic agencies in the executive branch rather than to the president. As we shall see, however, contemporary presidents have found ways to capture a good deal of this delegated power for themselves.

delegated powers constitutional powers that are assigned to one governmental agency but that are exercised by another agency with the express permission of the first

Presidents have claimed a third source of power beyond expressed and delegated powers. These are powers not specified in the Constitution or the law but said to stem from "the rights, duties and obligations of the presidency."[1] They are referred to as the **inherent powers** of the presidency and are most often asserted by presidents in times of war or national emergency. For example, after the fall of Fort Sumter and the outbreak of the Civil War, President Abraham Lincoln

inherent powers powers claimed by a president that are not expressed in the Constitution, but are inferred from it

The term imperial presidency *was popularized in 1973 by a book of that name written during the Vietnam era. President Lyndon B. Johnson, pictured here greeting American troops in Vietnam, believed that his presidential powers allowed the Gulf of Tonkin Resolution to mean that any of the nation's resources could be used to fight the war in Vietnam.*

issued a series of executive orders for which he had no clear legal basis. Without even calling Congress into session, Lincoln combined the state militias into a ninety-day national volunteer force, called for 40,000 new volunteers, enlarged the regular army and navy, diverted $2 million in unspent appropriations to military needs, instituted censorship of the U.S. mails, ordered a blockade of southern ports, suspended the writ of *habeas corpus* in the border states, and ordered the arrest by military police of individuals whom he deemed to be guilty of engaging in or even contemplating treasonous actions.[2] Lincoln asserted that these extraordinary measures were justified by the president's inherent power to protect the nation.[3] Subsequent presidents, including Franklin Delano Roosevelt and George W. Bush, have had similar views.

Expressed Powers

The president's expressed powers, as defined by Sections 2 and 3 of Article II, fall into several categories:

1. *Military.* Article II, Section 2, provides for the power as "Commander in Chief of the Army and Navy of the United States, and of the Militia of the several States, when called in to the actual Service of the United States."
2. *Judicial.* Article II, Section 2, also provides the power to "grant Reprieves and Pardons for Offences against the United States, except in Cases of Impeachment."
3. *Diplomatic.* Article II, Section 2, also provides the power "by and with the Advice and Consent of the Senate to make Treaties." Article II, Section 3, provides the power to "receive Ambassadors and other public Ministers."
4. *Executive.* Article II, Section 3, authorizes the president to see to it that all the laws are faithfully executed; Section 2 gives the chief executive power to appoint, remove, and supervise all executive officers and to appoint all federal judges.
5. *Legislative.* Article I, Section 7 and Article II, Section 3 give the president the power to participate authoritatively in the legislative process.

commander in chief the role of the president as commander of the national military and the state national guard units (when called into service)

MILITARY The president's military powers are among the most important exercised by the chief executive. The position of **commander in chief** makes the president the highest military authority in the United States, with control of the entire defense establishment. The president is also head of the nation's intelligence network, which includes not only the Central Intelligence Agency (CIA) but also the National Security Council (NSC), the National Security Agency (NSA), the Federal Bureau of Investigation (FBI), and a host of less well known but very powerful international and domestic security agencies.

War and Inherent Presidential Power The Constitution gives Congress the power to declare war. Presidents, however, have gone a long way toward capturing this power for themselves. Congress has not declared war since December 1941, but, since then American military forces have engaged in numerous campaigns throughout the world under the orders of the president. When North Korean forces invaded South Korea in June 1950, Congress was actually prepared to declare war, but President Harry S. Truman decided not to ask for congressional action. Instead, Truman asserted that the president and not Congress could decide when and where to deploy America's military might. Truman dispatched American

The President versus the World: How Presidents Seized Control of the War Power

The 1973 War Powers Resolution provided that presidents could not deploy military forces for more than sixty days without securing congressional authorization. Many in Congress saw this time limit as a restraint on presidential action, though it gave the president more discretion than the framers of the Constitution had provided. President Gerald Ford had carefully followed the letter of the law when organizing a military effort to rescue American sailors held by North Korea. But this was the first and last time that the War Powers Act was fully observed. Between 1982 and 1986, President Reagan presented Congress with a set of military *faits accomplis* that undermined the War Powers Act and, in effect, asserted a doctrine of sole presidential authority in the security realm.

In October 1983, while American forces were still in Lebanon, President Reagan ordered an invasion of the Caribbean island of Grenada after a coup had led to the installation of a pro-Cuban government on the island. Congress threatened to invoke the War Powers Act, but Reagan withdrew American troops before the Senate acted. In 1986, Reagan ordered the bombing of Libya in response to a terrorist attack in Berlin that the administration blamed on Libyan agents. In all three cases, Reagan acted without consulting Congress and claimed that his authority had come directly from the Constitution.

Reagan's successor, George H. W. Bush, ordered an invasion of Panama designed to oust the Panamanian strongman General Manuel Noriega. Congress made no official response to the invasion. In 1990–91, the Bush administration sent a huge American military force into the Persian Gulf in response to Iraq's invasion and occupation of Kuwait. Both houses of Congress voted to authorize military action against Iraq—the Senate by the narrowest of margins—but the president made it clear that he did not feel bound by any congressional declaration. Indeed, the president later pointed out that he had specifically avoided asking Capitol Hill for "authorization" since such a request might improperly imply that Congress "had the final say in . . . an executive decision."[a]

In 1994, President Clinton planned an invasion of Haiti under the cover of a UN Security Council resolution. Congress expressed strong opposition to Clinton's plans, but he pressed forward nonetheless, claiming that he did not need congressional approval. In a similar vein, between 1994 and 1998, the administration undertook a variety of military actions in the former Yugoslavia without formal congressional authorization.

In 2001, President George W. Bush ordered an attack that soon toppled Afghanistan's Taliban regime. In 2003, Bush sent American forces to oust Saddam Hussein's government in Iraq. Bush had congressional support for his actions but, like his predecessors, asserted that he did not need Congress's permission to undertake military action. When the Democrats took control of Congress in 2006, they sought to bring the Iraq war to an end but were unable to prevail against the president.

At the start of a new administration, it is not clear what war powers, if any, remain in the hands of Congress.

FOR CRITICAL ANALYSIS

1. Article I of the Constitution gives Congress the power to declare war. Why have modern presidents consistently refrained from asking Congress for such a declaration?
2. The late Edward Corwin said that the Constitution invited the president and Congress to struggle over war powers. What advantages have allowed presidents gradually to prevail in this struggle over the past century?

a. George H. W. Bush and Brent Scowcroft, *A World Transformed* (New York: Knopf, 1998), 441.

forces to Korea without a congressional declaration, and in the face of the emergency, Congress felt it had to acquiesce. Congress passed a resolution approving the president's actions, and this became the pattern for future congressional-executive relations in the military realm. The wars in Vietnam, Bosnia, Afghanistan, and Iraq, as well as a host of lesser conflicts, were all fought without declarations of war.

War Powers Resolution a resolution of Congress that the president can send troops into action abroad only by authorization of Congress, or if American troops are already under attack or serious threat

In 1973, Congress responded to presidential unilateralism by passing the **War Powers Resolution** over President Nixon's veto. This resolution reasserted the principle of congressional war power, required the president to inform Congress of any planned military campaign, and stipulated that forces must be withdrawn within sixty days in the absence of a specific congressional authorization for their continued deployment. Presidents, however, have generally ignored the War Powers Resolution, claiming inherent executive power to defend the nation. Thus, President George W. Bush responded to the 2001 attacks by Islamic terrorists by organizing a major military campaign to overthrow the Taliban regime in Afghanistan, which had sheltered the terrorists. In 2003, Bush ordered a major American campaign against Iraq, which he accused of posing a threat to the United States. U.S. forces overthrew the government of the Iraqi dictator, Saddam Hussein, and occupied the country. In both instances, Congress passed resolutions approving the president's actions, but the president was careful to assert that he did not need congressional authorization. The War Powers Resolution was barely mentioned on Capitol Hill and was ignored by the White House.

Politics Today

The framers of the Constitution gave Congress the power to declare war. Some commentators have asserted that this implies that Congress also has the power to "undeclare" war. Should Congress be able to declare, through legislation, that the president must cease military activities in Iraq?

Military Sources of Domestic Power The president's military powers extend into the domestic sphere. Article IV, Section 4, provides that the "United States shall [protect] every State . . . against Invasion . . . and . . . domestic Violence." Congress has made this an explicit presidential power through statutes directing the president as commander in chief to discharge these obligations.[4] The Constitution restrains the president's use of domestic force by providing that a state legislature (or governor when the legislature is not in session) must request federal troops before the president can send them into the state to provide public order. Yet this proviso is not absolute. First, presidents are not obligated to deploy national troops merely because the state legislature or governor makes such a request. And more important, the president may deploy troops in a state or city without a specific request from the state legislature or governor if the president considers it necessary to maintain an essential national service during an emergency, to enforce a federal judicial order, or to protect federally guaranteed civil rights.

One historic example of the unilateral use of presidential emergency power to protect the states against domestic disorder, even when the states don't request it, was the decision by President Dwight Eisenhower in 1957 to send troops into Little Rock, Arkansas, literally against the wishes of the state of Arkansas, to enforce court orders to integrate Little Rock's Central High School. The governor of Arkansas, Orval Faubus, had posted the Arkansas National Guard at the entrance of Central High School to prevent the court-ordered admission of nine black students. After an effort to negotiate with Governor Faubus failed, President Eisenhower reluctantly sent a thousand paratroopers to Little Rock; they stood watch while the black students took their places in the all-white classrooms. This case makes quite clear that the president does not have to wait for a request by a state legislature or governor before acting as a domestic commander in chief.[5]

However, in most instances of domestic disorder—whether from human or from natural causes—presidents tend to exercise unilateral power by declaring a

Although President George W. Bush sought Congress's approval before taking action in Iraq, his subsequent actions provoked criticism that the "imperial presidency" had returned to the White House. Critics charged that he had led the United States into war under false pretenses and without a realistic plan for ending the war. Here, Bush addresses U.S. troops in Iraq during a surprise visit intended to boost morale.

"state of emergency," thereby making available federal grants, insurance, and direct assistance. In 1992, in the aftermath of the devastating riots in Los Angeles and the hurricanes in Florida, American troops were very much in evidence, sent in by the president, but more in the role of good Samaritans than of military police. In 2005, President Bush declared a state of emergency to allow the Federal Emergency Management Agency (FEMA) to coordinate the government's response to Hurricane Katrina, an immense storm that devastated the city of New Orleans. Bush sent federal troops to bolster local efforts.

Military emergencies have typically also led to expansion of the domestic powers of the executive branch. This was true during the First and Second World Wars and has been true in the wake of the "war on terrorism" as well. Within a month of the September 11 attacks, the White House had drafted and Congress had enacted the USA PATRIOT Act, expanding the power of government agencies to engage in domestic surveillance activities, including electronic surveillance, and restricting judicial review of such efforts. The act also gave the attorney general greater authority to detain and deport aliens suspected of having terrorist affiliations. The following year, Congress created the Department of Homeland Security, combining offices from twenty-two federal agencies into one huge new cabinet department that would be responsible for protecting the nation from attack. The new agency includes the Coast Guard, Transportation Safety Administration, Federal Emergency Management Administration, Immigration and Naturalization Service, and offices from the departments of Agriculture, Energy, Transportation, Justice, Health and Human Services, Commerce, and the General Services Administration. The actual reorganization plan was drafted by the White House, but Congress weighed in to make certain that the new agency's workers had civil service and union protections.

When wildfires threatened large areas of California, President Bush used his powers to declare a state of emergency and sent Homeland Security Secretary Michael Chertoff to the scene.

JUDICIAL The presidential power to grant reprieves, pardons, and amnesties involves power over all individuals who may be a threat to the security of the United States. Presidents may use this power on behalf of a particular individual, as did Gerald Ford when he pardoned Richard Nixon in 1974 "for all offenses against the United States which he . . . has committed or may have committed." Or they may use it on a large scale, as did President Andrew Johnson in 1868, when he gave full amnesty to all southerners who had participated in the "Late Rebellion," and President Carter in 1977, when he declared an amnesty for all the draft evaders of the Vietnam War. President Clinton issued a number of controversial pardons during his last weeks in office. This power of life and death over others helped elevate the president to the level of earlier conquerors and kings by establishing him or her as the person before whom supplicants might come to make their pleas for mercy.

DIPLOMATIC The president is America's "head of state"—its chief representative in dealings with other nations. As head of state the president has the power to make treaties for the United States (with the advice and consent of the Senate). When President Washington received Edmond Genêt ("Citizen Genêt") as the formal emissary of the revolutionary government of France in 1793 and had his cabinet officers and Congress back his decision, he established a greatly expanded interpretation of the power to "receive Ambassadors and other public Ministers," extending it to the power to "recognize" other countries. That power gives the president the almost unconditional authority to review the claims of any new ruling groups to determine whether they indeed control the territory and population of their country, so that they can commit it to treaties and other agreements.

executive agreement an agreement, made between the president and another country, that has the force of a treaty but does not require the Senate's "advice and consent"

In recent years, presidents have expanded the practice of using executive agreements instead of treaties to establish relations with other countries.[6] An **executive agreement** is exactly like a treaty because it is a contract between two countries, but an executive agreement does not require a two-thirds vote of approval by the Senate. There are actually two types of executive agreements. One is the executive-congressional agreement. For this type of agreement, the president will submit the proposed arrangement to Congress for a simple majority vote in both houses, usually easier for presidents to win than the two-thirds approval of the Senate that is required. The other type of executive agreement is the sole executive agreement, which is simply an understanding between the president and a foreign state and is not submitted to Congress for its approval. In the past, sole executive agreements were used to flesh out commitments already made in treaties or to arrange for matters well below the level of policy. Since the 1930s, however, presidents have entered into sole executive agreements on important issues when they were uncertain about their prospects for securing congressional approval of an agreement. For example, the General Agreement on Tariffs and Trade (GATT), one of the cornerstones of U.S. international economic policy in the post–World War II era, was based on an executive agreement. The courts have held that executive agreements have the force of law, as though they were formal treaties.

The President and Warrantless Wiretapping

Soon after the September 11 terrorist attacks, the president issued directives authorizing the National Security Agency (NSA) to eavesdrop on Americans and others inside the United States who communicated via telephone or e-mail with persons outside the United States. These directives permitted the NSA to engage in what is sometimes called "data mining," a process of sifting through millions of calls and e-mails searching for words and phrases that might signal terrorist involvement. Under the Foreign Intelligence Surveillance Act (FISA), the government is required to obtain warrants for such surveillance from the Foreign Intelligence Surveillance Court, which holds secret sessions at the Justice Department. President Bush, however, decided to bypass statutory restrictions. Encountering a firestorm of protest when the existence of the secret orders was leaked to the press in 2005, President Bush and his advisers asserted that the president had acted properly.

The president said he based his actions on Article II of the Constitution and Congress's 2001 resolution giving the president the authority to use "all necessary and appropriate force against those nations, organizations or persons he determines planned, authorized, committed or aided" the September 11 attacks against the United States. The White House also asserted that FISA does not apply during wartime. A 2006 Justice Department memorandum asserted that the president's position was supported by the *Federalist Papers*, numerous court cases, the writings of Republican and Democratic presidents, and many scholarly papers.[a] One important federal court decision that seemed to support the president's view was the case of *Campbell v. Clinton*, decided in 2000. In this case, the court said that the president's authority as commander in chief extends to the "independent authority to repel aggressive acts . . . without specific congressional authorization" and without court review of the level of force selected. In 2007, a federal appeals court declined to halt the NSA's eavesdropping program on the grounds that the group challenging the program lacked standing. The court did not comment on the program itself.

Some legal scholars have echoed the administration's position. The presidential legal advisor John Yoo said in a 2001 memorandum that no statute enacted by Congress "can place any limits on the president's determinations as to any terrorist threat, the amount of military force to be used in response, or the method, timing and nature of the response."[b] Another expert who defended the president's actions is the former associate attorney general John Schmidt. The president, in Schmidt's view, has a constitutional duty to gather foreign intelligence and argues that the enactment of FISA did not alter the president's constitutional authority.

Many top legal scholars, however, believe that the president's actions were illegal. They argue that FISA clearly makes warrantless wiretapping illegal and that the president knowingly violated the law through his orders. Similarly, in 2006, the American Bar Association issued a statement denouncing the warrantless domestic surveillance program and accusing the president of exceeding his constitutional power.

Critics of the program contend that the dangers of unfettered presidential power inherent in President Bush's actions outweigh the likely benefits. Some critics have said that the president's logic in defending his actions seemed to suggest that there are no restrictions on presidential power. The Georgetown law professor Jonathon Turley said, "There's no limiting principle to that theory."[c]

FOR CRITICAL ANALYSIS

1. Article II of the Constitution establishes the president as commander in chief. Article I, however, gives Congress the power to declare war. What roles should the two branches play in exercising war powers?
2. Past presidents have often assumed expanded powers during times of war. Should the threat of terrorism influence our debates about the Constitution and the laws, particularly as they relate to presidential power?

---

a. Eric Lichtblau and James Risen, "Legal Rationale By Justice Department On Spying Effort," *New York Times*, January 20, 2006, p. 1.

b. Scott Shane, "Behind Power, One Principle," *New York Times*, December 17, 2005, p. 1. Yoo's views are more fully spelled out in his book *The Powers of War and Peace* (Chicago: University of Chicago Press, 2005).

c. Joseph Curl, "Legal Scholars Split on Wiretaps," *Washington Times*, January 18, 2006, p. A4.

The Supreme Court's decision in U.S. vs. Nixon *is often seen as a blow to presidential power because President Nixon was required to turn over secret tapes related to the Watergate scandal, despite his claim of executive privilege. Nixon later announced his resignation on national television. However, the Court's decision implied that executive privilege might be valid in other cases.*

During the 1960s, Congress discovered that several presidents had entered into agreements with foreign governments and not informed Congress. This discovery led to the enactment of the 1972 Case-Zablocki Act, requiring the president to provide Congress each year with a complete list of all executive agreements signed during the course of that year. Presidents have not fully complied with this law. If they wish to keep an agreement secret, they call it by another name, such as "national security memorandum," and claim that it is not covered by the Case act.

EXECUTIVE POWER The most important basis of the president's power as chief executive is to be found in Article II, Section 3, which stipulates that the president must see that all the laws are faithfully executed, and Section 2, which provides that the president will appoint, remove, and supervise all executive officers, and appoint all federal judges (with Senate approval). The power to appoint the principal executive officers and to require each of them to report to the president on subjects relating to the duties of their departments makes the president the true chief executive officer (CEO) of the nation. In this manner, the Constitution focuses executive power and legal responsibility on the president. The famous sign on President Truman's desk, "The buck stops here," was not merely an assertion of Truman's personal sense of responsibility but was in fact his recognition of the legal and constitutional responsibility of the president. The president is subject to some limitations, because the appointment of all such officers, including ambassadors, ministers, and federal judges, is subject to a majority approval by the Senate. But these appointments are at the discretion of the president, and the loyalty and the responsibility of each appointee are presumed to be directed toward the president.

executive privilege the claim that confidential communications between a president and close advisers should not be revealed without the consent of the president

Another component of the president's power as chief executive is **executive privilege.** Executive privilege is the claim that confidential communications between a president and close advisers should not be revealed without the consent of the president. Presidents have made this claim ever since George Washington refused a request from the House of Representatives to deliver documents concerning negotiations of an important treaty. Washington refused (successfully) on the grounds that, first, the House was not constitutionally part of the treaty-making process and that, second, that diplomatic negotiations required secrecy.

Although many presidents have claimed executive privilege, the concept was not tested in the courts until the 1971 "Watergate" affair. President Richard Nixon refused congressional demands that he turn over secret White House tapes that congressional investigators thought would establish Nixon's complicity in illegal activities. In *United States v. Nixon* (418 U.S. 683, 1974), the Supreme Court ordered Nixon to turn over the tapes. The president complied with the order and was forced to resign from office. The *U.S. v. Nixon* case is often seen as a blow to presidential power but, in actuality, the Court's ruling recognized for the first time the validity of a claim of executive privilege, though holding that it did not apply in this particular instance. Subsequent presidents have cited *U.S. v. Nixon* in support of their claims of executive privilege. For example, the Bush administration successfully invoked executive privilege when it refused congressional demands for records of Vice President Dick Cheney's 2001 energy task force meetings.

Politics Today

In December, 2007, the Senate Judiciary Committee voted contempt citations against the former presidential adviser Karl Rove and the former White House chief of staff Joshua Bolten. The White House claimed that both officials were protected by executive privilege. Members of Congress called this action an abuse of executive power. Do you agree?

THE PRESIDENT'S LEGISLATIVE POWER The president plays a role not only in the administration of government but also in the legislative process. Two constitutional provisions are the primary sources of the president's power in the legislative arena. The first of these is the portion of Article II, Section 3, providing that the president "shall from time to time give to the Congress Information of the State of the Union, and recommend to their Consideration such Measures as he shall judge necessary and expedient." The second of the president's legislative powers is the veto power assigned by Article I, Section 7.[7]

Delivering a "State of the Union" address does not at first appear to be of any great import. It is a mere obligation on the part of the president to make recommendations for Congress's consideration. But as political and social conditions began to favor an increasingly prominent role for presidents, each president, especially since Franklin Delano Roosevelt, began to rely on this provision to become the primary initiator of proposals for legislative action in Congress and the principal source for public awareness of national issues, as well as the most important single individual participant in legislative decisions. Few today doubt that the president and the executive branch together are the primary source for many important congressional actions.[8]

veto the president's constitutional power to turn down acts of Congress. A presidential veto may be overridden by a two-thirds vote of each house of Congress

pocket veto a presidential veto that is automatically triggered if the president does not act on a given piece of legislation passed during the final ten days of a legislative session

The **veto** is the president's constitutional power to turn down acts of Congress (see Figure 13.1). It makes the president the most important single legislative leader.[9] No bill vetoed by the president can become law unless both the House and Senate override the veto by a two-thirds vote. In the case of a **pocket veto,** Congress does not even have the option of overriding the veto, but must reintroduce the bill in the next session. A pocket veto can occur when the president is presented with a bill during the last ten days of a legislative session. Usually, if a president does not sign a bill within ten days, it automatically becomes law. But this is true only while Congress is in session. If a president chooses not to sign a bill presented within the last ten days that Congress is in session, then the ten-day limit does not expire until Congress is out of session, and instead of becoming law, the bill is vetoed. Use of the veto varies according to the political situation that each president confronts. During Bill Clinton's first two years in office, when Democrats controlled both houses of Congress, he vetoed no bills. Following the congressional elections of 1994, however, Clinton confronted a Republican-controlled Congress with a definite agenda, and he began to use his veto power more vigorously. In a similar vein, George W. Bush did not find it necessary to use his veto until 2007, when the Democrats controlled both houses of Congress.

legislative initiative the president's inherent power to bring a legislative agenda before Congress

Although this power is not explicitly stated, the Constitution also provides the president with the power of **legislative initiative.** The framers of the Constitution clearly saw legislative initiative as one of the keys to executive power. Initiative implies the ability to formulate proposals for important policies, and the president, as an individual with a great deal of staff assistance, is able to initiate decisive action more frequently than Congress, with its large assemblies that have to deliberate and debate before taking action. With some important exceptions, Congress banks on the president to set the agenda of public policy. And quite clearly, initiative confers power; there is power in being able to set the terms of discourse in the making of public policy.

FIGURE 13.1 ★
The Veto Process

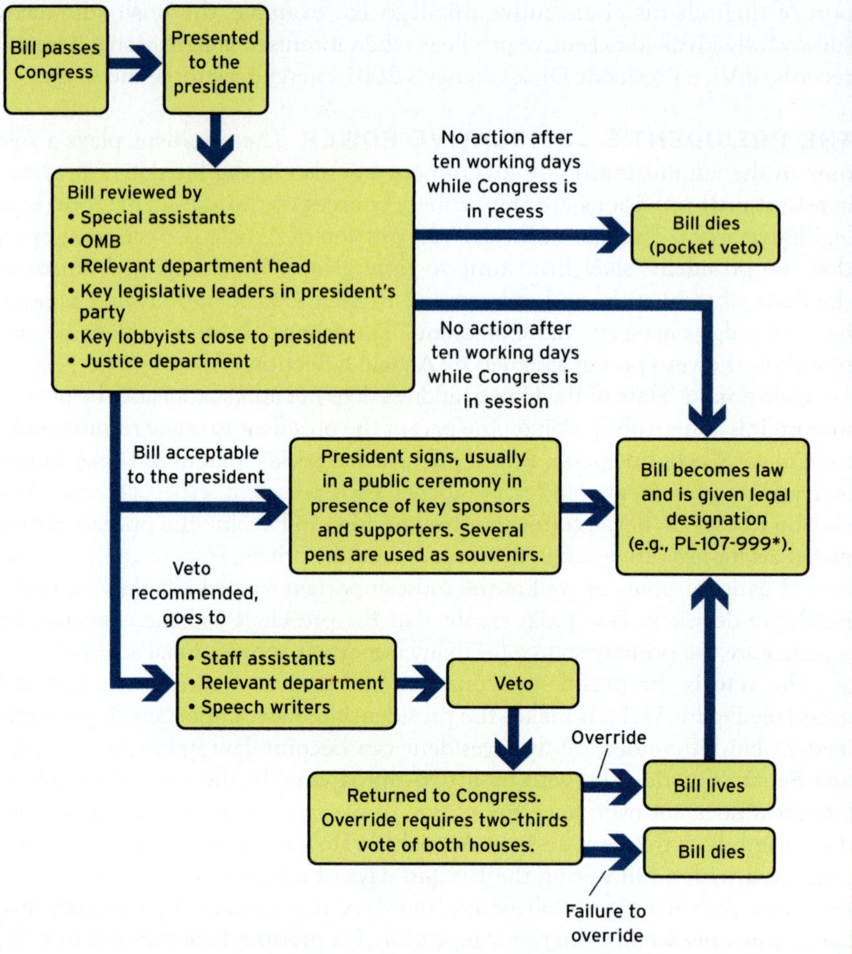

*PL = public law; 107 = number of Congress (107th was 2000–2001); 999 = number of the law.

For example, during the weeks immediately following September 11, George W. Bush took many presidential initiatives to Congress, and each was given almost unanimous support—from commitments to pursue al Qaeda and to the removal of the Taliban, the reconstitution of the Afghanistan regime, all the way to almost unlimited approval for mobilization of both military force and power over the regulation of American civil liberties. After winning re-election in 2004, Bush sought to push forward his legislative domestic agenda, including changes in the nation's Social Security system and comprehensive tax reform. Over the next year, though, the president's political stock plummeted as the administration seemed bewildered by the tenacity of insurgent forces in Iraq and the scope of such domestic calamities as Hurricane Katrina. Bush's policy initiatives in such areas as Social Security and tax reform floundered. After the 2006 elections, Democrats vowed to use their new congressional power to substitute their own agenda for the president's. Although President Bush declared his readiness to work with a Democratic Congress, it seemed clear that the president was also prepared to use his veto power to block Democratic initiatives as well as his executive powers to circumvent the Congress.

The president's initiative does not end with policy making involving Congress and the making of laws in the ordinary sense of the term. The president has still another legislative role (in all but name) within the executive branch. This is designated as the power to issue **executive orders.** The executive order is first and foremost simply a normal tool of management, a power that virtually any CEO has to make "company policy"—rules setting procedures, etiquette, chains of command, functional responsibilities, and so on. But evolving out of this normal management practice is a recognized presidential power to promulgate rules that have the effect and the formal status of legislation. Most presidential executive orders provide for the reorganization of structures and procedures or otherwise direct the affairs of the executive branch—either to be applied across the board to all agencies or applied in some important respect to a single agency or department. One of the most important examples is Executive Order No. 8248, September 8, 1939, establishing the divisions of the Executive Office of the President. Another one of equal importance is President Nixon's executive order establishing the Environmental Protection Agency in 1970–71, which included establishment of the Environmental Impact Statement.

executive order a rule or regulation issued by the president that has the effect and formal status of legislation

This legislative or policy leadership role of the presidency is an institutionalized feature of the office that exists independent of the occupant of the office. That is to say, anyone duly elected president would possess these powers regardless of his or her individual energy or leadership characteristics.[10]

Delegated Powers

Many of the powers exercised by the president and the executive branch are not found in the Constitution but are the products of congressional statutes and resolutions. Over the past century, Congress has voluntarily delegated a great deal of its own legislative authority to the executive branch. To some extent, this delegation of power has been an almost inescapable consequence of the expansion of government activity in the United States since the New Deal. Given the vast range of the federal government's responsibilities, Congress cannot execute and administer all the programs it creates and the laws it enacts. Inevitably, Congress must turn to the hundreds of departments and agencies in the executive branch or, when necessary, create new agencies to implement its goals. Thus, for example, in 2002, when Congress sought to protect America from terrorist attacks, it established a Department of Homeland Security and gave it broad powers in the realms of law enforcement, public health, and immigration. Similarly, in 1970, when Congress enacted legislation designed to improve the nation's air and water quality, it assigned the task of implementing its goals to a new Environmental Protection Agency (EPA) created by an executive order issued by President Nixon. Congress gave the EPA substantial power to set and enforce air- and water-quality standards.

As they implement congressional legislation, federal agencies collectively develop thousands of rules and regulations and issue thousands of orders and findings every year. Agencies interpret Congress's intent, promulgate rules aimed at implementing that intent, and issue orders to individuals, firms, and organizations throughout the nation designed to impel them to conform to the law. When it establishes an agency, Congress sometimes grants it only limited discretionary authority, providing very specific guidelines and standards that must be followed by the administrators charged with the program's implementation. Take the Internal

THE ROLES OF THE PRESIDENT

Chief of State (acting on behalf of all Americans)
Commander in Chief (in charge of military)
Chief Jurist (judicial responsibilities)
Chief Diplomat (managing our relations with other nations)
Chief Executive (as "boss" of executive branch)
Chief Legislator (legislative powers)
Chief Politician (party leadership)

For Critical Analysis

Presidents have expressed, delegated, and inherent sources of power. Which of the three do you think most accounts for the powers of the presidency?

Revenue Service (IRS), for example. Most Americans view the IRS as a powerful agency whose dictates can have an immediate and sometimes unpleasant impact on their lives. Yet congressional tax legislation is very specific and detailed and leaves little to the discretion of IRS administrators.[11] The agency certainly develops numerous rules and procedures to enhance tax collection. It is Congress, however, that establishes the structure of tax liabilities, tax exemptions, and tax deductions that determine each taxpayer's burdens and responsibilities.

In most instances, however, congressional legislation is not very detailed. Often, Congress defines a broad goal or objective and delegates enormous discretionary power to administrators to determine how that goal is to be achieved. For example, the 1970 act creating the Occupational Safety and Health Administration (OSHA) states, as Congress's purpose, "to assure so far as is possible every working man and woman in the nation safe and healthful working conditions." The act, however, neither defines such conditions nor suggests how they might be achieved.[12] The result is that agency administrators have enormous discretionary power to draft rules and regulations that have the effect of law. Indeed, the courts treat these administrative rules like congressional statutes. For all intents and purposes, when Congress creates an agency such as OSHA or the Department of Homeland Security, giving it a broad mandate to achieve some desirable outcome, it transfers its own legislative power to the executive branch.

During the nineteenth and early twentieth centuries, Congress typically wrote laws that provided fairly clear principles and standards to guide executive implementation. For example, the 1923 tariff act empowered the president to increase or decrease duties on certain manufactured goods in order to reduce the difference in costs between domestically produced products and those manufactured abroad. The act authorized the president to make the final determination, but his discretionary authority was quite constrained. The statute listed the criteria the president was to consider, fixed the permissible range of tariff changes, and outlined the procedures to be used to calculate the cost differences between foreign and domestic goods. When an importer challenged a particular executive decision as an abuse of delegated power, the Supreme Court had no difficulty finding that the president was merely acting in accordance with Congress's directives.[13]

At least since the New Deal, however, Congress has tended to give executive agencies broad mandates and to draft legislation that offers few clear standards or guidelines for implementation by the executive. For example, the 1933 National Industrial Recovery Act gave the president the authority to set rules to bring about *fair competition* in key sectors of the economy without ever defining what the term meant or how it was to be achieved.[14] Similarly, the 1938 Agricultural Adjustment Act, which led to a system of commodity price supports and agricultural production restrictions, authorized the secretary of agriculture to make agricultural marketing "orderly" without offering any guidance regarding the commodities to be affected, how markets were to be organized, or how prices should be determined. All these decisions were left to the discretion of the secretary and his agents.[15] This pattern of broad delegation became typical in the ensuing decades. The 1972 Consumer Product Safety Act, for example, authorizes the Consumer Product Safety Commission to reduce unreasonable risk of injury from household products but offers no suggestions to guide the commission's determination of what constitutes reasonable and unreasonable risks or how these are to be reduced.[16]

This shift from the nineteenth-century pattern of relatively well-defined congressional guidelines for administrators to the more contemporary pattern of broad

Movies, Television, and Perceptions of the American Presidency

Since the 1990s, numerous films and at least one television program have focused on the personal lives of fictional presidents and the inner workings of the White House. Whether dramas, thrillers, or comedies, these stories have depicted the president as a human being with personal flaws, insecurities, and often, romantic love interests. While such fictional portrayals are designed to entertain, research suggests that they may also inadvertently shape our perceptions of real-world presidents.

In 1993, Kevin Kline played "Dave," a presidential look-alike recruited to substitute for the actual president, Bill Mitchell, who was incapacitated by a stroke. 1995's *The American President*, starring Michael Douglas, portrays the president struggling with human situations such as raising a child and trying to impress a new love interest, and concludes with his principled defense of his romantic relationship, in spite of its possible effects on his popularity. Although primarily an action-thriller, 1997's *Air Force One*, starring Harrison Ford as the fictional President Marshall, also reveals a family man behind the persona of the commander in chief.

In addition to the many films portraying the private life of the president, the television drama *The West Wing* featured the public and personal life of fictional president Josiah Bartlet (played by Martin Sheen). Among the various plotlines focusing on the president's personal life are his struggle with multiple sclerosis, his relationship with his wife, and his relationship with his grown children. *The West Wing* is particularly notable for the extent to which it emphasizes President Bartlet's personal characteristics—his sense of humor, his warmth towards his friends, family, and staff, his intelligence, and his strong principles. As the political communication scholar Lance Holbert and his coauthors note, "Put simply, *The West Wing* is most directly about character."[a]

Holbert and his colleagues conducted an experiment exploring how exposure to *The West Wing* affects the way people think about public officials and the presidency. They also looked at how the program affected people's views on the traits necessary to be a successful president. The researchers found that after viewing *The West Wing*, participants in the experiment saw President George W. Bush and former President Bill Clinton more favorably than they had prior to watching the show. They also found that watching *The West Wing* made viewers more inclined to judge public officials on the basis of personal character. "*The West Wing* viewers, after viewing the show, tended to think being compassionate, warm, funny, and loving is more important to being a successful president."[b]

Although fictional portrayals of the presidency as in *The West Wing* certainly entertain viewers, they also seem to promote a more positive view of the executive branch. These findings support the claim that movies and entertainment television may "prime" viewers to look at politics and politicians in a certain way.

FOR CRITICAL ANALYSIS

1. In recent presidential elections, many voters have reported basing their decision on the candidates' "character" rather than policy positions and experience. What are the pros and cons of choosing a president based on his or her perceived character?
2. Do fictional portrayals of the presidency that emphasize personal character have a negative effect on democracy by discouraging viewers from thinking about serious policy issues? Or do they engage viewers in politics and thus encourage participation?

a. R. L. Holbert, W. Pillion, D. A. Tschida, G. G. Armfield, K. Kinder, D. L. Cherry, and A. R. Daulton, "*The West Wing* as Endorsement of the U.S. Presidency: Expanding the Bounds of Priming in Political Communication," *Journal of Communication* 53 (2003): 427–43.
b. Holbert et al., "*The West Wing* as Endorsement of the U.S. Presidency."

delegations of congressional power to the executive branch is, to be sure, partially a consequence of the great scope and complexity of the tasks that America's contemporary government has undertaken. During much of the nineteenth century, the federal government had relatively few domestic responsibilities and Congress could pay close attention to details. Today, the operation of an enormous executive establishment and literally thousands of programs under varied and changing circumstances requires that administrators be allowed some considerable measure of discretion to carry out their jobs. Nevertheless, the end result is to shift power from Congress to the executive branch.

THE CABINET DEPARTMENTS

DEPARTMENT	YEAR CREATED
State	1789
Treasury	1789
Defense[*]	1947
Justice	1789
Interior[†]	1862
Agriculture	1889
Commerce	1913
Labor	1913
Health and Human Services[‡]	1953
Housing and Urban Development	1965
Transportation	1966
Energy	1977
Education	1979
Veterans Affairs	1989
Homeland Security	2002

[*]Formerly the War and Navy Departments, created in 1789 and 1798, respectively.
[†]Created in 1862; made part of Cabinet in 1889.
[‡]Formerly Health, Education, and Welfare; reorganized in 1979 (when separate Department of Education was created).

The Presidency as an Institution

The framers of the Constitution, as we saw, created a unitary executive because they thought this would make the presidency a more energetic institution. Nevertheless, since the ratification of the Constitution, the president has been joined by thousands of officials and staffers who work for, assist, or advise the chief executive (see Figure 13.2). Collectively, these individuals could be said to make up the institutional presidency and to give the president a capacity for action that no single individual, however energetic, could duplicate. The first component of the institutional presidency is the president's Cabinet.

The Cabinet

In the American system of government, the **Cabinet** is the traditional but informal designation for the heads of all the major federal government departments. The Cabinet has no constitutional status. Unlike in Great Britain and many other parliamentary countries, where the cabinet *is* the government, the American Cabinet is not a collective body. It meets but makes no decisions as a group. Each appointment must be approved by the Senate, but Cabinet members are not responsible to the Senate or to Congress at large. Cabinet appointments help build party and popular support, but the Cabinet is not a party organ. The Cabinet is made up of directors, but is not a true board of directors.

Since Cabinet appointees generally have not shared political careers with the president or with each other, and since they may meet literally for the first time after their selection, the formation of an effective governing group out of this motley collection of appointments is unlikely. Although President Clinton's insistence on a Cabinet diverse enough to resemble American society could be considered an act of political wisdom, it virtually guaranteed that few of his appointees had ever spent much time working together or even knew the policy positions or beliefs of the other appointees.[17]

Some presidents have relied more heavily on an "inner Cabinet," the **National Security Council (NSC).** The NSC, established by law in 1947, is composed of the president, the vice president, the secretaries of state, defense, and the treasury, the attorney general, and other officials invited by the president. It has its own staff of foreign-policy specialists run by the special assistant to the president for national security affairs. For these highest appointments, presidents often turn to people from outside Washington, usually longtime associates. Former president George W. Bush's "inner Cabinet" was composed largely of former senior staffers and Cabinet members of previous Republican administrations, notably Vice President Dick Cheney, Defense Secretary Robert

Cabinet the secretaries, or chief administrators, of the major departments of the federal government. Cabinet secretaries are appointed by the president with the consent of the Senate

National Security Council (NSC) a presidential foreign-policy advisory council composed of the president; the vice president; the secretaries of state, defense, and the treasury; the attorney general; and other officials invited by the president

FIGURE 13.2 ★ The Institutional Presidency

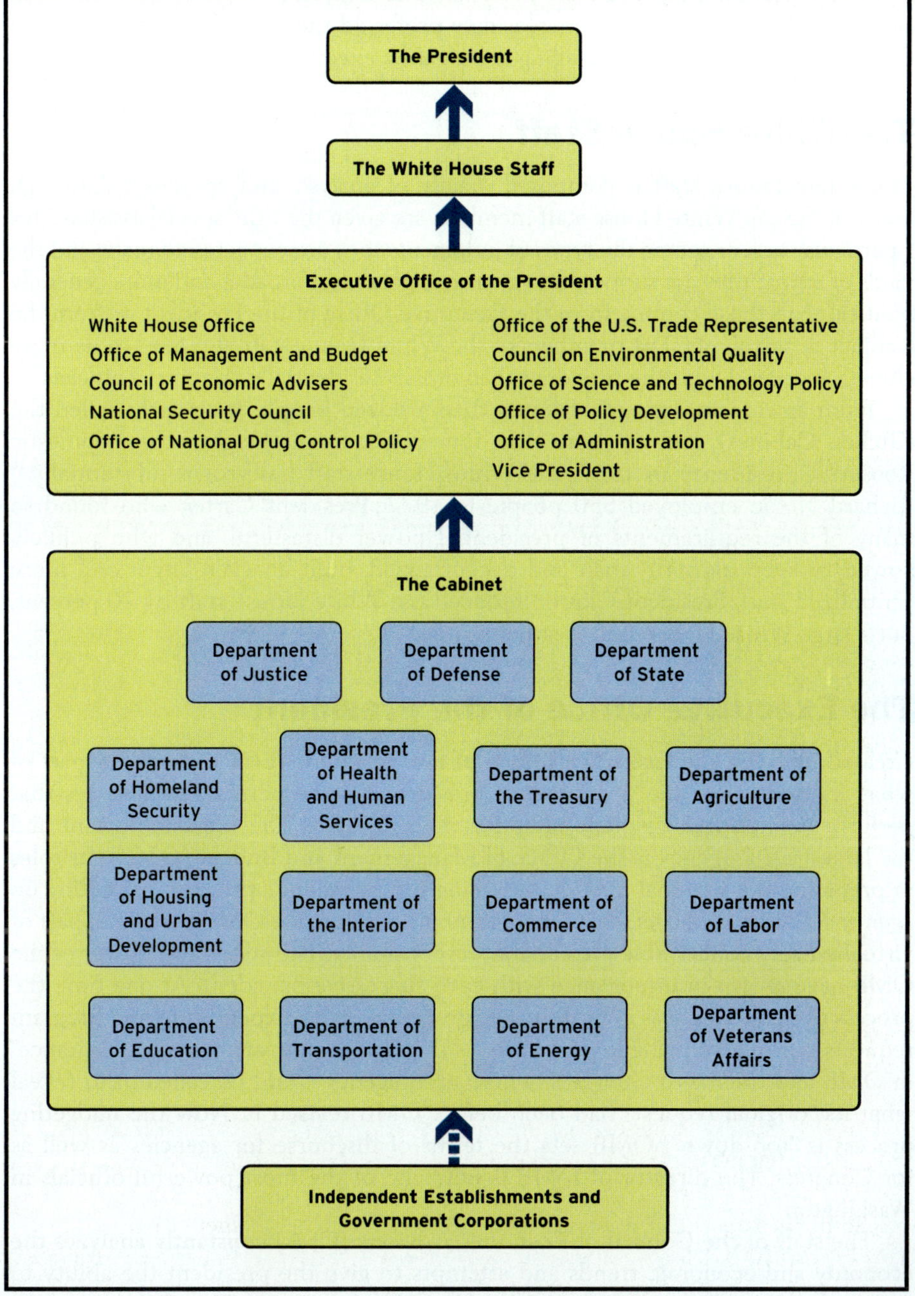

Gates, and Secretary of State Condoleezza Rice. President Bush's penchant for relying on trusted staffers to fill important posts became especially apparent in 2005 when he nominated his long-time legal adviser, Harriet Miers, to the Supreme Court. Miers seemed unqualified for the appointment, and the president was forced to withdraw the nomination after even many of his allies accused him of "cronyism."

Presidents have obviously been uneven and unpredictable in their reliance on the NSC and other subcabinet bodies because executive management is inherently a personal matter. Despite all the personal variations, however, one generalization can be made: presidents have increasingly preferred the White House staff to the Cabinet as their means of managing the gigantic executive branch.

The White House Staff

White House staff analysts and advisers to the president, often given the title "special assistant"

The **White House staff** is composed mainly of analysts and advisers.[18] Although many of the top White House staff members are given the title "special assistant" for a particular task or sector, the types of judgments they are expected to make and the kinds of advice they are supposed to give are a good deal broader and more generally political than those coming from the Executive Office of the President or from the Cabinet departments. The members of the White House staff also tend to be more closely associated with the president than other presidentially appointed officials.

Kitchen Cabinet an informal group of advisers to whom the president turns for counsel and guidance. Members of the official Cabinet may or may not also be members of the Kitchen Cabinet

From an informal group of fewer than a dozen people (popularly called the **Kitchen Cabinet**), and no more than four dozen at the height of the domestic Roosevelt presidency in 1937, the White House staff has grown substantially.[19] Richard Nixon employed 550 people in 1972. President Carter, who found so many of the requirements of presidential power distasteful, and who publicly vowed to keep his staff small and decentralized, built an even larger and more centralized staff. President Clinton reduced the White House staff by 20 percent, but a large White House staff is still essential.

The Executive Office of the President

Executive Office of the President (EOP) the permanent agencies that perform defined management tasks for the president. Created in 1939, the EOP includes the Office of Management and Budget, the Council of Economic Advisers, the National Security Council, and other agencies

Created in 1939, the **Executive Office of the President (EOP)** is a major part of what is often called the "institutional presidency"—the permanent agencies that perform defined management tasks for the president. The most important and the largest EOP agency is the Office of Management and Budget (OMB). Its roles in preparing the national budget, designing the president's program, reporting on agency activities, and overseeing regulatory proposals make OMB personnel part of virtually every conceivable presidential responsibility. The status and power of the OMB have grown in importance with each successive president. At one time the process of budgeting was a "bottom-up" procedure, with expenditure and program requests passing from the lowest bureaus through the departments to "clearance" in OMB and thence to Congress, where each agency could be called in to reveal what its "original request" had been before OMB revised it. Now the budgeting process is "top-down": OMB sets the terms of discourse for agencies as well as for Congress. The director of OMB is now one of the most powerful officials in Washington.

The staff of the Council of Economic Advisers (CEA) constantly analyzes the economy and economic trends and attempts to give the president the ability to anticipate events rather than waiting and reacting to events. The Council on Environmental Quality was designed to do for environmental issues what the CEA does for economic issues. The National Security Council (NSC) is composed of designated Cabinet officials who meet regularly with the president to give advice on the large national security picture. The staff of the NSC assimilates and analyzes data from all intelligence-gathering agencies (CIA, etc.). Other EOP agencies perform more specialized tasks.

Somewhere between 1,500 and 2,000 highly specialized people work for EOP agencies.[20] The importance of each agency in the EOP varies according to the personal orientation of each president. For example, the NSC staff was of immense importance under President Nixon, especially because it served essentially as the personal staff of the presidential assistant Henry Kissinger. But it was of less importance to President George H. W. Bush, who looked outside the EOP altogether for military policy matters, turning much more to the Joint Chiefs of Staff and its chair at the time, General Colin Powell. Powell later served as Secretary of State under President George W. Bush.

The Vice Presidency

The vice presidency is a constitutional anomaly even though the office was created along with the presidency by the Constitution. The vice president exists for two purposes only: to succeed the president in case of death, resignation, or incapacitation and to preside over the Senate, casting a tie-breaking vote when necessary.[21]

The main value of the vice presidency as a political resource for the president is electoral. Traditionally, a presidential candidate's most important guideline in choosing a running mate is that he or she bring the support of at least one state (preferably a large one) not otherwise likely to support the ticket. Another guideline holds that the vice-presidential nominee should provide some regional balance and, wherever possible, some balance among various ideological or ethnic subsections of the party. It is very doubtful that John Kennedy would have won in 1960 without his vice-presidential candidate, Lyndon Johnson, and the contribution Johnson made to winning in Texas. Barack Obama chose Senator Joseph Biden of Delaware to be his running mate for a number of reasons. To begin with, Biden is Catholic and has blue-collar origins. Obama hoped that Biden would appeal to these important groups in such must-win states as Pennsylvania and Ohio. Perhaps

Vice President Joseph Biden had thirty-five years' experience in the Senate before Barack Obama nominated him as his running mate. In particular, Biden's foreign policy experience was seen as an important strength in the campaign and the Obama administration.

Throughout history, presidential spouses have played an important role in White House initiatives. Eleanor Roosevelt was the first first lady to hold regular press conferences; she served as the administration's spokesperson on matters pertaining to race relations and human rights.

even more important, Biden possessed enormous foreign policy experience and chaired the Senate Foreign Relations Committee. The Republicans had often pointed to Obama's lack of experience in the international realm as indicating that he was not ready to be president. Democrats hoped that Biden's presence on the ticket would put the "experience" issue to rest. Indeed, after John McCain designated Sarah Palin to be his vice-presidential running mate, Republicans found it difficult to claim that their ticket was more experienced than that of the Democrats.

As the institutional presidency has grown in size and complexity, most presidents of the past twenty-five years have sought to use their vice presidents as a management resource after the election. George H. W. Bush, as vice president, was "kept within the loop" of decision making because President Reagan delegated so much power. A copy of virtually everything made for Reagan was made for Bush, especially during the first term, when Bush's close friend James Baker was chief of staff. Former President Bush did not take such pains to keep Dan Quayle "in the loop," but President Clinton relied greatly on his vice president, Al Gore, and Gore emerged as one of the most trusted and effective figures in the Clinton White House. Gore's most important task was to oversee the National Performance Review (NPR), an ambitious program to "reinvent" the way the federal government conducts its affairs. The presidency of George W. Bush resulted in unprecedented power and responsibility for his vice president, Dick Cheney, who is viewed as one of the most influential, if not the most influential, vice presidents in American history.

The vice president is also important because, in the event of the death or incapacity of the president, he or she will succeed to the nation's highest office. During the course of American history, six vice presidents have had to replace presidents who died in office. One vice president—Gerald Ford—found himself at the head of the nation when President Richard Nixon was forced to resign as a result of the Watergate scandal. During the 2004 vice-presidential debates, Dick Cheney reminded Americans of the importance of the succession when he sought to distinguish himself from the Democratic vice-presidential nominee, John Edwards, by averring that he, unlike the less-experienced Edwards, had been chosen for his ability to serve as president if that became necessary.

Until the ratification of the Twenty-fifth Amendment in 1965, the succession of the vice president to the presidency was a tradition, launched by John Tyler when he assumed the presidency after William Henry Harrison's death, rather than a constitutional or statutory requirement. The Twenty-fifth Amendment codified this tradition by providing that the vice president would assume the presidency in the event of the chief executive's death or incapacity and setting forth the procedures that would be followed. In the event that both the president and vice president are killed, the Presidential Succession Act of 1947 establishes an order of succession, beginning with the Speaker of the House and continuing with the president of the Senate and the cabinet secretaries. This piece of legislation was adopted during the Cold War and prompted by fear of a nuclear attack. It has, however, taken on new importance in an age of global terrorism.

The First Spouse

During the 2008 presidential race, Michelle Obama campaigned for her husband, speaking at rallies and appearing on talk shows. Her legal and policy background suggested that she would likely take an active role as first lady.

The president serves as both chief executive and chief of state—the equivalent of Great Britain's prime minister and king rolled into one, simultaneously leading the government and serving as a symbol of the nation at official ceremonies and functions. Traditionally, most first ladies limited their activities to the ceremonial portion of the presidency. They greeted foreign dignitaries, visited other countries, and attended important national ceremonies.

Because they are generally associated exclusively with the head-of-state aspect of America's presidency, presidential spouses are usually not subject to the same sort of media scrutiny or partisan attack as that aimed at the president. However, some first spouses have had more influence over policy. Franklin Roosevelt's wife, Eleanor, was widely popular, but also widely criticized, for her active role in many elements of her husband's presidency. She was a tireless advocate for the poor, the working class, and African Americans. She was also the first first lady to hold a government post—assistant director of the Office of Civilian Defense (an agency that existed during World War II). Lyndon Johnson's wife, Lady Bird, headed the national campaign to beautify America. Hillary Clinton played a major political and policy role in Bill Clinton's presidency. During the 1992 campaign, Bill Clinton often implied that she would be active in the administration by joking that voters would get "two for the price of one." After the election, Hillary took a leading role in many policy areas, most notably heading the administration's health care reform effort. Like Eleanor Roosevelt, Hillary Clinton was fiercely criticized for exercising too much influence over her husband's administration. She also became the first first lady to seek public office on her own when she won a seat in the U.S. Senate in 2000 and then ran for president in 2008. President George W. Bush's wife, Laura, assumed the more traditional role of behind-the-scenes adviser and spokesperson for worthy causes such as the improvement of school libraries. Barack Obama's wife, Michelle, is an attorney and served for a number of years as a senior administrator at the University of Chicago's Pritzker School of Medicine. Given her legal and policy background, Michelle Obama seemed likely to become a visible and activist first lady on the Hillary Clinton model.

The President and Policy

The president's powers and institutional resources, taken together, give the chief executive a substantial voice in the nation's policy-making processes. Strictly speaking, presidents cannot introduce legislation. Only members of Congress can formally propose new programs and policies. Nevertheless, a great many of the major bills acted on by the Congress are crafted by the president and his aides and then introduced by friendly legislators. Congress has come to expect the president to propose the government's budget, and the nation has come to expect presidential initiatives to deal with major problems. Some of these initiatives have come in the form of huge packages of programs—Franklin Roosevelt's "New Deal" and Lyndon Johnson's "Great Society." Sometimes presidents craft a single program they hope will have a significant impact on the nation and on their political fortunes. For example, Bill Clinton developed a major health-care reform initiative whose political defeat marked a significant setback for his presidency. George W. Bush made the "war on terrorism" the centerpiece of his administration. To fight this war, Bush brought about the creation of a new cabinet department—the Department of Homeland Security—and the enactment of such pieces of legislation as the USA PATRIOT Act to give the executive branch more power to deal with the terrorist threat. Going beyond terrorism, Bush also presided over a huge expansion of the Medicare program to provide prescription drug benefits for senior citizens. All this was achieved by a president who was said to lack a popular **mandate** in the wake of the controversial 2000 election. Bush may have lacked a mandate, but the expressed and delegated powers of the office gave him the resources through which to prevail.

mandate a claim by a victorious candidate that the electorate has given him or her special authority to carry out promises made during the campaign

At one time, historians and journalists liked to debate the question of strong versus weak presidents. Some presidents, such as Lincoln and FDR, were called "strong" for their leadership and their ability to guide the nation's political agenda. Others, such as Buchanan and Coolidge, were seen as "weak" for failing to develop significant legislative programs and seeming to observe rather than shape political events. Today, the strong-versus-weak categorization has become moot. *Every president is strong.* This strength is not so much a function of personal charisma or political savvy as it is a reflection of the increasing power of the institution of the presidency. Let us see how this came about.

The Contemporary Bases of Presidential Power

During the nineteenth century, Congress was America's dominant institution of government, and members of Congress sometimes treated the president with disdain. Today, however, no one would assert that the presidency is an unimportant institution. Presidents seek to dominate the policy-making process and claim the inherent power to lead the nation in time of war. The expansion of presidential power over the course of the past century has not come about by accident but as the result of an ongoing effort by successive presidents to enlarge the powers of the office. Some of these efforts have succeeded and others have failed. As the framers of the Constitution predicted, presidential *ambition* has been a powerful and unrelenting force in American politics.

Generally, presidents can expand their power in three ways: party, popular mobilization, and administration. In the first instance, presidents may construct or strengthen national partisan institutions with which to exert influence in the legislative process and through which to implement their programs. Alternatively, or in addition to the first tactic, presidents may use popular appeals to create a mass base of support that will allow them to subordinate their political foes. This tactic is called "going public."[22] Third, presidents may seek to bolster their control of established executive agencies or to create new administrative institutions and procedures that will reduce their dependence on Congress and give them a more independent governing and policy-making capability. Presidents' use of executive orders to achieve their policy goals in lieu of seeking to persuade Congress to enact legislation is, perhaps, the most obvious example.

Party as a Source of Power

All presidents have relied on the members and leaders of their own party to implement their legislative agendas. President George W. Bush, for example, worked closely with congressional GOP leaders on such matters as energy policy and Medicare reform. But the president does not control his own party; party members have considerable autonomy. Moreover, in America's system of separated powers, the president's party may be in the minority in Congress and unable to do much for the chief executive's programs (see Figure 13.3). Consequently, although their party is valuable to chief executives, it has not been a fully reliable presidential tool. As a result, contemporary presidents are more likely to use two other methods—popular mobilization and executive administration—to achieve their political goals.

Going Public

Popular mobilization as a technique of presidential power has its historical roots in the presidencies of Theodore Roosevelt and Woodrow Wilson and has, subsequently, become a weapon in the political arsenals of most presidents since the mid-twentieth century. During the nineteenth century, it was considered inappropriate for presidents to engage in personal campaigning on their own behalf or in support of programs and policies. When Andrew Johnson broke this unwritten rule and made a series of speeches vehemently seeking public support for his Reconstruction program, even

FIGURE 13.3 ★ The Presidential Batting Average: Presidential Success on Congressional Votes* (1953–2007)

Presidents have more success in Congress when their party is in the majority. Can you identify the periods when presidents had majority support in Congress and when they did not?

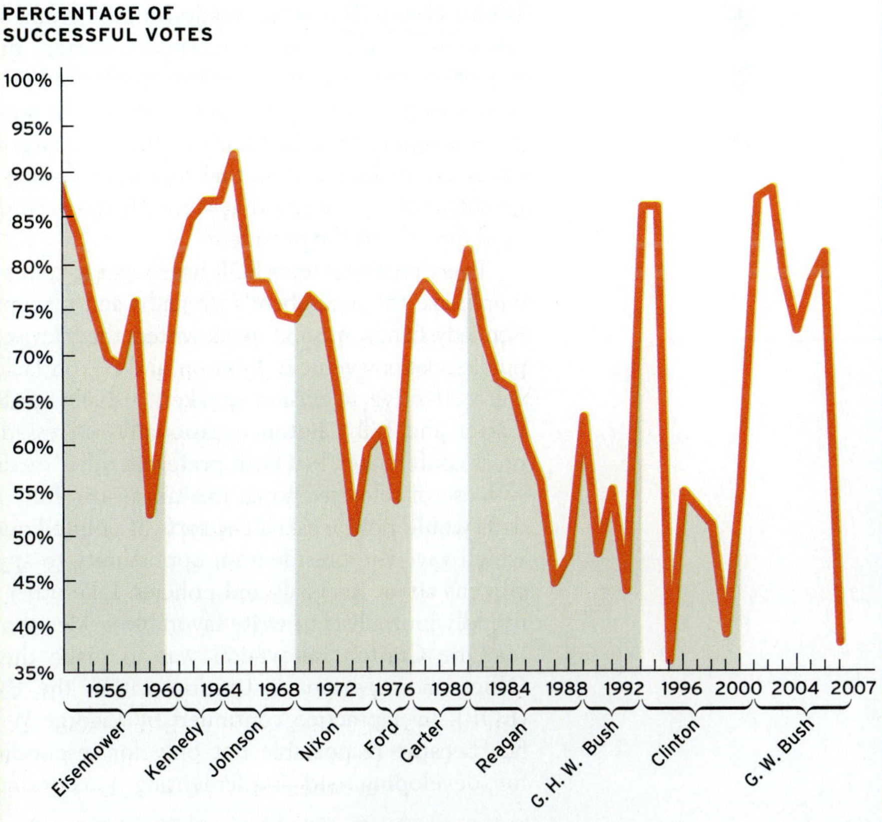

*Percentages based on votes on which presidents took a position.
SOURCE: *Congressional Quarterly Weekly Report*, January 14, 2008, p. 133

some of Johnson's most ardent supporters were shocked at what they saw as his lack of decorum and dignity. The president's opponents cited his "inflammatory" speeches in one of the articles of impeachment drafted by the Congress pursuant to the first effort in American history to oust an incumbent president.[23]

The first presidents to make systematic use of appeals to the public were Theodore Roosevelt and Woodrow Wilson, but the president who used public appeals most effectively was Franklin Delano Roosevelt. The political scientist Sydney Milkis observes that FDR was "firmly persuaded of the need to form a direct link between the executive office and the public."[24] Roosevelt developed a number of tactics aimed at forging such a link. Like his predecessors, he often embarked on speaking trips around the nation to promote his programs. On one such tour, he told a crowd, "I regain strength just by meeting the American people."[25] In addition, FDR made limited but important use of the new electronic medium, the radio, to reach millions of Americans. In his famous "fireside chats," the president, or at least his voice, came into every living room in the country to discuss programs and policies and generally to assure Americans that Franklin Delano Roosevelt was aware of their difficulties and working diligently toward solutions.

Roosevelt was also an innovator in the realm of what now might be called press relations. When he entered the White House, FDR faced a mainly hostile press typically controlled by conservative members of the business establishment. As the president wrote, "All the fat-cat newspapers—85 percent of the whole—have been utterly opposed to everything the Administration is seeking."[26] Roosevelt hoped to be able to use the press to mold public opinion, but to do so he needed to circumvent the editors and publishers who were generally unsympathetic to his goals. To this end, the president worked to cultivate the reporters who covered the White House. Roosevelt made himself available for biweekly press conferences where he offered candid answers to reporters' questions and made certain to make important policy announcements that would provide the reporters with significant stories to file with their papers.[27] Roosevelt was the first president to designate a press secretary (Stephen Early) who was charged with organizing the press conferences and making certain that reporters observed the informal rules distinguishing presidential comments that were off the record from those that could be attributed directly to the president.

Every president since FDR has sought to craft a public-relations strategy that would emphasize the incumbent's strengths and maximize his popular appeal. For John F. Kennedy, handsome and quick witted, the televised press conference was an excellent public-relations vehicle. Johnson and Nixon lacked Kennedy's charisma, but both were effective television speakers, usually reading from a prepared text. Jimmy Carter and Bill Clinton occasionally addressed the nation and sometimes held press conferences, but both preferred other media formats. Both men made extensive use of televised town meetings—carefully staged events in which the president would not be asked the sorts of pointed questions preferred by reporters and which gave the president an opportunity to appear to consult with rank-and-file citizens about his goals and policies. Like other presidents, Clinton also relied on friendly journalists to write favorable stories about the administration.

One Clinton innovation was to make the White House Communications Office an important institution within the Executive Office of the President (EOP). In a practice continued by George W. Bush, the Communications Office became responsible not only for responding to reporters' queries but also for developing and implementing a coordinated communications strategy—

promoting the president's policy goals, developing responses to unflattering news stories, and making certain that a favorable image of the president would, insofar as possible, dominate the news. The Communications Office, in effect, institutionalized the functions undertaken on an ad hoc basis by media-savvy presidents, such as the Roosevelts, and their staffers. George W. Bush's first communications director, Karen Hughes, sought to put the office "ahead of the news," constantly developing stories that would dominate the headlines, present the president in a favorable light, and deflect criticism.

President Franklin Delano Roosevelt's direct appeals to the American people allowed FDR to "reach over the heads" of congressional opponents and force them to follow his lead because their constituents demanded it.

THE LIMITS OF GOING PUBLIC Some presidents have been able to make effective use of popular appeals to overcome congressional opposition. Popular support, though, has not been a firm foundation for presidential power. The public is notoriously fickle. President George W. Bush maintained an approval rating of over 70 percent for more than a year following the September 11 terrorist attacks. By the end of 2005, however, President Bush's approval rating had dropped to 39 percent as a result of the growing unpopularity of the Iraq war, the administration's inept handling of hurricane relief, and several White House scandals, including the conviction of Vice President Cheney's chief of staff on charges of lying to a federal grand jury. After America's triumph in the 1990 Persian Gulf War, President George H. W. Bush scored a remarkable 90 percent approval rating in the polls. Two years later, however, after the 1991 budget crisis, Bush's support plummeted and the president was defeated in his bid for re-election. During his first two years in office, Ronald Reagan's approval score ranged from a high of 59 percent in 1981 to a low of 37 percent in early 1983.[28] As Reagan's poll standing fell, his ability to overawe Democratic opponents and retain the support of wavering Republicans diminished sharply. Such declines in popular approval during a president's term in office are nearly inevitable and follow a predictable pattern (see Figure 13.4).[29] Presidents generate popular support by promising to undertake important programs that will contribute directly to the well-being of large numbers of Americans. Almost inevitably, presidential performance falls short of promises and popular expectations, leading to a sharp decline in public support and the ensuing collapse of presidential influence.[30]

Presidents have certainly not abandoned "going public," but they no longer do so as frequently as they once did—there has been, for example, a decline in presidential appearances on prime-time television over the past five administrations.[31] Instead, presidents have employed institutionalized public and media relations efforts more to create a generally favorable public image than to promote specific policies. Thus, in 2002, President George W. Bush made several speeches to boost the proposed creation of a Homeland Security department. Similarly, in 2007, President Bush made a number of speeches promoting his "surge" strategy, which entailed sending more troops to Iraq. At the same time, however, the White House Communications office was engaged in a nonstop, seven-day-a-week effort to promote news and feature stories aimed at bolstering the president's more general public image. Stories emphasized the president's empathy for retirees hurt by the downturn of stock prices; the president's anger over corporate abuses; the president's concern for the environment; the president's determination to prevent terrorism; the president's support for Israel;

FIGURE 13.4 ★ Presidential Performance Ratings from Kennedy to Bush

In presidential performance rating polls, respondents are asked, "Do you approve of the way the president is handling his job?" This graph shows the percentage of positive responses. As we can see, presidents generally experience broad shifts in popular approval. What factors help to explain changes in presidential approval ratings? Does popular approval really affect presidential power? How can popular feelings about the president affect the president's conduct and influence?

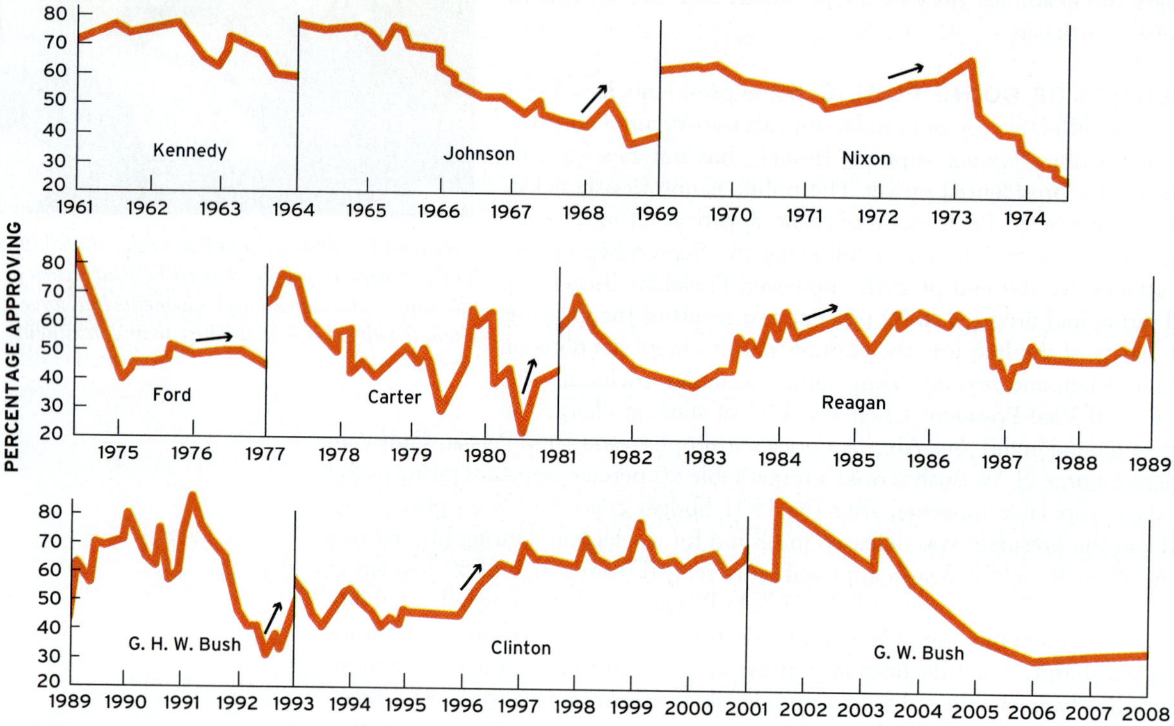

NOTE: Arrows indicate pre-election upswings.

SOURCES: Courtesy of the Gallup Organization and Louis Harris & Associates; 2006 information from CBS/*New York Times* poll, May 9, 2006.

and so forth. These are all examples of image polishing rather than going public on behalf of specific programs. Confronted with the limitations of a strategy of popular mobilization, presidents have shifted from an offensive strategy to a more defensive mode in this domain. The limitations of going public as a route to presidential power have also led contemporary presidents to make use of a third technique: expansion of their administrative capabilities.

The Administrative State

Contemporary presidents have increased the administrative capabilities of their office in three ways. First, they have enhanced the reach and power of the Executive Office of the President (EOP). Second, they have sought to increase White House control over the federal bureaucracy. Third, they have expanded the role of execu-

President Bill Clinton was a master of the televised town meeting, in which the president gives the appearance of consulting average citizens on important policy issues. Clinton's technique illustrated how campaign-style events could become tools to shape and sell national policy.

tive orders and other instruments of direct presidential governance. Taken together, these three components of what might be called the White House "administrative strategy" have given presidents a capacity to achieve their programmatic and policy goals even when they are unable to secure congressional approval. Indeed, some recent presidents have been able to accomplish quite a bit without much congressional, partisan, or even public support.

THE EXECUTIVE OFFICE OF THE PRESIDENT The Executive Office of the President has grown from six administrative assistants in 1939 to today's 400 employees working directly for the president in the White House office along with some 1,400 individuals staffing the several (currently eight) divisions of the Executive Office.[32] The creation and growth of the White House staff gives the president an enormously enhanced capacity to gather information, plan programs and strategies, communicate with constituencies, and exercise supervision over the executive branch. The staff multiplies the president's eyes, ears, and arms, becoming a critical instrument of presidential power.[33]

In particular, the Office of Management and Budget (OMB) serves as a potential instrument of presidential control over federal spending and hence a mechanism through which the White House has greatly expanded its power. The OMB has the capacity to analyze and approve all legislative proposals, not only budgetary requests, emanating from all federal agencies before being submitted to Congress. This procedure, now a matter of routine, greatly enhances the president's control over the entire executive branch. All legislation emanating from the White House as well as all executive orders also go through the OMB.[34] Thus, through one White House agency, the president has the means to exert major influence over the flow of money as well as the shape and content of national legislation.

REGULATORY REVIEW A second tactic that presidents have used to increase their power and reach is the process of regulatory review, through which presidents have sought to seize control of rule making by the agencies of the executive branch (see also Chapter 14). Whenever Congress enacts a statute, its actual implementation requires the promulgation of hundreds of rules by the agency charged with administering the law and giving effect to the will of Congress. Some congressional statutes are quite detailed and leave agencies with relatively little discretion. Typically, however, Congress enacts a relatively broad statement of legislative intent and delegates to the appropriate administrative agency the power to fill in many important details.[35] In other words, Congress typically says to an administrative agency, "Here is the problem: deal with it."[36]

The discretion Congress delegates to administrative agencies has provided recent presidents with an important avenue for expanding their own power. For example, President Clinton believed the president had full authority to order agencies of the executive branch to adopt such rules as the president thought appropriate.

During the course of his presidency, Clinton issued 107 directives to administrators ordering them to propose specific rules and regulations. In some instances, the language of the rule to be proposed was drafted by the White House staff; in other cases, the president asserted a priority but left it to the agency to draft the precise language of the proposal. Presidential rule-making directives covered a wide variety of topics. For example, Clinton ordered the Food and Drug Administration (FDA) to develop rules designed to restrict the marketing of tobacco products to children. White House and FDA staffers then spent several months preparing nearly 1,000 pages of new regulations affecting tobacco manufacturers and vendors.[37] Republicans, of course, denounced Clinton's actions as a usurpation of power.[38] However, after he took office, President George W. Bush made no move to surrender the powers Clinton had claimed—quite the contrary. Bush continued the Clinton-era practice of issuing presidential directives to agencies to spur them to issue new rules and regulations.

GOVERNING BY DECREE: EXECUTIVE ORDERS A third mechanism through which contemporary presidents have sought to enhance their power to govern unilaterally is through the use of executive orders and other forms of presidential decrees, including executive agreements, national security findings and directives, proclamations, reorganization plans, the signing of statements, and a host of others.[39] Executive orders have a long history in the United States and have been the vehicles for a number of important government policies, including the purchase of Louisiana, the annexation of Texas, the emancipation of the slaves, the internment of the Japanese, the desegregation of the military, the initiation of affirmative action, and the creation of important federal agencies, among them the EPA, the FDA, and the Peace Corps.[40]

Although wars and national emergencies produce the highest volume of executive orders, such presidential actions also occur frequently in peacetime (see Figure 13.5). In the realm of foreign policy, unilateral presidential actions in the form of executive agreements have virtually replaced treaties as the nation's chief foreign-policy instruments.[41] Presidential decrees, however, are often used for purely domestic purposes.

FIGURE 13.5 ★
Significant Executive Orders, 1900–1996

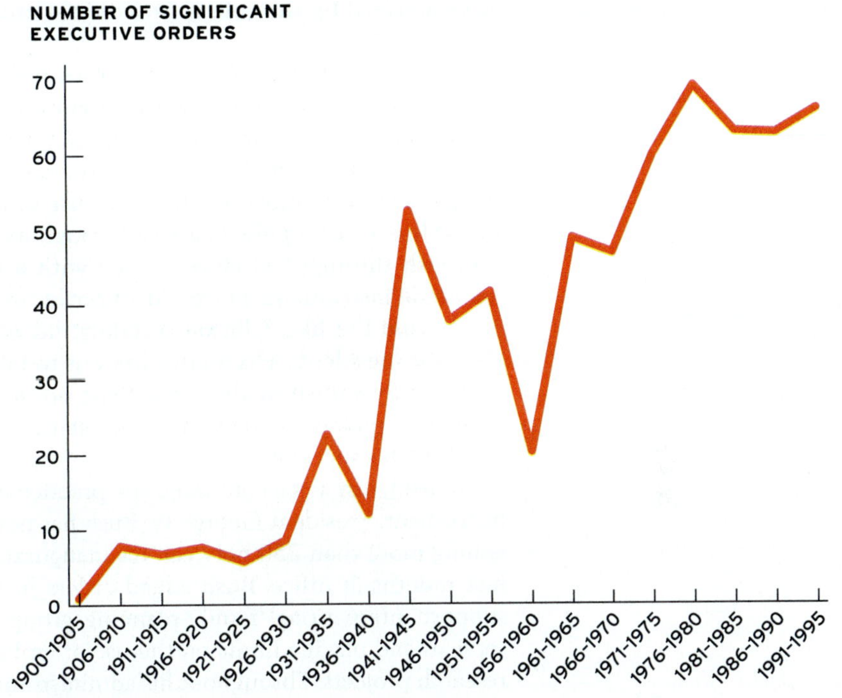

Over the past century, presidents have made increasingly frequent use of executive orders to accomplish their policy goals. What factors explain this development? How has Congress responded to increased presidential assertiveness? What might explain the large number of executive orders issued during the 1940s?

SOURCE: William Howell, "The President's Powers of Unilateral Action: The Strategic Advantages of Acting Alone" (Ph.D. diss., Stanford University, 1999).

Presidents may not use executive orders to issue whatever commands they please. The use of such decrees is bound by law. If a president issues an executive order, proclamation, directive, or the like, in principle he does so pursuant to the powers granted to him by the Constitution or delegated to him by Congress, usually through a statute. When presidents issue such orders, they generally state the constitutional or statutory basis for their actions. For example, when President Truman ordered the desegregation of the armed services, he did so pursuant to his constitutional powers as commander in chief. In a similar vein, when President Johnson issued Executive Order No. 11246, he asserted that the order was designed to implement the 1964 Civil Rights Act, which prohibited employment discrimination. Where an executive order has no statutory or constitutional basis, the courts have held it to be void. The most important case on this point is *Youngstown Co. v. Sawyer*, the so-called steel seizure case of 1952.[42] Here, the Supreme Court ruled that President Truman's seizure of the nation's steel mills during the Korean War had no statutory or constitutional basis and was thus invalid.

A number of court decisions, though, have established broad boundaries that leave considerable room for presidential action. For example, the courts have held that Congress might approve presidential action after the fact or, in effect, ratify presidential action through "acquiescence," by not objecting for long periods of time or by continuing to provide funding for programs established by executive orders. In addition, the courts have indicated that some areas, most notably the realm of military policy, are presidential in character and have allowed presidents wide latitude to make policy by executive decree. Thus, within the very broad limits established by the courts, presidential orders can be and have been important policy tools.

President Clinton issued numerous orders designed to promote a coherent set of policy goals: protecting the environment, strengthening federal regulatory power, shifting America's foreign policy from a unilateral to a multilateral focus, expanding affirmative action programs, and helping organized labor in its struggles with employers.[43] As in his use of regulatory review, President Clinton was able to craft a policy agenda through executive orders that he could not accomplish through legislation. Faced with a hostile Congress, Clinton turned to unilateral instruments of executive power including regulatory review, executive orders, and the like. Clinton certainly did not issue more executive orders than previous presidents. His innovation was to take an instrument that had been used sporadically and show that an activist president could develop and implement a significant policy agenda without legislation—a lesson that surely will not be lost on Clinton's successors.

Indeed, just as he continued the practice of using regulatory review as a policy instrument, President George W. Bush has not hesitated to use executive orders—issuing more than 250 between his inauguration and the end of 2007. During his first months in office, Bush issued orders prohibiting the use of federal funds to support international family-planning groups that provided abortion-counseling services and placing limits on the use of embryonic stem cells in federally funded research projects. Throughout his administration, Bush made very aggressive use of executive orders in response to the threat of terrorism. In November 2001, for example, Bush issued a directive authorizing the creation of military tribunals to try noncitizens accused of involvement in acts of terrorism against the United States. As recently as May 2007, Bush issued controversial national security directives that gave the president sole responsibility for determining when and how constitutional government could be reestablished in the event of a catastrophic attack on the United States.

Although terrorism was certainly at the top of President Bush's agenda, he also issued a number of executive orders having to do with domestic policy. For example, the president was able to overcome congressional resistance to his efforts to increase domestic energy exploration and the rapid exploitation of domestic energy resources. Like Clinton, however, President Bush discovered that an executive order can often substitute for legislation. In May 2001, Bush signed an executive order that closely followed a recommendation from the American Petroleum Institute, an oil industry trade association, to free energy companies from a number of federal regulations. In April 2004, the president signed another executive order supported by the energy industry, expediting the approval process for energy-production and energy-transmission projects.

THE ADVANTAGES OF THE ADMINISTRATIVE STRATEGY Through the course of American history, party leadership and popular appeals have played important roles in presidential efforts to overcome political opposition. Both party and appeals to the people continue to be instruments of presidential power. Reagan's tax cuts and Clinton's budget victories were achieved with strong partisan support. George W. Bush, lacking the oratorical skills of a Reagan or a Roosevelt, nevertheless made good use of sophisticated communications strategies to promote his agenda. Yet, as we saw, in the modern era parties have waned in institutional strength, and the effects of popular appeals have often proven evanescent. The limitations of the alternatives have increasingly impelled presidents to try to expand the administrative capabilities of the office and their own capacity for unilateral action as means of achieving their policy goals. And in recent decades, the expansion of the Executive Office, the development of regulatory review, the use of executive orders, the signing of statements, and the like have given presidents a substantial capacity to achieve significant policy results despite congressional opposition to their legislative agendas.

To be sure, the administrative strategy does not always succeed. In some instances over the years the federal courts have struck down unilateral actions by the president. And, occasionally, Congress acts to reverse presidential orders. For example, in 1999, Congress enacted legislation prohibiting the Department of Education from carrying out a presidential directive to administer national education tests.[44] In 2000, Congress went even a step further. In response to President Clinton's aggressive regulatory review program, the Republican-controlled Congress moved to strengthen its capacity to block the president's use of administrative directives by enacting the Congressional Review Act (CRA). This piece of legislation requires federal agencies to send all proposed regulations to Congress for review sixty days before they take effect. The act also creates a fast-track procedure to allow the House and Senate to enact a joint resolution of disapproval that not only would void the regulation but also would prohibit the agency from subsequently issuing any substantially similar rule. The first test of the act came after Clinton left office. In the early weeks of the Bush administration, Congress passed a joint resolution repealing an ergonomics standard that had been supported by the Clinton administration and adopted by the Occupational Safety and Health Administration (OSHA). President Bush, who opposed the standard, signed the resolution, and the ergonomics standard was voided. Although this outcome may be seen as an effective effort by Congress to thwart a presidential directive, it seems clear that Congress was successful only because Clinton had left office. Had his term not expired, Clinton would almost certainly have vetoed the resolution. Indeed, one reason Clinton was willing to sign CRA into law in the first place was that the president retained the power to veto any action undertaken by Congress under the statute's authority.

In principle, perhaps, Congress could respond more vigorously to unilateral policy making by the president than it has. Certainly a Congress willing to impeach a president should have the mettle to overturn his administrative directives. But the president has significant advantages in such struggles with Congress. In battles over presidential directives and orders, Congress is on the defensive, reacting to presidential initiatives. The framers of the Constitution saw "energy," or the ability to take the initiative, as a key feature of executive power.[45] When the president takes action by issuing an order or an administrative directive, Congress must initiate the cumbersome and time-consuming lawmaking process, overcome internal divisions, and enact legislation that the president may ultimately veto. Moreover, as the political scientist Terry Moe has argued, in such battles Congress faces a significant collective-action problem insofar as members are likely to be more sensitive to the substance of a president's actions and its effects on their constituents than to the more general implications of presidential power for the long-term vitality of their institution.[46]

For Critical Analysis

In recent years, presidents have expanded their power through increased use of executive orders, executive agreements, and other unilateral instruments. Is the United States becoming a "presidential republic"? Is this a development to be feared or welcomed?

In fall 2002, President George W. Bush held several meetings with members of Congress, such as the one shown here in the White House, briefing them on U.S. intelligence on Iraq. In October 2002, Congress adopted a resolution giving the president complete discretion to decide whether to attack Iraq, but the White House made it clear that the president didn't actually need Congress's approval.

Thinking Critically about Presidential Power and Democracy

The framers of the Constitution created a system of government in which the Congress and the executive branch were to share power. At least since the New Deal, however, the powers of Congress have waned, whereas those of the presidency have expanded dramatically. To begin with a recent instance of congressional retreat in the face of presidential assertiveness, in October 2002, pressed by President George W. Bush, both houses of Congress voted overwhelmingly to authorize the White House to use military force against Iraq. The resolution adopted by Congress allowed the president complete discretion to determine whether, when, and how to attack Iraq. The president had rejected language that might have implied even the slightest limitations on his prerogatives. Indeed, Bush's legal advisers had pointedly declared that the president did not actually need specific congressional authorization to attack Iraq if he deemed such action to be in America's interest. "We don't want to be in the legal position of asking Congress to authorize the use of force when the president already has that full authority," said one senior administration official. Few members of Congress even bothered to object to this apparent rewriting of the U.S. Constitution. When the Democrats took control of Congress in 2006, they vowed to bring an end to the Iraq war. Congressional Democrats soon discovered, however, that they possessed little ability to interfere with the president's war policies.

There is no doubt that Congress continues to be able to harass presidents and even, on occasion, to hand the White House a sharp rebuff. In the larger view, however, presidents' occasional defeats—however dramatic—have to be seen as temporary setbacks in a gradual and decisive shift toward increased presidential power in the twenty-first century. Louis Fisher, America's leading authority on the separation of powers, recently observed that in what are arguably the two most important policy arenas, national defense and the federal budget, the powers

Work in the White House

Johanna Atienza was a twenty-year-old junior majoring in political science at a West Coast university when she learned from other students that her school had a Washington, D.C., internship program—and that it included the possibility of working in the White House. She was immediately interested: "What better way is there to learn about politics than from the inside?" She also felt that a semester in the nation's capital would help her to understand if the people who worked in the federal government really cared about the average citizen.

Johanna spent considerable time and effort on the application and then waited for the response. When she received the letter informing her of her acceptance, she was thrilled. In early January, she moved to Washington, D.C., and was assigned to work with the people who scheduled travel for the president and the first lady. Over the next three months, Johanna met and worked with some of the top officials in the White House. She also had the opportunity to meet the president and first lady. Although it was exciting to wander around the maze of offices in the White House, Johanna reports, she was often so busy that she had little time to realize that she was indeed wandering through White House corridors.

What did Johanna learn from her three-month participation in the day-to-day life of White House politics that she was unlikely to learn in a classroom? First, she was struck by the incredible complexity of the presidency and Washington politics. Procedures were detailed and time-consuming. Things moved remarkably slowly, if at all. Second, however, she gained tremendous respect for the people who work in the White House. They were dedicated people who worked long hours, often for little money. Even the older aides worked long hours and devoted themselves to public service.

- ★ If this type of hands-on experience appeals to you, you can apply for the White House internship online at www.whitehouse.gov/government/wh-intern.html. Although each presidential administration varies the exact requirements, in general, students will have to complete an application form that includes several essay questions and is accompanied by two or three letters of recommendation. Once selected, interns must agree to a background check and a random drug test.
- ★ Find out if your college offers course credit for internships in government. Although the internship is unpaid, students can usually arrange to earn course credits for their time and, if they work with their home institution, they can use student loans to help cover the cost of room and board.

If a semester in Washington, D.C., does not fit into your schedule, there are a lot of other ways to learn about the administration's policies and practices.

- ★ Use the White House Web site to learn more about the president's policies. The WH Web page, www.whitehouse.gov, has links to at least a dozen top policy areas, where you can read what the president sees as the problem—and his proposed solution. This is only one side of the story, of course, but it is a good launching pad for further investigation.
- ★ Ask questions through the WH Web site. There are also links that will allow you to ask a question about the historical background for various presidential traditions or submit a more policy-based query about the current administration's stance on a particular issue. If you're unsure what to ask, you can always read through the archive of others' questions—and the answers provided by the president's staff.
- ★ Listen to the president. The president records a weekly radio address that is broadcast on radio stations across the country. You can listen to the most recent recording, or search the archives to hear what the president has to say—in his own words and in his own voice. While some addresses may seem only loosely connected to top issues of the day, others, particularly on key dates or anniversaries, will address more important issues. Both should give you a sense of the range of topics facing our nation's top administrator.

For more than a year after September 11, 2001, President Bush's approval rating remained over 70 percent as the nation rallied behind the president in the war on terror. By 2004, mounting casualties in Iraq led to a significant drop in approval for the president, and by 2006 Bush's approval rating reached a record low of 31 percent.

of Congress have shown a "precipitous decline" for at least the past fifty years. The last occasion on which Congress exercised its constitutional power to declare war was December 8, 1941, and yet, since that time, American forces have been committed to numerous battles on every continent by order of the president. The much-hailed 1973 War Powers Resolution, far from limiting presidential power, actually allowed the president considerably more discretionary authority than he was granted by the Constitution. The War Powers Act gave the president the authority to deploy forces abroad without congressional authority for sixty days. The Constitution, though, seems to require congressional authorization before troops can be deployed for even one day. And presidents have ignored even these stipulations.

As to spending powers, the framers of the Constitution conceived the "power of the purse" to be Congress's most fundamental prerogative. For more than a century this power was jealously guarded by powerful congressional leaders such as the Taft-era House Speaker "Uncle" Joe Cannon, who saw congressional control of the budget as a fundamental safeguard against "Prussian-style" militarism and autocracy. Since the New Deal, however, successive Congresses have yielded to steadily increasing presidential influence over the budget process. In 1939, Congress allowed Franklin D. Roosevelt to take a giant step toward presidential control of the nation's purse strings when it permitted him to bring the Bureau of the Budget (BoB) into the newly created Executive Office of the President. Roosevelt and his successors used the BoB (now called the OMB) effectively to seize the nation's legislative and budgetary agenda. In 1974, Congress attempted to respond to Richard Nixon's efforts to further enhance presidential control of spending when it enacted the Budget and Impoundment Control Act. This piece of legislation centralized Congress's own budgetary process and seemed to reinforce congressional power. Yet, less than ten years later, Congress watched as President Ronald Reagan essentially seized control over the congressional budget process. Subsequently, as Fisher observes, lacking confidence in its own ability to maintain budgetary discipline, Congress has surrendered more and more power to the president.

For Critical Analysis

What factors contributed to the dominance of Congress during the nineteenth century? What factors contributed to the resurgence of the presidency? Which branch of government dominates now? Why do you think so?

Representative assemblies such as the United States Congress derive their influence from the support of groups and forces in civil society that believe these institutions serve their interests. Britain's Parliament ultimately overcame the Crown because it gradually won the confidence and support of the most important forces in civil society. A chief executive, such as the president of the United States, on the other hand, fundamentally derives power from the command of bureaucracies, armies, and the general machinery of the state. Presidents can certainly benefit from popular support. If we imagine, however, a fully demobilized polity in which neither institution could count on much support from forces in civil society, the president would still command the institutions of the state, whereas Congress would be without significant resources. In a fully mobilized polity, on the other hand, Congress might have a chance to counterbalance the president's institutional powers with the support of significant social forces.

A powerful presidency, a weak Congress, and a partially demobilized electorate are a dangerous mix. Presidents have increasingly asserted the right to govern unilaterally and now appear able to overcome most institutional and political constraints. Presidential power, to be sure, can be a force for good. To cite one example from the not-so-distant past, it was President Lyndon Johnson, more than Congress or the judiciary, who faced up to the task of smashing America's apartheid system. Yet, as the framers knew, unchecked power is always dangerous. Americans of the founding generation feared that unchecked presidential power would lead to *monocracy*—a republican form of monarchy without a king. Have we not taken more than one step in that direction? Inevitably, we will pay a price for our undemocratic politics.

For Critical Analysis

The presidency and the Congress are both democratic institutions. Which is the more democratic of the two? Why?

FOR FURTHER READING

Aberbach, Joel, and Mark Peterson, eds. *The Executive Branch.* New York: Oxford University Press, 2005.

Barber, James David. *The Presidential Character.* Englewood Cliffs, NJ: Prentice-Hall, 1992.

Crenson, Matthew, and Benjamin Ginsberg. *Presidential Power: Unchecked and Unbalanced.* New York: Norton, 2007.

Draper, Robert. *Dead Certain: The Presidency of George Bush.* New York: Free Press, 2007.

Edwards, George. *Why the Electoral College is Bad for America.* New Haven, CT: Yale University Press, 2004.

Hayes, Stephen F. *Cheney: The Untold Story of America's Most Powerful and Controversial Vice President.* New York: HarperCollins, 2007.

Lowi, Theodore J. *The Personal President: Power Invested, Promise Unfulfilled.* Ithaca, NY: Cornell University Press, 1985.

Milkis, Sidney M. *The President and the Parties: The Transformation of the American Party System since the New Deal.* New York: Oxford University Press, 1993.

Neustadt, Richard E. *Presidential Power: The Politics of Leadership from Roosevelt to Reagan.* Rev. ed. New York: Free Press, 1990.

Savage, Charles. *Takeover: The Return of the Imperial Presidency.* Boston: Little, Brown, 2007.

Skowronek, Stephen. *The Politics Presidents Make: Leadership from John Adams to Bill Clinton.* Cambridge, MA: The Belknap Press of Harvard University Press, 1997.

Yoo, John. *The Powers of War and Peace.* Chicago: University of Chicago Press, 2005.

RECOMMENDED WEB SITES

Almanac of Policy Issues: War Powers Resolution
www.policyalmanac.org/world/archive/war_powers_resolution.shtml

The War Powers Resolution was passed in 1973 to define and limit the president's power during times of war. Read the full text of the resolution at this Web page.

Dave Leip's Atlas of U.S. Presidential Elections
www.uselectionatlas.org

For information on upcoming and past presidential elections, refer to this Web page. Experiment with the electoral college calculator to see how your state could affect the electoral outcome.

The National Archives: Executive Branch
www.archives.gov/executive/

Research official executive branch documents at the Executive Branch Web page, provided by the U.S. National Archives and Records Administration.

Vicepresidents.com
www.vicepresidents.com

This Web site is dedicated to providing lots of interesting facts and archives about vice presidents, along with some lively humor.

The White House
www.whitehouse.gov
This is the official Web site of the White House. Here you can read about current presidential news, the president's Cabinet, executive orders, and presidential appointments.

White House Historical Association
www.whitehousehistory.org
The White House Historical Association is dedicated to the understanding, appreciation, and preservation of the White House. At its Web site you can find historical facts and take a detailed online tour of the numerous rooms and the property.

The White House: Past First Ladies
www.whitehouse.gov/history/firstladies/
The first lady is an important resource for the president in his role as head of state. Read about the current and past first ladies on this Web site.

STUDY OUTLINE

www.wwnorton.com/wtp7e

The Constitutional Basis of the Presidency

1. The framers thought a unitary executive would be energetic and thus better able to protect the nation's interests.
2. Presidents are selected in indirect elections through the electoral college.

The Constitutional Powers of the Presidency

1. The president's expressed powers fall into five categories—military, judicial, diplomatic, executive, and legislative—that are the source of some of the most important powers on which the president can draw.
2. The position of commander in chief makes the president the highest military authority in the United States, with control of the entire military establishment.
3. The Constitution delegates to the president, as commander in chief, the obligation to protect every state against invasion and domestic violence.
4. The presidential power to grant reprieves, pardons, and amnesties allows the president to choose freedom or confinement, and even life or death for all individuals who have violated, or are suspected of having violated, federal laws, including people who directly threaten the security of the United States.
5. The power to receive representatives of foreign countries allows the president almost unconditional authority to determine whether a new ruling group can indeed commit its country to treaties and other agreements.
6. The president's executive power consists of the ability to appoint and supervise all executive officers.
7. The president's legislative power consists of the obligation to make recommendations for consideration by Congress and the ability to veto legislation.

The Presidency as an Institution

1. Presidents have at their disposal a variety of institutional resources—such as the power to fill high-level political positions—that directly affect their ability to govern.
2. Presidents increasingly have preferred the White House staff to the Cabinet as a tool for managing the gigantic executive branch.
3. The White House staff, which is composed primarily of analysts and advisers, has grown from an informal group of fewer than a dozen people to a new presidential bureaucracy.
4. The Executive Office of the President, often called the institutional presidency, is larger than the White House staff, and comprises the president's permanent management agencies.
5. As the institutional presidency has grown in size and complexity, most presidents of the past twenty-five years have sought to use their vice presidents as a management resource after the election.

The Contemporary Bases of Presidential Power

1. Generally, presidents have expanded their power in three ways: party, popular mobilization, and administration.
2. Although all presidents rely on the members and leaders of their own party to implement their legislative agendas, during periods of divided government, the president's party is in the minority in Congress.
3. "Going public" as a source of presidential power has been especially significant in the past fifty years. But popular support for the president can be fickle and tends to decline over the course of a president's administration.

4. Contemporary presidents have increased the administrative capabilities and power of their office by enhancing the reach and power of the Executive Office of the President, increasing White House control over the federal bureaucracy, and expanding the role of executive orders and other instruments of direct presidential governance.

Thinking Critically about Presidential Power and Democracy

1. The decline of voting and other forms of popular involvement in American political life reduces congressional influence while enhancing the power of the presidency.

PRACTICE QUIZ

www.wwnorton.com/wtp7e

1. Which article of the Constitution establishes the presidency?
   a) Article I
   b) Article II
   c) Article III
   d) none of the above
2. Which of the following war powers does the Constitution *not* assign to the president?
   a) command of the army and navy of the United States
   b) the power to declare war
   c) command of the state militias
   d) The Constitution assigns all of the powers above to the president.
3. Which of the following does not require the advice and consent of the Senate?
   a) an executive agreement
   b) a treaty
   c) Supreme Court nominations
   d) All of the above require the advice and consent of the Senate.
4. Which of the following terms has been used to describe the presidency as presidents have used constitutional and other powers to make themselves more powerful?
   a) "the delegated presidency"
   b) "the imperial presidency"
   c) "the personal presidency"
   d) "the preemptive presidency"
5. By what process can Congress reject a presidential veto?
   a) veto override
   b) pocket veto
   c) executive delegation
   d) impeachment
6. Which of the following describes the presidential foreign-policy advisory council composed of the president; the vice president; the secretaries of state, defense, and the treasury; the attorney general; and others?
   a) the "inner Cabinet"
   b) the National Security Council
   c) both a and b
   d) neither a nor b
7. The Office of Management and Budget is part of
   a) the Executive Office of the President.
   b) the White House staff.
   c) the Kitchen Cabinet.
   d) both a and b.
8. Which twentieth-century presidency transformed the American system of government from a Congress-centered to a president-centered system?
   a) Woodrow Wilson's
   b) Franklin Roosevelt's
   c) Richard Nixon's
   d) Jimmy Carter's
9. How many people work for agencies within the Executive Office of the President?
   a) 25 to 50
   b) 700 to 1,000
   c) 1,500 to 2,000
   d) 4,500 to 5,000

KEY TERMS

www.wwnorton.com/wtp7e

Cabinet (p. 520)
caucus (political) (p. 506)
commander in chief (p. 508)
delegated powers (p. 507)
executive agreement (p. 512)
Executive Office of the President (EOP) (p. 522)
executive order (p. 517)
executive privilege (p. 514)
expressed powers (p. 507)
inherent powers (p. 507)
Kitchen Cabinet (p. 522)
legislative initiative (p. 515)
mandate (p. 526)
National Security Council (NSC) (p. 520)
pocket veto (p. 515)
veto (p. 515)
War Powers Resolution (p. 510)
White House staff (p. 522)

14 Bureaucracy in a Democracy

- Bureaucracy and Bureaucrats
- The Organization of the Executive Branch
- Can Bureaucracy Be Reinvented?
- Can the Bureaucracy Be Reduced?
- Can Bureaucracy Be Controlled?
- Thinking Critically about Responsible Bureaucracy in a Democracy

WHAT GOVERNMENT DOES AND WHY IT MATTERS

Americans depend on government bureaucracies to accomplish the most spectacular achievements as well as the most mundane. Yet they often do not realize that public bureaucracies are essential for providing the services that they use every day and that they rely on in emergencies. On a typical day, a college student might check the weather forecast, drive on an interstate highway, mail the rent check, drink from a public water fountain, check the calories on the side of a yogurt container, attend a class, log on to the Internet, and meet a relative at the airport. Each of these activities is possible because of the work of a government bureaucracy: the U.S. Weather Service, the U.S. Department of Transportation, the U.S. Postal Service, the Environmental Protection Agency, the Food and Drug Administration, the student loan programs of the U.S. Department of Education, the Advanced Research Projects Agency (which developed the Internet in the 1960s), and the Federal Aviation Administration. Without the ongoing work of these agencies, many of these common activities would be impossible, unreliable, or more expensive. Even though bureaucracies provide essential services that all Americans rely on, they are often disparaged by politicians and the general public alike. Criticized as "big government," many federal bureaucracies come into public view only when they are charged with fraud, waste, and abuse.

In emergencies, the national perspective on bureaucracy and, indeed, on "big government" shifts. After the September 11 terrorist attacks, all eyes turned to Washington. The federal government responded by strengthening and reorganizing the bureaucracy to undertake a whole new set of responsibilities designed to keep America safe.

In the biggest government reorganization in over half a century, Congress created the Department of Homeland Security in 2002. The massive new department merged twenty-two existing agencies into a single department employing nearly 170,000 workers. The operation of the new department is a gargantuan management challenge. The Department of Homeland Security combined under one umbrella established agencies with vastly different cultures and no history of working together. For example, the Coast Guard, the old Immigration and Naturalization Service, and the Federal Emergency Management Agency (FEMA) are all part of the new department.

The new department faced its first great challenge with Hurricane Katrina in 2005. Its woefully inadequate response highlighted the severe management problems that resulted from combining so many disparate agencies into a single department.

At the same time that it created a vast new federal department, the Bush administration launched a major push to contract out government jobs to private employers. In fact, in an era marked by new security needs, the desire to limit the size of government and promote the use of private contractors has led to an explosion of contracting. Reliance on government contractors has spread throughout the federal bureaucracy, but it has been especially common in the Department of Homeland Security, which has had to expand its capacities very quickly.

The two initiatives, apparently headed in opposite directions, illustrate the conflicts that arise in an era when most Americans believe that government is more necessary than ever but have significant doubts about whether the existing government is up to the job. Privatization raises questions about whether the private sector is, in fact, more cost effective than government and whether such extensive privatization is compatible with our national security needs and with democratic accountability.

In fact, as we shall see in this chapter, Americans have a love/hate relationship with the federal bureaucracy. This ambivalence prompts politicians at times to promise that they will slash the federal bureaucracy or move government responsibilities to the private sector. Yet, they rarely follow through on such promises. Because Americans rely on government in so many aspects of their lives, significant reductions in the federal bureaucracy would create disruptions that no one wishes to experience. As a result, over the years, the number of federal employees has kept pace with the growth of the economy and the population. Nor has privatization offered a silver bullet to cure the ills of bureaucracy. Instead, it creates new challenges for ensuring accountability and efficiency in meeting public needs.

- **We begin this chapter by clarifying what we mean by "bureaucracy."** We first examine why bureaucracy is necessary. From there, we turn to the size, role, functions, and characteristics of the federal bureaucracy.
- **We next examine the organization of the executive branch as a whole, looking at the Cabinet departments, agencies, and bureaus that make up its operating parts.** Since the executive branch is vast and there are far too many agencies for us to identify here, we will instead evaluate the different broad purposes that federal agencies serve.
- **We next turn to ways in which the size and role of the federal bureaucracy can be reduced.** Although efforts to downsize government have been popular in recent years, we examine whether these attempts are effective or even address the most pressing problem regarding the control of the federal bureaucracy.

Bureaucracy and Bureaucrats

Bureaucracy is nothing more nor less than a form of organization, a complex structure of offices, tasks, and rules. To gain some objectivity, and to appreciate the universality of bureaucracy, let us take the word and break it into its two main parts—*bureau* and *cracy. Bureau*, a French word, can mean either "office" or "desk." *Cracy* is from the Greek word for "rule" or "form of rule." Taken together, *bureau* and *cracy* produce a very interesting definition: **Bureaucracy** is a form of rule by offices and desks. Each member of an organization has an office, meaning a place as well as a set of responsibilities. That is, each "office" comprises a set of tasks that are specialized to the needs of the organization, and the person holding that office (or position) performs those specialized tasks. Specialization and repetition are essential to the efficiency of any organization. Therefore, when an organization is inefficient, it is often because it is not bureaucratized enough!

bureaucracy the complex structure of offices, tasks, rules, and principles of organization that are employed by all large-scale institutions to coordinate the work of their personnel

Both routine and exceptional tasks require the organization, specialization, and expertise found in bureaucracies. To provide services, government bureaucracies employ specialists such as meteorologists, doctors, and scientists. To do their jobs effectively, these specialists require resources and tools (ranging from paper to blood samples); they have to coordinate their work with others (for example, the traffic engineers must communicate with construction engineers); and there must be effective outreach to the public (for example, private doctors must be made aware of health warnings). Bureaucracy offers a way to coordinate the many different parts that must work together for the government to provide good services.

The Size of the Federal Service

For over two decades, politicians from both parties have asserted that the federal government is too big. Ronald Reagan led the way with his 1981 statement that government was the problem, not the solution. Fifteen years later President Bill Clinton abandoned the traditional Democratic defense of government, declaring that "the era of big government is over." President George W. Bush voiced similar sentiments when he accepted his party's nomination for president in 2000, proclaiming "Big government is not the answer!" Despite fears of bureaucratic growth getting out of hand, however, the federal service has hardly grown at all during the past thirty-five years; it reached its peak postwar level in 1968 with 3.0 million civilian employees plus an additional 3.6 million military personnel (a figure swollen by Vietnam). The number of civilian federal employees has since fallen to approximately 2.7 million in 2006; the number of military personnel totals only 1.4 million.[1]

The growth of the federal service over the past fifty years is even less imposing when placed in the context of the total workforce and when compared with the size of state and local public employment. Figure 14.1 indicates that since 1950, the ratio of federal employment to the total workforce has been steady, and in fact has *declined* slightly in the past thirty years. In 1950, there were 4.3 million state and local civil service employees (about 6.5 percent of the country's workforce). In 2006, there were just over 19 million (nearly 14 percent of the workforce). Federal employment, in contrast, exceeded 5 percent of the workforce only during World War II (not shown), and almost all of that momentary growth was military.

FIGURE 14.1 ★ Employees in the Federal Service and in the National Workforce, 1946–2006

Since 1950, the ratio of federal employment to the total workforce has gradually declined. The lower line in this figure shows that the federal service has tended to grow at a rate that keeps pace with the economy and society. The upper line shows that variations in federal employment since 1946 have been in the military and are directly related to war and the Cold War. When did military employment begin its sharp decline?

SOURCES: Office of Management and Budget, www.whitehouse.gov/omb/budget/fy2008/pdf/hist.pdf; Bureau of Labor Statistics, ftp://ftp.bls.gov/pub/suppl/empsit.ceseebl.txt (accessed 3/8/08); and U.S. Department of Labor, Bureau of Labor Statistics, *Employment and Earnings* (monthly).

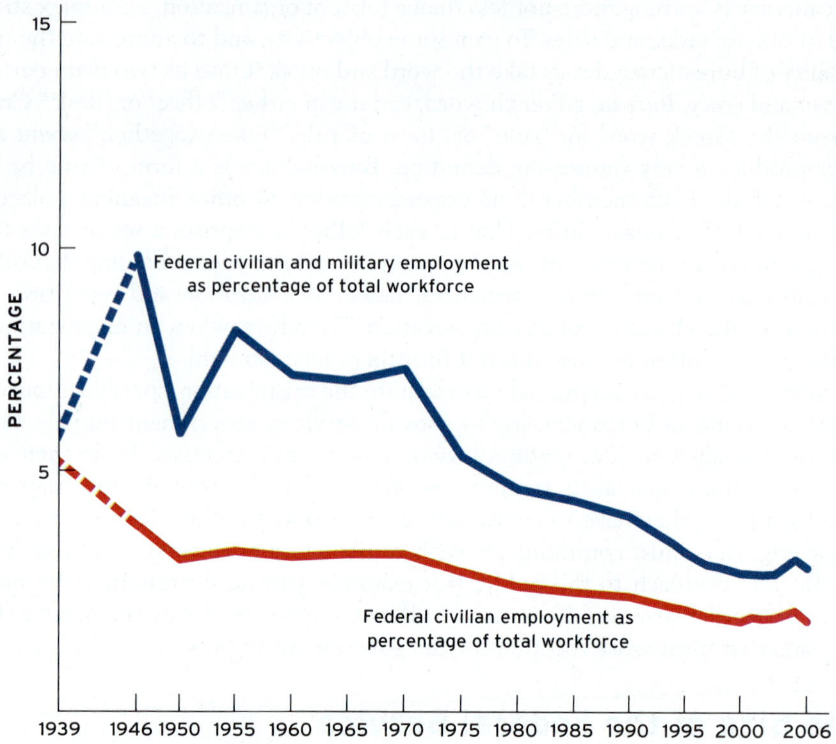

Another useful comparison is to be found in Figure 14.2. Although the dollar increase in federal spending shown by the bars looks impressive, the trend line indicating the relation of federal spending to the Gross Domestic Product (GDP) shows that in 2008, this percentage was barely higher than in 1960.

In sum, the national government is indeed "very large," but it has not been growing any faster than the economy or society. The same is roughly true of the growth pattern of state and local public personnel. Bureaucracy keeps pace with society, despite people's seeming dislike of it, because the control towers, the prisons, the Social Security system, and other essential elements cannot be operated without bureaucracy. The United States certainly could not hope to protect the nation against terrorism without a large military and civilian bureaucracy.

Although the federal executive branch is large and complex, everything about it is commonplace. Bureaucracies are commonplace because they touch so many aspects of daily life. Government bureaucracies implement the decisions made through the political process. Bureaucracies are full of routine because that ensures the regular delivery of services and also ensures that each agency fulfills its man-

FIGURE 14.2 ★
Annual Federal Outlays, 1960–2008

As the bars on this figure indicate, when measured in dollars, federal government spending, which supports the federal bureaucracy, shows dramatic increases over time. But as the trend line shows, federal spending as a percentage of gross domestic product has increased only slightly since 1960. Since 1960, when did federal spending as a proportion of GDP peak?

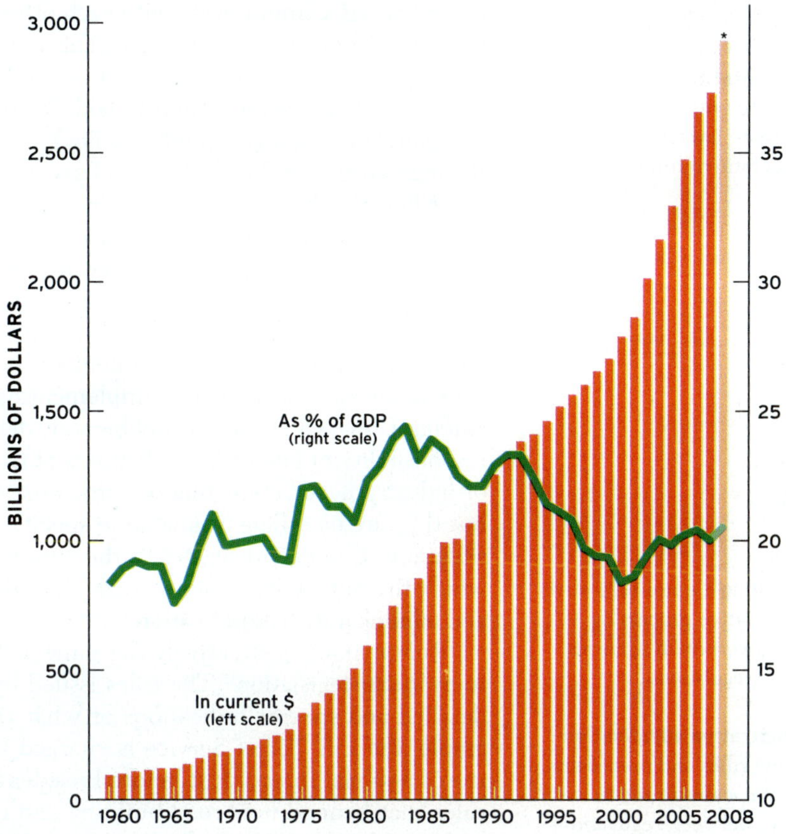

*Data from 2008 is estimated.
SOURCE: Office of Management and Budget, www.whitehouse.gov/omb/budget/fy2009/pdf/hist.pdf (accessed 3/27/08).

date. Public bureaucracies are powerful because legislatures and chief executives, and indeed the people, delegate vast power to them to make sure a particular job is done—enabling citizens to be freer to pursue their private ends.

Bureaucrats

"Government by offices and desks" conveys to most people a picture of hundreds of office workers shuffling millions of pieces of paper. There is a lot of truth in that image, but we have to look more closely at what papers are being shuffled and why. More than seventy years ago, an astute observer defined bureaucracy as "continuous routine business."[2] As we saw at the beginning of this chapter, almost any organization succeeds by reducing its work to routines, with each routine being given to a different specialist. But specialization separates people from each other; one worker's output becomes another worker's input. The timing of such relationships is essential, and timing requires these workers to stay in communication with each other. In fact, bureaucracy was the first information network.

WHAT DO BUREAUCRATS DO? Bureaucrats, whether in public or in private organizations, communicate with each other in order to coordinate all the specializations within their organization. This coordination is necessary to carry out the primary task of bureaucracy, which is **implementation,** that is, implementing the objectives of the organization as laid down by its board of directors (if a private company) or by law (if a public agency). In government, the "bosses" are ultimately the legislature and the elected chief executive.

implementation the efforts of departments and agencies to translate laws into specific bureaucratic routines

When the bosses—Congress, in particular, when it is making the law—are clear in their instructions to bureaucrats, implementation is a fairly straightforward process. Bureaucrats translate the law into specific routines for each of the employees of an agency. This requires yet another job for bureaucrats: interpretation. Interpretation is a form of implementation, in that the bureaucrats still have to carry out what they believe to be the intentions of their superiors. But when bureaucrats have to interpret a law before implementing it, they are in effect engaging in *lawmaking.* Congress frequently deliberately delegates to an administrative agency the responsibility of lawmaking. Members of Congress often conclude that some area of industry needs regulating or some area of the environment needs protection, but they are unwilling or unable to specify just how that should be done. In such situations, Congress delegates to the appropriate agency a broad authority within which the bureaucrats have to make law, through the procedures of **rule making** and **administrative adjudication.**

rule making a quasi-legislative administrative process by which government agencies produce regulations

administrative adjudication applying rules and precedents to specific cases to settle disputes between regulated parties

Rule making is effectively the same as legislation; in fact, it is often referred to as "quasi-legislation." The rules issued by government agencies provide more detailed and specific indications of what the policy actually will mean. For example, the U.S. Forest Service is charged with making policies that govern the use of national forests. Just before President Clinton left office, the agency issued rules that banned new road building and development in the forests. This goal had long been sought by environmentalists and conservationists. In 2005, the Forest Service relaxed the rules, allowing states to make proposals for building new roads within the national forests. Just as the timber industry opposed the Clinton rule banning road building, environmentalists have challenged the new ruling and have sued the U.S. Forest Service in federal court for violating clean water and endangered species legislation. The rule-making process is thus a highly political one. Once rules are approved, they are published in the *Federal Register* and have the force of law.

Administrative adjudication is very similar to what the judiciary ordinarily does: apply rules and precedents to specific cases to settle disputes. In administrative adjudication, the agency charges the person or business suspected of violating the law. The ruling in an adjudication dispute applies only to the specific case being considered. Many regulatory agencies use administrative adjudication to make decisions about specific products or practices. For example, the Consumer Product Safety Commission, which is charged with establishing guidelines to ensure the safety of a wide range of consumer items, often uses administrative adjudication to recall unsafe products. In 2007, when concern about the safety of children's toys grabbed national headlines, the commission negotiated forty-three recalls of children's products, including toys, jewelry, and school supplies.[3] These guidelines have the force of law.

Government bureaucrats do essentially the same things that bureaucrats in large private organizations do, and neither type deserves the disrespect embodied in the term *bureaucrat.* But because of the authoritative, coercive nature of government, far more constraints are imposed on public bureaucrats than on private bureaucrats, even when their jobs are the same. During the 1970s and 1980s, the length of time required to develop an administrative rule from a proposal to actual publication in the *Federal Register* (when it takes on full legal status) grew from an average of fifteen months to an average of thirty-five to forty months. Inefficiency? No. Most of the increased time is attributable to new procedures requiring more public notice, more public hearings, more hearings held out in the field rather than in Washington, more cost-benefit analysis, and stronger legal obligations to prepare "environmental impact statements" demonstrating that the proposed rule or agency action will not have an unacceptably large negative impact on the human or physical environment.[4] Thus, a great deal of what is popularly paraded as the lower efficiency of public agencies can be attributed to the political, judicial, legal, and public-opinion restraints and extraordinarily high expectations imposed on public bureaucrats.

Politics Today

In 2007 the Consumer Product Safety Commission did not appear strong enough to protect American consumers when it was discovered that numerous products manufactured abroad—including toys, food, and medicines—were unsafe. Why do you think many Americans nonetheless feel we have "too much" bureaucracy?

We will have more to say at the end of this chapter about bureaucratic accountability and the potential role of citizens in it. Suffice it to say here that if a private company such as Microsoft were required to open up all its decision processes and management practices to full view by the media, their competitors, and all interested citizens, Microsoft—despite its profit motive and the pressure of competition—would likely appear far less efficient, perhaps no more efficient than public bureaucracies.

A good case study of the important role agencies can play is the story of how ordinary federal bureaucrats created the Internet. Yes, it's true: what became the Internet was developed largely by the U.S. Department of Defense, and defense considerations still shape the basic structure of the Internet. In 1957, immediately following the profound American embarrassment over the Soviet Union's launching of *Sputnik*, Congress authorized the establishment of the Advanced Research Projects Agency (ARPA) to develop, among other things, a means of maintaining communications in the event the existing telecommunications network (the telephone system) was disabled by a strategic attack. Since the telephone network was highly centralized and therefore could have been completely disabled by a single attack, ARPA developed a decentralized, highly redundant network. Redundancy in this case improved the probability of functioning after an attack. The full design, called by the acronym of ARPANET, took almost a decade to create. By 1971, around twenty universities were connected to the ARPANET. The forerunner to the Internet was born.[5]

The rules established by regulatory agencies have the force of law. In 2007, the Consumer Product Safety Commission found that numerous toys did not meet its safety guidelines, and the toys had to be recalled.

THE MERIT SYSTEM: HOW TO BECOME A BUREAUCRAT

Although they face more inconveniences than their counterparts in the private sector, public bureaucrats are rewarded in part with greater job security than employees of most private organizations. More than a century ago, the federal government attempted to imitate business by passing the Civil Service Act of 1883, which was followed by almost universal adoption of equivalent laws in state and local governments. These laws required that appointees to public office be qualified for the job to which

merit system a product of civil service reform, in which appointees to positions in public bureaucracies must objectively be deemed qualified for those positions

they are appointed. This policy came to be called the **merit system**; its ideal was not merely to put an end to political appointments under the "spoils system" but also to require adequate preparation for every job by holding competitive examinations through which the very best candidates were to be hired. At the higher levels of government agencies, including such posts as cabinet secretaries and assistant secretaries, many jobs are filled with political appointees and are not part of the merit system.

As a further safeguard against political interference (and to compensate for the lower-than-average pay given to public employees), merit system employees—genuine civil servants—were given a form of tenure: legal protection against being fired without a show of cause. Reasonable people may disagree about the value of job tenure and how far it should extend in the civil service, but the justifiable objective of tenure—cleansing bureaucracy of political interference while upgrading performance—cannot be disputed.

The Organization of the Executive Branch

department the largest subunit of the executive branch. The secretaries of the fifteen departments form the Cabinet

Cabinet departments, agencies, and bureaus are the operating parts of the bureaucratic whole. Figure 14.3 is an organizational chart of one of the largest and most important of the fifteen **departments,** the Department of Agriculture. At the top is the head of the department, who in the United States is called the "secretary" of the department.[6] Below the secretary and the deputy secretary is a second tier of "undersecretaries" who have management responsibilities for one or more operating agencies, shown in the smaller print directly below each undersecretary's title. Those operating agencies are the third tier of the department, yet they are the highest level of responsibility for the actual programs around which the entire department is organized. This third tier is generally called the "bureau level." Each bureau-level agency usually operates under a statute, enacted by Congress, that set up the agency and gave it its authority and jurisdiction. The names of these bureau-level agencies are often quite well known to the public—the Forest Service and the Food Safety and Inspection Service, for example. These are the so-called line agencies, those that deal directly with the public. Sometimes these agencies are officially called "bureaus," such as the Federal Bureau of Investigation (FBI), which is a part of the third tier of the Department of Justice. But "bureau" is also the conventional term for this level of administrative agency, even though many agencies or their supporters have preferred over the years to adopt a more palatable designation, such as "service" or "administration." Each bureau is, of course, even further subdivided into divisions, offices, or units—all are parts of the bureaucratic hierarchy.

independent agency an agency that is not part of a Cabinet department

government corporation a government agency that performs a service normally provided by the private sector

Not all government agencies are part of Cabinet departments. Some **independent agencies** are set up by Congress outside the departmental structure altogether, even though the president appoints and directs the heads of these agencies. Independent agencies usually have broad powers to provide public services that are either too expensive or too important to be left to private initiatives. Some examples of independent agencies are the National Aeronautics and Space Administration (NASA), the Central Intelligence Agency (CIA), and the Environmental Protection Agency (EPA). **Government corporations** are a third type of govern-

FIGURE 14.3 ★ Organizational Chart of the Department of Agriculture, 2008

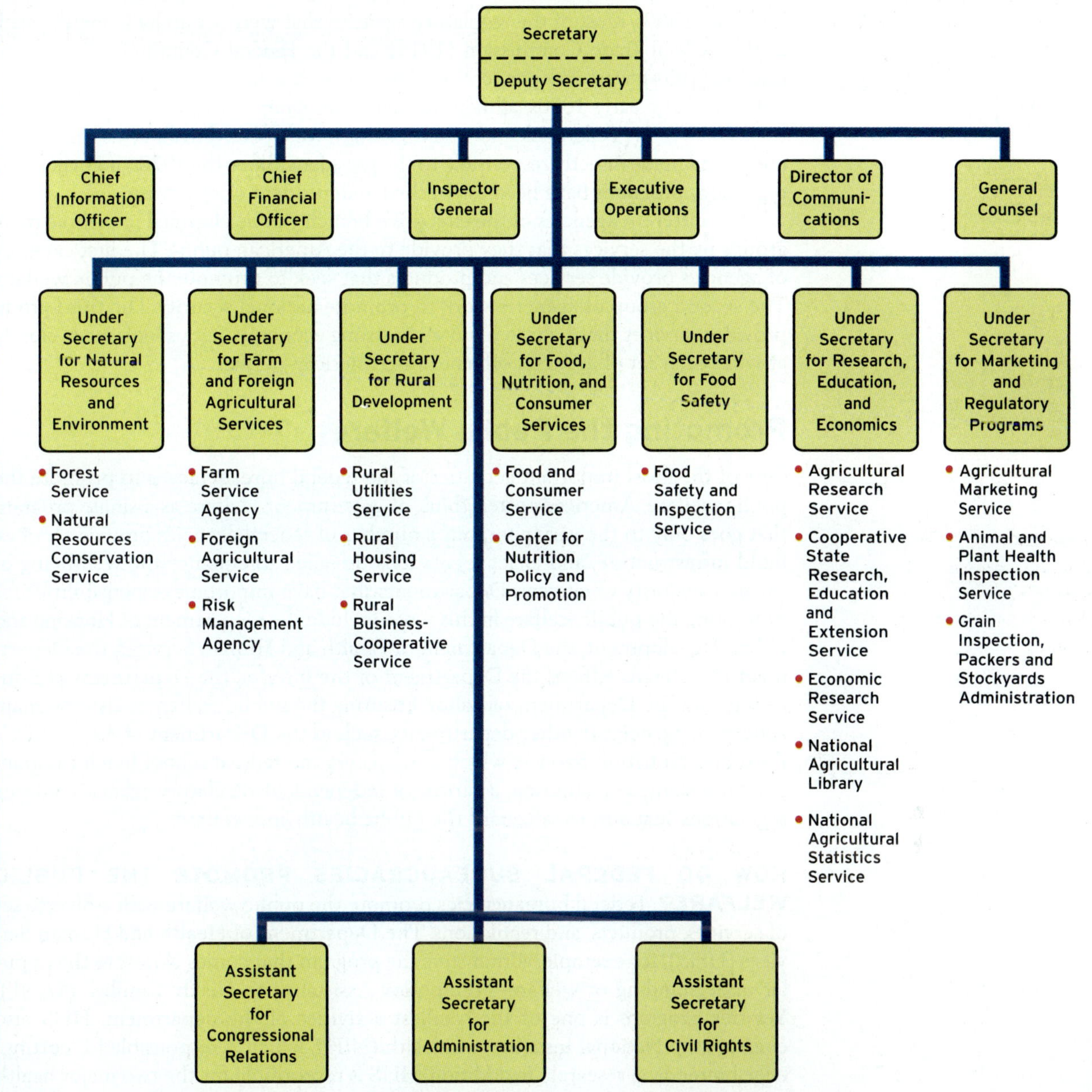

SOURCE: U.S. Department of Agriculture, www.usda.gov/img/content/org_chart_enlarged.jpg (accessed 3/8/08).

ment agency, but are more like private businesses performing and charging for a market service, such as delivering the mail (the United States Postal Service) or transporting railroad passengers (Amtrak).

Yet a fourth type of agency is the independent regulatory commission, given broad discretion to make rules. The first regulatory agencies established by Congress, beginning with the Interstate Commerce Commission in 1888, were set up as independent regulatory commissions because Congress recognized that regulatory agencies are "minilegislatures," whose rules are exactly the same as legislation but require the kind of expertise and full-time attention that is beyond the capacity of Congress. Until the 1960s, most of the regulatory agencies that were set up by Congress, such as the Federal Trade Commission (1914) and the Federal Communications Commission (1934), were independent regulatory commissions. But beginning in the late 1960s and the early 1970s, all new regulatory programs, with two or three exceptions (such as the Federal Election Commission), were placed within existing departments and made directly responsible to the president. Since the 1970s, no major new regulatory programs have been established, independent or otherwise.

The different agencies of the executive branch can be classified into three main groups by the services that they provide to the American public. The first category of agencies provide services and products that seek to promote the public welfare. The second group of agencies work to promote national security. The third group provides services that help to maintain a strong economy. Let us look more closely at what each set of agencies offers to the American public.

Promoting the Public Welfare

One of the most important activities of the federal bureaucracy is to promote the public welfare. Americans often think of government welfare as a single program that goes only to the very poor; but a number of federal agencies provide services, build infrastructure, and enact regulations designed to enhance the well-being of the vast majority of citizens. Departments that have important responsibilities for promoting the public welfare in this sense include the Department of Housing and Urban Development, the Department of Health and Human Services, the Department of Veterans Affairs, the Department of the Interior, the Department of Education, and the Department of Labor. Ensuring the public welfare is also the main activity of agencies in other departments, such as the Department of Agriculture's Food and Nutrition Service, which administers the federal school lunch program and food stamps. In addition, a variety of independent regulatory agencies enforce regulations that aim to safeguard the public health and welfare.

HOW DO FEDERAL BUREAUCRACIES PROMOTE THE PUBLIC WELFARE? Federal bureaucracies promote the public welfare with a diverse set of services, products, and regulations. The Department of Health and Human Services (HHS), for example, administers the program that comes closest to the popular understanding of welfare—Temporary Assistance to Needy Families (TANF). Yet this program is one of the smallest activities of the department. HHS also oversees the National Institutes of Health (NIH), which is responsible for cutting-edge biomedical research. In addition, HHS is responsible for the two major health programs of the federal government: Medicaid, which provides health care for low-income families and for many elderly and disabled people in nursing homes, and Medicare, which is the health insurance available to all elderly people in the United States.

A different notion of the public welfare but one highly valued by most Americans is provided by the National Park Service, which is under the Department of the Interior. First created in 1916, the National Park Service is responsible for the care and upkeep of national parks. Since the nineteenth century, Americans have seen protection of the natural environment as an important public goal and have looked to federal agencies to implement laws and administer programs that preserve natural areas and keep them open to the public.

The United States has no "Department of Regulation" but has many **regulatory agencies.** Some of these are bureaus within departments, such as the Food and Drug Administration (FDA) within the Department of Health and Human Services and the Occupational Safety and Health Administration (OSHA) in the Department of Labor. As we saw earlier, other regulatory agencies are independent regulatory commissions, such as the Consumer Product Safety Commission, Federal Communications Commission (FCC) and the EPA. But whether departmental or independent, an agency or commission is regulatory if Congress delegates to it relatively broad powers over a sector of the economy or a type of commercial activity and authorizes it to make rules restricting the conduct of people and businesses within that jurisdiction. Rules made by regulatory agencies have the force and effect of law.

regulatory agencies
departments, bureaus, or independent agencies whose primary mission is to impose limits, restrictions, or other obligations on the conduct of individuals or companies in the private sector

Through their activities, these agencies seek to promote the welfare of all Americans, often working behind the scenes. The FDA, for example, works to protect public health by setting standards for food processing and inspecting plants to ensure that those standards are met. The EPA sets standards to limit polluting emissions from automobiles, among other functions. EPA regulations required automobile manufacturers to change the way they designed cars. The result has been cleaner air in many metropolitan areas.

BUREAUCRACIES, CLIENTELES, AND THE PUBLIC Some of the public agencies that provide services that enhance well-being are tied to a specific group or segment of American society that is often thought of as the main clientele of that agency. For example, the Department of Agriculture was established in 1862 to promote the interests of farmers. Likewise, the Department of Veterans Affairs has strong links to veterans' organizations, such as the American Legion and the Veterans of Foreign Wars. The Department of Education relies on teachers' organizations for support.

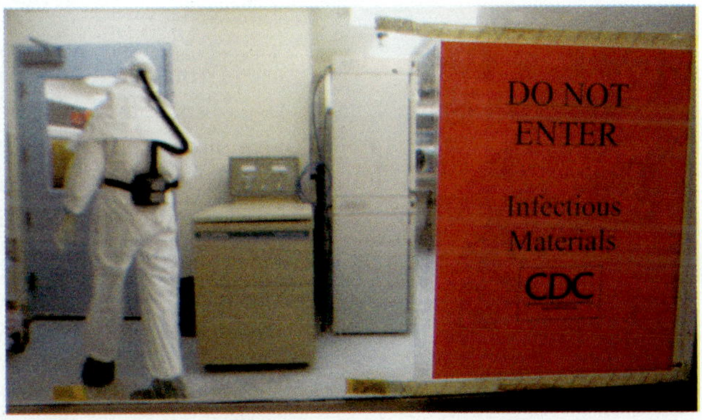

The federal bureaucracy plays an important role in promoting public welfare. The EPA creates and enforces regulations related to the environment—for instance, preventing the pollution of groundwater. At left, an EPA manager examines a plastic liner that catches acid runoff from an abandoned copper mine in Nevada. The Centers for Disease Control and Prevention (at right), part of the Department of Health and Human Services, protects the health and safety of people through its work to reduce and eliminate infectious diseases, including those caused by bioterrorism and chemical terrorism, and avian flu.

FIGURE 14.4 ★
Iron Triangles

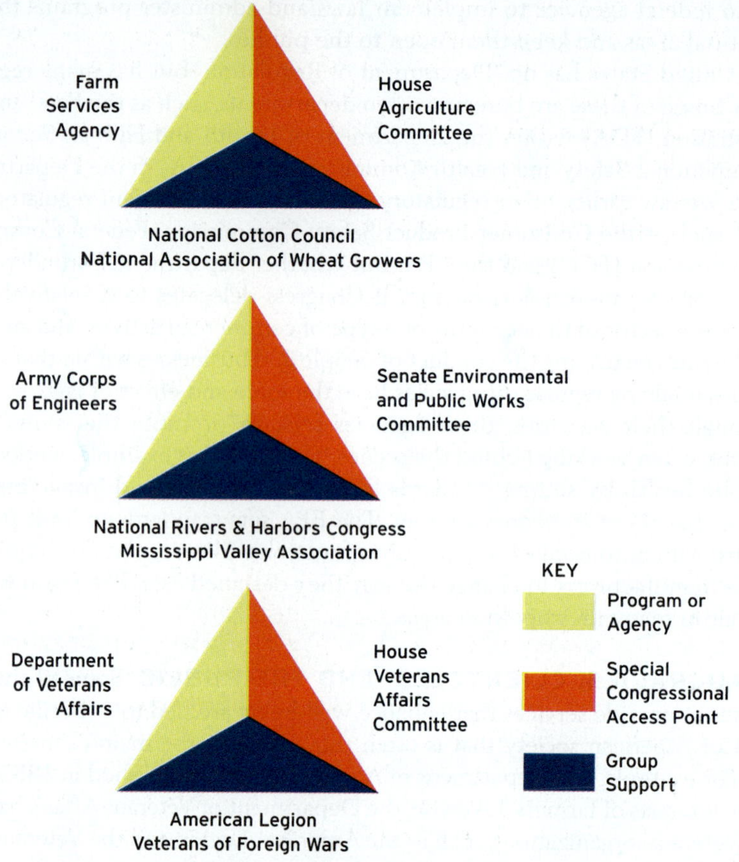

SOURCES: Adapted from U.S. House of Representatives, *Report of the Subcommittee for Special Investigations of the Committee on Armed Services*, 86th Cong., 1st sess. (Washington, DC: Government Printing Office, 1960), 7. Reprinted from Theodore J. Lowi, *Incomplete Conquest: Governing America*, 2nd ed. (New York: Holt, Rinehart and Winston, 1981), 139.

iron triangle the stable, cooperative relationship that often develops among a congressional committee, an administrative agency, and one or more supportive interest groups. Not all of these relationships are triangular, but the iron triangle is the most typical

Figure 14.4 is a representation of this type of politics. This configuration is known as an **iron triangle,** a pattern of stable relationships among an agency in the executive branch, a congressional committee or subcommittee, and one or more organized groups of agency clientele. (Iron triangles were discussed in detail in Chapter 11.)

These relationships with particular clienteles are often important in preserving agencies from political attack. During his 1980 campaign, Ronald Reagan promised to dismantle the Department of Education as part of his commitment to get government "off people's backs." After his election, President Reagan even appointed a secretary of the department who was publicly committed to eliminating it. Yet, by the end of his administration, the Department of Education was still standing and barely touched. In 1995, the Republican Congress vowed to eliminate the Department of Education, along with two other departments, but it, too, failed. The educational constituency of the department (its clientele) mobilized to save it each time.

Such clientele groups generally have more influence over federal agencies than do people who are not part of the clientele group. But the ability of clientele groups to get their way is not automatic, as agencies have to balance limited resources, competing interests, and political pressures. For example, the Department of Veterans Affairs long resisted the efforts of Vietnam veterans to be compensated for exposure to Agent Orange, a chemical defoliant used extensively during the Vietnam War. Veterans charged that exposure to Agent Orange had left them with a variety of diseases ranging from cancer to severe birth defects in their children. Only after decades of lobbying, lawsuits, and federally sponsored studies did the Department of Veterans Affairs provide assistance to affected veterans.

Moreover, federal agencies increasingly seek public support outside their direct clients for their activities. In some cases, key clientele groups will work to build more widespread support for agency activities. For example, the AFL-CIO, which represents organized labor, built a broad coalition of student organizations, church groups, consumer groups, and civil rights activists opposed to sweatshops in the United States. These groups helped to support the Department of Labor's campaign to uncover and eliminate such manufacturing practices in the United States. Agency failure to consider public opinion can result in embarrassing incidents, which bureaucrats prefer to avoid. In 1981, the Department of Agriculture's Food and Nutrition Service, which administers the federal school lunch program, had to retract its cost-cutting decision to classify ketchup as a vegetable after a public outcry that the agency was harming children.

For Critical Analysis

What is the impact of iron triangles on inequality in the United States? Do the ties among agencies, congressional committees, and organized groups promote inequality?

Attentiveness to the public often means making the public aware of services and improving the way services are delivered. The Social Security Administration is an independent agency that administers old-age and disability insurance, the federal government's most important and expensive welfare program. Old-age insurance, or Social Security, is supported by the AARP, an interest group representing people over fifty, generally considered to be the most powerful interest group operating in the United States today. But worried that younger workers are losing confidence in Social Security, the agency has recently begun to issue annual statements to each worker, outlining the benefits that they can count on from Social Security when they retire and indicating what benefits are available if they become disabled before retirement.

Providing National Security

One of the remarkable features of American federalism is that the most vital agencies for providing security for the American people are located in state and local governments—namely the police. But some agencies vital to maintaining national security are located in the national government, and they can be grouped into two categories: (1) agencies for control of conduct defined as a threat to internal national security and (2) agencies for defending American security from external threats. The departments of greatest influence in these two areas are Homeland Security, Justice, Defense, and State.

AGENCIES FOR INTERNAL SECURITY The task of maintaining domestic security changed dramatically after the terrorist attacks of September 11, 2001. The creation of the Department of Homeland Security in late 2002 signaled the high priority that domestic security would now have. The orientation of domestic agencies shifted as well, as agencies geared up to prevent terrorism, a task that differed greatly from their former charge of investigating crime. Along with this shift in responsibility, these agencies have acquired broad new powers—many of them controversial—including the power to detain terrorist suspects and to engage in extensive domestic intelligence-gathering about possible terrorists.

Crime, Violence, and National Security on Television

Government agencies that are charged with providing national security, such as the Justice Department and the Department of Homeland Security, affect the lives of Americans every day. But the extent to which Americans accept the authority of these security agencies has varied over time. Violent real-world events may increase Americans' level of fear and result in increased support for security measures. After September 11, many Americans were willing to grant security agencies greater powers. Interestingly, mass media—particularly television—may also play a role in this process. Whether national news, local news, or entertainment programs, television's powerful images seem in some cases to increase viewers' fear of crime and terrorism, and thus their support for security agencies.

In the 1970s, George Gerbner and his colleagues at the Annenberg School of Communication began a line of research regarding the effects of violent television content on fear of crime, and the acceptance of authority and security presence. Gerbner showed through various studies that a strong correlation existed between television viewing and the belief that the world was a mean and dangerous place. Because the television world is rife with crime and violence, Gerbner contends that viewers of television will see the world as a dangerous place. Gerbner warns that this causes citizens to favor martial policies of law and order, including a greater security presence and tougher punishment for criminals.[a]

Indeed, recent studies have confirmed that viewing television can increase citizens' fear of violence, crime, and terrorism. While exploring the effects of television viewing on fear and anxiety after the September 11 attacks, at least two studies found that the more television content people watched after the attacks, the greater their self-reported fear and anxiety. Yet both studies found that people who read the newspaper and people who watched television had different levels of support for expanded police authority and restrictions on privacy in the interest of national security. Specifically, hours spent watching television in general and watching television news in particular were associated with greater support for such policies, whereas reading the newspaper was associated with less support.

Violence, crime, and terrorism in entertainment programming may also affect viewers' attitudes about security and governmental authority. Another study analyzed the effects of exposure to crime dramas such as *NYPD Blue* on viewers' perceptions of crime as an important problem, and the extent to which viewers judged public officials on their performance on crime-related issues. The authors argued that crime dramas frequently "activate" the concept of crime in the mind of the viewers, causing viewers to think more about it when making political judgments.

Consider programs like the popular drama 24 starring Kiefer Sutherland as Jack Bauer, a stubborn counter-terrorism expert who plays by his own rules. The show takes place in real time, creating a heightened sense of urgency, with a major criminal or terrorist threat always imminent. Each episode is laden with back-to-back violent encounters with thugs, spies, and terrorists. To what extent these images increase citizens' acceptance of the authority of police and security agencies is still being debated. However, studies such as those described here certainly point to television's important contributing role in shaping Americans' response to security measures and to the authority of policing agencies.

FOR CRITICAL ANALYSIS

1. If television content increases viewers' fear and subsequent support for security agencies, is that good or bad for the functioning of American democracy? What if the television content makes the world seem more dangerous than it actually is?
2. After September 11, Americans were generally more willing to accept increased powers of security agencies. Why have critics argued that some of the measures these agencies have taken in the fight against terrorism are at odds with democracy?

a. G. Gerbner, L. Gross, M. Morgan, and N. Signorielli, "The 'Mainstreaming' of America: Violence Profile No. 11," *Journal of Communication* 30 (1980): 10–29.

Prior to September 11, most of the effort put into maintaining national security took the form of legal work related to prosecuting federal crimes. The largest and most important unit of the Justice Department is the Criminal Division. Lawyers in the Criminal Division represent the United States government when it is the plaintiff enforcing the federal criminal laws, except for those cases (about 25 percent) specifically assigned to other divisions or agencies. Criminal litigation is handled by U.S. attorneys, who are appointed by the president. There is one U.S. attorney in each of the ninety-four federal judicial districts; he or she supervises the work of a number of assistant U.S. attorneys.

The Civil Division of the Justice Department deals with litigation in which the United States is the defendant being sued for injury and damages allegedly inflicted by a government official or agency. The missions of the other divisions of the Justice Department—Antitrust, Civil Rights, Environment and Natural Resources, and Tax—are described by their names.

When terrorism prevention took center stage, the Justice Department reoriented its activities accordingly. It was aided in its new mission by the USA PATRIOT Act, enacted soon after September 11. The act gave the Justice Department broad new powers, allowing the attorney general to detain any foreigner suspected of posing a threat to internal security. The Patriot Act also expanded the government's ability to use wiretaps and to issue search warrants without notifying suspects immediately. It required public libraries to keep lists of the public's book and Internet usage for federal inspection. Although initially popular with most Americans, these measures created concern about civil liberties. Despite these concerns, Congress renewed the act with only modest revisions in 2006.

Since 2001, the Justice Department has played a central role in setting the balance between national security and civil liberties. In 2007, high-profile congressional hearings revealed extensive conflicts between the Justice Department and the White House over the use of warrantless wiretapping in the United States. These included a dramatic hospital scene in 2005 in which White House officials sought—unsuccessfully—to persuade the gravely ill former attorney general, John Ashcroft, to approve the continuation of the wiretapping program over the wishes of Justice Department officials. The hearings also exposed the fact that in 2005 the former attorney general, Alberto Gonzales, secretly approved the use of severe methods of interrogation—many classified as torture under the Geneva Convention—even after Congress had passed a law forbidding torture.[7]

Since its creation in 2002, the Department of Homeland Security has joined the Justice Department as the major bureaucracy charged with domestic security. The new department took over some of the security-oriented agencies previously controlled by other departments (see Table 14.1). For example, the Immigration and Naturalization Service (INS) was moved from Justice to Homeland Security. Once inside the new department, the INS was abolished. Immigration services were consolidated into U.S. Citizenship and Immigration Services. The enforcement functions of the old INS were combined with the U.S. Customs Services (formerly part of the Treasury Department) to create a new Bureau of Immigration and Customs Enforcement, known as ICE, in the Department of Homeland Security. ICE has extensive investigative capacities, with field offices around the United States and bureaus in over thirty countries. Other agencies that were transferred to the Department of Homeland Security include the Coast Guard, the Secret Service, and the Federal Emergency Management Agency.

TABLE 14.1 ★ The Shape of a Domestic Security Department

DEPARTMENT OF HOMELAND SECURITY	The agencies and departments that were moved to the main divisions of the Department of Homeland Security under the legislation creating the new department:	Department or agency they were previously under:	*From the 2008 budget request:* Budget request, in millions:	Estimated number of employees:
Border and Transportation Security	U.S. Customs and Border Protection	Treasury Department	$10,174	48,551
	Immigration and Customs Enforcement	Justice Department	$5,014	17,463
	U.S. Citizenship and Immigration Services	Justice Department	$2,568	10,714
	National Protection and Program Directorate (includes domestic preparedness)	General Services Administration	$1,046	646
	Transportation Security Administration	Transportation Department	$6,401	50,173
	Federal Law Enforcement Training Center	Treasury Department	$263	1,049
Emergency Preparedness and Response	Federal Emergency Management Agency	Independent agency	$8,020	6,651
Domestic Nuclear Detection Office	(new)		$561	121
Science and Technology	(multiple programs)	Department of Energy	$799	381
Secret Service	Secret Service, including presidential protection units	Treasury Department	$1,608	6,700
Coast Guard	Coast Guard	Transportation Department	$8,726	48,124
Total DHS			$46,399	192,760*

*Includes additional employees from central management and oversight.
SOURCES: The White House; U.S. Department of Homeland Security, www.dhs.gov/interweb/assetlibrary/reorganization_plan.pdf; and www.dhs.gov/xlibrary/assets/budget_bib-fy2008.pdf (accessed 3/28/08).

The Justice Department plays a central role in determining the balance between national security and civil liberties. When questions about unwarranted wiretapping and harsh interrogation methods arose in 2005, critics charged that former attorney general Alberto Gonzales had not done enough to protect civil liberties.

Growing pains were evident in the department's first years as different bureaucratic cultures, now part of a single operation, sought to work together. The new department also quickly became embroiled in turf battles with the FBI (which remained in the Justice Department) as the two departments attempted to sort out their respective responsibilities for homeland security. The department's most public failure was its terrible performance during Hurricane Katrina. Not only did the agency fail to move quickly to assist stranded residents of New Orleans, but it also mismanaged contracts and grants associated with the recovery efforts. The heavy reliance of the Department of Homeland Security on private contractors has contributed to its failings. Without the staff to supervise the contractors adequately, the department has become known for massive cost overruns and poor performance. Concerns about conflicts of interest between contractors and the agency have mounted. Alarm bells went off in 2007 when the Coast Guard, the largest agency under Homeland Security, renewed a $24 billion contract for fleet modernization only eleven days after department officials testified about major flaws in the program.[8]

For Critical Analysis

Why was the Department of Homeland Security created? What problems has the new agency faced?

AGENCIES FOR EXTERNAL NATIONAL SECURITY Two departments occupy center stage in maintaining external national security: the departments of State and Defense.

The State Department's primary mission is diplomacy. As the United States geared up to invade Afghanistan in 2001 and Iraq in 2003, Secretary of State Colin Powell took the lead in building the case for American action. Although diplomacy is the primary task of the State Department, diplomatic missions are only one of its organizational dimensions. As of 2008, the State Department comprised twenty-seven bureau-level units, each under the direction of an assistant secretary.

These bureaus support the responsibilities of the elite of foreign affairs, the foreign service officers (FSOs), who staff U.S. embassies around the world and who hold almost all of the most powerful positions in the department below the rank of ambassador.[9] The ambassadorial positions, especially the plum positions in the major capitals of the world, are filled by presidential appointees, many of whom get their posts by having been important donors to the victorious political campaign.

Despite the importance of the State Department in foreign affairs, fewer than 20 percent of all U.S. government employees working abroad are directly under its authority. By far the largest number of career government professionals working abroad are under the authority of the Defense Department.

The creation of the Department of Defense by legislation between 1947 and 1949 was an effort to unify the two historic military departments, the War Department and the Navy Department, and to integrate them with a new department, the Air Force. Real unification, however, did not occur. The Defense Department simply added more pluralism to an already pluralistic national security establishment. That establishment became more complex in 1952, with the creation of the National Security Agency, charged with electronic surveillance and intelligence gathering.

The American military, following worldwide military tradition, is organized according to a "chain of command"—a tight hierarchy of clear responsibility and rank, made clearer by uniforms, special insignia, and detailed organizational charts and rules of order and etiquette. At the top of the military chain of command are chiefs of staff (called chief of naval operations in the navy, and commandant in the marines). These chiefs of staff also constitute the membership of the Joint Chiefs of Staff—the center of military policy and management.

In 2002, for the first time in our nation's history, the Defense Department created a regional commander in chief charged with homeland defense and command of military operations inside the nation's borders. The U.S. Northern Command is charged with providing emergency backup to state and local governments, which are the first responders to any security disaster. It also provides security when military personnel or equipment is needed. For example, during the 2004 Super Bowl the Northern Command deployed aircraft to patrol airspace above Houston's Reliant Stadium, which had been declared a no-fly zone. The creation of a regional command within the United States is an unprecedented move, breaching a long-standing line between domestic law enforcement and foreign military operations.

As the creation of a military capacity within the United States suggests, addressing the threat of terrorism calls for greater coordination of internal and external security. In 2004, the National Commission on Terrorist Attacks upon the United States (the 9/11 Commission) issued a widely read report that called for a major reorganization of bureaucratic responsibilities for internal and external security.[10] The report revealed that different departments of the American government had information that, if handled properly, might have prevented the attacks of September 11, 2001. To correct this, the commission made major recommendations designed to promote unity of effort across the bureaucracy.

The 9/11 Commission's work prompted a major reorganization of the fragmented intelligence community. In 2005, a new office, the Office of the Director of National Intelligence, took over responsibility for coordinating the efforts of the sixteen different agencies that gather intelligence. The DNI reports directly to the president each morning.

There is considerable disagreement about whether the reorganization has built more effective intelligence capacities. In 2007, the Director of National Intelligence issued a surprising report declaring that Iran no longer had an active nuclear program. Called "one of the biggest reversals in the history of U.S. nuclear intelligence," the new report directly contradicted earlier accounts about the nuclear threat in Iran.[11] Although some members of Congress viewed the revised report as a sign that the intelligence reorganization was working, others charged that the conclusions were politically motivated.[12]

After September 11, the federal government assumed a new role in airport security. With the passage of the Secure Aviation and Transportation Act, the federal government became involved with screening passengers and baggage.

NATIONAL SECURITY AND DEMOCRACY Of all the agencies in the federal bureaucracy, those charged with providing national security most often come into tension with the norms and expectations of American democracy. Two issues in particular arise as these agencies work to ensure the national security: (1) the trade-offs between respecting the personal rights of individuals versus protecting the general public and (2) the need for secrecy in matters of national security versus the public's right to know what the government is doing. Standards of what is an acceptable trade-off in each area vary depending on whether the country is at war or peace. The nature of the threat facing national security also affects judgments about the appropriate trade-offs. Needless to say, Americans often disagree about such threats and therefore take different views about what activities the government should be able to pursue to defend our national security. At the outset of the war on terrorism, the nation was unusually united in its support for a wide range of government security measures that would have been highly controversial in any other circumstance.

When national security is at stake, federal agencies have taken actions that are normally considered incompatible with individual rights. For example, in World War II, thousands of American citizens of Japanese descent were interned for national security reasons. Although the Supreme Court declared this action justified, the federal government has since acknowledged that it constituted unjustified discrimination and has offered reparations to those who were interned. In the 1960s, the FBI director J. Edgar Hoover authorized extensive wiretaps to eavesdrop on telephone calls of the civil rights leader Martin Luther King, Jr.; most people today would regard this an illegal invasion of his personal privacy. With the advent of the war on terrorism, the government gained unprecedented powers to detain foreign suspects, carry out wiretaps and searches, conduct secret military tribunals, and build an integrated law enforcement and intelligence system. Congress hastily enacted many of these sweeping provisions of the USA PATRIOT Act several weeks after the terrorist attacks, with little debate. Since then, extensive doubts about the broad powers of the Patriot Act have emerged. As denunciations of the act spread from civil libertarians on the left to libertarians on the right and to groups such as librarians and city governments, who objected to its surveillance provisions, Congress began to consider measures that would restrict federal power in order to protect individual liberties. When Congress debated renewing the Patriot Act in 2005–06, these concerns about individual liberties threatened to block renewal. The act that was finally approved in 2006 protected most libraries from having to turn over information to the government. Nonetheless, many in Congress felt the safeguards to individual liberties did not go far enough.

Protecting national security often requires the government to conduct its activities in secret. Yet, as Americans have come to expect a more open government in the past three decades, many critics believe that federal agencies charged with national security keep too many secrets from the American public. As one critic put it, "the United States government must rest, in the words of the Declaration of Independence, on 'the consent of the governed.' And there can be no meaningful consent where those who are governed do not know to what they are consenting."[13] The effort to make information related to national security more available to the public began in 1966 with the passage of the Freedom of Information Act (FOIA). Strengthened in 1974 after Watergate, the act allows any person to request classified information from any federal agency. It is estimated that the federal government spends $398 million a year responding to 21,412,571 requests for information.[14] The information obtained through the Freedom of Information Act often reveals unflattering or unsuccessful aspects of national security activities. One private organization, the National Security Archive, makes extensive use of the Freedom of Information Act to obtain information about the activities of national security agencies. The National Security Archive has published many of these documents on its Web site and maintains an archive in Washington, D.C. that is open to the public.

The tension between secrecy and democracy has sharpened dramatically with the war on terrorism. The Freedom of Information Act has been curtailed, and the range of information deemed sensitive has greatly expanded. President Bush defended the new secrecy, declaring, "We're an open society, but we're at war. Foreign terrorists and agents must never again be allowed to use our freedoms against us." Although most Americans agreed that enhanced secrecy was needed to ensure domestic security, concerns about excessive secrecy mounted. Some analysts worried that secrecy would prevent Congress from carrying out its basic oversight responsibilities. They also claimed that much of the secrecy had nothing to do with national security. As head of the commission appointed to investigate the events of September 11, including related intelligence failures, former New Jersey governor Tom Kean became a critic of the level of secrecy in the Bush administration. "I've been reading these highly, highly classified documents. In most cases, I finish with them, I look up and say, 'Why is this classified?' And so one of the things that I hope is that maybe out of our work and maybe others, a lot of these documents that are classified will be unclassified."[15] Others charged that the Bush administration was reversing the trend toward a more open government on issues that had nothing to do with domestic security (see Figure 14.5). For example, the White House has attempted to keep secret the names of those attending meetings with administration officials. In an unprecedented move, the Government Accountability Office, the investigative arm of Congress, sued the administration for failing to disclose information about Vice President Dick Cheney's task force on energy. In 2005, the courts ruled that Cheney did have the right to keep the task force secret. A similar issue arose in 2007, when an

FIGURE 14.5 ★
Keeping Secrets

The number of classified documents has increased substantially since 2001, whereas the pages of material that have been declassified has declined sharply. Meanwhile, requests to declassify material under the Freedom of Information Act have increased at a rate that agencies have found difficult to manage. During what years was there a move toward more openness in government?

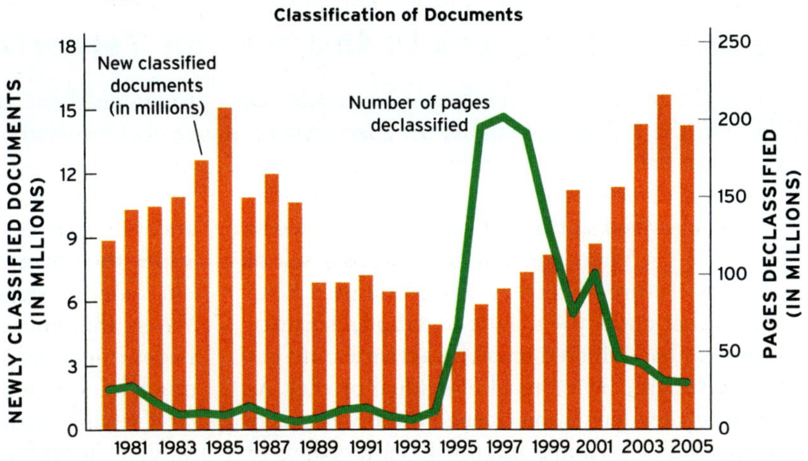

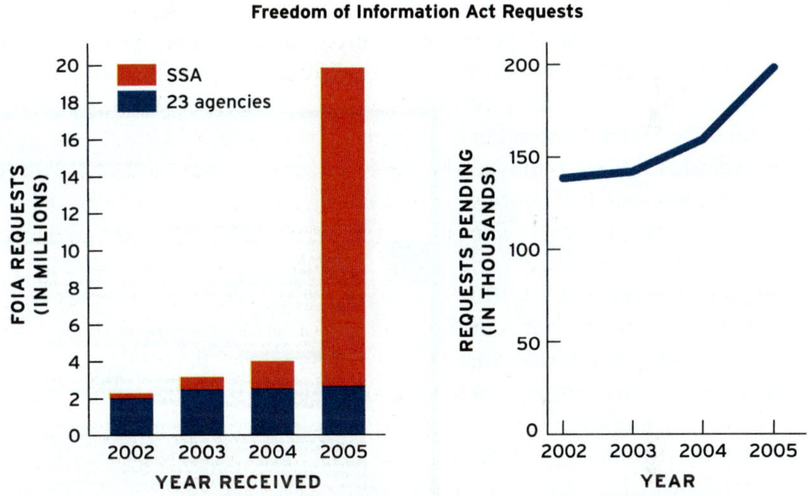

SOURCES: Information Security Oversight Office, www.openthegovernment.org/otg/SRC2006.pdf; and U.S. Government Accountability Office, www.gao.gov/new.items/d07491t.pdf (accessed 3/10/08).

outside group sought to make the White House visitor logs public. This time the courts held that the information should be released, although the White House appealed the ruling in an effort to keep the logs private.[16]

There are no easy answers to the questions about how the needs for national security should be reconciled with the values of a democratic society. It is clear, however, that in an era when national security is foremost in the public's mind, conflicts between democracy and secrecy are sure to increase.

Maintaining a Strong Economy

In our capitalist economic system, the government does not directly run the economy. Yet many federal government activities are critical to maintaining a strong economy. Foremost among these are the agencies responsible for fiscal and monetary policy. Other agencies, such as the Internal Revenue Service (IRS), transform

Secrecy and Openness in the War on Terrorism

During the 1950s and 1960s, in the early decades of the Cold War, the federal government argued that secrecy was essential to ensure national security. Information about a diverse range of government activities was routinely classified so that the public had no access to it. The 1973–74 Watergate scandal marked a sea of change in this culture of secrecy. The Watergate hearings revealed that under the mantle of national security, the government had initiated unlawful activities and engaged in unjustifiable invasions of individual privacy. As a consequence, new legislation opened the bureaucracy up to greater public scrutiny, and the 1974 Freedom of Information Act allowed individuals to request access to classified information.

In the aftermath of the September 11 terrorist attacks, President W. Bush defended the need to reimpose greater secrecy in the interests of national security. After September 11, the administration removed hundreds of thousands of public documents from the Internet. The administration also refused to reveal the identities of more than 1,100 people held in custody—but not charged—for suspected terrorism. And in a move designed to weaken one of the most important tools promoting public disclosure, Attorney General John Ashcroft issued a directive to government agencies to use greater caution in responding to freedom of information requests.

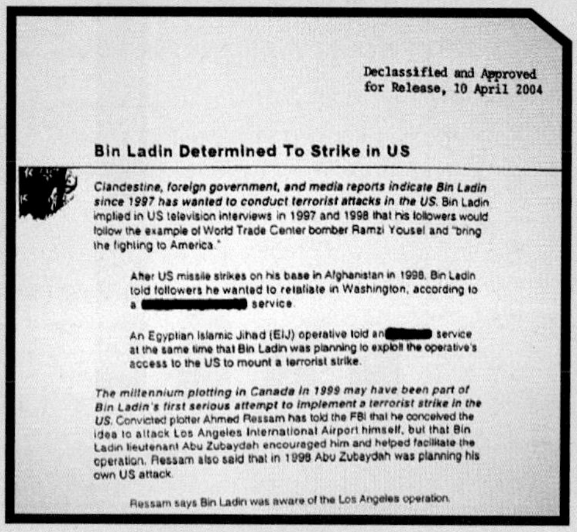

Declassified and Approved for Release, 10 April 2004

Bin Ladin Determined To Strike in US

Clandestine, foreign government, and media reports indicate Bin Ladin since 1997 has wanted to conduct terrorist attacks in the US. Bin Ladin implied in US television interviews in 1997 and 1998 that his followers would follow the example of World Trade Center bomber Ramzi Yousef and "bring the fighting to America."

After US missile strikes on his base in Afghanistan in 1998, Bin Ladin told followers he wanted to retaliate in Washington, according to a [redacted] service.

An Egyptian Islamic Jihad (EIJ) operative told an [redacted] service at the same time that Bin Ladin was planning to exploit the operative's access to the US to mount a terrorist strike.

The millennium plotting in Canada in 1999 may have been part of Bin Ladin's first serious attempt to implement a terrorist strike in the US. Convicted plotter Ahmed Ressam has told the FBI that he conceived the idea to attack Los Angeles International Airport himself, but that Bin Ladin lieutenant Abu Zubaydah encouraged him and helped facilitate the operation. Ressam also said that in 1998 Abu Zubaydah was planning his own US attack.

Ressam says Bin Ladin was aware of the Los Angeles operation.

The issue of secrecy and the war on terrorism reignited in late 2005 when the *New York Times* revealed that the Bush administration had been conducting unauthorized wiretaps on U.S. citizens since 2002. Although administration officials defended their actions as constitutional and essential to fighting terrorism, critics across the political spectrum charged that such eavesdropping was not lawful.

Supporters of enhanced secrecy contend that standards of openness prevalent in peacetime must give way during a war. Although most of the war on terrorism is not visible to the public, the need for secrecy may be even greater than in other wars in which the United States has been involved. Terrorists rely on publicly available sources of information to plan their attacks. Apparently innocuous information about the location of facilities, such as nuclear power plants or water-treatment facilities, provides terrorists with vulnerable targets. Furthermore, counterterrorism is a delicate task. If the sources of information on which counterintelligence agencies rely become public, these sources may become unavailable in the future. For example, until 1998, the government tracked the activities of Osama bin Laden through calls he made on his satellite phone. When this knowledge became publicly available, bin Laden apparently stopped using the phone, making him much harder to track.

Critics contend that the administration has gone too far in its quest for secrecy. They charge that the administration has claimed a right to secrecy on issues that have nothing to do with national security, as in its refusal to divulge the proceedings of its energy task force. Even in matters of national security, the administration has gone overboard, according to critics. Without access to information, Congress cannot exercise its oversight responsibilities, which are vital to democratic accountability. And, the secrecy surrounding those jailed as part of the terrorism probe distorts the American system of justice, since very few of these individuals were actually charged with a crime. Finally, critics charge that secrecy will eventually erode public confidence in the government, thus undermining the war on terrorism. Thomas Kean, the co-chair of the 9/11 Commission, stressed the importance of open government to national security, arguing, "The best ally we have in protecting ourselves against terrorism is an informed public."[a]

FOR CRITICAL ANALYSIS

1. Why do some argue that greater government secrecy is necessary since the terrorist attacks in 2001?
2. Does secrecy undermine basic American values? How can the United States guard against terrorism without destroying the fundamental liberties that define our nation?

---

a. "The Dangerous Comfort of Secrecy," *New York Times*, July 12, 2005, p. A20.

private resources into use for public purposes. Tax policy may also strengthen the economy through decisions about whom to tax, how much, and when. Finally, the federal government, through such agencies as the Department of Transportation, the Commerce Department, and the Energy Department may directly provide services or goods that bolster the economy.

FISCAL AND MONETARY AGENCIES The best term for government activity affecting or relating to money is **fiscal policy.** "Fiscal" can refer to anything and everything having to do with public finance. However, we in the United States often reserve *fiscal* for taxing and spending policies and use *monetary* for policies having to do with banks, credit, and currency. Yet a third term, *welfare,* deserves to be treated as an equal member of this redistributive category.[17]

fiscal policy the government's use of taxing, monetary, and spending powers to manipulate the economy

The administration of fiscal policy occurs primarily in the Treasury Department. In addition to collecting income, corporate, and other taxes, the Treasury also manages the enormous national debt—$5.8 trillion in 2008.[18] The debt is a fiscal instrument in the hands of the federal government that can be used—through manipulation of interest rates and through the buying and selling of government bonds—to slow down or to speed up the activity of the entire national economy, as well as to defend the value of the dollar in international trade. The Treasury Department is also responsible for printing U.S. currency, but currency is only a tiny proportion of the entire money economy. Most of the trillions of dollars used in the transactions of the private and public sectors of the U.S. economy exist in computerized accounts, not in actual currency.

Another important fiscal agency (although for technical reasons it is called an agency of monetary policy) is the **Federal Reserve System,** which is headed by the Federal Reserve Board. The Federal Reserve System (called simply the Fed) has authority over the interest rates and lending activities of the nation's most important banks. Congress established the Fed in 1913 as a clearinghouse responsible for adjusting the supply of money and credit to the needs of commerce and industry in different regions of the country. The Fed is also responsible for ensuring that banks do not overextend themselves, a policy that guards against a chain of bank failures during a sudden economic scare, such as occurred in 1929 and again in 2008. The Federal Reserve Board directs the operations of the twelve district Federal Reserve Banks, which are essentially "bankers' banks," serving the monetary needs of the hundreds of member banks in the national banking system.[19] The Treasury and the Federal Reserve took center stage when a string of bank failures threatened economic catastrophe in 2008. These agencies designed a $700 billion bailout package and persuaded Congress that a rapid response was needed to avert a worldwide depression. Although the Treasury and the Federal Reserve sprang into action when economic calamity loomed, critics charged that the crisis could have been prevented if these agencies had exercised more regulatory oversight over the financial sector during the previous decade.

Federal Reserve System a system of twelve Federal Reserve Banks that facilitates exchanges of cash, checks, and credit; regulates member banks; and uses monetary policies to fight inflation and deflation

REVENUE AGENCIES One of the first actions Congress took under President George Washington was to create the Department of the Treasury, and probably its oldest function is the collection of taxes on imports, called tariffs. Now part of the United States Customs Service, federal customs agents are located at every U.S. seaport and international airport to oversee the collection of tariffs. But far and away the most important of the **revenue agencies** is the Internal Revenue Service. The Customs Service and the IRS are two of at least twelve bureaus within the Treasury Department.

revenue agencies agencies responsible for collecting taxes. Examples include the Internal Revenue Service for income taxes, the U.S. Customs Service for tariffs and other taxes on imported goods, and the Bureau of Alcohol, Tobacco, and Firearms for collection of taxes on the sales of those particular products

In recent years, there have been several attempts to "reinvent" government. In 1993, President Bill Clinton and Vice President Al Gore established the National Performance Review to reinvent government. Gore promoted this on David Letterman's show, where he railed against the government's procurement requirements, which even specified the number of pieces into which a government ashtray may shatter.

The IRS is the government agency that Americans love to hate. As one expert put it, "probably no organization in the country, public or private, creates as much clientele *dis*favor as the Internal Revenue Service. The very nature of its work brings it into an adversary relationship with vast numbers of Americans every year."[20] Taxpayers complain about the IRS's needless complexity, its lack of sensitivity and responsiveness to individual taxpayers, and its overall lack of efficiency. Such complaints led Congress to pass the IRS Restructuring and Reform Act of 1998, which instituted a number of new protections for taxpayers. The law aimed to make IRS agents more "customer friendly" and limit the agency's ability to collect money owed through liens on individual income or wages. It also mandated the firing of IRS employees who harass taxpayers or violate their rights. By 2005, however, concern was shifting toward the problem of tax dodgers. Critics charged that the reduction in the IRS budget and its heightened scrutiny of low-income workers had created new problems of tax avoidance among high earners. When a 2005 report indicated that the gap between true income and income reported to the IRS was at an all-time high, the IRS vowed to step up enforcement activities, focusing especially on foreign tax shelters favored by the wealthy.

The politics of the IRS is most interesting because although thousands upon thousands of individual corporations and wealthy individuals have a strong and active interest in American tax policy, key taxation decisions are set by agreements among the president, the Treasury Department, and the leading members of the two tax committees in Congress, the House Ways and Means Committee and the Senate Finance Committee. External influence is not spread throughout the fifty states but is much more centralized in the majority political party, a few key figures in Congress, and a handful of professional lobbyists. Suspicions of unfair exemptions and favoritism are widespread, and they do exist, but these exemptions come largely from Congress, *not* from the IRS itself.

ECONOMIC DEVELOPMENT AGENCIES Federal agencies also conduct programs designed to strengthen particular segments of the economy or to provide specific services aimed at strengthening the entire economy. Created in 1889, the Department of Agriculture is the fourth oldest cabinet department. Its initial mission, to strengthen American agriculture through research and to assist farmers by providing information about effective farming practices, reflected the enormous importance of agriculture in the American economy. Through its Agricultural Extension Service, the Department of Agriculture established an important presence in rural areas throughout the country. It also built strong support for its activities among the nation's farmers and at the many land-grant colleges, where agricultural research has been conducted for over one hundred years.

At first glance, the Department of Transportation, which oversees the nation's highway and air traffic systems, may seem to have little to do with economic development. But effective transportation is the backbone of a strong economy. The interstate highway system, for example, is widely acknowledged as a key factor in promoting economic growth in the decades after World War II. The Departments of Commerce and Energy also oversee programs designed to ensure a strong economy. The Small Business Administration in the Department of Commerce provides loans and technical assistance to small businesses across the country.

In recent decades dissatisfaction with government has led to calls to keep government out of the economy. Yet if the federal government were to disappear, chances are high that the economy would fall into chaos. Agreement is widespread that the federal government should set the basic rules for economic activity and intervene—through such measures as setting interest rates—to keep the economy strong. Some analysts argue that the government's role should go beyond rule setting to include more active measures such as investment in infrastructure. These advocates of government action point to the economic benefits of government investments in the interstate highway system and the government research in the 1960s that led to the creation of the Internet.

Can Bureaucracy Be Reinvented?

When citizens complain that government is too bureaucratic, what they often mean is that government bureaucracies seem inefficient and waste money. The epitome of such bureaucratic inefficiency in the late 1980s was the Department of Defense, which was revealed to have spent $640 apiece for toilet seats and $435 apiece for hammers.[21] Many citizens also had personal experience with the federal government: a mountain of forms to fill out, lengthy waits, and unsympathetic service. Why can't government do better? many citizens asked. The application of new technologies and innovative management strategies in the private sector during the 1980s made government agencies look even more lumbering and inefficient by comparison. People were coming to expect faster service and more customer-friendly interactions in the private sector. But how can public-sector bureaucracies change their ways when they are not subject to tests of efficiency and cost effectiveness that often prompt innovation in the private sector?

In 1993, President Clinton launched the National Performance Review (NPR)—a part of his promise to "reinvent government"—to make the federal bureaucracy more efficient, accountable, and effective. Vice President Al Gore took charge of

The latest case of reinventing government is the largest and most complex yet, the creation of the Department of Homeland Security. Reorganizing the bureaucracy on this level has been a complicated procedure, as the organizational chart being held by Representative Jane Harman (D-Calif.) attests.

the new effort. The National Performance Review sought to prod federal agencies into adopting flexible, goal-driven practices. Clinton promised that the result would be a government that would "work better and cost less." Virtually all observers agreed that the NPR made substantial progress. Its original goal was to save more than $100 billion over five years, in large part by cutting the federal workforce by 12 percent (more than 270,000 jobs) by the end of 1999. Actually, by 2000, $136 billion in savings were already assured through legislative or administrative action, and the federal workforce had been cut by 426,200.[22]

The NPR also focused on cutting red tape, streamlining procurement (how the government purchases goods and services), improving the coordination of federal management, and simplifying federal rules. For instance, the Office of Management and Budget (OMB) abolished the notorious 10,000-page Federal Personnel Manual and the Standard Form 171, the government's lengthy job application form. Another example, even more revealing of the nature of the NPR's work, was the employee-designed reform of the Defense Department's method for reimbursing its employees' travel expenses: a process that used to take seventeen steps and two months was streamlined to a four-step, computer-based procedure taking less than fifteen minutes, with anticipated savings of $1 billion over five years.

Another fact about administrative reform is that no reform movement will survive a change of administration. Thus, although Republicans have an equal or better record than Democrats in the history of administrative reform, one of the first things that happened as President Bush took the oath of office in January 2001 was the termination of NPR. Reform of public bureaucracies is always complex because strong constituencies may attempt to block changes that they believe will harm them. Instead Bush sought to fulfill his promise of smaller government by launching a far-reaching effort to contract out government jobs. The president introduced new procedures that would subject more than 800,000 federal jobs—nearly half the federal civilian workforce—to competitive outsourcing. If it were determined that a private company could do the job more efficiently, the work would be contracted out. Not surprisingly, Bush's effort aroused considerable opposition from government workers. It also caused controversy in Congress, where it sparked a countermovement to restrict the conditions under which federal jobs could be contracted out.

Bush's efforts to streamline the federal bureaucracy were further complicated by the new demands put on the federal government by the war on terrorism. As we have already seen, the Department of Homeland Security presents a massive management challenge and may take many years to achieve its goal of greater coordination of domestic security agencies. At the same time, the new demands of domestic and international security have made it difficult to reduce the size of government. Although the number of federal civil servants has declined by about 2 percent since Bush took office, the numbers of people employed under federal contracts and grants has grown substantially. The political scientist Paul C. Light estimates that the "true size" of government, including both federal civil service and contract and grant-generated jobs, grew by 32 percent from 1999 to 2005.[23] Light estimates that at the end of the Cold War in 1990, there were three and a half contractors and grantees for every civil servant; by 2005, the buildup for the war on terror had altered the ratio to five and a half contractors and grantees for every civil servant.[24] As we will see, the growth in government contractors raises difficult questions about how to ensure that these private actors are serving the public interest.

Can the Bureaucracy Be Reduced?

Does bureaucracy serve the interests of all the American people? Or does it provide special benefits for influential interest groups, ignoring public needs? Or does bureaucracy mainly benefit government workers themselves, wasting public money by providing inefficient services? During the 1980s and 1990s, the reputation of the federal bureaucracy was at a low point. The belief that bureaucracy benefited entrenched interests and wasted taxpayer dollars was widespread. The negative image of the federal bureaucracy led to numerous efforts to reduce (or to use the popular contemporary word, "downsize") the bureaucracy. This downsizing could be achieved in at least three ways: termination, devolution, or privatization.

Termination

The only *certain* way to reduce the size of the bureaucracy is to eliminate programs. Variations in the levels of federal personnel and expenditures (as were shown in Figures 14.1 and 14.2) demonstrate the futility of trying to make permanent cuts in existing agencies. Furthermore, most agencies have a supportive constituency that will fight to reinstate any cuts that are made. Termination is the only way to ensure an agency's reduction; this is a rare occurrence, even in the Reagan administration and the first Bush administration, both of which proclaimed a strong commitment to the reduction of the national government. In fact, not a single national government agency or program was terminated during the twelve years of Reagan and Bush.

The Republican-led 104th Congress (1995–96) was even more committed to the termination of programs. Newt Gingrich, Speaker of the House, took Congress by storm with his promises of a virtual revolution in government. But when the dust had settled at the end of the first session of the first Gingrich-led Congress, no significant progress had been made toward downsizing through termination of agencies and programs.[25] The only two agencies eliminated were the Office of Technology Assessment, which provided research for Congress, and the Advisory Council on Intergovernmental Relations, which studied the relationship between the federal government and the states. Significantly, neither of these agencies had a strong constituency to defend it.

The overall lack of success in terminating bureaucracy is a reflection of Americans' love/hate relationship with the national government. As antagonistic as Americans may be toward bureaucracy in general, they benefit from the services being rendered and protections being offered by particular bureaucratic agencies; that is, they fiercely defend their favorite agencies while perceiving no inconsistency between that defense and their antagonistic attitude toward the bureaucracy in general. A good case in point is the agonizing problem of closing military bases in the wake of the Cold War with the former Soviet Union, when the United States no longer needed so many bases. Since every base was in some congressional member's district, it proved impossible for Congress to decide to close any of them. Consequently, between 1988 and 1990, Congress established a Defense Base Closure and Realignment Commission to decide on base closings, taking the matter out of Congress's hands altogether.[26] And even so, the process was slow and agonizing.

Elected leaders have come to rely on a more incremental approach to downsizing the bureaucracy. Much has been done by budgetary means, reducing the budgets of all agencies across the board by small percentages, and cutting some less-supported agencies by larger amounts. Yet these changes are still incremental, leaving the existence of agencies unaddressed.

An additional approach has been taken to thwart the highly unpopular regulatory agencies, which are so small (relatively) that cutting their budgets contributes virtually nothing to reducing the deficit. This approach is called **deregulation,** simply defined as a reduction in the number of rules promulgated by regulatory agencies. President Reagan used this strategy successfully and was very proud of it. Presidents Bush, Clinton, and George W. Bush have proudly followed Reagan's lead.

deregulation a policy of reducing or eliminating regulatory restraints on the conduct of individuals or private institutions

Devolution

The next best approach to genuine reduction of the size of the bureaucracy is **devolution**—downsizing the federal bureaucracy by delegating the implementation of programs to state and local governments. Devolution often alters the pattern of who benefits most from government programs. Opponents of devolution in social policy, for example, charge that it reduces the ability of the government to remedy inequality. They argue that state governments, which cannot run deficits as does the federal government and which have more limited taxing capabilities, will inevitably cut spending on programs that serve low-income residents. They point to the State Child Health Insurance Program, which was created in 1997 to extend health insurance to low-income children. When the economy was booming,

devolution a policy to remove a program from one level of government by delegating it or passing it down to a lower level of government, such as from the national government to the state and local governments

The State Children's Health Insurance Program helps pay for health insurance for families with children. When Congress proposed renewing and expanding the program in 2007, President Bush vetoed both bills passed by Congress, but did sign an extension of the program through 2009.

Creating the Capabilities for Nation Building

As the world's strongest democracy, the United States has consistently regarded its international role as one that should not only project the country's military power but also embody American values. The federal government's goals in promoting democracy abroad—previously focused on containing communism—have steadily grown to include all the different tasks that fall under the problem of nation building.

During the Cold War, the United States tried to contain the Soviet Union's efforts to establish communist ideology in the satellite regimes of Eastern Europe and the developing world. In the war on terrorism, by contrast, the United States confronted terrorist groups that wanted control in societies divided by fierce religious and ethnic conflicts. Instead of the tightly controlled governments of the Soviet satellite countries, these countries had only the most fragile political institutions. They were called fragile or failed states.

As the conflicts in Afghanistan and Iraq made clear, such conditions called for the creation of new capabilities. Increasingly doubtful that the use of military force alone could create stable democracies in either country, Congress and the Executive Branch began to ask what skills were needed in order to strengthen political institutions and national cohesion in these countries. In August 2004, Congress authorized the State Department to create the Office of the Coordinator for Reconstruction and Stabilization (S/CRS).

The core mission of the S/CRS is to lead civilian capacity for stabilizing and reconstructing postconflict societies. In concrete terms, this mission involves many specialized tasks that have to be pursued in careful sequence. As military units establish day-to-day security, the new office is responsible for mobilizing experts in areas including municipal administration; reconstruction of water supply, electricity, and telecommunications; humanitarian relief; housing; education; banking; agriculture; and the innumerable other specialties required for stabilizing war-torn countries. Other professionals were simultaneously charged with responsibility for strengthening political institutions and, where necessary, planting the seeds of entirely new institutions such as political parties, legislative assemblies, courts, and local governments. The role of the S/CRS is to mobilize civilian resources to respond rapidly when a crisis occurs.

Despite its overarching goals, the new office commands modest personnel and financial resources. Its core staff is relatively small because it is primarily charged with planning and coordinating other agencies. Equally important, under this new arrangement, the State Department office is expected to develop a civilian reserve corps of several hundred individuals drawn from federal agencies and nongovernmental organizations who can apply their expertise quickly to postconflict trouble spots.

Some observers question whether the State Department is the best location for the new S/CRS. Even though its mission rests on planning and coordinating, the tasks involved in postconflict reconstruction are far different from the customary reporting and liaison work familiar to the State Department's Foreign Service officers. Meanwhile, supporters of the Defense Department argued that the Pentagon was a more natural place to locate such postconflict planning capabilities. These observers noted that the Pentagon's capabilities extended well beyond the narrow use of military force. The Defense Department had far more personnel, many of them trained in the engineering and logistical disciplines that were central to postconflict reconstruction.

Given the fact that postconflict reconstruction will remain an ongoing task for the United States abroad, such questions are only likely to become more, rather than less, pressing.

FOR CRITICAL ANALYSIS

1. Why does the United States need so many different kinds of expertise to promote political stability in fragile and failed states?
2. What are the pros and cons of assigning responsibility for postconflict stabilization to the State Department instead of the Department of Defense?

states added children to the rolls and some even extended benefits to their parents. By 2002, however, as states faced their worst budget crisis in decades, many cut back on the state Children's Health Insurance Program. Although the federal government was initially able to compensate for state funding problems, states have found it difficult to keep pace with the rising number of children without health insurance. Moreover, because state revenues can fluctuate widely from year to year, states are often forced to cut back on expensive health coverage programs. For example, even as California debated a plan for providing universal health coverage in 2008, the state was considering significant cutbacks in medical programs for the poor.

For Critical Analysis

Dissatisfied citizens have supported a range of bureaucratic reforms, including termination of agencies, devolution of responsibility to lower levels of government, and privatization. Are such reforms likely to make the bureaucracy more responsive to public wishes?

Often the central aim of devolution is to provide more efficient and flexible government services. Yet by its very nature, devolution entails variation across the states. In some states, government services may improve as a consequence of devolution. In other states, services may deteriorate as the states use devolution as an opportunity to cut spending and reduce services. This has been the pattern in the implementation of the welfare reform passed in 1996, the most significant devolution of federal government social programs in many decades. Some states, such as Wisconsin, have used the flexibility of the reform to design innovative programs that respond to clients' needs; other states, such as Idaho, have virtually dismantled their welfare programs. Because the legislation placed a five-year lifetime limit on receiving welfare, the states will take on an even greater role in the future as current clients lose their eligibility for federal benefits. Welfare reform has been praised by many for reducing welfare rolls and responding to the public desire that welfare be a temporary program. At the same time, it has placed more low-income women and their children at risk for being left with no form of assistance at all, depending on the state in which they live.

This is the dilemma that devolution poses. Up to a point, variation can be considered one of the virtues of federalism. But dangers are inherent in large variations in the provisions of services and benefits in a democracy.

Privatization

Most of what is called "privatization" is the provision of government goods and services by private contractors under direct government supervision. Except for top-secret strategic materials, virtually all military hardware, from boats to bullets, is produced on a privatized basis by private contractors. Research services worth billions of dollars are bought under contract by governments; these private contractors are universities as well as ordinary industrial corporations and private "think tanks." **Privatization** simply means that a formerly public activity is picked up under contract by a private company or companies. But such programs are still very much government programs; they are paid for by government and supervised by government. Privatization downsizes the government only in that the workers providing the service are no longer counted as part of the government bureaucracy.

privatization removing all or part of a program from the public sector to the private sector

The central aim of privatization is to reduce the cost of government. Depending on how it is conducted, competitive outsourcing may not lead to extensive privatization; instead, competition may improve government performance by forcing federal agencies to reexamine how they can do their work more efficiently. When private contractors can perform a task as well as government can but for less money, taxpayers win. But private firms may not be more efficient or less costly than government. This is especially likely when there is little competition among private firms and when public bureaucracies are not granted a fair chance to bid in the contracting competition. When private firms have a monopoly on service provision, they may be less efficient than government and more expensive. In fact, there is no good evidence that privatization saves the government money. And problems of accountability arise with private contractors just as they do with government workers.

Concerns about adequate government oversight and accountability have escalated in recent years as the scale of contracting has dramatically increased. Payments for federal contracts grew from $207 billion in 2000 to $400 billion in 2007. In 2005, only 48 percent of existing contracts were subject to competition, whereas 79 percent were open to competition in 2001 (Figure 14.6).[27] Although military contracts account for much of the growth, contracting is common throughout the federal bureaucracy. In fact, contracting is now so widespread that it has been called a "virtual fourth branch of government."[28]

FIGURE 14.6 ★ Outsourcing the Government

As spending on federal contracts has grown, the number of contracts subject to open competition has declined substantially. At the same time, the rise in spending by private contractors on lobbying and campaign contributions raises questions about improper political influence on government contracting decisions.

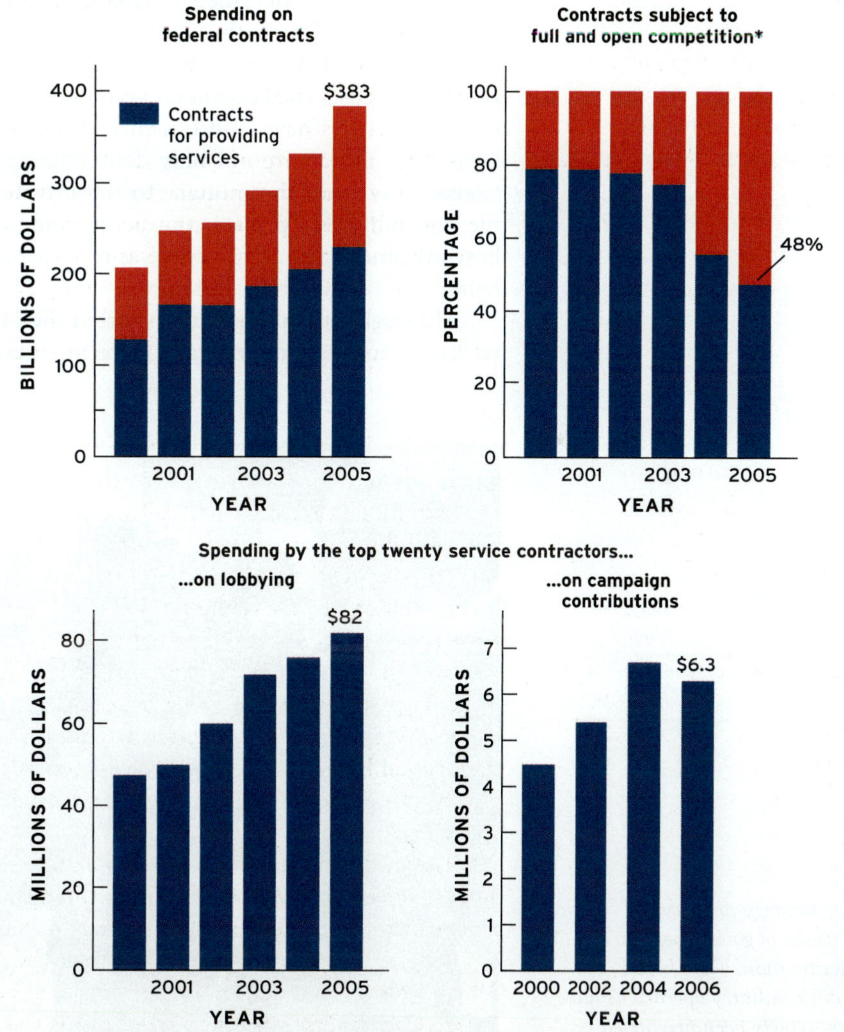

*Includes both new contracts and payments against existing contracts.
SOURCES: Scott Shane and Ron Nixon, "In Washington, Contractors Take on Biggest Role Ever," *New York Times*, February 4, 2007, p. A1. From Federal Procurement Data Center; Center for Responsive Politics; Senate Office of Public Records.

Much of the public attention to contracting has focused on the use of private contractors in Iraq. Congressional hearings revealed massive cost overruns by KBR (formerly a subsidiary of Halliburton, the firm that former vice president Dick Cheney headed), which held $9 billion in no-bid contracts to provide services ranging from supplying fuel for the military to cafeteria meals in Iraq. Army auditors have challenged $1.9 billion of KBR's bills as improper, citing violations ranging from unserved meals to inflated gas prices.[29]

Private security firms pose even more serious oversight issues. Estimates in 2007 showed that there were some 48,000 employees of private security firms in Iraq compared to 160,000 troops.[30] High profile congressional hearings into the role of Blackwater, a private security firm, in civilian killings in Iraq illustrated the difficulties of relying on private contractors to conduct a war. With a billion dollars of government contracts, Blackwater played an essential role in providing security in Iraq. But many argue that its effectiveness came at a high cost. Because they are not bound by the same rules of conduct as the military, private security forces have been accused of being more likely than the regular military to kill civilians who posed little threat. Similarly, because the private military is not subject to the military code of justice, illegal behavior is difficult to sanction. The private military is also costlier. Noting that "sergeants in the military generally cost the Government between $50,000 to $70,000 per year" and that "a comparable position at Blackwater costs the Federal Government over $400,000, six times as much," congressional critics have questioned whether the private military is cost effective.[31] Disparities in pay are not only demoralizing to the troops, they also lure trained troops away from the military to the private contractors. Even more troubling is the possibility that private contractors undermined the mission in Iraq by creating hostility among the Iraqi people as reports of unprovoked civilian killings came to light.[32]

Although federal regulations forbid the outsourcing of "inherently governmental work," no clear line separates governmental and nongovernmental work. In most

One strategy to carry out the tasks of government is privatization. The United States's military operations have increasingly been privatized.

aspects of government activity, contract employees work side by side with government employees in what has been called a "blended workforce."[33] For example, many agencies that rely on technical expertise, such as the National Oceanographic and Atmospheric Administration, routinely rely on contractors. The rule against using contractors for inherently governmental work seems to have little impact. For example, in 2006 the General Services Administration hired a private firm, CACI International, to help it examine cases of fraud by other private contractors. Not only did the contract workers cost double their public counterparts, they were engaged in oversight of other private contractors, a clear conflict of interest.[34]

In 2007, there were some signs that the pendulum was swinging back, if only a little, toward increasing the numbers of government workers. A congressional conference committee on intelligence, concerned about inappropriate use of contractors, ordered a comprehensive review of the role that contractors play in intelligence activities. Congress allowed most intelligence agencies to increase their staffing levels by 10 percent as they reduced the use of contractors in areas of intelligence work deemed too sensitive for private contractors.[35]

Politics Today

Private security firms played a significant role in the Iraq war and its aftermath. What are the advantages and disadvantages of relying on private firms in wartime? Can government provide adequate oversight of these private companies?

Can Bureaucracy Be Controlled?

By their very nature, bureaucracies pose challenges to democratic governance. Bureaucracies provide the expertise needed to implement the public will, but they can also become entrenched organizations that serve their own interests. The task is neither to retreat from bureaucracy nor to attack it, but to take advantage of its strengths while making it more accountable to the demands of democratic politics and representative government. This task will be the focus of the remainder of this chapter.

Over two hundred years, millions of employees, and trillions of dollars after the Founding, we must return to James Madison's observation, "You must first enable the government to control the governed; and in the next place oblige it to control itself."[36] Today the problem is the same, only now the process has a name: administrative accountability. Accountability implies that some higher authority will guide and judge the actions of the bureaucracy. The highest authority in a democracy is *demos*—the people—and the guidance for bureaucratic action is the popular will. But that ideal of accountability must be translated into practical terms by the president and Congress.

The President as Chief Executive

In 1937, President Franklin Roosevelt's Committee on Administrative Management gave official sanction to an idea that had been growing increasingly urgent: "The president needs help." The national government had grown rapidly during the preceding twenty-five years, but the structures and procedures necessary to manage the burgeoning executive branch had not yet been established. The response to the call for "help" for the president initially took the form of three management policies: (1) All communications and decisions that related to executive policy decisions must pass through the White House. (2) In order to cope with such a flow, the White House must have adequate staffs of specialists in research, analysis, legislative and legal writing, and public affairs. (3) The White House must have additional staff to follow through on presidential decisions—to ensure that those decisions are made, communicated to Congress, and carried out by the appropriate agency.

MAKING THE MANAGERIAL PRESIDENCY Establishing a management capacity for the presidency began in earnest with FDR, but it did not stop there.[37] The story of the modern presidency can be told largely as a series of responses to the plea for managerial help. Indeed, each expansion of the national government into new policies and programs in the twentieth century was accompanied by a parallel expansion of the president's management authority. This pattern began even before FDR's presidency, with the policy innovations of President Woodrow Wilson between 1913 and 1920. Congress responded to Wilson's policies with the 1921 Budget and Accounting Act, which turned over the prime legislative power of budgeting to the White House. Each successive president has continued this pattern, creating what we now know as the "managerial presidency."

Presidents John Kennedy and Lyndon Johnson were committed both to government expansion and to management expansion, in the spirit of their party's hero, FDR. President Nixon also strengthened and enlarged the managerial presidency, but for somewhat different reasons. He sought the strongest possible managerial hand because he had to assume that the overwhelming majority of federal employees had sympathies with the Democratic Party, which had controlled the White House and had sponsored governmental growth for twenty-eight of the previous thirty-six years.[38]

President Jimmy Carter was probably more preoccupied with administrative reform and reorganization than any other president in the twentieth century. His reorganization of the civil service will long be recognized as one of the most significant contributions of his presidency. The Civil Service Reform Act of 1978 was the first major revamping of the federal civil service since its creation in 1883. The 1978 act abolished the century-old Civil Service Commission (CSC) and replaced it with three agencies, each designed to handle one of the CSC's functions on the theory that the competing demands of these functions had given the CSC an "identity crisis." The Merit Systems Protection Board (MSPB) was created to defend competitive merit recruitment and promotion from political encroachment. A separate Federal Labor Relations Authority (FLRA) was set up to administer collective bargaining and individual personnel grievances. The third new agency, the Office of Personnel Management (OPM), was created to manage recruiting, testing, training, and the retirement system. The Senior Executive Service was also created at this time to recognize and foster "public management" as a profession and to facilitate the movement of top, "supergrade" career officials across agencies and departments.[39]

Carter also tried to impose a stringent budgetary process on all executive agencies. Called "zero-base budgeting," it was a method of budgeting from the bottom up, whereby each agency was required to rejustify its entire mission rather than merely its next year's increase. Zero-base budgeting did not succeed, but the effort was not lost on President Reagan. Although Reagan gave the impression of being a laid-back president, he actually centralized management to an unprecedented degree. From Carter's "bottom-up" approach, Reagan went to a "top-down" approach, whereby the initial budgetary decisions would be made in the White House and the agencies would be required to fit within those decisions. This process converted

Following the government's slow and inadequate response to Hurricane Katrina in 2005, some questioned President Bush's management of executive agencies. When Hurricane Rita threatened the Gulf states a month later, Bush worked closely with FEMA to make sure that the error was not repeated.

the OMB into an agency of policy determination and presidential management.[40] President George H. W. Bush took Reagan's centralization strategy even further in using the White House staff instead of cabinet secretaries for managing the executive branch.[41]

President Clinton was often criticized for the way he managed his administration. His easygoing approach to administration led critics to liken his management style to college "bull sessions" complete with pizza and "all-nighters." Yet, as we have seen, Clinton also inaugurated one of the most systematic efforts "to change the way government does business" in his National Performance Review. Heavily influenced by the theories of management consultants who prized decentralization, customer responsiveness, and employee initiative, Clinton sought to infuse these new practices into government.[42]

George W. Bush was the first president with a degree in business. His management strategy followed a standard business school dictum: select skilled subordinates and delegate responsibility to them. Bush followed this model closely in his appointment of highly experienced officials to cabinet positions and in his selection of Dick Cheney for vice president. Indeed, at the outset of his term, Bush often appeared overshadowed by these appointees (and by the vice president in particular). Many observers had the impression that Bush did not lead his own administration. Concern about Bush's managerial skills escalated after the administration's inadequate response to Hurricane Katrina, new revelations about flawed intelligence in the lead-up to the Iraq war, and the prolonged conflict in Iraq.

Critics also contended that the Bush administration exercised inappropriate political control over the bureaucracy. For example, in 2006, NASA scientists charged that the NASA public affairs office had suppressed the views of scientists when they differed from Bush administration policy. Political appointees barred scientists from using the term "global warming" and instructed them instead to use the more neutral term "climate change."[43] In a 2007 incident, the Office of Management and Budget heavily edited the congressional testimony of the Director of the Centers for Disease Control and Prevention on the topic of climate change and public health. More than half of her testimony was deleted, sparking charges that the "White House has denied a congressional committee's access to scientific information about health and global warming."[44]

Decades of reform have increased the managerial capacity of the presidency, but such reforms themselves do not ensure democratic accountability—presidents must put their managerial powers to use. Although Ronald Reagan was an enormously popular president, he was faulted for his disengaged management style. During his administration, the National Security Council staff was not prevented from running its own policies toward Iran and Nicaragua for at least two years (1985–86) after Congress had explicitly restricted activities toward Nicaragua and the president had forbidden negotiations with Iran. The Tower Commission, appointed to investigate the Iran-Contra affair, concluded that although there was nothing fundamentally wrong with the institutions involved in foreign-policy making there had been a "flawed process," "a failure of responsibility," and a thinness of the president's personal engagement in the issues. The Tower Commission found that "at no time did [President Reagan] insist upon accountability and performance review."[45] In 2008, Congress held hearings to investigate the financial crisis. Members grilled banking and insurance executives as well former chairman of the Federal Reserve, Alan Greenspan. Greenspan, once hailed as a financial wizard, memorably admitted that inadequate regulation of lending practices played a role in causing the crisis.

executive privilege the claim that confidential communications between a president and close advisers should not be revealed without the consent of the president

Presidents may also use their managerial capacities to limit democratic accountability if they believe it is a hindrance to effective government. Even in the unusual circumstances of the war on terrorism, critics question whether the Bush administration has been too quick to assert **executive privilege** and shield its actions from public scrutiny. In such circumstances, the separation of powers among the branches of government may be the best way to ensure democratic accountability.

Thinking Critically about Responsible Bureaucracy in a Democracy

Congress is constitutionally essential to responsible bureaucracy because ultimately the key to bureaucratic responsibility is legislation. When a law is passed and its intent is clear, the accountability for implementation of that law is also clear. Then the president knows what to "faithfully execute," and the responsible agency understands what is expected of it. But when Congress enacts vague legislation, agencies must resort to their own interpretations. The president and the federal courts often step in to tell agencies what the legislation intended. And so do the most intensely interested groups. Yet when everybody, from president to courts to interest groups, gets involved in the actual interpretation of legislative intent, to whom and to what is the agency accountable?

oversight the effort by Congress, through hearings, investigations, and other techniques, to exercise control over the activities of executive agencies

Congress's answer is **oversight.** The more power Congress has delegated to the executive, the more it has sought to reinvolve itself in directing the interpretation of laws through committee and subcommittee oversight of each agency. The standing committee system in Congress is well suited to oversight, inasmuch as most of the congressional committees and subcommittees have jurisdictions roughly parallel to one or more departments and agencies, and members of Congress who sit on these committees can develop expertise equal to that of the bureaucrats. The exception is the Department of Homeland Security, whose activities are now overseen by more than twenty committees. One of the central recommendations of the 9/11 Commission—as yet unimplemented—was to create a single committee with oversight of the DHS. Appropriations committees, as well as authorization committees, have oversight powers—as do their respective subcommittees. In addition to these, the Committee on Oversight and Government Reform in the House and the Homeland Security and Governmental Affairs Committee in the Senate have oversight powers not limited by departmental jurisdiction.

The best indication of Congress's oversight efforts is the use of public hearings, before which bureaucrats and other witnesses are summoned to discuss and defend agency budgets and past decisions. In 2007, for example, Congress held high-profile hearings on topics as diverse as the use of military contractors in Iraq, potentially improper dismissals of U.S. attorneys, and the failures of the Consumer Products Safety Commission to keep lead out of children's toys.

Politics Today

What are some of the important topics on which Congress has held oversight hearings? What was Congress trying to achieve by holding oversight hearings?

The data drawn from systematic studies of congressional committee and subcommittee hearings and meetings show quite dramatically that Congress has tried through oversight to keep pace with the expansion of the executive branch. The annual number of oversight hearings grew over time as the bureaucracy expanded. Oversight hearings in both the Senate and the House increased dramatically in the 1970s in the aftermath of Watergate. In recent years, oversight has become a topic of substantial political concern. After the Republicans took over Congress in 1995, they concentrated their oversight power on investigating scandal. When George W. Bush became president in 2001, congressional oversight virtually disappeared. From 2001 to 2006, the number of oversight hearings declined dramatically. In the House the number of oversight hearings decreased significantly from their highs during the Clinton administration, while the Senate virtually ceased holding oversight hearings during the same time. In the words of the congressional scholars Thomas Mann and Norman Ornstein, Republican members of Congress saw "themselves as field lieutenants in the president's army far more than they [did] as members of a separate and independent branch of government."[46] In their view, Congress's failure to exercise its oversight role led to poor government performance and bureaucracies that were not accountable to the American people.

Since winning back Congress in 2006, the Democrats have revived the oversight role. Compared with the Republican Congress in 2005, Democrats held many more oversight hearings in 2007: in 2005 the House held a total of 579 oversight hearings; in only the first half of 2007 the number was 942. In 2005 the Republican Senate held 346 oversight hearings, whereas the Democrats in the first half of 2007 held 451.[47] The true test of whether the Congress will reassert its oversight responsibility will come when Congress next faces a president from the same party.

Although congressional oversight is potent because of Congress's power to make, and therefore to change, the law, often the most effective and influential lever over bureaucratic accountability is "the power of the purse"—the ability of the House and Senate committees and subcommittees on appropriations to look at agency performance through the microscope of the annual appropriations process (see Chapter 12). This annual process makes bureaucrats attentive to Congress because they know that Congress has a chance each year to reduce their funding.[48]

Individual members of Congress can also carry out oversight. Such inquiries addressed to bureaucrats are considered standard congressional "case work" and can turn up significant questions of public responsibility even when the motivation is only to meet the demand of an individual constituent. Oversight also takes place

Navigate the Bureaucracy

To some, the idea of "getting involved" in something as complex as the federal, state, or even local bureaucracy can seem daunting. As you probably know by now, the bureaucracy has grown considerably in size in the last thirty five or so years and now touches aspects of daily life ranging from protecting citizens from terrorist attacks, to protecting the environment, to making sure the food you eat is safe. These are all important issues that citizens should easily be able to get involved with, but given the size of bureaucracies these days, where do you jump in?

It's not that hard, actually, to make a difference in how bureaucracies respond to social and political problems. Often it's as simple as volunteering your efforts in order to bring greater attention to a problem so that a relevant bureaucratic agency does something to fix the problem.

For example, you may see news stories about people working together locally in order to help the homeless. College students are often part of volunteer efforts to count the homeless in order to provide government agencies with a good idea of how widespread the homeless problem is in a given area. This information is then used to help lobby health and human service agencies to provide increased and better housing and resources for those on the streets.

College students have also fought, with some success, bureaucracies on their own campuses over issues like peer-to-peer file sharing and music downloads on the campus network. Recognizing that this is a practice that's here to stay and students expect schools to not restrict access, colleges and universities across the country have begun offering free or cheap access to legal sites such as Napster, Rhapsody, and Ruckus.

So, even though the old adage "you can't fight city hall" is the conventional wisdom, there is room for people such as yourself to have an impact on the bureaucracy at all levels. Here are a few suggestions for getting involved in ways that range from limited to more concentrated activism.

- ★ Start with something fairly simple. Ask yourself what political or social issue interests you and find out what bureaucratic agency is responsible for oversight and administering programs for that issue. Just trying to find out who to turn to with questions about your issue could be a lesson in and of itself. For example, you may be concerned with the treatment of veterans returning from active service in places like Iraq and Afghanistan. The Department of Veterans Affairs (www.va.gov) would be a good place to start for information on what the government is doing to help those returning with physical and psychological injuries.
- ★ If you're interested in more active involvement in the bureaucracy, you should consider interning with a government agency in Washington, D.C. For example, you could spend a summer or even an entire semester earning academic credit while interning at bureaucratic agencies ranging from the Food and Drug Administration, to the Department of Housing and Urban Development, to the Department of Defense. This is probably the best way to get hands-on experience with the bureaucracy. One way to intern while earning academic credit is through attending the Washington Center (www.twc.edu).
- ★ Finally, you could think about being an "ombudsperson" to help people deal with the bureaucracy. Grandparents and other elderly relatives often need help navigating the Social Security system, new immigrants are often in the dark about what to do in order to become legal citizens, and many high school students need help filling out forms for financial aid. Try visiting VolunteerMatch (www.volunteermatch.org), a Web site that puts people together with individuals and groups who are in need of unpaid assistance. You might even be able to use your affiliation with a campus organization, such as a fraternity or sorority, to encourage others to become volunteer ombudspersons, especially if charitable work is one of the organization's goals.

through communications between congressional staff and agency staff. In addition, Congress has created for itself three large agencies whose obligations are to engage in constant research on problems taking place in or confronted by the executive branch. These are the Government Accountability Office (GAO), the Congressional Research Service (CRS), and the Congressional Budget Office (CBO). Each of these agencies is designed to give Congress information independent of the information it can get directly from the executive branch through hearings and other communications.[49] Normally a low-visibility agency, the GAO stepped into the national spotlight in 2002 when it sued the Bush administration for the release of information about its energy-policy task force. This was the first time the GAO had ever sued an administration in its eighty-year history. Another source of information for oversight is directly from citizens through the Freedom of Information Act, which, as we have seen, gives ordinary citizens the right to gain access to agency files and agency data to determine whether derogatory information exists in the file about the citizens themselves and to learn about what the agency is doing in general. Nevertheless, the information citizens gain through FOIA can be effective only through the institutionalized channels of congressional committees and, on a few occasions, through public-interest litigation in the federal courts.

For Critical Analysis

Through elected officials (that is, the president and the Congress) the public can achieve some control over the bureaucracy. What are the relative advantages and disadvantages of presidential and congressional control of the bureaucracy?

The Bush administration's effort to expand the scope of contracting out raised new questions about democratic accountability. When government work is contracted out, federal monitoring is essential to ensure that funds are spent in accordance with the public will and to confirm that the costs are fair. Yet government contracting is now so extensive that such monitoring has become extremely difficult. Even with monitoring, accountability may be hard to achieve. Many of the mechanisms of democratic accountability do not apply to private firms that contract to perform public work. For example, private corporations can resist FOIA requests, and they are not constrained by the same ethics rules as public employees. Moreover, because private firms do not have to disclose information about their operations in the same way that public bureaucracies do, Congress has much more limited oversight. The move to contracting out clearly presents major challenges to democratic accountability in the future.

One of the most troubling aspects of contracting is that private contractors donate millions of dollars each year to political campaigns and lobbying. As Figure 14.6 shows, the top twenty service contractors have substantially increased their spending on lobbying and political campaigns since 2000. These expenditures raise troubling questions about how assertive members of Congress are likely to be in scrutinizing the business practices of important political donors or in moving business from the private to the public sector.

As the president and Congress seek to translate the ideal of democratic accountability into practice, they struggle to find the proper balance between administrative discretion and the public's right to know. An administration whose every move is subject to intense public scrutiny may be hamstrung in its efforts to carry out the public interest. On the other hand, a bureaucracy that is shielded from the public eye may wind up pursuing its own interests rather than those of the public. The last century has seen a double movement toward strengthening the managerial capacity of the presidency and ensuring that bureaucratic decision making is more transparent. The purpose of these reforms has been to create an effective, responsive bureaucracy. But reforms alone cannot guarantee democratic accountability. Presidential and congressional vigilance in defense of the public interest is essential.

FOR FURTHER READING

Aberbach, Joel D., and Mark A. Peterson, eds. *Institutions of American Democracy: The Executive Branch* (Institutions of American Democracy Series). New York: Oxford University Press, 2006.

Arnold, Peri E. *Making the Managerial Presidency: Comprehensive Organization Planning.* Princeton, NJ: Princeton University Press, 1986.

Fesler, James W., and Donald F. Kettl. *The Politics of the Administrative Process.* Chatham, NJ: Chatham House, 1991.

Light, Paul C. *A Government Ill Executed: The Decline of the Federal Service and How to Reverse It.* Cambridge, MA: Harvard University Press, 2008.

Weiner, Tom. *Legacy of Ashes: The History of the CIA.* New York: Doubleday, 2007.

Wildavsky, Aaron. *The New Politics of the Budget Process.* 2nd ed. New York: HarperCollins, 1992.

Wilson, James Q. *Bureaucracy: What Government Agencies Do and Why They Do It.* New York: Basic Books, 1989.

Wood, Dan B. *Bureaucratic Dynamics: The Role of Bureaucracy in a Democracy.* Boulder, CO: Westview, 1994.

RECOMMENDED WEB SITES

Central Intelligence Agency
www.cia.gov/about-cia/faqs/index.html
The Central Intelligence Agency (CIA) is one of several bureaucracies responsible for providing national security. A major problem facing this clandestine agency is how to provide security and meet the public's right to know what the government is doing. At the official Web site for the CIA, see what questions are often asked.

Department of Homeland Security
www.dhs.gov
The Department of Homeland Security was created after 9/11 to promote bureaucratic communication and domestic security. See what the department is doing to protect America from foreign threats.

Federal Emergency Management Agency
www.fema.org
In the aftermath of Hurricane Katrina, the Federal Emergency Management Agency (FEMA) became infamous for its role in the disaster relief efforts. View the disaster history of your state and see what FEMA is currently doing to prevent disasters and assist Americans in need.

Official U.S. Executive Branch Web Sites
www.loc.gov/rr/news/fedgov.html
This resource page at the Library of Congress Web site provides links to every federal department, independent agency, and regulatory commission in the federal bureaucracy.

Privatization.org
www.privatization.org
Privatization is the removal of all or part of a program from the public sector to the private sector. This Web page, part of the Reason Foundation's Web site, promotes privatization and reform in all levels of the U.S. government.

Project on Government Oversight
www.pogo.org
The Project on Government Oversight is an independent, nonprofit organization that seeks to make government more accountable by investigating corruption and misconduct. Originally set up to focus on the military, this organization now examines all types of government bureaucracies.

U.S. Agency for International Development
www.usaid.gov
In 1961 Congress created the U.S. Agency for International Development (USAID) to provide economic and social development assistance to foreign countries. Often criticized for promoting American values and foreign policy objectives, USAID is currently involved in numerous global issues.

STUDY OUTLINE

www.wwnorton.com/wtp7e

Bureaucracy and Bureaucrats

1. Bureaucracy is simply a form of organization. Specialization and repetition are essential to the efficiency of any organization.
2. Despite fears of bureaucratic growth, the federal service has grown little during the past twenty-five years. The national government is large, but the federal service has not been growing any faster than the economy or the society.
3. The primary task of bureaucracy is to implement the laws passed by Congress.
4. Because statutes and executive orders often provide only vague instructions, one important job of the bureaucracy is to interpret the intentions of Congress and the president prior to implementation of orders.
5. The lower efficiency of public agencies can be attributed to the added constraints put on them, as compared with those put on private agencies.
6. Through civil service reform, national and state governments have attempted to reduce political interference in public bureaucracies by granting certain public bureaucrats legal protection from being fired without a show of cause.

The Organization of the Executive Branch

1. Cabinet departments, agencies, and bureaus are the operating parts of the bureaucracy. Not all government agencies are part of Cabinet departments. Independent agencies, government corporations, and independent regulatory commissions also are part of the executive branch.
2. The different agencies of the executive branch can be classified into three main groups according to the services that they provide to the American public. The first category of agencies provides services and products that seek to promote the public welfare. Some of these agencies are particularly tied to a specific group or segment of American society that is often thought of as the main clientele of that agency.
3. The second category of agencies work to promote national security from internal and external threat.
4. The third group of agencies provides services that help to maintain a strong economy. Foremost among these are the agencies that are responsible for fiscal and monetary policy. In addition, the federal government may directly provide services or goods that bolster the economy.

Can Bureaucracy Be Reinvented?

1. The National Performance Review was an effort to make the bureaucracy more efficient, accountable, and effective.
2. Although government bureaucracies can be made more responsive and efficient, reform is not simply a matter of management techniques but also a political matter.

Can the Bureaucracy Be Reduced?

1. The bureaucracy can be reduced in three ways: termination, devolution, and privatization.

Can Bureaucracy Be Controlled?

1. Each expansion of the national government during the twentieth century was accompanied by a parallel expansion of presidential management authority, but the expansion of presidential power cannot guarantee responsible bureaucracy.
2. Although Congress attempts to control the bureaucracy through oversight, a more effective way to ensure accountability may be to clarify legislative intent.

PRACTICE QUIZ

www.wwnorton.com/wtp7e

1. Which of the following best describes the growth of the federal service in the past twenty-five years?
   a) rampant, exponential growth
   b) little growth at all
   c) decrease in the total number of federal employees
   d) vast, compared to the growth of the economy and the society
2. What task must bureaucrats perform if Congress charges them with enforcing a law through explicit directions?
   a) implementation
   b) interpretation
   c) lawmaking
   d) quasi-judicial decision making

3. Which of the following was *not* a component of the Civil Service Act of 1883?
   a) the merit system
   b) a type of tenure system
   c) a spoils system
   d) All of the above were associated with the Civil Service Act of 1883.
4. Which of the following is a way in which the bureaucracy might be reduced?
   a) devolution
   b) termination
   c) privatization
   d) all of the above
5. Which of the following is *not* an example of a clientele agency?
   a) Department of Justice
   b) Department of Commerce
   c) Department of Agriculture
   d) Department of Housing and Urban Development
6. The concept of oversight refers to the effort made by
   a) Congress to make executive agencies accountable for their actions.
   b) the president to make Congress accountable for its actions.
   c) the courts to make executive agencies responsible for their actions.
   d) the states to make the executive branch accountable for its actions.
7. Which president instituted the bureaucratic reform of the National Performance Review?
   a) Richard Nixon
   b) Lyndon Johnson
   c) Jimmy Carter
   d) Bill Clinton
8. Which of the following are *not* part of the executive branch?
   a) Cabinet departments
   b) government corporations
   c) independent regulatory commissions
   d) All of the above are parts of the executive branch.

KEY TERMS

www.wwnorton.com/wtp7e

administrative adjudication (p. 550)
bureaucracy (p. 547)
department (p. 552)
deregulation (p. 572)
devolution (p. 572)
executive privilege (p. 580)
Federal Reserve System (p. 567)
fiscal policy (p. 567)
government corporation (p. 552)
implementation (p. 550)
independent agency (p. 552)
iron triangle (p. 556)
merit system (p. 552)
oversight (p. 580)
privatization (p. 574)
regulatory agencies (p. 555)
revenue agencies (p. 567)
rule making (p. 550)

15 The Federal Courts

- ★ The Legal System
- ★ Federal Jurisdiction
- ★ The Power of the Supreme Court: Judicial Review
- ★ Judicial Power and Politics
- ★ Thinking Critically about the Judiciary, Liberty, and Democracy

WHAT GOVERNMENT DOES AND WHY IT MATTERS

Young Americans may think of the Supreme Court as a distant and mysterious institution whose decisions affect giant corporations, wealthy individuals, and powerful politicians. They see no direct relationship between the black-robed justices and the everyday lives of ordinary people. Occasionally, however, the Supreme Court is asked to hear questions that touch students' lives in a very direct way. One recent example is the 2007 case of *Morse v. Frederick*.[1] This case dealt with the policies of Juneau-Douglas High School in Juneau, Alaska. In 2002, the Olympic torch relay passed through Juneau on its way to Salt Lake City for the opening of the Winter Olympics. As the torch passed Juneau-Douglas High, a senior, Joseph Frederick, unfurled a banner that read, "Bong Hits 4 Jesus." The school's principal promptly suspended Frederick, who then brought suit for reinstatement, alleging that his free speech rights had been violated.[2]

Like most of America's public schools, Juneau-Douglas High prohibits assemblies or expressions on school grounds that advocate illegal drug use. Schools say that some federal aid is contingent on this policy. Civil libertarians see such policies as restricting students' right to free speech—a right that has been recognized by the Supreme Court since a 1969 case when it said an Iowa public school could not prohibit students from wearing antiwar armbands. Unfortunately for Frederick, today's Supreme Court has a more conservative cast than it did in 1969. Speaking for the Court's majority, Chief Justice Roberts said that the First Amendment did not require schools to permit students to advocate illegal drug use. This decision affected not only Joseph Frederick, but millions of other students whose views might be seen as inappropriate by school administrators. Far from being a remote institution, the Supreme Court turns out to have reached into every public school in America.

Every year, nearly 25 million cases are tried in American courts, and one American in every nine is directly involved in litigation. Cases can arise from disputes between citizens, from efforts by government agencies to punish wrongdoing, or from citizens' efforts to prove that a right provided them by law has been infringed on as a result of government action—or inaction. Many critics of the U.S. legal system assert that Americans have become much too litigious (ready to use the courts for all purposes), and perhaps that is true. But the heavy use that Americans make of the courts is also an indication of the extent of conflict in American society. And given the existence of social conflict, it is far better that Americans seek to settle their differences through the courts rather than by fighting or feuding.

During the 2008 presidential campaign, Democrats asserted that a victory by Republican candidate, John McCain would have dire consequences for the makeup of the nation's judiciary. In particular, Democrats declared that if elected president, McCain might be in a position to appoint two Supreme Court justices when John Paul Stevens, who was nearly ninety years old, and Ruth Bader Ginsburg, who was in poor health, retired. Stevens and Ginsburg are members of the Court's liberal wing. Currently, the Court consists of four liberal justices (Breyer, Ginsburg, Souter, and Stevens), four conservative justices (Alito, Roberts, Scalia, and Thomas) and one middle-of-the-road "swing vote," Justice Anthony Kennedy. If Stevens or Ginsburg or both were replaced by conservatives, the Court might swing more sharply to the right. Democrats asserted that such a shift might have major long-term consequences, including the overturning of *Roe v. Wade,* the 1973 decision that prohibited the states from writing laws to outlaw abortion. Democrats' fears were increased when McCain chose Alaska governor, Sarah Palin, as his vice-presidential running mate. Palin was known as a staunch foe of abortion. For their part, Republicans were concerned that a victory by Democratic candidate, Barack Obama, would leave the Supreme Court stalemated on the abortion issue, allowing the practice of abortion to continue. Thus, though we do not elect federal judges and Supreme Court justices, the question of who might be appointed as judges and justices became an important electoral issue.

The framers of the American Constitution called the Supreme Court the "least dangerous branch" of American government. Today, it is not unusual to hear the Court described as an all-powerful "imperial judiciary." Before we can understand this transformation and its consequences, we must look in some detail at America's judicial process.

- **In this chapter, we first examine the legal system, including the types of cases that the federal courts consider and the types of law with which they deal.**
- **Second, we assess the organization and structure of the federal court system as well as the flow of cases through the courts.**
- **Third, we consider judicial review and how it makes the Supreme Court a "lawmaking body."** We also analyze the procedures of and influences on the Supreme Court.
- **Finally, we consider the role and power of the federal courts in the American political process, looking in particular at the growth of judicial power in the United States.** We conclude by looking at how this changing role affects liberty and democracy.

The Legal System

Originally, a "court" was the place where a sovereign ruled—where the king and his entourage governed. Settling disputes between citizens was part of governing. According to the Bible, King Solomon had to settle a dispute between two women over which of them was the mother of the child both claimed. Judging is the settling of disputes, a function that was slowly separated from the king and the king's court and made into a separate institution of government. Courts have taken over from kings the power to settle controversies by hearing the facts on both sides and deciding which side possesses the greater merit. But since judges are not kings, they must have a basis for their authority. That basis in the United States is the Constitution and the law. Courts decide cases by hearing the facts on both sides of a dispute and applying the relevant law or principle to the facts. This can be a sensitive matter because courts have been given the authority to settle disputes not only between citizens but also between citizens and the government itself, where the courts are obliged to maintain the same neutrality and impartiality as they do in disputes involving two citizens. This is the essence of the "rule of law"—that "the state" and its officials must be judged by the same laws as the citizenry.

Cases and the Law

Court cases in the United States proceed under two broad categories of law: criminal law and civil law, each with myriad subdivisions.

Cases of **criminal law** are those in which the government charges an individual with violating a statute that has been enacted to protect public health, safety, morals, or welfare. In criminal cases, the government is always the **plaintiff** (the party that brings charges) and alleges that a criminal violation has been committed by a named **defendant.** Most criminal cases arise in state and municipal courts and

criminal law the branch of law that regulates the conduct of individuals, defines crimes, and specifies punishment for criminal acts

plaintiff the individual or organization who brings a complaint in court

defendant the one against whom a complaint is brought in a criminal or civil case

The courts have the authority to settle disputes not only between individuals and other private entities but also between individuals and the government. In recent "enemy combatant" cases, the Supreme Court has ruled on the rights of prisoners being held in the U.S. base in Guantánamo, Cuba.

involve matters ranging from traffic offenses to robbery and murder. Although the great bulk of criminal law is still a state matter, a large and growing body of federal criminal law deals with matters ranging from tax evasion and mail fraud to the sale of narcotics and acts of terrorism. Defendants found guilty of criminal violations may be fined or sent to prison.

civil law the branch of law that deals with disputes that do not involve criminal penalties

Cases of **civil law** involve disputes among individuals, groups, corporations, and other private entities, or between such litigants and the government in which no criminal violation is charged. Unlike criminal cases, the losers in civil cases cannot be fined or sent to prison, although they may be required to pay monetary damages for their actions. In a civil case, the one who brings a complaint is the plaintiff and the one against whom the complaint is brought is the defendant. The two most common types of civil cases involve contracts and torts. In a typical contract case, an individual or corporation charges that it has suffered because of another's violation of a specific agreement between the two. For example, the Smith Manufacturing Corporation may charge that Jones Distributors failed to honor an agreement to deliver raw materials at a specified time, causing Smith to lose business. Smith asks the court to order Jones to compensate it for the damage allegedly suffered. In a typical tort case, one individual charges that he or she has been injured by another's negligence or malfeasance. Medical malpractice suits are one example of tort cases. Another important area of civil law is administrative law, which involves disputes over the jurisdiction, procedures or authority of administrative agencies. A plaintiff may assert, for example, that an agency did not follow proper procedures when issuing new rules and regulations. A court will then examine the agency's conduct in light of the Administrative Procedure Act, the legislation that governs agency rule making.

precedent prior case whose principles are used by judges as the basis for their decision in a present case

In deciding cases, courts apply statutes (laws) and legal **precedents** (prior decisions). State and federal statutes, for example, often govern the conditions under which contracts are and are not legally binding. Jones Distributors might argue that it was not obliged to fulfill its contract with the Smith Corporation because actions by Smith, such as the failure to make promised payments, constituted fraud under state law. Attorneys for a physician being sued for malpractice, on the other hand, may search for prior instances in which courts ruled that actions similar to those of their client did not constitute negligence. Such precedents are applied under the doctrine of ***stare decisis,*** a Latin phrase meaning "let the decision stand."

stare decisis literally, "let the decision stand." The doctrine that a previous decision by a court applies as a precedent in similar cases until that decision is overruled

If a case involves the actions of the federal government or a state government, a court may also be asked to examine whether the government's conduct was consistent with the Constitution. In a criminal case, for example, defendants might assert that their constitutional rights were violated when the police searched their property. Similarly, in a civil case involving federal or state restrictions on land development, plaintiffs might assert that government actions violated the Fifth Amendment's prohibition against taking private property without just compensation. Thus, both civil and criminal cases may raise questions of constitutional law.

Types of Courts

In the United States, systems of courts have been established both by the federal government and by the governments of the individual states. Both systems have several levels, as shown in Figure 15.1. More than 99 percent of all court cases in the United States are heard in state courts. The overwhelming majority of criminal cases, for example, involve violations of state laws prohibiting such actions as murder, robbery,

FIGURE 15.1 ★
The U.S. Court System

The state and federal court systems parallel each other until they reach the U.S. Supreme Court. The Supreme Court hears appeals from both systems.

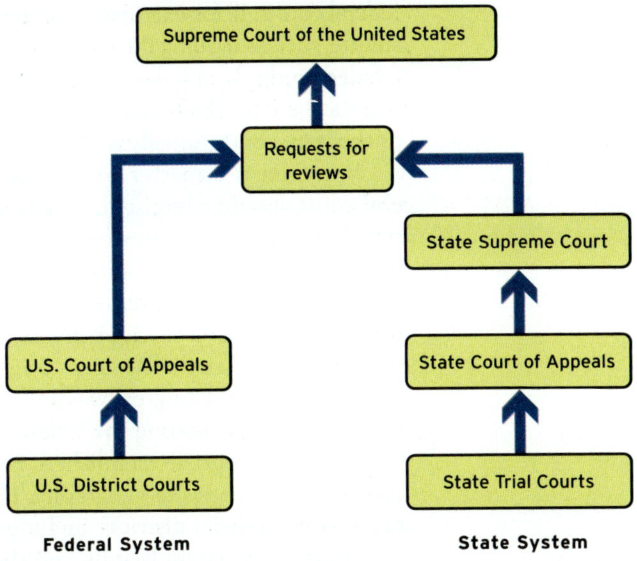

fraud, theft, and assault. If such a case is brought to trial, it will be heard in a state **trial court,** in front of a judge and sometimes a jury, who will determine whether the defendant violated state law. If the defendant is convicted, he or she may appeal the conviction to a higher court, such as a state **court of appeals,** and from there to a court of last resort, usually called the state's **supreme court.** Similarly, in civil cases, most litigation is brought in the courts established by the state in which the activity in question took place. For example, a patient bringing suit against a physician for malpractice would file the suit in the appropriate court in the state where the alleged malpractice occurred. The judge hearing the case would apply state law and state precedent to the matter at hand. There is some variation in court structure among the fifty states. Several states lack an intermediate appellate level. In these states, the court of last resort is the only appellate court. Two states, Oklahoma and Texas, have established two state courts of last resort, one for civil appeals and the other for criminal appeals. It should be noted that in both criminal and civil matters, most cases are settled before trial through negotiated agreements between the parties. In criminal cases these agreements are called **plea bargains.**

Although each state has its own set of laws, these laws have much in common from state to state. Murder and robbery, obviously, are illegal in all states, although the range of possible punishments for those crimes varies from state to state. Some states, for example, provide for capital punishment (the death penalty) for murder and other serious offenses; other states do not. However, some acts that are criminal offenses in one state may be legal in another state. Prostitution, for example, is legal in some Nevada counties, although it is outlawed in all other states. Considerable similarity among the states is also found in the realm of civil law. In the case of contract law, most states have adopted the **Uniform Commercial Code** in order to reduce interstate differences. In areas such as family law, however, which covers such matters as divorce and child custody arrangements, state laws vary greatly.

Cases are heard in the federal courts if they involve federal laws, treaties with other nations, or the U.S. Constitution; these areas are the official **jurisdiction** of the federal

trial court the first court to hear a criminal or civil case

court of appeals a court that hears appeals of trial court decisions

supreme court the highest court in a particular state or in the United States. This court primarily serves an appellate function

plea bargain a negotiated agreement in a criminal case in which a defendant agrees to plead guilty in return for the state's agreement to reduce the severity of the criminal charge or prison sentence the defendant is facing

Uniform Commercial Code code used in many states in the area of contract law to reduce interstate differences in judicial decisions

jurisdiction the sphere of a court's power and authority courts. In addition, any case in which the U.S. government is a party is heard in the federal courts. If, for example, an individual is charged with violating a federal criminal statute, such as evading the payment of income taxes, charges would be brought before a federal judge by a federal prosecutor. Civil cases involving the citizens of more than one state and in which more than $75,000 is at stake may be heard in either the federal or the state courts, usually depending on the preference of the plaintiff.

But even if a matter belongs in federal court, how do we know which federal court should exercise jurisdiction over the case? The answer to this seemingly simple question is somewhat complex. The jurisdiction of each federal court is derived from the U.S. Constitution and federal statutes. Article III of the Constitution gives the Supreme Court appellate jurisdiction in all federal cases and original jurisdiction in cases involving foreign ambassadors and issues in which a state is a party. Article III assigns original jurisdiction in all other federal cases to the lower courts that Congress was authorized to establish. Over the years, as Congress enacted statutes creating the federal judicial system, it specified the jurisdiction of each type of court it established. For the most part, Congress has assigned jurisdictions on the basis of geography. The nation is currently, by statute, divided into ninety-four judicial districts, including one court for each of three U.S. territories: Guam, the U.S. Virgin Islands, and the Northern Marianas. Each of the ninety-four U.S. district courts exercises jurisdiction over federal cases arising within its territorial domain. The judicial districts are, in turn, organized into eleven regional circuits and the D.C. circuit. Each circuit court exercises appellate jurisdiction over cases heard by the district courts within its region.

Geography, however, is not the only basis for federal court jurisdiction. Congress has also established several specialized courts that have nationwide original jurisdiction in certain types of cases. These include the U.S. Court of International Trade, created to deal with trade and customs issues, and the U.S. Court of Federal Claims, which handles damage suits against the United States. Congress has, in addition, established a court with nationwide appellate jurisdiction. This is the U.S. Court of Appeals for the Federal Circuit, which hears appeals involving patent law and those arising from the decisions of the trade and claims courts. Other federal courts assigned specialized jurisdictions by Congress include the U.S. Court of Veterans Appeals, which exercises exclusive jurisdiction over cases involving veterans' claims, and the U.S. Court of Military Appeals, which deals with questions of law arising from trials by court-martial.

With the exception of the claims court and the Court of Appeals for the Federal Circuit, these specialized courts were created by Congress on the basis of the powers the legislature exercises under Article I, rather than Article III, of the Constitution. Article III is designed to protect judges from political pressure by granting them life tenure and prohibiting reduction of their salaries while they serve. The judges of Article I courts, by contrast, are appointed by the president for fixed terms of fifteen years and are not protected by the Constitution from salary reduction. As a result, these "legislative courts" are generally viewed as less independent than the courts established under Article III of the Constitution. The three territorial courts were also established under Article I, and their judges are appointed for ten-year terms.

The appellate jurisdiction of the federal courts also extends to cases originating in the state courts. In both civil and criminal cases, a decision of the highest state court can be appealed to the U.S. Supreme Court by raising a federal issue. Appellants might assert, for example, that they were denied the right to counsel or otherwise deprived of the **due process of law** guaranteed by the federal Constitu-

due process of law the right of every citizen against arbitrary action by national or state governments tion, or they might assert that important issues of federal law were at stake in the case. The U.S. Supreme Court is not obligated to accept such appeals and will do so only if it believes that the matter has considerable national significance. We will return to this topic later in the chapter. In addition, in criminal cases, defendants who have been convicted in a state court may request a **writ of *habeas corpus*** from a federal district court. Sometimes known as the "Great Writ," *habeas corpus* is a court order to the authorities to release a prisoner deemed to be held in violation of his or her legal rights. In 1867, its distrust of southern courts led Congress to authorize federal district judges to issue such writs to prisoners whom they believed had been deprived of constitutional rights in state court. Generally speaking, state defendants seeking a federal writ of *habeas corpus* must show that they have exhausted all available state remedies and must raise issues not previously raised in their state appeals. Federal courts of appeals and, ultimately, the U.S. Supreme Court have appellate jurisdiction for federal district court *habeas* decisions.

Although the federal courts hear only a small fraction of all the civil and criminal cases decided each year in the United States, their decisions are extremely important. It is in the federal courts that the Constitution and federal laws that govern all Americans are interpreted and their meaning and significance established. Moreover, it is in the federal courts that the powers and limitations of the increasingly powerful national government are tested. Finally, through their power to review the decisions of the state courts, it is ultimately the federal courts that dominate the American judicial system.

Considerable controversy surrounded the 2005 case of Terri Schiavo, whose husband wanted to remove the feeding tube that was keeping her alive in a permanent vegetative state. Despite objections from Schiavo's parents and conservative politicians, the courts ruled that the feeding tube could be removed. The Supreme Court refused to hear the case, implying that the lower courts had applied the law properly.

Federal Jurisdiction

In 2007, federal district courts (the lowest federal level) received 278,272 cases. Though large, this number is approximately 1 percent of the number of cases heard by state courts. The federal courts of appeal listened to 60,668 cases in 2007 and about 15 percent of the verdicts were appealed to the U.S. Supreme Court. Most of the cases filed with the Supreme Court are dismissed without a ruling on their merits. The Court has broad latitude to decide what cases it will hear and generally listens to only those cases it deems to raise the most important issues. Only seventy-three cases were given full-dress Supreme Court review in 2007–08.[3]

writ of *habeas corpus* a court order that the individual in custody be brought into court and shown the cause for detention. *Habeas corpus* is guaranteed by the Constitution and can be suspended only in cases of rebellion or invasion

original jurisdiction the authority to initially consider a case. Distinguished from appellate jurisdiction, which is the authority to hear appeals from a lower court's decision

Federal Trial Courts

Most of the cases of original federal jurisdiction are handled by the federal district courts. Courts of **original jurisdiction** are the courts that are responsible for discovering the facts in a controversy and creating the record on which a judgment is based. Although the Constitution gives the Supreme Court original jurisdiction in several types of cases, such as those affecting ambassadors and those in which a state is one of the parties, most original jurisdiction goes to the lowest courts—the trial courts. (In courts that have appellate jurisdiction, judges receive cases after the factual record is established by the trial court. Ordinarily, new facts cannot be presented before appellate courts.)

There are eighty-nine district courts in the fifty states, plus one in the District of Columbia and one in Puerto Rico, and three territorial courts. These courts are staffed by 679 federal district judges. District judges are assigned to district courts according to the workload; the busiest of these courts may have as many as twenty-eight judges. Only one judge is assigned to each case, except where statutes provide for three-judge courts to deal with special issues. The routines and procedures of the federal district courts are essentially the same as those of the lower state courts, except that federal procedural requirements tend to be stricter. States, for example, do not have to provide a grand jury, a twelve-member trial jury, or a unanimous jury verdict. Federal courts must provide all these things.

Federal Appellate Courts

Politics Today

The 2006 Military Commissions Act declared that enemy combatants held by the United States at Guantánamo could not bring *habeas corpus* petitions challenging their detention to the federal courts. Does Congress have the power to strip the federal courts of their jurisdiction in this matter?

Roughly 20 percent of all lower court cases, along with appeals from some federal agency decisions, are subsequently reviewed by federal appeals courts. As noted, the country is divided geographically into twelve judicial circuits, each of which has a U.S. Court of Appeals. Every state, the District of Columbia, and each of the territories is assigned to the circuit in the continental United States that is closest to it. A thirteenth appellate court, the U.S. Court of Appeals for the Federal Circuit, has a subject matter, rather than a geographical, jurisdiction.

Except for cases selected for review by the Supreme Court, decisions made by the appeals courts are final. Because of this finality, certain safeguards have been built into the system. The most important is the provision of more than one judge for every appeals case. Each court of appeals has from six to twenty-eight permanent judgeships, depending on the workload of the circuit. Although normally three judges hear appealed cases, in some instances a larger number of judges sit together *en banc*.

Another safeguard is provided by the assignment of a Supreme Court justice as the circuit justice for each of the twelve circuits. The circuit justice deals with requests for special action by the Supreme Court. The most frequent and best-known action of circuit justices is that of reviewing requests for stays of execution when the full Court is unable to do so—primarily during the summer, when the Court is in recess.

The Supreme Court

The Supreme Court is America's highest court. Article III of the Constitution vests "the judicial power of the United States" in the Supreme Court, and this court is supreme in fact as well as form. The Supreme Court is the only federal court established by the Constitution. The lower federal courts are created by statute and can be restructured or, presumably, even abolished by the Congress. The Supreme Court is made up of a chief justice and eight associate justices. The **chief justice** presides over the Court's public sessions and conferences. In the Court's actual deliberations and decisions, however, the chief justice has no more authority than his colleagues. Each justice casts one vote. The chief justice, though, is always the first to speak and the last to vote when the justices deliberate. In addition, if the chief justice has voted with the majority, he

chief justice justice on the Supreme Court who presides over the Court's public sessions decides which of the justices will write the formal opinion for the court. The character of the opinion can be an important means of influencing the evolution of the law beyond the mere affirmation or denial of the appeal on hand. To some extent, the influence of the chief justice is a function of his or her own leadership ability. Some chief justices, such as the late Earl Warren, have been able to lead the court in a new direction. In other instances, forceful associate justices, such as the late Felix Frankfurter, are the dominant figures on the Court.

The Constitution does not specify the number of justices who should sit on the Supreme Court; Congress has the authority to change the Court's size. In the early nineteenth century, there were six Supreme Court justices; later there were seven. Congress set the number of justices at nine in 1869, and the Court has remained that size ever since. In 1937, President Franklin D. Roosevelt, infuriated by several Supreme Court decisions that struck down New Deal programs, asked Congress to enlarge the Court so that he could add a few sympathetic justices to the bench. Although Congress balked at Roosevelt's "court packing" plan, the Court gave in to FDR's pressure and began to take a more favorable view of his policy initiatives. The president, in turn, dropped his efforts to enlarge the Court.

How Judges Are Appointed

Federal judges are appointed by the president and confirmed by the Senate. They are generally selected from among the more prominent or politically active members of the legal profession. Many federal judges previously served as state court judges or state or local prosecutors. Before the president makes a formal nomination, however, the senators from the candidate's own state must indicate that they support the nominee. This is an informal but seldom violated practice called **senatorial courtesy.** If one or both senators from a prospective nominee's home state belong to the president's political party, the president will almost invariably consult them and secure their blessing for the nomination. Because the president's party in the Senate will rarely support a nominee opposed

senatorial courtesy the practice whereby the president, before formally nominating a person for a federal judgeship, seeks the indication that senators from the candidate's own state support the nomination

As of 2008, the members of the Supreme Court are: Standing (left to right), Justice Stephen Breyer, Justice Clarence Thomas, Justice Ruth Bader Ginsburg, and Justice Samuel Alito. Seated (left to right), Justice Anthony Kennedy, Justice John Paul Stevens, Chief Justice John Roberts, Jr., Justice Antonin Scalia, and Justice David Souter.

President Bush nominated John Roberts (left photo, center) first as a Supreme Court justice, and then as chief justice after the death of former Chief Justice William Rehnquist. Although Roberts's nomination was approved fairly easily in the Senate, President Bush's next nominee, Samuel Alito (right) was subjected to harsher questioning before being confirmed. Democratic senators were worried that Alito, who was replacing a more moderate justice, would shift the overall balance of the Court toward the right.

by a home-state senator from their ranks, this arrangement gives these senators virtual veto power over appointments to the federal bench in their own states. Senators also see nominations to the judiciary as a way to reward important allies and contributors in their states. If the state has no senator from the president's party, the governor or members of the state's House delegation may make suggestions. The practice of "courtesy" generally does not apply to Supreme Court appointments, only to district and circuit court nominations.

Federal appeals court nominations follow much the same pattern. Since appeals court judges preside over jurisdictions that include several states, however, senators do not have so strong a role in proposing potential candidates. Instead, potential appeals court candidates are generally suggested to the president by the Justice Department or by important members of the administration. The senators from the nominee's own state are still consulted before the president will formally act.

There are no formal qualifications for service as a federal judge. In general, presidents endeavor to appoint judges who possess legal experience and good character and whose partisan and ideological views are similar to the president's own. During the presidencies of Ronald Reagan and George H. W. Bush, most federal judicial appointees were conservative Republicans. Bush established an advisory committee to screen judicial nominees to make certain that their legal and political philosophies were sufficiently conservative. Bill Clinton's appointees to the federal bench, on the other hand, tended to be liberal Democrats. Clinton also made a major effort to appoint women and African Americans to the federal courts. Nearly half of his nominees were drawn from these groups.

Once the president has formally nominated an individual, the nominee must be considered by the Senate Judiciary Committee and confirmed by a majority vote in the full Senate. In recent years, the Senate Judiciary Committee has sought to signal the president when it has had qualms about a judicial nomination. After the Republicans won control of the Senate in 1994, for example, the Judiciary

Committee chairman Orrin Hatch of Utah let President Clinton know that he considered two of Clinton's nominees to be too liberal. The president withdrew the nominations.

During President George W. Bush's first two years in office, Democrats controlled the Senate and used their majority on the Judiciary Committee to block eight of the president's first eleven federal court nominations. After the GOP won a narrow Senate majority in the 2002 national elections, Democrats used a filibuster to block action on Bush federal appeals court nominees. On two occasions early in 2004, Bush skirted the Senate confirmation process during a congressional recess and used his power to make appointments when Congress is not in session. Bush named Charles W. Pickering, Sr., and William H. Pryor, Jr., directly to the federal appeals court bench. Both had earlier been blocked by Senate Democrats. Under the Constitution, these appointments last only until the end of the next session of Congress. Throughout the history of the federal judiciary, there have been more than 300 such judicial recess appointments, though few have occurred in recent years. Both Democrats and Republicans saw struggles over lower court slots as practice and preparation for all-out partisan warfare over the next Supreme Court vacancy.

If political factors play an important role in the selection of district and appellate court judges, they are decisive when it comes to Supreme Court appointments. Because the high court has so much influence over American law and politics, virtually all presidents have made an effort to select justices who share their own political philosophies. Presidents Ronald Reagan and George H. W. Bush, for example, appointed five justices whom they believed to have conservative perspectives: Sandra Day O'Connor, Antonin Scalia, Anthony Kennedy, David Souter, and Clarence Thomas. For his part, President Bill Clinton endeavored to appoint liberal justices. Clinton named Ruth Bader Ginsburg and Stephen Breyer to the Court, hoping to counteract the influence of the Reagan and Bush appointees. President George W. Bush appointed two conservative justices—Chief Justice John G. Roberts and Justice Samuel Alito. (Table 15.1 shows information about the current Supreme Court justices.)

TABLE 15.1 ★ Supreme Court Justices, 2008 (in Order of Seniority)

NAME	YEAR OF BIRTH	PRIOR EXPERIENCE	APPOINTED BY	YEAR OF APPOINTMENT
John Paul Stevens	1920	Federal judge	Ford	1975
Antonin Scalia	1936	Law professor, federal judge	Reagan	1986
Anthony Kennedy	1936	Federal judge	Reagan	1988
David Souter	1939	Federal judge	G. H. W. Bush	1990
Clarence Thomas	1948	Federal judge	G. H. W. Bush	1991
Ruth Bader Ginsburg	1933	Federal judge	Clinton	1993
Stephen Breyer	1938	Federal judge	Clinton	1994
John Roberts, Jr. *Chief Justice*	1955	Federal judge	G. W. Bush	2005
Samuel Alito	1950	Federal judge	G. W. Bush	2006

In 2008, the Supreme Court decided that race could not be used as a criterion in assigning students to public schools, even if the goal was greater diversity. Liberals worried that the Court's conservative majority was turning back progress on racial integration.

It is important to note that as of the beginning of 2008, seven of the nine justices had been appointed by Republican presidents. Though two of these seven, Justices Souter and Stevens, turned out to have liberal leanings, the appointment process has led to a fairly reliable conservative majority on the high court. This majority, consisting of Chief Justice Roberts and Justices Alito, Kennedy, Scalia, and Thomas, has propelled the Court in a more conservative direction in a variety of areas. During its 2006–07 term, for example, in a series of 5-to-4 decisions, the Court invalidated school integration plans in Seattle and Louisville, upheld a state limitation on abortion, and overturned portions of the Bipartisan Campaign Finance Reform Act.[4] Three members of the conservative bloc—Justices Alito, Thomas, and Roberts—are relatively young individuals who will likely serve on the Court for years, if not decades, to come. Through such judicial appointments, presidents continue to exercise influence long after they have passed from the political scene.

In recent decades, Supreme Court nominations have come to involve intense partisan struggle. Typically, after the president has named a nominee, interest groups opposed to the nomination have mobilized opposition in the media, the public, and the Senate. When President George H. W. Bush proposed the conservative judge Clarence Thomas for the Court, for example, liberal groups launched a campaign to discredit Thomas. After extensive research into his background, opponents of the nomination were able to produce evidence suggesting that Thomas had sexually harassed a former subordinate, Anita Hill. Thomas denied the charge. After contentious Senate Judiciary Committee hearings, highlighted by testimony from both Thomas and Hill, Thomas narrowly won confirmation.

Likewise, conservative interest groups carefully scrutinized Bill Clinton's somewhat more liberal nominees, hoping to find information about them that would sabotage their appointments. During his two opportunities to name Supreme Court justices, Clinton was compelled to drop several potential appointees because of information unearthed by political opponents.

From the liberal perspective, the danger of a conservative judiciary was underlined by the Supreme Court's decision in the Florida election case, *Bush v. Gore.* The court's conservative bloc, in recent years, has argued that the states deserve considerable deference from the federal courts. In this instance, however, the Supreme Court overturned a decision of the Florida supreme court regarding Florida election law. By voting to overrule the Florida court, the Supreme Court's conservative justices appeared to disregard the logic of their own decisions, which had expanded the authority of the states over the past two decades (see Chapter 3).

During the 2008 campaign, possible Supreme Court appointments again became an issue, particularly in relation to the question of abortion. The McCain campaign told its supporters that if vacancies arose on the High Court, a Democratic president would appoint liberal justices who would expand abortion rights. The Obama campaign, on the other hand, warned its supporters that a Republican president would use vacancies on the Court to appoint conservatives who might overturn *Roe v. Wade*. During their third debate, McCain and Obama both claimed that if called upon to fill the two judicial vacancies both seemed to expect, they would seek the best qualified individuals and would employ no political "litmus test" in gauging the qualifications of potential appointees. Each, however, intimated that his opponent was not so broad-minded and might appoint ideologues to the Court.

The Power of the Supreme Court: Judicial Review

The phrase **judicial review** refers to the power of the judiciary to examine and, if necessary, invalidate actions undertaken by the legislative and executive branches if it finds them unconstitutional. The phrase is sometimes also used to describe the scrutiny that appellate courts give to the actions of trial courts, but, strictly speaking, this is an improper usage. A higher court's examination of a lower court's decisions might be called "appellate review," but it is not judicial review.

judicial review the power of the courts to review and, if necessary, declare actions of the legislative and executive branches invalid or unconstitutional. The Supreme Court asserted this power in *Marbury v. Madison*

Judicial Review of Acts of Congress

Because the Constitution does not give the Supreme Court the power of judicial review over congressional enactments, the Court's exercise of it is something of a usurpation. It is not known whether the framers of the Constitution opposed judicial review, but "if they intended to provide for it in the Constitution, they did so in a most obscure fashion."[5] Disputes over the intentions of the framers were settled in 1803 in the case of *Marbury v. Madison*.[6] Although Congress and the president have often been at odds with the Court, its legal power to review acts of Congress has not been seriously questioned since 1803. One reason is that judicial power has been accepted as natural, if not intended. Another reason is that over more than two centuries, the Supreme Court has struck down only some 160 acts of Congress. When such acts do come up for review, the Court makes a self-conscious effort to give them an interpretation that will make them constitutional. In some instances, however, the Court reaches the conclusion that a congressional enactment directly violates the Constitution. For example, in 2007, the high court struck down key portions of the Bipartisan Campaign Finance Reform Act, through which Congress had sought to regulate spending in political campaigns.[7] The Court found that provisions of the act limiting political advertising violated the First Amendment.

Judicial Review of State Actions

The power of the Supreme Court to review state legislation or other state action and to determine its constitutionality is neither granted by the Constitution nor inherent in the federal system. But the logic of the **supremacy clause** of Article VI of the Constitution, which declares the Constitution itself and laws made under its authority to be the supreme law of the land, is very strong. Furthermore, in the Judiciary Act of 1789, Congress conferred on the Supreme Court the power to reverse state constitutions and laws whenever they are clearly in conflict with the U.S. Constitution,

supremacy clause Article VI of the Constitution, which states that laws passed by the national government and all treaties are the supreme law of the land and superior to all laws adopted by any state or any subdivision

In Marbury v. Madison *(1803), Chief Justice John Marshall established the Supreme Court's power to rule on the constitutionality of federal and state laws. This power makes the Court a lawmaking body.*

federal laws, or treaties.[8] This power gives the Supreme Court appellate jurisdiction over all of the millions of cases that American courts handle each year.

The supremacy clause of the Constitution not only established the federal Constitution, statutes, and treaties as the "supreme Law of the Land," but also provided that "the Judges in every State shall be bound thereby, any Thing in the Constitution or Laws of the State to the Contrary notwithstanding." Under this authority, the Supreme Court has frequently overturned state constitutional provisions or statutes and state court decisions it deems to contravene rights or privileges guaranteed under the federal Constitution or federal statutes.

The civil rights arena abounds with examples of state laws that the Supreme Court has overturned because the statutes violated guarantees of due process and equal protection contained in the Fourteenth Amendment to the Constitution. For example, in the 1954 case of *Brown v. Board of Education*, the Court overturned statutes from Kansas, South Carolina, Virginia, and Delaware that either required or permitted segregated public schools on the basis that such statutes denied black schoolchildren equal protection of the law. In 1967, in *Loving v. Virginia*, the Court invalidated a Virginia statute prohibiting interracial marriages.[9]

State statutes in other subject matter areas are equally subject to challenge. In *Griswold v. Connecticut*, the Court invalidated a Connecticut statute prohibiting the general distribution of contraceptives to married couples on the basis that the statute violated the couples' rights to marital privacy.[10] In *Brandenburg v. Ohio*, the Court overturned an Ohio statute forbidding any person to urge criminal acts as a means of inducing political reform. The statute had also prohibited joining any association that advocated such activities. The Court found that the statute punished "mere advocacy" and therefore violated the free speech provisions of the Constitution.[11]

Judicial Review of Federal Agency Actions

Although Congress makes the law, as we saw in Chapters 12 and 14, Congress can hardly administer the thousands of programs it has enacted and must delegate power to the president and to a huge bureaucracy to achieve its purposes. For example, if Congress wishes to improve air quality, it cannot possibly anticipate all the conditions and circumstances that may arise with respect to that general goal. Inevitably, Congress must delegate to the executive substantial discretionary power to make judgments about the best ways to bring about improved air quality in the face of changing circumstances. Thus, over the years, almost any congressional program will result in thousands and thousands of pages of administrative regulations developed by executive agencies nominally seeking to implement the will of the Congress.

Delegation of power to the executive poses a number of problems for Congress and the federal courts. If Congress delegates broad authority to the president, it risks seeing its goals subordinated to and subverted by those of the executive branch.[12] If Congress attempts to limit executive discretion by enacting precise rules and standards to govern the conduct of the president and the executive branch, it risks writing laws that do not conform to real-world conditions and that are too rigid to be adapted to changing circumstances.[13]

The issue of delegation of power has led to a number of court decisions over the past two centuries, generally revolving around the question of the scope of the delegation. Courts have also been called on to decide whether the rules and regulations adopted by federal agencies are consistent with Congress's express or implied intent.

As presidential power expanded during the New Deal era, one measure of increased congressional subordination to the executive was the enactment of laws that contained few, if any, principles limiting executive discretion. Congress enacted legislation, often at the president's behest, that gave the executive virtually unfettered authority to address a particular concern. For example, the Emergency Price Control Act of 1942 authorized the executive to set "fair and equitable" prices without offering any indication of what those terms might mean.[14] Although the Court initially challenged these delegations of power to the president during the New Deal, a confrontation with President Franklin D. Roosevelt caused the Court to retreat from its position. Perhaps as a result, since then no congressional delegation of power to the president has been struck down as impermissibly broad. Particularly in recent years, the Supreme Court has found that so long as federal agencies developed rules and regulations "based upon a permissible construction" or "reasonable interpretation" of Congress's statute, the judiciary would accept the views of the executive branch. Generally, the courts give considerable deference to administrative agencies as long as those agencies have engaged in a formal rule-making process and can show that they have carried out the conditions prescribed by the various statutes governing agency rule making.

Judicial Review and Presidential Power

The federal courts are also called on to review the actions of the president. On many occasions, members of Congress and individuals and groups opposing the president's policies have challenged presidential orders and actions in the federal courts. In recent years, the federal bench has, more often than not, upheld assertions of presidential power in such realms as foreign policy, war and emergency powers, legislative power, and administrative authority. In June 2004, however, the Supreme Court ruled on three cases involving President George W. Bush's anti-terrorism initiatives and claims of executive power and in two of the three cases appeared to place some limits on presidential authority.

One important case the Court decided was *Hamdi v. Rumsfeld*.[15] Yaser Esam Hamdi, apparently a Taliban soldier, was captured by American forces in Afghanistan and brought to the United States, where he was incarcerated at the Norfolk Naval Station. Hamdi was classified as an enemy combatant and denied civil rights, including the right to counsel, despite the fact that he had been born in Louisiana and held American citizenship. A federal district court scheduled a hearing on Hamdi's *habeas* petition and ordered that he be given unmonitored access to counsel. This ruling, however, was reversed by the U.S. Court of Appeals for the Fourth Circuit. In its opinion, the court held that, in the national security realm, the president wields "plenary and exclusive power." In essence, said the court, the president had virtually unfettered discretion to deal with emergencies, and it was inappropriate for the judiciary to saddle presidential decisions with what the court called the "panoply of encumbrances associated with civil litigation."

In June 2004, the Supreme Court ruled that Hamdi was entitled to a lawyer and "a fair opportunity to rebut the government's factual assertions." However, the Supreme Court affirmed that the president possessed the authority to declare a U.S. citizen an enemy combatant and to order that such an individual be held in federal detention. Several of the justices intimated that once designated an enemy combatant, a U.S. citizen might by tried before a military tribunal and the normal presumption of innocence be suspended. One government legal adviser indicated

Protesters charged that the Supreme Court's decision in Bush v. Gore *unfairly handed the presidency to George W. Bush. However, in several cases related to presidential power in the war on terror, the Court ruled against the Bush administration's programs and procedures.*

that the effect of the Court's decision was minimal. "They are basically upholding the whole enemy combatant status and tweaking the evidence test," he said.[16] Thus the Supreme Court did assert that presidential actions were subject to judicial scrutiny and placed some constraints on the president's unfettered power. But at the same time, the Court affirmed the president's single most important claim—the unilateral power to declare individuals, including U.S. citizens, "enemy combatants" who could be detained by federal authorities under adverse legal circumstances. Indeed, whatever Hamdi's fate, future presidents are likely to cite the Court's decisions as precedents for, rather than limits on, the exercise of executive power.

Politics Today

During his 2005 confirmation hearings, senators asked Chief Justice Roberts why the Supreme Court was more willing to declare acts of Congress unconstitutional than it was to confront the president on the constitutionality of his actions. What reasons might you identify?

Another important Supreme Court decision came in the 2006 case of *Hamdan v. Rumsfeld* (126 S.Ct. 2749). Salim Hamdan was a Taliban fighter captured in Afghanistan and held at the Guantánamo Bay naval base. The Bush administration planned to try Hamdan before a military commission authorized by a 2002 presidential order. The Supreme Court ruled that the commissions created by the president planned to use procedures that violated federal law and U.S. treaty obligations. President Bush responded by demanding that Congress rewrite the law. Congress quickly obliged and enacted the Military Commissions Act, which gave the president statutory authority for his actions. In Section 7 of the Act, Congress declared that Guantánamo prisoners could not bring *habeas corpus* petitions to federal courts to seek their release. In the 2008 case of *Boumediene v. Bush* 06-1195 (2008), however, the Supreme Court struck down Section 7 and declared *habeas corpus* to be a fundamental right.

Judicial Review and Lawmaking

Much of the work of the courts involves the application of statutes to the particular case at hand. Over the centuries, judges have also developed a body of rules and principles of interpretation that are not grounded in specific statutes. This body of judge-made law is called common law.

The appellate courts, however, are in another realm. Their rulings can be considered laws, but they are laws governing the behavior only of the judiciary. The written opinion of an appellate court is about halfway between common law and statutory law. It is judge-made and draws heavily on the precedents of previous cases. But it tries to articulate the rule of law controlling the case in question and future cases like it. In this respect, it is like a statute. But it differs from a statute in that a statute addresses itself to the future conduct of citizens, whereas a written opinion addresses itself mainly to the willingness or ability of courts in the future to take cases and render favorable opinions. Decisions by appellate courts affect citizens by giving them a cause of action or by taking it away from them. That is, they open or close access to the courts.

A specific case may help clarify the distinction. Before the Second World War, one of the most insidious forms of racial discrimination was the "restrictive covenant," a clause in a contract whereby the purchasers of a house agreed that if they later decided to sell it, they would sell only to a Caucasian. When a test case finally reached the Supreme Court in 1948, the Court ruled unanimously that citizens had a right to discriminate with restrictive covenants in their sales contracts but that the courts could not enforce these contracts. Its argument was that enforcement would constitute violation of the Fourteenth Amendment provision that no state shall "deny to any person within its jurisdiction equal protection under the law."[17] The Court was thereby predicting what it would and would not do in future cases of this sort. Most states have now enacted statutes that forbid homeowners to place such covenants in sales contracts.

The 1963 case *Gideon v. Wainwright* extends the point. When the Supreme Court ordered a new trial for Clarence Earl Gideon because he had been denied the right to legal counsel,[18] it said to all trial judges and prosecutors that henceforth they would be wasting their time if they cut corners in trials of indigent defendants. It also invited thousands of prisoners to appeal their convictions. (See Chapter 4 for a further discussion of this case.)

Many areas of civil law have been constructed in the same way—by judicial messages to other judges, some of which are codified eventually into legislative enactments. An example of great concern to employees and employers is that of liability for injuries sustained at work. Courts have sided with employees so often that it has become virtually useless for employers to fight injury cases. It has become "the law" that employers are liable for such injuries, without regard to negligence. But the law in this instance is simply a series of messages to lawyers that they should advise their corporate clients not to appeal injury decisions. In recent years, the Supreme Court has also been developing law in the realm of sexual harassment in the workplace. In a 2006 case, for example, the Supreme Court said that a victim of sexual harassment who was transferred from her job could sue her employer even though the company disciplined the perpetrator when the harassment was reported.[19]

The appellate courts cannot decide what types of behavior will henceforth be a crime. They cannot directly prevent the police from forcing confessions from suspects or intimidating witnesses. In other words, they cannot directly change the behavior of citizens or eliminate abuses of government power. What they can do, however, is make it easier for mistreated persons to gain redress.

In redressing wrongs, the appellate courts—and even the Supreme Court itself—often call for a radical change in legal principle. Changes in race relations, for example, would probably have taken a great deal longer if the Supreme Court had

Due process of law is another area in which federal courts have been critical in "making law" since the 1960s. In 2002, the issue of random drug testing of high school students who participate in extracurricular activities came before the Court. Lindsey Earls (second from right), a member of the Tecumseh, Oklahoma, high school choir and marching band, challenged the constitutionality of this policy; Sharon Smith, holding the sign, supported it.

not rendered the 1954 decision *Brown v. Board of Education*, which redefined the rights of African Americans.

Similarly, the Supreme Court interpreted the doctrine of the separation of church and state so as to alter significantly the practice of religion in public institutions. For example, in a 1962 case, *Engel v. Vitale*, the Court declared that a once widely observed ritual—the recitation of a prayer by students in a public school—was unconstitutional under the establishment clause of the First Amendment. Almost all the dramatic changes in the treatment of criminals and of persons accused of crimes have been made by the appellate courts, especially the Supreme Court. The Supreme Court brought about a veritable revolution in the criminal process with three cases over less than five years: *Gideon v. Wainwright*, in 1963, was just discussed. *Escobedo v. Illinois*, in 1964, gave suspects the right to remain silent and the right to have counsel present during questioning. But the *Escobedo* decision left confusions that allowed differing decisions to be made by lower courts. In *Miranda v. Arizona*, in 1966, the Supreme Court cleared up these confusions by setting forth what is known as the ***Miranda* rule**: arrested people have the right to remain silent, the right to be informed that anything they say can be held against them, and the right to counsel before and during police interrogation (see Chapter 4).[20] In 2000, the Supreme Court considered overruling *Miranda* in *Dickerson v. United States*, but it decided that the wide acceptance of Miranda rights in the legal culture is "adequate reason not to overrule" it.

***Miranda* rule** the requirement, articulated by the Supreme Court in *Miranda v. Arizona*, that persons under arrest must be informed prior to police interrogation of their rights to remain silent and to have the benefit of legal counsel

One of the most significant changes brought about by the Supreme Court was the revolution in legislative representation unleashed by the 1962 case of *Baker v. Carr.*[21] In this landmark case, the Supreme Court held that it could no longer avoid reviewing complaints about the apportionment of seats in state legislatures. Following that decision, the federal courts went on to force reapportionment of all state, county, and local legislatures in the country.

The Supreme Court in Action

Given the millions of disputes that arise every year, the job of the Supreme Court would be impossible if it were not able to control the flow of cases and its own caseload. The Supreme Court has original jurisdiction in a limited variety of cases defined by the Constitution. The original jurisdiction includes (1) cases between the United States and one of the fifty states, (2) cases between two or more states, (3) cases involving foreign ambassadors or other ministers, and (4) cases brought by one state against citizens of another state or against a foreign country. The most important of these cases are disputes between states over land, water, or old debts. Generally, the Supreme Court deals with these cases by appointing a "special master," usually a retired judge, to actually hear the case and present a report. The Supreme Court then allows the states involved in the dispute to present arguments for or against the master's opinion.[22] The fact that a matter falls within the Supreme Court's jurisdiction does not mean that the Court will necessarily hear the case.

RULES OF ACCESS Over the years, the courts have developed specific rules that govern which cases within their jurisdiction they will and will not hear. In order to be heard by the courts, cases must meet certain criteria that are initially applied by the trial court but may be reconsidered by appellate courts. These rules of access can be broken down into three major categories: case or controversy, standing, and mootness.

Article III of the Constitution and Supreme Court decisions define judicial power as extending only to "cases and controversies." This means that the case before a court must be an actual controversy, not a hypothetical one, with two truly adversarial parties. The courts have interpreted this language to mean that they do not have the power to render advisory opinions to legislatures or agencies about the constitutionality of proposed laws or regulations. Furthermore, even after a law is enacted, the courts will generally refuse to consider its constitutionality until it is actually applied.

Parties to a case must also have **standing**—that is, they must show that they have a substantial stake in the outcome of the case. The traditional requirement for standing has been to show injury to oneself; that injury can be personal, economic, or even aesthetic. In order for a group or class of people to have standing (as in class-action suits), each member must show specific injury. This means that a general interest in the environment, for instance, does not provide a group with sufficient basis for standing.

standing the right of an individual or organization to initiate a court case, on the basis of their having a substantial stake in the outcome

The Supreme Court also uses a third criterion in determining whether it will hear a case: that of **mootness.** In theory, this requirement disqualifies cases that are brought too late—after the relevant facts have changed or the problem has been resolved by other means. The criterion of mootness, however, is subject to the discretion of the courts, which have begun to relax the rules of mootness, particularly in cases where a situation that has been resolved is likely to come up again. In the abortion case *Roe v. Wade,* for example, the Supreme Court rejected the lower court's argument that because the pregnancy had already come to term, the case was moot. The Court agreed to hear the case because no pregnancy was likely to outlast the lengthy appeals process.

mootness a criterion used by courts to screen cases that no longer require resolution

Putting aside the formal criteria, the Supreme Court is most likely to accept cases that involve conflicting decisions by the federal circuit courts, cases that present important questions of civil rights or civil liberties, and cases in which the federal government is the appellant. Ultimately, however, the question of which cases to accept can come down to the preferences and priorities of the justices. If a group of justices believes that the Court should intervene in a particular area of policy or politics, they are likely to look for a case or cases that will serve as vehicles for judicial intervention. For many years, for example, the Court was not interested in considering challenges to affirmative action or other programs designed to provide particular benefits to minorities. In recent years, however, several of the Court's more conservative justices have been eager to push back the limits of affirmative action and racial preference, and have therefore accepted a number of cases that would allow them to do so. In 1995, the Court's decisions in *Adarand Constructors v. Pena, Missouri v. Jenkins,* and *Miller v. Johnson* placed new restrictions on federal affirmative action programs, school desegregation efforts, and attempts to increase minority representation in Congress through the creation of "minority districts" (see Chapter 10).[23]

writ of *certiorari* a decision of at least four of the nine Supreme Court justices to review a decision of a lower court; from the Latin "to make more certain"

WRITS Most cases reach the Supreme Court through a **writ of *certiorari*** (Figure 15.2). *Certiorari* is an order to a lower court to deliver the records of a particular case to be reviewed for legal errors. The term *certiorari* is sometimes shortened to *cert,* and cases deemed to merit certiorari are referred to as "certworthy." An individual who loses in a lower federal court or state court and wants the Supreme Court to review the decision has ninety days to file a petition for a writ of *certiorari* with the clerk of the U.S. Supreme Court. There are two types of petitions, paid petitions and petitions *in forma pauperis* (in the form of a pauper). The former requires payment of filing fees, submission of a certain number of copies, and compliance with a variety of other rules. For *in forma pauperis* petitions, usually filed by prison inmates, the Court waives the fees and most other requirements. Petitions for thousands of cases are filed with the Court every year (Figure 15.3).

Since 1972, most of the justices have participated in a "*certiorari* pool" in which their law clerks work together to evaluate the petitions. Each petition is reviewed by one clerk who writes a memo for all the justices participating in the pool summarizing the facts and issues and making a recommendation. Clerks for the other justices add their comments to the memo. After the justices have reviewed the memos, any one of them may place any case on the discuss list, which is circulated by the chief justice. If a case is not placed on the discuss list, it is automatically denied *certiorari*. Cases placed on the discuss list are considered and voted on during the justices' closed-door conference.

For *certiorari* to be granted, four justices must be convinced that the case satisfies Rule 10 of the Rules of the U.S. Supreme Court. Rule 10 states that *certiorari* is not a matter of right but is to be granted only when there are special and compelling reasons. These include conflicting decisions by two or more circuit courts, conflicts between circuit courts and state courts of last resort, conflicting decisions by two or more state courts of last resort, decisions by circuit courts on matters of federal law that should be settled by the Supreme Court, and a circuit court decision on an important question that conflicts with Supreme Court decisions. It should be clear from this list that the Court will usually take action under only the most compelling circumstances—when there are conflicts among the lower courts about what the law should be, when an important legal question has been raised in the lower courts but not definitively answered, or when a lower court deviates from the principles and precedents established by the high court. The support of four justices is needed for *certiorari*, and few cases are able to satisfy this requirement. In recent sessions, although thousands of petitions were filed, the Court

FIGURE 15.2 ★ How Cases Reach the Supreme Court

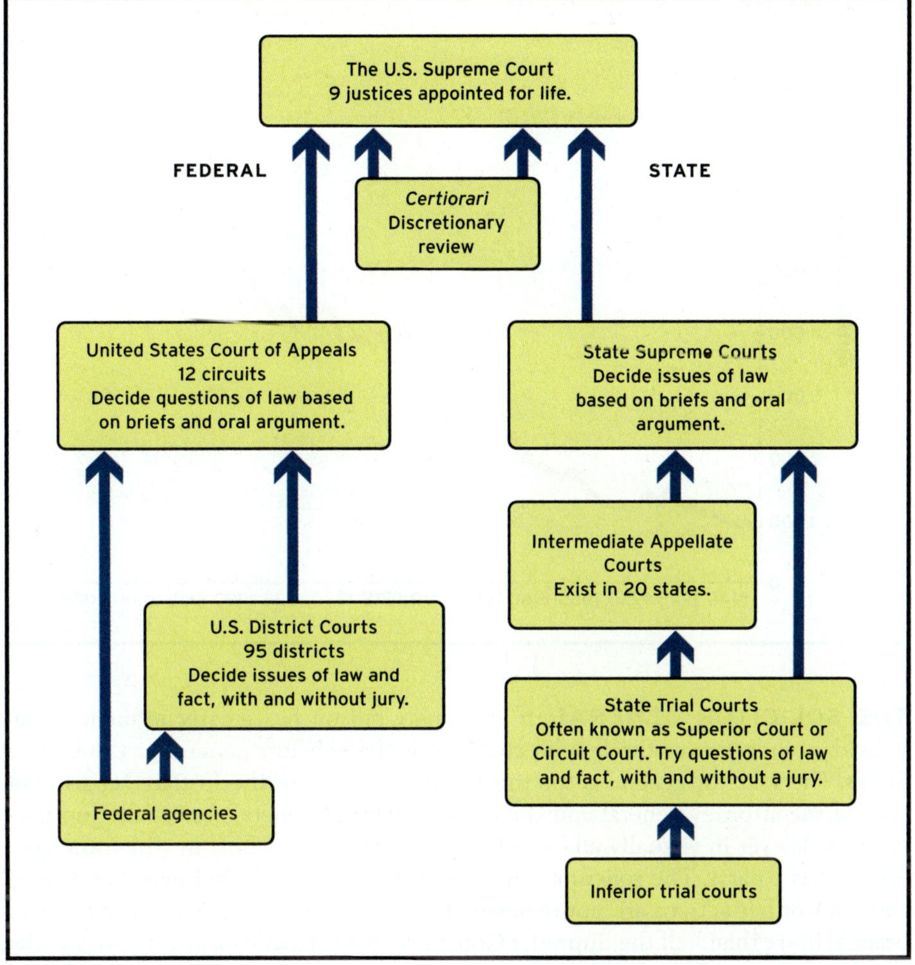

has granted *certiorari* to hardly more than eighty petitioners each year—about 1 percent of those seeking a Supreme Court review.

A handful of cases reach the Supreme court through avenues other than *certiorari*. One of these is the writ of certification. This writ can be used when a U.S. court of appeals asks the Supreme Court for instructions on a point of law that has never been decided. A second alternative avenue is the writ of appeal, which is used to appeal the decision of a three-judge district court.

Controlling the Flow of Cases

In addition to the judges themselves, other actors play important roles in shaping the flow of cases through the federal courts: the solicitor general and federal law clerks.

FIGURE 15.3 ★
Cases Filed in the U.S. Supreme Court, 1938–2005 Terms*

*Number of cases filed in term starting in year indicated.
SOURCES: Years 1938–1969: successive volumes of U.S. Bureau of the Census, *Statistical Abstract of the United States* (Washington, DC: Government Printing Office); 1970–1983: Office of the Clerk of the Supreme Court; 1984–1999: reprinted with permission from *The United States Law Week* (Washington, DC: Bureau of National Affairs), vol. 56, 3102; vol. 59, 3064; vol. 61, 3098; vol. 63, 3134; vol. 65, 3100; vol. 67, 3167; vol. 69, 3134 (copyright © Bureau of National Affairs Inc.); and 2000–2005: successive volumes of U.S. Bureau of the Census, *Statistical Abstract of the United States* (Washington, DC: Government Printing Office).

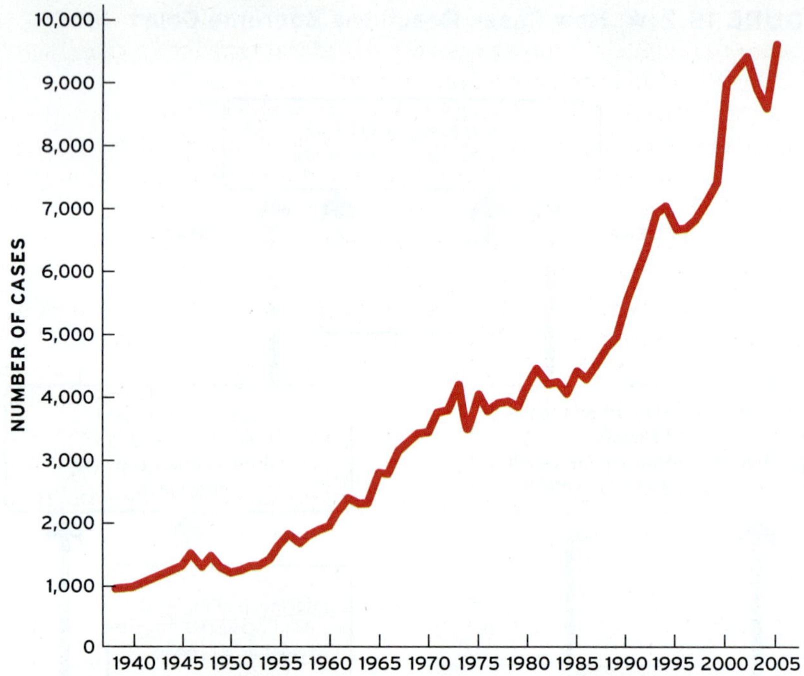

solicitor general the top government lawyer in all cases before the Supreme Court where the government is a party

per curiam a brief, unsigned decision by an appellate court, usually rejecting a petition to review the decision of a lower court

amicus curiae literally, "friend of the court"; individuals or groups who are not parties to a lawsuit but who seek to assist the Supreme Court in reaching a decision by presenting additional briefs

THE SOLICITOR GENERAL If any single person has greater influence than individual judges over the federal courts, it is the **solicitor general** of the United States. The solicitor general is the third-ranking official in the Justice Department (below the attorney general and the deputy attorney general) but is the top government lawyer in virtually all cases before the Supreme Court in which the government is a party. The solicitor general has the greatest control over the flow of cases; his or her actions are not reviewed by any higher authority in the executive branch. More than half the Supreme Court's total workload consists of cases under the direct charge of the solicitor general.

The solicitor general exercises especially strong influence by screening cases before any agency of the federal government can appeal them to the Supreme Court; indeed, the justices rely on the solicitor general to "screen out undeserving litigation and furnish them with an agenda to government cases that deserve serious consideration."[24] Typically, more requests for appeals are rejected than are accepted by the solicitor general. Agency heads may lobby the president or otherwise try to circumvent the solicitor general, and a few of the independent agencies have a statutory right to make direct appeals, but without the solicitor general's support, these requests are seldom reviewed by the Court. At best, they are doomed to ***per curiam*** rejection—rejection through a brief, unsigned opinion by the whole Court. Congress has given only a few agencies, including the Federal Communications Commission, the Federal Maritime Commission, and in some cases the Department of Agriculture (even though it is not an independent agency), the right to appeal directly to the Supreme Court without going through the solicitor general.

The solicitor general can enter a case even when the federal government is not a direct litigant by writing an ***amicus curiae*** ("friend of the court") brief. A friend of the court is not a direct party to a case but has a vital interest in its outcome. Thus, when the government has such an interest, the solicitor general can file an *amicus* brief, or a federal court can invite such a brief because it wants an opinion in writing. Other interested parties may file briefs as well.

In addition to exercising substantial control over the flow of cases, the solicitor general can shape the arguments used before the federal courts. Indeed, the Supreme Court tends to give special attention to the way the solicitor general characterizes the issues. The solicitor general is the person who appears most frequently before the Court and, theoretically at least, is the most disinterested. The credibility of the solicitor general is not hurt when several times each year he or she comes to the Court to withdraw a case with the admission that the government has made an error.

The solicitor general's sway over the flow of cases does not, however, entirely overshadow the influence of the other agencies and divisions in the Department of Justice. The solicitor general is counsel for the major divisions in the department, including the Antitrust, Tax, Civil Rights, and Criminal divisions. Their activities generate a great part of the solicitor general's agenda. This is particularly true of the Criminal Division, whose cases are appealed every day. These cases are generated by initiatives taken by the United States attorneys and the district judges before whom they practice.

LAW CLERKS Every federal judge employs law clerks to research legal issues and assist with the preparation of opinions. Each Supreme Court justice is assigned four clerks. The clerks are almost always honors graduates of the nation's most prestigious law schools. A clerkship with a Supreme Court justice is a great honor and generally indicates that the fortunate individual is likely to reach the very top of the legal profession. The work of the Supreme Court clerks is a closely guarded secret, but it is likely that some justices rely heavily on their clerks for advice in writing opinions and in deciding whether the Court should hear an individual case. In a recent book, a former law clerk to the late justice Harry Blackmun charged that Supreme Court justices yielded "excessive power to immature, ideologically driven clerks, who in turn use that power to manipulate their bosses."[25]

Lobbying for Access: Interests and the Court

At the same time that the Court exercises discretion over which cases it will review, groups and forces in society often seek to persuade the justices to listen to their problems. Interest groups use several different strategies to get the Court's attention. Lawyers representing these groups try to choose the proper client and the proper case, so that the issues in question are most dramatically and appropriately portrayed. They also have to pick the right district or jurisdiction in which to bring the case. Sometimes they even have to wait for an appropriate political climate.

Group litigants have to plan carefully when to use and when to avoid publicity. They must also attempt to develop a proper record at the trial court level, one that includes some constitutional arguments and even, when possible, errors on the part of the trial court. One of the most effective strategies that litigants use in getting cases accepted for review by the appellate courts is to bring the same type of suit in more than one circuit (that is, to develop a "pattern of cases"), in the hope that inconsistent treatment by two different courts will improve the chance of a Supreme Court review.

Congress will sometimes provide interest groups with legislation designed to facilitate their use of litigation. One important recent example is the 1990 Americans with

Abortion and the Right to Privacy

Although the word *privacy* does not appear in the Bill of Rights, the courts have agreed that such a fundamental right exists. They disagree, however, about exactly from where the protection arises and about how far it should be applied. Nowhere is this disagreement more protracted than on the issue of abortion.

Since its 1973 landmark ruling in *Roe v. Wade,* the Supreme Court has repeatedly found that the right to privacy protects the right of a woman to end a pregnancy via abortion, subject to some court-approved restrictions. Abortion opponents, of course, have rejected the premise of *Roe* that privacy protects an act they consider murder. For example, members of Congress who oppose abortion have succeeded in restricting federal Medicaid funding for abortions. Today's more conservative Supreme Court has allowed states to impose restrictions such as parental notification for minors and twenty-four-hour waiting periods for those seeking abortions.

Supporters of privacy-based protection for abortion argue that, as a matter of law and tradition, a developing fetus cannot be accorded the same legal status as the woman carrying a fetus. If privacy means anything, it must extend to the right of a woman to decide, at least during the early months of pregnancy, whether or not to have an abortion. For the government to require women to carry most or all pregnancies to term represents extreme government intrusion into the innately personal decision over procreation. The principle of individual liberty must allow women to make such fundamental decisions themselves.

Further, supporters of abortion rights argue that the idea that all abortions are murder means that a fertilized egg does and should possess the same traits as a full-term baby, an idea that is rejected by medical science, most Americans, and many religions. Abortion laws properly reflect these differences. Finally, the Constitution addresses to the issue by noting that citizenship, and therefore the rights stemming from it, begins at birth.

Opponents of abortion argue that the relative differences observed in fetal development do not change the fact that, by genetic makeup, even a fertilized egg is a person. The absence of birth does not, in and of itself, mean that a fetus is without rights. Even if the Constitution's framers had all agreed that the Bill of Rights protected the right to privacy, there is no reason to believe that they would have countenanced its extension to abortion. Furthermore, to say that such issues are purely a matter of personal choice is to turn a blind eye to the sort of evil that government has every right to regulate or prohibit. And although pregnancy is a developmental process for the fetus, it is precisely because there is no magic, agreed-on point at which a fetus becomes a person that the fetus must be protected as a person at all stages.

Opponents of abortion believe that women who become pregnant, whether by accident or intent, assume a special obligation to the innocent life they carry. Although some who oppose abortions are willing to allow exceptions for cases of rape or incest, such cases account for only a tiny percentage of all abortions. Legal abortion is harmful in other respects. It demeans respect for life by allowing, even encouraging, abortion as a means of birth control. Above all, the right of a fetus to live must supersede the privacy rights, however defined, of pregnant women.

FOR CRITICAL ANALYSIS

1. If *Roe* were reversed and states made abortion a crime, how would protection of the fetus, beginning with the fertilized egg, be implemented? If a "miscarriage" was induced by abortion, what should be the charge against the mother? Murder? Criminal negligence? Manslaughter?
2. Thousands of childless couples engage in great effort and endure delays and disappointments in adopting a child. Should government provide incentives to pregnant women to go to term so that more children are available for adoption?

Disabilities Act (ADA), enacted after intense lobbying by public interest and advocacy groups. The ADA, in conjunction with the 1991 Civil Rights Act, opened the way for disabled individuals to make effective use of the courts to press their interests.

The two most notable users of the pattern of cases strategy in recent years have been the National Association for the Advancement of Colored People (NAACP) and the American Civil Liberties Union (ACLU). For many years, the NAACP (and its Defense Fund—now a separate group) has worked through local chapters and with many individuals to encourage litigation on issues of racial discrimination and segregation. Sometimes it distributes petitions to be signed by parents and filed with local school boards and courts, deliberately sowing the seeds of future litigation. The NAACP and the ACLU often encourage private parties to bring suit and then join the suit as *amici curiae.*

One illustration of an interest group employing a carefully crafted litigation strategy to pursue its goals through the judiciary was the Texas-based effort to establish a right to free public school education for children of illegal aliens. The issue arose in 1977 when the Texas state legislature, responding to a sudden public backlash against illegal immigration from Mexico, enacted a law permitting school districts to charge undocumented children hefty tuition for the privilege of attending public school. A public-interest law organization, the Mexican American Legal Defense Fund, prepared to challenge the law in court after determining that public opposition precluded any chance of persuading the legislature to change its own law.

Part of the defense fund's litigation strategy was to bring a lawsuit in the northern section of Texas, far from the Mexican border, where illegal immigration would be at a minimum. Thus, in Tyler, Texas, where the complaint was initially filed, the trial court found only sixty undocumented alien students in a school district composed of 16,000. This strategy effectively contradicted the state's argument that the Texas law was necessary to reduce the burdens on educational resources created by masses of incoming aliens. Another useful litigation tactic was to select plaintiffs who, although illegal aliens, were nevertheless clearly planning to remain in Texas even without free public education for their children. Thus, all of the plaintiffs came from families that had already lived in Tyler for several years and included at least one child who was an American citizen by virtue of birth in the United States. By emphasizing the stability of such families, the defense fund argued convincingly that the Texas law would not motivate families to return to the poverty in Mexico from which they had fled, but would more likely result in the creation of a subclass of illiterate people who would add to the state's unemployment and crime rates. Five years after the lawsuit on behalf of the Tyler children began, the U.S. Supreme Court in the case of *Plyler v. Doe* held that the Texas law was unconstitutional under the equal protection clause of the Fourteenth Amendment.[26]

More recently, a conservative advocacy group, the Washington, D.C.–based Center for Individual Rights, has launched an active campaign of litigation to challenge affirmative action programs in college admissions and employment. In the case of *Hopwood v. Texas,* the center won a major victory against affirmative action, with the Fifth Circuit Court invalidating the University of Texas law school's program of preferential minority admissions.[27] In two very important subsequent cases, the center challenged the University of Michigan's minority admissions programs, which gave preferential treatment to minority applicants to the college of arts and sciences and to the law school. In 2003, the U.S. Supreme Court upheld the law school's program with certain changes. But the justices struck down the affirmative action rules that the undergraduate college applied.[28] In so doing, the Court forced colleges throughout the nation to place new restrictions on their affimative action efforts. The center has also sued

MGM v. Grokster: Digital Media and the Federal Courts

As digital technology evolves, America's federal courts find themselves bombarded by questions of intellectual property and copyright law. Some of the most recent high-profile cases involving the fate of digital technologies in the federal courts have involved P2P (peer-to-peer) networks such as Napster or Grokster, which are best known for facilitating the sharing of audio and video files between users.

Napster, the first well-known P2P file-sharing service, became popular soon after it was launched in 1999. Napster's creator, Shawn Fanning, was a student at Northeastern University when he began writing the program that would allow quick and convenient sharing of MP3 music files. Artists such as Metallica and Madonna criticized Napster, and music industry executives, fearing that Napster's distribution network was encouraging illegal exchanges of music and costing the industry millions, filed a lawsuit in 1999. In spring of 2001, with over 25 million users, Napster was forced by the Ninth Circuit Court of Appeals to cease operations.

But with the shutdown of Napster, P2P technologies only became larger, less centralized and more difficult to regulate. One example of the next generation of P2P networks was Grokster, a P2P file-sharing service without a centralized search engine. In 2003, Grokster was challenged by large media companies including AOL, Sony, Viacom, and Disney over the legality of their service. The U.S. District Court ruled in favor of Grokster, arguing that the company had no say over how its users chose to actually employ the technology. Judge Stephen Wilson pointed out that the service Grokster provided was similar to that of a VCR, in that it could be used for many *legal* purposes. "Grokster and Streamcast are not significantly different from companies that sell home video recorders or copy machines, both of which can be and are used to infringe copyrights," said Judge Wilson.[a]

After industry executives appealed the decision, the Ninth Circuit Court of Appeals—the same one that shut down Napster three years earlier—heard the Grokster case. But unlike the Napster case in 2004, this time the court ruled in favor of the P2P network, citing the precedent of the 1984 Betamax case, which deemed VCR manufacturers not responsible for how individuals used their product. The court found that Grokster's file-sharing service was legal because it was decentralized, hence the company was not liable for the copyright infringements made by its users.[b] Frustrated by the ruling, the movie and music companies appealed to the Supreme Court.

In response to the court's ruling, the Recording Industry Association of America began filing lawsuits against individual P2P users (many of them teenagers) for copyright infringement.

In 2005, the Supreme Court judged in favor of the music and movie industries, arguing that the legality of Grokster was not so much a function of the details of the technology but rather that Grokster's business model was predicated on the notion that users would share copyrighted material.

FOR CRITICAL ANALYSIS

1. When the Supreme Court issued its decision on the *MGM v. Grokster* case, it did so based not on the technology behind the P2P service, but on the company's business model. Why is this an important distinction? How might this decision contribute to setting a precedent in a way that a decision based on the technology itself might not have?
2. Should the courts be more accommodating of innovative technologies? Or should they do more to protect artists and "traditional" businesses?

---

a. R. Naraine, "Judge Rules In Favor of File-Swapping Sites," Internet News.com, April 25, 2003, www.internetnews.com/bus-news/article .php/2197111 (accessed 3/12/08).

b. R. Smolla, "You Say Napster, I Say Grokster: What Do You Do When Technology Outpaces the Law?" Slate.com, December 13, 2004, www .slate.com/id/2110982/ (accessed 3/12/08).

the University of Washington over minority admissions, Alabama State University (a historically black school) over preferential treatment for whites, and a school district in Minnesota over preferential treatment for minorities in magnet school admissions.[29] Through this pattern of suits in federal and state courts, the center has sought to challenge and undermine the legal underpinnings of affirmative action.

In many states, it is considered unethical and illegal for attorneys to engage in "fomenting and soliciting legal business in which they are not parties and have no pecuniary right or liability." The NAACP was sued by the state of Virginia in the late 1950s in an attempt to restrict or eliminate its efforts to influence the pattern of cases. The Supreme Court reviewed the case in 1963, recognized that the strategy was being utilized, and held that the NAACP strategy was protected by the First and Fourteenth Amendments, just as other forms of speech and petition are protected.[30]

Thus, many pathbreaking cases are eventually granted *certiorari* because continued refusal to review one or more of them would amount to a rule of law just as much as if the courts had handed down a written opinion. In this sense, the flow of cases, especially the pattern of significant cases, influences the behavior of the appellate judiciary.

The Supreme Court's Procedures

THE PREPARATION The Supreme Court's decision to accept a case is the beginning of what can be a lengthy and complex process (see Figure 15.4). First, the attorneys on both sides must prepare **briefs**—written documents in which the attorneys explain why the Court should rule in favor of their client. Briefs are filled with referrals to precedents specifically chosen to show that other courts have frequently ruled in the same way the attorneys are asking the Supreme Court. The attorneys for both sides muster the most compelling precedents they can in support of their arguments.

brief a written document in which attorneys explain, using case precedents, why the court should find in favor of their client

FIGURE 15.4 ★ The Supreme Court's Decision-Making Process

Thousands of petitions for *certiorari* are filed each year, but the Supreme Court accepts and decides only the handful of cases it deems to be especially important.

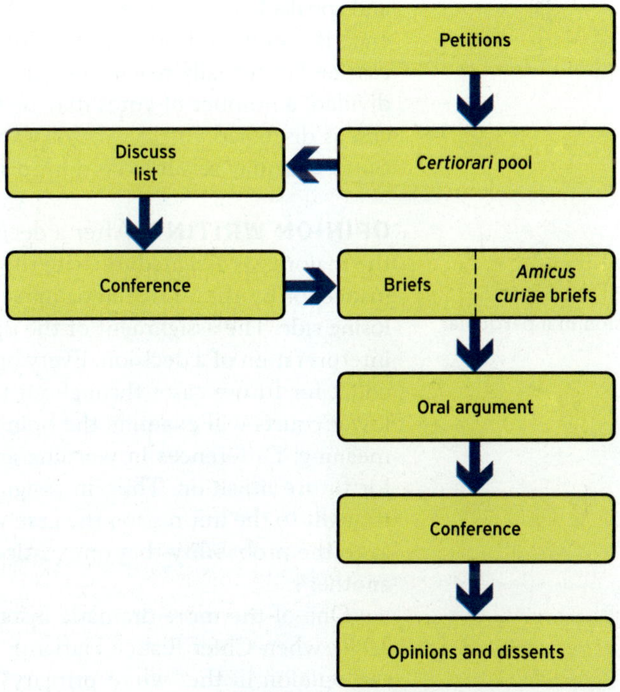

As the attorneys prepare their briefs, they often ask sympathetic interest groups for their help. These groups are asked to file *amicus curiae* briefs that support the claims of one or the other litigant. In a case involving separation of church and state, for example, liberal groups such as the ACLU and Citizens for the American Way are likely to be asked to file *amicus* briefs in support of strict separation, whereas conservative religious groups are likely to file *amicus* briefs advocating increased public support for religious ideas. Often, dozens of briefs will be filed on each side of a major case. *Amicus* filings are one of the primary methods used by interest groups to lobby the Court. By filing these briefs, groups indicate to the Court where they stand and signal to the justices that they believe the case to be an important one.

oral argument stage in Supreme Court procedure in which attorneys for both sides appear before the Court to present their positions and answer questions posed by justices

ORAL ARGUMENT The next stage of a case is **oral argument,** in which attorneys for both sides appear before the Court to present their positions and answer the justices' questions. Each attorney has only a half hour to present his or her case, and this time includes interruptions for questions. Certain members of the Court, such as Justice Antonin Scalia, are known to interrupt attorneys dozens of times. Others, such as Justice Clarence Thomas, seldom ask questions. For an attorney, the opportunity to argue a case before the Supreme Court is a singular honor and a mark of professional distinction. It can also be a harrowing experience, as justices interrupt a carefully prepared presentation. Nevertheless, oral argument can be very important to the outcome of a case. It allows justices better to understand the heart of the case and to raise questions that might not have been addressed in the opposing sides' briefs. It is not uncommon for justices to go beyond the strictly legal issues and ask opposing counsel to discuss the implications of the case for the Court and the nation at large.

THE CONFERENCE Following oral argument, the Court discusses the case in its Wednesday or Friday conference. The chief justice presides over the conference and speaks first; the other justices follow in order of seniority. The Court's conference is secret, and no outsiders are permitted to attend. The justices discuss the case and eventually reach a decision on the basis of a majority vote. If the Court is divided, a number of votes may be taken before a final decision is reached. As the case is discussed, justices may try to influence or change each other's opinions. At times, this may result in compromise decisions.

opinion the written explanation of the Supreme Court's decision in a particular case

OPINION WRITING After a decision has been reached, one of the members of the majority is assigned to write the **opinion.** This assignment is made by the chief justice, or by the most senior justice in the majority if the chief justice is on the losing side. The assignment of the opinion can make a significant difference to the interpretation of a decision. Every opinion of the Supreme Court sets a major precedent for future cases throughout the judicial system. Lawyers and judges in the lower courts will examine the opinion carefully to ascertain the Supreme Court's meaning. Differences in wording and emphasis can have important implications for future litigation. Thus, in assigning an opinion, the justices must give serious thought to the impression the case will make on lawyers and on the public, as well as to the probability that one justice's opinion will be more widely accepted than another's.

One of the more dramatic instances of this tactical consideration occurred in 1944, when Chief Justice Harlan F. Stone chose Justice Felix Frankfurter to write the opinion in the "white primary" case *Smith v. Allwright.* The chief justice be-

In 2005, the Supreme Court decided two cases involving displays of the Ten Commandments on government property. Christian activists paid close attention to the wording of the decisions, which allowed such displays in some circumstances.

lieved that this sensitive case, which overturned the southern practice of prohibiting black participation in nominating primaries, required the efforts of the most brilliant and scholarly jurist on the Court. But the day after Stone made the assignment, Justice Robert H. Jackson wrote a letter to Stone urging a change of assignment. In his letter, Jackson argued that Frankfurter, a foreign-born Jew from New England, would not win the South with his opinion, regardless of its brilliance. Stone accepted the advice and substituted Justice Stanley Reed, an American-born Protestant from Kentucky and a southern Democrat in good standing.[31]

Once the majority opinion is drafted, it is circulated to the other justices. Some members of the majority may agree with both the outcome and the rationale, but wish to emphasize or highlight a particular point. For that purpose, they draft a concurring opinion, called a *regular concurrence.* In other instances, one or more justices may agree with the majority but disagree with the rationale presented in the majority opinion. These justices may draft *special concurrences,* explaining their disagreements with the majority.

DISSENT Justices who disagree with the majority decision of the Court may choose to publicize the character of their disagreement in the form of a **dissenting opinion.** The dissenting opinion is generally assigned by the senior justice among the dissenters. Dissents can be used to express irritation with an outcome or to signal to defeated political forces in the nation that their position is supported by at least some members of the Court. Ironically, the most dependable way an individual justice can exercise a direct and clear influence on the Court is to write a dissent. Because there is no need to please a majority, dissenting opinions can be more eloquent and less guarded than majority opinions. The current Supreme Court often produces 5-to-4 decisions, with dissenters writing long and detailed opinions that, they hope, will help them to convince a swing justice to join their side on the next round of cases dealing with a similar topic. During the Court's 2006–07 term, Justice Ruth Bader Ginsburg was so unhappy about the majority's

dissenting opinion a decision written by a justice in the minority in a particular case in which the justice wishes to express his or her reasoning in the case

On several recent occasions, Justice Ruth Bader Ginsburg read her dissenting opinions aloud from the bench, to emphasize her strong disagreement with the majority. Dissenting opinions can encourage lawyers to bring similar cases in the future by letting the public know that not all of the justices support the majority decision.

decisions in a number of cases that she violated her own long-standing practice and read forceful dissents from the bench in two cases. Reading a dissent from the bench is one way that a justice can underscore his or her disagreement with current legal trends and point the way toward other possibilities.

Dissent plays a special role in the work and impact of the Court because it amounts to an appeal to lawyers all over the country to keep bringing cases of the sort at issue. Therefore, an effective dissent influences the flow of cases through the Court as well as the arguments that lawyers will use in later cases. Even more important, dissent points out that although the Court speaks with a single opinion, it is the opinion only of the majority—and one day the majority might go the other way.

Explaining Supreme Court Decisions

The Supreme Court explains its decisions in terms of law and precedent. But although law and precedent do have an effect on the Court's deliberations and eventual decisions, it is the Supreme Court that decides what laws actually mean and what importance precedent will actually have. Throughout its history, the Court has shaped and reshaped the law. In the late nineteenth and early twentieth centuries, for example, the Supreme Court held that the Constitution, law, and precedent permitted racial segregation in the United States. Beginning in the late 1950s, however, the Court found that the Constitution prohibited segregation on the basis of race and indicated that the use of racial categories in legislation was always suspect. By the 1970s and 1980s, the Court once again held that the Constitution permitted the use of racial categories—when such categories were needed to help members of minority groups achieve full participation in American society. Since the 1990s, the Court has retreated from this position, too, indicating that governmental efforts to provide extra help to racial minorities could represent an unconstitutional infringement on the rights of the majority.

ACTIVISM AND RESTRAINT One element of judicial philosophy is the issue of activism versus restraint. Over the years, some justices have believed that courts should interpret the Constitution according to the stated intentions of its framers and defer to the views of Congress when interpreting federal statutes. The late justice Felix Frankfurter, for example, advocated judicial deference to legislative bodies and avoidance of the "political thicket" in which the Court would entangle itself by deciding questions that were essentially political rather than legal in character. Advocates of **judicial restraint** are sometimes called "strict constructionists," because they look strictly to the words of the Constitution in interpreting its meaning.

judicial restraint judicial philosophy whose adherents refuse to go beyond the clear words of the Constitution in interpreting its meaning

judicial activism judicial philosophy that posits that the Court should go beyond the words of the Constitution or a statute to consider the broader societal implications of its decisions

The alternative to restraint is **judicial activism.** Activist judges such as the late chief justice Earl Warren believed that the Court should go beyond the words of the Constitution or a statute to consider the broader societal implications of its decisions. Activist judges sometimes strike out in new directions, promulgating new interpretations or inventing new legal and constitutional concepts when they believe these to be socially desirable. For example, Justice Harry Blackmun's opinion in *Roe v. Wade* was based on a constitutional right to privacy that is not found in the words of the Constitution but was, rather, from the Court's prior decision in *Griswold v. Connecticut.*[32] Blackmun and the other members of the majority in the *Roe* case argued that the right to privacy was implied by other constitutional provisions. In this instance of judicial activism, the Court knew the result it wanted to achieve and was not afraid to make the law conform to the desired outcome.

Activism and restraint are sometimes confused with liberalism and conservatism. For example, conservative politicians often castigate "liberal activist" judges and call for the appointment of conservative jurists who will refrain from reinterpreting the law. To be sure, some liberal jurists are activists and some conservatives have been advocates of restraint, but the relationships are by no means synonymous. Indeed, the Rehnquist court, dominated by conservatives, was among the most activist courts in American history, striking out in new directions in such areas as federalism and election law. The Roberts court is continuing along the same route.

Politics Today

In its 2008 decision in the case of *District of Columbia v. Heller*, the Supreme Court struck down a District of Columbia law that prohibited most private citizens from keeping handguns in their homes. How does the *Heller* decision affect gun laws outside the District of Columbia?

POLITICAL IDEOLOGY The second component of judicial philosophy is political ideology. The liberal or conservative attitudes of justices play an important role in their decisions.[33] Indeed, the philosophy of activism versus restraint is sometimes a smokescreen for political ideology. In the past, liberal judges have often been activists, willing to use the law to achieve social and political change, whereas conservatives have been associated with judicial restraint. Interestingly, however, in recent years some conservative justices who have long called for restraint have actually become activists in seeking to undo some of the work of liberal jurists over the past three decades.

From the 1950s to the 1980s, the Supreme Court took an activist role in such areas as civil rights, civil liberties, abortion, voting rights, and police procedures. For example, the Supreme Court was more responsible than any other governmental institution for breaking down America's system of racial segregation. The Supreme Court virtually prohibited states from interfering with the right of a woman to seek an abortion and sharply curtailed state restrictions on voting rights. And it was the Supreme Court that placed restrictions on the behavior of local police and prosecutors in criminal cases. Since that time, however, the conservative justices appointed by presidents Ronald Reagan, George H. W. Bush, and George W. Bush have become the dominant bloc on the Court and, as we saw earlier, have moved the Court to the right on a number of issues, including affirmative action and abortion.

The political struggles of recent years amply illustrate the importance of judicial ideology. Is abortion a fundamental right or a criminal activity? How much separation must there be between church and state? Does application of the Voting Rights Act to increase minority representation constitute a violation of the rights of whites? The answers to these and many other questions cannot be found in the words of the Constitution. They must be located, instead, in the hearts and minds of the judges who interpret that text.

Judicial Power and Politics

One of the most important institutional changes to occur in the United States during the past half-century has been the striking transformation of the role and power of the federal courts, and of the Supreme Court in particular. Understanding how this transformation came about is the key to understanding the contemporary role of the courts in America.

The Supreme Court and International Law

For most of its history the American judiciary has been a particularly domestic institution. But in this epoch of globalization, the Court has had to give up what Justice Ruth Bader Ginsburg in 2003 called "our 'island' or 'lone ranger' mentality." Ginsburg went on to note that increasingly the justices were considering the perspectives of comparative and international law.

Along one path of change, numerous cases involving such things as interpreting the terms of an international treaty have arisen over "cross-border transactions" in which international law is not only relevant but could be the governing law. Such cases have given rise to the adoption of the United Nations Convention on Contracts for the International Sale of Goods (CISG), which the United States ratified in 1986. By the mid-1990s, U.S. courts had to deal with an increasing number of such cases, and the lower judges as well as the Supreme Court justices and their law clerks had a difficult time with these because they required research on international law and decisions by foreign courts. In 2003, Justice Stephen Breyer confessed in a speech to the Society of International Law that he and his colleagues had to rely on the lawyers involved in the litigation for applicable foreign precedents to apply. And our various courts continually disagree over the weight to put on the rulings of foreign tribunals: Are these foreign decisions to be taken as precedents in our courts? Or do U.S. courts apply U.S. law to such transnational cases?

A second path of change, more diffuse and harder to measure, is the extent to which our courts, all the way to the top, can permit themselves to be influenced not only by precedents in cases of international law but also by international opinion and the decisions by foreign legislators and courts in their domestic disputes. The most striking was the 2003 decision that a Texas statute making it a crime for two persons of the same sex to engage in consensual sexual conduct violates the due process clause (*Lawrence v. Texas*, 123 S.Ct. 2472). This opinion overruled a case that had been the leading opinion since 1986 (*Bowers v. Hardwick*, 478 U.S. 186). More controversial than the ruling itself was part of its argument—that other nations, including Great Britain, had repealed such laws ten years earlier. Another decision of equal import was the 2002 decision in which the majority opinion noted that "within the world community the imposition of the death penalty for crimes committed by mentally retarded offenders is overwhelmingly disapproved." Chief Justice Rehnquist and Justice Scalia vigorously dissented on this point: "The viewpoints of other countries simply are not relevant . . . [and foreign] notions of justice are not always those of our people" (*Atkins v. Virginia*, 536 U.S. 304).

More recently, in 2005, the International Task Force on Euthanasia and Assisted Suicide (ITFEA) filed an *amicus* brief in the case of *Gonzales v. Oregon*. This case involved Oregon's assisted suicide law, which allows individuals to end their own lives under certain circumstances. The ITFEA sought to convince the U.S. Supreme Court that the federal government should be prohibited from prosecuting Oregon physicians who cooperated with suicides permitted by the state law.

Another international influence is the UN Treaty to establish an International Criminal Court (ICC), to be given jurisdiction over the conduct of military personnel in any international campaign. Since its creation in 1998, 130 countries have signed the treaty. Although President Clinton signed for the United States, he continued to bargain over terms, and the U.S. Senate has never had to confront a vote on ratification. However, Clinton's signature committed the United States to avoid acting in any way that would undermine the treaty. Consequently, fears persist that U.S. military personnel could be subject to prosecution if one of the ratifying states comes forward with an allegation that a "war crime" has been committed.

FOR CRITICAL ANALYSIS

1. Who should have jurisdiction if American soldiers at Abu Ghraib Prison in Baghdad are charged by the new Iraqi government with war crimes for mistreating Iraqi prisoners? Iraqi courts? American courts? the ICC?
2. Who should have jurisdiction if an American soldier is arrested by Iraqi police and charged with molesting an Iraqi woman?

Traditional Limitations on the Federal Courts

For much of American history, the power of the federal courts was subject to a number of limitations.[34] To begin with, unlike other governmental institutions, courts cannot exercise power on their own initiative. Judges must wait until a case is brought to them before they can make authoritative decisions. Traditionally, moreover, courts were constrained by judicial rules of standing that limited access to the bench. Claimants who simply disagreed with governmental action or inaction could not obtain access. Access to the courts was limited to individuals who could show that they were particularly affected by the government's behavior in some area. This limitation on access to the courts diminished the judiciary's capacity to forge links with important political and social forces.

Second, courts were traditionally limited in the character of the relief they could provide. In general, courts acted only to offer relief or assistance to individuals and not to broad social classes, again inhibiting the formation of alliances between the courts and important social forces. Third, courts lacked enforcement powers of their own and were compelled to rely on executive or state agencies to ensure compliance with their edicts. If the executive or state agencies were unwilling to assist the courts, judicial enactments could go unheeded, as when President Andrew Jackson declined to enforce Chief Justice John Marshall's 1832 order to the state of Georgia to release two missionaries it had arrested on Cherokee lands. Marshall asserted that the state had no right to enter the Cherokee lands without their assent.[35] Jackson is reputed to have said, "John Marshall has made his decision, now let him enforce it." Congress and the president have ignored Supreme Court rulings in recent years as well. For example, in 1983 the Supreme Court declared that a practice known as the one-house legislative veto was unconstitutional. This practice entailed the enactment of legislation that could later be rescinded by either house of Congress if it was dissatisfied with the results. In the case of *Immigration and Naturalization Service v. Chadha*, the Court ruled that this amounted to the usurpation of executive power by the legislature.[36] Congress and the president, however, find the legislative veto procedure convenient and continue to use it by other names, despite the Court's ruling.

Fourth, federal judges are, of course, appointed by the president (with the consent of the Senate). As a result, the president and Congress can shape the composition of the federal courts and ultimately, perhaps, the character of judicial decisions. Finally, Congress has the power to change both the size and jurisdiction of the Supreme Court and other federal courts. In many areas, federal courts obtain their jurisdiction not from the Constitution but from congressional statutes. On a number of occasions, Congress has threatened to take matters out of the Court's hands when it was unhappy with the Court's policies.[37] For example, in 1996 Congress enacted several pieces of legislation designed to curb the jurisdiction of the federal courts. One of these laws was the Prison Litigation Reform Act, which limits the ability of federal judges to issue "consent decrees" under which the judges could take control of state prison systems. Another jurisdictional curb was included in the Immigration Reform Act, which prohibited the federal courts from hearing class-action suits against Immigration and Naturalization Service deportation orders. As to the size of the Court, on one memorable occasion, presidential and congressional threats to expand the size of the Supreme Court—Franklin Roosevelt's "court packing" plan—encouraged the justices to drop their opposition to New Deal programs.

For Critical Analysis

Are the federal courts "imperial," or are they merely handmaidens of the elected branches of government? In what respect does the federal judiciary still play a "checks and balances" role?

As a result of these limitations on judicial power, through much of their history the chief function of the federal courts was to provide judicial support for executive agencies and to legitimize acts of Congress by declaring them to be consistent with constitutional principles. Only on rare occasions have the federal courts dared to challenge Congress or the executive branch.[38]

Two Judicial Revolutions

Since the Second World War, however, the role of the federal judiciary has been strengthened and expanded. There have been two judicial revolutions in the United States since World War II. The first and more visible of these was the substantive revolution in judicial policy. As we saw earlier in this chapter and in Chapters 4 and 5, in policy areas, including school desegregation, legislative apportionment, and criminal procedure, as well as obscenity, abortion, and voting rights, the Supreme Court was at the forefront of a series of sweeping changes in the role of the U.S. government, and ultimately, in the character of American society.[39]

But at the same time that the courts were introducing important policy innovations, they were also bringing about a second, less visible revolution. During the 1960s and 1970s, the Supreme Court and other federal courts instituted a series of changes in judicial procedures that fundamentally expanded the power of the courts in the United States. First, the federal courts liberalized the concept of standing to permit almost any group that seeks to challenge the actions of an administrative agency to bring its case before the federal bench. In 1971, for example, the Supreme Court ruled that public interest groups could use the National Environmental Policy Act to challenge the actions of federal agencies by claiming that the agencies' activities might have adverse environmental consequences.[40]

When the Supreme Court upheld Oregon's assisted suicide law in October 2005, the Court's most conservative justices—Chief Justice Roberts, Justice Scalia, and Justice Thomas—dissented from the majority opinion. Ideology often plays a major role in Supreme Court decisions.

Congress helped to make it even easier for groups dissatisfied with government policies to bring their cases to the courts by adopting Section 1983 of the U.S. Code, which permits the practice of "fee shifting"—that is, allowing citizens who successfully bring a suit against a public official for violating their constitutional rights to collect their attorneys' fees and costs from the government. Thus, Section 1983 encourages individuals and groups to bring their problems to the courts rather than to Congress or the executive branch. These changes have given the courts a far greater role in the administrative process than ever before. Many federal judges are concerned that federal legislation in areas such as health care reform would create new rights and entitlements that would give rise to a deluge of court cases. "Any time you create a new right, you create a host of disputes and claims," warned Barbara Rothstein, chief judge of the federal district court in Seattle, Washington.[41]

class-action suit a legal action by which a group or class of individuals with common interests can file a suit on behalf of everyone who shares that interest

Second, the federal courts broadened the scope of relief to permit themselves to act on behalf of broad categories or classes of persons in "class action" cases, rather than just on behalf of individuals.[42] A **class-action suit** is a procedural device that permits large numbers of persons with common interests to join together under a representative party to bring or defend a lawsuit. One example of a class-action suit is the

Become an Advocate for Justice

Do you think you can't affect the outcome of justice? Think again. Thousands of socially conscious youth convened in Jena, Louisiana in 2007 to protest the sentences of the so-called "Jena 6." After black students at a local high school sat beneath a campus tree that was historically claimed by white students, nooses were found dangling from the same tree. The heightened racial tensions were only exacerbated when the justice system appeared to treat white students lightly while coming down hard on black students who behaved similarly. In order to protest the perceived injustice of the criminal justice system to black defendants, more than 10,000 demonstrators, including a large number of young people, descended on the city of Jena for marches and vigils. Their presence helped to overturn the original sentences of the "Jena 6."

If protesting what you believe to be an injustice in the court system isn't for you, there are plenty of other things that you can do to take a more active role in understanding and helping to shape the outcome of court cases in this country.

- ★ Help wrongfully convicted inmates. The Innocence Project identifies and assists prison inmates who may be vindicated through the use of DNA testing and has helped to exonerate more than 200 inmates who were serving lengthy sentences or even facing the death penalty in prisons around the country. You don't have to be an attorney or someone skilled in the science of DNA testing in order to help to ensure that innocent people aren't sitting in prisons or even on death row. By visiting their Web site (www.innocentproject.org), you can find out about things that you can do to help, including spreading the word about the plight of wrongfully incarcerated individuals by hosting a screening of their recommended list of movies and television programs.

- ★ Draw attention to the courts' role in key issues. Recent decisions by the California, Connecticut, and Massachusetts Supreme Courts to declare legislation that defines marriage as a union between a man and woman unconstitutional have drawn considerable criticism from those opposed to what some call "legislating from the bench." By this, some accuse justices of using the courts to become policy makers rather than arbiters of justice. Gay marriage isn't the only issue that critics have used to argue against this practice. Others include abortion, because the right to privacy isn't mentioned in the Constitution, and medical marijuana.

  Talk to friends and family about what role the courts should play in settling policy disputes. If you feel comfortable enough, consider writing a letter to a newspaper editor about whether the courts should take a more active role in settling a certain issue or an area in which they have intervened too much.

- ★ Along similar lines, you can explore various perspectives on the court's role in society. There are a variety of membership groups who are organized around a very clear idea of how the courts should interface with civil society. Some of them even have campus chapters nationwide in order to bring together like-minded young people around the principles of either judicial activism or judicial restraint. If exploring this dimension of the courts sounds interesting, you can check out the Web sites for the Federalist Society for Law and Public Policy Studies (www.fed-soc.org) and the People for the American Way (www.pfaw.org). You might even consider joining a campus chapter or starting one if it doesn't already exist, or even attending events that are sponsored by these groups nationwide.

- ★ Listen to Supreme Court media files. The Web site for Oyez (www.oyez.org) has links to Supreme Court oral arguments and opinion announcements. Listening to how things unfold once a case makes its way to the Supreme Court can help to demystify what is often perceived as the most remote branch of government.

case of *In re Agent Orange Product Liability Litigation*, in which a federal judge in New York certified Vietnam War veterans as a class with standing to sue a manufacturer of herbicides for damages allegedly incurred from exposure to the defendant's product while in Vietnam.[43] The class potentially numbered in the tens of thousands.

Third, the federal courts began to employ so-called structural remedies, in effect retaining jurisdiction of cases until the court's mandate had actually been implemented to its satisfaction.[44] The best known of these instances was federal judge W. Arthur Garrity's effort to operate the Boston school system from his bench in order to ensure its desegregation. Between 1974 and 1985, Judge Garrity issued fourteen decisions relating to different aspects of the Boston school desegregation plan that had been developed under his authority and put into effect under his supervision.[45] In another recent case, federal judge Leonard B. Sand imposed fines that would have forced the city of Yonkers, New York, into bankruptcy if it had refused to accept his plan to build public housing in white neighborhoods. After several days of fines, the city gave in to the judge's ruling.

For Critical Analysis

In what ways are courts, judges, and justices shielded from politics and political pressure? In what ways are they vulnerable to political pressure? Are the courts an appropriate place for politics?

Through these three judicial mechanisms, the federal courts paved the way for an unprecedented expansion of national judicial power. In essence, liberalization of the rules of standing and expansion of the scope of judicial relief drew the federal courts into linkages with important social interests and classes, while the introduction of structural remedies enhanced the courts' ability to serve these constituencies. Thus, during the 1960s and 1970s, the power of the federal courts expanded in the same way the power of the executive expanded during the 1930s—through links with constituencies, such as civil rights, consumer, environmental, and feminist groups, that staunchly defended the Supreme Court in its battles with Congress, the executive, and other interest groups.

Thinking Critically about the Judiciary, Liberty, and Democracy

In the original conception of the framers, the judiciary was to be the institution that would protect individual liberty from the government. As we saw in Chapter 2, the framers believed that in a democracy the great danger was what they termed "tyranny of the majority"—the possibility that a popular majority, "united or actuated by some common impulse or passion," would "trample on the rules of justice."[46] The framers hoped that the courts would protect liberty from the potential excesses of democracy. And for most of American history, this was precisely the role the federal courts played. The courts' most important decisions were those that protected the freedoms—to speak, worship, publish, vote, and attend school—of groups and individuals whose political views, religious beliefs, or racial or ethnic backgrounds made them unpopular.

Today, Americans of all political persuasions seem to view the courts as useful instruments through which to pursue their goals rather than protectors of individual rights. Liberals and conservatives alike hope to use the courts as instruments of social policy. One side wants to ban abortion and the other to promote school integration. One side hopes to help business maintain its profitability, whereas the other wants to enhance the power of workers in the workplace. These may all be noble goals, but they present a basic dilemma for students of American government. If the courts are simply one more set of policy-making institutions, then who is left to protect the liberty of individuals?

FOR FURTHER READING

Baum, Lawrence. *The Supreme Court.* Washington, DC: Congressional Quarterly Press, 2006.

Cross, Frank. *Decision Making in the U.S. Courts of Appeals.* Stanford: Stanford University Press, 2007.

Epstein, Lee. *Constitutional Law for a Changing America.* Washington, DC: Congressional Quarterly Press, 2007.

Ginsburg, Ruth Bader. *Supreme Court Decisions and Womens' Rights.* Washington DC: Congressional Quarterly Press, 2000.

Greenberg, Jan Crawford. *Supreme Conflict: The Inside Story of the United States Supreme Court.* New York: Penguin, 2008.

Hall, Kermit L., James W. Ely, Jr., and Joel B. Grossman. *The Oxford Companion to the Supreme Court of the United States.* 2nd ed. New York: Oxford University Press, 2005.

Irons, Peter. *A People's History of the Supreme Court.* New York: Penguin, 2006.

McClosky, Robert, and Sanford Levinson. *The American Supreme Court.* Chicago: University of Chicago Press, 2004.

O'Brien, David M. *Storm Center: The Supreme Court in American Politics.* 7th ed. New York: Norton, 2005.

Raskin, Jamin B. *We the Students: Supreme Court Decisions for and about Students.* Washington, DC: Congressional Quarterly Press, 2003.

Rehnquist, William H. *The Supreme Court.* New York: Vintage, 2002.

Rosen, Jeffrey. *The Supreme Court: The Personalities and Rivalries That Defined America.* New York: Henry Holt, 2007.

Rosenberg, Gerald. *The Hollow Hope: Can Courts Bring about Social Change?* Chicago: University of Chicago Press, 1991.

Rossum, Ralph. *Antonin Scalia's Jurisprudence.* Lawrence: University Press of Kansas, 2006.

Silverstein, Mark. *Judicious Choices: The New Politics of Supreme Court Confirmations.* New York: Norton, 1994.

Sunstein, Cass. *Are Judges Political?* Washington, DC: Brookings Institution Press, 2006.

Toobin, Jefrey. *The Nine: Inside the Secret World of the Supreme Court.* New York: Doubleday, 2007.

RECOMMENDED WEB SITES

Concourts
www.concourts.net
The U.S. Supreme Court has the responsibility of examining and interpreting the Constitution. The Concourts Web site assumes a comparative perspective and looks at systems of constitutional review in over 150 countries.

FindLaw
http://findlaw.com
FindLaw's Web site provides answers to most legal questions and helps individuals find legal counsel.

Justice Talking
justicetalking.org
Justice Talking is a public radio program that examines current legal issues and important court cases.

Legal Information Institute
www.law.cornell.edu
The Legal Information Institute at Cornell University is a wonderful Web site for conducting legal research.

Office of the Solicitor General
www.usdoj.gov/osg
The solicitor general conducts litigation on behalf of the U.S. Supreme Court and has a tremendous amount of control over the cases that it hears. See what cases are currently being considered by this powerful official of the Justice Department.

U.S. Courts
www.uscourts.gov
The U.S. court system consists of trial, appellate, and supreme courts. The U.S. Courts Web site provides a look at the different types of courts in the federal judiciary.

U.S. Supreme Court
www.supremecourtus.gov
The Web site for the U.S. Supreme Court provides information on recent decisions. Take a moment to read some oral arguments, briefs, or court opinions.

U.S. Supreme Court Media
www.oyez.com
The Web site for U.S. Supreme Court Media has a great search engine for finding information on such landmark cases as *Marbury v. Madison*, *Miranda v. Arizona*, and *Roe v. Wade*.

STUDY OUTLINE

www.wwnorton.com/wtp7e

The Legal System

1. Court cases in the United States proceed under three categories of law: criminal, civil, and public.
2. In the area of criminal law, either a state government or the federal government is the plaintiff, who alleges that someone has committed a crime.
3. Civil cases are those between individuals or between individuals and the government in which no criminal violation is charged. In deciding these cases, courts apply statutes and legal precedent.
4. Public law involves questions of whether the government has the constitutional or statutory authority to take action.
5. By far, most cases are heard by state courts.
6. Cases are heard in federal courts if the U.S. government is a party in the case or if the case involves federal statutes, treaties with other nations, or the U.S. Constitution.
7. Although the federal courts hear only a fraction of all the cases decided every year in the United States, federal court decisions are extremely important.

Federal Jurisdiction

1. The eighty-nine federal district courts are trial courts of original jurisdiction and their cases are, in form, indistinguishable from cases in the state trial courts.
2. The twelve U.S. courts of appeals review and render decisions in approximately 10 percent of all lower-court and agency cases.
3. Federal judges are appointed by the president and confirmed by a majority vote of the full Senate.
4. The Supreme Court is the highest court in the country and has the power and the obligation to review any lower court decision involving a substantial issue of public law, state legislation, or act of Congress.
5. The Constitution does not specify the number of justices who should sit on the Supreme Court, although since 1869 there have been nine—one chief justice and eight associate justices.
6. The solicitor general can influence the Court by screening cases before they reach the Supreme Court, submitting *amicus* briefs, and shaping the arguments used before the Court.

The Power of the Supreme Court: Judicial Review

1. The Supreme Court's power to review acts of Congress, although accepted as natural and rarely challenged, is not specifically granted by the Constitution.
2. The Supreme Court's power to review state action or legislation derives from the Constitution's supremacy clause, although it is neither granted specifically by the Constitution nor inherent in the federal system.
3. Appeals of lower court decisions can reach the Supreme Court in one of two ways: through a writ of *certiorari*, or, in the case of convicted state prisoners, through a writ of *habeas corpus.*
4. Over the years, courts have developed specific rules that govern which cases within their jurisdiction they hear. These rules of access can be broken down into three categories: case or controversy, standing, and mootness.
5. Groups and forces in society attempt to influence justices' rulings on particular issues.
6. After filing written arguments, or briefs, attorneys present oral argument to the Supreme Court. After oral argument, the justices discuss the case and vote on a final decision.
7. The Supreme Court always explains its decisions in terms of law and precedent.
8. Despite the rule of precedent, the Court often reshapes law. Such changes in the interpretation of law can be explained, in part, by changes in the judicial philosophy of activism versus restraint and by changes in political ideology.

Judicial Power and Politics

1. For much of American history, the power of the federal courts was subject to several limitations: standing, the limited relief courts could provide, the lack of enforcement powers, political appointment, the power of Congress to change the size and jurisdiction of federal courts, and the fact that courts can't exercise power on their own initiative.
2. The role of the federal judiciary has been strengthened since World War II by two judicial revolutions. The first revolution was a substantive revolution in several policy areas. The second revolution involved changes in judicial procedures that decreased traditional limitations on the courts.

PRACTICE QUIZ

www.wwnorton.com/wtp7e

1. Which of the following is a brief submitted to the Supreme Court by someone other than one of the parties in the case?
   a) *amicus curiae*
   b) *habeas corpus*
   c) solicitor general
   d) *ex post* brief
2. By what term is the practice of the courts to uphold precedent known?
   a) *certiorari*
   b) *stare decisis*
   c) rule of four
   d) senatorial courtesy
3. Which government official is responsible for arguing the federal government's position in cases before the Supreme Court?
   a) the vice president
   b) the attorney general
   c) the U.S. district attorney
   d) the solicitor general
4. Which of the following helps to explain the expanded power of the judiciary since World War II?
   a) changes in judicial procedure
   b) changes in judicial policy areas
   c) Neither a nor b is correct.
   d) Both a and b are correct.
5. What is the name for the body of law that involves disputes between private parties?
   a) civil law
   b) privacy law
   c) household law
   d) common law
6. Under what authority is the number of Supreme Court justices decided?
   a) the president
   b) the chief justice
   c) Congress
   d) the Constitution
7. Which of the following does not influence the flow of cases heard by the Supreme Court?
   a) the Supreme Court itself
   b) the solicitor general
   c) the attorney general
   d) the FBI
8. Which of the following cases involved the "right to privacy"?
   a) *Griswold v. Connecticut*
   b) *Brown v. Board of Education*
   c) *Schneckloth v. Bustamante*
   d) *Marbury v. Madison*
9. Which of the following Supreme Court cases from the 1960s involved the rights of criminal suspects?
   a) *Gideon v. Wainwright*
   b) *Miranda v. Arizona*
   c) *Escobedo v. Illinois*
   d) all of the above
10. Where do most trials in America take place?
    a) state and local courts
    b) appellate courts
    c) federal courts
    d) the Supreme Court

KEY TERMS

www.wwnorton.com/wtp7e

amicus curiae (p. 610)
brief (p. 615)
chief justice (p. 596)
civil law (p. 592)
class-action suit (p. 622)
court of appeals (p. 593)
criminal law (p. 591)
defendant (p. 591)
dissenting opinion (p. 617)
due process of law (p. 594)
judicial activism (p. 618)
judicial restraint (p. 618)
judicial review (p. 601)
jurisdiction (p. 593)
Miranda rule (p. 606)
mootness (p. 607)
opinion (p. 616)
oral argument (p. 616)
original jurisdiction (p. 595)
per curiam (p. 610)
plaintiff (p. 591)
plea bargain (p. 593)
precedent (p. 592)
senatorial courtesy (p. 597)
solicitor general (p. 610)
standing (p. 607)
stare decisis (p. 592)
supremacy clause (p. 601)
supreme court (p. 593)
trial court (p. 593)
Uniform Commercial Code (p. 593)
writ of *certiorari* (p. 608)
writ of *habeas corpus* (p. 595)

PART IV Policy

16 Government and the Economy

- The Goals of Economic Policy
- The Tools of Economic Policy
- The Environment and the Economy
- The Politics of Economic Policy Making
- Thinking Critically about Economic Policy

WHAT GOVERNMENT DOES AND WHY IT MATTERS

Since the 1930s, Americans have counted on the federal government to ensure a prosperous economy. Political leaders have a wide variety of tools they can use to improve economic performance. Among the most widely used are spending, tax cuts, and interest rate changes, all of which aim to stimulate economic activity or reduce inflation; and regulations that influence competition among firms. Political leaders' choice of economic tools depends on their perceptions about what the most pressing economic problem is, beliefs about which tools are most likely to be effective, and considerations about who is likely to benefit from the policy and who is likely to be hurt. Although economic policy is a highly technical field, the choice of policy tools is fundamentally a political decision.

During the 2008 elections, the economy emerged as the central issue as the fallout over the subprime mortgage lending threatened to plunge the world economy into a deep recession. As major investment banks and insurance companies collapsed or teetered on the brink of failure, the federal government devised a $700 billion rescue package to prevent further economic damage. Using federal dollars to buy public shares in these private institutions, the federal government quickly became a major stakeholder in the financial sector. How far this extraordinary government role in the economy would go and how long it would last was anyone's guess. Faced with an unprecedented challenge, federal officials and the Congress threw the rule book out in the effort to rescue the economy.

These developments raised fundamental questions about the role of the government in the economy. On the side of the spectrum are those who believe that the government should have a minimal role in the economy. Government's main purpose should be to set and enforce rules that ensure economic stability. This perspective is sometimes called the night watchman state.[1] At the other end of the spectrum are those who want to see the state actively engaged in shaping economic outcomes. Not only should the government promote economic growth in this perspective, it should step in to protect individuals from economic harm. The government's role in the economy should be actively to shape the kind of society we want.

Although political leaders discuss economic policy in terms of fundamental principles and justify their decisions on grounds of technical effectiveness, most economic policy choices reflect political goals as well as economic objectives. For example, during the Great Depression, President Franklin Roosevelt expanded public spending to boost the economy but also to provide jobs to the unemployed workers whose votes he hoped to win. Throughout his administration, President George W. Bush supported tax cuts that disproportionately benefited upper-income taxpayers, on the grounds that their investments would help the economy grow. Such taxpayers were also more likely to cast their votes for Republican candidates. On occasion, new economic problems lead politicians to support policies that seem out of step with their party's traditional positions. For example, President Clinton backed free trade policies, hoping they would bring a more prosperous economy, despite the opposition of many Democrats. In 2008, many Republicans charged that the plan to send all taxpayers a cash rebate was wasteful spending that would not stimulate the economy but they eventually supported the legislation as the prospect of an economic recession grew more worrisome.

American economic policy has historically reflected the belief that individual liberty is the key to a thriving economy. In this view, the government's role is to set the basic rules that govern economic transactions and then stand back and let individuals engage in the market. However, periodically, Americans have demanded restrictions on market freedoms in order to protect the public. An array of laws governing competition and protecting consumers and the environment are the consequence of these democratic demands. Although American economic policy has not traditionally sought to reduce inequality, the growth in inequality over the past three decades has spurred new interest in understanding the impact of government policy on economic inequality.

› **In this chapter, we will first look at the goals of economic policy.** These include promoting stable markets, promoting economic prosperity, promoting business development, and protecting employees and consumers. We then examine four schools of economic thought that government officials have relied on as they formulate priorities and strategies for economic policy.

› **We will then classify and review the tools of economic policy.** Our discussion will focus on four major categories: monetary policies, fiscal policies, regulatory policies, and subsidies and contracting.

› **The chapter then assesses the politics of economic policy making.** We will look at the debate among political leaders over the priorities of economic policy and the role that interest groups play in that debate. We will also examine whether economic policies serve special interests or the public interest.

› **We then examine the environment and the economy.** Although environmental goals have intersected with economic policy concerns in the past, concern about global warming has brought new prominence to this issue. We will examine the profound economic consequences and opportunities posed by global climate change.

› **We will conclude by looking at how citizens can evaluate the ways that economic policies affect them.**

The Goals of Economic Policy

The job of this chapter and the following chapter is to step beyond the politics and the institutions to look at the goals of government—the public policies. **Public policy** can be defined simply as an officially expressed purpose or goal backed by a sanction (a reward or a punishment). Public policy can be embodied in a law, a rule, a regulation, or an order. This chapter will focus on policies toward the economy.

public policy a law, rule, statute, or edict that expresses the government's goals and provides for rewards and punishments to promote their attainment

At the most basic level, government makes it possible for the economy to function efficiently by setting the rules for economic exchange and punishing those who violate those rules. Among the most important rules for the economy are those that define property rights, contracts, and standards for goods. This kind of government rule making allows markets to expand by making it easier for people who do not know each other to engage in economic transactions. They no longer have to rely only on personal trust to do business. Likewise, government helps markets expand by creating money and standing behind its value. Money allows diverse goods to be traded and greatly simplifies economic transactions. The importance of government to basic market transactions is evident in periods when government authority is very weak. Governments that are on the losing side of wars, for example, are often so weak that they cannot enforce the basic rules needed for markets to function. In these settings, markets often break down, money loses its value, and economies contract as the basic conditions for doing business disappear.

Government involvement in the economy now extends far beyond these basic market-creating functions. As we shall see in this section, government has become involved in many aspects of the economy in order to promote the public well-being. Of course, there is often vigorous disagreement about the extent to which government should intervene in the economy to promote the public welfare. In addition, beliefs about which forms of government intervention in the economy are most necessary and most effective have changed over time. Although the policies have changed government intervention in the economy has sought to achieve four fundamental goals. The first goal is to promote economic stability, the second is to stimulate economic growth, the third is to promote business development, and the fourth is to protect employees and consumers.

One way that the government promotes economic stability is by regulating competition and preventing monopolies. Monopolistic "trusts" became a particular concern in the late 1800s, and in 1904 President Teddy Roosevelt was depicted taking a swing at the railroad trust, the oil trust, and others that he believed were stifling competition.

Promoting Stable Markets

One of the central reasons for government involvement in the economy is to protect the welfare and property of individuals and businesses. Because the threats to welfare and property change as the economy grows and new technologies emerge, government actions are constantly being updated and adapted to meet new conditions.

Maintenance of law and order is one of the most important ways that government can protect welfare and property. The federal government has also enacted laws designed to protect individuals and businesses in economic transactions. Federal racketeering laws, for example, aim to end criminal efforts to control businesses through such illegal means as extortion and kickbacks.

Another way in which the government promotes economic stability is by regulating competition. Beginning in the nineteenth century, as many sectors of the national economy flourished, certain companies began to exert monopolistic control over those sectors. Decreased competition threatened the efficiency of the market and the equitable distribution of its benefits. As a result, the national government stepped in to "level the playing field."

Another major reason that Congress began to adopt national business regulatory policies was that the regulated companies themselves felt burdened by the inconsistencies among the states. These companies often preferred a single, national regulatory authority, no matter how burdensome, because it would ensure consistency throughout the United States; the companies could thereby treat the nation as a single market.[2]

Political shifts and advances in technology make the regulation of competition a moving target. In 1913, when telephone service was becoming widely available, the federal government sanctioned AT&T's status as a publicly regulated monopoly. It believed that a single company—publicly regulated—could provide the best service in this industry. By the 1980s, views about the necessity and effectiveness of such monopoly control had changed, and the federal government moved to break up AT&T and open the field to new competitors. Creating competition in the telephone industry, it was hoped, would reduce prices and make the industry more responsive to consumers. And indeed, although consumers have many complaints

The government also provides public goods that support and stimulate the economy. The Grand Coulee Dam—a government facility in the state of Washington—was built to provide irrigation and electricity that were vital to economic development in the West.

about telephone companies, prices dropped dramatically as competitors arose. In the late 1990s, there was considerable concern about emerging monopolies in high technology. A federal lawsuit charged that Microsoft Corporation's monopoly position would stifle future innovation in software. The subsequent settlement, however, did little to alter Microsoft's market dominance.

The government also promotes economic stability by providing **public goods.** This term refers to facilities the state provides, because no single participant can afford to provide those facilities. The provision of public goods may entail supplying the physical marketplace itself—such as the commons in New England towns or the provision of an interstate highway system to stimulate the trucking industry. The provision of public goods is essential to market operation, and the manner in which the government provides those goods will affect the market's character.

public good a good or service that is provided by the government because it either is not supplied by the market or is not supplied in sufficient quantities

In the United States, public goods related to transportation have been particularly important in promoting economic development. From the first canal systems that spread commerce into the interior of the country to the contemporary public role in supporting and regulating air transportation, government has created the conditions for reliable and efficient business activity. In some cases, government will supply a public good to stimulate the economy and then allow private companies to take over. The federal government brought electricity to rural areas in the 1930s to promote economic development, but over time the provision of electricity has been taken over by private companies. Government often supplies public goods that are too big or too risky for private actors to tackle. Major dams and hydroelectric projects are an example. By bringing water and energy to new areas, such public projects transformed the American West. More recently, government-supplied public goods have enhanced public security through such measures as the federal takeover of airport security, the creation of a pharmaceutical stockpile to protect against bioterrorism, and the support for research to develop vaccines to counter bioterrorism agents.

Promoting Economic Prosperity

In addition to setting the basic conditions that allow markets to function, governments may actively intervene in the economy to promote economic growth. Although the idea that government should stimulate economic growth can be traced back to Alexander Hamilton's views about promoting industry, it was not until the twentieth century that the federal government assumed a central role in promoting economic growth.

MEASURING ECONOMIC GROWTH Since the 1930s, the federal government has carefully tracked national economic growth. Economic growth is measured in several different ways. The two most important measures are the Gross National Product (GNP), which is the market value of the goods and services produced in the economy, and the **Gross Domestic Product (GDP),** the same measure but excluding income from foreign investments. In the late 1990s, the American economy grew at a rate of over 4 percent a year, a rate considered high by modern standards (see Figure 16.1). Growth fell to 0.5 percent during the recession in 2001. It briefly rose but began to fall again, rising by a modest 2.2 percent in 2007.

Gross Domestic Product (GDP) the total value of goods and services produced within a country

The engine of American economic growth has shifted over the centuries. In the 1800s, our nation's rich endowment of natural resources was especially important in propelling growth. Manufacturing industries became the driving force of economic

FIGURE 16.1 ★ Changes in Real Gross Domestic Product, 1960–2007

The rates of growth in gross domestic product have varied over time. They were particularly volatile during the 1980s as the economy first plunged into recession and then rapidly recovered with high rates of growth. What was the pattern of growth during the last five presidential election years?

SOURCE: U.S. Department of Commerce, www.bea.gov/national/index.htm#gdp (accessed 4/8/08).

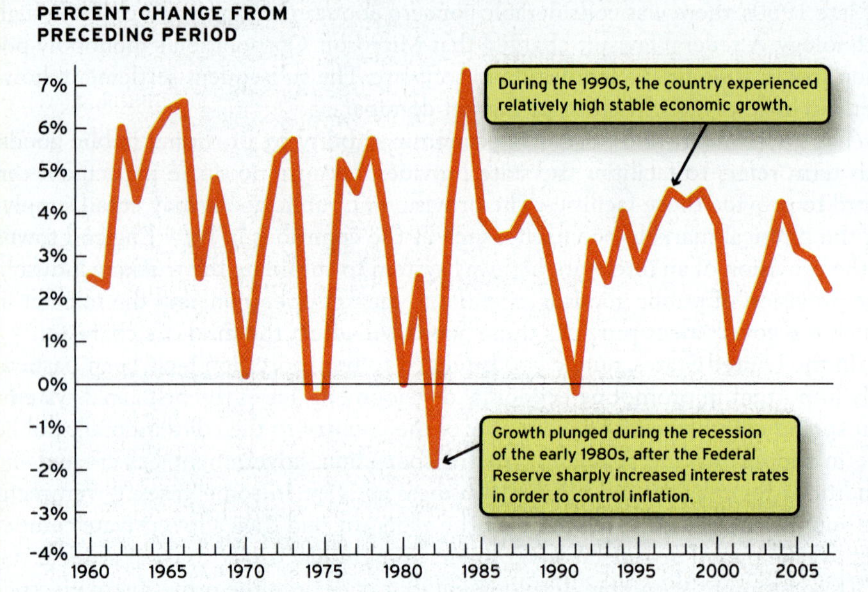

growth during the late nineteenth century as mass production made it possible to manufacture goods at a pace that was once unimaginable. In more recent times, the high-technology boom fostered unanticipated and vigorous economic growth that made the United States the envy of the world. Despite these very different economic engines, the basic prerequisites of growth are similar in each case: strong investment, technological innovation, and a productive workforce. Throughout the nation's history, the federal government has adopted policies to promote each of these conditions needed to sustain economic growth.

The most fundamental way that government affects investment is by promoting business, investor, and consumer confidence. When businesses fear political instability, unpredictable government action, or widespread disregard of the law, they are unlikely to invest. When consumers are insecure about the future, they are unlikely to spend. Government officials monitor surveys of business and consumer confidence as they devise economic policy. After the terrorist attacks of 2001, the federal government moved quickly to reassure the financial markets, businesses, and consumers. The Federal Reserve responded with interest-rate cuts aimed at promoting spending and investment. In 2008, the federal government enacted a $700 billion rescue plan in order to restore investor confidence after several large banks failed.

Businesses also need access to new sources of capital in order to grow. The federal government promotes reliable access to new investment through its regulation of financial markets. The most important federal agency in this regard is the Securities and Exchange Commission (SEC), created after the stock market crash of 1929. The SEC requires companies to disclose information about the stocks and bonds they are selling, inform buyers of the investment risks, and protect investors against fraud. In this way, the SEC helps to maintain investor confidence and a strong supply of capital for American business. The SEC came in for harsh criticism during the financial crisis in 2008. Analysts pointed to weak SEC oversight and regulation as an important factor in driving the financial sector to the brink of collapse. Congressional critics called for tougher SEC regulation of Wall Street in the future.

Public investment is another important source of growth in the American economy. Such investment can be expressly designed to promote growth in accordance with the Keynesian principles outlined later in this chapter. In the 1930s and again in the late 1970s, the federal government promoted public investment as a means to spark economic growth. Some kinds of public investment promote growth as a byproduct of other more central objectives. One of the most important of these is military spending. Many analysts credited the rise in military spending associated with the war in Iraq with helping to spur economic growth in 2003.

The second important condition for economic growth is innovation. The federal government has sought to support innovation in a variety of ways. One of the most important is through the National Science Foundation. Created in 1950, the National Science Foundation supports basic research across a range of scientific fields. The aim is to advance fundamental knowledge that may be useful in many different applications.[3] Federal government sponsorship of health research began in the late 1800s. Today, the National Institutes of Health (NIH) conduct basic and applied research in biomedicine. The Human Genome Project—the effort to map the basic genetic structure of human life—was initiated by government researchers and only later taken up by private corporations. Recently, the NIH has taken the lead in basic research to counter bioterrorism. Its efforts to understand the biology of various infectious agents and to develop vaccines are expected to produce important new knowledge about the human immune system. Research sponsored by the military has long been an important source of innovation for the American economy. Such key twentieth-century innovations as radar and nuclear power stemmed from military research. And as we saw in Chapter 14, military research also created the technology for the twenty-first century with ARPANET, the precursor of the Internet.

A third fundamental condition for economic growth is a sufficient and productive workforce. Federal immigration policy has played a key role in ensuring an adequate supply of labor throughout American history. Immigration laws routinely give special priority to workers who have skills that are in demand among American employers. Immigrants with nursing degrees, for example, have long received special priority.

Today, a productive workforce is a highly educated workforce. Education, as we will see in Chapter 17, is primarily the responsibility of state and local governments. The federal government, however, supports the development of a productive workforce with a variety of programs to support higher education, such as educational grants, tax breaks, and loans. The federal government also sponsors a limited array of job-training programs that focus primarily on low-skilled workers. Some analysts argue that the federal government must do much more to support the development of a highly skilled workforce if the United States is to sustain economic growth in the future.

FULL EMPLOYMENT Before the 1930s, neither the federal nor the state governments sought to promote full employment. Unemployment was widely viewed as an unfortunate occurrence that government could do little to alter. The New Deal response to the prolonged and massive unemployment of the

The government's role in creating job growth was a sore point for the Bush administration. The Bush administration called its 2003 tax-cut package its "Jobs and Growth" plan, projecting that the plan would result in 5.5 million new jobs by the end of 2004. Economic predictions are risky, however: the plan fell well short of this goal.

Great Depression changed that view. The federal government put millions of people back to work on public projects sponsored by such programs as the Works Progress Administration (WPA). The bridges, walkways, and buildings they constructed can still be seen across the United States today. The federal government viewed these programs as temporary measures, however. As the buildup for World War II boosted the economy and unemployment melted away, the employment programs were dismantled.

The New Deal and government wartime spending, however, showed that government could help ensure full employment. Public expectations changed as well: Americans looked to the federal government to reduce unemployment after the war. Moreover, economic theory now supported their expectations. Keynes's theories that government could boost employment by stimulating demand had become very influential.

Federal policy placed the most emphasis on achieving full employment during the 1960s. Keynesian economists in the Council of Economic Advisers convinced President Kennedy to enact the first tax cut designed to stimulate the economy and promote full employment.[4] The policy was widely seen as a success, and unemployment declined to a low of 3.4 percent in 1968.

Favorable economic conditions in the 1990s reduced unemployment to record lows once again. Many analysts contended that the economy had changed so much that the old trade-offs between inflation and unemployment had ceased to exist. When the economy fell into recession in 2001, it was apparent that the boom of the 1990s—and many of the economic speculations it generated—were only temporary. The new economic worry was the "jobless recovery." Throughout 2003, as economic growth surged, job creation lagged far behind. Economists and politicians alike remained puzzled by the sluggish job market, speculating about the impact of foreign trade and growing productivity on limiting new hires. Not until the middle of 2005 did the number of private-sector jobs surpass the level in March 2001, the peak of the last economic expansion. As the economy fell into recession in 2008, unemployment began once again to climb.

inflation a consistent increase in the general level of prices

LOW INFLATION During the 1970s and early 1980s, **inflation,** a consistent increase in the general level of prices, was one of America's most vexing problems. There was much disagreement over what to do about it—what public policies were most appropriate and effective. The first effort, beginning in 1971, was the adoption of strict controls over wages, prices, dividends, and rents—that is, authorizing an agency in the executive branch to place limits on what wage people could be paid for their work, what rent their real estate could bring, and what interest they could get on their money. After two years of effort, these particular policies were fairly well discredited, and the search resumed for one or more other policies to fight inflation. Since oil prices had become so clearly a major source of inflation in the late 1970s, President Carter experimented with the licensing of imports of oil from the Middle East, with tariffs and excise taxes on unusually large oil profits made by producers, and with sales taxes on gasoline at the pump to discourage all casual consumption of gasoline. President Carter also attempted to reduce consumer spending in general by raising income taxes, especially Social Security taxes on employees.

In the 1970s, the government tried to rein in high inflation that made many everyday goods too expensive for ordinary Americans. Unable to afford regularly priced food, these New York residents lined up to buy wholesale food from a warehouse.

The continuing high rate of inflation paved the way to an entirely different approach by President Reagan in the early 1980s. In place of oil import licensing and selective tax increases, President Reagan proposed and got a general tax cut. The Reagan theory was that if tax cuts were deep enough and were guaranteed to endure, they would increase the "supply" of money, would change people's psychology from pessimism to optimism, and would thereby encourage individuals and corporations to invest enough and produce enough to get the country out of inflation. At the same time, President Reagan supported the continuation of the high Social Security taxes enacted during the Carter administration, which probably went further than any other method to fight inflation by discouraging consumption. Inflation is caused by too many dollars chasing too few goods, bidding up prices. Any tax will take dollars out of consumption, but since the Social Security tax hits middle- and lower-middle-income people the heaviest, and since these middle-income people are the heaviest consumers, such a tax reduces consumer dollars. Another policy supported by the Reagan administration was restraining the amount of credit in the economy by pushing up interest rates.

Inflation was finally reduced from its historic highs of nearly 20 percent down toward 2 and 3 percent each year. Noting that the 1970s were America's only "peacetime inflation," the economist Bradford DeLong contends that it wasn't until inflation had risen to dizzying heights late in the decade that the Federal Reserve truly had a mandate to reduce inflation.[5] Once it had full political support for reducing inflation in 1979, the Federal Reserve raised interest rates sharply and brought inflation rates down at the same time that it provoked a sharp recession.

Promoting Business Development

During the nineteenth century, the national government was a promoter of markets. National roads and canals were built to tie states and regions together. National tariff policies promoted domestic markets by restricting imported goods; a tax on an import raised its price and weakened its ability to compete with similar domestic products. The national government also heavily subsidized the railroad system. Until the 1840s, railroads were thought to be of limited commercial value. But between 1850 and 1872, Congress granted over 100 million acres of public-domain land to railroad interests, and state and local governments pitched in an estimated $280 million in cash and credit. Before the end of the century, 35,000 miles of track existed—almost half the world's total at the time.

Railroads were not the only clients of federal support for the private markets. Many sectors of agriculture began receiving federal subsidies during the nineteenth century. Agriculture remains highly subsidized. In 2001, an environmental group caused a stir by putting the exact amounts of subsidies received by individual farmers on a widely publicized Web site. In 2005, 40 percent of farms in the United States received subsidies; by 2006 the total subsidy was estimated at more than $20 billion. One of the many criticisms of the farm subsidy program is that it disproportionately supports large-scale farmers rather than small family farmers. The list of farm subsidy recipients includes many large corporations.

categorical grants
congressional grants given to states and localities on the condition that expenditures be limited to a problem or group specified by the law

The national government also promotes business development indirectly through **categorical grants** (see Chapter 3), whereby the national government offers grants to states on condition that the state (or local) government undertake a particular activity. Thus, in order to use motor transportation to improve national markets, a 900,000-mile national highway system was built during the 1930s, based on a formula whereby the national government would pay 50 percent of the cost if the state would provide the other 50 percent. Over twenty years, beginning in the late 1950s, the federal government constructed an additional 45,000 miles of interstate highways. In this program, the national government agreed to pay 90 percent of the construction costs on the condition that each state provide 10 percent of the costs of any portion of a highway built within its boundaries.[6] The tremendous growth of highways was a major boon to the automobile and trucking industries.

The federal government supports specific business sectors with direct subsidies, loans, and tax breaks. In 1953, the Small Business Administration (SBA) was created to offer loans, loan guarantees, and disaster assistance to small businesses. Recognizing that such businesses often find it harder to obtain financing and to recover from unexpected events such as fires, the federal government has provided assistance where the market would not. Today, the SBA provides more than $45 billion in such assistance to small businesses.

Among the many contemporary examples of policies promoting private industry, Sematech may be the most instructive. Sematech is a nonprofit, research and development (R&D) consortium of major U.S. computer microchip manufacturers, set up in 1987 to work with government and academic institutions to reestablish U.S. leadership in semiconductor manufacturing. (The United States appeared to be in danger of losing out to the Japanese in this area during the 1980s.) The results of its research were distributed among the fourteen consortium members.[7] For nine years, industry and government together spent $1.7 billion to make the American microchip industry the leader in the world. The government contributed about half of the total expenditures. In 1997, federal funding was phased out. Industry leaders, convinced they no longer needed federal support, themselves initiated the break with government. At a critical moment, the federal government had stepped in to save the chip industry; it stepped out once that goal had been achieved.

Since the early nineteenth century, the government has been an important promoter of business development in the United States. Beginning around 1850, federal, state, and local governments gave railroad companies the land on which to lay tracks and financial aid to construct the railroads. Railroads also received additional land from the government that they could sell at low prices to attract settlers to build along their lines.

Since September 11, 2001, the federal government has taken on a major role in promoting technological innovation related to national security. Even before the September 11 terrorist attacks, the CIA had set up its own venture-capital firm, In-Q-Tel (the "Q" stands for a character in the James Bond movies), to invest in high-tech start-ups whose work could enhance intelligence efforts. With defense and homeland security at the top of the national agenda, military spending increased by 20 percent during the first two years of the George W. Bush administration. A new emphasis on technological innovation accompanied the increase in spending. As a way to promote its access to the latest technology, the Department of Defense runs a $1.1 billion program that funds the early stages of research and development for innovative small firms.

Protecting Employees and Consumers

Stable relations between business and labor are important elements of a productive economy. During the latter half of the nineteenth century, strikes over low wages or working conditions became a standard feature of American economic life. In fact, the United States has one of the most violent histories of labor relations in the world. Yet for most of American history, the federal government did little to regulate relations between business and labor. Local governments and courts often weighed in on the side of business by prohibiting strikes and arresting strikers.

As the economic depression enveloped the United States in the 1930s, massive strikes for union recognition and plummeting wages prompted the federal government to take action. Congress passed the 1935 National Labor Relations Act, which set up a new framework for industrial relations. The new law created a permanent agency, the National Labor Relations Board (NLRB), charged with overseeing union elections and collective bargaining between labor and industry. The federal government weighed in further on the side of organized labor in 1938, when it passed the Fair Labor Standards Act, which created the minimum wage.

Protecting consumers has been a central goal of economic policy since the early twentieth century. In 1906, Congress passed the New Meat Inspection Act, which required that all meat intended for interstate commerce meet federal health standards. This photo shows a Chicago slaughterhouse immediately following the passage of the act.

Because it is not indexed to inflation, the value of the minimum wage declines if it is not raised periodically. Since 1938, conflicts over increasing the minimum wage have been a regular feature of American politics.

During the 1950s and 1960s, the federal government played an active role in industrial relations. The Department of Labor and occasionally even the president directly intervened in labor-management disputes to ensure peaceful industrial relations. Although Democrats were generally seen as more supportive of labor, both parties sought to achieve a balance between business and labor that would promote a strong stable economy.

President Reagan made a decisive break with this tradition of compromise in 1981 when he fired striking air traffic controllers and hired permanent replacements to take their jobs. Politicians are now much less likely to intervene in labor relations.

Politics Today

What does the American government do to ensure that the products that Americans buy are safe? What challenges does it face in making certain that products are safe?

Economic policies also protect consumers. The idea that the federal government should protect consumers emerged in the first decade of the 1900s. Upton Sinclair's graphic exposé about the unsanitary practices of the meatpacking industry, *The Jungle*, published in 1906, galvanized public concern about unsanitary food processing. These concerns prompted the U.S. Department of Agriculture to inspect packing plants and the meat they produced, stamping approved meats with the now familiar "USDA" certification. Similar concern about food and drug safety led to the creation of the Food and Drug Administration in 1927.

The movement for consumer protection took off again in the 1960s. The consumer advocate Ralph Nader's 1965 book *Unsafe at Any Speed* helped spark new demands for federal action. Nader's book showed that design flaws in the Corvair, a popular car model, had caused deaths that could have been prevented. Nader's book not only led to the demise of the Corvair but also galvanized calls for more federal action to protect consumers. The first response was the 1966 National Traffic and Motor Vehicle Safety Act, which gave the Department of Transportation responsibility for ensuring vehicle safety. Federal responsibility for consumer safety expanded in 1972 when Congress created the Consumer Product Safety Commission. The Commission, which is an independent agency, informs consumers about hazards associated with products and works with industry to set product standards. In cases where safety concerns are severe, it will see that such products are recalled. Through the Consumer Product Safety Commission, the Department of Transportation, and the Food and Drug Administration (which regulates food, drugs, and cosmetics), the federal government continues to play an active role in protecting the public from unsafe products.

In 2007, the Consumer Product Safety Commission became the target of vigorous criticism for failing to protect consumers from hazardous products. Recalls of popular children's toys, reports of injuries to children from magnetic toys, dogs and cats dying from tainted pet food, and reported dangers from imported toothpaste all raised questions about the agency's effectiveness. Congressional hearings probed the capacity of the agency to monitor consumer safety, given that its staff had declined from more than 800 in 1980 to 420 in 2007. At the same time that the staff declined, the growth of consumer products manufactured in China made the agency's job tougher. In 2006, 20 percent of America's consumer goods had been manufactured in China, and 55 percent of all recalled products came from China, where rapid economic expansion and fewer consumer protections contributed to the problem.[8] Ensuring the safety of goods manufactured in China is a formidable challenge that will require a much greater capacity than currently exists at the Consumer Product Safety Commission.

laissez-faire capitalism an economic system in which the means of production and distribution are privately owned and operated for profit with minimal or no government interference

Four Schools of Economic Thought

Not surprisingly, there are deep differences of opinion about whether, how much, and in what ways government should be involved in the economy. Ideas about the appropriate role for government have shifted in response to unanticipated or tenacious economic problems such as recession or inflation. As politicians, interest groups, and the public debate which goals are most important and appropriate for economic policy to achieve, their views are informed by underlying theories. Different theories about how the economy works present quite distinct roles for government.

The Scottish economist Adam Smith revolutionized economic thinking in the eighteenth century by arguing that government should limit its involvement in the economy because "the invisible hand" of the market would create economic prosperity if left to operate without government interference.

The idea that government should have only a minimal role in the economy is often called **laissez-faire capitalism.** Proponents of laissez-faire (literally, "let to do") argue that the economy will flourish if the government leaves it alone. The argument for laissez-faire was first elaborated in the late 1700s by the great Scottish economist Adam Smith. Smith believed that most government involvement in the economy—such as the government-authorized monopolies that dominated trade in his day—depressed economic growth. Instead, he argued that competition among free enterprises would unleash economic energy, fostering growth and innovation. In his view, the self-seeking behavior of individuals, when subject to the discipline of market competition, would create products that consumers want at the best possible price. Smith praised "the invisible hand" of the market, by which he meant that millions of individual economic transactions together create

The economist John Maynard Keynes influenced economic policy with the idea that governments could remedy economic downturns by increasing public spending or cutting taxes.

Keynesians followers of the economic theories of John Maynard Keynes, who argued that the government can stimulate the economy by increasing public spending or by cutting taxes

monetarists followers of economic theories that contend that the role of the government in the economy should be limited to regulating the supply of money

supply-side economics posits that reducing the marginal rate of taxation will create a productive economy by promoting levels of work and investment that would otherwise be discouraged by higher taxes

a greater good—far better than the government could create. Smith believed that the government role should be restricted to national defense, establishing law and order (including the protection of private property), and providing basic public goods (such as roads) that facilitate commerce.

In the 1930s, the ideas of the British economist John Maynard Keynes laid the foundation for a revolution in thinking about the role of the government in the economy during periodic downturns. **Keynesians** argue that by pumping money into the economy, government can stimulate demand and create a cycle of increased production and jobs that will pull the economy out of recession. Governments can do this in several ways. For one, they can increase public spending through such measures as public works or public employment. Alternatively, governments can stimulate demand through temporary tax cuts. Tax cuts will allow workers to keep more of their earnings; their increased spending power will boost consumption and increase demand.[9]

After World War II, Keynesian ideas guided economic policy making across the industrialized world. By the 1960s, Keynesians believed they could ensure ongoing prosperity by "fine-tuning" the economy: policy makers could stimulate demand with spending or tax cuts when recession loomed and then cut back on spending or increase taxes when inflation threatened. Then Republican president Richard Nixon reflected the strong consensus behind Keynesian ideas when he remarked, "I am now a Keynesian."

Yet, by the time Keynesian ideas became the accepted wisdom, new economic conditions threatened their effectiveness. Many observers argued that increased international trade made Keynesian remedies less useful. Confidence that the government can fine-tune the economy had diminished, and Keynesians lost the great influence they once had in economic policy.

In contrast to Keynesians, **monetarists** believe that the role of the government in managing the economy should be limited to regulating the supply of money. More active government management of the economy, monetarists argue, either has little effect or actually makes the economy worse. Monetarists do not believe that government can act quickly enough to fine-tune the economy. Instead, they maintain that government should promote economic stability by regulating the money supply. The most prominent monetarist in the United States, the late economist Milton Friedman, recommended that the federal government let the growth in the money supply match the rate of economic growth. In this way, inflation could be kept low even as economic growth continued. This strict version of monetarism envisions a hands-off approach for the government; the theory calls for little exercise of discretion on the part of government officials. Instead, they must follow a simple rule about how much to increase the supply of money.

In the late 1970s, when high levels of inflation plagued the American economy, monetarists became especially influential in economic policy making. However, today it is impractical to implement a strict version of monetarism. Instead, economic policy makers have sought to manipulate interest rates to ensure a healthy and stable economy.

Proponents of **supply-side economics** believe that reducing the role of government in the economy will promote investment and spur economic growth. Reducing tax rates is the centerpiece of the supply-side economic strategy. Supply-side arguments maintain that lower tax rates create incentives for more productive and efficient use of resources. When individuals know they can keep more of their earnings, they are more likely to be productive workers and creative investors. The ideas behind supply-side economics emerged in the 1970s, when Keynesian solutions appeared to have little impact on the high rates of inflation and a sluggish economy.

Key thinkers associated with developing the ideas behind supply-side economics include the economists Robert Mundell, who won the Nobel Prize, and Arthur B. Laffer. Laffer became know for the "Laffer curve," which posited that there was an optimal rate of taxation. If taxes went above the optimal rate, tax revenues would shrink because economic activity would decline. In this perspective, decreasing taxes could yield more tax revenue by spurring economic activity. This view marked a shift for conservatives by placing more emphasis on tax cuts and less on budget deficits. Supply-side ideas were very influential in the administrations of the Republican presidents Ronald Reagan and George W. Bush, both of whom pointed to supply-side ideas as a sound reason for enacting significant tax cuts.

Monetarists such as the late economist Milton Friedman call for limiting government involvement in the economy. Monetarists tend to emphasize economic stability and controlling inflation over promoting equality and curbing unemployment.

The Tools of Economic Policy

The U.S. economy is no accident; it is the result of specific policies that have expanded American markets and sustained massive economic growth. The Constitution provides that Congress shall have the power

> To lay and collect Taxes, . . . to pay the Debts and provide for the common Defence and general Welfare; . . . To borrow Money; . . . To coin Money [and] regulate the Value thereof. . . .

These clauses of Article I, Section 8, are the constitutional sources of the fiscal and monetary policies of the national government. The Constitution says nothing, however, about *how* these powers can be used, although the way they are used shapes the economy. As it works to meet the multiple goals of economic policy outlined above, the federal government relies on a broad set of tools that has evolved over time. Let us now turn to the actual tools designed to accomplish the goals of economic policy.

Monetary Policies

monetary policy an effort to regulate the economy through the manipulation of the supply of money and credit. America's most powerful institution in this area of monetary policy is the Federal Reserve Board

Monetary policies manipulate the growth of the entire economy by controlling the availability of money to banks. With a very few exceptions, banks in the United States are privately owned and locally operated. Until well into the twentieth century, banks were regulated, if at all, by state legislatures. Each bank was granted a charter, giving it permission to make loans, hold deposits, and make investments within that state. Although more than 25,000 banks continue to be state-chartered banks, they are less important than they used to be in the overall financial picture, as the most important banks now are members of the federal banking system.

But banks did not become the core of American capitalism without intense political controversy. The Federalist majority in Congress, led by Alexander Hamilton, did in fact establish a Bank of the United States in 1791, but it was vigorously opposed by agrarian interests led by Thomas Jefferson, who feared that the interests of urban, industrial capitalism would dominate such a bank. The Bank of the

United States was terminated during the administration of Andrew Jackson, but the fear of a central, public bank lingered eight decades later, when Congress in 1913 established an institution—the **Federal Reserve System**—to integrate private banks into a single national system. The Federal Reserve System did not become a central bank in the European tradition but rather is composed of twelve Federal Reserve banks, each located in a major commercial city. The Federal Reserve banks are not ordinary banks; they are banker's banks that make loans to other banks, clear checks, and supply the economy with currency and coins. They also play a regulatory role over the member banks. Every national bank must be a member of the Federal Reserve System and must follow national banking rules. State banks and savings and loan associations may also join if they accept national rules. At the top of the system is the Federal Reserve Board—"the Fed"—comprising seven members appointed by the president (with Senate confirmation) for fourteen-year terms. The chairman of the Fed is selected by the president from among the seven members of the board for a four-year term. In all other concerns, however, the Fed is an independent agency (see Chapter 14) inasmuch as its members cannot be removed during their terms except "for cause," and the president's executive power does not extend to them or their policies. Nonetheless, observers charged the longtime Federal Reserve chairman, Alan Greenspan, with being attentive to politics, for example, in his endorsement of President George W. Bush's tax cuts. In his 2005 confirmation hearings to head the Fed, economist Ben Bernanke promised Congress that he would be "strictly independent of all political influences."[10]

Federal Reserve System a system of twelve Federal Reserve Banks that facilitates exchanges of cash, checks, and credit; regulates member banks; and uses monetary policies to fight inflation and deflation

For Critical Analysis

Why is the Federal Reserve so important to economic policy?

The major advantage that a bank gains from being in the Federal Reserve System is that it can borrow from the system. This enables banks to expand their loan operations continually, as long as there is demand for loans in the economy. On the other hand, it is this very access of member banks to the Federal Reserve System that gives the Fed its power: the ability to expand and contract the *amount of credit* available in the United States.

The Fed can affect the total amount of credit through the interest (called the discount rate) it charges on the loans it extends to member banks. If the Fed significantly decreases the discount rate, it can give a boost to a sagging economy. During 2001, the Fed cut interest rates eleven times to combat the combined effects of recession and the terrorist attacks. As the economy began to sag in late 2007, all eyes were on the Fed to reduce interest rates. By March 2008, the Fed had cut rates six times from their high in September 2007. If the Fed raises the discount rate, it can put a brake on the economy because the higher discount rate also increases the general interest rates charged by leading private banks to their customers. Although the Federal Reserve is responsible for ensuring high employment as well as price stability, it has been particularly important in fighting inflation. During the late 1970s and early 1980s, with inflation at record high levels, Federal Reserve Chairman Paul Volcker aggressively raised interest rates in order to dampen inflation. Although his actions provoked a sharp recession, they raised the stature of the Fed, demonstrating its ability to manage the economy. Because the Fed is so closely associated with inflation fighting, Senate Democrats pressed Ben Bernanke, President Bush's nominee to head the Fed, to indicate that he would view maximum employment as a goal of equal importance to that of fighting inflation.

reserve requirement the amount of liquid assets and ready cash that banks are required to hold to meet depositors' demands for their money

A second power of the Fed is control over the **reserve requirement**—the amount of cash and negotiable securities every bank must hold readily available to cover withdrawals and checks written by its depositors. When the Fed decides to increase the reserve requirement, it can decrease significantly the amount of

Ben Bernanke, appointed by President Bush to chair the Federal Reserve Board in 2005, promised Congress that he would not be influenced by politics. The Fed seeks to regulate the U.S. economy by manipulating the supply of money and credit.

money banks have to lend; conversely, if the Fed lowers the reserve requirement, banks can be more liberal in extending more loans.[11]

A third power of the Fed is called **open-market operations,** whereby the Fed buys and sells government securities to increase or decrease the supply of money in the economy. When the Fed buys government securities in the open market, it increases the amount of money available to consumers to spend or invest; when it sells securities, it is reducing the money supply.

open-market operations method by which the Open Market Committee of the Federal Reserve System buys and sells government securities, etc., to help finance government operations and to reduce or increase the total amount of money circulating in the economy

Finally, a fourth power is derived from one of the important services the Federal Reserve System renders, which is the opportunity for member banks to borrow from each other. One of the original reasons for creating a Federal Reserve System was to balance regions of the country that might be vigorously expanding with other areas that might be fairly dormant: the national system would enable the banks in a growing region, facing great demand for credit, to borrow money from banks in regions of the country where the demand for credit is much lower. This exchange is called the "federal funds market," and the interest rate charged by one bank to another, the **federal funds rate,** can be manipulated just like the discount rate, to expand or contract credit.[12]

federal funds rate the interest rate on loans between banks that the Federal Reserve Board influences by affecting the supply of money available

The federal government also provides insurance to foster credit and encourage private capital investment. The Federal Deposit Insurance Corporation (FDIC) insures bank deposits up to $100,000. Another important promoter of investment is the federal insurance of home mortgages through the Department of Housing and Urban Development (HUD). By guaranteeing mortgages, the government can reduce the risks that banks run in making such loans, thus allowing banks to lower their interest rates and make such loans more affordable to middle- and lower-income families. Such programs have enabled millions of families who could not have otherwise afforded it to finance the purchase of a home.

This system began to unravel in the first decade of the 2000s with the growth of the subprime market for lending. This market made home loans available to people who could not otherwise afford to buy a home. At the same time, however, it created new instabilities in the market by offering risky loans that would become more costly due to adjustable interest rates. The slowing housing market in 2007 set off a wave of foreclosures as many homeowners discovered that they could not pay back their loans. Some analysts predicted that as many as 2 million homeowners could lose their homes by the end of 2009.[13]

Politics Today

Why were economic policymakers so concerned about the crisis in the home mortgage market in 2007 and 2008? How did the Federal Reserve respond to the crisis?

The foreclosure crisis in turn set shock waves through the financial system, as investment banks found themselves holding worthless loans. One casualty of the home loan meltdown was the Wall Street investment bank Bear Stearns, which faced bankruptcy early in March 2008. Seeking to limit the harm to the broader economy that such a bankruptcy would cause, Fed chairman Bernanke arranged for Bear Stearns to be bought—at basement bargain prices—by JP Morgan Chase, another investment bank. In making this move, Bernanke was exercising powers of the Federal Reserve Act that had not been used since the 1930s.[14] By the fall of 2008 several other investment banks and insurance companies were close to insolvency. Suddenly in September 2008, the Treasury and the Federal Reserve announced a rescue package in which the federal government made up to $700 billion dollars in emergency credit and capital available.

Fiscal Policies

fiscal policy the government's use of taxing, monetary, and spending powers to manipulate the economy

Fiscal policy includes the government's taxing and spending powers. Personal and corporate income taxes, which raise most of the U.S. government's revenues, are the most prominent examples. Although the direct purpose of an income tax is to raise revenue, each tax has a different impact on the economy, and government can attempt to plan for that impact. After passing major tax cuts in 2001, President Bush proposed and Congress passed a sweeping new round of cuts in 2003. Bush's plan was intended to promote investment by reducing taxes on most stock dividends, to spur business activity by offering tax breaks to small businesses, and to stimulate the economy by reducing the tax rates for all taxpayers. In 2006, Congress extended the rate reductions on dividends and capital gains, a move that estimates show will cost the treasury $70 billion over five years. The Bush administration tax cuts have been criticized on several grounds. Many Democrats argued that the tax cuts were simply a giveaway to the weatlhy and to corporations, and that they did nothing to promote growth. There has been concern that the tax cuts are responsible for the large federal deficits: the federal budget moved from running surpluses in 2000 to steep deficits only four years later.

tariff a tax on imported goods

TAXATION During the nineteenth century, the federal government received most of its revenue from a single tax, the **tariff**. It also relied on excise taxes, which are taxes levied on specific products, such as tobacco and alcohol. As federal activities expanded in the 1900s, the federal government added new sources of tax revenue. The most important was the income tax, proposed by Congress in 1909, ratified by the states, and added to the Constitution in 1913 as the Sixteenth Amendment. The income tax is levied on individuals as well as corporations. With the creation of the Social Security system in 1935, social insurance taxes became an additional source of federal revenue.

Before World War II, individual income taxes accounted for only 14 percent of federal revenues.[15] The need to raise revenue for World War II made the income tax much more important. Congress expanded the base of the income tax so that

TABLE 16.1 ★ Federal Revenues by Type of Tax as Percentage of Total Receipts, 1960–2008

The federal government collects revenue from a variety of different taxes. Most important is the individual income tax. Since 1960, revenues from the corporation income tax have fallen significantly. At the same time, taxes for social insurance and retirement programs have grown substantially. Does the federal government draw more of its revenue from progressive taxes or from regressive taxes?

YEAR	INDIVIDUAL INCOME TAX	CORPORATION INCOME TAX	SOCIAL INSURANCE AND RETIREMENT RECEIPTS	EXCISE TAXES	OTHER
1960	44.0	23.2	15.9	12.6	4.2
1970	46.9	17.1	23.0	8.1	4.9
1980	47.2	12.5	30.5	4.7	5.1
1990	45.2	9.1	36.8	3.4	5.4
2000	49.6	10.2	32.2	3.4	4.5
2004	43.0	10.1	39.0	3.7	4.2
2005	43.0	12.9	36.9	3.4	3.8
2006	43.4	14.7	34.8	3.1	4.1
2007	45.3	14.4	33.9	2.5	3.9
2008 (est)	48.4	13.7	36.1	2.7	−0.9

SOURCE: Office of Management and Budget, www.whitehouse.gov/omb/budget/fy2009/pdf/hist.pdf (accessed 5/9/08).

most Americans paid income taxes after World War II. Table 16.1 shows several notable shifts that have occurred in taxes since 1960. Social insurance taxes now comprise a much greater share of federal revenues, rising from 15.9 percent of revenues in 1960 to 36.1 percent in 2008. Receipts from corporate income taxes have declined over the same time period, dropping from 23.2 percent of receipts in 1960 to 13.7 in 2008. The share of the federal individual income tax has remained fairly stable; it was 44 percent in 1960 and 48.4 percent in 2008.

One of the most important features of the American income tax is that it is a "progressive" or a "graduated" tax, with the heaviest burden carried by those most able to pay. A tax is called **progressive** if the rate of taxation goes up with each higher income bracket. A tax is called **regressive** if people in lower income brackets pay a higher proportion of their income toward the tax than people in higher income brackets. For example, a sales tax is deemed regressive because everybody pays at the same rate, so that the proportion of total income paid in taxes goes down as the total income goes up (assuming, as is generally the case, that as total income goes up the amount spent on sales-taxable purchases increases at a lower

progressive taxation taxation that hits upper income brackets more heavily

regressive taxation taxation that hits lower income brackets more heavily rate). The Social Security tax is another example of a regressive tax. In 2008, Social Security law applied a tax of 6.2 percent on the first $102,000 of income for the retirement program and an additional 1.45 percent on all income (without limit) for Medicare benefits, for a total of 7.65 percent in Social Security taxes. This means that a person earning an income of $102,000 pays $7,803 in Social Security taxes, a rate of 7.65 percent. But someone earning twice that income, $204,000, pays a total of $10,761 in Social Security taxes, a rate of 5.3 percent. As one's income continues to rise, the amount of Social Security taxes also rises (until the cap is reached), but the rate, or the percentage of one's income that goes to taxes, declines.

redistribution a policy whose objective is to tax or spend in such a way as to reduce the disparities of wealth between the lowest and the highest income brackets

loophole incentive to individuals and businesses to reduce their tax liabilities by investing their money in areas that the government designates

Although the primary purpose of the graduated income tax is, of course, to raise revenue, an important second objective is to collect revenue in such a way as to reduce the disparities of wealth between the lowest and the highest income brackets. We call this a policy of **redistribution.** Another policy objective of the income tax is the encouragement of the capitalist economy by rewarding investment. The tax laws allow individuals or companies to deduct from their taxable income any money they can justify as an investment or a "business expense"; this gives an incentive to individuals and companies to spend money to expand their production, their advertising, or their staff, and reduces the income taxes businesses have to pay. These kinds of deductions are called incentives or "equity" by those who support them; others call them **"loopholes."** The tax laws of the 1980s actually closed a number of important loopholes in U.S. tax laws. But others still exist—on home mortgages and on business expenses, for example—and others will return, because there is a strong consensus among members of Congress, both Democrats and Republicans, that businesses often need such incentives. The differences between the two parties focus largely on which incentives are justifiable.[16]

For Critical Analysis

What are the multiple goals of tax policy in America? How else might some of these goals be achieved? In what ways is the tax system in the United States progressive? In what ways is it regressive?

The tax reform laws of 1981 and 1986 significantly reduced the progressiveness of the federal income tax. Drastic rate reductions were instituted in 1986. Before George W. Bush's 2001 reform, there were five tax brackets, ranging from a 15 percent tax on those in the lowest income bracket to 39.6 percent on those in the highest income bracket. Prior to the 1980s, the highest tax brackets sometimes were taxed at a rate of 90 percent on the last $1 million of taxable income earned in a given year. Meanwhile, Social Security taxes—the most regressive taxes of all—remain high and are likely to be increased.[17]

Taxes became a controversial issue during the George W. Bush administration. As we have seen, the president made tax reduction the centerpiece of his administration and enacted major tax cuts. The argument for the tax cuts was largely a supply-side argument: the cuts would make for a prosperous economy. The president and his supporters pointed to the expanding economy and lower taxes for all as the fruit of the tax cuts. Opponents charged that it made no sense to cut taxes since the benefits of the tax cuts primarily go to the wealthy. They argue that not only do the rich already benefit from unequal patterns of growth that have sent their income skyrocketing, tax cuts that disproportionately benefit the wealthy do not stimulate the economy, as supply-side theory predicts. Critics also charge that the tax cuts have caused the federal budget, which was in surplus when Bush took office, to fall into deficit.[18]

The decision about whether these tax breaks should be made permanent must be made before 2010, when they are scheduled to expire. As the economy dipped into recession in early 2008, Bush urged making the cuts permanent: "The smartest thing we can do is to keep taxes low. In a time of economic uncertainty, we don't need to be taking money out of your pocket."[19] Democratic candidates, on the other hand, argued that the tax cuts benefited the rich too much. They argued that moving back to higher tax rates on the wealthy would help fund crucial public programs, such as improving the health care system.

SPENDING AND BUDGETING The federal government's power to spend is one of the most important tools of economic policy. Decisions about how much to spend affect the overall health of the economy. They also affect every aspect of American life from the distribution of income to the availability of different modes of transportation to the level of education in society. Not surprisingly, the fight for control over spending is one of the most contentious in Washington, as interest groups and politicians strive to determine the priorities and appropriate levels of spending. Decisions about spending are made as part of the annual budget process. During the 1990s, when the federal **budget deficit** first became a major political issue and when parties were deeply split on spending, the budget process became the focal point of the entire policy-making process. Even though the budget deficit disappeared in the late 1990s, the budget continued to dominate the attention of policy makers (Figure 16.2). With the rapid swing from budget surpluses in 2000 to record deficits by 2003, deficits once again emerged as a political issue. This time, however, Republican leaders, who had made deficits the focal point of politics in the mid-1990s, largely dismissed their importance.

budget deficit amount by which government spending exceeds government revenue in a fiscal year

FIGURE 16.2 ★
U.S. Budget Deficits and Surpluses, 1962–2008*

The federal deficit grew substantially during the 1980s under President Ronald Reagan. During the 1990s, the budget deficit declined significantly but then grew dramatically in the first half of the 2000s. When was the last time that the federal budget showed a surplus? Why did the budget deficit grow so much after 2001?

*Estimate
SOURCE: Office of Management and Budget, http://origin.www.gpoaccess.gov/usbudget/fy09/hist.html (accessed 5/9/08).

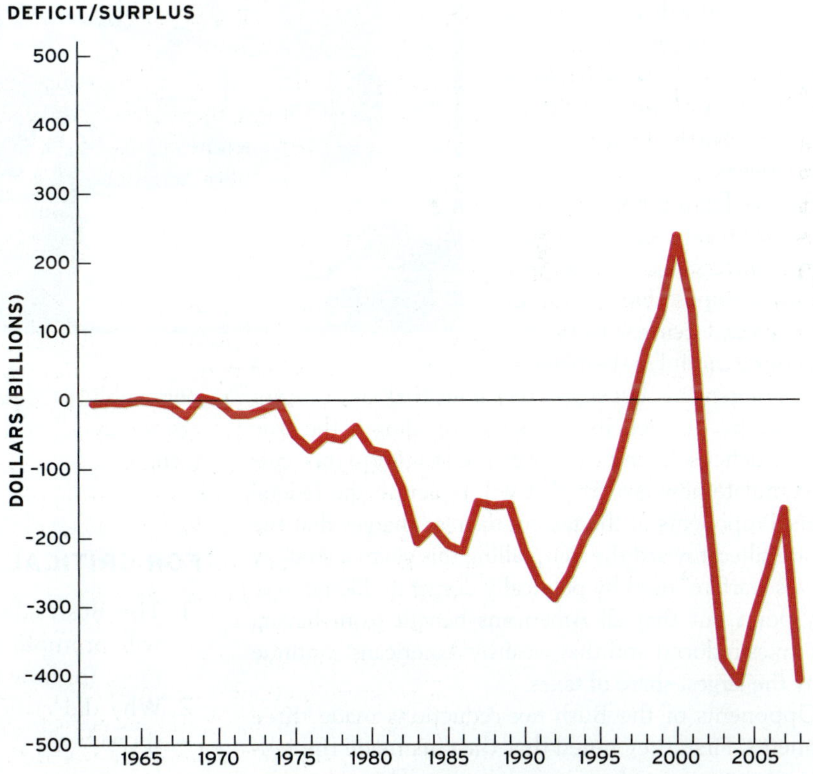

Tax Cuts and the American Economy

No one enjoys paying taxes, but nearly everyone agrees that taxes are necessary. Without tax revenue, the government would not be able to fund the basic public goods that all Americans rely on in their daily lives. Yet disagreement is widespread about how high taxes should be, how they should be distributed across individuals and corporations, and what types of taxes government should impose. President George W. Bush's major tax reductions of 2001 and 2003 reignited fundamental debates about the purposes and consequences of federal tax policy. This debate is ongoing because unless the tax cuts are made permanent, they will expire in 2010.

Supporters defended Bush's tax-reduction policy on two grounds. First, they argued that taxes should be as low as possible because the individual taxpayer, not the government, is the best judge of how his or her money should be spent. Second, they claimed that taxes should be especially low on investments and on corporations because a vibrant economy depends on the investment decisions of wealthy individuals and corporations. This supply-side rationale for tax policy maintains that lower taxes encourage investment and stimulate growth, which benefits all Americans.

Reduced government revenues are not a problem, according to tax-cut supporters. Lower tax revenues will impose fiscal discipline on Congress, forcing it to become much more careful in spending the public's money. Tax-cut supporters argue that tax cuts cannot cause budget deficits; excessive spending is the true cause of deficits. In any case, over the long term, tax cuts will stimulate new growth that will replenish the federal coffers. Proponents of the tax cut dismiss charges that the cuts are tilted toward the rich, calling this claim a strategy of "class warfare" used by politically desperate Democrats. They point out that all Americans benefit from having their taxes reduced and that wealthy Americans continue to pay the largest share of taxes.

Opponents of the Bush tax reductions made three arguments. First, they noted that the cuts made the federal tax system much more regressive. Thus, the cuts created a permanent bias in favor of business and the very wealthy. Tax cuts for the very rich cost more than support for K–12 education, veterans' medical care, and the National Institutes of Health in 2006.[a] We should be spending our money on these important public purposes, not on tax cuts for those who don't need the money, according to this perspective. Second, critics point to the large deficits that have occurred as a result of the tax cuts. These deficits will ultimately harm the economy by driving up interest rates. Moreover, the deficits will saddle future generations with the consequences of Bush's policy. Thirdly, critics charge that the administration's tax cuts were little more than a political ploy to reward President Bush's wealthy supporters and corporate allies, not a policy designed to achieve broad economic goals.

Taxes became a major issue in the closing weeks of the presidential race in 2008. Republican candidate John McCain pledged not to raise taxes and he labeled Barack Obama a "redistributionist." Using the example of "Joe the Plumber," an Ohio man concerned that Obama would raise his taxes, McCain made the taxes his central issue in the waning days of the campaign. Obama, for his part, defended his plan to roll back the Bush cuts and stuck with his pledge to raise taxes on the 3 percent of households who make more than $250,000 a year. He pointed out that Joe the Plumber, who made far less than $250,000 a year, would in fact benefit more from his plan than McCain's. The debate recapped a classic partisan division, with Republicans arguing that any tax increase harms the economy and Democrats contending that taxes are needed to support public programs and that it is only fair for high earners to pay a larger share of taxes than those with lower incomes.

FOR CRITICAL ANALYSIS

1. The Bush administration claimed that its tax cuts will promote economic growth. What is its argument for how tax cuts spur economic growth?
2. Why did critics call President Bush's tax cuts irresponsible?

a. Aviva Aron-Dine, "Have the 2001 and 2003 Tax Cuts Made the Tax Code More Progressive?" Center on Budget and Policy Priorities, March 19, 2007, www.cbpp.org/3-19-07tax.htm (accessed 3/20/08).

As then House Majority Leader Tom DeLay put it, "The Soviet Union had a balanced budget. Well, you can raise taxes until you balance it, but the economy will go into the toilet."[20] Nonetheless, with deficits identified as causing future reductions in Social Security and other programs, deficits are likely to remain on the political agenda.

The president and Congress have each created institutions to assert control over the budget process. The Office of Management and Budget (OMB) in the Executive Office of the President is responsible for preparing the president's budget. This budget contains the president's spending priorities and the estimated costs of the president's policy proposals. It is viewed as the starting point for the annual debate over the budget. When different parties control the presidency and Congress, the president's budget may have little influence on the budget that is ultimately adopted. Members of the president's own party also may have different priorities. In 2002, members of Congress from both parties resisted the president's efforts to cut spending for domestic programs. A key Republican staffer defended congressional prerogatives to shape the budget, declaring, "Our job is not to rubber-stamp what OMB says."[21]

Congress has its own budget institutions. Congress created the Congressional Budget Office (CBO) in 1974 so that it could have reliable information about the costs and economic impact of the policies it considers. At the same time, Congress established a budget process designed to establish spending priorities and to consider individual expenditures in light of the entire budget. A key element of the process is the annual budget resolution, which designates broad targets for spending. By estimating the costs of policy proposals, Congress hoped to control spending and to reduce deficits. When the congressional budget process proved unable to hold down deficits in the 1980s, Congress established stricter measures to control spending, including "spending caps" that limit spending on some types of programs.

A very large and growing proportion of the annual federal budget is **mandatory spending,** expenditures that are, in the words of the OMB, "relatively uncontrollable." Interest payments on the national debt, for example, are determined by the actual size of the national debt. Legislation has mandated payment rates for such programs as retirement under Social Security, retirement for federal employees, unemployment assistance, Medicare, and farm price supports (see Figures 16.3 and 16.4). These payments increase with the cost of living; they increase as the average age of the population goes up; they increase as national and world agricultural surpluses go up. In 1970, 38.5 percent of the total federal budget was made up of these **uncontrollables;** in 1975, 52.5 percent fell into that category; and by 2008, around 61.2 percent was in the uncontrollable category. This means that the national government now has very little **discretionary spending,** which will allow it to counteract fluctuations in the business cycle.

Government spending as a fiscal policy works fairly well when deliberate deficit spending is used to stop a recession and to speed up the recovery period, but it does not work very well in fighting inflation, because elected politicians are politically unable to make the drastic expenditure cuts necessary to balance the budget, much less to produce a budgetary surplus.

mandatory spending federal spending that is made up of "uncontrollables," budget items that cannot be controlled through the regular budget process

uncontrollable a budgetary item that is beyond the control of budgetary committees and can be controlled only by substantive legislative action in Congress. Some uncontrollables, such as interest on the debt, are beyond the power of Congress, because the terms of payments are set in contracts

discretionary spending federal spending on programs that are controlled through the regular budget process

Regulation and Antitrust Policy

Americans have long been suspicious of concentrations of economic power. Federal economic regulation aims to protect the public against potential abuses by

FIGURE 16.3 ★ Uncontrollables as a Percentage of Total Federal Budget, 1962–2008

Spending on mandatory programs—such as Social Security and Medicare—has grown dramatically since 1970. These popular programs accounted for over 60 percent of the federal budget in 2008. What drives the increase in spending on these programs?

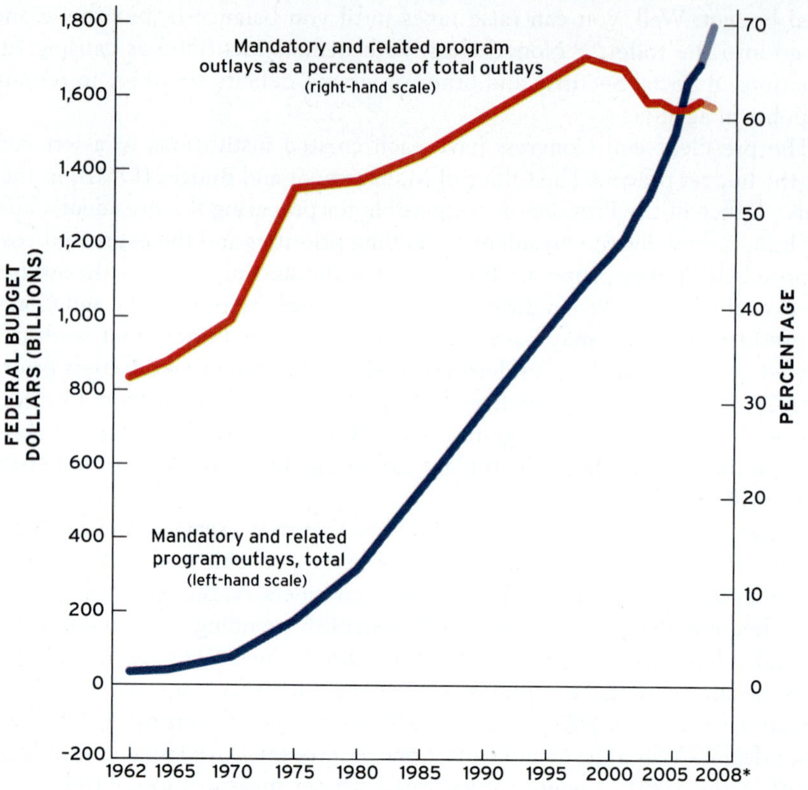

*Estimate

SOURCE: Office of Management and Budget, http://origin.www.gpoaccess.gov/usbudget/fy09/hist.html (accessed 5/9/08).

concentrated economic power in two ways. First, the federal government can establish conditions that govern the operation of big businesses to ensure fair competition. For example, it can require business to make information about its activities and account books available to the public. Second, the federal government can force a large business to break up into smaller companies if it finds that the company has established a **monopoly.** This is called **antitrust policy.** In addition to economic regulation, the federal government engages in social regulation. Social regulation establishes conditions on businesses in order to protect workers, the environment, and consumers.

monopoly the existence of a single firm in a market that controls all the goods and services of that market; absence of competition

antitrust policy government regulation of large businesses that have established monopolies

Federal regulatory policy was a reaction to public demands. As the American economy prospered throughout the nineteenth century, some companies grew so large that they were recognized as possessing "market power." This meant that they were powerful enough to eliminate competitors and to impose conditions on consumers rather than catering to consumer demand. The growth of billion-dollar corporations led to collusion among companies to control prices, much to the dismay of smaller businesses and ordinary consumers. Small businesses, laborers, farmers, and consumers all began to clamor for protective regulation. Although the states had been regulating businesses in one way or another all along, interest groups turned to Washington as economic problems appeared to be beyond the reach of the individual state governments. If markets were national, there would have to be national regulation.[22]

FIGURE 16.4 ★ Budget Outlays of the Federal Government by Function, 2008*

The biggest items in the federal budget are mandatory programs, including Social Security and Medicare. These programs are supported by contributory taxes and enjoy broad support. It is easier to cut discretionary spending, because appropriations must be approved each year. With rising budget deficits and congressional unwillingness to raise taxes, discretionary spending—including defense, but especially domestic programs—are the easiest programs to cut.

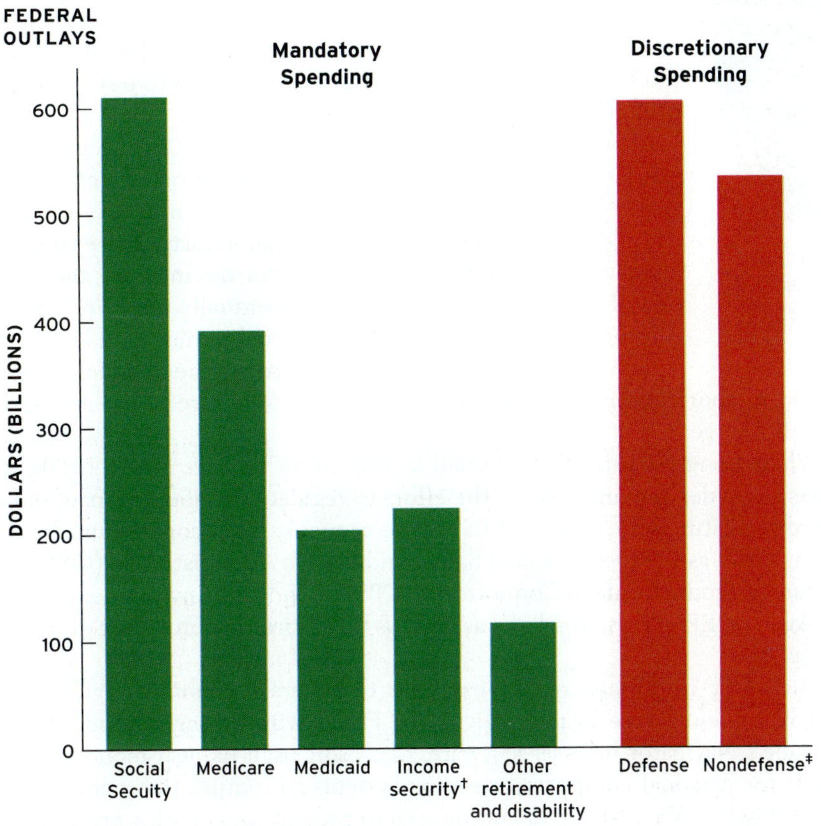

*Estimate

†Includes unemployment compensation, food and nutrition assistance, Supplemental Security Income, earned income tax credits, family and other support assistance, foster care and adoption assistance, and housing assistance.

‡Includes appropriations for all domestic programs, for example, agriculture, transportation, labor, interior, Health and Human Services, education, housing, and homeland security.

SOURCE: Office of Management and Budget, www.whitehouse.gov/omb/budget/fy2009/pdf/hist.pdf (accesssed 5/9/08).

The first national regulatory policy was the Interstate Commerce Act of 1887, which created the first national independent regulatory commission, the Interstate Commerce Commission (ICC), designed to control the monopolistic practices of the railroads. Two years later, the Sherman Antitrust Act extended regulatory power

In 1969, Cleveland's Cuyahoga River caught fire due to the industrial waste dumped into the water and became a symbol of the need for government regulation of polluting industries.

to cover all monopolistic practices, including "trusts" or any other agreement between companies to eliminate competition. These were strengthened in 1914 with the enactment of the Federal Trade Act (creating the Federal Trade Commission, or FTC) and the Clayton Act. The only significant addition of economic regulatory policy beyond regulation of interstate trade, however, was the establishment in 1913 of the Federal Reserve System, which was given powers to regulate the banking industry along with its general monetary powers. At the same time, public demands to protect consumers led the federal government to enact a more limited number of social regulations. As we have seen, Upton Sinclair's best-seller about the meatpacking industry, *The Jungle,* led to the federal meat inspection program in 1906. Two decades later, the Food and Drug Administration was set up to test and regulate products viewed as essential to public health.

The modern epoch of comprehensive national regulation began in the 1930s. Most of the regulatory programs of the 1930s were established to regulate the conduct of companies within specifically designated sectors of American industry. For example, the jurisdiction of one agency was the securities industry; the jurisdiction of another was the radio (and eventually television) industry. Another was banking. Another was coal mining; still another was agriculture. At this time, Congress also set the basic framework of American labor regulation, including the rules for collective bargaining and the minimum wage.

When Congress turned once again to regulatory policies in the 1970s, it became still bolder, moving beyond the effort to regulate specific sectors of industry toward regulating some aspect of the entire economy. The scope or jurisdiction of such agencies as the Occupational Safety and Health Administration (OSHA), the Consumer Product Safety Commission (CPSC), and the Environmental Protection Agency (EPA) is as broad and as wide as the entire economy, indeed the entire society.

The most important recent example of federal economic regulation was the government's case against Microsoft. Faced with strong competition from Netscape's Navigator browser software, Microsoft used its near-monopoly of the market for personal computer operating systems to require that computers run by Microsoft's Windows 98 operating system present users with a preloaded icon for Internet Explorer. Computer manufacturing companies would have to comply or they would "lose their Windows license and thus lose their business."[23] The Justice Department's Antitrust Division charged Microsoft with "product tying," a violation of antitrust law (the oldest of federal economic regulations). Initial court rulings found Microsoft guilty of using its monopoly power to harm the consumer by reducing competition and stifling innovation. At first it appeared that Microsoft would be subject to severe penalties, including possibly splitting the company in two. Instead, the Justice Department settled the case, requiring only minor concessions on Microsoft's part. Microsoft now has to disclose parts of its Windows code and allow computer manufacturers to install competing software on their machines. Critics charged that these measures would do little to change Microsoft's anticompetitive business practices. The changes did not help Netscape Navigator, which went off line in 2008.

Despite occasional high-profile regulatory cases such as the one against Microsoft, the trend since the late 1970s has been against regulation. Businesses complained about the burden of the new regulations they confronted, and many economists began to argue that excessive regulation was hurting the economy. Congress and the president responded with a wave of **deregulation.** For example, President Reagan went about the task of changing the direction of regulation by way of "presidential oversight." Shortly after taking office, he gave the OMB authority to review all executive-branch proposals for new regulations. By this means, Reagan reduced the total number of regulations issued by federal agencies, dropping the number of pages in the *Federal Register* from 74,000 in 1980 to 49,600 in 1987.[24] By 2007 the *Federal Register* had grown again to more than 74,000 pages. Nonetheless, the movement for deregulation became steadily more controversial during the presidency of George W. Bush. In the late 1980s and 1990s, many states had opened their electrical power markets to competition, resulting in lower prices. But in 2001, severe energy shortages in California caused power outages and skyrocketing prices. California officials charged that Enron and other out-of-state suppliers had used their market power to drive up the price of energy and then used their political clout to dissuade federal regulators from intervening.

deregulation a policy of reducing or eliminating regulatory restraints on the conduct of individuals or private institutions

For Critical Analysis

Regulation is a key tool of economic policy. What are the purposes of government regulation? Why is regulation often controversial?

Calls for tighter regulation of the finance industry peaked in 2008, when weaknesses in the subprime mortgage business triggered a worldwide crisis of confidence. Banks and other companies had devised new ways of bundling individual mortgage loans into complex securities known as derivatives. Since mortgages were thought to be solid investments, the investment banks borrowed capital to purchase and resell them in high volume. As some homeowners started finding it difficult to keep up with their payments, however, the banks suddenly appeared overextended. Other investors became reluctant to lend. Congress decided it had little choice but to approve the massive rescue plan proposed by the Treasury and the Federal Reserve. But an unmistakable movement had by then taken shape for a thorough overhaul of the country's regulatory architecture of the financial system.

Subsidies and Contracting

Subsidies and contracting are the carrots of economic policy. Their purpose is to encourage people to do something they might not otherwise do or to get people to do more of what they are already doing. Sometimes the purpose is merely to compensate people for something done in the past.

SUBSIDIES **Subsidies** are simply government grants of cash or other valuable commodities, such as land. Although subsidies are often denounced as "giveaways," they have played a fundamental role in the history of government in the United States. Subsidies were the dominant form of public policy of the national government and the state and local governments throughout the nineteenth century. They continue to be an important category of public policy at all levels of government. The first planning document ever written for the national government, Alexander Hamilton's *Report on Manufactures,* was based almost entirely on Hamilton's assumption that American industry could be encouraged by federal subsidies and that these were not only desirable but constitutional.

subsidy a government grant of cash or other valuable commodities, such as land, to an individual or an organization; used to promote activities desired by the government, to reward political support, or to buy off political opposition

The thrust of Hamilton's plan was not lost on later policy makers. Subsidies in the form of land grants were given to farmers and to railroad companies to encourage western settlement. Substantial cash subsidies have traditionally been given to shipbuilders to help build the commercial fleet and to guarantee the use of their ships as military personnel carriers in time of war. Policies using the subsidy technique continued to be plentiful in the twentieth century, even after the 1990s when there was widespread public and official hostility toward subsidies. For example, in 2005, the annual value of corporate subsidies not including agriculture was estimated at more than $75 billion.[25] Crop subsidies alone, implemented by the Department of Agriculture, amounted to about $18 billion in 2007.

Politicians have always favored subsidies because subsidies can be treated as "benefits" that can be spread widely in response to many demands that might otherwise produce profound political conflict. Subsidies can, in other words, be used to buy off the opposition.

Another secret to the popularity of subsidies is that those who receive the benefits do not perceive the controls inherent in them. In the first place, most of the resources available for subsidies come from taxation. (During the nineteenth century, there was a lot of public land to distribute, but that is no longer the case.) Second, the effect of any subsidy has to be measured somewhat indirectly in terms of what people *would be doing* if the subsidy were not available. For example, many thousands of people settled in lands west of the Mississippi only because land subsidies were available. Similarly, hundreds of research laboratories exist in universities and corporations only because certain types of research subsidies from the government are available to fund them.

CONTRACTING Like any corporation, a government agency must purchase goods and services by contract. The law requires open bidding for a substantial proportion of these contracts because government contracts are extremely valuable to businesses in the private sector and because the opportunities and incentives for abuse surrounding contracting are very great. But contracting is more than a method of buying goods and services. Contracting is also an important technique of policy because government agencies are often authorized to use their **contracting power** as a means of encouraging corporations to improve themselves, as a means of helping to build up whole sectors of the economy, and as a means of encouraging certain desirable goals or behavior, such as equal employment opportunity. For example, the infant airline industry of the 1930s was nurtured by the national government's lucrative contracts to carry airmail. A more recent example is the use of government contracting to encourage industries, universities, and other organizations to engage in research and development on a wide range of issues in basic and applied science.

contracting power the power of government to set conditions on companies seeking to sell goods or services to government agencies

For Critical Analysis

Think about a specific instance of government intervention in the American economy since the New Deal. What economic policy tool was used? What other tools might have been used? In your opinion, when is government action in the economy necessary?

Military contracting has long been a major element in government spending. So tight was the connection between defense contractors and the federal government during the Cold War that as he was leaving office, President Eisenhower warned the nation to beware of the powerful "military-industrial complex." After the Cold War, as military spending and production declined, major defense contractors began to look for alternative business activities to supplement the reduced demand for weapons. For example, Lockheed Martin, the nation's largest defense contractor, began to bid on contracts related to welfare reform. Since the terrorist attacks of 2001, however, the military budget has been awash in new funds and military contractors are flooded with business. President Bush increased the Pentagon budget by more than 7 percent a year, requesting so many weapons systems that one observer called the budget a "weapons smorgasbord."[26] Military contractors geared up to produce not only weapons for foreign warfare but also surveillance systems to enhance domestic security.

The Environment and the Economy

Federal interest in environmental conservation stretches back to the early 1900s, with the creation of the National Park Service and other efforts to preserve natural beauty. But it was not until the 1970s that environmental policy emerged as a major component of federal action, with the passage of new laws reaching into many aspects of the economy. Today, concern about global warming has put environmental issues front and center in debates about the economy. Not only must policy makers grapple with the costs of combating global warming, they must also assess the long-term impact of warming on the American economy and society. This is a fundamental challenge because the effects of global warming are likely to be very widely felt. At the same time, however, the specific consequences and the timing of their impact remain very uncertain.

The wave of environmental policy enacted in the 1970s stemmed in large part from American prosperity in the 1960s. An affluent America with more time for leisure grew concerned about the quality of the environment and the need to preserve natural beauty. The consequences of economic growth that paid little attention to environmental impact were evident all over America. In 1969, Cleveland's Cayuhoga River, long a dumping ground for industrial waste, caught fire. Images of the burning river became especially vivid symbols of environmental neglect. The first "Earth Day" in 1970 celebrated this new set of concerns which would become a major feature of American politics in the coming decades.[27]

A wave of new laws wrote environmental goals into policy. The 1969 National Environmental Policy Act (NEPA), the Clean Air Act Amendments of 1970, the 1972 Clean Water Act, and the 1974 Safe Drinking Water Act together established a new set of goals and procedures for protecting the environment.

Former vice president Al Gore's 2006 film An Inconvenient Truth *attracted broad attention to the issue of global warming. The film won an Academy Award, and Gore was a corecipient of the Nobel Peace Prize for his efforts to raise public awareness.*

They are properly considered part of economic policy because they regulate the activities of virtually every aspect of the economy. NEPA, for example, requires federal agencies to prepare an environmental impact statement for every major development project that they propose. In this way, environmental impacts routinely become factored into considerations about whether a particular project is feasible or desirable.

Environmental disasters have often drawn attention to new environmental hazards and have prompted greater federal regulation. For example, during the mid-1970s the residents of the Love Canal neighborhood in Buffalo, New York, discovered that their neighborhood had been built on a toxic waste dump. Many of the chemicals in the soil were suspected carcinogens. At federal and state cost, residents were moved to new homes. Partly as a result of this highly publicized incident, Congress passed legislation to facilitate cleanup of hazardous waste sites. Yet government action and corporate liability are often bitterly contested issues in this area. As the book and film *A Civil Action*—about toxic waste in a Massachusetts community—demonstrated, identifying the sources of toxic pollution and linking such pollution to health hazards can be very difficult.[28]

Protecting the environment presents policy makers with difficult trade-offs. Compliance with environmental regulations can be very costly. Moreover, critics maintain that federal standards are sometimes too high. How clean should the air be? What is the difference between pure drinking water and safe drinking water? Who should bear the costs of providing environmental benefits? Not only do citizens, consumers, and businesses take different perspectives on these questions but the goals themselves often present a moving target. As new scientific evidence shows (or fails to find evidence for) new or suspected environmental hazards, conflicts over the proper government role emerge.

The Debate on Global Warming

Nowhere have these conflicts been more acute than in the debate over global warming. A large and growing body of scientific evidence suggests that greenhouse gas emissions from cars, power plants and other human-made sources are causing temperatures on Earth to rise.[29] The projected environmental consequences are dire: melting polar ice caps, extreme weather, droughts, fire, rising sea levels, and disease. All would have profound economic consequences. Yet these projections come with considerable uncertainty: how likely are most catastrophic scenarios? Should we prepare for the most damaging outcomes or only the most likely outcomes of global warming?[30] These questions are important because the costs of transforming the world's carbon-based technologies through lower energy use and newer green technologies are enormous. These questions are especially salient for the United States, which has the world's largest economy and is responsible for 25 percent of the world's greenhouse gas emissions but has only 10 percent of the world's population.[31] And because the United States relies so heavily on fossil fuels for its energy sources, the effort to reduce carbon emission requires a major shift in how we obtain and use energy.

As scientists have learned more about the effects of human activity on the climate, the issue of global warming has risen on the national agenda. The issue attracted broad attention in 2006 with the success of former vice president Al Gore's film *An Inconvenient Truth*. In 2007, the film won an Academy Award, and Gore, along with the UN's International Panel on Climate Change, received the Nobel

Peace Prize for arousing public awareness about the dangers of global warming. American public opinion reflected the growing salience of global warming as a policy issue. For example, in 2007, 84 percent of Americans reported believing that human activity was at least a contributing factor in global warming.[32] In the same survey, just over half of the public said that they would support protecting the environment over stimulating the economy, while 36 percent chose the economy.[33] When asked whether or not the issue would affect their votes, just under half of the public said that global warming would be "extremely" or "very important" to their vote for president.[34] Some corporate leaders have also become increasingly concerned about global warming, sponsoring events to learn more about the problem and joining coalitions to press for solutions. Moreover, many political leaders who have been skeptical about the reality and causes of global warming have come to accept that it poses a threat that must be addressed. For much of his administration, former president George W. Bush resisted pressure to address global warming. Instead, concern about the availability and cost of energy drove his administration to press for securing new oil resources, such as the controversial and unsuccessful effort to open the Arctic Natural Wildlife Refuge to oil drilling. But by the end of his term, Bush had come to accept the importance of addressing global warming, warding off critics with his declaration, "I take the issue seriously."[35]

Environmental Policies

But how can the goal of a "greener America" be reached? Agreeing on policies to reduce greenhouse gas emissions remains extremely difficult. Policy makers charged with devising approaches to global warming have identified three basic policy approaches. The first is mitigation, or reduction of greenhouse gas emissions. The second is large-scale research and development to promote alternative technologies. The third consists of measures that allow us to adapt to a warmer

Politics Today

What are some of the policies that can be used to address global warming? Which policies have the best chance of being enacted?

In 2008, soaring gasoline prices contributed to calls for alternative energy technologies. Supporters of alternative fuels argued that they would reduce American's dependency on foreign oil.

The United States and Global Climate Change

Concerns about global warming began to surface more than two decades ago. The international scope of the question became apparent when more than 150 countries, including the United States, signed the United Nations Framework Convention on Climate Change (UNFCCC) in 1992 at the so-called Earth Summit in Rio de Janeiro. By 1997, the signatory parties agreed on the Kyoto Protocol for reducing the level of heat trapping gases in the earth's atmosphere. To achieve this goal, the Kyoto Protocol set binding targets for greenhouse gas emissions to be met by each country by the year 2012 at levels 5.2 percent lower than their 1990 levels.

Since the Kyoto Protocol, the United States has been a hesitant participant in international climate negotiations. The United States signed the protocol during the Clinton presidency, but disagreement quickly erupted over the economic costs that industry would incur if forced to lower greenhouse emissions. As a result, President Clinton never submitted the protocol to the Senate for ratification. On taking office in 2001, President Bush then announced he would not submit the Kyoto agreement to the Senate because it exempted China and other developing countries from binding limits while imposing excessive costs on the U.S. economy.

Even as the scientific basis for global warming gained wider acceptance, the politics of implementing binding limits produced a growing split between wealthy industrialized countries and the developing world. China and Brazil argued that the industrialized countries and especially the United States had contributed far more to global warming over time than developing countries. The industrialized leaders, especially the United States, should therefore shoulder the burden of limiting worldwide emissions while giving poorer countries a chance to develop their economies.

In the ensuing debates, many other Kyoto signatories also came to see the United States as a laggard in international efforts to control global warming. With only 10 percent of the world's population, the United States emitted approximately 25 percent of greenhouse gases, more than any other single country. At the Montréal conference of Kyoto signatories in 2005, the U.S. delegation participated only as observers and refused to accept binding frameworks that did not include China, Brazil, and other developing countries.

With the Kyoto Protocol set to expire in 2012, many countries wanted to lay the groundwork for a new international agreement. Given the key role of the United States in any such agreement, hopes for full U.S. participation grew steadily. In December 2007, representatives from 180 countries met in Bali, Indonesia, to discuss whether the Kyoto Protocol should be extended or whether a new agreement would provide a better framework for dealing with global climate change.

In the initial sessions in Bali, the United States appeared increasingly isolated. Many companies within the United States—including the Detroit car makers—were beginning to voice support for nationwide caps on greenhouse gases.[a] The complexion of international debate was clearly changing. When the official U.S. representative at Bali announced the administration's continued resistance to mandatory caps on carbon emissions, her statement was audibly booed by the audience.[b]

But behind the scenes at Bali, the United States, as well as the key developing countries, showed greater flexibility. On the last day of the conference, the U.S. delegation announced that other countries had softened their positions enough for the United States to join the consensus in favor of pursuing mandatory emissions caps at subsequent meetings. The specific mechanisms for limiting future emissions were sure to provoke vehement negotiations, but the door to meaningful international cooperation was opened far more decisively than many observers would have predicted.

FOR CRITICAL ANALYSIS

1. Why did many countries that signed the Kyoto Protocol come to see the United States as a laggard in efforts to control global warming?
2. Why was it so important to U.S. negotiators that mandatory limits on greenhouse gas emissions be applied to China as well as to the developed countries?

a. Environmental Defense Fund, "Big Three Automakers Endorse Cap on Global Warming Pollution," press release, March 14, 2007.

b. *The Newshour,* "Bali Climate Conference Ends with Compromise," December 17, 2007, www.pbs.org/newshour/bb/environment/july-dec 07/bali_12-17.html (accessed 3/21/08).

climate. Each of these strategies entails potentially gargantuan costs in the form of higher energy prices, subsidies to industry, infrastructure projects, and relocation decisions. When specific policy proposals are discussed and these costs become apparent, the consensus for addressing global warming breaks down.

MITIGATION: REDUCING EMISSIONS The mitigation approach, which seeks to reduce greenhouse gas emissions, has garnered the most attention from policy makers. Two policies that aim to achieve this goal are tougher standards for auto fuel mileage and higher taxes on gasoline. Both have been very controversial. Although the public strongly supports higher gas-mileage standards, auto companies resisted such standards for nearly thirty years after they were first put into place in the early 1970s. The 2007 energy bill's requirement that automobiles raise fuel efficiency rates by 40 percent—to 35 miles per gallon by 2020—was a breakthrough on this issue. Even so, when California and fifteen other states sought to require even tougher standards for fuel mileage, the Environmental Protection Agency rejected their request, citing the need for a single national standard. Proposals to increase gasoline taxes have so far been political nonstarters. Public opinion polls routinely show that a majority of Americans oppose a tax on gasoline as a way to reduce emissions, and few politicians want to sponsor such an unpopular policy.[36]

International agreements on climate change, such as the Kyoto Protocol, seek to reduce carbon emissions by establishing mandatory caps on the total amount of emissions developed countries can emit. Although the United States signed the protocol in 1997, congressional and presidential opposition prevented any effort to implement its provisions. Policy makers have since considered several ways to reduce carbon emissions. One of the most effective is a "carbon tax," which would tax the producers of energy. The higher costs would then be passed onto consumers. Yet only a handful of politicians have expressed interest in supporting carbon taxes, which could substantially raise the costs of all sorts of consumer products.

Perhaps the most politically feasible strategy for reducing carbon emissions is a cap-and-trade system. This approach sets a target for carbon emissions for each industry but allows companies to trade "carbon credits" with each other. This market-based system is attractive to political leaders because it achieves its goals by creating incentives for private actors and allows them flexibility as they seek to reduce emissions. More than twenty-three large firms, including leading auto makers, have joined environmentalists in a coalition called the U.S. Climate Action Partnership (USCAP) to press for a cap-and-trade system to reduce carbon emissions.[37] In 2007, Senators Joe Lieberman (Ind.-Conn.) and John Warner (R-Va.) introduced a cap-and-trade bill. Dubbed "America's Climate Security Act," the measure reflected the growing consensus on this market-based approach, which effectively "puts a price on pollution" to reduce greenhouse gas emissions.[38] The Lieberman-Warner bill sets the stage for future debates over how to attack global warming through mitigation.

PROMOTING ALTERNATIVE TECHNOLOGIES Many analysts and politicians, however, prefer a second strategy, which centers on increasing research and development to promote alternative technologies. Former president Bush supported this approach in his 2007 State of the Union address, which called for a 22 percent increase in funding for clean energy initiatives.[39] A particularly popular type of green technology has been the hybrid car. In 2007, almost every major auto manufacturer had plans for producing a hybrid car, and over 350,000 hybrid vehicles were sold in the United States.[40] Other kinds of green technologies include recycling, solar power, and hydrogen fuel cells.

Green technologies may prove to be a boon for the American economy. Because highly skilled labor is required to produce most green technologies, America has a competitive advantage over many other countries. To be more precise, the production of green technologies—unlike other kinds of goods—cannot be outsourced to developing countries.

In addition to enhancing environmental quality and promoting economic growth, a move toward green technologies could significantly improve American national security. Indeed, because most oil money goes to Saudi Arabia and Iran, some argue that adopting more fuel-efficient technologies would take money away from regimes that support terrorism against the United States. As the *New York Times* columnist Thomas Friedman put it, "Green is the new red, white and blue."[41]

Part of the attraction of green technologies is that they appear to entail fewer politically difficult costs. A closer look, however, reveals that green technologies do impose unpopular costs. For example, the search for cleaner technologies has renewed interest in nuclear power. But nuclear power has long suffered from NIMBY (Not In My Backyard) problems: few people want a nuclear power plant close by. The question of how to dispose of nuclear waste poses similar problems. Current plans to deposit nuclear waste in Nevada's Yucca Mountain have been the target of considerable controversy, not only by people close by but also by those concerned with the dangers of transporting nuclear waste to Nevada. Even less dangerous technologies, such as wind farms, attract opposition, as the effort to establish a large wind farm off Cape Cod demonstrated. Other alternatives, such as the use of ethanol to replace gasoline, have different problems. In 2007, as corn farmers sought to produce corn for the ethanol market, Americans experienced rising food prices.[42]

Development of green technologies will no doubt be an important component of America's efforts to combat climate change. However, opposition to some of the new technologies and the time required to develop these alternatives mean that they are not the magic bullet that many proponents wish they were.

ADAPTATION POLICIES A final approach to climate change is adaptation to a warmer climate. Adaptation would entail a diverse set of policies, including establishment of green corridors, pest and disease control, water conservation to deal with drought, and new infrastructure such as seawalls to cope with rising sea levels.[43] Even more controversial measures, such as moving people away from low-lying areas, would be part of an adaptation strategy.

Many aspects of a deliberate adaptation strategy would be difficult to implement in the market-oriented, decentralized context of the United States. Although some European countries, such as the low-lying Netherlands, are relocating people as part of their adaptation strategy, American politicians have little stomach for initiating such controversial measures. Moreover, the combination of conservation and new infrastructure requires considerable public resources and broad coordination across multiple public agencies. Both are hard to achieve in the context of American politics. For example, the environmentally sensitive Sacramento Delta is extremely vulnerable to rising sea levels. The delta, a swath of land that lies below sea level, is economically important because it supplies much of northern

California, including California agribusiness, with water. Yet decisions about what happens in the delta involve more than 200 government agencies.[44]

When deliberate adaptation does not occur, de facto adaptation may. Although no single event such as Hurricane Katrina can be attributed to climate change, the consequences of Katrina are relevant to global-warming scenarios. As in New Orleans, the most vulnerable people with the fewest resources will suffer the worst consequences of adaptation as they lose their homes and livelihoods. As in New Orleans and in recent urban heat waves, many will die. Many scientists believe that deliberate adaptation has to be part of our approach to climate change because even if we take major steps to mitigate carbon emissions and pour resources into developing new technologies, global warming has already arrived.[45]

Global climate change poses a difficult economic challenge for the United States. It presents the opportunity for American industry to take the lead in developing green technologies, placing the nation's economic prosperity on a fundamentally new base. Yet it also calls for government to enforce the reduction of carbon emissions and adapt current practices to a changing world. Many industries have expressed support for action to address climate change, but such a major economic transformation creates winners and losers. Firms, such as the auto companies, whose profits are jeopardized and workers whose jobs are threatened by change have successfully blocked bold action in the past. The diffuse long-term harms that global warming poses are hard to pit against the specific concentrated costs that face industries today. Nonetheless, growing recognition that climate change is real and poses potentially catastrophic consequences ensures that economic policy and environmental policy will be ever more closely intertwined in the future.

Since the 1930s, the American people have expected the government to provide emergency relief during economic downturns. During the Great Depression, the Works Progress Administration put 3.5 million unemployed people to work on a wide range of public projects, from construction to the arts.

The Politics of Economic Policy Making

Addressing economic challenges and maintaining a healthy economy are extremely important to political leaders. As presidents from Herbert Hoover (who presided over the beginning of the Great Depression of the 1930s) to Jimmy Carter (who faced double-digit inflation) discovered, voters will punish politicians for poor economic performance. Yet even though all politicians want a healthy economy, they often differ in their views about how to attain it. Moreover, politicians disagree about what the priorities of economic policy should be. Democrats and Republicans alike want to promote economic growth, but Democrats are generally more concerned about equality and unemployment than are Republicans. Republicans stress the importance of economic freedom for maintaining a healthy economy, whereas Democrats are often more willing to support economic regulation to attain social objectives. Such differences along party lines are not hard and fast divisions, however. The politics of economic policy making are also greatly influenced by economic ideas.

Until 1929, most Americans believed that government had little to do with actively managing the economy. The world was guided by the theory that the economy, if left to its own devices, would produce full employment and maximum production. This traditional view of the relationship between government and the economy crumbled in 1929 before the stark reality of the Great Depression of 1929–33. Some misfortune befell nearly everyone. Around 20 percent of the workforce became unemployed, and few of these individuals had any monetary resources or the old family farm to fall back on. Banks failed, wiping out the savings of millions who had been prudent enough or fortunate enough to have any. Thousands of businesses failed, throwing middle-class Americans onto the bread lines alongside unemployed laborers and dispossessed farmers. The Great Depression proved to Americans that imperfections in the economic system could exist.

Demands grew for the federal government to act. In Congress, some Democrats proposed that the federal government finance public works to aid the economy and put people back to work. Other members introduced legislation to provide federal grants to the states to assist their relief efforts.

When President Franklin D. Roosevelt took office in 1933, he energetically threw the federal government into the business of fighting the Depression. He proposed a variety of temporary measures to provide federal relief and work programs. Most of the programs he proposed were to be financed by the federal government but administered by the states. In addition to these temporary measures, Roosevelt presided over the creation of several important federal programs designed to provide future economic security for Americans. Since that time, the government has been instrumental in ensuring that the economy will never again collapse as it did during the Depression.

The experience of the 1930s transformed public expectations about federal government involvement in the economy. Since that time, the public has held the government—and the president in particular—responsible for ensuring a healthy economy.

As we have seen, Keynesian ideas, which used spending and tax policy to promote growth and low unemployment, dominated economic policy during the 1960s and during the first half of the 1970s. The Council of Economic Advisers

Coca-Cola and the Middle East: Brands as American Icons

"That's as American as apple pie," or so the expression goes. But perhaps a more accurate simile for contemporary American culture would be, "that's as American as Coca-Cola," or McDonalds, or Starbucks, or Microsoft, or Marlboro. As the American government helps promote American goods and services abroad, increasing numbers of people from around the world experience American culture through its brands. However, the world has long been engaged in a love/hate relationship with the ubiquity of American brands and the popular culture that accompanies them. While in many cases, people abroad are simply worried about American brands competing with local businesses, consumers around the globe also use their wallets to respond to American foreign policy and international economic policy.

Although the United States remains a leader in exports, in August 2005, the *Financial Times* reported that "anti-Americanism is hurting companies whose products are considered to be distinctly 'American.'" At the start of the 2003 war in Iraq, sales of Coca-Cola dropped 10 percent in the Middle East and McDonalds's sales fell 7.5 percent. According to the *San Francisco Chronicle*, a 2005 study revealed that substantial proportions of opinion leaders in Canada, the United Kingdom, France, and Germany reported that they were less likely to buy American goods as a result of American foreign policy.

In some cases, local entrepreneurs in Europe and the Middle East have begun to offer goods and services to replace American brands. Take Coca-Cola, for example. Since it was placed on the Arab League's official boycott list in 1967 for doing business in Israel, Coca-Cola has had hurdles to overcome with its public relations in the Middle East. Once placed on the list, Coca-Cola was perceived by some in the Middle East as a supporter of the Israeli military and of the Jewish religion. So strong was this rumor, in fact, that The Coca-Cola Company has a section on its Web site entitled "Middle East Rumors" where the company states that it "is not affiliated with any specific religion or ethnic group . . . [and] does not support or oppose governments, political or religious causes." Nonetheless, to many people around the world, Coke represents America—American culture, interests, and policy. Entrepreneurs have responded by offering alternatives to American goods, such as Mecca Cola, which was launched by Tawfik Mathlouthi. Mathlouthi explains that Mecca Cola "is not just a drink. It is an act of protest against Bush and Rumsfeld and their policies."[a] The company has pledged to give 10 percent of profits to Palestinian children's charities and an additional 10 percent to European Nongovernmental Organizations (NGOs). Mecca Cola has quickly grown in popularity in Belgium, France, and Germany and is currently being introduced in the Middle East.

Many U.S. companies that have felt the effects of foreign boycotts abroad are engaging in campaigns to bring consumers back. One argument against local consumers' boycotts of American goods is that the bulk of the impact will not be felt in America, but in the local communities where the boycotts take place. American companies are trying to convey the message that the people who will be hurt are local farmers, suppliers, and employees of the local plants—not American executives or politicians. However, they have had limited success in finding a solution. The shape of this solution, whether economic, political, or merely a matter of good public relations, has yet to emerge.

FOR CRITICAL ANALYSIS

1. Do you think that boycotts of American products abroad will ultimately be successful in influencing American foreign policy? Why or why not?
2. Do you choose to buy or not buy certain goods or services for political reasons? To what extent do you believe your personal purchasing choices affect the company behind the products?

a. Jon Fasman, "Freedom Coke: The Arab World's Foolish Boycott of American Food," Slate.com, March 25, 2003, www.slate.com/id/2080611/ (accessesd 3/22/08).

(CEA) played a central role in economic policy during that time because the president relied on its advice about whether to stimulate or depress the economy. As Keynesian prescriptions became less effective, however, the CEA began to lose its central role. Since the late 1970s, when President Carter began to emphasize monetary policy, the chairman of the Federal Reserve has occupied the pivotal position in economic policy making. The long run of economic prosperity in the 1990s made the former Fed chairman Alan Greenspan into something of a cult figure. Universally praised by Democrats and Republicans alike for his management of the economy, Greenspan served four four-year terms as head of the Federal Reserve. As the economy fell into recession in the early 2000s, critics complained that Greenspan had lost his touch and had helped create the conditions for recession.

Presidents who preside over periods of economic downturn are generally punished by the electorate. In 1992, economic recession and relatively high levels of unemployment greatly improved the challenger Bill Clinton's presidential prospects, even though he was not widely known when he started campaigning. Clinton's campaign took as a central theme the unofficial slogan, "It's the economy, stupid." The uncertain direction of the economy made it an issue in the 2004 presidential campaign. Anxious not to repeat his father's experience in 1992, President George W. Bush claimed in 2004 that his policies were creating new jobs and touted the benefits of his tax cuts for middle-income families. Democrats countered that Bush's policies benefited the wealthy but left most Americans economically worse off.

The groups that influence decisions about economic policy are as wide ranging as the objectives of policy. Consumer groups, environmentalists, businesses, and labor all attempt to shape economic policy. Of these groups, organized labor and business are the most consistent actors who weigh in across the spectrum of policies. In the past, organized labor was much more important in influencing economic policy than it is today. At the height of their strength in the 1950s, unions represented some 35 percent of the labor force. Today, labor unions, representing 12.5 percent of the labor force, are much less powerful in influencing economic policy. Democratic presidents continue to court labor because unions control resources and votes important to Democratic politicians, but labor's overall power has waned. On particular issues, organized labor can still exercise significant influence. For example, labor played a key role in Congress's decision to increase the minimum wage in 1996. Labor has recently sought to boost its political profile and has particularly sought to influence trade policy.

Business organizations are the most consistently powerful actors in economic policy. Business groups are most united around the goal of reducing government regulation. Organizations such as the U.S. Chamber of Commerce, which represents small business, and the Business Roundtable and the National Association of Manufacturers, which represent big business, actively worked to roll back government regulation in the 1970s and 1980s.

In addition to subsidies and tax breaks, business also relies on the federal government for protection against unfair foreign competition. For example, over the past several years, the film-production industry has lobbied Washington to help it compete with other countries where films can be made more cheaply than in the United States. This country loses an estimated $10 billion in annual revenues to these foreign competitors. Television shows and films with American locales are routinely filmed in Canada, where tax incentives and lower costs make produc-

Your Money and Politics

In the summer of 1998, a group of students formed the United Students Against Sweatshops. These young men and women were concerned about the working conditions of the laborers who made the apparel bearing their universities' logos. They argued that when schools and then students bought goods made in sweatshops, they were implicitly lending support to unjust labor practices. They wanted their universities to only purchase products from suppliers who agreed to a code of conduct that protected workers.

Many university administrations were reluctant to adopt anti-sweatshop policies, so students put on more pressure, sponsoring debates, holding street theater events, and in some instances even occupying the university president's office and staging hunger strikes. This persistence, amid constant negotiations, paid off, and by 2006, more than 150 universities had signed on to the Workers' Rights Commission, an independent organization that monitors the working conditions of apparel factories.

At the heart of these efforts was the belief that how students spend their money has an effect on other people throughout the world—and that they can use their money wisely, to reflect their values. Although the effort was aimed at workers in factories around the globe, the action was local—starting with their own campuses.

Individual citizens can have an impact on economic policies at any level and from any ideological direction.

★ *Join an organization that promotes fiscal responsibility.* There are numerous organizations that are concerned about federal budgeting decisions. One of the most prominent is the Concord Coalition (www.concordcoalition.org), a bipartisan group that uses grassroots advocacy and public information campaigns to lobby for more efficient federal spending, which means taking steps to eliminate annual deficits and paying down the national debt.

★ *Join an organization that promotes economic justice.* The Sargent Shriver National Center on Poverty Law (www.povertylaw.org), for example, provides information about the impact of economic policies on poor people in the United States. They advocate for policies that will provide greater economic security (such as living wages and health care) for the poor.

★ *Work to fight poverty.* There are a host of organizations that will connect you with opportunities to volunteer your time and effort with the less fortunate. The Corporation for National and Community Service (www.nationalservice.gov) is the federal government's clearinghouse for volunteer opportunities. You can also try www.dosomething.org or the U.S. Department of Education's Web site (www.ed.gov/students/involve/service/edpicks.jhtml).

★ *Work for economic justice on campus.* Find out if your university has signed on to the Workers' Rights Commission. If they haven't done so, and you feel they should, United Students Against Sweatshops (www.usas.org) can help you (or your school organization) to start a movement on campus. If your school is in compliance, you may want to follow the lead of students on other campuses and advocate for the rights (such as living wages) and benefits (such as health insurance) of service employees of the college or university.

★ *Spend your money judiciously.* Every day, consumers make decisions about what companies to support (by buying their products) and what companies to oppose (by boycotting their goods or services) with every purchase they make. Some people will drink only fair-trade coffee, which is produced in a way that protects small farmers in coffee-producing countries. Others have boycotted Coca-Cola products to pressure the company to allow their workers in Colombia to unionize.

tion considerably cheaper. Industry representatives, fearing that Los Angeles could turn into a "rust belt" for film production, have sought legislation to secure wage credits.[46] The Screen Actors Guild went so far as to ask the federal government to investigate Canada for unfair trade practices.

Thinking Critically about Economic Policy

Historically, Americans have been more concerned with ensuring economic liberty than with promoting economic equality. The widespread perception of openness and opportunity in American society has made Americans more tolerant of economic inequality than Europeans. American economic policy has rarely aimed to promote economic equality. Instead, economic policy has sought to ensure fairness in the marketplace and protect against the worst side effects of the free market. One of the central ways to ensure fair markets is to guard against the emergence of businesses so large that they can control markets. As we have seen, antitrust policy aims to break up such concentrations of power in the name of free and fair competition. The laws designed to strengthen labor in the 1930s likewise aimed to limit the power of big business by creating a countervailing power; they did not attempt directly to create equality. Consumer and environmental regulations are key economic policy protections against the worst side effects of the free market. Over time, as Americans have grown more concerned about the quality of life, policies in these areas have placed greater restrictions on the market. In a sense, economic prosperity and market success laid the foundation for such restrictions. As Americans felt more economically secure, they could afford to worry about how the economy affected the nonmaterial aspects of their lives, such as the environment. It is no accident that social regulation of the economy took off after the unprecedented prosperity of the 1960s.

The growth in economic inequality over the past three decades raises new questions about economic policy. Increased global competition, computerization, and the decline of unions and worker skills have all been identified as sources of the growth of inequality.[47] Taxes are another policy area that affects inequality. Depending on how they are designed, tax policies put relatively more money in the pockets of people with lower incomes or people with higher incomes. For example, tax cuts on investment income and reductions in the estate tax are more likely to increase the after-tax income of the wealthy because this group derives more of its income from investments and inheritances than do people with lower incomes.[48] Likewise, income-tax rates can be reduced for all groups, but depending on the proportion of tax cuts for each group, some income brackets may benefit more than others. One of the major criticisms of the tax cuts of 2001, 2003, and 2006 is that they increased the gap between rich and poor. They did so by allowing the rich to retain a greater proportion of their after-tax income than did middle- and lower-income taxpayers. The liberal Center for Budget and Policy Priorities analyzed the impact of these tax cuts. As Figure 16.5 shows, the tax cuts allowed households in the bottom fifth of the income range to keep an additional 0.5 percent of their pretax income. For the middle-income group, after-tax income grew by 2.3 percent, while the top 20 percent gained 4.6 in after-tax income. The gains for the top 1 percent of households was much larger: an increase of 6.8 percent of after-tax income each year.[49] These differences matter because long-terms trends in growth are widening the gap between

For Critical Analysis

How does economic policy affect inequality among Americans? Should economic policy makers take equality into account as they decide among different economic tools?

FIGURE 16.5 ★
Two Perspectives on Tax Cuts

Liberals and conservatives take different perspectives on the tax cuts introduced by President George W. Bush. Liberals charge that the cuts are regressive because they allow wealthy people to keep much more of their pretax income, as the top chart shows. Conservatives contend that the tax cuts benefited less-wealthy taxpayers because their share of the total tax burden declined while the tax burden of the richest taxpayers increased, as the bottom chart shows.

SOURCES: Center on Budget and Policy Priorities, www.cbpp.org/3-19-07tax.htm; Congressional Budget Office, www.cbo.gov/ftpdocs/61xx/doc6133/03-01-EffectiveTaxRates.pdf; and www.cbo.gov/ftpdocs/88xx/doc8885/EffectiveTaxRates.shtml (accessed 3/22/08).

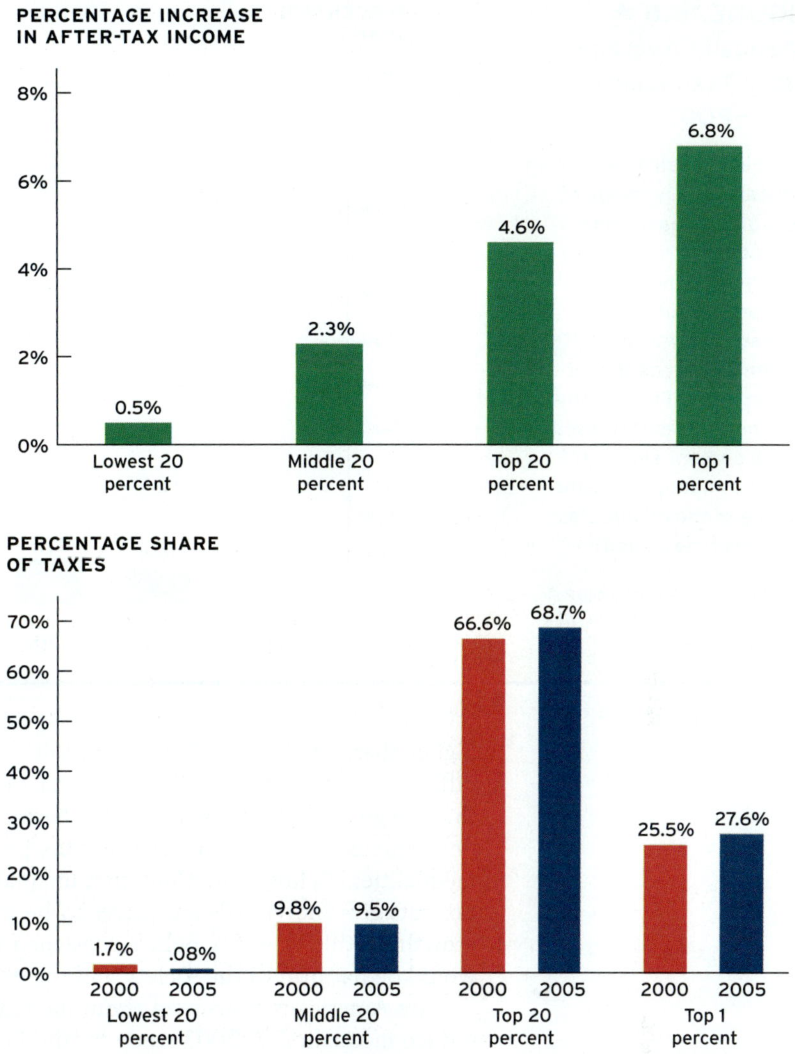

rich and poor, as Figure 16.6 shows. Because after-tax incomes are *more unequal* as a consequence of the tax changes, liberals identify them as a regressive tax change.

Conservatives take a different view. They argue that even with these changes, the rich paid by far the greatest share of federal taxes. In fact, as the second half of Figure 16.5 shows, in 2005, the top fifth of households paid 68.7 percent of all taxes, whereas the bottom fifth paid less than 1 percent. Most crucial in judging the impact of the tax cuts, the rich paid a *larger share* of the total federal tax bill after the tax cuts than before. As Figure 16.5 shows, the share of the total tax bill fell for households in the lowest- and middle-income categories, but it increased for the top categories. Therefore, although the lowest group paid .09 percent *less* as a share of total taxes, the top 20 percent of earners paid 2.1 percent *more.*

What is fair? So long as the rich still pay a higher proportion of their income in taxes, should we worry that the tax cuts are making after-tax income distribution more unequal? After all, as the rich have gotten richer, they have paid an ever

FIGURE 16.6 ★
Change in Average After-Tax Income, 1979–2005

Income inequality has grown substantially as the gains from growth have gone disproportionately to the wealthy. The income of the top 1 percent of earners increased by well over 200 percent, whereas that of the bottom fifth of the income distribution has increased by only 6 percent since 1979. What has happened to the income of the middle class over this time period?

SOURCE: Center on Budget and Policy Priorities, www.cbpp.org/12-14-07inc.htm (accessed 3/19/08).

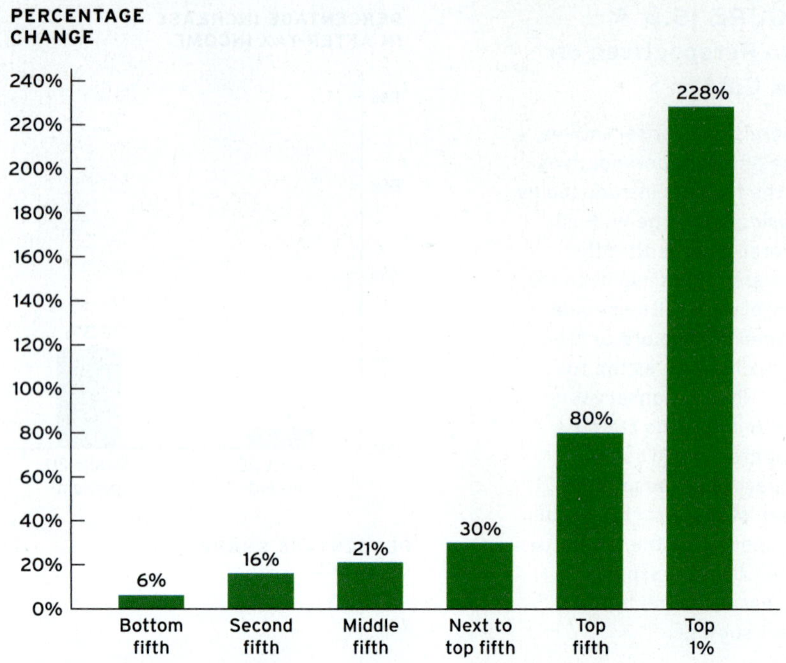

higher share of the total federal tax bill. The answer to this question depends on different views about the consequences of income inequality. Those who believe that the growth of income inequality harms the middle class by increasing prices or undermines democracy believe that tax policy should be designed to lessen these inequalities.[50] Those who think that inequality is not a major problem believe that tax cuts give individuals incentives to be productive and thus promote economic growth. In this view, tax policies designed to reduce after-tax income inequalities would be harmful to the society and the economy.[51]

Are Americans concerned about inequality? Do they want economic policy to reduce inequality? A 2003 study by the Princeton political scientist Larry Bartels showed that the public is indeed aware of rising inequality and that a majority think it is a bad thing. Nonetheless, his research showed that people "fail to connect inequality and public policy." Part of the reason is that many people do not understand where they fit in the tax system. One survey showed that half of the respondents thought that "most families" have to pay the estate tax, when in fact only 2 percent of estates had to pay the tax. Americans' aversion to taxes can make it difficult to have a national debate about raising taxes on higher-income earners. This became evident in the waning days of the 2008 campaign. Questioned about his tax plan, Barack Obama defended his proposal to increase taxes for high earners. Obama's casual remark that it made sense to "spread the wealth around" ignited a firestorm of criticism from his opponent John McCain, who had pledged not to raise taxes at all. The debate that ensued highlighted the difficulties in conducting a public debate about taxes and inequality.

If widespread concern about inequality is to drive changes in economic policy, the American public needs a better understanding of the relationship between economic policy and inequality.

FOR FURTHER READING

Auerbach, Alan J., David Card, and John M. Quigley, eds. *Public Policy and the Income Distribution.* New York: Russell Sage Foundation, 2006.

Bryner, Gary C. *Blue Skies, Green Politics: The Clean Air Act of 1990.* Rev. ed. Washington, DC: Congressional Quarterly Press, 1995.

Frank, Robert H. *Falling Behind: How Rising Inequality Harms the Middle Class.* Berkeley: University of California Press, 2007.

Friedman, Milton, and Walter Heller. *Monetary versus Fiscal Policy.* New York: Norton, 1969.

Greider, William. *Secrets of the Temple: How the Federal Reserve Runs the Country.* New York: Simon & Schuster, 1987.

Harris, Richard A., and Sidney M. Milkis. *The Politics of Regulatory Change.* 2nd ed. New York: Oxford University Press, 1996.

Jacobs, Lawrence, and Theda Skocpol, eds. *Inequality and American Democracy: What We Know and What We Need to Learn.* New York: Russell Sage Foundation, 2005.

Schick, Alan. *The Federal Budget: Politics, Policy, Process.* Washington, DC: Brookings Institution Press, 1995.

Stein, Robert M., and Kenneth N. Bickers. *Perpetuating the Pork Barrel: Policy Subsystems and American Democracy.* New York: Cambridge University Press, 1995.

Stiglitz, Joseph E. *Globalization and Its Discontents.* New York: Norton, 2003.

Uchitelle, Louis. *The Disposable American: Layoffs and Their Consequences.* New York: Knopf, 2006.

Weir, Margaret. *Politics and Jobs: The Boundaries of Employment Policy in the United States.* Princeton, NJ: Princeton University Press, 1992.

RECOMMENDED WEB SITES

Board of Governors of the Federal Reserve System
www.federalreserve.gov
The Federal Reserve System consists of twelve banks that utilize monetary policy to fight inflation and deflation. Visit the "Fed's" official Web site to see how it is working to maintain a strong economy.

Citizens for Tax Justice
www.ctj.org
Review federal, state, and local tax laws at the Web site of Citizens for Tax Justice. This nonprofit organization is dedicated to educating ordinary citizens about tax laws and reducing the tax burden on low- and middle-income Americans.

National Bureau of Economic Research
www.nber.org
The National Bureau of Economic Research (NBER) is a nonprofit, nonpartisan organization dedicated to creating a better understanding of the economy. Take a minute to review some of their free research publications.

Tax Foundation
www.taxfoundation.org/research/topic/9.html
The Tax Foundation is a respected organization that has been providing Americans with information about tax policy for over fifty years. Click on your state to learn about current tax and spending policies.

Treasury Direct
www.treasurydirect.gov/govt/govt.htm
Treasury Direct, part of the U.S. Department of the Treasury, provides a statistical look at federal, state, and public debt.

U.S. Census Bureau: The 2008 Statistical Abstract
www.census.gov/compendia/statab/brief.html
The Annual Statistical Abstract, provided by the U.S. Census Bureau, makes available an abundance of statistics on education, welfare, housing, employment, and agriculture.

U.S. Department of Commerce
www.commerce.gov
The U.S. Department of Commerce promotes domestic and international commerce to foster economic progress. Review the initiatives and programs designed to encourage economic development.

STUDY OUTLINE

www.wwnorton.com/wtp7e

The Goals of Economic Policy

1. Public policy is an officially expressed intention backed by a sanction, which can be a reward or a punishment.
2. At the most basic level, government makes it possible for markets to function efficiently by setting the rules for economic exchange and punishing those who violate the rules.

3. Government promotes stable markets by protecting the welfare and property of individuals, maintaining law and order, providing protection of private property, and regulating competition.
4. Government makes the market economy possible by providing public goods.
5. A strong and prosperous economy is the basic goal of all economic policy. But the key elements of a strong economy—economic growth, full employment, and low inflation—often appear to conflict with each other.
6. Government promotes business development indirectly through categorical grants and supports specific business sectors with direct subsidies, loans, and tax breaks.
7. From the 1930s to the 1980s, the government regulated industrial relations by overseeing union elections and collective bargaining between labor groups and management. But more recently, with the exception of the minimum wage, the government has significantly reduced its involvement in industrial relations.
8. The federal government plays an active role in protecting consumers from unsafe products.
9. There are different theories about whether, how much, and in what ways government should be involved in the economy.
10. Proponents of laissez-faire argue that the economy will flourish if the government leaves it alone.
11. Proponents of Keynesianism argue for an ongoing role for government in the economy by redistributing money and stimulating consumer demand.
12. Proponents of monetarism argue that the role of government in the economy should be limited to regulating the supply of money.
13. Proponents of supply-side economics argue that reducing the government's role in the economy, particularly through tax cuts, will promote investment and spur economic growth.

The Tools of Economic Policy

1. Monetary policies manipulate the growth of the entire economy by controlling the availability of money to banks through the Federal Reserve System.
2. Fiscal policies include the government's taxing and spending powers.
3. During the nineteenth century, the federal government received most of its revenue from a single tax, the tariff. Since then, the federal government has added new sources of tax revenue, the most important being the income tax and social insurance taxes. One of the most important features of the American income tax is that it is a progressive tax.
4. The federal government's power to spend is one of the most important tools of economic policy because spending decisions affect every aspect of the economy. These decisions, which are typically contentious, are made as part of the annual budget process involving the president and Congress.
5. The federal government can establish conditions that regulate the operation of big businesses to ensure fair competition and can force large monopolies to break up into smaller companies. In addition to economic regulation, the federal government can also impose conditions on businesses to protect workers, the environment, and consumers.
6. By the late 1970s, a reaction against regulation set in. Although the deregulation movement has resulted in a reduction in the amount of regulatory laws, few regulatory programs have actually been terminated.
7. Subsidies and contracting are the carrots of economic policy. Their purpose is to encourage people to do something they might not otherwise do or to get people to do more of what they are already doing.

The Environment and the Economy

1. During the 1970s, environmental policy emerged as a major component of federal action, with the passage of new laws reaching into many aspects of the economy. During this time Congress enacted the National Environmental Policy Act (which created the Environmental Protection Agency), the Clean Air Act, the Clean Water Act, and the Safe Drinking Water Act.
2. Concerns about climate change pose complex new challenges for economic policy. Policymakers are considering a variety of solutions including policies designed to reduce greenhouse gases, development of alternative technologies, and policies that promote adaptation to a changed climate.

The Politics of Economic Policy Making

1. Since the Great Depression of the 1930s, the public has held the government responsible for maintaining a healthy economy.
2. Politicians disagree about what the priorities of economic policy should be. Both Democrats and Republicans want to promote economic growth, but Republicans stress the importance of maintaining economic freedom whereas Democrats are more willing to support economic regulation to attain social or environmental objectives.
3. Consumer groups, environmentalists, businesses, and labor all attempt to shape economic policy, though business groups are the most consistently influential today.
4. Historically, Americans have been more concerned about ensuring economic liberty than with promoting economic equality, although debates about the appropriate balance between the two are an ongoing feature of economic policy in the United States.

PRACTICE QUIZ

www.wwnorton.com/wtp7e

1. The argument for laissez-faire was first elaborated by
   a) James Madison.
   b) Adam Smith.
   c) Alan Greenspan.
   d) Milton Friedman.
2. Which of the following economic perspectives argues for an ongoing role for government in the economy?
   a) laissez-faire
   b) Keynesianism
   c) monetarism
   d) rational expectations
3. The theories of which economist were used to help justify the increase in government spending during the New Deal?
   a) John Maynard Keynes
   b) Milton Friedman
   c) Robert Lucas
   d) Alan Greenspan
4. Monetary policy is handled largely by
   a) Congress.
   b) the president.
   c) the Department of the Treasury.
   d) the Federal Reserve System.
5. Monetary policy seeks to influence the economy through
   a) taxing and spending.
   b) the availability of credit and money.
   c) foreign exchange of currency.
   d) administrative regulation.
6. A situation in which the government attempts to affect the economy through taxing and spending is an example of
   a) an expropriation policy.
   b) a monetary policy.
   c) a fiscal policy.
   d) eminent domain.
7. A tax that places a greater burden on those who are better able to afford it is called
   a) regressive.
   b) progressive.
   c) a flat tax.
   d) voodoo economics.
8. Which groups currently have the most political influence in economic policy making?
   a) consumer groups
   b) labor unions
   c) business groups
   d) environmental groups
9. Which of the following is *not* a reason that government forms and changes regulatory policies?
   a) public opinion
   b) politics
   c) morality
   d) budget surplus
10. Which of the following is *not* one of the reasons that government is involved in the economy?
    a) to guarantee economic equality
    b) to protect property
    c) to regulate competition
    d) to provide public goods

KEY TERMS

www.wwnorton.com/wtp7e

antitrust policy (p. 654)
budget deficit (p. 651)
categorical grants (p. 640)
contracting power (p. 658)
deregulation (p. 657)
discretionary spending (p. 653)
federal funds rate (p. 647)
Federal Reserve System (p. 646)
fiscal policy (p. 648)
Gross Domestic Product (GDP) (p. 635)
inflation (p. 638)
Keynesians (p. 644)
laissez-faire capitalism (p. 643)
loophole (p. 650)
mandatory spending (p. 653)
monetarists (p. 644)
monetary policy (p. 645)
monopoly (p. 654)
open-market operations (p. 647)
progressive taxation (p. 649)
public good (p. 635)
public policy (p. 633)
redistribution (p. 650)
regressive taxation (p. 649)
reserve requirement (p. 646)
subsidy (p. 657)
supply-side economics (p. 644)
tariff (p. 648)
uncontrollable (p. 653)

17 Social Policy

- ★ The Welfare State
- ★ Opening Opportunity
- ★ Who Gets What from Social Policy?
- ★ Thinking Critically about Social Policy and Equality

WHAT GOVERNMENT DOES AND WHY IT MATTERS

Social policies promote a range of public goals. The first is to protect against the risks and insecurities that most people face over the course of their lives. These include illness, disability, temporary unemployment, and the reduced earning capability that comes with old age. Most spending on social welfare in the United States goes to programs, such as Social Security and medical insurance for the elderly, that serve these purposes. These programs are widely regarded as successful and popular. Although large projected deficits in both programs have generated conflict about these policies, they are the least controversial areas of social spending.

Comprehensive health-care reform is more controversial. Most Americans support universal access to health care, but when it comes to specific proposals, they often express doubts. Fear that reform will be too costly and will jeopardize current health-care arrangements makes it difficult to devise a plan that can survive the political process. Nonetheless, politicians continue to put comprehensive health-care reform on the national agenda, hoping that widespread concern about access to medical care will eventually lead to success.

Two other goals of social policy have also been controversial: promoting equality of opportunity and assisting the poor. Although Americans admire the ideal of equal opportunity, there is no general agreement about what government should do to address inequalities of results: groups that have suffered from past inequality generally support much more extensive government action to promote equality of opportunity than do others. Yet most Americans support some government action, especially in the area of education.

The third goal of social policy—to alleviate poverty—has long generated controversy in the United States. Americans take pride in their strong work ethic and prize the value of self-sufficiency. As a result, the majority of Americans express suspicions that the able-bodied poor will not try hard enough to support themselves if they are offered too much assistance or if they receive the wrong kind of assistance. Yet Americans also recognize that poverty may be the product of past inequality of opportunity. Since the 1960s, a variety of educational programs and income-assistance policies have sought to end poverty and promote equal opportunity. Much progress has been made toward these goals. However, the disproportionate rates of poverty among minorities suggest that our policies have not solved the problem of unequal opportunity. Likewise, the high rates of child poverty challenge us to find new ways to assist the poor.

American social policy reflects the nation's views about which risks should be borne by the individual and which should be shared by society as a whole. As such, social policy reflects public wishes, as would be expected in a democracy. However, Americans often have quite different views about whether social policy should advance the value of equality. There is a broad consensus that equality of opportunity is not only desirable but also an essential part of American culture. There is much less agreement about which social policies are needed to promote equality of opportunity. Americans also have different views about how social policy affects liberty. Some argue that it entails no significant curtailment of liberty, whereas others believe that social policy reduces liberty by increasing the size of government and by raising taxes.

Americans judge social policy issues in relation to deeply held convictions including their views about what is fair and what is not fair, what the appropriate role of government should be, and what is the individual's responsibility and what is a social responsibility. Even so, public views about social policy shift as the economy creates new needs. For example, Americans looked to the federal government to provide economic security for the first time when faced with the massive unemployment of the Great Depression of the 1930s. Today, the increasing number of working Americans who are poor or near poor and who lack health insurance has boosted support for programs that help working people. Changes in families and gender roles can also transform views about the appropriate social role of government. For example, the growing number of working women since the 1970s led to the creation of tax and subsidy programs to help pay for child care. Thus, the debate about social policy is constantly shifting as new economic and social challenges cause Americans to reconsider which social policies support their values.

- **The first section of this chapter will deal with policies concerned with economic insecurity.** We will also look at how the "welfare state" is financed.
- **The second section looks at policies aimed at permanently changing the status of America's poorest citizens.** Through education, job training, housing assistance, and health care, governments in America promote equality of opportunity.
- **The third section analyzes who benefits from social policies.** In this section, we also assess how effectively welfare policies help the poor.
- **Last, we will consider how the welfare state in America reflects (or does not reflect) the values of liberty, equality, and democracy.** Citizens have an opportunity to influence the debate over social policies, although most Americans tend to take a pragmatic perspective that strikes a balance among these core political ideals.

The Welfare State

For much of American history, local governments and private charities were in charge of caring for the poor. During the 1930s, when this largely private system of charity collapsed in the face of widespread economic destitution, the federal government created the beginnings of an American welfare state. The idea of the welfare state was new; it meant that the national government would oversee programs designed to promote economic security for all Americans—not just for the poor. The American system of social welfare comprises many different policies enacted over the years since the Great Depression. Because each program is governed by distinct rules, the kind and level of assistance available varies widely.

The History of the Social Welfare System

America has always had a welfare system, but until 1935, it was almost entirely private, composed of an extensive system of voluntary donations through churches and other religious groups, ethnic and fraternal societies, communities and neighborhoods, and philanthropically inclined wealthy individuals. Most often it was called "charity," and although it was private and voluntary, it was thought of as a public obligation.

There were great variations in the generosity of charity from town to town, but one thing seems to have been universal: the tradition of distinguishing between two classes of poverty—the "deserving poor" and the "undeserving poor." The deserving poor were the widows and orphans and others rendered dependent by some misfortune, such as the death or serious injury of the family's breadwinner in the course of honest labor. The undeserving poor were able-bodied persons unwilling to work, transients new to the community, and others of whom, for various reasons, the community did not approve. This private charity was a very subjective matter: the givers and their agents spent a great deal of time and resources examining the qualifications, both economic and moral, of the seekers of charity.

Before the Great Depression, much of the private charity was given in cash, called "outdoor relief." But because of fears that outdoor relief spawned poverty rather than relieving or preventing it, many communities set up settlement houses and other "indoor relief" institutions. Some of America's most dedicated and unselfish citizens worked in the settlement houses, and their efforts made a significant contribution to the development of the field of social work.

A still larger institution of indoor relief was the police station, where many of America's poor sought temporary shelter. But even in the severest weather, the homeless could not stay in police stations for many nights without being jailed as vagrants.[1] Indeed, the settlement houses and the police departments were not all that different in their approaches, since social workers in those days tended to consider "all social case work [to be] mental hygiene."[2] And even though not all social workers were budding psychiatrists, "it was true that they focused on counseling and other preventive techniques, obscuring and even ignoring larger structural problems."[3]

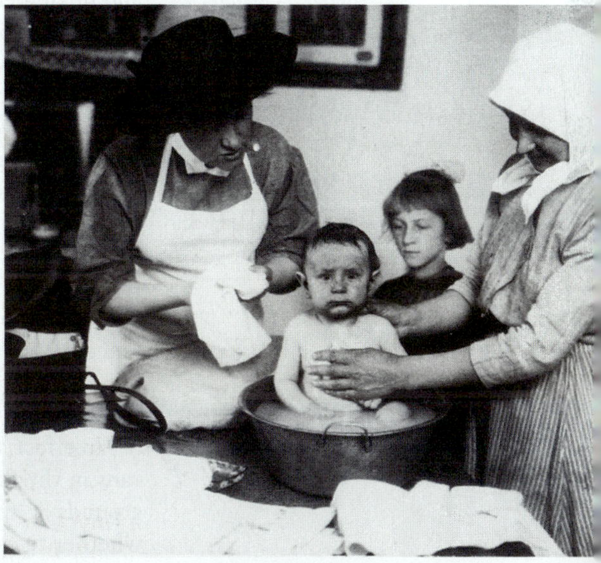

The creation of the modern welfare state in the 1930s shifted responsibility for alleviating poverty from private charities, such as settlement houses, to the government. Chicago's Hull House was one of the most famous settlement houses in the early twentieth century. There, social workers instructed the poor in methods of hygiene and child rearing.

In the early days of the Depression, much of the assistance for the destitute was provided by private groups, through projects such as New York City soup kitchens. Just a few years later, the government became responsible for providing food to needy families.

The severe limitations on financing faced by private charitable organizations and settlement houses slowly produced a movement by many groups toward public assumption of some of these charitable or welfare functions. Workers' compensation laws were enacted in a few states, for example, but the effect of such laws was limited because they benefited only workers injured on the job, and of them, only those who worked for certain types of companies. A more important effort, one that led more directly to the modern welfare state, was public aid to mothers with dependent children. Beginning in Illinois in 1911, the movement for mothers' pensions spread to include forty states by 1926. Initially, such aid was viewed as simply an inexpensive alternative to providing "indoor relief" to mothers and their children. Moreover, applicants not only had to pass a rigorous means test but also had to prove that they were deserving, because the laws provided that assistance would be given only to individuals who were deemed "physically, mentally, and morally fit." In most states, a mother was deemed unfit if her children were illegitimate.[4]

In effect, these criteria proved to be racially discriminatory. Many African Americans in the South and ethnic immigrants in the North were denied benefits on the grounds of "moral unfitness." Furthermore, local governments were allowed to decide whether to establish such pension programs. In the South, many counties with large numbers of African American women refused to implement assistance programs.

Despite the spread of state government programs to assume some of the obligation to relieve the poor, the private sector remained dominant until the 1930s. Even as late as 1928, only 11.6 percent of all relief granted in fifteen of the largest cities came from public funds.[5] Nevertheless, the various state and local public experiences provided guidance and precedents for the national government's welfare system, once it was developed.

The traditional approach, dominated by the private sector with its severe distinction between deserving and undeserving poor, crumbled in 1929 before the stark reality of the Great Depression. During the depression, misfortune became so widespread and private wealth shrank so drastically that private charity was out of the question, and the distinction between deserving and undeserving became impossible to draw. Around 20 percent of the workforce immediately became unemployed; this figure grew as the depression stretched into years. Moreover, few of these individuals had any monetary resources or any family farm on which to fall back. Banks failed, wiping out the savings of millions who had been fortunate enough to have any savings at all. Thousands of businesses failed as well, throwing middle-class Americans onto the bread lines along with unemployed laborers, dispossessed farmers, and those who had never worked in any capacity whatever. The Great Depression proved to Americans that poverty could be a result of imperfections in the economic system as well as of individual irresponsibility. It also forced Americans to alter drastically their standards regarding who was deserving and who was not.

Once poverty and dependency were accepted as problems inherent in the economic system, a large-scale public-policy approach was not far away. By the time the Roosevelt administration took office in 1933, the question was not whether there was to be a public welfare system, but how generous or restrictive that system would be.

Foundations of the Welfare State

If the welfare state were truly a state, its founding would be the Social Security Act of 1935. This act created two separate categories of welfare: contributory and noncontributory. Table 17.1 lists the key programs in each of these categories, with the year of their enactment, the most recent figures on the number of Americans they benefit, and their cost to the federal government.

CONTRIBUTORY PROGRAMS The category of welfare programs that are financed by taxation can justifiably be called "forced savings"; these programs force working Americans to set aside a portion of their current earnings to provide income and benefits during their retirement years. These **contributory programs** are what most people have in mind when they refer to **Social Security** or social insurance. Under the original contributory program, old-age insurance, the employer and the employee were each required to pay equal amounts, which in 1937 were set at 1 percent of the first $3,000 of wages, to be deducted from the paycheck of each employee and matched by the same amount from the employer. This percentage has increased over the years; the contribution in 2008 was 7.65 percent subdivided as follows: 6.2 percent on the first $102,000 of income for Social Security benefits, plus 1.45 percent on all earnings for Medicare.[6]

contributory programs social programs financed in whole or in part by taxation or other mandatory contributions by their present or future recipients

Social Security a contributory welfare program into which working Americans contribute a percentage of their wages, and from which they receive cash benefits after retirement

Social Security may seem to be a rather conservative approach to welfare. In effect, the Social Security tax, as a forced saving, sends a message that people cannot be trusted to save voluntarily to take care of their own needs. But in another sense, it is quite radical. Social Security is not real insurance; workers' contributions do not accumulate in a personal account, as they would in an annuity. Consequently, contributors do not receive benefits in proportion to their own contributions, and this means that a redistribution of wealth is occurring. In brief, Social Security mildly redistributes wealth from higher- to lower-income people, and it quite significantly redistributes wealth from younger workers to older retirees.

TABLE 17.1 ★ Public Welfare Programs

The biggest public welfare programs are the insurance or contributory programs, including old age insurance (what we commonly call Social Security), Medicare (health care for seniors), and unemployment insurance. The noncontributory programs of the public assistance system are generally smaller and less expensive. Which group does the government spend more money on—the elderly or poor families with children?

TYPE OF PROGRAM	YEAR ENACTED	NUMBER OF RECIPIENTS IN 2005 (IN MILLIONS)	FEDERAL AND STATE OUTLAYS IN 2005 (IN BILLIONS)
Contributory (Insurance) System			
Old-Age, Survivors, and Disability Insurance	1935	48.4	$520.6
Medicare	1965	42.4	$336.9
Unemployment Compensation	1935	5.8	$32.3
Noncontributory (Public Assistance) System			
Medicaid	1965	55.1	$257.7
Food Stamps	1964	25.7	$28.5
Supplemental Security Income (cash assistance for aged, blind, disabled)	1974	7.1	$37.2
Housing Assistance to Low-Income Families	1937	4.5*	$31.8
School Lunch Program	1946	29.6	$7.4
Temporary Assistance to Needy Families	1996	4.5	$25.4
State Children's Health Insurance Policy†	1997	6.6	7.0

*Number of units, Section 8 Housing and low-cost public housing; 2002 data.
†2006 data.
SOURCE: U.S. Census Bureau, www.census.gov/compendia/statab/2008edition.html (accessed 5/15/08).

Medicare a form of national health insurance for the elderly and the disabled

indexing periodic process of adjusting social benefits or wages to account for increases in the cost of living

cost-of-living adjustment (COLA) a change made to the level of benefits of a government program based on the rate of inflation

Congress increased Social Security benefits every two or three years during the 1950s and 1960s. The biggest single expansion in contributory programs since 1935 was the establishment in 1965 of **Medicare,** which provides substantial medical services to elderly persons who are already eligible to receive old-age, survivors', and disability insurance under the original Social Security system. In 1972, Congress decided to end the grind of biennial legislation to increase benefits by establishing **indexing,** whereby benefits paid out under contributory programs would be modified annually by **cost-of-living adjustments (COLAs)** designed to increase benefits to keep up with the rate of inflation. But, of course, Social Security taxes (contributions) also increased after almost every benefit increase. This made Social Security, in the words of one observer, "a politically ideal program. It bridged partisan conflict by providing liberal benefits under conservative financial auspices."[7] In other words, conservatives could more readily yield to the demands of the well-organized and ever-growing constituency of elderly voters if benefit

After 1935, the federal government created new programs to help poor families. For example, the federally funded school lunch program provides nutritious meals for needy children.

increases were automatic; liberals could cement conservative support by agreeing to finance the increased benefits through increases in the regressive Social Security tax rather than out of the general revenues coming from the more progressive income tax. (See Chapter 16 for a discussion of regressive and progressive taxes.)

NONCONTRIBUTORY PROGRAMS Programs to which beneficiaries do not have to contribute—**noncontributory programs**—are also known as "public assistance programs," or, derisively, as "welfare." Until 1996, the most important noncontributory program was Aid to Families with Dependent Children (AFDC)—originally called Aid to Dependent Children, or ADC—which was founded in 1935 by the original Social Security Act. In 1996, Congress abolished AFDC and replaced it with the Temporary Assistance to Needy Families (TANF) block grant. Eligibility for public assistance is determined by **means testing,** a procedure that requires applicants to show a financial need for assistance. Between 1935 and 1965, the government created programs to provide housing assistance, school lunches, and food stamps to other needy Americans.

noncontributory programs social programs that provide assistance to people on the basis of demonstrated need rather than any contribution they have made

means testing a procedure by which potential beneficiaries of a public-assistance program establish their eligibility by demonstrating a genuine need for the assistance

Medicaid a federally and state-financed, state-operated program providing medical services to low-income people

Like contributory programs, the noncontributory public assistance programs also made their most significant advances during the 1960s and 1970s. The largest single category of expansion was the establishment in 1965 of **Medicaid,** a program that provides extended medical services to all low-income persons who have already established eligibility through means testing under AFDC or TANF. Noncontributory programs underwent another major transformation during the 1970s in the level of benefits they provide. Besides being means tested, noncontributory programs are federal rather than national; grants-in-aid are provided by the national government to the states as incentives to establish the programs (see Chapter 3). Thus, from the beginning there were considerable disparities in benefits from state to state. The national government sought to rectify the disparities in levels of old-age benefits in 1974 by creating the Supplemental

FIGURE 17.1 ★
Monthly Spending on TANF Benefits

Spending on TANF benefits varies widely across the country. In thirteen states, monthly benefits for a family of three are below $300; in fourteen states, they are above $500 a month. In which regions does spending on TANF benefits tend to be higher? In which regions is it generally lower?

SOURCE: National Center for Children in Poverty, www.nccp.org/tools/policy, based on data from The Urban Institute, www.acf.hhs.gov/programs/opre/welfare_employ/state_tanf/reports/wel_rules05/databook_2005.pdf (accessed 4/9/08).

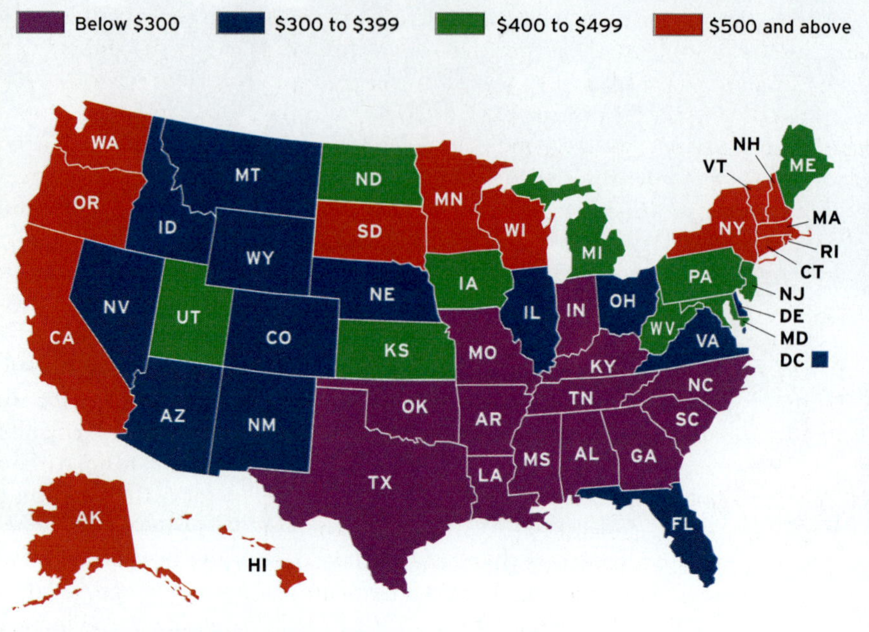

Security Income (SSI) program to augment benefits for the aged, the blind, and the disabled. SSI provides uniform minimum benefits across the entire nation and includes mandatory COLAs. States are allowed to be more generous if they wish, but no state is permitted to provide benefits below the minimum level set by the national government. As a result, twenty-five states increased their own SSI benefits to the mandated level.

The TANF program is also administered by the states and, as with the old-age benefits just discussed, benefit levels vary widely from state to state (see Figure 17.1). For example, in 2003, the states' monthly TANF benefits for a family of three varied from $170 in Mississippi to $923 in Alaska.[8] Even the most generous TANF payments are well below the federal poverty line. In 2007, the poverty level for a family of three included those earning less than $17,170 a year or $1,430 a month.[9]

The number of people receiving AFDC benefits expanded in the 1970s, in part because new welfare programs had been established during the mid-1960s: Medicaid (discussed earlier) and **food stamps,** which were formerly coupons that could be exchanged for food at most grocery stores and now come in the form of a debit card. These programs provide what are called **in-kind benefits**—noncash goods and services that would otherwise have to be paid for in cash by the beneficiary. Because AFDC recipients automatically received Medicaid and food stamps, these new programs created an incentive for poor Americans to establish their eligibility for AFDC.

food stamps a debit card that can be used for food at most grocery stores; the largest in-kind benefits program

in-kind benefits noncash goods and services provided to needy individuals and families by the federal government

Another, more complex reason for the growth of AFDC in the 1970s was that it became more difficult for the government to terminate people's AFDC benefits for lack of eligibility. In the 1970 case of *Goldberg v. Kelly*, the Supreme

Court held that the financial benefits of AFDC could not be revoked without due process—that is, a hearing at which evidence is presented, and so on.[10] This ruling inaugurated the concept of the **entitlement,** a class of government benefits with a status similar to that of property (which, according to the Fourteenth Amendment, cannot be taken from people "without due process of law"). *Goldberg v. Kelly* did not provide that the beneficiary had a "right" to government benefits; it provided that once a person's eligibility for AFDC was established, and as long as the program was still in effect, that person could not be denied benefits without due process. The decision left open the possibility that Congress could terminate the program and its benefits by passing a piece of legislation. If the welfare benefit were truly a property right, Congress would have no authority to deny it by a mere majority vote.

entitlement a legal obligation of the federal government to provide payments to individuals, or groups of individuals according to eligibility criteria or benefit rules

Thus the establishment of in-kind benefit programs and the legal obstacles involved in terminating benefits contributed to the growth of the welfare state. But it is important to note that real federal spending on AFDC itself did not rise after the mid-1970s. Unlike Social Security, AFDC was not indexed to inflation; without cost of living adjustments, the value of AFDC benefits fell by more than one-third. Moreover, the largest noncontributory welfare program, Medicaid (as shown by Table 17.1), actually devotes less than one-third of its expenditures to poor families; the rest goes to the disabled and the elderly in nursing homes.[11] Together, these programs have significantly increased the security of the poor and the vulnerable and must be included in a genuine assessment of the redistributive influence and the cost of the welfare state today.

Welfare Reform

The unpopularity of welfare led to widespread calls for reform as early as the 1960s. Public-opinion polls consistently showed that Americans disliked welfare more than any other government program. Although a series of modest reforms were implemented starting in the late 1960s, it took thirty years for Congress to enact a major transformation in the program. Why did welfare become so unpopular, and why was it so hard to reform? How has the 1996 law that replaced AFDC with TANF changed welfare?

From the 1960s to the 1990s, opinion polls consistently showed that the public viewed welfare beneficiaries as "undeserving."[12] Underlying that judgment was the belief that welfare recipients did not want to work. The Progressive-era reformers who first designed AFDC wanted single mothers to stay at home with their children. Motivated by horror stories of children killed in accidents while their mothers were off working or of children tied up at home all day in order to keep them safe, these reformers believed that it was better for the child if the mother did not work. By the 1960s, as more women entered the labor force and as welfare rolls rose, welfare recipients appeared in a more unfavorable light. Common criticisms charged that welfare recipients were taking advantage of the system, that they were irresponsible people who refused to work. These negative assessments were amplified by racial stereotypes. By 1973, 46 percent of welfare recipients were African American. Although the majority of recipients were white, media portrayals helped to create the widespread perception that the vast majority of welfare recipients were black. A careful study by Martin Gilens has shown how racial stereotypes of blacks as uncommitted to the work ethic reinforced public opposition to welfare.[13]

Despite public opposition, it proved difficult to reform welfare. Congress added modest work requirements in 1967 but little changed in the administration of welfare. A more significant reform in 1988 imposed stricter work requirements but also provided additional support services, such as child care and transportation assistance. This compromise legislation reflected a growing consensus that effective reform entailed a combination of sticks (work requirements) and carrots (extra services to make work possible). The 1988 reform also created a new system to identify the absent parent (usually the father) and enforce child-support payments.

These reforms were barely implemented when welfare rolls rose again with the recession of the early 1990s, reaching an all-time high in 1994. Sensing continuing public frustration with welfare, presidential candidate Bill Clinton vowed "to end welfare as we know it," an unusual promise for a Democrat. Once in office, Clinton found it difficult to design a plan that would provide an adequate safety net for recipients who were unable to find work. One possibility—to provide government jobs as a last resort—was rejected as too expensive. Clinton's major achievement in the welfare field was to increase the Earned Income Tax Credit. This credit allows working parents whose annual income falls below approximately $37,000 to file through their income tax return for an income supplement of up to $4,536, depending on their income and family size. It was a first step toward realizing Clinton's campaign promise to ensure that "if you work, you shouldn't be poor."

For Critical Analysis

Why was AFDC—commonly called "welfare"—such an unpopular program? How did welfare reform alter the way poor people are assisted? What direction should future reforms to the welfare law take?

Congressional Republicans proposed a much more dramatic reform of welfare, which Clinton, faced with re-election in 1996, signed. The Personal Responsibility and Work Opportunity Reconciliation Act (PRWORA) repealed AFDC. In place of the individual entitlement to assistance, the new law created block grants to the states and allowed states much more discretion in designing their cash-assistance programs to needy families. The new law also established time limits, restricting recipients to two years of assistance and creating a lifetime limit of five years. It imposed new work requirements on those receiving welfare, and it restricted most legal immigrants from receiving benefits. The aim of the new law was to reduce welfare caseloads, promote work, and reduce out-of-wedlock births. Notably, reducing poverty was not one of its stated objectives.

After this law was enacted, the number of families receiving assistance dropped by 60 percent nationwide (see Figure 17.2). The sharp decline in the number of recipients was widely hailed as a sign that the welfare reform was working. Indeed, former welfare recipients have been more successful at finding and keeping jobs than many critics of the law predicted. One important indicator of how welfare has changed is the proportion of funds it provides in cash assistance. Before the 1996 reform, assistance was provided largely in the form of a cash grant. By 2006, 65 percent of welfare funds were allocated for noncash assistance and 35 percent for cash assistance. This means that an increasing proportion of welfare funds is spent on such costs as assistance with transportation to work, temporary shelter, or one-time payments for emergencies so that people do not go on the welfare rolls. The orientation of assistance has shifted away from subsidizing people who are not in the labor force toward addressing temporary problems that low-income people face and providing assistance that facilitates work.[14] The law has been less successful in other respects: researchers have found no clear evidence that it has helped reduce out-of-wedlock births. And critics point out that most former welfare recipients are not paid enough to pull their families out of poverty. Moreover, many families eligible for food stamps and Medicaid stopped receiving these benefits when they left the welfare rolls. The law has helped reduce welfare caseloads, but it has done little to reduce poverty.[15]

FIGURE 17.2 ★
Welfare Caseload, 1982–2006

Welfare caseloads began to decline even before the 1996 reform. They have continued to plummet in the years since welfare reform. Welfare caseloads remained low even during the recession of the early 2000s. Does the decline in the welfare caseload show that the 1996 reform was successful?

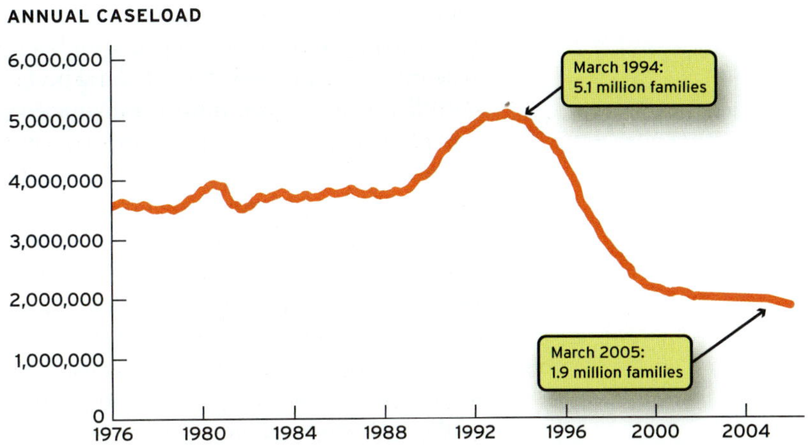

SOURCE: U.S. Department of Health and Human Services, www.acf.hhs.gov/programs/opre/welfare_employ/tanf_caseload/reports/tanf_caseload_comp/tanf_csld_ch3.html (accessed 3/25/08).

Since 1996, two different perspectives on TANF reform have emerged. Democrats have proposed changes that would make the welfare law "an antipoverty weapon."[16] They hope to increase spending on child care, allow more education and training, and relax time limits for those working and receiving welfare benefits. Republicans, by contrast, have proposed stricter work requirements and advocated programs designed to promote marriage among welfare recipients.[17] In his 2004 State of the Union address, President Bush proposed expanding the government role in promoting marriage. These disagreements about the direction of welfare prevented Congress from reauthorizing the TANF legislation until 2005. Changes introduced that year increased the work requirements for participants in the TANF program. Despite these differences, neither party has challenged the fundamental features—especially the work orientation—of the 1996 welfare reform.

How Do We Pay for the Welfare State?

Since the 1930s, when the main elements of the welfare state were first created, spending on social policy has grown dramatically. Most striking has been the growth of entitlement programs, the largest of which are Social Security and Medicare. The costs of entitlement programs grew from 26 percent of the total federal budget in 1962 to 53 percent by 2008. Funds to pay for these social programs have come disproportionately from increases in payroll taxes. In 1970, social insurance taxes accounted for 23 percent of all federal revenues; in 2008 they had grown to 36 percent of all federal revenues.[18] During the same time period, corporate taxes fell from 17 percent to 13 percent of all federal revenues. Because the payroll tax is regressive, low- and middle-income families have carried the burden for funding increased social spending.

Although much public attention has centered on welfare and other social spending programs for the poor, such as food stamps, these programs account for only a small proportion of social spending. For example, even at its height AFDC made up only 1 percent of the federal budget. In recent years, Congress has tightly controlled spending on most means-tested programs, and lawmakers and government officials currently express little concern that spending on such programs is out of control. The biggest spending increases have come in social insurance programs that provide broad-based benefits. Such expenditures are hard to control because these programs are entitlements, and the government has promised to cover all people who fit the category of beneficiary. So, for example, the burgeoning elderly population will require that spending on Social Security automatically increase in the future. Furthermore, because Social Security benefits are indexed to inflation, there is no easy way to reduce benefits. Spending on medical programs—Medicare and Medicaid—has also proven difficult to control, in part because of the growing numbers of people eligible for the programs but also because of rising health-care costs. Health-care expenditures have risen much more sharply than inflation in recent years (Figure 17.3).

Concern about social spending has centered on Social Security because the aging of the baby-boom generation will force spending up sharply in the coming

FIGURE 17.3 ★ Federal Social Spending, 1962–2013

Social Security and Medicare, the main entitlement programs that provide pensions and health insurance for people over sixty-five, have grown dramatically since 1962. The federal government spends far more on these two programs, which benefit all elderly people regardless of income, than it does on means-tested programs, which benefit the poor.

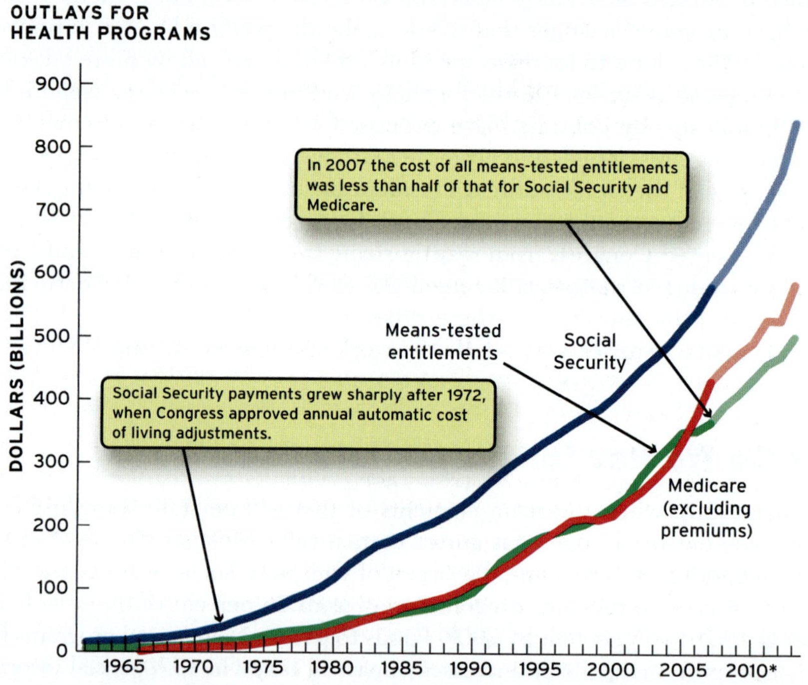

*2008–2013 are estimates.
SOURCE: Office of Management and Budget, www.gpoaccess.gov/usbudget/fy09/pdf/hist.pdf (accessed 5/15/08).

decades. Indeed, under current law, the Social Security Trust Fund—the special government account from which Social Security payments are made—is projected to experience a shortfall beginning in 2041. Critics also contend that Americans are not getting their money's worth from Social Security and that workers would be better off if they could take at least part of the payroll tax that currently pays for Social Security and invest it in individual accounts. They highlight unfavorable rates of return in the current system, noting for example, that a single male worker born in 2000 can expect to see a return of only 0.86 percent on his Social Security contributions. This is well below what an insured bank account would pay and far below stock market returns over the past decades.[19]

Former president George W. Bush came to office supporting Social Security reforms, including the creation of private retirement accounts. Soon after taking office, the president appointed a Social Security Commission whose final report prominently featured individual accounts as a reform strategy. The commission recommended three reform plans, each of which offered workers the choice of contributing a portion (ranging from 2 to 4 percent) of the payroll tax to an individual account. The worker's traditional benefits would be reduced by the amount diverted to the individual account. According to the commission, individual plans would create a better system because they would allow workers to accumulate assets and build wealth, wealth that could be passed on to their children.[20]

Because Social Security is such a popular program, proposed changes that might weaken it are generally greeted with suspicion. Given the politically volatile character of debates about Social Security, the president backed off from proposing any changes in the program during his first term. Nonetheless, in 2004, immediately after his reelection, Bush announced that he would make Social Security reform a centerpiece of his next administration. Although the president did not put forth a precise plan, private accounts were at the heart of his approach to reform. During the first half of 2005, the president toured the country attempting to win support for his ideas. But he immediately faced huge opposition as unions and the AARP mobilized to oppose him. The AARP launched a national advertising campaign against private accounts with slogans designed to highlight the risks and radical nature of the president's proposal: "If we feel like gambling, we'll play the slots," and "If you have a problem with the sink, you don't tear down the entire house." Senate Democrats, displaying unusual unity, closed ranks against the president's ideas. By October 2005, the president had to admit that Social Security reform was dead.

Supporters of the current Social Security system contend that the system's financial troubles are exaggerated. They dispute arguments that deficits require cuts in Social Security. They point out that Social Security taxes were raised in 1983 and its trust funds officially placed "off budget" so that the program would be prepared to serve the aging baby-boom generation.[21] They argue that instead of saving that money, however, the federal government cut taxes on the wealthy and used Social Security taxes to finance the deficit. Advocates of the current system believe that many of Social Security's troubles could be solved by raising income taxes on the wealthy and eliminating the cap on payroll taxes. In 2008, only the first $102,000 of income was subject to the payroll tax. If this cap were lifted, these critics argue, the resulting revenues would cut the expected shortfall in the Social Security Trust Fund in half.

Politics Today

Is Social Security a policy "in crisis"? What changes are policy makers discussing to alter Social Security so that future generations can have a secure retirement?

Recent reports have estimated that the Social Security system will be unable to pay full benefits by 2041. Former president Bush advocated creating private retirement accounts as a way of reforming Social Security. However, opponents of the president's plan successfully argued that private accounts were too risky and would not address the budget shortfall Social Security currently faces.

Immigration and American Society

In the 2008 election, immigration became one of the most controversial issues, arousing passionate debate on different sides of the issue. After efforts to reform immigration law failed in 2006, many states and localities enacted their own tough laws, punishing employers who hired undocumented workers and landlords who rented to them. The new laws reflected fears that immigration had gotten out of control and was harming America. Opponents of tougher laws argued that they unfairly punish law-abiding people who have been in the United States working and paying taxes, many of them for much of their lives. Moreover, they argue, the American economy depends on the work that undocumented immigrants do and the taxes they pay. These two poles in the immigration debate reflect starkly different views about the costs and contributions of the estimated 12 million undocumented immigrants currently living in the United States.

Those who advocate taking a tough stand on immigration emphasize the fundamental importance of securing the nation's borders in an era of unprecedented threat from terrorists. In order to reduce the number of illegal immigrants currently living in the United States and to discourage others from coming, illegal immigrants should be treated as the lawbreakers that they are, in this view. In 2006, Congress passed legislation that reflected this line of reasoning. The bill approved construction of a 700-mile fence along the Mexican border.

Proponents of getting tough on immigration also point to the problems that the large immigrant community poses for American society. Noting that the vast majority of illegal immigrants from Mexico and Central America are low-wage workers, they cite studies showing that immigrants depress the wages of low-skilled American workers.[a] They also highlight the financial burdens that immigrants place on state and local governments with their use of social services and schools. Finally, those who favor getting tough on immigration often express fears about the difficulty of assimilating such a large group of newcomers. At worst, they fear that the United States will become partitioned into areas dominated by Spanish-speaking immigrants whose culture is fundamentally different from that of the rest of Americans. The existence of such different social groups in one country will undermine American political culture and American democracy.

Pro-immigration advocates argue that it is impractical to seal off the Mexican border. Instead, the United States needs to find ways to regulate the entry of noncitizens to work in the United States. Proponents of this view contend that illegal immigrants do not harm native workers because they are doing jobs that Americans will not do. They point to studies showing that illegal immigrants have minimal impact on the wages of less-skilled American workers.[b] They also emphasize that many illegal workers pay income taxes and Social Security taxes, as well as sales taxes.

The central policy goal of immigrant advocates is to create a path to earned citizenship for undocumented immigrants living in the United States. Although proposals differ, most would require immigrants to demonstrate proficiency in English and pay a fine for having entered the country illegally. Such a path toward citizenship is essential to the health of American democracy, which suffers from having large communities of people who cannot vote and are fearful of public authorities.

There is much less agreement on the pro-immigrant side about how or whether the United States should regulate the entry of noncitizen workers. Some support a guest worker program, which would allow non-citizens to work temporarily in the United States. Others oppose creating a guest worker program, fearing that it could create a permanent subclass of workers in the United States.

FOR CRITICAL ANALYSIS

1. What are the arguments for significantly tightening border security? What do you think is the most effective way to secure the border?
2. What are the arguments in favor of a path toward earned citizenship for immigrants? Do you think that such a provision would help or hurt American society in the long run?

a. Kathleen Pender, "Labor's Complex Situation," *San Francisco Chronicle*, April 27, 2006, p. C1.
b. Pender, "Labor's Complex Situation."

Supporters of the current system are also deeply skeptical about the benefits of individual accounts. They charged that the president's commission presented a rosy scenario that overestimated likely gains through the stock market. When more realistic assumptions are adopted and the costs of the private accounts are considered, they argue, individual accounts do not provide higher benefits than the current system. Moreover, these critics note that individual accounts would do nothing to solve the budget crisis that Social Security will face.[22]

Finally, supporters of the present system emphasize that Social Security is not just a retirement account, it is a social insurance program that provides "income protection to workers and their families if the wage earner retires, becomes disabled or dies."[23] Because it provides this social insurance protection, supporters argue, Social Security's returns should not be compared with those of a private retirement account.

Opening Opportunity

The welfare state not only supplies a measure of economic security but also provides opportunity. The American belief in **equality of opportunity** makes such programs particularly important. Programs that provide opportunity keep people from falling into poverty, and they offer a hand up to those who are poor. At their best, opportunity policies allow all individuals to rise as high as their talents will take them. Four types of policies are most significant in opening opportunity: education policies, employment policies, health policies, and housing policies.

equality of opportunity a widely shared American ideal that all people should have the freedom to use whatever talents and wealth they have to reach their fullest potential

Education Policies

Those who understand American federalism from Chapter 3 already are aware that most of the education of the American people is provided by the public policies of state and local governments. What may be less obvious is that these education policies—especially the policy of universal compulsory public education—are the most important single force in the distribution and redistribution of opportunity in America.

For most of American history, the federal government has played only a minor role in education. In the early years of the nation, the federal government assisted schools through the Land Ordinance of 1785 and the Northwest Ordinance of 1787, both of which ensured that lands were set aside for public schools and their maintenance. In 1862 Congress established land-grant colleges with the Morrill Act. After World War II, the federal government stepped up its role in education policy with the enactment of the GI Bill of Rights of 1944, the National Defense Education Act (NDEA) of 1958, the Elementary and Secondary Education Act of 1965 (ESEA), and various youth and adult vocational training acts since 1958. Note, however, that since the GI Bill was aimed almost entirely at postsecondary schooling, the national government did not really enter the field of elementary education until after 1957.[24]

For Critical Analysis

What factors led to the expansion of governmental power (both state and national) over social policy? What factors might lead to a decrease of governmental activity in social policy? How do you think social policy in the United States will change in the future?

What finally brought the national government into elementary education was embarrassment that the Soviet Union had beaten the United States into space with the launching of *Sputnik*. The national policy under NDEA was aimed specifically at improving education in science and mathematics. General federal aid for education did not come until ESEA in 1965, which allocated funds to school districts with substantial numbers of children from families who were unemployed or earning less than $2,000 a year. By the early 1970s, federal expenditures for elementary and secondary education were running over $4 billion per year, and rose to a peak in 1980 at $4.8 billion.[25]

Politics Today

Why is the No Child Left Behind Act, initially passed with bipartisan support, so controversial today? Should the federal government be involved in setting standards for educational progress? Or is this a job better left to the states?

Ronald Reagan's administration signaled a new focus for federal education policy: the pursuit of higher standards. In 1983, the Department of Education issued *A Nation at Risk*, an influential report that identified low educational standards as the cause of America's declining international economic competitiveness. The report did not suggest any changes in federal policy but it urged states to make excellence in education their primary goal. This theme was picked up again by President George H. W. Bush. Because Republicans have historically opposed a strong federal role in education, the initiatives of Reagan and Bush remained primarily advisory. But they were very influential in focusing educational reform on standards and testing, now widely practiced across the states.

The federal role was substantially increased by President George W. Bush's signature education act, the No Child Left Behind Act of 2001. This act created stronger federal requirements for testing and school accountability. It requires that every child in grades 3 through 8 be tested yearly for proficiency in math and reading. For a school to be judged a success, it has to show positive test results for all subcategories of children—minority race and ethnicity, English learners, and disability—not just overall averages. Parents whose child is in a failing school have the right to transfer the child to a better school. Because of strong congressional opposition to creating a national test, the states were made responsible for setting standards and devising appropriate tests.

Education policy is the most important means of providing equal opportunity for all Americans. President George W. Bush's 2001 "No Child Left Behind" Act, an education reform bill passed by overwhelmingly bipartisan majorities in Congress, imposes stronger national requirements for school accountability and testing.

As we saw in Chapter 3, No Child Left Behind initially attracted broad bipartisan support, but it quickly generated considerable controversy. Many states branded it an unfunded mandate, noting that the law placed expensive new obligations on the schools to improve their performance but provided woefully inadequate resources. Teachers objected that "teaching to the test" undermined critical-thinking skills. In some states, up to half the schools failed to meet the new standards, presenting a costly remedial challenge. Under the federal law, they were required to improve student performance by providing such new services as supplemental tutoring, longer school days, and additional summer school. By 2004, some fiscally strapped states were beginning to rebel, refusing to implement No Child Left Behind. These conflicts meant that when No Child Left Behind came up for reauthorization in 2007, Congress was unable to reach agreement on a new bill. The current provisions of the act remained in effect. It will be up to a future Congress to work out the difficult compromises needed to reauthorize the legislation.

One of the hottest areas of controversy in education is school choice. For over 200 years, schools have been public institutions in the United States, and many name public schooling as the most important social policy in America. Today, however, there are serious challenges to the public monopoly on education. Some critics of public schools argue that government should simply provide parents with vouchers that they can use to send their children to the school of their choice, public or private. Supporters of vouchers claim that the public education system is too bureaucratic to provide quality education and does not allow parents enough control over their children's education. Voucher plans have so far been implemented on only a very small scale in a few places (Cleveland, Milwaukee, and Florida). In Cleveland, where most of the students using vouchers attend Catholic schools, opponents have charged that vouchers violate the constitutional separation between church and state. Uncertainty about the constitutionality of vouchers had put a damper on the movement supporting vouchers. In 2002, however, the Supreme Court ruled that the Cleveland program was constitutional because it allowed parents to exercise true choices about where their children went to school. Since that decision, a number of states have sought to introduce voucher programs, but only Colorado has adopted a statewide voucher program. In 2003, Congress approved a voucher program for the District of Columbia, the first federally funded voucher program.

Pressures to change the organization of schooling have led to the creation of charter schools across the country. Charter schools are publicly funded schools that are free from the bureaucratic rules and regulations of the school district in which they are located. Charter schools are free to design specialized curricula and to use resources in ways they think most effective. Since the creation of the first charter schools in Minnesota in 1990, states across the country have passed legislation to allow charter schools. The great popularity of such schools suggests that reforms allowing more flexibility and responsiveness to parents may well be possible within the existing public system.

Employment and Training Programs

Considering the importance that Americans attach to work and the high value they place on education, it is somewhat surprising that the United States does not have a strong system for employment and job training. Such programs have two goals. One is to prepare entry-level workers for new jobs or to retrain workers whose jobs have disappeared. A second goal is to provide public jobs during economic downturns when sufficient private employment is not available. Since the 1930s, the American employment and training systems have fared poorly in terms of expenditures, stability, and results.[26]

The first public employment programs were launched during the New Deal. These programs were created to use the power of the federal government to get people back to work again. An "alphabet soup" of federal programs sought to employ those who did not have jobs: the Civilian Conservation Corps (CCC) put young men to work on environmental projects in rural areas; and the Works Progress Administration (WPA) employed many different kinds of workers, from writers and artists to manual laborers. In the desperate circumstances of the Great Depression, these public employment programs enjoyed widespread support. But by the end of the 1930s, questions about corruption and inefficiency in employment programs reduced support for them.

Not until the 1960s did the federal government try again. This time, as part of the War on Poverty, government programs were designed to train and retrain workers, primarily the poor, rather than providing them with public employment. For the most part, the results of these programs were disappointing. It proved very difficult to design effective training policies in the federal system; lack of coordination

For Critical Analysis

How did the WPA assist unemployed workers during the Depression of the 1930s? What does the government do to assist workers who lose their jobs today? Do you think that, with increasing outsourcing of American jobs, the federal government should do more to help American workers?

and poor administration plagued the Great Society training programs. Concern about such administrative problems led Congress to combine funds for all the different training programs into a single block grant in 1973, via the Comprehensive Employment and Training Act (CETA). In doing this, Congress hoped that more local flexibility would create more effective programs.

CETA expanded greatly and, as unemployment rose sharply during the 1970s, became primarily a public-service employment program. The federal government provided state and local governments funds to create jobs for the unemployed. At its peak, CETA had a budget of more than $10 billion and provided jobs for nearly 739,000 workers—12 percent of the nation's unemployed. But complaints soon arose that CETA was providing jobs primarily to people who were the most job ready and was doing little for the most disadvantaged. This practice of selecting the best prepared as participants—called "creaming"—has been a persistent problem with other job-training programs as well. Critics also charged that localities were simply using CETA money to perform tasks they would have paid for out of their own funds if federal money had not been available. Congress abolished CETA in 1981, making it one of the only federal programs totally eliminated in the past thirty or so years.[27]

But job training remained a popular idea, and in 1982, Congress created a new program that supported local efforts: the Job Training Partnership Act (JTPA) became the primary federal program. In addition to retraining adult workers, JTPA provided funding for summer jobs for youth. President Clinton placed an especially high value on creating a strong system of job training. During the last years of the Clinton administration, the Workforce Investment Act sought to create a more flexible and accessible job-training system, allowing individual workers to select their own training programs. Replacing the maze of job programs inherited from the past are "one-stop centers" where workers can learn about a range of training possibilities, register for unemployment insurance, and find assistance with job placement. The act also created local "workforce investment boards" that allow employers a greater say in determining what kind of training is needed in particular areas. The aim of this provision was to make sure that job training programs fit the needs of the local labor market. The law also provides job training for at-risk youth and for the disabled. As the American economy changes and many corporations transfer operations out of the country or downsize their workforces, the need for retraining has become more pressing. Such training is particularly important for the three-quarters of American workers who have not finished four years of college. Enhancing the ability of the federal government to assist American workers, who face increasing economic insecurity, is one of the most important challenges confronting policy makers today.

Health Policies

Until recent decades, no government in the United States—national, state, or local—concerned itself directly with individual health. But public responsibility was always accepted for *public* health. After New York City's newly created Board of Health was credited with holding down a cholera epidemic in 1867, most states followed with the creation of statewide public health agencies. Within a decade, the results were obvious. Between 1884 and 1894, for example, Massachusetts's rate of infant mortality dropped from 161.3 per 1,000 to 141.4 per 1,000.[28] Reductions in mortality rates during the late nineteenth century may be the most significant contribution ever made by government to human welfare.

POLITICS & POPULAR CULTURE

Health Policy in Television and Film

For many Americans, issues surrounding health policy are complicated and may seem somewhat abstract until they affect friends, family, or themselves. While politicians and the news media can highlight important health policy issues, another less direct route of information and influence comes in the form of entertainment programming.

Primetime medical dramas like NBC's *ER* or Fox's *House, M.D.* often illustrate how health policy affects individual citizens' lives, without abstractions or statistics. Programs like *ER* and *House* portray individual characters struggling with issues like malpractice, whether or not to resuscitate a loved one, or how they are going to afford their medical treatment. The plots reveal the practical and emotional implications of these issues, and may make them more meaningful to the audience. Because of this potential influence on viewers, in some cases researchers have even worked with the writers and producers of medical dramas to make certain that the health information presented is accurate and helpful.

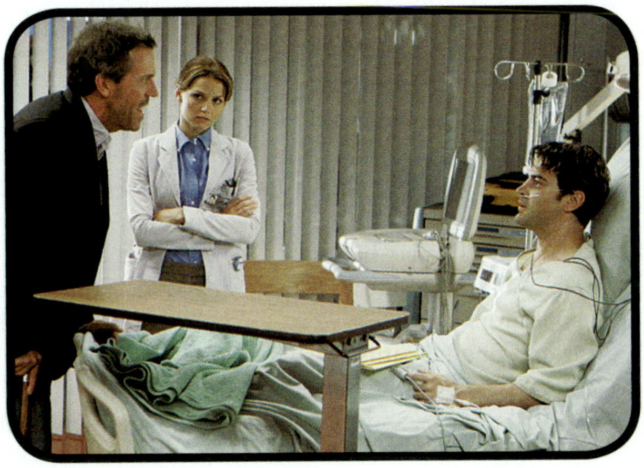

In addition, researchers are studying the content of medical dramas to determine how health policy debates are presented, who is engaged in the debates, and whether or not they are balanced. A report by the Kaiser Family Foundation from July 2002 concluded that the kinds of health policy debates presented in American medical dramas fell into two main categories: (1) resource issues like HMOs, Medicare, Medicaid, and disparities in insurance coverage, and (2) ethical issues such as patients' rights, end-of-life options, stem-cell research, and clinical drug trials. However, ethical issues, with their dramatic content, were far more likely to receive attention than were resource issues. Some issues such as the problems of long-term care or problems of the uninsured received little attention in these programs. Most policy debates presented in the programs were relevant to current legislative debates or other health policy discussions in the news. In general, the study found that medical shows present balanced portrayals of health policy debates, with both sides equally represented in the discussions.

The controversial filmmaker Michael Moore tackled health care in his 2007 film *Sicko*. Rather than attempting to balance both sides, Moore's message was very clear—the American system is deeply flawed and in desperate need of reform. *Sicko* relied on a series of vignettes to illustrate that the American health-care system fails to serve not only those without health insurance but also those who pay for it. Moore introduces, for example, a man who saws off two fingers but can only afford to have one of the fingers sewn back on. Another story follows a 9/11 volunteer who is denied the treatment he needs for a lung condition he developed while digging through the rubble of the World Trade Center.

There is some evidence to suggest that *Sicko* may have had a significant impact on the debate about health care in America. A survey by the Kaiser Family Foundation found that although only 4 percent of the public had seen *Sicko*, 42 percent had heard or read about it. More importantly, of those who had seen, heard about, or read about *Sicko*, 43 percent said the movie made them more likely to think that the health-care system in America needs reform and 27 percent said they were paying closer attention to the positions of presidential candidates on health care as a result of the film.[a]

FOR CRITICAL ANALYSIS

1. What are some of the drawbacks of getting information about complex health policies from entertainment television and movies? What are some possible advantages?
2. Most Americans believe that the government should ensure that all citizens receive adequate health care. What are some of the obstacles to implementing universal health care? What are some possible solutions?

a. Survey by Henry J. Kaiser Family Foundation, Princeton Survey Research Associates International, August 2–8, 2007. [USPSRA .082707HTP.R12]

The U.S. Public Health Service (USPHS) has been in existence since 1798 but was a small part of public health policy until after World War II. Established in 1937 but little noticed for twenty years was the National Institutes of Health (NIH), an agency within the USPHS that was created to do biomedical research. Between 1950 and 2007, NIH expenditures by the national government increased from $160 million to $28 billion. NIH research on the link between smoking and disease led to one of the most visible public-health campaigns in American history. The Centers for Disease Control and Prevention (CDC), which monitors outbreaks of disease and implements prevention measures, coordinates such public-health campaigns. Subsequently, NIH's focus turned to cancer and acquired immunodeficiency syndrome (AIDS). As with smoking, this work on AIDS resulted in massive public-health education as well as new products and regulations.

Other recent commitments to the improvement of public health are the numerous laws aimed at cleaning up and defending the environment (including the creation in 1970 of the Environmental Protection Agency) and laws attempting to improve the health and safety of consumer products (regulated by the Consumer Product Safety Commission, created in 1972). Health policies aimed directly at the poor include Medicaid and nutritional programs, particularly food stamps and the school lunch program.

In 2007, federal grants to states for Medicaid totaled $190.6 billion, up from $41 billion in 1990. Federal programs for AIDS research, treatment, prevention, and income support had a budget of $23.3 billion in 2008, a major increase from the $2.9 billion spent in 1990.[29] President Clinton put greater emphasis on AIDS by appointing an "AIDS czar" to coordinate federal AIDS policy, and by giving this position Cabinet status. Bush continued the practice, appointing his own AIDS czar. However, the position has been a difficult balancing act between advocates, health-care professionals, and the realities of government finances.

In 2007, Congress approved a bill to reauthorize and expand the State Children's Insurance Program, which helps cover health insurance costs for families with children. President Bush vetoed the bill but eventually approved extending the existing program through March 2009.

The United States is the only advanced industrial nation without universal access to health care. Opposition from the American Medical Association, the main lobbying organization of doctors, prevented President Roosevelt from proposing national health insurance during the 1930s, when other elements of the welfare state became law. As a result, the United States developed a patchwork system: approximately 80 percent of workers are offered health insurance through their jobs, older Americans are covered through Medicare, and the poor and disabled are assisted with Medicaid. This system has become frayed in recent decades. The growing costs of employer-provided insurance means that increasing numbers of workers cannot afford it. Many small employers cannot even afford to offer benefits because they are so expensive. And both Medicaid and Medicare face severe fiscal strain due to rising costs.

President Clinton's major attempt to reshape federal health policy, and the boldest policy initiative of his administration, was his effort to reform America's health-care system. In September 1993, Clinton announced a plan with two key objectives: to limit the rising costs of the American health-care system (1991 per capita health spending, $2,932, was 83 percent higher than in twenty-one other industrialized nations)[30] and to provide universal health insurance coverage for all Americans (more than 41 million Americans lacked health insurance). Clinton's plan at first garnered enormous public support and seemed likely to win congressional approval in some form. But the plan, which entailed a major expansion of federal administration of the health-care system, gradually lost momentum as resistance to it took root among those who feared changes in a system that worked well for them. Although Clinton had pledged to make health care the centerpiece of his 1994 legislative agenda, no health care bill even came up for a full congressional vote that year. Following the failure of President Clinton's health care initiative, Congress passed a much smaller program expanding health insurance coverage for low-income children not already receiving Medicaid, called the State Children's Health Insurance Program.

In 2003, Congress enacted a major reform of the Medicare program, which has provided health care to seniors since 1964. Most notably, Congress added a prescription drug benefit to the package of health benefits for the elderly. The high cost of prescription drugs had been an issue of growing concern to millions of older Americans. State and city governments, too, worried about rising drug costs, and some of them approved buying prescription drugs in Canada, where the national health insurance program made them available at lower prices.

Politics Today

Why does the United States have such a patchwork approach to health coverage? Is it possible to provide health-care benefits to everyone?

The Medicare reform bill passed under very unusual circumstances: House leaders held the floor open for three hours—instead of the usual 15 minutes—while they rounded up the necessary votes. The controversy over Medicare reform did not end with the bill's passage. Many Democrats argued that the complex provisions in the prescription benefit would actually reduce coverage for some seniors who already had private plans and would leave some income groups with little drug benefit coverage. Moreover, critics charged that the bill included a sweetheart deal with drug companies, because the legislation contained a provision prohibiting the federal government from using its purchasing power to reduce drug prices. Many Democrats also objected to the legislation because it opened the door for private health plans to play a significant role in health care provision for the elderly. They feared that the entry of such plans would significantly weaken Medicare, which has been one of the most strongly supported federal social programs. Fiscal conservatives worried about the costs of the prescription drug package. This

The American Health-Care System in Comparison

When compared with other advanced industrialized democracies, the United States is unique: it is the only one that does not provide universal access to health care. The American approach to health care is a patchwork of different programs. About 60 percent of Americans under the age of 65 receive health care from their employers who contract with private insurance companies to provide care. There is also a large federal role—accounting for half of all medical expenditures—composed of three different programs: Medicare, which provides health insurance for people over 65; Medicaid, which covers low-income people, the disabled, and elderly people who need long-term care; and the State Children's Health Insurance Plan (SCHIP), a federal-state program for uninsured children.

The trouble with the American approach is twofold: it leaves some people without coverage, and it is expensive. Not all employers provide health insurance for their workers, and not all workers opt to purchase the health plans that employers offer. The number of uninsured in 2007 was 45.7 million, or around 16 percent of the population. Moreover, the American system is the world's most expensive. The costs of health care in the United States have made it increasingly difficult for individuals to pay for care, even with employer help. And employers complain that the costs of providing health care are making them uncompetitive in world markets. Can we do better?

The health systems in Europe and Canada rely on two fundamentally different models to offer universal coverage at much lower cost than in the United States. The first model is the single-payer approach; the second is the compulsory insurance model.

In single-payer systems, the government plays the central role in collecting revenues to fund health care, and it pays for the care that is supplied. The fact that the government is the "single payer" allows it to bargain for the lowest prices from providers. The French system has been called the best in the world because of the broad coverage it provides at low costs, along with provisions that allow those who want to pay more for extra services to do so.[a]

The compulsory insurance model is used in Germany, the Netherlands, and Switzerland. In these countries, individuals make contributions to "sickness funds," which are public-private organizations that pay for and provide health care. Many of the funds are attached to work settings, similar to employer-provided health insurance in the United States. What is different in these systems is that the sickness funds are highly regulated by the government: funds are required to provide specific basic services and are not allowed to expel individuals if they lose their jobs. The funds that cover healthier people—who cost less—are required to subsidize the funds for the less healthy, which ensures that the costs of the sick are spread through out the system. All of these compulsory insurance systems have an emphasis on preventive care and ensuring access to primary care.

Since the 1930s, efforts to reform health care in the United States have been defeated by fears that "socialized medicine" would lead to poorer care. A common claim is that Americans have the best system in the world. Yet, today the United States pays more for health care—over $6,000 a year per capita, compared with $2,500 in low-cost Britain and approximately $3,000 in France, Canada, and Germany[b]—and does not appear to do better than countries that spend far less.

FOR CRITICAL ANALYSIS

1. What is a single-payer system of health care? How does it differ from that of the United States? What are some of the political obstacles to creating a single-payer system in the United States?
2. How do compulsory health-insurance systems work? Do you think this system could work in the United States? Why or why not?

a. Victor G. Rodwin, "The Health Care System under French National Health Insurance: Lessons for Health Reform in the United States," *American Journal of Public Health* 93, no. 1 (2003): 31–37.

b. Chris L. Peterson and Rachel Burton, "U.S. Health Care Spending: Comparison with Other OECD Countries," Congressional Research Service, September 17, 2007, http://assets.opencrs.com/rpts/RL34175_20070917.pdf (accessed 3/25/08).

concern escalated several months after the bill's passage, when the administration issued new, much higher cost estimates for the prescription drug benefit than the estimates presented when the bill was being debated. Adding fuel to the growing controversy over drug prices was the disclosure that the former Medicare administrator had prevented his chief actuary from releasing the higher cost estimates to Congress as it was considering the Medicare bill.

The conflict over Medicare reform highlights the problems surrounding health care more generally. A majority of Americans believe that government should ensure that all people receive adequate health care. Yet how to deliver such benefits and how to pay for them are extremely contentious issues. In the 2008 presidential campaign, once again, the old question captured political attention: why can't the richest country in the world provide access to health care for all its citizens?[31] In the past, liberals had sought to answer this question with proposals for top-to-bottom reform of the health-care system. In 2008, by contrast, they sought to provide universal coverage by patching the existing system of employer-provided benefits and public coverage offered through Medicaid, SCHIP, and Medicare. Drawing on a plan adopted in Massachusetts, most liberal plans required employers to provide health insurance or pay a premium. They also offered financial assistance to small businesses, which find it more difficult to pay for insurance. Some of these proposals also required uninsured individuals to purchase their own coverage. To make this more possible, the federal government would provide tax credits and allow people to enroll in a public plan similar to Medicare or any other private insurance. Conservatives rejected this approach as too much federal-government involvement in health care and too expensive. Instead, they proposed to extend health savings accounts, tax-shielded accounts that allow individuals to save for their health needs and spend when they require care. This approach, they argue, makes individuals more responsible for their own health care decisions, creating a more cost-effective system. Even if either of these approaches to reform is successful, health care policy will remain a work in progress: advances in medical technology and the longer lives of Americans ensure that the question of how to afford quality health care will remain on the public agenda.

Politics Today

Health-care reform was a hot issue in the 2008 presidential campaign. What steps have President Obama and Congress taken to address the challenge of providing affordable health care for all Americans?

Housing Policies

The United States has one of the highest rates of home ownership in the world, and the central thrust of federal housing policy has been to promote home ownership. The federal government has traditionally done much less to provide housing for low-income Americans who cannot afford to buy homes. Federal housing programs were first created in the 1930s depression period, when many Americans found themselves unable to afford housing.

Through public housing for low-income families, which originated in 1937 with the Wagner-Steagall National Housing Act, and subsidized private housing after 1950, the percentage of American families living in overcrowded conditions was reduced from 20 percent in 1940 to 9 percent in 1970. Federal policies made an even greater contribution to reducing "substandard" housing, defined by the U.S. Census Bureau as dilapidated houses without hot running water and without some other plumbing. In 1940, almost 50 percent of American households lived in substandard housing. By 1950, this had been reduced to 35 percent; by 1975, to 8 percent.[32] Despite these improvements in housing standards, federal housing policy until the 1970s was largely seen as a failure. Restricted to the poorest of the poor,

In 2008, as a growing number of Americans found they could not afford the mortgages on their homes, the government authorized measures to help people keep their homes. Critics of the government's response said that the measures did not do enough to help homeowners and were intended mainly to help big financial companies.

marked by racial segregation and inadequate spending, public housing contributed to the problems of the poor by isolating them from shopping, jobs, and urban amenities. Dilapidated high-rise housing projects stood as a symbol of the failed American policy of "warehousing the poor." By the 1980s, the orientation of housing policy had changed: most federal housing policy for low-income Americans came in the form of housing vouchers (called Section 8 vouchers) that provided recipients with support to rent in the private market. Although this program did not promote the same kind of isolation of the poor, it was often useless in very active housing markets where the vouchers provided too little money to cover rental costs.

The Clinton administration at first showed a strong ideological commitment to encouraging housing policies and combating homelessness. For instance, in 1994, the Department of Housing and Urban Development (HUD) launched a comprehensive plan to increase emergency shelter availability, access to transitional and rehabilitative services, and the amount of affordable permanent housing. Federal appropriations nearly doubled in 1995, to $1.7 billion. But especially after 1994, the Clinton administration began to retreat. HUD Secretary Henry Cisneros continually had to waive, virtually to the point of abandonment, a long-standing one-for-one HUD rule that provided that for every public housing unit destroyed, another would have to be built. The Bush administration placed less emphasis on housing policy. It proposed transforming the federal voucher program into a block grant to the states. The initiative, which never came to a vote in Congress, faced opposition from housing proponents who feared that it would greatly reduce assistance to low-income renters.

In 2007 and 2008, a home loan foreclosure crisis presented the government with a different kind of housing problem. During the housing boom of the early 2000s, many homeowners received loans that they later could not afford to repay. As a result, millions of homeowners were in danger of losing their homes as they defaulted on their mortgage payments. Moreover, the magnitude of bad debt harmed banks and threatened to destabilize the entire economy. The federal government responded with a plan that would postpone the rising interest rates that were the cause of the problem for some homeowners. Even so, many people lost their homes, and the broader economy felt the strain as the effects of the defaulted loans filtered through the economic system.

Who Gets What from Social Policy?

The two categories of social policy—contributory and noncontributory—generally serve different groups of people. We can understand much about the development of social policy by examining which constituencies benefit from different policies.

The strongest and most generous programs are those in which the beneficiaries are widely perceived as deserving of assistance and also are politically powerful. Because Americans prize work, constituencies that have "earned" their benefits in some way or those who cannot work because of a disability are usually seen as most deserving of government assistance. Politically powerful constituencies are those who vote as a group, lobby effectively, and mobilize to protect the programs from which they benefit.

When we study social policies from a group perspective, we can see that the elderly and the middle class receive the most benefits from the government's social policies and that children and the working poor receive the fewest. In addition, America's social policies do little to change the fact that minorities and women are more likely to be poor than white men.

The Elderly

The elderly are the beneficiaries of the two strongest and most generous social policies: old-age pensions (what we call Social Security) and Medicare (medical care for the elderly). As these programs have grown, they have provided most elderly Americans with economic security and have dramatically reduced the poverty rate among the elderly. In 1959, before very many people over the age of sixty-five received social insurance, the poverty rate for the elderly was 35 percent; by 2006, it had dropped to 9.4 percent.[33] Because of this progress, many people call Social Security the most effective antipoverty program in the United States.[34] This does not mean that the elderly are rich, however; in 2006, the median income of elderly households was $27,798, well below the national median income. The aim of these programs is to provide security and prevent poverty rather than to assist people once they have become poor. And they succeeded in preventing poverty among most of the aged.

One reason that Social Security and Medicare are politically strong is that the elderly are widely seen as a deserving population. They are not expected to work, because of their age. Moreover, both programs are contributory, and a work history is a requirement for receiving a Social Security pension. But these programs are also strong because they serve a constituency that has become quite powerful. The elderly are a very large group: in 2008, there were 37 million Americans over the age of sixty-five. Because Social Security and Medicare are not means tested, they are available to nearly all people over the age of sixty-five, whether they are poor or not. The size of this group is of great political importance because the elderly turn out to vote in higher numbers than the rest of the population.

In 1995, the Republican-led Congress proposed cuts in Medicare spending, prompting vigorous protests from senior citizens. Fearing negative political repercussions in the 1996 elections, Congressional Republicans retreated from their efforts to overhaul the Medicare system. In 2003, the support of senior groups like the AARP was critical to the passage of a new Medicare prescription drug plan.

In addition, the elderly have developed strong and sophisticated lobbying organizations that can influence policy making and mobilize elderly Americans to defend these programs against proposals to cut them. One important and influential organization that defends the interests of older people in Washington is the AARP. The initials stood for the American Association of Retired Persons, but in 1999, the organization changed its name to its initials only. This is because 44 percent of AARP members work full or part time. The AARP had over 35 million members in 2008, amounting to one-fifth of all voters. It also has a sophisticated lobbying organization in Washington, which employs twenty-eight lobbyists and a staff of 165 policy analysts.[35] (See Chapter 11 for more discussion of the AARP's lobbying efforts.) Although the AARP is the largest and the strongest organization of the elderly, other groups, such as the Alliance for Retired Americans, to which many retired union members belong, also lobby Congress on behalf of the elderly.

When Congress considers changes in programs that affect the elderly, these lobbying groups pay close attention. They mobilize their supporters and work with legislators to block changes they believe will hurt the elderly.[36] As we saw in Chapters 11 and 16, the power of this lobby was apparent in 2003, and in 2005, during the effort to reform Social Security. The AARP had long opposed any reform that allowed private health-care firms to provide Medicare benefits. But in 2003, it changed its position and supported the president's bill, which combined prescription drug benefits and an opening for private firms. The AARP's vocal support—including its television advertisements in favor of the bill—was widely credited with making the legislative victory possible. In 2005 the AARP switched sides and opposed the president's proposals to reform Social Security. AARP opposition was a key factor in the proposal's failure to attract political support.

The Middle Class

Americans don't usually think of the middle class as benefiting from social policies, but government action promotes the social welfare of the middle class in a variety of ways. First, medical care and pensions for the elderly help the middle class by relieving them of the burden of caring for elderly relatives. Before these programs existed, old people were more likely to live with and depend financially on their adult children. Many middle-class families whose parents and grandparents are in nursing homes rely on Medicaid to pay nursing-home bills.

In addition, the middle class benefits from what some analysts call the shadow welfare state.[37] These are the social benefits that private employers offer to their workers: medical insurance and pensions, for example. The federal government subsidizes such benefits by not taxing the payments that employers and employees make for health insurance and pensions. These **tax expenditures,** as they are called, are an important way the federal government helps ensure the social welfare of the middle class. (Such programs are called "tax expenditures" because the federal government helps finance them through the tax system rather than by direct spending.) Another key tax expenditure that helps the middle class is the tax exemption on mortgage interest payments: taxpayers can deduct the amount they have paid in interest on a mortgage from the income they report on their tax return. By not taxing these payments, the government makes home ownership less expensive.

tax expenditures government subsidies provided to employers and employees through tax deductions for amounts spent on health insurance and other benefits

People often don't think of these tax expenditures as part of social policy because they are not as visible as the programs that provide direct payments or services to beneficiaries. But tax expenditures represent a significant federal investment: they cost the national treasury some $945 billion a year and make it easier and less expensive for working Americans to obtain health care, save for retirement, and buy homes.[38] These programs are very popular with the middle class, and Congress rarely considers reducing them. On the few occasions when public officials have tried to limit these programs—with proposals to limit the amount of mortgage interest that can be deducted, for example—they have quickly retreated. These programs are simply too popular among Americans whose power comes from their numbers at the polling booth.

The Working Poor

People who are working but are poor or are just above the poverty line receive only limited assistance from government social programs. This is somewhat surprising, given that Americans value work so highly. But the working poor are typically employed in jobs that do not provide pensions or health care; often they are renters because they cannot afford to buy homes. This means they cannot benefit from the shadow welfare state that subsidizes the social benefits enjoyed by most middle-class Americans. At the same time, however, they cannot get assistance through programs such as Medicaid and TANF, which are largely restricted to the nonworking poor.

Two government programs do assist the working poor: the Earned Income Tax Credit (EITC) and food stamps. The EITC was implemented in 1976 to provide poor workers some relief from increases in the taxes that pay for Social Security. As it has expanded, the EITC has provided a modest wage supplement for the working poor, allowing them to catch up on utility bills or pay for children's clothing.

For Critical Analysis

The American welfare state is very generous to some groups and much less generous to others. How did these patterns of social welfare policy become established over time? In what way do these benefit patterns reflect American values?

Poor workers can also receive food stamps. These two programs help supplement the income of poor workers, but they offer only modest support. Because the wages of less-educated workers have declined significantly over the past fifteen years and minimum wages have not kept pace with inflation, the problems of the working poor remain acute.

Even though the working poor may be seen as deserving, they are not politically powerful because they are not organized. There is no equivalent to the AARP for the poor. Nonetheless, because work is highly valued in American society, politicians find it difficult to cut the few social programs that help the working poor. In 1995, efforts to cut the EITC were defeated by coalitions of Democrats and moderate Republicans, although Congress did place new restrictions on food stamps and also reduced the level of spending on this type of aid.

The Nonworking Poor

The only nonworking, able-bodied poor people who receive federal cash assistance are parents who are caring for children. The primary source of cash assistance for these families was AFDC and now is the state-run TANF program, but they also rely on food stamps and Medicaid. Able-bodied adults who are not caring for children are not eligible for federal assistance other than food stamps. Many states provide small amounts of cash assistance to such individuals through programs called "general assistance," but in the past decade, many states have abolished or greatly reduced their general assistance programs in an effort to encourage these adults to work. Thus, the primary reason the federal government provides any assistance to able-bodied adults is that they are caring for children. Although Americans don't like to subsidize adults who are not working, they do not want to harm children.

AFDC was the most unpopular social spending program ever undertaken by the federal government; as a result, spending on it declined after 1980. Under TANF, states receive a fixed amount of federal funds, whether the welfare rolls rise or fall. Because the numbers of people on welfare have declined so dramatically since 1994—by over 50 percent—states have had generous levels of federal resources for the remaining welfare recipients. Many states, however, have used the windfall of federal dollars to cut taxes and indirectly support programs that benefit the middle class, not the poor.[39] Welfare recipients have little political power to resist cuts in their benefits. During the late 1960s and early 1970s, the short-lived National Welfare Rights Organization sought to represent the interests of welfare recipients. But keeping the organization in operation proved difficult because its members and its constituents had few resources and were difficult to organize.[40] Because welfare recipients are widely viewed as undeserving, and because they are not politically organized, they have played little part in recent debates about welfare.

For Critical Analysis

Two factors that seem to influence a particular group's ability to get what it wants from social policy are: (1) the perception that the group is deserving; and (2) the political organization and power of the group. How has each of these factors affected social policy in recent years?

Minorities, Women, and Children

Minorities, women, and children are disproportionately poor. Much of this poverty is the result of disadvantages that stem from the position of these groups in the labor market. African Americans and Latinos tend to be economically less well off than the rest of the American population. In 2006, the poverty rate for African Americans was 24.3 percent, and for Latinos it was 20.6 percent. Both rates are more than double the poverty rate for non-Hispanic whites, which was 10.3

FIGURE 17.4 ★ Poverty Level in the United States, 1960–2006

Poverty among all Americans has declined markedly since 1960. However, the rate of progress has varied significantly across groups. Female headed households have made the slowest progress, although poverty rates for this group have dropped sharply since 1994. Which group has seen the greatest reduction in its poverty level since 1960?

SOURCE: U.S. Census Bureau, www.census.gov/prod/2007pubs/p60-233.pdf (accessed 3/26/08).

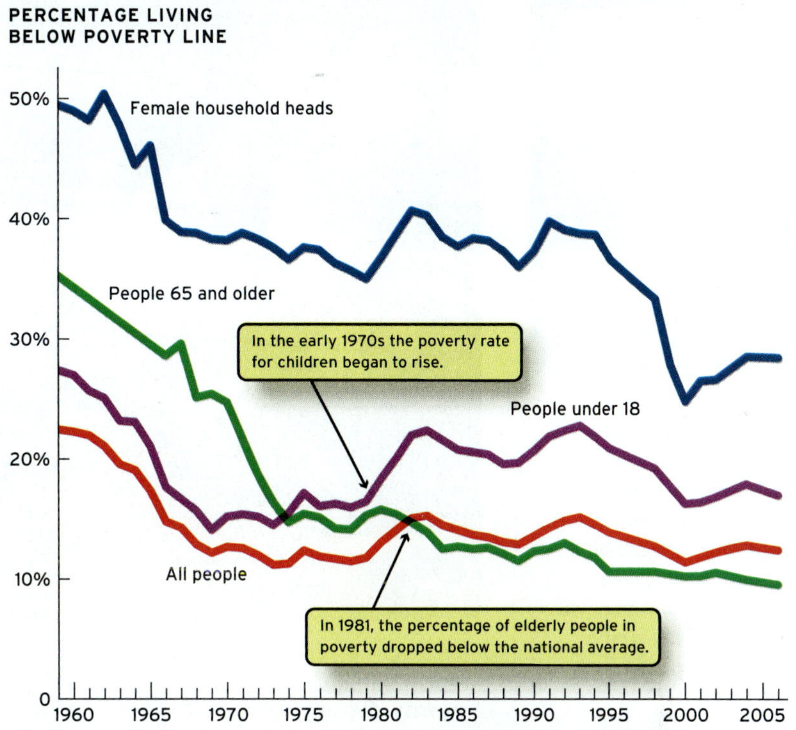

percent.[41] The median income for black households in 2006 was $31,969. For Hispanics it was $37,781, whereas for non-Hispanic white households the median household income was $52,423.[42] Much of this economic inequality occurs because minority workers tend to have low-wage jobs. Minorities are also more likely to become unemployed and to remain unemployed for longer periods of time than are white Americans. African Americans, for example, typically have experienced twice as much unemployment as other Americans have. The combination of low-wage jobs and unemployment often means that minorities are less likely to have jobs that give them access to the shadow welfare state. They are more likely to fall into the precarious categories of the working poor or the nonworking poor.

In the past several decades, policy analysts have begun to talk about the "feminization of poverty," or the fact that women are more likely than men to be poor. This problem is particularly acute for single mothers, who are more than twice as likely to fall below the poverty line than the average American (see Figure 17.4). When the Social Security Act was passed in 1935, the main programs for poor women were Aid to Dependent Children (ADC) and survivors' insurance for widows. The framers of the act believed that ADC would gradually disappear as more women became eligible for survivors' insurance. The social model behind the Social Security Act was that of a male breadwinner with a wife and children. Women were not expected to work, and if a woman's husband died, ADC or survivors' insurance would help her stay at home and raise her children. The framers of Social

The poor and working poor (including many single mothers with children) have little influence on government. Although organized protests representing the interests of the poor and working poor occasionally do occur, they fail to have the impact of similar protests by other groups, such as senior citizens.

Security did not envision today's large number of single women heading families. At the same time, they did not envision that so many women with children would also be working. This combination of changes helped make AFDC (the successor program to ADC) more controversial. Many people asked, Why shouldn't welfare recipients work, if the majority of women who are not on welfare work? Such questions led to the welfare reform of 1996, which created TANF, specifically meant as a means of temporary assistance to families.

The need to combine work and child care is a problem for most single parents. This problem is more acute for single mothers than for single fathers, because on average, women still earn less than men, and because working creates new expenses such as child-care and transportation costs. Many women working in low-wage jobs do not receive health insurance as a benefit of their jobs; they must pay the cost of such insurance themselves. As a result, many poor women found that once they were working, the expenses of child care, transportation, insurance, and other needs left them with less cash per month than they would have received if they had not worked and had instead collected AFDC and Medicaid benefits. These women concluded that it was not "worth it" for them to leave AFDC and work. Some states are now experimenting with programs to encourage women to work by allowing them to keep some of their welfare benefits even when they are working. Although Americans want individuals to be self-sufficient, research suggests that single mothers with low-wage jobs are likely to need continuing assistance to make ends meet.[43]

One of the most troubling issues related to American social policy is the number of American children who live in poverty. The rate of child poverty in 2006 was 16.9 percent—4.6 percent higher than that of the population as a whole. These high rates of poverty stem in part from the design of American social policies. Because these policies do not generously assist able-bodied adults who aren't working, and because these policies offer little help to the working poor, the children of these adults are likely to be poor as well.

As child poverty has grown, several lobbying groups have emerged to represent children's interests; the best known of these is the Children's Defense Fund. But even with a sophisticated lobbying operation and although their numbers are large, poor children do not vote and therefore cannot wield much political power.[44]

Thinking Critically about Social Policy and Equality

The development of social policy in the United States reflects shifts in our views about how government can best help accomplish fundamental national goals. Until the 1930s, the federal government did very little in the domain of social policy. The country's major social policy was free public education, which was established by the states and administered locally. Americans placed especially strong emphasis on education because an educated citizenry was seen as an essential component of a strong democracy.[45] Given the strength of these beliefs, it is not surprising that free public education was available in the United States well before European nations established public education systems.

Other public social policies, established from the 1930s on, have stirred up much more controversy. Liberals often argue that more generous social policies are needed if America is to truly ensure equality of opportunity. Some liberals have argued that the government needs to go beyond simply providing opportunity and should ensure more equal conditions, especially where children are concerned. Conservative critics, on the other hand, often argue that social policies that offer income support take the ideal of equality too far and, in the process, do for individuals what they should be doing for themselves. From this perspective, social policies make the government too big, and big government is seen as a fundamental threat to Americans' liberties.

For Critical Analysis

Critics of American social policy argue that social policy does more harm than good. What negative consequences of social policy do they point to? Do you agree with their arguments?

Yet conservatives do not agree about how best to achieve a balance between the ideals of liberty, equality, and democracy. Two different conservative perspectives can be distinguished. The **libertarian** view holds that government social policy interferes with society too much and, in the process, has created more problems than it has solved.[46] Many libertarians believe that the mere existence of social policies is an infringement on individual liberties: the government forces some citizens to pay taxes for the benefit of other citizens. The most extreme policy prescription that emerges from this perspective advocates the elimination of all social policies. For example, the political scientist Charles Murray has proposed eliminating all social programs except temporary unemployment insurance. In his view, such a move would both enhance the freedom of all Americans and improve society, because individuals would recover their own initiative if they had to take care of themselves.[47] A less sweeping approach would reduce social programs to a bare minimum or make them temporary.

libertarian the political philosophy that is skeptical of any government intervention as a potential threat to individual liberty

Other conservatives see things differently. They want to use the power of the government to enforce certain standards of behavior among beneficiaries of government social programs. Many people with these views call themselves "new paternalists."[48] They believe that government social programs have not forced recipients

Take an Active Stance on Social Problems

In June 2008, a small group of young people from across the country went to Washington, D.C., for a two-day "Youth Entitlement Summit." These young men and women spent their days in congressional hearing rooms, conducting their own hearings, where they questioned leading experts about the current and future state of Social Security, the health care crisis, and the underrepresentation of youth voices in current debates. At the end of the summit, they had developed a series of policy statements on these key issues—and a blueprint for continuing to educate themselves and others. Their goal was to help shape the debate, rather than simply react to the plans offered by elected officials or other organizations.

As this chapter illustrates, social policy affects all aspects of our lives. The decisions we make as a society concerning issues such as these reflect our national values. So, when we increase spending on federal grants for higher education we make a commitment to expanding access to college for low- and middle-income students. When we require welfare recipients to move to work or risk losing their benefits, we emphasize our commitment to self-reliance. And if we allow individuals to invest some of their Social Security taxes in the private market, we underscore our faith in liberty and choice.

Social policy also reflects what we believe about responsibility. It illustrates what we think about our responsibility to each other and what we are willing to do for each other as members of a shared polity. With so many issues (and with limits on our ability to fund everything), it may be hard to decide what to support or what you want the government to do. Certainly, many people feel so overwhelmed or intimidated that they opt out of the debate altogether. But others, like the young people at the YES summit, decide to educate themselves about the issues and take an active role in the national conversation. You can do so as well.

- You can start by thinking through debates over major social policies and finding out where you fit. Two issues that have been debated recently are the future of the Social Security system and health-care reform. Some want to privatize a portion of workers' contributions to Social Security while others think this is too risky. And as for health-care, should the United States move toward a government-sponsored, universal health-care system like other western democracies? A good place to start developing a deeper understanding of these issues is the Public Agenda Foundation (www.publicagenda.org/issues/issuehome.cfm), which provides background on various issues.

- Many people across the political spectrum see an important role for nonprofit organizations, including faith-based groups, to work with (or instead of) government in providing key services to those in need. The Roundtable on Religion and Social Policy (from SUNY Rochester), www.religionandsocialpolicy.org/, provides independent analysis of this phenomenon. The Web site includes an overview of what faith-based initiatives mean, an analysis of their effectiveness in addressing social problems, and insight into key state initiatives.
- Immigration reform is a perennial issue in American politics. As much as we like to think of ourselves as the proverbial "melting pot," the influx of immigrants, many of whom are here illegally, challenges our embrace of diversity. By working through a campus organization (student government, campus Democrats or Republicans, etc.), you might consider staging a debate with experts on both sides of the issue. Groups that you might consider contacting for speakers include the American Civil Liberties Union (www.aclu.org), American Conservative Union (www.conservative.org), National Council of La Raza (www.nclr.org), and the Asian American Legal Defense and Education Fund (www.aaldef.org).

to behave responsibly. They reject the idea that social programs should simply be abandoned because they fear the consequences for our democracy. New paternalists do not believe that individuals will behave more responsibly if government programs are withdrawn; instead they fear that social disorder will simply continue. In their view, such disorder will inevitably undermine a healthy democracy, and the primary role of government social policy should be to restore the social order.

Some of the measures supported by new paternalists are also backed by many liberals. These include requiring work in exchange for welfare benefits and compelling absent parents (usually fathers) to make child support payments to the families they have abandoned. Many people from varying political perspectives applauded in 1995 when the federal government tracked down and arrested a prominent investment banker who had fled from state to state in order to avoid paying child support.[49] Other measures are more controversial. For example, some states have enacted reforms denying additional welfare benefits to women who bear a child while on welfare. Liberals charge that such measures violate a most basic individual liberty: the right to have children.[50] New paternalists argue that infringement of individual liberties is simply the price that beneficiaries of government programs have to pay in return for receiving public support.

Conservatives share the view that the primary problems that many social policies address are not economic in origin but instead stem from individual deficiencies. If people behaved more responsibly—if they saved for their retirement, if they did not have children they couldn't afford to support—there would be little need for government social policy. Liberals, in contrast, believe that the root of many social problems is economic. They believe that opportunities for economic success are not equally available to all Americans and that it is the government's responsibility to open opportunities for all. Thus, liberals are far more likely than conservatives to believe that the ideal of equality compels the state to provide social programs. But, like conservatives, liberals do not all agree: some liberals place a greater emphasis on achieving equality as a *result;* others believe that government should do all it can to provide opportunity but that it should not go beyond providing opportunity.

Some liberals who believe that the government should do more to promote equal outcomes have argued that social benefits should be provided as a right of citizenship and that all Americans should be entitled to a basic standard of living. At particular historical moments, there have been social movements arguing in favor of such approaches to social policy in the United States, but views arguing in favor of equality of result have always been disadvantaged in the American political system. The idea of "social rights," prevalent in many European nations, has no counterpart in American politics. Moreover, the Supreme Court repeatedly refused to acknowledge social or economic rights in the 1960s and 1970s, even as it was making strong efforts to ensure political and civil rights.[51]

For Critical Analysis

How does American social policy attempt to promote equality of opportunity? Do its various programs succeed in making opportunity more available to all Americans? Why or why not?

Most liberals, then, argue that the aim of social policy should be to provide equality of opportunity. They believe that it is particularly important to ensure that all children have an equal chance to succeed. The sharpest liberal criticism of current social policy has been directed at its failure to address the growth of child poverty. This criticism stems from the belief that poor children have far less opportunity to succeed than the children of the well-off and that such inequalities are incompatible with fundamental American ideals. Liberals also believe that the government has an important role in creating opportunities for adults.

Where do average Americans fit in all these debates? Americans are often said to be philosophical conservatives and operational liberals.[52] When asked about government social policy in the abstract, they say they disapprove of activist government—a decidedly conservative view. But when they must evaluate particular programs, Americans generally express support—a more liberal perspective. Some programs, of course, are preferred over others. Policies in which the recipients are regarded as deserving, such as programs for the elderly, receive more support than those that assist working-age people. Programs that have a reputation for effectiveness and programs that require people to help themselves through work are also viewed favorably.[53]

In sum, most Americans take a pragmatic approach to social welfare policies: they favor programs that work, and they want to reform those that seem not to work. By rejecting the policy extremes, Americans signal their awareness of the tensions that social policies generate among their most deeply held values of liberty, equality, and democracy. Political debates about social policy connect most closely with the public when they consider which mix of policies represents the appropriate balance among these three ideals, rather than when they ask the public to choose among them.

FOR FURTHER READING

Campbell, Andrea Louise. *How Policies Make Citizens: Senior Political Activism and the American Welfare State.* Princeton, NJ: Princeton University Press, 2005.

Hacker, Jacob S. *The Great Risk Shift: Why American Jobs, Families, Health Care, and Retirement Aren't Secure—and How We Can Fight Back.* New York: Oxford University Press, 2006.

Howard, Christopher. *The Welfare State Nobody Knows: Debunking Myths about U.S. Social Policy.* Princeton, NJ: Princeton University Press, 2007.

Katz, Michael. *In the Shadow of the Poorhouse: A Social History of Welfare in America.* New York: Basic Books, 1986.

Katznelson, Ira, and Margaret Weir. *Schooling for All: Race, Class, and the Democratic Ideal.* New York: Basic Books, 1985.

Light, Paul. *Artful Work: The Politics of Social Security Reform.* New York: Random House, 1985.

Mettler, Suzanne. *Soldiers to Citizens: The GI Bill and the Making of the Greatest Generation.* New York: Oxford University Press, 2005.

Murray, Charles. *Losing Ground: American Social Policy, 1950–1980.* New York: Basic Books, 1984.

Patterson, James T. *America's Struggle against Poverty in the Twentieth Century.* Cambridge, MA: Harvard University Press, 2000.

Rank, Mark Robert. *One Nation, Underprivileged: Why American Poverty Affects Us All.* New York: Oxford University Press, 2004.

Skocpol, Theda. *The Missing Middle: Working Families and the Future of American Social Policy.* New York: Norton, 2000.

Weir, Margaret, Ann Orloff, and Theda Skocpol, eds. *The Politics of Social Policy in the United States.* Princeton, NJ: Princeton University Press, 1988.

RECOMMENDED WEB SITES

Center on Budget and Policy Priorities
www.cbpp.org

The Center on Budget and Policy Priorities is a nonpartisan, liberal-leaning, nonprofit organization that provides timely data and analysis of social programs that serve low-income Americans. It also studies economic and social changes that affect the well-being of low-income people. Areas of research include the Earned Income Tax Credit, Food Assistance, Social Security, and climate change. It focuses on national programs as well as state and local policies.

Center for Retirement Research
http://crr.bc.edu/index.php

Americans pay for their retirement with a mix of Social Security, employer-sponsored savings plans, and private savings. This Web site provides analyses of the challenges that face all aspects of the current arrangements and includes a downloadable "Social Security Fix-It Book."

Libertarian Party
www.lp.org

Contrary to many other Americans, libertarians believe that social programs pose a threat to personal freedom and should be eliminated. Go to the Libertarian Party's Web site to read the organization's opinions and positions on most current social policies.

Medicare
www.medicare.gov

Health care is one of the largest and most controversial social programs in the United States. At the Medicare Web site, find out what services the Department of Health and Human Services provides.

Modern American Poetry: The Great Depression
www.english.uiuc.edu/maps/depression/depression.htm

The Great Depression changed American opinion about the causes of and responsibility for poverty. This Web site, by Carey Norton at the University of Illinois at Urbana-Champaign, provides information, statistics, and photos of this historical period as well as analysis of poems by depression-era writers.

Poverty.com
www.poverty.com

Poverty is a problem that exists in the United States and around the world. Read about how poverty, hunger, and related problems affect people in other areas of the globe.

Public Agenda
www.publicagenda.com

Public Agenda is a nonpartisan organization that tries to bridge the gap between American leaders and public opinion on current social, domestic, and foreign-policy issues.

U.S. Department of Education
www.ed.gov

The U.S. Department of Education is dedicated to providing equal access to education and improving academic programs throughout America. At the department's Web site, you can learn about the No Child Left Behind Act and other policies.

STUDY OUTLINE

www.wwnorton.com/wtp7e

1. Equality of opportunity, a widely shared American ideal, was enshrined by Thomas Jefferson in the Declaration of Independence, but problems associated with this ideal persist.
2. The lowest income brackets are disproportionately composed of members of groups who have been deprived of opportunities.

The Welfare State

1. Prior to 1935, the welfare system in America was composed of private groups rather than government. State governments gradually assumed some of the obligation to relieve the poor.
2. The founding of the welfare state can be dated to the Social Security Act of 1935; this act provided for both contributory and noncontributory welfare programs.
3. Contributory programs—such as Social Security and unemployment compensation—provide "forced savings" for individuals who, as a consequence of making a contribution, can receive program benefits at a later time.
4. Noncontributory programs—such as food stamps and Temporary Assistance to Needy Families (TANF)—provide assistance to people based on demonstrated need rather than on any contribution they may have made.
5. Spending on social policies, especially Social Security and Medicare, has increased dramatically in recent decades, raising concerns about how entitlement programs will be paid for in future decades.

Opening Opportunity

1. Education, employment, health, and housing policies are four ways to break the cycle of poverty and redistribute opportunities.
2. The education policies of state and local governments are the most important single force in the distribution and redistribution of opportunity in America.
3. Employment and job training programs have not been a consistent goal of the modern welfare state.
4. Although states also took the early lead in the arena of public-health policy, the federal government began to adopt policies during the early 1900s to protect citizens from the effects of pollution and other health hazards.
5. Federal housing policy consists of many pork-barrel programs, but it also is a commitment to improving the conditions and opportunities of the poor.

Who Gets What from Social Policy?

1. The elderly are the beneficiaries of generous social policies in part because they are perceived as being a deserving population and because they have become a strong interest group.

2. The middle class benefits from social policies in many ways; one way is through the use of tax expenditures, which provide that certain payments made by employers and employees are not taxed by the government.
3. People who are working but are still poor receive limited assistance from government social programs. Although they may be seen as deserving, they receive only limited assistance because they lack organization and political power.
4. Medicaid and TANF are programs aimed at the able-bodied, nonworking poor, but they receive assistance only if they are parents caring for children. The unpopularity of such programs has prompted efforts to decrease spending in recent years.

Thinking Critically about Social Policy and Equality

1. The development of social policy in the United States reflects the tensions among the values of liberty, equality, and democracy. Various conservative and liberal perspectives attempt to reconcile these tensions with differing views on social policy. Each of these approaches seems out of step, however, with the more pragmatic view held by most Americans.

PRACTICE QUIZ

www.wwnorton.com/wtp7e

1. Which of the following is *not* an example of a contributory program?
   a) Social Security
   b) Medicare
   c) food stamps
   d) All of the above are examples of contributory programs.
2. Prior to 1935, the private welfare system in the United States made a distinction between
   a) contributory and noncontributory programs.
   b) citizens and recent immigrants.
   c) the deserving poor and the undeserving poor.
   d) religious and secular assistance.
3. America's welfare state was constructed initially in response to
   a) World War II.
   b) political reforms of the Progressive era.
   c) the Great Depression.
   d) the growth of the military-industrial complex.
4. Which of the following are examples of in-kind benefits?
   a) Medicaid and food stamps
   b) Social Security payments and cost-of-living adjustments
   c) Medicare and unemployment compensation
   d) none of the above
5. Means testing requires that applicants for welfare benefits show
   a) that they are capable of getting to and from their workplace.
   b) that they have the ability to store and prepare food.
   c) some definite need for assistance plus an inability to provide for it.
   d) that they have the time and resources to take full advantage of federal educational opportunities.
6. In 1996, as part of welfare reform, Aid to Families with Dependent Children was abolished and replaced by
   a) the Earned Income Tax Credit.
   b) Aid to Dependent Children.
   c) Supplemental Security Income.
   d) Temporary Assistance to Needy Families.
7. In terms of receiving benefits of social policies, what distinguishes the elderly from the working poor?
   a) The elderly are perceived as deserving, whereas the working poor are not.
   b) There is no significant difference between these two groups.
   c) The elderly are more organized and more politically powerful than are the working poor.
   d) The elderly are less organized and less politically powerful than are the working poor.
8. Who are the chief beneficiaries of the "shadow welfare state"?
   a) the rich
   b) the nonworking poor
   c) the working poor
   d) the middle class
9. Which of the following is *not* aimed at breaking the cycle of poverty?
   a) drug policies
   b) education policies
   c) employment training programs
   d) health policies

KEY TERMS

www.wwnorton.com/wtp7e

contributory programs (p. 681)
cost-of-living adjustment (COLA) (p. 682)
entitlement (p. 685)
equality of opportunity (p. 691)
food stamps (p. 684)
indexing (p. 682)
in-kind benefits (p. 684)
libertarian (p. 707)
means testing (p. 683)
Medicaid (p. 683)
Medicare (p. 682)
noncontributory programs (p. 683)
Social Security (p. 681)
tax expenditures (p. 703)

18 Foreign Policy and Democracy

★ The Nature of Foreign Policy

★ The Goals of Foreign Policy

★ Who Makes American Foreign Policy?

★ The Instruments of Modern American Foreign Policy

★ Foreign Policy and America's Place in the World

★ Thinking Critically about America's Role in the World Today

WHAT GOVERNMENT DOES AND WHY IT MATTERS

In the immediate aftermath of the September 11, 2001 terrorist attacks, Americans seemed united in their convictions that the United States should mount a strong military response against Afghanistan's Taliban regime. A year later, when President George W. Bush ordered the invasion of Iraq that led to the ouster of Saddam Hussein, a majority of Americans still agreed that military action was necessary, even though few of America's allies supported the Bush administration's policies. However, by the start of the 2008 presidential campaign, public opinion had shifted sharply. Most Americans wanted an end to the fighting in the Middle East and wanted American troops brought home. Many believed that years of costly warfare had hurt the domestic economy, undermined America's alliances, and weakened rather than bolstered the nation's security.

Concerns about foreign policy have been common in our history. Americans have usually been dubious about protracted involvement in world affairs, particularly if it meant war and the use of force. Though Europeans and others around the world call the United States a "superpower" or even a "hyperpower," constantly meddling in the affairs of other nations, most Americans believe that other nations should take care of their own problems. For better or worse, however, the United States *is* a superpower whose actions and even failures to act have enormous consequences for Americans and all the people of the world. American foreign policy affects global security, the global economy, and the global environment.

In 2008, one of the main criticisms that Republicans made of the Democratic presidential candidate, Barack Obama, was that Obama lacked the foreign policy experience of the Republican candidate, John McCain. When Obama selected Senator Joseph Biden, who chaired the Senate Foreign Relations Committee, as his vice-presidential running mate, many observers assumed it was a response to this concern. Although the economy became the most prominent issue in the fall before the election, foreign policy and domestic affairs are inextricably linked. For example, our foreign policies have an impact on domestic energy costs. Our foreign policies affect employment and wages at home. And, of course, our foreign policies affect the security of every American.

› **This chapter examines the three main dimensions of American foreign policy.**

› **First, what are the main goals and purposes of U.S. foreign policy?** We will see that even though America's policy makers are mainlyy concerned with national security, other purposes are important as well.

› **Second, who makes and shapes foreign policy in the United States?** Among the major actors, we will see that the president is most influential.

› **Third, what instruments do policy makers use to conduct foreign policy?** We will examine the institutions and programs that enable the government to pursue America's interests.

The Nature of Foreign Policy

Generally speaking, the term *foreign policy* refers to the programs and policies that determine America's relations with other nations and foreign entities. Foreign policy includes diplomacy, military and security policy, international human rights policies, and various forms of economic policy, such as trade policy and international energy policy. Of course, foreign policy and domestic policy are not completely separate categories but are instead closely intertwined. Take security policy, for example. Defending the nation requires the design and manufacture of tens of billions of dollars worth of military hardware. The construction and procurement of this military equipment involves a host of economic policies, and paying for it shapes America's fiscal policies.

At first glance, the basic contours of the foreign-policy arena seem similar to those of America's other policy domains. The nation's chief foreign-policy makers are the president, Congress, and the bureaucracy. Just as in the cases of economic and social policy, battles over foreign policy often erupt between and within these institutions as competing politicians and a variety of organized groups and rival political forces pursue their own versions of the national interest or their own narrower purposes, which they seek to present as the national interest. In many instances, the outcome of these battles among competing forces depends on the relative power of the institutions they control. Institutions affect foreign as well as domestic policy outcomes. In the foreign-policy arena, the institutional powers of the presidency give presidents and their allies an advantage over political forces based in Congress, although Congress is not without institutional resources of its own through which to influence the conduct of foreign policy. Moreover, like domestic-policy matters, foreign-policy issues often figure prominently in public debate and national election campaigns as competing forces seek to mobilize popular support for their positions or at least to castigate the opposition for the putative shortcomings of its policies.

Despite these similarities, the foreign- and domestic-policy arenas differ in at least three important ways. The first is history. History always matters, but history and historical memory generally play a larger role in the foreign-policy realm than in most areas of domestic policy. Foreign policy, as we shall see, is often guided by historical events, experiences, and commitments. Debates over foreign policy tend to be strongly affected by competing historical perceptions. For example, those who argue in favor of confronting Iran, North Korea, and other potentially hostile powers often refer to the disastrous consequences of pre-World War II efforts by Britain and France to "appease" Nazi Germany. On the other hand, those who favor withdrawing American forces from Iraq cite the parallels to America's failed efforts in Vietnam. Each group's view of the present is strongly shaped by its understanding of the past.

Second, in the foreign-policy arena, questions of the national interest figure more prominently than in most domestic-policy debates. To be sure, advocates of competing social and economic policies argue that their preferred programs promote the interests of the nation as a whole. Yet such pronouncements are usually taken with a grain of salt, and we are usually prepared to forgive advocates whose preferred economic or social policies turn out to serve discrete constituencies rather than the entire nation. In the realm of foreign policy, though, the public interest looms larger. In a world where entities ranging from rival nation-states to shadowy terrorist groups present genuine threats to the security of the entire nation, advocates of particular foreign policies are more likely than their domestic counterparts to be asked to demonstrate that the policies they espouse serve broad national interests. In the realm of foreign policy, unlike, say, the arena of health-care reform, advocates can and do accuse one another of threatening the nation's security and demonstrating outright disloyalty.

Finally, the foreign-policy arena is affected by America's historic wariness of foreign commitments and the difficulties of making and justifying what are often cold, harsh, calculating foreign-policy decisions in a democratic context. Ever since George Washington, in his Farewell Address, warned the American people "to have . . . as little political connection as possible" to foreign nations and to "steer clear of permanent alliances," Americans have been distrustful of foreign policy. Despite this distrust, the United States has been forced to pursue its national interests in the world, even when this has meant fighting a war. As a result of its foreign

Foreign policy often intersects with domestic policy. As the government has taken steps to protect Americans from foreign terrorists, such as monitoring borders more closely, this has also affected domestic-level debates about issues like immigration. Here, a Homeland Security official watches video feeds of the U.S.-Canadian border.

entanglements, the United States emerged as a world power, but not without maintaining some misgivings about foreign entanglements.

The Goals of Foreign Policy

Although U.S. foreign policy has a number of purposes, three main goals stand out. These are security, prosperity, and the creation of a better world. These goals are, of course, closely intertwined and can never be pursued fully in isolation from each other.

Security

To many Americans, the chief purpose of the nation's foreign policy is protection of America's security in an often hostile world. Traditionally, the United States has been concerned about threats that might emanate from other nations, such as Nazi Germany during the 1940s and then Soviet Russia until the Soviet Union's collapse in the late 1980s. Today, American security policy is concerned not only with the actions of other nations but also with the activities of terrorist groups and other hostile **non-state actors.**[1] To protect the nation's security from foreign threats, the United States has built an enormous military apparatus and a complex array of intelligence-gathering institutions, such as the Central Intelligence Agency (CIA), charged with evaluating and anticipating challenges from abroad.[2]

non-state actor groups other than nation-states that attempt to play a role in the international system. Terrorist groups are one type of non-state actor

Security is, of course, a broad term. Policy makers must be concerned with Americans' physical security. The 9/11 terrorist attacks killed and injured thousands of Americans and the government constantly fears that new attacks could be even more catastrophic. Policy makers must also be concerned with such matters as the security of America's food supplies, transportation infrastructure, and energy supplies. Many of our efforts in the Middle East, for example, are aimed at ensuring continuing American access to vital oil fields. In recent years, cyberspace has become a new security concern. The nation's dependence on computers means that the government must be alert to efforts by hostile governments, groups, or even individual "hackers" to damage computer networks.

During the nineteenth century, the United States believed that its security was based on its geographic isolation. We were separated by two oceans from European and Asian powers, and many Americans thought that our security would be best preserved by remaining aloof from international power struggles. This policy was known as **isolationism.** In the twentieth century, technology made oceans less of a barrier to foreign threats, and the world's growing economic interdependence meant that the United States could no longer ignore events abroad. At the beginning of the twentieth century, despite its isolationist sentiments, the United States entered World War I on the side of Great Britain when the Wilson administration concluded that America's economic and security interests would be adversely affected by a German victory. In 1941, America was drawn into World War II when Japan attacked the U.S. Pacific fleet anchored at Pearl Harbor, Hawaii. Even before the Japanese attack forced America to fight, the Roosevelt administration had already concluded that the United States must come to Britain's aid to prevent a victory by the German-Japanese-Italian Axis alliance. Until the Japanese attack, however, President Roosevelt had not been able to overcome proponents of American isolationism, who declared that our security was best served by leaving

isolationism desire to avoid involvement in the affairs of other nations foreigners to their own devices. With their attack, the Japanese proved that the Pacific Ocean could not protect the United States from foreign foes and effectively discredited isolationism as a security policy.

In the aftermath of World War II, the United States developed a new security policy known as **deterrence.** Following the war, the power of the Soviet Union seemed to grow exponentially. By the end of the 1940s, the Soviets had built a huge empire and enormous military forces. Most threatening of all, the Soviet Union had built nuclear weapons and intercontinental bombers capable of attacking the United States. Some Americans argued that we should attack the Soviets before it was too late. This policy is known as **preventive war.** Others said that we should show our peaceful intentions and attempt to placate the Soviets. This policy is called **appeasement.**

The policy that the United States actually adopted, deterrence, could be seen as midway between preventive war and appeasement. A nation pursuing a policy of deterrence, on the one hand, signals its peaceful intentions, but on the other hand indicates its willingness and ability to fight if attacked. Thus, during the era of confrontation with the Soviet Union, known as the **Cold War,** the United States frequently asserted that it had no intention of attacking the Soviet Union. At the same time, however, the United States built a huge military force, including an arsenal of nuclear weapons and intercontinental missiles, and frequently asserted that in the event of a Soviet attack, it had the ability and will to respond with overwhelming force. The Soviet Union announced that its nuclear weapons were also intended for deterrent purposes. Eventually the two sides possessed such enormous arsenals of nuclear missiles that each potentially had the ability to destroy the other in the event of war. This heavily armed standoff came to be called a posture of mutually assured destruction.

A policy of deterrence not only requires the possession of large military forces but also requires the nation pursuing such a policy to convince potential adversaries that it is willing to fight. France had a large army in the 1930s, but Nazi Germany was not deterred from pursuing its expansionist goals in Europe because the German chancellor, Adolf Hitler, did not believe that the French were actually willing to fight. Thus, as part of its policy of deterrence, the United States engaged in wars in Korea, Vietnam, and elsewhere in response to what it believed to be Soviet aggression. Though the United States had no particular interests in Korea or Vietnam, American policy makers believed that if the United States did not fight in these areas, the Soviets would be emboldened to pursue an expansionist policy elsewhere, thinking that the Americans would not respond. Through military deterrence, the United States hoped to "contain" the Soviet Union and prevent futher increases in its power and territory.

During the 1990s, the Soviet Union collapsed, partly because its huge military expenditures undermined its creaky and inefficient centrally planned economy. The new Russia, though still a formidable and sometimes unfriendly power, seemed to pose less of a threat to the United States. Americans celebrated the end of the Cold War and believed that the enormous expense of America's own military forces might be reduced. Within a few years of the Soviet collapse, however, a new set of security threats emerged, requiring new policy responses. The September 11 terrorist attacks demonstrated a threat against which security scholars had long warned. The threat was that non-state actors and so-called rogue states might acquire significant military capabilities, including nuclear weapons, and would not be affected by America's deterrent capabilities.

A policy of deterrence assumes certainty and rationality. Certainty means that a potential adversary must know for sure that the United States will reply with force if attacked. Rationality means that, to be deterred, a potential adversary

deterrence the development and maintenance of military strength as a means of discouraging attack

preventive war policy of striking first when a nation fears that a foreign foe is comtemplating hostile action

appeasement effort to forestall war by giving in to the demands of a hostile power

Cold War the period of struggle between the United States and the former Soviet Union between the late 1940s and about 1990

During the Cold War, the United States and the Soviet Union engaged in an arms race, each acquiring a massive arsenal of nuclear weapons in an effort to deter the other from attacking. A policy of deterrence relies on military strength to discourage attacks.

nation-state a political entity consisting of a people with some common cultural experience (nation) who also share a common political authority (state), recognized by other sovereignties (nation-states)

preemption willingness to strike first in order to prevent an enemy attack

must be capable of rationally assessing the risks and costs of aggression against the United States. These two assumptions, which were valid when we faced the Soviet Union, may not be appropriate in the face of contemporary security threats. Unlike **nation-states,** countries with governments and fixed borders, terrorist groups are non-state actors having no fixed geographic location that can be attacked. Terrorists may believe that they can attack and melt away, leaving the United States with no one against whom to retaliate. Hence, the threat of massive retaliation does not deter them. Rogue states are nations with unstable and erratic leaders who seem to pursue policies driven by ideological or religious fervor rather than careful consideration of economic or human costs. The United States considers North Korea and Iran to be rogue states. Such states are difficult to deter because they may be willing to accept or may not fully grasp the potential costs of their actions.

To counter these new security threats, the United States has shifted from a policy of deterrence to one of **preemption.** Preemption is often used as another name for preventive war or willingness to strike first in order to prevent an enemy attack. The United States has declared that it will not wait to be attacked but will, if necessary, take action to disable terrorist groups and rogue states before they can do us harm. The Bush administration's "global war on terror" is an expression of this notion of preemption, as was the U.S. invasion of Iraq. The United States has also refused to rule out the possibility that it would attack North Korea or Iran if it deemed those nations' nuclear programs to be an imminent threat to American security interests. Accompanying this shift in military doctrines has been an enormous increase in overall U.S. military spending (see Figure 18.1). It remains to be seen whether America's doctrine of preemption will successfully counter threats or merely convince the world that America is, itself, a hostile and aggressive power.

The U.S. invasion of Iraq was an example of preemptive war. The Bush administration argued that it had to strike Iraq first, before Iraq used weapons of mass destruction to attack American interests.

FIGURE 18.1 ★ U.S. Military Expenditure since 2001

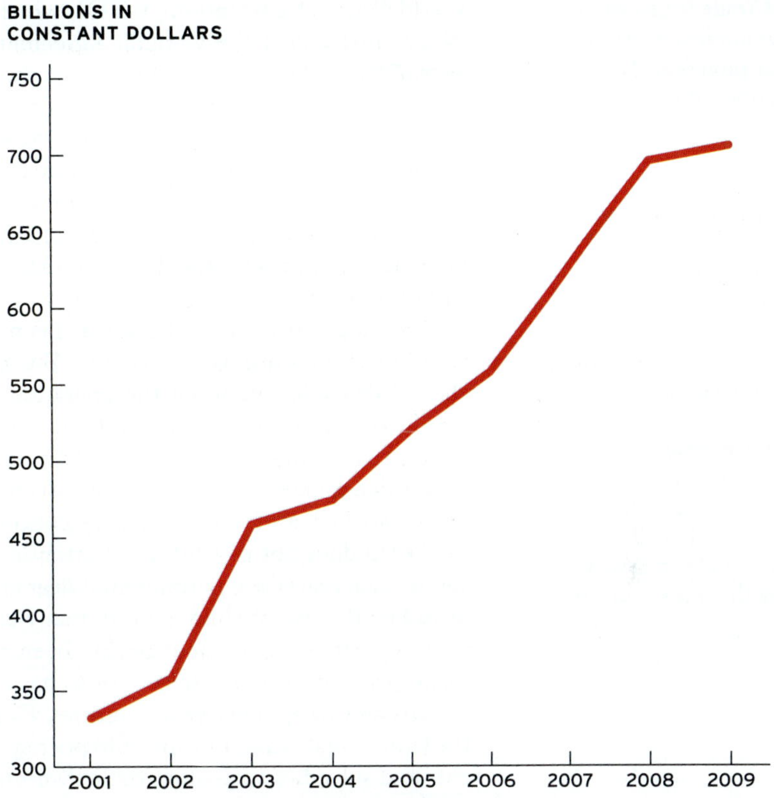

NOTE: Figure includes Department of Defense spending, Department of Energy's nuclear weapons program, the costs of the wars in Iraq and Afghanistan, and DOD-related spending by other agencies.
SOURCE: Center for Arms Control and Non-Proliferation, www.armscontrolcenter.org/policy/securityspending/articles/defense_spending_since_2001/index.html (accessed 5/19/08).

Economic Prosperity

A second major goal of U.S. foreign policy is promoting American prosperity. America's international economic policies are intended to expand employment opportunities in the United States, to maintain access to foreign energy supplies at a reasonable cost, to promote foreign investment in the United States, and to lower the prices Americans pay for goods and services.

Among the most visible and important elements of U.S. international economic policy is trade policy. The promotion and advertising of American goods and services abroad is a long-standing goal of U.S. trade policy, and it is one of the major obligations of the Department of Commerce. Yet modern trade policy involves a complex arrangement of treaties, tariffs, and other mechanisms of policy formation. For example, the United States has a long-standing policy of granting **most favored nation status** to certain countries—that is, the United States offers to another country the same tariff rate it already gives to its most favored trading partner, in return for trade (and sometimes other) concessions. In 1998, to avoid any suggestion that "most favored nation" implied some special relationship with an undemocratic country (China, for example), President Clinton changed the term from "most favored nation" to "normal trade relations."[3]

most favored nation status
agreement to offer a trading partner the lowest tariff rate offered to other trading partners

World Trade Organization (WTO) international trade agency promoting free trade that grew out of the General Agreement on Tariffs and Trade

General Agreement on Tariffs and Trade (GATT) international trade organization, in existence from 1947 to 1995, that set many of the rules governing international trade

North American Free Trade Agreement (NAFTA) trade treaty among the United States, Canada, and Mexico to lower and eliminate tariffs among the three countries

The most important international organization for promoting free trade is the **World Trade Organization (WTO),** which officially came into being in 1995. The WTO grew out of the **General Agreement on Tariffs and Trade (GATT).** Since World War II, GATT had brought together a wide range of nations for regular negotiations designed to reduce barriers to trade. Such barriers, many believed, had contributed to the breakdown of the world economy in the 1930s and had helped to cause World War II. The WTO has 151 members worldwide; decisions about trade are made by the Ministerial Conference, which meets every two years. Similar policy goals are pursued in regional arrangements, such as the **North American Free Trade Agreement (NAFTA),** a trade treaty among the United States, Canada, and Mexico.

Working toward freer trade has been an important goal of each presidential administration since World War II. Yet as globalization has advanced, concerns about free trade and about the operation of the WTO, in particular, have grown. The WTO meetings held in Seattle in 1999 provoked unprecedented protests by groups that included environmentalists and labor unions. Tens of thousands of protesters denounced the undemocratic decision-making process of the WTO, which, they charged, was dominated by the concerns of business. These critics believe that the WTO does not pay sufficient attention to the concerns of developing nations and to such issues as environmental degradation, human rights, and labor practices, including the use of child labor in many countries. The Seattle meetings were adjourned with no agreement having been reached. Since the Seattle meeting, the major problem in WTO negotiations has been conflicts between poor, developing nations and rich, developed countries. Countries in the developing world accuse the United States and Europe of hypocrisy, preaching free trade but then using patents and subsidies to protect their own markets. There have been some successes on these issues, notably new WTO guidelines that allow poor countries to override expensive patents. Such patents make desperately needed drugs unavailable to most of the developing world. It has been more difficult to reach agreement on agricultural subsidies. Both the United States and Europe provide massive subsidies

At the WTO's convention in Hong Kong in 2005, agricultural subsidies were especially controversial. Some developing countries accused the United States and Europe of preaching free trade while still offering subsidies to their own farmers.

FIGURE 18.2 ★
U.S. International Trade in Goods and Services

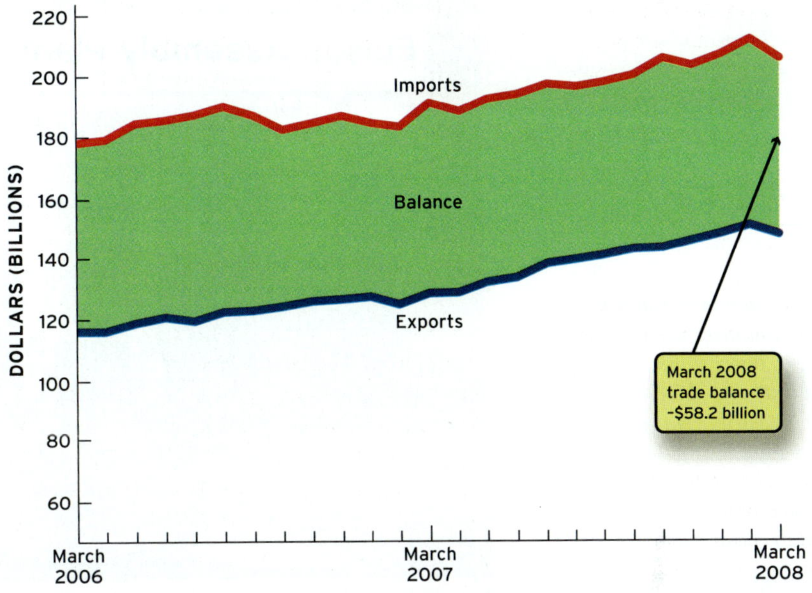

SOURCE: U.S. Census Bureau, www.census.gov/indicator/www/ustrade.html (accessed 5/19/08).

to their own agricultural industries. The prospects for resolving this issue are dim. The developed world has been reluctant to confront the economic dislocations and political costs of reducing the subsidies.

For over a half-century, the United States has led the world in supporting free trade as the best route to growth and prosperity. Yet the American government, too, has sought to protect domestic industry when it is politically necessary. Subsidies, as we have seen, have long boosted American agriculture, artificially lowering the price of American products on world markets. In 2002 President George W. Bush, a vocal advocate of free trade, angered the rest of the world when he imposed protective tariffs on imported steel. Accused of hypocrisy and faced with retaliation from trading partners, the administration defended its actions by pointing to the damage that imports were doing to the domestic steel industry. When the WTO ruled that the steel tariffs violated WTO rules, Bush faced an unhappy choice. He could allow the European Union to retaliate by imposing tariffs, many of them on goods produced in politically important states. Or he could lift the tariffs, thus angering steel producers and workers. The president chose to lift the steel tariffs.

Trade was also an issue in the 2008 election. During their third debate, John McCain accused Barack Obama of promoting protectionist policies, while Obama said Republicans had exported American jobs abroad and allowed an enormous trade deficit to develop. The U.S. trade deficit was projected to reach $60 billion (see Figure 18.2) and jobs growth in the United States had been low for several years. Analysts predicted that many of the 2.8 million manufacturing jobs lost in the recession of the early 2000s would never return to the United States. Moreover, outsourcing—the practice of moving jobs to other countries—began to hit the white-collar workforce, as jobs for workers such as call center operators and computer programmers moved to India and other countries with cheaper labor forces. There is much disagreement about the impact that outsourcing will have on American jobs. Some studies suggest that 20 percent of all jobs in the developed world could be affected by outsourcing including "all American librarians, statisticians, chemical engineers and air traffic controllers."[4] Other

For Critical Analysis

What are the arguments in favor of free trade (versus restrictions on trade)? Do the advocates of restrictions on trade always favor narrow special interests, or can they too be seen as favoring the public interest?

As more manufacturing jobs move to countries where labor is cheaper, American workers have raised concerns about their wages and job security. This is just one of numerous U.S. plants that Ford has shut down. Meanwhile, the company has increasingly turned to cheaper labor in Mexico.

observers say that the impact will be felt more as pressure to reduce American wages. Still others suggest that concern about outsourcing has been overblown, arguing that it will be many decades before outsourcing has a major impact on American workers. All of these uncertainties have made trade a controversial policy area. As one political observer declared, "Trade is the new third rail of U.S. politics—touch it and die."[5]

International Humanitarian Policies

A third goal of American policy is to make the world a better place for all its inhabitants. The main forms of policy that address this goal are international environmental policy, international human rights policy, and international peacekeeping. The United States also contributes to international organizations such as the World Health Organization that work for global health and against hunger. These policies are often seen as secondary to the other goals of American foreign policy, forced to give way if they interfere with security or foreign economic policy. Moreover, although the United States spends billions annually on security policy and hundreds of millions on trade policy, we spend relatively little on environmental, human rights and peacekeeping efforts. Some critics charge that America has the wrong priorities, spending far more to make war than to protect human rights and the global environment. Nevertheless, a number of important American foreign policy efforts are, at least in part, designed to make the world a better place.

In the realm of international environmental policy, the United States supports a number of international efforts to protect the environment. These include the United Nations Framework Convention on Climate Change, an international agreement to study and ameliorate harmful changes in the global environment, and the Montréal Protocol, an agreement signed by more than 150 countries to limit the production of substances potentially harmful to the world's ozone layer.

The United States and the World Trade Organization

The United States has been the strongest proponent of free trade on the world stage for more than half a century. The American government played a central role in creating international institutions, designed to reduce barriers to trade, most recently the World Trade Organization. Formed in 1995, the WTO is a forum for enforcing international rules to promote free trade. Member countries can appeal to the WTO when they believe another nation is violating international rules by imposing excessive tariffs or protective subsidies. If the WTO decides in favor of the challengers, it allows them to retaliate by imposing their own tariffs on the offending country.

One of the most controversial areas of trade liberalization is agriculture. Since 2001, the WTO trade talks—called the Doha Round because they began in Qatar in 2001—have especially focused on reducing trade barriers in agriculture. Since the formation of the WTO, the United States has pressured the developing world to reduce trade barriers. At the same time, however, the United States and Europe have offered heavy subsidies to their own agricultural industries. Such subsidies keep the prices of commodities high, helping to ensure that farmers make a profit. Developing countries have long imposed tariffs to limit the entry of these artificially cheap products, which would otherwise destroy their agricultural sector. During the Doha Round, the developing world charged the richer nations with hypocrisy for demanding that poor countries lower tariffs while the rich countries refused to reduce their agriculture subsidies. This conflict led to the embarrassing public collapse of the trade summit held in Cancun in 2003. Reflecting the despair in the developing world, one protester—a South Korean who blamed the loss of his farm on reduced tariffs—killed himself after shouting "The WTO kills farmers."[a]

Both the United States and Europe have been reluctant to reduce subsidies and tariffs because farmers are important political constituencies. During the mid-1990s, the United States began to cut agricultural subsidies, but in the lead-up to the 2002 elections, President Bush signed a very generous farm bill that reinstated many of these subsidies. By 2006, American farm subsidies neared record highs. U.S. trade officials have sought to persuade American farmers that the costs of reduced subsidies will be far outweighed by the benefits gained from opening new markets for their products.

American farmers are not the only constituency blocking more liberalized trade in agricultural products. European nations also have highly subsidized agricultural industries. Despite years of trade talks on the issue, by 2005 the European Union (EU) continued to resist making substantial changes in its tariff levels. Frustrated with European proposals, U.S. trade officials derided the EU offer to reduce protection on the import of chicken legs, saying it "would amount to 'one Chicken McNugget' per person per year in the EU."[b] European officials in turn castigated Americans for pressing too hard.

In July 2006, the Doha Round of trade talks finally collapsed. Five years of negotiations had yielded very little in the way of trade liberalization because rich nations proved unable to wrest sufficient concessions from powerful domestic agricultural interests. The deep conflicts over liberalizing agricultural trade underscore the high stakes involved in promoting free trade. The United States and the rest of the developed world must be willing to bear the domestic economic and political costs of reducing trade barriers if world trade is to occur on a more level playing field.

FOR CRITICAL ANALYSIS

1. What is the role of the World Trade Organization? What have been some of the obstacles to promoting open markets around the world?
2. Why do agricultural protections pose a particularly difficult problem for advocates of liberalizing world trade? Why have the richer countries, which espouse free trade, been so reluctant to reduce protections for their own agricultural sectors?

a. Bill Lambrecht, "Upcoming World Trade Organization Summit May Draw Protests by Farmers," *St. Louis Post-Dispatch*, October 30, 2005, p. A14.

b. Alan Beattie and Frances Williams, "Last Round? Intransigence on Trade Calls into Questions the Multilateral Approach," *Financial Times*, November 16, 2005, p. 17.

Many Americans believe that protecting human rights around the world should be a goal of U.S. foreign policy. These protesters called for U.S. government action to stop human rights abuses by China in Tibet. However, humanitarian goals in foreign policy sometimes conflict with other political and economic goals.

Other nations have severely criticized the United States for withdrawing from the 1997 Kyoto Protocol, an agreement setting limits on emissions of greenhouse gases from industrial countries. The United States has asserted that the Kyoto Protocol would be harmful to American economic interests. Although the United States is concerned with the global environment, national economic interests took precedence in this case.

The same national priorities seem apparent in the area of human rights policy. The United States has a long-standing commitment to human rights and is a party to most major international agreements concerning human rights. These include the International Covenant on Civil and Political Rights, the International Convention Against Torture, the Convention on the Elimination of All Forms of Racial Discrimination, and various agreements to protect children. The State Department's Bureau of Democracy, Human Rights and Labor works cooperatively with international organizations to investigate and focus attention on human rights abuses. In 1998, the United States enacted the International Religious Freedom Act, which calls on all governments to respect religious freedom. The act lists a number of sanctions that the United States and other signatories may employ to punish nations found to be in violation.

Although the United States is committed to promoting human rights, this commitment has a lower priority in American foreign policy than the nation's security concerns and economic interests. Thus, the United States is likely to overlook human rights violations by its major trading partners, such as China, and remain silent in the face of human rights violations by such allies as Saudi Arabia. Nevertheless, human rights concerns do play a role in American foreign policy. For example, beginning in 2007, the United States has made available several million dollars annually in small grants to pay medical and legal expenses incurred by individuals who have been the victims of retaliation in their own countries for working against their governments' repressive practices. In this small way, the United States is backing its often-asserted principles.

Another form of U.S. policy designed to improve the condition of the world is support for international peacekeeping efforts. At any point in time, a number of border wars, civil wars, and guerilla conflicts flare somewhere in the world, usually in its poorer regions. These wars often generate humanitarian crises in the form of casualties, disease, and refugees. In cooperation with international agencies and other nations, the United States funds a number of efforts to keep the peace in volatile regions and to deal with the health-care and refugee problems associated with conflict. In 2007, the United States provided more than $1 billion in funding for United Nations peacekeeping operations in Bosnia, Kosovo, Sierra Leone, Lebanon, the Democratic Republic of Congo, and East Timor.

America's humanitarian policies are important. Without American efforts and funding, many international humanitarian programs would be far less successful than they are today. In general, though, security and economic interests take precedence in the eyes of U.S. policy makers over humanitarian concerns. The U.S. government is far more likely to decry abuses of religious freedom in Iran—an adversary—than in Saudi Arabia—an ally.

Who Makes American Foreign Policy?

As we have seen, domestic policies are made by governmental institutions and influenced by a variety of interest groups, political movements, and even the mass media. The same is true in the realm of foreign policy. The president and his chief advisors are the principal architects of U.S. foreign policy. However, the Congress, the bureaucracy, the courts, political parties, interest groups, and trade associations also play important roles in this realm. Often, the president and Congress are at odds over foreign policy. When the Democrats took control of Congress in 2006, they vowed to force the president to end the war in Iraq. The president vowed to resist the Democrats' efforts and generally prevailed. Ethnic lobbies such as the pro-Israel lobby and the Armenian lobby also seek to affect foreign policy. In 2007, the Armenian lobby persuaded Congress to condemn Turkey's actions in 1915, which led to the deaths of more than one million Armenians. The president feared that Turkey, an important U.S. ally, would be offended and blocked the effort. Let us examine the major institutions and forces shaping American foreign policy.

The President

Most American presidents have been domestic politicians who set out to make their place in history through achievements in domestic policy. The standard joke during Bill Clinton's 1992 campaign, extending well into his first year, was that he had learned his foreign policy at the International House of Pancakes. Thus, it was not unusual that President George W. Bush had virtually no foreign-policy preparation prior to taking office. He had traveled very little outside the United States, and he had had virtually no foreign experience as governor of Texas.

Politics Today

In 2008, voters said the economy was the most important issue affecting their presidential choice. Given the problems facing the United States in the world today, should foreign policy be more important to American voters?

Nonetheless, Bush was decisive in the initiatives he took to define America's national interest for his administration. Examples include revival of the controversial nuclear missile shield ("Star Wars"); his readiness to abandon the Anti-Ballistic Missile (ABM) treaty, which meant a serious and ugly confrontation with the Russians; changes in policy priorities away from humanitarian and environmental goals with a far stronger emphasis on goals more specifically within the realm of national security; and turning America's concerns (by degree or emphasis) away from Europe toward an "Asia-first" policy.

September 11 and its aftermath immensely accentuated the president's role and his place in foreign policy.[6] By 2002, foreign policy was the centerpiece of the Bush administration's agenda. In a June 1 speech at West Point, the **"Bush Doctrine"** of preemptive war was announced. Bush argued that "our security will require all Americans . . . to be ready for preemptive action when necessary to defend our liberty and to defend our lives." Bush's statement was clearly intended to justify his administration's plans to invade Iraq, but it had much wider implications for international relations, including the central role of the American president in guiding foreign policy.

Bush Doctrine foreign policy based on the idea that the United States should take preemptive action against threats to its national security

In 2008, the Republican presidential candidate John McCain was an exception to the usual rule emphasing domestic priorities. McCain had specialized in foreign policy matters in the Senate. During his presidential race, McCain emphasized his foreign-policy expertise. Democrats countered by naming Senator Joseph Biden, chairman of the Senate Foreign Relations Committee, as their vice-presidential candidate.

The National Security Council (NSC), which includes the secretary of state, the secretary of defense, the vice president, and other officials, advises the president on foreign policy. Here, the former secretary of state Condoleezza Rice meets with the Iraqi president Jalal Talabani.

The Bureaucracy

The major foreign-policy actors in the bureaucracy are the secretaries of the departments of State, Defense, and the Treasury; the Joint Chiefs of Staff (JCOS), especially the chair of the JCOS; and the director of the Central Intelligence Agency (CIA). Since 1947, a separate unit in the White House has overseen the vast foreign-policy establishment for the purpose of synthesizing all the messages arising out of the bureaucracy and helping the president make his own foreign policy. This is the National Security Council (NSC). It is a "subcabinet" made up of the major players just listed, plus two or three others each president was given the authority to add. Since the profound shake-up of September 11, two additional key players have been added. The first of these was the secretary of the new Department of Homeland Security (DHS), composed of twenty-two existing agencies relocated from all over the executive branch on the theory that their expertise could be better coordinated, more rational, and more efficient in a single organization designed to fight international terrorism and domestic natural disasters. The second was imposed at the top as the war in Iraq was becoming a quagmire: a director of national intelligence, to collate and coordinate intelligence coming in from multiple sources and to report a synthesis of all this to the president, on a daily basis.

Since the creation of the CIA and the Department of Defense in 1947, the secretary of defense and the director of the CIA have often been rivals engaged in power struggles for control of the intelligence community.[7] For the most part, secretaries of defense have prevailed in these battles, and the Defense Department today controls more than 80 percent of the nation's intelligence capabilities and funds. The creation of the position of director of national intelligence in 2005 to coordinate all intelligence activities set off new Washington power struggles as the "intelligence czar" faced opposition from both the CIA and the Department of Defense. As of 2008, the Defense Department has continued to resist cooperating with civilian intelligence agencies and moved to expand its own intelligence capabilities at their expense, though in a 2008 executive order the president sought to increase the power of the director of national intelligence.

In addition to these top cabinet-level officials, key lower-level staff members have policy-making influence as strong as that of the Cabinet secretaries. Some may occasionally exceed Cabinet influence. These include the two or three specialized national security advisers in the White House, the staff of the NSC (headed by the national security adviser), and a few other career bureaucrats in the departments of State and Defense whose influence varies according to their specialty and to the foreign policy issue at hand. A few civilian intelligence agencies are also involved in foreign policy and national security, the most important of which are the Federal Bureau of Investigation (FBI), the U.S. Citizenship and Immigration Services, and the Internal Revenue Service (IRS).

Politicians may turn to military leaders for information and advice as they formulate foreign policy. General David Petraeus, the leader of coalition forces in Iraq, testified before Congress on the situation in Iraq and American strategy.

In the wake of 9/11, military and law-enforcement agencies have increased their role in America's foreign policy making.[8] To a significant extent, American foreign policy is driven by military and antiterrorist concerns, and the agencies deemed capable of addressing these concerns are coming to play a larger and larger role in American foreign policy. For example, in recent years, American ambassadors have complained that they have been relegated to secondary status as the White House has looked to military commanders for information, advice, and policy implementation. For every region of the world, the U.S. military has assigned a "combatant commander," usually a senior general or admiral, to take charge of operations in that area. In many instances, these combatant commanders, who control troops, equipment, and intelligence capabilities, have become the real eyes, ears, and spokespersons for American foreign policy in their designated regions.

Congress

Although the Constitution gives Congress the power to declare war (see Table 18.1), Congress has exercised this power on only five occasions: the War of 1812, the Mexican War (1846), the Spanish-American War (1898), World War I (1917), and World War II (1941). For the first 150 years of American history, Congress's role was limited because the United States' role in world affairs was limited. During this time, the Senate was the only important congressional foreign-policy player because of its constitutional role in reviewing and approving treaties. The treaty power is still the primary entrée of the Senate into foreign-policy making. But since World War II and the continual involvement of the United States in international security and foreign aid, Congress as a whole has become a major foreign-policy maker because most modern foreign policies require financing, which requires action by both the House of Representatives and the Senate. For example, Congress's first act after September 11 was to authorize the president to use "all necessary and appropriate force," coupled with a $40 billion emergency appropriations bill for homeland defense. And although President Bush believed he possessed the constitutional authority to invade Iraq, he still sought congressional approval, which he received in October 2002. After the Democrats took control of Congress in 2007, the Democratic leadership proposed a new resolution opposing President Bush's policies in Iraq. The president asserted that he would not be bound by such a vote.

Politics Today

In 2008, Congressional Democrats again acceded to most of President Bush's demands in the realm of military and intelligence powers. What factors might make Congress unable or unwilling to take on the president in these realms?

TABLE 18.1 ★ Principal Foreign-Policy Provisions of the Constitution		
	POWER GRANTED TO: PRESIDENT	CONGRESS
War power	Commander in chief of armed forces	Provide for the common defense; declare war
Treaties	Negotiate treaties	Ratification of treaties, by two-thirds majority (Senate)
Appointments	Nominate high-level government officials	Confirm president's appointments (Senate)
Foreign commerce	No explicit powers, but treaty negotiation and appointment powers pertain	Explicit power "to regulate foreign commerce"
General powers	Executive power; veto	Legislative power; power of the purse; oversight and investigation

Democratic leaders also discussed ways of reducing at least some funding for the war. In principle, Congress's "power of the purse" is its ultimate weapon. However, reducing funding for troops already in battle is a difficult undertaking, one that can leave Congress vulnerable to the charge of endangering American lives. The president's 2007 budget proposal demanded increased funding for the war in Iraq. Initially, Congress sought to tie increased funding to a timetable for troop withdrawal. After a battle with the president, however, it was Congress that was forced to withdraw and in May 2007, Congress acceded to Bush's demands.

Not only does the president need Congress to provide funding for foreign and military policy initiatives but, under the Constitution, many presidential agreements with foreign nations also have to be approved by Congress. Article II, Section 2 of the Constitution declares that proposed treaties with other nations must be submitted by the president to the Senate and approved by a two-thirds vote. Because this "supermajority" is usually difficult to achieve, presidents generally prefer a different type of agreement with other nations called an **executive agreement.** An executive agreement is similar to a treaty and has the force of law but usually requires only a plurality vote (that is, 50 percent plus one) in both houses of Congress for approval. In recent years, Congress has approved thousands of executive agreements including such cornerstones of American trade policy as the North American Free Trade Agreement (NAFTA).

executive agreement an agreement, made between the president and another country, that has the force of a treaty but does not require the Senate's "advice and consent"

Another aspect of Congress's role in foreign policy is the Senate's power to confirm the president's nominations of Cabinet members, ambassadors, and other high-ranking officials (such as the director of the CIA, but not the director of the NSC). A final constitutional power of Congress is the regulation of "commerce with foreign nations."

Other congressional players are the foreign-policy and military-policy committees: In the Senate, these are the Foreign Relations Committee, the Armed Services Committee, and the Homeland Security and Governmental Affairs Committee; in the House, these are the Foreign Affairs and Homeland Security Committee and the Armed Services Committee. Usually, a few members of these committees who have spent years specializing in foreign affairs become trusted members of the foreign-policy establishment and are influential makers of foreign policy. In fact, several members of Congress have left the legislature to become key foreign-affairs cabinet members. After September 11, congressional committees conducted hearings on the failure of the intelligence agencies, but at the time most members of Congress were reluctant to take on these agencies or a popular president. In 2007, though, with Congress under Democratic control and the president's popularity fading, a number of congressional committees launched inquiries into the conduct of the war in Iraq and the more general operations of the intelligence and defense communities. Within weeks, congressional testimony revealed flaws in military procurement procedures, military planning, and other aspects of the administration's programs and policies. Congressional investigations and the publicity they generate are weapons Congress frequently uses to blunt presidential power.

Interest Groups

Although the president, the executive-branch "bureaucracy," and Congress are the true makers of foreign policy, the "foreign-policy establishment" is a much larger arena, including what can properly be called the shapers of foreign policy—a host of unofficial, informal players, people who possess varying degrees of influence, depending on their prestige, their reputation, their socioeconomic standing, and—most important—the party and ideology that are dominant at a given moment.

By far the most important category of nonofficial player is the interest group—that is, the interest group to which one or more foreign-policy issues are of long-standing and vital relevance. The type of interest group with the reputation for the most influence is the economic interest group. Yet the myths about its influence far outnumber and outweigh the realities. The actual influence of organized economic interest groups in foreign policy varies enormously from issue to issue and year to year. Most of these groups are "single-issue" groups and are therefore most active when their particular issue is on the agenda. On many of the broader and more sustained policy issues—such as the North American Free Trade Agreement (NAFTA) or the general question of American involvement in international trade—the larger interest groups, sometimes called peak associations, find it difficult to maintain tight enough control of their many members to speak with a single voice. The most systematic study of international trade policies and their interest groups concluded that the leaders of these large economic interest groups spend more time maintaining consensus among their members than they do lobbying Congress or pressuring major players in the executive branch.[9] The more successful economic interest groups, in terms of influencing foreign policy, are the narrower, single-issue groups such as the tobacco industry, which over the years has successfully kept American foreign policy from putting heavy restrictions on international trade in and advertising of tobacco products; and the computer hardware and software industries, which have successfully hardened the American attitude toward Chinese piracy of intellectual property rights.

Members of Amnesty International asked the U.S. government to take action to end the violence in the Darfur region of Sudan. Interest groups like Amnesty International may influence foreign policy by lobbying the government directly and by raising public awareness of certain issues.

Another type of interest group with a well-founded reputation for influence in foreign policy is made up of people with strong attachments to and identification with their country of national origin. The interest group with the reputation for the greatest influence is Jewish Americans, whose family and emotional ties to Israel make them one of the most alert and active interest groups in the whole field of foreign policy. But note once again how narrowly specialized that interest is—it focuses almost entirely on policies toward Israel. Similarly, Americans of Irish heritage, despite having lived in the United States for two, three, or four generations, still maintain vigilance about American policies toward Ireland and Northern Ireland; some even contribute to the Irish Republican Army. Many other ethnic and national interest groups wield similar influence over American foreign policy.

These ethnic or national-origin interest groups are more influential than their counterparts in other democratic countries. This is a kind of dual loyalty that Americans generally welcome as a worthy sentiment. But there are limits, especially when national origin is coupled with or tied to countries in which a single religion is dominant. For example, Jews with strong ties to Israel and Catholics with connections to Ireland have on occasion been blocked from group influence on foreign policy because "dual loyalty" can be taken by other groups as "doubtful loyalty."[10] Nevertheless, Irish and Jewish groups, as well as a variety of other ethnic American interest groups, are vigorously involved in salient aspects of foreign policy, and it is an irrational or nonrational elected politician who disregards their signals. It is quite possible that the "electoral connection"[11] and the politics of representation in Congress (and the White House) are at their most intense when national origin is linked to a foreign-policy issue. Many will argue that the rationality principle "need not . . . be equated with such narrowly self-serving actions."[12] However, the nationality interest is often the strongest electoral connection.

A third type of interest group, one with a reputation that has been growing in the past two decades, is devoted to human rights. Such groups are made up of people who, instead of having self-serving economic or ethnic interests in foreign policy, are genuinely concerned about the welfare and treatment of people throughout the world—particularly those who suffer under harsh political regimes. A relatively small but often quite influential example is Amnesty International, whose exposés of human-rights abuses have altered the practices of many regimes around the world. In recent years, the Christian right has been a vocal advocate for the human rights of Christians who are persecuted in other parts of the world, most notably in China, for their religious beliefs. For example, the Christian Coalition joined groups such as Amnesty International in lobbying Congress to restrict trade with countries that permit attacks against religious believers.

A related type of group with rapidly growing influence is the ecological or environmental group, sometimes collectively called greens. Groups of this nature often depend more on demonstrations than on the usual forms and strategies of influence in Washington—lobbying and using electoral politics, for example. Demonstrations in strategically located areas can have significant influence on American foreign policy. The most recent examples were the 1999 protests in Seattle and the

2001 protest in Genoa, Italy, against the World Trade Organization (WTO) and its authority to impose limits and restrictions on sovereign nations (even the United States).

The Media

Each part of the media has its own character and mode of operations, and as a consequence each may represent a different source of anguish and a different source of opportunity in making and implementing foreign policy. This makes the media a very special problem for every president because—as George Washington warned—once we become "entangled" with other nations, the media have to be "managed" to a certain extent, or persuaded to present a single, national voice. And managing can come close to a violation of the First Amendment's freedom of the press guarantee. Such management, then, becomes an overwhelming problem during times of war, cold war, or any other sustained threat to national security, including these years following September 11.

The balancing of security against freedom of the press has become increasingly difficult with the increased power of the media that has resulted from significant developments in communications and information technology. Iraq is of course the most important case in point. During the first few weeks of the invasion in 2003, nearly 600 embedded journalists (plus a number of "free-floating" U.S. and non-U.S. journalists) provided the most intensive coverage in the history of war, and without any question for the first time the coverage was instantaneous, visual, annotated, and in color—not only on television but on the front pages of the major newspapers.

Take special note of the word *embedded*. No matter how delicately put, embedding involved the management of the journalists in a deal to provide access and protection in return for "responsible" reporting, a deal that led to the widespread suspicion and fear that not only the journalists but also the news itself was being managed. The suspicion grew as the war changed after the regime of Saddam Hussein was deposed, the Iraqi armed forces dispersed, and the entire civil government that had been dominated by the Hussein Baathist party was decommissioned. Quite simply, the situation changed from a conventional, organized war to an ambiguous, insurgent war. This was the end of any practice of embedding and the beginning of fewer but freer-floating journalists, a change that also meant the expansion of dissent and open criticism accompanying the reports. "News management" to any degree was no longer possible.

As casualties mounted and the insurgency dragged on, reporting from Iraq (and the entire Middle East) began to demonstrate the true plurality of the term *media*. Considerable support remained—among Americans at home and journalists reporting from the scene—for maintaining America's commitment to Iraq and for sustaining and increasing American military and economic support of Iraq. But as reports critical of America's policy—and, even more, of the policy's implementation—expanded in number, scale, and intensity, the reaction to the unmanaged reporting also increased. Inevitably, self-designated conservative and neoconservative critics were charging that ideology was driving the opposition to the war and that the media—especially certain national newspapers, periodicals, and television syndicates—were nothing more than channels for "liberal bias."

Putting It Together

What can we say about who really makes American foreign policy? First, except for the president, the influence of players and shapers varies from case to case—this is a good reason to look with some care at each example of foreign policy in this chapter. Second because the one constant influence is the centrality of the president in foreign-policy making, it is best to evaluate other actors and factors as they interact with the president.[13] Third, the reason influence varies from case to case is that each case arises under different conditions and with vastly different time constraints: For issues that arise and are resolved quickly, the opportunity for influence is limited. Fourth, foreign-policy experts will usually disagree about the level of influence any player or type of player has on policy making.

But just to get started, let's make a few tentative generalizations and then put them to the test with the substance and experience reported in the remainder of this chapter. First, when an important foreign-policy decision has to be made under conditions of crisis—where time is of the essence—the influence of the presidency is at its strongest. Second, within those time constraints, access to the decision is limited almost exclusively to the narrowest definition of the foreign-policy establishment. The arena for participation is tiny; any discussion at all is limited to the officially and constitutionally designated players. To put this another way, in a crisis the foreign-policy establishment works as it is supposed to.[14] As time becomes less restricted, even when the decision to be made is of great importance, the arena of participation expands to include more government players and more nonofficial, informal players—the most concerned interest groups and the most important journalists. In other words, the arena becomes more pluralistic and, therefore, less distinguishable from the politics of domestic-policy making. Third, because there are so many other countries with power and interests on any given issue, there are severe limits on the choices the United States can make. That is, in sharp contrast to domestic politics, U.S. policy makers in the foreign-policy realm are engaged not only in infighting but also in strategic interaction with policy makers in other nations; their choices are made both in reaction to and in anticipation of these strategic interactions. As one author concludes, in foreign affairs, "policy takes precedence over politics."[15] Thus even though foreign-policy making in noncrisis situations may closely resemble the pluralistic politics of domestic-policy making, foreign-policy making is still a narrower arena with fewer participants.

The Instruments of Modern American Foreign Policy

Any government has at hand certain instruments, or tools, to use in implementing its foreign policy. An instrument is neutral, capable of serving many goals. There have been many instruments of American foreign policy, and we can deal here only with those instruments we deem to be most important in the modern epoch: diplomacy, the United Nations, the international monetary structure, economic aid, collective security, and military deterrence. Each of these instruments will be evaluated in this section for its utility in the conduct of American foreign policy, and each will be assessed in light of the history and development of American values.

Diplomacy

We begin this treatment of instruments with diplomacy because it is the instrument to which all other instruments should be subordinated, although they seldom are. **Diplomacy** is the representation of a government to other foreign governments. Its purpose is to promote national values or interests by peaceful means. According to Hans Morgenthau, "a diplomacy that ends in war has failed in its primary objective."[16]

diplomacy the representation of a government to other foreign governments

The first effort to create a modern diplomatic service in the United States was made through the Rogers Act of 1924, which established the initial framework for a professional foreign service staff. But it took World War II and the Foreign Service Act of 1946 to forge the foreign service into a fully professional diplomatic corps.

Diplomacy, by its very nature, is overshadowed by spectacular international events, dramatic initiatives, and meetings among heads of state or their direct personal representatives. The traditional American distrust of diplomacy continues today, albeit in weaker form. Impatience with or downright distrust of diplomacy has been built not only into all the other instruments of foreign policy but also into the modern presidential system itself.[17] So much personal responsibility has been heaped on the presidency that it is difficult for presidents to entrust any of their authority or responsibility in foreign policy to professional diplomats in the State Department and other bureaucracies.

Distrust of diplomacy has also produced a tendency among all recent presidents to turn frequently to military and civilian personnel outside the State Department to take on a special diplomatic role as direct personal representatives of the president. As discouraging as it is to those who have dedicated their careers to foreign service to have personal appointees chosen over their heads, it is probably even more discouraging when they are displaced from a foreign-policy issue as soon as relations with the country they are posted in begin to heat up. When a special personal representative is sent abroad to represent the president, that envoy holds a status higher than that of the local ambassador, and the embassy becomes the envoy's temporary residence and base of operation. Despite the impressive professionalization of the American foreign service—with advanced training,

The United Nations is not always but can be an important instrument of American foreign policy. In trying to build international support for the U.S. case against Iraq, President Bush went before the General Assembly and urged the United Nations to compel Iraq to disarm. Two months later, the UN Security Council gave its qualified support to Bush's position.

competitive exams, language requirements, and career commitment—this practice of displacing career ambassadors with political appointees and with special personal presidential representatives continues. For instance, when President Clinton in 1998 sought to boost the peace process in Northern Ireland, he called on the former senator George Mitchell. Mitchell received almost unanimous praise for his skill and patience in chairing the Northern Ireland peace talks. The caliber of his work in Northern Ireland led to Senator Mitchell's becoming involved in another of the world's apparently unsolvable conflicts, that between the Israelis and the Palestinians.

Despite the United States' track record of distrust of diplomacy, immediately following the terrorist attacks of September 11, 2001, questions arose about how we could go after terrorist networks without the active cooperation of dozens of governments. Getting access to terrorists in various countries, plus putting together and keeping together the worldwide alliance of governments to fight terrorism, was a diplomatic, not a military, chore. In calls to more than eighty nations, former Secretary of State Colin Powell helped to extract dozens of pledges that would have been more difficult to get months later, when sympathy for America began to wane. In short, global unity and success in fighting terrorism required constant diplomatic efforts, not only by Powell, but also by other leading players, including President Bush himself.

In 2008, both parties' presidential candidates criticized the Bush administration for having failed to use diplomacy to secure greater international support for the Iraq war. Both promised to revitalize American diplomacy.

The significance of diplomacy and its vulnerability to politics may be better appreciated as we proceed to the other instruments. Diplomacy was an instrument more or less imposed on Americans as the prevailing method of dealing among nation-states in the nineteenth century. The other instruments to be identified and assessed below are instruments that Americans self-consciously crafted for themselves to take care of their own chosen place in the world affairs of the second half of the twentieth century and beyond. They therefore better reflect American culture and values than diplomacy does.

The United Nations

United Nations (UN) an organization of nations founded in 1945 to serve as a channel for negotiation and a means of settling international disputes peaceably. The UN has had frequent successes in providing a forum for negotiation and on some occasions a means of preventing international conflicts from spreading. On a number of occasions, the UN has been a convenient cover for U.S. foreign-policy goals

The utility of the **United Nations (UN)** to the United States as an instrument of foreign policy can be too easily underestimated, because the United Nations is a very large and unwieldy institution with few powers and no armed forces to implement its rules and resolutions. Its supreme body is the UN General Assembly, comprising one representative of each of the 191 member states; each member representative has one vote, regardless of the size of the country. Important issues require a two-thirds majority vote, and the annual session of the General Assembly runs only from September to December (although it can call extra sessions). It has little organization that can make it an effective decision-making body, with only six standing committees, few tight rules of procedure, and no political parties to provide priorities and discipline. Its defenders are quick to add that although it lacks armed forces, it relies on the power of world opinion; and this is not to be taken lightly. The powers of the United Nations devolve mainly to its "executive committee," the UN Security Council, which alone has the real power to make decisions and rulings that member states are obligated by the UN Charter to implement. The Security Council may be called into session at any time, and each member (or

POLITICS & POPULAR CULTURE

Popular Culture and America's Reputation Abroad

In the past few years, scholars and journalists have been discussing America's "image problem" across the globe. In Chapter 16 we looked at how foreign policy decisions were affecting the global marketplace and consumption of American brands. But how does American popular culture itself contribute to the image of what America is like and who Americans are as people? Does American popular culture help or hurt perceptions of America around the globe?

Although perceptions of American foreign policy may be negative in numerous countries, appreciation for America's popular culture has remained relatively high. Andrew Kohut of the Pew Global Attitudes Project reports that in countries with large Muslim populations, where U.S. foreign policy is often seen unfavorably, appreciation for American popular culture is greater than one might expect. In Lebanon, for example, approval of U.S. foreign policy is particularly low, and yet 65 percent of the population still report liking American films, television, and music.

However, some scholars and researchers are concerned about the potentially negative impact of American popular culture on global perceptions of the United States. The humanities scholar Martha Bayles is a critic of the export of American culture abroad due to the impression that violent and sexually explicit content may make on foreign viewers of American media. "Along with worrying about what popular culture is teaching our children about life," writes Bayles, "we need also to worry about what it is teaching the world about America."[a] One set of studies directly addressed the question of what impact American media may have on the international community's opinions of American culture. Through surveys administered to high school students in twelve countries, the authors determined that perceptions of Americans as violent, criminal, and sexually immoral were significantly influenced by the violent and sexual images that bombarded them through American media."[b]

Interestingly, television programmers in international markets report that the violence in American media is often what international television viewers want the most. Klaus Hallig, who purchases American media for various eastern European television markets, explained to *The Washington Post* that central Europeans want big, violent television. "They want cars to be exploded fourteen stories high—blow 'em up, kill 'em, stab 'em."[c]

Some researchers have observed that positive aspects of American television and film speak to global audiences. The quintessentially American narrative of the underdog protagonist who triumphs over hardship has broad appeal. The sociologist Todd Gitlin stated in a *Washington Post* interview that the United States is particularly skilled at "producing themes and story lines that appeal to a global sensibility: freedom, freedom of movement, freedom from family, from place, from earth, from roles."[d]

FOR CRITICAL ANALYSIS

1. Do you think that American popular culture contributes to positive or negative opinions of America abroad? Should the government try to regulate or influence the image of the United States that is conveyed through popular culture?
2. Why do you think that American popular culture remains fairly popular in countries where American foreign policy is distinctly unpopular?

a. M. Bayles, "Now Showing: The Good, the Bad and the Ugly Americans," *Washington Post*, August 28, 2005, p. B1.
b. M. DeFleur and M. DeFleur, *Learning to Hate Americans: How the U.S. Media Shape Negative Attitudes among Teenagers in Twelve Countries* (Spokane, WA: Marquette Books, 2003).
c. P. Farhi and M. Rosenfeld, "American Pop Penetrates Worldwide," *Washington Post*, October 25, 1998, p. A1.
d. Farhi and Rosenfeld, "American Pop Penetrates Worldwide."

a designated alternate) must be present at UN Headquarters in New York at all times. It is composed of fifteen members: five are permanent (the victors of World War II), and ten are elected by the General Assembly for two-year, nonrepeatable terms. The five permanent members are China, France, Russia, the United Kingdom, and the United States. Each of the fifteen members has only one vote, and a nine-vote majority of the fifteen is required on all substantive matters. But each of the five permanent members also has a negative vote, a "veto," and one veto is sufficient to reject any substantive proposal.

The UN can serve as a useful forum for international discussions and an instrument for multilateral action. Most peacekeeping efforts to which the United States contributes, for example, are undertaken under UN auspices.

The International Monetary Structure

Fear of a repeat of the economic devastation that followed World War I brought the United States together with its allies (except the USSR) to Bretton Woods, New Hampshire, in 1944 to create a new international economic structure for the postwar world. The result was two institutions: the International Bank for Reconstruction and Development (commonly called the World Bank) and the International Monetary Fund.

The World Bank was set up to finance long-term capital. Leading nations took on the obligation of contributing funds to enable the World Bank to make loans to capital-hungry countries. (The U.S. quota has been about one-third of the total.)

International Monetary Fund (IMF) an institution established in 1944 that provides loans and facilitates international monetary exchange

The **International Monetary Fund (IMF)** was set up to provide for the short-term flow of money. After the war, the dollar, instead of gold, was the chief means by which the currencies of one country would be "changed into" currencies of another country for purposes of making international transactions. To permit debtor countries with no international balances to make purchases and investments, the IMF was set up to lend dollars or other appropriate currencies to needy member countries to help them overcome temporary trade deficits. For many years after World War II, the IMF, along with U.S. foreign aid, in effect constituted the only international medium of exchange.

During the 1990s, the IMF returned to a position of enhanced importance through its efforts to reform some of the largest debtor nations and formerly communist countries, to bring them more fully into the global capitalist economy. For example, in the early 1990s, Russia and thirteen other former Soviet republics were invited to join the IMF and the World Bank with the expectation of receiving $10.5 billion from these two agencies, primarily for a currency-stabilization fund. Each republic was to get a permanent IMF representative, and the IMF increased its staff by at least 10 percent to provide the expertise necessary to cope with the problems of these emerging capitalist economies.[18]

The IMF, with $93 billion, has more money to lend poor countries than do the United States, Europe, or Japan (the three leading IMF shareholders) individually. It makes its policy decisions in ways that are generally consonant with the interests of the leading shareholders.[19] Two weeks after September 11, 2001, the IMF had approved a $135 million loan to economically troubled Pakistan, a key player in the war against the Taliban government of Afghanistan because of its strategic location. Turkey, also because of its strategic location in the Middle East, was likewise put back in the IMF pipeline.[20] The future of the IMF, the World Bank, and all other private sources of international investment will depend in part on extension

Multilateralism versus Unilateralism

After the sudden end of the Cold War, everyone knew international relations would never be the same, but no one could guess how they would be different. The first intimation came on August 2, 1990, when Iraq invaded Kuwait and occupied a substantial amount of Kuwaiti territory. President George H. W. Bush used diplomatic means behind the scenes to create a multinational alliance of twenty-nine nations against Iraq.

Ten years later, President George W. Bush's foreign policy behavior was quickly defined as that of a classic go-it-alone, cowboy president. Disregarding ten presidential predecessors over fifty-two years, Bush mostly acted unilaterally. He denounced arms control, rejected the Kyoto Protocol on global warming, and opposed treaties or international agreements in principle. He and his advisers saw multilateralism not as a beneficial alliance but as a "straitjacket."

But a revolution in American foreign policy came about immediately after September 11, 2001. Pakistan, Russia, and other nations cooperated when it was clear that the United States was ready to go to war against world terrorism. Although President Bush sounded quite unilateral when he warned that those nations who weren't with us were against us, most of his actions were multilateral. The Russian president Vladimir Putin dropped all objections to the deployment of American and NATO counterterrorism forces in the former Soviet republic key states on the long border between Russia and the Middle East. The possibility was even emerging that Russia would seek and might gain admission to NATO. President Bush also reversed other facets of his earlier unilateralism, including paying all back dues to the United Nations and making then Secretary of State Colin Powell, who earlier had been losing out to the go-it-alone phalanx of the administration, a prominent player in building this alliance.

But there's a price for multilateralism. One lesson to be learned from the 1991 Gulf war alliance is that a genuine alliance can be a restraint on the United States. In 1991, the influence of many of the twenty-nine-nation Desert Storm members shaped the decision to interrupt the advance to Baghdad and the eradication of the entire Saddam Hussein regime. Our termination of the war at that point was regarded as a grievous error even by a number of high-ranking American military officers. And it was a lesson taken seriously by the advisers around President George W. Bush ten years later.

In October 2002, Bush went to the United Nations with a different attitude from his unilateral position and agreed to abide by a stern UN Security Council resolution that Iraq disarm and subject itself to unconditional weapons inspection, with serious consequences if it did not cooperate within one month's time. But Bush balked at the provision for a second UN Security Council resolution if Iraq did not cooperate and asserted his conviction that the United States would proceed if it was not satisfied that complete disarmament was taking place. Although the UN resolution had put the United States on course to form another multilateral alliance, the Bush administration reserved the option of going it alone if necessary. Officially, the war was conducted by a "coalition of the willing," but in reality that was a euphemism for a unilateral American offensive. The British contribution was fairly substantial, but not enough to characterize the war as a "bilateral" effort. The Iraq war of 2003 was American, and the war went quickly. But the occupation, the reconstruction of the economy, the development of a government, and the achievement of democracy all took vastly more time and lives than the American strategic planners had anticipated.

FOR CRITICAL ANALYSIS

1. Given American experience in Iraq, is it necessary to conclude that unilateralism is always the worst choice and multilateralism always the best? Is a multilateral alliance genuine only when supported by a UN resolution?
2. Is bilateralism a genuine midpoint between the two extremes of unilateralism and multilateralism? When and under what conditions would bilateralism be the best choice?

of more credit to the Third World and other developing countries, because credit means investment and productivity. But the future may depend even more on reducing the debt that is already there from previous extensions of credit.

Economic Aid and Sanctions

Every year, the United States provides nearly $30 billion in economic assistance to other nations. Some aid has a humanitarian purpose, such as helping to provide health care, shelter for refugees, or famine relief. A good deal of American aid, however, is designed to promote American security interests or economic concerns. For example, the United States provides military assistance to a number of its allies in the form of advanced weapons or loans to help them purchase advanced weapons. Such loans generally stipulate that the recipient must purchase the designated weapons from American firms. In this way, the United States hopes to bolster its security and economic interests with one grant. The two largest recipients of American military assistance are Israel and Egypt, American allies that fought two wars against one another. The United States believes that its military assistance allows both to feel sufficiently secure to remain at peace with one another.

Politics Today

There has been a good deal of debate about whether economic sanctions can convince North Korea or Iran to halt their nuclear weapons programs. What factors might determine the effectiveness of sanctions?

Aid is an economic carrot. Sanctions are an economic stick. Economic sanctions that the United States employs against other nations include trade embargoes, bans on investment, and efforts to prevent the World Bank or other international institutions from extending credit to a nation against which the United States has a grievance. Sanctions are most often employed when the United States seeks to weaken what it considers a hostile regime or when it is attempting to compel some particular action by another regime. Thus, for example, in order to weaken the Castro government, the United States has long prohibited American firms from doing business with Cuba. In recent years, the United States has maintained economic sanctions against Iran and North Korea in an effort to prevent those nations from pursuing nuclear weapons programs.

Unilateral sanctions by the United States usually have little effect, since the target can usually trade elsewhere, sometimes even with foreign affiliates of U.S. firms. If, however, the United States is able to convince its allies to cooperate, sanctions have a better chance of success. International sanctions applied to Libya, for example, played a role in the regime's decision to enter into negotiations with the United States over Libyan responsibility for a number of terrorist attacks.

Collective Security

In 1947, most Americans hoped that the United States could meet its world obligations through the United Nations and economic structures alone. But most foreign policy makers recognized that was a vain hope even as they were permitting and encouraging Americans to believe it. They had anticipated the need for military entanglements at the time of drafting the original UN Charter by insisting on language that recognized the right of all nations to provide for their mutual defense independent of the United Nations. And almost immediately after enactment of the Marshall Plan, designed to promote European economic recovery, the White House and a parade of State and Defense Department officials followed up with an urgent request to the Senate to ratify, and to both houses of Congress to finance, mutual defense alliances.

At first quite reluctant to approve treaties providing for national security alliances, the Senate ultimately agreed with the executive branch. The first collective security agreement was the Rio Treaty (ratified by the Senate in September 1947), which created the Organization of American States (OAS). This was the model treaty, anticipating all succeeding collective security treaties by providing that an armed attack against any of its members "shall be considered as an attack against all the American States," including the United States. A more significant break with U.S. tradition against peacetime entanglements came with the North Atlantic Treaty (signed in April 1949), which created the **North Atlantic Treaty Organization (NATO).** ANZUS, a treaty tying Australia and New Zealand to the United States, was signed in September 1951. Three years later, the Southeast Asia Treaty created the Southeast Asia Treaty Organization (SEATO).

North Atlantic Treaty Organization (NATO) a treaty organization, comprising the United States, Canada, and most of Western Europe, formed in 1948 to counter the perceived threat from the Soviet Union

bilateral treaty treaty made between two nations

In addition to these multilateral treaties, the United States entered into a number of **bilateral treaties**—treaties between two countries. As one author has observed, the United States has been a *producer* of security, whereas most of its allies have been *consumers* of security.[21]

This pattern has continued in the post–Cold War era, and its best illustration is in the Persian Gulf War, where the United States provided the initiative, the leadership, and most of the armed forces, even though its allies were obliged to reimburse over 90 percent of the cost.

It is difficult to evaluate collective security and its treaties, because the purpose of collective security as an instrument of foreign policy is prevention, and success of this kind has to be measured in terms of what did *not* happen. Critics have argued that U.S. collective security treaties posed a threat of encirclement to the Soviet Union, forcing it to produce its own collective security, particularly the Warsaw Pact.[22] Nevertheless, no one can deny the counterargument that more than sixty years have passed without a world war.

In 1998, the expansion of NATO took its first steps toward former Warsaw Pact members, extending membership to Poland, Hungary, and the Czech Republic. Most of Washington embraced this expansion as the true and fitting end of the Cold

Military force is the most visible instrument of foreign policy and may become necessary when other options fail. The use of force, however, almost always engenders unanticipated consequences and problems, as America's experience in Iraq has shown.

War, and the U.S. Senate echoed this with a resounding 80-to-19 vote to induct these three former Soviet satellites into NATO. The expansion was also welcomed among European member nations, who quickly approved the move, hailing it as the final closing of the book on Yalta, the 1945 treaty that divided Europe into Western and Soviet spheres of influence after the defeat of Germany. Expanded membership seems to have made NATO less threatening and more acceptable to Russia. Russia became a partner when the NATO-Russia Council was formed in 2002. Finally, although the expanded NATO membership (now nineteen countries) reduces the threat to Russia, it also reduces the utility of NATO as a military alliance. The September 11 attack on the United States was the first time in its fifty-plus-year history that Article 5 of the North Atlantic Treaty had to be invoked; it provides that an attack on one country is an attack on all the member countries. In fighting the war on terror, the Bush administration recognized that no matter how preponderant American power was, some aspects of its foreign policy could not be achieved without multilateral cooperation. On the other hand, the United States did not want to be constrained by its alliances. The global coalition initially forged after September 11 numbered over 170 countries. Not all joined the war effort in Afghanistan, but most if not all provided some form of support for some aspect of the war on terrorism, such as economic sanctions and intelligence. The war in Iraq, however, put the "coalition of the willing" to a test. The Bush administration was determined not to make its decision to go to war subject to the UN or NATO or any other international organization. The breadth of the United States' coalition was deemed secondary to its being nonconstraining. As a result, other than the British government, no major power supported the United States' actions.

Military Force

The most visible instrument of foreign policy is, of course, military force. The United States has built the world's most imposing military, with army, navy, marine and air force units stationed in virtually every corner of the globe. The United States spends nearly as much on military might as the rest of the world combined (Figure 18.3). The famous Prussian military strategist Carl von Clausewitz called war "politics by other means." By this he meant that nations used force not simply to demonstrate their capacity for violence. Rather, force or the threat of force is a tool nations must sometimes use to achieve their foreign-policy goals. Military force may be needed to protect a nation's security interests and economic concerns. Ironically, force may also be needed to achieve humanitarian goals. For example, without international military protection, the Africans who have taken refuge in Darfur camps would be at the mercy of the violent Sudanese regime.

Though force is sometimes necessary, military force is generally seen as a last resort and avoided if possible because of a number of problems commonly associated with its use. First, the use of military force is extremely costly in both human and financial terms. In the past fifty years, tens of thousands of Americans have been killed and hundreds of billions of dollars spent in America's military operations. Before they employ military force to achieve national goals, policy makers must be certain that achieving these goals is essential and that other means are unlikely to succeed.

Second, the use of military force is inherently fraught with risk. However carefully policy makers and generals plan for military operations, results can seldom be fully anticipated. Variables ranging from the weather to unexpected weapons and

FIGURE 18.3 ★ Military Spending, 2008 (in Billions of U.S. Dollars and Percentage of World Total)

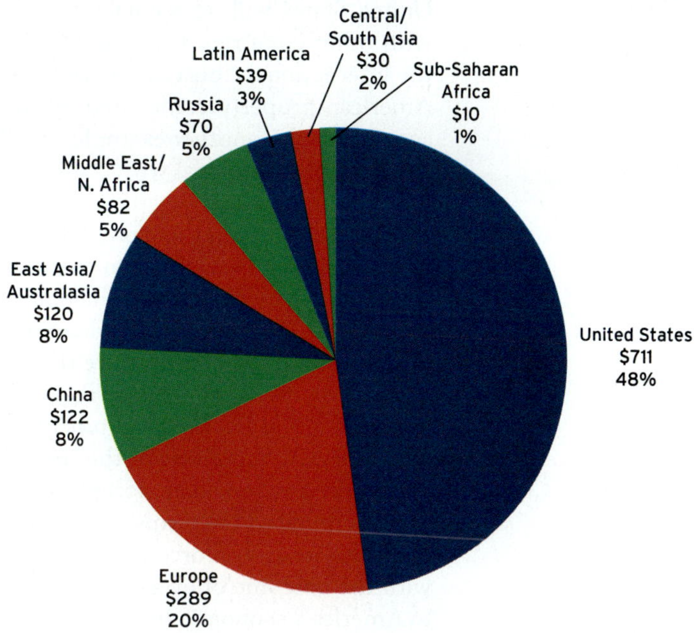

NOTE: 2008 total military spending: $1. 473 trillion
SOURCE: Center for Arms Control and Non-Proliferation, www.armscontrolcenter.org/policy/securityspending/articles/fy09_dod_request_global/ (accessed 5/19/08).

tactics deployed by opponents may upset the most careful calculations and turn military operations into costly disasters or convert maneuvers that were expected to be quick and decisive into long, drawn-out, expensive struggles. For example, American policy makers expected to defeat the Iraqi army quickly and easily in 2003—and they did. Policy makers did not anticipate, however, that American forces would still be struggling years later to defeat the insurgency that arose in the war's aftermath.

Finally, in a democracy, the use of military force is almost certain to engender political difficulties for any government that chooses to address policy problems through military means. Generally speaking, the American public will support relatively short and decisive military engagements. If, however, a conflict drags on, producing casualties and expenses with no clear outcome, the public loses patience and opposition politicians point to the government's lies and ineptitude. Korea, Vietnam, and Iraq are all examples of protracted conflicts whose domestic political repercussions brought down the governments that decided military force was needed.

Thus, military force remains a major foreign policy tool, and the United States currently possesses a more powerful and effective set of military forces than any other nation. Nevertheless, even for the United States, the use of military force is fraught with risk and is not to be undertaken lightly.

Arbitration

The final foreign-policy tool we shall consider is dispute arbitration. Arbitration means referring an international disagreement to a neutral third party for resolution. Arbitration is sometimes seen as a form of "soft power" as distinguished from military force, economic sanctions, and other coercive foreign policy instruments. The United States will occasionally turn to international tribunals to resolve disputes with other countries. For example, in February 2008, the U.S. government asked the International Court of Justice to resolve a long-standing dispute with Italy over American property confiscated by the Italian government more than forty years ago. Or, to take another example, in 1981 the United States and Iran established an arbitral tribunal to deal with claims arising from Iran's seizure of the U.S. embassy in Tehran in 1979.

More important, the United States relies heavily on the work of arbitral panels to maintain the flow of international trade on which America's economy depends. American firms would be reluctant to do business abroad if they could not be certain that their property and contractual rights would be honored by other nations. Arbitration helps produce that certainty. Almost every international contract contains an arbitration clause requiring that disputes between the parties will be resolved not by foreign governments, but by impartial arbitral panels accepted by both sides. By the terms of the "New York Convention," virtually every nation in the world has agreed to accept and enforce arbitral verdicts. The United States has incorporated the terms of the New York Convention into federal law, and U.S. courts vigorously enforce arbitral judgements. The United States may not be happy with the outcome of every arbitral proceeding, but the arbitral system is essential to America's economic interests.

Foreign Policy and America's Place in the World

When policy makers choose courses of action and select the policy instruments they will employ, they do not begin with a blank slate. Presidents and other policy makers are generally guided by some overall vision of America's national interest and the nation's place in the world. Some recent presidents, Jimmy Carter for example, have seen America as a great power in decline, compelled to act cautiously on the world stage. Others, such as Ronald Reagan, have seen America as a rising power—"It's morning in America" was Reagan's slogan—capable of undertaking bold and decisive foreign policy moves.

Four Visions of America's Role in the World

In general terms, it is possible to identify four distinct visions of America's world role that, at various times, have guided recent presidents. These are:

Napoleonic role a strategy pursued by a powerful nation to prevent aggressive actions against it by improving the internal state of affairs of a particular country, even if this means encouraging revolution in that country

THE NAPOLEONIC ROLE The **Napoleonic role** takes its name from the role that postrevolutionary France played under Napoleon. The French at that time felt not only that their new democratic system of government was the best on earth but also that France would not be safe until democracy was adopted universally. If this meant intervention in the internal affairs of France's neighbors, and if that meant warlike reactions, then so be it. President Woodrow Wilson expressed a similar viewpoint when he supported the U.S. declaration of war in 1917 with his argument that "the world must be made safe for democracy." Obviously any powerful nation can adopt such a position as a rationalization for intervening at its convenience in the internal affairs of another country. But it can also be sincerely espoused, and in the United States it has from time to time enjoyed broad popular consensus. We played the Napoleonic role most recently in ousting the Philippine dictator Ferdinand Marcos (February 1986), the Panamanian leader Manuel Noriega (December 1989), the Sandinista government of Nicaragua (February 1990), the military rulers of Haiti (September 1994), the Taliban government of Afghanistan (2001), and Iraq's Saddam Hussein (2003).

THE HOLY ALLIANCE ROLE The concept of the **Holy Alliance role** emerged out of the defeat of Napoleon and the agreement by the leaders of Great Britain, Russia, Austria, and Prussia to preserve the social order against *all* revolution, including democratic revolution, at whatever cost. (Post-Napoleonic France also joined it.) The Holy Alliance made use of every kind of political instrument available—including political suppression, espionage, sabotage, and outright military intervention—to keep existing governments in power. The Holy Alliance role is comparable to the Napoleonic role in that each is based on the assumption that intervention into the internal affairs of other countries is justified for the maintenance of peace. But Napoleonic intervention is motivated by fear of dictatorship, and it can accept and even encourage revolution. In contrast, Holy Alliance intervention is antagonistic to any form of political change, even when this means supporting an existing dictatorship.[23]

Holy Alliance role a strategy pursued by a superpower to prevent any change in the existing distribution of power among nation-states, even if this requires intervention into the internal affairs of another country in order to keep a ruler from being overthrown

THE BALANCE-OF-POWER ROLE The **balance-of-power role** is basically an effort by the major powers to play off each other so that no great power or combination of great and lesser powers can impose conditions on others. The most relevant example of the use of this strategy is found in the nineteenth century, especially the latter half. What makes the balance-of-power role most distinct from the two previously identified roles is that this role accepts the political system of each country, asking no questions except whether the country will join an alliance and will use its resources to ensure that each country will respect the borders and interests of all the others.[24]

balance-of-power role the strategy whereby many countries form alliances with one or more countries in order to counterbalance the behavior of other, usually more powerful, nation-states

In preparing for a potential war against Iraq, the United States tried to enlist multilateral support through the U.N. However, among the world's leaders only Britain's prime minister, Tony Blair, explicitly endorsed the United States's preemptive intervention in Iraq. Blair's decision to support the United States and send troops to Iraq angered many British citizens.

economic expansionist role the strategy often pursued by capitalist countries to adopt foreign policies that will maximize the success of domestic corporations in their dealings with other countries

THE ECONOMIC EXPANSIONIST ROLE The **economic expansionist role**, also called the capitalist role, shares with the balance-of-power role the attitude that the political system or ideology of a country is irrelevant; the only questions are whether a country has anything to buy or sell and whether its entrepreneurs, corporations, and government agencies will honor their contracts. Governments and their armies are occasionally drawn into economic expansionist relationships in order to establish, reopen, or expand trade relationships, and to keep the lines of commerce open. But the role is political, too. For example, the United States played an economic expansionist role in Latin and Central America until the Cold War pushed us toward a Holy Alliance role with most Latin nations.

Like arms control, however, economic expansion does not happen spontaneously. In the past, economic expansion owed a great deal to military backing because contracts do not enforce themselves, trade deficits are not paid automatically, and new regimes do not always honor the commitments made by regimes they replace. The only way to expand economic relationships is through diplomacy.

Thinking Critically about America's Role in the World Today

Let us examine how each of these visions of America's world role has helped policy makers shape America's actions on the international stage.

The Cold War and the Holy Alliance Role

For Critical Analysis

What values have been most important to American foreign policy? How have these priorities changed during major epochs of American history?

The emergence of the Soviet Union as a superpower had an overwhelming influence on American foreign policy thinking in the post–World War II era. The distribution of power in the world was "bipolar," and Americans saw the world separated in two, with an "iron curtain" dividing the communist world from the free world. Immediately after the war, America's foreign-policy goal had been "prodemocracy," a Napoleonic role dominated by the Marshall Plan and the genuine hope for a democratic world. This quickly shifted toward a Holy Alliance role, with "containment" as the primary foreign policy criterion.[25] Containment was fundamentally a Holy Alliance concept. According to the foreign-policy expert Richard Barnet, during the 1950s and 1960s, "the United States used its military or paramilitary power on an average of once every eighteen months either to prevent a government deemed undesirable from coming to power or to overthrow a revolutionary or reformist government considered inimical to America's interests."[26] Although Barnet did not refer to a Holy Alliance, his description fits the model perfectly.

During the 1970s, the United States played the Holy Alliance role less frequently, not so much because of the outcome of the Vietnam War as because of the emergence of a multipolar world. In 1972, the United States accepted (and later recognized) the communist government of the People's Republic of China and broke forever its pure bipolar, Cold War view of world-power distribution. Other powers became politically important as well, including Japan, the European Economic Community (now the European Union), India, and, depending on their

Following the end of the Cold War, a multilateral approach to tackling the world's trouble spots guided American foreign policy. Efforts to keep the peace in Bosnia involved a NATO peace force working with the Russian military. This photo shows a live-fire artillery exercise from 1997, the first time since World War II that U.S. and Russian troops fired live ammunition together.

own resolve, the countries making up the Organization of Petroleum Exporting Countries (OPEC). The United States experimented with all four of the previously identified roles, depending on which was appropriate to a specific region of the world. In the Middle East, America tended to play an almost classic balance-of-power role, appearing sometimes cool in its relations with Israel and playing off one Arab country against another. The United States has been able to do this despite the fact that every country in the Middle East recognizes that for cultural, domestic, and geostrategic reasons, the United States has always considered Israel its most durable and important ally in the region and has unwaveringly committed itself to Israel's survival in a very hostile environment. President Nixon introduced balance-of-power considerations in the Far East by "playing the China card." In other parts of the world, particularly in Latin America, we tended to hold to the Holy Alliance and Napoleonic roles.

This multipolar phase ended after 1989, with the collapse of the Soviet Union and the end of the Cold War. Soon thereafter the Warsaw Pact collapsed too, ending armed confrontation in Europe. With almost equal suddenness, the popular demand for "self-determination" produced several new nation-states and the demand for still more. On the one hand, it was indeed encouraging to witness the reemergence of some twenty-five major nationalities after anywhere from forty-five to seventy-five years of suppression. On the other hand, policy makers with a sense of history are aware that this new world order bears a strong resemblance to the world of 1914. Then, the trend was known as "Balkanization." Balkanization meant nationhood and self-determination, but it also meant war. The Soviet Union after World War I and Yugoslavia after World War II kept more than twenty nationalities from making war against each other for several decades. In 1989 and the years that followed, the world was caught unprepared for the dangers of a new disorder that the reemergence of these nationalities produced.

The Post–Cold War Era and Global Capitalism

The abrupt end of the Cold War unleashed another dynamic factor, the globalization of markets; one could call it the globalization of capitalism. This is good news, but it has its problematic side because the free market can disrupt nationhood. Although the globalization of markets is enormously productive, countries like to enjoy its benefits while attempting at the same time to prevent international economic influences from affecting local jobs, local families, and established class and tribal relationships.

This struggle between capitalism and nationhood produces a new kind of bipolarity in the world. The old world order was shaped by *external bipolarity*—of West versus East. This seems to have been replaced by *internal bipolarity*, wherein each country is struggling to make its own hard policy choices to preserve its cultural uniqueness while competing effectively in the global marketplace.

Approval of the North American Free Trade Agreement (NAFTA) is the best example of this struggle within the United States. NAFTA was supported by a majority of Democrats and Republicans on the grounds that a freer, global market was in America's national interest. But even as large bipartisan majorities in Congress were embracing NAFTA, three important factions were rising to fight it. The former presidential candidate Pat Buchanan led a large segment of conservative Americans to fight NAFTA because, he argued, communities and families would be threatened by job losses and by competition from legal and illegal immigrant workers. Another large faction, led by Ross Perot, opposed NAFTA largely on the theory that American companies would move their operations to Mexico, where labor costs are lower. Organized labor also joined the fight against NAFTA.

Another form of internal bipolarity became evident in 1999 over the World Trade Organization (WTO) and its authority to impose limits and restrictions on sovereign nations, even the United States. The WTO had been around since 1994, when it was set up by the major trading nations to facilitate implementation of

Another controversial aspect of the United States' international economic policy has been its trade relations with China. At home, normalizing trade relations with China has been the subject of frequent criticism and protests from those who argue that it threatens the welfare of American workers and ignores human rights violations committed by the Chinese government.

treaties made under the General Agreement on Tariffs and Trade (GATT). But protesters in Seattle saw the WTO as a threat to local ways of life and a contributor to job loss, environmental degradation, and violation of human rights.

These battles are examples of the "internal bipolarity" that is coming to the fore around the world. As the *New York Times* foreign affairs columnist Thomas Friedman put it, "Now that the free market is triumphing on a global basis, the most interesting conflicts are between the winners and losers within countries. It is these internal battles that will increasingly shape international affairs."[27]

The global market is here to stay. American values have changed enough to incorporate it, despite the toll it may take on community and family tradition. Meanwhile, many of the elements of foreign policy created during the Cold War have persisted because they turned out to be good adjustments to the modern era. The Marshall Plan and the various forms of international economic aid that succeeded it continue to this day. Although appropriations for foreign aid have been shrinking, only a small minority of members of the Senate and the House favor the outright abolition of foreign aid programs. NATO and other collective security arrangements continue, as do some aspects of containment, even though there is no longer a Soviet Union, because collective security arrangements have, as we shall see, proven useful in dealing with new democracies and other nations seeking to join the global market. Even though the former Soviet Union is now more often an ally than an adversary, the United States still quite frequently uses unilateral and multilateral means of keeping civil wars contained within their own borders, so that conflict does not spread into neighboring states. America is practicing a new form of containment, but one that is based on the values and institutions of Cold War containment.

The quest for a global market is more than a search for world prosperity. Economic globalization carries with it the hope that economic competition will displace armed conflict, perhaps even reducing if not eliminating the need for traditional diplomacy. But since there are too many instances in world history when economic competition actually led to war rather than avoided it, the United States has added democratization to the recipe of globalization because of the fairly well-supported hypothesis that democracies never go to war against each other. Thus, democratization is a genuine and strongly committed goal of U.S. foreign policy, even if it is secondary to economic expansion. Meanwhile, we play the economic card in hopes that capitalism will contribute not only to world prosperity but also to the expansion of democratization.

One of the first indications of the post–Cold War American foreign policy was President George H. W. Bush's conciliatory approach to the dictatorial regime of the People's Republic of China after its brutal military suppression of the democratic student movement in Tienanmen Square in June 1989. Subsequently, President Clinton also maintained friendly relations with the dictatorial regime, and both presidents continued to grant the Chinese "normal trade relations" status. Their policy was to separate China's trade status from its human rights record, arguing that economic growth provided the only effective means to bring about political reform in a country as large and as powerful as China.

The Holy Alliance or the Napoleonic Role in the Post–Cold War Era?

During the Cold War era, the purpose of the Holy Alliance role was to keep regimes in power as long as they did not espouse Soviet foreign-policy goals. In the post–Cold War world, the purpose of the Holy Alliance role is still to keep regimes in power, but only as long as they maintain general stability, keep their nationalities contained within their own borders, and encourage their economies to attain some level of participation in the global market. If countries fail to satisfy these conditions, the United States has shown signs of reverting to its Napoleonic role. The United States has also continued to confront unfriendly dictators by adopting a Napoleonic strategy of intervention.

One case of the Holy Alliance role in the post–Cold War era is Iraq's invasion of Kuwait and our Desert Storm response to it. Iraq's invasion of Kuwait occurred in July 1990, but Desert Storm was not undertaken until January 1991. In the interim, President Bush was mobilizing Congress and the American people, not only in case the United States had to intervene militarily, but also in hopes that the possibility of such action might convince Saddam Hussein to withdraw voluntarily. President Bush was also putting together a worldwide alliance of twenty-nine nations—he had no intention of leading the United States into Desert Storm without this alliance, even though most of its members did not send troops but instead sent political approval plus what amounted to a monetary subscription. Bush had initially taken a Napoleonic position, urging the people of Iraq to "take matters into their own hands" and to force Hussein to "step aside." But after America withdrew its troops and uprisings inside Iraq began to emerge, President Bush backed away. It was enough that the Iraqis stayed within their borders, although regular overflights and occasional shootings by American pilots in the northern and southern "no-fly" zones of Iraq later appeared to be Napoleonic departures from the Holy Alliance role.

Regarding Bosnia, at first the United States refused to exert leadership, and it deferred to the European nations when civil war erupted after Croatia and Bosnia-Herzegovina declared independence from Yugoslavia. When Europe failed to address the problem adequately, the United States and the United Kingdom stepped in, again to no avail. Although the Americans' surprise bombing in 1995 was virtually unilateral, what emerged was a new alliance of twenty-five nations acting "in concert" to separate the warring factions from one another. And although one-third of the sixty thousand occupying troops and virtually all the navy and air force units were American, twenty-four other nations established and maintained a physical presence in the field, all in order to maintain the status quo, including leaving the Yugoslav president Slobodan Milosevic in power. Almost everything about the Bosnian operation was an acting out of the traditional Holy Alliance role.

Kosovo (part of Yugoslavia) in 1999 was perhaps the most spectacular case of post–Cold War Holy Alliance policy—although history may prove that the United States and virtually the entire Western world stumbled into this war.[28] Throughout 1998 and early 1999, ethnic cleansing proceeded in Kosovo, but the United States would not go it alone, and the NATO nations (except for Great Britain) were not willing to intervene in Kosovo. As late as January 1999, the CIA reported to President Clinton that "[Yugoslav President Milosevic] doesn't believe NATO is going to bomb."[29] It is clear that these delays were due less to American indecision than to America's or President Clinton's inability to forge a European, multicountry alliance. Prospects of embarrassment at the upcoming fiftieth anniversary of NATO may have forced some European leaders to reconsider an alliance—but even so, only if the United States took the lead, and then only if it promised to limit the assault to an air war, which guaranteed a minimum of casualties, especially on the allied side.

Make Your Voice Heard in Foreign Policy

On April 4, 2008, a group of students at the University of Utah staged a "die in" to raise awareness about the genocide in Darfur, Sudan. Following in the footsteps of thousands of students nationwide, these young men and women spent five minutes lying in silence to symbolize the victims who have died or been displaced since the conflict began. The students were part of a local chapter of STAND, an acronym for "Students Taking Action NOW: Darfur." Formed in 2004, the anti-genocide student-run organization has chapters in over 600 colleges and high schools throughout the United States. These students have been motivated to action by stories of the hundreds of thousands of Sudanese who have died from violence, disease, and starvation, as well as the 2.5 million refugees who have fled their homes since the conflict began.

The students in STAND fall in line with a history of student activism that is associated with divestment strategies. In the 1980s college students nationwide, horrified by the apartheid system in South Africa, urged their colleges and universities to divest from the country—and pushed for U.S. sanctions against the South African government. Just like the STAND activists, anti-apartheid groups educated their fellow students about the issue, staged protests, and lobbied policymakers. Some even lived in makeshift shanties on campus quads, to serve as symbols of the conditions of blacks under apartheid.

You may feel you do not know enough about U.S. foreign policy to get involved in the debate. Fortunately, there are many easily accessible resources available to help you learn, and, once you've educated yourself, many outlets for action.

- ★ *Take the test.* You can test your own geographic knowledge by taking a quiz from National Geographic at www.nationalgeographic.com/roper2006/. You can see how well you do—and how you compare to other young adults worldwide.
- ★ *Educate yourself.* The Council on Foreign Relations (www.cfr.org) is a nonpartisan, nonprofit organization that has numerous resources for educating yourself about the key issues in U.S. foreign policy. You can link to background materials to learn about the key issues facing the nation and the world.
- ★ *Join an advocacy group.* As you learn more about key issues, you may find yourself developing support for a particular perspective or side in the debate. There are groups working to influence public policy from every perspective. Visiting their Web sites and taking advantage of their educational materials, as well as the opportunities they offer to get more involved, will provide you a means of adding your voice to others who share your values. For example, if you are concerned about the war in Iraq, you could check out the National Youth & Student Peace Coalition (www.nyspc.org). Or, if you think U.S. foreign policy should be more oriented toward reflecting key American values of equality and justice, then you can read the materials and sign the petitions at www.justforeignpolicy.org. Finally, if you want to work to ensure that the American troops in Afghanistan and Iraq receive the support they need, look into www.moveamericaforward.org.
- ★ *Educate your fellow students.* You may find that you are so moved by some of the foreign policy issues that you want to share your knowledge with other students. Many of the national organizations have resources to help students start campus chapters. STAND, for example, will provide you with training in establishing a group on campus, instructions on how to advocate effectively, and even help you to find speakers to bring to campus.

So the United States got its alliance—for NATO, a precedent-setting one—but without any ground troops.[30] But there are inherent limits to multinational coalitions. NATO is simply a more formalized version of a multicountry alliance with the same fundamental problem of any such alliance: *The power of decision tends toward the weakest member.* Opposition within the NATO alliance to intervene in Kosovo came mostly from the weaker and more internally divided Italy and Greece rather than from Britain, France, or Germany.

The Kosovo campaign validates what we have been observing throughout this chapter: Holy Alliance politics has been the prevailing American role internationally since the Cold War, and the United States draws virtually all its allies and potential allies into that role at one point or another. In 2008, Russia reacted to American efforts to draw states along its borders into the American alliance structure by invading Georgia, a formed Soviet republic. Georgia had welcomed close relations with the United States and even discussed possibly joining NATO. The Russians saw an attack on Georgia as a warning to other former Soviet republics and satellite states, Poland in particular, against linking themselves closely to America.

The War on Terror: From Holy Alliance to Napoleonic Unilateralism

In the immediate aftermath of the 9/11 terrorist attacks, the United States had no difficulty in securing pledges of support from a number of other nations. Although the United States took the lead in launching attacks against Afghanistan's Taliban regime, which had harbored the leadership of the Al Qaeda terrorist group that planned the attacks, many other nations contributed diplomatic, military, and financial support.

However, when the Bush administration made it clear that it intended to invade Iraq to topple the dictator Saddam Hussein, only Great Britain offered unequivocal support and significant military cooperation. Most of the world's leaders expressed doubt about the wisdom of America's actions and declined to endorse or support the Bush administration's policies. President Bush averred that America was prepared to lead a "coalition of the willing" into battle. In other words, the president indicated that he did not care whether other nations joined the United States or not. Those who were willing were welcome to participate. Those not willing were welcome to stay home.

Most Europeans and many Americans were dismayed by the administration's unilateralism, but Congress supported the president, and American forces struck into Iraq. The Iraqi army was quickly defeated and, after a search, Saddam Hussein was located, placed under arrest, and eventually tried and executed for his brutal crimes against the Iraqi people. Thus, initially, the Bush administration's unilateralist foreign policy appeared to be succeeding. Not long after the Iraqi army collapsed, and continuing to the present time though, a guerilla insurgency, aided by terrorist groups and armed by Iran, began to harass American and British occupation forces, inflicting casualties on British and American troops on a daily basis. Even the steadfast British began to waver. It seemed more and more likely that the "coalition of the willing" would consist of the United States, alone.

The Bush administration's policies in Iraq illustrate the advantages and disadvantages of Napoleonic unilateralism. The major advantage is that not having to deal with allies allows the United States to do as it sees fit. The disadvantage, though, is that as problems develop, the capacity of even a great power such as the United States to go it alone becomes more and more doubtful. During the 2008 presidential campaign, candidates presented their formulae to resolve America's problems in Iraq. We shall see how a new president deals with the fallout from Napoleonic unilateralism.

FOR FURTHER READING

Bacevich, Andrew. *The New American Militarism: How Americans Are Seduced by War.* New York: Oxford University Press, 2006.

Berman, Paul. *Terror and Liberalism.* New York: Norton, 2004.

Daalder, Ivo H., and James M. Lindsay. *American Unbound—The Bush Revolution in Foreign Policy.* Washington, DC: Brookings Institution Press, 2003.

Fisk, Robert. *The Great War for Civilization: The Conquest of the Middle East.* New York: Knopf, 2007.

Gaddis, John L. *The Cold War: A New History.* New York: Penguin, 2005.

Hook, Stephen, and John Spanier. *American Foreign Policy since World War II.* Washington, DC: Congressional Quarterly Press, 2006.

Jentleson, Bruce. *American Foreign Policy—The Dynamics of Choice in the Twenty-First Century.* 3rd ed. New York: Norton, 2007.

Johnson, Chalmers. *The Sorrows of Empire.* New York: Henry Holt, 2004.

Johnson, Loch K. *Seven Sins of American Foreign Policy.* New York: Longman, 2006.

Kagan, Robert. *Dangerous Nation.* New York: Knopf, 2006.

Kennan, George F. *Around the Cragged Hill. A Personal and Political Philosophy.* New York: Norton, 1993.

Mandelbaum, Michael. *The Case for Goliath: How America Acts as the World's Government in the Twenty-First Century.* Washington, DC: Public Affairs Press, 2005.

Mann, James. *Rise of the Vulcans.* New York: Penguin, 2004.

Pillar, Paul R. *Terrorism and American Foreign Policy.* Washington, DC: Brookings Institution Press, 2003.

Reid, T. R. *The United States of Europe—The New Superpower and the End of American Supremacy.* New York: Penguin, 2004.

Smith, Rupert. *The Utility of Force: The Art of War in the Modern World.* New York: Vintage, 2008.

U.S. Congress. *Report of the Congressional Committees Investigating the Iran-Contra Affair.* Washington, DC: U.S. Government Printing Office, 1987.

Yoo, John. *The Powers of War and Peace.* Chicago: University of Chicago Press, 2005.

RECOMMENDED WEB SITES

American Israel Public Affairs Committee
www.aipac.org

Interest groups are some of the main shapers of foreign policy. One of the top lobbies in the nation, the American Israel Public Affairs Committee (AIPAC) works to strengthen the U.S.-Israel relationship.

Foreign Policy Association
www.fpa.org

This nonprofit organization tries to generate interest in and draw attention to global issues and policies.

International Monetary Fund
www.imf.org
World Trade Organization
www.wto.org

The International Monetary Fund (IMF) and the World Trade Organization (WTO) have been considered instruments of modern American foreign policy. Read about how these organizations are trying to promote capitalism, free trade, and economic development.

National Security Council
www.whitehouse.gov/nsc/

The National Security Council was formed in 1947 and consists of senior advisors and Cabinet officials who keep the president informed on all matters of national security and foreign policy.

Peterson Institute for International Economics
www.iie.com

The Peterson Institute for International Economics is dedicated to analyzing international economic policy. Take a minute to review some of the studies that have influenced the policies of such international organizations as NAFTA, the WTO, and the IMF.

United Nations
www.un.org

Founded in 1945, the United Nations (UN) promotes international peace and security. Visit the UN Web site for information on the General Assembly, the Security Council, economic and social development, and humanitarian issues.

U.S. Department of State
www.state.gov

The U.S. Department of State is the primary bureaucratic department for American diplomacy and national security.

U.S. Senate: Treaties
http://senate.gov/pagelayout/legislative/d_three_sections_with_teasers/treaties.htm

The most important foreign-policy task of the Senate is reviewing and approving treaties. Learn more about the Senate's treaty-making powers and find information about treaty action at this U.S. Senate Web site.

STUDY OUTLINE

www.wwnorton.com/wtp7e

The Nature of Foreign Policy

1. Foreign policy refers to the programs and policies that determine America's relations with other nations and foreign entities. Foreign policy includes diplomacy, military and security policy, international human rights policies, and various forms of economic policy.
2. The foreign-policy arena seems similar to America's other policy domains, but differs in at least three ways: history, questions of national interest are more predominant in the foreign-policy arena, and the foreign-policy arena is affected by America's wariness of foreign commitments and the difficulty of foreign-policy decision making.

The Goals of Foreign Policy

1. Today, American security policy is concerned not only with the actions of other nations, but with the activities of terrorist groups and other hostile non-state actors, as well as with food and energy supplies and transportation and electronic infrastructures.
2. America's international economic policies are intended to expand employment opportunities in the United States, maintain access to foreign energy supplies at a reasonable cost, promote foreign investment in the United States, and lower the prices Americans pay for goods and services.
3. International environmental policy, international human rights policy, and international peacekeeping, in addition to American contributions to international organizations, are important U.S. foreign policy goals but are often forced to give way if they interfere with security or economic policy goals.

Who Makes American Foreign Policy?

1. All foreign policy decisions must be made and implemented in the name of the president.
2. The key players in foreign policy in the bureaucracy are the secretaries of state, defense, homeland security, and treasury; the Joint Chiefs of Staff (especially the chair); and the director of the Central Intelligence Agency.
3. Although the Senate traditionally has more foreign-policy power than the House, since World War II, the House and the Senate have both been important players in foreign policy.
4. Many types of interest groups help shape American foreign policy. These groups include economic interest groups, ethnic or national interest groups, and human-rights and environmental interest groups.
5. The media communicate issues and policies to the American people, and communicate the public's opinions back to the president. One definite influence of television on foreign policy has been to make the American people more cynical and skeptical than they otherwise would be.
6. Individual or group influence in foreign policy varies from case to case and from situation to situation.

The Instruments of Modern American Foreign Policy

1. Diplomacy is the representation of a government to other foreign governments, and it is the foreign-policy instrument to which all other instruments must be subordinated.
2. The United Nations is an instrument whose usefulness to American foreign policy can too easily be underestimated.

3. The international monetary structure, which consists of the World Bank and the International Monetary Fund, was created to avoid the economic devastation that followed World War I.
4. Economic aid has been important as an instrument of American foreign policy, but it was put together as a balance between traditional values and the modern needs of a great, imperial power.
5. After World War II, the United States recognized the importance of collective security, and subsequently entered into multilateral collective security treaties and other bilateral treaties.
6. World War II broke the American cycle of demobilization-remobilization and led to a new policy of military preparedness.
7. Military force is sometimes necessary, but it is a response of last resort because of its extreme risk and high cost in both financial and human terms.
8. Dispute arbitration, which allows neutral third parties to settle international disputes, ensures the flow of international trade by providing for the protection of property and contractual rights.

Foreign Policy and America's Place in the World

1. There are four roles available to a nation in the conduct of its foreign policy: the Napoleonic role, the Holy Alliance role, the balance-of-power role, and the economic expansionist role.
2. Although the United States played the Napoleonic role during the postwar era and then switched to the Holy Alliance role during the Cold War, it is now beginning to adopt all four roles, playing whichever one is appropriate to a particular region and set of circumstances.

PRACTICE QUIZ

www.wwnorton.com/wtp7e

1. The making of American foreign policy is
   a) dominated entirely by the president.
   b) dominated entirely by Congress.
   c) dominated entirely by interest groups.
   d) highly pluralistic, involving a large mix of both official and unofficial players.
2. The Constitution assigns the power to declare war to
   a) the president.
   b) Congress.
   c) the secretary of defense.
   d) the chief justice of the United States.
3. The "Cold War" refers to the
   a) competition between the United States and Canada over Alaska.
   b) the years between World War I and World War II when the United States and Germany were hostile to one another.
   c) the period of struggle between the United States and the Soviet Union between the late 1940s and the late 1980s.
   d) the economic competition between the United States and Japan today.
4. The North Atlantic Treaty Organization was formed in 1948 by the United States,
   a) Canada, and most of Eastern Europe.
   b) Canada, and Mexico.
   c) Canada, and most of Western Europe.
   d) Canada, and the United Kingdom.
5. Which of the following terms best describes the American posture toward the world prior to the middle of the twentieth century?
   a) interventionist
   b) isolationist
   c) appeasement
   d) none of the above
6. Which of the following are important international economic institutions created after World War II?
   a) the Federal Reserve
   b) the World Bank
   c) the International Monetary Fund
   d) Both b and c are correct.
7. Which of the following terms describes the idea that the development and maintenance of military strength discourages attack?
   a) deterrence
   b) containment
   c) "Minuteman" theory of defense
   d) detente
8. Which of the following was dedicated to the relief, reconstruction, and economic recovery of Western Europe?
   a) the Marshall Plan
   b) the Lend-Lease Act
   c) the General Agreement on Tariffs and Trade
   d) the North American Free Trade Agreement

KEY TERMS

www.wwnorton.com/wtp7e

appeasement (p. 719)
balance-of-power role (p. 745)
bilateral treaty (p. 741)
Bush Doctrine (p. 727)
Cold War (p. 719)
deterrence (p. 719)
diplomacy (p. 735)
economic expansionist role (p. 746)
executive agreement (p. 730)
General Agreement on Trade and Tariffs (GATT) (p. 722)
Holy Alliance role (p. 745)
International Monetary Fund (IMF) (p. 738)
isolationism (p. 718)
most favored nation status (p. 721)
Napoleonic role (p. 744)
nation-state (p. 720)
non-state actor (p. 718)
North American Free Trade Agreement (NAFTA) (p. 722)
North Atlantic Treaty Organization (NATO) (p. 741)
preemption (p. 720)
preventive war (p. 719)
United Nations (UN) (p. 736)
World Trade Organization (WTO) (p. 722)

The Declaration of Independence

In Congress, July 4, 1776

The unanimous Declaration of the thirteen united States of America,

When in the Course of human events, it becomes necessary for one people to dissolve the political bands which have connected them with another, and to assume among the powers of the earth, the separate and equal station to which the Laws of Nature and of Nature's God entitle them, a decent respect to the opinions of mankind requires that they should declare the causes which impel them to the separation.

We hold these truths to be self-evident, that all men are created equal, that they are endowed by their Creator with certain unalienable Rights, that among these are Life, Liberty and the pursuit of Happiness.—That to secure these rights, Governments are instituted among Men, deriving their just powers from the consent of the governed. —That whenever any Form of Government becomes destructive of these ends, it is the Right of the People to alter or to abolish it, and to institute new Government, laying its foundation on such principles and organizing its powers in such form, as to them shall seem most likely to effect their Safety and Happiness. Prudence, indeed, will dictate that Governments long established should not be changed for light and transient causes; and accordingly all experience hath shewn, that mankind are more disposed to suffer, while evils are sufferable, than to right themselves by abolishing the forms to which they are accustomed. But when a long train of abuses and usurpations, pursuing invariably the same Object evinces a design to reduce them under absolute Despotism, it is their right, it is their duty, to throw off such Government, and to provide new Guards for their future security.—Such has been the patient sufferance of these Colonies; and such is now the necessity which constrains them to alter their former Systems of Government. The history of the present King of Great Britain is a history of repeated injuries and usurpations, all having in direct object the establishment of an absolute Tyranny over these States. To prove this, let Facts be submitted to a candid world.

He has refused his Assent to Laws, the most wholesome and necessary for the public good.

He has forbidden his Governors to pass Laws of immediate and pressing importance, unless suspended in their operation till his Assent should be obtained; and when so suspended, he has utterly neglected to attend to them.

He has refused to pass other Laws for the accommodation of large districts of people, unless those people would relinquish the right of Representation in the Legislature, a right inestimable to them and formidable to tyrants only.

He has called together legislative bodies at places unusual, uncomfortable, and distant from the depository of their public Records, for the sole purpose of fatiguing them into compliance with his measures.

He has dissolved Representative Houses repeatedly, for opposing with manly firmness his invasions on the rights of the people.

He has refused for a long time, after such dissolutions, to cause others to be elected; whereby the Legislative powers, incapable of Annihilation, have returned to the People at large for their exercise; the State remaining in the mean time exposed to all the dangers of invasion from without, and convulsions within.

He has endeavoured to prevent the population of these States; for that purpose obstructing the Laws for Naturalization of Foreigners; refusing to pass others to encourage their migrations hither, and raising the conditions of new Appropriations of Lands.

He has obstructed the Administration of Justice, by refusing his Assent to Laws for establishing Judiciary powers.

He has made Judges dependent on his Will alone, for the tenure of their offices, and the amount and payment of their salaries.

He has erected a multitude of New Offices, and sent hither swarms of Officers to harrass our people, and eat out their substance.

He has kept among us, in times of peace, Standing Armies without the Consent of our legislatures.

He has affected to render the Military independent of and superior to the Civil power.

He has combined with others to subject us to a jurisdiction foreign to our constitution, and unacknowledged by our laws; giving his Assent to their Acts of pretended Legislation:

For Quartering large bodies of armed troops among us:

For protecting them, by a mock Trial, from punishment for any Murders which they should commit on the Inhabitants of these States:

For cutting off our Trade with all parts of the world:

For imposing Taxes on us without our Consent:

For depriving us in many cases, of the benefits of Trial by Jury:

For transporting us beyond Seas to be tried for pretended offences:

For abolishing the free System of English Laws in a neighboring Province, establishing therein an Arbitrary government, and enlarging its Boundaries so as to render it at once an example and fit instrument for introducing the same absolute rule into these Colonies:

For taking away our Charters, abolishing our most valuable Laws, and altering fundamentally the Forms of our Governments:

For suspending our own Legislatures, and declaring themselves invested with power to legislate for us in all cases whatsoever.

He has abdicated Government here, by declaring us out of his Protection and waging War against us.

He has plundered our seas, ravaged our Coasts, burnt our towns, and destroyed the lives of our people.

He is at this time transporting large Armies of foreign Mercenaries to compleat the works of death, desolation and tyranny, already begun with circumstances of Cruelty & perfidy scarcely paralleled in the most barbarous ages, and totally unworthy the Head of a civilized nation.

He has constrained our fellow Citizens taken Captive on the high Seas to bear Arms against their Country, to become the executioners of their friends and Brethren, or to fall themselves by their Hands.

He has excited domestic insurrections amongst us, and has endeavoured to bring on the inhabitants of our frontiers, the merciless Indian Savages, whose known rule of warfare, is an undistinguished destruction of all ages, sexes and conditions.

In every stage of these Oppressions We have Petitioned for Redress in the most humble terms: Our repeated Petitions have been answered only by repeated injury. A Prince whose character is thus marked by every act which may define a Tyrant, is unfit to be the ruler of a free people.

Nor have We been wanting in attentions to our Brittish brethren. We have warned them from time to time of attempts by their legislature to extend an unwarrantable jurisdiction over us. We have reminded them of the circumstances of our emigration and settlement here. We have appealed to their native justice and magnanimity, and we have conjured them by the ties of our common kindred to disavow these usurpations, which, would inevitably interrupt our connections and correspondence. They too have been deaf to the voice of justice and of consanguinity. We must, therefore, acquiesce in the necessity, which denounces our Separation, and hold them, as we hold the rest of mankind, Enemies in War, in Peace Friends.

We, Therefore, the Representatives of the United States of America, in General Congress, Assembled, appealing to the Supreme Judge of the world for the rectitude of our intentions, do, in the Name, and by Authority of the good People of these Colonies, solemnly publish and declare, That these United Colonies are, and of Right ought to be Free and Independent States; that they are Absolved from all Allegiance to the British Crown, and that all political connection between them and the State of Great Britain, is and ought to be totally dissolved; and that as Free and Independent States, they have full Power to levy War, conclude Peace, contract Alliances, establish Commerce, and to do all other Acts and Things which Independent States may of right do. And for the support of this Declaration, with a firm reliance on the protection of divine Providence, we mutually pledge to each other our Lives, our Fortunes and our sacred Honor.

The foregoing Declaration was, by order of Congress, engrossed, and signed by the following members:

John Hancock

NEW HAMPSHIRE
Josiah Bartlett
William Whipple
Matthew Thornton

MASSACHUSETTS BAY
Samuel Adams
John Adams
Robert Treat Paine
Elbridge Gerry

RHODE ISLAND
Stephen Hopkins
William Ellery

CONNECTICUT
Roger Sherman
Samuel Huntington
William Williams
Oliver Wolcott

NEW YORK
William Floyd
Philip Livingston
Francis Lewis
Lewis Morris

NEW JERSEY
Richard Stockton
John Witherspoon
Francis Hopkinson
John Hart
Abraham Clark

PENNSYLVANIA
Robert Morris
Benjamin Rush
Benjamin Franklin
John Morton
George Clymer
James Smith
George Taylor
James Wilson
George Ross

DELAWARE
Caesar Rodney
George Read
Thomas M'Kean

MARYLAND
Samuel Chase
William Paca
Thomas Stone
Charles Carroll, of Carrollton

VIRGINIA
George Wythe
Richard Henry Lee
Thomas Jefferson
Benjamin Harrison
Thomas Nelson, Jr.
Francis Lightfoot Lee
Carter Braxton

NORTH CAROLINA
William Hooper
Joseph Hewes
John Penn

SOUTH CAROLINA
Edward Rutledge
Thomas Heyward, Jr.
Thomas Lynch, Jr.
Arthur Middleton

GEORGIA
Button Gwinnett
Lyman Hall
George Walton

Resolved, That copies of the Declaration be sent to the several assemblies, conventions, and committees, or councils of safety, and to the several commanding officers of the continental troops; that it be proclaimed in each of the United States, at the head of the army.

The Articles of Confederation

Agreed to by Congress November 15, 1777; ratified and in force March 1, 1781

To all whom these Presents shall come, we the undersigned Delegates of the States affixed to our Names, send greeting. Whereas the Delegates of the United States of America, in Congress assembled, did, on the fifteenth day of November, in the Year of Our Lord One thousand Seven Hundred and Seventy seven, and in the Second Year of the Independence of America, agree to certain articles of Confederation and perpetual Union between the States of Newhampshire, Massachusetts-bay, Rhodeisland and Providence Plantations, Connecticut, New-York, New-Jersey, Pennsylvania, Delaware, Maryland, Virginia, North-Carolina, South-Carolina and Georgia in the words following, viz. "Articles of Confederation and perpetual Union between the states of Newhampshire, Massachusetts-bay, Rhodeisland and Providence Plantations, Connecticut, New-York, New-Jersey, Pennsylvania, Delaware, Maryland, Virginia, North-Carolina, South-Carolina and Georgia.

Art. I. The Stile of this confederacy shall be "The United States of America."

Art. II. Each state retains its sovereignty, freedom and independence, and every Power, Jurisdiction and right, which is not by this confederation expressly delegated to the United States, in Congress assembled.

Art. III. The said states hereby severally enter into a firm league of friendship with each other, for their common defence, the security of their Liberties, and their mutual and general welfare, binding themselves to assist each other, against all force offered to, or attacks made upon them, or any of them, on account of religion, sovereignty, trade, or any other pretence whatever.

Art. IV. The better to secure and perpetuate mutual friendship and intercourse among the people of the different states in this union, the free inhabitants of each of these states, paupers, vagabonds and fugitives from Justice excepted, shall be entitled to all privileges and immunities of free citizens in the several states; and the people of each state shall have free ingress and regress to and from any other state, and shall enjoy therein all the privileges of trade and commerce, subject to the same duties, impositions and restrictions as the inhabitants thereof respectively, provided that such restriction shall not extend so far as to prevent the removal of property imported into any state, to any other state, of which the Owner is an inhabitant; provided also that no imposition, duties or restriction shall be laid by any state, on the property of the united states, or either of them.

If any Person guilty of, or charged with treason, felony, or other high misdemeanor in any state, shall flee from Justice, and be found in any of the united states, he shall, upon demand of the Governor or executive power, of the state from which he fled, be delivered up and removed to the state having jurisdiction of his offence.

Full faith and credit shall be given in each of these states to the records, acts and judicial proceedings of the courts and magistrates of every other state.

Art. V. For the more convenient management of the general interests of the united states, delegates shall be annually appointed in such manner as the legislature of each state shall direct, to meet in Congress on the first Monday in November, in every year, with a power reserved to each state, to recall its delegates, or any of them, at any time within the year, and to send others in their stead, for the remainder of the Year.

No state shall be represented in Congress by less than two, nor by more than seven Members; and no person shall be capable of being a delegate for more than three years in any term of six years; nor shall any person, being a delegate, be capable of holding any office under the united states, for which he, or another for his benefit receives any salary, fees or emolument of any kind.

Each state shall maintain its own delegates in a meeting of the states, and while they act as members of the committee of the states.

In determining questions in the united states, in Congress assembled, each state shall have one vote.

Freedom of speech and debate in Congress shall not be impeached or questioned in any Court, or place out of Congress, and the members of congress shall be protected in their persons from arrests and imprisonments, during the time of their going to and from, and attendance on congress, except for treason, felony, or breach of the peace.

Art. VI. No state without the Consent of the united states in congress assembled, shall send any embassy to, or receive any embassy from, or enter into any conference, agreement, or alliance or treaty with any King, prince or state; nor shall any person holding any office or profit or trust under the united states, or any of them, accept of any present, emolument, office or title of any kind whatever from any king, prince or foreign state; nor shall the united states in congress assembled, or any of them, grant any title of nobility.

No two or more states shall enter into any treaty, confederation or alliance whatever between them, without the consent of the united states in congress assembled, specifying accurately the purposes for which the same is to be entered into, and how long it shall continue.

No state shall lay any imposts or duties, which may interfere with any stipulations in treaties, entered into by the united states in congress assembled, with any king, prince or state, in pursuance of any treaties already proposed by congress, to the courts of France and Spain.

No vessels of war shall be kept up in time of peace by any state, except such number only, as shall be deemed necessary by the united states in congress assembled, for the defence of such state, or its trade; nor shall any body of forces be kept up by any state, in time of peace, except such number only, as in the judgment of the united states, in congress assembled, shall be deemed requisite to garrison the forts necessary for the defence of such state; but every state shall always keep up a well regulated and disciplined militia, sufficiently armed and accoutred, and shall provide and constantly have ready for use, in public stores, a due number of field pieces and tents, and a proper quantity of arms, ammunition and camp equipage.

No state shall engage in any war without the consent of the united states in congress assembled, unless such state be actually invaded by enemies, or shall have received certain advice of a resolution being formed by some nation of Indians to invade such state, and the danger is so imminent as not to admit of a delay, till the united states in congress asssembled can be consulted; nor shall any state grant commissions to any ships or vessels of war, nor letters of marque or reprisal, except it be after a declaration of war by the united states in congress assembled, and then only against the kingdom or state and the subjects thereof, against which war has been so declared, and under such regulations as shall be established by the united states in congress assembled, unless such state be infested by pirates; in which case vessels of war may be fitted out for that occasion, and kept so long as the danger shall continue, or until the united states in congress assembled shall determine otherwise.

Art. VII. When land-forces are raised by any state for the common defence, all officers of or under the rank of colonel, shall be appointed by the legislature of each state respectively, by whom such forces shall be raised, or in such manner as such state shall direct, and all vacancies shall be filled up by the state which first made the appointment.

Art. VIII. All charges of war, and all other expences that shall be incurred for the common defence or general welfare, and allowed by the united states in congress assembled, shall be defrayed out of a common treasury, which shall be supplied by the several states in proportion to the value of all land within each state, granted to or surveyed for any Person, as such land and the buildings and improvements thereon shall be estimated according to such mode as the united states in congress assembled, shall from time to time direct and appoint.

The taxes for paying that proportion shall be laid and levied by the authority and direction of the legislatures of the several states within the time agreed upon by the united states in congress assembled.

Art. IX. The united states in congress assembled, shall have the sole and exclusive right and power of determining on peace and war, except in the cases mentioned in the sixth article—of sending and receiving ambassadors—entering into treaties and alliances, provided that no treaty of commerce shall be made whereby the legislative power of the respective states shall be restrained from imposing such imposts and duties on foreigners, as their own people are subjected to, or from prohibiting the exportation of any species of goods or commodities whatsoever—of establishing rules for deciding in all cases, what captures on land or water shall be legal, and in what manner prizes taken by land or naval forces in the service of the united states shall be divided or appropriated—of granting letters of marque and reprisal in times of peace—appointing courts for the trial of piracies and felonies committed on the high seas and establishing courts for receiving and determining finally appeals in all cases of captures, provided that no member of congress shall be appointed a judge of any of the said courts.

The united states in congress assembled shall also be the last resort on appeal in all disputes and differences now subsisting or that hereafter may arise between two or more states concerning boundary, jurisdiction or any other cause whatever; which authority shall always be exercised in the manner following. Whenever the legislative or executive authority or lawful agent of any state in controversy with another shall present a petition to congress stating the matter in question and praying for a hearing, notice thereof shall be given by order of congress to the legislative or executive authority of the other state in controversy, and a day assigned for the appearance of the parties by their lawful agents, who shall then be directed to appoint by joint consent, commissioners or judges to constitute a court for hearing and determining the matter in question: but if they cannot agree, congress shall name three persons out of each of the united states, and from the list of such persons each party shall alternately strike out one, the petitioners beginning, until the number shall be reduced to thirteen; and from that number not less than seven, nor more than nine names as congress shall direct, shall in the presence of congress be drawn out by lot, and the persons whose names shall be so drawn or any five of them, shall be commissioners or judges, to hear and finally determine the controversy, so always as a major part of the judges who shall hear the cause shall agree in the determination: and if either party shall neglect to attend at the day appointed, without shewing reasons, which congress shall judge sufficient, or being present shall refuse to strike, the congress shall proceed to nominate three persons out of each state, and the secretary of congress shall strike in behalf of such party absent or refusing; and the judgment and sentence of the court to be appointed, in the manner before prescribed, shall be final and conclusive; and if any of the parties shall refuse to submit to the authority of such court, or to appear to defend their claim or cause, the court shall nevertheless proceed to pronounce sentence, or judgment, which shall in like manner be final and decisive, the judgment or sentence and other proceedings being in either case transmitted to congress, and lodged among the acts of congress for the security of the parties concerned: provided that every commissioner, before he sits in judgment, shall take an oath to be administered by one of the judges of the supreme or superior court of the state, where the cause shall be tried, "well and truly to hear and determine the matter in question, according to the best of his judgment, without favour, affection or hope of reward:" provided also, that no state shall be deprived of territory for the benefit of the united states.

All controversies concerning the private right of soil claimed under different grants of two or more states, whose jurisdictions as they may respect such lands, and the states which passed such grants are adjusted, the said grants or either of them being at the same time claimed to have originated antecedent to such settlement of jurisdiction, shall on the petition of either party to the congress of the united states, be finally determined as near as may be in the same manner as is before prescribed for deciding disputes respecting territorial jurisdiction between different states.

The united states in congress assembled shall also have the sole and exclusive right and power of regulating the alloy and value of coin struck by their own authority, or by that of the respective states—fixing the standard of weights and measures throughout the united states—regulating the trade and managing all affairs with the Indians, not members of any of the states, provided that the legislative right of any state within its own limits be not infringed or violated—establishing and regulating post-offices from one state to another, throughout all the united states, and exacting such postage on the papers passing thro' the same as may be requisite to defray the expences of the said office—appointing all officers of the land forces, in the service of the united states, excepting regimental officers—appointing all the officers of the naval forces, and commissioning all officers whatever in the service of the united states—making rules for the government and regulation of the said land and naval forces, and directing their operations.

The united states in congress assembled shall have authority to appoint a committee, to sit in the recess of congress, to be denominated "A Committee of the States," and to consist of one delegate from each state; and to appoint such other committees and civil officers as may be necessary for managing the general affairs of the united states under their direction—to appoint one of their number to preside, provided that no person be allowed to serve in the office of president more than one year in any term of three years; to ascertain the necessary sums of Money to be raised for the service of the united states, and to appropriate and apply the same for defraying the public expenses—to borrow money, or emit bills on the credit of the united states, transmitting every half year to the respective states an account of the sums of money so borrowed or emitted,—to build and equip a navy—to agree upon the number of land forces, and to make requisitions from each state for its quota, in proportion to the number of white inhabitants in such state; which requisition shall be binding, and thereupon the legislature of each state shall appoint the regimental officers, raise the men and cloath, arm and equip them in a soldier like manner, at the expense of the united states; and the officers and men so cloathed, armed and equipped shall march to the place appointed, and within the time agreed on by the united states in congress assembled: But if the united states in congress assembled shall, on consideration of circumstances judge proper that any state should not raise men, or should raise a smaller number than its quota, and that any other state should raise a greater number of men than the quota thereof, such extra number shall be raised, officered, cloathed, armed and equipped in the same manner as the quota of such state, unless the legislature of such state shall judge that such extra number cannot be safely spared out of the same, in which case they shall raise officer, cloath, arm and equip as many of such extra number as they judge can be safely spared. And the officers and men so cloathed, armed and equipped, shall march to the place appointed, and within the time agreed on by the united states in congress assembled.

The united states in congress assembled shall never engage in a war, nor grant letters of marque and reprisal in time of peace, nor enter into any treaties or alliances, nor coin money, nor regulate the value thereof, nor ascertain the sums and expenses necessary for the defence and welfare of the united states, or any of them, nor emit bills, nor borrow money on the credit of the united states, nor appropriate money, nor agree upon the number of vessels of war, to be built or purchased, or the number of land or sea forces to be raised, nor appoint a commander in chief of the army or navy, unless nine states assent to the same: nor shall a question on any other point, except for adjourning from day to day be determined, unless by the votes of a majority of the united states in congress assembled.

The congress of the united states shall have power to adjourn to any time within the year, and to any place within the united states, so that no period of adjournment be for a longer duration than the space of six Months, and shall publish the Journal of their proceedings monthly, except such parts thereof relating to treaties, alliances or military operations, as in their judgment require secrecy; and the yeas and nays of the delegates of each state on any question shall be entered on the Journal, when it is desired by any delegate; and the delegates of a state, or any of them, at his or their request shall be furnished with a transcript of the said Journal, except such parts as are above excepted, to lay before the legislatures of the several states.

Art. X. The committee of the states, or any nine of them, shall be authorised to execute, in the recess of congress, such of the powers of congress as the united states in congress assembled, by the consent of nine states, shall from time to time think expedient to vest them with; provided that no power be delegated to the said committee, for the exercise of which, by the articles of confederation, the voice of nine states in the congress of the united states assembled is requisite.

Art. XI. Canada acceding to this confederation, and joining in the measures of the united states, shall be admitted into, and entitled to all the advantages of this union: but no other colony shall be admitted into the same, unless such admission be agreed to by nine states.

Art. XII. All bills of credit emitted, monies borrowed and debts contracted by, or under the authority of congress, before the assembling of the united states, in pursuance of the present confederation, shall be deemed and considered as a charge against the united states, for payment and satisfaction whereof the said united states and the public faith are hereby solemnly pledged.

Art. XIII. Every state shall abide by the determinations of the united states in congress assembled, on all questions which by this confederation are submitted to them. And the Articles of this confederation shall be inviolably observed by every state, and the union shall be perpetual; nor shall any alteration at any time hereafter be made in any of them; unless such alteration be agreed to in a congress of the united states, and be afterwards confirmed by the legislatures of every state.

And Whereas it hath pleased the Great Governor of the World to incline the hearts of the legislatures we respectively represent in congress, to approve of, and to authorize us to ratify the said articles of confederation and perpetual union. Know Ye that we the undersigned delegates, by virtue of the power and authority to us given for that purpose, do by these presents, in the name and in behalf of our respective constituents, fully and entirely ratify and confirm each and every of the said articles of confederation and perpetual union, and all and singular the matters and things therein contained: And we do further solemnly plight and engage the faith of our respective constituents, that they shall abide by the determinations of the united states in congress assembled, on all questions, which by the said confederation are submitted to them. And that the articles thereof shall be inviolably observed by the states we respectively represent, and that the union shall be perpetual. In Witness whereof we have hereunto set our hands in Congress. Done at Philadelphia in the state of Pennsylvania the ninth day of July, in the Year of our Lord one Thousand seven Hundred and Seventy-eight, and in the third year of the independence of America.

The Constitution of the United States of America

[PREAMBLE]
We the People of the United States, in Order to form a more perfect Union, establish Justice, insure domestic Tranquility, provide for the common defence, promote the general Welfare, and secure the Blessings of Liberty to ourselves and our Posterity, do ordain and establish this Constitution for the United States of America.

Article I

SECTION 1

[LEGISLATIVE POWERS]

All legislative Powers herein granted shall be vested in a Congress of the United States, which shall consist of a Senate and House of Representatives.

SECTION 2

[HOUSE OF REPRESENTATIVES, HOW CONSTITUTED, POWER OF IMPEACHMENT]

The House of Representatives shall be composed of Members chosen every second Year by the People of the several States, and the Electors in each State shall have the Qualifications requisite for Electors of the most numerous Branch of the State Legislature.

No Person shall be a Representative who shall not have attained to the Age of twenty five Years, and been seven Years a Citizen of the United States, and who shall not, when elected, be an Inhabitant of that State in which he shall be chosen.

Representatives and *direct Taxes*[1] shall be apportioned among the several States which may be included within this Union, according to their respective Numbers, *which shall be determined by adding to the whole Number of free Persons, including those bound to Service for a Term of Years, and excluding Indians not taxed, three fifths of all other Persons.*[2] The actual Enumeration shall be made within three Years after the first Meeting of the Congress of the United States, and within every subsequent Term of ten Years, in such Manner as they shall by Law direct. The Number of Representatives shall not exceed one for every thirty Thousand, but each State shall have at Least one Representative; *and until such enumeration shall be made, the State of New Hampshire shall be entitled to chuse three, Massachusetts eight, Rhode-Island and Providence Plantations one, Connecticut five, New-York six, New Jersey four, Pennsylvania eight, Delaware one, Maryland six, Virginia ten, North Carolina five, South Carolina five, and Georgia three.*[3]

When vacancies happen in the Representation from any State, the Executive Authority thereof shall issue Writs of Election to fill such Vacancies.

The House of Representatives shall chuse their Speaker and other Officers; and shall have the sole Power of Impeachment.

SECTION 3

[THE SENATE, HOW CONSTITUTED, IMPEACHMENT TRIALS]

The Senate of the United States shall be composed of two Senators from each State, *chosen by the Legislature thereof,*[4] for six Years; and each Senator shall have one Vote.

Immediately after they shall be assembled in Consequence of the first Election, they shall be divided as equally as may be into three Classes. The Seats of the Senators of the first Class shall be vacated at the Expiration of the second Year, of the second Class at the Expiration of the fourth Year, and of the third Class at the Expiration of the sixth Year, so that one third may be chosen every second Year; *and if Vacancies happen by Resignation, or otherwise, during the Recess of the Legislature of any State, the Executive thereof may make temporary Appointments until the next Meeting of the Legislature, which shall then fill such Vacancies.*[5]

No Person shall be a Senator who shall not have attained to the Age of thirty Years, and been nine Years a Citizen of the United States, and who shall not, when elected, be an Inhabitant of that State for which he shall be chosen.

The Vice President of the United States shall be President of the Senate, but shall have no Vote, unless they be equally divided.

The Senate shall chuse their other Officers, and also a President pro tempore, in the Absence of the Vice President,

[1]Modified by Sixteenth Amendment.

[2]Modified by Fourteenth Amendment.

[3]Temporary provision.

[4]Modified by Seventeenth Amendment.

[5]Modified by Seventeenth Amendment.

or when he shall exercise the Office of President of the United States.

The Senate shall have the sole Power to try all Impeachments. When sitting for that Purpose, they shall be on Oath or Affirmation. When the President of the United States is tried, the Chief Justice shall preside: And no Person shall be convicted without the Concurrence of two thirds of the Members present.

Judgment in Cases of Impeachment shall not extend further than to removal from Office, and disqualification to hold and enjoy any Office of honor, Trust or Profit under the United States: but the Party convicted shall nevertheless be liable and subject to Indictment, Trial, Judgment and Punishment, according to Law.

SECTION 4

[ELECTION OF SENATORS AND REPRESENTATIVES]

The Times, Places and Manner of holding Elections for Senators and Representatives, shall be prescribed in each State by the Legislature thereof; but the Congress may at any time by Law make or alter such Regulations, except as to the Places of chusing Senators.

The Congress shall assemble at least once in every Year, and such Meeting shall be on the first Monday in December, unless they shall by Law appoint a different Day.[6]

SECTION 5

[QUORUM, JOURNALS, MEETINGS, ADJOURNMENTS]

Each House shall be the Judge of the Elections, Returns and Qualifications of its own Members, and a Majority of each shall constitute a Quorum to do Business; but a smaller Number may adjourn from day to day, and may be authorized to compel the Attendance of absent Members, in such Manner, and under such Penalties as each House may provide.

Each House may determine the Rules of its Proceedings, punish its Members for disorderly Behaviour, and, with the Concurrence of two thirds, expel a Member.

Each House shall keep a Journal of its Proceedings, and from time to time publish the same, excepting such Parts as may in their Judgment require Secrecy; and the Yeas and Nays of the Members of either House on any questions shall, at the Desire of one fifth of those Present, be entered on the Journal.

Neither House, during the Session of Congress, shall, without the Consent of the other, adjourn for more than three days, nor to any other Place than that in which the two Houses shall be sitting.

SECTION 6

[COMPENSATION, PRIVILEGES, DISABILITIES]

The Senators and Representatives shall receive a Compensation for their Services, to be ascertained by Law, and paid out of the Treasury of the United States. They shall in all Cases, except Treason, Felony and Breach of the Peace, be privileged from Arrest during their Attendance at the Session of their respective Houses, and in going to and returning from the same; and for any Speech or Debate in either House, they shall not be questioned in any other Place.

No Senator or Representative shall, during the Time for which he was elected, be appointed to any civil Office under the Authority of the United States, which shall have been created, or the Emoluments whereof shall have been encreased during such time; and no Person holding any Office under the United States, shall be a Member of either House during his Continuance in Office.

SECTION 7

[PROCEDURE IN PASSING BILLS AND RESOLUTIONS]

All Bills for raising Revenue shall originate in the House of Representatives; but the Senate may propose or concur with Amendments as on other Bills.

Every Bill which shall have passed the House of Representatives and the Senate, shall, before it become a Law, be presented to the President of the United States: If he approve he shall sign it, but if not he shall return it, with his Objections to that House in which it shall have originated, who shall enter the Objections at large on their Journal, and proceed to reconsider it. If after such Reconsideration two thirds of that House shall agree to pass the Bill, it shall be sent, together with the Objections, to the other House, by which it shall likewise be reconsidered, and if approved by two thirds of that House, it shall become a Law. But in all such Cases the Votes of both Houses shall be determined by yeas and Nays, and the Names of the Persons voting for and against the Bill shall be entered on the Journal of each House respectively. If any Bill shall not be returned by the President within ten Days (Sundays excepted) after it shall have been presented to him, the Same shall be a Law, in like Manner as if he had signed it, unless the Congress by their Adjournment prevent its Return, in which Case it shall not be a Law.

Every Order, Resolution, or Vote to which the Concurrence of the Senate and House of Representatives may be necessary (except on a question of Adjournment) shall be presented to the President of the United States; and before the Same shall take Effect, shall be approved by him, or being disapproved by him, shall be repassed by two thirds of the Senate and House of Representatives, according to the Rules and Limitations prescribed in the Case of a Bill.

SECTION 8

[POWERS OF CONGRESS]

The Congress shall have Power

To lay and collect Taxes, Duties, Imposts and Excises, to pay the Debts and provide for the common Defence and general Welfare of the United States; but all Duties, Imposts and Excises shall be uniform throughout the United States;

[6]Modified by Twentieth Amendment.

To borrow Money on the credit of the United States;

To regulate Commerce with foreign Nations, and among the several States, and with the Indian Tribes;

To establish an uniform Rule of Naturalization, and uniform Laws on the subject of Bankruptcies throughout the United States;

To coin Money, regulate the Value thereof, and of foreign Coin, and fix the Standard of Weights and Measures;

To provide for the Punishment of counterfeiting the Securities and current Coin of the United States;

To establish Post Offices and post Roads;

To promote the Progress of Science and useful Arts, by securing for limited Times to Authors and Inventors the exclusive Right to their respective Writings and Discoveries;

To constitute Tribunals inferior to the supreme Court;

To define and punish Piracies and Felonies committed on the high Seas, and Offences against the Law of Nations;

To declare War, grant Letters of Marque and Reprisal, and make Rules concerning Captures on Land and Water;

To raise and support Armies, but no Appropriation of Money to that Use shall be for a longer Term than two Years;

To provide and maintain a Navy;

To make Rules for the Government and Regulation of the land and naval Forces;

To provide for calling forth the Militia to execute the Laws of the Union, suppress Insurrections and repel Invasions;

To provide for organizing, arming, and disciplining, the Militia, and for governing such Part of them as may be employed in the Service of the United States, reserving to the States respectively, the Appointment of the Officers, and the Authority of training the Militia according to the discipline prescribed by Congress;

To exercise exclusive Legislation in all Cases whatsoever, over such District (not exceeding ten Miles square) as may, by Cession of particular States, and the Acceptance of Congress, become the Seat of the Government of the United States, and to exercise like Authority over all Places purchased by the Consent of the Legislature of the State in which the Same shall be, for the Erection of Forts, Magazines, Arsenals, dock-Yards, and other needful Buildings;—And

To make all Laws which shall be necessary and proper for carrying into Execution the foregoing Powers, and all other Powers vested by this Constitution in the Government of the United States, or in any Department or Officer thereof.

SECTION 9

[SOME RESTRICTIONS ON FEDERAL POWER]

The Migration or Importation of such Persons as any of the States now existing shall think proper to admit, shall not be prohibited by the Congress prior to the Year one thousand eight hundred and eight, but a Tax or duty may be imposed on such Importation, not exceeding ten dollars for each Person.[7]

The Privilege of the Writ of Habeas Corpus shall not be suspended, unless when in Cases of Rebellion or Invasion the public Safety may require it.

No Bill of Attainder or ex post facto Law shall be passed.

No Capitation, or other direct, Tax shall be laid, unless in Proportion to the Census or Enumeration herein before directed to be taken.[8]

No Tax or Duty shall be laid on Articles exported from any State.

No Preference shall be given by any Regulation of Commerce or Revenue to the Ports of one State over those of another; nor shall Vessels bound to, or from, one State, be obliged to enter, clear, or pay Duties in another.

No Money shall be drawn from the Treasury, but in Consequence of Appropriations made by Law; and a regular Statement and Account of the Receipts and Expenditures of all public Money shall be published from time to time.

No Title of Nobility shall be granted by the United States: And no Person holding any Office of Profit or Trust under them, shall, without the Consent of the Congress, accept of any present, Emolument, Office, or Title, of any kind whatever, from any King, Prince, or foreign State.

SECTION 10

[RESTRICTIONS UPON POWERS OF STATES]

No State shall enter into any Treaty, Alliance, or Confederation; grant Letters of Marque and Reprisal; coin Money; emit Bills of Credit; make any Thing but gold and silver Coin a Tender in Payment of Debts; pass any Bill of Attainder, ex post facto Law, or Law impairing the Obligation of Contracts, or grant any Title of Nobility.

No State shall, without the Consent of the Congress, lay any Imposts or Duties on Imports or Exports, except what may be absolutely necessary for executing its inspection Laws: and the net Produce of all Duties and Imposts, laid by any State on Imports or Exports, shall be for the Use of the Treasury of the United States; and all such Laws shall be subject to the Revision and Control of the Congress.

No State shall, without the Consent of Congress, lay any Duty of Tonnage, keep Troops, or Ships of War in time of Peace, enter into any Agreement or Compact with another State, or with a foreign Power, or engage in War, unless actually invaded, or in such imminent Danger as will not admit of delay.

Article II

SECTION 1

[EXECUTIVE POWER, ELECTION, QUALIFICATIONS OF THE PRESIDENT]

---

[7]Temporary provision.

[8]Modified by Sixteenth Amendment.

The executive Power shall be vested in a President of the United States of America. *He shall hold his Office during the Term of four Years, and, together with the Vice President, chosen for the same Term, be elected, as follows*[9]

Each State shall appoint, in such Manner as the Legislature thereof may direct, a Number of Electors, equal to the whole Number of Senators and Representatives to which the State may be entitled in the Congress: but no Senator or Representative, or Person holding an Office of Trust or Profit under the United States, shall be appointed an Elector.

The electors shall meet in their respective States, and vote by ballot for two Persons, of whom one at least shall not be an Inhabitant of the same State with themselves. And they shall make a List of all the Persons voted for, and of the Number of Votes for each; which List they shall sign and certify, and transmit sealed to the Seat of the Government of the United States, directed to the President of the Senate. The President of the Senate shall, in the Presence of the Senate and House of Representatives, open all the Certificates, and the Votes shall then be counted. The Person having the greatest Number of Votes shall be the President, if such Number be a Majority of the whole Number of Electors appointed; and if there be more than one who have such Majority, and have an equal Number of Votes, then the House of Representatives shall immediately chuse by Ballot one of them for President; and if no Person have a Majority, then from the five highest on the List the said House shall in like Manner chuse the President. But in chusing the President, the Votes shall be taken by States, the Representation from each State having one Vote; A quorum for this Purpose shall consist of a Member or Members from two thirds of the States, and a Majority of all the States shall be necessary to a Choice. In every Case, after the Choice of the President, the person having the greatest Number of Votes of the Electors shall be the Vice President. But if there should remain two or more who have equal Votes, the Senate shall chuse from them by Ballot the Vice President.[10]

The Congress may determine the Time of chusing the Electors, and the Day on which they shall give their Votes; which Day shall be the same throughout the United States.

No Person except a natural born Citizen, or a Citizen of the United States, at the time of the Adoption of this Constitution, shall be eligible to the Office of President; neither shall any Person be eligible to that Office who shall not have attained to the Age of thirty five Years, and been fourteen Years a Resident within the United States.

In Case of the Removal of the President from Office, or his Death, Resignation, or Inability to discharge the Powers and Duties of the said Office, the Same shall devolve on the Vice President, and the Congress may by Law provide for the Case of Removal, Death, Resignation or Inability, both of the President and Vice President, declaring what Officer shall then act as President, and such Officer shall act accordingly, until the Disability be removed, or a President shall be elected.

The President shall, at stated Times, receive for his Services, a Compensation, which shall neither be increased nor diminished during the Period for which he shall have been elected, and he shall not receive within that Period any other Emolument from the United States, or any of them.

Before he enter on the Execution of his Office, he shall take the following Oath or Affirmation:—"I do solemnly swear (or affirm) that I will faithfully execute the Office of President of the United States, and will to the best of my Ability, preserve, protect and defend the Constitution of the United States."

SECTION 2

[POWERS OF THE PRESIDENT]

The President shall be Commander in Chief of the Army and Navy of the United States, and of the Militia of the several States, when called into the actual Service of the United States; he may require the Opinion, in writing, of the principal Officer in each of the executive Departments, upon any Subject relating to the Duties of their respective Offices, and he shall have Power to grant Reprieves and Pardons for Offences against the United States, except in Cases of Impeachment.

He shall have Power, by and with the Advice and Consent of the Senate, to make Treaties, provided two thirds of the Senators present concur; and he shall nominate, and by and with the Advice and Consent of the Senate, shall appoint Ambassadors, other public Ministers and Consuls, Judges of the supreme Court, and all other Officers of the United States, whose Appointments are not herein otherwise provided for, and which shall be established by Law: but the Congress may by Law vest the Appointment of such inferior Officers, as they think proper, in the President alone, in the Courts of Law, or in the Heads of Departments.

The President shall have Power to fill up all Vacancies that may happen during the Recess of the Senate, by granting Commissions which shall expire at the End of their next Session.

SECTION 3

[POWERS AND DUTIES OF THE PRESIDENT]

He shall from time to time give to the Congress Information of the State of the Union, and recommend to their Consideration such Measures as he shall judge necessary and expedient; he may, on extraordinary Occasions, convene both Houses, or either of them, and in Case of Disagreement between them, with Respect to the Time of Adjournment, he may adjourn them to such Time as he shall think proper; he shall receive Ambassadors and other public Ministers; he shall take Care that the Laws be faithfully executed, and shall Commission all the Officers of the United States.

SECTION 4

[IMPEACHMENT]

[9]Number of terms limited to two by Twenty-second Amendment.

[10]Modified by Twelfth and Twentieth Amendments.

The President, Vice President and all civil Officers of the United States, shall be removed from Office on Impeachment for, and Conviction of, Treason, Bribery, or other high Crimes and Misdemeanors.

Article III

SECTION 1

[JUDICIAL POWER, TENURE OF OFFICE]

The judicial Power of the United States, shall be vested in one supreme Court, and in such inferior Courts as the Congress may from time to time ordain and establish. The Judges, both of the supreme and inferior Courts, shall hold their Offices during good Behaviour, and shall, at stated Times, receive for their Services, a Compensation, which shall not be diminished during their Continuance in Office.

SECTION 2

[JURISDICTION]

The judicial Power shall extend to all Cases, in Law and Equity, arising under this Constitution, the Laws of the United States, and Treaties made, or which shall be made, under their Authority;—to all Cases affecting Ambassadors, other public Ministers and Consuls;—to all Cases of admiralty and maritime Jurisdiction;—to Controversies to which the United States shall be a Party;—to Controversies between two or more States;*—between a State and Citizens of another State;*—between Citizens of different States,—between Citizens of the same State claiming Lands under Grants of different States, *and between a State*, or the Citizens thereof, *and foreign States, Citizens or Subjects.*[11]

In all Cases affecting Ambassadors, other public Ministers and Consuls, and those in which a State shall be Party, the supreme Court shall have original Jurisdiction. In all the other Cases before mentioned, the supreme Court shall have appellate Jurisdiction, both as to Law and Fact, with such Exceptions, and under such Regulations as the Congress shall make.

The Trial of all Crimes, except in Cases of Impeachment, shall be by Jury; and such Trial shall be held in the State where the said Crimes shall have been committed; but when not committed within any State, the Trial shall be at such Place or Places as the Congress may by Law have directed.

SECTION 3

[TREASON, PROOF, AND PUNISHMENT]

Treason against the United States, shall consist only in levying War against them, or in adhering to their Enemies, giving them Aid and Comfort. No Person shall be convicted of Treason unless on the Testimony of two Witnesses to the same overt Act, or on Confession in open Court.

The Congress shall have Power to declare the Punishment of Treason, but no Attainder of Treason shall work Corruption of Blood, or Forfeiture except during the Life of the Person attainted.

Article IV

SECTION 1

[FAITH AND CREDIT AMONG STATES]

Full Faith and Credit shall be given in each State to the public Acts, Records, and judicial Proceedings of every other State. And the Congress may by general Laws prescribe the Manner in which such Acts, Records and Proceedings shall be proved, and the Effect thereof.

SECTION 2

[PRIVILEGES AND IMMUNITIES, FUGITIVES]

The Citizens of each State shall be entitled to all Privileges and Immunities of Citizens in the several States.

A Person charged in any State with Treason, Felony or other Crime, who shall flee from Justice, and be found in another State, shall on Demand of the executive Authority of the State from which he fled, be delivered up, to be removed to the State having Jurisdiction of the Crime.

No person held to Service or Labour in one State, under the Laws thereof, escaping into another, shall, in Consequence of any Law or Regulation therein, be discharged from such Service or Labour, but shall be delivered up on Claim of the Party to whom such Service or Labour may be due.[12]

SECTION 3

[ADMISSION OF NEW STATES]

New States may be admitted by the Congress into this Union; but no new State shall be formed or erected within the Jurisdiction of any other State; nor any State be formed by the Junction of two or more States, or Parts of States, without the Consent of the Legislatures of the States concerned as well as of the Congress.

The Congress shall have Power to dispose of and make all needful Rules and Regulations respecting the Territory or other Property belonging to the United States; and nothing in this Constitution shall be so construed as to Prejudice any Claims of the United States, or of any particular State.

SECTION 4

[GUARANTEE OF REPUBLICAN GOVERNMENT]

The United States shall guarantee to every State in this Union a Republican Form of Government, and shall protect each of them against Invasion; and on Application of the Legislature, or of the Executive (when the Legislature cannot be convened), against domestic Violence.

---

[11]Modified by Eleventh Amendment.

[12]Repealed by the Thirteenth Amendment.

Article V

[AMENDMENT OF THE CONSTITUTION]

The Congress, whenever two thirds of both Houses shall deem it necessary, shall propose Amendments to this Constitution, or, on the Application of the Legislatures of two thirds of the several States, shall call a Convention for proposing Amendments, which, in either Case, shall be valid to all Intents and Purposes, as Part of this Constitution, when ratified by the Legislatures of three fourths of the several States, or by Conventions in three fourths thereof, as the one or the other Mode of Ratification may be proposed by the Congress; *Provided that no Amendment which may be made prior to the Year One thousand eight hundred and eight shall in any Manner affect the first and fourth Clauses in the Ninth Section of the first Article;*[13] and that no State, without its Consent, shall be deprived of its equal Suffrage in the Senate.

Article VI

[DEBTS, SUPREMACY, OATH]

All Debts contracted and Engagements entered into, before the Adoption of this Constitution, shall be as valid against the United States under this Constitution, as under the Confederation.

This Constitution, and the Laws of the United States which shall be made in Pursuance thereof; and all Treaties made, or which shall be made, under the Authority of the United States, shall be the supreme Law of the Land; and the Judges in every State shall be bound thereby, any Thing in the Constitution or Laws of any State to the Contrary notwithstanding.

The Senators and Representatives before mentioned, and the Members of the several State Legislatures, and all executive and judicial Officers, both of the United States and of the several States, shall be bound by Oath or Affirmation, to support this Constitution; but no religious Test shall be required as a Qualification to any Office or public Trust under the United States.

Article VII

[RATIFICATION AND ESTABLISHMENT]

The Ratification of the Conventions of nine States, shall be sufficient for the Establishment of this Constitution between the States so ratifying the Same.[14]

Done in Convention by the Unanimous Consent of the States present the Seventeenth Day of September in the Year of our Lord one thousand seven hundred and Eighty seven and of the Independence of the United States of America the Twelfth. *In Witness* whereof We have hereunto subscribed our Names,

[13]Temporary provision.

[14]The Constitution was submitted on September 17, 1787, by the Constitutional Convention, was ratified by the conventions of several states at various dates up to May 29, 1790, and became effective on March 4, 1789.

G:[o] WASHINGTON—
Presidt. and deputy from Virginia

NEW HAMPSHIRE
John Langdon
Nicholas Gilman

MASSACHUSETTS
Nathaniel Gorham
Rufus King

CONNECTICUT
Wm. Saml. Johnson
Roger Sherman

NEW YORK
Alexander Hamilton

NEW JERSEY
Wil: Livingston
David Brearley
Wm. Paterson
Jona: Dayton

PENNSYLVANIA
B Franklin
Thomas Mifflin
Robt. Morris
Geo. Clymer
Thos. FitzSimons
Jared Ingersoll
James Wilson
Gouv Morris

DELAWARE
Geo: Read
Gunning Bedford jun
John Dickinson
Richard Bassett
Jaco: Broom

MARYLAND
James McHenry
Dan of St Thos. Jenifer
Danl. Carroll

VIRGINIA
John Blair—
James Madison Jr.

NORTH CAROLINA
Wm. Blount
Richd. Dobbs Spaight
Hu Williamson

SOUTH CAROLINA
J. Rutledge
Charles Cotesworth Pinckney
Charles Pinckney
Pierce Butler

GEORGIA
William Few
Abr Baldwin

Amendments to the Constitution

Proposed by Congress and Ratified by the Legislatures of the Several States, Pursuant to Article V of the Original Constitution.

Amendments I–X, known as the Bill of Rights, were proposed by Congress on September 25, 1789, and ratified on December 15, 1791.

Amendment I

[FREEDOM OF RELIGION, OF SPEECH, AND OF THE PRESS]

Congress shall make no law respecting an establishment of religion, or prohibiting the free exercise thereof; or abridging the freedom of speech, or of the press; or the right of the people peaceably to assemble, and to petition the Government for a redress of grievances.

Amendment II

[RIGHT TO KEEP AND BEAR ARMS]

A well regulated Militia, being necessary to the security of a free State, the right of the people to keep and bear Arms, shall not be infringed.

Amendment III

[QUARTERING OF SOLDIERS]

No Soldier shall, in time of peace be quartered in any house, without the consent of the Owner, nor in time of war, but in a manner to be prescribed by law.

Amendment IV

[SECURITY FROM UNWARRANTABLE SEARCH AND SEIZURE]

The right of the people to be secure in their persons, houses, papers, and effects, against unreasonable searches and seizures, shall not be violated, and no Warrants shall issue, but upon probable cause, supported by Oath or affirmation, and particularly describing the place to be searched, and the persons or things to be seized.

Amendment V

[RIGHTS OF ACCUSED PERSONS IN CRIMINAL PROCEEDINGS]

No person shall be held to answer for a capital, or otherwise infamous crime, unless on a presentment or indictment of a Grand Jury, except in cases arising in the land or naval forces, or in the Militia, when in actual service in time of War or in public danger; nor shall any person be subject for the same offence to be twice put in jeopardy of life or limb; nor shall be compelled in any criminal case to be a witness against himself, nor be deprived of life, liberty, or property, without due process of law; nor shall private property be taken for public use, without just compensation.

Amendment VI

[RIGHT TO SPEEDY TRIAL, WITNESSES, ETC.]

In all criminal prosecutions, the accused shall enjoy the right to a speedy and public trial, by an impartial jury of the State and district wherein the crime shall have been committed, which district shall have been previously ascertained by law, and to be informed of the nature and cause of the accusation; to be confronted with the witnesses against him; to have compulsory process for obtaining witnesses in his favor, and to have the Assistance of Counsel for his defence.

Amendment VII

[TRIAL BY JURY IN CIVIL CASES]

In suits at common law, where the value in controversy shall exceed twenty dollars, the right of trial by jury shall be preserved, and no fact tried by a jury, shall be otherwise reexamined in any Court of the United States, than according to the rules of the common law.

Amendment VIII

[BAILS, FINES, PUNISHMENTS]

Excessive bail shall not be required, nor excessive fines imposed, nor cruel and unusual punishments inflicted.

Amendment IX

[RESERVATION OF RIGHTS OF PEOPLE]

The enumeration in the Constitution, of certain rights, shall not be construed to deny or disparage others retained by the people.

Amendment X

[POWERS RESERVED TO STATES OR PEOPLE]

The powers not delegated to the United States by the Constitution, nor prohibited by it to the States, are reserved to the States respectively, or to the people.

Amendment XI

[*Proposed by Congress on March 4, 1794; declared ratified on January 8, 1798.*]

[RESTRICTION OF JUDICIAL POWER]

The Judicial power of the United States shall not be construed to extend to any suit in law or equity, commenced or prosecuted against one of the United States by Citizens of another State, or by Citizens or Subjects of any Foreign State.

Amendment XII

[*Proposed by Congress on December 9, 1803; declared ratified on September 25, 1804.*]

[ELECTION OF PRESIDENT AND VICE PRESIDENT]

The Electors shall meet in their respective states and vote by ballot for President and Vice-President, one of whom, at least, shall not be an inhabitant of the same state with themselves; they shall name in their ballots the person voted for as President, and in distinct ballots the person voted for as Vice-President, and they shall make distinct lists of all persons voted for as President, and of all persons voted for as Vice-President, and of the number of votes for each, which lists they shall sign and certify, and transmit sealed to the seat of the government of the United States, directed to the President of the Senate;—the President of the Senate shall, in presence of the Senate and House of Representatives, open all the certificates and the votes shall then be counted;—The person having the greatest number of votes for President, shall be the President, if such number be a majority of the whole number of Electors appointed; and if no person have such majority, then from the persons having the highest numbers not exceeding three on the list of those voted for as President, the House of Representatives shall choose immediately, by ballot, the President. But in choosing the President, the votes shall be taken by states, the representation from each state having one vote; a quorum for this purpose shall consist of a member or members from two-thirds of the states, and a majority of all the states shall be necessary to a choice. And if the House of Representatives shall not choose a President whenever the right of choice shall devolve upon them, before the fourth day of March next following, then the Vice-President shall act as President, as in the case of the death or other constitutional disability of the President.—The person having the greatest number of votes as Vice-President, shall be the Vice-President, if such number be a majority of the whole number of Electors appointed, and if no person have a majority, then from the two highest numbers on the list, the Senate shall choose the Vice-President; a quorum for the purpose shall consist of two-thirds of the whole number of Senators, and a majority of the whole number shall be necessary to a choice. But no person constitutionally ineligible to the office of President shall be eligible to that of Vice-President of the United States.

Amendment XIII

[*Proposed by Congress on January 31, 1865; declared ratified on December 18, 1865.*]

SECTION 1

[ABOLITION OF SLAVERY]

Neither slavery nor involuntary servitude, except as a punishment for crime whereof the party shall have been duly convicted, shall exist within the United States, or any place subject to their jurisdiction.

SECTION 2

[POWER TO ENFORCE THIS ARTICLE]

Congress shall have power to enforce this article by appropriate legislation.

Amendment XIV

[*Proposed by Congress on June 13, 1866; declared ratified on July 28, 1868.*]

SECTION 1

[CITIZENSHIP RIGHTS NOT TO BE ABRIDGED BY STATES]

All persons born or naturalized in the United States, and subject to the jurisdiction thereof, are citizens of the United States and of the State wherein they reside. No State shall make or enforce any law which shall abridge the privileges or immunities of citizens of the United States; nor shall any State deprive any person of life, liberty, or property, without due process of law; nor deny to any person within its jurisdiction the equal protection of the laws.

SECTION 2

[APPORTIONMENT OF REPRESENTATIVES IN CONGRESS]

Representatives shall be apportioned among the several States according to their respective numbers, counting the whole number of persons in each State, excluding Indians not taxed. But when the right to vote at any election for the choice of electors for President and Vice-President of the United States, Representatives in Congress, the Executive and Judicial officers of a State, or the members of the Legislature thereof, is denied to any of the male inhabitants of such State, being twenty-one years of age, and citizens of the United States, or in any way abridged, except for participation in rebellion, or other crime, the basis of representation therein shall be reduced in the proportion which the number of such male citizens shall bear to the whole number of male citizens twenty-one years of age in such State.

SECTION 3

[PERSONS DISQUALIFIED FROM HOLDING OFFICE]

No person shall be a Senator or Representative in Congress, or elector of President and Vice-President, or hold any office, civil or military, under the United States, or under any State, who, having previously taken an oath, as a member of Congress, or as an officer of the United States, or as a member of any State legislature, or as an executive or judicial officer of any State, to support the Constitution of the United States, shall have engaged in insurrection or rebellion against the same, or given aid or comfort to the enemies thereof. But Congress may by a vote of two-thirds of each House, remove such disability.

SECTION 4

[WHAT PUBLIC DEBTS ARE VALID]

The validity of the public debt of the United States, authorized by law, including debts incurred for payment of pensions and bounties for services in suppressing insurrection or rebellion, shall not be questioned. But neither the United States nor any State shall assume or pay any debt or obligation incurred in aid of insurrection or rebellion against the United States, or any claim for the loss or emancipation of any slave; but all such debts, obligations and claims shall be held illegal and void.

SECTION 5

[POWER TO ENFORCE THIS ARTICLE]

The Congress shall have power to enforce, by appropriate legislation, the provisions of this article.

Amendment XV

[*Proposed by Congress on February 26, 1869; declared ratified on March 30, 1870.*]

SECTION 1

[NEGRO SUFFRAGE]

The right of citizens of the United States to vote shall not be denied or abridged by the United States or by any State on account of race, color, or previous condition of servitude.

SECTION 2

[POWER TO ENFORCE THIS ARTICLE]

The Congress shall have power to enforce this article by appropriate legislation.

Amendment XVI

[*Proposed by Congress on July 2, 1909; declared ratified on February 25, 1913.*]

[AUTHORIZING INCOME TAXES]

The Congress shall have power to lay and collect taxes on incomes, from whatever source derived, without apportionment among the several States, and without regard to any census or enumeration.

Amendment XVII

[*Proposed by Congress on May 13, 1912; declared ratified on May 31, 1913.*]

[POPULAR ELECTION OF SENATORS]

The Senate of the United States shall be composed of two Senators from each State, elected by the people thereof, for six years; and each Senator shall have one vote. The electors in each State shall have the qualifications requisite for electors of the most numerous branch of the State legislatures.

When vacancies happen in the representation of any State in the Senate, the executive authority of such State shall issue writs of election to fill such vacancies: *Provided*, That the legislature of any State may empower the executive thereof to make temporary appointments until the people fill the vacancies by election as the legislature may direct.

This amendment shall not be so construed as to affect the election or term of any Senator chosen before it becomes valid as part of the Constitution.

Amendment XVIII

[*Proposed by Congress December 18, 1917; declared ratified on January 29, 1919.*]

SECTION 1

[NATIONAL LIQUOR PROHIBITION]

After one year from the ratification of this article the manufacture, sale, or transportation of intoxicating liquors within, the importation thereof into, or the exportation thereof from the United States and all territory subject to the jurisdiction thereof for beverage purposes is hereby prohibited.

SECTION 2

[POWER TO ENFORCE THIS ARTICLE]

The Congress and the several States shall have concurrent power to enforce this article by appropriate legislation.

SECTION 3

[RATIFICATION WITHIN SEVEN YEARS]

This article shall be inoperative unless it shall have been ratified as an amendment to the Constitution by the legislatures of the several States, as provided in the Constitution, within seven years from the date of the submission hereof to the States by the Congress.[1]

---

[1]Repealed by the Twenty-first Amendment.

Amendment XIX

[Proposed by Congress on June 4, 1919; declared ratified on August 26, 1920.]

[WOMAN SUFFRAGE]

The right of citizens of the United States to vote shall not be denied or abridged by the United States or by any State on account of sex.

Congress shall have power to enforce this article by appropriate legislation.

Amendment XX

[Proposed by Congress on March 2, 1932; declared ratified on February 6, 1933.]

SECTION 1

[TERMS OF OFFICE]

The terms of the President and Vice President shall end at noon on the 20th day of January, and the terms of Senators and Representatives at noon on the 3d day of January, of the years in which such terms would have ended if this article had not been ratified; and the terms of their successors shall then begin.

SECTION 2

[TIME OF CONVENING CONGRESS]

The Congress shall assemble at least once in every year, and such meeting shall begin at noon on the 3d day of January, unless they shall by law appoint a different day.

SECTION 3

[DEATH OF PRESIDENT-ELECT]

If, at the time fixed for the beginning of the term of the President, the President elect shall have died, the Vice President elect shall become President. If a President shall not have been chosen before the time fixed for the beginning of his term, or if the President elect shall have failed to qualify, then the Vice President elect shall act as President until a President shall have qualified; and the Congress may by law provide for the case wherein neither a President elect nor a Vice President elect shall have qualified, declaring who shall then act as President, or the manner in which one who is to act shall be selected, and such person shall act accordingly until a President or Vice President shall have qualified.

SECTION 4

[ELECTION OF THE PRESIDENT]

The Congress may by law provide for the case of the death of any of the persons from whom the House of Representatives may choose a President whenever the right of choice shall have devolved upon them, and for the case of the death of any of the persons from whom the Senate may choose a Vice President whenever the right of choice shall have devolved upon them.

SECTION 5

[AMENDMENT TAKES EFFECT]

Sections 1 and 2 shall take effect on the 15th day of October following the ratification of this article.

SECTION 6

[RATIFICATION WITHIN SEVEN YEARS]

This article shall be inoperative unless it shall have been ratified as an amendment to the Constitution by the legislatures of three-fourths of the several States within seven years from the date of its submission.

Amendment XXI

[Proposed by Congress on February 20, 1933; declared ratified on December 5, 1933.]

SECTION 1

[NATIONAL LIQUOR PROHIBITION REPEALED]

The eighteenth article of amendment to the Constitution of the United States is hereby repealed.

SECTION 2

[TRANSPORTATION OF LIQUOR INTO "DRY" STATES]

The transportation or importation into any State, Territory, or Possession of the United States for delivery or use therein of intoxicating liquors, in violation of the laws thereof, is hereby prohibited.

SECTION 3

[RATIFICATION WITHIN SEVEN YEARS]

This article shall be inoperative unless it shall have been ratified as an amendment to the Constitution by conventions in the several States, as provided in the Constitution, within seven years from the date of the submission hereof to the States by the Congress.

Amendment XXII

[Proposed by Congress on March 21, 1947; declared ratified on February 27, 1951.]

SECTION 1

[TENURE OF PRESIDENT LIMITED]

No person shall be elected to the office of President more than twice, and no person who has held the office of President or acted as President, for more than two years of a term to which some other person was elected President shall be elected to the office of the President more than once. But this Article shall not apply to any person holding the office of President when this Article was proposed by the Congress, and shall not prevent any person who may be holding the office of President, or acting as President, during the term within which this

Article becomes operative from holding the office of President or acting as President during the remainder of such term.

SECTION 2

[RATIFICATION WITHIN SEVEN YEARS]

This article shall be inoperative unless it shall have been ratified as an amendment to the Constitution by the legislatures of three-fourths of the several States within seven years from the date of its submission to the States by the Congress.

Amendment XXIII

[*Proposed by Congress on June 16, 1960; declared ratified on March 29, 1961.*]

SECTION 1

[ELECTORAL COLLEGE VOTES FOR THE DISTRICT OF COLUMBIA]

The District constituting the seat of Government of the United States shall appoint in such manner as the Congress may direct:

A number of electors of President and Vice President equal to the whole number of Senators and Representatives in Congress to which the District would be entitled if it were a State, but in no event more than the least populous State; they shall be in addition to those appointed by the States, but they shall be considered, for the purposes of the election of President and Vice President, to be electors appointed by a State; and they shall meet in the District and perform such duties as provided by the twelfth article of amendment.

SECTION 2

[POWER TO ENFORCE THIS ARTICLE]

The Congress shall have power to enforce this article by appropriate legislation.

Amendment XXIV

[*Proposed by Congress on August 27, 1962; declared ratified on January 23, 1964.*]

SECTION 1

[ANTI-POLL TAX]

The right of citizens of the United States to vote in any primary or other election for President or Vice President, for electors for President or Vice President, or for Senator or Representative of Congress, shall not be denied or abridged by the United States or any State by reason of failure to pay any poll tax or other tax.

SECTION 2

[POWER TO ENFORCE THIS ARTICLE]

The Congress shall have power to enforce this article by appropriate legislation.

Amendment XXV

[*Proposed by Congress on July 6, 1965; declared ratified on February 10, 1967.*]

SECTION 1

[VICE PRESIDENT TO BECOME PRESIDENT]

In case of the removal of the President from office or his death or resignation, the Vice President shall become President.

SECTION 2

[CHOICE OF A NEW VICE PRESIDENT]

Whenever there is a vacancy in the office of the Vice President, the President shall nominate a Vice President who shall take the office upon confirmation by a majority vote of both houses of Congress.

SECTION 3

[PRESIDENT MAY DECLARE OWN DISABILITY]

Whenever the President transmits to the President pro tempore of the Senate and the Speaker of the House of Representatives his written declaration that he is unable to discharge the powers and duties of his office, and until he transmits to them a written declaration to the contrary, such powers and duties shall be discharged by the Vice President as Acting President.

SECTION 4

[ALTERNATE PROCEDURES TO DECLARE AND TO END PRESIDENTIAL DISABILITY]

Whenever the Vice President and a majority of either the principal officers of the executive departments, or of such other body as Congress may by law provide, transmit to the President pro tempore of the Senate and the Speaker of the House of Representatives their written declaration that the President is unable to discharge the powers and duties of his office, the Vice President shall immediately assume the powers and duties of the office as Acting President.

Thereafter, when the President transmits to the President pro tempore of the Senate and the Speaker of the House of Representatives his written declaration that no inability exists, he shall resume the powers and duties of his office unless the Vice President and a majority of either the principal officers of the executive department, or of such other body as Congress may by law provide, transmit within four days to the President pro tempore of the Senate and the Speaker of the House of Representatives their written declaration that the President is unable to discharge the powers and duties of his office. Thereupon Congress shall decide the issue, assembling within forty eight hours for that purpose if not in session. If the Congress, within twenty one days after receipt of the latter written declaration, or, if Congress is not in session, within twenty one days after Congress is required to assemble, determines by two-thirds vote of both Houses that the President is unable to discharge the powers and duties of his office, the Vice President shall continue to discharge the same as Acting President; otherwise, the President shall resume the powers and duties of his office.

Amendment XXVI

[Proposed by Congress on March 23, 1971; declared ratified on July 1, 1971.]

SECTION 1

[EIGHTEEN-YEAR-OLD VOTE]

The right of citizens of the United States, who are eighteen years of age or older, to vote shall not be denied or abridged by the United States or by any State on account of age.

SECTION 2

[POWER TO ENFORCE THIS ARTICLE]

The Congress shall have power to enforce this article by appropriate legislation.

Amendment XXVII

[Proposed by Congress on September 25, 1789; declared ratified on May 8, 1992.]

[CONGRESS CANNOT RAISE ITS OWN PAY]

No law varying the compensation for the services of the Senators and Representatives, shall take effect, until an election of representatives shall have intervened.

The Federalist Papers

No. 10: Madison

Among the numerous advantages promised by a well constructed Union, none deserves to be more accurately developed than its tendency to break and control the violence of faction. The friend of popular governments never finds himself so much alarmed for their character and fate, as when he contemplates their propensity to this dangerous vice. He will not fail therefore to set a due value on any plan which, without violating the principles to which he is attached, provides a proper cure for it. The instability, injustice, and confusion introduced into the public councils have, in truth, been the mortal diseases under which popular governments have everywhere perished, as they continue to be the favorite and fruitful topics from which the adversaries to liberty derive their most specious declamations. The valuable improvements made by the American constitutions on the popular models, both ancient and modern, cannot certainly be too much admired; but it would be an unwarrantable partiality to contend that they have as effectually obviated the danger on this side, as was wished and expected. Complaints are everywhere heard from our most considerate and virtuous citizens, equally the friends of public and private faith and of public and personal liberty, that our governments are too unstable, that the public good is disregarded in the conflicts of rival parties, and that measures are too often decided, not according to the rules of justice and the rights of the minor party, but by the superior force of an interested and overbearing majority. However anxiously we may wish that these complaints had no foundation, the evidence of known facts will not permit us to deny that they are in some degree true. It will be found, indeed, on a candid review of our situation, that some of the distresses under which we labor have been erroneously charged on the operation of our governments; but it will be found, at the same time, that other causes will not alone account for many of our heaviest misfortunes; and, particularly, for that prevailing and increasing distrust of public engagements and alarm for private rights which are echoed from one end of the continent to the other. These must be chiefly, if not wholly, effects of the unsteadiness and injustice with which a factious spirit has tainted our public administration.

By a faction I understand a number of citizens, whether amounting to a majority or minority of the whole, who are united and actuated by some common impulse of passion, or of interest, adverse to the rights of other citizens, or to the permanent and aggregate interests of the community.

There are two methods of curing the mischiefs of faction: the one, by removing its causes; the other, by controlling its effects.

There are again two methods of removing the causes of faction: the one, by destroying the liberty which is essential to its existence; the other, by giving to every citizen the same opinions, the same passions, and the same interests.

It could never be more truly said than of the first remedy, that it is worse than the disease. Liberty is to faction what air is to fire, an aliment without which it instantly expires. But it could not be a less folly to abolish liberty, which is essential to political life, because it nourishes faction, than it would be to wish the annihilation of air, which is essential to animal life, because it imparts to fire its destructive agency.

The second expedient is as impracticable, as the first would be unwise. As long as the reason of man continues fallible, and he is at liberty to exercise it, different opinions will be formed. As long as the connection subsists between his reason and his self-love, his opinions and his passions will have a reciprocal influence on each other; and the former will be objects to which the latter will attach themselves. The diversity in the faculties of men, from which the rights of property originate, is not less an insuperable obstacle to a uniformity of interests. The protection of these faculties is the first object of Government. From the protection of different and unequal faculties of acquiring property, the possession of different degrees and kinds of property immediately results; and from the influence of these on the sentiments and views of the respective proprietors, ensues a division of the society into different interests and parties.

The latent causes of faction are thus sown in the nature of man; and we see them everywhere brought into different degrees of activity, according to the different circumstances of civil society. A zeal for different opinions concerning religion, concerning Government, and many other points, as well of speculation as of practice; an attachment to different leaders ambitiously contending for pre-eminence and power; or to persons of other descriptions whose fortunes have been interesting to the human passions, have in turn divided mankind into parties, inflamed them with mutual animosity, and rendered them much more disposed to vex and oppress each other, than to co-operate for their common good. So strong is this propensity of mankind to fall into mutual animosities, that where no substantial occasion presents itself, the most frivolous and fanciful distinctions have been sufficient to kindle their unfriendly passions, and excite their most violent conflicts. But the most common and durable source of factions has been the various and unequal distribution of property. Those who hold and those who are without property have ever formed distinct interests in society. Those who are creditors, and those who are debtors, fall under a like discrimination. A landed interest, a manufacturing interest, a mercantile interest, a moneyed interest, with many lesser interests, grow up of necessity in civilized nations, and divide them into different classes, actuated by different sentiments and views. The regulation of these various and interfering interests forms the principal task of modern Legislation, and involves the spirit of party and faction in the necessary and ordinary operations of Government.

No man is allowed to be judge in his own cause, because his interest would certainly bias his judgment and, not improbably, corrupt his integrity. With equal, nay with greater reason, a body of men are unfit to be both judges and parties at the same time; yet what are many of the most important acts of legislation but so many judicial determinations, not indeed concerning the rights of single persons, but concerning the rights of large bodies of citizens; and what are the different classes of legislators but advocates and parties to the causes which they determine? Is a law proposed concerning private debts? It is a question to which the creditors are parties on one side and the debtors on the other. Justice ought to hold the balance between them. Yet the parties are, and must be, themselves the judges; and the most numerous party, or in other words, the most powerful faction must be expected to prevail. Shall domestic manufacturers be encouraged, and in what degree, by restrictions on foreign manufacturers? are questions which would be differently decided by the landed and the manufacturing classes, and probably by neither with a sole regard to justice and the public good. The apportionment of taxes on the various descriptions of property is an act which seems to require the most exact impartiality; yet there is, perhaps, no legislative act in which greater opportunity and temptation are given to a predominant party to trample on the rules of justice. Every shilling with which they overburden the inferior number is a shilling saved to their own pockets.

It is in vain to say that enlightened statesmen will be able to adjust these clashing interests and render them all subservient to the public good. Enlightened statesmen will not always be at the helm. Nor, in many cases, can such an adjustment be made at all without taking into view indirect and remote considerations, which will rarely prevail over the immediate interest which one party may find in disregarding the rights of another or the good of the whole.

The inference to which we are brought is that the *causes* of faction cannot be removed and that relief is only to be sought in the means of controlling its *effects.*

If a faction consists of less than a majority, relief is supplied by the republican principle, which enables the majority to defeat its sinister views by regular vote. It may clog the administration, it may convulse the society; but it will be unable to execute and mask its violence under the forms of the Constitution. When a majority is included in a faction, the form of popular government, on the other hand, enables it to sacrifice to its ruling passion or interest both the public good and the rights of other citizens. To secure the public good and private rights against the danger of such a faction, and at the same time to preserve the spirit and the form of popular government, is then the great object to which our enquiries are directed. Let me add that it is the great desideratum by which alone this form of government can be rescued from the opprobrium under which it has so long labored and be recommended to the esteem and adoption of mankind.

By what means is this object attainable? Evidently by one of two only. Either the existence of the same passion or interest in a majority at the same time must be prevented, or the majority, having such co-existent passion or interest, must be rendered, by their number and local situation, unable to concert and carry into effect schemes of oppression. If the impulse and the opportunity be suffered to coincide, we well know that neither moral nor religious motives can be relied on as an adequate control. They are not found to be such on the injustice and violence of individuals, and lose their efficacy in proportion to the number combined together, that is, in proportion as their efficacy becomes needful.

From this view of the subject it may be concluded that a pure Democracy, by which I mean a Society consisting of a small number of citizens, who assemble and administer the Government in person, can admit of no cure for the mischiefs of faction. A common passion or interest will, in almost every case, be felt by a majority of the whole; a communication and concert results from the form of Government itself; and there is nothing to check the inducements to sacrifice the weaker party or an obnoxious individual. Hence it is that such Democracies have ever been spectacles of turbulence and contention; have ever been found incompatible with personal security or the rights of property; and have in general been as short in their lives as they have been violent in their deaths. Theoretic politicians, who have patronized this species of Government, have erroneously supposed that by reducing mankind to a perfect equality in their political rights, they would at the same time be perfectly equalized and assimilated in their possessions, their opinions, and their passions.

A Republic, by which I mean a Government in which the scheme of representation takes place, opens a different prospect and promises the cure for which we are seeking. Let us examine the points in which it varies from pure Democracy, and we shall comprehend both the nature of the cure and the efficacy which it must derive from the Union.

The two great points of difference between a Democracy and a Republic are: first, the delegation of the Government, in the latter, to a small number of citizens elected by the rest; secondly, the greater number of citizens and greater sphere of country over which the latter may be extended.

The effect of the first difference is, on the one hand, to refine and enlarge the public views by passing them through the medium of a chosen body of citizens, whose wisdom may best discern the true interest of their country and whose patriotism and love of justice will be least likely to sacrifice it to temporary or partial considerations. Under such a regulation it may well happen that the public voice, pronounced by the representatives of the people, will be more consonant to the public good than if pronounced by the people themselves, convened for the purpose. On the other hand, the effect may be inverted. Men of factious tempers, of local prejudices, or of sinister designs, may, by intrigue, by corruption, or by other means, first obtain the suffrages, and then betray the interests of the people. The question resulting is, whether small or extensive Republics are most favorable to the election of proper guardians of the public weal; and it is clearly decided in favor of the latter by two obvious considerations.

In the first place it is to be remarked that however small the Republic may be, the Representatives must be raised to a certain number in order to guard against the cabals of a few; and that however large it may be they must be limited to a certain number in order to guard against the confusion of a multitude. Hence, the number of Representatives in the two cases not being in proportion to that of the Constituents, and being proportionally greatest in the small Republic, it follows that if the proportion of fit characters be not less in the large than in the small Republic, the former will present a greater option, and consequently a greater probability of a fit choice.

In the next place, as each Representative will be chosen by a greater number of citizens in the large than in the small Republic, it will be more difficult for unworthy candidates to practise with success the vicious arts by which elections are too often carried; and the suffrages of the people being more free, will be more likely to centre on men who possess the most attractive merit and the most diffusive and established characters.

It must be confessed that in this, as in most other cases, there is a mean, on both sides of which inconveniencies will be found to lie. By enlarging too much the number of electors, you render the representative too little acquainted with all their local circumstances and lesser interests; as by reducing it too much, you render him unduly attached to these, and too little fit to comprehend and pursue great and national objects. The Federal Constitution forms a happy combination in this respect; the great and aggregate interests being referred to the national, the local and particular to the State legislatures.

The other point of difference is the greater number of citizens and extent of territory which may be brought within the compass of Republican than of Democratic Government; and it is this circumstance principally which renders factious combinations less to be dreaded in the former than in the latter. The smaller the society, the fewer probably will be the distinct parties and interests composing it; the fewer the distinct parties and interests, the more frequently will a majority be found of the same party; and the smaller the number of individuals composing a majority, and the smaller the compass within which they are placed, the more easily will they concert and execute their plans of oppression. Extend the sphere and you take in a greater variety of parties and interests; you make it less probable that a majority of the whole will have a common motive to invade the rights of other citizens; or if such a common motive exists, it will be more difficult for all who feel it to discover their own strength and to act in unison with each other. Besides other impediments, it may be remarked, that where there is a consciousness of unjust or dishonorable purposes, communication is always checked by distrust in proportion to the number whose concurrence is necessary.

Hence, it clearly appears that the same advantage which a Republic has over a Democracy in controlling the effects of faction is enjoyed by a large over a small republic—is enjoyed by the Union over the States composing it. Does this advantage consist in the substitution of representatives whose enlightened views and virtuous sentiments render them superior to local prejudices and to schemes of injustice? It will not be denied that the representation of the Union will be most likely to possess these requisite endowments. Does it consist in the greater security afforded by a greater variety of parties, against the event of any one party being able to outnumber and oppress the rest? In an equal degree does the increased variety of parties comprised within the Union increase this security? Does it, in fine, consist in the greater obstacles opposed to the concert and accomplishment of the secret wishes of an unjust and interested majority? Here again the extent of the Union gives it the most palpable advantage.

The influence of factious leaders may kindle a flame within their particular States but will be unable to spread a general conflagration through the other States: a religious sect may degenerate into a political faction in a part of the Confederacy; but the variety of sects dispersed over the entire face of it must secure the national Councils against any danger from that source: a rage for paper money, for an abolition of debts, for an equal division of property, or for any other improper or wicked project, will be less apt to pervade the whole body of the Union than a particular member of it; in the same proportion as such a malady is more likely to taint a particular county or district than an entire State.

In the extent and proper structure of the Union, therefore, we behold a republican remedy for the diseases most incident to Republican Government. And according to the degree of pleasure and pride we feel in being republicans ought to be our zeal in cherishing the spirit and supporting the character of federalist.

PUBLIUS

No. 51: Madison

To what expedient, then, shall we finally resort, for maintaining in practice the necessary partition of power among the several departments as laid down in the constitution? The only answer that can be given is that as all these exterior provisions are found to be inadequate the defect must be supplied, by so contriving the interior structure of the government as that its several constituent parts may, by their mutual relations, be the means of keeping each other in their proper places. Without presuming to undertake a full development of this important idea I will hazard a few general observations which may perhaps place it in a clearer light, and enable us to form a more correct judgment of the principles and structure of the government planned by the convention.

In order to lay a due foundation for that separate and distinct exercise of the different powers of government, which to a certain extent is admitted on all hands to be essential to the preservation of liberty, it is evident that each department should have a will of its own; and consequently should be so constituted that the members of each should have as little agency as possible in the appointment of the members of the others. Were this principle rigorously adhered to, it would require that all the appointments for the supreme executive, legislative, and judiciary magistracies should be drawn from the same fountain of authority, the people, through channels having no communication whatever with one another. Perhaps such a plan of constructing the several departments would be less difficult in practice than it may in contemplation appear. Some difficulties, however, and some additional expense would attend the execution of it. Some deviations, therefore, from the principle must be admitted. In the constitution of the judiciary department in particular, it might be inexpedient to insist rigorously on the principle: first, because peculiar qualifications being essential in the members, the primary consideration ought to be to select that mode of choice which best secures these qualifications; second, because the permanent tenure by which the appointments are held in that department must soon destroy all sense of dependence on the authority conferring them.

It is equally evident that the members of each department should be as little dependent as possible on those of the others for the emoluments annexed to their offices. Were the executive magistrate, or the judges, not independent of the legislature in this particular, their independence in every other would be merely nominal.

But the great security against a gradual concentration of the several powers in the same department consists in giving to those who administer each department the necessary constitutional means and personal motives to resist encroachments of the others. The provision for defence must in this, as in all other cases, be made commensurate to the danger of attack. Ambition must be made to counteract ambition. The interest of the man must be connected with the constitutional rights of the place. It may be a reflection on human nature that such devices should be necessary to control the abuses of government. But what is government itself but the greatest of all reflections on human nature? If men were angels, no government would be necessary. If angels were to govern men, neither external nor internal controls on government would be necessary. In framing a government which is to be administered by men over men, the great difficulty lies in this: You must first enable the government to control the governed; and in the next place oblige it to control itself. A dependence on the people is, no doubt, the primary control on the government; but experience has taught mankind the necessity of auxiliary precautions.

This policy of supplying, by opposite and rival interests, the defect of better motives, might be traced through the whole system of human affairs, private as well as public. We see it particularly displayed in all the subordinate distributions of power, where the constant aim is to divide and arrange the several offices in such a manner as that each may be a check on the other; that the private interest of every individual may be a sentinel over the public rights. These inventions of prudence cannot be less requisite in the distribution of the supreme powers of the State.

But it is not possible to give to each department an equal power of self-defense. In republican government, the legislative authority necessarily predominates. The remedy for this inconveniency is to divide the legislature into different branches; and to render them, by different modes of election and different principles of action, as little connected with each other as the nature of their common functions and their common dependence on the society will admit. It may even be necessary to guard against dangerous encroachments by still further precautions. As the weight of the legislative authority requires that it should be thus divided, the weakness of the executive may require, on the other hand, that it should be fortified. An absolute negative on the legislature appears, at first view, to be the natural defense with which the executive magistrate should be armed. But perhaps it would be neither altogether safe nor alone sufficient. On ordinary occasions it might not be exerted with the requisite firmness, and on extraordinary occasions it might be perfidiously abused. May not this defect of an absolute negative be supplied by some qualified connection between this weaker branch of the stronger department, by which the latter may be led to support the constitutional rights of the former, without being too much detached from the rights of its own department?

If the principles on which these observations are founded be just, as I persuade myself they are, and they be applied as a criterion to the several State constitutions, and to the federal Constitution, it will be found that if the latter does not perfectly correspond with them, the former are infinitely less able to bear such a test.

There are, moreover, two considerations particularly applicable to the federal system of America, which place that system in a very interesting point of view.

First. In a single republic, all the power surrendered by the people is submitted to the administration of a single government; and usurpations are guarded against by a division of the government into distinct and separate departments. In the compound republic of America, the power surrendered by the people is first divided between two distinct governments, and then the portion allotted to each subdivided among distinct and separate departments. Hence a double security arises to the rights of the people. The different governments will control each other, at the same time that each will be controlled by itself.

Second. It is of great importance in a republic not only to guard the society against the oppression of its rulers, but to guard one part of the society against the injustice of the other part. Different interests necessarily exist in different classes of citizens. If a majority be united by a common interest, the rights of the minority will be insecure. There are but two methods of providing against this evil: The one by creating a will in the community independent of the majority—that is, of the society itself; the other, by comprehending in the society so many separate descriptions of citizens as will render an unjust combination of a majority of the whole very improbable, if not impracticable. The first method prevails in all governments possessing an hereditary or self-appointed authority. This, at best, is but a precarious security; because a power independent of the society may as well espouse the unjust views of the major as the rightful interests of the minor party, and may possibly be turned against both parties. The second method will be exemplified in the federal republic of the United States. Whilst all authority in it will be derived from and dependent on the society, the society itself will be broken into so many parts, interests and classes of citizens, that the rights of individuals, or of the minority, will be in little danger from interested combinations of the majority. In a free government the security for civil rights must be the same as that for religious rights. It consists in the one case in the multiplicity of interests, and in the other in the multiplicity of sects. The degree of security in both cases will depend on the number of interests and sects; and this may be presumed to depend on the extent of country and number of people comprehended under the same government. This view of the subject must particularly recommend a proper federal system to all the sincere and considerate friends of republican government: Since it shows that in exact proportion as the territory of the Union may be formed into more circumscribed Confederacies, or States, oppressive combinations of a majority will be facilitated; the best security, under the republican form, for the rights of every class of citizens, will be diminished; and consequently the stability and independence of some member of the government, the only other security, must be proportionally increased. Justice is the end of government. It is the end of civil society. It ever has been and ever will be pursued until it be obtained, or until liberty be lost in the pursuit. In a society under the forms of which the stronger faction can readily unite and oppress the weaker, anarchy may as truly be said to reign as in a state of nature, where the weaker individual is not secured against the violence of the stronger: And as, in the latter state, even the stronger individuals are prompted, by the uncertainty of their condition, to submit to a government which may protect the weak as well as themselves: So, in the former state, will the more powerful factions or parties be gradually induced, by a like motive, to wish for a government which will protect all parties, the weaker as well as the more powerful. It can be little doubted that if the State of Rhode Island was separated from the Confederacy and left to itself, the insecurity of rights under the popular form of government within such narrow limits would be displayed by such reiterated oppressions of factious majorities that some power altogether independent of the people would soon be called for by the voice of the very factions whose misrule had proved the necessity of it. In the extended republic of the United States, and among the great variety of interests, parties, and sects which it embraces, a coalition of a majority of the whole society could seldom take place on any other principles than those of justice and the general good; and there being thus less danger to a minor from the will of the major party, there must be less pretext, also, to provide for the security of the former, by introducing into the government a will not dependent on the latter, or, in other words, a will independent of the society itself. It is no less certain than it is important, notwithstanding the contrary opinions which have been entertained, that the larger the society, provided it lie within a practicable sphere, the more duly capable it will be of self-government. And happily for the *republican cause,* practicable sphere may be carried to a very great extent by a judicious modification and mixture of the *federal principle.*

PUBLIUS

Presidents and Vice Presidents

	PRESIDENT	VICE PRESIDENT
1	George Washington *(Federalist 1789)*	John Adams *(Federalist 1789)*
2	John Adams *(Federalist 1797)*	Thomas Jefferson *(Dem.-Rep. 1797)*
3	Thomas Jefferson *(Dem.-Rep. 1801)*	Aaron Burr *(Dem.-Rep. 1801)* George Clinton *(Dem.-Rep. 1805)*
4	James Madison *(Dem.-Rep. 1809)*	George Clinton *(Dem.-Rep. 1809)* Elbridge Gerry *(Dem.-Rep. 1813)*
5	James Monroe *(Dem.-Rep. 1817)*	Daniel D. Tompkins *(Dem.-Rep. 1817)*
6	John Quincy Adams *(Dem.-Rep. 1825)*	John C. Calhoun *(Dem.-Rep. 1825)*
7	Andrew Jackson *(Democratic 1829)*	John C. Calhoun *(Democratic 1829)* Martin Van Buren *(Democratic 1833)*
8	Martin Van Buren *(Democratic 1837)*	Richard M. Johnson *(Democratic 1837)*
9	William H. Harrison *(Whig 1841)*	John Tyler *(Whig 1841)*
10	John Tyler *(Whig and Democratic 1841)*	
11	James K. Polk *(Democratic 1845)*	George M. Dallas *(Democratic 1845)*
12	Zachary Taylor *(Whig 1849)*	Millard Fillmore *(Whig 1849)*
13	Millard Fillmore *(Whig 1850)*	
14	Franklin Pierce *(Democratic 1853)*	William R. D. King *(Democratic 1853)*
15	James Buchanan *(Democratic 1857)*	John C. Breckinridge *(Democratic 1857)*
16	Abraham Lincoln *(Republican 1861)*	Hannibal Hamlin *(Republican 1861)* Andrew Johnson *(Unionist 1865)*
17	Andrew Johnson *(Unionist 1865)*	
18	Ulysses S. Grant *(Republican 1869)*	Schuyler Colfax *(Republican 1869)* Henry Wilson *(Republican 1873)*
19	Rutherford B. Hayes *(Republican 1877)*	William A. Wheeler *(Republican 1877)*
20	James A. Garfield *(Republican 1881)*	Chester A. Arthur *(Republican 1881)*
21	Chester A. Arthur *(Republican 1881)*	
22	Grover Cleveland *(Democratic 1885)*	Thomas A. Hendricks *(Democratic 1885)*

	PRESIDENT	VICE PRESIDENT
23	Benjamin Harrison *(Republican 1889)*	Levi P. Morton *(Republican 1889)*
24	Grover Cleveland *(Democratic 1893)*	Adlai E. Stevenson *(Democratic 1893)*
25	William McKinley *(Republican 1897)*	Garret A. Hobart *(Republican 1897)* Theodore Roosevelt *(Republican 1901)*
26	Theodore Roosevelt *(Republican 1901)*	Charles W. Fairbanks *(Republican 1905)*
27	William H. Taft *(Republican 1909)*	James S. Sherman *(Republican 1909)*
28	Woodrow Wilson *(Democratic 1913)*	Thomas R. Marshall *(Democratic 1913)*
29	Warren G. Harding *(Republican 1921)*	Calvin Coolidge *(Republican 1921)*
30	Calvin Coolidge *(Republican 1923)*	Charles G. Dawes *(Republican 1925)*
31	Herbert Hoover *(Republican 1929)*	Charles Curtis *(Republican 1929)*
32	Franklin D. Roosevelt *(Democratic 1933)*	John Nance Garner *(Democratic 1933)* Henry A. Wallace *(Democratic 1941)* Harry S. Truman *(Democratic 1945)*

	PRESIDENT	VICE PRESIDENT
33	Harry S. Truman *(Democratic 1945)*	Alben W. Barkley *(Democratic 1949)*
34	Dwight D. Eisenhower *(Republican 1953)*	Richard M. Nixon *(Republican 1953)*
35	John F. Kennedy *(Democratic 1961)*	Lyndon B. Johnson *(Democratic 1961)*
36	Lyndon B. Johnson *(Democratic 1963)*	Hubert H. Humphrey *(Democratic 1965)*
37	Richard M. Nixon *(Republican 1969)*	Spiro T. Agnew *(Republican 1969)* Gerald R. Ford *(Republican 1973)*
38	Gerald R. Ford *(Republican 1974)*	Nelson Rockefeller *(Republican 1974)*
39	James E. Carter *(Democratic 1977)*	Walter Mondale *(Democratic 1977)*
40	Ronald Reagan *(Republican 1981)*	George H. W. Bush *(Republican 1981)*
41	George H. W. Bush *(Republican 1989)*	J. Danforth Quayle *(Republican 1989)*
42	William J. Clinton *(Democratic 1993)*	Albert Gore, Jr. *(Democratic 1993)*
43	George W. Bush *(Republican 2001)*	Richard Cheney *(Republican 2001)*
44	Barack H. Obama *(Democratic 2009)*	Joseph R. Biden, Jr. *(Democratic 2009)*

GLOSSARY

administrative adjudication applying rules and precedents to specific cases to settle disputes between regulated parties

affirmative action government policies or programs that seek to redress past injustices against specified groups by making special efforts to provide members of these groups with access to educational and employment opportunities

agencies of socialization social institutions, including families and schools, that help to shape individuals' basic political beliefs and values

agency representation the type of representation in which a representative is held accountable to a constituency if he or she fails to represent that constituency properly. This is the incentive for good representation when the personal backgrounds, views, and interests of the representative differ from those of his or her constituency

agenda setting the power of the media to bring public attention to particular issues and problems

amendment a change added to a bill, law, or constitution

American political community citizens who are eligible to vote and who participate in American political life

amicus curiae literally, "friend of the court"; individuals or groups who are not parties to a lawsuit but who seek to assist the Supreme Court in reaching a decision by presenting additional briefs

Antifederalists those who favored strong state governments and a weak national government and who were opponents of the Constitution proposed at the American Constitutional Convention of 1787

antitrust policy government regulation of large businesses that have established monopolies

appeasement effort to forestall war by giving in to the demands of a hostile power

apportionment the process, occurring after every decennial census, that allocates congressional seats among the fifty states

appropriations the amounts of money approved by Congress in statutes (bills) that each unit or agency of government can spend

Articles of Confederation America's first written constitution; served as the basis for America's national government until 1789

attitude (or opinion) a specific preference on a particular issue

authoritarian government a system of rule in which the government recognizes no formal limits but may nevertheless be restrained by the power of other social institutions

autocracy a form of government in which a single individual—a king, queen, or dictator—rules

balance-of-power role the strategy whereby many countries form alliances with one or more countries in order to counterbalance the behavior of other, usually more powerful, nation-states

bandwagon effect a shift in electoral support to the candidate whom public opinion polls report as the front-runner

benign gerrymandering attempts to draw district boundaries so as to create districts made up primarily of disadvantaged or underrepresented minorities

bicameral having a legislative assembly composed of two chambers or houses; opposite of unicameral

bilateral treaty a treaty made between two nations

bill a proposed law that has been sponsored by a member of Congress and submitted to the clerk of the House or Senate

Bill of Rights the first ten amendments to the U.S. Constitution, ratified in 1791; they ensure certain rights and liberties to the people

bill of attainder a law that declares a person guilty of a crime without a trial

block grants federal grants-in-aid that allow states considerable discretion in how the funds are spent

brief a written document in which attorneys explain, using case precedents, why the court should find in favor of their client

Brown v. Board of Education the 1954 Supreme Court decision that struck down the "separate but equal" doctrine as fundamentally unequal. This case eliminated state power to use race as a criterion of discrimination in law and provided the national government with the power to intervene by exercising strict regulatory policies against discriminatory actions

budget deficit amount by which government spending exceeds government revenue in a fiscal year

bureaucracy the complex structure of offices, tasks, rules, and principles of organization that are employed by all large-scale institutions to coordinate the work of their personnel

Bush Doctrine foreign policy based on the idea that the United States should take preemptive action against threats to its national security

Cabinet the secretaries, or chief administrators, of the major departments of the federal government. Cabinet secretaries are appointed by the president with the consent of the Senate

campaign an effort by political candidates and their staffs to win the backing of donors, political activists, and voters in the quest for political office

categorical grants congressional grants given to states and localities on the condition that expenditures be limited to a problem or group specified by law

caucus (congressional) an association of members of Congress based on party, interest, or social group, such as gender or race

caucus (political) a normally closed meeting of a political or legislative group to select candidates, plan strategy, or make decisions regarding legislative matters

checks and balances mechanisms through which each branch of government is able to participate in and influence the activities of the other branches. Major examples include the presidential veto power over congressional legislation, the power of the Senate to approve presidential appointments, and judicial review of congressional enactments

chief justice justice on the Supreme Court who presides over the Court's public sessions

citizenship informed and active membership in a political community

civic engagement a sense of concern among members of the political community about public, social, and political life, expressed through participation in social and political organizations

civil law the branch of law that deals with disputes that do not involve criminal penalties

civil liberties areas of personal freedom with which governments are constrained from interfering

civil rights obligation imposed on government to take positive action to protect citizens from any illegal action of government agencies as well as of other private citizens

class-action suit a legal action by which a group or class of individuals with common interests can file a suit on behalf of everyone who shares that interest

"clear and present danger" test test to determine whether speech is protected or unprotected, based on its capacity to present a "clear and present danger" to society

closed caucus a presidential nominating caucus open only to registered party members

closed primary a primary election in which voters can participate in the nomination of candidates, but only of the party in which they are enrolled for a period of time prior to primary day

closed rule a provision by the House Rules Committee limiting or prohibiting the introduction of amendments during debate

cloture a rule allowing a majority of two-thirds or three-fifths of the members of a legislative body to set a time limit on debate over a given bill

coattail effect the result of voters casting their ballot for president or governor and "automatically" voting for the remainder of the party's ticket

Cold War the period of struggle between the United States and the former Soviet Union between the late 1940s and about 1990

collective goods benefits, sought by groups, that are broadly available and cannot be denied to nonmembers

commander in chief the role of the president as commander of the national military and the state national guard units (when called into service)

commerce clause Article I, Section 8, of the Constitution, which delegates to Congress the power "to regulate commerce with foreign nations, and among the several States and with the Indian tribes." This clause was interpreted by the Supreme Court in favor of national power over the economy

committee markup session in which a congressional committee rewrites legislation to incorporate changes discussed during hearings on the bill

concurrent powers authority possessed by *both* state and national governments, such as the power to levy taxes

confederation a system of government in which states retain sovereign authority except for the powers expressly delegated to the national government

conference a gathering of House Republicans every two years to elect their House leaders. Democrats call their gathering the caucus

conference committee a joint committee created to work out a compromise on House and Senate versions of a piece of legislation

conservative today this term refers to those who generally support the social and economic status quo and are suspicious of efforts to introduce new political formulae and economic arrangements. Conservatives believe that a large and powerful government poses a threat to citizens' freedom

constituency the residents in the area from which an official is elected

constitutional government a system of rule in which formal and effective limits are placed on the powers of the government

contracting power the power of government to set conditions on companies seeking to sell goods or services to government agencies

contributory programs social programs financed in whole or in part by taxation or other mandatory contributions by their present or future recipients

cooperative federalism a type of federalism existing since the New Deal era in which grants-in-aid have been used strategically to encourage states and localities (without commanding them) to pursue nationally defined goals. Also known as "intergovernmental cooperation"

cost-of-living adjustment (COLA) change made to the level of benefits of a government program based on the rate of inflation

court of appeals a court that hears appeals of trial court decisions

criminal law the branch of law that regulates the conduct of individuals, defines crimes, and specifies punishment for criminal acts

de facto literally, "by fact"; practices that occur even when there is no legal enforcement, such as school segregation in much of the United States today

de jure literally, "by law"; legally enforced practices, such as school segregation in the South before the 1960s

defendant the one against whom a complaint is brought in a criminal or civil case

delegate a representative who votes according to the preferences of his or her constituency

delegated powers constitutional powers that are assigned to one governmental agency but that are exercised by another agency with the express permission of the first

delegates political activists selected to vote at a party's national convention

democracy a system of rule that permits citizens to play a significant part in the governmental process, usually through the election of key public officials

department the largest subunit of the executive branch. The secretaries of the fifteen departments form the Cabinet

deregulation a policy of reducing or eliminating regulatory restraints on the conduct of individuals or private institutions

deterrence the development and maintenance of military strength as a means of discouraging attack

devolution a policy to remove a program from one level of government by delegating it or passing it down to a lower level of government, such as from the national government to the state and local governments

diplomacy the representation of a government to other foreign governments

direct democracy a system of rule that permits citizens to vote directly on laws and policies

discretionary spending federal spending on programs that are controlled through the regular budget process

discrimination use of any unreasonable and unjust criterion of exclusion

dissenting opinion a decision written by a justice in the minority in a particular case in which the justice wishes to express his or her reasoning in the case

divided government the condition in American government wherein the presidency is controlled by one party while the opposing party controls one or both houses of Congress

double jeopardy the Fifth Amendment right providing that a person cannot be tried twice for the same crime

dual federalism the system of government that prevailed in the United States from 1789 to 1937, in which most fundamental governmental powers were shared between the federal and state governments

due process of law the right of every citizen against arbitrary action by national or state governments

economic expansionist role the strategy often pursued by capitalist countries to adopt foreign policies that will maximize the success of domestic corporations in their dealings with other countries

elastic clause Article I, Section 8, of the Constitution (also known as the necessary and proper clause), which enumerates the powers of Congress and provides Congress with the authority to make all laws "necessary and proper" to carry them out

electoral college the presidential electors from each state who meet after the popular election to cast ballots for president and vice president

electoral realignment the point in history when a new party supplants the ruling party, becoming in turn the dominant political force. In the United States, this has tended to occur roughly every thirty years

eminent domain the right of government to take private property for public use

entitlement a legal obligation of the federal government to provide payments to individuals, or groups of individuals according to eligibility criteria or benefit rules

equal protection clause provision of the Fourteenth Amendment guaranteeing citizens "the equal protection of the laws." This clause has been the basis for the civil rights of African Americans, women, and other groups

equal time rule the requirement that broadcasters provide candidates for the same political office equal opportunities to communicate their messages to the public

equality of opportunity a widely shared American ideal that all people should have the freedom to use whatever talents and wealth they have to reach their fullest potential

establishment clause the First Amendment clause that says that "Congress shall make no law respecting an establishment of religion." This law means that a "wall of separation" exists between church and state

***ex post facto* law** a law that declares an action to be illegal after it has been committed

exclusionary rule the ability of courts to exclude evidence obtained in violation of the Fourth Amendment

executive agreement an agreement, made between the president and another country, that has the force of a treaty but does not require the Senate's "advice and consent"

Executive Office of the President (EOP) the permanent agencies that perform defined management tasks for the president. Created in 1939, the EOP includes the Office of Management and Budget, the Council of Economic Advisers, the National Security Council, and other agencies

executive order a rule or regulation issued by the president that has the effect and formal status of legislation

executive privilege the claim that confidential communications between a president and close advisers should not be revealed without the consent of the president

expressed powers specific powers granted by the Constitution to Congress (Article I, Section 8), and to the president (Article II)

fairness doctrine a Federal Communications Commission requirement for broadcasters who air programs on controversial issues to provide time for opposing views. The FCC ceased enforcing this doctrine in 1985

federal funds rate the interest rate on loans between banks that the Federal Reserve Board influences by affecting the supply of money available

Federal Reserve System a system of twelve Federal Reserve Banks that facilitates exchanges of cash, checks, and credit; regulates member banks; and uses monetary policies to fight inflation and deflation

federal system a system of government in which the national government shares power with lower levels of government, such as states

federalism a system of government in which power is divided, by a constitution, between a central government and regional governments

Federalist Papers a series of essays written by Alexander Hamilton, James Madison, and John Jay supporting the ratification of the Constitution

Federalists those who favored a strong national government and supported the Constitution proposed at the American Constitutional Convention of 1787

Fifteenth Amendment one of three Civil War amendments; guaranteed voting rights for African American men

fighting words speech that directly incites damaging conduct

filibuster a tactic used by members of the Senate to prevent action on legislation they oppose by continuously holding the floor and speaking until the majority backs down. Once given the floor, senators have unlimited time to speak, and it requires a vote of three-fifths of the Senate to end a filibuster

fiscal policy the government's use of taxing, monetary, and spending powers to manipulate the economy

501c(4) committees nonprofit groups that also engage in issue advocacy. Under Section 501c(4) such a group may spend up to half its revenue for political purposes

527 committees nonprofit independent groups that receive and disburse funds to influence the nomination, election, or defeat of candidates. Named after Section 527 of the Internal Revenue Code, which defines and provides tax-exempt status for nonprofit advocacy groups

food stamps a debit card that can be used for food at most grocery stores; the largest in-kind benefits program

formula grants grants-in-aid in which a formula is used to determine the amount of federal funds a state or local government will receive

Fourteenth Amendment one of three Civil War amendments; guaranteed equal protection and due process

framing the power of the media to influence how events and issues are interpreted

free exercise clause the First Amendment clause that protects a citizen's right to believe and practice whatever religion he or she chooses

free riders those who enjoy the benefits of collective goods but did not participate in acquiring them

full faith and credit clause provision from Article IV, Section 1, of the Constitution, requiring that the states normally honor the public acts and judicial decisions that take place in another state

gender gap a distinctive pattern of voting behavior reflecting the differences in views between women and men

General Agreement on Tariffs and Trade (GATT) international trade organization, in existence from 1947 to 1995, that set many of the rules governing international trade

general revenue sharing the process by which one unit of government yields a portion of its tax income to another unit of government, according to an established formula. Revenue sharing typically involves the national government providing money to state governments

gerrymandering apportionment of voters in districts in such a way as to give unfair advantage to one racial or ethnic group or political party

government institutions and procedures through which a territory and its people are ruled

government corporation a government agency that performs a service normally provided by the private sector

grand jury jury that determines whether sufficient evidence is available to justify a trial; grand juries do not rule on the accused's guilt or innocence

grants-in-aid programs through which Congress provides money to state and local governments on the condition that the funds be employed for purposes defined by the federal government

grassroots mobilization a lobbying campaign in which a group mobilizes its membership to contact government officials in support of the group's position

Great Compromise the agreement reached at the Constitutional Convention of 1787 that gave each state an equal number of senators regardless of its population, but linked representation in the House of Representatives to population

Gross Domestic Product (GDP) the total value of goods and services produced within a country

habeas corpus a court order demanding that an individual in custody be brought into court and shown the cause for detention

Holy Alliance role a strategy pursued by a superpower to prevent any change in the existing distribution of power among nation-states, even if this requires intervention into the internal affairs of another country in order to keep a ruler from being overthrown

home rule power delegated by the state to a local unit of government to manage its own affairs

illusion of saliency the impression conveyed by polls that something is important to the public when actually it is not

impeachment the formal charge by the House of Representatives that a government official has committed "Treason, Bribery, or other high Crimes and Misdemeanors"

implementation the efforts of departments and agencies to translate laws into specific bureaucratic routines

implied powers powers derived from the necessary and proper clause of Article I, Section 8, of the Constitution. Such powers are not specifically expressed, but are implied through the expansive interpretation of delegated powers

in-kind benefits noncash goods and services provided to needy individuals and families by the federal government

incumbency holding a political office for which one is running

incumbent a candidate running for re-election to a position that he or she already holds

independent agency an agency that is not part of a Cabinet department

indexing periodic process of adjusting social benefits or wages to account for increases in the cost of living

inflation a consistent increase in the general level of prices

informational benefits special newsletters, periodicals, training programs, conferences, and other information provided to members of groups to entice others to join

inherent powers powers claimed by a president that are not expressed in the Constitution, but are inferred from it

institutional advertising advertising designed to create a positive image of an organization

interest group individuals who organize to influence the government's programs and policies

intermediate scrutiny test used by the Supreme Court in gender discrimination cases, which places the burden of proof partially on the government and partially on the challengers to show that the law in question is unconstitutional

International Monetary Fund (IMF) an institution established in 1944 that provides loans and facilitates international monetary exchange

iron triangle the stable, cooperative relationship that often develops among a congressional committee, an administrative agency, and one or more supportive interest groups. Not all of these relationships are triangular, but the iron triangle is the most typical

isolationism desire to avoid involvement in the affairs of other nations.

issue network a loose network of elected leaders, public officials, activists, and interest groups drawn together by a specific policy issue

"Jim Crow" laws laws enacted by southern states following Reconstruction that discriminated against African Americans

joint committee a legislative committee formed of members of both the House and the Senate

judicial activism judicial philosophy that posits that the Court should go beyond the words of the Constitution or a statute to consider the broader societal implications of its decisions

judicial restraint judicial philosophy whose adherents refuse to go beyond the clear words of the Constitution in interpreting its meaning

judicial review the power of the courts to review and, if necessary, declare actions of the legislative and executive branches invalid or unconstitutional. The Supreme Court asserted this power in *Marbury v. Madison*

jurisdiction the sphere of a court's power and authority

Keynesians followers of the economic theories of John Maynard Keynes, who argued that the government can stimulate the economy by increasing public spending or by cutting taxes

Kitchen Cabinet an informal group of advisers to whom the president turns for counsel and guidance. Members of the official Cabinet may or may not also be members of the Kitchen Cabinet

laissez-faire capitalism an economic system in which the means of production and distribution are privately owned and operated for profit with minimal or no government interference

legislative initiative the president's inherent power to bring a legislative agenda before Congress

***Lemon* test** a rule articulated in *Lemon v. Kurtzman* that government action toward religion is permissible if it is secular in purpose, neither promotes nor inhibits the practice of religion, and does not lead to "excessive entanglement" with religion

libel a written statement made in "reckless disregard of the truth" that is considered damaging to a victim because it is "malicious, scandalous, and defamatory"

liberal today this term refers to those who generally support social and political reform; extensive governmental intervention in the economy; the expansion of federal social services; more vigorous efforts on behalf of the poor, minorities, and women; and greater concern for consumers and the environment

libertarian the political philosophy that is skeptical of any government intervention as a potential threat to individual liberty; one who favors minimal government and maximum individual freedom

liberty freedom from governmental control

limited government a principle of constitutional government; a government whose powers are defined and limited by a constitution

litigation a lawsuit or legal proceeding; as a form of political participation, an attempt to seek relief in a court of law

lobbying a strategy by which organized interests seek to influence the passage of legislation by exerting direct pressure on members of the legislature

logrolling a legislative practice whereby agreements are made between legislators in voting for or against a bill; vote trading

loophole incentive to individuals and businesses to reduce their tax liabilities by investing their money in areas that the government designates

machines strong party organizations in late-nineteenth- and early-twentieth-century American cities. These machines were led by "bosses" who controlled party nominations and patronage

majority leader the elected leader of the majority party in the House of Representatives or in the Senate. In the House, the majority leader is subordinate in the party hierarchy to the Speaker of the House

majority/minority district a gerrymandered voting district that improves the chances of minority candidates by making selected minority groups the majority within the district

majority party the party that holds the majority of legislative seats in either the House or the Senate

majority rule, minority rights the democratic principle that a government follows the preferences of the majority of voters but protects the interests of the minority

majority system a type of electoral system in which, to win a seat in the parliament or other representative body, a candidate must receive a majority of all the votes cast in the relevant district

mandate a claim by a victorious candidate that the electorate has given him or her special authority to carry out promises made during the campaign

mandatory spending federal spending that is made up of "uncontrollables," budget items that cannot be controlled through the regular budget process

marketplace of ideas the public forum in which beliefs and ideas are exchanged and compete

material benefits special goods, services, or money provided to members of groups to entice others to join

means testing a procedure by which potential beneficiaries of a public-assistance program establish their eligibility by demonstrating a genuine need for the assistance

measurement error failure to identify the true distribution of opinion within a population because of errors such as ambiguous or poorly worded questions

Medicaid a federally and state-financed, state-operated program providing medical services to low-income people

Medicare a form of national health insurance for the elderly and the disabled

membership association an organized group in which members actually play a substantial role, sitting on committees and engaging in group projects

merit system a product of civil service reform, in which appointees to positions in public bureaucracies must objectively be deemed qualified for those positions

midterm elections congressional elections that do not coincide with a presidential election; also called off-year elections

minority leader the elected leader of the minority party in the House or Senate

minority party the party that holds a minority of legislative seats in either the House or the Senate

***Miranda* rule** the requirement, articulated by the Supreme Court in *Miranda v. Arizona*, that persons under arrest must be informed prior to police interrogation of their rights to remain silent and to have the benefit of legal counsel

mobilization the process by which large numbers of people are organized for a political activity

monetarists followers of economic theories that contend that the role of the government in the economy should be limited to regulating the supply of money

monetary policy an effort to regulate the economy through the manipulation of the supply of money and credit. America's most powerful institution in this area of monetary policy is the Federal Reserve Board

monopoly the existence of a single firm in a market that controls all the goods and services of that market; absence of competition

mootness a criterion used by courts to screen cases that no longer require resolution

most favored nation status agreement to offer a trading partner the lowest tariff rate offered to other trading partners

multiple-member district an electorate that selects all candidates at large from the whole district; each voter is given the number of votes equivalent to the number of seats to be filled

Napoleonic role a strategy pursued by a powerful nation to prevent aggressive actions against it by improving the internal state of affairs of a particular country, even if this means encouraging revolution in that country

nation-state a political entity consisting of a people with some common cultural experience (nation) who also share a common political authority (state), recognized by other sovereignties (nation-states)

national convention a national party political institution that nominates the party's presidential and vice presidential candidates, establishes party rules, and writes and ratifies the party's platform

National Security Council (NSC) a presidential foreign-policy advisory council composed of the president; the vice president; the secretaries of state, defense, and the treasury; the attorney general; and other officials invited by the president

necessary and proper clause Article I, Section 8, of the Constitution, it provides Congress with the authority to make all laws "necessary and proper" to carry out its expressed powers

New Federalism attempts by Presidents Nixon and Reagan to return power to the states through block grants

New Jersey Plan a framework for the Constitution, introduced by William Paterson, which called for equal state representation in the national legislature regardless of population

New Politics movement a political movement that began in the 1960s and 1970s, made up of professionals and intellectuals for whom the civil rights and antiwar movements were formative experiences. The New Politics movement strengthened public interest groups

nomination the process through which political parties select their candidates for election to public office

noncontributory programs social programs that provide assistance to people on the basis of demonstrated need rather than any contribution they have made

non-state actors groups other than nation-states that attempt to play a role in the international system. Terrorist groups are one type of non-state actor

North American Free Trade Agreement (NAFTA) trade treaty among the United States, Canada, and Mexico to lower and eliminate tariffs among the three countries

North Atlantic Treaty Organization (NATO) a treaty organization, comprising the United States, Canada, and most of Western Europe, formed in 1948 to counter the perceived threat from the Soviet Union

oligarchy a form of government in which a small group—landowners, military officers, or wealthy merchants—controls most of the governing decisions

open caucus a presidential nominating caucus open to anyone who wishes to attend

open-market operations method by which the Open Market Committee of the Federal Reserve System buys and sells government securities, etc., to help finance government operations and to reduce or increase the total amount of money circulating in the economy

open primary a primary election in which the voter can wait until the day of the primary to choose which party to enroll in to select candidates for the general election

open rule a provision by the House Rules Committee that permits floor debate and the addition of new amendments to a bill

opinion the written explanation of the Supreme Court's decision in a particular case

oral argument stage in Supreme Court procedure in which attorneys for both sides appear before the Court to present their positions and answer questions posed by justices

original jurisdiction the authority to initially consider a case. Distinguished from appellate jurisdiction, which is the authority to hear appeals from a lower court's decision

oversight the effort by Congress, through hearings, investigations, and other techniques, to exercise control over the activities of executive agencies

party activists partisans who contribute time, energy, and effort to support their party and its candidates

party identification an individual voter's psychological ties to one party or another

party organization the formal structure of a political party, including its leadership, election committees, active members, and paid staff

party unity vote a roll-call vote in the House or Senate in which at least 50 percent of the members of one party take a particular position and are opposed by at least 50 percent of the members of the other party

patronage the resources available to higher officials, usually opportunities to make partisan appointments to offices and to confer grants, licenses, or special favors to supporters

per curiam a brief, unsigned decision by an appellate court, usually rejecting a petition to review the decision of a lower court

plaintiff the individual or organization who brings a complaint in court

platform a party document, written at a national convention, that contains party philosophy, principles, and positions on issues

plea bargain a negotiated agreement in a criminal case in which a defendant agrees to plead guilty in return for the state's agreement to reduce the severity of the criminal charge or prison sentence the defendant is facing

pluralism the theory that all interests are and should be free to compete for influence in the government. The outcome of this competition is compromise and moderation

plurality system a type of electoral system in which, to win a seat in the parliament or other representative body, a candidate need only receive the most votes in the election, not necessarily a majority of the votes cast

pocket veto a presidential veto that is automatically triggered if the president does not act on a given piece of legislation passed during the final ten days of a legislative session

police power power reserved to the state government to regulate the health, safety, and morals of its citizens

policy entrepreneur an individual who identifies a problem as a political issue and brings a policy proposal into the political agenda

political action committee (PAC) a private group that raises and distributes funds for use in election campaigns

political culture broadly shared values, beliefs, and attitudes about how the government should function. American political culture emphasizes the values of liberty, equality, and democracy

political efficacy the ability to influence government and politics

political equality the right to participate in politics equally, based on the principle of "one person, one vote"

political ideology a cohesive set of beliefs that forms a general philosophy about the role of government

political participation political activities, such as voting, contacting political officials, volunteering for a campaign, or participating in a protest, whose purpose is to influence government

political parties organized groups that attempt to influence the government by electing their members to important government offices

political socialization the induction of individuals into the political culture; learning the underlying beliefs and values on which the political system is based

politics conflict over the leadership, structure, and policies of governments

poll tax a state-imposed tax on voters as a prerequisite for registration. Poll taxes were rendered unconstitutional in national elections by the Twenty-fourth Amendment, and in state elections by the Supreme Court in 1966

popular sovereignty a principle of democracy in which political authority rests ultimately in the hands of the people

pork barrel (or **pork**) appropriations made by legislative bodies for local projects that are often not needed but that are created so that local representatives can win re-election in their home districts

power influence over a government's leadership, organization, or policies

precedent a prior case whose principles are used by judges as the basis for their decision in a present case

preemption the principle that allows the national government to override state or local actions in certain policy areas. In foreign policy, the willingness to strike first in order to prevent an enemy attack

preventive war policy of striking first when a nation fears that a foreign foe is contemplating hostile action

priming process of preparing the public to take a particular view of an event or political actor

primary elections elections held to select a party's candidate for the general election

prior restraint an effort by a governmental agency to block the publication of material it deems libelous or harmful in some other way; censorship. In the United States, the courts forbid prior restraint except under the most extraordinary circumstances

private bill a proposal in Congress to provide a specific person with some kind of relief, such as a special exemption from immigration quotas

privatization removing all or part of a program from the public sector to the private sector

privileges and immunities clause provision from Article IV, Section 2, of the Constitution, that a state cannot discriminate against someone from another state or give its own residents special privileges

probability sampling a method used by pollsters to select a representative sample in which every individual in the population has an equal probability of being selected as a respondent

progressive taxation taxation that hits upper income brackets more heavily

project grants grant programs in which state and local governments submit proposals to federal agencies and for which funding is provided on a competitive basis

proportional representation a multiple-member district system that allows each political party representation in proportion to its percentage of the total vote

prospective voting voting based on the imagined future performance of a candidate

protest participation that involves assembling crowds to confront a government or other official organization

public good a good or service that is provided by the government because it either is not supplied by the market or is not supplied in sufficient quantities

public interest groups groups that claim they serve the general good rather than only their own particular interest

public opinion citizens' attitudes about political issues, leaders, institutions, and events

public-opinion polls scientific instruments for measuring public opinion

public policy a law, rule, statute, or edict that expresses the government's goals and provides for rewards and punishments to promote their attainment

public relations an attempt, usually through the use of paid consultants, to establish a favorable relationship with the public and influence its political opinions

purposive benefits selective benefits of group membership that emphasize the purpose and accomplishments of the group

push polling a polling technique in which the questions are designed to shape the respondent's opinion

random digit dialing a polling method in which respondents are selected at random from a list of ten-digit telephone numbers, with every effort made to avoid bias in the construction of the sample

recall procedure to allow voters an opportunity to remove state officials from office before their terms expire

redistribution a policy whose objective is to tax or spend in such a way as to reduce the disparities of wealth between the lowest and the highest income brackets

redistributive programs economic policies designed to control the economy through taxing and spending, with the goal of benefiting the poor

redistricting the process of redrawing election districts and redistributing legislative representatives. This happens every ten years to reflect shifts in population or in response to legal challenges to existing districts

redlining a practice in which banks refuse to make loans to people living in certain geographic locations

referendum the practice of referring a measure proposed or passed by a legislature to the vote of the electorate for approval or rejection

regressive taxation taxation that hits lower income brackets more heavily

regulated federalism a form of federalism in which Congress imposes legislation on states and localities, requiring them to meet national standards

regulatory agencies departments, bureaus, or independent agencies whose primary mission is to impose limits, restrictions, or other obligations on the conduct of individuals or companies in the private sector

representative democracy/republic a system of government in which the populace selects representatives, who play a significant role in governmental decision making

reserve requirement the amount of liquid assets and ready cash that banks are required to hold to meet depositors' demands for their money

reserved powers powers, derived from the Tenth Amendment to the Constitution, that are not specifically delegated to the national government or denied to the states

responsible party government a set of principles that idealizes a strong role for parties in defining their stance on issues, mobilizing voters, and fulfilling their campaign promises once in office

retrospective voting voting based on the past performance of a candidate

revenue agencies agencies responsible for collecting taxes. Examples include the Internal Revenue Service for income taxes, the U.S. Customs Service for tariffs and other taxes on imported goods, and the Bureau of Alcohol, Tobacco, and Firearms for collection of taxes on the sales of those particular products

right of rebuttal a Federal Communications Commission regulation giving individuals the right to have the opportunity to respond to personal attacks made on a radio or television broadcast

right to privacy the right to be left alone, which has been interpreted by the Supreme Court to entail free access to birth control and abortions

roll-call vote a vote in which each legislator's yes or no vote is recorded as the clerk calls the names of the members alphabetically

rule making a quasi-legislative administrative process by which government agencies produce regulations

salient interests attitudes and views that are especially important to the individual holding them

sample a small group selected by researchers to represent the most important characteristics of an entire population

sampling error polling error that arises based on the small size of the sample

select committee a (usually) temporary legislative committee set up to highlight or investigate a particular issue or address an issue not within the jurisdiction of existing committees

selection bias polling error that arises when the sample is not representative of the population being studied, which creates errors in overrepresenting or underrepresenting some opinions

selective incorporation the process by which different protections in the Bill of Rights were incorporated into the Fourteenth Amendment, thus guaranteeing citizens protection from state as well as national governments

senatorial courtesy the practice whereby the president, before formally nominating a person for a federal judgeship, seeks the indication that senators from the candidate's own state support the nomination

seniority ranking given to an individual on the basis of length of continuous service on a committee in Congress

"separate but equal" rule doctrine that public accommodations could be segregated by race but still be equal

separation of powers the division of governmental power among several institutions that must cooperate in decision making

single-member district an electorate that is allowed to select only one representative from each district; the normal method of representation in the United States

slander an oral statement, made in "reckless disregard of the truth," which is considered damaging to the victim because it is "malicious, scandalous, and defamatory"

Social Security a contributory welfare program into which working Americans contribute a percentage of their wages, and from which they receive cash benefits after retirement

socioeconomic status status in society based on level of education, income, and occupational prestige

sociological representation a type of representation in which representatives have the same racial, gender, ethnic, religious, or educational backgrounds as their constituents. It is based on the principle that if two individuals are similar in background, character, interests, and perspectives, then one could correctly represent the other's views

soft money money contributed directly to political parties for political activities that is not regulated by federal campaign spending laws

solicitor general the top government lawyer in all cases before the Supreme Court where the government is a party

solidary benefits selective benefits of group membership that emphasize friendship, networking, and consciousness raising

sound bites short snippets of information aimed at dramatizing a story rather than explaining its substantive meaning

Speaker of the House the chief presiding officer of the House of Representatives. The Speaker is the most important party and House leader, and can influence the legislative agenda, the fate of individual pieces of legislation, and members' positions within the House

"speech plus" speech accompanied by conduct such as sit-ins, picketing, and demonstrations; protection of this form of speech under the First Amendment is conditional, and restrictions imposed by state or local authorities are acceptable if properly balanced by considerations of public order

spot advertisement a fifteen-, thirty-, or sixty-second television campaign commercial that permits a candidate's message to be delivered to a target audience

staff agency a legislative support agency responsible for policy analysis

staff organization a type of membership group in which a professional staff conducts most of the group's activities

standing the right of an individual or organization to initiate a court case, on the basis of their having a substantial stake in the outcome

standing committee a permanent committee with the power to propose and write legislation that covers a particular subject, such as finance or agriculture

stare decisis literally, "let the decision stand." The doctrine that a previous decision by a court applies as a precedent in similar cases until that decision is overruled

states' rights the principle that the states should oppose the increasing authority of the national government. This principle was most popular in the period before the Civil War

strict scrutiny test used by the Supreme Court in racial discrimination cases and other cases involving civil liberties and civil rights, which places the burden of proof on the government rather than on the challengers to show that the law in question is constitutional

subsidy a government grant of cash or other valuable commodities, such as land, to an individual or an organization; used to promote activities desired by the government, to reward political support, or to buy off political opposition

suffrage the right to vote; also called franchise

superdelegate a convention delegate position, in Democratic conventions, reserved for party officials

supply-side economics posits that reducing the marginal rate of taxation will create a productive economy by promoting levels of work and investment that would otherwise be discouraged by higher taxes

supremacy clause Article VI of the Constitution, which states that laws passed by the national government and all treaties are the supreme law of the land and superior to all laws adopted by any state or any subdivision

supreme court the highest court in a particular state or in the United States. This court primarily serves an appellate function

tariff a tax on imported goods

tax expenditures government subsidies provided to employers and employees through tax deductions for amounts spent on health insurance and other benefits

term limits legally prescribed limits on the number of terms an elected official can serve

third parties parties that organize to compete against the two major American political parties

Thirteenth Amendment one of three Civil War amendments; abolished slavery

Three-fifths Compromise the agreement reached at the Constitutional Convention of 1787 that stipulated that for purposes of the apportionment of congressional seats, every slave would be counted as three-fifths of a person

totalitarian government a system of rule in which the government recognizes no formal limits on its power and seeks to absorb or eliminate other social institutions that might challenge it

town meeting a media format in which candidates meet with ordinary citizens. Allows candidates to deliver messages without the presence of journalists or commentators

trial court the first court to hear a criminal or civil case

trustee a representative who votes based on what he or she thinks is best for his or her constituency

turnout the percentage of eligible individuals who actually vote

two-party system a political system in which only two parties have a realistic opportunity to compete effectively for control

tyranny oppressive government that employs cruel and unjust use of power and authority

uncontrollable a budgetary item that is beyond the control of budgetary committees and can be controlled only by substantive legislative action in Congress. Some uncontrollables, such as interest on the debt, are beyond the power of Congress, because the terms of payments are set in contracts

unfunded mandates regulations or conditions for receiving grants that impose costs on state and local governments for which they are not reimbursed by the federal government

Uniform Commercial Code code used in many states in the area of contract law to reduce interstate differences in judicial decisions

unitary system a centralized government system in which lower levels of government have little power independent of the national government

United Nations (UN) an organization of nations founded in 1945 to serve as a channel for negotiation and a means of settling international disputes peaceably. The UN has had frequent successes in providing a forum for negotiation and on some occasions a means of preventing international conflicts from spreading. On a number of occasions, the UN has been a convenient cover for U.S. foreign-policy goals

values (or beliefs) basic principles that shape a person's opinions about political issues and events

veto the president's constitutional power to turn down acts of Congress. A presidential veto may be overridden by a two-thirds vote of each house of Congress

Virginia Plan a framework for the Constitution, introduced by Edmund Randolph, which called for representation in the national legislature based on the population of each state

War Powers Resolution a resolution of Congress that the president can send troops into action abroad only by authorization of Congress, or if American troops are already under attack or serious threat

whip a party member in the House or Senate responsible for coordinating the party's legislative strategy, building support for key issues, and counting votes

White House staff analysts and advisers to the president, often given the title "special assistant"

winner-take-all system a system in which all of a state's presidential nominating delegates are awarded to the candidate who wins the most votes, while runners-up receive no delegates

World Trade Organization (WTO) international trade agency promoting free trade that grew out of the General Agreement on Tariffs and Trade

writ of *certiorari* a decision of at least four of the nine Supreme Court justices to review a decision of a lower court; from the Latin "to make more certain"

writ of *habeas corpus* a court order that the individual in custody be brought into court and shown the cause for detention. *Habeas corpus* is guaranteed by the Constitution and can be suspended only in cases of rebellion or invasion

ENDNOTES

Chapter 1

1. Gary Orren, "Fall from Grace: The Public's Loss of Trust in Government," in *Why People Don't Trust Government*, ed. Joseph S. Nye, Jr., Philip D. Zelikow, and David C. King (Cambridge, MA: Harvard University Press, 1997), 80–81.
2. Robert J. Blendon et al., "Changing Attitudes in America," in *Why People Don't Trust Government*, ed. Nye, Zelikow, and King, 207–8.
3. Michael A. Fletcher, "Trust and Interest in Government Soar on College Campuses," *Washington Post*, November 23, 2001, p. A3.
4. Amelia Gruber, "Public Finds Government Inefficient, Study Shows," GovExec.com, August 8, 2003.
5. iPOLL Databank, The Roper Center for Public Opinion Research, University of Connecticut, "Survey by CBS News/New York Times, July 9–July 17, 2007," www.ropercenter.uconn.edu/ipoll.html (accessed 2/25/08).
6. iPOLL Databank, The Roper Center for Public Opinion Research, University of Connecticut, "Survey by Cable News Network and Opinion Research Corporation, March 9–March 11, 2007," www.ropercenter.uconn.edu/ipoll.html (accessed 2/25/08); iPOLL Databank, The Roper Center for Public Opinion Research, University of Connecticut, "Survey by Cable News Network, USA Today and Gallup Organization, June 9–June 10, 2003," www.ropercenter.uconn.edu/ipoll.html (accessed 2/25/08); iPOLL Databank, The Roper Center for Public Opinion Research, University of Connecticut, "Survey by NBC News, Wall Street Journal and Hart and Newhouse Research Companies, April 20–April 23, 2007," www.ropercenter.uconn.edu/ipoll.html (accessed 2/25/08.
7. Joseph S. Nye, Jr., "Introduction: The Decline of Confidence in Government," in *Why People Don't Trust Government*, ed. Nye, Zelikow, and King, 4.
8. The Pew Research Center for the People and the Press, "Trends in Political Attitudes and Core Values: 1987–2007, news release, March 22, 2007, http://people-press.org/reports/pdf/312.pdf (accessed 3/8/08).
9. This definition is taken from Norman H. Nie, Jane Junn, and Kenneth Stehlik-Barry, *Education and Democratic Citizenship in America* (Chicago: University of Chicago Press, 1996).
10. See Eugen Weber, *Peasants into Frenchmen: The Modernization of Rural France, 1870–1914* (Stanford, CA: Stanford University Press, 1976), chap. 5.
11. See V. O. Key, *Politics, Parties, and Pressure Groups* (New York: Crowell, 1964), 201.
12. Harold Lasswell, *Politics: Who Gets What, When, How* (New York: Meridian Books, 1958).
13. Susan B. Carter, Scott Sigmund Gartner, Michael R. Haines, Alan L. Olmsted, Richard Sutch, and Gavin Wright, eds., *Historical Statistics of the United States: Millennial Edition Online*, Table Aa145-184, Population, by Sex and Race: 1790–1990 (New York: Cambridge University Press, 2006). 2007 data available at U.S. Census Bureau, www.census.gov.
14. Carter et al., *Historical Statistics of the United States*, Table Aa145-184, Population, by Sex and Race: 1790–1990.
15. Carter et al., *Historical Statistics of the United States*, Table Aa145-184, Population, by Sex and Race: 1790–1990; Table Aa2189-2215, Hispanic Population Estimates.
16. U.S. Census Bureau, www.census.gov; Claude S. Fischer and Michael Hout, *A Century of Difference: How America Changed in the Last One Hundred Years* (New York: Russell Sage Foundation, 2006), 36.
17. Carter et al., *Historical Statistics of the United States*, Table Aa22-35, Selected Population Characteristics.
18. Fischer and Hout, *A Century of Difference*, 24.
19. Michael B. Katz and Mark J. Stern, *One Nation Divisible: What America Was and What It Is Becoming* (New York: Russell Sage Foundation, 2006), 16.
20. Carter et al., *Historical Statistics of the United States*, Table Aa145-184, Population, by Sex and Race: 1790–1990.
21. U.S. Census Bureau, "Table 3: Annual Estimates of the Population by Sex, Race, and Hispanic Origin for the United States: April 1, 2000 to July 1, 2007 (NC-EST2007-03)," www.census.gov/popest/national/asrh/NC-EST2007-srh.html (accessed 7/13/08).
22. U.S. Census Bureau, "Population Profile of the United States: Dynamic Version," www.census.gov/population/pop-profile/dynamic/ForeignBorn.pdf (accessed 2/5/08).
23. Jeffrey S. Passel, "Size and Characteristics of the Unauthorized Migrant Population in the U.S.," Pew Hispanic Center, March 7, 2006, www.pewhispanic.org/files/reports/61.pdf (accessed 2/5/08).

24 Anthony Faiola, "States' Immigrant Policies Diverge," *Washington Post*, October 15, 2007, p. A1.

25. Fischer and Hout, *A Century of Difference*, 187; Pew Forum on Religion and Public Life, "Religious Demographic Profile: United States," www.pewforum.org/world-affairs/countries/?CountryID=222 (accessed 2/5/08).

26. Pew Forum, "Religious Demographic Profile."

27. Carter et al., *Historical Statistics of the United States*, Table Aa125-144, Population, by Age: 1900–2000; U.S. Census Bureau, "National Population Estimates," www.census.gov/popest/national/asrh/ (accessed 3/18/08).

28 Carter et al., *Historical Statistics of the United States*, Table Aa22-35, Selected Population Characteristics; Kevin Kinsella and Victoria A. Velkoff, *An Aging World: 2001* (November 2001), www.census.gov/prod/200pubs/p95-01-1.pdf (accessed 3/18/08).

29. Michael R. Haines, "Population Characteristics," in *Historical Statistics of the United States*, ed. Carter et al., 1–21.

30. Constitution of the United States of America, Article I, Section 2; Karen M. Mills, *Congressional Apportionment: Census 2000 Brief* (U.S. Census Bureau, 2001), www.census.gov/prod/2001pubs/c2kbr01-7.pdf (accessed 2/5/08).

31. Herbert McClosky and John Zaller, *The American Ethos: Public Attitudes toward Capitalism and Democracy* (Cambridge, MA: Harvard University Press, 1984), 19.

32. J. R. Pole, *The Pursuit of Equality in American History* (Berkeley: University of California Press, 1978), 3.

33. See Judith N. Shklar, *American Citizenship: The Quest for Inclusion* (Cambridge, MA: Harvard University Press, 1991).

34. See Rogers M. Smith, *Liberalism and American Constitutional Law* (Cambridge, MA: Harvard University Press, 1985), chap. 6.

35. The case was *San Antonio Independent School District v. Rodriguez*, 411 U.S. 1 (1973). See the discussion in Smith, *Liberalism and American Constitutional Law*, 163–64.

36. See the discussion in Eileen McDonagh, "Gender Political Change," in *New Perspectives on American Politics*, ed. Lawrence C. Dodd and Calvin Jillson (Washington, DC: Congressional Quarterly Press, 1994), 58–73. The argument for moving women's issues into the public sphere is made by Jean Bethke Elshtain, *Public Man, Private Woman* (Princeton, NJ: Princeton University Press, 1981).

37. Roger Lowenstein, "The Way We Live Now: The Inequality Conundrum," *New York Times Magazine*, June 10, 2007, p. 11.

38. Steve Greenhouse, "Taxpayers Would Get a Bigger Break, Over All, in Obama's Plan," October 31, 2008, *New York Times*, p. A14.

39. Kevin Phillips, *Arrogant Capital: Washington, Wall Street, and the Frustration of American Politics* (Boston: Little, Brown, 1994).

40. Joe Stephens, "Hard Money, Strong Arms and 'Matrix'," *Washington Post*, February 10, 2002, p. 1.

Chapter 2

1. Michael Kammen, *A Machine That Would Go of Itself* (New York: Vintage, 1986), 22.

2. The social makeup of colonial America and some of the social conflicts that divided colonial society are discussed in Jackson Turner Main, *The Social Structure of Revolutionary America* (Princeton, NJ: Princeton University Press, 1965).

3. George B. Tindall and David E. Shi, *America: A Narrative History*, 3rd ed. (New York: Norton, 1992), 194.

4. For a discussion of events leading up to the Revolution, see Charles M. Andrews, *The Colonial Background of the American Revolution* (New Haven, CT: Yale University Press, 1924).

5. See Carl Becker, *The Declaration of Independence* (New York: Knopf, 1942).

6. An excellent and readable account of the development from the Articles of Confederation to the Constitution will be found in Alfred H. Kelly, Winfred A. Harbison, and Herman Belz, *The American Constitution: Its Origins and Development*, 7th ed. (New York: Norton, 1991), vol. I, chap. 5.

7. Reported in Samuel E. Morrison, Henry Steele Commager, and William Leuchtenberg, *The Growth of the American Republic* (New York: Oxford University Press, 1969), vol. 1, 244.

8. Quoted in Morrison et al., *The Growth of the American Republic*, vol. 1, 242.

9. Charles A. Beard, *An Economic Interpretation of the Constitution of the United States* (New York: Macmillan, 1913).

10. Madison's notes, along with the somewhat less complete records kept by several other participants in the convention, are available in a four-volume set. See Max Farrand, ed., *The Records of the Federal Convention of 1787*, 4 vols., rev. ed. (New Haven, CT: Yale University Press, 1966).

11. Farrand, ed., *The Records of the Federal Convention of 1787*, vol. 1, 476.

12. Farrand, ed., *The Records of the Federal Convention of 1787*, vol. 2, 10.

13. Alexander Hamilton, James Madison, and John Jay, *The Federalist*, ed. E. M. Earle (New York: Modern Library, 1937), No. 71.

14. Earle, ed., *The Federalist*, No. 62.

15. Earle, ed., *The Federalist*, No. 70.

16. Max Farrand, *The Framing of the Constitution of the United States* (New Haven, CT: Yale University Press, 1962), 49.

17. Melancthon Smith, quoted in Herbert J. Storing, *What the Anti-Federalists Were For* (Chicago: University of Chicago Press, 1981), 17.

18. "Essays of Brutus," No. 1, in Herbert Storing, ed., *The Complete Anti-Federalist* (Chicago: University of Chicago Press, 1981).

19. Earle, ed., *The Federalist*, No. 57.

20. "Essays of Brutus," No. 15, in Storing, ed., *The Complete Anti-Federalist.*
21. Earle, ed., *The Federalist,* No. 10.
22. "Essays of Brutus," No. 7, in Storing, ed., *The Complete Anti-Federalist.*
23. "Essays of Brutus," No. 6, in Storing, ed., *The Complete Anti-Federalist.*
24. Storing, *What the Anti-Federalists Were For,* 28.
25. Earle, ed., *The Federalist,* No. 51.
26. Quoted in Storing, *What the Anti-Federalists Were For,* 30.
27. See Marcia Lee, "The Equal Rights Amendment: Public Policy by Means of a Constitutional Amendment," in *The Politics of Policy Making in America,* ed. David Caputo (San Francisco: Freeman, 1977); Jane Mansbridge, *Why We Lost the ERA* (Chicago: University of Chicago Press, 1986); and Donald Mathews and Jane Sherron DeHart, *Sex, Gender, and the Politics of the ERA* (New York: Oxford University Press, 1990).
28. Earle, ed., *The Federalist,* No. 10.

Chapter 3

1. Donald Kettl, *The Next Government of the United States* (New York: Norton, forthcoming); U.S. House of Representatives, Select Bipartisan Committee to Investigate the Preparation for and Response to Hurricane Katrina, "A Failure of Initiative: The Final Report of the Select Bipartisan Committee to Investigate the Preparation for and Response to Hurricane Katrina," www.katrina.house.gov/full_katrina_report.htm (accessed 7/14/08).
2. Robert D. McFadden, "State Court Recognizes Gay Marriages from Elsewhere," *New York Times,* February 2, 2008, www.nytimes.com/2008/02/02/nyregion/02samesex.html?fta=y (accessed 3/26/08).
3. P. J. Huffstutter, "An 'I Do' on Same-Sex Marriage is Stayed," *Los Angeles Times,* September 1, 2007, p. A16. See also National Conference of State Legislatures, "Same Sex Marriage, Civil Unions and Domestic Partnerships," www.ncsl.org/programs/cyf/samesex.htm (accessed 2/11/08).
4. Ken I. Kersch, "Full Faith and Credit for Same-Sex Marriages?" *Political Science Quarterly* 112 (Spring 1997): 117–36; Joan Biskupic, "Once Unthinkable, Now Under Debate," *Washington Post,* September 3, 1996, p. A1.
5. Barbara Hoberock, "State Won't Fight Same-Sex Adoption Ruling," *Tulsa World,* August 17, 2007, p. A9.
6. *Hicklin v. Orbeck,* 437 U.S. 518 (1978).
7. *Sweeny v. Woodall,* 344 U.S. 86 (1953).
8. Marlise Simons, "France Won't Extradite American Convicted of Murder," *New York Times,* December 5, 1997, p. A9.
9. Patricia S. Florestano, "Past and Present Utilization of Interstate Compacts in the United States," *Publius* 24 (Fall 1994): 13–26.
10. A good discussion of the constitutional position of local governments is in York Willbern, *The Withering Away of the City* (Bloomington: Indiana University Press, 1971). For more on the structure and theory of federalism, see Thomas R. Dye, *American Federalism: Competition among Governments* (Lexington, MA: Lexington Books, 1990), chap. 1; and Martha Derthick, "Up-to-Date in Kansas City: Reflections on American Federalism" (the 1992 John Gaus Lecture), *PS: Political Science & Politics* 25 (December 1992): 671–75.
11. For a good treatment of the contrast between national political stability and social instability, see Samuel P. Huntington, *Political Order in Changing Societies* (New Haven, CT: Yale University Press, 1968), chap. 2.
12. *McCulloch v. Maryland,* 4 Wheaton 316 (1819).
13. *Gibbons v. Ogden,* 9 Wheaton 1 (1824).
14. The Sherman Antitrust Act, adopted in 1890, for example, was enacted not to restrict commerce, but rather to protect it from monopolies, or trusts, in order to prevent unfair trade practices, and to enable the market again to become self-regulating. Moreover, the Supreme Court sought to uphold liberty of contract to protect businesses. For example, in *Lochner v. New York,* 198 U.S. 45 (1905), the Court invalidated a New York law regulating the sanitary conditions and hours of labor of bakers on the grounds that the law interfered with liberty of contract.
15. The key case in this process of expanding the power of the national government is generally considered to be *NLRB v. Jones & Laughlin Steel Corporation,* 301 U.S. 1 (1937), in which the Supreme Court approved federal regulation of the workplace and thereby virtually eliminated interstate commerce as a limit on the national government's power.
16. *United States v. Darby Lumber Co.,* 312 U.S. 100 (1941).
17. W. John Moore, "Pleading the 10th," *National Journal,* July 29, 1995, p. 1940.
18. *United States v. Lopez,* 115 S.Ct. 1624 (1995).
19. *Printz v. United States,* 117 S.Ct. 2365 (1997).
20. *Seminole Indian Tribe v. Florida,* 116 S.Ct. 1114 (1996).
21. See the poll reported in Guy Gugliotta, "Scaling Down the American Dream," *Washington Post,* April 19, 1995, p. A21. See also Richard Cole, John Kincaid, and Alejandro Rodriguez, "Public Opinion on Federalism and Federal Political Culture in Canada, Mexico and the United States, 2004," *Publius: The Journal of Federalism* 34:3 (2004): 201–21, http://publius.oxfordjournals.org/cgi/reprint/34/3/201 (accessed 2/12/08).
22. Kenneth T. Palmer, "The Evolution of Grant Policies," in *The Changing Politics of Federal Grants,* ed. Lawrence D. Brown, James W. Fossett, and Kenneth T. Palmer (Washington, DC: Brookings Institutional Press, 1984), 15.

23. Palmer, "The Evolution of Grant Policies," 6.
24. Morton Grozdins, *The American System*, ed. Daniel J. Elazar (Chicago: Rand McNally, 1966).
25. See Terry Sanford, *Storm over the States* (New York: McGraw-Hill, 1967).
26. James L. Sundquist with David W. Davis, *Making Federalism Work* (Washington, DC: Brookings, 1969), 271. George Wallace was mistrusted by the architects of the War on Poverty because he was a strong proponent of racial segregation and "states' rights."
27. See Don Kettl, *The Regulation of American Federalism* (Baton Rouge: Louisiana State University Press, 1983).
28. Cindy Skrzycki, "Trial Lawyers on the Offensive in Fight Against Preemptive Rules," *Washington Post*, September 11, 2007, p. D2.
29. Skrzycki, "Trial Lawyers."
30. See U.S. Advisory Commission on Intergovernmental Relations, *Federal Regulation of State and Local Governments: The Mixed Record of the 1980s* (Washington, DC: Advisory Commission on Intergovernmental Relations, July 1993).
31. U.S. Advisory Commission on Intergovernmental Relations, *Federal Regulation of State and Local Governments*, iii.
32. Utah State Legislature, "Resolution Opposing Real ID Act," 2007 General Session, www.le.state.ut.us/~2007/bills/hbillint/hr0002.htm (accessed 2/11/08).
33. CNN.com/politics, "The Reality Behind the Real ID Act," August 16, 2007, www.cnn.com/2007/POLITICS/08/16/real.id.details/ (accessed 2/11/08).
34. Quoted in Timothy Conlon, *New Federalism: Intergovernmental Reform from Nixon to Reagan* (Washington, DC: Brookings Institution Press, 1988), 25.
35. For the emergence of complaints about federal categorical grants, see Palmer, "The Evolution of Grant Policies," 17–18. On the governors' efforts to gain more control over federal grants after the 1994 congressional elections, see Dan Balz, "GOP Governors Eager to Do Things Their Way," *Washington Post*, November 22, 1994, p. A4.
36. U.S. Advisory Commission on Intergovernmental Relations, *Federal Regulation of State and Local Governments.*
37. For an assessment of the achievements of the 104th and 105th Congresses, see Timothy Conlan, *From New Federalism to Devolution: Twenty-Five Years of Intergovernmental Reform* (Washington, DC: Brookings Institution Press, 1998).
38. Robert Frank, "Proposed Block Grants Seen Unlikely to Cure Management Problems," *Wall Street Journal*, May 1, 1995, p. 1.
39. Sarah Kershaw, "U.S. Rule Limits Emergency Care for Immigrants," *New York Times*, Sepember 22, 2007, p. A1.
40. U.S. Committee on Federalism and National Purpose, *To Form a More Perfect Union* (Washington, DC: National Conference on Social Welfare, 1985). See also the discussion in Paul E. Peterson, *The Price of Federalism* (Washington, DC: Brookings, 1995), esp. chap. 8.
41. Malcolm Gladwell, "In States' Experiments, a Cutting Contest," *New York Times*, March 10, 1995, p. 6.
42. The phrase *laboratories of democracy* was coined by Supreme Court Justice Louis Brandeis in his dissenting opinion in *New State Ice Co. v. Liebman*, 285 U.S. 262 (1932).
43. Christopher Lee, "New Jersey's Corzine to Defy New Health Care Rules," *Washington Post*, September 14, 2007, p. A4.
44. "Motor Vehicle Fatalities in 1996 Were 12 Percent Higher on Interstates, Freeways in 12 States that Raised Speed Limits," Insurance Institute for Highway Safety, press release, October 10, 1997.
45. Adam Nagourney, "G.O.P. Right Is Splintered on Schiavo Intervention," *New York Times*, March 23, 2005, p. A14.
46. *Massachusetts v. Environmental Protection Agency*, 549 U.S. 497 (2007). The petitioners were the states of California, Connecticut, Illinois, Maine, Massachusetts, New Jersey, New Mexico, New York, Oregon, Rhode Island, Vermont, and Washington; the cities of New York, Baltimore, and Washington, D.C.; the territory of American Samoa; and the organizations the Center for Biological Diversity, the Center for Food Safety, the Conservation Law Foundation, the Environmental Advocates, the Environmental Defense Fund, Friends of the Earth, Greenpeace, the International Center for Technology Assessment, the National Environmental Trust, the Natural Resources Defense Council, the Sierra Club, the Union of Concerned Scientists, and the U.S. Public Interest Research Group. See Linda Greenhouse, "Justices Say E.P.A. Has Power to Act on Harmful Gases," *New York Times*, April 2, 2007, p. A1.
47. Emily Bazar, "Fewer Licenses for Illegal Migrants; More States Require Legal Status to Drive," *USA Today*, January, 30, 2008, p. 3A.
48. Karin Brulliard, "Immigrant Laws Tread Uncharted Legal Path," *Washington Post*, August 28, 2007, p. B1.
49. This was a comment from Walter E. Dellinger, President Clinton's acting solicitor general. Linda Greenhouse, "Will the Court Reassert National Authority?" *New York Times*, September 30, 2001, sect. 4, p. 14.
50. iPOLL Databank, The Roper Center for Public Opinion Research, University of Connecticut, "Survey by Gallup Organization, February 1–February 4, 2007," www.ropercenter.uconn.edu/ipoll.html (accessed 2/26/08).

Chapter 4

1. Alexander Hamilton, James Madison, and John Jay, *The Federalist Papers*, ed. Clinton Rossiter (New York: New American Library, 1961), No. 84, 513.
2. Rossiter, ed., *The Federalist Papers*, No. 84, 513.
3. Clinton Rossiter, *1787: The Grand Convention* (New York: Norton, 1987), 302.
4. Rossiter, *1787*, 303. Rossiter also reports that "in 1941 the States of Connecticut, Massachusetts and Georgia celebrated the sesquicentennial of the Bill of Rights by giving their hitherto withheld and unneeded assent."
5. *Barron v. Baltimore*, 7 Peters 243, 246 (1833).
6. The Fourteenth Amendment also seems designed to introduce civil rights. The final clause of the all-important Section 1 provides that no state can "deny to any person within its jurisdiction the equal protection of the laws." It is not unreasonable to conclude that the purpose of this provision was to obligate the state governments as well as the national government to take positive actions to protect citizens from arbitrary and discriminatory actions, at least those based on race. This will be explored in Chapter 5.
7. For example, *The Slaughterhouse Cases*, 16 Wallace 36 (1883).
8. *Chicago, Burlington and Quincy Railroad Company v. Chicago*, 166 U.S. 226 (1897).
9. *Gitlow v. New York*, 268 U.S. 652 (1925).
10. *Near v. Minnesota*, 283 U.S. 697 (1931); *Hague v. C.I.O.*, 307 U.S. 496 (1939).
11. *Palko v. Connecticut*, 302 U.S. 319 (1937).
12. All of these were implicitly included in the *Palko* case as "not incorporated" into the Fourteenth Amendment as limitations on the powers of the states.
13. There is one interesting exception, which involves the Sixth Amendment right to public trial. In the 1948 case *In re Oliver*, 33 U.S. 257, the right to the public trial was, in effect, incorporated as part of the Fourteenth Amendment. However, the issue in that case was put more generally as "due process," and public trial itself was not actually mentioned in so many words. Later opinions, such as *Duncan v. Louisiana*, 391 U.S. 145 (1968), cited the *Oliver* case as the precedent for more explicit incorporation of public trials as part of the Fourteenth Amendment.
14. *Parker v. District of Columbia*, 478 F3d 370 (D.C. Cir. 2007).
15. *Abington School District v. Schempp*, 374 U.S. 203 (1963).
16. *Engel v. Vitale*, 370 U.S. 421 (1962).
17. *Wallace v. Jaffree*, 472 U.S. 38 (1985).
18. *Lynch v. Donnelly*, 465 U.S. 668 (1984).
19. *Lemon v. Kurtzman*, 403 U.S. 602 (1971). The *Lemon* test is still good law, but as recently as the 1994 Court term, four justices have urged that the *Lemon* test be abandoned. Here is a settled area of law that may soon become unsettled.
20. *Rosenberger v. Rector and Visitors of the University of Virginia*, 115 S.Ct. 2510 (1995).
21. *Agostini v. Felton*, 117 S.Ct. 1997 (1997). The case being overruled was *Aguilar v. Felton*, 473 U.S. 402 (1985).
22. *Zelman v. Simmons-Harris*, 536 U.S. 639 (2002).
23. *Van Orden v. Perry*, 545 U.S. 677 (2005).
24. *McCreary v. ACLU*, 545 U.S. 844 (2005).
25. *West Virginia State Board of Education v. Barnette*, 319 U.S. 624 (1943). The case it reversed was *Minersville School District v. Gobitus*, 310 U.S. 586 (1940).
26. *Employment Division, Department of Human Resources of Oregon v. Smith*, 494 U.S. 872 (1990).
27. *City of Boerne v. Flores*, 117 S.Ct. 293 (1996).
28. *Wisconsin v. Yoder*, 406 U.S. 205 (1972).
29. *Abrams v. U.S.*, 250 U.S. 616 (1919).
30. *U.S. v. Carolene Products Company*, 304 U.S. 144 (1938), note 4. This footnote is one of the Court's most important doctrines. See Alfred H. Kelly, Winfred A. Harbison, and Herman Belz, *The American Constitution: Its Origins and Development*, 7th ed. (New York: Norton, 1991), vol. 2, 519–23.
31. *Schenk v. U.S.*, 249 U.S. 47 (1919).
32. *Brandenburg v. Ohio*, 395 U.S. 444 (1969).
33. *McConnell v. FEC*, 124 S.Ct. 34 (2003).
34. *Federal Election Commission v. Wisconsin Right to Life*, No. 06-969 (2007).
35. *Stromberg v. California*, 283 U.S. 359 (1931).
36. *Texas v. Johnson*, 488 U.S. 884 (1989).
37. *United States v. Eichman*, 496 U.S. 310 (1990).
38. Lizette Alvarez, "Measure to Ban Flag Burning Falls 4 Votes Short in the Senate," *New York Times*, March 30, 2000, p. A24; Adam Clymer, "House, in Ritual Vote, Opposes Flag Burning," *New York Times*, July 18, 2001, p. A20.
39. *Virginia v. Black*, 528 U.S. 343 (2003).
40. For a good general discussion of speech plus, see Louis Fisher, *American Constitutional Law* (New York: McGraw-Hill, 1990), 544–46. The case upholding the buffer zone against the abortion protesters is *Madsen v. Women's Health Center*, 114 S.Ct. 2516 (1994).
41. *Rumsfeld v. FAIR*, No. 04-11152 (2006).
42. *Near v. Minnesota*, 283 U.S. 697 (1931).
43. *New York Times v. U.S.*, 403 U.S. 731 (1971).
44. *Branzburg v. Hayes*, 408 U.S. 656 (1972).
45. *New York Times v. Sullivan*, 376 U.S. 254 (1964).
46. *Hustler Magazine v. Falwell*, 108 S.Ct. 876 (1988).
47. See *Zeran v. America Online*, 129 F3d 327 (4th Cir. 1977).
48. *Roth v. U.S.*, 354 U.S. 476 (1957).
49. Concurring opinion in *Jacobellis v. Ohio*, 378 U.S. 184 (1964).
50. *Miller v. California*, 413 U.S. 15 (1973).

51. *Reno v. American Civil Liberties Union*, 117 S.Ct. 2329 (1997).
52. *U.S. v. American Library Association*, 539 U.S. 194 (2003).
53. *Chaplinsky v. State of New Hampshire*, 315 U.S. 568 (1942).
54. *Dennis v. United States*, 341 U.S. 494 (1951), which upheld the infamous Smith Act of 1940, which provided criminal penalties for those who "willfully and knowingly conspire to teach and advocate the forceful and violent overthrow and destruction of the government."
55. "The Penn File: An Update," *Wall Street Journal*, April 11, 1994, p. A14.
56. *Meritor Savings Bank, FBD v. Vinson*, 477 U.S. 57 (1986).
57. Charles Fried, "The New First Amendment Jurisprudence: A Threat to Liberty," in *The Bill of Rights in the Modern State*, ed. Geoffrey R. Stone, Cass R. Sunstein, and Richard A. Epstein (Chicago: University of Chicago Press, 1992), 249.
58. *Bethel School District No. 403 v. Fraser*, 478 U.S. 675 (1986).
59. *Hazelwood School District v. Kuhlmeier*, 108 S. Ct. 562 (1988).
60. *Morse v. Frederick*, No. 06-278 (2007).
61. *Broadcasting Company v. Acting Attorney General*, 405 U.S. 1000 (1972).
62. *Board of Trustees of the State University of New York v. Fox*, 109 S.Ct. 3028 (1989).
63. *City Council v. Taxpayers for Vincent*, 466 U.S. 789 (1984).
64. *Posadas de Puerto Rico Associates v. Tourism Company of Puerto Rico*, 479 U.S. 328 (1986).
65. Fisher, *American Constitutional Law*, 546.
66. *Bigelow v. Virginia*, 421 U.S. 809 (1975).
67. *Virginia State Board of Pharmacy v. Virginia Citizens Consumer Council*, 425 U.S. 748 (1976). Later cases restored the rights of lawyers to advertise their services.
68. *44 Liquormart, Inc. and Peoples Super Liquor Stores Inc., Petitioners v. Rhode Island and Rhode Island Liquor Stores Association*, 116 S.Ct. 1495 (1996).
69. *Lorillard Tobacco v. Reilly*, 121 S.Ct. 2404 (2001).
70. *Presser v. Illinois*, 116 U.S. 252 (1886).
71. *District of Columbia v. Heller*, No. 07-290 (2008).
72. *In re Winship*, 397 U.S. 361 (1970). An outstanding treatment of due process in issues involving the Fourth through Seventh Amendments will be found in Fisher, *American Constitutional Law*, chap. 13.
73. *Horton v. California*, 496 U.S. 128 (1990).
74. *Mapp v. Ohio*, 367 U.S. 643 (1961). Although Ms. Mapp went free in this case, she was later convicted in New York on narcotics trafficking charges and served nine years of a twenty-year sentence.
75. For a good discussion of the issue, see Fisher, *American Constitutional Law*, 884–89.
76. *U.S. v. Grubbs*, No. 04-1414 (2006).
77. *National Treasury Employees Union v. Von Raab*, 39 U.S. 656 (1989).
78. *Skinner v. Railroad Labor Executives Association*, 489 U.S. 602 (1989).
79. *Vernonia School District 47J v. Acton*, 115 S.Ct. 2386 (1985).
80. *Chandler et al. v. Miller, Governor of Georgia et al.*, 117 S.Ct. 1295 (1997).
81. *Indianapolis v. Edmund*, 531 U.S. 32 (2000), 121 S.Ct. 447 (2000).
82. *Brendlin v. California*, 06-8120 (2007).
83. *Ferguson v. Charleston*, 121 S.Ct. 1281 (2001).
84. *Kyllo v. U.S.*, 121 S.Ct. 2038 (2001).
85. Corwin and Peltason, *Understanding the Constitution* (New York: Holt, 1967), 286.
86. *Miranda v. Arizona*, 348 U.S. 436 (1966).
87. *Berman v. Parker*, 348 U.S. 26 (1954). For a thorough analysis of the case see Benjamin Ginsberg, "*Berman v. Parker:* Congress, the Court, and the Public Purpose," *Polity* 4 (1971): 48–75. For a later application of the case that suggests that "just compensation"—defined as something approximating market value—is about all a property owner can hope for protection against a public taking of property, see Theodore Lowi et al., *Poliscide; Big Government, Big Science, Lilliputian Politics*, 2nd ed. (Lanham, MD: University Press of America, 1990), 267–70.
88. *Kelo v. City of New London*, 545 U.S. 469 (2005).
89. *Gideon v. Wainwright*, 372 U.S. 335 (1963). For a full account of the story of the trial and release of Clarence Earl Gideon, see Anthony Lewis, *Gideon's Trumpet* (New York: Random House, 1964). See also David O'Brien, *Storm Center*, 2nd ed. (New York: Norton, 1990).
90. *Wiggins v. Smith*, 123 S.Ct. 2527 (2003).
91. For further discussion of these issues, see Corwin and Peltason, *Understanding the Constitution*, 319–23.
92. *U.S. v. Gonzalez-Lopez*, No. 05-352 (2006).
93. *Furman v. Georgia*, 408 U.S. 238 (1972).
94. *Gregg v. Georgia*, 428 U.S. 153 (1976).
95. *Panetti v. Quarterman*, No. 04-6407 (2007).
96. Robert Barnes and Jerry Markon, "Supreme Court Halts Virginia Inmate's Execution," *Washington Post*, Oct. 18, 2007, p. 1.
97. *Olmstead v. U.S.*, 227 U.S. 438 (1928). See also David M. O'Brien, *Constitutional Law and Politics*, 6th ed. (New York: Norton, 2005), vol. 1, 76–84.
98. *West Virginia State Board of Education v. Barnette*, 319 U.S. 624 (1943).
99. *NAACP v. Alabama ex rel. Patterson*, 357 U.S. 447 (1958).
100. *Griswold v. Connecticut*, 381 U.S. 479 (1965).
101. *Griswold v. Connecticut*, concurring opinion. In 1972, the Court extended the privacy right to unmarried women: *Eisenstadt v. Baird*, 405 U.S. 438 (1972).

102. *Roe v. Wade*, 410 U.S. 113 (1973).
103. *Webster v. Reproductive Health Services*, 109 S.Ct. 3040 (1989), which upheld a Missouri law that restricted the use of public medical facilities for abortion. The decision opened the way for other states to limit the availability of abortion.
104. *Planned Parenthood of Southeastern Pennsylvania v. Casey*, 112 S.Ct. 2791 (1992).
105. *Stenberg v. Carhart*, 120 S.Ct. 2597 (2000).
106. *Ayotte v. Planned Parenthood*, No. 546 U.S. 320 (2006).
107. *Gonzales v. Carhart*, No. 05-380 (2007).
108. *Bowers v. Hardwick*, 478 U.S. 186 (1986).
109. The dissenters were quoting an earlier case, *Olmstead v. United States*, 27 U.S. 438 (1928), to emphasize the nature of their disagreement with the majority in the *Bowers* case.
110. *Lawrence v. Texas*, 123 S.Ct. 2472 (2003).
111. It is worth recalling here the provision of the Ninth Amendment: "The enumeration in the Constitution, of certain rights, shall not be construed to deny or disparage others retained by the people."
112. *Gonzales v. Oregon*, No. 04-623 (2006).
113. *Hamdi v. Rumsfeld*, 542 U.S. 507 (2004).
114. *Hamdan v. Rumsfeld*, No. 05-184 (2006).
115. *ACLU v. NSA*, 06-2095 (6th Cir. 2007).

Chapter 5

1. Paula Baker, "The Domestication of Politics: Women and American Political Society, 1780–1920," *American Historical Review* 89 (June 1984): 620–47.
2. Oscar Handlin, *America—A History* (New York: Holt, Rinehart & Winston, 1968), 474.
3. *Dred Scott v. Sandford*, 19 Howard 393 (1857).
4. August Meier and Elliot Rudwick, *From Plantation to Ghetto* (New York: Hill and Wang, 1976), 184–88.
5. Jill Dupont, "Susan B. Anthony," New York Notes (Albany, NY: New York State Commission on the Bicentennial of the U.S. Constitution, 1988), 3.
6. *Plessy v. Ferguson*, 163 U.S. 537 (1896).
7. Dupont, "Susan B. Anthony," 4.
8. The prospect of a Fair Employment Practices law tied to the commerce power produced the Dixiecrat break with the Democratic Party in 1948. The Democratic Party organization of the States of the Old Confederacy seceded from the national party and nominated its own candidate, the then-Democratic governor of South Carolina, Strom Thurmond, who later became a Republican senator. This almost cost President Truman the election.
9. This was based on the provision in Article VI of the Constitution that "all treaties made, . . . under the Authority of the United States," shall be the "supreme Law of the Land." The committee recognized that if the U.S. Senate ratified the Human Rights Covenant of the United Nations—a treaty—then that power could be used as the constitutional umbrella for effective civil rights legislation. The Supreme Court had recognized in *Missouri v. Holland*, 252 U.S. 416 (1920), that a treaty could enlarge federal power at the expense of the states.
10. *Missouri ex rel. Gaines v. Canada*, 305 U.S. 337 (1938).
11. *Sweatt v. Painter*, 339 U.S. 629 (1950).
12. *Smith v. Allwright*, 321 U.S. 649 (1944).
13. *Shelley v. Kraemer*, 334 U.S. 1 (1948).
14. Kermit L. Hall, *The Magic Mirror: Law in American History* (New York: Oxford University Press, 1989), 322–24. See also Richard Kluger, *Simple Justice* (New York: Random House, Vintage Edition, 1977), 530–37.
15. The District of Columbia case came up too, but since the District of Columbia is not a state, this case did not directly involve the Fourteenth Amendment and its "equal protection" clause. It confronted the Court on the same grounds, however—that segregation is inherently unequal. Its victory in effect was "incorporation in reverse," with equal protection moving from the Fourteenth Amendment to become part of the Bill of Rights. See *Bolling v. Sharpe*, 347 U.S. 497 (1954).
16. *Brown v. Board of Education of Topeka, Kansas*, 347 U.S. 483 (1954).
17. The Supreme Court first declared that race was a suspect classification requiring strict scrutiny in the decision *Korematsu v. United States*, 323 U.S. 214 (1944). In this case, the Court upheld President Roosevelt's executive order of 1941 allowing the military to exclude persons of Japanese ancestry from the West Coast and to place them in internment camps. It is one of the few cases in which classification based on race survived strict scrutiny.
18. The two most important cases were *Cooper v. Aaron*, 358 U.S. 1 (1958), which required Little Rock, Arkansas, to desegregate; and *Griffin v. Prince Edward County School Board*, 377 U.S. 218 (1964), which forced all the schools of that Virginia county to reopen after five years of closing to avoid desegregation.
19. In *Cooper v. Aaron*, the Supreme Court ordered immediate compliance with the lower court's desegregation order and went beyond that with a stern warning that it is "emphatically the province and duty of the judicial department to say what the law is."
20. *Shuttlesworth v. Birmingham Board of Education*, 358 U.S. 101 (1958), upheld a "pupil placement" plan purporting to assign pupils on various bases, with no mention of race. This case interpreted *Brown* to mean that school districts must stop explicit racial discrimination but were under no obligation to take positive steps to desegregate. For a while black parents were doomed to case-by-case approaches.
21. For good treatments of this long stretch of the struggle of the federal courts to integrate the schools, see Paul Brest and Sanford Levinson, *Processes of Constitutional*

Decision-Making: Cases and Materials, 2nd ed. (Boston: Little, Brown, 1983), 471–80; and Alfred Kelly et al., *The American Constitution: Its Origins and Development*, 6th ed. (New York: Norton, 1983), 610–16.

22. Pierre Thomas, "Denny's to Settle Bias Cases," *Washington Post*, May 24, 1994, p. A1.
23. See Hamil Harris, "For Blacks, Cabs Can Be Hard to Get," *Washington Post*, July 21, 1994, p. J1.
24. For a thorough analysis of the Office for Civil Rights, see Jeremy Rabkin, "Office for Civil Rights," in *The Politics of Regulation*, ed. James Q. Wilson (New York: Basic Books, 1980).
25. This was an accepted way of using quotas or ratios to determine statistically that blacks or other minorities were being excluded from schools or jobs, and then on the basis of that statistical evidence to authorize the Justice Department to bring suits in individual cases and in class action suits as well. In most segregated situations outside the South, it is virtually impossible to identify and document an intent to discriminate.
26. *Swann v. Charlotte-Mecklenberg Board of Education*, 402 U.S. 1 (1971).
27. *Milliken v. Bradley*, 418 U.S. 717 (1974).
28. For a good evaluation of the Boston effort, see Gary Orfield, *Must We Bus? Segregated Schools and National Policy* (Washington: Brookings Institution, 1978), 144–46. See also Bob Woodward and Scott Armstrong, *The Brethren: Inside the Supreme Court* (New York: Simon & Schuster, 1979), 426–27; and J. Anthony Lukas, *Common Ground* (New York: Random House, 1986).
29. *Board of Education v. Dowell*, 498 U.S. 237 (1991).
30. *Missouri v. Jenkins*, 115 S.Ct. 2038 (1995).
31. john a. powell, "Segregated Schools Ruling Not All Bad: In Rejecting Seattle's Integration Bid, Top Court Majority Also Held that Avoiding Racial Isolation Is a Legitimate Public Goal," *Newsday* (July 16, 2007), p. A33.
32. See especially *Katzenbach v. McClung*, 379 U.S. 294 (1964). Almost immediately after passage of the Civil Rights Act of 1964, a case was brought challenging the validity of Title II, which covered discrimination in public accommodations. Ollie's Barbecue was a neighborhood restaurant in Birmingham, Alabama. It was located eleven blocks away from an interstate highway and even farther from railroad and bus stations. Its table service was for whites only; there was only a take-out service for blacks. The Supreme Court agreed that Ollie's was strictly an intrastate restaurant, but since a substantial proportion of its food and other supplies were bought from companies outside the state of Alabama, there was a sufficient connection to interstate commerce; therefore, racial discrimination at such restaurants would "impose commercial burdens of national magnitude upon interstate commerce." Although this case involved Title II, it had direct bearing on the constitutionality of Title VII.
33. *Griggs v. Duke Power Company*, 401 U.S. 24 (1971). See also Allan Sindler, *Bakke, DeFunis, and Minority Admissions* (New York: Longman, 1978), 180–89.
34. For a good treatment of these issues, see Charles O. Gregory and Harold A. Katz, *Labor and the Law* (New York: Norton, 1979), chap. 17.
35. In 1970, this act was amended to outlaw for five years literacy tests as a condition for voting in all states.
36. Joint Center for Political Studies, *Black Elected Officials: A National Roster—1988* (Washington, DC: Joint Center for Political Studies Press, 1988), 9–10. For a comprehensive analysis and evaluation of the Voting Rights Act, see Bernard Grofman and Chandler Davidson, eds., *Controversies in Minority Voting: The Voting Rights Act in Perspective* (Washington, DC: Brookings Institution Press, 1992).
37. Ford Fessenden, "Ballots Cast by Blacks and Older Voters Were Tossed in Far Greater Numbers," *New York Times*, November 12, 2001, p. A17.
38. See Douglas S. Massey and Nancy A. Denton, *American Apartheid: Segregation and the Making of the Underclass* (Cambridge, MA: Harvard University Press, 1993), chap. 7.
39. "Countrywide Sued in Race Bias Case," *Los Angeles Times*, July 13, 2007, p. C2.
40. See Jane J. Mansbridge, *Why We Lost the ERA* (Chicago: University of Chicago Press, 1986); and Gilbert Steiner, *Constitutional Inequality* (Washington, DC: Brookings Institution Press, 1985).
41. See *Frontiero v. Richardson*, 411 U.S. 677 (1973).
42. See *Craig v. Boren*, 423 U.S. 1047 (1976).
43. *Franklin v. Gwinnett County Public Schools*, 503 U.S. 60 (1992).
44. Jennifer Halperin, "Women Step Up to Bat," *Illinois Issues* 21 (September 1995): 11–14.
45. Joan Biskupic and David Nakamura, "Court Won't Review Sports Equity Ruling," *Washington Post*, April 22, 1997, p. A1.
46. *U.S. v. Virginia*, 116 S.Ct. 2264 (1996).
47. Judith Havemann, "Two Women Quit Citadel over Alleged Harassment," *Washington Post*, January 13, 1997, p. A1.
48. *Meritor Savings Bank v. Vinson*, 477 U.S. 57 (1986). See also Gwendolyn Mink, *Hostile Environment—The Political Betrayal of Sexually Harassed Women* (Ithaca, NY: Cornell University Press, 2000), 28–32.
49. *Harris v. Forklift Systems, Inc.*, 510 U.S. 17 (1993).
50. *Burlington Industries v. Ellerth*, 118 S.Ct. 2257 (1998); *Faragher v. City of Boca Raton*, 118 S.Ct. 2275 (1998).
51. New Mexico had a different history because not many Anglos settled there initially. ("Anglo" is the term for a non-Hispanic white, generally of European background.) Mexican Americans had considerable power in territorial legislatures between 1865 and 1912. See Lawrence H. Fuchs, *The American Kaleidoscope* (Hanover, NH: University Press of New England, 1990), 239–40.

52. *Salvatierra v. Del Rio Independent School District*, 1931 (Texas).
53. David Montgomery, "A First Class Civil Rights Lesson," *Washington Post*, October 9, 2007, p. C01; *Mendez v. Westminster School District, et al.*, 64 F. Supp. 544 (S.D. Cal. 1946), 64 F. Supp. 544 (D.C.CAL. 1946), http://w3.uchastings.edu/wingate/Mendez%20v.htm (accessed 3/28/08).
54. On La Raza Unida Party, see "La Raza Unida Party and the Chicano Student Movement in California," in *Latinos in the American Political System*, ed. F. Chris Garcia (Notre Dame, IN: University of Notre Dame Press, 1988), 213–35.
55. *United States v. Wong Kim Ark*, 169 U.S. 649 (1898).
56. *Korematsu v. United States*, 323 U.S. 214 (1944).
57. Children of the Camps, http://pbs.org/childofcamp/history/civilact.html (accessed 2/17/08).
58. *Lau v. Nichols*, 414 U.S. 563 (1974).
59. Dick Kirschten, "Not Black and White," *National Journal*, March 2, 1991, p. 497.
60. Anthony Faiola, "States' Immigrant Policies Diverge," *Washington Post*, October 15, 2007, p. A1.
61. Not all Indian tribes agreed with this, including the Navajos. See Ronald Takaki, *A Different Mirror: A History of Multicultural America* (Boston: Little, Brown: 1993), 238–45.
62. On the resurgence of Indian political activity, see Stephen Cornell, *The Return of the Native: American Indian Political Resurgence* (New York: Oxford University Press, 1990); and Dee Brown, *Bury My Heart at Wounded Knee* (New York: Holt, 1971).
63. See the discussion in Robert A. Katzmann, *Institutional Disability: The Saga of Transportation Policy for the Disabled* (Washington, DC: Brookings Institution Press, 1986).
64. For example, after pressure from the Justice Department, one of the nation's largest rental-car companies agreed to make special hand controls available to any customer requesting them. See "Avis Agrees to Equip Cars for Disabled," *Los Angeles Times*, September 2, 1994, p. D1.
65. The case and the interview with Stephen Bokat were reported in Margaret Warner, "Expanding Coverage," *The News-Hour with Jim Lehrer*, July 1, 1998, www.pbs.org/newshour/bb/law/jan-june98/hiv_6-30.html (accessed 2/18/08).
66. *Bowers v. Hardwick*, 478 U.S. 186 (1986).
67. Quoted in Joan Biskupic, "Gay Rights Activists Seek a Supreme Court Test Case," *Washington Post*, December 19, 1993, p. A1.
68. *Romer v. Evans*, 116 S.Ct. 1620 (1996).
69. *Lawrence v. Texas*, 123 S.Ct. 2472 (2003).
70. From Lyndon B. Johnson, *The Vantage Point* (New York: Holt, Rinehart, and Winston, 1971), 166.
71. The Department of Health, Education, and Welfare (HEW) was the cabinet department charged with administering most federal social programs. In 1980, when education programs were transferred to the newly created Department of Education, HEW was renamed the Department of Health and Human Services.
72. *Regents of the University of California v. Bakke*, 438 U.S. 265 (1978).
73. See, for example, *United Steelworkers v. Weber*, 443 U.S. 193 (1979); and *Fullilove v. Klutznick*, 100 S.Ct. 2758 (1980).
74. *Ward's Cove v. Atonio*, 109 S.Ct. 2115 (1989).
75. *Adarand Constructors v. Pena*, 115 S.Ct. 2097 (1995).
76. *Gratz v. Bollinger*, 123 S.Ct. 2411 (2003).
77. *Grutter v. Bollinger*, 123 S.Ct. 2325 (2003).
78. Michael A. Fletcher, "Opponents of Affirmative Action Heartened by Court Decision," *Washington Post*, April 13, 1997, p. A21.
79. See Sam Howe Verhovek, "Houston Vote Underlined Complexity of Rights Issue," *New York Times*, November 6, 1997, p. A1.
80. There are still many genuine racists in America, but with the exception of a lunatic fringe, made up of neo-Nazis and members of the Ku Klux Klan, most racists are too ashamed or embarrassed to take part in normal political discourse. They are not included in either category here.
81. *Slaughterhouse Cases*, 16 Wallace 36 (1873).
82. See Paul M. Sniderman and Edward G. Carmines, *Reaching beyond Race* (Cambridge, MA: Harvard University Press, 1997).

Chapter 6

1. Carol Glynn, et al., *Public Opinion*, 2nd ed. (Boulder, CO: Westview, 2004), 293.
2. Benjamin Ginsberg, *The American Lie: Government by the People and Other Political Fables* (Boulder, CO: Paradigm, 2007), 79.
3. Erika Falk, et al., "Legislative Issue Advertising in the 108th Congress," Annenberg Public Policy Center, March 2005.
4. Morris Fiorina, *Culture War: The Myth of a Polarized America* (New York: Longman, 2005).
5. For a discussion of the political beliefs of Americans, see Harry Holloway and John George, *Public Opinion* (New York: St. Martin's, 1986). See also Paul R. Abramson, *Political Attitudes in America* (San Francisco: Freeman, 1983).
6. See Paul M. Sniderman and Edward G. Carmines, *Reaching beyond Race* (Cambridge, MA: Harvard University Press, 1997).
7. See Angus Campbell et al., *The American Voter* (New York: Wiley, 1960), 147.

8. Richard Morin, "Poll Reflects Division over Simpson Case," *Washington Post*, October 8, 1995, p. A31.
9. Paul Farhi, "Black Media Barons Back Sharpton Bid," *Washington Post*, November 9, 2003, p. A4.
10. "Middle-Class Views in Black and White," *Washington Post*, October 9, 1995, p. A22.
11. For data, see Rutgers University, Eagleton Institute of Politics, Center for the American Woman in Politics, "Sex Differences in Voter Turnout," August 1994.
12. Donald Green, Bradley Palmquist, and Eric Schickler, *Partisan Hearts and Minds: Political Parties and the Social Identities of Voters* (New Haven, CT: Yale University Press, 2002).
13. David S. Broder, "Partisan Gap Is at a High, Poll Finds," *Washington Post*, November 9, 2003, p. A6.
14. Pamela Johnston Conover, "The Role of Social Groups in Political Thinking," *British Journal of Political Science* 18 (1988): 51–78.
15. See Michael C. Dawson, "Structure and Ideology: The Shaping of Black Opinion," paper presented at the annual meeting of the Midwest Political Science Association, Chicago, Illinois, April 7–9, 1995. See also Michael C. Dawson, *Behind the Mule: Race, Class, and African American Politics* (Princeton, NJ: Princeton University Press, 1994).
16. Elisabeth Noelle-Neumann, *The Spiral of Silence* (Chicago: University of Chicago Press, 1984).
17. O. R. Holsti, "A Widening Gap Between the Military and Society? Some Evidence, 1976–1996" *International Security* 23 (Winter 1998–1999): 5–42.
18. Michael X. Delli Carpini and Scott Keeter, *What Americans Know about Politics and Why It Matters* (New Haven, CT: Yale University Press, 1996).
19. For a discussion of the role of information in democratic politics, see Arthur Lupia and Matthew D. McCubbins, *The Democratic Dilemma: Can Citizens Learn What They Need to Know?* (New York: Cambridge University Press, 1998).
20. Larry M. Bartels, "Homer Gets a Tax Cut: Inequality and Public Policy in the American Mind." Paper prepared for presentation at the annual meeting of the American Political Science Association, Philadelphia, August 2003.
21. Sniderman and Carmines, *Reaching beyond Race*, chap. 4.
22. For an interesting discussion of opinion formation, see John Zaller, *The Nature and Origins of Mass Opinion* (New York: Cambridge University Press, 1992).
23. Benjamin Ginsberg, *The American Lie: Government By the People and Other Political Fables* (Boulder, CO: Paradigm, 2007).
24. Gerald F. Seib and Michael K. Frisby, "Selling Sacrifice," *Wall Street Journal*, February 5, 1993, p. 1.
25. Michael K. Frisby, "Clinton Seeks Strategic Edge with Opinion Polls," *Wall Street Journal*, June 24, 1996, p. A16.
26. Joshua Green, "The Other War Room," *Washington Monthly*, April 2002.
27. Peter Marks, "Adept in Politics and Advertising, 4 Women Shape a Campaign," *New York Times*, November 11, 2001, p. B6.
28. See Gillian Peele, *Revival and Reaction* (Oxford, U.K.: Clarendon, 1985). Also see Connie Paige, *The Right-to-Lifers* (New York: Summit, 1983).
29. See David Vogel, "The Power of Business in America: A Reappraisal," *British Journal of Political Science* 13 (January 1983): 19–44.
30. See David Vogel, "The Public Interest Movement and the American Reform Tradition," *Political Science Quarterly* 96 (Winter 1980): 607–27.
31. Jason DeParle, "The Clinton Welfare Bill Begins Trek in Congress," *New York Times*, July 15, 1994, p. 1.
32. Joe Queenan, "Birth of a Notion," *Washington Post*, September 20, 1992, p. C1.
33. Zaller, *The Nature and Origins of Mass Opinion*.
34. See Shanto Iyengar, *Is Anyone Responsible? How Television Frames Political Issues* (Chicago: University of Chicago Press, 1991); and Shanto Iyengar, *Do the Media Govern?* (Thousand Oaks, CA: Sage, 1997).
35. Herbert Asher, *Polling and the Public* (Washington, DC: CQ Press, 2001), 64.
36. Anna Greenberg and Michael Bocian, "Uncertainty in Internet-Based Polling," paper presented at the Annual Meeting of the American Association of Public Opinion Research, 2000.
37. Carl Cannon, "A Pox on Both Our Parties," in David C. Canon et al., eds., *The Enduring Debate*, (New York: Norton, 2000), 389.
38. John Goyder, Keith Warriner, and Susan Miller, "Evaluating Socio-economic Status Bias in Survey Nonresponse," *Journal of Official Statistics* 18, no. 1 (2002).
39. Michael Kagay and Janet Elder, "Numbers Are No Problem for Pollsters, Words Are," *New York Times*, August 9, 1992, p. E6.
40. "Dial S for Smear," *Memphis Commercial Appeal*, September 22, 1996, p. 6B.
41. Amy Keller, "Subcommittee Launches Investigation of Push Polls," *Roll Call*, October 3, 1996, p. 1.
42. For a discussion of the growing difficulty of persuading people to respond to surveys, see John Brehm, *Phantom Respondents* (Ann Arbor: University of Michigan Press, 1993).
43. See Richard Morin, "Is Bush's Bounce a Boom or a Bust?" *Washington Post National Weekly Edition*, August 31–September 6, 1992, p. 37.
44. See Thomas E. Mann and Gary Orren, eds., *Media Polls in American Politics* (Washington, DC: Brookings Institution Press, 1992).
45. For an excellent and reflective discussion by a journalist, see Richard Morin, "Clinton Slide in Survey Shows Perils of Polling," *Washington Post*, August 29, 1992, p. A6.

46. See Michael Traugott, "The Impact of Media Polls on the Public," in *Media Polls in American Politics*, ed. Mann and Orren, 125–49.
47. Benjamin I. Page and Robert Y. Shapiro, "Effects of Public Opinion on Policy," *American Political Science Review* 77 (March 1983): 175–90.
48. Robert A. Erikson, Gerald Wright, and John McIver, *Statehouse Democracy: Public Opinion and Democracy in the American States* (New York: Cambridge University Press, 1994).
49. The results of separate studies by the political scientists Lawrence Jacobs, Robert Shapiro, and Alan Monroe were reported by Richard Morin in "Which Comes First, the Politician or the Poll?" *Washington Post National Weekly Edition*, February 10, 1997, p. 35.
50. David S. Broder, *Democracy Derailed: Initiative Campaigns and the Power of Money* (New York: Harcourt, 2000).
51. Robert Tomsho, "Liberals Take a Cue from Conservatives: This Election, the Left Tries to Make Policy with Ballot Initiatives," *Wall Street Journal*, November 6, 2000, p. A12.

Chapter 7

1. Benjamin Ginsberg and Martin Shefter, *Politics by Other Means* (New York: Basic Books, 1990), 24.
2. Dan Baltz and Anne E. Kornblut, "Public Voice Adds Edge to Debate," *Washington Post*, July 24, 2007, p. 1.
3. Jose Antonio Vargas, "For Candidates, Web Is Power and Poison," *Washington Post*, November 8, 2007, p. A6.
4. Amy Schatz, "BO, UR So Gr8: How a Young Tech Entrepreneur Translated Barack Obama into the Idiom of Facebook," *Wall Street Journal*, May 26, 2007, p. 1.
5. Samantha M. Shapiro, "The Dean Connection," *New York Times Magazine*, December 7, 2003, p. 58.
6. Amy Schatz, "Local Politics, Web Money," *Wall Street Journal*, September 28, 2007, p. A6.
7. Leslie Wayne, "A Fund-Raising Rainmaker Arises Online," *New York Times*, November 29, 2007, p. A22.
8. June Kronholz and Amy Schatz, "How Conservatives Enhanced Online Voice," *Wall Street Journal*, July 3, 2007, p. A5.
9. *Red Lion Broadcasting Company v. FCC*, 395 U.S. 367 (1969).
10. U.S. Census Bureau, *Statistical Abstract of the United States: 2007* (Washington, DC: U.S. Government Printing Office, 2007); "How Much Information? 2003" www2.sims.berkeley.edu/research/projects/how-much-info-2003/broadcast.htm (accessed 2/20/08).
11. For a criticism of the increasing consolidation of the media, see the essays in Patricia Aufderheide et al., *Conglomerates and the Media* (New York: New Press, 1997).
12. See Ben Bagdikian, *The New Media Monopoly* (Boston: Beacon Press, 2004).
13. See Benjamin Ginsberg, *The Captive Public* (New York: Basic Books, 1986).
14. Pew Research Center for the People and the Press, May 2004.
15. University of Connecticut, Department of Public Policy, May 2005.
16. Katherine Q. Seelye, "Citizen-Journalism Project Gains a Voice in the Campaign," *The New York Times*, July 25, 2008, p. A14.
17. *New York Times v. U.S.*, 403 U.S. 713 (1971).
18. Michael Massing, "The Press: The Enemy Within," *New York Review of Books*, December 15, 2005, p. 6.
19. Jim Rutenberg, "Clinton Gets an Instant Chance to Wield a New Weapon," *New York Times*, November 9, 2007, p. A19.
20. See Tom Burnes, "The Organization of Public Opinion," in *Mass Communication and Society*, ed. James Curran (Beverly Hills, CA: Sage, 1979), 44–230. See also David Altheide, *Creating Reality* (Beverly Hills, CA: Sage, 1976).
21. David J. Garrow, *Protest at Selma: Martin Luther King, Jr., and the Voting Rights Act of 1965* (New Haven, CT: Yale University Press, 2001).
22. See Todd Gitlin, *The Whole World Is Watching* (Berkeley: University of California Press, 1980).
23. For a discussion of framing, see Amy Jasperson, et al., "Framing and the Public Agenda," *Political Communication* 15, no. 2 (1998): 205–24.
24. Katherine Q. Seelye, "Obama Plays Convincing Obama in a Skit Mocking Clinton," *New York Times*, November 5, 2007, p. A17.
25. Jim Rutenberg, "Student Paper Upsets the Edwards Camp," *New York Times*, October 27, 2007, p. A13.
26. See Martin Linsky, *Impact: How the Press Affects Federal Policymaking* (New York: Norton, 1986).

Chapter 8

1. Joanne Laucius, "Vote or Die?" *Ottawa Citizen*, November 4, 2004, p. A8.
2. The OnLine News Hour, Generation Next: Speak Up Be Heard, "Iraq, Economy Weigh on Minds of Young Voters," August 31, 2007, www.pbs.org/newshour/generation-next/demographic/youthvote_08-31.html (accessed 2/21/08).
3. For a discussion of the decline of voting turnout over time, see Ruy A. Teixeira, *The Disappearing American Voter* (Washington, DC: Brookings Institution Press, 1992). On the 1994 elections, see Paul Taylor, "Behind the Broom of '94: Wealthier, Educated Voters," *Washington Post*, June 8, 1995, p. A12.

4. Sidney Verba, Kay Lehman Schlozman, and Henry E. Brady, *Voice and Equality: Civic Voluntarism in American Politics* (Cambridge, MA: Harvard University Press, 1995), chap. 3, for kinds of participation, and pp. 66–67 for prevalence of local activity.
5. For a discussion of citizen lobbying, see Jeffrey M. Berry, *The New Liberalism: The Rising Power of Citizen Groups* (Washington, DC: Brookings Institution Press, 1999).
6. Nina Bernstein, "In the Streets, Suddenly, An Immigrant Groundswell," *New York Times*, March 27, 2006, p. 14.
7. Verba, Schlozman, and Brady, *Voice and Equality*, p. 51.
8. Robert Jackman, "Political Institutions and Voter Turnout in the Democracies," *American Political Science Review* 81 (June 1987): 420.
9. See William Julius Wilson, *The Truly Disadvantaged: The Inner City, the Underclass, and Public Policy* (Chicago: University of Chicago Press, 1987); and Douglas Massey and Nancy Denton, *American Apartheid: Segregation and the Making of the American Underclass* (Cambridge, MA: Harvard University Press, 1993).
10. See Michael C. Dawson, *Behind the Mule: Race and Class in African-American Politics* (Princeton, NJ: Princeton University Press, 1994), chaps. 5 and 6.
11. Dawson, *Behind the Mule.*
12. See the discussion in David L. Leal, Matt Barreto, Jongho Lee, and Rodolfo O. de la Garza, "The Latino Vote in the 2004 Election," *PS: Political Science and Politics* 38 (January 2005): 41–49.
13. Pew Hispanic Center, "Latinos and the 2006 Mid-Term Elections, November 27, 2006, http://pewhispanic.org/files/factsheets/26.pdf (accessed 2/21/08).
14. CNN.com, "America Votes, 2006," www.cnn.com/ELECTION/2006/pages/results/states/US/H/00/epolls.0.html (accessed 3/8/08).
15. Anne E. Kornblut, "Bush Plan to Win over Democratic Voters Lags," *Boston Globe* (April 27, 2003), p. A1.
16. CNN.com, "America Votes, 2006."
17. Ronald Browstein, "Response to Terror: The Times Poll," *Los Angeles Times*, November 15, 2001, p. A1.
18. Dan Balz and Jon Cohen, "Majority in Poll Favor Deadline for Iraq Pullout," *Washington Post*, Feburary 27, 2007, p. A1.
19. Gallup Poll, January 2003.
20. Center for American Women and Politics, "Gender Gap in 2004 Presidential Race is Widespread" (November 10, 2004), www.cawp.rutgers.edu/Facts/Elections/GG2004widespread.pdf (accessed 2/22/08).
21. Center for American Women and Politics, "Women in Elective Office 2008," www.cawp.rutgers.edu/Facts.html#elective (accessed 2/22/08).
22. David S. Broder, "Key to Women's Political Parity: Running," *Washington Post*, September 8, 1994, p. A17.
23. Center for American Women and Politics, "The Impact of Women in Public Office: Findings at a Glance" (New Brunswick, NJ: Rutgers University, n.d.).
24. *Engel v. Vitale*, 370 U.S. 421 (1962); *Abington School District v. Schempp*, 374 U.S. 203 (1963); *Roe v. Wade*, 410 U.S. 113 (1973).
25. Laurie Goodstein, "Bush's Charity Plan Is Raising Concerns for Religious Right," *New York Times*, March 3, 2001, p. A1.
26. Mark Hugo Lopez, Karlo Barrios Marcelo, and Emily Hoban Kirby, "Youth Voter Turnout Increases in 2006" (Circle: The Center for Information and Research on Civic Learning and Engagement, June 2007), www.civicyouth.org/PopUps/FactSheets/FS07_2006MidtermCPS.pdf (accessed 2/22/08); and U.S. Census Bureau, "Statistical Abstract of the United States: 2008," Table 404: Voting-Age Population, Percent Reporting Registered, and Voted: 1994 to 2006, www.census.gov/compendia/statab/tables/08s0404.pdf (accessed 4/8/08).
27. Michael DeCourcy Hinds, "Youth Vote 2000: They'd Rather Volunteer," *Carnegie Reporter* 1, no. 2 (Spring 2001): 2.
28. Kristen Oshyn and Tova Andrea Wang, "Issue Brief: Youth Vote 2008," (Century Foundation), www.tcf.org/publications/electionreform/youthvote.pdf (accessed 2/21/08).
29. Hinds, "Youth Vote 2000," p. 3.
30. U.S. Census Bureau, "Statistical Abstract of the United States: 2008," Table 404: Voting-Age Population, Percent Reporting Registered, and Voted: 1994 to 2006.
31. See Richard A. Brody, "The Puzzle of Political Participation in America," in *The New American Political System*, ed. Anthony King (Washington, DC: American Enterprise Institute, 1978), chap. 8.
32. On the nineteenth century, see Michael E. McGerr, *The Decline of Popular Politics: The American North, 1865–1928* (New York: Oxford University Press, 1986).
33. Verba, Schlozman, and Brady, *Voice and Equality.*
34. See Alexis de Tocqueville, *Democracy in America* (New York: Vintage, 1945).
35. Robert D. Putnam, "Bowling Alone: America's Declining Social Capital," *Journal of Democracy* 6, no. 1 (January 1995): 65–78.
36. On television see Robert D. Putnam, "Tuning In, Tuning Out: The Strange Disappearance of Social Capital in America," *PS: Political Science and Politics* 28, no. 4 (December 1995): 664–83; for a reply see Pippa Norris, "Does Television Erode Social Capital? A Reply to Putnam," *PS: Political Science and Politics* 29, no. 3 (September 1996): 474–80.
37. Michael Schudson, "What If Civic Life Didn't Die?" *American Prospect* 25 (March–April 1996): 17–20.
38. Rosenstone and Hansen, *Mobilization, Participation, and Democracy in America*, (New York: Macmillan Pub. Co.; Toronto: Maxwell Macmillan Canada; New York: Maxwell Macmillan International, c1993), 59.

39. Robert A. Jackson, Robert D. Brown, and Gerald C. Wright, "Registration, Turnout and the Electoral Representativeness of U.S. State Electorates," *American Politics Quarterly* 26, no. 3 (July 1998): 259–87. Also, Benjamin Highton, "Easy Registration and Voter Turnout," *Journal of Politics* 59, no. 2 (April 1997): 565–87.
40. Connie Cass, "'Motor Voter' Impact Slight," *Chattanooga News-Free Press*, June 20, 1997, p. A5. On the need to motivate voters see Marshall Ganz, "Motor Voter or Motivated Voter?" *American Prospect*, no. 28 (September–October 1996): 41–49. On the hopes for Motor Voter, see Frances Fox Piven and Richard A. Cloward, "Northern Bourbons: A Preliminary Report on the National Voter Registration Act," *PS: Political Science and Politics* 29, no. 1 (March 1996): 39–42. On turnout in the 1996 election, see Barbara Vobejda, "Just under Half of Possible Voters Went to the Polls," *Washington Post*, November 7, 1996, p. A3.
41. The data in this paragraph are drawn from The Sentencing Project and Human Rights Watch, "Losing the Vote: The Impact of Felony Disfranchisement Laws in the United States" (October 1998), www.sentencingproject.org/tmp/File/FVR/fd_losingthevote.pdf (accessed 2/22/08).
42. Ryan S. King, "A Decade of Reform: Felony Disenfranchisement Policy in the United States" (The Sentencing Project, October 2006), www.sentencingproject.org/Admin/Documents/publications/fd_decade_reform.pdf (accessed 2/21/08).
43. Chris Uggen and Jeffrey Manza, "Democratic Contraction: Political Consequences of Felon Disenfranchisement in the United States," *American Sociological Review 2002* 67, no. 6: 777–803.
44. U.S. Election Assistance Commission, Election Day Survey, www.eac.gov/clearinghouse/2004-election-day-survey/ (accessed 2/22/08).
45. Paul Gronke, Eva Galanes-Rosenbaum, and Peter Miller. "Early Voting and Turnout." *PS: Political Science and Politics* XL, no. 4 (October 2007): 639–45.
46. Lawrence Bobo and Franklin D. Gilliam, "Race, Sociopolitical Participation, and Black Empowerment," *American Political Science Review* 24, no. 2 (June 1990): 377–93.
47. Rosenstone and Hansen, *Mobilization, Participation, and Democracy in America*, 59.
48. Alan S. Gerber and Donald P. Green, "The Effects of Canvassing, Telephone Calls, and Direct Mail on Voter Turnout: A Field Experiment," *The American Political Science Review* 94, no. 3 (September 2000): 660.
49. Donald P. Green and Alan S. Gerber, "Getting Out the Youth Vote: Results from Randomized Field Experiments," December 29, 2001, pp. 26–27, www.youngvoterstrategies.org/index.php?tg=fileman&idx=get&id=1&gr=Y&path=Research&file=Green+-+Getting+Out+the+Youth+Vote%2C+Results+from+Field+Experiments.pdf (accessed 3/8/08).
50. Jared Wadley, "Text Messages Encourage Young Voters to Cast Their Ballots," (University Record Online, September 21, 2007), www.ur.umich.edu/0708/Sept17_07/01.shtml (accessed 2/21/08).
51. Erik Austin and Jerome Chubb, *Political Facts of the United States since 1789* (New York: Columbia University Press, 1986), 378–79.
52. Kenneth N. Weine, "Campaigns without a Human Face," *Washington Post*, October 27, 1996, p. C1; see also Margaret Weir and Marshall Ganz, "Reconnecting People and Politics," in *The New Majority: Toward Popular Progressive Politics*, ed. Stanley B. Greenberg and Theda Skocpol, (New Haven, CT: Yale University Press, 1997), 149–71.
53. *Buckley v. Valeo*, 424 U.S. 1 (1976).
54. Schudson, "What If Civic Life Didn't Die?" p. 18.
55. See Christopher Lasch, *The Revolt of the Elites and the Betrayal of American Democracy* (New York: Norton, 1995). The idea of the "secession of the rich" comes from Robert Reich, *The Work of Nations* (New York: Knopf, 1991), chaps. 23 and 24.

Chapter 9

1. Nicole Gaouette, "Congress Boosts Financial Aid to Students, Takes from Lenders," *Los Angeles Times*, September 8, 2007, p. A1.
2. See Matthew Crenson and Benjamin Ginsberg, *Downsizing Democracy* (Baltimore, MD: Johns Hopkins University Press, 2002).
3. See Morris Fiorina, "Parties and Partisanship: A Forty Year Retrospective," *Political Behavior* 24, no. 2 (June 2002): 93–115.
4. Benjamin Ginsberg, *The Consequences of Consent* (New York: Random House, 1982), chap. 4.
5. For a discussion of third parties in the United States, see Daniel Mazmanian, *Third Parties in Presidential Election* (Washington, DC: Brookings Institution Press, 1974).
6. See Maurice Duverger, *Political Parties* (New York: Wiley, 1954).
7. Glen Justice, "F.E.C. Declines to Curb Independent Fund Raisers," *New York Times*, May 14, 2004, p. A16.
8. Jim Rutenberg and David D. Kirkpatrick, "A New Channel for Soft Money Appears in Race," *New York Times*, November 12, 2007, p. A1.
9. See Harold Gosnell, *Machine Politics Chicago Model*, rev. ed. (Chicago: University of Chicago Press, 1968).
10. For a useful discussion, see John Bibby and Thomas Holbrook, "Parties and Elections," in *Politics in the American States*, ed. Virginia Gray and Herbert Jacob (Washington, DC: Congressional Quarterly Press, 1996), 78–121.
11. Kyle L. Saunders and Alan I. Abramowitz, "Ideological Realignment and Active Partisans in the American Electorate," *American Politics Research* 32 (May 2004): 285–309.

12. John C. Green, "Religion and the Presidential Vote: A Tale of Two Gaps" (Pew Forum on Religion and Public Life, August, 21, 2007), www.pewforum.org/docs/?DocID=240 (accessed 2/24/08).
13. Christopher Shea, "Who Are You Calling Working Class?" *Boston Globe*, February 12, 2006, www.boston.com/news/globe/ideas/articles/2006/02/12/who_are_you_calling_working_class/ (accessed 2/24/08).
14. For an excellent analysis of the parties' role in recruitment, see Paul Herrnson, *Congressional Elections: Campaigning at Home and in Washington* (Washington, DC: CQ Press, 1995).
15. Duverger, *Political Parties*, 426.
16. Duverger, *Political Parties*, chap. 1.
17. Stanley Kelley, Jr., Richard E. Ayres, and William Bowen, "Registration and Voting: Putting First Things First," *American Political Science Review* 61 (June 1967): 359–70.
18. David H. Fischer, *The Revolution of American Conservatism* (New York: Harper & Row, 1965), 93.
19. Fischer, *The Revolution of American Conservatism*, 109.
20. Henry Jones Ford, *The Rise and Growth of American Politics* (1898 reprint; New York: Da Capo Press, 1967 edition), chap. 9.
21. Ford, *The Rise and Growth of American Politics*, 125.
22. Ford, *The Rise and Growth of American Politics*, 125.
23. Ford, *The Rise and Growth of American Politics*, 126.

Chapter 10

1. *League of United Latin American Citizens v. Wilson*, CV-94-7569 (C.D. Calif. 1995).
2. *Gray v. Sanders*, 372 U.S. 368 (1963); *Wesberry v. Sanders*, 376 U.S. 1 (1964); *Reynolds v. Sims*, 377 U.S. 533 (1964).
3. *Thornburg v. Gingles*, 478 U.S. 613 (1986).
4. *Shaw v. Reno*, 509 U.S. 113 (1993).
5. State legislatures determine the system by which electors are selected. Almost all states use this "winner-take-all" system. Maine and Nebraska, however, provide that one electoral vote goes to the winner in each congressional district and two electoral votes go to the winner statewide.
6. Stephen Ansolabehere and James Snyder, "Campaign War Chests and Congressional Elections," *Business and Politics* 2 (2000): 9–34.
7. Gary W. Cox and Eric Magar, "How Much Is Majority Status in the U.S. Congress Worth?" *American Political Science Review* 93 (1999): 299–309.
8. Howard Kurtz, "Presidential Ad Wars Heat Up," *Washington Post*, September 20, 2007, p. A4.
9. Amy Schatz, "BO,URSoGr8," *Wall Street Journal*, May 26, 2007.
10. M. Ostrogorski, *Democracy and the Organization of Political Parties* (New York: Macmillan, 1902).
11. Timothy Clark, "The RNC Prospers, the DNC Struggles as They Face the 1980 Election," *National Journal*, October 27, 1980, 1619.
12. For discussions of the consequences, see Thomas Edsall, *The New Politics of Inequality* (New York: Norton, 1984). Also see Thomas Edsall, "Both Parties Get the Company's Money—But the Boss Backs the GOP," *Washington Post*, National Weekly Edition, September 16, 1986, p. 14; and Benjamin Ginsberg, "Money and Power: The New Political Economy of American Elections," in *The Political Economy*, ed. Thomas Ferguson and Joel Rogers (Armonk, NY: M. E. Sharpe, 1984).
13. Leslie Wayne, "A Fund-Raising Rainmaker Arises Online," *New York Times*, November 29, 2007, p. A22.
14. Michael Luo and Jeff Zeleny, "Straining to Reach Money Goal, Obama Presses Donors" *New York Times*, September 9, 2008, p. 1.

Chapter 11

1. John M. Broder, "Senate Approves Energy Bill Without Tax Increase," *New York Times*, December 13, 2007, p. 1.
2. Clinton Rossiter, ed., *The Federalist Papers* (New York: New American Library, 1961), No. 10, p. 83.
3. Rossiter, ed., *Federalist Papers*, No. 10.
4. The best statement of the pluralist view is in David Truman, *The Governmental Process* (New York: Knopf, 1951), chap. 2.
5. Betsy Wagner and David Bowermaster, "B.S. Economics," *Washington Monthly*, (November 1992): 19–21.
6. Truman, *The Governmental Process*.
7. Mancur Olson, *The Logic of Collective Action* (Cambridge, MA: Harvard University Press, 1965).
8. Timothy Penny and Steven Schier, *Payment Due: A Nation in Debt, a Generation in Trouble* (Boulder, CO: Westview, 1996), 64–65.
9. Kay Lehman Schlozman and John T. Tierney, *Organized Interests and American Democracy* (New York: Harper & Row, 1986), 60.
10. John Herbers, "Special Interests Gaining Power as Voter Disillusionment Grows," *New York Times*, November 14, 1978.
11. Erika Falk, Erin Grizard, and Gordon McDonald, "Legislative Issue Advertising in the 108th Congress: Pluralism or Peril?" *Harvard International Journal of Press/Politics* 11, no. 4 (Fall 2006): 148–64, http://hij.sagepub.com/cgi/reprint/11/4/148 (accessed 3/2/08).
12. Jeffrey Birnbaum, "The Road to Riches Is Called K Street," *Washington Post*, June 22, 2005, p. 1.

13. For discussions of lobbying, see Allan J. Cigler and Burdett A. Loomis, eds., *Interest Group Politics* (Washington, DC: Congressional Quarterly Press, 1983). See also Jeffrey M. Berry, *Lobbying for the People* (Princeton, NJ: Princeton University Press, 1977).
14. "The Swarming Lobbyists," *Time*, August 7, 1978, p. 15.
15. See Frank Baumgartner and Beth Leech, *Basic Interests* (Princeton, NJ: Princeton University Press, 1998).
16. Steven Brill, *After: How America Confronted the September 12 Era* (New York: Simon & Schuster, 2003).
17. Daniel Franklin, "Tommy Boggs and the Death of Health Care Reform," *Washington Monthly* (April 1995): 36.
18. Marie Jojnacki, "Interest Groups' Decisions to Join Alliances or Work Alone," *American Journal of Political Science* 41 (1997): 61–87; Kevin W. Hula, *Lobbying Together: Interest Groups Coalitions in Legislative Politics* (Washington, DC: Georgetown University Press, 1999).
19. Peter H. Stone, "Follow the Leaders," *National Journal*, June 24, 1995, p. 1641.
20. "The Microsoft Playbook: A Report from Common Cause," www.commoncause.org, September 25, 2000.
21. Michael Barbaro, "A New Weapon for Wal-Mart: A War Room," *New York Times*, November 1, 2005, p. 1.
22. "Edison Electric Institute Lobbying to Weaken Toxic Mercury Standards," http://tristatenews.com, February 28, 2003.
23. John P. Heinz et al., *The Hollow Core: Private Interests in National Policy Making* (Cambridge, MA: Harvard University Press, 1993).
24. For an excellent discussion of the political origins of the Administrative Procedure Act, see Martin Shapiro, "APA: Past, Present, Future," 72 *Virginia Law Review* 377 (March 1986): 447–92.
25. David Kirkpatrick, "Congress Finds Ways of Avoiding Lobbyist Limits," *Washington Post*, February 11, 2007, p. 1.
26. *Roe v. Wade*, 93 S.Ct. 705 (1973).
27. *Webster v. Reproductive Health Services*, 109 S.Ct. 3040 (1989).
28. *Brown v. Board of Education of Topeka, Kansas*, 74 S.Ct. 686 (1954).
29. See, for example, *Duke Power Co. v. Carolina Environmental Study Group*, 438 U.S. 59 (1978).
30. E. Pendleton Herring, *Group Representation before Congress* (New York: McGraw-Hill, 1936).
31. Michael Weisskopf, "Energized by Pulpit or Passion, the Public Is Calling," *Washington Post*, February 1, 1993, p. 1.
32. Julia Preston, "Grass Roots Roared and Immigration Bill Collapsed," *New York Times*, June 10, 2007, p. 1.
33. Jane Fritsch, "The Grass Roots, Just a Free Phone Call Away," *New York Times*, June 23, 1995, pp. A1, A22.
34. Richard L. Burke, "Religious-Right Candidates Gain as GOP Turnout Rises," *New York Times*, November 12, 1994, p. 10.
35. Some Americans and even more Europeans would stress only the negative aspect of the softening and adulterating effect of the two-party system on class and other basic subdivisions of society. For a discussion of how the working class was divided and softened, with native workers joining the Democratic Party and new immigrant workers becoming Republicans, see Gwendolyn Mink, *Old Labor and New Immigrants in American Political Development: Union, Party, and State, 1875–1920* (Ithaca, NY: Cornell University Press, 1986).
36. Elisabeth R. Gerber, *The Populist Paradox* (Princeton, NJ: Princeton University Press, 1999).
37. Rossiter, ed., *The Federalist Papers*, No. 10.
38. Olson, *The Logic of Collective Action*.

Chapter 12

1. See Mildred L. Amer, "Membership of the 110th Congress: A Profile," CRS Report RS22555, December 15, 2006.
2. See Amer, "Membership of the 110th Congress."
3. Amer, "Membership of the 110th Congress."
4. For a discussion, see Benjamin Ginsberg, *The Consequences of Consent* (New York: Random House, 1982), chap. 1.
5. For some interesting empirical evidence, see Angus Campbell, Philip Converse, Warren Miller, and Donald Stokes, *Elections and the Political Order* (New York: Wiley, 1966), chap. 11.
6. Congressional Management Foundation, "Communicating with Congress Conference," October 2007, www.cmfweborg/index.php?option=com_content&task=view&id=230 (accessed 3/5/08).
7. John S. Saloma, *Congress and the New Politics* (Boston: Little, Brown, 1969), 184–85. A 1977 official report using less detailed categories came up with almost the same impression of Congress's workload. Commission on Administrative Review, *Administrative Reorganization and Legislative Management*, House Doc. #95-232 (September 28, 1977), vol. 2, esp. pp. 17–19.
8. See Linda Fowler and Robert McClure, *Political Ambition: Who Decides to Run for Congress* (New Haven, CT: Yale University Press, 1989); and Alan Ehrenhalt, *The United States of Ambition: Politicians, Power, and the Pursuit of Office* (New York: Three Rivers Press, 1992).
9. See Barbara C. Burrell, *A Woman's Place Is in the House: Campaigning for Congress in the Feminist Era* (Ann Arbor: University of Michigan Press, 1994), chap. 6; and the essays in Elizabeth Adell Cook, Sue Thomas, and Clyde Wilcox, eds., *The Year of the Woman: Myths and Realities* (Boulder, CO: Westview, 1994).
10. Joe Hallett, "Kilroy Vs. Pryce: Can Grass Roots Withstand the Big Pull for Change?" *Columbus Dispatch*, October 23, 2005, p. 7C.

11. Michael Leahy, "House Rules," Washington Post, June 10, 2007, p. W12.
12. See Burrell, *A Woman's Place Is in the House*; and David Broder, "Key to Women's Political Parity: Running," *Washington Post*, September 8, 1994, p. A17.
13. "Did Redistricting Sink the Democrats?" *National Journal*, December 17, 1994, p. 2984.
14. *Miller v. Johnson*, 115 S.Ct. 2475 (1995).
15. Tom Hamburger and Richard Simon, "Everybody Will Know If It's Pork," *Los Angeles Times*, January 6, 2007, p. A1
16. Marilyn W. Thompson and Ron Nixon, "Even Cut 50%, Earmarks Clog a Military Bill," *New York Times*, November 4, 2007, p. A1.
17. Timothy Eagan, "Built with Steel, Perhaps, But Greased with Pork," *New York Times*, April 10, 2004, p. A1.
18. Congressman Pete Stark, "Constituent Services: Federal Grants," www.house.gov/stark/webarchives/Stark%20Web%20Page/services/grants.html (accessed 3/5/08).
19. Kelly McCormack, "Private Bills," *The Hill*, May 9, 2007, http://thehill.com/cover-stories/private-bills-2007-05-08.html (accessed 3/20/08).
20. Richard Fenno, Jr., *Home Style: House Members in Their Districts* (Boston: Little, Brown, 1978).
21. Edward Epstein, "Pelosi Proud of Dems' Work in First 100 Days," *San Francisco Chronicle*, March 29, 2007, p. A1.
22. Carl Hulse, "In Conference: Process Undone By Partisanship," *New York Times*, September 26, 2007, p. A1.
23. Derek Willis, "Republicans Mix It Up When Assigning House Chairmen for the 108th," *Congressional Quarterly Weekly*, January 11, 2003, p. 89.
24. Rebecca Kimitch, "CQ Guide to the Committees: Democrats Opt to Spread the Power," CQ *Weekly*, April 16, 2007, p. 1080.
25. Richard E. Cohen, "Crackup of the Committees," *National Journal*, July 31, 1999, pp. 2210–16.
26. David W. Rhode, "Committees and Policy Formulation," in *Institutions of American Democracy: The Legislative Branch*, ed. Paul J. Quirk and Sarah A. Binder (New York: Oxford University Press, 2005), 201–23.
27. See Robert Pear, "Senator X Kills Measure on Anonymity," *New York Times*, November 11, 1997, p. 12.
28. Jonathan Weisman, "House Votes 411–18 to Pass Ethics Overhaul," *Washington Post*, August 1, 2007, p. A1.
29. Manu Raju, "Ensign Scrambles to Explain Objections to Disclosure Bill, *The Hill*, September 26, 2007, p. 4.
30. See John W. Kingdon, *Congressmen's Voting Decisions* (New York: Harper & Row, 1973), chap. 3; and R. Douglas Arnold, *The Logic of Congressional Action* (New Haven, CT: Yale University Press, 1990).
31. Jane Fritsch, "The Grass Roots, Just a Free Phone Call Away," *New York Times*, June 23, 1995, p. A1.
32. Holly Idelson, "Signs Point to Greater Loyalty on Both Sides of the Aisle," *Congressional Quarterly Weekly Report*, December 19, 1992, p. 3849.
33. "GOP Leadership PACs' Fundraising Far Outstrips 1997–98," *Congressional Quarterly Weekly Report*, August 15, 1999, p. 1991.
34. Kimitch, "CQ Guide to the Committees," p. 1080.
35. Leahy, "House Rules," p. W12.
36. James J. Kilpatrick, "Don't Overlook Corn for Porn Plot," *Chicago Sun-Times*, January 3, 1992, p. 23.
37. Dennis McDougal, "Cattle Are Bargaining Chip of the NEA," *Los Angeles Times*, November 2, 1991, p. F1.
38. Susan Milligan, "Congress Reduces Its Oversight Role; Since Clinton, a Change in Focus," *Boston Globe*, November 20, 2005, p. A1; Bill Shaikin, "Clemens is Star Attraction at Hearing," *Lost Angeles Times*, February 12, 2008, p. D1.
39. Elizabeth Williamson, "Revival of Oversight Role Sought; Congress Hires More Investigators, Plans Subpeonas," *Washington Post*, April 25, 2007, p. A1.
40. Thomas E. Mann, Molly Reynolds, and Peter Hoey, "A New, Improved Congress?" *New York Times*, August 26, 2007, p. 11.
41. Williamson, "Revival of Oversight Role Sought."
42. *United States v. Pink*, 315 U.S. 203 (1942). For a good discussion of the problem, see James W. Davis, *The American Presidency* (New York: Harper & Row, 1987), chap. 8.
43. Carroll J. Doherty, "Impeachment: How It Would Work," *Congressional Quarterly Weekly Report*, January 31, 1998, p. 222.
44. See Kenneth A. Shepsle, "Representation and Governance: The Great Legislative Trade-off," *Political Science Quarterly* 103:3 (1988): 461–84.
45. Role of the Public in Government Decisions Survey, January 1999, Roper Center Public Opinion Online, Accession number 0325495; Role of the Public in Government Decisions Survey, January 1999, Roper Center Public Opinion Online, Accession number 0325490.
46. John R. Hibbing and Elizabeth Theiss-Morse, *Congress as Public Enemy: Public Attitudes toward American Political Institutions* (New York: Cambridge University Press, 1996), 105.
47. Jeanne Cummings, "Lobbying Lucre Awaits Lott," *Politico*, November 27, 2007, www.politico.com/news/stories/1107/7051.html (accessed 3/4/08).
48. Larry M. Bartels, "Economic Inequality and Political Representation" (unpublished paper, Department of Politics and Woodrow Wilson School of Public and International Affairs, Princeton University, November 2002).

Chapter 13

1. *In re Neagle*, 135 U.S. 1 (1890).
2. James G. Randall, *Constitutional Problems under Lincoln* (New York: Appleton, 1926), chap. 1.
3. Edward S. Corwin, *The President: Office and Powers*, 4th rev. ed. (New York: New York University Press, 1957), 229.
4. These statutes are contained mainly in Title 10 of the United States Code, Sections 331, 332, and 333.
5. The best study covering all aspects of the domestic use of the military is that of Adam Yarmolinsky, *The Military Establishment* (New York: Harper & Row, 1971). Probably the most famous instance of a president's unilateral use of the power to protect a state "against domestic violence" was in dealing with the Pullman Strike of 1894. The famous Supreme Court case that ensued was *In re Debs*, 158 U.S. 564 (1895).
6. In *United States v. Pink*, 315 U.S. 203 (1942), the Supreme Court confirmed that an executive agreement is the legal equivalent of a treaty, despite the absence of Senate approval. This case approved the executive agreement that was used to establish diplomatic relations with the Soviet Union in 1933. An executive agreement, not a treaty, was used in 1940 to exchange "fifty over-age destroyers" for ninety-nine-year leases on some important military bases.
7. A third source of presidential power is implied from the provision for "faithful execution of the laws." This is the president's power to impound funds—that is, to refuse to spend money Congress has appropriated for certain purposes. One author referred to this as a "retroactive veto power" (Robert E. Goosetree, "The Power of the President to Impound Appropriated Funds," *American University Law Review*, January 1962). This impoundment power was used freely and to considerable effect by many modern presidents, and Congress occasionally delegated such power to the president by statute. But in reaction to the Watergate scandal, Congress adopted the Budget and Impoundment Control Act of 1974 and designed this act to circumscribe the president's ability to impound funds by requiring that the president must spend all appropriated funds unless both houses of Congress consent to an impoundment within forty-five days of a presidential request. Therefore, since 1974, the use of impoundment has declined significantly. Presidents have had either to bite their tongues and accept unwanted appropriations or to revert to the older and more dependable but politically limited method of vetoing the entire bill.
8. For a different perspective, see William F. Grover, *The President as Prisoner: A Structural Critique of the Carter and Reagan Years* (Albany: State University of New York Press, 1988).
9. For more on the veto, see Chapter 13 and Robert J. Spitzer, *The Presidential Veto: Touchstone of the American Presidency* (Albany: State University of New York Press, 1989).
10. For a good review of President Clinton's legislative leadership in the first session of his last Congress, see *Congressional Quarterly Weekly*, November 13, 1999, especially the cover story by Andrew Taylor, "Clinton Gives Republicans a Gentler Year-End Beating," pp. 2698–2700.
11. Kenneth F. Warren, *Administrative Law*, 3rd ed. (Upper Saddle River, NJ: Prentice Hall, 1996), 250.
12. Theodore J. Lowi, *The End of Liberalism*, 2nd ed. (New York: Norton, 1979), 117–18.
13. *J. W. Hampton & Co. v. U.S.*, 276 U.S. 394 (1928).
14. 48 Stat. 200.
15. David Schoenbrod, *Power without Responsibility: How Congress Abuses the People through Delegation* (New Haven, CT: Yale University Press, 1993), 49–50.
16. Lowi, *The End of Liberalism*, 117.
17. Adam Clymer, "The Transition: Push for Diversity May Cause Reversal on Interior Secretary," *New York Times*, December 23, 1992, p. 1.
18. A substantial portion of this section is taken from Theodore J. Lowi, *The Personal President* (Ithaca, NY: Cornell University Press, 1985), 141–50.
19. All the figures since 1967, and probably 1957, are understated, because additional White House staff members were on "detail" service from the military and other departments (some secretly assigned) and are not counted here because they were not on the White House payroll.
20. The actual number is difficult to estimate because, as with White House staff, some EOP personnel, especially in national security work, are detailed to EOP from outside agencies.
21. Article I, Section 3, provides that "The Vice-President . . . shall be President of the Senate, but shall have no Vote, unless they be equally divided." This is the only vote the vice president is allowed.
22. Samuel Kernell, *Going Public: New Strategies of Presidential Leadership*, 3rd ed. (Washington, DC: Congressional Quarterly Press, 1997); also, Jeffrey K. Tulis, *The Rhetorical Presidency* (Princeton, NJ: Princeton University Press, 1987).
23. Tulis, *The Rhetorical Presidency*, 91.
24. Sidney M. Milkis, *The President and the Parties* (New York: Oxford, 1993), 97.
25. James MacGregor Burns, *Roosevelt: The Lion and the Fox* (New York: Harcourt, Brace, 1956), 317.
26. Burns, *Roosevelt*, 317.
27. Kernell, *Going Public*, 79.
28. Tulis, *The Rhetorical Presidency*, 161.
29. Lowi, *The Personal President*.
30. Lowi, *The Personal President*, 11.
31. Kernell, *Going Public*, 114.
32. Harold W. Stanley and Richard G. Niemi, *Vital Statistics on American Politics, 2001–2002* (Washington, DC: Congressional Quarterly Press, 2001), 250–51.
33. Milkis, *The President and the Parties*, 128.

34. Milkis, *The President and the Parties*, 160.
35. The classic critique of this process is Theodore J. Lowi, *The End of Liberalism* (New York: Norton, 1969).
36. Kenneth Culp Davis, *Administrative Law Treatise* (St. Paul: West Publishing, 1958), 9.
37. Elena Kagan, "Presidential Administration," 114 *Harvard Law Review 2245* (2001): 2265.
38. For example, Douglas W. Kmiec, "Expanding Power," in Roger Pilon, ed., *The Rule of Law in the Wake of Clinton* (Washington, DC: Cato Institute Press, 2000), 47–68.
39. A complete inventory is provided in Harold C. Relyea, "Presidential Directives: Background and Review," Congressional Research Service Report 98–611 (Washington, DC: Library of Congress, November 9, 2001).
40. Terry M. Moe and William G. Howell, "The Presidential Power of Unilateral Action," *Journal of Law, Economics and Organization*, 15, no. 1 (January 1999): 133–34.
41. Moe and Howell, "The Presidential Power of Unilateral Action," 164.
42. *Youngstown Sheet & Tube Co. v. Sawyer*, 346 U.S. 579 (1952).
43. Todd Gaziano, "The New 'Massive Resistance,'" *Policy Review* (May–June 1998): 283.
44. Kagan, "Presidential Administration," p. 2351.
45. Alexander Hamilton, James Madison, and John Jay, *The Federalist Papers*, ed. Clinton Rossiter (New York: New American Library, 1961), No. 70, 423–30.
46. Terry Moe, "The Presidency and the Bureaucracy: The Presidential Advantage," in Michael Nelson, ed., *The Presidency and the Political System* (Washington, DC: Congressional Quarterly Press, 2002), 416–20.

Chapter 14

1. U.S. Census Bureau, "Statistical Abstract of the United States, 2006," Table 482: Federal Civilian Employment and Annual Payroll by Branch: 1970 to 2006, www.census.gov/compendia/statab/tables/08s0482.pdf (accessed 3/11/08); Table 498: Department of Defense Personnel: 1960 to 2006, www.census.gov/compendia/statab/tables/08s0498.pdf (accessed 3/11/08).
2. Arnold Brecht and Comstock Glaser, *The Art and Techniques of Administration in German Ministries* (Cambridge, MA: Harvard University Press, 1940), 6.
3. OMB Watch, "Congress Hears Pleas for Expanded Authority and Resources at CPSC" (September 25, 2007), www.ombwatch.org/article/articleview/3990 (accessed 3/8/08).
4. Gary Bryner, Bureaucratic Discretion (New York: Pergamon, 1987).
5. This account is drawn from Alan Stone, *How America Got On-Line: Politics, Markets, and the Revolution in Telecommunications* (Armonk, NY: M. E. Sharpe, 1997), 184–87.
6. There are historical reasons that American cabinet-level administrators are called "secretaries." During the Second Continental Congress and the subsequent confederal government, standing committees were formed to deal with executive functions related to foreign affairs, military and maritime issues, and public financing. The heads of those committees were called "secretaries" because their primary task was to handle all correspondence and documentation related to their areas of responsibility.
7. David Johnston, "Bush Intervened in Dispute over N.S.A. Eavesdropping," *New York Times*, May 16, 2007, p. A1; Scott Shane, David Johnston, and James Risen, "Secret U.S. Endorsement of Severe Interrogations," *New York Times*, October 4, 2007, p. A1.
8. Rob Margetta, "Homeland Security for Hire," *Congressional Quarterly Weekly*, November 12, 2007, pp. 3392–99, http://library.cqpress.com/cqweekly/weeklyreport 110-000002625610 (accessed 11/14/07).
9. For more detail, consult John E. Harr, *The Professional Diplomat* (Princeton, NJ: Princeton University Press, 1972), 11; and Nicholas Horrock, "The CIA Has Neighbors in the 'Intelligence Community,'" *New York Times*, June 29, 1975, sec. 4, p. 2. See also Morton H. Halperin and Priscilla Clapp, with Arnold Kanter, *Bureaucratic Politics and Foreign Policy*, 2nd ed. (Washington, DC: Brookings Institution Press, 2007).
10. *The 9/11 Commission Report: Final Report of the National Commission on Terrorist Attacks upon the United States* (New York: Norton, 2004).
11. David E. Sanger and Steven Lee Myers, "Notes from Secret Iran Talks Led to U.S. Reversal," *New York Times*, December 7, 2007, p. 4.
12. Mark Mazzetti, "New Data, New Methods, New Conclusion," *New York Times*, December 5, 2007, p. 12; Peter Baker and Dafna Linzer, "Diving Deep, Unearthing a Surprise," *Washington Post*, December 8, 2007, p. A9; Jon Ward, "NIE Authors Accused of Partisan Politics," *Washington Times*, December 7, 2007, p. A1.
13. Daniel Patrick Moynihan, "The Culture of Secrecy," *Public Interest*, (Summer 1997): 55–71.
14. The total number of FOIA requests includes 18,691,031 from the Social Security Administration; all other agencies combined reported 2,721,540 requests. See the U.S. Department of Justice, Office of Information and Privacy, FOIA Post, "Summary of Annual FOIA Reports for Fiscal Year 2006" www.usdoj.gov/oip.foiapost/2007foiapost11.htm#fl (accessed 3/28/08).
15. Dana Milbank, "Under Bush, Expanding Secrecy," *Washington Post*, December 23, 2003, p. A19.

16. "White House to Appeal Visitor Log Ruling," *San Francisco Chronicle*, December 20, 2007, www.sfgate.com/cgi-bin/article.cgi?f=/n/a/2007/12/17/national/w100931S95.DTL (accessed 12/28/07).
17. See Paul Peterson, *The Price of Federalism* (Washington, DC: Brookings Institution Press, 1995) for a recent argument that "redistribution" is the distinctive function of the national government in the American federal system.
18. U.S. Department of the Treasury, "The Debt to the Penny and Who Holds It," www.treasurydirect.gov/NP/BPDLogin?application=np (accessed 8/6/08). This figure does not include the "intragovernmental holdings," which include the debts in government accounts. This debt has little impact on the overall economy. The total national debt, including intragovernmental holdings, was $9.6 trillion in 2008.
19. For an excellent political analysis of the Fed, see Donald Kettl, *Leadership at the Fed* (New Haven, CT: Yale University Press, 1986).
20. George E. Berkley, *The Craft of Public Administration* (Boston: Allyn & Bacon, 1975), 417 (emphasis added).
21. Eric Schmitt, "Washington Talk: No $435 Hammers, but Questions," *New York Times*, October 23, 1990, p. A16.
22. Vice President Gore's National Partnership for Reinventing Government, "Appendix F, History of the National Partnership for Reinventing Government Accomplishments, 1993–2000, A Summary," http://govinfo.library.unt.edu/npr/whoweare/appendixf.html (accessed 3/28/08).
23. Paul C. Light, "The New True Size of Government," Organizational Performance Initiative, Research Brief no. 2, Wagner School of Public Service, New York University, http://wagner.nyu.edu/performance/files/True_Size.pdf (accessed 3/11/08).
24. Light, "The New True Size of Government," p. 8.
25. A thorough review of the first session of the 104th Congress will be found in "Republican's Hopes for 1996 Lie in Unfinished Business," *Congressional Quarterly Weekly Report*, January 6, 1996, pp. 6–18.
26. Public Law 101-510, Title XXIX, Sections 2,901 and 2,902 of Part A (Defense Base Closure and Realignment Commission).
27. Scott Shane and Ron Nixon, "In Washington, Contractors Take on Biggest Role Ever," *New York Times*, February 4, 2007, p. A1.
28. Shane and Nixon, "In Washington, Contractors Take on Biggest Role Ever."
29. Matt Kelly, "GAO challenges $150B Contract Awarded By Army," *USA Today*, November 30, 2007, p. 5A.
30. Steve Fainaru, "Warnings Unheeded on Guards in Iraq," *Washington Post*, December 24, 2007, p. A1.
31. Committee on Oversight and Government Reform, Hearings on Blackwater USA, preliminary transcript, October 2, 2007, http://oversight.house.gov/documents/20071127131151.pdf (accessed 3/10/08).
32. Committee on Oversight and Government Reform, Hearings on Blackwater USA.
33. Shane and Nixon, "In Washington, Contractors Take on Biggest Role Ever."
34. Shane and Nixon, "In Washington, Contractors Take on Biggest Role Ever."
35. Walter Pincus, "Conferees Want a Hard Look at Contractors," *Washington Post*, December 17, 2007, p. A19.
36. Alexander Hamilton, James Madison, and John Jay, *The Federalist Papers*, ed. Clinton Rossiter (New York: New American Library, 1961), No. 51, 322.
37. The title of this section was inspired by Peri Arnold, *Making the Managerial Presidency* (Princeton, NJ: Princeton University Press, 1986).
38. See Richard Nathan, *The Plot that Failed: Nixon and the Administrative Presidency* (New York: Wiley, 1975), 68–76.
39. For more details and evaluations, see David Rosenbloom, *Public Administration* (New York: Random House, 1986), 186–221; Charles H. Levine with the assistance of Rosslyn S. Kleeman, *The Quiet Crisis of the Civil Service: The Federal Personnel System at the Crossroads* (Washington, DC: National Academy of Public Administration, 1986).
40. Lester Salamon and Alan Abramson, "Governance: The Politics of Retrenchment," in *The Reagan Record*, ed. John Palmer and Isabel Sawhill (Cambridge, MA: Ballinger, 1984), 40.
41. Colin Campbell, "The White House and the Presidency under the 'Let's Deal' President," in *The Bush Presidency: First Appraisals*, ed. Colin Campbell and Bert A. Rockman (Chatham, NJ: Chatham House, 1991), 185–222.
42. See John Micklethwait, "Managing to Look Attractive," *New Statesman* 125, November 8, 1996, p. 24.
43. Andrew C. Revkin, "Calls for Openness at NASA Add to Reports of Pressure," *New York Times*, February 16, 2006, p. 20.
44. Juliet Eilperin, "Sen. Boxer Seeks Answers on Redacted Testimony," *Washington Post*, October 25, 2007, p. A2.
45. Quoted in I. M. Destler, "Reagan and the World: An 'Awesome Stubbornness,'" in *The Reagan Legacy: Promise and Performance*, ed. Charles O. Jones (Chatham, NJ: Chatham House, 1988), 244, 257. The source of the quote is *Report of the President's Special Review Board* (Washington, DC: U.S. Government Printing Office, 1987).
46. Thomas E. Mann and Norman J. Ornstein, *The Broken Branch: How Congress is Failing America and How to Get It Back on Track* (New York: Oxford University Press, 2006), 155.
47. Thomas E. Mann, Sarah A. Binder, and Molly Reynolds, "Is the Broken Branch on the Mend? An Early Report on the 110th Congress," Mending the Broken Branch Project,

no. 1 (Washington, DC: Brookings Institution Press, October 2007), 11–12, www.brookings.edu/~/media/Files/rc/papers/2007/0904governance_mann/0904governance_mann.pdf (accessed 3/11/08).

48. See Aaron Wildavsky, *The New Politics of the Budgetary Process*, 2nd ed. (New York: HarperCollins, 1992), 15–16.

49. The Office of Technology Assessment (OTA) was a fourth research agency serving Congress until 1995. It was one of the first agencies scheduled for elimination by the 104th Congress. Until 1983, Congress had still another tool of legislative oversight: the legislative veto. Each agency operating under such provisions was obliged to submit to Congress every proposed decision or rule, which would then lie before both chambers for thirty to sixty days. If Congress took no action by one-house or two-house resolution explicitly to veto the proposed measure during the prescribed period, it became law. The legislative veto was declared unconstitutional by the Supreme Court in 1983 on the grounds that it violated the separation of powers—the resolutions Congress passed to exercise its veto were not subject to presidential veto, as required by the Constitution. See *Immigration and Naturalization Service v. Chadha*, 462 U.S. 919 (1983).

Chapter 15

1. *Morse v. Frederick*, No. 06-278 (2007).
2. Charles Lane, "Court Backs School On Speech Curbs," *Washington Post*, June 26, 2007, p. A6.
3. U.S. Bureau of the Census, *Statistical Abstract of the United States* (Washington, DC: Government Printing Office, 2008).
4. Linda Greenhouse, "In Steps Big and Small the Supreme Court Moved Right," *New York Times*, July 1, 2007, p. 1.
5. *Marbury v. Madison*, 1 Cr. 137 (1803).
6. *Clinton v. City of New York*, 55 U.S.L.W. 4543 (1998).
7. *Federal Election Commission v. Wisconsin Right to Life*, No. 09-969 (2007).
8. This review power was affirmed by the Supreme Court in *Martin v. Hunter's Lessee*, 1 Wheat. 304 (1816).
9. *Brown v. Board of Education*, 347 U.S. 483 (1954); *Loving v. Virginia*, 388 U.S. 1 (1967).
10. *Griswold v. Connecticut*, 381 U.S. 479 (1965).
11. *Brandenburg v. Ohio*, 395 U.S. 444 (1969).
12. See Theodore J. Lowi, *The End of Liberalism*, 2nd ed. (New York: Norton, 1979); also, David Schoenbrod, *Power without Responsibility: How Congress Abuses the People through Delegation* (New Haven, CT: Yale University Press, 1993).
13. Kenneth Culp Davis, *Discretionary Justice* (Baton Rouge: Louisiana State University Press, 1969), 15–21.
14. Emergency Price Control Act, 56 Stat. 23 (January 30, 1942).
15. *Hamdi v. Rumsfeld*, 2004 Westlaw 1431951.
16. Charles Lane, "Justices Back Detainee Access to U.S. Courts," *Washington Post*, June 29, 2004, p. 1.
17. *Shelley v. Kraemer*, 334 U.S. 1 (1948).
18. *Gideon v. Wainwright*, 372 U.S. 335 (1963).
19. *Burlington Northern v. White*, No. 05-259 (2006).
20. *Engel v. Vitale*, 370 U.S. 421 (1962); *Gideon v. Wainwright*, 372 U.S. 335 (1963); *Escobedo v. Illinois*, 378 U.S. 478 (1964); and *Miranda v. Arizona*, 384 U.S. 436 (1966).
21. *Baker v. Carr*, 369 U.S. 186 (1962).
22. Walter F. Murphy, "The Supreme Court of the United States," in *Encyclopedia of the American Judicial System*, ed. Robert J. Janosik (New York: Scribner's, 1987).
23. *Adarand Constructors v. Pena*, 115 S.Ct. 2097 (1995); *Missouri v. Jenkins*, 115 S.Ct. 2573 (1995); *Miller v. Johnson*, 115 S.Ct. 2475 (1995).
24. Robert Scigliano, *The Supreme Court and the Presidency* (New York: Free Press, 1971), 162. For an interesting critique of the solicitor general's role during the Reagan administration, see Lincoln Caplan, "Annals of the Law," *New Yorker*, August 17, 1987, pp. 30–62.
25. Edward Lazarus, *Closed Chambers* (New York: Times Books, 1998), 6.
26. *Plyler v. Doe*, 457 U.S. 202 (1982).
27. *Hopwood v. State of Texas*, 78 F3d 932 (Fifth Circuit, 1996).
28. *Gratz v. Bollinger*, 123 S.Ct. 2411 (2003).
29. *Jacobs v. Independent School District No.* 625, 99-CV-542 (D. Minn., filed April 6, 1999).
30. *NAACP v. Button*, 371 U.S. 415 (1963). The quotation is from the opinion in this case.
31. *Smith v. Allwright*, 321 U.S. 649 (1994).
32. *Griswold v. Connecticut*, 381 U.S. 479 (1965).
33. R. W. Apple, Jr., "A Divided Government Remains, and with It the Prospect of Further Combat," *New York Times*, November 7, 1996, p. B6.
34. For limits on judicial power, see Alexander Bickel, *The Least Dangerous Branch* (Indianapolis: Bobbs-Merrill, 1962).
35. *Worcester v. Georgia*, 6 Pet. 515 (1832).
36. *Immigration and Naturalization Service v. Chadha*, 462 U.S. 919 (1983).
37. See Walter Murphy, *Congress and the Court* (Chicago: University of Chicago Press, 1962).
38. Robert Dahl, "The Supreme Court and National Policy Making," *Journal of Public Law* 6 (1958): 279.
39. Martin Shapiro, "The Supreme Court: From Warren to Burger," in *The New American Political System*, ed. Anthony King (Washington, DC: American Enterprise Institute, 1978).

40. *Citizens to Preserve Overton Park v. Volpe*, 401 U.S. 402 (1971).
41. Toni Locy, "Bracing for Health Care's Caseload," *Washington Post*, August 22, 1994, p. A15.
42. See "Developments in the Law—Class Actions," *Harvard Law Review* 89 (1976): 1318.
43. *In re Agent Orange Product Liability Litigation*, 100 F.R.D. 718 (D.C.N.Y. 1983).
44. See Donald Horowitz, *The Courts and Social Policy* (Washington, DC: Brookings Institution Press, 1977).
45. *Moran v. McDonough*, 540 F2d 527 (1 Cir., 1976; *cert. denied*, 429 U.S. 1042 [1977]).
46. Alexander Hamilton, James Madison, and John Jay, *The Federalist Papers*, ed. Clinton Rossiter (New York: New American Library, 1961), No. 10, 78.

Chapter 16

1. Robert Nozick, *Anarchy, State and Utopia (*New York: Basic Books, 1974; reprint, Oxford: Blackwell, 2003).
2. Compare with Gabriel Kolko, *The Triumph of Conservatism* (New York: Free Press, 1963), chap. 6.
3. See David M. Hart, *Forged Consensus: Science, Technology and Economic Policy in the United States, 1921–1953* (Princeton, NJ: Princeton University Press, 1998).
4. See Margaret Weir, *Politics and Jobs: The Boundaries of Employment Policy in the United States* (Princeton, NJ: Princeton University Press, 1992).
5. Bradford DeLong, "America's Only Peacetime Inflation: The 1970s" (University of California at Berkeley and National Bureau of Economic Research, December 19, 1995), www.j-bradford-delong.net/pdf_files/Peacetime_Inflation.pdf (accessed 3/18/08).
6. The act of 1955 officially designated the interstate highways as the National System of Interstate and Defense Highways. It was indirectly a major part of President Dwight Eisenhower's defense program. But it was just as obviously a "pork barrel" policy as any rivers and harbors legislation.
7. The members were AMD, Digital, Hewlett-Packard, Intel, IBM, Lucent, Motorola, National Semiconductor, Rockwell, and Texas Instruments.
8. Eric Lipton, "Safety Agency Faces Scrutiny Amid Changes," *New York Times*, September 2, 2007, p. A1.
9. For a good summary of Keynes's ideas see Robert Lekachman, *The Age of Keynes* (New York: McGraw-Hill, 1966).
10. Kevin G. Hall, "Bernanke to Stay on Greenspan Path, But Not All the Way," *Seattle Times*, November 16, 2005, p. C1.
11. As a rule of thumb, in a growing economy where there is demand for credit, and assuming a reserve requirement of 20 percent, a deposit of $100 will create nearly $500 of new credit. This is called the "multiplier effect," because the bank can lend out $80 of the original $100 deposit to a new borrower; that becomes another $80 deposit, 20 percent of which ($64) can be lent to another borrower, and so on until the original $100 grows to approximately $500 of new credit.
12. Good treatments of the Federal Reserve System and monetary policy can be found in Donald Kettl, *Leadership at the Fed* (New Haven: Yale University Press, 1986); and Albert T. Sommers, *The U.S. Economy Demystified* (Lexington, MA: Lexington Books, 1988), especially chap. 5.
13. Majority Staff of the Joint Economic Committee, Senator Charles E. Schumer, Chairman Rep. Carolyn B. Maloney, Vice Chair, *The Subprime Lending Crisis: The Economic Impact on Wealth, Property Values and Tax Revenues, and How We Got Here*, Report and Recommendations, October 2007, p. 1, http://jec.senate.gov/index.cfm?FuseAction=Files.View&FileStore_id=148eaf7c-ee62-42f0-b215-006db6a11d65 (accessed 5/8/08).
14. Steven R. Wesiman, "Bernanke Faces Bear Stearns Queries," *New York Times*, April 2, 2008, p. C1.
15. Executive Office of the President of the United States, GPO Access, "Budget of the United States Government: Historical Tables Fiscal Year 2009," Table 2.2—Percentage Composition of Receipts by Source: 1934–2013, http://origin.www.gpoaccess.gov/usbudget/fy09/hist.html (accessed 5/9/08).
16. For a systematic account of the role of government in providing incentives and inducements to business, see C. E. Lindblom, *Politics and Markets* (New York: Basic Books, 1977), chap. 13. For a detailed account of the dramatic Reagan tax cuts and reforms, see Jeffrey Birnbaum and Alan Murray, *Showdown at Gucci Gulch: Lawmakers, Lobbyists, and the Unlikely Triumph of Tax Reform* (New York: Random House, 1987).
17. For further background, see David E. Rosenbaum, "Cutting the Deficit Overshadows Clinton's Promise to Cut Taxes," *New York Times*, January 12, 1993, p. A1; and "Clinton Weighing Freeze or New Tax on Social Security," *New York Times*, January 31, 1993, p. A1.
18. Center on Budget and Policy Priorities, "Tax Cuts, Myths and Realities," November 16, 2007, www.cbpp.org/9-27-06tax.htm (accessed 3/20/08).
19. "Bush Urges Permanent Tax Cuts Amid 'Economic Uncertainty,'" *New York Times*, January 8, 2008.
20. Andrew Taylor, "With Half-Trillion in Red Ink, U.S. Inc. Looks Bad on Paper," *Congressional Quarterly Weekly*, January 17, 2004, p. 132.
21. Karen Masterson, "Bush's Budget Promise Goes Bust," *Houston Chronicle*, May 7, 2002, p. A1.
22. For an account of the relationship between mechanization and law, see Lawrence Friedman, *A History of American Law* (New York: Simon & Schuster, 1973), 409–29.

23. Quotes are drawn from the *Economist*, January 31, 1998, pp. 65–66.
24. The *Federal Register* is the daily publication of all official acts of Congress, the president, and the administrative agencies. A law or executive order is not legally binding until it is published in the *Federal Register*.
25. Cato Institute, Cato Handbook for Congress 6th ed., 9. Corporate Welfare (2005), www.cato.org/pubs/handbook/hb105-9.html (accessed 3/24/08).
26. James Dao, "The Nation; Big Bucks Trip Up the Lean New Army," *New York Times*, February 10, 2002, sec. 4, p. 5.
27. See Samuel P. Hays, *Beauty, Health, and Permanence: Environmental Politics in the United States, 1955–1985* (Cambridge: Cambridge University Press, 1987).
28. Jonathan Harr, *A Civil Action* (New York: Vintage, 1996).
29. Pew Center on Global Climate Change, "Climate Change 101: The Science and Impacts," www.pewclimate.org/docUploads/101_Science_Impacts.pdf (accessed 3/21/08).
30. See the discussion in Peter R. Orszag, "Issues in Climate Change," Congressional Budget Office, November 16, 2007, www.cbo.gov/ftpdocs/88xx/doc8819/11-16-ClimateChangeConf.pdf (accessed 3/21/08).
31. Energy Information Administration, "Greenhouse Gases, Climate Change, and Energy," www.eia.doe.gov/oiaf/1605/ggccebro/chapter1.html (accessed 3/21/08).
32. John M. Broder and Marjorie Connelly, "Public Says Warming Is a Problem, But Remains Split on Response," *New York Times*, April 27, 2007, p. 20.
33. Broder and Connelly, "Public Says Warming Is a Problem."
34. Survey by Cable News Network, conducted by Opinion Research Corporation, November 2–November 4, 2007 and based on telephone interviews with a national adult sample of 1,024. [USORC.110707.R05L]
35. Peter Baker, "In Bush's Final Year, the Agenda Gets Greener," *Washington Post*, December 29, 2007, p. A1.
36. Broder and Connelly, "Public Says Warming Is a Problem."
37. Environmental Defense Fund, "Top Firms Call for Climate Action," www.edf.org/article.cfm?contentID=5828&bclid=CJjkwl_p-5ACFSoWiQodHGVGhA (accessed 3/21/08).
38. "Climate Change on Capitol Hill," *Washington Post*, October 22, 2007, p. A22.
39. White House, "President Bush Delivers State of the Union Address," January 31, 2006, www.whitehouse.gov/news/releases/2006/01/20060131-10.html (accessed3/21/08).
40. HybridCars, "December 2007 Dashboard," www.hybridcars.com/market-dashboard/dec07-overview.html (accessed 4/8/08).
41. Thomas L. Friedman, "The Power of Green," *New York Times*, April 15, 2007.
42. Andrew Martin, "Food and Fuel Compete for Land," *New York Times*, December 18, 2007.
43. Orszag, "Issues in Climate Change."
44. Joe Palca, "California Turns to Holland for Flood Expertise," National Public Radio, January 14, 2008. www.npr.org/templates/story/story.php?storyId=18080442 (accessed 3/21/08).
45. Roger Pielke, Jr., Gwyn Prins, Steve Rayner, and Daniel Sarewitz, "Climate Change 2007: Lifting the Taboo on Adaptation," *Nature*, February 8, 2007, pp. 597–98.
46 Megan Garvey, "Company Town; SAG Says Canada Film Policies Illegal, Seeks Federal Inquiry," *Los Angeles Times*, August 22, 2001, part 3, p. 5.
47. David H. Autor, Lawrence F. Katz, and Melissa S. Kearney, "The Polarization of the U.S. Labor Market," *American Economic Review* 96, no. 2, (May 2006): 189–94 (6).
48. Thomas Piketty and Emmanuel Saez credit the progressive income tax with reducing income inequality in the United States since the 1930s. See their argument in "Income Inequality in the United States, 1913–1998" *Quarterly Journal of Economics* 118, no. 1 (February 2003): 1–39.
49. Tax Policy Center, Table T06-0279 Combined Effect of the 2001–2006 Tax Cuts, Distribution of Federal Tax Change by Cash Income Percentile, 2006, November 13, 2006, www.taxpolicycenter.org/numbers/displayatab.cfm?DocID=1361 (accessed 3/22/08).
50. Robert H. Frank, *Falling Behind: How Rising Inequality Harms the Middle Class* (Berkeley: University of California Press, 2007).
51. For a classic statement, see Milton Friedman and Rose Friedman, *Free to Choose* (New York: Harvest Books, 1990). See also Bruce Bartlett, "Is Income Inequality Really a Problem?" *New York Times*, January 24, 2007, http://bartlett.blogs.nytimes.com/2007/01/24/is-income-inequality-really-a-problem/ (accessed 3/22/08).

Chapter 17

1. A good source of pre-1930s welfare history is James T. Patterson, *America's Struggle against Poverty, 1900–1994* (Cambridge, MA: Harvard University Press, 1994), chap. 2.
2. Quoted in Patterson, *America's Struggle against Poverty*, 26.
3. Patterson, *America's Struggle against Poverty*, 26.
4. Patterson, *America's Struggle against Poverty*, 27.
5. This figure is based on a WPA study by Ann E. Geddes, reported in Merle Fainsod et al., *Government and the American Economy*, 3rd ed. (New York: Norton, 1959), 769.
6. Social Security Online, "Contribution and Benefit Base," www.ssa.gov/OACT/COLA/cbb.html (accessed 4/9/08).
7. Edward J. Harpham, "Fiscal Crisis and the Politics of Social Security Reform," in *The Attack on the Welfare State*, eds. Anthony Champagne and Edward Harpham (Prospect Heights, IL: Waveland, 1984), 13.

8. National Center for Children in Poverty, "State Profiles," www.nccp.org/profiles/ (accessed 3/26/08); Gretchen Rowe with Mary Murphy and Meghan Williamson, *The Welfare Rules Databook: State Policies as of July 2005* (Washington, DC: The Urban Institute, 2006), www.acf.hhs.gov/programs/opre/welfare_employ/state_tanf/reports/wel_rules05/databook_2005.pdf (accessed 4/9/08).
9. Department of Health and Human Services, "The 2007 HHS Poverty Guidelines," http://aspe.hhs.gov/poverty/07poverty.shtml (accessed 3/26/08).
10. *Goldberg v. Kelly*, 397 U.S. 254 (1970).
11. Henry J. Kaiser Family Foundation, Statehealthfacts.org, "Distribution of Medicaid Payments by Enrollment Group (in millions), FY2005," www.statehealthfacts.org/comparetable.jsp?ind=182&cat=4 (accessed 4/9/08).
12. See Martin Gilens, *Why Americans Hate Welfare* (Chicago: University of Chicago Press, 1999), chaps. 3, 4.
13. Gilens, *Why Americans Hate Welfare.*
14. Center for Law and Social Policy, "Analysis of Fiscal Year 2006 TANF and MOE Spending by States," http://clasp.org/WelfarePolicy/pdf/map100907us.pdf (accessed 4/9/08).
15. See the discussion of the law and the data presented in House Ways and Means Committee Print, WMCP: 106-14, 2000 Green Book, Section 7, Temporary Assistance for Needy Families (TANF), http://frwebgate.access.gpo.gov/cgi-bin/useftp.cgi?IPaddress=162.140.64.181&filename=wm014_07.wais&directory=/data/wais/data/106_green_book (accessed 3/26/08); Rebecca M. Blank, "Evaluating Welfare Reform in the United States," *Journal of Economic Literature* 40 (December 2002): 1105–66.
16. Robert Pear, "House Democrats Propose Making the '96 Welfare Law an Antipoverty Weapon," *New York Times*, January 24, 2002, p. A22.
17. Robin Toner, "Welfare Chief Is Hoping to Promote Marriage," *New York Times*, February 19, 2002, p. A1.
18. Office of Management and Budget, "Historical Tables, Budget of the United States Government, Fiscal Year 2009," Table 8.3—Percentage Distribution of Outlays by Budget Enforcement Act Category: 1962–2013, and Table 2.2—Percentage Composition of Receipts by Source: 1934–2013, www.whitehouse.gov/omb/budget/fy2009/pdf/hist.pdf (accessed 4/9/08).
19. President's Commission to Strengthen Social Security, "Strengthening Social Security and Creating Personal Wealth for All Americans," December 21, 2001, 5, www.csss.gov/reports/Final_report.pdf (accessed 3/26/08).
20. President's Commission to Strengthen Social Security, "Strengthening Social Security."
21. Alicia H. Munnell, "Are the Social Security Trust Funds Meaningful?" Center for Retirement Research, Boston College, May 2005, no. 30, p. 4, http://crr.bc.edu/images/stories/Briefs/ib_30.pdf (accessed 3/25/08); see also Social Security Online, Summary of P.L. 98-21, (H.R. 1900) Social Security Amendments of 1983—Signed on April 20, 1983, www.ssa.gov/history/1983amend.html (accessed 3/25/08).
22. Christian E. Weller, "Undermining Social Security with Private Accounts," Economic Policy Institute Issue Brief, December 11, 2001, www.epi.org/content.cfm/issuebriefs_ib172 (accessed 3/26/08); Robert Greenstein, "Social Security Commission Proposals Contain Serious Weaknesses but May Improve the Debate in an Important Respect," Center on Budget and Policy Priorities, December 26, 2001, www.centeronbudget.org/12-11-01socsec.htm (accessed 3/26/08).
23. Quoted in Jill Quadragno, "Social Security Policy and the Entitlement Debate," in *Social Policy and the Conservative Agenda*, eds. Clarence Y. H. Lo and Michael Schwartz (Malden, MA: Blackwell, 1998), 111.
24. There were a couple of minor precedents. One was the Smith-Hughes Act of 1917, which made federal funds available to the states for vocational education at the elementary and secondary levels. Second, the Lanham Act of 1940 made federal funds available to schools in "federally impacted areas," that is, areas with an unusually large number of government employees and/or where the local tax base was reduced by large amounts of government-owned property.
25. Office of Management and Budget, *Budget of the United States Government, Fiscal Year 1982* (Washington, DC: Government Printing Office, 1981), 427.
26. For an analysis of employment and training initiatives since the 1930s, see Margaret Weir, *Politics and Jobs* (Princeton, NJ: Princeton University Press, 1992).
27. On CETA, see Donald C. Baumer and Carl E. Van Horn, *The Politics of Unemployment* (Washington, DC: Congressional Quarterly Press, 1985).
28. Morton Keller, *Affairs of State: Public Life in Nineteenth Century America* (Cambridge, MA: Belknap Press, 1977), 500.
29. Office of Management and Budget, "Historical Tables, Budget of the United States Government, Fiscal Year 2009," Table 16.1—Outlays for Health Programs: 1962–2013, www.gpoaccess.gov/usbudget/fy09/pdf/hist.pdf (accessed 5/15/08); Henry J. Kaiser Family Foundation HIV/AIDS Policy Fact Sheet (March 2008), www.kff.org/hivaids/upload/3029_08.pdf (accessed 4/13/08).
30. U.N. Development Program, Organization for Economic Cooperation and Development, cited in Paul Spector, "Failure, by the Numbers," *New York Times*, September 24, 1994.
31. For a description of the 2008 candidates' statements on health care, see "The Front Runners," *Washingtonpost.com*, http://projects.washingtonpost.com/2008-presidential-candidates/ (accessed 1/4/08); see also Atul Gawande, "The Obama Health Plan," *New York Times*, May 31, 2007, p. A19.
32. John E. Schwarz, *America's Hidden Success*, 2nd ed. (New York: Norton, 1988), 41–42.

33. Carmen DeNavas-Walt, Bernadette D. Proctor, and Jessica Smith, "Income, Poverty, and Health Insurance Coverage in the United States: 2006," U.S. Census Bureau, Current Population Reports, P60-233 (Washington, DC: U.S. Government Printing Office, August 2007), www.census.gov/prod/2007pubs/p60-233.pdf (accessed 3/26/08).
34. See, for example, Theodore R. Marmor, Jerry L. Mashaw, and Philip L. Harvey, *America's Misunderstood Welfare State* (New York: Basic Books, 1990), 156.
35. Burdett A. Loomis and Allan J. Cigler, "Introduction: The Changing Nature of Interest Group Politics," in *Interest Group Politics*, 4th ed., eds. Burdett A. Loomis and Allan J. Cigler (Washington, DC: Congressional Quarterly Press, 1995), 12.
36. See Senator Bob Kerrey's remarks quoted in David S. Broder, "Deficit Doomsday," *Washington Post*, August 7, 1994, p. C9.
37. Christopher Howard, *The Hidden Welfare State: Tax Expenditures and Social Policy in the United States* (Princeton, NJ: Princeton University Press, 1999); Jacob S. Hacker, *The Divided Welfare State: The Battle over Public and Private Benefits in the United States* (New York: Cambridge University Press, 2002).
38. Thomas L. Hungerford, "Tax Expenditures: Trends and Critiques," Congressional Research Service, September 13, 2006, http://assets.opencrs.com/rpts/RL33641_20060913.pdf (accessed 3/25/08).
39. Raymond Hernandez, "Federal Welfare Overhaul Allows Albany to Shift Money Elsewhere," *New York Times*, April 23, 2000, p.1.
40. Frances Fox Piven and Richard Cloward, *Poor People's Movements* (New York: Pantheon, 1977), chap. 5.
41. DeNavas-Walt, Proctor, and Smith, "Income, Poverty, and Health Insurance Coverage in the United States: 2006."
42. DeNavas-Walt, Proctor, and Smith, "Income, Poverty, and Health Insurance Coverage in the United States: 2006."
43. See for example, Sharon Hayes, *Flat Broke with Children: Women in the Age of Welfare Reform* (New York: Oxford University Press, 2004).
44. For an argument that children should be given the vote, see Paul E. Peterson, "An Immodest Proposal," *Daedalus* 121 (Fall 1992): 151–74.
45. On the relationship between education and democracy in the United States, see Ira Katznelson and Margaret Weir, *Schooling for All: Race, Class, and the Democratic Ideal* (New York: Basic Books, 1985).
46. For a description of these different views among conservatives, see David Frum, *Dead Right* (New York: Basic Books, 1994).
47. See, for example, Charles Murray, *Losing Ground* (New York: Basic Books, 1984).
48. See, for example, Lawrence Mead, *Beyond Entitlement: The Social Obligations of Citizenship* (New York: Free Press, 1986).
49. See James C. McKinley, Jr., "Father Faces U.S. Charges over Support," *New York Times*, August 9, 1995, p. B1.
50. See Christopher Jencks and Kathryn Edin, "Do Poor Women Have the Right to Bear Children?" *American Prospect* 20 (Winter 1995): 43–52.
51. See Elizabeth Bussiere, "The Failure of Constitutional Welfare Rights in the Warren Court," *Political Science Quarterly* 109 (Winter 1994): 105–31.
52. See L. Free and Hadley Cantril, *The Political Beliefs of Americans* (New York: Simon & Schuster, 1968).
53. See Fay Lomax Cook and Edith Barrett, *Support for the American Welfare State* (New York: Columbia University Press, 1992); and Hugh Heclo, "The Political Foundations of Antipoverty Policy," in *Fighting Poverty: What Works and What Doesn't*, eds. Sheldon H. Danziger and Daniel H. Weinberg (Cambridge, MA: Harvard University Press, 1986), 312–40.

Chapter 18

1. Rupert Smith, *The Utility of Force: The Art of War in the Modern World* (New York: Vintage, 2008).
2. D. Robert Worley, *Shaping U.S. Military Forces: Revolution or Relevance in a Post–Cold War World* (Westport, CT: Praeger Security International, 2006).
3. This was done quietly in an amendment to the Internal Revenue Service Reform Act (PL 105-206), June 22, 1998. But it was not accomplished easily. See Bob Gravely, "Normal Trade with China Wins Approval," *Congressional Quarterly Weekly Report*, July 25, 1998; and Richard Dunham, "MFN by any other name is . . . NTR?," Business Week online news flash, June 19, 1997.
4. Eduardo Porter, "True or False: Outsourcing Is a Crisis," *New York Times*, June 19, 2005, sec. 3, p. 4.
5. Deborah McGregor, "Democrats Set Trail Alight with Attacks on Free Trade," *Financial Times*, February 4, 2004, p. 9.
6. Matthew Crenson and Benjamin Ginsberg, *Presidential Power: Unchecked and Unbalanced* (New York: Norton, 2007).
7. Benjamin Ginsberg, *The American Lie: Government by the People and Other Political Fables* (Boulder, CO: Paradigm, 2007).
8. Paul R. Pillar, *Terrorism and American Foreign Policy* (Washington, DC: Brookings Institution Press, 2003).
9. Raymond A. Bauer, Ithiel de Sola Pool, and Lewis Anthony Dexter, *American Business and Public Policy: The Politics of Foreign Trade*, 2nd ed. (Chicago: Aldine-Atherton, 1972).

10. For a good treatment of this in regard to Irish Catholics and Catholics in general, see Timothy Byrnes, *Catholic Bishops and American Politics* (Princeton, NJ: Princeton University Press, 1991). For a (controversial) discussion of the role of Jewish groups, see John J. Mearsheimer and Stephen M. Walt, *The Israel Lobby and U.S. Foreign Policy* (New York: Farrar, Straus and Giroux, 2007).
11. This felicitous term is from David R. Mayhew, *Congress: The Electoral Connection* (New Haven: Yale University Press, 1974).
12. John H. Aldrich, *Why Parties? The Origin and Transformation of Political Parties in America* (Chicago: University of Chicago Press, 1995), 278.
13. A very good brief outline of the centrality of the president in foreign policy is found in Paul E. Peterson, "The President's Dominance in Foreign Policy Making," *Political Science Quarterly* 109 (Summer 1994): 215–34.
14. One confirmation of this is found in Theodore Lowi, *The End of Liberalism: The Second Republic of the United States*, 2nd ed. (New York: Norton, 1979), 127–30; another is found in Stephen Krasner, "Are Bureaucracies Important?" *Foreign Policy* 7 (Summer 1972): 159–79. However, it should be noted that Krasner was writing his article in disagreement with Graham T. Allison, "Conceptual Models and the Cuban Missile Crisis," *American Political Science Review* 63, no. 3 (September 1969): 689–718.
15. Peterson, "The President's Dominance in Foreign Policy Making," 232.
16. Hans Morgenthau, *Politics among Nations*, 2nd ed. (New York: Knopf, 1956), 505.
17. See Theodore Lowi, *The Personal President: Power Invested, Promise Unfulfilled* (Ithaca, NY: Cornell University Press, 1985), 167–69.
18. "IMF: Sleeve-Rolling Time," *Economist*, May 2, 1992, pp. 98–99.
19. James Dao and Patrick E. Tyler, "U.S. Says Military Strikes Are Just a Part of Big Plan," *The Alliance*, September 27, 2001; and Joseph Kahn, "A Nation Challenged: Global Dollars," *New York Times*, September 20, 2001, p. B1.
20. Turkey was desperate for help to extricate its economy from its worst recession since 1945. The Afghanistan crisis was going to hurt Turkey all the more; its strategic location helped its case with IMF. "Official Says Turkey Is Advancing in Drive for I.M.F. Financing," *New York Times*, October 6, 2001, p. A7.
21. George Quester, *The Continuing Problem of International Politics* (Hinsdale, IL: Dryden Press, 1974), 229.
22. The Warsaw Pact was signed in 1955 by the Soviet Union, the German Democratic Republic (East Germany), Poland, Hungary, Czechoslovakia, Romania, Bulgaria, and Albania. Albania later dropped out. The Warsaw Pact was terminated in 1991.
23. For a thorough and instructive exposition of the original Holy Alliance pattern, see Paul M. Kennedy, *The Rise and Fall of the Great Powers: Economic Change and Military Conflict from 1500 to 2000* (New York: Random House, 1987), 159–60. And for a comparison of the Holy Alliance role with the balance-of-power role, to be discussed next, see Karl Polanyi, *The Great Transformation* (New York: Rinehart, 1944; Beacon paperback edition, 1957), 5–11 and 259–62.
24. Felix Gilbert et al., *The Norton History of Modern Europe* (New York: Norton, 1971), 1222–24.
25. The original theory of containment was articulated by former ambassador and scholar George Kennan in a famous article published under the pseudonym X, "The Sources of Soviet Conduct," *Foreign Affairs* 25 (1947): 556.
26. Richard Barnet, "Reflections," *New Yorker*, March 9, 1987, p. 82.
27. Thomas L. Friedman, "14 Big Macs Later . . . ," *New York Times*, December 31, 1995, sec. 4, p. 9.
28. See, for example, the cover story of the *Economist*, "Stumbling into War," March 27–April 2, 1999, pp. 17, 27, 49, 50.
29. Quoted in Elaine Sciolino and Ethan Bronner, "How a President, Distracted by Scandal, Entered Balkan War," *New York Times*, April 18, 1999, p. 12.
30. Note once again the title of the previously cited article, "How a President, Distracted by Scandal, Entered Balkan War."

ANSWER KEY

CHAPTER 1
1. d
2. b
3. c
4. d
5. c
6. d
7. d
8. a
9. a
10. a

CHAPTER 2
1. b
2. b
3. b
4. d
5. c
6. c
7. d
8. d
9. d
10. a

CHAPTER 3
1. b
2. c
3. d
4. c
5. c
6. b
7. a
8. d
9. c
10. d

CHAPTER 4
1. a
2. c
3. b
4. a
5. d
6. d
7. b
8. a
9. a
10. c

CHAPTER 5
1. b
2. a
3. b
4. b
5. c
6. b
7. d
8. d
9. d
10. a

CHAPTER 6
1. c
2. a
3. d
4. c
5. d
6. b
7. d
8. b
9. a
10. b

CHAPTER 7
1. c
2. b
3. d
4. a and c
5. d
6. a
7. b
8. a
9. d
10. a

CHAPTER 8
1. d
2. d
3. a
4. c
5. d
6. d
7. a
8. c
9. c
10. d

CHAPTER 9
1. a
2. d
3. c
4. d
5. b
6. c
7. c
8. a
9. c
10. d

CHAPTER 10
1. a
2. b
3. c
4. d
5. a
6. a
7. b
8. a
9. d
10. c

CHAPTER 11
1. a
2. d
3. c
4. a
5. a
6. c
7. d
8. d
9. a

CHAPTER 12
1. a
2. d
3. c
4. c
5. a
6. c
7. b
8. a
9. a
10. c

CHAPTER 13
1. b
2. b
3. a
4. b
5. a
6. c
7. a
8. b
9. c

CHAPTER 14
1. b
2. a
3. c
4. d
5. a
6. a
7. d
8. d

CHAPTER 15
1. a
2. b
3. d
4. d
5. a
6. c
7. c
8. a
9. d
10. a

CHAPTER 16
1. b
2. b
3. a
4. d
5. b
6. c
7. b
8. c
9. d
10. a

CHAPTER 17
1. c
2. c
3. c
4. a
5. c
6. d
7. c
8. d
9. a

CHAPTER 18
1. d
2. b
3. c
4. c
5. b
6. d
7. a
8. a

PHOTO CREDITS

Chapter 1: 2–3: AP Images/Stefano Paltera; 5: Scott J. Ferrell/Congressional Quarterly/Getty Images; 10: AP Images; 11: REUTERS/Stefano Rellandini; 13: Comedy Central/Everett Collection; 15: Bettmann/Corbis; 16: Corbis; 19: Library of Congress; 20: Library of Congress; 21: New York Times; 24: Gilles Mingasson/Getty Images; 26: Bettmann/Corbis; 27: Library Company of Philadelphia; 28: KAREN BLEIER/AFP/Getty Images; 29: From the Art Collection of the Boatmen's National Bank of St. Louis; 31: Getty Images; 33 (top): Bettmann/Corbis; 33 (bottom): Marc Serota/Reuters/Corbis; 30: AP Images/Hussein Mulla; 35: AP Images; 34: Ian Shaw/Alamy. **Chapter 2:** 40–41: Bettmann/Corbis; 43: Library of Congress; 44: Bettmann/Corbis; 45: The Metropolitan Museum of Art, Arthur Hoppock Hearn Fund, 1950 (50.117). Photograph © 1988 The Metropolitan Museum of Art; © Estate of Grant Wood/Licensed by VAGA, New York, NY; 46: Library of Congress; 48: Bettmann/Corbis; 49: Historical Society of Pennsylvania; 51: Library of Congress; 52: Library of Congress; 57: The Granger Collection, New York; 62: Library of Congress; 65: AP Images/Brennan Linsley; 67 (right): Rick Friedman/Corbis; 67 (left): AP Images/Susan Ragan; 68: Frederic Larson/San Francisco Chronicle/Corbis; 70: Bettmann/Corbis; 75: Bettmann/Corbis; 74: Cynthia Johnson/Time Life Pictures/Getty Images. **Chapter 3:** 80–81: Larry Downing/Reuters; 85: AP Images/Devork Djansezian; 89: Collection of the New York Historical Society; 90: Library of Congress; 93: AP Images/David Zalubowski; 94: AP Images; 95: Reuters/Corbis; 97: PEMCO Webster and Stevens Collection, Museum of History and Industry, Seattle/Corbis; 101: Kim Kulish/Corbis; 103: UPI Photo/Roger L. Wollenberg; 104: Photo by Alex Wong/Getty Images; 108: AP Images; 109: AP Images; 110: AFP/Getty Images; 112: AP Images/Topeka Capital-Journal, Anthony S. Bush. **Chapter 4:** 118–119: AP Images/David J. Phillip; 122: Mike Simons/Corbis; 125: AP Images; 126: AP Images; 127: Bob Daemmrich/Corbis; 130: AP Images/Rick Bowmer; 132: American Broadcasting Companies, Inc.; 134: Random House, Inc.; 139 (top): Win McNamee/Getty Images;139 (bottom): AP Images/Steve Helber; 141: AP Images; 142: Bettmann/Corbis; 143: Bettmann/Corbis; 146: AP Images/Chuck Robinson; 147: Clay McLachlan/Corbis; 149: AP Images/Lynne Sladky; 151: AP Images/Chris O'Meara, File; 150: Stefan Zaklin/epa/Corbis; 136: Nick Ut/AP Images. **Chapter 5:** 156–157: AP Images; 159: Bettmann/Corbis; 160: Bettmann/Corbis; 162: Warder Collection; 164 (top): Corbis; 164 (bottom): Corbis; 167: AP Images; 172: Stanley J. Forman, Pulitzer Prize 1977; 174: AP Images/Manuel Balce Ceneta; 178: Bettmann/Corbis; 180: Mitchell Smith/Corbis; 181: RAFIQUR RAHMAN/Reuters/Corbis; 183: AP Images/USPS; 184: Corbis; 187: AP Images/Eric Risberg; 189: AP Images; 190: Alex Wong/Getty Images; 194: The Kobal Collection; 197: AP Images/John F. Martin. **Chapter 6:** 204–205: REUTERS/Joshua Roberts; 209: Jessica Rinaldi/Stringer/Reuters/Corbis; 214: Richard B. Levine/Newscom; 217: Raedle/Getty Images; 218: Wally McNamee/Corbis; 219: Lawrence Jackson/AP Images; 220: Alex Wong/Getty Images; 223: Rob Crandall/Newscom; 226: Swim Ink 2, LLC/Corbis; 229: By permission of Bob Gorrell and Creators Syndicate; 230: AP Images/Gerald Herbert; 232: Bettmann/Corbis; 237: AP Images/Mark Lennihan; 238: Photo by Majid/Getty Images; 241: AP Images/J. Scott Applewhite; 240: Ron Sachs/CNP/Newscom. **Chapter 7:** 246–247: REUTERS/Kevin Lamarque; 250: Guerrucci/Pool/Sipa Press; 255: Frederic Larson/San Francisco Chronicle/Corbis; 253: AP Images/Charles Dharapa; 254: Shannon Stapleton/Reuters/Corbis; 256: NICHOLAS KAMM/AFP/Getty Images/Newscom; 259: AP Images/Richard Lewis; 260: AP Images; 268: AP Images; 262: REUTERS/Larry Downing; 264: Reuters TV/Reuters/Corbis; 266: David McNew/Getty Images; 269: AP Images/Nick Ut; 272: NEW YORK TIMES/REDUX TIME; 265: Charles Moore/Black Star; 270: Koichi Kamoshida/Liaison/Getty Images; 274: AP Images/Trinity United Church of Christ; 273 (right): AP Images/Margaret Norton/NBCU Photo Bank; 273 (left): AP Images/Dennis Cook; 277: AP Images; 275: Mario Tama/Getty Images. **Chapter 8:** 282–283: Adrian Sanchez Gonzalez/EFE/Corbis; 287: AP Images/Mike Derer; 289: AP Images/J. Pat Carver; 292: AP Images/Yahya Ahmed; 295: Chicago Historical Society; 296: REUTERS/Mike Carlson; 298: Library of Congress; 297: CAUSE (www.causeusa.org); 302: Linda Spillers/WireImage; 304: AP Images/Kelley McCall; 309: Brown Brothers, Sterling, PA; 310: AP Images/Charles Dharapak; 311 (right): Courtesy of Simon & Schuster, Inc.; 311 (left): Courtesy of Simon & Schuster, Inc.; 313: AP Images/Ben Margot. **Chapter 9:** 318–319: Scott J. Ferrell/Congressional Quarterly/Getty Images; 321: Library of Congress; 324: Chip Somodevilla/Getty Images; 327: The Granger Collection, New York; 325: AP Images/John Duricka, File; 328: Library of Congress; 330: Nancy Kaszerman/Newscom; 332: The Granger Collection, New York; 334: AP Images/Lawrence Jackson; 339: AP Images; 337: Michal Czerwonka/epa/Corbis; 341: AP Images/Mark Humphrey; 351 (left): Jim Sulley/epa/Corbis; 351 (right): Max Whittaker/Reuters/Corbis; 353: AFP/Getty

Images; 355: Eric Thayer/Getty Images; 344: Andrew Gombert/epa/Corbis; 345: AP Images/Don Petersen; 357: AP Images/Don Ryan. **Chapter 10:** 362–363: PAUL J. RICHARDS/AFP/Getty Images; 365: AP Images/Andy Manis; 367 (right): Bettmann/Cobis; 367 (left): The Granger Collection, New York; 368 (left): AP Images/Harry Cabluck; 368 (right): AP Images; 372 (left): Reuters/Corbis; 372 (right): AP Images/Rich Pedroncelli; 380: Win McNamee/Getty Images; 383: Margaret Norton/NBCU Photo Bank; 385: Eric Thayer/Getty Images; 388: Public Domain; 387: AP Images/Michel Euler; 393–404: SAUL LOEB/AFP/Getty Images; AP Images/Ron Edmonds; CBS /Landov; Dana Edelson/NBCU Photo Bank; Joe Corrigan/Getty Images; AP Images/Jae C. Hong; 405: AP Images/Tyler Morning Telegraph, Tom Turner; 411: AP Images; 412: Getty Images. **Chapter 11:** 416–417: AP Images/J. Scott Applewhite; 419: The Granger Collection, New York; 421: Zunique/Newscom; 422: Chip Somodevilla/Getty Images; 423: AP Images; 426: AP Images; 432: AP Images/Stephan Savoia; 433: AP Images; 434: Corbis; 437: AP Images/J. Scott Applewhite; 439: AP Images/Rick Bowmer; 441: Reuters/Corbis; 444: Public Domain; 446: AP Images/Jean-Marc Bouju; 448: AP Images. **Chapter 12:** 454–455: Mark Wilson/Getty Images; 458: Bettmann/Corbis; 459: Alex Wong/Getty Images; 469: Olivier Douliery/ABACAUSA/Newscom; 473: Scott J. Ferrell/Congressional Quarterly/Newscom; 475: Zuma Press/Newscom; 479: Mark Wilson/Getty Images; 481: Rockstar Games/Handout/Reuters/Corbis; 483: Photo by Jay Tinker/Courtesy of Maryland Society for Sight, founded in 1909 with the mission of saving sight; 484: AP Images/The Indianapolis Star, Charlie Nye; 487: Courtesy Congresswoman Kathy Castor/FedNet; 488: Tim Sloan/AFP/Getty Images; 489: Roger L. Wollenberg/UPI /Landov; 490: AP Images; 491: Getty Images; 492: AP Images/Dennis Cook; 493: AP Images/Greg Gibson; 494: AP Images/APTN; 496: Courtesy of Armenian Assembly of America. **Chapter 13:** 502–503: Ozier Muhammad/The New York Times; 505: The Granger Collection, New York; 507: AFP/Getty Images; 509: Brooks Kraft/Corbis; 511: Larry Downing/Reuters/Corbis; 512: Mike Blake/Reuters/Landov; 513: Reuters; 514: Pierre Manevy/Hulton Archive/Getty Images; 519: Everett Collection; 523: AP Images/Christina Jamison/NBC NewsWire; 524: Bettmann/Corbis; 525: AP Images/Jim Mone; 529: Bettmann/Corbis; 531: AP Images; 536: AP Images/Doug Mills; 537: RAFAEL SUANES/MCT /Landov; 538: Time Life Pictures/Getty Images. **Chapter 14:** 544–545: AP Images/Tyler Morning Telegraph, D.J. Peters; 551: Chip Somodevilla/Getty Images; 555 (left): AP Images; 555 (right): Courtesy of IMC Global, Inc.; 558: 20th Century Fox Film Corp. All rights reserved; 561: AP Images/Charles Dharapak; 563: Stephen Crowley/The New York Times/Redux; 566: Luje Frazza/AFP/Getty Images; 568: Photo by Alan F. Singer; CBS 1995; 570: AP Images/Richard Drew; 572: Mark Wilson/Getty Images; 573: Scott Peterson/Getty Images; 576: Scott Peterson/Getty Images; 579: Ron Sachs/CNP/Corbis; 582: Jeff Greenberg/Alamy. **Chapter 15:** 588–589: Mark Wilson/Getty Images; 591: Tim Sloan/AFP/Getty Images; 595: Rick Fowler/Reuters/Corbis; 597: Courtesy of The Supreme Court Historical Society. Photo by Richard Stauss, Smithsonian Institution; 598 (left): AP Images/Ken Heinen; 598 (right): AP Images/Pablo Martinez Monsivais; 600: John Mathews II; 602: Bettmann/Corbis; 604: AP Images; 606: AP Images/Susan Walsh; 612: AP Images/Joe Marquette; 614: NICHOLAS KAMM/AFP/Getty Images; 617: AP Images/J. Scott Applewhite; 618: Collection of the Supreme Court of the United States, photo by Steve Petteway; 620: AP Images/Shawn Baldwin; 622: AP Images/Charles Dharapak; 623: Chris Graythen/Getty Images. **Chapter 16:** 630–631: Brendan Smialowski/Getty Images; 633: The Granger Collection, New York; 634: Harald Sund/Getty Images; 638: Reuters/Corbis; 639: Bettmann/CORBIS; 641 (left): The Granger Collection, New York; 641 (right): Bettmann/Corbis; 643: North Wind Picture Archives/Alamy; 644: Bettmann/Corbis; 645: Brooks Kraft/Corbis; 647: Scull/BloombergNews/Landov; 642: Bettmann/Corbis; 652: Paul J. Richards/AFP/Getty Images; 655: Bettmann/Corbis; 656: AP Images; 659: Paramount Classics/Photofest; 661: Flores/AFP/Getty Images/Newscom; 662: AP Images/Binsar Bakkara; 667: Bazuki Muhammad/Reuters/Corbis; 669: Steve Liss/Time Life Pictures/Getty Images. **Chapter 17:** 676–677: AP Images/Jennifer Graylock; 679: Chicago Historical Society; 680: AP Images; 683: AP Images/Toby Talbot; 689: AP Images/Eric Draper; 690: SHANNON STAPLETON/Reuters; 692: Chip Somodevilla/Getty Images; 695: Fox/Photofest; 696: Mark Wilson/Getty Images; 698: David Hoffman Photo Library/Alamy; 700: AP Images/Matt Rourke; 702: AP Images/Denis Paquin; 706 (left): AP Images; 706 (right): AP Images/Dawn Villella; 708: Seth Wenig/Star Ledger/Corbis. **Chapter 18:** 741–715: Jim Watson/AFP/Getty Images; 717: AP Images/David Duprey; 719: Bettmann/CORBIS; 720: AP Images/Rahmat Gul; 722: Ryan Pyle/Corbis; 724: AP Images/The News-Gazette, Robert K. O'Daniell; 725: AP/KEYSTONE/Martial Trezzini; 726: Darcy Padilla/Redux; 728: AP Imagess/Mohammed Hato; 729: AP Images/Susan Walsh; 732: Mandel Ngan/AFP/Getty Images; 735: AP Images; 737: PARAMOUNT PICTURES/THE KOBAL COLLECTION/VAUGHAN, STEPHEN; 739: Reuters/Corbis; 741: U.S. Marine Corps photo by Cpl. Tyler Hill; 745: AP Images; 747: AP Images; 748: AP Images/Lefteris Pitarakis; 751: Somodevilla/Getty Images.

INDEX

Page numbers in *italics* refer to tables, figures, and photos.

Political Map of the World

Arctic Ocean
Franz Josef Land
Severnaya Zemlya
Svalbard (Norway)
Novaya Zemlya
Kara Sea
Laptev Sea
New Siberian Islands
East Siberian Sea
Wrangel Island
Barents Sea
RUSSIA
FINLAND
SWEDEN
Oslo
Stockholm
ESTONIA
Baltic Sea
LATVIA
LITHUANIA
RUS.
Moscow
Bering Sea
Sea of Okhotsk
BELARUS
Berlin
POLAND
CZECH REP.
SLOVAKIA
UKRAINE
AUSTRIA
HUNGARY
MOLDOVA
SL.
CROATIA
ROMANIA
B.H.
SERBIA
MONT.
ITALY
Rome
ALBANIA
MAC.
BULGARIA
GREECE
Black Sea
GEORGIA
ARMENIA
AZERBAIJAN
TURKEY
Caspian Sea
Astana
KAZAKHSTAN
Aral Sea
Lake Balkhash
UZBEKISTAN
TURKMENISTAN
KYRGYZSTAN
TAJIKISTAN
Lake Baikal
Ulan Bator
MONGOLIA
Aleutian Islands
Kuril Islands
NORTH KOREA
Beijing
Sea of Japan
Seoul
SOUTH KOREA
JAPAN
Tokyo
North Pacific Ocean
CHINA
Yellow Sea
East China Sea
TAIWAN
Mediterranean Sea
CYPRUS
SYRIA
LEBANON
ISRAEL
Tripoli
Tehrān
IRAQ
IRAN
Kabul
AFGHANISTAN
Islamabad
PAKISTAN
New Delhi
Kathmandu
NEPAL
BHUTAN
Thimphu
BANGLADESH
Dhaka
INDIA
Cairo
JORDAN
KUWAIT
Persian Gulf
BAHRAIN
QATAR
UNITED ARAB EMIRATES
SAUDI ARABIA
Muscat
OMAN
LIBYA
EGYPT
Red Sea
MYANMAR
LAOS
THAILAND
South China Sea
Philippine Sea
Northern Mariana Islands (U.S.)
Bay of Bengal
Arabian Sea
YEMEN
ERITREA
Khartoum
SUDAN
CHAD
N'Djamena
DJIBOUTI
Gulf of Aden
Socotra (Yemen)
Andaman Islands (India)
Manila
VIETNAM
CAMBODIA
PHILIPPINES
Guam (U.S.)
MARSHALL ISLANDS
FEDERATED STATES OF MICRONESIA
PALAU
Adis Ababa
ETHIOPIA
CENTRAL AFRICAN REP.
CAMEROON
SRI LANKA
Gulf of Thailand
BRUNEI
MALDIVES
MALAYSIA
SINGAPORE
Celebes Sea
UGANDA
SOMALIA
Mogadishu
KENYA
Nairobi
CONGO
RWANDA
DEMOCRATIC REP. OF CONGO
BURUNDI
TANZANIA
Dar es Salaam
SEYCHELLES
Chagos Archipelago (U.K.)
Sumatra
Jakarta
Java Sea
INDONESIA
PAPUA NEW GUINEA
NAURU
KIRIBATI
SOLOMON ISLANDS
Java
EAST TIMOR
Timor
Timor Sea
Arafura Sea
Diego Garcia
Luanda
ANGOLA
COMOROS
MALAWI
ZAMBIA
TUVALU
Coral Sea
Indian Ocean
Mozambique Channel
ZIMBABWE
MOZAMBIQUE
Antananarivo
MADAGASCAR
MAURITIUS
Réunion (Fr.)
FIJI
VANUATU
NAMIBIA
Windhoek
BOTSWANA
Gaborone
Pretoria
Johannesburg
SWAZILAND
Maseru
LESOTHO
SOUTH AFRICA
Cape Town
AUSTRALIA
New Caledonia (Fr.)
South Pacific Ocean
Norfolk Island (Aus.)
Kermadec Islands (N.Z.)
Sydney
Canberra, A.C.T.
Tasman Sea
Great Australian Bight
North Island
NEW ZEALAND
South Island
Prince Edward Islands (So. Africa)
Crozet Islands
French Southern and Antarctic Lands (Fr.)
Kerguélen Islands
Heard Island and McDonald Islands (Aus.)
Southern Ocean